THE
SRC ORANGE BOOK®
OF
12-YEAR
NASDAQ CHARTS®

January 2013

Published by

Securities Research Company

P.O. Box 180250, Boston, MA 02118

Toll Free (800)921-3950; Outside U.S. (508)832-4509

www.srcstockcharts.com

THE SRC ORANGE BOOK OF 12-YEAR NASDAQ CHARTS

THE SRC ORANGE BOOK OF 12-YEAR NASDAQ CHARTS

THE SRC ORANGE BOOK OF 12-YEAR NASDAQ CHARTS

THE SRC ORANGE BOOK OF 12-YEAR NASDAQ CHARTS

NAME CHANGE

21st Century Holding Co	now	Federated National Holding
Angeion Corp	now	MGC Diagnostic Corp
CompuCredit Corp.	now	Atlanticus Holdings
DG Fast Channel	now	Digital Generation
Kaiser financialGrp	now	SIMPLICITY BANCORP, INC.
Kraft Foods Inc.	now	Mondelez International, Inc
Nabi Pharmaceuticals	now	Biota Pharmaceuticals
OYO Geospace Corp.	now	GeoSpace Technologies, Inc.
Petroleum Development	now	PDC Energy Inc.
Shuffle Master, Inc.	now	SHFL Entertainment, Inc.

REMOVED THIS EDITION

A123 System, Inc.	
Ariba Inc.	BIDZ.com Inc
Brightpoint, Inc.	Central Bancorp Mass
Ceradyne Inc.	Credo Pete Corp
Ditech Networks, Inc.	Deltek Inc
DUSA Pharmaceuticals	ecommerce China Dangdang
Edelman Financial Group	Fidelity Bancorp.
FSI International Inc	IntegraMed America Inc.
IRIS International, Inc	J Alexanders Corp
JDA Software Group Inc	Jones Soda Co.
KSW Inc	Medcath Corp.
Mediware Info Systems	New Frontier Media Inc
OPNET Technologies Inc.	Pacific Capital Bancorp
Peet's Coffee & Tea	Penson Worldwide
Physicians Formula Hldgs	Presstek, Inc
Quest Software Inc.	
Union Drilling Inc.	Versant Corp.

Charted data in this edition completed through December 31, 2012

THE SRC SECTOR & INDUSTRY CODE REFERENCE

SECTORS & INDUSTRIES

Consumer Discretionary Sector........SPCCS

Industries
Advertising	ADVER
Apparel Accessories & Luxury Goods	APPRL
Auto Parts & Equipment	AUTOP
Automobile Manufacturers	AUTOS
Automotive Retail	AUTOR
Broadcasting & Cable TV	MEDIA
Casinos & Gaming	CSINO
Consumer Electronics	CELEC
Department Stores	RTDEP
Distributors	DISTR
Education Services	EDSER
Footwear	SHOES
General Merchandise Stores	RTGEN
Home Furnishings	HMFRN
Homebuilding	HMBLD
Home Furnishing Retail	HOMEF
Hotels, Resorts & Cruise Lines	HOTEL
Household Appliances	HSAPP
Housewares & Specialties	HSWRE
Leisure Facilities	LEISF
Leisure Products	LEISP
Motorcycle Manufacturers	MOTOC
Movies & Entertainment	ENTMT
Photographic Products	PHOTO
Publishing	PUBPR
Restaurants	RESTR
Retail – Apparel	RTAPP
Retail – Catalog	RTCAT
Retail – Computers & Electronics	RTCOM
Retail – Home Improvement	RTHOM
Retail – Internet	RTNET
Special Consumer Services	SPECS
Specialty Stores	RTSPE
Tires & Rubber Goods	TIRES

Consumer Staples Sector................SPCNS

Industries
Agricultural Products	AGPRD
Brewers	BRWRS
Distillers & Vintners	DSTLR
Food Distributors	FOODD
Household Products	HSHLD
Hypermarkets & Supercenters	HYPMK
Packaged Foods & Meats	PKGFD
Personal Products	CSMTG
Retail – Drugs	RTDRG
Retail – Food	FOODR
Soft Drinks	BEVGS
Tobacco	TBACO

Energy Sector.............................SPENS

Industries
Coal & Consumer Fuels	COCOF
Oil & Gas – Drilling	OGDRL
Oil & Gas – Equipment & Services	OGEQP
Oil & Gas – Exploration & Products	OGEXP
Oil & Gas – Integrated	OGINT
Oil & Gas – Refining & Marketing	OGREF
Oil & Gas – Storage	OGSTO

Financials Sector............................SPFN

Industries
Asset Management	ASMGT
Banks – Diversified	BANKS
Banks – Regional	RBANK
Consumer Finance	FINAN
Diversified Financial Services	DIVFN
Diversified REITs (old)	DREIT
Exchange Traded Funds	EXTFS
Industrial REITs (old)	IREIT
Insurance – Brokers	INSBR
Insurance – Life & Health	INSLH
Insurance – Multi-Line	INSML
Insurance – Property & Casualty	INSPC
Investment Banking & Brokerage	IBANK
Mortgage REITs (old)	MREIT
Multi-Sector Holdings	MSHLD
Office REITs (old)	OREIT
Real Estate Mgmt & Development	REMDV
Reinsurance	REINS
REITS Equity Diversified	REQDV
REITS Equity Residential	REQRS
REITS Equity Retail	REQRT
REITS Industrial	REQIR
REITS Mortgage Backed	RMOMB
REITS Office	REQOR
REITS Specialized	REQSR
Residential REITs (old)	LREIT
Retail REITs (old)	EREIT
Specialized Finance	SPCFN
Specialized REITs (old)	ZREIT
Thrifts & Mortgage Finance	THRFT

Health Care Sector.........................HCX

Industries
Biotechnology	BIOTK
Healthcare Distributors & Services	HCDIS
Healthcare Equipment	HCEQP
Healthcare Facilities	HCFAC
Healthcare Managed Care	HCMAN
Healthcare Services	HCSVS
Healthcare Supplies	HCSUP
Healthcare Tech	HCTFC
Life Science Tools	LFSCT
Pharmaceuticals	DRUGS

Industrials Sector...........................SPIN

Industries
Aerospace & Defense	AEROD
Air Freight & Logistics	AIRFR
Airlines	ARLNS
Building Products	BLDGP
Commercial Printing	PRINT
Construction & Engineering	ENGNR
Electrical Components & Equipment	EEQPM
Industrial Conglomerates	CONGL
Machinery – Construction & Farm	TRKPT
Machinery – Industrial	MACHN
Marine	SHIPP
Railroads	RAILR
Services – Diversified Commercial	DCMSR
Services – Employment	SRVEM
Services – Environmental	PCTRL
Services – Office & Supplies	OFICE
Trading Companies & Distributors	TRADE
Trucking	TRUCK

Information Technology Sector.........SPHTI

Industries
Application Software	APPSF
Communications Equipment	TELEQ
Computer Hardware	CMPTR
Computer Storage & Peripherals	DISKS
Electronic Equipment	ELEEQ
Electronic Manufacturing Services	EMSVC
Home Entertainment Software	HSOFT
Internet Software & Services	ITSOF
IT Consulting & Services	ITCON
Office Electronics	OFCEL
Semiconductor Equipment	SEMIQ
Semiconductors	SEMIC
Services – Data Processing	DPSVS
Systems Software	SYSSF
Technology Distribution	TDSTR

Materials Sector..........................SPBMS

Industries
Aluminum	ALUMN
Chemicals – Commodity	CCHEM
Chemicals – Diversified	DCHEM
Chemicals – Fertilizers & Agricultural	FERTL
Chemicals – Specialty	SCHEM
Construction Materials	CONST
Containers – Metal & Glass	CONTM
Diverse Metals & Mining	METAL
Forest Products	FPROD
Gold	GOLDM
Industrial Gases	INGAS
Paper Packaging	PPACK
Paper Products	PPROD
Steel	STEEL

Telecommunication Services Sector...SPCSS

Industries
Integrated Telecommunications Srvc	PHONE
Wireless Telecommunications Service	TLCEL

Utilities Sector.............................SPUT

Industries
Electric Utilities	EUTIL
Gas Utilities	GUTIL
Independent Power Products	IPPET
Multi-Utilities & Unregulated Power	MUTIL
Water Utilities	WUTIL

NOTE: Ticker symbol is obtained from Thomson Financials 'Baseline' product.

DOW JONES COMPOSITE 65 (DJC)

30 Industrials + 20 Transportation + 15 Utility Stocks

Growth Performance Measurement				
Years	Price	Earn.	Div.	Tot Ret
Last 1	5.0	6.7	3.3	7.6
Last 5	.2	2.2	4.5	2.4
Last 10	6.5	---	---	8.3

Copyright 2012 Securities Research Company

'01 '02 '03 '04 '05 '06 '07 '08 '09 '10 '11 '12

Bonds $.0 Mil Com .000 Mil BV .00 /sh P/E 14.44 (Ind P/E N/A) Ctry US

DOW JONES INDUSTRIAL AVERAGE (DJIA)

An index of 30 "blue chip" stocks of U.S. "Industrial" companies

Growth Performance Measurement				
Years	Price	Earn.	Div.	Tot Ret
Last 1	7.3	2.3	8.4	10.1
Last 5	-.2	3.7	3.6	2.0
Last 10	4.6	7.9	7.0	6.6

Copyright 2012 Securities Research Company

'01 '02 '03 '04 '05 '06 '07 '08 '09 '10 '11 '12

Bonds $.0 Mil Com .000 Mil BV .00 /sh P/E 13.15 (Ind P/E N/A) Ctry US

DOW JONES TRANSPORTATION AVERAGE (DJTA)

(D)

An index of 20 "blue chip" stocks of U.S. "Transportation" companies

Growth Performance Measurement				
Years	Price	Earn.	Div.	Tot Ret
Last 1	5.7	33.2	-6.9	7.3
Last 5	3.0	1.0	6.1	4.5
Last 10	8.7	---	10.2	9.8

(309.33)(176.17)(27.08)   2.09   3.4
(255.20)(294.73)(98.09)   (10.86) (66.43)
(107.43)(344.72)(151.31) -2.13 (145.58)

Copyright 2012 Securities Research Company

'01 '02 '03 '04 '05 '06 '07 '08 '09 '10 '11 '12

Bonds $.0 Mil Com .000 Mil BV .00 /sh P/E 16.83 (Ind P/E N/A) Ctry US

DOW JONES UTILITY AVERAGE (DJUA)

An index of 15 "blue chip" stocks of U.S. "Utility" companies

Growth Performance Measurement				
Years	Price	Earn.	Div.	Tot Ret
Last 1	-2.5	-3.3	-.9	1.4
Last 5	-3.2	-.4	4.0	.1
Last 10	7.7	2.7	4.9	10.6

Copyright 2012 Securities Research Company

'01 '02 '03 '04 '05 '06 '07 '08 '09 '10 '11 '12

Bonds $.0 Mil Com .000 Mil BV .00 /sh P/E 15.40 (Ind P/E N/A) Ctry US

AMEX COMPOSITE INDEX (XAX)

Index reflects the aggregate market value of all its components

Growth Performance Measurement				
Years	Price	Earn.	Div.	Tot Ret
Last 1	3.4	---	---	3.4
Last 5	-.5	---	---	-.5
Last 10	11.1	---	---	11.1

NASDAQ COMPOSITE INDEX (COMPQ)

Broad-based market capitalization weighted methodology index

Growth Performance Measurement				
Years	Price	Earn.	Div.	Tot Ret
Last 1	15.9	6.9	38.2	17.2
Last 5	2.6	13.1	20.9	3.3
Last 10	8.5	18.0	22.7	9.0

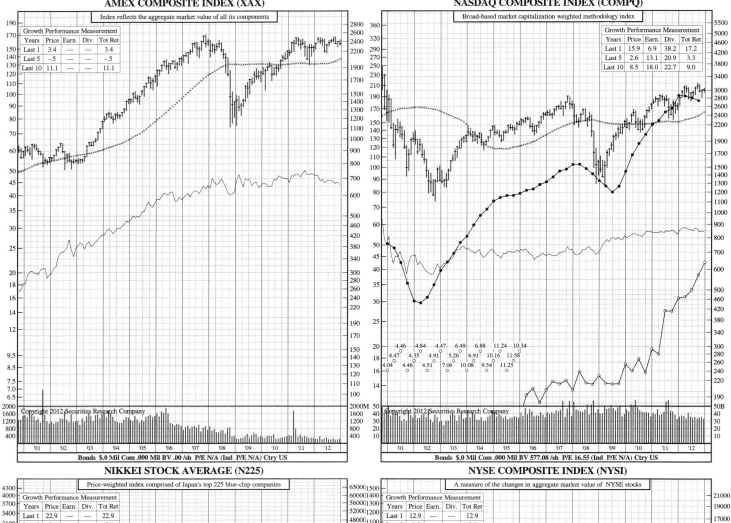

Copyright 2012 Securities Research Company

AMEX: Bonds $.0 Mil Com .000 Mil BV .00 /sh P/E N/A (Ind P/E N/A) Ctry US

NASDAQ: Bonds $.0 Mil Com .000 Mil BV 577.08 /sh P/E 16.55 (Ind P/E N/A) Ctry US

NIKKEI STOCK AVERAGE (N225)

Price-weighted index comprised of Japan's top 225 blue-chip companies

Growth Performance Measurement				
Years	Price	Earn.	Div.	Tot Ret
Last 1	22.9	---	---	22.9
Last 5	-7.4	---	---	-7.4
Last 10	1.9	---	---	1.9

NYSE COMPOSITE INDEX (NYSI)

A measure of the changes in aggregate market value of NYSE stocks

Growth Performance Measurement				
Years	Price	Earn.	Div.	Tot Ret
Last 1	12.9	---	---	12.9
Last 5	-2.8	---	---	-2.8
Last 10	5.4	---	---	5.4

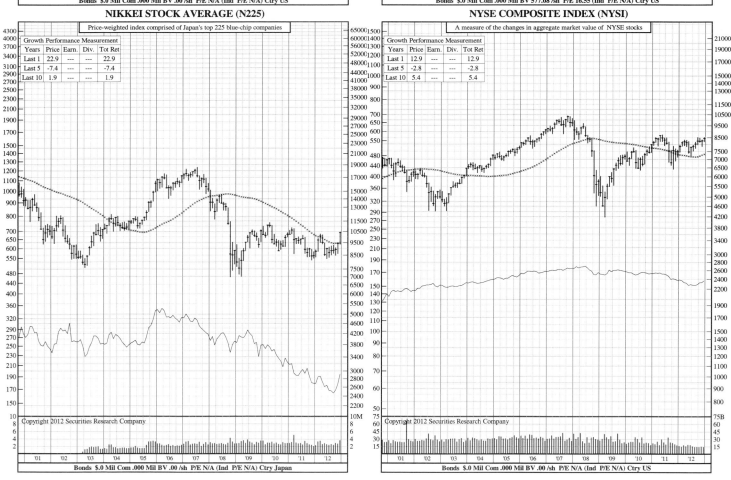

Copyright 2012 Securities Research Company

Nikkei: Bonds $.0 Mil Com .000 Mil BV .00 /sh P/E N/A (Ind P/E N/A) Ctry Japan

NYSE: Bonds $.0 Mil Com .000 Mil BV .00 /sh P/E N/A (Ind P/E N/A) Ctry US

RUSSELL FRANK INVESTMENTS 3000 INDEX (RUA)

Large-cap index and Small-cap Index of the Russell 3000 Index

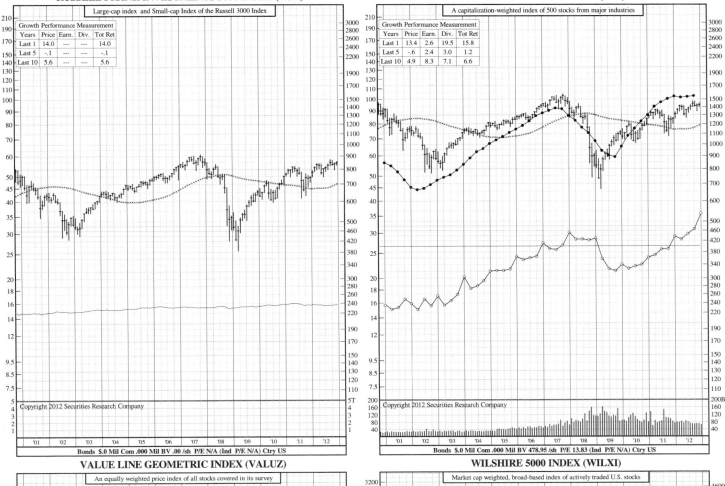

Growth Performance Measurement

Years	Price	Earn.	Div.	Tot Ret
Last 1	14.0	---	---	14.0
Last 5	-.1	---	---	-.1
Last 10	5.6	---	---	5.6

Bonds $.0 Mil Com .000 Mil BV .00 /sh P/E N/A (Ind P/E N/A) Ctry US

S&P 500 COMPOSITE INDEX (SPX)

A capitalization-weighted index of 500 stocks from major industries

Growth Performance Measurement

Years	Price	Earn.	Div.	Tot Ret
Last 1	13.4	2.6	19.5	15.8
Last 5	-.6	2.4	3.0	1.2
Last 10	4.9	8.3	7.1	6.6

Bonds $.0 Mil Com .000 Mil BV 478.95 /sh P/E 13.83 (Ind P/E N/A) Ctry US

VALUE LINE GEOMETRIC INDEX (VALUZ)

An equally weighted price index of all stocks covered in its survey

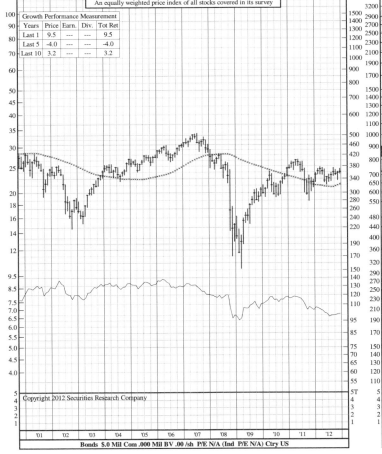

Growth Performance Measurement

Years	Price	Earn.	Div.	Tot Ret
Last 1	9.5	---	---	9.5
Last 5	-4.0	---	---	-4.0
Last 10	3.2	---	---	3.2

Bonds $.0 Mil Com .000 Mil BV .00 /sh P/E N/A (Ind P/E N/A) Ctry US

WILSHIRE 5000 INDEX (WILXI)

Market cap weighted, broad-based index of actively traded U.S. stocks

Growth Performance Measurement

Years	Price	Earn.	Div.	Tot Ret
Last 1	8.5	---	---	7.7
Last 5	-1.0	---	---	-1.0
Last 10	5.5	---	---	5.4

Bonds $.0 Mil Com .000 Mil BV .00 /sh P/E N/A (Ind P/E N/A) Ctry US

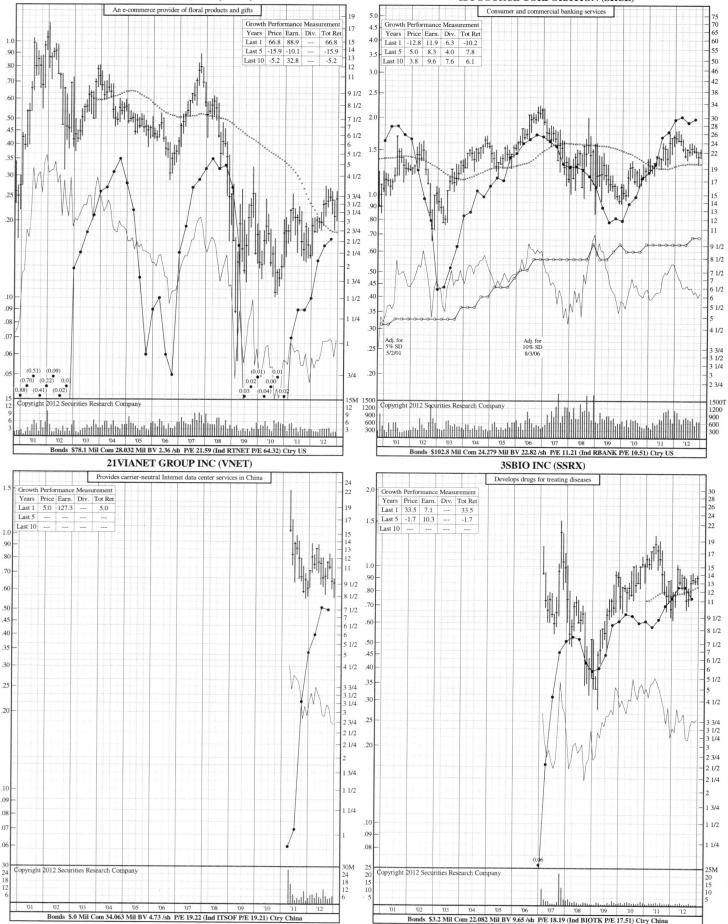

4

1 800 FLOWERS COM (FLWS)

An e-commerce provider of floral products and gifts

Bonds $78.1 Mil Com 28.032 Mil BV 2.36 /sh P/E 21.59 (Ind RTNET P/E 64.32) Ctry US

1ST SOURCE CORPORATION (SRCE)

Consumer and commercial banking services

Adj. for
5% SD
5/2/01

Adj. for
10% SD
8/3/06

Bonds $102.8 Mil Com 24.279 Mil BV 22.82 /sh P/E 11.21 (Ind RBANK P/E 10.51) Ctry US

21VIANET GROUP INC (VNET)

Provides carrier-neutral Internet data center services in China

Bonds $.0 Mil Com 34.063 Mil BV 4.73 /sh P/E 19.22 (Ind ITSOF P/E 19.21) Ctry China

3SBIO INC (SSRX)

Develops drugs for treating diseases

Bonds $3.2 Mil Com 22.082 Mil BV 9.65 /sh P/E 18.19 (Ind BIOTK P/E 17.51) Ctry China

8X8 INCORPORATED (EGHT)

(P)

Engaged in sale of telecommunication technology and services

65% SCALE

Growth Performance Measurement				
Years	Price	Earn.	Div.	Tot Ret
Last 1	132.8	88.9	---	132.8
Last 5	52.7	---	---	52.7
Last 10	42.1	---	---	42.1

(2.46) (0.24) (0.40) (0.18) (0.21) (0.46) (0.43) (0.27) (0.12)   (0.03)
(1.11) (0.33) (0.35) (0.29) (0.11) (0.43) (0.47) (0.35) 0.00   (0.05)
(0.96) (2.05) (0.23) (0.37) (0.09) (0.32) (0.48) (0.41) (0.22) (0.05) (0.04) (0.01)

Copyright 2012 Securities Research Company

'01 '02 '03 '04 '05 '06 '07 '08 '09 '10 '11 '12

Bonds $.0 Mil Com 71.471 Mil BV 1.93 /sh P/E 43.41 (Ind PHONE P/E 15.99) Ctry US

AAON INC (AAON)

Markets rooftop air-conditioning and heating

Growth Performance Measurement				
Years	Price	Earn.	Div.	Tot Ret
Last 1	1.9	19.7	.0	3.0
Last 5	9.6	2.4	22.0	10.7
Last 10	9.8	6.5	---	10.4

Adj. for
3 for 2
6/5/02

Adj. for
3 for 2
10/1/01

Adj. for
3 for 2
8/22/07

Adj. for
3 for 2
6/14/11

Copyright 2012 Securities Research Company

'01 '02 '03 '04 '05 '06 '07 '08 '09 '10 '11 '12

Bonds $.0 Mil Com 24.526 Mil BV 5.58 /sh P/E 22.93 (Ind BLDGP P/E 87.92) Ctry US

AASTROM BIOSCIENCES INC (ASTM)

Cell production equipment

65% SCALE

Growth Performance Measurement				
Years	Price	Earn.	Div.	Tot Ret
Last 1	-30.8	-13.6	---	-30.8
Last 5	-21.2	4.8	---	-21.2
Last 10	-10.4	4.1	---	-10.4

Adj. for
1 for 8
2/18/10

(1.36) (1.20) (1.52)   (1.28) (1.04) (1.04) (1.28) (1.20) (1.28) (1.28) (1.04) (0.88) (0.79) (1.04) (1.00)
(1.04) (1.60) (1.52) (1.44) (1.12) (0.96) (1.12) (1.20) (1.20) (1.28) (1.12) (0.88) (0.74) (0.96) (0.88) (1.00)
(1.12) (1.44) (1.52) (1.52) (1.76) (1.04) (1.04) (1.20) (1.28) (1.28) (1.20) (0.96) (0.80) (0.99) (0.88) (1.00)

Copyright 2012 Securities Research Company

'01 '02 '03 '04 '05 '06 '07 '08 '09 '10 '11 '12

Bonds $.0 Mil Com 43.784 Mil BV -.49 /sh P/E N/A (Ind BIOTK P/E 17.51) Ctry US

ABAXIS INC (ABAX)

(P)(E)

Makes/markets portable blood analysis systems

Growth Performance Measurement				
Years	Price	Earn.	Div.	Tot Ret
Last 1	34.1	14.0	---	34.1
Last 5	.7	4.2	---	.7
Last 10	25.1	36.0	---	25.1

Special
$1.00

0.00 0.03 0.06
0.04 0.02 0.02
0.06 0.00 0.03 0.08

Copyright 2012 Securities Research Company

'01 '02 '03 '04 '05 '06 '07 '08 '09 '10 '11 '12

Bonds $.0 Mil Com 21.950 Mil BV 8.47 /sh P/E 57.08 (Ind HCEQP P/E 14.39) Ctry US

6

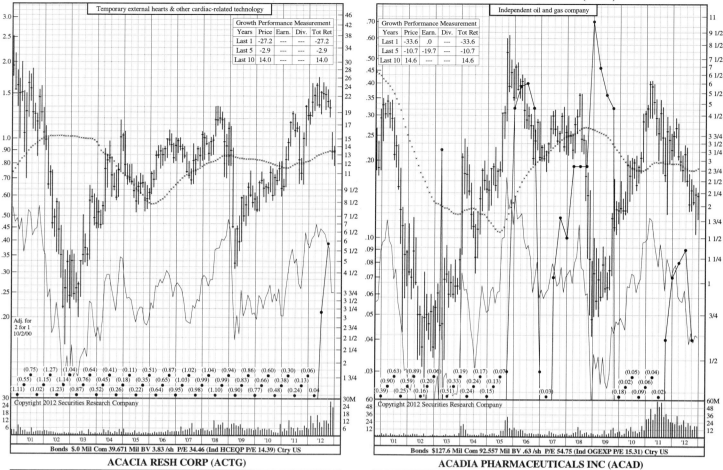

ABIOMED INC (ABMD)

Temporary external hearts & other cardiac-related technology

Growth Performance Measurement				
Years	Price	Earn.	Div.	Tot Ret
Last 1	-27.2	---	---	-27.2
Last 5	-2.9	---	---	-2.9
Last 10	14.0	---	---	14.0

Adj. for
2 for 1
10/2/00

(0.75) (1.27) (1.04) (0.64) (0.41) (0.11) (0.51) (0.87) (1.02) (1.04) (0.94) (0.86) (0.60) (0.30) (0.06)
(0.55) (1.15) (1.14) (0.76) (0.45) (0.18) (0.35) (0.65) (1.03) (0.99) (0.99) (0.83) (0.66) (0.38) (0.13)
(1.11) (1.02) (1.23) (0.87) (0.52) (0.26) (0.22) (0.64) (0.95) (0.98) (1.10) (0.90) (0.77) (0.48) (0.24) 0.04

Copyright 2012 Securities Research Company

'01 '02 '03 '04 '05 '06 '07 '08 '09 '10 '11 '12

Bonds $.0 Mil Com 39.671 Mil BV 3.83 /sh P/E 34.46 (Ind HCEQP P/E 14.39) Ctry US

ABRAXAS PETE CORP (AXAS)

Independent oil and gas company

Growth Performance Measurement				
Years	Price	Earn.	Div.	Tot Ret
Last 1	-33.6	.0	---	-33.6
Last 5	-10.7	-19.7	---	-10.7
Last 10	14.6	---	---	14.6

(0.63) (0.89) (0.06) (0.19) (0.17) (0.07) (0.05) (0.04)
(0.90) (0.59) (0.33) (0.24) (0.13) (0.02) (0.06)
(0.39) (0.25) (0.16) (0.51) (0.24) (0.15) (0.03) (0.18) (0.09) (0.02)

Copyright 2012 Securities Research Company

'01 '02 '03 '04 '05 '06 '07 '08 '09 '10 '11 '12

Bonds $127.6 Mil Com 92.557 Mil BV .63 /sh P/E 54.75 (Ind OGEXP P/E 15.31) Ctry US

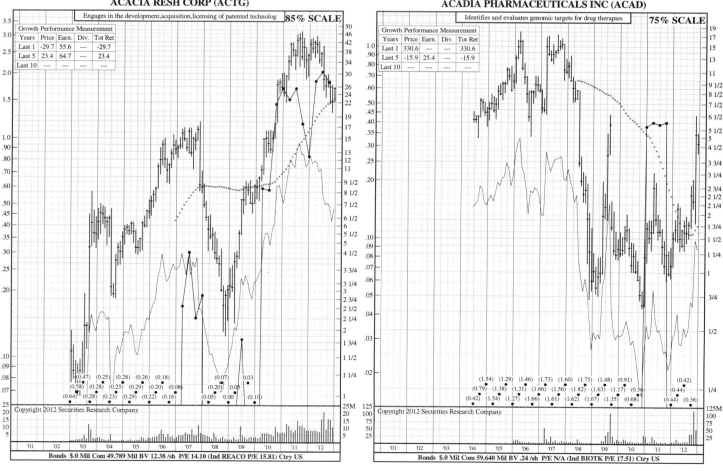

ACACIA RESH CORP (ACTG)

Engages in the development,acquisition,licensing of patented technolog **85% SCALE**

Growth Performance Measurement				
Years	Price	Earn.	Div.	Tot Ret
Last 1	-29.7	55.6	---	-29.7
Last 5	23.4	64.7	---	23.4
Last 10	---	---	---	---

(0.47) (0.25) (0.28) (0.26) (0.18) (0.07) 0.03
(0.58) (0.28) (0.25) (0.29) (0.20) (0.08) (0.20) 0.05
(0.64) (0.28) (0.23) (0.29) (0.22) (0.16) (0.05) 0.00 (0.10)

Copyright 2012 Securities Research Company

'01 '02 '03 '04 '05 '06 '07 '08 '09 '10 '11 '12

Bonds $.0 Mil Com 49.789 Mil BV 12.38 /sh P/E 14.10 (Ind REACO P/E 15.81) Ctry US

ACADIA PHARMACEUTICALS INC (ACAD)

Identifies and evaluates genomic targets for drug therapies **75% SCALE**

Growth Performance Measurement				
Years	Price	Earn.	Div.	Tot Ret
Last 1	330.6	---	---	330.6
Last 5	-15.9	25.4	---	-15.9
Last 10	---	---	---	---

(1.54) (1.29) (1.46) (1.73) (1.60) (1.75) (1.48) (0.91) (0.42)
(0.79) (1.38) (1.31) (1.66) (1.56) (1.82) (1.63) (1.17) (0.56) (0.44)
(0.42) (1.54) (1.27) (1.66) (1.61) (1.62) (1.67) (1.35) (0.68) (0.44) (0.36)

Copyright 2012 Securities Research Company

'01 '02 '03 '04 '05 '06 '07 '08 '09 '10 '11 '12

Bonds $.0 Mil Com 59.640 Mil BV .24 /sh P/E N/A (Ind BIOTK P/E 17.51) Ctry US

ACCELRYS INC (ACCL)

Develops software for managing data studies of genomes and proteins

Dist. 1 sh. Pharmacopeia Drug Discovery
for ea. 2 shs. ACCl held 4/30/04

Growth Performance Measurement				
Years	Price	Earn.	Div.	Tot Ret
Last 1	34.7	.0	---	34.7
Last 5	3.7	19.4	---	3.7
Last 10	.1	---	---	.1

Copyright 2012 Securities Research Company

Bonds $.0 Mil Com 55.638 Mil BV 4.44 /sh P/E 26.62 (Ind LFSCT P/E 13.82) Ctry US

ACCURAY INC (ARAY)

Radiosurgery system that zaps tumors with radiation

Growth Performance Measurement				
Years	Price	Earn.	Div.	Tot Ret
Last 1	52.0	-560.0	---	52.0
Last 5	-15.8	-8.4	---	-15.8
Last 10	---	---	---	---

Copyright 2012 Securities Research Company

Bonds $.0 Mil Com 72.273 Mil BV 2.17 /sh P/E N/A (Ind HCEQP P/E 14.39) Ctry US

ACETO CORPORATION (ACET)

Distribution and marketing of Pharmaceutical and Specialty Chemicals

Growth Performance Measurement				
Years	Price	Earn.	Div.	Tot Ret
Last 1	45.7	45.8	.0	48.6
Last 5	4.7	9.2	5.9	6.6
Last 10	7.8	8.8	8.1	9.4

Adj. for
3 for 2
1/3/03

Adj. for
3 for 2
1/5/04

Adj. for
3 for 2
1/11/05

Copyright 2012 Securities Research Company

Bonds $.0 Mil Com 27.185 Mil BV 6.39 /sh P/E 14.36 (Ind TRADE P/E 25.46) Ctry US

ACHILLION PHARMACEUTICALS IN (ACHN)

(E)

Develops biopharmaceutical treatments for infectious diseases

Growth Performance Measurement				
Years	Price	Earn.	Div.	Tot Ret
Last 1	5.1	-8.1	---	5.1
Last 5	9.9	21.4	---	9.9
Last 10	---	37.0	---	---

Copyright 2012 Securities Research Company

Bonds $.0 Mil Com 79.517 Mil BV 1.03 /sh P/E N/A (Ind BIOTK P/E 17.51) Ctry US

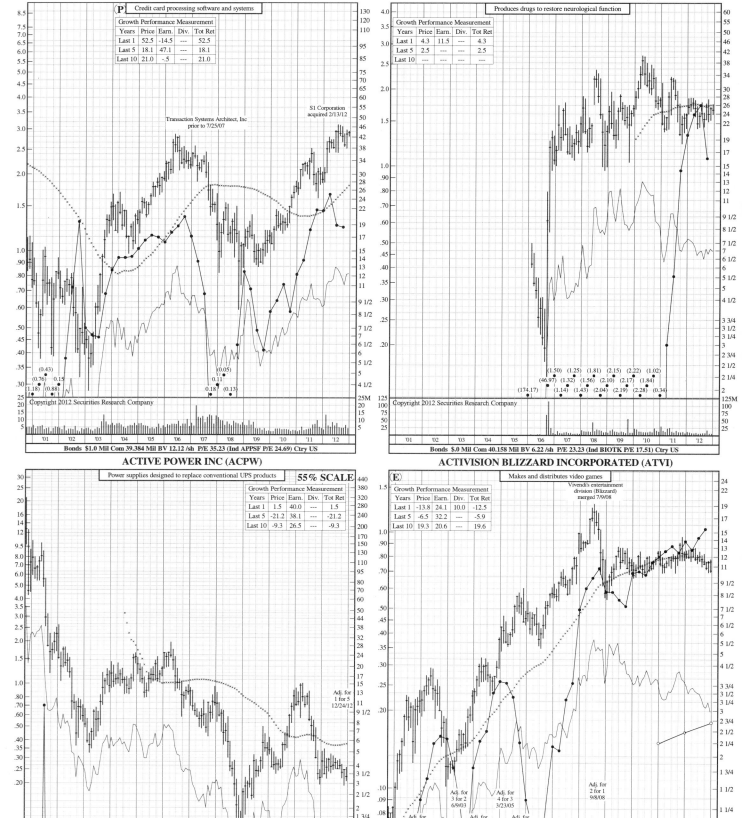

8

ACI WORLDWIDE INC (ACIW)

Credit card processing software and systems

Growth Performance Measurement				
Years	Price	Earn.	Div.	Tot Ret
Last 1	52.5	-14.5	---	52.5
Last 5	18.1	47.1	---	18.1
Last 10	21.0	-.5	---	21.0

Transaction Systems Architect, Inc
prior to 7/25/07

S1 Corporation
acquired 2/13/12

(0.43)
(0.76) 0.15
(1.18) (0.88)
(0.05)
0.11
0.18 (0.13)

Bonds $1.0 Mil Com 39.384 Mil BV 12.12 /sh P/E 35.23 (Ind APPSF P/E 24.69) Ctry US

ACORDA THERAPEUTICS INC (ACOR)

Produces drugs to restore neurological function

Growth Performance Measurement				
Years	Price	Earn.	Div.	Tot Ret
Last 1	4.3	11.5	---	4.3
Last 5	2.5	---	---	2.5
Last 10	---	---	---	---

(1.50) (1.25) (1.81) (2.15) (2.22) (1.02)
(46.97) (1.32) (1.56) (2.10) (2.17) (1.84)
(174.17) (1.14) (1.43) (2.04) (2.19) (2.28) (0.34)

Bonds $.0 Mil Com 40.158 Mil BV 6.22 /sh P/E 23.23 (Ind BIOTK P/E 17.51) Ctry US

ACTIVE POWER INC (ACPW)

Power supplies designed to replace conventional UPS products

55% SCALE

Growth Performance Measurement				
Years	Price	Earn.	Div.	Tot Ret
Last 1	1.5	40.0	---	1.5
Last 5	-21.2	38.1	---	-21.2
Last 10	-9.3	26.5	---	-9.3

Adj. for
1 for 5
12/24/12

(1.35) (3.35) (3.30) (2.60) (3.20) (3.00) (2.30) (2.15) (1.65) (1.15) (0.85) (0.85) (0.45) (0.15) (0.35)
(4.70) (3.45) (3.35) (3.00) (2.55) (2.40) (2.40) (2.00) (1.25) (1.00) (0.75) (0.65) (0.15) (0.35) (0.15)
(9.60) (3.50) (3.35) (3.25) (3.25) (2.50) (2.30) (2.45) (1.55) (1.25) (0.80) (0.85) (0.30) (0.25) (0.20)

Bonds $.0 Mil Com 19.111 Mil BV 1.37 /sh P/E N/A (Ind EEQPM P/E 16.88) Ctry US

ACTIVISION BLIZZARD INCORPORATED (ATVI)

Makes and distributes video games

Growth Performance Measurement				
Years	Price	Earn.	Div.	Tot Ret
Last 1	-13.8	24.1	10.0	-12.5
Last 5	-6.5	32.2	---	-5.9
Last 10	19.3	20.6	---	19.6

Vivendi's entertainment
division (Blizzard)
merged 7/9/08

Adj. for
3 for 2
6/9/03

Adj. for
4 for 3
3/23/05

Adj. for
2 for 1
9/8/08

Adj. for
3 for 2
11/21/01

Adj. for
3 for 2
3/16/04

Adj. for
4 for 3
10/25/05

Adj. for
3 for 2

Bonds $.0 Mil Com 1112.705 Mil BV 9.78 /sh P/E 10.31 (Ind HSOFT P/E 16.13) Ctry US

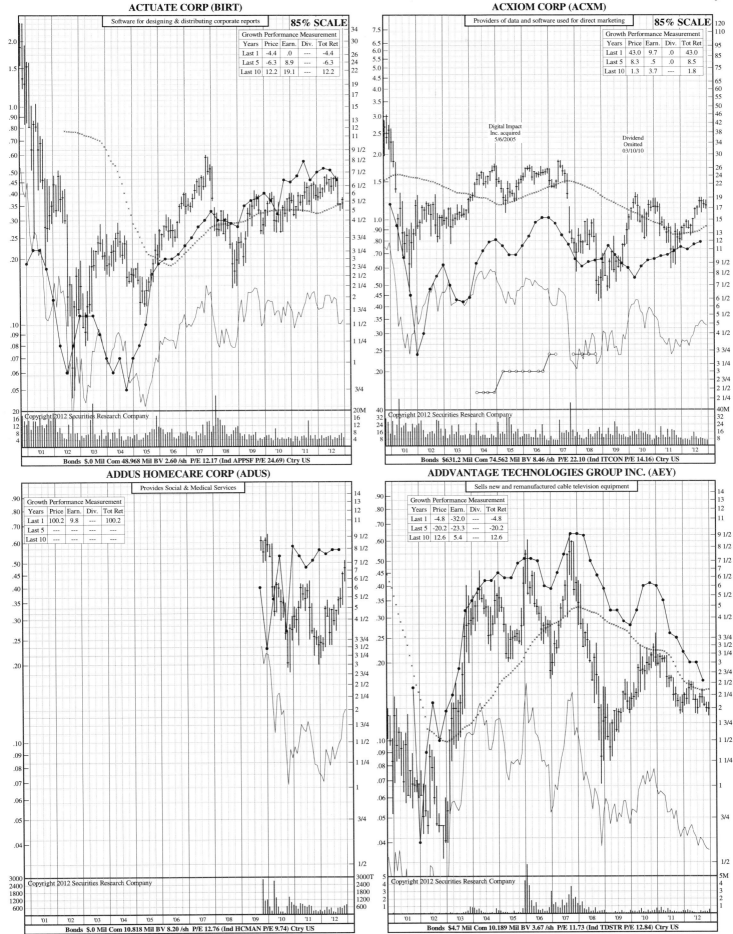

9

ACTUATE CORP (BIRT)

Software for designing & distributing corporate reports

85% SCALE

Growth Performance Measurement				
Years	Price	Earn.	Div.	Tot Ret
Last 1	-4.4	.0	---	-4.4
Last 5	-6.3	8.9	---	-6.3
Last 10	12.2	19.1	---	12.2

Copyright 2012 Securities Research Company

Bonds $.0 Mil Com 48.968 Mil BV 2.60 /sh P/E 12.17 (Ind APPSF P/E 24.69) Ctry US

ACXIOM CORP (ACXM)

Providers of data and software used for direct marketing

85% SCALE

Growth Performance Measurement				
Years	Price	Earn.	Div.	Tot Ret
Last 1	43.0	9.7	.0	43.0
Last 5	8.3	.5	.0	8.5
Last 10	1.3	3.7	---	1.8

Digital Impact
Inc. acquired
5/6/2005

Dividend
Omitted
03/10/10

Copyright 2012 Securities Research Company

Bonds $631.2 Mil Com 74.562 Mil BV 8.46 /sh P/E 22.10 (Ind ITCON P/E 14.16) Ctry US

ADDUS HOMECARE CORP (ADUS)

Provides Social & Medical Services

Growth Performance Measurement				
Years	Price	Earn.	Div.	Tot Ret
Last 1	100.2	9.8	---	100.2
Last 5	---	---	---	---
Last 10	---	---	---	---

Copyright 2012 Securities Research Company

Bonds $.0 Mil Com 10.818 Mil BV 8.20 /sh P/E 12.76 (Ind HCMAN P/E 9.74) Ctry US

ADDVANTAGE TECHNOLOGIES GROUP INC. (AEY)

Sells new and remanufactured cable television equipment

Growth Performance Measurement				
Years	Price	Earn.	Div.	Tot Ret
Last 1	-4.8	-32.0	---	-4.8
Last 5	-20.2	-23.3	---	-20.2
Last 10	12.6	5.4	---	12.6

Copyright 2012 Securities Research Company

Bonds $4.7 Mil Com 10.189 Mil BV 3.67 /sh P/E 11.73 (Ind TDSTR P/E 12.84) Ctry US

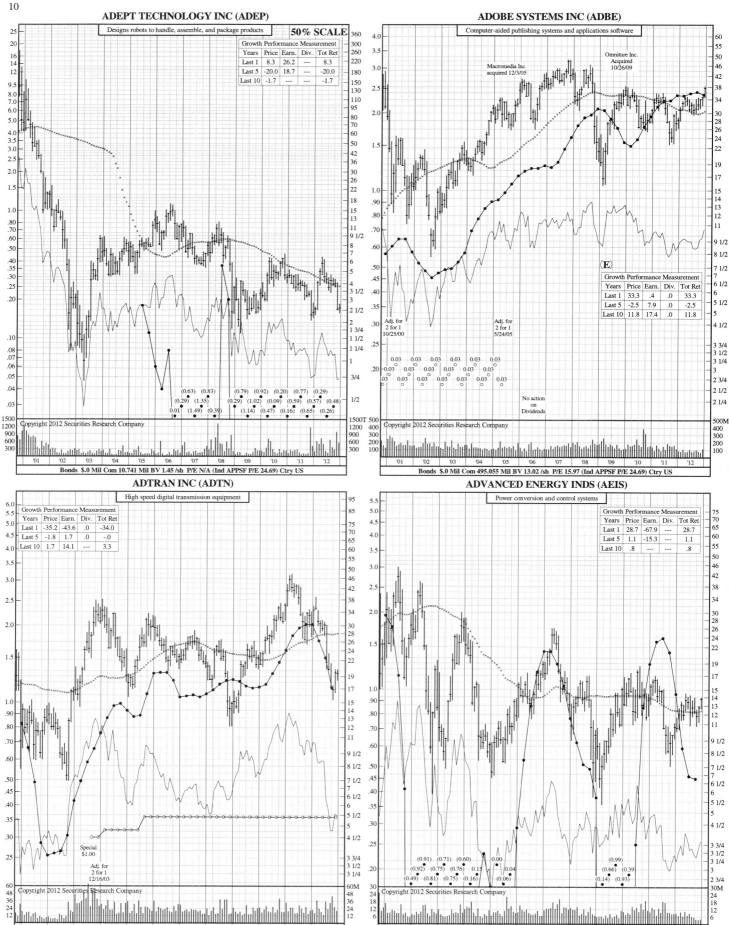

10

ADEPT TECHNOLOGY INC (ADEP)

Designs robots to handle, assemble, and package products

50% SCALE

Growth Performance Measurement

Years	Price	Earn.	Div.	Tot Ret
Last 1	8.3	26.2	---	8.3
Last 5	-20.0	18.7	---	-20.0
Last 10	-1.7	---	---	-1.7

(0.63) (0.83) (0.79) (0.92) (0.20) (0.77) (0.29)
(0.29) (1.35) (0.29) (1.02) (0.09) (0.59) (0.57) (0.48)
0.01 (1.49) (0.39) (1.14) (0.47) (0.16) (0.65) (0.26)

Copyright 2012 Securities Research Company

Bonds $.0 Mil Com 10.741 Mil BV 1.45 /sh P/E N/A (Ind APPSF P/E 24.69) Ctry US

ADOBE SYSTEMS INC (ADBE)

Computer-aided publishing systems and applications software

Macromedia Inc.
acquired 12/3/05

Omniture Inc.
Acquired
10/26/09

Adj. for
2 for 1
10/25/00

Adj. for
2 for 1
5/24/05

(E)

Growth Performance Measurement

Years	Price	Earn.	Div.	Tot Ret
Last 1	33.3	.4	.0	33.3
Last 5	-2.5	7.9	.0	-2.5
Last 10	11.8	17.4	.0	11.8

.03 .03 .03 .03 .03 .03
.03 .03 .03 .03 .03 .03
.03 .03 .03 .03 .03

No action
on
Dividends

Copyright 2012 Securities Research Company

Bonds $.0 Mil Com 495.055 Mil BV 13.02 /sh P/E 15.97 (Ind APPSF P/E 24.69) Ctry US

ADTRAN INC (ADTN)

High speed digital transmission equipment

Growth Performance Measurement

Years	Price	Earn.	Div.	Tot Ret
Last 1	-35.2	-43.6	.0	-34.0
Last 5	-1.8	1.7	.0	-.0
Last 10	1.7	14.1	---	3.3

Special
$1.00

Adj. for
2 for 1
12/16/03

Copyright 2012 Securities Research Company

Bonds $50.0 Mil Com 62.671 Mil BV 11.22 /sh P/E 17.14 (Ind TELEQ P/E 13.72) Ctry US

ADVANCED ENERGY INDS (AEIS)

Power conversion and control systems

Growth Performance Measurement

Years	Price	Earn.	Div.	Tot Ret
Last 1	28.7	-67.9	---	28.7
Last 5	1.1	-15.3	---	1.1
Last 10	.8	---	---	.8

(0.91) (0.71) (0.60)   0.00   (0.99)
(0.92) (0.75) (0.76) (0.15)   (0.04) (0.66) (0.39)
(0.49) (0.81) (0.75) (0.16) (0.06) (0.14) (0.93)

Copyright 2012 Securities Research Company

Bonds $135.1 Mil Com 37.875 Mil BV 10.00 /sh P/E 30.69 (Ind SEMIQ P/E 13.46) Ctry US

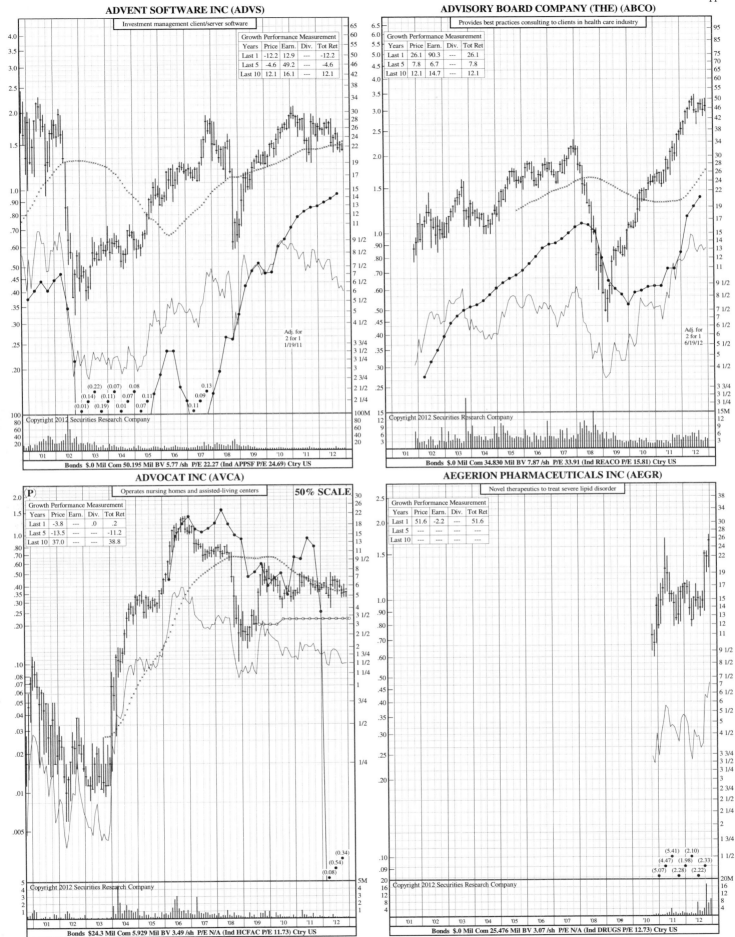

ADVENT SOFTWARE INC (ADVS)

Investment management client/server software

Growth Performance Measurement				
Years	Price	Earn.	Div.	Tot Ret
Last 1	-12.2	12.9	---	-12.2
Last 5	-4.6	49.2	---	-4.6
Last 10	12.1	16.1	---	12.1

(0.22) (0.07) 0.08
(0.14) (0.11) 0.07   0.13
(0.01) (0.19) 0.07 0.09
        0.07 0.11 0.11

Adj. for
2 for 1
1/19/11

Copyright 2012 Securities Research Company

Bonds $.0 Mil Com 50.195 Mil BV 5.77 /sh P/E 22.27 (Ind APPSF P/E 24.69) Ctry US

ADVISORY BOARD COMPANY (THE) (ABCO)

Provides best practices consulting to clients in health care industry

Growth Performance Measurement				
Years	Price	Earn.	Div.	Tot Ret
Last 1	26.1	90.3	---	26.1
Last 5	7.8	6.7	---	7.8
Last 10	12.1	14.7	---	12.1

Adj. for
2 for 1
6/19/12

Copyright 2012 Securities Research Company

Bonds $.0 Mil Com 34.830 Mil BV 7.87 /sh P/E 33.91 (Ind REACO P/E 15.81) Ctry US

ADVOCAT INC (AVCA)

(P)

Operates nursing homes and assisted-living centers

50% SCALE

Growth Performance Measurement				
Years	Price	Earn.	Div.	Tot Ret
Last 1	-3.8	---	.0	.2
Last 5	-13.5	---	---	-11.2
Last 10	37.0	---	---	38.8

(0.34)
(0.54)
(0.08)

Copyright 2012 Securities Research Company

Bonds $24.3 Mil Com 5.929 Mil BV 3.49 /sh P/E N/A (Ind HCFAC P/E 11.73) Ctry US

AEGERION PHARMACEUTICALS INC (AEGR)

Novel therapeutics to treat severe lipid disorder

Growth Performance Measurement				
Years	Price	Earn.	Div.	Tot Ret
Last 1	51.6	-2.2	---	51.6
Last 5	---	---	---	---
Last 10	---	---	---	---

(5.41) (2.10)
(4.47) (1.98) (2.33)
(5.07) (2.28) (2.22)

Copyright 2012 Securities Research Company

Bonds $.0 Mil Com 25.476 Mil BV 3.07 /sh P/E N/A (Ind DRUGS P/E 12.73) Ctry US

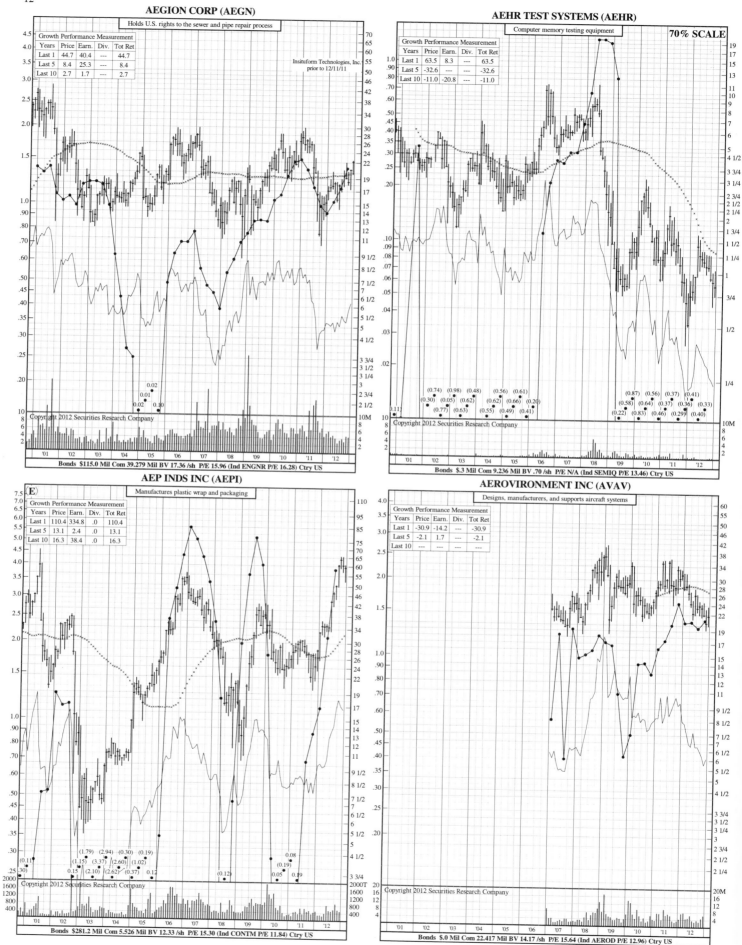

12

AEGION CORP (AEGN)

Holds U.S. rights to the sewer and pipe repair process

Insituform Technologies, Inc. prior to 12/11/11

Growth Performance Measurement				
Years	Price	Earn.	Div.	Tot Ret
Last 1	44.7	40.4	---	44.7
Last 5	8.4	25.3	---	8.4
Last 10	2.7	1.7	---	2.7

0.02
0.01
0.02 0.10

Copyright 2012 Securities Research Company

Bonds $115.0 Mil Com 39.279 Mil BV 17.36 /sh P/E 15.96 (Ind ENGNR P/E 16.28) Ctry US

AEHR TEST SYSTEMS (AEHR)

Computer memory testing equipment

70% SCALE

Growth Performance Measurement				
Years	Price	Earn.	Div.	Tot Ret
Last 1	63.5	8.3	---	63.5
Last 5	-32.6	---	---	-32.6
Last 10	-11.0	-20.8	---	-11.0

0.11

(0.74) (0.98) (0.48)   (0.56) (0.61)
(0.30) (0.05) (0.62)   (0.62) (0.66) (0.20)
    (0.77) (0.63)   (0.55) (0.49) (0.41)

(0.87) (0.56) (0.37) (0.41)
(0.58) (0.64) (0.37) (0.36) (0.33)
(0.22) (0.83) (0.46) (0.29) (0.40)

Copyright 2012 Securities Research Company

Bonds $.3 Mil Com 9.236 Mil BV .70 /sh P/E N/A (Ind SEMIQ P/E 13.46) Ctry US

AEP INDS INC (AEPI)

(E)

Manufactures plastic wrap and packaging

Growth Performance Measurement				
Years	Price	Earn.	Div.	Tot Ret
Last 1	110.4	334.8	.0	110.4
Last 5	13.1	2.4	.0	13.1
Last 10	16.3	38.4	.0	16.3

(0.11)
(0.30)

(1.79) (2.94) (0.30) (0.19)
(1.15) (3.37) (2.60) (1.02)
0.15 (2.10) (2.62) (0.37) 0.12

0.08
0.19
(0.12)   0.05 0.19

Copyright 2012 Securities Research Company

Bonds $281.2 Mil Com 5.526 Mil BV 12.33 /sh P/E 15.30 (Ind CONTM P/E 11.84) Ctry US

AEROVIRONMENT INC (AVAV)

Designs, manufacturers, and supports aircraft systems

Growth Performance Measurement				
Years	Price	Earn.	Div.	Tot Ret
Last 1	-30.9	-14.2	---	-30.9
Last 5	-2.1	1.7	---	-2.1
Last 10	---	---	---	---

Copyright 2012 Securities Research Company

Bonds $.0 Mil Com 22.417 Mil BV 14.17 /sh P/E 15.64 (Ind AEROD P/E 12.96) Ctry US

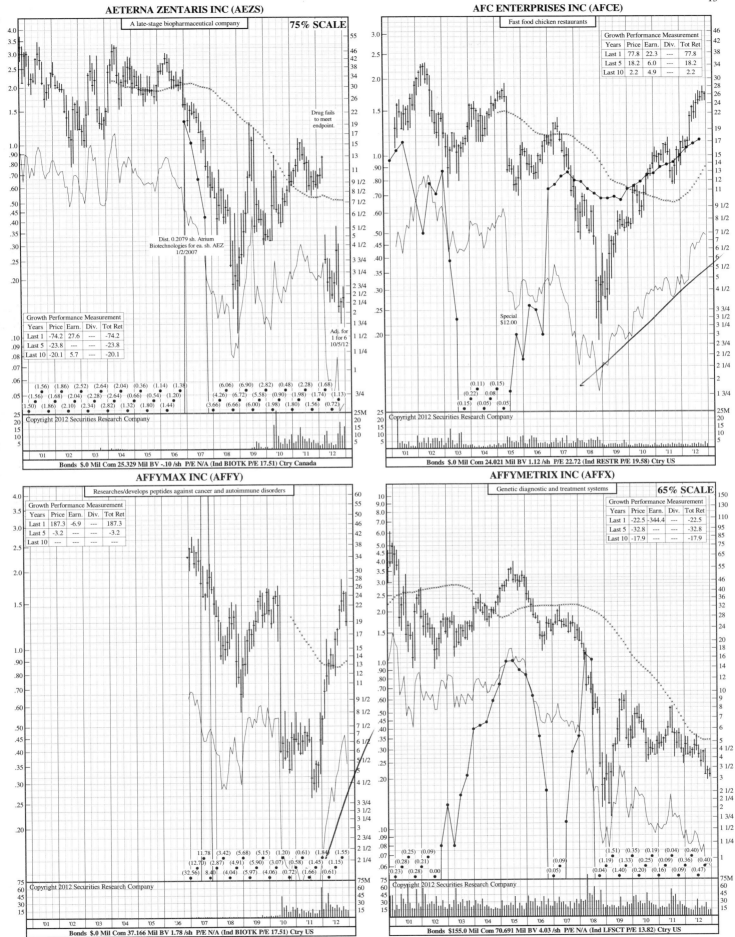

AETERNA ZENTARIS INC (AEZS)

A late-stage biopharmaceutical company

75% SCALE

Drug fails to meet endpoint.

Dist. 0.2079 sh. Atrium Biotechnologies for ea. sh. AEZ 1/2/2007

Adj. for 1 for 6 10/5/12

Growth Performance Measurement				
Years	Price	Earn.	Div.	Tot Ret
Last 1	-74.2	27.6	---	-74.2
Last 5	-23.8	---	---	-23.8
Last 10	-20.1	5.7	---	-20.1

(1.56) (1.86) (2.52) (2.64) (2.04) (0.36) (1.14) 1.38
(1.56) (1.68) (2.04) (2.28) (2.64) (0.66) (0.54) (1.20)
(1.50) (1.86) (2.10) (2.34) (2.82) (1.32) (1.80) (1.44)

(6.06) (6.90) (2.82) (0.48) (2.28) (1.68)
(4.26) (6.72) (5.58) (0.90) (1.98) (1.74) (1.13)
(3.66) (6.66) (6.00) (1.98) (1.80) (1.56) (0.72)

Copyright 2012 Securities Research Company

'01 '02 '03 '04 '05 '06 '07 '08 '09 '10 '11 '12

Bonds $.0 Mil Com 25.329 Mil BV -.10 /sh P/E N/A (Ind BIOTK P/E 17.51) Ctry Canada

AFC ENTERPRISES INC (AFCE)

Fast food chicken restaurants

Growth Performance Measurement				
Years	Price	Earn.	Div.	Tot Ret
Last 1	77.8	22.3	---	77.8
Last 5	18.2	6.0	---	18.2
Last 10	2.2	4.9	---	2.2

Special $12.00

(0.11) (0.15)
(0.22) 0.08
(0.15) (0.05) (0.05)

Copyright 2012 Securities Research Company

'01 '02 '03 '04 '05 '06 '07 '08 '09 '10 '11 '12

Bonds $.0 Mil Com 24.021 Mil BV 1.12 /sh P/E 22.72 (Ind RESTR P/E 19.58) Ctry US

AFFYMAX INC (AFFY)

Researches/develops peptides against cancer and autoimmune disorders

Growth Performance Measurement				
Years	Price	Earn.	Div.	Tot Ret
Last 1	187.3	-6.9	---	187.3
Last 5	-3.2	---	---	-3.2
Last 10	---	---	---	---

11.78 (3.42) (5.68) (5.15) (1.20) (0.61) 1.84 (1.55)
(12.70) (2.87) (4.91) (5.90) (3.07) (0.58) (1.45) (1.15)
(32.56) 8.40 (4.04) (5.97) (4.06) (0.72) (1.66) (0.61)

Copyright 2012 Securities Research Company

'01 '02 '03 '04 '05 '06 '07 '08 '09 '10 '11 '12

Bonds $.0 Mil Com 37.166 Mil BV 1.78 /sh P/E N/A (Ind BIOTK P/E 17.51) Ctry US

AFFYMETRIX INC (AFFX)

Genetic diagnostic and treatment systems

65% SCALE

Growth Performance Measurement				
Years	Price	Earn.	Div.	Tot Ret
Last 1	-22.5	-344.4	---	-22.5
Last 5	-32.8	---	---	-32.8
Last 10	-17.9	---	---	-17.9

(0.25) (0.09)
(0.28) (0.21)
(0.23) (0.28) 0.00

(0.09)
(0.05)

(1.51) (0.35) (0.19) (0.04) (0.40)
(1.19) (1.33) (0.25) (0.09) (0.36) (0.40)
(0.04) (1.40) (0.20) (0.16) (0.09) (0.47)

Copyright 2012 Securities Research Company

'01 '02 '03 '04 '05 '06 '07 '08 '09 '10 '11 '12

Bonds $155.0 Mil Com 70.691 Mil BV 4.03 /sh P/E N/A (Ind LFSCT P/E 13.82) Ctry US

14

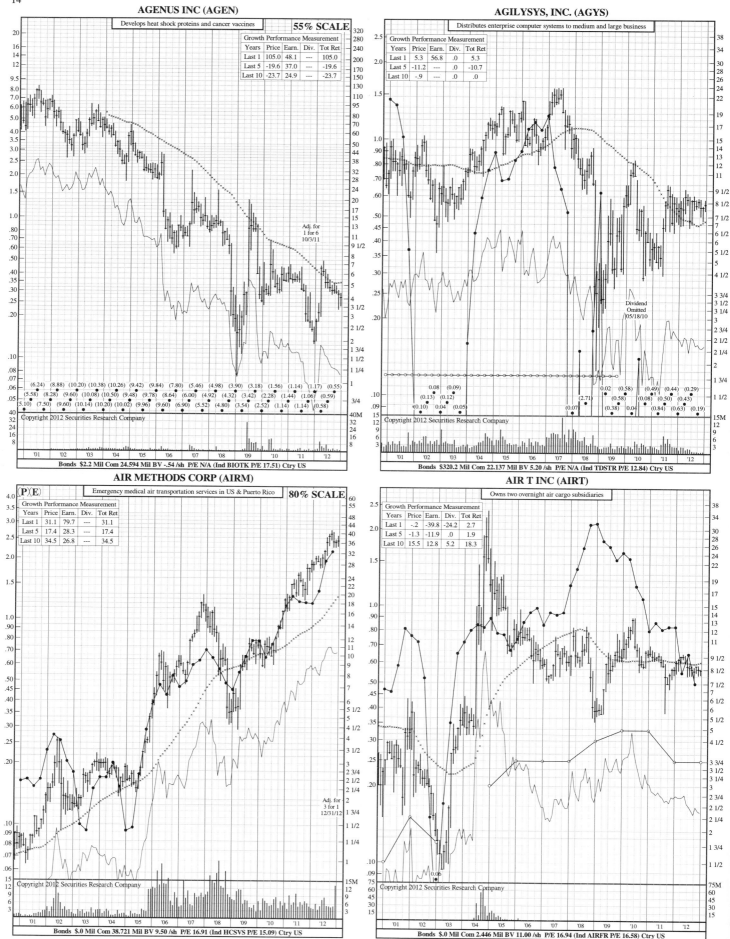

AGENUS INC (AGEN)

Develops heat shock proteins and cancer vaccines

55% SCALE

Growth Performance Measurement				
Years	Price	Earn.	Div.	Tot Ret
Last 1	105.0	48.1	---	105.0
Last 5	-19.6	37.0	---	-19.6
Last 10	-23.7	24.9	---	-23.7

Adj. for
1 for 6
10/3/11

(6.24) (8.88) (10.20) (10.38) (10.26) (9.42) (9.84) (7.80) (5.46) (4.98) (3.90) (3.18) (1.56) (1.14) (1.17) (0.55)
(5.58) (8.28) (9.60) (10.08) (10.50) (9.48) (9.78) (8.64) (6.00) (4.92) (4.32) (3.42) (2.28) (1.44) (1.06) (0.59)
(5.10) (7.50) (9.60) (10.14) (10.20) (10.02) (9.96) (9.60) (6.90) (5.52) (4.80) (3.54) (2.52) (1.14) (1.14) (0.58)

Copyright 2012 Securities Research Company

'01 '02 '03 '04 '05 '06 '07 '08 '09 '10 '11 '12

Bonds $2.2 Mil Com 24.594 Mil BV -.54 /sh P/E N/A (Ind BIOTK P/E 17.51) Ctry US

AGILYSYS, INC. (AGYS)

Distributes enterprise computer systems to medium and large business

Growth Performance Measurement				
Years	Price	Earn.	Div.	Tot Ret
Last 1	5.3	56.8	.0	5.3
Last 5	-11.2	---	.0	-10.7
Last 10	-.9	---	.0	.0

Dividend
Omitted
05/18/10

0.08 (0.09)
(0.13) (0.12) 0.02 (0.58) (0.49) (0.44) (0.29)
(0.10) 0.04 (0.05) (2.71) (0.58) (0.08) (0.50) (0.43)
0.07 (0.38) 0.04 (0.84) (0.63) (0.19)

Copyright 2012 Securities Research Company

'01 '02 '03 '04 '05 '06 '07 '08 '09 '10 '11 '12

Bonds $320.2 Mil Com 22.137 Mil BV 5.20 /sh P/E N/A (Ind TDSTR P/E 12.84) Ctry US

(P/E) **AIR METHODS CORP (AIRM)**

Emergency medical air transportation services in US & Puerto Rico

80% SCALE

Growth Performance Measurement				
Years	Price	Earn.	Div.	Tot Ret
Last 1	31.1	79.7	---	31.1
Last 5	17.4	28.3	---	17.4
Last 10	34.5	26.8	---	34.5

Adj. for
3 for 1
12/31/12

Copyright 2012 Securities Research Company

'01 '02 '03 '04 '05 '06 '07 '08 '09 '10 '11 '12

Bonds $.0 Mil Com 38.721 Mil BV 9.50 /sh P/E 16.91 (Ind HCSVS P/E 15.09) Ctry US

AIR T INC (AIRT)

Owns two overnight air cargo subsidiaries

Growth Performance Measurement				
Years	Price	Earn.	Div.	Tot Ret
Last 1	-.2	-39.8	-24.2	2.7
Last 5	-1.3	-11.9	.0	1.9
Last 10	15.5	12.8	5.2	18.3

0.06

Copyright 2012 Securities Research Company

'01 '02 '03 '04 '05 '06 '07 '08 '09 '10 '11 '12

Bonds $.0 Mil Com 2.446 Mil BV 11.00 /sh P/E 16.94 (Ind AIRFR P/E 16.58) Ctry US

AKAMAI TECHNOLOGIES INC (AKAM)

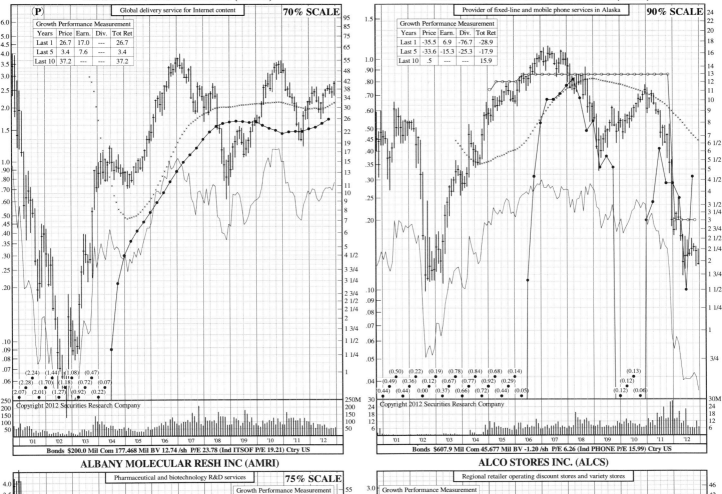

(P) Global delivery service for Internet content — **70% SCALE**

Growth Performance Measurement				
Years	Price	Earn.	Div.	Tot Ret
Last 1	26.7	17.0	---	26.7
Last 5	3.4	7.6	---	3.4
Last 10	37.2	---	---	37.2

(2.24) (1.44) (1.08) (0.47)
(2.28) (1.70) (1.18) (0.72) (0.07)
(2.07) (2.01) (1.27) (0.92) (0.22)

Copyright 2012 Securities Research Company

Bonds $200.0 Mil Com 177.468 Mil BV 12.74 /sh P/E 23.78 (Ind ITSOF P/E 19.21) Ctry US

ALASKA COMMUNICATIONS SYS GR (ALSK)

Provider of fixed-line and mobile phone services in Alaska — **90% SCALE**

Growth Performance Measurement				
Years	Price	Earn.	Div.	Tot Ret
Last 1	-35.5	6.9	-76.7	-28.9
Last 5	-33.6	-15.3	-25.3	-17.9
Last 10	.5	---	---	15.9

(0.50) (0.22) (0.19) (0.78) (0.84) (0.68) (0.14)   (0.13)
(0.49) (0.36) (0.12) (0.67) (0.77) (0.92) (0.29)   (0.12)
(0.44) (0.44) (0.00) (0.37) (0.66) (0.72) (0.44) (0.05)   (0.12) (0.06)

Copyright 2012 Securities Research Company

Bonds $607.9 Mil Com 45.677 Mil BV -1.20 /sh P/E 6.26 (Ind PHONE P/E 15.99) Ctry US

ALBANY MOLECULAR RESH INC (AMRI)

Pharmaceutical and biotechnology R&D services — **75% SCALE**

Growth Performance Measurement				
Years	Price	Earn.	Div.	Tot Ret
Last 1	80.2	66.7	---	80.2
Last 5	-18.2	---	---	-18.2
Last 10	-9.8	---	---	-9.8

0.00 (0.24) (0.42) (0.13)
(0.01) (0.20) (0.39) (0.30)
0.03 (0.10) (0.32) (0.38)

Copyright 2012 Securities Research Company

Bonds $.2 Mil Com 30.924 Mil BV 6.65 /sh P/E N/A (Ind LFSCT P/E 13.82) Ctry US

ALCO STORES INC. (ALCS)

Regional retailer operating discount stores and variety stores

Growth Performance Measurement				
Years	Price	Earn.	Div.	Tot Ret
Last 1	13.0	-54.3	---	13.0
Last 5	-22.0	-28.1	---	-22.0
Last 10	-1.5	-19.0	---	-1.5

Duckwall-Alco Stores, Inc.
prior to 7/5/12

(0.46)   (1.13)
(0.64) (0.83)   (0.94) (0.49)
(0.06) (0.39)   (0.81) (1.16)

Copyright 2012 Securities Research Company

Bonds $27.9 Mil Com 3.258 Mil BV 25.83 /sh P/E 58.85 (Ind RTGEN P/E 13.91) Ctry US

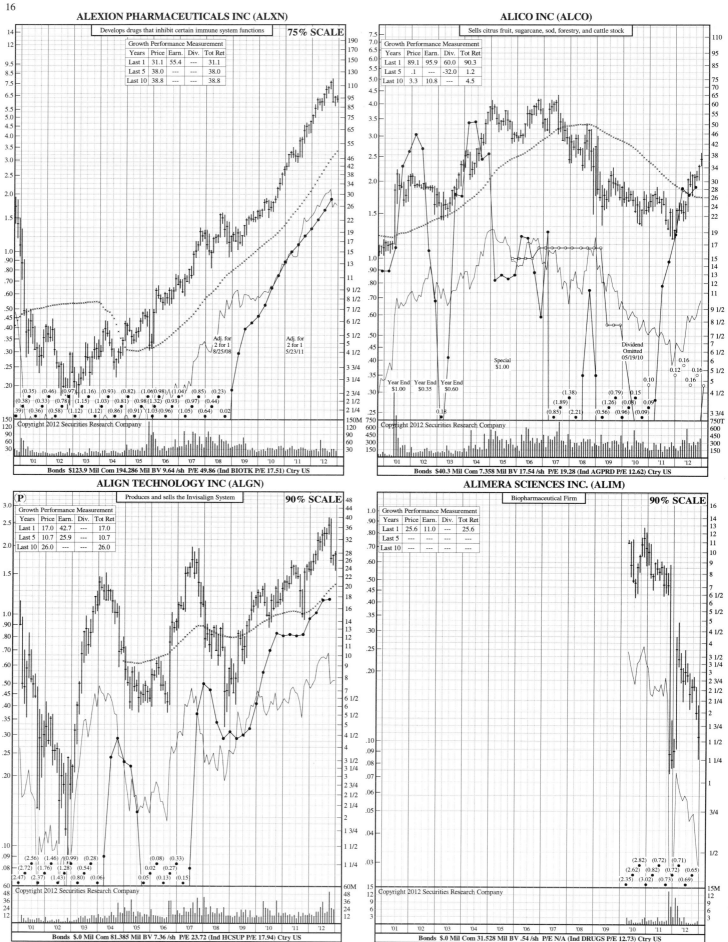

ALKERMES PLC (ALKS)

Therapeutics and drug delivery systems

Growth Performance Measurement				
Years	Price	Earn.	Div.	Tot Ret
Last 1	6.7	---	---	6.7
Last 5	3.5	12.1	---	3.5
Last 10	11.4	---	---	11.4

(0.69) (0.96) (1.29) (1.32) (1.07) (0.71) (0.17) 0.02   (0.01) (0.27) (0.32) (0.46) (0.37)
(0.43) (0.83) (1.37) (1.42) (1.22) (0.83) (0.29) 0.10 0.03   0.05 (0.22) (0.20) (0.44) (0.41)
(0.90) (0.72) (1.16) (1.31) (1.35) (0.92) (0.57) 0.03 0.04   0.10 (0.15) (0.22) (0.35) (0.37) (0.25)

Copyright 2012 Securities Research Company

Bonds $222.8 Mil Com 131.930 Mil BV 7.22 /sh P/E 47.49 (Ind BIOTK P/E 17.51) Ctry US

ALLEGIANT TRAVEL CO (ALGT)

Travel agency

Growth Performance Measurement				
Years	Price	Earn.	Div.	Tot Ret
Last 1	37.6	31.4	---	37.6
Last 5	18.0	21.0	---	18.0
Last 10	---	---	---	---

Copyright 2012 Securities Research Company

Bonds $.0 Mil Com 19.290 Mil BV 21.94 /sh P/E 21.16 (Ind ARLNS P/E 18.30) Ctry US

ALLIANCE FINANCIAL CORP NY (ALNC)

Bank holding company

Growth Performance Measurement				
Years	Price	Earn.	Div.	Tot Ret
Last 1	40.9	-15.1	3.2	44.9
Last 5	10.8	4.4	7.8	13.6
Last 10	4.8	1.6	4.8	7.0

Bridge Street Financial
acquired 10/6/06

Copyright 2012 Securities Research Company

Bonds $205.4 Mil Com 4.782 Mil BV 30.95 /sh P/E 18.36 (Ind RBANK P/E 10.51) Ctry US

ALLIANCE HOLDINGS GP LP (AHGP)

Production and marketing of coal to utilities and industrial users

Growth Performance Measurement				
Years	Price	Earn.	Div.	Tot Ret
Last 1	-8.5	5.4	18.0	-3.2
Last 5	14.9	19.4	22.1	19.4
Last 10	---	---	---	---

Copyright 2012 Securities Research Company

Bonds $.0 Mil Com 59.863 Mil BV 7.05 /sh P/E 12.89 (Ind COCOF P/E 16.47) Ctry US

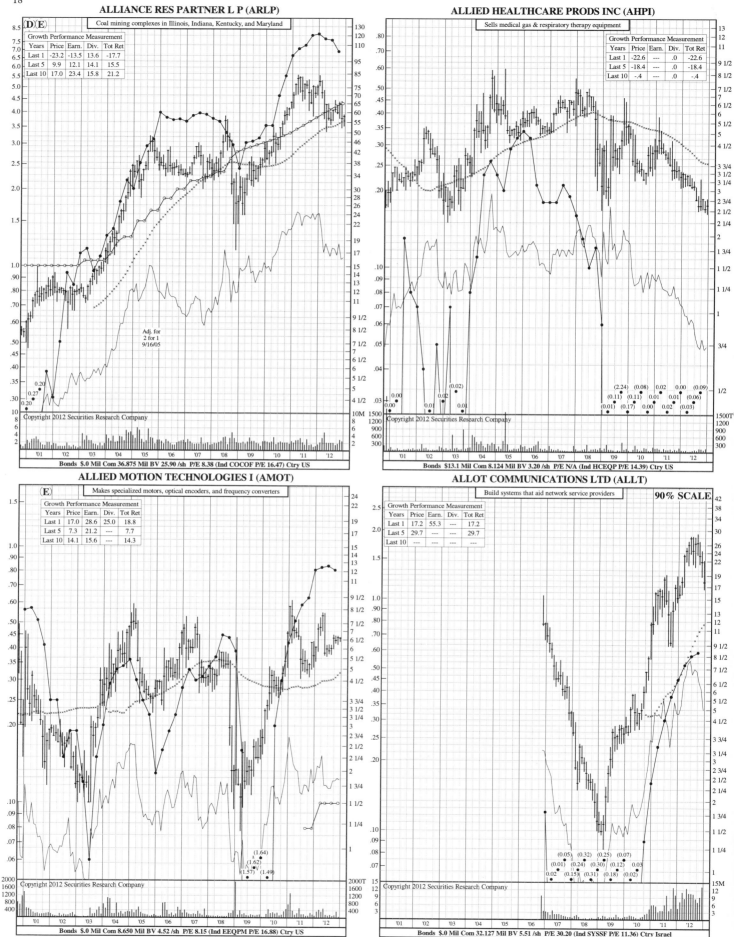

18

ALLIANCE RES PARTNER L P (ARLP)
Coal mining complexes in Illinois, Indiana, Kentucky, and Maryland

(D)(E)

Growth Performance Measurement

Years	Price	Earn.	Div.	Tot Ret
Last 1	-23.2	-13.5	13.6	-17.7
Last 5	9.9	12.1	14.1	15.5
Last 10	17.0	23.4	15.8	21.2

Adj. for
2 for 1
9/16/05

0.20
0.27
0.20

Copyright 2012 Securities Research Company

'01 '02 '03 '04 '05 '06 '07 '08 '09 '10 '11 '12

Bonds $.0 Mil Com 36.875 Mil BV 25.90 /sh P/E 8.38 (Ind COCOF P/E 16.47) Ctry US

ALLIED HEALTHCARE PRODS INC (AHPI)
Sells medical gas & respiratory therapy equipment

Growth Performance Measurement

Years	Price	Earn.	Div.	Tot Ret
Last 1	-22.6	---	.0	-22.6
Last 5	-18.4	---	.0	-18.4
Last 10	-.4	---	.0	-.4

0.00
0.00

0.01
0.02

(0.02)
0.01

(2.24) (0.08) 0.02 0.00 (0.09)
(0.11) (0.11) 0.01 0.01 (0.06)
(0.01) (0.17) 0.00 0.02 (0.03)

Copyright 2012 Securities Research Company

'01 '02 '03 '04 '05 '06 '07 '08 '09 '10 '11 '12

Bonds $13.1 Mil Com 8.124 Mil BV 3.20 /sh P/E N/A (Ind HCEQP P/E 14.39) Ctry US

ALLIED MOTION TECHNOLOGIES I (AMOT)
Makes specialized motors, optical encoders, and frequency converters

(E)

Growth Performance Measurement

Years	Price	Earn.	Div.	Tot Ret
Last 1	17.0	28.6	25.0	18.8
Last 5	7.3	21.2	---	7.7
Last 10	14.1	15.6	---	14.3

(1.64)
(1.62)
(1.57) (1.49)

Copyright 2012 Securities Research Company

'01 '02 '03 '04 '05 '06 '07 '08 '09 '10 '11 '12

Bonds $.0 Mil Com 8.650 Mil BV 4.52 /sh P/E 8.15 (Ind EEQPM P/E 16.88) Ctry US

ALLOT COMMUNICATIONS LTD (ALLT)
Build systems that aid network service providers

90% SCALE

Growth Performance Measurement

Years	Price	Earn.	Div.	Tot Ret
Last 1	17.2	55.3	---	17.2
Last 5	29.7	---	---	29.7
Last 10	---	---	---	---

(0.05) (0.32) (0.25) (0.07)
(0.01) (0.24) (0.30) (0.12) 0.03
0.02 (0.15) (0.31) (0.18) (0.02)

Copyright 2012 Securities Research Company

'01 '02 '03 '04 '05 '06 '07 '08 '09 '10 '11 '12

Bonds $.0 Mil Com 32.127 Mil BV 5.51 /sh P/E 30.20 (Ind SYSSF P/E 11.36) Ctry Israel

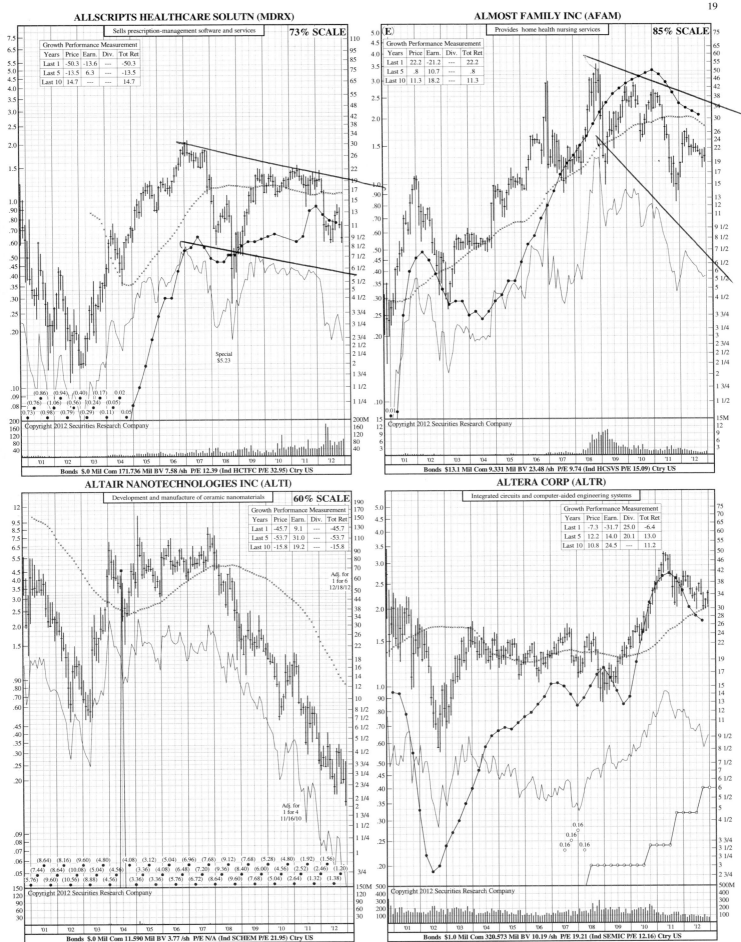

ALLSCRIPTS HEALTHCARE SOLUTN (MDRX)

Sells prescription-management software and services

73% SCALE

Growth Performance Measurement				
Years	Price	Earn.	Div.	Tot Ret
Last 1	-50.3	-13.6	---	-50.3
Last 5	-13.5	6.3	---	-13.5
Last 10	14.7	---	---	14.7

Special $5.23

(0.86) (0.94) (0.40) (0.17) 0.02
(0.76) (1.06) (0.56) (0.24) (0.05)
(0.73) (0.98) (0.79) (0.29) (0.11) 0.05

Copyright 2012 Securities Research Company

Bonds $.0 Mil Com 171.736 Mil BV 7.58 /sh P/E 12.39 (Ind HCTFC P/E 32.95) Ctry US

ALMOST FAMILY INC (AFAM)

(E) Provides home health nursing services

85% SCALE

Growth Performance Measurement				
Years	Price	Earn.	Div.	Tot Ret
Last 1	22.2	-21.2	---	22.2
Last 5	.8	10.7	---	.8
Last 10	11.3	18.2	---	11.3

0.01

Copyright 2012 Securities Research Company

Bonds $13.1 Mil Com 9.331 Mil BV 23.48 /sh P/E 9.74 (Ind HCSVS P/E 15.09) Ctry US

ALTAIR NANOTECHNOLOGIES INC (ALTI)

Development and manufacture of ceramic nanomaterials

60% SCALE

Growth Performance Measurement				
Years	Price	Earn.	Div.	Tot Ret
Last 1	-45.7	9.1	---	-45.7
Last 5	-53.7	31.0	---	-53.7
Last 10	-15.8	19.2	---	-15.8

Adj. for
1 for 6
12/18/12

Adj. for
1 for 4
11/16/10

(8.64) (8.16) (9.60) (4.80) (4.08) (3.12) (5.04) (6.96) (7.68) (9.12) (7.68) (5.28) (4.80) (1.92) (1.56)
(7.44) (8.64) (10.08) (5.04) (4.56) (3.36) (4.08) (6.48) (7.20) (9.36) (8.40) (6.00) (4.56) (2.52) (2.46) (1.20)
(5.76) (9.60) (10.56) (8.88) (4.56) (3.36) (3.36) (5.76) (6.72) (8.64) (9.60) (7.68) (5.04) (2.64) (1.32) (1.38)

Copyright 2012 Securities Research Company

Bonds $.0 Mil Com 11.590 Mil BV 3.77 /sh P/E N/A (Ind SCHEM P/E 21.95) Ctry US

ALTERA CORP (ALTR)

Integrated circuits and computer-aided engineering systems

Growth Performance Measurement				
Years	Price	Earn.	Div.	Tot Ret
Last 1	-7.3	-31.7	25.0	-6.4
Last 5	12.2	14.0	20.1	13.0
Last 10	10.8	24.5	---	11.2

0.16
0.16 0.16
0.16 0.16

Copyright 2012 Securities Research Company

Bonds $1.0 Mil Com 320.573 Mil BV 10.19 /sh P/E 19.21 (Ind SEMIC P/E 12.16) Ctry US

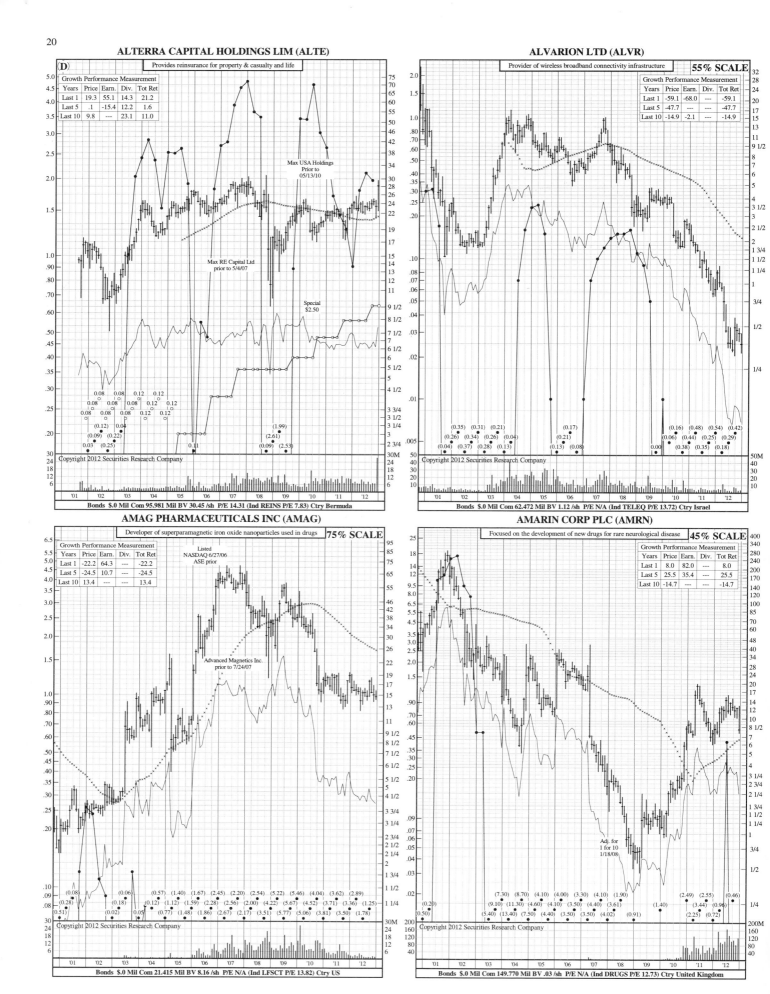

ALTERRA CAPITAL HOLDINGS LIM (ALTE)

Provides reinsurance for property & casualty and life

(D)

Growth Performance Measurement

Years	Price	Earn.	Div.	Tot Ret
Last 1	19.3	55.1	14.3	21.2
Last 5	.1	-15.4	12.2	1.6
Last 10	9.8	---	23.1	11.0

Max USA Holdings Prior to 05/13/10

Max RE Capital Ltd prior to 5/4/07

Special $2.50

Copyright 2012 Securities Research Company

Bonds $.0 Mil Com 95.981 Mil BV 30.45 /sh P/E 14.31 (Ind REINS P/E 7.83) Ctry Bermuda

ALVARION LTD (ALVR)

Provider of wireless broadband connectivity infrastructure

55% SCALE

Growth Performance Measurement

Years	Price	Earn.	Div.	Tot Ret
Last 1	-59.1	-68.0	---	-59.1
Last 5	-47.7	---	---	-47.7
Last 10	-14.9	-2.1	---	-14.9

Copyright 2012 Securities Research Company

Bonds $.0 Mil Com 62.472 Mil BV 1.12 /sh P/E N/A (Ind TELEQ P/E 13.72) Ctry Israel

AMAG PHARMACEUTICALS INC (AMAG)

Developer of superparamagnetic iron oxide nanoparticles used in drugs

75% SCALE

Growth Performance Measurement

Years	Price	Earn.	Div.	Tot Ret
Last 1	-22.2	64.3	---	-22.2
Last 5	-24.5	10.7	---	-24.5
Last 10	13.4	---	---	13.4

Listed NASDAQ 6/27/06 ASE prior

Advanced Magnetics Inc. prior to 7/24/07

Copyright 2012 Securities Research Company

Bonds $.0 Mil Com 21.415 Mil BV 8.16 /sh P/E N/A (Ind LFSCT P/E 13.82) Ctry US

AMARIN CORP PLC (AMRN)

Focused on the development of new drugs for rare neurological disease

45% SCALE

Growth Performance Measurement

Years	Price	Earn.	Div.	Tot Ret
Last 1	8.0	82.0	---	8.0
Last 5	25.5	35.4	---	25.5
Last 10	-14.7	---	---	-14.7

Adj. for 1 for 10 1/18/08

Copyright 2012 Securities Research Company

Bonds $.0 Mil Com 149.770 Mil BV .03 /sh P/E N/A (Ind DRUGS P/E 12.73) Ctry United Kingdom

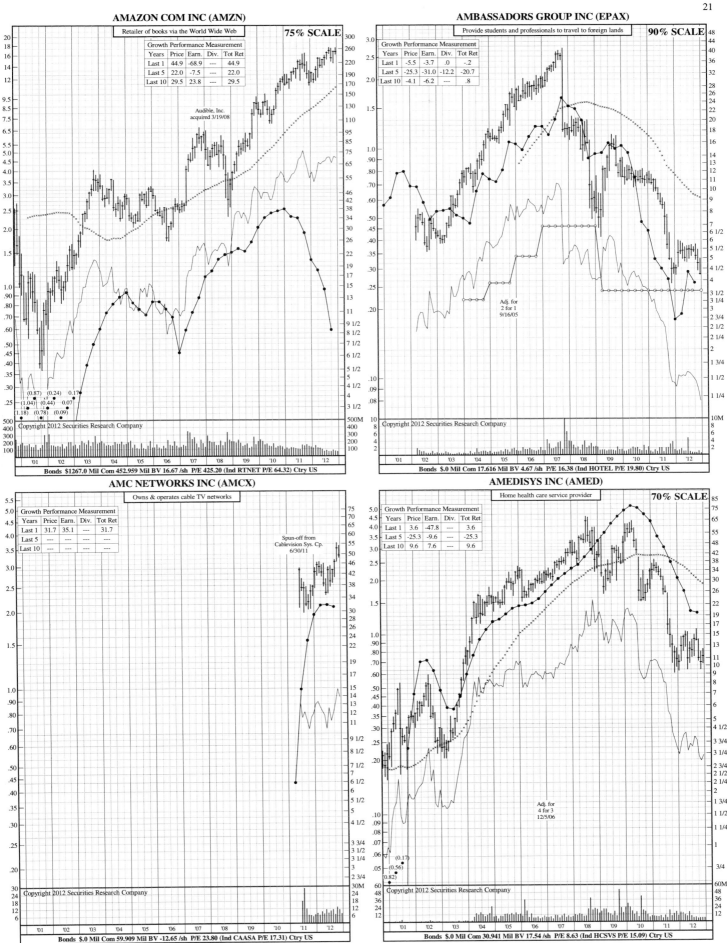

21

AMAZON COM INC (AMZN)

Retailer of books via the World Wide Web

75% SCALE

Growth Performance Measurement

Years	Price	Earn.	Div.	Tot Ret
Last 1	44.9	-68.9	---	44.9
Last 5	22.0	-7.5	---	22.0
Last 10	29.5	23.8	---	29.5

Audible, Inc.
acquired 3/19/08

(0.87) (0.24) 0.17
(1.04) (0.44) 0.07
(1.18) (0.78) 0.09

Copyright 2012 Securities Research Company

Bonds $1267.0 Mil Com 452.959 Mil BV 16.67 /sh P/E 425.20 (Ind RTNET P/E 64.32) Ctry US

AMBASSADORS GROUP INC (EPAX)

Provide students and professionals to travel to foreign lands

90% SCALE

Growth Performance Measurement

Years	Price	Earn.	Div.	Tot Ret
Last 1	-5.5	-3.7	.0	-.2
Last 5	-25.3	-31.0	-12.2	-20.7
Last 10	-4.1	-6.2	---	.8

Adj. for
2 for 1
9/16/05

Copyright 2012 Securities Research Company

Bonds $.0 Mil Com 17.616 Mil BV 4.67 /sh P/E 16.38 (Ind HOTEL P/E 19.80) Ctry US

AMC NETWORKS INC (AMCX)

Owns & operates cable TV networks

Growth Performance Measurement

Years	Price	Earn.	Div.	Tot Ret
Last 1	31.7	35.1	---	31.7
Last 5	---	---	---	---
Last 10	---	---	---	---

Spun-off from
Cablevision Sys. Cp.
6/30/11

Copyright 2012 Securities Research Company

Bonds $.0 Mil Com 59.909 Mil BV -12.65 /sh P/E 23.80 (Ind CAASA P/E 17.31) Ctry US

AMEDISYS INC (AMED)

Home health care service provider

70% SCALE

Growth Performance Measurement

Years	Price	Earn.	Div.	Tot Ret
Last 1	3.6	-47.8	---	3.6
Last 5	-25.3	-9.6	---	-25.3
Last 10	9.6	7.6	---	9.6

Adj. for
4 for 3
12/5/06

(0.17)
(0.56)
(0.82)

Copyright 2012 Securities Research Company

Bonds $.0 Mil Com 30.941 Mil BV 17.54 /sh P/E 8.63 (Ind HCSVS P/E 15.09) Ctry US

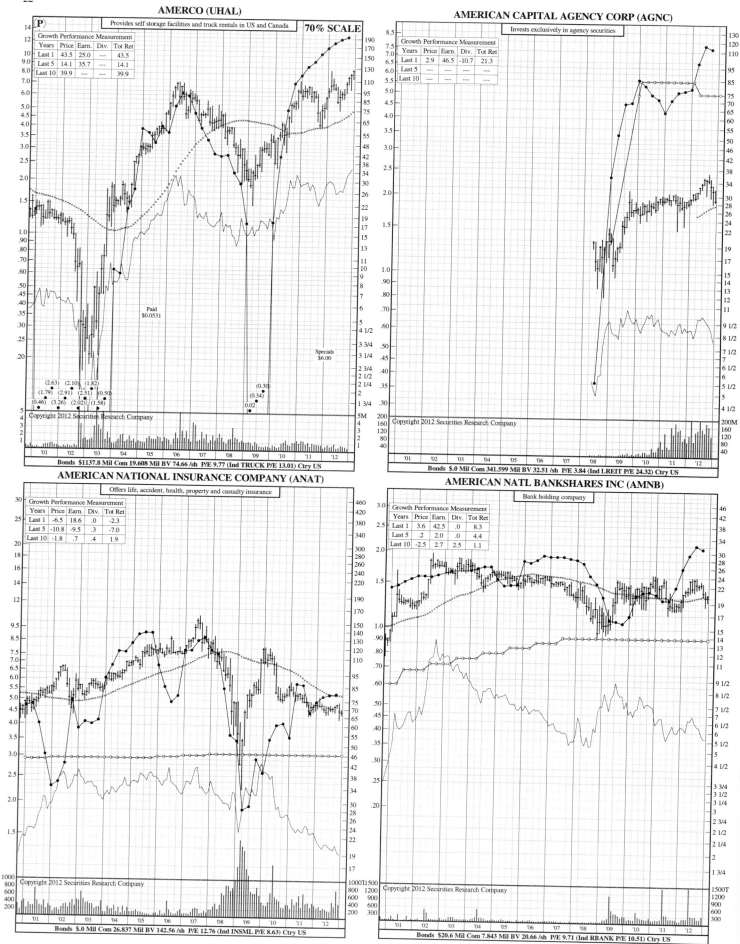

22

AMERCO (UHAL)

Provides self storage facilities and truck rentals in US and Canada

70% SCALE

Growth Performance Measurement				
Years	Price	Earn.	Div.	Tot Ret
Last 1	43.5	25.0	---	43.5
Last 5	14.1	35.7	---	14.1
Last 10	39.9	---	---	39.9

Paid
$0.0531

Specials
$6.00

(2.63) (2.10) (1.82)
(1.79) (2.91) (2.51) (0.50)
(0.46) (3.26) (2.02) (1.58)

(0.30)
(0.34)
0.02

Copyright 2012 Securities Research Company

Bonds $1137.8 Mil Com 19.608 Mil BV 74.66 /sh P/E 9.77 (Ind TRUCK P/E 13.01) Ctry US

AMERICAN CAPITAL AGENCY CORP (AGNC)

Invests exclusively in agency securities

Growth Performance Measurement				
Years	Price	Earn.	Div.	Tot Ret
Last 1	2.9	46.5	-10.7	21.3
Last 5	---	---	---	---
Last 10	---	---	---	---

Copyright 2012 Securities Research Company

Bonds $.0 Mil Com 341.599 Mil BV 32.51 /sh P/E 3.84 (Ind LREIT P/E 24.32) Ctry US

AMERICAN NATIONAL INSURANCE COMPANY (ANAT)

Offers life, accident, health, property and casualty insurance

Growth Performance Measurement				
Years	Price	Earn.	Div.	Tot Ret
Last 1	-6.5	18.6	.0	-2.3
Last 5	-10.8	-9.5	.3	-7.0
Last 10	-1.8	.7	.4	1.9

Copyright 2012 Securities Research Company

Bonds $.0 Mil Com 26.837 Mil BV 142.56 /sh P/E 12.76 (Ind INSML P/E 8.63) Ctry US

AMERICAN NATL BANKSHARES INC (AMNB)

Bank holding company

Growth Performance Measurement				
Years	Price	Earn.	Div.	Tot Ret
Last 1	3.6	42.5	.0	8.3
Last 5	.2	2.0	.0	4.4
Last 10	-2.5	2.7	2.5	1.1

Copyright 2012 Securities Research Company

Bonds $20.6 Mil Com 7.843 Mil BV 20.66 /sh P/E 9.71 (Ind RBANK P/E 10.51) Ctry US

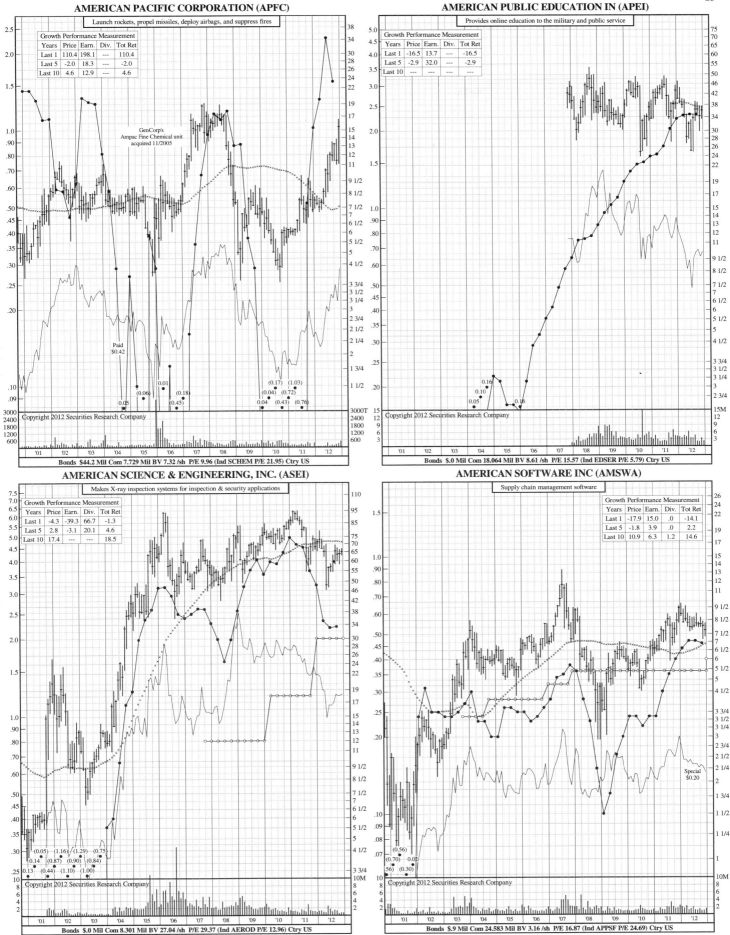

AMERICAN PACIFIC CORPORATION (APFC)

Launch rockets, propel missiles, deploy airbags, and suppress fires

Growth Performance Measurement				
Years	Price	Earn.	Div.	Tot Ret
Last 1	110.4	198.1	---	110.4
Last 5	-2.0	18.3	---	-2.0
Last 10	4.6	12.9	---	4.6

GenCorp's
Ampac Fine Chemical unit
acquired 11/2005

Paid
$0.42

(0.01)
(0.06)   (0.18)   (0.17)   (1.03)
0.05   (0.04)   (0.72)
              (0.45)   0.04 (0.43) (0.76)

Copyright 2012 Securities Research Company

Bonds $44.2 Mil Com 7.729 Mil BV 7.32 /sh P/E 9.96 (Ind SCHEM P/E 21.95) Ctry US

AMERICAN PUBLIC EDUCATION IN (APEI)

Provides online education to the military and public service

Growth Performance Measurement				
Years	Price	Earn.	Div.	Tot Ret
Last 1	-16.5	13.7	---	-16.5
Last 5	-2.9	32.0	---	-2.9
Last 10	---	---	---	---

0.16
0.10
0.05   0.16

Copyright 2012 Securities Research Company

Bonds $.0 Mil Com 18.064 Mil BV 8.61 /sh P/E 15.57 (Ind EDSER P/E 5.79) Ctry US

AMERICAN SCIENCE & ENGINEERING, INC. (ASEI)

Makes X-ray inspection systems for inspection & security applications

Growth Performance Measurement				
Years	Price	Earn.	Div.	Tot Ret
Last 1	-4.3	-39.3	66.7	-1.3
Last 5	2.8	-3.1	20.1	4.6
Last 10	17.4	---	---	18.5

(0.05) (1.16) (1.29) (0.75)
0.14   (0.87) (0.90) (0.84)
0.13   (0.44) (1.10) (1.00)

Copyright 2012 Securities Research Company

Bonds $.0 Mil Com 8.301 Mil BV 27.04 /sh P/E 29.37 (Ind AEROD P/E 12.96) Ctry US

AMERICAN SOFTWARE INC (AMSWA)

Supply chain management software

Growth Performance Measurement				
Years	Price	Earn.	Div.	Tot Ret
Last 1	-17.9	15.0	.0	-14.1
Last 5	-1.8	3.9	.0	2.2
Last 10	10.9	6.3	1.2	14.6

Special
$0.20

(0.56)
(0.70)   0.02
56   (0.30)

Copyright 2012 Securities Research Company

Bonds $.9 Mil Com 24.583 Mil BV 3.16 /sh P/E 16.87 (Ind APPSF P/E 24.69) Ctry US

23

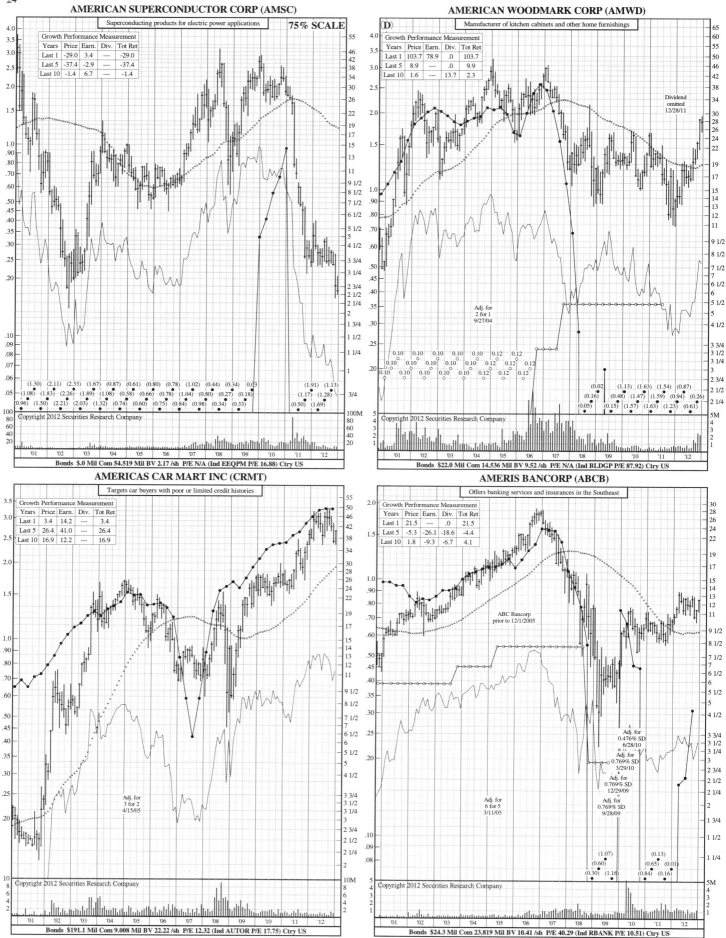

24

AMERICAN SUPERCONDUCTOR CORP (AMSC)
Superconducting products for electric power applications

75% SCALE

Growth Performance Measurement				
Years	Price	Earn.	Div.	Tot Ret
Last 1	-29.0	3.4	---	-29.0
Last 5	-37.4	-2.9	---	-37.4
Last 10	-1.4	6.7	---	-1.4

Copyright 2012 Securities Research Company

Bonds $.0 Mil Com 54.519 Mil BV 2.17 /sh P/E N/A (Ind EEQPM P/E 16.88) Ctry US

AMERICAN WOODMARK CORP (AMWD)
Manufacturer of kitchen cabinets and other home furnishings

(D)

Growth Performance Measurement				
Years	Price	Earn.	Div.	Tot Ret
Last 1	103.7	78.9	.0	103.7
Last 5	8.9	---	.0	9.9
Last 10	1.6	---	13.7	2.3

Dividend
omitted
12/28/11

Adj. for
2 for 1
9/27/04

Copyright 2012 Securities Research Company

Bonds $22.0 Mil Com 14.536 Mil BV 9.52 /sh P/E N/A (Ind BLDGP P/E 87.92) Ctry US

AMERICAS CAR MART INC (CRMT)
Targets car buyers with poor or limited credit histories

Growth Performance Measurement				
Years	Price	Earn.	Div.	Tot Ret
Last 1	3.4	14.2	---	3.4
Last 5	26.4	41.0	---	26.4
Last 10	16.9	12.2	---	16.9

Adj. for
3 for 2
4/15/05

Copyright 2012 Securities Research Company

Bonds $191.1 Mil Com 9.008 Mil BV 22.22 /sh P/E 12.32 (Ind AUTOR P/E 17.75) Ctry US

AMERIS BANCORP (ABCB)
Offers banking services and insurances in the Southeast

Growth Performance Measurement				
Years	Price	Earn.	Div.	Tot Ret
Last 1	21.5	---	.0	21.5
Last 5	-5.3	-26.1	-18.6	-4.4
Last 10	1.8	-9.3	-6.7	4.1

ABC Bancorp
prior to 12/1/2005

Adj. for
0.476% SD
6/28/10

Adj. for
0.769% SD
3/29/10

Adj. for
0.769% SD
12/29/09

Adj. for
0.769% SD
9/28/09

Adj. for
6 for 5
3/11/05

Copyright 2012 Securities Research Company

Bonds $24.3 Mil Com 23.819 Mil BV 10.41 /sh P/E 40.29 (Ind RBANK P/E 10.51) Ctry US

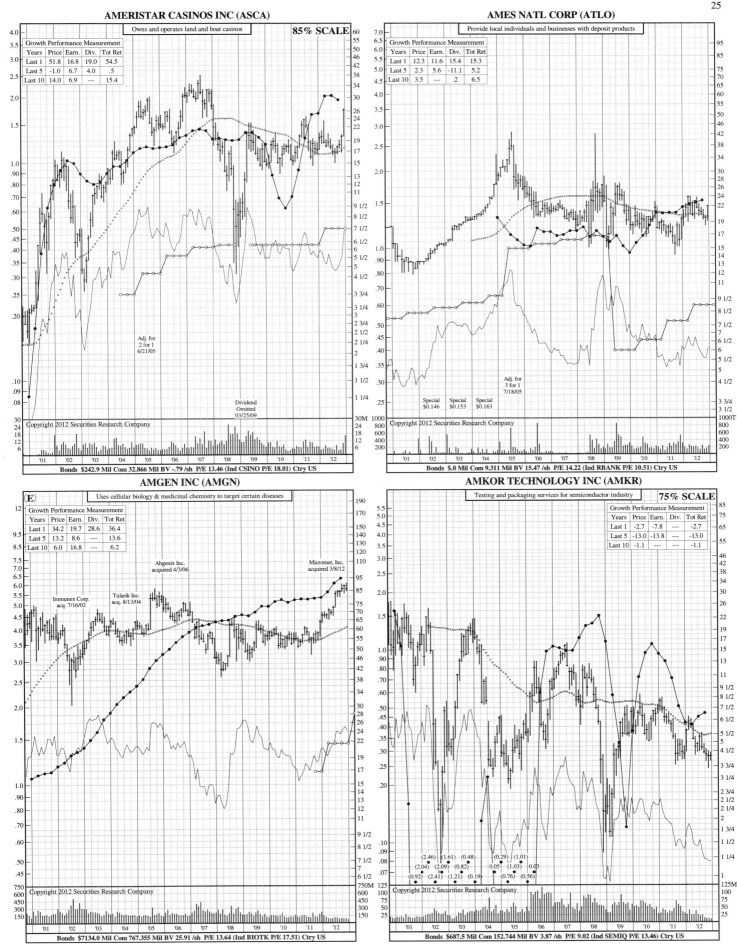

AMERISTAR CASINOS INC (ASCA)

Owns and operates land and boat casinos

85% SCALE

Growth Performance Measurement

Years	Price	Earn.	Div.	Tot Ret
Last 1	51.8	16.8	19.0	54.5
Last 5	-1.0	6.7	4.0	.5
Last 10	14.0	6.9	---	15.4

Adj. for
2 for 1
6/21/05

Dividend
Omitted
03/25/09

Copyright 2012 Securities Research Company

Bonds $242.9 Mil Com 32.866 Mil BV -.79 /sh P/E 13.46 (Ind CSINO P/E 18.01) Ctry US

AMES NATL CORP (ATLO)

Provide local individuals and businesses with deposit products

Growth Performance Measurement

Years	Price	Earn.	Div.	Tot Ret
Last 1	12.3	11.6	15.4	15.3
Last 5	2.3	5.6	-11.1	5.2
Last 10	3.5	---	.2	6.5

Adj. for
3 for 1
7/18/05

Special $0.146	Special $0.153	Special $0.163

Copyright 2012 Securities Research Company

Bonds $.0 Mil Com 9.311 Mil BV 15.47 /sh P/E 14.22 (Ind RBANK P/E 10.51) Ctry US

AMGEN INC (AMGN)

Uses cellular biology & medicinal chemistry to target certain diseases

E

Growth Performance Measurement

Years	Price	Earn.	Div.	Tot Ret
Last 1	34.2	19.7	28.6	36.4
Last 5	13.2	8.6	---	13.6
Last 10	6.0	16.8	---	6.2

Immunex Corp.
acq. 7/16/02

Tularik Inc.
acq. 8/13/04

Abgenix Inc.
acquired 4/3/06

Micromet, Inc,
acquired 3/8/12

Copyright 2012 Securities Research Company

Bonds $7134.0 Mil Com 767.355 Mil BV 25.91 /sh P/E 13.64 (Ind BIOTK P/E 17.51) Ctry US

AMKOR TECHNOLOGY INC (AMKR)

Testing and packaging services for semiconductor industry

75% SCALE

Growth Performance Measurement

Years	Price	Earn.	Div.	Tot Ret
Last 1	-2.7	-7.8	---	-2.7
Last 5	-13.0	-13.8	---	-13.0
Last 10	-1.1	---	---	-1.1

(2.46) (1.61) (0.48)   (0.29) (1.01)
(2.04) (2.09) (0.82)   (0.05) (1.03) (0.03)
(0.92) (2.41) (1.21) (0.19)   (0.76) (0.56)

Copyright 2012 Securities Research Company

Bonds $687.5 Mil Com 152.744 Mil BV 3.87 /sh P/E 9.02 (Ind SEMIQ P/E 13.46) Ctry US

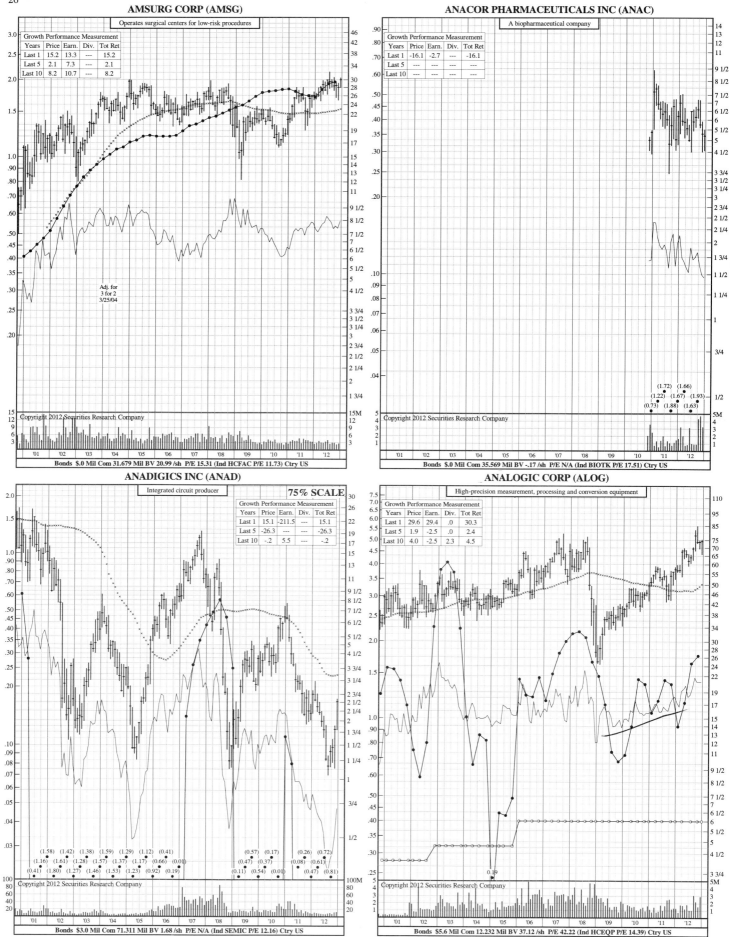

26

AMSURG CORP (AMSG)

Operates surgical centers for low-risk procedures

Growth Performance Measurement

Years	Price	Earn.	Div.	Tot Ret
Last 1	15.2	13.3	---	15.2
Last 5	2.1	7.3	---	2.1
Last 10	8.2	10.7	---	8.2

Adj. for
3 for 2
3/25/04

Copyright 2012 Securities Research Company

Bonds $.0 Mil Com 31.679 Mil BV 20.99 /sh P/E 15.31 (Ind HCFAC P/E 11.73) Ctry US

ANACOR PHARMACEUTICALS INC (ANAC)

A biopharmaceutical company

Growth Performance Measurement

Years	Price	Earn.	Div.	Tot Ret
Last 1	-16.1	-2.7	---	-16.1
Last 5	---	---	---	---
Last 10	---	---	---	---

(1.72) (1.66)
(1.22) (1.67) (1.93)
(0.73) (1.88) (1.63)

Copyright 2012 Securities Research Company

Bonds $.0 Mil Com 35.569 Mil BV -.17 /sh P/E N/A (Ind BIOTK P/E 17.51) Ctry US

ANADIGICS INC (ANAD)

Integrated circuit producer

75% SCALE

Growth Performance Measurement

Years	Price	Earn.	Div.	Tot Ret
Last 1	15.1	-211.5	---	15.1
Last 5	-26.3	---	---	-26.3
Last 10	-.2	5.5	---	-.2

(1.58) (1.42) (1.38) (1.59) (1.29) (1.12) (0.41)   (0.57) (0.17)   (0.26) (0.72)
(1.16) (1.61) (1.28) (1.57) (1.37) (1.17) (0.66) (0.01) (0.47) (0.37)   (0.08) (0.61)
(0.41) (1.80) (1.27) (1.46) (1.53) (1.23) (0.92) (0.19) (0.11) (0.54) (0.01) (0.47) (0.81)

Copyright 2012 Securities Research Company

Bonds $3.0 Mil Com 71.311 Mil BV 1.68 /sh P/E N/A (Ind SEMIC P/E 12.16) Ctry US

ANALOGIC CORP (ALOG)

High-precision measurement, processing and conversion equipment

Growth Performance Measurement

Years	Price	Earn.	Div.	Tot Ret
Last 1	29.6	29.4	.0	30.3
Last 5	1.9	-2.5	.0	2.4
Last 10	4.0	-2.5	2.3	4.5

0.19

Copyright 2012 Securities Research Company

Bonds $5.6 Mil Com 12.232 Mil BV 37.12 /sh P/E 42.22 (Ind HCEQP P/E 14.39) Ctry US

ANALYSTS INTL CORP (ANLY)

Computer analytical and programming services

80% SCALE

Growth Performance Measurement				
Years	Price	Earn.	Div.	Tot Ret
Last 1	-43.2	-62.7	.0	-43.2
Last 5	-16.3	---	.0	-16.3
Last 10	-10.8	---	.0	-10.8

Dividend suspended 10/22/01

Adj. for 1 for 5 3/1/10

(0.35) (0.20)
(0.50) (0.20) (0.15)
(0.25) (0.30) (0.30)
(0.35) (0.65) (0.40)
(0.55) (0.20) (0.60)
(0.45) (0.25) (0.65)
(1.60) (3.05) (1.36)
0.00 (2.50) (1.70) (0.01)
0.00 (2.20) (1.95) (0.60)

Copyright 2012 Securities Research Company

Bonds $33.9 Mil Com 5.083 Mil BV 3.80 /sh P/E 11.33 (Ind ITCON P/E 14.16) Ctry US

ANAREN INC (ANEN)

Makes microwave components, assemblies, and subsystems

80% SCALE

Growth Performance Measurement				
Years	Price	Earn.	Div.	Tot Ret
Last 1	17.0	-30.9	---	17.0
Last 5	3.4	-4.1	---	3.4
Last 10	8.3	25.2	---	8.3

Adj. for 2 for 1 11/28/00

Copyright 2012 Securities Research Company

Bonds $.0 Mil Com 13.775 Mil BV 13.51 /sh P/E 22.88 (Ind TELEQ P/E 13.72) Ctry US

ANCESTRY COM INC (ACOM1)

Online Source For Family History

Growth Performance Measurement				
Years	Price	Earn.	Div.	Tot Ret
Last 1	39.6	26.3	---	39.6
Last 5	---	---	---	---
Last 10	---	---	---	---

Acquired by Permira Advisers LLP 12/31/2012

Copyright 2012 Securities Research Company

Bonds $.0 Mil Com 43.365 Mil BV 8.67 /sh P/E 18.53 (Ind ITSOF P/E 19.21) Ctry US

ANDATEE CHINA MARINE FUEL SVCS CORP (AMCF)

Production & Distiribution of Marine Fuel

75% SCALE

Growth Performance Measurement				
Years	Price	Earn.	Div.	Tot Ret
Last 1	-84.2	---	---	-84.2
Last 5	---	---	---	---
Last 10	---	---	---	---

(0.38)

Copyright 2012 Securities Research Company

Bonds $.0 Mil Com 9.519 Mil BV 5.41 /sh P/E N/A (Ind SHIPP P/E 23.24) Ctry China

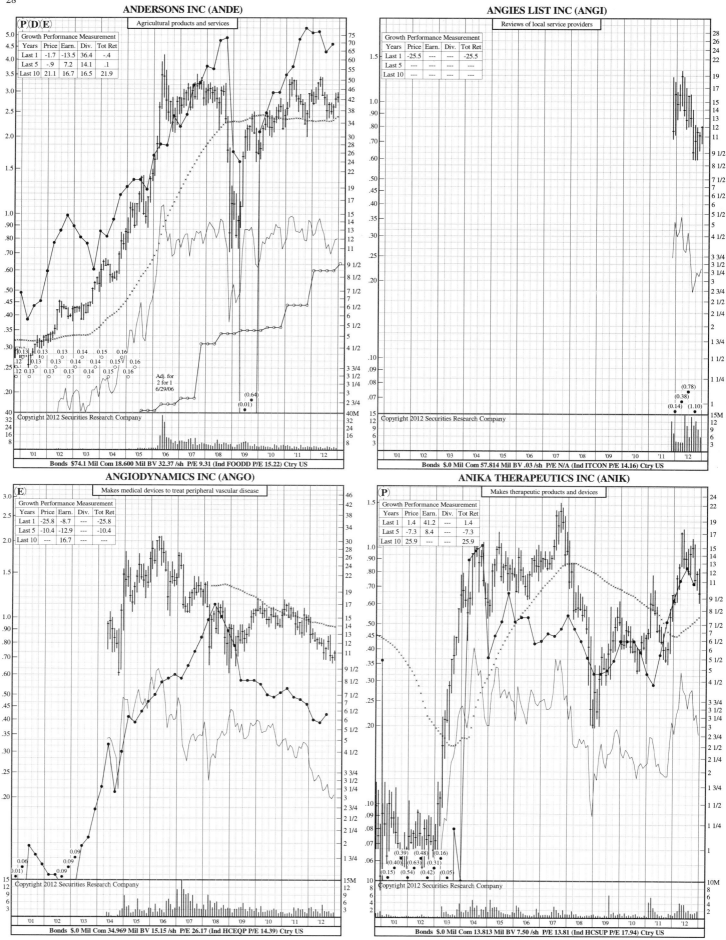

28

ANDERSONS INC (ANDE)
Agricultural products and services

(P)(D)(E)

Growth Performance Measurement				
Years	Price	Earn.	Div.	Tot Ret
Last 1	-1.7	-13.5	36.4	-.4
Last 5	-.9	7.2	14.1	.1
Last 10	21.1	16.7	16.5	21.9

Adj. for
2 for 1
6/29/06

(0.64)
(0.01)

Copyright 2012 Securities Research Company

Bonds $74.1 Mil Com 18.600 Mil BV 32.37 /sh P/E 9.31 (Ind FOODD P/E 15.22) Ctry US

ANGIES LIST INC (ANGI)
Reviews of local service providers

Growth Performance Measurement				
Years	Price	Earn.	Div.	Tot Ret
Last 1	-25.5	---	---	-25.5
Last 5	---	---	---	---
Last 10	---	---	---	---

(0.78)
(0.38)
(0.14) (1.10)

Copyright 2012 Securities Research Company

Bonds $.0 Mil Com 57.814 Mil BV .03 /sh P/E N/A (Ind ITCON P/E 14.16) Ctry US

ANGIODYNAMICS INC (ANGO)
Makes medical devices to treat peripheral vascular disease

(E)

Growth Performance Measurement				
Years	Price	Earn.	Div.	Tot Ret
Last 1	-25.8	-8.7	---	-25.8
Last 5	-10.4	-12.9	---	-10.4
Last 10	---	16.7	---	---

0.09
0.06   0.09
0.09
0.01   0.09

Copyright 2012 Securities Research Company

Bonds $.0 Mil Com 34.969 Mil BV 15.15 /sh P/E 26.17 (Ind HCEQP P/E 14.39) Ctry US

ANIKA THERAPEUTICS INC (ANIK)
Makes therapeutic products and devices

(P)

Growth Performance Measurement				
Years	Price	Earn.	Div.	Tot Ret
Last 1	1.4	41.2	---	1.4
Last 5	-7.3	8.4	---	-7.3
Last 10	25.9	---	---	25.9

(0.39) (0.48) (0.16)
(0.40) (0.63) (0.31)
(0.15) (0.54) (0.42) (0.05)

Copyright 2012 Securities Research Company

Bonds $.0 Mil Com 13.813 Mil BV 7.50 /sh P/E 13.81 (Ind HCSUP P/E 17.94) Ctry US

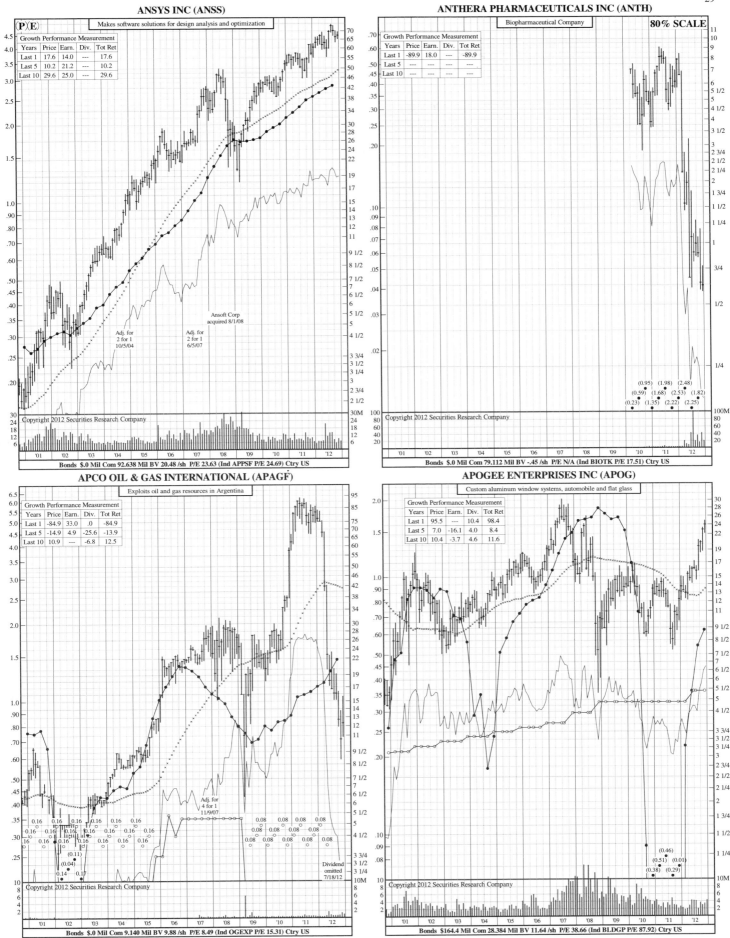

ANSYS INC (ANSS)

Makes software solutions for design analysis and optimization

Growth Performance Measurement				
Years	Price	Earn.	Div.	Tot Ret
Last 1	17.6	14.0	---	17.6
Last 5	10.2	21.2	---	10.2
Last 10	29.6	25.0	---	29.6

Ansoft Corp
acquired 8/1/08

Adj. for
2 for 1
10/5/04

Adj. for
2 for 1
6/5/07

Copyright 2012 Securities Research Company

Bonds $.0 Mil Com 92.638 Mil BV 20.48 /sh P/E 23.63 (Ind APPSF P/E 24.69) Ctry US

ANTHERA PHARMACEUTICALS INC (ANTH)

Biopharmaceutical Company

80% SCALE

Growth Performance Measurement				
Years	Price	Earn.	Div.	Tot Ret
Last 1	-89.9	18.0	---	-89.9
Last 5	---	---	---	---
Last 10	---	---	---	---

(0.95) (1.98) (2.48)
(0.59) (1.68) (2.53) (1.82)
(0.23) (1.35) (2.22) (2.25)

Copyright 2012 Securities Research Company

Bonds $.0 Mil Com 79.112 Mil BV -.45 /sh P/E N/A (Ind BIOTK P/E 17.51) Ctry US

APCO OIL & GAS INTERNATIONAL (APAGF)

Exploits oil and gas resources in Argentina

Growth Performance Measurement				
Years	Price	Earn.	Div.	Tot Ret
Last 1	-84.9	33.0	.0	-84.9
Last 5	-14.9	4.9	-25.6	-13.9
Last 10	10.9	---	-6.8	12.5

Adj. for
4 for 1
11/9/07

0.16 0.16 0.16 0.16 0.16 0.16   0.08 0.08 0.08 0.08
0.16 0.16 0.16 0.16 0.16 0.16   0.08 0.08 0.08 0.08
0.16   0.16 0.16 0.16 0.16   0.08 0.08 0.08 0.08 0.08
(0.11)
0.14 0.17

Dividend
omitted
7/18/12

Copyright 2012 Securities Research Company

Bonds $.0 Mil Com 9.140 Mil BV 9.88 /sh P/E 8.49 (Ind OGEXP P/E 15.31) Ctry US

APOGEE ENTERPRISES INC (APOG)

Custom aluminum window systems, automobile and flat glass

Growth Performance Measurement				
Years	Price	Earn.	Div.	Tot Ret
Last 1	95.5	---	10.4	98.4
Last 5	7.0	-16.1	4.0	8.4
Last 10	10.4	-3.7	4.6	11.6

(0.46)
(0.51) (0.01)
(0.38) (0.29)

Copyright 2012 Securities Research Company

Bonds $164.4 Mil Com 28.384 Mil BV 11.64 /sh P/E 38.66 (Ind BLDGP P/E 87.92) Ctry US

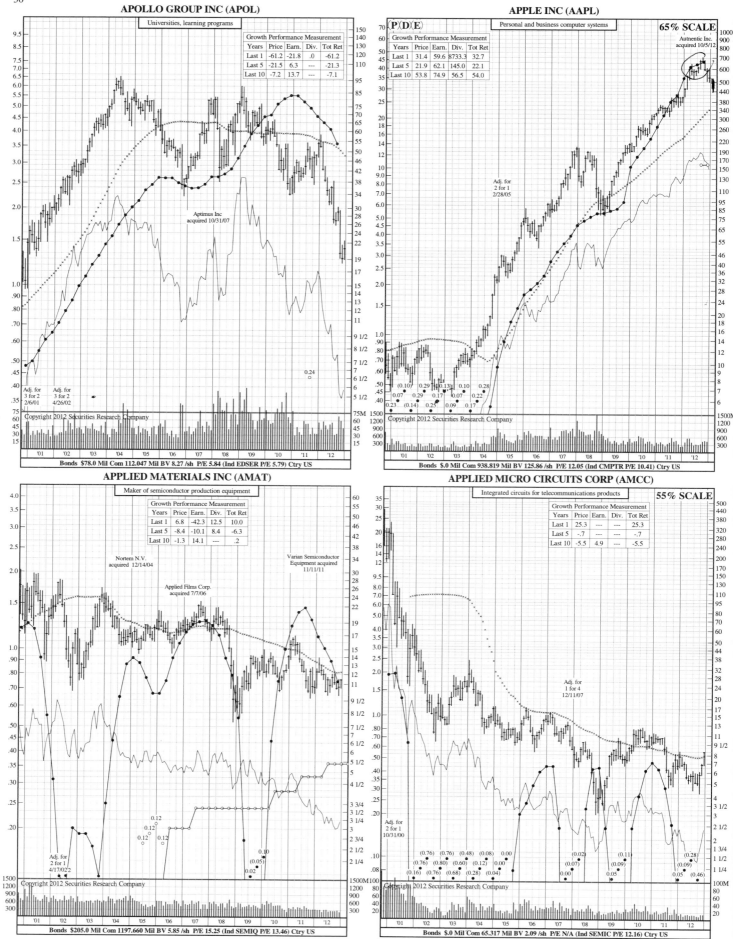

30

APOLLO GROUP INC (APOL)

Universities, learning programs

	Growth Performance Measurement			
Years	Price	Earn.	Div.	Tot Ret
Last 1	-61.2	-21.8	.0	-61.2
Last 5	-21.5	6.3	---	-21.3
Last 10	-7.2	13.7		-7.1

Aptimus Inc
acquired 10/31/07

Adj. for
3 for 2
2/6/01

Adj. for
3 for 2
4/26/02

0.24

Copyright 2012 Securities Research Company

Bonds $78.0 Mil Com 112.047 Mil BV 8.27 /sh P/E 5.84 (Ind EDSER P/E 5.79) Ctry US

APPLE INC (AAPL)

(P)(D)(E)

Personal and business computer systems

65% SCALE

Autnentic Inc.
acquired 10/5/12

	Growth Performance Measurement			
Years	Price	Earn.	Div.	Tot Ret
Last 1	31.4	59.6	8733.3	32.7
Last 5	21.9	62.1	145.0	22.1
Last 10	53.8	74.9	56.5	54.0

Adj. for
2 for 1
2/28/05

(0.10) 0.29 0.13 0.10 0.28
0.07 0.17 0.07 0.22
0.23 (0.14) 0.25 0.17 0.17

Copyright 2012 Securities Research Company

Bonds $.0 Mil Com 938.819 Mil BV 125.86 /sh P/E 12.05 (Ind CMPTR P/E 10.41) Ctry US

APPLIED MATERIALS INC (AMAT)

Maker of semiconductor production equipment

	Growth Performance Measurement			
Years	Price	Earn.	Div.	Tot Ret
Last 1	6.8	-42.3	12.5	10.0
Last 5	-8.4	-10.1	8.4	-6.3
Last 10	-1.3	14.1	---	.2

Nortem N.V.
acquired 12/14/04

Varian Semiconductor
Equipment acquired
11/11/11

Applied Films Corp.
acquired 7/7/06

0.12
0.12
0.12 0.12

0.10
(0.05)
0.02

Adj. for
2 for 1
4/17/02

Copyright 2012 Securities Research Company

Bonds $205.0 Mil Com 1197.660 Mil BV 5.85 /sh P/E 15.25 (Ind SEMIQ P/E 13.46) Ctry US

APPLIED MICRO CIRCUITS CORP (AMCC)

Integrated circuits for telecommunications products

55% SCALE

	Growth Performance Measurement			
Years	Price	Earn.	Div.	Tot Ret
Last 1	25.3	---	---	25.3
Last 5	-.7	---	---	-.7
Last 10	-5.5	4.9	---	-5.5

Adj. for
1 for 4
12/11/07

Adj. for
2 for 1
10/31/00

(0.76) (0.76) (0.48) (0.08) 0.00   (0.02)   (0.11)   (0.28)
(0.76) (0.80) (0.60) (0.12) 0.00   (0.07)   (0.09)   (0.09)
(0.16) (0.76) (0.68) (0.28) (0.04)   0.00   0.05   0.05 (0.46)

Copyright 2012 Securities Research Company

Bonds $.0 Mil Com 65.317 Mil BV 2.09 /sh P/E N/A (Ind SEMIC P/E 12.16) Ctry US

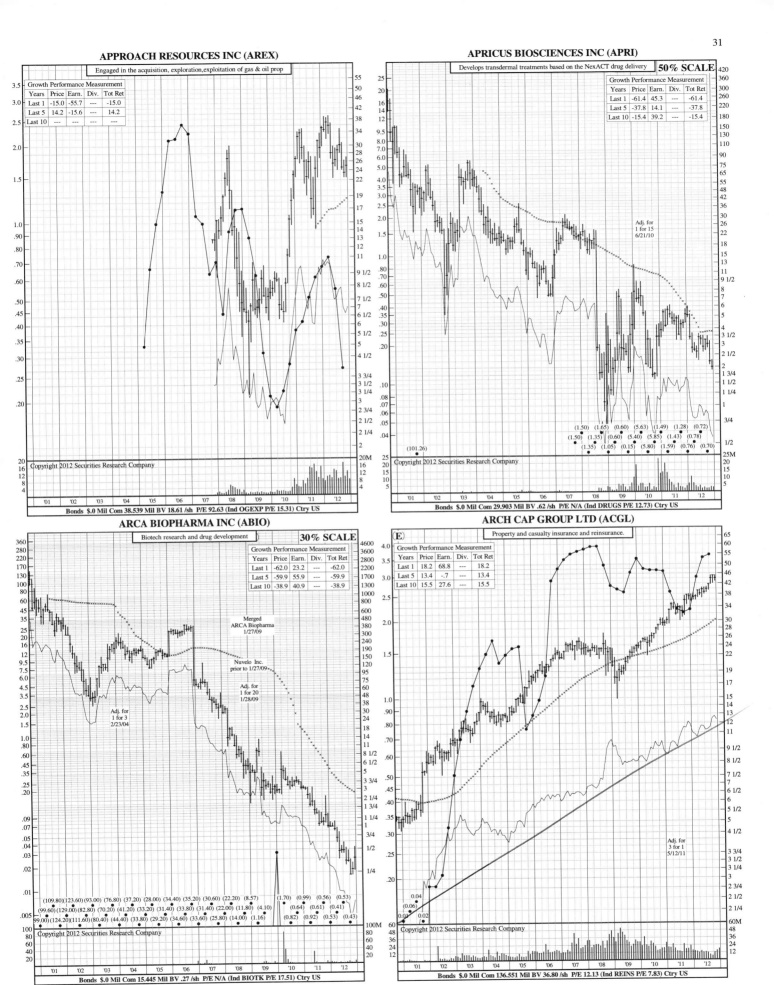

APPROACH RESOURCES INC (AREX)

Engaged in the acquisition, exploration,exploitation of gas & oil prop

Growth Performance Measurement				
Years	Price	Earn.	Div.	Tot Ret
Last 1	-15.0	-55.7	---	-15.0
Last 5	14.2	-15.6	---	14.2
Last 10	---	---	---	---

Copyright 2012 Securities Research Company

Bonds $.0 Mil Com 38.539 Mil BV 18.61 /sh P/E 92.63 (Ind OGEXP P/E 15.31) Ctry US

APRICUS BIOSCIENCES INC (APRI)

Develops transdermal treatments based on the NexACT drug delivery **50% SCALE**

Growth Performance Measurement				
Years	Price	Earn.	Div.	Tot Ret
Last 1	-61.4	45.3	---	-61.4
Last 5	-37.8	14.1	---	-37.8
Last 10	-15.4	39.2	---	-15.4

Adj. for
1 for 15
6/21/10

(1.50) (1.65) (0.60) (5.63) (1.49) (1.28) (0.72)
(1.50) (1.35) (0.60) (5.40) (5.85) (1.43) (0.78)
(101.26)
(1.35) (1.05) (0.15) (5.80) (1.59) (0.76) (0.70)

Copyright 2012 Securities Research Company

Bonds $.0 Mil Com 29.903 Mil BV .62 /sh P/E N/A (Ind DRUGS P/E 12.73) Ctry US

ARCA BIOPHARMA INC (ABIO)

Biotech research and drug development   **30% SCALE**

Growth Performance Measurement				
Years	Price	Earn.	Div.	Tot Ret
Last 1	-62.0	23.2	---	-62.0
Last 5	-59.9	55.9	---	-59.9
Last 10	-38.9	40.9	---	-38.9

Merged
ARCA Biopharma
1/27/09

Nuvelo Inc.
prior to 1/27/09

Adj. for
1 for 20
1/28/09

Adj. for
1 for 3
2/23/04

(109.80)(123.60) (93.00) (76.80) (37.20) (28.00) (34.40) (35.20) (30.60) (22.20) (8.57)   (1.70) (0.99) (0.56) (0.53)
(99.60)(129.00) (82.80) (70.20) (41.20) (33.20) (31.40) (33.80) (31.40) (22.00) (11.80) (4.10)   (0.64) (0.61) (0.41)
99.00)(124.20)(111.60) (80.40) (44.40) (33.80) (29.20) (34.60) (33.60) (25.80) (14.00) (1.16)   (0.82) (0.92) (0.53) (0.43)

Copyright 2012 Securities Research Company

Bonds $.0 Mil Com 15.445 Mil BV .27 /sh P/E N/A (Ind BIOTK P/E 17.51) Ctry US

ARCH CAP GROUP LTD (ACGL)

(E)   Property and casualty insurance and reinsurance.

Growth Performance Measurement				
Years	Price	Earn.	Div.	Tot Ret
Last 1	18.2	68.8	---	18.2
Last 5	13.4	-.7	---	13.4
Last 10	15.5	27.6	---	15.5

Adj. for
3 for 1
5/12/11

0.04
(0.06)
0.02

Copyright 2012 Securities Research Company

Bonds $.0 Mil Com 136.551 Mil BV 36.80 /sh P/E 12.13 (Ind REINS P/E 7.83) Ctry US

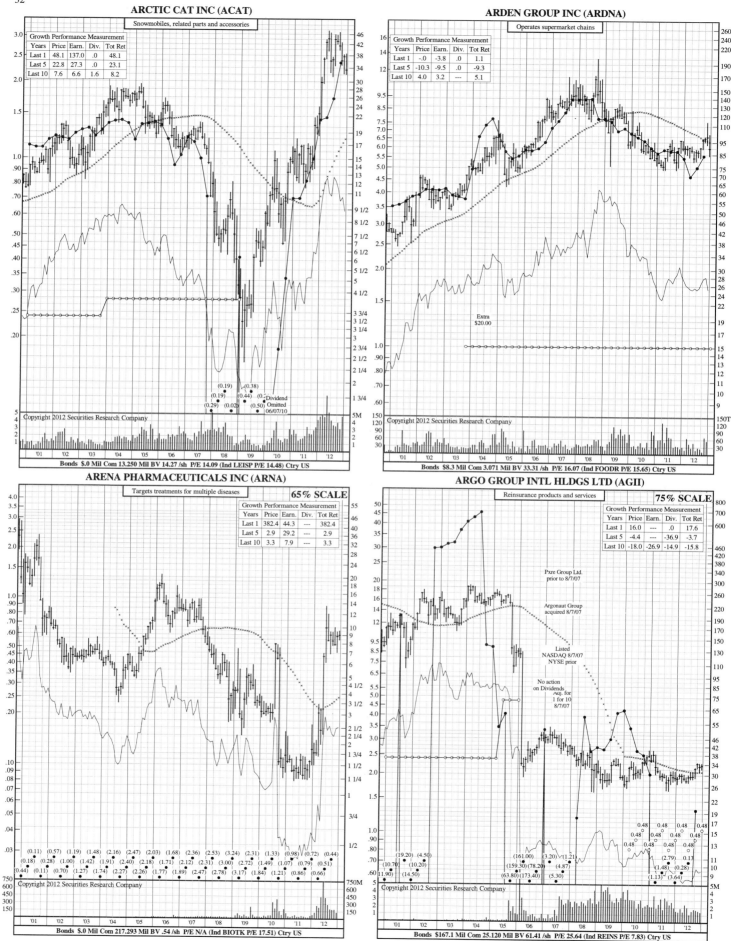

32

ARCTIC CAT INC (ACAT)

Snowmobiles, related parts and accessories

Bonds $.0 Mil Com 13.250 Mil BV 14.27 /sh P/E 14.09 (Ind LEISP P/E 14.48) Ctry US

Growth Performance Measurement				
Years	Price	Earn.	Div.	Tot Ret
Last 1	48.1	137.0	.0	48.1
Last 5	22.8	27.3	.0	23.1
Last 10	7.6	6.6	1.6	8.2

(0.19)
(0.19)   (0.44)   (0.38)
(0.29) (0.02)   (0.50)   Dividend
Omitted
06/07/10

ARDEN GROUP INC (ARDNA)

Operates supermarket chains

Bonds $8.3 Mil Com 3.071 Mil BV 33.31 /sh P/E 16.07 (Ind FOODR P/E 15.65) Ctry US

Growth Performance Measurement				
Years	Price	Earn.	Div.	Tot Ret
Last 1	-.0	-3.8	.0	1.1
Last 5	-10.3	-9.5	.0	-9.3
Last 10	4.0	3.2	---	5.1

Extra
$20.00

ARENA PHARMACEUTICALS INC (ARNA)

Targets treatments for multiple diseases

65% SCALE

Bonds $.0 Mil Com 217.293 Mil BV .54 /sh P/E N/A (Ind BIOTK P/E 17.51) Ctry US

Growth Performance Measurement				
Years	Price	Earn.	Div.	Tot Ret
Last 1	382.4	44.3	---	382.4
Last 5	2.9	29.2	---	2.9
Last 10	3.3	7.9	---	3.3

(0.11) (0.57) (1.19) (1.48) (2.16) (2.47) (2.03) (1.68) (2.36) (2.53) (3.24) (2.31) (1.33) (0.98) (0.72) (0.44)
(0.18) (0.28) (1.00) (1.42) (1.91) (2.40) (2.18) (1.71) (2.12) (2.31) (3.00) (2.72) (1.49) (1.07) (0.79) (0.51)
(0.44) (0.11) (0.70) (1.27) (1.74) (2.27) (2.26) (1.77) (1.89) (2.47) (2.78) (3.17) (1.84) (1.21) (0.86) (0.66)

ARGO GROUP INTL HLDGS LTD (AGII)

Reinsurance products and services

75% SCALE

Bonds $167.1 Mil Com 25.120 Mil BV 61.41 /sh P/E 25.64 (Ind REINS P/E 7.83) Ctry US

Growth Performance Measurement				
Years	Price	Earn.	Div.	Tot Ret
Last 1	16.0	---	.0	17.6
Last 5	-4.4	---	-36.9	-3.7
Last 10	-18.0	-26.9	-14.9	-15.8

Pxre Group Ltd.
prior to 8/7/07

Argonaut Group
acquired 8/7/07

Listed
NASDAQ 8/7/07
NYSE prior

No action
on Dividends
Aug. for
1 for 10
8/7/07

0.48   0.48   0.48   0.48
0.48   0.48   0.48   0.48
(2.79)   0.13
0.48   0.48   0.48   0.48
(1.48) (0.28)
(19.20) (4.50)   (161.00)   (3.20) 1.21   (1.13) (3.64)
(10.70) (10.20)   (159.30) (78.20) (4.87)
(11.90) (14.50)   (63.80)(173.40) (5.30)

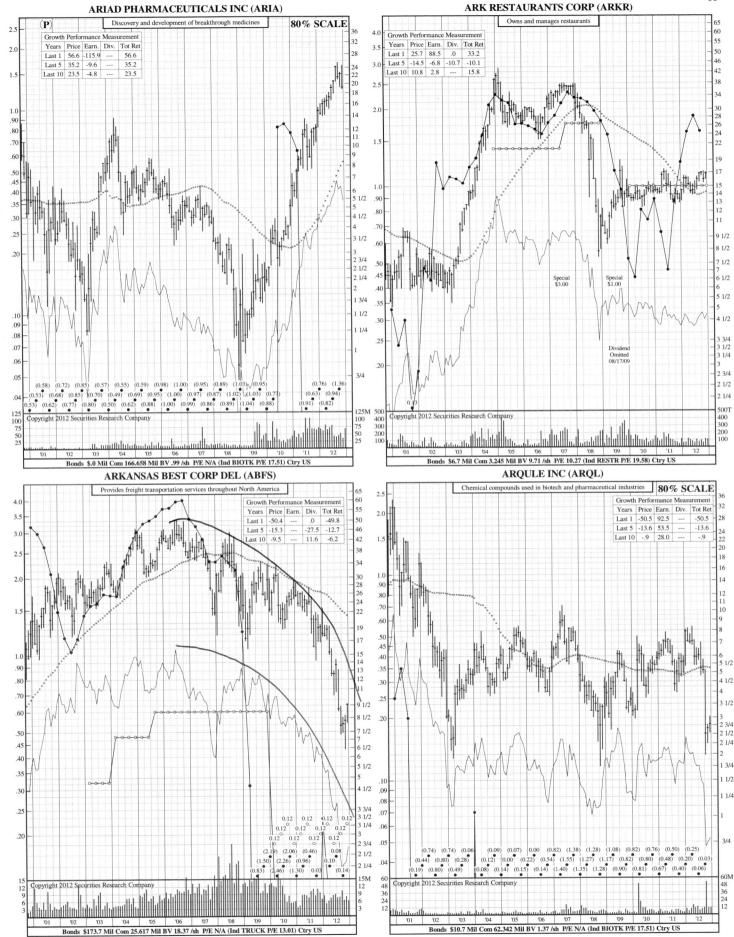

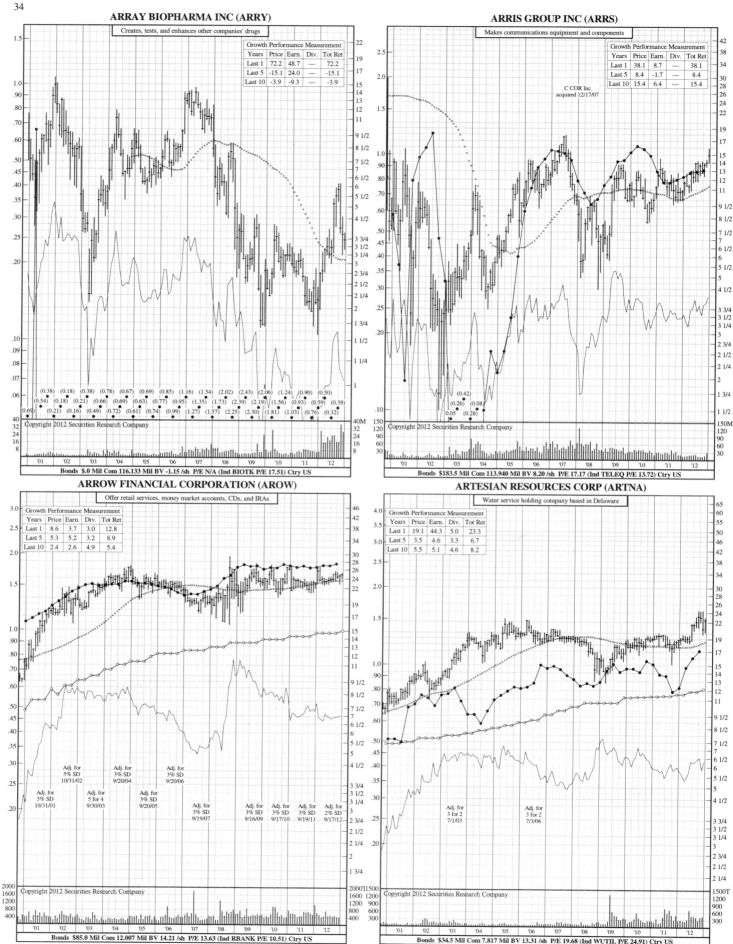

ARRAY BIOPHARMA INC (ARRY)

Creates, tests, and enhances other companies' drugs

Growth Performance Measurement				
Years	Price	Earn.	Div.	Tot Ret
Last 1	72.2	48.7	---	72.2
Last 5	-15.1	24.0	---	-15.1
Last 10	-3.9	-9.3	---	-3.9

(0.38) (0.18) (0.38) (0.78) (0.67) (0.69) (0.85) (1.16) (1.54) (2.02) (2.43) (2.06) (1.24) (0.90) (0.50)
(0.54) (0.18) (0.21) (0.66) (0.69) (0.63) (0.77) (0.95) (1.35) (1.73) (2.39) (2.19) (1.56) (0.93) (0.59) (0.39)
(0.69) (0.21) (0.16) (0.49) (0.72) (0.61) (0.74) (0.99) (1.27) (1.57) (2.25) (2.30) (1.81) (1.03) (0.76) (0.32)

Copyright 2012 Securities Research Company

Bonds $.0 Mil Com 116.133 Mil BV -1.15 /sh P/E N/A (Ind BIOTK P/E 17.51) Ctry US

ARRIS GROUP INC (ARRS)

Makes communications equipment and components

Growth Performance Measurement				
Years	Price	Earn.	Div.	Tot Ret
Last 1	38.1	8.7	---	38.1
Last 5	8.4	-1.7	---	8.4
Last 10	15.4	6.4	---	15.4

C COR Inc
acquired 12/17/07

(0.42)
(0.26) (0.08)
0.05 (0.28)

Copyright 2012 Securities Research Company

Bonds $183.5 Mil Com 113.940 Mil BV 8.20 /sh P/E 17.17 (Ind TELEQ P/E 13.72) Ctry US

ARROW FINANCIAL CORPORATION (AROW)

Offer retail services, money market accounts, CDs, and IRAs

Growth Performance Measurement				
Years	Price	Earn.	Div.	Tot Ret
Last 1	8.6	3.7	3.0	12.8
Last 5	5.3	5.2	3.2	8.9
Last 10	2.4	2.6	4.9	5.4

Adj. for
5% SD
10/31/02

Adj. for
3% SD
9/20/04

Adj. for
3% SD
9/20/06

Adj. for
5% SD
10/31/01

Adj. for
5 for 4
9/30/03

Adj. for
3% SD
9/20/05

Adj. for
3% SD
9/19/07

Adj. for
3% SD
9/16/09

Adj. for
3% SD
9/17/10

Adj. for
3% SD
9/19/11

Adj. for
2% SD
9/17/12

Copyright 2012 Securities Research Company

Bonds $85.0 Mil Com 12.007 Mil BV 14.21 /sh P/E 13.63 (Ind RBANK P/E 10.51) Ctry US

ARTESIAN RESOURCES CORP (ARTNA)

Water service holding company based in Delaware

Growth Performance Measurement				
Years	Price	Earn.	Div.	Tot Ret
Last 1	19.1	44.3	5.0	23.3
Last 5	3.5	4.6	3.3	6.7
Last 10	5.5	5.1	4.6	8.2

Adj. for
3 for 2
7/1/03

Adj. for
3 for 2
7/3/06

Copyright 2012 Securities Research Company

Bonds $34.5 Mil Com 7.817 Mil BV 13.31 /sh P/E 19.68 (Ind WUTIL P/E 24.91) Ctry US

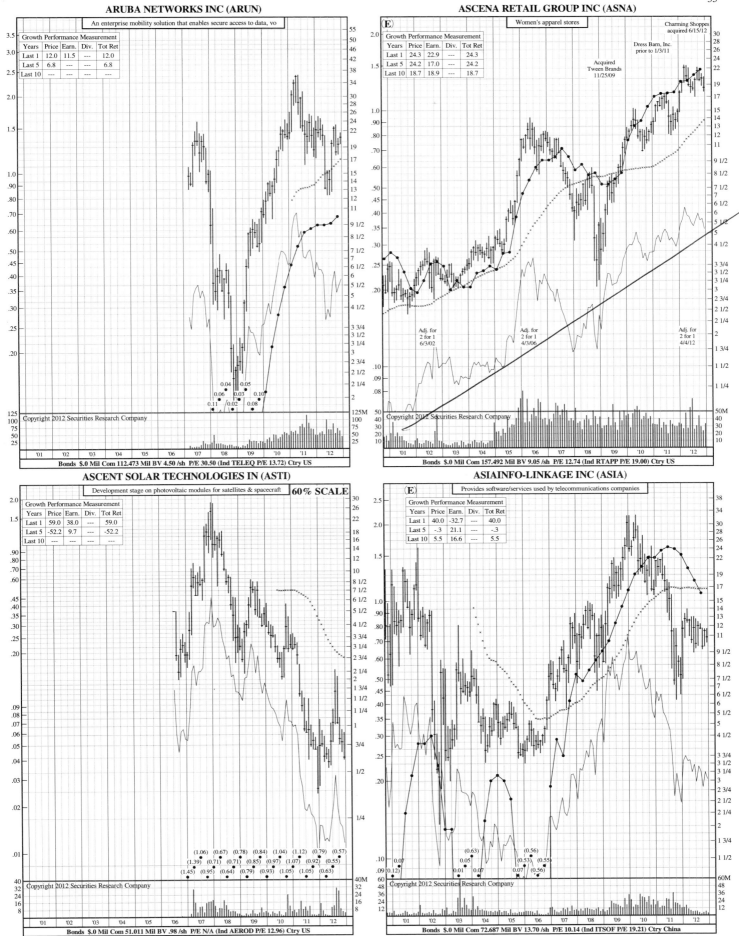

ARUBA NETWORKS INC (ARUN)

An enterprise mobility solution that enables secure access to data, vo

Growth Performance Measurement

Years	Price	Earn.	Div.	Tot Ret
Last 1	12.0	11.5	---	12.0
Last 5	6.8	---	---	6.8
Last 10	---	---	---	---

0.04 0.05
0.06 0.03 0.10
0.11 0.02 0.08

Copyright 2012 Securities Research Company

Bonds $.0 Mil Com 112.473 Mil BV 4.50 /sh P/E 30.50 (Ind TELEQ P/E 13.72) Ctry US

ASCENA RETAIL GROUP INC (ASNA)

(E)   Women's apparel stores

Charming Shoppes
acquired 6/15/12

Dress Barn, Inc.
prior to 1/3/11

Acquired
Tween Brands
11/25/09

Growth Performance Measurement

Years	Price	Earn.	Div.	Tot Ret
Last 1	24.3	22.9	---	24.3
Last 5	24.2	17.0	---	24.2
Last 10	18.7	18.9	---	18.7

Adj. for
2 for 1
6/3/02

Adj. for
2 for 1
4/3/06

Adj. for
2 for 1
4/4/12

Copyright 2012 Securities Research Company

Bonds $.0 Mil Com 157.492 Mil BV 9.05 /sh P/E 12.74 (Ind RTAPP P/E 19.00) Ctry US

ASCENT SOLAR TECHNOLOGIES IN (ASTI)

Development stage on photovoltaic modules for satellites & spacecraft   **60% SCALE**

Growth Performance Measurement

Years	Price	Earn.	Div.	Tot Ret
Last 1	59.0	38.0	---	59.0
Last 5	-52.2	9.7	---	-52.2
Last 10	---	---	---	---

(1.06) (0.67) (0.78) (0.84) (1.04) (1.12) (0.79) (0.57)
(1.39) (0.71) (0.71) (0.85) (0.97) (1.07) (0.92) (0.55)
(1.45) (0.95) (0.64) (0.79) (0.93) (1.05) (1.05) (0.63)

Copyright 2012 Securities Research Company

Bonds $.0 Mil Com 51.011 Mil BV .98 /sh P/E N/A (Ind AEROD P/E 12.96) Ctry US

ASIAINFO-LINKAGE INC (ASIA)

(E)   Provides software/services used by telecommunications companies

Growth Performance Measurement

Years	Price	Earn.	Div.	Tot Ret
Last 1	40.0	-32.7	---	40.0
Last 5	-.3	21.1	---	-.3
Last 10	5.5	16.6	---	5.5

0.07
(0.12)

0.05
0.01

0.07

(0.63)

(0.56)
(0.53) (0.55)
0.07 (0.56)

Copyright 2012 Securities Research Company

Bonds $.0 Mil Com 72.687 Mil BV 13.70 /sh P/E 10.14 (Ind ITSOF P/E 19.21) Ctry China

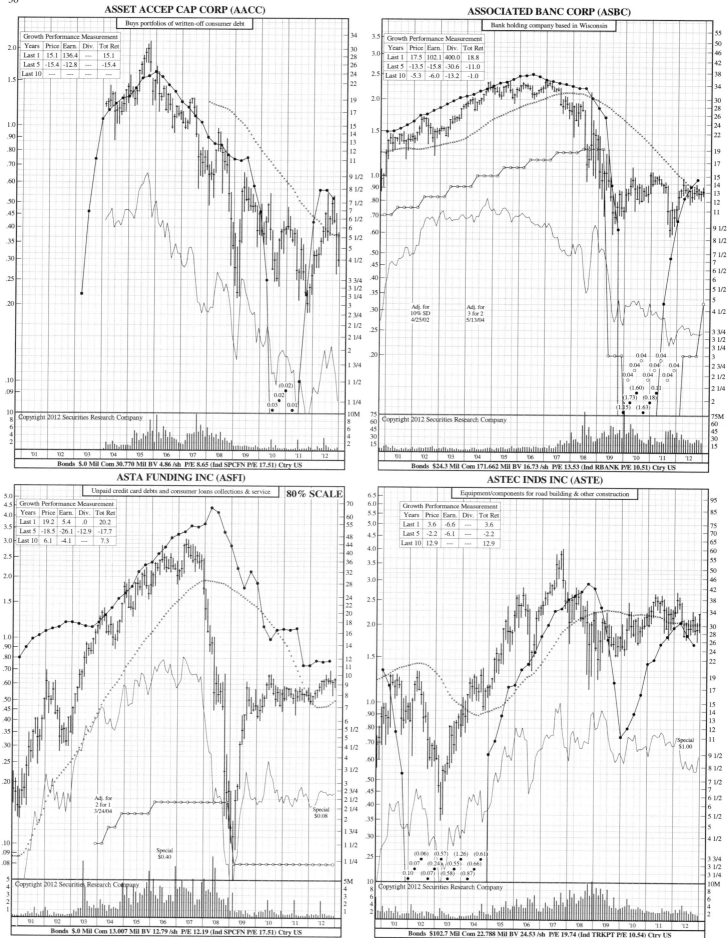

ASSET ACCEP CAP CORP (AACC)

Buys portfolios of written-off consumer debt

Growth Performance Measurement				
Years	Price	Earn.	Div.	Tot Ret
Last 1	15.1	136.4	---	15.1
Last 5	-15.4	-12.8	---	-15.4
Last 10	---	---	---	---

(0.02)
0.02
0.03 0.01

Copyright 2012 Securities Research Company

Bonds $.0 Mil Com 30.770 Mil BV 4.86 /sh P/E 8.65 (Ind SPCFN P/E 17.51) Ctry US

ASSOCIATED BANC CORP (ASBC)

Bank holding company based in Wisconsin

Growth Performance Measurement				
Years	Price	Earn.	Div.	Tot Ret
Last 1	17.5	102.1	400.0	18.8
Last 5	-13.5	-15.8	-30.6	-11.0
Last 10	-5.3	-6.0	-13.2	-1.0

Adj. for
10% SD
4/25/02

Adj. for
3 for 2
5/13/04

0.04   0.04
0.04 0.04 0.04
0.04 0.04 0.04

(1.60) 0.11
(1.73) (0.18)
(1.15) (1.63)

Copyright 2012 Securities Research Company

Bonds $24.3 Mil Com 171.662 Mil BV 16.73 /sh P/E 13.53 (Ind RBANK P/E 10.51) Ctry US

ASTA FUNDING INC (ASFI)

Unpaid credit card debts and consumer loans collections & service   **80% SCALE**

Growth Performance Measurement				
Years	Price	Earn.	Div.	Tot Ret
Last 1	19.2	5.4	.0	20.2
Last 5	-18.5	-26.1	-12.9	-17.7
Last 10	6.1	-4.1	---	7.3

Adj. for
2 for 1
3/24/04

Special
$0.40

Special
$0.08

Copyright 2012 Securities Research Company

Bonds $.0 Mil Com 13.007 Mil BV 12.79 /sh P/E 12.19 (Ind SPCFN P/E 17.51) Ctry US

ASTEC INDS INC (ASTE)

Equipment/components for road building & other construction

Growth Performance Measurement				
Years	Price	Earn.	Div.	Tot Ret
Last 1	3.6	-6.6	---	3.6
Last 5	-2.2	-6.1	---	-2.2
Last 10	12.9	---	---	12.9

Special
$1.00

(0.06) (0.57) (1.26) (0.61)
0.07   (0.24) (0.55) (0.66)
0.10   (0.07) (0.58) (0.87)

Copyright 2012 Securities Research Company

Bonds $102.7 Mil Com 22.788 Mil BV 24.53 /sh P/E 19.74 (Ind TRKPT P/E 10.54) Ctry US

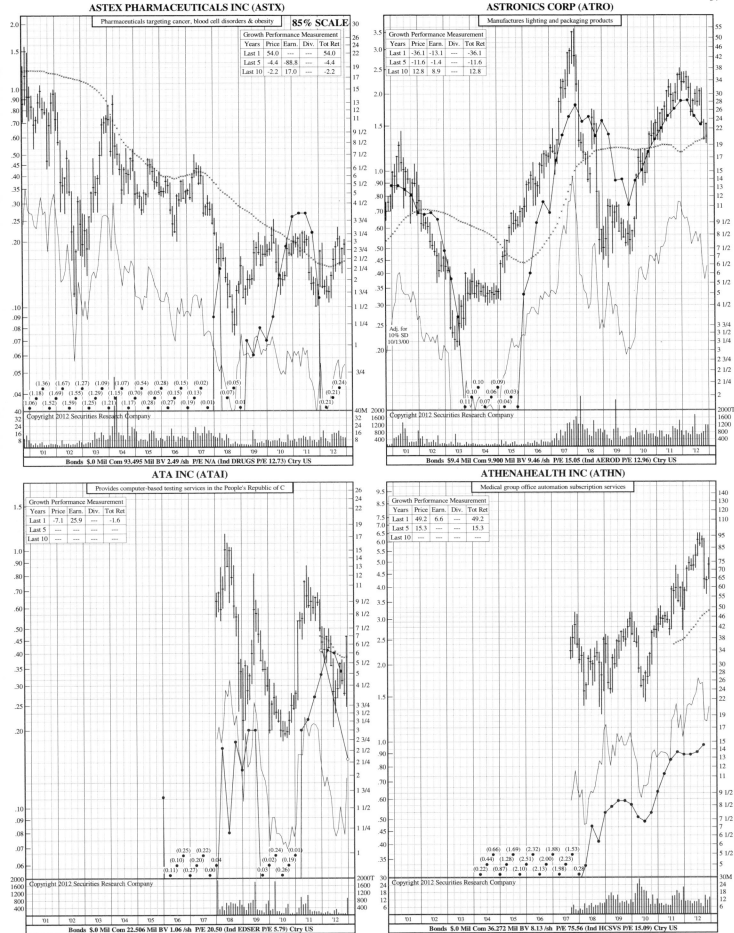

ASTEX PHARMACEUTICALS INC (ASTX)

Pharmaceuticals targeting cancer, blood cell disorders & obesity

85% SCALE

Growth Performance Measurement				
Years	Price	Earn.	Div.	Tot Ret
Last 1	54.0	---	---	54.0
Last 5	-4.4	-88.8	---	-4.4
Last 10	-2.2	17.0	---	-2.2

(1.36) (1.67) (1.27) (1.09) (1.07) (0.54) (0.28) (0.15) (0.02) (0.05) (0.24)
(1.18) (1.69) (1.55) (1.29) (1.15) (0.70) (0.05) (0.13) (0.07) (0.21)
(1.06) (1.52) (1.59) (1.25) (1.21) (1.17) (0.28) (0.27) (0.19) (0.01) (0.01) (0.21)

Copyright 2012 Securities Research Company

Bonds $.0 Mil Com 93.495 Mil BV 2.49 /sh P/E N/A (Ind DRUGS P/E 12.73) Ctry US

ASTRONICS CORP (ATRO)

Manufactures lighting and packaging products

Growth Performance Measurement				
Years	Price	Earn.	Div.	Tot Ret
Last 1	-36.1	-13.1	---	-36.1
Last 5	-11.6	-1.4	---	-11.6
Last 10	12.8	8.9	---	12.8

Adj. for
10% SD
10/13/00

0.10 (0.09)
0.10 0.06 (0.03)
0.11 0.07 0.04

Copyright 2012 Securities Research Company

Bonds $9.4 Mil Com 9.900 Mil BV 9.46 /sh P/E 15.05 (Ind AEROD P/E 12.96) Ctry US

ATA INC (ATAI)

Provides computer-based testing services in the People's Republic of C

Growth Performance Measurement				
Years	Price	Earn.	Div.	Tot Ret
Last 1	-7.1	25.9	---	-1.6
Last 5	---	---	---	---
Last 10	---	---	---	---

(0.25) (0.22) (0.24) (0.01)
(0.10) (0.20) 0.04 (0.02) (0.19)
(0.11) (0.27) 0.00 0.03 (0.26)

Copyright 2012 Securities Research Company

Bonds $.0 Mil Com 22.506 Mil BV 1.06 /sh P/E 20.50 (Ind EDSER P/E 5.79) Ctry US

ATHENAHEALTH INC (ATHN)

Medical group office automation subscription services

Growth Performance Measurement				
Years	Price	Earn.	Div.	Tot Ret
Last 1	49.2	6.6	---	49.2
Last 5	15.3	---	---	15.3
Last 10	---	---	---	---

(0.66) (1.69) (2.32) (1.88) (1.53)
(0.44) (1.28) (2.51) (2.00) (2.23)
(0.22) (0.87) (2.10) (2.13) (1.98) (0.28)

Copyright 2012 Securities Research Company

Bonds $.0 Mil Com 36.272 Mil BV 8.13 /sh P/E 75.56 (Ind HCSVS P/E 15.09) Ctry US

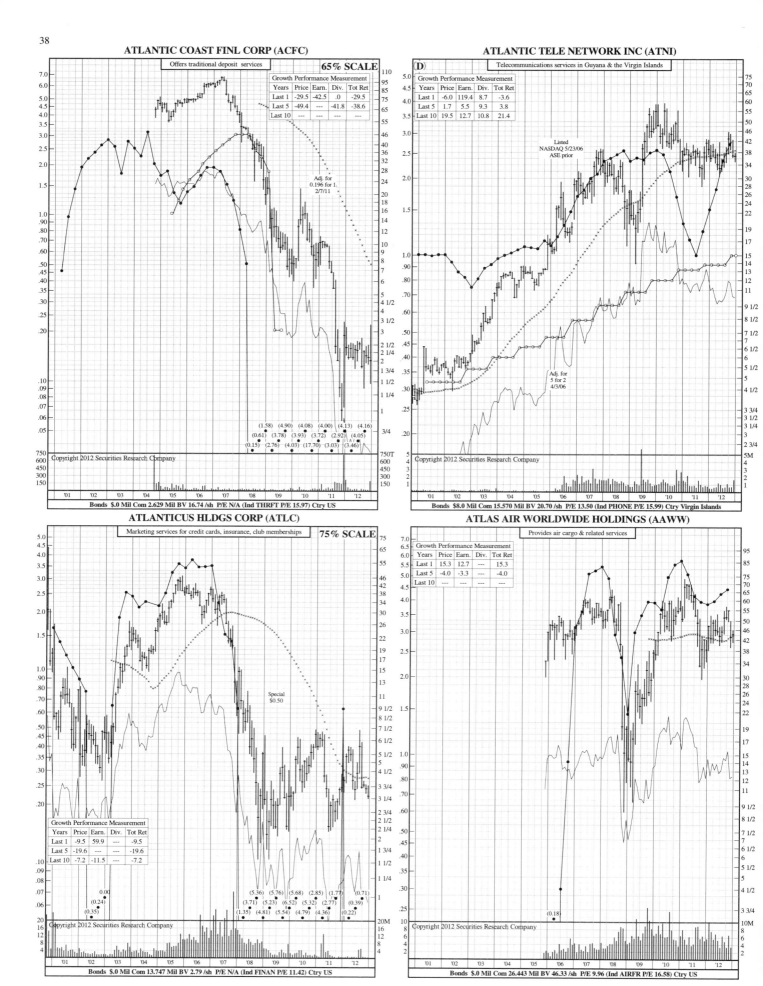

ATLANTIC COAST FINL CORP (ACFC)

Offers traditional deposit services

65% SCALE

Growth Performance Measurement				
Years	Price	Earn.	Div.	Tot Ret
Last 1	-29.5	-42.5	.0	-29.5
Last 5	-49.4	---	-41.8	-38.6
Last 10	---	---	---	---

Adj. for
0.196 for 1.
2/7/11

(1.58) (4.90) (4.08) (4.00) (4.13) (4.16)
(0.61) (3.78) (3.93) (3.72) (2.92) (4.05)
(0.15) (2.76) (4.03) (17.70) (3.03) (3.46)

Copyright 2012 Securities Research Company

'01 '02 '03 '04 '05 '06 '07 '08 '09 '10 '11 '12

Bonds $.0 Mil Com 2.629 Mil BV 16.74 /sh P/E N/A (Ind THRFT P/E 15.97) Ctry US

ATLANTIC TELE NETWORK INC (ATNI)

Telecommunications services in Guyana & the Virgin Islands

(D)

Growth Performance Measurement				
Years	Price	Earn.	Div.	Tot Ret
Last 1	-6.0	119.4	8.7	-3.6
Last 5	1.7	5.5	9.3	3.8
Last 10	19.5	12.7	10.8	21.4

Listed
NASDAQ 5/23/06
ASE prior

Adj. for
5 for 2
4/3/06

Copyright 2012 Securities Research Company

'01 '02 '03 '04 '05 '06 '07 '08 '09 '10 '11 '12

Bonds $8.0 Mil Com 15.570 Mil BV 20.70 /sh P/E 13.50 (Ind PHONE P/E 15.99) Ctry Virgin Islands

ATLANTICUS HLDGS CORP (ATLC)

Marketing services for credit cards, insurance, club memberships

75% SCALE

Special
$0.50

Growth Performance Measurement				
Years	Price	Earn.	Div.	Tot Ret
Last 1	-9.5	59.9	---	-9.5
Last 5	-19.6	---	---	-19.6
Last 10	-7.2	-11.5	---	-7.2

0.00
(0.24)
(0.35)

(5.36) (5.76) (5.68) (2.85) (1.77) (0.71)
(3.71) (5.23) (6.52) (5.32) (2.77) (0.39)
(1.35) (4.81) (5.54) (4.79) (4.36) (0.22)

Copyright 2012 Securities Research Company

'01 '02 '03 '04 '05 '06 '07 '08 '09 '10 '11 '12

Bonds $.0 Mil Com 13.747 Mil BV 2.79 /sh P/E N/A (Ind FINAN P/E 11.42) Ctry US

ATLAS AIR WORLDWIDE HOLDINGS (AAWW)

Provides air cargo & related services

Growth Performance Measurement				
Years	Price	Earn.	Div.	Tot Ret
Last 1	15.3	12.7	---	15.3
Last 5	-4.0	-3.3	---	-4.0
Last 10	---	---	---	---

(0.18)

Copyright 2012 Securities Research Company

'01 '02 '03 '04 '05 '06 '07 '08 '09 '10 '11 '12

Bonds $.0 Mil Com 26.443 Mil BV 46.33 /sh P/E 9.96 (Ind AIRFR P/E 16.58) Ctry US

38

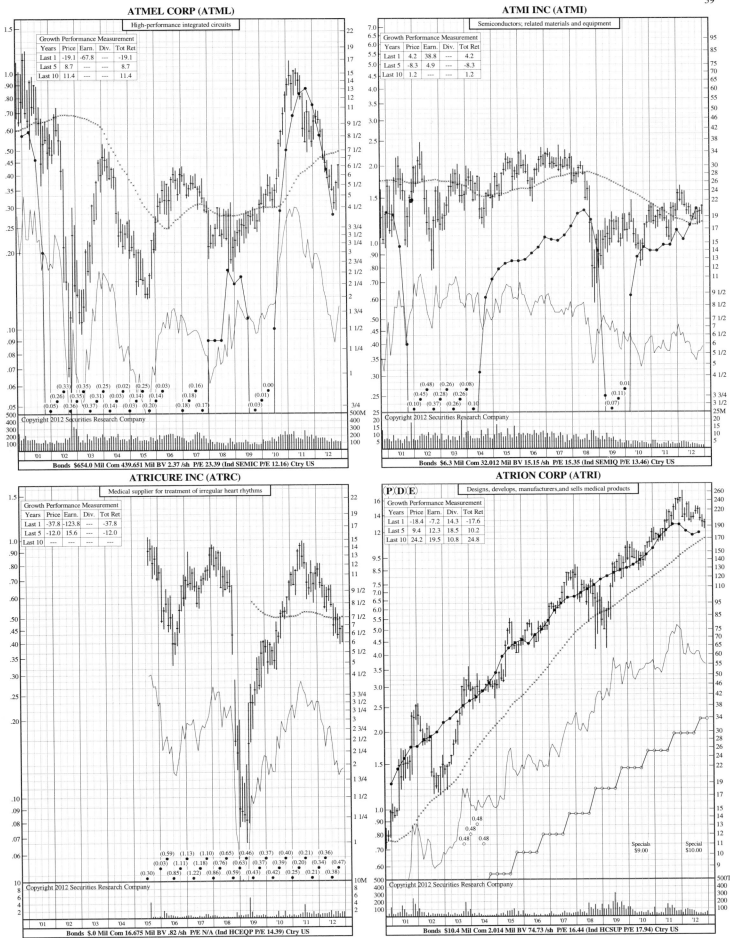

ATMEL CORP (ATML)

High-performance integrated circuits

Growth Performance Measurement

Years	Price	Earn.	Div.	Tot Ret
Last 1	-19.1	-67.8	---	-19.1
Last 5	8.7	---	---	8.7
Last 10	11.4	---	---	11.4

(0.33) (0.35) (0.25) (0.02) (0.25) (0.03)   (0.16)   0.00
(0.26) (0.35) (0.31) (0.03) (0.14) (0.14)   (0.18)   (0.01)
(0.05) (0.36) (0.37) (0.14) (0.03) (0.20) (0.18) (0.17) (0.03)

Copyright 2012 Securities Research Company

Bonds $654.0 Mil Com 439.651 Mil BV 2.37 /sh P/E 23.39 (Ind SEMIC P/E 12.16) Ctry US

ATMI INC (ATMI)

Semiconductors; related materials and equipment

Growth Performance Measurement

Years	Price	Earn.	Div.	Tot Ret
Last 1	4.2	38.8	---	4.2
Last 5	-8.3	4.9	---	-8.3
Last 10	1.2	---	---	1.2

(0.48) (0.26) (0.08)   0.01
(0.45) (0.28) (0.26)   (0.11)
(0.10) (0.37) (0.26) 0.10   (0.07)

Copyright 2012 Securities Research Company

Bonds $6.3 Mil Com 32.012 Mil BV 15.15 /sh P/E 15.35 (Ind SEMIQ P/E 13.46) Ctry US

ATRICURE INC (ATRC)

Medical supplier for treatment of irregular heart rhythms

Growth Performance Measurement

Years	Price	Earn.	Div.	Tot Ret
Last 1	-37.8	-123.8	---	-37.8
Last 5	-12.0	15.6	---	-12.0
Last 10	---	---	---	---

(0.59) (1.13) (1.10) (0.65) (0.46) (0.37) (0.40) (0.21) (0.36)
(0.03) (1.11) (1.18) (0.76) (0.63) (0.37) (0.39) (0.20) (0.34) (0.47)
(0.30) (0.85) (1.22) (0.86) (0.59) (0.43) (0.42) (0.25) (0.21) (0.38)

Copyright 2012 Securities Research Company

Bonds $.0 Mil Com 16.675 Mil BV .82 /sh P/E N/A (Ind HCEQP P/E 14.39) Ctry US

ATRION CORP (ATRI)

(P)(D)(E)   Designs, develops, manufacturers,and sells medical products

Growth Performance Measurement

Years	Price	Earn.	Div.	Tot Ret
Last 1	-18.4	-7.2	14.3	-17.6
Last 5	9.4	12.3	18.5	10.2
Last 10	24.2	19.5	10.8	24.8

0.48
0.48
0.48 0.48

Specials   Special
$9.00 $10.00

Copyright 2012 Securities Research Company

Bonds $10.4 Mil Com 2.014 Mil BV 74.73 /sh P/E 16.44 (Ind HCSUP P/E 17.94) Ctry US

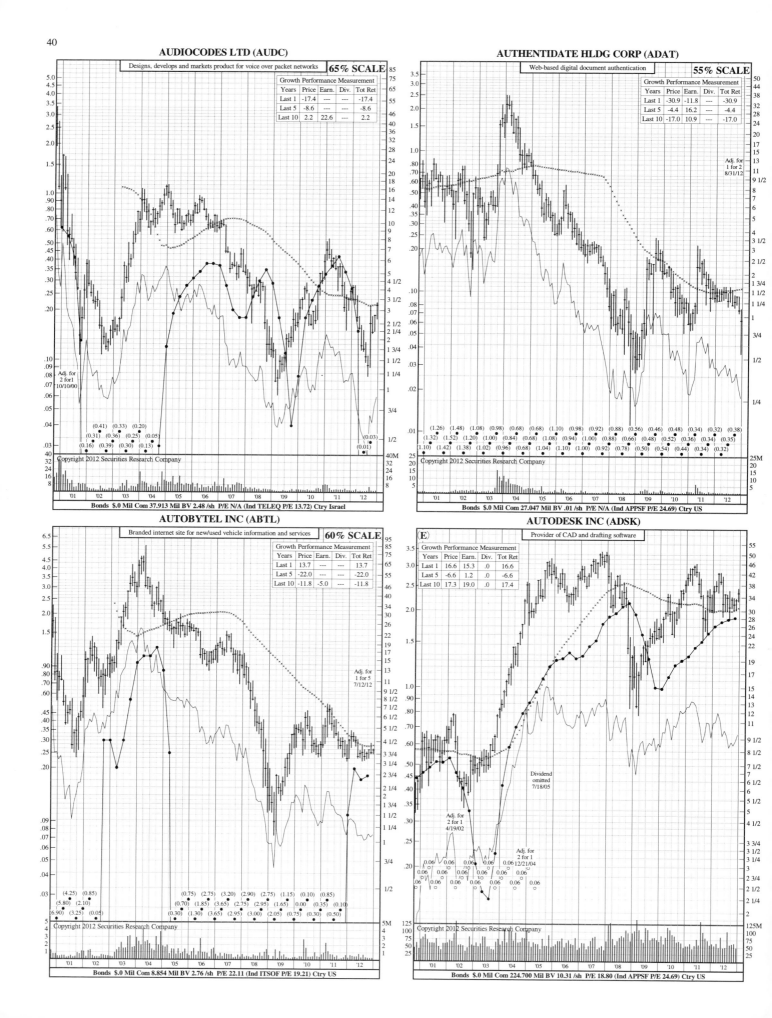

40

AUTOMATIC DATA PROCESSING IN (ADP)

Wide variety of computer services

(D)

Growth Performance Measurement				
Years	Price	Earn.	Div.	Tot Ret
Last 1	5.4	7.4	9.7	8.3
Last 5	5.0	6.9	11.4	7.5
Last 10	3.8	4.4	13.1	5.5

Added to
NASDAQ 100
12/12/08

Dist. 1 sh. Broadridge Financial Solutions
for ea. 4 shs. ADP held 3/23/07

Copyright 2012 Securities Research Company

Bonds $17861.7 Mil Com 485.474 Mil BV 13.22 /sh P/E 20.70 (Ind DPSVS P/E 20.19) Ctry US

AUXILIUM PHARMACEUTICALS INC (AUXL)

Developing treatments for urology and sexual health

Growth Performance Measurement				
Years	Price	Earn.	Div.	Tot Ret
Last 1	-7.0	56.4	---	-7.0
Last 5	-9.2	21.4	---	-9.2
Last 10	---	---	---	---

(9.41) (1.55) (1.37) (1.48) (1.06) (1.12) (1.16) (1.10) (1.07) (0.78) (0.21)
(9.07) (1.92) (1.38) (1.50) (1.13) (1.05) (1.13) (1.23) (0.98) (0.97) (0.48)
(8.56) (10.07) (1.59) (1.52) (1.35) (1.03) (1.12) (1.27) (1.06) (1.14) (0.69) (0.34)

Copyright 2012 Securities Research Company

Bonds $.0 Mil Com 49.208 Mil BV 2.11 /sh P/E N/A (Ind DRUGS P/E 12.73) Ctry US

AV HOMES INC (AVHI)

Develops upscale living communities; water & wastewater services

65% SCALE

Growth Performance Measurement				
Years	Price	Earn.	Div.	Tot Ret
Last 1	98.1	-294.1	---	98.1
Last 5	-19.4	---	---	-19.4
Last 10	-4.7	-25.0	---	-4.7

Avatar Holdings, Inc.
prior to 2/16/12

(0.36)
(0.17)
0.03

(1.88) (3.59) (2.58) (2.98) (2.97) (3.35)
(1.20) (3.16) (3.20) (3.07) (0.85) (3.54)
(0.27) (2.80) (3.29) (2.41) (3.80) (2.85)

Copyright 2012 Securities Research Company

Bonds $119.5 Mil Com 13.020 Mil BV 17.16 /sh P/E N/A (Ind REEDV P/E N/A) Ctry US

AVIAT NETWORKS INC. (AVNW)

Digital microwave radio and fiber optic products

55% SCALE

Growth Performance Measurement				
Years	Price	Earn.	Div.	Tot Ret
Last 1	79.8	175.0	---	79.8
Last 5	-27.7	-30.9	---	-27.7
Last 10	-9.4	---	---	-9.4

DMC Stratex Networks
prior to 9/13/02
Digital Microwave
prior to 8/15/00

Harris Starex Inc.
Prior To
01/29/10

Stratex Networks Inc.
prior to 1/29/07
Merged Harris Corp
&
Stratex Networks
1/26/07

Adj. for
1 for 4
1/29/07

(1.92) (0.76) (1.12) (1.60) (1.36) (0.04)   (0.24) (0.40)
(1.68) (1.24) (0.80) (1.60) (1.56) (0.72)   (0.02) (0.50)
(0.84) (1.68) (0.68) (1.56) (1.44) (1.08)   (6.40) (0.49) (0.22)

Copyright 2012 Securities Research Company

Bonds $.0 Mil Com 61.256 Mil BV 2.62 /sh P/E 29.91 (Ind TELEQ P/E 13.72) Ctry US

42

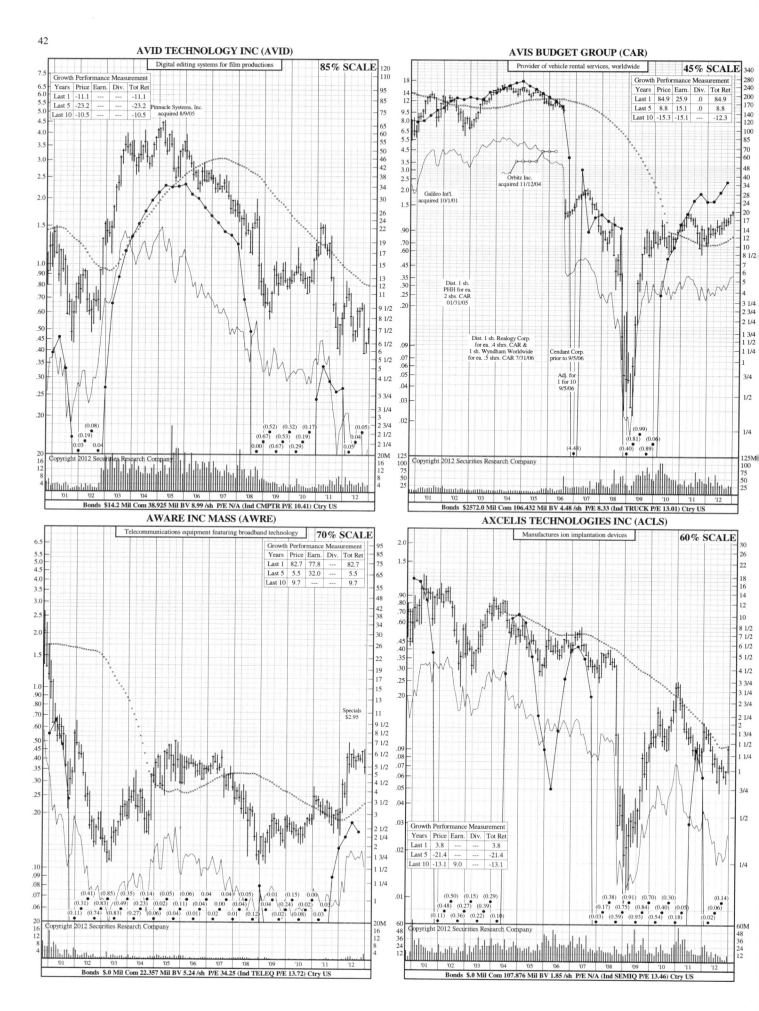

AVID TECHNOLOGY INC (AVID)

Digital editing systems for film productions

85% SCALE

Pinnacle Systems, Inc.
acquired 8/9/05

Growth Performance Measurement				
Years	Price	Earn.	Div.	Tot Ret
Last 1	-11.1	---		-11.1
Last 5	-23.2	---		-23.2
Last 10	-10.5	---		-10.5

(0.08)
(0.19)
0.03   0.04

(0.52) (0.32) (0.17)
(0.67) (0.53) (0.19)   (0.05)
0.00   (0.67) (0.29)   0.04
       0.05   0.05

Copyright 2012 Securities Research Company

Bonds $14.2 Mil Com 38.925 Mil BV 8.99 /sh P/E N/A (Ind CMPTR P/E 10.41) Ctry US

AVIS BUDGET GROUP (CAR)

Provider of vehicle rental services, worldwide

45% SCALE

Growth Performance Measurement				
Years	Price	Earn.	Div.	Tot Ret
Last 1	84.9	25.9	.0	84.9
Last 5	8.8	15.1	.0	8.8
Last 10	-15.3	-15.1	---	-12.3

Orbitz Inc.
acquired 11/12/04

Galileo Intl.
acquired 10/1/01

Dist. 1 sh.
PHH for ea.
2 shs. CAR
01/31/05

Dist. 1 sh. Realogy Corp.
for ea. .4 shrs. CAR &
1 sh. Wyndham Worldwide
for ea. .5 shrs. CAR 7/31/06

Cendant Corp.
prior to 9/5/06

Adj. for
1 for 10
9/5/06

(0.99)
(0.81) (0.06)
(4.48)   (0.40) (0.89)

Copyright 2012 Securities Research Company

Bonds $2572.0 Mil Com 106.432 Mil BV 4.48 /sh P/E 8.33 (Ind TRUCK P/E 13.01) Ctry US

AWARE INC MASS (AWRE)

Telecommunications equipment featuring broadband technology

70% SCALE

Growth Performance Measurement				
Years	Price	Earn.	Div.	Tot Ret
Last 1	82.7	77.8	---	82.7
Last 5	5.5	32.0	---	5.5
Last 10	9.7	---	---	9.7

Specials
$2.95

(0.41) (0.85) (0.35) (0.14) (0.05) (0.06) 0.04   0.04 (0.05) (0.01) (0.15) 0.00
(0.31) (0.83) (0.49) (0.23) (0.02) (0.11) (0.04)   (0.04) 0.04 (0.24) (0.02) (0.03)
(0.11) (0.74) (0.83) (0.27) (0.06) (0.04) (0.01)   0.01   0.12 (0.02) (0.08) 0.03

Copyright 2012 Securities Research Company

Bonds $.0 Mil Com 22.357 Mil BV 5.24 /sh P/E 34.25 (Ind TELEQ P/E 13.72) Ctry US

AXCELIS TECHNOLOGIES INC (ACLS)

Manufactures ion implantation devices

60% SCALE

Growth Performance Measurement				
Years	Price	Earn.	Div.	Tot Ret
Last 1	3.8	---		3.8
Last 5	-21.4	---		-21.4
Last 10	-13.1	9.0		-13.1

(0.50) (0.15) (0.29)   (0.38) (0.91) (0.70) (0.30)   (0.14)
(0.48) (0.27) (0.39)   (0.17) (0.75) (0.84) (0.40) (0.05) (0.06)
(0.11) (0.36) (0.22) (0.10)   (0.03) (0.59) (0.93) (0.54) (0.18) (0.02)

Copyright 2012 Securities Research Company

Bonds $.0 Mil Com 107.876 Mil BV 1.85 /sh P/E N/A (Ind SEMIQ P/E 13.46) Ctry US

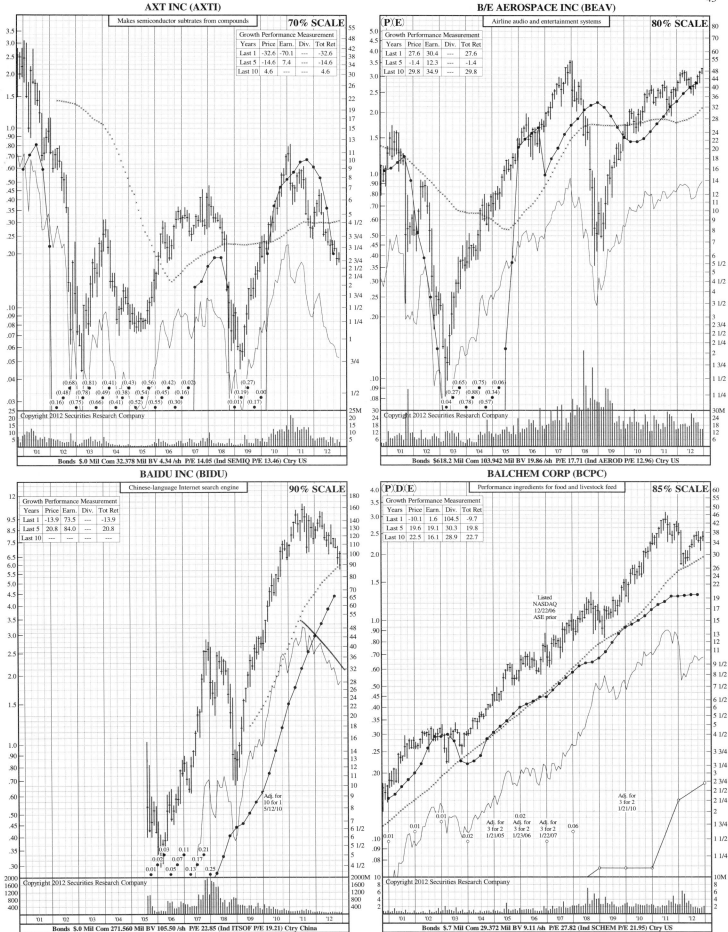

AXT INC (AXTI)

Makes semiconductor subtrates from compounds

70% SCALE

Growth Performance Measurement				
Years	Price	Earn.	Div.	Tot Ret
Last 1	-32.6	-70.1	---	-32.6
Last 5	-14.6	7.4	---	-14.6
Last 10	4.6	---	---	4.6

(0.68) (0.81) (0.41) (0.43) (0.56) (0.42) (0.02)   (0.27)
(0.48) (0.78) (0.49) (0.38) (0.54) (0.45) (0.16)   (0.19) 0.00
(0.16) (0.75) (0.66) (0.41) (0.52) (0.55) (0.30)   (0.01) (0.17)

Copyright 2012 Securities Research Company

Bonds $.0 Mil Com 32.378 Mil BV 4.34 /sh P/E 14.05 (Ind SEMIQ P/E 13.46) Ctry US

B/E AEROSPACE INC (BEAV)

Airline audio and entertainment systems

(P)(E)   **80% SCALE**

Growth Performance Measurement				
Years	Price	Earn.	Div.	Tot Ret
Last 1	27.6	30.4	---	27.6
Last 5	-1.4	12.3	---	-1.4
Last 10	29.8	34.9	---	29.8

(0.65) (0.75) (0.06)
(0.27) (0.88) (0.34)
0.04 (0.78) (0.57)

Copyright 2012 Securities Research Company

Bonds $618.2 Mil Com 103.942 Mil BV 19.86 /sh P/E 17.71 (Ind AEROD P/E 12.96) Ctry US

BAIDU INC (BIDU)

Chinese-language Internet search engine

90% SCALE

Growth Performance Measurement				
Years	Price	Earn.	Div.	Tot Ret
Last 1	-13.9	73.5	---	-13.9
Last 5	20.8	84.0	---	20.8
Last 10	---	---	---	---

Adj. for
10 for 1
5/12/10

0.03 0.11 0.21
0.02 0.07 0.17
0.01 0.05 0.13 0.25

Copyright 2012 Securities Research Company

Bonds $.0 Mil Com 271.560 Mil BV 105.50 /sh P/E 22.85 (Ind ITSOF P/E 19.21) Ctry China

BALCHEM CORP (BCPC)

Performance ingredients for food and livestock feed

(P)(D)(E)   **85% SCALE**

Growth Performance Measurement				
Years	Price	Earn.	Div.	Tot Ret
Last 1	-10.1	1.6	104.5	-9.7
Last 5	19.6	19.1	30.3	19.8
Last 10	22.5	16.1	28.9	22.7

Listed
NASDAQ
12/22/06
ASE prior

Adj. for
3 for 2
1/21/10

0.01
0.01   0.02
0.01   Adj. for   Adj. for   Adj. for
3 for 2   3 for 2   3 for 2   0.06
0.02   1/21/05 1/23/06 1/22/07
0.01

Copyright 2012 Securities Research Company

Bonds $.7 Mil Com 29.372 Mil BV 9.11 /sh P/E 27.82 (Ind SCHEM P/E 21.95) Ctry US

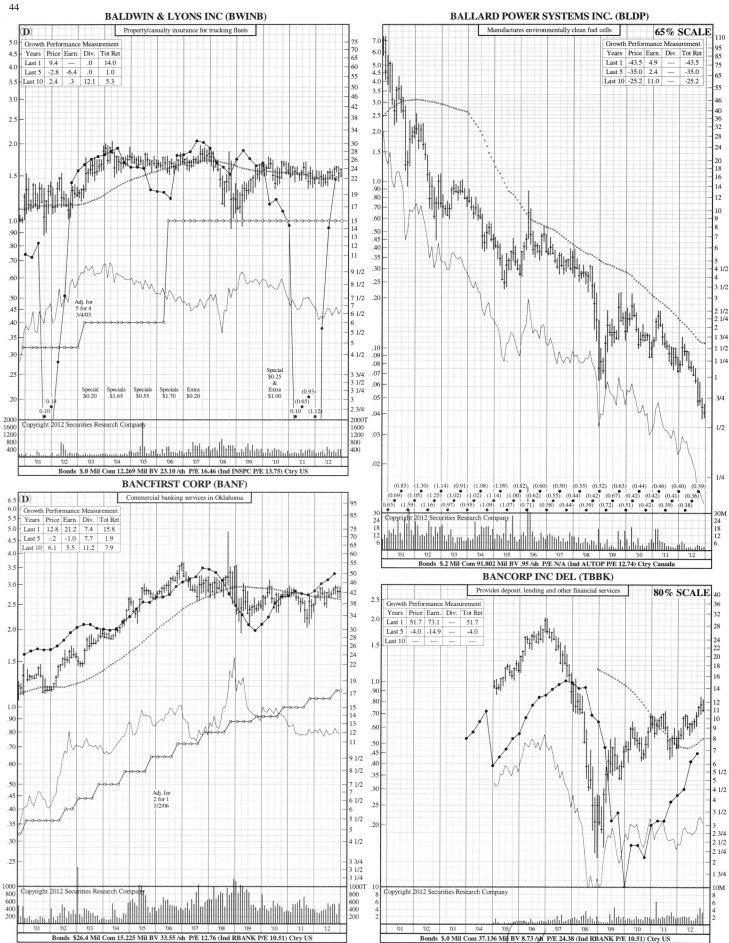

44

BALDWIN & LYONS INC (BWINB)

Property/casualty insurance for trucking fleets

Growth Performance Measurement

Years	Price	Earn.	Div.	Tot Ret
Last 1	9.4	---	.0	14.0
Last 5	-2.8	-6.4	.0	1.0
Last 10	2.4	.3	12.1	5.3

Adj. for 5 for 4 3/4/03

Special $0.20   Specials $1.65   Specials $0.55   Specials $1.70   Extra $0.20

Special $0.25 & Extra $1.00

(0.93)
(0.65)
0.10   (1.12)

0.1
0.10

Copyright 2012 Securities Research Company

Bonds $.0 Mil Com 12.269 Mil BV 23.10 /sh P/E 16.46 (Ind INSPC P/E 13.75) Ctry US

BALLARD POWER SYSTEMS INC. (BLDP)

Manufactures environmentally clean fuel cells

65% SCALE

Growth Performance Measurement

Years	Price	Earn.	Div.	Tot Ret
Last 1	-43.5	4.9	---	-43.5
Last 5	-35.0	2.4	---	-35.0
Last 10	-25.2	11.0	---	-25.2

(0.85) (1.30) (1.14) (0.91) (1.08) (1.09) (0.82) (0.60) (0.50) (0.33) (0.52) (0.63) (0.44) (0.46) (0.40) (0.39)
(0.69) (1.05) (1.25) (1.02) (1.02) (1.14) (1.00) (0.62) (0.55) (0.44) (0.42) (0.67) (0.42) (0.42) (0.41) (0.36)
(0.65) (1.59) (1.16) (0.97) (0.95) (1.09) (1.07) (0.71) (0.58) (0.44) (0.39) (0.72) (0.51) (0.42) (0.39) (0.38)

Copyright 2012 Securities Research Company

Bonds $.2 Mil Com 91.802 Mil BV .95 /sh P/E N/A (Ind AUTOP P/E 12.74) Ctry Canada

BANCFIRST CORP (BANF)

Commercial banking services in Oklahoma

Growth Performance Measurement

Years	Price	Earn.	Div.	Tot Ret
Last 1	12.8	21.2	7.4	15.8
Last 5	-.2	-1.0	7.7	1.9
Last 10	6.1	5.5	11.2	7.9

Adj. for 2 for 1 3/2/06

Copyright 2012 Securities Research Company

Bonds $26.4 Mil Com 15.225 Mil BV 33.55 /sh P/E 12.76 (Ind RBANK P/E 10.51) Ctry US

BANCORP INC DEL (TBBK)

Provides deposit, lending and other financial services

80% SCALE

Growth Performance Measurement

Years	Price	Earn.	Div.	Tot Ret
Last 1	51.7	73.1	---	51.7
Last 5	-4.0	-14.9	---	-4.0
Last 10	---	---	---	---

Copyright 2012 Securities Research Company

Bonds $.0 Mil Com 37.136 Mil BV 8.73 /sh P/E 24.38 (Ind RBANK P/E 10.51) Ctry US

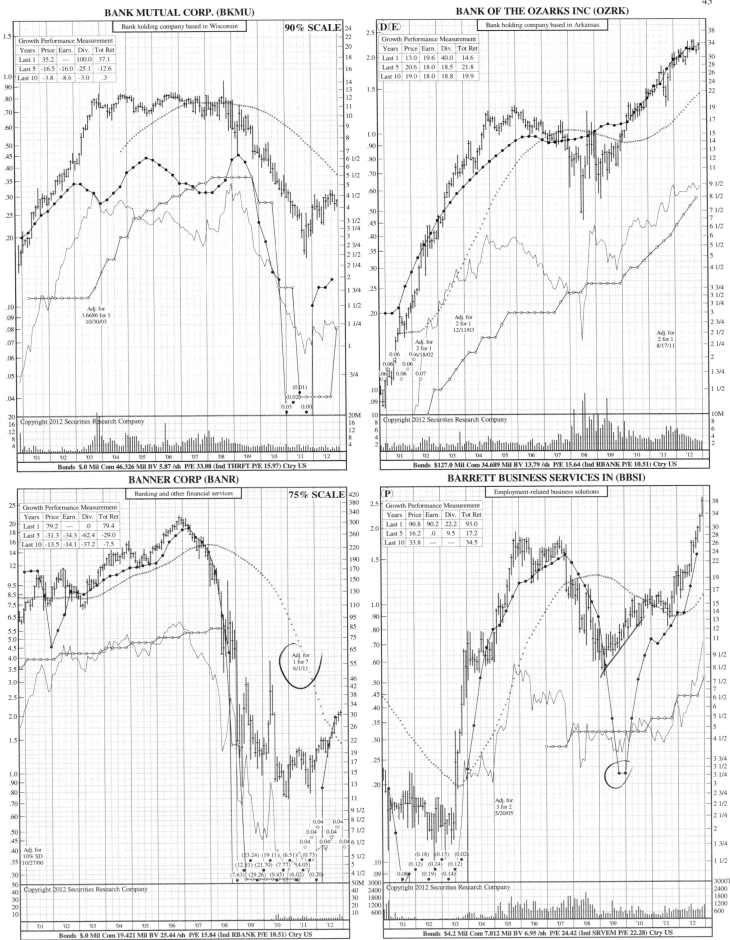

45

BANK MUTUAL CORP. (BKMU)

Bank holding company based in Wisconsin

90% SCALE

Growth Performance Measurement

Years	Price	Earn.	Div.	Tot Ret
Last 1	35.2	---	100.0	37.1
Last 5	-16.5	-16.0	-25.1	-12.6
Last 10	-3.8	-8.6	-3.0	.3

Adj. for
3.6686 for 1
10/30/03

(0.01)
(0.02)
0.03 0.00

Copyright 2012 Securities Research Company

Bonds $.0 Mil Com 46.326 Mil BV 5.87 /sh P/E 33.08 (Ind THRFT P/E 15.97) Ctry US

BANK OF THE OZARKS INC (OZRK)

Bank holding company based in Arkansas

(D)(E)

Growth Performance Measurement

Years	Price	Earn.	Div.	Tot Ret
Last 1	13.0	19.6	40.0	14.6
Last 5	20.6	18.0	18.5	21.8
Last 10	19.0	18.0	18.8	19.9

Adj. for
2 for 1
12/11/03

Adj. for
2 for 1
06/18/02

0.06 0.06
0.06 0.06
0.06   0.07

Adj. for
2 for 1
8/17/11

Copyright 2012 Securities Research Company

Bonds $127.0 Mil Com 34.689 Mil BV 13.79 /sh P/E 15.64 (Ind RBANK P/E 10.51) Ctry US

BANNER CORP (BANR)

Banking and other financial services

75% SCALE

Growth Performance Measurement

Years	Price	Earn.	Div.	Tot Ret
Last 1	79.2	---	.0	79.4
Last 5	-31.3	-34.3	-62.4	-29.0
Last 10	-13.5	-14.1	-37.2	-7.5

Adj. for
1 for 7
6/1/11

Adj. for
10% SD
10/27/00

0.04   0.04
0.04   0.04
0.04   0.04
0.04   0.04

(23.24) (19.11) (6.51) (0.73)
(12.81) (21.70) (7.77) (4.05)
(7.63) (29.26) (9.45) (6.02) (0.20)

Copyright 2012 Securities Research Company

Bonds $.0 Mil Com 19.421 Mil BV 25.44 /sh P/E 15.84 (Ind RBANK P/E 10.51) Ctry US

BARRETT BUSINESS SERVICES IN (BBSI)

Employment-related business solutions

(P)

Growth Performance Measurement

Years	Price	Earn.	Div.	Tot Ret
Last 1	90.8	90.2	22.2	93.0
Last 5	16.2	.0	9.5	17.2
Last 10	33.8	---	---	34.5

Adj. for
3 for 2
5/20/05

(0.18) (0.15) (0.02)
(0.12) (0.24) (0.12)
0.08 (0.19) (0.14)

Copyright 2012 Securities Research Company

Bonds $4.2 Mil Com 7.012 Mil BV 6.95 /sh P/E 24.42 (Ind SRVEM P/E 22.28) Ctry US

BARRY R G CORP OHIO (DFZ)

Footwear and thermal products

Growth Performance Measurement				
Years	Price	Earn.	Div.	Tot Ret
Last 1	17.3	33.0	14.3	19.9
Last 5	15.0	5.4	34.8	16.3
Last 10	13.2	---	16.1	13.8

Listed
Nasdaq 3/11/08
Amex prior

Special
$0.25

(0.30)　(0.23)　(1.27)　(0.84)　(4.14)
(0.30)　(0.11)　(1.23)　(0.94)　(3.87)　(0.70)
(0.09)　(0.03)　(0.48)　(1.06)　(3.26)　(2.05)

Copyright 2012 Securities Research Company

'01 '02 '03 '04 '05 '06 '07 '08 '09 '10 '11 '12

Bonds $.4 Mil Com 11.265 Mil BV 7.54 /sh P/E 11.71 (Ind SHOES P/E 22.44) Ctry US

BASSETT FURNITURE INDS INC (BSET)

Wood and upholstered furniture manufacturer

75% SCALE

Growth Performance Measurement				
Years	Price	Earn.	Div.	Tot Ret
Last 1	66.5	160.0	66.7	69.0
Last 5	6.0	---	-24.2	7.9
Last 10	-1.4	4.8	-12.9	2.1

Dividend
Omitted
06/07/10

Special
$1.25

(0.21)　(0.27)　(2.56)　(0.67)
(0.08)　(0.02)　(1.85)　(1.52)
(0.10)　(0.01)　(1.05)　(2.51)

Copyright 2012 Securities Research Company

'01 '02 '03 '04 '05 '06 '07 '08 '09 '10 '11 '12

Bonds $18.0 Mil Com 10.892 Mil BV 14.23 /sh P/E 11.99 (Ind HMFRN P/E 19.93) Ctry US

BBCN BANCORP INC (BBCN)

Holding company serving small and mid-sized businesses and consumers **70% SCALE**

Growth Performance Measurement				
Years	Price	Earn.	Div.	Tot Ret
Last 1	22.4	21.9	81.8	23.0
Last 5	-.2	-9.9	12.7	.1
Last 10	8.4	5.2	7.2	9.1

Center Financial Cp
acquired 11/30/11

Nara Bancorp, Inc.
prior to 11/30/11

Adj. for
2 for 1
3/18/03

Adj. for
2 for1
6/16/04

Dividend
Omitted
04/20/10

(0.75)　(0.14)
(0.64)　(0.33)
(0.34)　(0.42)　(0.16)

Copyright 2012 Securities Research Company

'01 '02 '03 '04 '05 '06 '07 '08 '09 '10 '11 '12

Bonds $.0 Mil Com 78.042 Mil BV 9.41 /sh P/E 14.83 (Ind RBANK P/E 10.51) Ctry US

BEASLEY BROADCAST GROUP INC (BBGI)

Owns and operates radio stations

Dividend
Omitted
01/21/10

Growth Performance Measurement				
Years	Price	Earn.	Div.	Tot Ret
Last 1	55.2	25.0	.0	55.2
Last 5	-1.2	11.4	-4.4	-.3
Last 10	-8.6	13.9	---	-7.3

Special
$0.085

(0.29)　(0.43)
(0.08)　(0.58)
(0.09)　(0.51)　(0.15)

Copyright 2012 Securities Research Company

'01 '02 '03 '04 '05 '06 '07 '08 '09 '10 '11 '12

Bonds $163.0 Mil Com 6.147 Mil BV 3.51 /sh P/E 8.89 (Ind MEDIA P/E 18.56) Ctry US

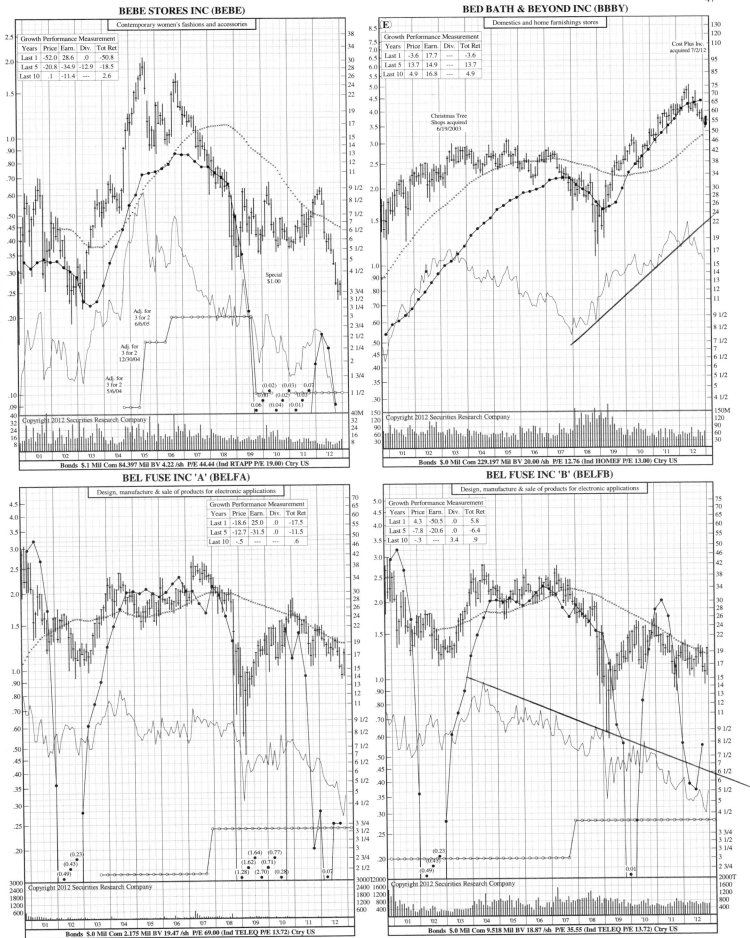

BEBE STORES INC (BEBE)

Contemporary women's fashions and accessories

Growth Performance Measurement				
Years	Price	Earn.	Div.	Tot Ret
Last 1	-52.0	28.6	.0	-50.8
Last 5	-20.8	-34.9	-12.9	-18.5
Last 10	.1	-11.4	---	2.6

Special $1.00

Adj. for 3 for 2 6/6/05

Adj. for 3 for 2 12/30/04

Adj. for 3 for 2 5/6/04

(0.02) (0.03) 0.07
0.00 (0.02) (0.03)
0.06 (0.04) (0.01)

Copyright 2012 Securities Research Company

Bonds $.1 Mil Com 84.397 Mil BV 4.22 /sh P/E 44.44 (Ind RTAPP P/E 19.00) Ctry US

BED BATH & BEYOND INC (BBBY)

Domestics and home furnishings stores

(E)

Cost Plus Inc. acquired 7/2/12

Growth Performance Measurement				
Years	Price	Earn.	Div.	Tot Ret
Last 1	-3.6	17.7	---	-3.6
Last 5	13.7	14.9	---	13.7
Last 10	4.9	16.8	---	4.9

Christmas Tree Shops acquired 6/19/2003

Copyright 2012 Securities Research Company

Bonds $.0 Mil Com 229.197 Mil BV 20.00 /sh P/E 12.76 (Ind HOMEF P/E 13.00) Ctry US

BEL FUSE INC 'A' (BELFA)

Design, manufacture & sale of products for electronic applications

Growth Performance Measurement				
Years	Price	Earn.	Div.	Tot Ret
Last 1	-18.6	25.0	.0	-17.5
Last 5	-12.7	-31.5	.0	-11.5
Last 10	-.5	---	---	.6

(0.23)
(0.43)
(0.49)

(1.64) (0.77)
(1.62) (0.71)
(1.28) (2.70) (0.28)
0.07

Copyright 2012 Securities Research Company

Bonds $.0 Mil Com 2.175 Mil BV 19.47 /sh P/E 69.00 (Ind TELEQ P/E 13.72) Ctry US

BEL FUSE INC 'B' (BELFB)

Design, manufacture & sale of products for electronic applications

Growth Performance Measurement				
Years	Price	Earn.	Div.	Tot Ret
Last 1	4.3	-50.5	.0	5.8
Last 5	-7.8	-20.6	.0	-6.4
Last 10	-.3	---	3.4	.9

(0.23)
(0.43)
(0.49)

0.01

Copyright 2012 Securities Research Company

Bonds $.0 Mil Com 9.518 Mil BV 18.87 /sh P/E 35.55 (Ind TELEQ P/E 13.72) Ctry US

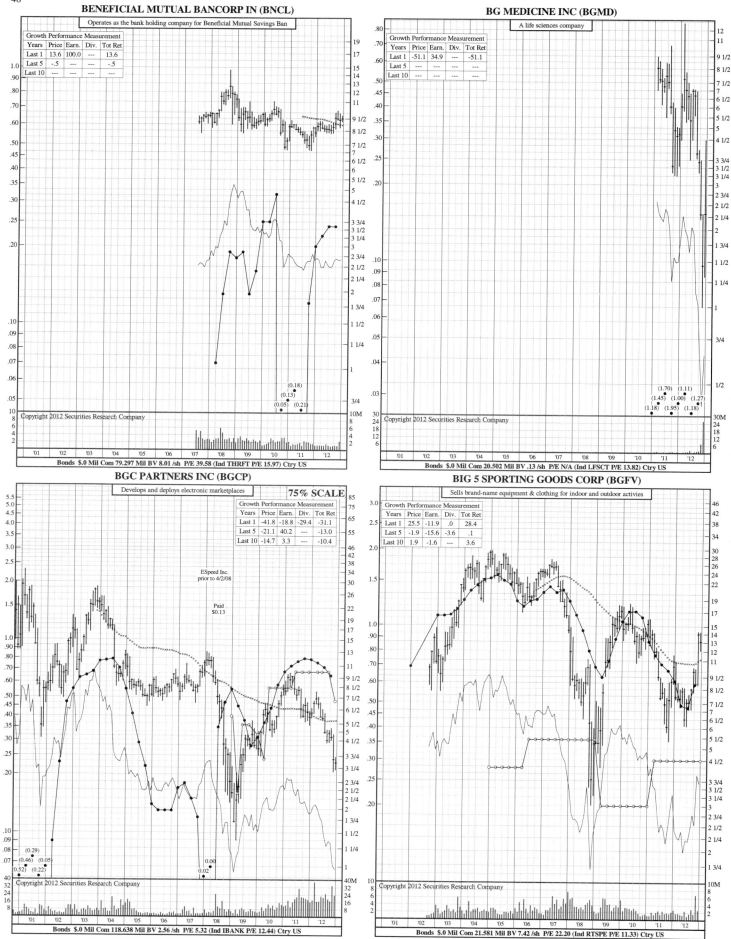

48

BENEFICIAL MUTUAL BANCORP IN (BNCL)

Operates as the bank holding company for Beneficial Mutual Savings Ban

Growth Performance Measurement				
Years	Price	Earn.	Div.	Tot Ret
Last 1	13.6	100.0	---	13.6
Last 5	-.5	---	---	-.5
Last 10	---	---	---	---

(0.18)
(0.13)
(0.05) (0.21)

Copyright 2012 Securities Research Company

Bonds $.0 Mil Com 79.297 Mil BV 8.01 /sh P/E 39.58 (Ind THRFT P/E 15.97) Ctry US

BG MEDICINE INC (BGMD)

A life sciences company

Growth Performance Measurement				
Years	Price	Earn.	Div.	Tot Ret
Last 1	-51.1	34.9	---	-51.1
Last 5	---	---	---	---
Last 10	---	---	---	---

(1.70) (1.11)
(1.45) (1.00) (1.27)
(1.18) (1.95) (1.18)

Copyright 2012 Securities Research Company

Bonds $.0 Mil Com 20.502 Mil BV .13 /sh P/E N/A (Ind LFSCT P/E 13.82) Ctry US

BGC PARTNERS INC (BGCP)

Develops and deploys electronic marketplaces

75% SCALE

Growth Performance Measurement				
Years	Price	Earn.	Div.	Tot Ret
Last 1	-41.8	-18.8	-29.4	-31.1
Last 5	-21.1	40.2	---	-13.0
Last 10	-14.7	3.3	---	-10.4

ESpeed Inc.
prior to 4/2/08

Paid
$0.13

(0.29)
(0.46) (0.05)
(0.52) (0.22)

0.00
0.02

Copyright 2012 Securities Research Company

Bonds $.0 Mil Com 118.638 Mil BV 2.56 /sh P/E 5.32 (Ind IBANK P/E 12.44) Ctry US

BIG 5 SPORTING GOODS CORP (BGFV)

Sells brand-name equipment & clothing for indoor and outdoor activies

Growth Performance Measurement				
Years	Price	Earn.	Div.	Tot Ret
Last 1	25.5	-11.9	.0	28.4
Last 5	-1.9	-15.6	-3.6	.1
Last 10	1.9	-1.6	---	3.6

Copyright 2012 Securities Research Company

Bonds $.0 Mil Com 21.581 Mil BV 7.42 /sh P/E 22.20 (Ind RTSPE P/E 11.33) Ctry US

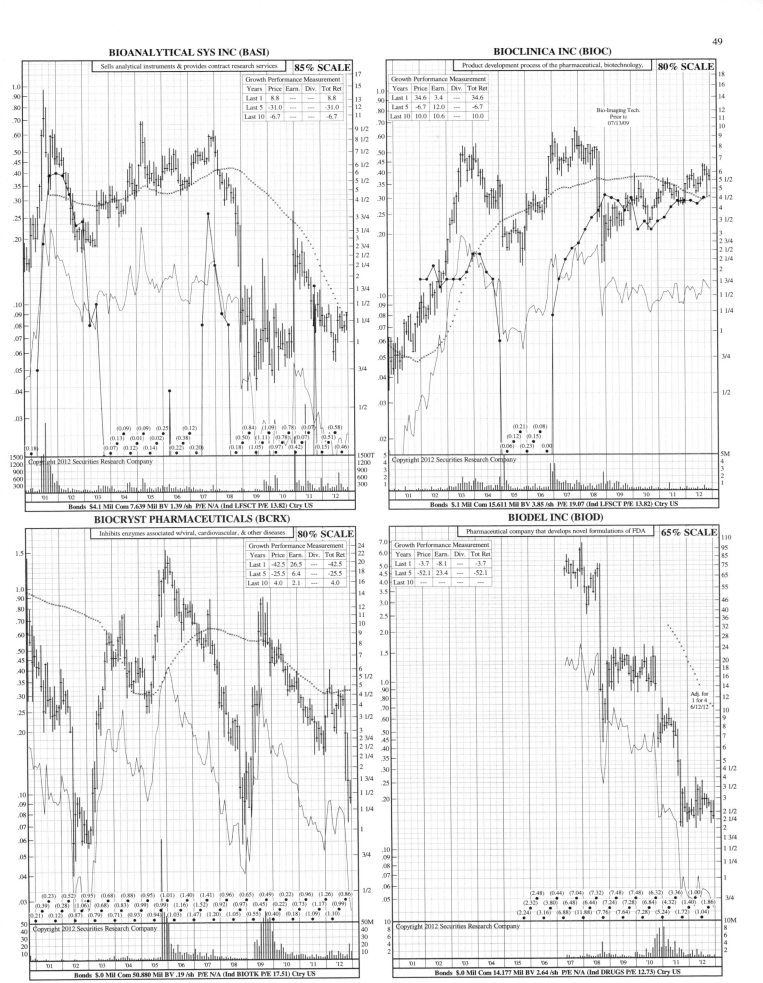

BIOANALYTICAL SYS INC (BASI)

Sells analytical instruments & provides contract research services

85% SCALE

Growth Performance Measurement

Years	Price	Earn.	Div.	Tot Ret
Last 1	8.8	---	---	8.8
Last 5	-31.0	---	---	-31.0
Last 10	-6.7	---	---	-6.7

(0.18)
(0.09) (0.09) (0.25) (0.12) (0.84) (1.09) (0.78) (0.07) (0.58)
(0.13) (0.01) (0.02) (0.38) (0.50) (1.11) (0.78) (0.07) (0.51)
(0.07) (0.12) (0.14) (0.22) (0.20) (0.18) (1.05) (0.97) (0.42) (0.15) (0.46)

1500
1200
900
600
300

Copyright 2012 Securities Research Company

1500T
900
600
300

Bonds $4.1 Mil Com 7.639 Mil BV 1.39 /sh P/E N/A (Ind LFSCT P/E 13.82) Ctry US

BIOCLINICA INC (BIOC)

Product development process of the pharmaceutical, biotechnology,

80% SCALE

Growth Performance Measurement

Years	Price	Earn.	Div.	Tot Ret
Last 1	34.6	3.4	---	34.6
Last 5	-6.7	12.0	---	-6.7
Last 10	10.0	10.6	---	10.0

Bio-Imaging Tech.
Prior to
07/13/09

(0.21) (0.08)
(0.12) (0.15)
(0.06) (0.23) 0.00

Copyright 2012 Securities Research Company

5M
4
3
2
1

Bonds $.1 Mil Com 15.611 Mil BV 3.85 /sh P/E 19.07 (Ind LFSCT P/E 13.82) Ctry US

BIOCRYST PHARMACEUTICALS (BCRX)

Inhibits enzymes associated w/viral, cardiovascular, & other diseases

80% SCALE

Growth Performance Measurement

Years	Price	Earn.	Div.	Tot Ret
Last 1	-42.5	26.5	---	-42.5
Last 5	-25.5	6.4	---	-25.5
Last 10	4.0	2.1	---	4.0

(0.23) (0.52) (0.95) (0.68) (0.88) (0.95) (1.01) (1.40) (1.41) (0.96) (0.65) (0.49) (0.22) (0.96) (1.26) (0.86)
(0.39) (0.28) (1.06) (0.68) (0.83) (0.99) (0.99) (1.16) (1.52) (0.92) (0.97) (0.45) (0.22) (0.73) (1.17) (0.99)
(0.21) (0.12) (0.87) (0.79) (0.71) (0.93) (0.94) (1.03) (1.47) (1.20) (0.55) (0.40) (0.18) (1.09) (1.10)

50
40
30
20
10

Copyright 2012 Securities Research Company

50M
40
30
20
10

Bonds $.0 Mil Com 50.880 Mil BV .19 /sh P/E N/A (Ind BIOTK P/E 17.51) Ctry US

BIODEL INC (BIOD)

Pharmaceutical company that develops novel formulations of FDA

65% SCALE

Growth Performance Measurement

Years	Price	Earn.	Div.	Tot Ret
Last 1	-3.7	-8.1	---	-3.7
Last 5	-52.1	23.4	---	-52.1
Last 10	---	---	---	---

Adj. for
1 for 4
6/12/12

(2.48) (0.44) (7.04) (7.32) (7.48) (7.48) (6.32) (3.36) (1.00)
(2.32) (3.80) (6.48) (6.44) (7.24) (7.28) (6.84) (4.32) (1.40) (1.86)
(2.24) (3.16) (6.88) (11.88) (7.76) (7.64) (7.28) (5.24) (1.72) (1.04)

10
8
6
4
2

Copyright 2012 Securities Research Company

10M
8
6
4
2

Bonds $.0 Mil Com 14.177 Mil BV 2.64 /sh P/E N/A (Ind DRUGS P/E 12.73) Ctry US

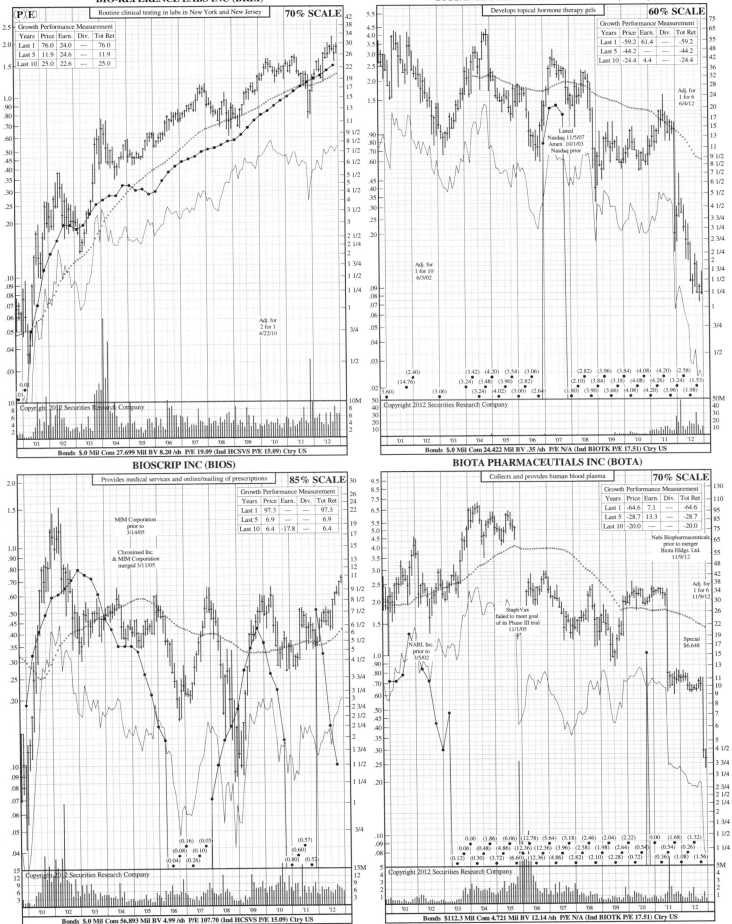

BIO-REFERENCE LABS INC (BRLI)

Routine clinical testing in labs in New York and New Jersey

70% SCALE

Growth Performance Measurement

Years	Price	Earn.	Div.	Tot Ret
Last 1	76.0	24.0	---	76.0
Last 5	11.9	24.6	---	11.9
Last 10	25.0	22.6	---	25.0

Adj. for 2 for 1 4/22/10

Copyright 2012 Securities Research Company

Bonds $.0 Mil Com 27.699 Mil BV 8.20 /sh P/E 19.09 (Ind HCSVS P/E 15.09) Ctry US

BIOSANTE PHARMACEUTICALS INC (BPAX)

Develops topical hormone therapy gels

60% SCALE

Growth Performance Measurement

Years	Price	Earn.	Div.	Tot Ret
Last 1	-59.2	61.4	---	-59.2
Last 5	-44.2	---	---	-44.2
Last 10	-24.4	4.4	---	-24.4

Adj. for 1 for 6 6/4/12

Listed Nasdaq 11/5/07 Amex 10/1/03 Nasdaq prior

Adj. for 1 for 10 6/3/02

(2.40) (3.42) (4.20) (3.54) (3.06) (2.82) (3.96) (3.84) (4.08) (4.20) (2.58)
(14.76) (3.24) (3.48) (3.90) (2.82) (2.10) (3.84) (3.18) (4.08) (4.26) (3.24) (1.53)
(3.60) (3.06) (3.24) (4.02) (3.00) (2.64) (1.80) (3.90) (3.66) (4.08) (4.20) (3.96) (1.98)

Copyright 2012 Securities Research Company

Bonds $.0 Mil Com 24.422 Mil BV .35 /sh P/E N/A (Ind BIOTK P/E 17.51) Ctry US

BIOSCRIP INC (BIOS)

Provides medical services and online/mailing of prescriptions

85% SCALE

Growth Performance Measurement

Years	Price	Earn.	Div.	Tot Ret
Last 1	97.3	---	---	97.3
Last 5	6.9	---	---	6.9
Last 10	6.4	-17.8	---	6.4

MIM Corporation prior to 3/14/05

Chronimed Inc. & MIM Corporation merged 3/11/05

(0.16) (0.05) (0.57)
(0.08) (0.10) (0.60)
(0.04) (0.26) (0.80) (0.52)

Copyright 2012 Securities Research Company

Bonds $.0 Mil Com 56.893 Mil BV 4.99 /sh P/E 107.70 (Ind HCSVS P/E 15.09) Ctry US

BIOTA PHARMACEUTIALS INC (BOTA)

Collects and provides human blood plasma

70% SCALE

Growth Performance Measurement

Years	Price	Earn.	Div.	Tot Ret
Last 1	-64.6	7.1	---	-64.6
Last 5	-28.7	13.3	---	-28.7
Last 10	-20.0	---	---	-20.0

Nabi Biopharmaceuticals prior to merger Biota Hldgs. Ltd. 11/9/12

Adj. for 1 for 6 11/9/12

StaphVax failed to meet goal of its Phase III trial 11/1/05

Special $6.648

NABI, Inc. prior to 3/5/02

0.00 (1.86) (6.06) (12.78) (5.64) (3.18) (2.46) (2.04) (2.22) 0.00 (1.68) (1.32)
0.06 (0.48) (4.86) (12.36) (12.36) (3.96) (2.58) (1.98) (2.64) (0.54) (0.54) (0.26)
(0.12) (0.30) (3.72) (6.60) (12.36) (4.86) (2.82) (2.10) (2.28) (0.72) (0.36) (1.08) (1.56)

Copyright 2012 Securities Research Company

Bonds $112.3 Mil Com 4.721 Mil BV 12.14 /sh P/E N/A (Ind BIOTK P/E 17.51) Ctry US

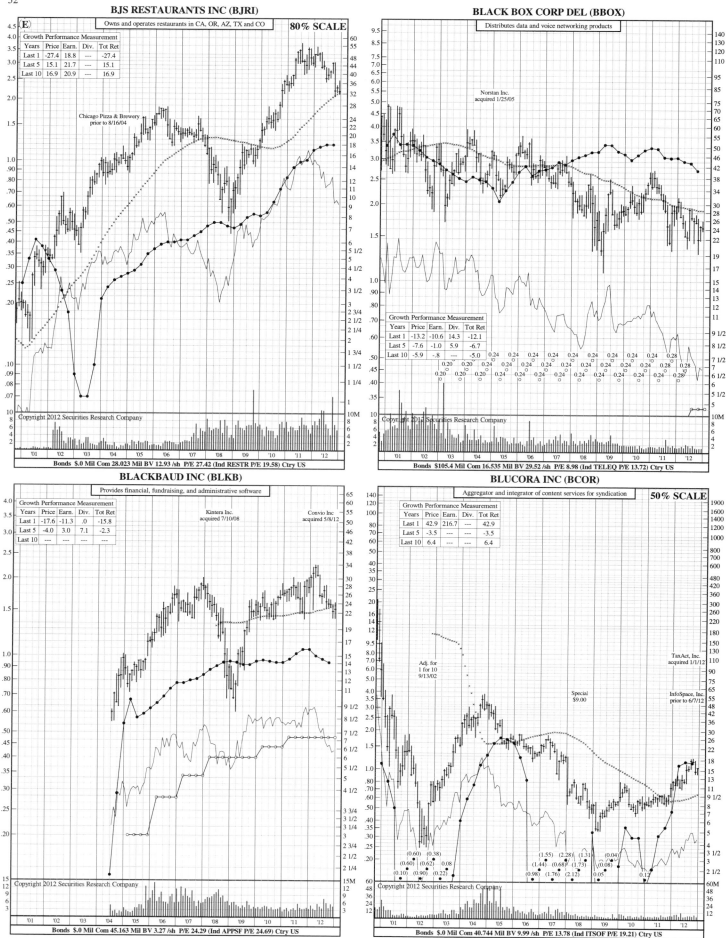

52

BJS RESTAURANTS INC (BJRI)

Owns and operates restaurants in CA, OR, AZ, TX and CO

80% SCALE

(E)

Growth Performance Measurement

Years	Price	Earn.	Div.	Tot Ret
Last 1	-27.4	18.8	---	-27.4
Last 5	15.1	21.7	---	15.1
Last 10	16.9	20.9	---	16.9

Chicago Pizza & Brewery
prior to 8/16/04

Copyright 2012 Securities Research Company

Bonds $.0 Mil Com 28.023 Mil BV 12.93 /sh P/E 27.42 (Ind RESTR P/E 19.58) Ctry US

BLACK BOX CORP DEL (BBOX)

Distributes data and voice networking products

Norstan Inc.
acquired 1/25/05

Growth Performance Measurement

Years	Price	Earn.	Div.	Tot Ret
Last 1	-13.2	-10.6	14.3	-12.1
Last 5	-7.6	-1.0	5.9	-6.7
Last 10	-5.9	-.8	---	-5.0

Copyright 2012 Securities Research Company

Bonds $105.4 Mil Com 16.535 Mil BV 29.52 /sh P/E 8.98 (Ind TELEQ P/E 13.72) Ctry US

BLACKBAUD INC (BLKB)

Provides financial, fundraising, and administrative software

Growth Performance Measurement

Years	Price	Earn.	Div.	Tot Ret
Last 1	-17.6	-11.3	.0	-15.8
Last 5	-4.0	3.0	7.1	-2.3
Last 10	---	---	---	---

Kintera Inc.
acquired 7/10/08

Convio Inc
acquired 5/8/12

Copyright 2012 Securities Research Company

Bonds $.0 Mil Com 45.163 Mil BV 3.27 /sh P/E 24.29 (Ind APPSF P/E 24.69) Ctry US

BLUCORA INC (BCOR)

Aggregator and integrator of content services for syndication

50% SCALE

Growth Performance Measurement

Years	Price	Earn.	Div.	Tot Ret
Last 1	42.9	216.7	---	42.9
Last 5	-3.5	---	---	-3.5
Last 10	6.4	---	---	6.4

Adj. for
1 for 10
9/13/02

Special
$9.00

TaxAct, Inc.
acquired 1/1/12

InfoSpace, Inc.
prior to 6/7/12

(0.60) (0.38)
(0.60) (0.62) 0.08
(0.10) (0.90) 0.22

(1.55) (2.28) (1.31) (0.04)
(1.44) (0.68) (1.73) (0.08)
(0.98) (1.76) (2.12) 0.05 0.13

Copyright 2012 Securities Research Company

Bonds $.0 Mil Com 40.744 Mil BV 9.99 /sh P/E 13.78 (Ind ITSOF P/E 19.21) Ctry US

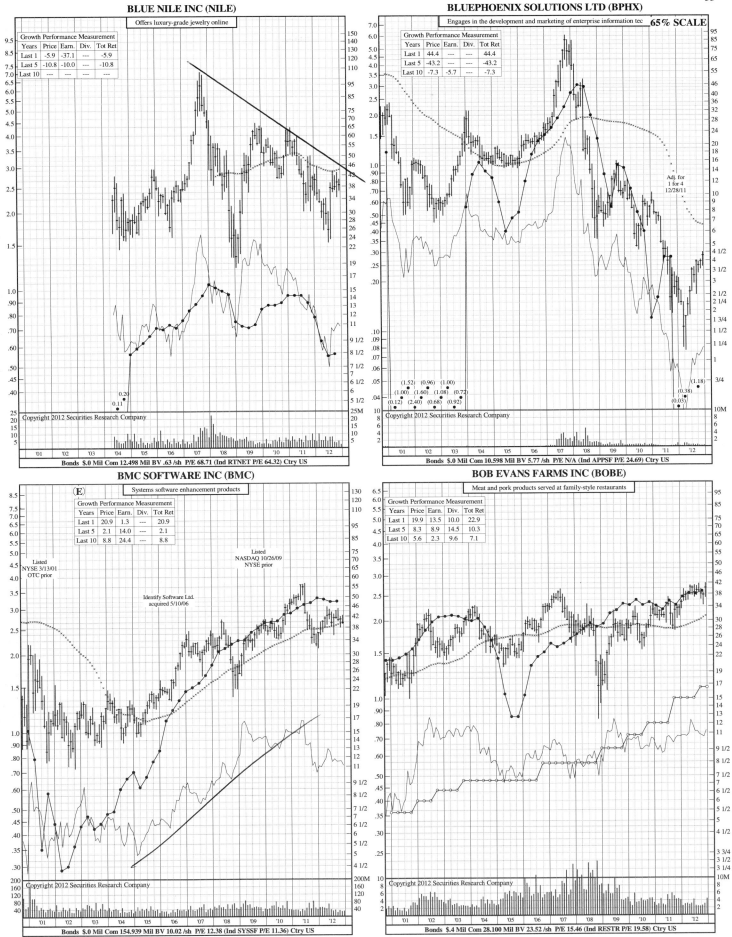

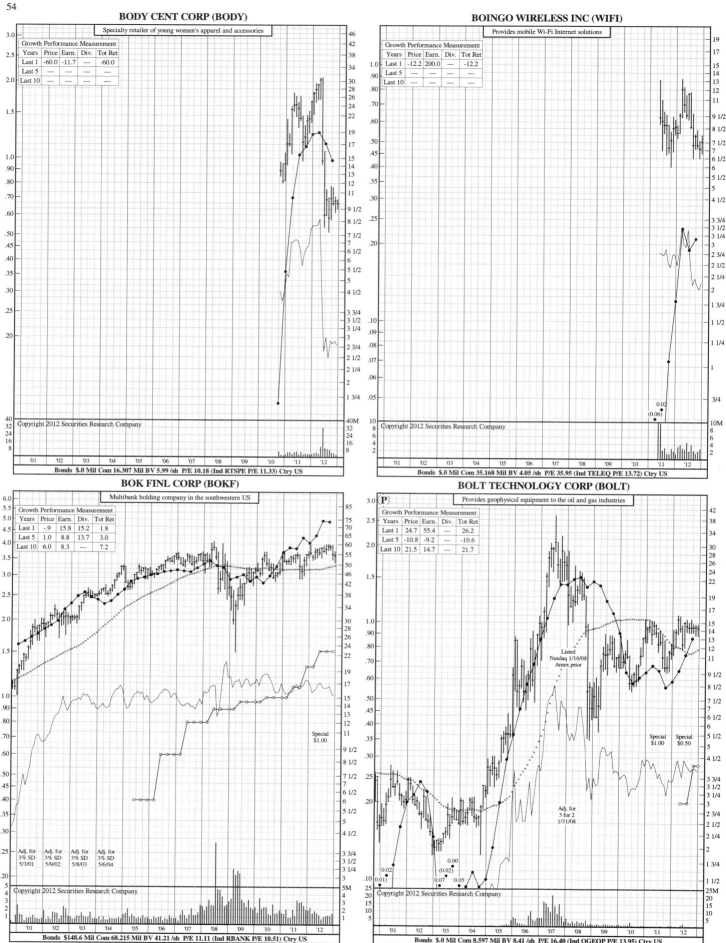

54

BODY CENT CORP (BODY)

Specialty retailer of young women's apparel and accessories

Growth Performance Measurement

Years	Price	Earn.	Div.	Tot Ret
Last 1	-60.0	-11.7	---	-60.0
Last 5	---	---	---	---
Last 10	---	---	---	---

Copyright 2012 Securities Research Company

Bonds $.0 Mil Com 16.307 Mil BV 5.99 /sh P/E 10.18 (Ind RTSPE P/E 11.33) Ctry US

BOINGO WIRELESS INC (WIFI)

Provides mobile Wi-Fi Internet solutions

Growth Performance Measurement

Years	Price	Earn.	Div.	Tot Ret
Last 1	-12.2	200.0	---	-12.2
Last 5	---	---	---	---
Last 10	---	---	---	---

0.02
(0.06)

Copyright 2012 Securities Research Company

Bonds $.0 Mil Com 35.168 Mil BV 4.05 /sh P/E 35.95 (Ind TELEQ P/E 13.72) Ctry US

BOK FINL CORP (BOKF)

Multibank holding company in the southwestern US

Growth Performance Measurement

Years	Price	Earn.	Div.	Tot Ret
Last 1	-.9	15.8	15.2	1.8
Last 5	1.0	8.8	13.7	3.0
Last 10	6.0	8.3		7.2

Special
$1.00

Adj. for
3% SD
5/3/01

Adj. for
3% SD
5/9/02

Adj. for
3% SD
5/8/03

Adj. for
3% SD
5/6/04

Copyright 2012 Securities Research Company

Bonds $148.6 Mil Com 68.215 Mil BV 41.21 /sh P/E 11.11 (Ind RBANK P/E 10.51) Ctry US

BOLT TECHNOLOGY CORP (BOLT)

(P)

Provides geophysical equipment to the oil and gas industries

Growth Performance Measurement

Years	Price	Earn.	Div.	Tot Ret
Last 1	24.7	55.4	---	26.2
Last 5	-10.8	-9.2	---	-10.6
Last 10	21.5	14.7	---	21.7

Listed
Nasdaq 1/16/08
Amex prior

Adj. for
3 for 2
1/31/08

Special
$1.00

Special
$0.50

0.02
(0.01)

0.00
(0.02)

0.07

0.05

Copyright 2012 Securities Research Company

Bonds $.0 Mil Com 8.597 Mil BV 8.41 /sh P/E 16.40 (Ind OGEQP P/E 13.95) Ctry US

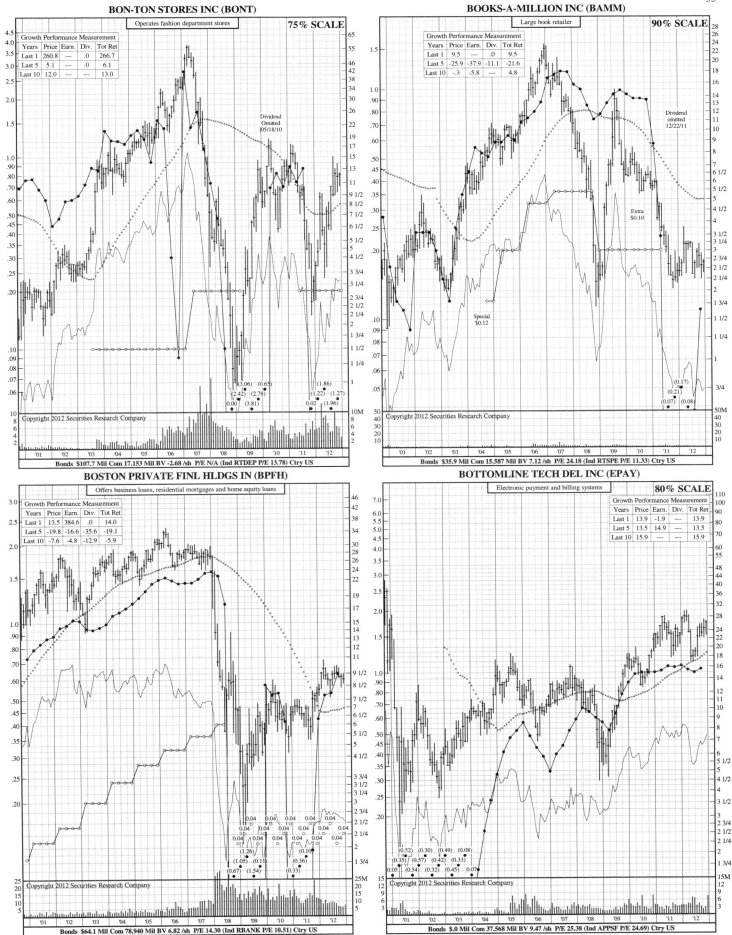

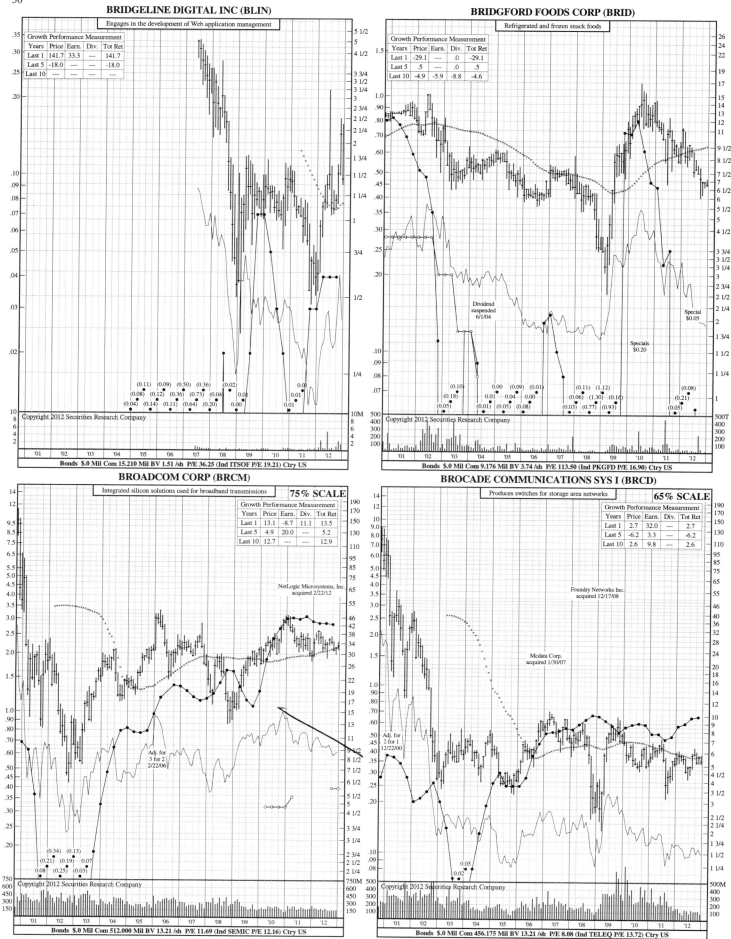

BRIDGELINE DIGITAL INC (BLIN)

Engages in the development of Web application management

Growth Performance Measurement

Years	Price	Earn.	Div.	Tot Ret
Last 1	141.7	33.3	---	141.7
Last 5	-18.0	---	---	-18.0
Last 10	---	---	---	---

(0.11) (0.09) (0.50) (0.36) (0.02) 0.0
(0.08) (0.12) (0.36) (0.73) (0.04) 0.0 0.01
(0.04) (0.14) (0.11) (0.64) (0.20) 0.00 0.01

Copyright 2012 Securities Research Company

'01 '02 '03 '04 '05 '06 '07 '08 '09 '10 '11 '12

Bonds $.0 Mil Com 15.210 Mil BV 1.51 /sh P/E 36.25 (Ind ITSOF P/E 19.21) Ctry US

BRIDGFORD FOODS CORP (BRID)

Refrigerated and frozen snack foods

Growth Performance Measurement

Years	Price	Earn.	Div.	Tot Ret
Last 1	-29.1	---	.0	-29.1
Last 5	.5	---	.0	.5
Last 10	-4.9	-5.9	-8.8	-4.6

Dividend
suspended
6/1/04

Special
$0.05

Specials
$0.20

(0.10) 0.00 (0.09) (0.01) (0.11) (1.12) (0.08)
(0.18) 0.01 0.04 0.01 (0.06) (1.30) (0.16) (0.21)
(0.05) (0.01) (0.05) (0.08) (0.03) (0.77) (0.93) (0.05)

Copyright 2012 Securities Research Company

'01 '02 '03 '04 '05 '06 '07 '08 '09 '10 '11 '12

Bonds $.0 Mil Com 9.176 Mil BV 3.74 /sh P/E 113.50 (Ind PKGFD P/E 16.90) Ctry US

BROADCOM CORP (BRCM)

Integrated silicon solutions used for broadband transmissions   75% SCALE

Growth Performance Measurement

Years	Price	Earn.	Div.	Tot Ret
Last 1	13.1	-8.7	11.1	13.5
Last 5	4.9	20.0	---	5.2
Last 10	12.7	---	---	12.9

NetLogic Microsystems, Inc.
acquired 2/22/12

Adj. for
3 for 2
2/22/06

(0.34) (0.13)
(0.21) (0.19) 0.07
0.08 (0.25) (0.03)

Copyright 2012 Securities Research Company

'01 '02 '03 '04 '05 '06 '07 '08 '09 '10 '11 '12

Bonds $.0 Mil Com 512.000 Mil BV 13.21 /sh P/E 11.69 (Ind SEMIC P/E 12.16) Ctry US

BROCADE COMMUNICATIONS SYS I (BRCD)

Produces switches for storage area networks   65% SCALE

Growth Performance Measurement

Years	Price	Earn.	Div.	Tot Ret
Last 1	2.7	32.0	---	2.7
Last 5	-6.2	3.3	---	-6.2
Last 10	2.6	9.8	---	2.6

Foundry Networks Inc.
acquired 12/17/08

Mcdata Corp.
acquired 1/30/07

Adj. for
2 for 1
12/22/00

0.05
0.02

Copyright 2012 Securities Research Company

'01 '02 '03 '04 '05 '06 '07 '08 '09 '10 '11 '12

Bonds $.0 Mil Com 456.175 Mil BV 13.21 /sh P/E 8.08 (Ind TELEQ P/E 13.72) Ctry US

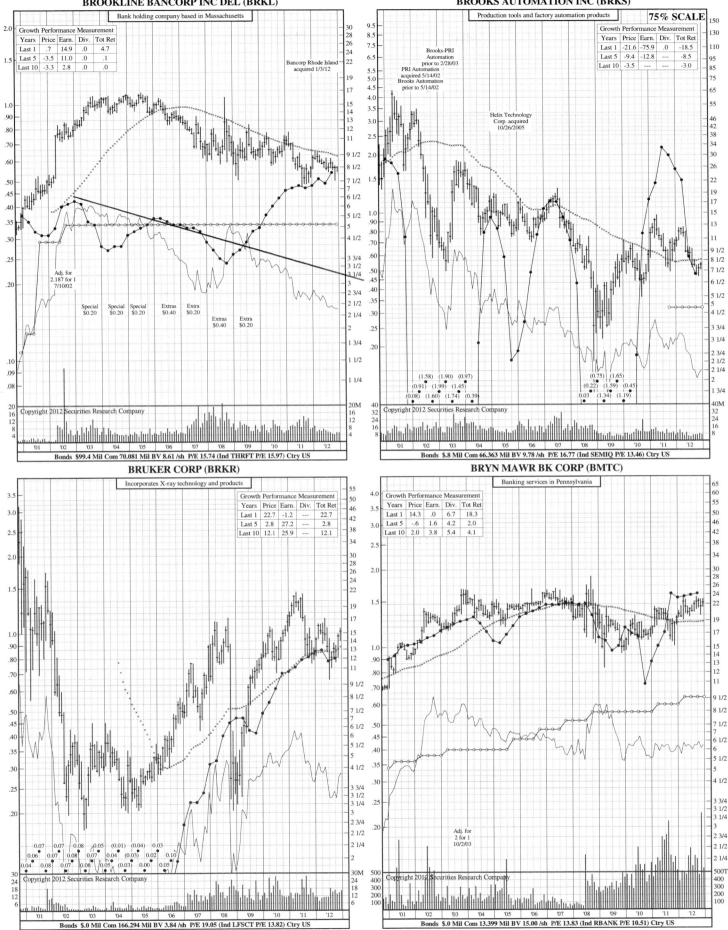

BROOKLINE BANCORP INC DEL (BRKL)

Bank holding company based in Massachusetts

Growth Performance Measurement				
Years	Price	Earn.	Div.	Tot Ret
Last 1	.7	14.9	.0	4.7
Last 5	-3.5	11.0	.0	.1
Last 10	-3.3	2.8	.0	.0

Bancorp Rhode Island acquired 1/3/12

Adj. for 2.187 for 1 7/10/02

Special $0.20   Special $0.20   Special $0.20   Extras $0.40   Extra $0.20

Extras $0.40   Extra $0.20

Copyright 2012 Securities Research Company

Bonds $99.4 Mil Com 70.081 Mil BV 8.61 /sh P/E 15.74 (Ind THRFT P/E 15.97) Ctry US

BROOKS AUTOMATION INC (BRKS)

Production tools and factory automation products   **75% SCALE**

Growth Performance Measurement				
Years	Price	Earn.	Div.	Tot Ret
Last 1	-21.6	-75.9	.0	-18.5
Last 5	-9.4	-12.8	---	-8.5
Last 10	-3.5	---	---	-3.0

Brooks-PRI Automation prior to 2/28/03
PRI Automation acquired 5/14/02
Brooks Automation prior to 5/14/02

Helix Technology Corp. acquired 10/26/2005

(1.58) (1.90) (0.97)
(0.91) (1.99) (1.45)
(0.08) (1.60) (1.74) (0.39)

(0.75) (1.65)
(0.22) (1.59) (0.45)
0.03 (1.34) (1.19)

Copyright 2012 Securities Research Company

Bonds $.8 Mil Com 66.363 Mil BV 9.78 /sh P/E 16.77 (Ind SEMIQ P/E 13.46) Ctry US

BRUKER CORP (BRKR)

Incorporates X-ray technology and products

Growth Performance Measurement				
Years	Price	Earn.	Div.	Tot Ret
Last 1	22.7	-1.2	---	22.7
Last 5	2.8	27.2	---	2.8
Last 10	12.1	25.9	---	12.1

0.07 0.07 0.08 0.05 (0.01) (0.04) 0.03
0.06 0.07 0.08 0.07 0.04 (0.03) 0.02 0.10
0.04 0.08 0.07 0.04 0.05 (0.03) 0.00 0.05

Copyright 2012 Securities Research Company

Bonds $.0 Mil Com 166.294 Mil BV 3.84 /sh P/E 19.05 (Ind LFSCT P/E 13.82) Ctry US

BRYN MAWR BK CORP (BMTC)

Banking services in Pennsylvania

Growth Performance Measurement				
Years	Price	Earn.	Div.	Tot Ret
Last 1	14.3	.0	6.7	18.3
Last 5	-.6	1.6	4.2	2.0
Last 10	2.0	3.8	5.4	4.1

Adj. for 2 for 1 10/2/03

Copyright 2012 Securities Research Company

Bonds $.0 Mil Com 13.399 Mil BV 15.00 /sh P/E 13.83 (Ind RBANK P/E 10.51) Ctry US

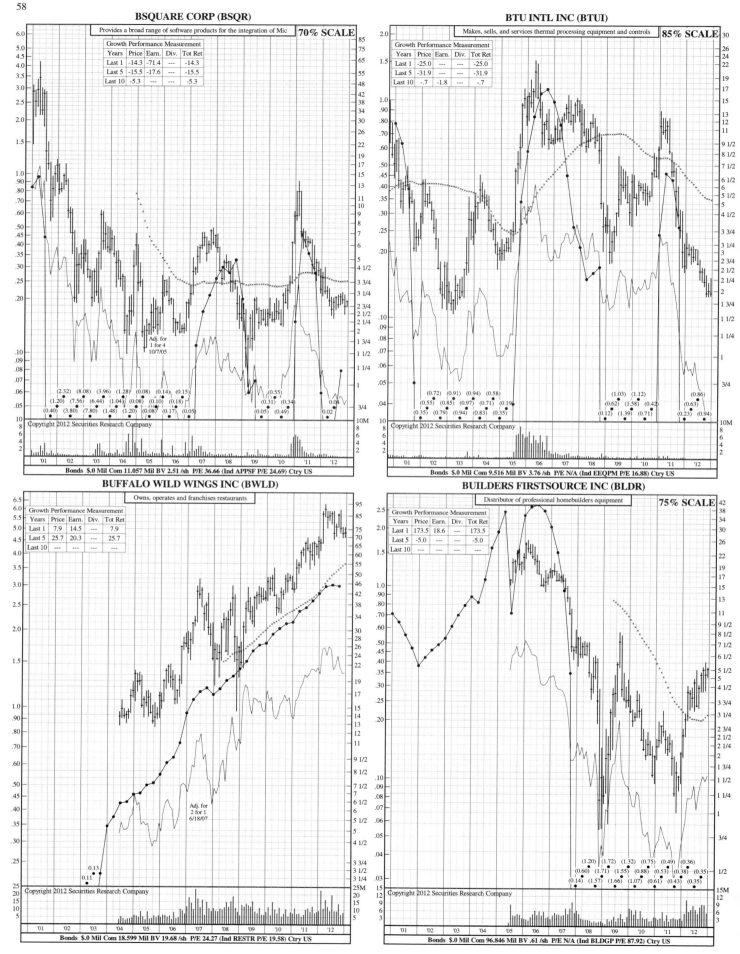

BSQUARE CORP (BSQR)

Provides a broad range of software products for the integration of Mic

70% SCALE

	Growth Performance Measurement			
Years	Price	Earn.	Div.	Tot Ret
Last 1	-14.3	-71.4	---	-14.3
Last 5	-15.5	-17.6	---	-15.5
Last 10	-5.3	---	---	-5.3

Adj. for
1 for 4
10/7/05

(2.32) (8.08) (3.96) (1.28) (0.08) (0.14) (0.15)   (0.55)
(1.20) (7.56) (6.44) (1.04) (0.08) (0.10) (0.18)   (0.31) (0.34)   (0.04)
(0.40) (3.80) (7.80) (1.48) (1.20) (0.08) (0.17) (0.05)   (0.05) (0.49)   (0.02)

Copyright 2012 Securities Research Company

'01 '02 '03 '04 '05 '06 '07 '08 '09 '10 '11 '12

Bonds $.0 Mil Com 11.057 Mil BV 2.51 /sh P/E 36.66 (Ind APPSF P/E 24.69) Ctry US

BTU INTL INC (BTUI)

Makes, sells, and services thermal processing equipment and controls

85% SCALE

	Growth Performance Measurement			
Years	Price	Earn.	Div.	Tot Ret
Last 1	-25.0	---	---	-25.0
Last 5	-31.9	---	---	-31.9
Last 10	-.7	-1.8	---	-.7

(0.72) (0.91) (0.94) (0.58)   (1.03) (1.12)   (0.86)
(0.55) (0.85) (0.97) (0.71) (0.19)   (0.62) (1.58) (0.42)   (0.63)
(0.35) (0.79) (0.94) (0.83) (0.35)   (0.12) (1.39) (0.71)   (0.23) (0.94)

Copyright 2012 Securities Research Company

'01 '02 '03 '04 '05 '06 '07 '08 '09 '10 '11 '12

Bonds $.0 Mil Com 9.516 Mil BV 3.76 /sh P/E N/A (Ind EEQPM P/E 16.88) Ctry US

BUFFALO WILD WINGS INC (BWLD)

Owns, operates and franchises restaurants

	Growth Performance Measurement			
Years	Price	Earn.	Div.	Tot Ret
Last 1	7.9	14.5	---	7.9
Last 5	25.7	20.3	---	25.7
Last 10	---	---	---	---

Adj. for
2 for 1
6/18/07

0.13
0.11

Copyright 2012 Securities Research Company

'01 '02 '03 '04 '05 '06 '07 '08 '09 '10 '11 '12

Bonds $.0 Mil Com 18.599 Mil BV 19.68 /sh P/E 24.27 (Ind RESTR P/E 19.58) Ctry US

BUILDERS FIRSTSOURCE INC (BLDR)

Distributor of professional homebuilders equipment

75% SCALE

	Growth Performance Measurement			
Years	Price	Earn.	Div.	Tot Ret
Last 1	173.5	18.6	---	173.5
Last 5	-5.0	---	---	-5.0
Last 10	---	---	---	---

(1.20) (1.72) (1.32) (0.75) (0.49) (0.36)
(0.60) (1.71) (1.55) (0.88) (0.53) (0.38) (0.35)
(0.14) (1.57) (1.66) (1.07) (0.61) (0.43) (0.35)

Copyright 2012 Securities Research Company

'01 '02 '03 '04 '05 '06 '07 '08 '09 '10 '11 '12

Bonds $.0 Mil Com 96.846 Mil BV .61 /sh P/E N/A (Ind BLDGP P/E 87.92) Ctry US

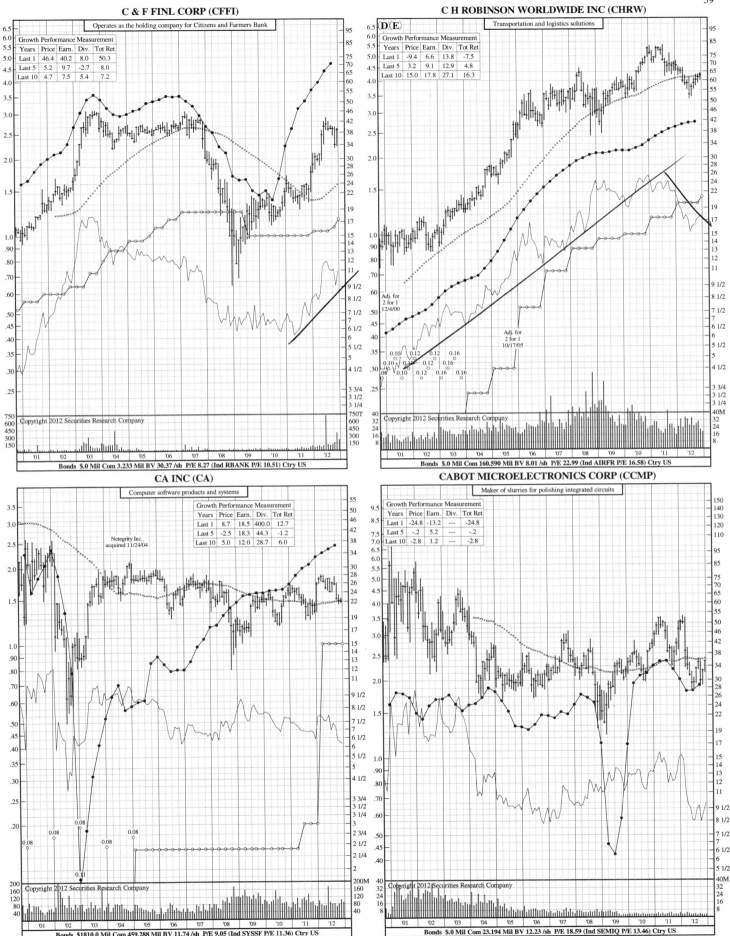

C & F FINL CORP (CFFI)

Operates as the holding company for Citizens and Farmers Bank

Growth Performance Measurement

Years	Price	Earn.	Div.	Tot Ret
Last 1	46.4	40.2	8.0	50.3
Last 5	5.2	9.7	-2.7	8.0
Last 10	4.7	7.5	5.4	7.2

Copyright 2012 Securities Research Company

Bonds $.0 Mil Com 3.233 Mil BV 30.37 /sh P/E 8.27 (Ind RBANK P/E 10.51) Ctry US

C H ROBINSON WORLDWIDE INC (CHRW)

(D)(E)

Transportation and logistics solutions

Growth Performance Measurement

Years	Price	Earn.	Div.	Tot Ret
Last 1	-9.4	6.6	13.8	-7.5
Last 5	3.2	9.1	12.9	4.8
Last 10	15.0	17.8	27.1	16.3

Adj. for
2 for 1
12/4/00

Adj. for
2 for 1
10/17/05

0.10 0.12   0.12   0.16
0.10   0.12   0.16
.08   0.10   0.12   0.16   0.16

Copyright 2012 Securities Research Company

Bonds $.0 Mil Com 160.590 Mil BV 8.01 /sh P/E 22.99 (Ind AIRFR P/E 16.58) Ctry US

CA INC (CA)

Computer software products and systems

Netegrity Inc.
acquired 11/24/04

Growth Performance Measurement

Years	Price	Earn.	Div.	Tot Ret
Last 1	8.7	18.5	400.0	12.7
Last 5	-2.5	18.3	44.3	-1.2
Last 10	5.0	12.0	28.7	6.0

0.08   0.08   0.08   0.08   0.08

0.11

Copyright 2012 Securities Research Company

Bonds $1810.0 Mil Com 459.288 Mil BV 11.74 /sh P/E 9.05 (Ind SYSSF P/E 11.36) Ctry US

CABOT MICROELECTRONICS CORP (CCMP)

Maker of slurries for polishing integrated circuits

Growth Performance Measurement

Years	Price	Earn.	Div.	Tot Ret
Last 1	-24.8	-13.2	---	-24.8
Last 5	-.2	5.2	---	-.2
Last 10	-2.8	1.2	---	-2.8

Copyright 2012 Securities Research Company

Bonds $.0 Mil Com 23.194 Mil BV 12.23 /sh P/E 18.59 (Ind SEMIQ P/E 13.46) Ctry US

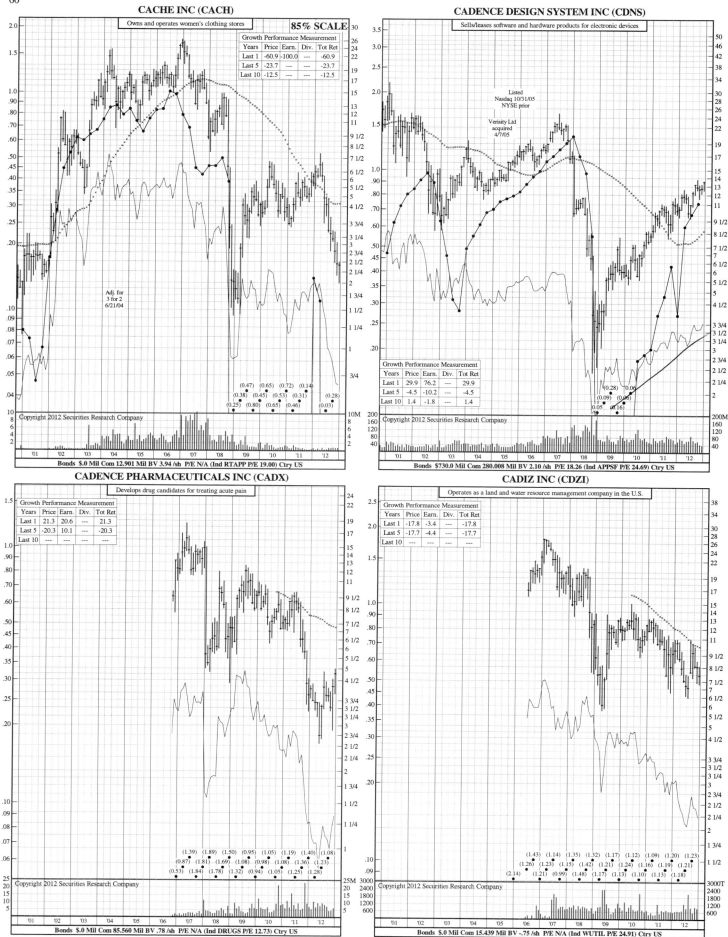

CACHE INC (CACH)

Owns and operates women's clothing stores

85% SCALE

Growth Performance Measurement				
Years	Price	Earn.	Div.	Tot Ret
Last 1	-60.9	-100.0	---	-60.9
Last 5	-23.7	---	---	-23.7
Last 10	-12.5	---	---	-12.5

Adj. for
3 for 2
6/21/04

(0.47) (0.65) (0.72) (0.14)
(0.38) (0.45) (0.53) (0.31) (0.28)
(0.25) (0.80) (0.65) (0.46) (0.03)

Copyright 2012 Securities Research Company

Bonds $.0 Mil Com 12.901 Mil BV 3.94 /sh P/E N/A (Ind RTAPP P/E 19.00) Ctry US

CADENCE DESIGN SYSTEM INC (CDNS)

Sells/leases software and hardware products for electronic devices

Listed
Nasdaq 10/31/05
NYSE prior

Verisity Ltd
acquired
4/7/05

Growth Performance Measurement				
Years	Price	Earn.	Div.	Tot Ret
Last 1	29.9	76.2	---	29.9
Last 5	-4.5	-10.2	---	-4.5
Last 10	1.4	-1.8	---	1.4

(0.28) (0.06)
(0.09) (0.05)
(0.05) (0.16)

Copyright 2012 Securities Research Company

Bonds $730.0 Mil Com 280.008 Mil BV 2.10 /sh P/E 18.26 (Ind APPSF P/E 24.69) Ctry US

CADENCE PHARMACEUTICALS INC (CADX)

Develops drug candidates for treating acute pain

Growth Performance Measurement				
Years	Price	Earn.	Div.	Tot Ret
Last 1	21.3	20.6	---	21.3
Last 5	-20.3	10.1	---	-20.3
Last 10	---	---	---	---

(1.39) (1.89) (1.50) (0.95) (1.05) (1.19) (1.40) (1.08)
(0.87) (1.81) (1.69) (1.08) (0.98) (1.08) (1.36) (1.23)
(0.53) (1.84) (1.78) (1.32) (0.94) (1.05) (1.25) (1.28)

Copyright 2012 Securities Research Company

Bonds $.0 Mil Com 85.560 Mil BV .78 /sh P/E N/A (Ind DRUGS P/E 12.73) Ctry US

CADIZ INC (CDZI)

Operates as a land and water resource management company in the U.S.

Growth Performance Measurement				
Years	Price	Earn.	Div.	Tot Ret
Last 1	-17.8	-3.4	---	-17.8
Last 5	-17.7	-4.4	---	-17.7
Last 10	---	---	---	---

(1.43) (1.14) (1.35) (1.32) (1.17) (1.12) (1.09) (1.20) (1.23)
(1.26) (1.23) (1.15) (1.42) (1.21) (1.24) (1.16) (1.19) (1.21)
(2.14) (1.21) (0.99) (1.48) (1.17) (1.13) (1.10) (1.13) (1.18)

Copyright 2012 Securities Research Company

Bonds $.0 Mil Com 15.439 Mil BV -.75 /sh P/E N/A (Ind WUTIL P/E 24.91) Ctry US

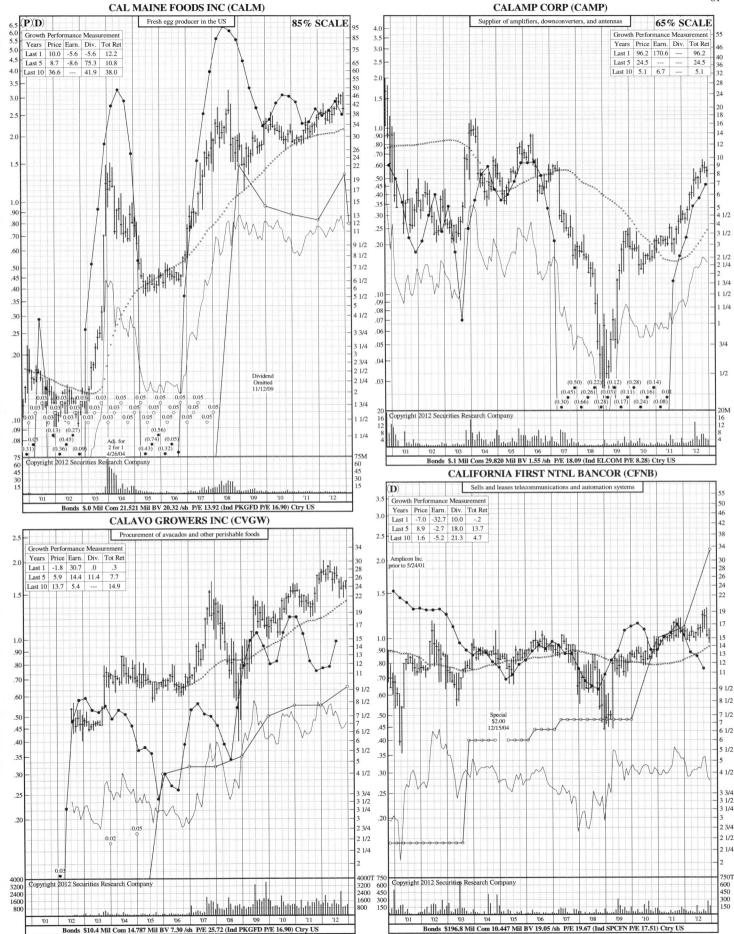

CAL MAINE FOODS INC (CALM)

Fresh egg producer in the US

85% SCALE

(P)(D)

Growth Performance Measurement

Years	Price	Earn.	Div.	Tot Ret
Last 1	10.0	-5.6	-5.6	12.2
Last 5	8.7	-8.6	75.3	10.8
Last 10	36.6	---	41.9	38.0

Dividend Omitted 11/12/09

Adj. for 2 for 1 4/26/04

Copyright 2012 Securities Research Company

Bonds $.0 Mil Com 21.521 Mil BV 20.32 /sh P/E 13.92 (Ind PKGFD P/E 16.90) Ctry US

CALAMP CORP (CAMP)

Supplier of amplifiers, downconverters, and antennas

65% SCALE

Growth Performance Measurement

Years	Price	Earn.	Div.	Tot Ret
Last 1	96.2	170.6	---	96.2
Last 5	24.5	---	---	24.5
Last 10	5.1	6.7	---	5.1

(0.50) (0.22) (0.12) (0.28) (0.14)
(0.45) (0.26) (0.03) (0.11) (0.16) (0.01)
(0.30) (0.66) (0.28) (0.17) (0.24) (0.08)

Copyright 2012 Securities Research Company

Bonds $.1 Mil Com 29.820 Mil BV 1.55 /sh P/E 18.09 (Ind ELCOM P/E 8.28) Ctry US

CALAVO GROWERS INC (CVGW)

Procurement of avacados and other perishable foods

Growth Performance Measurement

Years	Price	Earn.	Div.	Tot Ret
Last 1	-1.8	30.7	.0	.3
Last 5	5.9	14.4	11.4	7.7
Last 10	13.7	5.4	---	14.9

Copyright 2012 Securities Research Company

Bonds $10.4 Mil Com 14.787 Mil BV 7.30 /sh P/E 25.72 (Ind PKGFD P/E 16.90) Ctry US

CALIFORNIA FIRST NTNL BANCOR (CFNB)

Sells and leases telecommunications and automation systems

(D)

Growth Performance Measurement

Years	Price	Earn.	Div.	Tot Ret
Last 1	-7.0	-32.7	10.0	-.2
Last 5	8.9	-2.7	18.0	13.7
Last 10	1.6	-5.2	21.3	4.7

Amplicon Inc. prior to 5/24/01

Special $2.00 12/15/04

Copyright 2012 Securities Research Company

Bonds $196.8 Mil Com 10.447 Mil BV 19.05 /sh P/E 19.67 (Ind SPCFN P/E 17.51) Ctry US

62

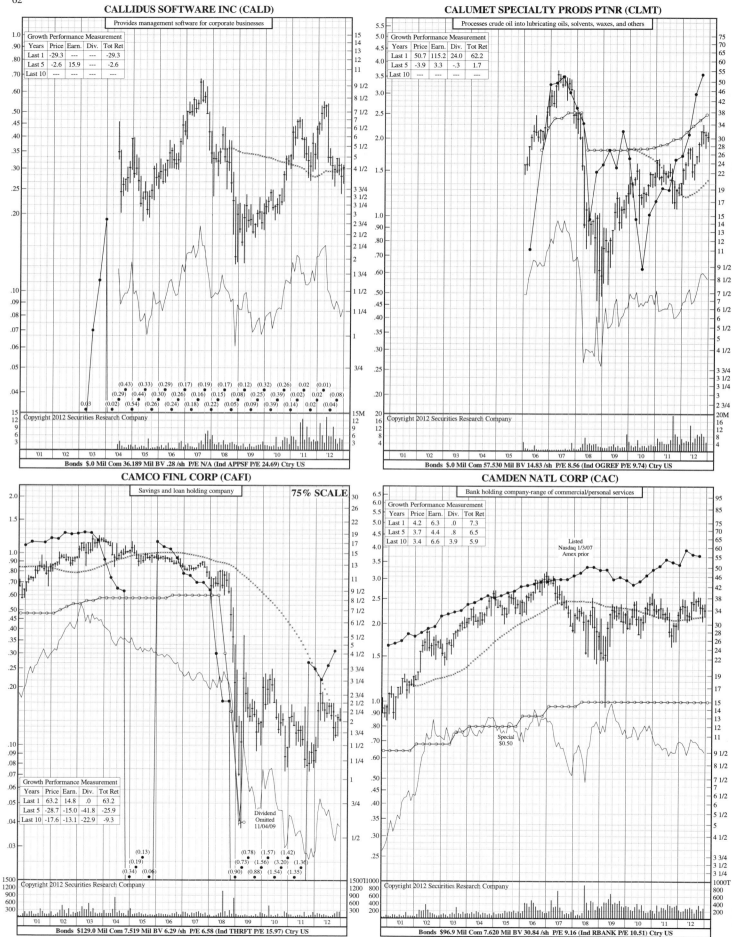

CALLIDUS SOFTWARE INC (CALD)

Provides management software for corporate businesses

Growth Performance Measurement				
Years	Price	Earn.	Div.	Tot Ret
Last 1	-29.3	---	---	-29.3
Last 5	-2.6	15.9	---	-2.6
Last 10	---	---	---	---

(0.43) (0.33) (0.29) (0.17) (0.19) (0.17) (0.12) (0.32) (0.26) 0.02 (0.01)
(0.29) (0.44) (0.30) (0.26) (0.16) (0.15) (0.08) (0.25) (0.39) (0.02) 0.02 (0.08)
0.03 (0.02) (0.54) (0.26) (0.24) (0.18) (0.22) (0.05) (0.09) (0.39) (0.14) 0.02 (0.04)

Copyright 2012 Securities Research Company

Bonds $.0 Mil Com 36.189 Mil BV .28 /sh P/E N/A (Ind APPSF P/E 24.69) Ctry US

CALUMET SPECIALTY PRODS PTNR (CLMT)

Processes crude oil into lubricating oils, solvents, waxes, and others

Growth Performance Measurement				
Years	Price	Earn.	Div.	Tot Ret
Last 1	50.7	115.2	24.0	62.2
Last 5	-3.9	3.3	-.3	1.7
Last 10	---	---	---	---

Copyright 2012 Securities Research Company

Bonds $.0 Mil Com 57.530 Mil BV 14.83 /sh P/E 8.56 (Ind OGREF P/E 9.74) Ctry US

CAMCO FINL CORP (CAFI)

Savings and loan holding company

75% SCALE

Growth Performance Measurement				
Years	Price	Earn.	Div.	Tot Ret
Last 1	63.2	14.8	.0	63.2
Last 5	-28.7	-15.0	-41.8	-25.9
Last 10	-17.6	-13.1	-22.9	-9.3

Dividend
Omitted
11/04/09

(0.13) (0.78) (1.57) (1.42)
(0.19) (0.73) (1.56) (3.20) (1.36)
(0.34) (0.06) (0.90) (0.88) (1.54) (1.35)

Copyright 2012 Securities Research Company

Bonds $129.0 Mil Com 7.519 Mil BV 6.29 /sh P/E 6.58 (Ind THRFT P/E 15.97) Ctry US

CAMDEN NATL CORP (CAC)

Bank holding company-range of commercial/personal services

Growth Performance Measurement				
Years	Price	Earn.	Div.	Tot Ret
Last 1	4.2	6.3	.0	7.3
Last 5	3.7	4.4	.8	6.5
Last 10	3.4	6.6	3.9	5.9

Listed
Nasdaq 1/3/07
Amex prior

Special
$0.50

Copyright 2012 Securities Research Company

Bonds $96.9 Mil Com 7.620 Mil BV 30.84 /sh P/E 9.16 (Ind RBANK P/E 10.51) Ctry US

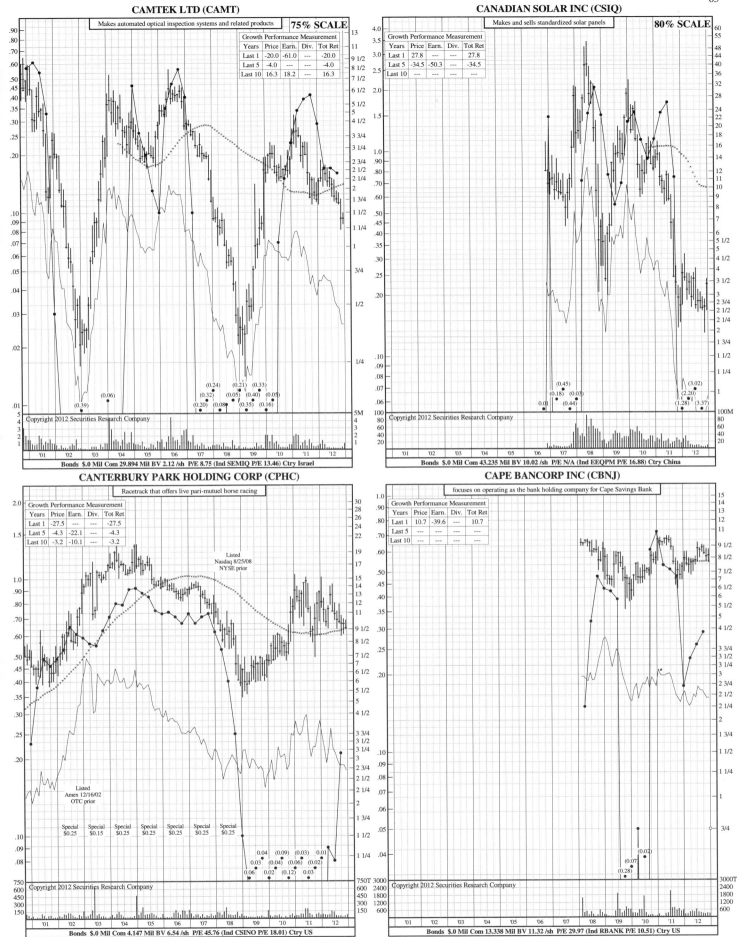

CAMTEK LTD (CAMT)

Makes automated optical inspection systems and related products

75% SCALE

Growth Performance Measurement				
Years	Price	Earn.	Div.	Tot Ret
Last 1	-20.0	-61.0	---	-20.0
Last 5	-4.0	---	---	-4.0
Last 10	16.3	18.2	---	16.3

(0.24) (0.21) (0.33)
(0.32) (0.05) (0.40) (0.05)
(0.06)
(0.20) (0.08) (0.35) (0.16)
(0.39)

Copyright 2012 Securities Research Company

Bonds $.0 Mil Com 29.894 Mil BV 2.12 /sh P/E 8.75 (Ind SEMIQ P/E 13.46) Ctry Israel

CANADIAN SOLAR INC (CSIQ)

Makes and sells standardized solar panels

80% SCALE

Growth Performance Measurement				
Years	Price	Earn.	Div.	Tot Ret
Last 1	27.8	---	---	27.8
Last 5	-34.5	-50.3	---	-34.5
Last 10	---	---	---	---

(0.45) (3.02)
(0.18) (0.03) (2.20)
0.01 (0.44) (1.28) (3.37)

Copyright 2012 Securities Research Company

Bonds $.0 Mil Com 43.235 Mil BV 10.02 /sh P/E N/A (Ind EEQPM P/E 16.88) Ctry China

CANTERBURY PARK HOLDING CORP (CPHC)

Racetrack that offers live pari-mutuel horse racing

Growth Performance Measurement				
Years	Price	Earn.	Div.	Tot Ret
Last 1	-27.5	---	---	-27.5
Last 5	-4.3	-22.1	---	-4.3
Last 10	-3.2	-10.1	---	-3.2

Listed
Nasdaq 8/25/08
NYSE prior

Listed
Amex 12/16/02
OTC prior

Special $0.25 Special $0.15 Special $0.25 Special $0.25 Special $0.25 Special $0.25 Special $0.25

0.04 (0.09) (0.03) 0.01
0.03 (0.04) (0.06) (0.02)
0.06 0.02 (0.12) 0.03

Copyright 2012 Securities Research Company

Bonds $.0 Mil Com 4.147 Mil BV 6.54 /sh P/E 45.76 (Ind CSINO P/E 18.01) Ctry US

CAPE BANCORP INC (CBNJ)

focuses on operating as the bank holding company for Cape Savings Bank

Growth Performance Measurement				
Years	Price	Earn.	Div.	Tot Ret
Last 1	10.7	-39.6	---	10.7
Last 5	---	---	---	---
Last 10	---	---	---	---

(0.02)
(0.07)
(0.28)

Copyright 2012 Securities Research Company

Bonds $.0 Mil Com 13.338 Mil BV 11.32 /sh P/E 29.97 (Ind RBANK P/E 10.51) Ctry US

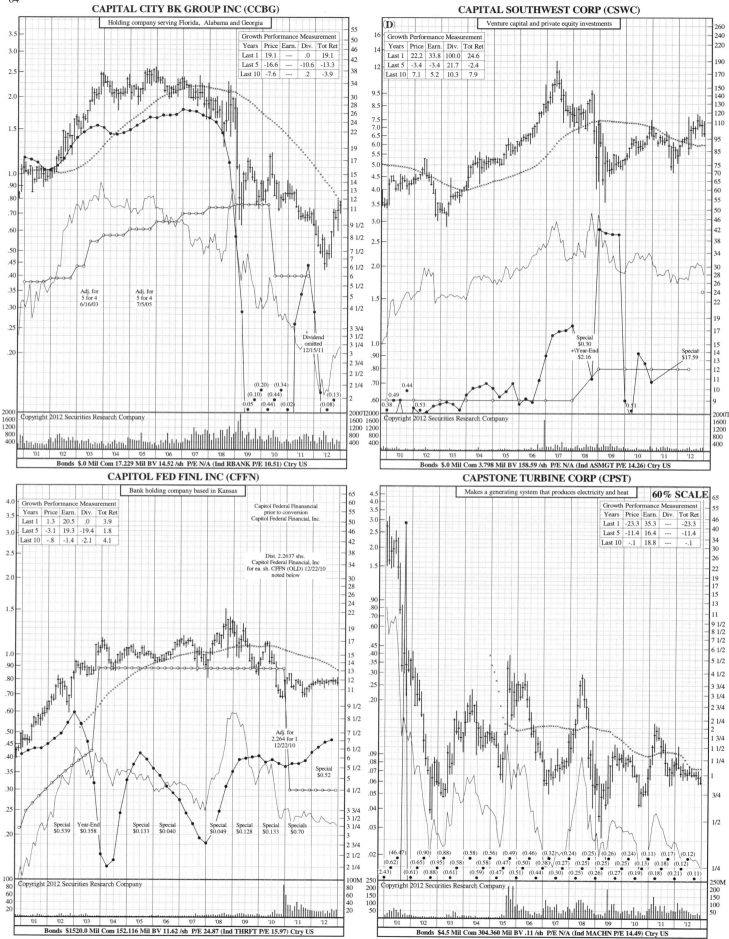

64

CAPITAL CITY BK GROUP INC (CCBG)

Holding company serving Florida, Alabama and Georgia

Growth Performance Measurement

Years	Price	Earn.	Div.	Tot Ret
Last 1	19.1	---	.0	19.1
Last 5	-16.6	---	-10.6	-13.3
Last 10	-7.6	---	.2	-3.9

Adj. for 5 for 4 6/16/03

Adj. for 5 for 4 7/5/05

Dividend omitted 12/15/11

(0.20) (0.34)
(0.10) (0.44)
0.05 (0.44) (0.02) (0.13)
(0.08)

Copyright 2012 Securities Research Company

Bonds $.0 Mil Com 17.229 Mil BV 14.52 /sh P/E N/A (Ind RBANK P/E 10.51) Ctry US

CAPITAL SOUTHWEST CORP (CSWC)

D

Venture capital and private equity investments

Growth Performance Measurement

Years	Price	Earn.	Div.	Tot Ret
Last 1	22.2	33.8	100.0	24.6
Last 5	-3.4	-3.4	21.7	-2.4
Last 10	7.1	5.2	10.3	7.9

Special $0.30 +Year-End $2.16

Special $17.59

0.44

0.49

0.38 0.53

0.51

Copyright 2012 Securities Research Company

Bonds $.0 Mil Com 3.798 Mil BV 158.59 /sh P/E N/A (Ind ASMGT P/E 14.26) Ctry US

CAPITOL FED FINL INC (CFFN)

Bank holding company based in Kansas

Growth Performance Measurement

Years	Price	Earn.	Div.	Tot Ret
Last 1	1.3	20.5	.0	3.9
Last 5	-3.1	19.3	-19.4	1.8
Last 10	-.8	-1.4	-2.1	4.1

Capitol Federal Finanancial prior to conversion Capitol Federal Financial, Inc.

Dist. 2.2637 shs.
Capitol Federal Financial, Inc for ea. sh. CFFN (OLD) 12/22/10 noted below

Adj. for 2.264 for 1 12/22/10

Special $0.52

Special $0.539

Year-End $0.358

Special $0.133

Special $0.040

Special $0.049

Special $0.128

Special $0.133

Specials $0.70

Copyright 2012 Securities Research Company

Bonds $1520.0 Mil Com 152.116 Mil BV 11.62 /sh P/E 24.87 (Ind THRFT P/E 15.97) Ctry US

CAPSTONE TURBINE CORP (CPST)

Makes a generating system that produces electricity and heat

60% SCALE

Growth Performance Measurement

Years	Price	Earn.	Div.	Tot Ret
Last 1	-23.3	35.3	---	-23.3
Last 5	-11.4	16.4	---	-11.4
Last 10	-.1	18.8	---	-.1

(46.47) (0.90) (0.88) (0.58) (0.56) (0.49) (0.46) (0.32) (0.24) (0.25) (0.26) (0.24) (0.11) (0.17) (0.12)
(0.62) (0.65) (0.95) (0.58) (0.58) (0.47) (0.50) (0.38) (0.27) (0.25) (0.25) (0.13) (0.18) (0.12)
2.43) (0.61) (0.88) (0.61) (0.59) (0.47) (0.51) (0.44) (0.30) (0.26) (0.27) (0.19) (0.18) (0.21) (0.11)

Copyright 2012 Securities Research Company

Bonds $4.5 Mil Com 304.360 Mil BV .11 /sh P/E N/A (Ind MACHN P/E 14.49) Ctry US

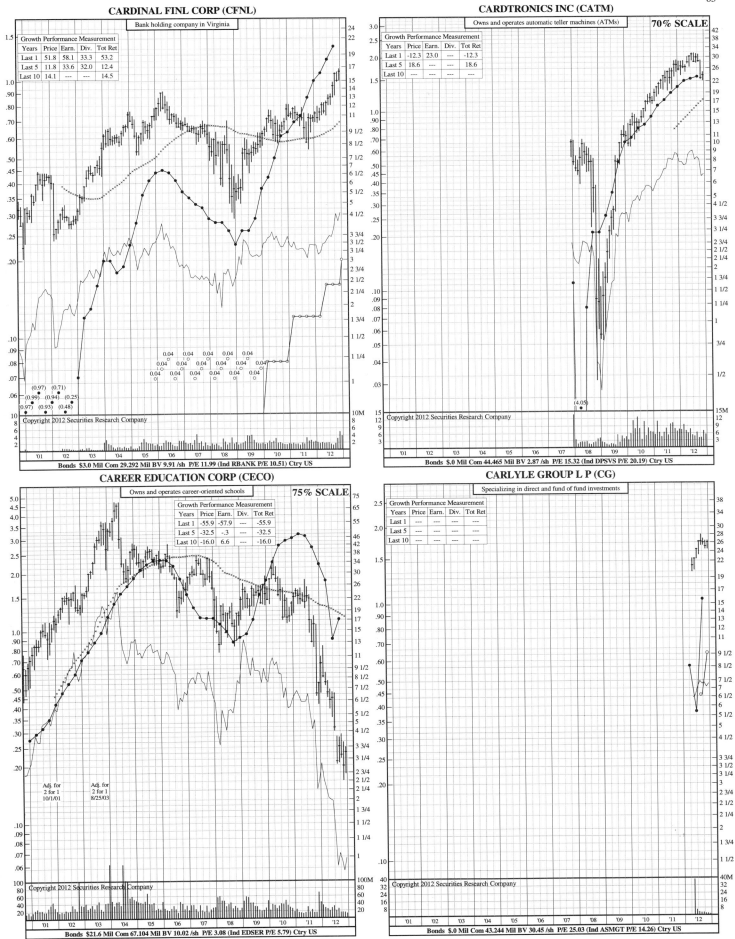

CARDINAL FINL CORP (CFNL)

Bank holding company in Virginia

Growth Performance Measurement				
Years	Price	Earn.	Div.	Tot Ret
Last 1	51.8	58.1	33.3	53.2
Last 5	11.8	33.6	32.0	12.4
Last 10	14.1	---	---	14.5

0.04 0.04 0.04 0.04 0.04
0.04 0.04 0.04 0.04 0.04
0.04 0.04 0.04 0.04 0.04
0.04 0.04 0.04 0.04 0.04

(0.97) (0.71)
(0.99) (0.94) (0.25)
(0.97) (0.93) (0.48)

Copyright 2012 Securities Research Company

Bonds $3.0 Mil Com 29.292 Mil BV 9.91 /sh P/E 11.99 (Ind RBANK P/E 10.51) Ctry US

CARDTRONICS INC (CATM)

Owns and operates automatic teller machines (ATMs)   **70% SCALE**

Growth Performance Measurement				
Years	Price	Earn.	Div.	Tot Ret
Last 1	-12.3	23.0	---	-12.3
Last 5	18.6	---	---	18.6
Last 10	---	---	---	---

(4.05)

Copyright 2012 Securities Research Company

Bonds $.0 Mil Com 44.465 Mil BV 2.87 /sh P/E 15.32 (Ind DPSVS P/E 20.19) Ctry US

CAREER EDUCATION CORP (CECO)

Owns and operates career-oriented schools   **75% SCALE**

Growth Performance Measurement				
Years	Price	Earn.	Div.	Tot Ret
Last 1	-55.9	-57.9	---	-55.9
Last 5	-32.5	-.3	---	-32.5
Last 10	-16.0	6.6	---	-16.0

Adj. for
2 for 1
10/1/01

Adj. for
2 for 1
8/25/03

Copyright 2012 Securities Research Company

Bonds $21.6 Mil Com 67.104 Mil BV 10.02 /sh P/E 3.08 (Ind EDSER P/E 5.79) Ctry US

CARLYLE GROUP L P (CG)

Specializing in direct and fund of fund investments

Growth Performance Measurement				
Years	Price	Earn.	Div.	Tot Ret
Last 1	---	---	---	---
Last 5	---	---	---	---
Last 10	---	---	---	---

Copyright 2012 Securities Research Company

Bonds $.0 Mil Com 43.244 Mil BV 30.45 /sh P/E 25.03 (Ind ASMGT P/E 14.26) Ctry US

'01 '02 '03 '04 '05 '06 '07 '08 '09 '10 '11 '12

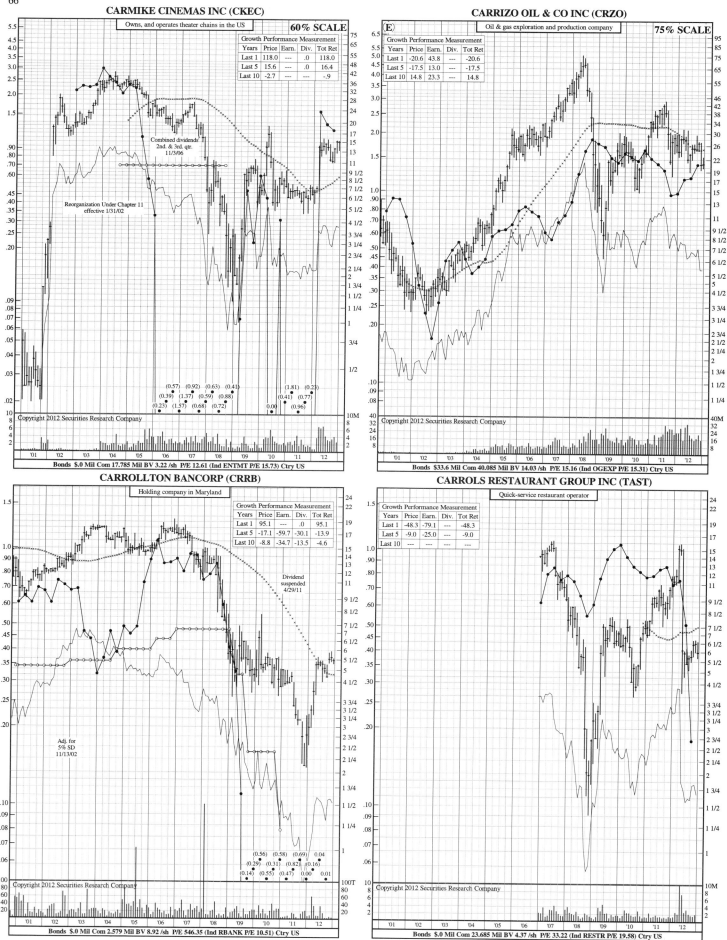

CARMIKE CINEMAS INC (CKEC)

Owns, and operates theater chains in the US

60% SCALE

Growth Performance Measurement				
Years	Price	Earn.	Div.	Tot Ret
Last 1	118.0	---	.0	118.0
Last 5	15.6	---	.0	16.4
Last 10	-2.7	---	---	-.9

Combined dividends
2nd. & 3rd. qtr.
11/3/06

Reorganization Under Chapter 11
effective 1/31/02

(0.57) (0.92) (0.63) (0.41)   (1.81) (0.23)
(0.39) (1.37) (0.59) (0.88)   (0.41) (0.77)
(0.23) (1.57) (0.68) (0.72)   0.00   (0.96)
                                0.04

Copyright 2012 Securities Research Company

Bonds $.0 Mil Com 17.785 Mil BV 3.22 /sh P/E 12.61 (Ind ENTMT P/E 15.73) Ctry US

CARRIZO OIL & CO INC (CRZO)

Oil & gas exploration and production company

75% SCALE

(E)

Growth Performance Measurement				
Years	Price	Earn.	Div.	Tot Ret
Last 1	-20.6	43.8	---	-20.6
Last 5	-17.5	13.0	---	-17.5
Last 10	14.8	23.3	---	14.8

Copyright 2012 Securities Research Company

Bonds $33.6 Mil Com 40.085 Mil BV 14.03 /sh P/E 15.16 (Ind OGEXP P/E 15.31) Ctry US

CARROLLTON BANCORP (CRRB)

Holding company in Maryland

Growth Performance Measurement				
Years	Price	Earn.	Div.	Tot Ret
Last 1	95.1	---	.0	95.1
Last 5	-17.1	-59.7	-30.1	-13.9
Last 10	-8.8	-34.7	-13.5	-4.6

Dividend
suspended
4/29/11

Adj. for
5% SD
11/13/02

(0.56) (0.58) (0.69) 0.04
(0.29) (0.31) (0.82) (0.16)
(0.14) (0.55) (0.47) 0.00 0.01

Copyright 2012 Securities Research Company

Bonds $.0 Mil Com 2.579 Mil BV 8.92 /sh P/E 546.35 (Ind RBANK P/E 10.51) Ctry US

CARROLS RESTAURANT GROUP INC (TAST)

Quick-service restaurant operator

Growth Performance Measurement				
Years	Price	Earn.	Div.	Tot Ret
Last 1	-48.3	-79.1	---	-48.3
Last 5	-9.0	-25.0	---	-9.0
Last 10	---	---	---	---

Copyright 2012 Securities Research Company

Bonds $.0 Mil Com 23.685 Mil BV 4.37 /sh P/E 33.22 (Ind RESTR P/E 19.58) Ctry US

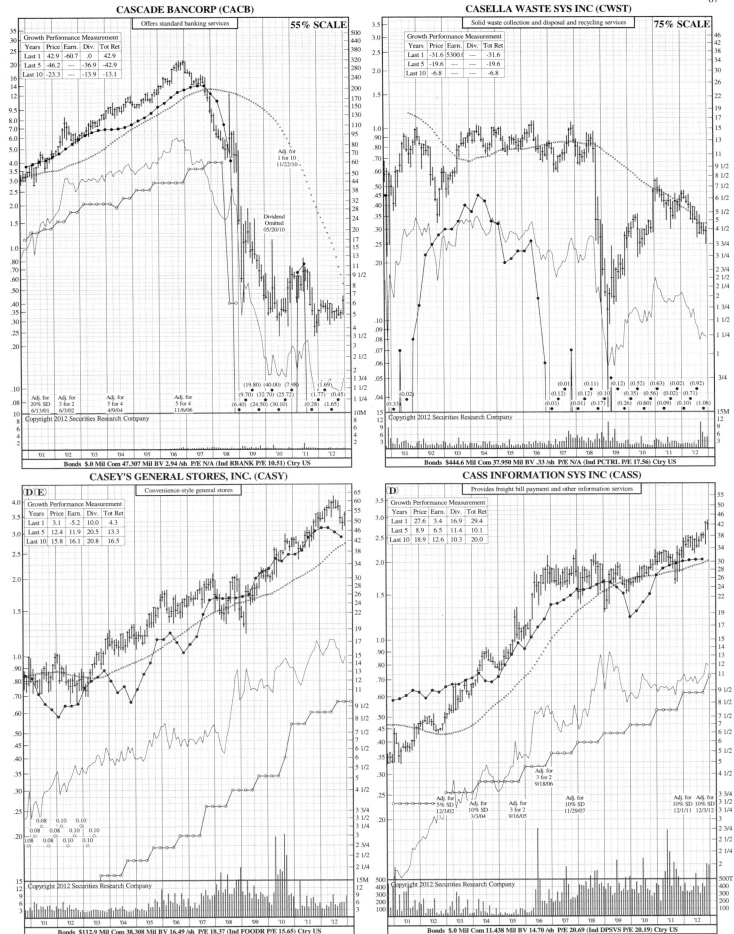

CASCADE BANCORP (CACB)

Offers standard banking services

55% SCALE

Growth Performance Measurement

Years	Price	Earn.	Div.	Tot Ret
Last 1	42.9	-60.7	.0	42.9
Last 5	-46.2	---	-36.9	-42.9
Last 10	-23.3	---	-13.9	-13.1

Adj. for
1 for 10
11/22/10

Dividend
Omitted
05/20/10

| Adj. for 20% SD 6/13/01 | Adj. for 3 for 2 6/3/02 | Adj. for 5 for 4 4/9/04 | Adj. for 5 for 4 11/6/06 |

(19.80) (40.00) (7.98) (1.69)
(9.70) (32.70) (25.72) (1.77) (0.45)
(6.40) (24.50) (30.10) (0.28) (1.65)

Copyright 2012 Securities Research Company

Bonds $.0 Mil Com 47.307 Mil BV 2.94 /sh P/E N/A (Ind RBANK P/E 10.51) Ctry US

CASELLA WASTE SYS INC (CWST)

Solid waste collection and disposal and recycling services

75% SCALE

Growth Performance Measurement

Years	Price	Earn.	Div.	Tot Ret
Last 1	-31.6	5300.0	---	-31.6
Last 5	-19.6	---	---	-19.6
Last 10	-6.8	---	---	-6.8

(0.01) (0.11) (0.12) (0.52) (0.63) (0.02) (0.92)
(0.12) (0.12) (0.10) (0.35) (0.56) (0.02) (0.71)
(0.02) (0.03) (0.01) (0.17) (0.26) (0.60) (0.09) (0.10) (1.08)
(0.33)

Copyright 2012 Securities Research Company

Bonds $444.6 Mil Com 37.950 Mil BV .33 /sh P/E N/A (Ind PCTRL P/E 17.56) Ctry US

CASEY'S GENERAL STORES, INC. (CASY)

(D)(E)

Convenience-style general stores

Growth Performance Measurement

Years	Price	Earn.	Div.	Tot Ret
Last 1	3.1	-5.2	10.0	4.3
Last 5	12.4	11.9	20.5	13.3
Last 10	15.8	16.1	20.8	16.5

0.08 0.10 0.10 0.10
0.08 0.08 0.10 0.10

Copyright 2012 Securities Research Company

Bonds $112.9 Mil Com 38.308 Mil BV 16.49 /sh P/E 18.37 (Ind FOODR P/E 15.65) Ctry US

CASS INFORMATION SYS INC (CASS)

D

Provides freight bill payment and other information services

Growth Performance Measurement

Years	Price	Earn.	Div.	Tot Ret
Last 1	27.6	3.4	16.9	29.4
Last 5	8.9	6.5	11.4	10.1
Last 10	18.9	12.6	10.3	20.0

Adj. for
3 for 2
9/18/06

| Adj. for 5% SD 12/3/02 | Adj. for 10% SD 3/3/04 | Adj. for 3 for 2 9/16/05 | Adj. for 10% SD 11/29/07 | Adj. for 10% SD 12/1/11 | Adj. for 10% SD 12/3/12 |

Copyright 2012 Securities Research Company

Bonds $.0 Mil Com 11.438 Mil BV 14.70 /sh P/E 20.69 (Ind DPSVS P/E 20.19) Ctry US

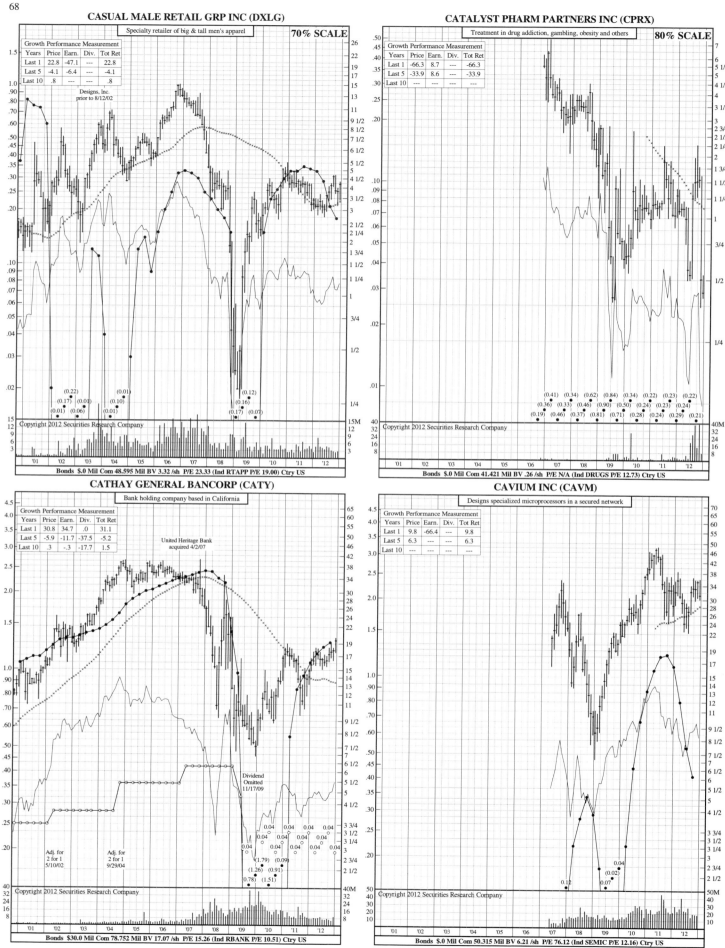

68

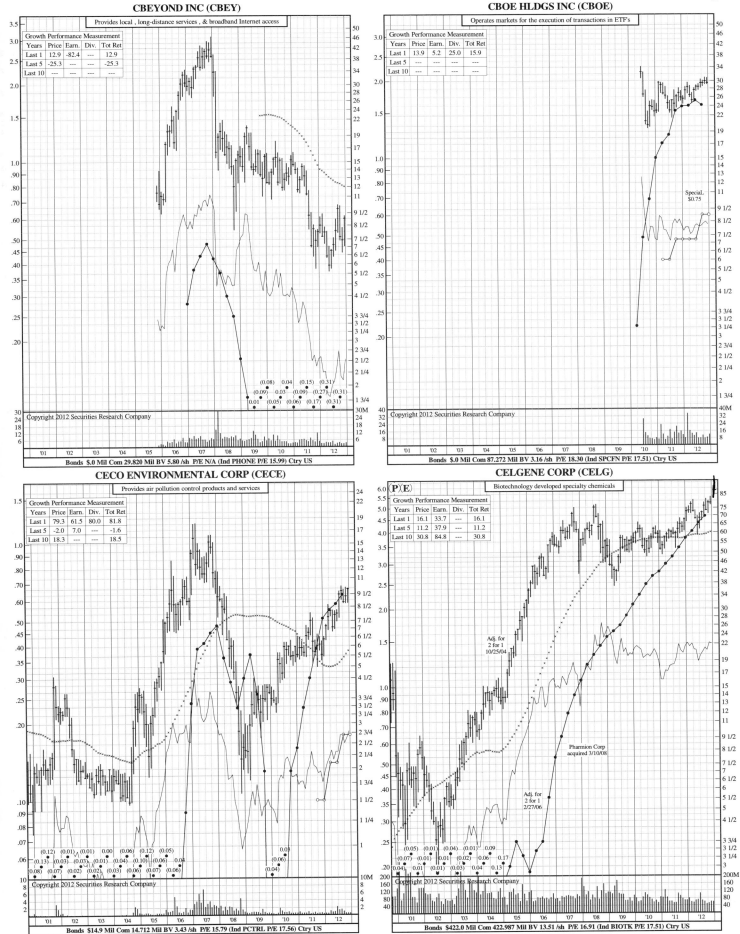

CBEYOND INC (CBEY)

Provides local , long-distance services , & broadband Internet access

Growth Performance Measurement

Years	Price	Earn.	Div.	Tot Ret
Last 1	12.9	-82.4	---	12.9
Last 5	-25.3	---	---	-25.3
Last 10	---	---	---	---

(0.08) 0.04 (0.15) 0.31
(0.09) 0.03 (0.09) (0.27) (0.31)
0.01 (0.05) (0.06) (0.17) (0.31)

Copyright 2012 Securities Research Company

Bonds $.0 Mil Com 29.820 Mil BV 5.80 /sh P/E N/A (Ind PHONE P/E 15.99) Ctry US

CBOE HLDGS INC (CBOE)

Operates markets for the execution of transactions in ETFs

Growth Performance Measurement

Years	Price	Earn.	Div.	Tot Ret
Last 1	13.9	5.2	25.0	15.9
Last 5	---	---	---	---
Last 10	---	---	---	---

Special
$0.75

Copyright 2012 Securities Research Company

Bonds $.0 Mil Com 87.272 Mil BV 3.16 /sh P/E 18.30 (Ind SPCFN P/E 17.51) Ctry US

CECO ENVIRONMENTAL CORP (CECE)

Provides air pollution control products and services

Growth Performance Measurement

Years	Price	Earn.	Div.	Tot Ret
Last 1	79.3	61.5	80.0	81.8
Last 5	-2.0	7.0	---	-1.6
Last 10	18.3	---	---	18.5

(0.12) (0.01) (0.01) 0.00 (0.06) (0.12) (0.05)   0.03
(0.13) (0.03) (0.03) (0.01) (0.04) (0.10) (0.06) 0.04   (0.06)
(0.08) (0.07) (0.02) (0.02) (0.03) (0.06) (0.07) (0.06)   (0.04)

Copyright 2012 Securities Research Company

Bonds $14.9 Mil Com 14.712 Mil BV 3.43 /sh P/E 15.79 (Ind PCTRL P/E 17.56) Ctry US

CELGENE CORP (CELG)

(P/E)

Biotechnology developed specialty chemicals

Growth Performance Measurement

Years	Price	Earn.	Div.	Tot Ret
Last 1	16.1	33.7	---	16.1
Last 5	11.2	37.9	---	11.2
Last 10	30.8	84.8	---	30.8

Adj. for
2 for 1
10/25/04

Pharmion Corp
acquired 3/10/08

Adj. for
2 for 1
2/27/06

(0.05) (0.01) (0.04) (0.01) 0.09
(0.07) (0.01) 0.01 (0.02) 0.06 0.17
(0.04) 0.01 (0.01) (0.03) 0.04 0.13

Copyright 2012 Securities Research Company

Bonds $422.0 Mil Com 422.987 Mil BV 13.51 /sh P/E 16.91 (Ind BIOTK P/E 17.51) Ctry US

70

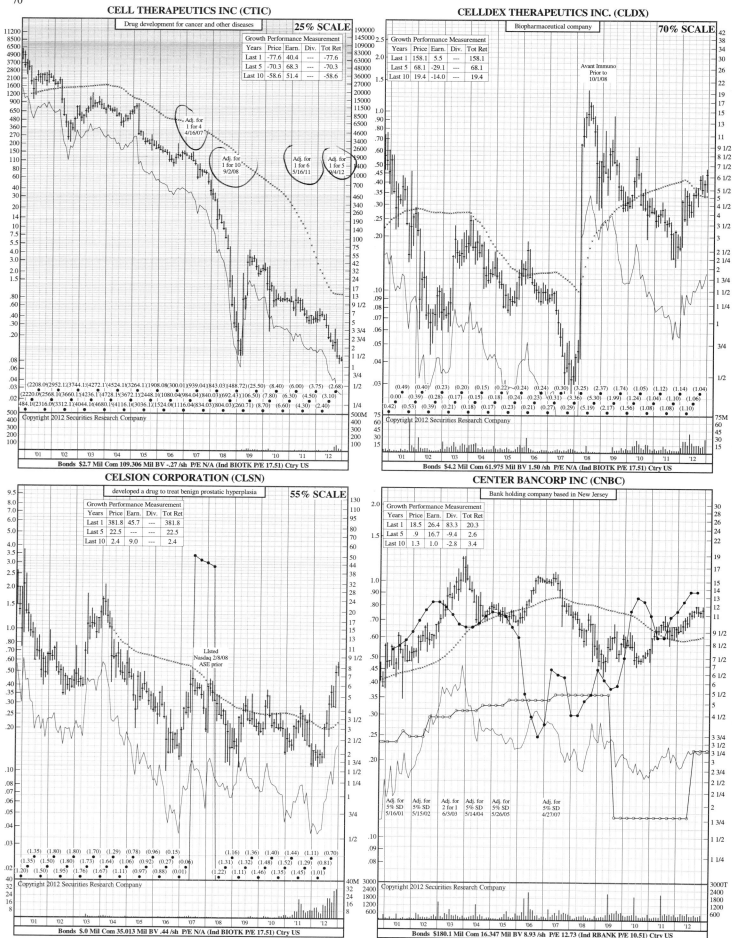

CELL THERAPEUTICS INC (CTIC)

Drug development for cancer and other diseases

25% SCALE

Growth Performance Measurement				
Years	Price	Earn.	Div.	Tot Ret
Last 1	-77.6	40.4	---	-77.6
Last 5	-70.3	68.3	---	-70.3
Last 10	-58.6	51.4	---	-58.6

Adj. for 1 for 4 4/16/07

Adj. for 1 for 10 9/2/08

Adj. for 1 for 6 5/16/11

Adj. for 1 for 5 9/4/12

(2208.0(2952.1(3744.1(4272.1(4524.1(3264.1(1908.08(300.01(939.04(843.03(488.72(25.50) (8.40) (6.00) (3.75) (2.68)
(2220.0(2568.1(3660.1(4236.1(4728.1(3672.1(2448.1(1080.04(984.04(840.03(692.43(106.50) (7.80) (6.30) (4.50) (3.10)
484.1(2316.0(3312.1(4044.1(4680.1(4116.1(3036.1(1524.0(1116.04(834.03(804.03(260.71) (8.70) (6.60) (4.00) (2.40)

Copyright 2012 Securities Research Company

Bonds $2.7 Mil Com 109.306 Mil BV -.27 /sh P/E N/A (Ind BIOTK P/E 17.51) Ctry US

CELLDEX THERAPEUTICS INC. (CLDX)

Biopharmaceutical company

70% SCALE

Growth Performance Measurement				
Years	Price	Earn.	Div.	Tot Ret
Last 1	158.1	5.5	---	158.1
Last 5	68.1	-29.1	---	68.1
Last 10	19.4	-14.0	---	19.4

Avant Immuno Prior to 10/1/08

(0.49) (0.40) (0.23) (0.20) (0.15) (0.22) (0.24) (0.24) (0.30) (3.25) (2.37) (1.74) (1.05) (1.12) (1.14) (1.04)
(0.40) (0.39) (0.28) (0.17) (0.15) (0.18) (0.24) (0.23) (0.31) (3.36) (5.30) (1.99) (1.24) (1.04) (1.10) (1.06)
(0.42) (0.53) (0.39) (0.21) (0.18) (0.17) (0.23) (0.21) (0.27) (0.29) (5.19) (2.17) (1.56) (1.08) (1.08) (1.10)

Copyright 2012 Securities Research Company

Bonds $4.2 Mil Com 61.975 Mil BV 1.50 /sh P/E N/A (Ind BIOTK P/E 17.51) Ctry US

CELSION CORPORATION (CLSN)

developed a drug to treat benign prostatic hyperplasia

55% SCALE

Growth Performance Measurement				
Years	Price	Earn.	Div.	Tot Ret
Last 1	381.8	45.7	---	381.8
Last 5	22.5	---	---	22.5
Last 10	2.4	9.0	---	2.4

LIsted Nasdaq 2/8/08 ASE prior

(1.35) (1.80) (1.80) (1.70) (1.29) (0.78) (0.96) (0.15) (1.16) (1.36) (1.40) (1.44) (1.11) (0.70)
(1.35) (1.50) (1.80) (1.73) (1.64) (1.06) (0.92) (0.27) (0.06) (1.31) (1.32) (1.48) (1.52) (1.29) (0.81)
(1.20) (1.50) (1.95) (1.76) (1.67) (1.11) (0.97) (0.88) (0.01) (1.22) (1.11) (1.46) (1.35) (1.45) (1.01)

Copyright 2012 Securities Research Company

Bonds $.0 Mil Com 35.013 Mil BV .44 /sh P/E N/A (Ind BIOTK P/E 17.51) Ctry US

CENTER BANCORP INC (CNBC)

Bank holding company based in New Jersey

Growth Performance Measurement				
Years	Price	Earn.	Div.	Tot Ret
Last 1	18.5	26.4	83.3	20.3
Last 5	.9	16.7	-9.4	2.6
Last 10	1.3	1.0	-2.8	3.4

Adj. for 5% SD 5/16/01

Adj. for 5% SD 5/15/02

Adj. for 2 for 1 6/3/03

Adj. for 5% SD 5/14/04

Adj. for 5% SD 5/26/05

Adj. for 5% SD 4/27/07

Copyright 2012 Securities Research Company

Bonds $180.1 Mil Com 16.347 Mil BV 8.93 /sh P/E 12.73 (Ind RBANK P/E 10.51) Ctry US

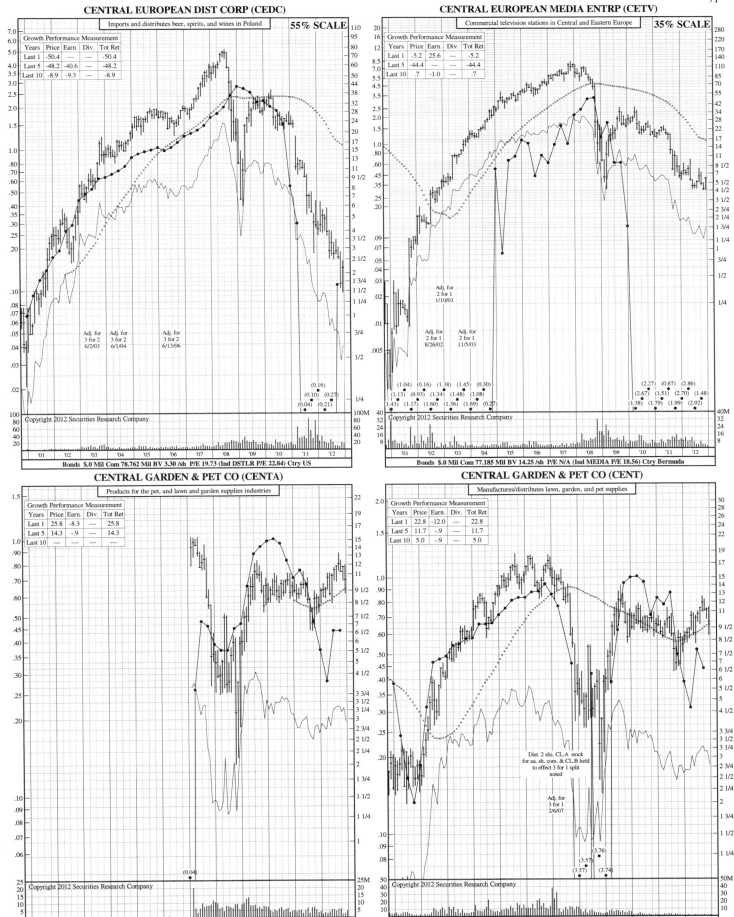

CENTRAL EUROPEAN DIST CORP (CEDC)

Imports and distributes beer, spirits, and wines in Poland   **55% SCALE**

Growth Performance Measurement				
Years	Price	Earn.	Div.	Tot Ret
Last 1	-50.4	---	---	-50.4
Last 5	-48.2	-40.6	---	-48.2
Last 10	-8.9	-9.3	---	-8.9

Adj. for 3 for 2 6/2/03
Adj. for 3 for 2 6/1/04
Adj. for 3 for 2 6/13/06

(0.16)
(0.10) (0.27)
(0.04) (0.21)

Copyright 2012 Securities Research Company

Bonds $.0 Mil Com 78.762 Mil BV 3.30 /sh P/E 19.73 (Ind DSTLR P/E 22.84) Ctry US

CENTRAL EUROPEAN MEDIA ENTRP (CETV)

Commercial television stations in Central and Eastern Europe   **35% SCALE**

Growth Performance Measurement				
Years	Price	Earn.	Div.	Tot Ret
Last 1	-5.2	25.6	---	-5.2
Last 5	-44.4	---	---	-44.4
Last 10	.7	-1.0	---	.7

Adj. for 2 for 1 1/10/03

Adj. for 2 for 1 8/26/02
Adj. for 2 for 1 11/5/03

(1.04) (0.16) (1.38) (1.45) (0.30)
(1.13) (0.93) (1.34) (1.48) (1.08)
(1.43) (1.17) (1.60) (1.36) (1.69) (0.27)

(2.27) (0.67) (2.86)
(2.67) (1.51) (2.70) (1.48)
(1.38) (1.79) (1.99) (2.92)

Copyright 2012 Securities Research Company

Bonds $.0 Mil Com 77.185 Mil BV 14.25 /sh P/E N/A (Ind MEDIA P/E 18.56) Ctry Bermuda

CENTRAL GARDEN & PET CO (CENTA)

Products for the pet, and lawn and garden supplies industries

Growth Performance Measurement				
Years	Price	Earn.	Div.	Tot Ret
Last 1	25.8	-8.3	---	25.8
Last 5	14.3	-.9	---	14.3
Last 10	---	---	---	---

(0.04)

Copyright 2012 Securities Research Company

Bonds $.0 Mil Com 34.753 Mil BV 9.59 /sh P/E 23.80 (Ind HSHLD P/E 17.60) Ctry US

CENTRAL GARDEN & PET CO (CENT)

Manufactures/distributes lawn, garden, and pet supplies

Growth Performance Measurement				
Years	Price	Earn.	Div.	Tot Ret
Last 1	22.8	-12.0	---	22.8
Last 5	11.7	-.9	---	11.7
Last 10	5.0	-.9	---	5.0

Dist. 2 shs. CL.A stock for ea. sh. com. & CL.B held to effect 3 for 1 split noted

Adj. for 3 for 1 2/6/07

(3.76)
(3.57)
(3.57) (3.74)

Copyright 2012 Securities Research Company

Bonds $123.9 Mil Com 12.247 Mil BV 9.77 /sh P/E 22.77 (Ind HSHLD P/E 17.60) Ctry US

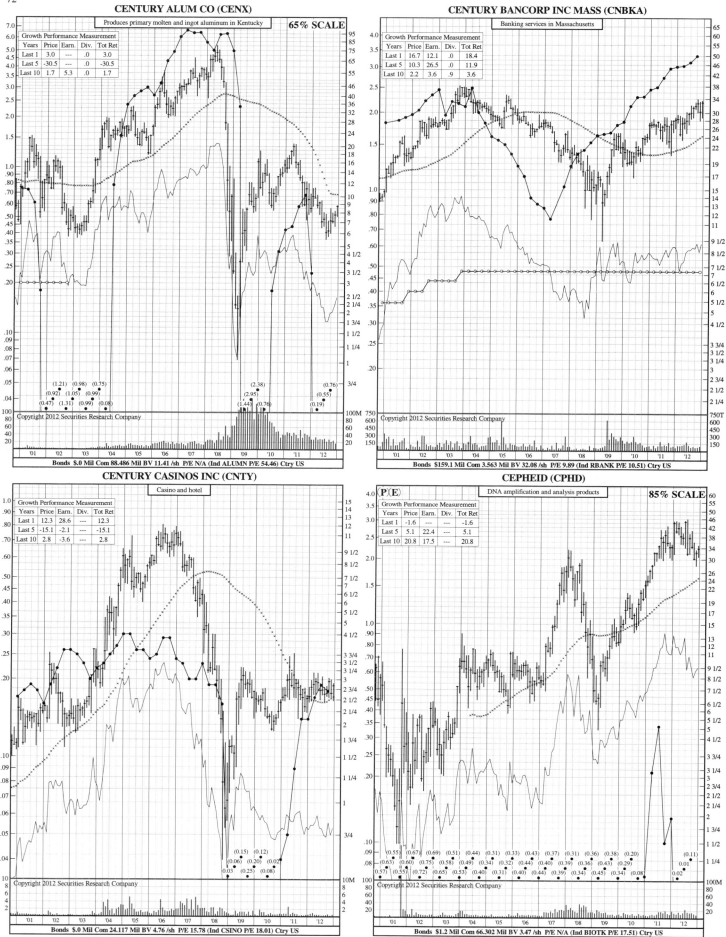

CENTURY ALUM CO (CENX)
Produces primary molten and ingot aluminum in Kentucky
65% SCALE

Growth Performance Measurement

Years	Price	Earn.	Div.	Tot Ret
Last 1	3.0	---	.0	3.0
Last 5	-30.5	---	.0	-30.5
Last 10	1.7	5.3	.0	1.7

(1.21) (0.98) (0.75)
(0.92) (1.05) (0.99)
(0.47) (1.31) (0.99) (0.08)

(2.38)
(2.95)
(1.44) (0.76)

(0.76)
(0.55)
(0.19)

Copyright 2012 Securities Research Company

Bonds $.0 Mil Com 88.486 Mil BV 11.41 /sh P/E N/A (Ind ALUMN P/E 54.46) Ctry US

CENTURY BANCORP INC MASS (CNBKA)
Banking services in Massachusetts

Growth Performance Measurement

Years	Price	Earn.	Div.	Tot Ret
Last 1	16.7	12.1	.0	18.4
Last 5	10.3	26.5	.0	11.9
Last 10	2.2	3.6	.9	3.6

Copyright 2012 Securities Research Company

Bonds $159.1 Mil Com 3.563 Mil BV 32.08 /sh P/E 9.89 (Ind RBANK P/E 10.51) Ctry US

CENTURY CASINOS INC (CNTY)
Casino and hotel

Growth Performance Measurement

Years	Price	Earn.	Div.	Tot Ret
Last 1	12.3	28.6	---	12.3
Last 5	-15.1	-2.1	---	-15.1
Last 10	2.8	-3.6	---	2.8

(0.15) (0.12)
(0.06) (0.20) (0.02)
0.03 (0.25) (0.08)

Copyright 2012 Securities Research Company

Bonds $.0 Mil Com 24.117 Mil BV 4.76 /sh P/E 15.78 (Ind CSINO P/E 18.01) Ctry US

CEPHEID (CPHD)
(P/E)
DNA amplification and analysis products
85% SCALE

Growth Performance Measurement

Years	Price	Earn.	Div.	Tot Ret
Last 1	-1.6	---	---	-1.6
Last 5	5.1	22.4	---	5.1
Last 10	20.8	17.5	---	20.8

(0.55) (0.67) (0.69) (0.51) (0.44) (0.31) (0.33) (0.43) (0.37) (0.31) (0.36) (0.38) (0.20) (0.11)
(0.63) (0.60) (0.75) (0.58) (0.49) (0.34) (0.32) (0.44) (0.40) (0.39) (0.36) (0.43) (0.29) 0.01
(0.57) (0.55) (0.72) (0.65) (0.53) (0.40) (0.31) (0.40) (0.44) (0.34) (0.45) (0.34) (0.08) 0.02

Copyright 2012 Securities Research Company

Bonds $1.2 Mil Com 66.302 Mil BV 3.47 /sh P/E N/A (Ind BIOTK P/E 17.51) Ctry US

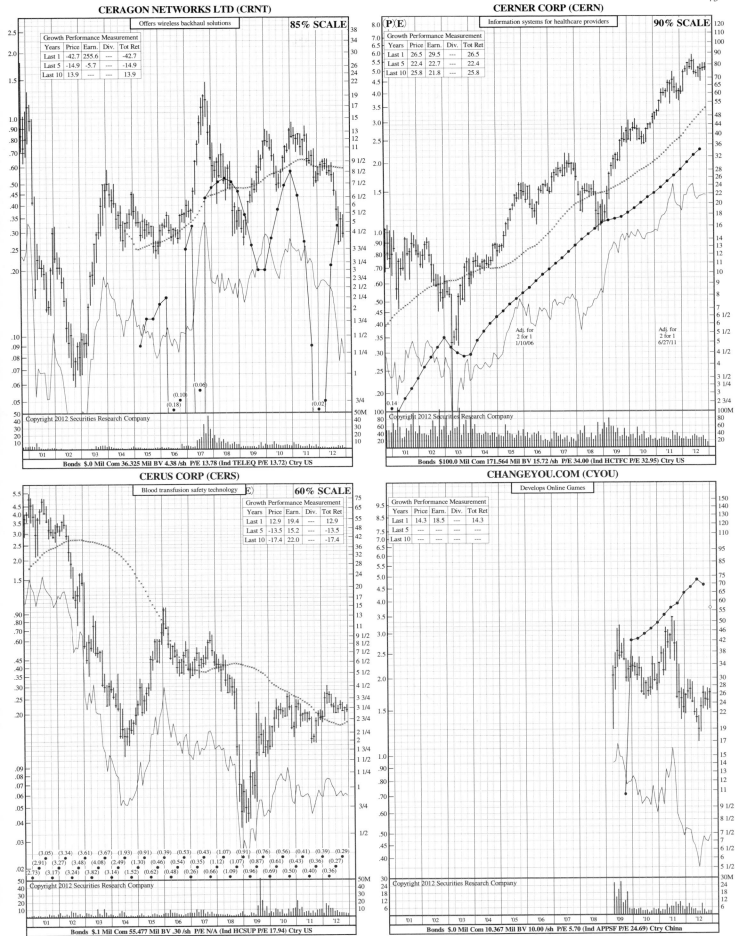

CERAGON NETWORKS LTD (CRNT)
Offers wireless backhaul solutions
85% SCALE

Growth Performance Measurement				
Years	Price	Earn.	Div.	Tot Ret
Last 1	-42.7	255.6	---	-42.7
Last 5	-14.9	-5.7	---	-14.9
Last 10	13.9	---	---	13.9

Copyright 2012 Securities Research Company

Bonds $.0 Mil Com 36.325 Mil BV 4.38 /sh P/E 13.78 (Ind TELEQ P/E 13.72) Ctry US

CERNER CORP (CERN)
Information systems for healthcare providers
90% SCALE

P/E

Growth Performance Measurement				
Years	Price	Earn.	Div.	Tot Ret
Last 1	26.5	29.5	---	26.5
Last 5	22.4	22.7	---	22.4
Last 10	25.8	21.8	---	25.8

Adj. for
2 for 1
1/10/06

Adj. for
2 for 1
6/27/11

0.14

Copyright 2012 Securities Research Company

Bonds $100.0 Mil Com 171.564 Mil BV 15.72 /sh P/E 34.00 (Ind HCTFC P/E 32.95) Ctry US

CERUS CORP (CERS)
Blood transfusion safety technology
60% SCALE

Growth Performance Measurement				
Years	Price	Earn.	Div.	Tot Ret
Last 1	12.9	19.4	---	12.9
Last 5	-13.5	15.2	---	-13.5
Last 10	-17.4	22.0	---	-17.4

Copyright 2012 Securities Research Company

Bonds $.1 Mil Com 55.477 Mil BV .30 /sh P/E N/A (Ind HCSUP P/E 17.94) Ctry US

CHANGEYOU.COM (CYOU)
Develops Online Games

Growth Performance Measurement				
Years	Price	Earn.	Div.	Tot Ret
Last 1	14.3	18.5	---	14.3
Last 5	---	---	---	---
Last 10	---	---	---	---

Copyright 2012 Securities Research Company

Bonds $.0 Mil Com 10.367 Mil BV 10.00 /sh P/E 5.70 (Ind APPSF P/E 24.69) Ctry China

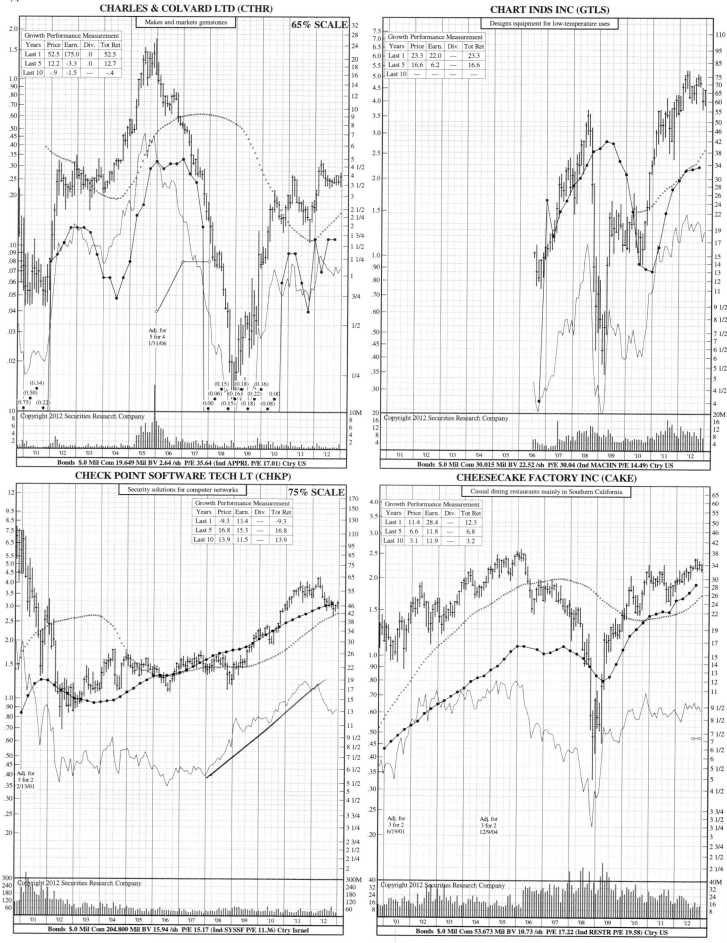

74

CHARLES & COLVARD LTD (CTHR)

Makes and markets gemstones

65% SCALE

Growth Performance Measurement

Years	Price	Earn.	Div.	Tot Ret
Last 1	52.5	175.0	.0	52.5
Last 5	12.2	-3.3	.0	12.7
Last 10	-.9	-1.5	---	-.4

Adj. for
5 for 4
1/31/06

(0.34)
(0.50)
(0.75) (0.22)
(0.15) (0.18) (0.16)
(0.06) (0.16) (0.22) 0.00
0.00 (0.15) (0.18) (0.08)

Copyright 2012 Securities Research Company

Bonds $.0 Mil Com 19.649 Mil BV 2.64 /sh P/E 35.64 (Ind APPRL P/E 17.01) Ctry US

CHART INDS INC (GTLS)

Designs equipment for low-temperature uses

Growth Performance Measurement

Years	Price	Earn.	Div.	Tot Ret
Last 1	23.3	22.0	---	23.3
Last 5	16.6	6.2	---	16.6
Last 10	---	---	---	---

Copyright 2012 Securities Research Company

Bonds $.0 Mil Com 30.015 Mil BV 22.52 /sh P/E 30.04 (Ind MACHN P/E 14.49) Ctry US

CHECK POINT SOFTWARE TECH LT (CHKP)

Security solutions for computer networks

75% SCALE

Growth Performance Measurement

Years	Price	Earn.	Div.	Tot Ret
Last 1	-9.3	13.4	---	-9.3
Last 5	16.8	15.3	---	16.8
Last 10	13.9	11.5	---	13.9

Adj. for
3 for 2
2/13/01

Copyright 2012 Securities Research Company

Bonds $.0 Mil Com 204.800 Mil BV 15.94 /sh P/E 15.17 (Ind SYSSF P/E 11.36) Ctry Israel

CHEESECAKE FACTORY INC (CAKE)

Casual dining restaurants mainly in Southern California

Growth Performance Measurement

Years	Price	Earn.	Div.	Tot Ret
Last 1	11.4	28.4	---	12.3
Last 5	6.6	11.8	---	6.8
Last 10	3.1	11.9	---	3.2

Adj. for
3 for 2
6/19/01

Adj. for
3 for 2
12/9/04

Copyright 2012 Securities Research Company

Bonds $.0 Mil Com 53.673 Mil BV 10.73 /sh P/E 17.22 (Ind RESTR P/E 19.58) Ctry US

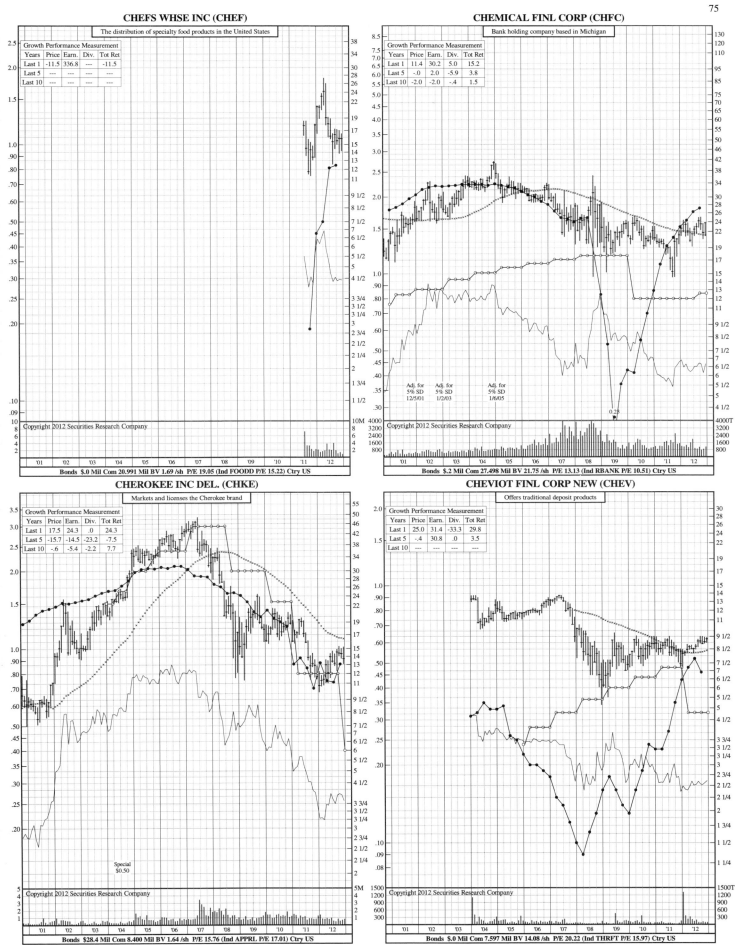

CHEFS WHSE INC (CHEF)

The distribution of specialty food products in the United States

Growth Performance Measurement

Years	Price	Earn.	Div.	Tot Ret
Last 1	-11.5	336.8	---	-11.5
Last 5	---	---	---	---
Last 10	---	---	---	---

Copyright 2012 Securities Research Company

Bonds $.0 Mil Com 20.991 Mil BV 1.69 /sh P/E 19.05 (Ind FOODD P/E 15.22) Ctry US

CHEMICAL FINL CORP (CHFC)

Bank holding company based in Michigan

Growth Performance Measurement

Years	Price	Earn.	Div.	Tot Ret
Last 1	11.4	30.2	5.0	15.2
Last 5	-.0	2.0	-5.9	3.8
Last 10	-2.0	-2.0	-.4	1.5

Adj. for 5% SD 12/5/01   Adj. for 5% SD 1/2/03   Adj. for 5% SD 1/6/05

0.25

Copyright 2012 Securities Research Company

Bonds $.2 Mil Com 27.498 Mil BV 21.75 /sh P/E 13.13 (Ind RBANK P/E 10.51) Ctry US

CHEROKEE INC DEL. (CHKE)

Markets and licenses the Cherokee brand

Growth Performance Measurement

Years	Price	Earn.	Div.	Tot Ret
Last 1	17.5	24.3	.0	24.3
Last 5	-15.7	-14.5	-23.2	-7.5
Last 10	-.6	-5.4	-2.2	7.7

Special $0.50

Copyright 2012 Securities Research Company

Bonds $28.4 Mil Com 8.400 Mil BV 1.64 /sh P/E 15.76 (Ind APPRL P/E 17.01) Ctry US

CHEVIOT FINL CORP NEW (CHEV)

Offers traditional deposit products

Growth Performance Measurement

Years	Price	Earn.	Div.	Tot Ret
Last 1	25.0	31.4	-33.3	29.8
Last 5	-.4	30.8	---	3.5
Last 10	---	---	---	---

Copyright 2012 Securities Research Company

Bonds $.0 Mil Com 7.597 Mil BV 14.08 /sh P/E 20.22 (Ind THRFT P/E 15.97) Ctry US

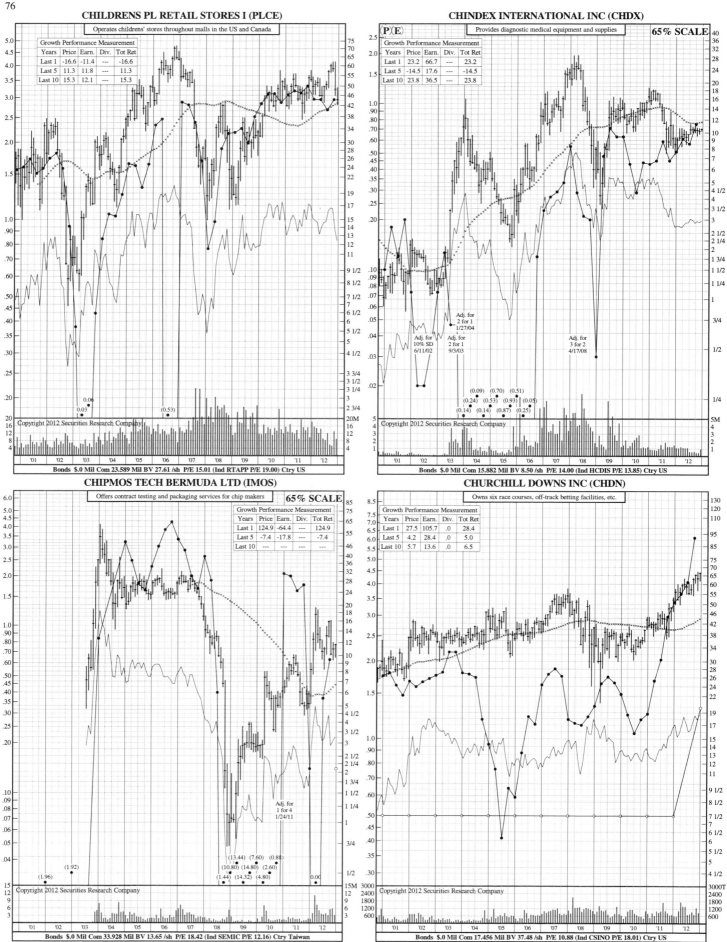

76

CHILDRENS PL RETAIL STORES I (PLCE)

Operates childrens' stores throughout malls in the US and Canada

Growth Performance Measurement

Years	Price	Earn.	Div.	Tot Ret
Last 1	-16.6	-11.4	---	-16.6
Last 5	11.3	11.8	---	11.3
Last 10	15.3	12.1	---	15.3

0.06
0.03
(0.53)

Copyright 2012 Securities Research Company

Bonds $.0 Mil Com 23.589 Mil BV 27.61 /sh P/E 15.01 (Ind RTAPP P/E 19.00) Ctry US

CHINDEX INTERNATIONAL INC (CHDX)

P/E   Provides diagnostic medical equipment and supplies   **65% SCALE**

Growth Performance Measurement

Years	Price	Earn.	Div.	Tot Ret
Last 1	23.2	66.7	---	23.2
Last 5	-14.5	17.6	---	-14.5
Last 10	23.8	36.5	---	23.8

Adj. for
2 for 1
1/27/04

Adj. for
10% SD
6/11/02

Adj. for
2 for 1
9/3/03

Adj. for
3 for 2
4/17/08

(0.09) (0.70) (0.51)
(0.24) (0.53) (0.93) (0.05)
(0.14) (0.14) (0.87) (0.25)

Copyright 2012 Securities Research Company

Bonds $.0 Mil Com 15.882 Mil BV 8.50 /sh P/E 14.00 (Ind HCDIS P/E 13.85) Ctry US

CHIPMOS TECH BERMUDA LTD (IMOS)

Offers contract testing and packaging services for chip makers   **65% SCALE**

Growth Performance Measurement

Years	Price	Earn.	Div.	Tot Ret
Last 1	124.9	-64.4	---	124.9
Last 5	-7.4	-17.8	---	-7.4
Last 10	---	---	---	---

Adj. for
1 for 4
1/24/11

(13.44) (7.60) (0.88)
(10.80) (14.80) (2.60)
(1.96)   (1.92)
(1.44) (14.32) (4.80)   0.00

Copyright 2012 Securities Research Company

Bonds $.0 Mil Com 33.928 Mil BV 13.65 /sh P/E 18.42 (Ind SEMIC P/E 12.16) Ctry Taiwan

CHURCHILL DOWNS INC (CHDN)

Owns six race courses, off-track betting facilities, etc.

Growth Performance Measurement

Years	Price	Earn.	Div.	Tot Ret
Last 1	27.5	105.7	.0	28.4
Last 5	4.2	28.4	.0	5.0
Last 10	5.7	13.6	.0	6.5

Copyright 2012 Securities Research Company

Bonds $.0 Mil Com 17.456 Mil BV 37.48 /sh P/E 10.88 (Ind CSINO P/E 18.01) Ctry US

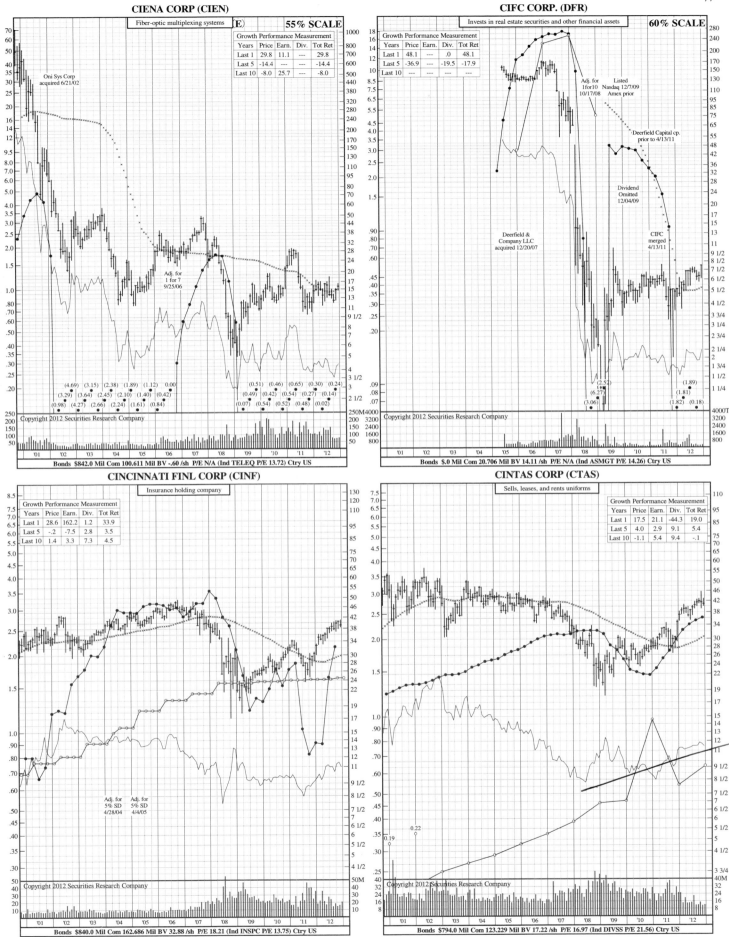

CIENA CORP (CIEN)

Fiber-optic multiplexing systems **E)** **55% SCALE**

Growth Performance Measurement				
Years	Price	Earn.	Div.	Tot Ret
Last 1	29.8	11.1	---	29.8
Last 5	-14.4	---	---	-14.4
Last 10	-8.0	25.7	---	-8.0

Oni Sys Corp acquired 6/21/02

Adj. for 1 for 7 9/25/06

(4.69) (3.15) (2.38) (1.89) (1.12) 0.00   (0.51) (0.46) (0.65) (0.30) (0.24)
(3.29) (3.64) (2.45) (2.10) (1.40) (0.42)   (0.49) (0.42) (0.54) (0.27) (0.14)
(0.98) (4.27) (2.66) (2.24) (1.61) (0.84)   (0.07) (0.54) (0.52) (0.48) (0.02)

Copyright 2012 Securities Research Company

Bonds $842.0 Mil Com 100.611 Mil BV -.60 /sh P/E N/A (Ind TELEQ P/E 13.72) Ctry US

CIFC CORP. (DFR)

Invests in real estate securities and other financial assets **60% SCALE**

Growth Performance Measurement				
Years	Price	Earn.	Div.	Tot Ret
Last 1	48.1	---	.0	48.1
Last 5	-36.9	---	-19.5	-17.9
Last 10	---	---	---	---

Adj. for 1 for 10 10/17/08

Listed Nasdaq 12/7/09 Amex prior

Deerfield Capital cp. prior to 4/13/11

Dividend Omitted 12/04/09

Deerfield & Company LLC acquired 12/20/07

CIFC merged 4/13/11

(2.52)   (1.89)
(6.27)   (1.81)
(3.06)   (1.82) (0.18)

Copyright 2012 Securities Research Company

Bonds $.0 Mil Com 20.706 Mil BV 14.11 /sh P/E N/A (Ind ASMGT P/E 14.26) Ctry US

CINCINNATI FINL CORP (CINF)

Insurance holding company

Growth Performance Measurement				
Years	Price	Earn.	Div.	Tot Ret
Last 1	28.6	162.2	1.2	33.9
Last 5	-.2	-7.5	2.8	3.5
Last 10	1.4	3.3	7.3	4.5

Adj. for 5% SD 4/28/04

Adj. for 5% SD 4/4/05

Copyright 2012 Securities Research Company

Bonds $840.0 Mil Com 162.686 Mil BV 32.88 /sh P/E 18.21 (Ind INSPC P/E 13.75) Ctry US

CINTAS CORP (CTAS)

Sells, leases, and rents uniforms

Growth Performance Measurement				
Years	Price	Earn.	Div.	Tot Ret
Last 1	17.5	21.1	-44.3	19.0
Last 5	4.0	2.9	9.1	5.4
Last 10	-1.1	5.4	9.4	-.1

0.22

0.19

Copyright 2012 Securities Research Company

Bonds $794.0 Mil Com 123.229 Mil BV 17.22 /sh P/E 16.97 (Ind DIVSS P/E 21.56) Ctry US

78

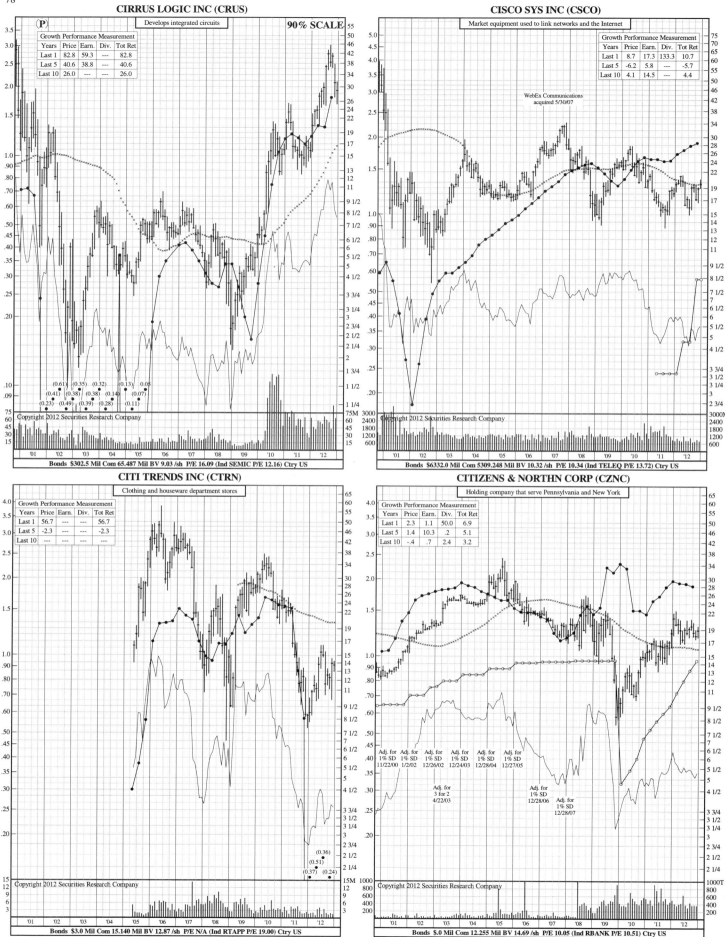

CIRRUS LOGIC INC (CRUS)

Develops integrated circuits

90% SCALE

(P)

Growth Performance Measurement

Years	Price	Earn.	Div.	Tot Ret
Last 1	82.8	59.3	---	82.8
Last 5	40.6	38.8	---	40.6
Last 10	26.0	---	---	26.0

(0.61) (0.35) (0.32) (0.13) 0.05
(0.41) (0.38) (0.38) (0.14) (0.07)
(0.23) (0.49) (0.39) (0.28) (0.11)

Copyright 2012 Securities Research Company

Bonds $302.5 Mil Com 65.487 Mil BV 9.03 /sh P/E 16.09 (Ind SEMIC P/E 12.16) Ctry US

CISCO SYS INC (CSCO)

Market equipment used to link networks and the Internet

WebEx Communications
acquired 5/30/07

Growth Performance Measurement

Years	Price	Earn.	Div.	Tot Ret
Last 1	8.7	17.3	133.3	10.7
Last 5	-6.2	5.8	---	-5.7
Last 10	4.1	14.5	---	4.4

Copyright 2012 Securities Research Company

Bonds $6332.0 Mil Com 5309.248 Mil BV 10.32 /sh P/E 10.34 (Ind TELEQ P/E 13.72) Ctry US

CITI TRENDS INC (CTRN)

Clothing and houseware department stores

Growth Performance Measurement

Years	Price	Earn.	Div.	Tot Ret
Last 1	56.7	---	---	56.7
Last 5	-2.3	---	---	-2.3
Last 10	---	---	---	---

(0.36)
(0.51)
(0.37) (0.24)

Copyright 2012 Securities Research Company

Bonds $3.0 Mil Com 15.140 Mil BV 12.87 /sh P/E N/A (Ind RTAPP P/E 19.00) Ctry US

CITIZENS & NORTHN CORP (CZNC)

Holding company that serve Pennsylvania and New York

Growth Performance Measurement

Years	Price	Earn.	Div.	Tot Ret
Last 1	2.3	1.1	50.0	6.9
Last 5	1.4	10.3	.2	5.1
Last 10	-.4	.7	2.4	3.2

Adj. for Adj. for Adj. for Adj. for Adj. for Adj. for
1% SD 1% SD 1% SD 1% SD 1% SD 1% SD
11/22/00 1/2/02 12/26/02 12/24/03 12/28/04 12/27/05

Adj. for
3 for 2
4/22/03

Adj. for
1% SD
12/28/06

Adj. for
1% SD
12/28/07

Copyright 2012 Securities Research Company

Bonds $.0 Mil Com 12.255 Mil BV 14.69 /sh P/E 10.05 (Ind RBANK P/E 10.51) Ctry US

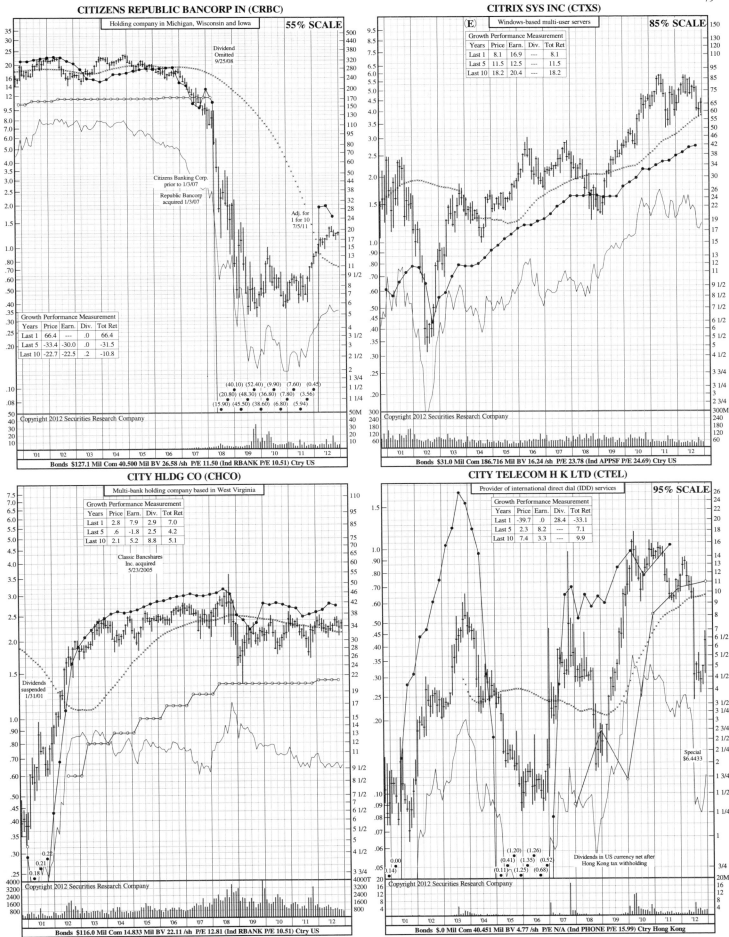

CITIZENS REPUBLIC BANCORP IN (CRBC)

Holding company in Michigan, Wisconsin and Iowa

55% SCALE

Dividend Omitted 9/25/08

Citizens Banking Corp. prior to 1/3/07

Republic Bancorp acquired 1/3/07

Adj. for 1 for 10 7/5/11

Growth Performance Measurement				
Years	Price	Earn.	Div.	Tot Ret
Last 1	66.4	---	.0	66.4
Last 5	-33.4	-30.0	.0	-31.5
Last 10	-22.7	-22.5	.2	-10.8

(40.10) (52.40) (9.90) (7.60) (0.45)
(20.80) (48.30) (36.80) (7.80) (3.56)
(15.90) (45.50) (38.60) (6.80) (5.94)

Copyright 2012 Securities Research Company

'01 '02 '03 '04 '05 '06 '07 '08 '09 '10 '11 '12

Bonds $127.1 Mil Com 40.500 Mil BV 26.58 /sh P/E 11.50 (Ind RBANK P/E 10.51) Ctry US

CITRIX SYS INC (CTXS)

Ⓔ Windows-based multi-user servers

85% SCALE

Growth Performance Measurement				
Years	Price	Earn.	Div.	Tot Ret
Last 1	8.1	16.9	---	8.1
Last 5	11.5	12.5	---	11.5
Last 10	18.2	20.4	---	18.2

Copyright 2012 Securities Research Company

'01 '02 '03 '04 '05 '06 '07 '08 '09 '10 '11 '12

Bonds $31.0 Mil Com 186.716 Mil BV 16.24 /sh P/E 23.78 (Ind APPSF P/E 24.69) Ctry US

CITY HLDG CO (CHCO)

Multi-bank holding company based in West Virginia

Growth Performance Measurement				
Years	Price	Earn.	Div.	Tot Ret
Last 1	2.8	7.9	2.9	7.0
Last 5	.6	-1.8	2.5	4.2
Last 10	2.1	5.2	8.8	5.1

Classic Bancshares Inc. acquired 5/23/2005

Dividends suspended 1/31/01

0.28
0.21
0.18

Copyright 2012 Securities Research Company

'01 '02 '03 '04 '05 '06 '07 '08 '09 '10 '11 '12

Bonds $116.0 Mil Com 14.833 Mil BV 22.11 /sh P/E 12.81 (Ind RBANK P/E 10.51) Ctry US

CITY TELECOM H K LTD (CTEL)

Provider of international direct dial (IDD) services

95% SCALE

Growth Performance Measurement				
Years	Price	Earn.	Div.	Tot Ret
Last 1	-39.7	.0	28.4	-33.1
Last 5	2.3	8.2	---	7.1
Last 10	7.4	3.3	---	9.9

Special $6.4433

(1.20) (1.26)
(0.41) (1.35) (0.52)
(0.11) (1.25) (0.68)
0.00
0.14

Dividends in US currency net after Hong Kong tax withholding

Copyright 2012 Securities Research Company

'01 '02 '03 '04 '05 '06 '07 '08 '09 '10 '11 '12

Bonds $.0 Mil Com 40.451 Mil BV 4.77 /sh P/E N/A (Ind PHONE P/E 15.99) Ctry Hong Kong

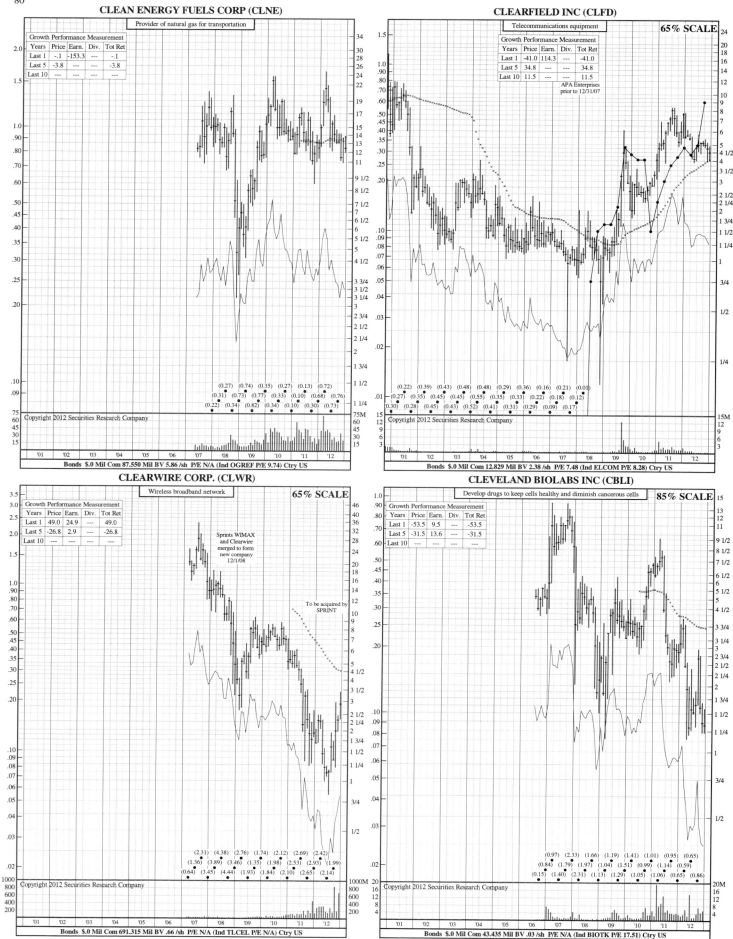

CLEAN ENERGY FUELS CORP (CLNE)

Provider of natural gas for transportation

Growth Performance Measurement

Years	Price	Earn.	Div.	Tot Ret
Last 1	-.1	-153.3	---	-.1
Last 5	-3.8	---	---	-3.8
Last 10	---	---	---	---

(0.27) (0.74) (0.35) (0.27) (0.13) (0.72)
(0.31) (0.73) (0.77) (0.33) (0.10) (0.68) (0.76)
(0.22) (0.34) (0.82) (0.34) (0.10) (0.30) (0.73)

Copyright 2012 Securities Research Company

Bonds $.0 Mil Com 87.550 Mil BV 5.86 /sh P/E N/A (Ind OGREF P/E 9.74) Ctry US

CLEARFIELD INC (CLFD)

Telecommunications equipment

65% SCALE

Growth Performance Measurement

Years	Price	Earn.	Div.	Tot Ret
Last 1	-41.0	114.3	---	-41.0
Last 5	34.8	---	---	34.8
Last 10	11.5	---	---	11.5

APA Enterprises
prior to 12/31/07

(0.22) (0.39) (0.43) (0.48) (0.48) (0.29) (0.36) (0.16) (0.21) (0.01)
(0.27) (0.35) (0.45) (0.45) (0.55) (0.35) (0.33) (0.22) (0.18) (0.12)
(0.30) (0.28) (0.43) (0.52) (0.41) (0.31) (0.29) (0.09) (0.17)

Copyright 2012 Securities Research Company

Bonds $.0 Mil Com 12.829 Mil BV 2.38 /sh P/E 7.48 (Ind ELCOM P/E 8.28) Ctry US

CLEARWIRE CORP. (CLWR)

Wireless broadband network

65% SCALE

Growth Performance Measurement

Years	Price	Earn.	Div.	Tot Ret
Last 1	49.0	24.9	---	49.0
Last 5	-26.8	2.9	---	-26.8
Last 10	---	---	---	---

Sprints WIMAX
and Clearwire
merged to form
new company
12/1/08

To be acquired by
SPRINT

(2.31) (4.38) (2.76) (1.74) (2.12) (2.69) (2.42)
(1.36) (3.89) (3.46) (1.35) (1.98) (2.53) (2.93) (1.99)
(0.64) (3.45) (4.44) (1.93) (1.84) (2.10) (2.65) (2.14)

Copyright 2012 Securities Research Company

Bonds $.0 Mil Com 691.315 Mil BV .66 /sh P/E N/A (Ind TLCEL P/E N/A) Ctry US

CLEVELAND BIOLABS INC (CBLI)

Develop drugs to keep cells healthy and diminish cancerous cells

85% SCALE

Growth Performance Measurement

Years	Price	Earn.	Div.	Tot Ret
Last 1	-53.5	9.5	---	-53.5
Last 5	-31.5	13.6	---	-31.5
Last 10	---	---	---	---

(0.97) (2.33) (1.66) (1.19) (1.41) (1.01) (0.95) (0.65)
(0.84) (1.79) (1.97) (1.04) (1.51) (0.99) (1.14) (0.59)
(0.15) (1.40) (2.31) (1.13) (1.29) (1.05) (1.06) (0.65) (0.86)

Copyright 2012 Securities Research Company

Bonds $.0 Mil Com 43.435 Mil BV .03 /sh P/E N/A (Ind BIOTK P/E 17.51) Ctry US

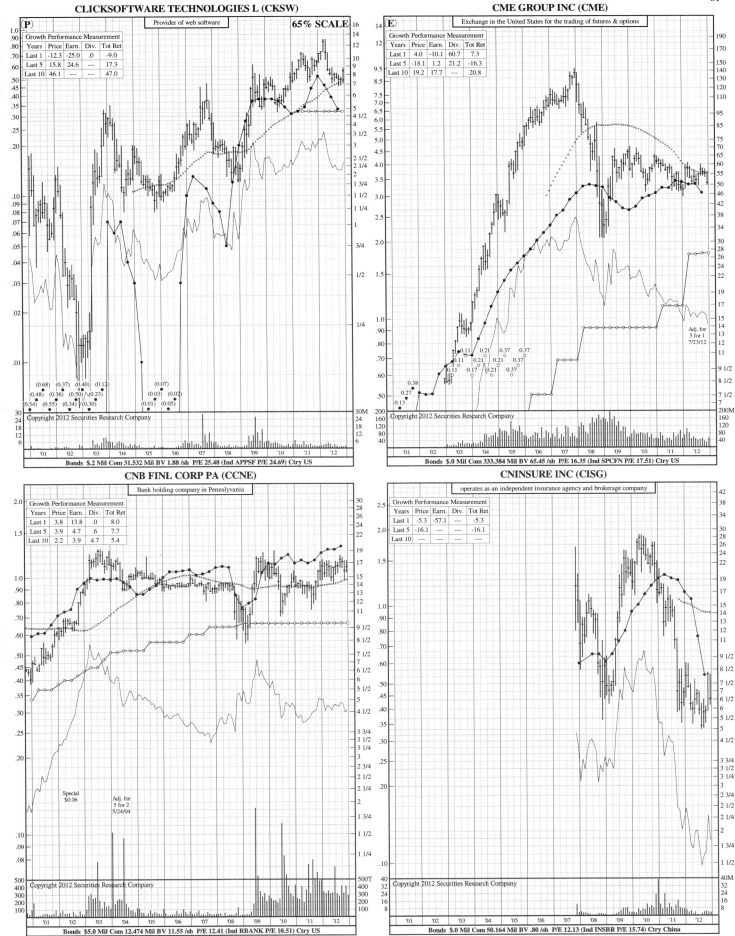

CLICKSOFTWARE TECHNOLOGIES L (CKSW)

Provider of web software

65% SCALE

Growth Performance Measurement				
Years	Price	Earn.	Div.	Tot Ret
Last 1	-12.3	-25.0	.0	-9.0
Last 5	15.8	24.6	---	17.3
Last 10	46.1	---	---	47.0

(0.68) (0.37) (0.40) (0.12) (0.07)
(0.48) (0.36) (0.50) (0.23) (0.03) (0.02)
(0.54) (0.55) (0.34) (0.30) (0.01) (0.05)

Copyright 2012 Securities Research Company

Bonds $.2 Mil Com 31.532 Mil BV 1.88 /sh P/E 25.48 (Ind APPSF P/E 24.69) Ctry US

CME GROUP INC (CME)

Exchange in the United States for the trading of futures & options

Growth Performance Measurement				
Years	Price	Earn.	Div.	Tot Ret
Last 1	4.0	-10.1	60.7	7.3
Last 5	-18.1	1.2	21.2	-16.3
Last 10	19.2	17.7	---	20.8

0.38
0.11 0.21 0.37 0.37
0.11 0.21 0.37
0.27 0.11 0.17 0.21 0.37
0.13

Adj. for
5 for 1
7/23/12

Copyright 2012 Securities Research Company

Bonds $.0 Mil Com 333.384 Mil BV 65.45 /sh P/E 16.35 (Ind SPCFN P/E 17.51) Ctry US

CNB FINL CORP PA (CCNE)

Bank holding company in Pennslyvania

Growth Performance Measurement				
Years	Price	Earn.	Div.	Tot Ret
Last 1	3.8	13.8	.0	8.0
Last 5	3.9	4.7	.6	7.7
Last 10	2.2	3.9	4.7	5.4

Special
$0.06

Adj. for
5 for 2
5/24/04

Copyright 2012 Securities Research Company

Bonds $5.0 Mil Com 12.474 Mil BV 11.55 /sh P/E 12.41 (Ind RBANK P/E 10.51) Ctry US

CNINSURE INC (CISG)

operates as an independent insurance agency and brokerage company

Growth Performance Measurement				
Years	Price	Earn.	Div.	Tot Ret
Last 1	-5.3	-57.1	---	-5.3
Last 5	-16.1	---	---	-16.1
Last 10	---	---	---	---

Copyright 2012 Securities Research Company

Bonds $.0 Mil Com 50.164 Mil BV .80 /sh P/E 12.13 (Ind INSBR P/E 15.74) Ctry China

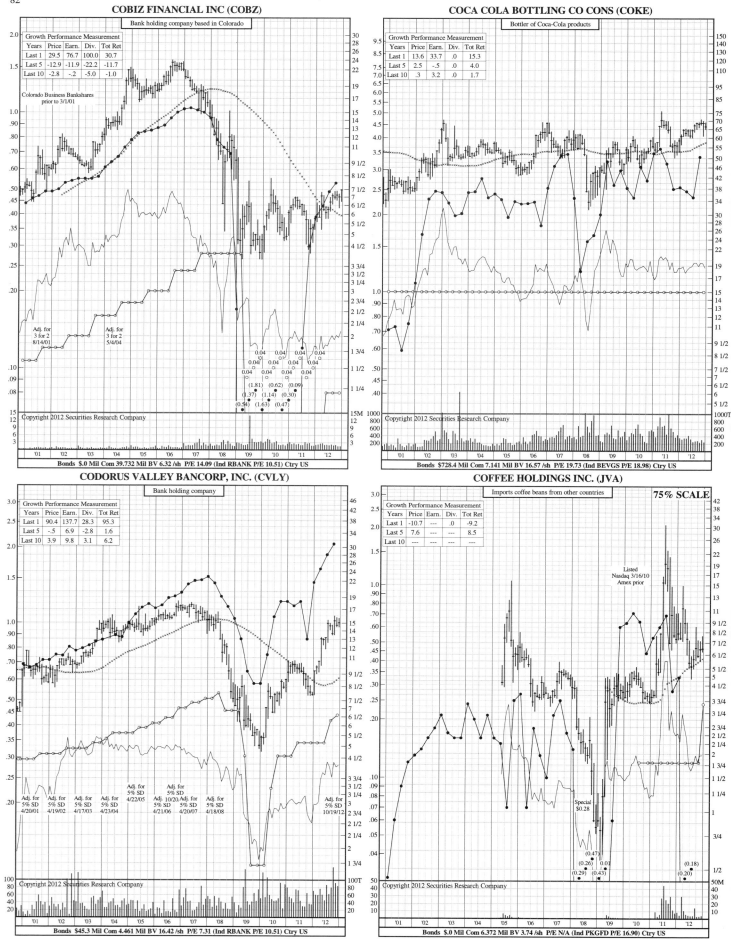

COBIZ FINANCIAL INC (COBZ)

Bank holding company based in Colorado

Growth Performance Measurement				
Years	Price	Earn.	Div.	Tot Ret
Last 1	29.5	76.7	100.0	30.7
Last 5	-12.9	-11.9	-22.2	-11.7
Last 10	-2.8	-.2	-5.0	-1.0

Colorado Business Bankshares prior to 3/1/01

Adj. for 3 for 2 8/14/01

Adj. for 3 for 2 5/4/04

Copyright 2012 Securities Research Company

Bonds $.0 Mil Com 39.732 Mil BV 6.32 /sh P/E 14.09 (Ind RBANK P/E 10.51) Ctry US

COCA COLA BOTTLING CO CONS (COKE)

Bottler of Coca-Cola products

Growth Performance Measurement				
Years	Price	Earn.	Div.	Tot Ret
Last 1	13.6	33.7	.0	15.3
Last 5	2.5	-.5	.0	4.0
Last 10	.3	3.2	.0	1.7

Copyright 2012 Securities Research Company

Bonds $728.4 Mil Com 7.141 Mil BV 16.57 /sh P/E 19.73 (Ind BEVGS P/E 18.98) Ctry US

CODORUS VALLEY BANCORP, INC. (CVLY)

Bank holding company

Growth Performance Measurement				
Years	Price	Earn.	Div.	Tot Ret
Last 1	90.4	137.7	28.3	95.3
Last 5	-.5	6.9	-2.8	1.6
Last 10	3.9	9.8	3.1	6.2

Adj. for 5% SD 4/20/01

Adj. for 5% SD 4/19/02

Adj. for 5% SD 4/17/03

Adj. for 5% SD 4/23/04

Adj. for 5% SD 4/22/05

Adj. for 5% SD 10/20/ 4/21/06

Adj. for 5% SD 4/20/07

Adj. for 5% SD 4/18/08

Adj. for 5% SD 10/19/12

Copyright 2012 Securities Research Company

Bonds $45.3 Mil Com 4.461 Mil BV 16.42 /sh P/E 7.31 (Ind RBANK P/E 10.51) Ctry US

COFFEE HOLDINGS INC. (JVA)

Imports coffee beans from other countries

75% SCALE

Growth Performance Measurement				
Years	Price	Earn.	Div.	Tot Ret
Last 1	-10.7	---	.0	-9.2
Last 5	7.6	---	---	8.5
Last 10	---	---	---	---

Listed Nasdaq 3/16/10 Amex prior

Special $0.28

Copyright 2012 Securities Research Company

Bonds $.0 Mil Com 6.372 Mil BV 3.74 /sh P/E N/A (Ind PKGFD P/E 16.90) Ctry US

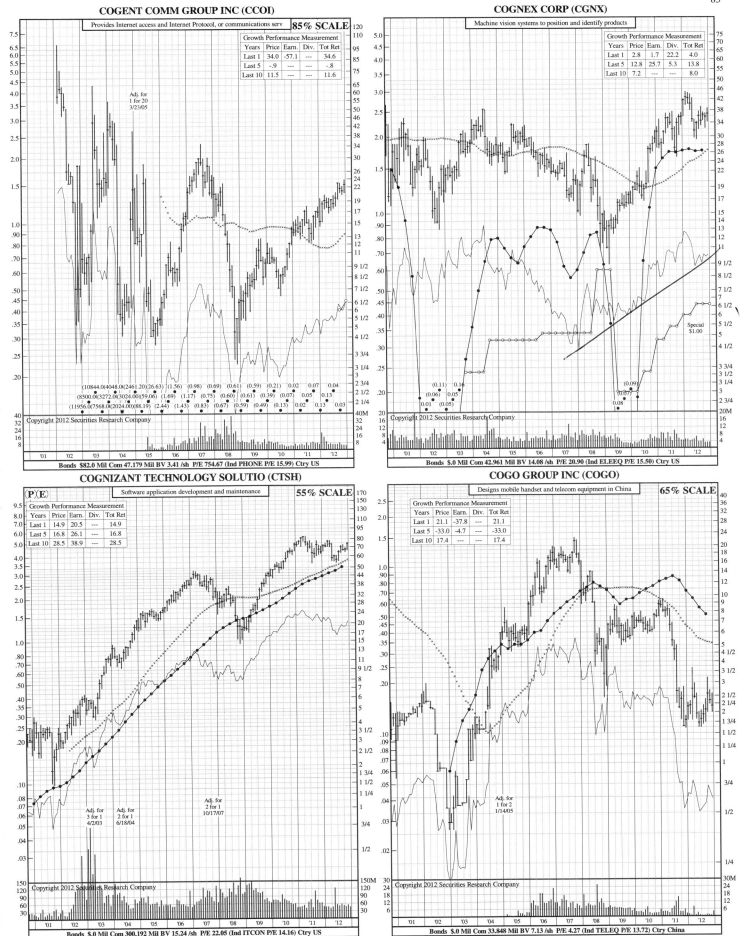

83

COGENT COMM GROUP INC (CCOI)

Provides Internet access and Internet Protocol, or communications serv **85% SCALE**

Growth Performance Measurement				
Years	Price	Earn.	Div.	Tot Ret
Last 1	34.0	-57.1	---	34.6
Last 5	-.9	---	---	-.8
Last 10	11.5	---	---	11.6

Adj. for
1 for 20
3/23/05

(10844.0)(4048.0)(2461.20)(26.63) (1.56) (0.98) (0.69) (0.61) (0.59) (0.21) 0.02 0.07 0.04
(8500.0)(3272.0)(3024.00)(59.06) (1.69) (1.17) (0.75) (0.60) (0.61) (0.39) (0.07) 0.05 0.13
(11956.0)(7568.0)(2024.00)(88.19) (2.44) (1.43) (0.83) (0.67) (0.59) (0.49) (0.13) 0.02 0.13 0.03

Copyright 2012 Securities Research Company

'01 '02 '03 '04 '05 '06 '07 '08 '09 '10 '11 '12

Bonds $82.0 Mil Com 47.179 Mil BV 3.41 /sh P/E 754.67 (Ind PHONE P/E 15.99) Ctry US

COGNEX CORP (CGNX)

Machine vision systems to position and identify products

Growth Performance Measurement				
Years	Price	Earn.	Div.	Tot Ret
Last 1	2.8	1.7	22.2	4.0
Last 5	12.8	25.7	5.3	13.8
Last 10	7.2	---	---	8.0

Special
$1.00

(0.11) 0.16
(0.06) 0.05
0.01 (0.05)

(0.09)
(0.07)
0.08

Copyright 2012 Securities Research Company

'01 '02 '03 '04 '05 '06 '07 '08 '09 '10 '11 '12

Bonds $.0 Mil Com 42.961 Mil BV 14.08 /sh P/E 20.90 (Ind ELEEQ P/E 15.50) Ctry US

COGNIZANT TECHNOLOGY SOLUTIO (CTSH)

Software application development and maintenance **55% SCALE**

(P)(E)

Growth Performance Measurement				
Years	Price	Earn.	Div.	Tot Ret
Last 1	14.9	20.5	---	14.9
Last 5	16.8	26.1	---	16.8
Last 10	28.5	38.9	---	28.5

Adj. for
3 for 1
4/2/03

Adj. for
2 for 1
6/18/04

Adj. for
2 for 1
10/17/07

Copyright 2012 Securities Research Company

'01 '02 '03 '04 '05 '06 '07 '08 '09 '10 '11 '12

Bonds $.0 Mil Com 300.192 Mil BV 15.24 /sh P/E 22.05 (Ind ITCON P/E 14.16) Ctry US

COGO GROUP INC (COGO)

Designs mobile handset and telecom equipment in China **65% SCALE**

Growth Performance Measurement				
Years	Price	Earn.	Div.	Tot Ret
Last 1	21.1	-37.8	---	21.1
Last 5	-33.0	-4.7	---	-33.0
Last 10	17.4	---	---	17.4

Adj. for
1 for 2
1/14/05

Copyright 2012 Securities Research Company

'01 '02 '03 '04 '05 '06 '07 '08 '09 '10 '11 '12

Bonds $.0 Mil Com 33.848 Mil BV 7.13 /sh P/E 4.27 (Ind TELEQ P/E 13.72) Ctry China

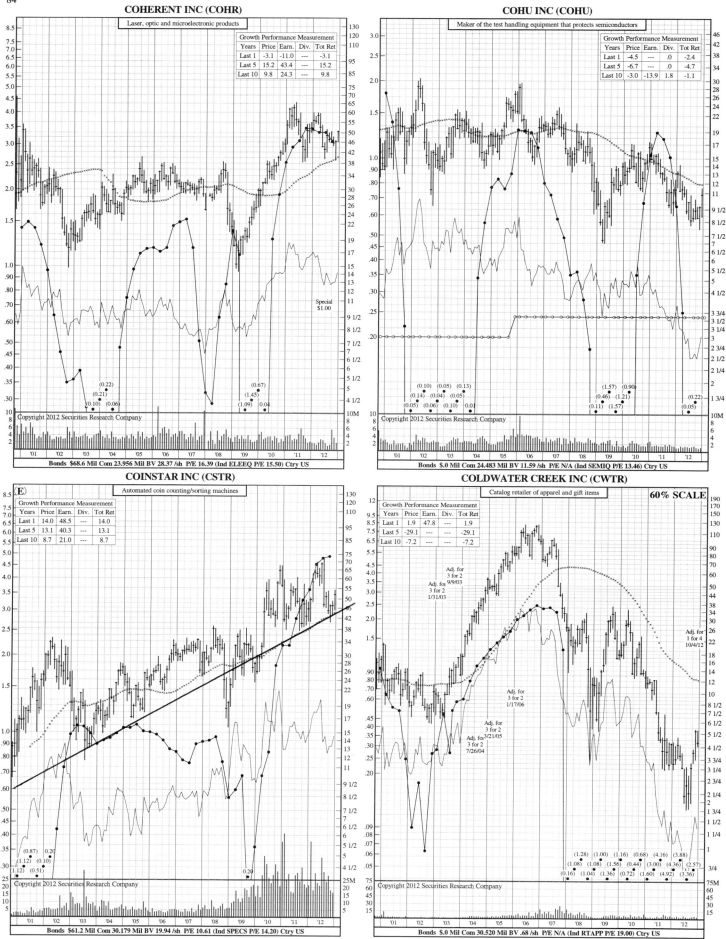

84

COHERENT INC (COHR)

Laser, optic and microelectronic products

Growth Performance Measurement				
Years	Price	Earn.	Div.	Tot Ret
Last 1	-3.1	-11.0	---	-3.1
Last 5	15.2	43.4	---	15.2
Last 10	9.8	24.3	---	9.8

Special $1.00

Copyright 2012 Securities Research Company

(0.22)
(0.21)
(0.67)
(0.10) (0.06)
(1.45)
(1.09) 0.04

Bonds $68.6 Mil Com 23.956 Mil BV 28.37 /sh P/E 16.39 (Ind ELEEQ P/E 15.50) Ctry US

COHU INC (COHU)

Maker of the test handling equipment that protects semiconductors

Growth Performance Measurement				
Years	Price	Earn.	Div.	Tot Ret
Last 1	-4.5	---	.0	-2.4
Last 5	-6.7	---	.0	-4.7
Last 10	-3.0	-13.9	1.8	-1.1

Copyright 2012 Securities Research Company

(0.10) (0.05) (0.13)
(0.14) (0.04) (0.05)
(1.57) (0.90)
(0.05) (0.06) (0.10) 0.01
(0.46) (1.21)
(0.11) (1.57)
(0.22)
(0.05)

Bonds $.0 Mil Com 24.483 Mil BV 11.59 /sh P/E N/A (Ind SEMIQ P/E 13.46) Ctry US

COINSTAR INC (CSTR)

(E)

Automated coin counting/sorting machines

Growth Performance Measurement				
Years	Price	Earn.	Div.	Tot Ret
Last 1	14.0	48.5	---	14.0
Last 5	13.1	40.3	---	13.1
Last 10	8.7	21.0	---	8.7

Copyright 2012 Securities Research Company

(0.87) 0.20
(1.12) (0.10)
(1.12)
(0.51)
0.20

Bonds $61.2 Mil Com 30.179 Mil BV 19.94 /sh P/E 10.61 (Ind SPECS P/E 14.20) Ctry US

COLDWATER CREEK INC (CWTR)

Catalog retailer of apparel and gift items

60% SCALE

Growth Performance Measurement				
Years	Price	Earn.	Div.	Tot Ret
Last 1	1.9	47.8	---	1.9
Last 5	-29.1	---	---	-29.1
Last 10	-7.2	---	---	-7.2

Adj. for
3 for 2
9/9/03

Adj. for
3 for 2
1/31/03

Adj. for
1 for 4
10/4/12

Adj. for
3 for 2
1/17/06

Adj. for
3 for 2
3/21/05

Adj. for
3 for 2
7/26/04

Copyright 2012 Securities Research Company

(1.28) (1.00) (1.16) (0.68) (4.16) (3.88)
(1.08) (1.08) (1.56) (0.44) (3.00) (4.36) (2.57)
(0.16) (1.04) (1.36) (0.72) (1.60) (4.92) (3.36)

Bonds $.0 Mil Com 30.520 Mil BV .68 /sh P/E N/A (Ind RTAPP P/E 19.00) Ctry US

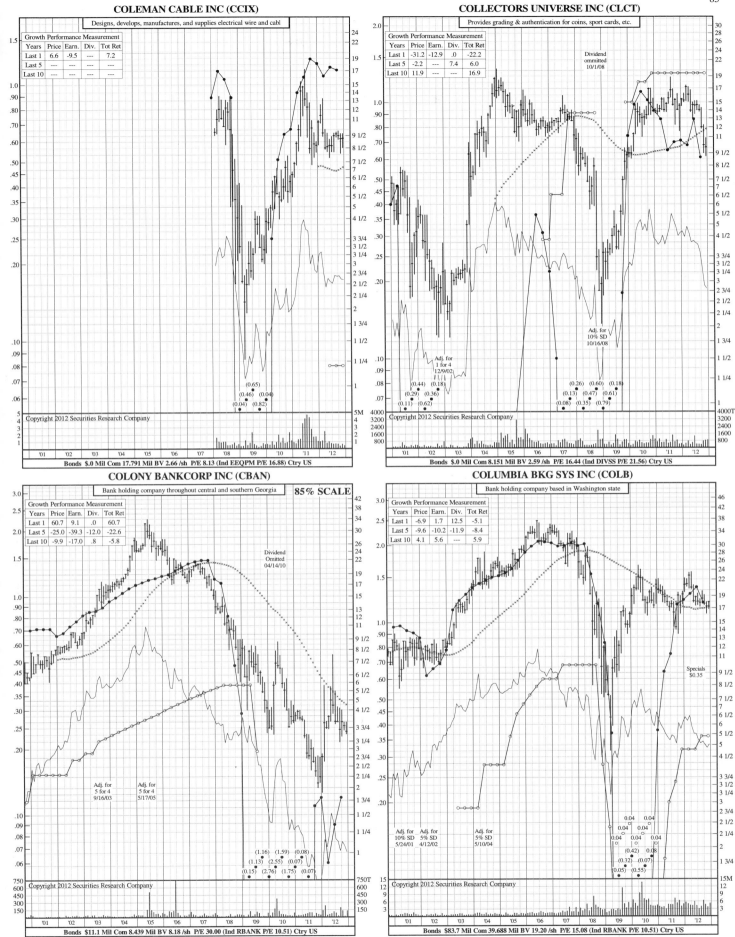

COLEMAN CABLE INC (CCIX)

Designs, develops, manufactures, and supplies electrical wire and cabl

Growth Performance Measurement

Years	Price	Earn.	Div.	Tot Ret
Last 1	6.6	-9.5	---	7.2
Last 5	---	---	---	---
Last 10	---	---	---	---

(0.65)
(0.46) (0.04)
(0.04) (0.82)

Copyright 2012 Securities Research Company

Bonds $.0 Mil Com 17.791 Mil BV 2.66 /sh P/E 8.13 (Ind EEQPM P/E 16.88) Ctry US

COLLECTORS UNIVERSE INC (CLCT)

Provides grading & authentication for coins, sport cards, etc.

Growth Performance Measurement

Years	Price	Earn.	Div.	Tot Ret
Last 1	-31.2	-12.9	.0	-22.2
Last 5	-2.2	---	7.4	6.0
Last 10	11.9	---	---	16.9

Dividend
ommitted
10/1/08

Adj. for
10% SD
10/16/08

Adj. for
1 for 4
12/9/02

(0.44) (0.18)
(0.29) (0.36)
(0.11) (0.62)

(0.26) (0.60) (0.18)
(0.13) (0.47) (0.61)
(0.08) (0.35) (0.79)

Copyright 2012 Securities Research Company

Bonds $.0 Mil Com 8.151 Mil BV 2.59 /sh P/E 16.44 (Ind DIVSS P/E 21.56) Ctry US

COLONY BANKCORP INC (CBAN)

85% SCALE

Bank holding company throughout central and southern Georgia

Growth Performance Measurement

Years	Price	Earn.	Div.	Tot Ret
Last 1	60.7	9.1	.0	60.7
Last 5	-25.0	-39.3	-12.0	-22.6
Last 10	-9.9	-17.0	.8	-5.8

Dividend
Omitted
04/14/10

Adj. for
5 for 4
9/16/03

Adj. for
5 for 4
5/17/05

(1.16) (1.59) (0.08)
(1.13) (2.55) (0.07)
(0.15) (2.76) (1.75) (0.07)

Copyright 2012 Securities Research Company

Bonds $11.1 Mil Com 8.439 Mil BV 8.18 /sh P/E 30.00 (Ind RBANK P/E 10.51) Ctry US

COLUMBIA BKG SYS INC (COLB)

Bank holding company based in Washington state

Growth Performance Measurement

Years	Price	Earn.	Div.	Tot Ret
Last 1	-6.9	1.7	12.5	-5.1
Last 5	-9.6	-10.2	-11.9	-8.4
Last 10	4.1	5.6	---	5.9

Specials
$0.35

Adj. for
10% SD
5/24/01

Adj. for
5% SD
4/12/02

Adj. for
5% SD
5/10/04

0.04 0.04
0.04 0.04
0.04 0.04 0.04

(0.42) 0.08
(0.32) (0.07)
(0.05) (0.55)

Copyright 2012 Securities Research Company

Bonds $83.7 Mil Com 39.688 Mil BV 19.20 /sh P/E 15.08 (Ind RBANK P/E 10.51) Ctry US

'01 '02 '03 '04 '05 '06 '07 '08 '09 '10 '11 '12

86

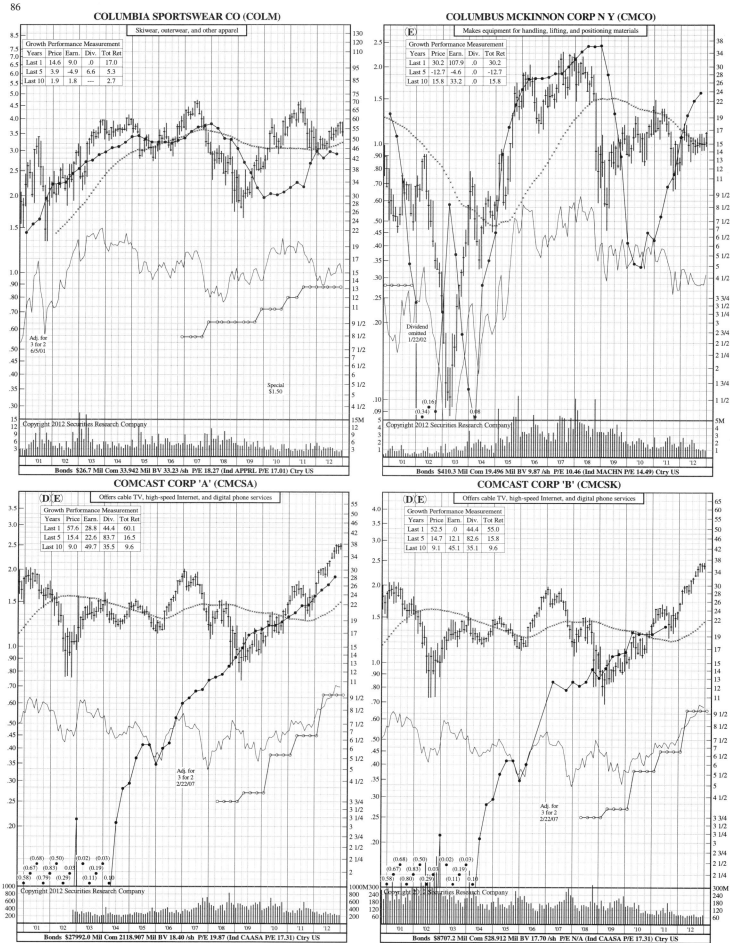

COLUMBIA SPORTSWEAR CO (COLM)

Skiwear, outerwear, and other apparel

Growth Performance Measurement				
Years	Price	Earn.	Div.	Tot Ret
Last 1	14.6	9.0	.0	17.0
Last 5	3.9	-4.9	6.6	5.3
Last 10	1.9	1.8	---	2.7

Adj. for
3 for 2
6/5/01

Special
$1.50

'01 '02 '03 '04 '05 '06 '07 '08 '09 '10 '11 '12

Bonds $26.7 Mil Com 33.942 Mil BV 33.23 /sh P/E 18.27 (Ind APPRL P/E 17.01) Ctry US

COLUMBUS MCKINNON CORP N Y (CMCO)

(E) Makes equipment for handling, lifting, and positioning materials

Growth Performance Measurement				
Years	Price	Earn.	Div.	Tot Ret
Last 1	30.2	107.9	.0	30.2
Last 5	-12.7	-4.6	.0	-12.7
Last 10	15.8	33.2	.0	15.8

Dividend
omitted
1/22/02

(0.16)
(0.34)   0.08

'01 '02 '03 '04 '05 '06 '07 '08 '09 '10 '11 '12

Bonds $410.3 Mil Com 19.496 Mil BV 9.87 /sh P/E 10.46 (Ind MACHN P/E 14.49) Ctry US

COMCAST CORP 'A' (CMCSA)

(D)(E) Offers cable TV, high-speed Internet, and digital phone services

Growth Performance Measurement				
Years	Price	Earn.	Div.	Tot Ret
Last 1	57.6	28.8	44.4	60.1
Last 5	15.4	22.6	83.7	16.5
Last 10	9.0	49.7	35.5	9.6

Adj. for
3 for 2
2/22/07

(0.68) (0.50) (0.02) (0.03)
(0.67) (0.83) 0.03 (0.19)
(0.58) (0.79) (0.29) (0.11) 0.10

'01 '02 '03 '04 '05 '06 '07 '08 '09 '10 '11 '12

Bonds $27992.0 Mil Com 2118.907 Mil BV 18.40 /sh P/E 19.87 (Ind CAASA P/E 17.31) Ctry US

COMCAST CORP 'B' (CMCSK)

(D)(E) Offers cable TV, high-speed Internet, and digital phone services

Growth Performance Measurement				
Years	Price	Earn.	Div.	Tot Ret
Last 1	52.5	.0	44.4	55.0
Last 5	14.7	12.1	82.6	15.8
Last 10	9.1	45.1	35.1	9.6

Adj. for
3 for 2
2/22/07

(0.68) (0.50) (0.02) (0.03)
(0.67) (0.83) 0.03 (0.19)
(0.58) (0.80) (0.29) (0.11) 0.10

'01 '02 '03 '04 '05 '06 '07 '08 '09 '10 '11 '12

Bonds $8707.2 Mil Com 528.912 Mil BV 17.70 /sh P/E N/A (Ind CAASA P/E 17.31) Ctry US

87

COMMERCE BANCSHARES INC (CBSH)

Large bank holding company in Missouri

Growth Performance Measurement

Years	Price	Earn.	Div.	Tot Ret
Last 1	-3.4	.3	5.0	-1.0
Last 5	-.1	3.5	3.3	2.2
Last 10	3.8	4.9	8.7	5.8

Adj. for
5% SD
11/27/06

Adj. for   Adj. for   Adj. for   Adj. for   Adj. for   Adj. for
5% SD   5% SD   5% SD   5% SD   5% SD   5% SD
11/27/07   11/12/08   11/25/09   12/2/10   11/28/11   11/28/12

Adj. fc Adj. for   Adj. for   Adj. for   Adj. for
5% SI   5% SD   5% SD   5% SD   5% SD
11/28/11/28/01   11/26/02   11/25/03   11/24/04   11/25/05

Copyright 2012 Securities Research Company

'01 '02 '03 '04 '05 '06 '07 '08 '09 '10 '11 '12

Bonds $25.7 Mil Com 91.666 Mil BV 24.99 /sh P/E 12.66 (Ind RBANK P/E 10.51) Ctry US

COMMTOUCH SOFTWARE LTD (CTCH)

(P)   Software for spam e-mail filtering and management applications   **65% SCALE**

Growth Performance Measurement

Years	Price	Earn.	Div.	Tot Ret
Last 1	-4.6	-16.0	---	-4.6
Last 5	-12.5	24.6	---	-12.5
Last 10	23.0	---	---	23.0

Adj. for
1 for 3
1/2/08

(11.13) (8.01) (0.81)   (0.54)   (0.27) (0.03)
(8.61) (10.68) (1.68) (0.75)   (0.42) (0.09)
(6.96) (13.98) (6.69) (0.69)   (0.51) (0.18) 0.00

Copyright 2012 Securities Research Company

'01 '02 '03 '04 '05 '06 '07 '08 '09 '10 '11 '12

Bonds $.0 Mil Com 24.916 Mil BV 1.31 /sh P/E 14.76 (Ind ITSOF P/E 19.21) Ctry US

COMMUNICATIONS SYS INC (JCS)

Telephone/telecommunications equipment, telephone companies

Growth Performance Measurement

Years	Price	Earn.	Div.	Tot Ret
Last 1	-26.0	-87.6	6.7	-21.6
Last 5	-2.6	-25.4	5.9	2.2
Last 10	2.7	-6.4	4.8	6.2

Listed
Nasdaq 6/3/08
ASE prior

Dividend
omitted
7/26/02

Copyright 2012 Securities Research Company

'01 '02 '03 '04 '05 '06 '07 '08 '09 '10 '11 '12

Bonds $.0 Mil Com 8.475 Mil BV 11.36 /sh P/E 57.78 (Ind TELEQ P/E 13.72) Ctry US

COMMUNITY TR BANCORP INC (CTBI)

Banking services in Kentucky

Growth Performance Measurement

Years	Price	Earn.	Div.	Tot Ret
Last 1	11.4	13.3	1.6	16.7
Last 5	3.6	4.3	3.1	7.3
Last 10	4.7	5.5	7.2	7.7

Adj. for   Adj. for   Adj. for
10% SD   10% SD   10% SD
11/26/02   11/26/03   11/29/04

Copyright 2012 Securities Research Company

'01 '02 '03 '04 '05 '06 '07 '08 '09 '10 '11 '12

Bonds $70.6 Mil Com 15.612 Mil BV 25.38 /sh P/E 11.62 (Ind RBANK P/E 10.51) Ctry US

87

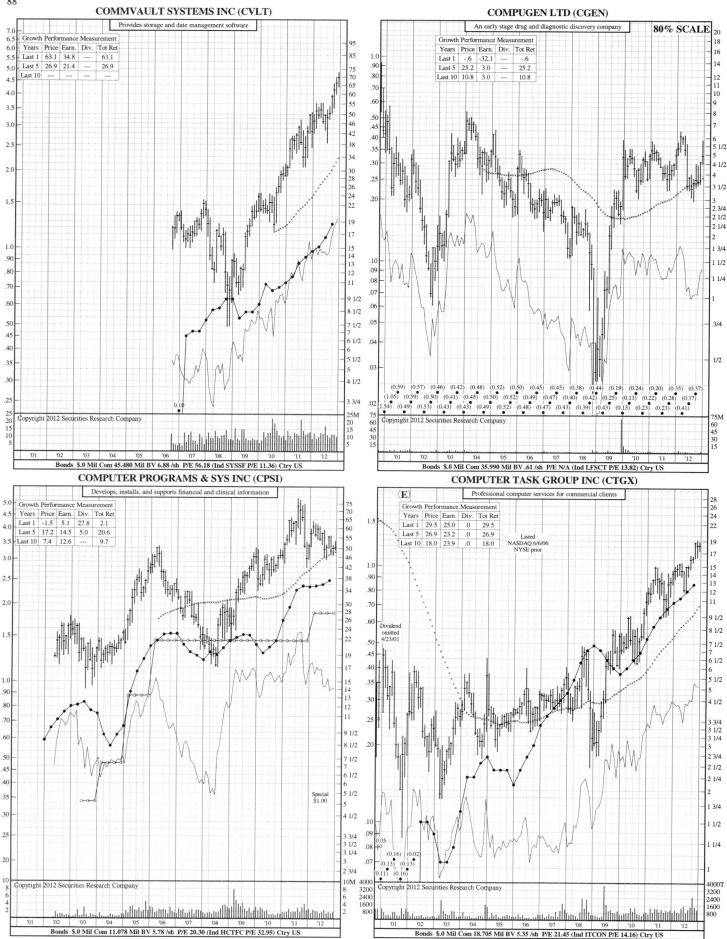

88

COMMVAULT SYSTEMS INC (CVLT)

Provides storage and date management software

Growth Performance Measurement

Years	Price	Earn.	Div.	Tot Ret
Last 1	63.1	34.8	---	63.1
Last 5	26.9	21.4	---	26.9
Last 10	---	---	---	---

0.10

Copyright 2012 Securities Research Company

Bonds $.0 Mil Com 45.480 Mil BV 6.88 /sh P/E 56.18 (Ind SYSSF P/E 11.36) Ctry US

COMPUGEN LTD (CGEN)

An early stage drug and diagnostic discovery company

80% SCALE

Growth Performance Measurement

Years	Price	Earn.	Div.	Tot Ret
Last 1	-.6	-32.1	---	-.6
Last 5	25.2	3.0	---	25.2
Last 10	10.8	3.0	---	10.8

(0.59) (0.57) (0.46) (0.42) (0.48) (0.52) (0.50) (0.45) (0.45) (0.38) (0.44) (0.19) (0.24) (0.20) (0.35) (0.37)
(1.05) (0.59) (0.49) (0.41) (0.45) (0.49) (0.52) (0.52) (0.49) (0.47) (0.40) (0.25) (0.13) (0.22) (0.28) (0.37)
(1.54) (0.49) (0.53) (0.43) (0.43) (0.49) (0.52) (0.48) (0.47) (0.43) (0.39) (0.43) (0.13) (0.23) (0.23) (0.41)

Copyright 2012 Securities Research Company

Bonds $.0 Mil Com 35.990 Mil BV .61 /sh P/E N/A (Ind LFSCT P/E 13.82) Ctry US

COMPUTER PROGRAMS & SYS INC (CPSI)

Develops, installs, and supports financial and clinical information

Growth Performance Measurement

Years	Price	Earn.	Div.	Tot Ret
Last 1	-1.5	5.1	27.8	2.1
Last 5	17.2	14.5	5.0	20.6
Last 10	7.4	12.6	---	9.7

Special
$1.00

Copyright 2012 Securities Research Company

Bonds $.0 Mil Com 11.078 Mil BV 5.78 /sh P/E 20.30 (Ind HCTFC P/E 32.95) Ctry US

COMPUTER TASK GROUP INC (CTGX)

(E) Professional computer services for commercial clients

Growth Performance Measurement

Years	Price	Earn.	Div.	Tot Ret
Last 1	29.5	25.0	.0	29.5
Last 5	26.9	23.2	.0	26.9
Last 10	18.0	23.9	.0	18.0

Listed
NASDAQ 6/6/06
NYSE prior

Dividend
omitted
4/23/01

0.05

(0.16) (0.02)
(0.13) (0.13)
(0.11) (0.16)
(0.13)

Copyright 2012 Securities Research Company

Bonds $.0 Mil Com 18.705 Mil BV 5.35 /sh P/E 21.45 (Ind ITCON P/E 14.16) Ctry US

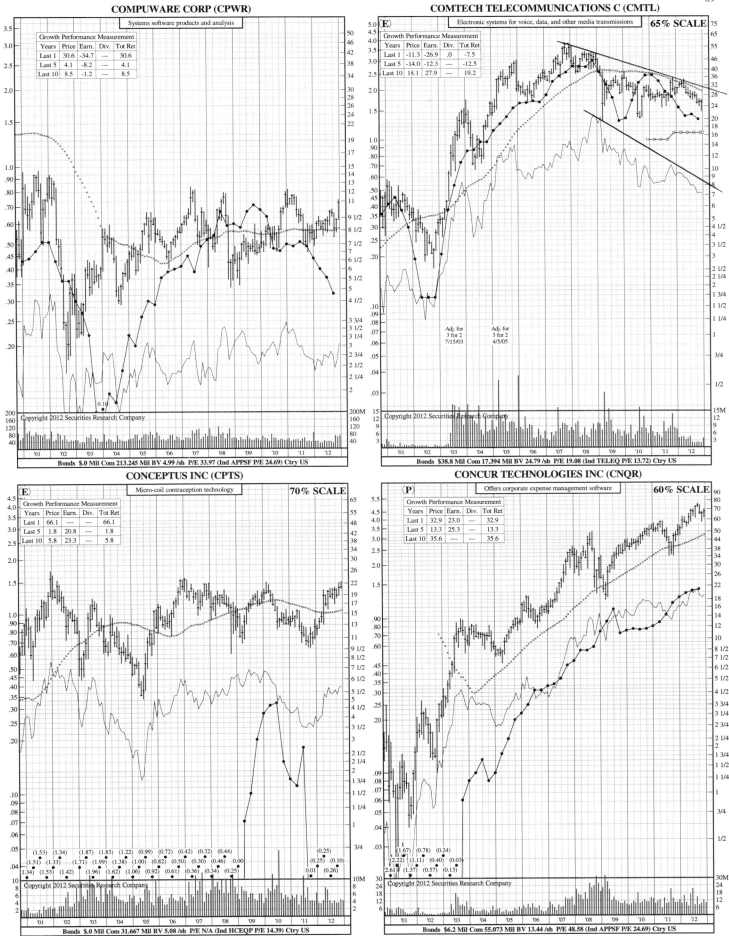

COMPUWARE CORP (CPWR)
Systems software products and analysis

Growth Performance Measurement				
Years	Price	Earn.	Div.	Tot Ret
Last 1	30.6	-34.7	---	30.6
Last 5	4.1	-8.2	---	4.1
Last 10	8.5	-1.2	---	8.5

Copyright 2012 Securities Research Company

Bonds $.0 Mil Com 213.245 Mil BV 4.99 /sh P/E 33.97 (Ind APPSF P/E 24.69) Ctry US

COMTECH TELECOMMUNICATIONS C (CMTL)
Electronic systems for voice, data, and other media transmissions

65% SCALE

Growth Performance Measurement				
Years	Price	Earn.	Div.	Tot Ret
Last 1	-11.3	-26.9	.0	-7.5
Last 5	-14.0	-12.3	---	-12.5
Last 10	18.1	27.9	---	19.2

Adj. for
3 for 2
7/15/03

Adj. for
3 for 2
4/5/05

Copyright 2012 Securities Research Company

Bonds $38.8 Mil Com 17.394 Mil BV 24.79 /sh P/E 19.08 (Ind TELEQ P/E 13.72) Ctry US

CONCEPTUS INC (CPTS)
Micro-coil contraception technology

70% SCALE

Growth Performance Measurement				
Years	Price	Earn.	Div.	Tot Ret
Last 1	66.1	---	---	66.1
Last 5	1.8	20.8	---	1.8
Last 10	5.8	23.3	---	5.8

(1.53) (1.34)   (1.87) (1.83) (1.22) (0.99) (0.72) (0.42) (0.32) (0.44)   (0.25)
(1.51) (1.33)   (1.71) (1.99) (1.06) (1.00) (0.82) (0.50) (0.30) (0.46) (0.00)   (0.25) (0.10)
(1.34) (1.53)   (1.42) (1.96) (1.62) (0.92) (0.61) (0.36) (0.34) (0.25)   0.01 (0.26)

Copyright 2012 Securities Research Company

Bonds $.0 Mil Com 31.667 Mil BV 5.08 /sh P/E N/A (Ind HCEQP P/E 14.39) Ctry US

CONCUR TECHNOLOGIES INC (CNQR)
Offers corporate expense management software

60% SCALE

Growth Performance Measurement				
Years	Price	Earn.	Div.	Tot Ret
Last 1	32.9	23.0	---	32.9
Last 5	13.3	25.3	---	13.3
Last 10	35.6	---	---	35.6

(1.67) (0.78) (0.24)
(2.22) (1.11) (0.40) (0.03)
(2.61) (1.37) (0.57) (0.13)

Copyright 2012 Securities Research Company

Bonds $6.2 Mil Com 55.073 Mil BV 13.44 /sh P/E 48.58 (Ind APPSF P/E 24.69) Ctry US

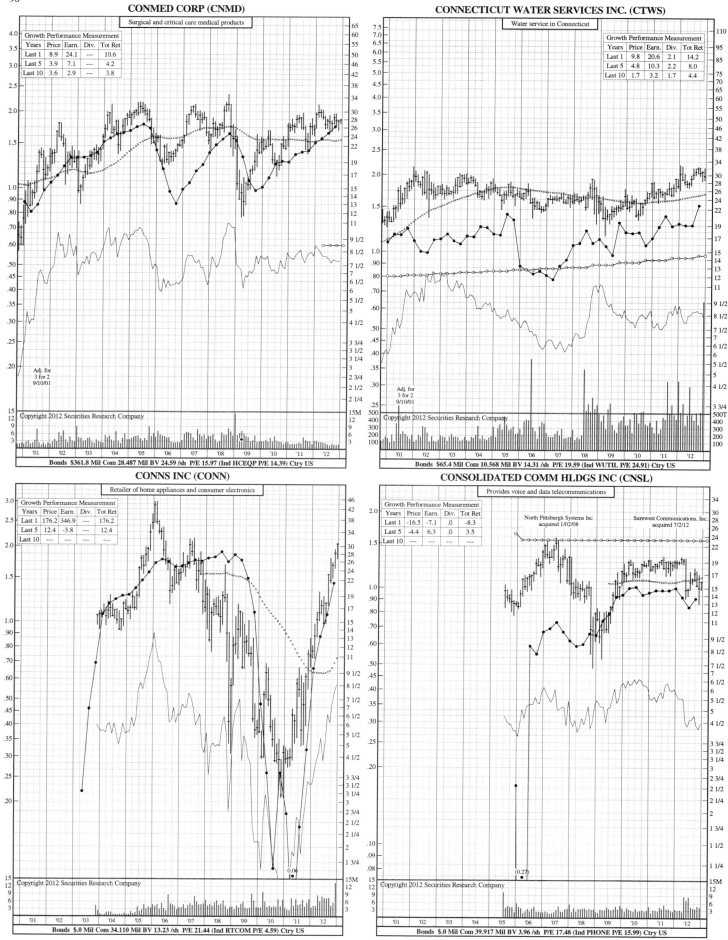

CONMED CORP (CNMD)

Surgical and critical care medical products

Growth Performance Measurement				
Years	Price	Earn.	Div.	Tot Ret
Last 1	8.9	24.1	---	10.6
Last 5	3.9	7.1	---	4.2
Last 10	3.6	2.9	---	3.8

Adj. for
3 for 2
9/10/01

Copyright 2012 Securities Research Company

Bonds $361.8 Mil Com 28.487 Mil BV 24.59 /sh P/E 15.97 (Ind HCEQP P/E 14.39) Ctry US

CONNECTICUT WATER SERVICES INC. (CTWS)

Water service in Connecticut

Growth Performance Measurement				
Years	Price	Earn.	Div.	Tot Ret
Last 1	9.8	20.6	2.1	14.2
Last 5	4.8	10.3	2.2	8.0
Last 10	1.7	3.2	1.7	4.4

Adj. for
3 for 2
9/10/01

Copyright 2012 Securities Research Company

Bonds $65.4 Mil Com 10.568 Mil BV 14.31 /sh P/E 19.59 (Ind WUTIL P/E 24.91) Ctry US

CONNS INC (CONN)

Retailer of home appliances and consumer electronics

Growth Performance Measurement				
Years	Price	Earn.	Div.	Tot Ret
Last 1	176.2	346.9	---	176.2
Last 5	12.4	-3.8	---	12.4
Last 10	---	---	---	---

0.06

Copyright 2012 Securities Research Company

Bonds $.0 Mil Com 34.110 Mil BV 13.23 /sh P/E 21.44 (Ind RTCOM P/E 4.59) Ctry US

CONSOLIDATED COMM HLDGS INC (CNSL)

Provides voice and data telecommunications

Growth Performance Measurement				
Years	Price	Earn.	Div.	Tot Ret
Last 1	-16.5	-7.1	.0	-8.3
Last 5	-4.4	6.3	.0	3.5
Last 10	---	---	---	---

North Pittsburgh Systems Inc
acquired 1/02/08

Surewest Communications, Inc.
acquired 7/2/12

(0.27)

Copyright 2012 Securities Research Company

Bonds $.0 Mil Com 39.917 Mil BV 3.96 /sh P/E 17.48 (Ind PHONE P/E 15.99) Ctry US

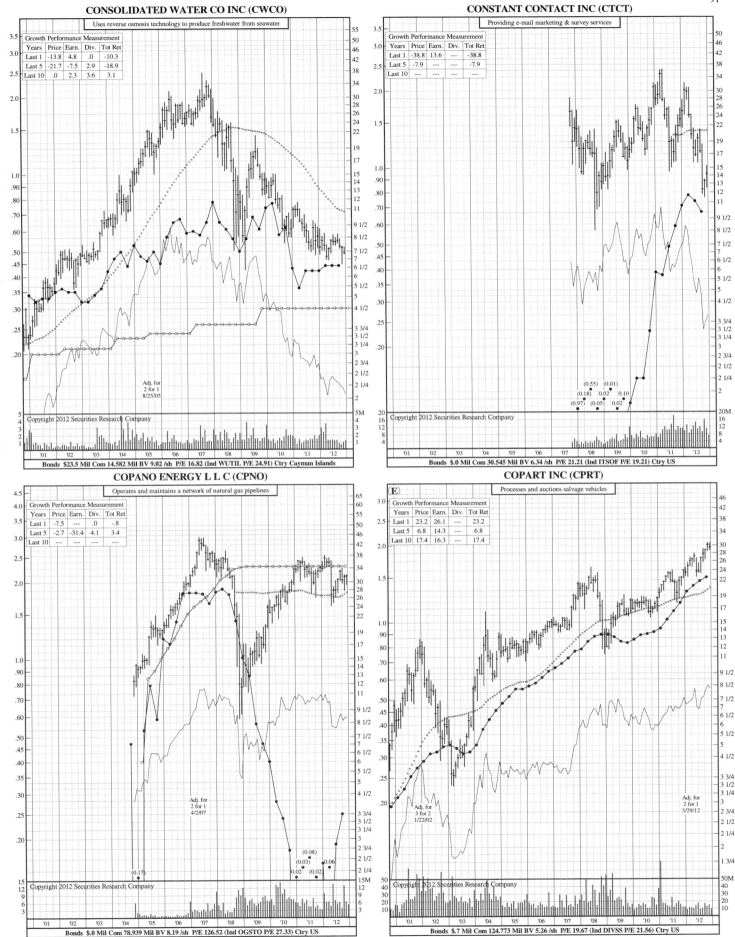

CONSOLIDATED WATER CO INC (CWCO)

Uses reverse osmosis technology to produce freshwater from seawater

Growth Performance Measurement

Years	Price	Earn.	Div.	Tot Ret
Last 1	-13.8	4.8	.0	-10.3
Last 5	-21.7	-7.5	2.9	-18.9
Last 10	.0	2.3	3.6	3.1

Adj. for
2 for 1
8/25/05

Copyright 2012 Securities Research Company

Bonds $23.5 Mil Com 14.582 Mil BV 9.02 /sh P/E 16.82 (Ind WUTIL P/E 24.91) Ctry Cayman Islands

CONSTANT CONTACT INC (CTCT)

Providing e-mail marketing & survey services

Growth Performance Measurement

Years	Price	Earn.	Div.	Tot Ret
Last 1	-38.8	13.6	---	-38.8
Last 5	-7.9	---	---	-7.9
Last 10	---	---	---	---

(0.55) (0.01)
(0.18) 0.02   0.10
(0.97) (0.05) 0.02

Copyright 2012 Securities Research Company

Bonds $.0 Mil Com 30.545 Mil BV 6.34 /sh P/E 21.21 (Ind ITSOF P/E 19.21) Ctry US

COPANO ENERGY L L C (CPNO)

Operates and maintains a network of natural gas pipelines

Growth Performance Measurement

Years	Price	Earn.	Div.	Tot Ret
Last 1	-7.5	---	.0	-.8
Last 5	-2.7	-31.4	4.1	3.4
Last 10	---	---	---	---

Adj. for
2 for 1
4/2/07

(0.08)
(0.03)
0.02   (0.02)   0.06

(0.17)

Copyright 2012 Securities Research Company

Bonds $.0 Mil Com 78.939 Mil BV 8.19 /sh P/E 126.52 (Ind OGSTO P/E 27.33) Ctry US

COPART INC (CPRT)

(E) Processes and auctions salvage vehicles

Growth Performance Measurement

Years	Price	Earn.	Div.	Tot Ret
Last 1	23.2	26.1	---	23.2
Last 5	6.8	14.3	---	6.8
Last 10	17.4	16.3	---	17.4

Adj. for
2 for 1
3/29/12

Adj. for
3 for 2
1/22/02

Copyright 2012 Securities Research Company

Bonds $.7 Mil Com 124.773 Mil BV 5.26 /sh P/E 19.67 (Ind DIVSS P/E 21.56) Ctry US

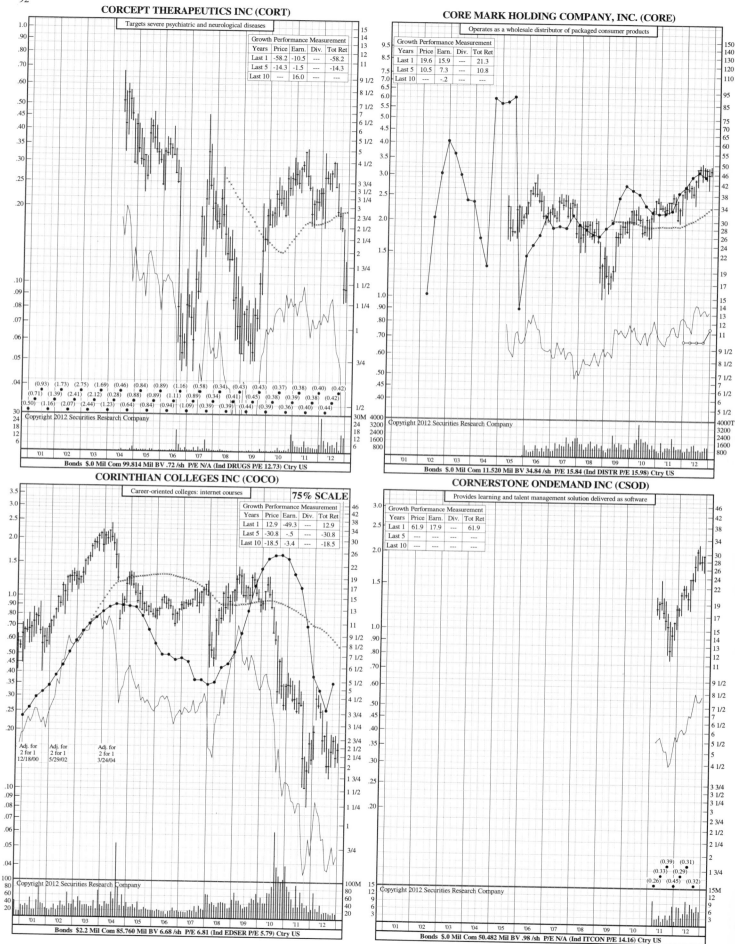

CORCEPT THERAPEUTICS INC (CORT)

Targets severe psychiatric and neurological diseases

Growth Performance Measurement				
Years	Price	Earn.	Div.	Tot Ret
Last 1	-58.2	-10.5	---	-58.2
Last 5	-14.3	-1.5	---	-14.3
Last 10	---	16.0	---	---

(0.93) (1.73) (2.75) (1.69) (0.46) (0.84) (0.89) (1.16) (0.58) (0.34) (0.43) (0.43) (0.37) (0.38) (0.40) (0.42)
(0.71) (1.39) (2.41) (2.12) (0.28) (0.88) (0.89) (1.11) (0.89) (0.34) (0.41) (0.45) (0.38) (0.39) (0.38) (0.42)
(0.50) (1.16) (2.07) (2.44) (1.23) (0.64) (0.84) (0.94) (1.09) (0.39) (0.44) (0.39) (0.36) (0.40) (0.44)

Copyright 2012 Securities Research Company

Bonds $.0 Mil Com 99.814 Mil BV .72 /sh P/E N/A (Ind DRUGS P/E 12.73) Ctry US

CORE MARK HOLDING COMPANY, INC. (CORE)

Operates as a wholesale distributor of packaged consumer products

Growth Performance Measurement				
Years	Price	Earn.	Div.	Tot Ret
Last 1	19.6	15.9	---	21.3
Last 5	10.5	7.3	---	10.8
Last 10	---	-.2	---	---

Copyright 2012 Securities Research Company

Bonds $.0 Mil Com 11.520 Mil BV 34.84 /sh P/E 15.84 (Ind DISTR P/E 15.98) Ctry US

CORINTHIAN COLLEGES INC (COCO)

Career-oriented colleges: internet courses

75% SCALE

Growth Performance Measurement				
Years	Price	Earn.	Div.	Tot Ret
Last 1	12.9	-49.3	---	12.9
Last 5	-30.8	-.5	---	-30.8
Last 10	-18.5	-3.4	---	-18.5

Adj. for
2 for 1
12/18/00

Adj. for
2 for 1
5/29/02

Adj. for
2 for 1
3/24/04

Copyright 2012 Securities Research Company

Bonds $2.2 Mil Com 85.760 Mil BV 6.68 /sh P/E 6.81 (Ind EDSER P/E 5.79) Ctry US

CORNERSTONE ONDEMAND INC (CSOD)

Provides learning and talent management solution delivered as software

Growth Performance Measurement				
Years	Price	Earn.	Div.	Tot Ret
Last 1	61.9	17.9	---	61.9
Last 5	---	---	---	---
Last 10	---	---	---	---

(0.39) (0.31)
(0.33) (0.29)
(0.26) (0.45) (0.32)

Copyright 2012 Securities Research Company

Bonds $.0 Mil Com 50.482 Mil BV .98 /sh P/E N/A (Ind ITCON P/E 14.16) Ctry US

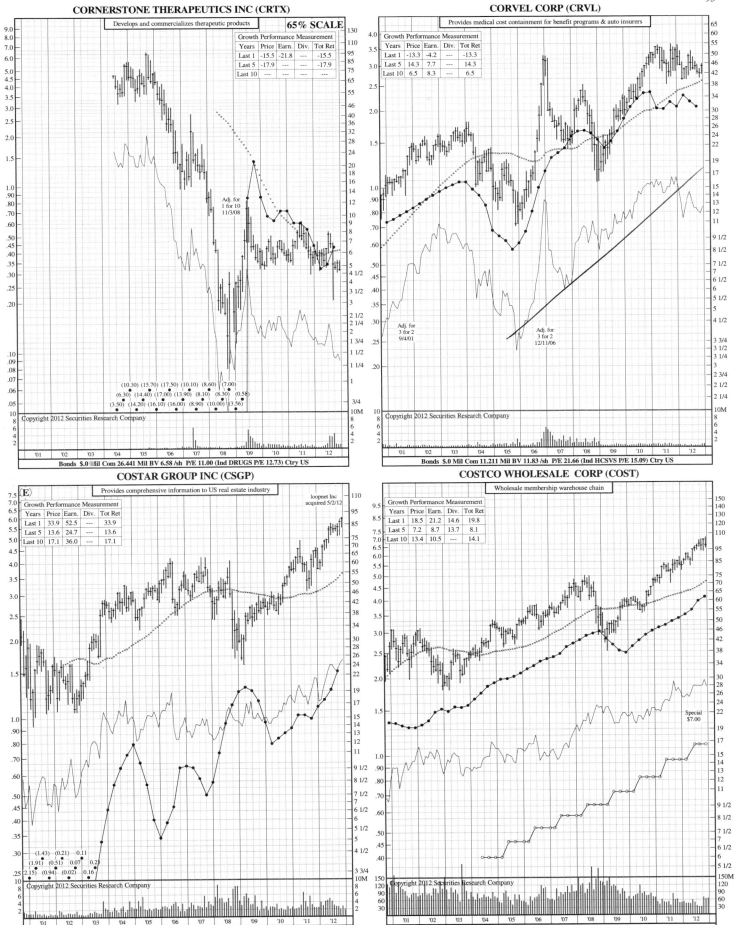

CORNERSTONE THERAPEUTICS INC (CRTX)

Develops and commercializes therapeutic products

65% SCALE

Growth Performance Measurement

Years	Price	Earn.	Div.	Tot Ret
Last 1	-15.5	-21.8	---	-15.5
Last 5	-17.9	---	---	-17.9
Last 10	---	---	---	---

Adj. for
1 for 10
11/3/08

(10.30) (15.70) (17.50) (10.10) (8.60) (7.00)
(6.30) (14.40) (17.00) (13.90) (8.10) (8.30) (0.58)
(3.50) (14.20) (16.10) (16.00) (8.90) (10.00) (3.56)

Copyright 2012 Securities Research Company

Bonds $.0 Mil Com 26.441 Mil BV 6.58 /sh P/E 11.00 (Ind DRUGS P/E 12.73) Ctry US

CORVEL CORP (CRVL)

Provides medical cost containment for benefit programs & auto insurers

Growth Performance Measurement

Years	Price	Earn.	Div.	Tot Ret
Last 1	-13.3	-4.2	---	-13.3
Last 5	14.3	7.7	---	14.3
Last 10	6.5	8.3	---	6.5

Adj. for
3 for 2
9/4/01

Adj. for
3 for 2
12/11/06

Copyright 2012 Securities Research Company

Bonds $.0 Mil Com 11.211 Mil BV 11.83 /sh P/E 21.66 (Ind HCSVS P/E 15.09) Ctry US

COSTAR GROUP INC (CSGP)

(E)

Provides comprehensive information to US real estate industry

loopnet Inc
acquired 5/2/12

Growth Performance Measurement

Years	Price	Earn.	Div.	Tot Ret
Last 1	33.9	52.5	---	33.9
Last 5	13.6	24.7	---	13.6
Last 10	17.1	36.0	---	17.1

(1.43) (0.21) 0.11
(1.91) (0.51) 0.07 0.28
(2.15) (0.94) (0.02) 0.16

Copyright 2012 Securities Research Company

Bonds $.0 Mil Com 28.260 Mil BV 28.87 /sh P/E 59.19 (Ind REACO P/E 15.81) Ctry US

COSTCO WHOLESALE CORP (COST)

Wholesale membership warehouse chain

Growth Performance Measurement

Years	Price	Earn.	Div.	Tot Ret
Last 1	18.5	21.2	14.6	19.8
Last 5	7.2	8.7	13.7	8.1
Last 10	13.4	10.5	---	14.1

Special
$7.00

Copyright 2012 Securities Research Company

Bonds $215.0 Mil Com 435.636 Mil BV 29.27 /sh P/E 23.96 (Ind HYPMK P/E 16.40) Ctry US

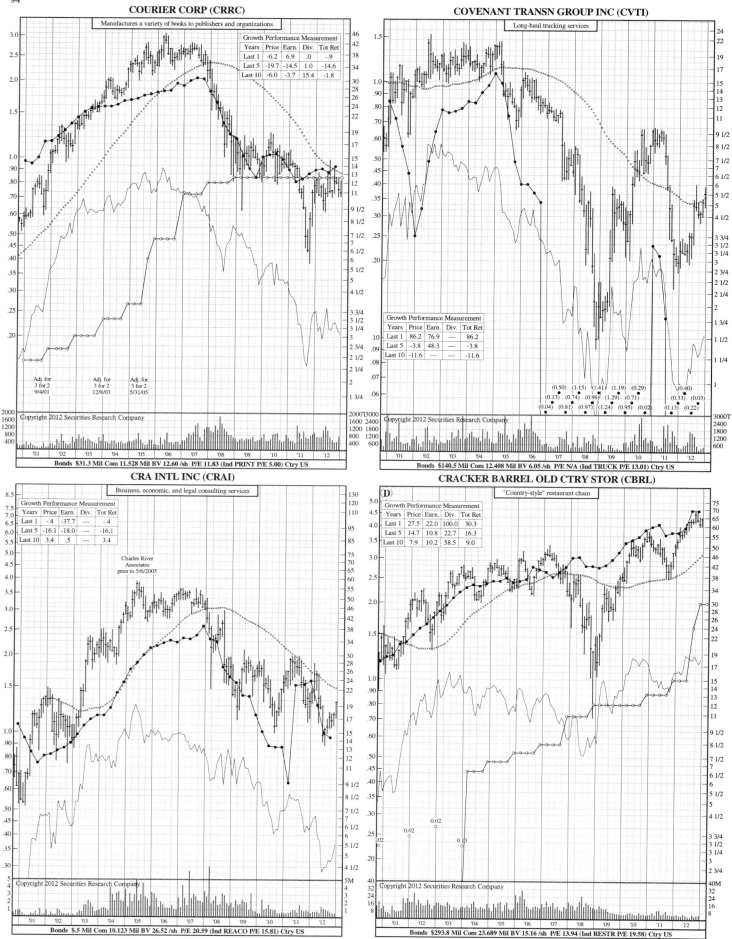

94

COURIER CORP (CRRC)

Manufactures a variety of books to publishers and organizations

Growth Performance Measurement				
Years	Price	Earn.	Div.	Tot Ret
Last 1	-6.2	6.9	.0	-.9
Last 5	-19.7	-14.5	1.0	-14.6
Last 10	-6.0	-3.7	15.4	-1.8

Adj. for
3 for 2
9/4/01

Adj. for
3 for 2
12/8/03

Adj. for
3 for 2
5/31/05

Copyright 2012 Securities Research Company

Bonds $31.3 Mil Com 11.528 Mil BV 12.60 /sh P/E 11.83 (Ind PRINT P/E 5.00) Ctry US

COVENANT TRANSN GROUP INC (CVTI)

Long-haul trucking services

Growth Performance Measurement				
Years	Price	Earn.	Div.	Tot Ret
Last 1	86.2	76.9	---	86.2
Last 5	-3.8	48.3	---	-3.8
Last 10	-11.6	---	---	-11.6

(0.50) (1.15) (1.41) (1.19) (0.29)   (0.40)
(0.13) (0.74) (0.96) (1.29) (0.71)   (0.33) (0.03)
(0.04) (0.81) (0.97) (1.24) (0.95) (0.02) (0.13) (0.22)

Copyright 2012 Securities Research Company

Bonds $140.5 Mil Com 12.408 Mil BV 6.05 /sh P/E N/A (Ind TRUCK P/E 13.01) Ctry US

CRA INTL INC (CRAI)

Business, economic, and legal consulting services

Growth Performance Measurement				
Years	Price	Earn.	Div.	Tot Ret
Last 1	-.4	-37.7	---	-.4
Last 5	-16.1	-18.0	---	-16.1
Last 10	3.4	.5	---	3.4

Charles River
Associates
prior to 5/6/2005

Copyright 2012 Securities Research Company

Bonds $.5 Mil Com 10.123 Mil BV 26.52 /sh P/E 20.59 (Ind REACO P/E 15.81) Ctry US

CRACKER BARREL OLD CTRY STOR (CBRL)

(D)

"Country-style" restaurant chain

Growth Performance Measurement				
Years	Price	Earn.	Div.	Tot Ret
Last 1	27.5	22.0	100.0	30.3
Last 5	14.7	10.8	22.7	16.3
Last 10	7.9	10.2	58.5	9.0

0.02
0.02
0.13

Copyright 2012 Securities Research Company

Bonds $293.8 Mil Com 23.689 Mil BV 15.16 /sh P/E 13.94 (Ind RESTR P/E 19.58) Ctry US

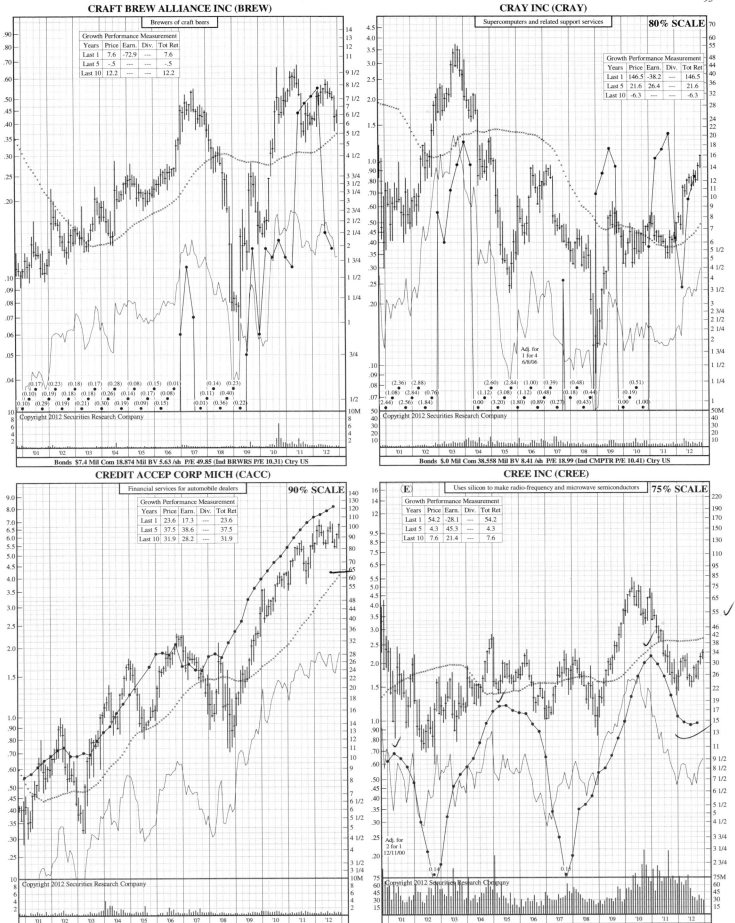

CRAFT BREW ALLIANCE INC (BREW)

Brewers of craft beers

Growth Performance Measurement				
Years	Price	Earn.	Div.	Tot Ret
Last 1	7.6	-72.9	---	7.6
Last 5	-.5		---	-.5
Last 10	12.2	---	---	12.2

(0.17) (0.23) (0.18) (0.17) (0.28) (0.08) (0.15) (0.01)   (0.14) (0.23)
(0.10) (0.19) (0.18) (0.18) (0.26) (0.14) (0.17) (0.08)   (0.11) (0.40)
(0.10) (0.29) (0.19) (0.21) (0.30) (0.19) (0.09) (0.15)   (0.01) (0.36) (0.22)

Copyright 2012 Securities Research Company

Bonds $7.4 Mil Com 18.874 Mil BV 5.63 /sh P/E 49.85 (Ind BRWRS P/E 10.31) Ctry US

CRAY INC (CRAY)

Supercomputers and related support services

80% SCALE

Growth Performance Measurement				
Years	Price	Earn.	Div.	Tot Ret
Last 1	146.5	-38.2	---	146.5
Last 5	21.6	26.4	---	21.6
Last 10	-6.3	---	---	-6.3

Adj. for
1 for 4
6/8/06

(2.36) (2.88)   (2.60) (2.84) (1.00) (0.39)   (0.48)   (0.51)
(1.08) (2.84) (0.76)   (1.12) (3.08) (1.12) (0.48) (0.18) (0.44)   (0.19)
(2.44) (2.56) (1.84)   0.00 (3.20) (1.80) (0.89) (0.27) (0.43)   0.00 (1.00)

Copyright 2012 Securities Research Company

Bonds $.0 Mil Com 38.558 Mil BV 8.41 /sh P/E 18.99 (Ind CMPTR P/E 10.41) Ctry US

CREDIT ACCEP CORP MICH (CACC)

Financial services for automobile dealers

90% SCALE

Growth Performance Measurement				
Years	Price	Earn.	Div.	Tot Ret
Last 1	23.6	17.3	---	23.6
Last 5	37.5	38.6	---	37.5
Last 10	31.9	28.2	---	31.9

Copyright 2012 Securities Research Company

Bonds $75.8 Mil Com 24.551 Mil BV 24.36 /sh P/E 12.49 (Ind FINAN P/E 11.42) Ctry US

CREE INC (CREE)

(E) Uses silicon to make radio-frequency and microwave semiconductors

75% SCALE

Growth Performance Measurement				
Years	Price	Earn.	Div.	Tot Ret
Last 1	54.2	-28.1	---	54.2
Last 5	4.3	45.3	---	4.3
Last 10	7.6	21.4	---	7.6

Adj. for
2 for 1
12/11/00

0.14   0.15

Copyright 2012 Securities Research Company

Bonds $.0 Mil Com 116.283 Mil BV 22.56 /sh P/E 35.03 (Ind SEMIC P/E 12.16) Ctry US

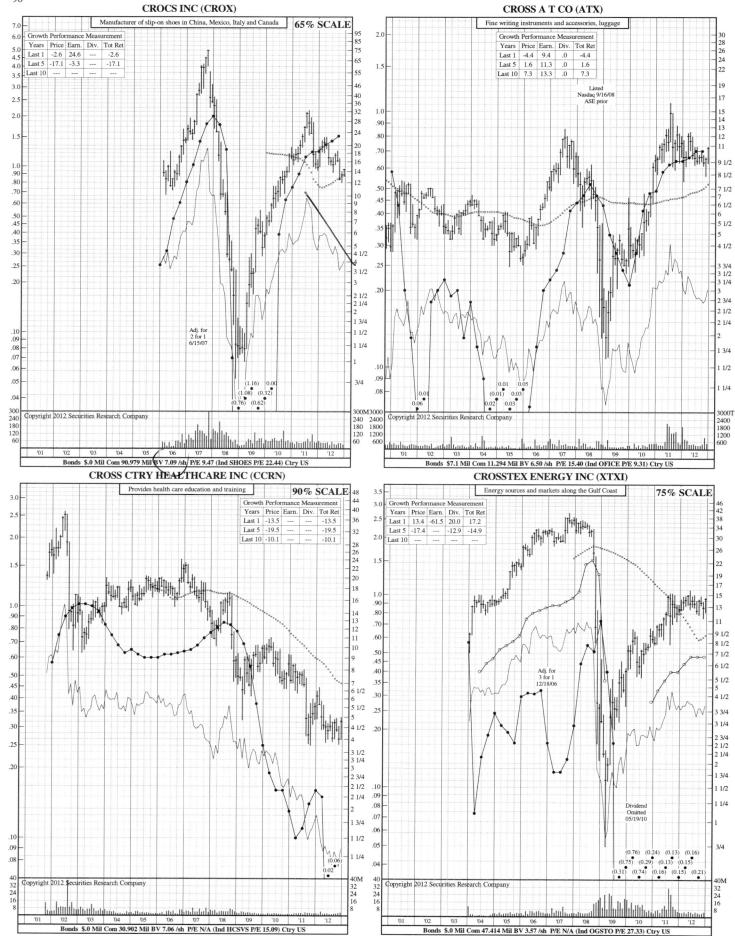

96

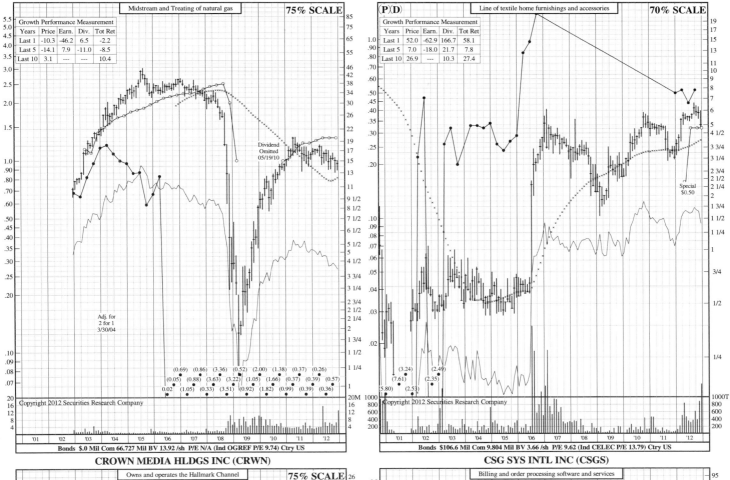

CROSSTEX ENERGY L P (XTEX)

Midstream and Treating of natural gas

75% SCALE

Growth Performance Measurement

Years	Price	Earn.	Div.	Tot Ret
Last 1	-10.3	-46.2	6.5	-2.2
Last 5	-14.1	7.9	-11.0	-8.5
Last 10	3.1	---	---	10.4

Dividend
Omitted
05/19/10

Adj. for
2 for 1
3/30/04

(0.69) (0.86) (3.36) (0.52) (2.00) (1.38) (0.37) (0.26)
(0.05) (0.88) (3.63) (3.22) (1.05) (1.66) (0.37) (0.39) (0.57)
0.02 (1.05) (0.33) (3.51) (0.92) (1.82) (0.99) (0.39) (0.36)

Copyright 2012 Securities Research Company

Bonds $.0 Mil Com 66.727 Mil BV 13.92 /sh P/E N/A (Ind OGREF P/E 9.74) Ctry US

CROWN CRAFTS INC (CRWS)

(P)(D)

Line of textile home furnishings and accessories

70% SCALE

Growth Performance Measurement

Years	Price	Earn.	Div.	Tot Ret
Last 1	52.0	-62.9	166.7	58.1
Last 5	7.0	-18.0	21.7	7.8
Last 10	26.9	---	10.3	27.4

Special
$0.50

(5.80)   (3.24)   (2.49)
(7.61) (2.35)
(2.53)

Copyright 2012 Securities Research Company

Bonds $106.6 Mil Com 9.804 Mil BV 3.66 /sh P/E 9.62 (Ind CELEC P/E 13.79) Ctry US

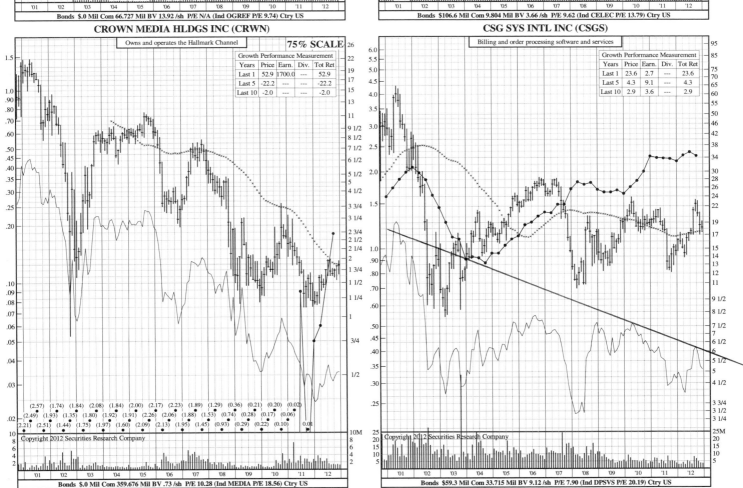

CROWN MEDIA HLDGS INC (CRWN)

Owns and operates the Hallmark Channel

75% SCALE

Growth Performance Measurement

Years	Price	Earn.	Div.	Tot Ret
Last 1	52.9	1700.0	---	52.9
Last 5	-22.2	---	---	-22.2
Last 10	-2.0	---	---	-2.0

(2.57) (1.74) (1.84) (2.08) (1.84) (2.00) (2.17) (2.23) (1.89) (1.29) (0.36) (0.21) (0.20) (0.02)
(2.49) (1.93) (1.35) (1.80) (1.92) (1.91) (2.26) (2.06) (1.88) (1.53) (0.74) (0.28) (0.17) (0.06)
(2.21) (2.51) (1.44) (1.75) (1.97) (1.60) (2.09) (2.13) (1.95) (1.45) (0.93) (0.29) (0.22) (0.10) 0.01

Copyright 2012 Securities Research Company

Bonds $.0 Mil Com 359.676 Mil BV .73 /sh P/E 10.28 (Ind MEDIA P/E 18.56) Ctry US

CSG SYS INTL INC (CSGS)

Billing and order processing software and services

Growth Performance Measurement

Years	Price	Earn.	Div.	Tot Ret
Last 1	23.6	2.7	---	23.6
Last 5	4.3	9.1	---	4.3
Last 10	2.9	3.6	---	2.9

Copyright 2012 Securities Research Company

Bonds $59.3 Mil Com 33.715 Mil BV 9.12 /sh P/E 7.90 (Ind DPSVS P/E 20.19) Ctry US

98

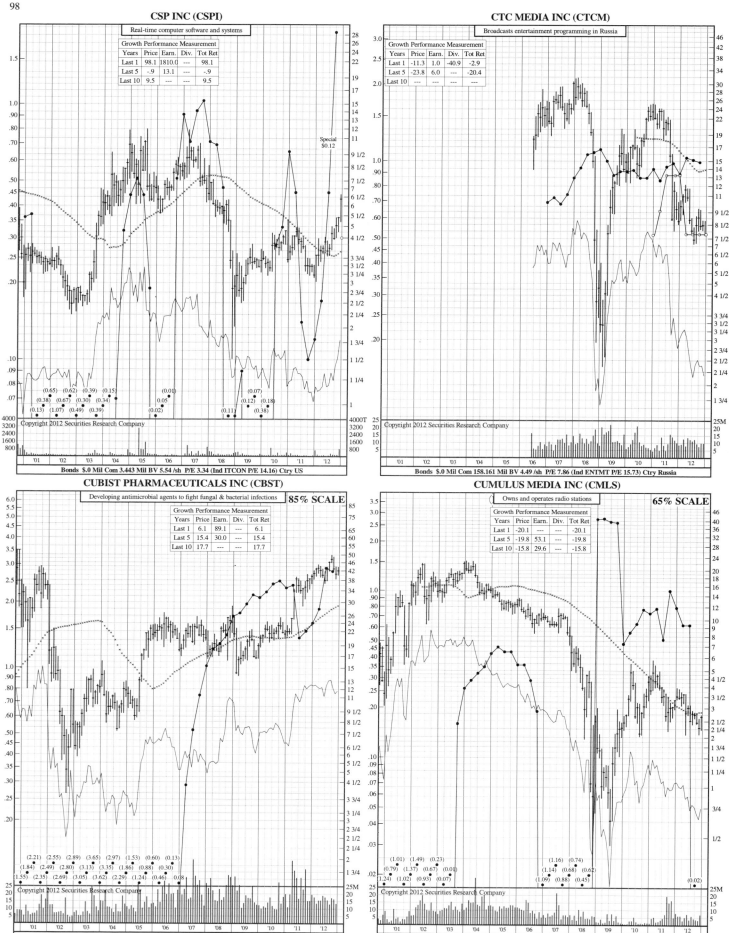

CSP INC (CSPI)

Real-time computer software and systems

Growth Performance Measurement

Years	Price	Earn.	Div.	Tot Ret
Last 1	98.1	1810.0	---	98.1
Last 5	-.9	13.1	---	-.9
Last 10	9.5	---	---	9.5

Special $0.12

(0.65) (0.62) (0.39) (0.15)   (0.01)   (0.07)
(0.38) (0.67) (0.30) (0.34) 0.05   (0.12) (0.18)
(0.13) (1.07) (0.49) (0.39) (0.02)   (0.11) (0.38)

Copyright 2012 Securities Research Company

Bonds $.0 Mil Com 3.443 Mil BV 5.54 /sh P/E 3.34 (Ind ITCON P/E 14.16) Ctry US

CTC MEDIA INC (CTCM)

Broadcasts entertainment programming in Russia

Growth Performance Measurement

Years	Price	Earn.	Div.	Tot Ret
Last 1	-11.3	1.0	-40.9	-2.9
Last 5	-23.8	6.0	---	-20.4
Last 10	---	---	---	---

Copyright 2012 Securities Research Company

Bonds $.0 Mil Com 158.161 Mil BV 4.49 /sh P/E 7.86 (Ind ENTMT P/E 15.73) Ctry Russia

CUBIST PHARMACEUTICALS INC (CBST)

Developing antimicrobial agents to fight fungal & bacterial infections   **85% SCALE**

Growth Performance Measurement

Years	Price	Earn.	Div.	Tot Ret
Last 1	6.1	89.1	---	6.1
Last 5	15.4	30.0	---	15.4
Last 10	17.7	---	---	17.7

(2.21) (2.55) (2.89) (3.65) (2.97) (1.53) (0.60) (0.13)
(1.84) (2.49) (2.80) (3.13) (3.35) (1.86) (0.88) (0.30)
(1.55) (2.35) (2.69) (3.05) (3.62) (2.29) (1.24) (0.46) 0.08

Copyright 2012 Securities Research Company

Bonds $.0 Mil Com 64.403 Mil BV 14.76 /sh P/E 15.13 (Ind BIOTK P/E 17.51) Ctry US

CUMULUS MEDIA INC (CMLS)

Owns and operates radio stations   **65% SCALE**

Growth Performance Measurement

Years	Price	Earn.	Div.	Tot Ret
Last 1	-20.1	---	---	-20.1
Last 5	-19.8	53.1	---	-19.8
Last 10	-15.8	29.6	---	-15.8

(1.01) (1.49) (0.23)   (1.16) (0.74)
(0.79) (1.37) (0.67) (0.01)   (1.14) (0.68) (0.62)
(1.24) (1.02) (0.93) (0.07)   (1.09) (0.88) (0.45)   (0.02)

Copyright 2012 Securities Research Company

Bonds $285.2 Mil Com 158.322 Mil BV 1.91 /sh P/E N/A (Ind MEDIA P/E 18.56) Ctry US

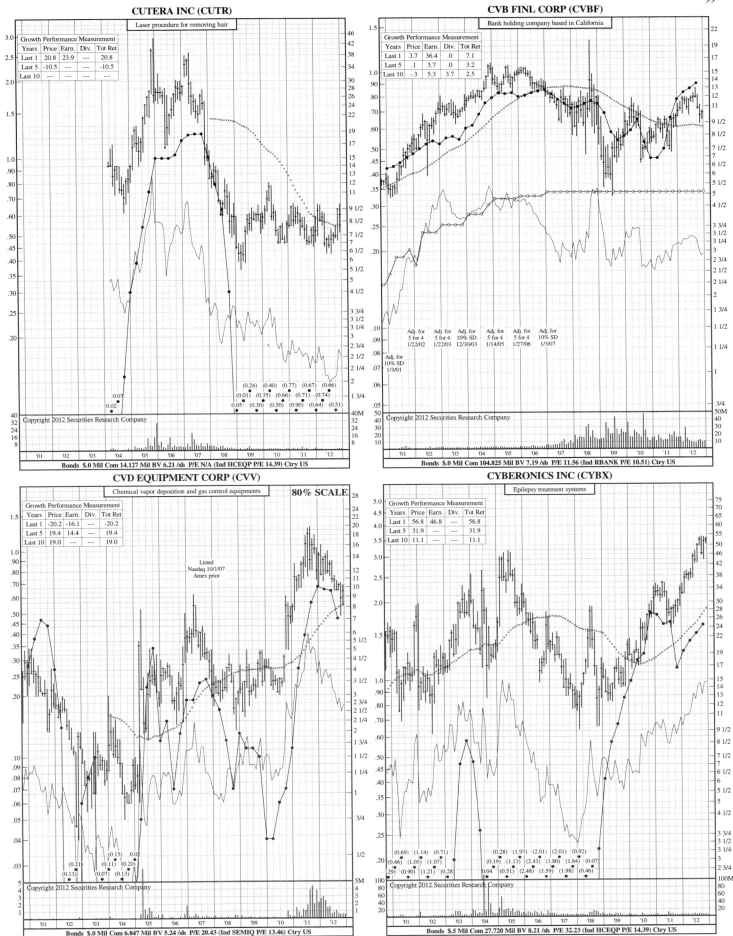

CUTERA INC (CUTR)

Laser procedure for removing hair

Growth Performance Measurement

Years	Price	Earn.	Div.	Tot Ret
Last 1	20.8	23.9	---	20.8
Last 5	-10.5	---	---	-10.5
Last 10	---	---	---	---

0.07
0.02

(0.24) (0.40) (0.77) (0.67) (0.66)
(0.01) (0.35) (0.66) (0.71) (0.74)
0.05 (0.30) (0.50) (0.90) (0.64) (0.51)

Copyright 2012 Securities Research Company

Bonds $.0 Mil Com 14.127 Mil BV 6.21 /sh P/E N/A (Ind HCEQP P/E 14.39) Ctry US

CVB FINL CORP (CVBF)

Bank holding company based in California

Growth Performance Measurement

Years	Price	Earn.	Div.	Tot Ret
Last 1	3.7	36.4	.0	7.1
Last 5	.1	3.7	.0	3.2
Last 10	-.3	5.3	3.7	2.5

| Adj. for 5 for 4 1/22/02 | Adj. for 5 for 4 1/22/03 | Adj. for 10% SD 12/30/03 | Adj. for 5 for 4 1/14/05 | Adj. for 5 for 4 1/27/06 | Adj. for 10% SD 1/3/07 |

Adj. for 10% SD 1/3/01

Copyright 2012 Securities Research Company

Bonds $.0 Mil Com 104.825 Mil BV 7.19 /sh P/E 11.56 (Ind RBANK P/E 10.51) Ctry US

CVD EQUIPMENT CORP (CVV)

Chemical vapor deposition and gas control equipments

80% SCALE

Growth Performance Measurement

Years	Price	Earn.	Div.	Tot Ret
Last 1	-20.2	-16.1	---	-20.2
Last 5	19.4	14.4	---	19.4
Last 10	19.0	---	---	19.0

Listed
Nasdaq 10/1/07
Amex prior

(0.15) 0.02
(0.21) (0.11) (0.20)
(0.13) (0.07) (0.13)

Copyright 2012 Securities Research Company

Bonds $.0 Mil Com 6.047 Mil BV 5.24 /sh P/E 20.43 (Ind SEMIQ P/E 13.46) Ctry US

CYBERONICS INC (CYBX)

Epilepsy treatment systems

Growth Performance Measurement

Years	Price	Earn.	Div.	Tot Ret
Last 1	56.8	46.8	---	56.8
Last 5	31.9	---	---	31.9
Last 10	11.1	---	---	11.1

(0.69) (1.14) (0.71)   (0.28) (1.93) (2.01) (2.01) (0.92)
(0.46) (1.05) (1.07)   (0.19) (1.13) (2.43) (1.80) (1.64) (0.07)
(29) (0.90) (1.21) (0.28) 0.04 (0.51) (2.48) (1.59) (1.98) (0.46)

Copyright 2012 Securities Research Company

Bonds $.5 Mil Com 27.720 Mil BV 8.21 /sh P/E 32.23 (Ind HCEQP P/E 14.39) Ctry US

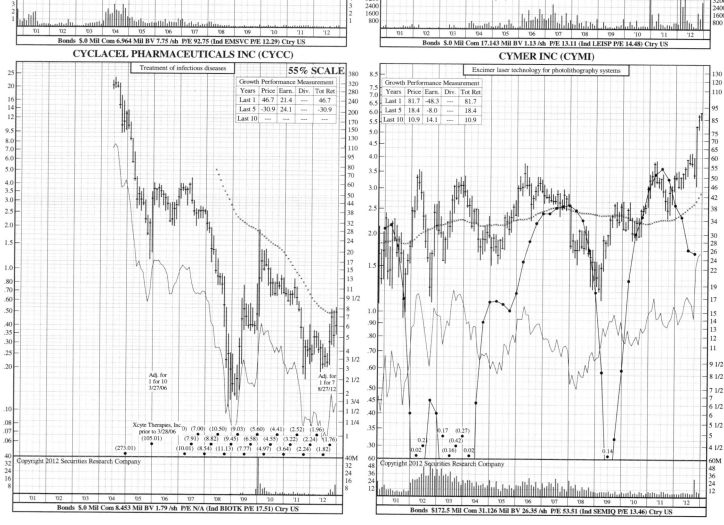

CYBEROPTICS CORP (CYBE)
Makes noncontact sensors and integrated systems

Growth Performance Measurement

Years	Price	Earn.	Div.	Tot Ret
Last 1	-4.9	-88.2	---	-4.9
Last 5	-9.1	-32.7	---	-9.1
Last 10	4.5	---	---	4.5

(1.26) (0.83) (0.32)
(1.01) (0.98) (0.63)
(0.52) (1.18) (0.69)
(0.91) (0.51)
(0.62) (0.86)
(0.25) (0.98) (0.10)   0.08

Copyright 2012 Securities Research Company

Bonds $.0 Mil Com 6.964 Mil BV 7.75 /sh P/E 92.75 (Ind EMSVC P/E 12.29) Ctry US

CYBEX INTL INC (CYBI)
Makes and sells premium-priced training and equipment

75% SCALE

Growth Performance Measurement

Years	Price	Earn.	Div.	Tot Ret
Last 1	492.9	-20.8	---	492.9
Last 5	-11.4	-18.9	---	-11.4
Last 10	5.9	---	---	5.9

Listed
NASDAQ 11/21/06
ASE prior

To be taken private by
UMK Hldgs & CEO

(0.49) (0.11) (0.12)
(0.55) (0.05) (0.04)
(0.51) (0.49) (0.17) (0.22)
(0.18) 0.00
(0.16) (0.10)
(0.03) (0.14) 0.00

Copyright 2012 Securities Research Company

Bonds $.0 Mil Com 17.143 Mil BV 1.13 /sh P/E 13.11 (Ind LEISP P/E 14.48) Ctry US

CYCLACEL PHARMACEUTICALS INC (CYCC)
Treatment of infectious diseases

55% SCALE

Growth Performance Measurement

Years	Price	Earn.	Div.	Tot Ret
Last 1	46.7	21.4	---	46.7
Last 5	-30.9	24.1	---	-30.9
Last 10	---	---	---	---

Adj. for
1 for 10
3/27/06

Adj. for
1 for 7
8/27/12

Xcyte Therapies, Inc
prior to 3/28/06   0) (7.00) (10.50) (9.03) (5.60) (4.41) (2.52) (1.96)
(105.01)   (7.91) (8.82) (9.45) (6.58) (4.55) (3.22) (2.24) (1.76)
(273.01)   (10.01) (8.54) (11.13) (7.77) (4.97) (3.64) (2.24) (1.82)

Copyright 2012 Securities Research Company

Bonds $.0 Mil Com 8.453 Mil BV 1.79 /sh P/E N/A (Ind BIOTK P/E 17.51) Ctry US

CYMER INC (CYMI)
Excimer laser technology for photolithography systems

Growth Performance Measurement

Years	Price	Earn.	Div.	Tot Ret
Last 1	81.7	-48.3	---	81.7
Last 5	18.4	-8.0	---	18.4
Last 10	10.9	14.1	---	10.9

0.21   0.17   (0.27)
0.02   (0.42)
0.02   (0.16) 0.02
0.14

Copyright 2012 Securities Research Company

Bonds $172.5 Mil Com 31.126 Mil BV 26.35 /sh P/E 53.51 (Ind SEMIQ P/E 13.46) Ctry US

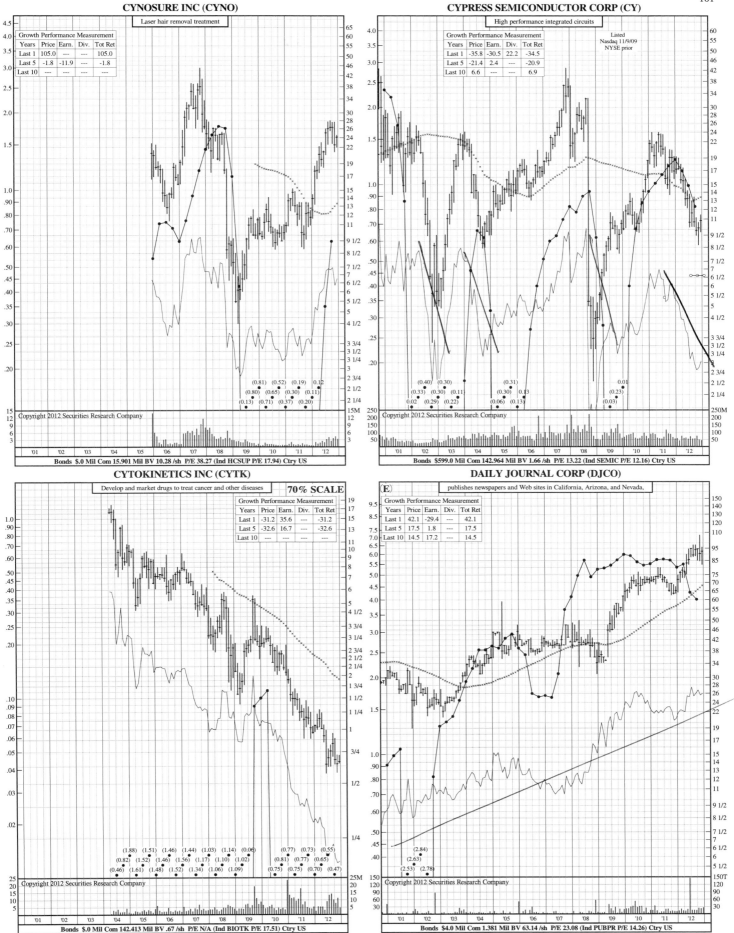

CYNOSURE INC (CYNO)

Laser hair removal treatment

Growth Performance Measurement				
Years	Price	Earn.	Div.	Tot Ret
Last 1	105.0	---	---	105.0
Last 5	-1.8	-11.9	---	-1.8
Last 10	---	---	---	---

(0.81) (0.52) (0.19) 0.12
(0.80) (0.65) (0.30) (0.11)
(0.13) (0.71) (0.37) (0.20)

Copyright 2012 Securities Research Company

Bonds $.0 Mil Com 15.901 Mil BV 10.28 /sh P/E 38.27 (Ind HCSUP P/E 17.94) Ctry US

CYPRESS SEMICONDUCTOR CORP (CY)

High performance integrated circuits

Listed
Nasdaq 11/9/09
NYSE prior

Growth Performance Measurement				
Years	Price	Earn.	Div.	Tot Ret
Last 1	-35.8	-30.5	22.2	-34.5
Last 5	-21.4	2.4	---	-20.9
Last 10	6.6	---	---	6.9

(0.40) (0.30)   (0.31)   0.01
(0.33) (0.30) (0.11)   (0.30) 0.13   (0.23)
0.02 (0.29) (0.22)   (0.06) (0.13)   (0.03)

Copyright 2012 Securities Research Company

Bonds $599.0 Mil Com 142.964 Mil BV 1.66 /sh P/E 13.22 (Ind SEMIC P/E 12.16) Ctry US

CYTOKINETICS INC (CYTK)

Develop and market drugs to treat cancer and other diseases

70% SCALE

Growth Performance Measurement				
Years	Price	Earn.	Div.	Tot Ret
Last 1	-31.2	35.6	---	-31.2
Last 5	-32.6	16.7	---	-32.6
Last 10	---	---	---	---

(1.88) (1.51) (1.46) (1.44) (1.03) (1.14) (0.06)   (0.77) (0.73) (0.55)
(0.82) (1.52) (1.46) (1.56) (1.17) (1.10) (1.02)   (0.81) (0.77) (0.65)
(0.46) (1.61) (1.48) (1.52) (1.34) (1.06) (1.09)   (0.75) (0.75) (0.70) (0.47)

Copyright 2012 Securities Research Company

Bonds $.0 Mil Com 142.413 Mil BV .67 /sh P/E N/A (Ind BIOTK P/E 17.51) Ctry US

DAILY JOURNAL CORP (DJCO)

(E) publishes newspapers and Web sites in California, Arizona, and Nevada,

Growth Performance Measurement				
Years	Price	Earn.	Div.	Tot Ret
Last 1	42.1	-29.4	---	42.1
Last 5	17.5	1.8	---	17.5
Last 10	14.5	17.2	---	14.5

(2.84)
(2.63)
(2.53) (2.78)

Copyright 2012 Securities Research Company

Bonds $4.0 Mil Com 1.381 Mil BV 63.14 /sh P/E 23.08 (Ind PUBPR P/E 14.26) Ctry US

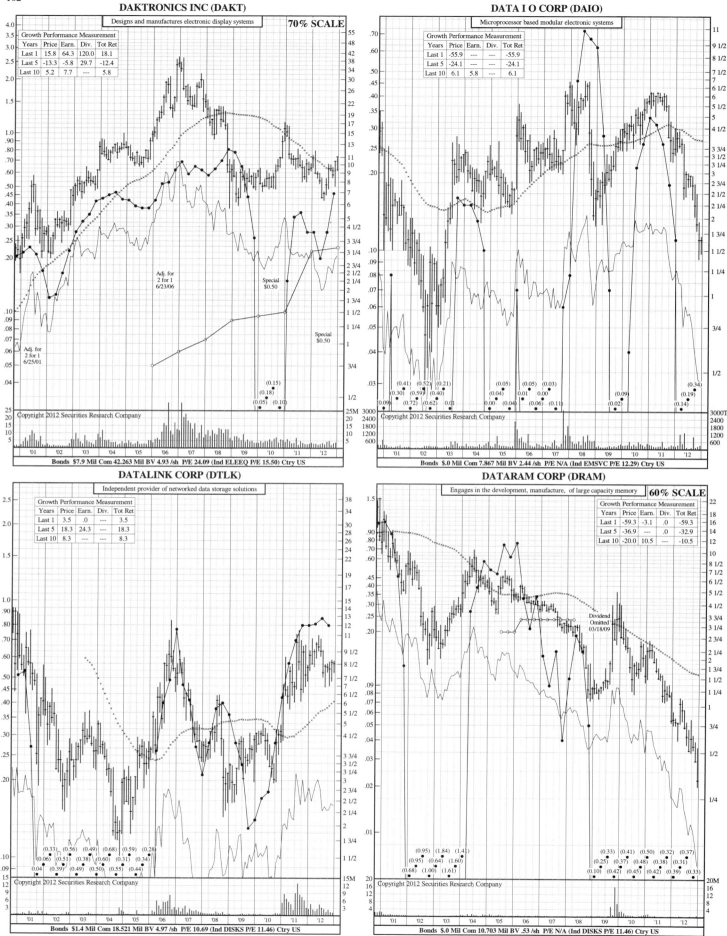

DAKTRONICS INC (DAKT)

Designs and manufactures electronic display systems

70% SCALE

Growth Performance Measurement

Years	Price	Earn.	Div.	Tot Ret
Last 1	15.8	64.3	120.0	18.1
Last 5	-13.3	-5.8	29.7	-12.4
Last 10	5.2	7.7	---	5.8

Adj. for
2 for 1
6/23/06

Special
$0.50

Adj. for
2 for 1
6/25/01

Special
$0.50

(0.15)
(0.18)
(0.05) (0.10)

Copyright 2012 Securities Research Company

Bonds $7.9 Mil Com 42.263 Mil BV 4.93 /sh P/E 24.09 (Ind ELEEQ P/E 15.50) Ctry US

DATA I O CORP (DAIO)

Microprocessor based modular electronic systems

Growth Performance Measurement

Years	Price	Earn.	Div.	Tot Ret
Last 1	-55.9	---	---	-55.9
Last 5	-24.1	---	---	-24.1
Last 10	6.1	5.8	---	6.1

(0.41) (0.52) (0.21)   (0.05) (0.05) (0.03)   (0.34)
(0.30) (0.59) (0.40)   (0.04) (0.01) (0.00)   (0.09)   (0.19)
(0.09)   (0.72) (0.62) (0.01) (0.00) (0.04) (0.06) (0.11)   (0.02)   (0.14)

Copyright 2012 Securities Research Company

Bonds $.0 Mil Com 7.867 Mil BV 2.44 /sh P/E N/A (Ind EMSVC P/E 12.29) Ctry US

DATALINK CORP (DTLK)

Independent provider of networked data storage solutions

Growth Performance Measurement

Years	Price	Earn.	Div.	Tot Ret
Last 1	3.5	.0	---	3.5
Last 5	18.3	24.3	---	18.3
Last 10	8.3	---	---	8.3

(0.33) (0.56) (0.49) (0.68) (0.59) (0.28)
(0.06) (0.51) (0.38) (0.60) (0.31) (0.34)
(0.04) (0.39) (0.49) (0.50) (0.55) (0.44)

Copyright 2012 Securities Research Company

Bonds $1.4 Mil Com 18.521 Mil BV 4.97 /sh P/E 10.69 (Ind DISKS P/E 11.46) Ctry US

DATARAM CORP (DRAM)

Engages in the development, manufacture, of large capacity memory

60% SCALE

Growth Performance Measurement

Years	Price	Earn.	Div.	Tot Ret
Last 1	-59.3	-3.1	.0	-59.3
Last 5	-36.9	---	.0	-32.9
Last 10	-20.0	10.5	---	-10.5

Dividend
Omitted
03/18/09

(0.95) (1.84) (1.41)   (0.33) (0.41) (0.50) (0.32) (0.37)
(0.68) (0.64) (1.60)   (0.25) (0.37) (0.48) (0.38) (0.31)
(0.68) (1.00) (1.61)   (0.10) (0.42) (0.45) (0.42) (0.39) (0.33)

Copyright 2012 Securities Research Company

Bonds $.0 Mil Com 10.703 Mil BV .53 /sh P/E N/A (Ind DISKS P/E 11.46) Ctry US

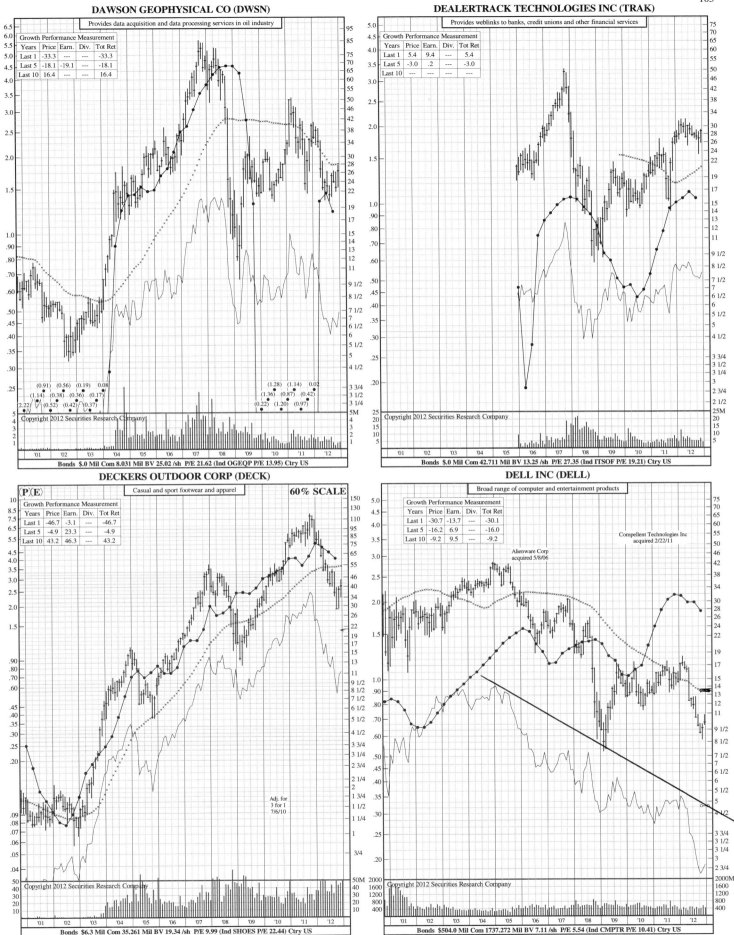

DAWSON GEOPHYSICAL CO (DWSN)

Provides data acquisition and data processing services in oil industry

Growth Performance Measurement

Years	Price	Earn.	Div.	Tot Ret
Last 1	-33.3	---	---	-33.3
Last 5	-18.1	-19.1	---	-18.1
Last 10	16.4	---	---	16.4

(0.91) (0.56) (0.19) 0.08
(1.14) (0.38) (0.36) (0.17)
2.22 (0.52) (0.42) (0.37)
(1.28) (1.14) 0.02
(1.36) (0.87) (0.42)
(0.22) (1.20) (0.97)

Copyright 2012 Securities Research Company

Bonds $.0 Mil Com 8.031 Mil BV 25.02 /sh P/E 21.62 (Ind OGEQP P/E 13.95) Ctry US

DEALERTRACK TECHNOLOGIES INC (TRAK)

Provides weblinks to banks, credit unions and other financial services

Growth Performance Measurement

Years	Price	Earn.	Div.	Tot Ret
Last 1	5.4	9.4	---	5.4
Last 5	-3.0	.2	---	-3.0
Last 10	---	---	---	---

Copyright 2012 Securities Research Company

Bonds $.0 Mil Com 42.711 Mil BV 13.25 /sh P/E 27.35 (Ind ITSOF P/E 19.21) Ctry US

DECKERS OUTDOOR CORP (DECK)

(P)(E)   Casual and sport footwear and apparel   60% SCALE

Growth Performance Measurement

Years	Price	Earn.	Div.	Tot Ret
Last 1	-46.7	-3.1	---	-46.7
Last 5	-4.9	23.3	---	-4.9
Last 10	43.2	46.3	---	43.2

Adj. for
3 for 1
7/6/10

Copyright 2012 Securities Research Company

Bonds $6.3 Mil Com 35.261 Mil BV 19.34 /sh P/E 9.99 (Ind SHOES P/E 22.44) Ctry US

DELL INC (DELL)

Broad range of computer and entertainment products

Growth Performance Measurement

Years	Price	Earn.	Div.	Tot Ret
Last 1	-30.7	-13.7	---	-30.1
Last 5	-16.2	6.9	---	-16.0
Last 10	-9.2	9.5	---	-9.2

Compellent Technologies Inc
acquired 2/22/11

Alienware Corp
acquired 5/8/06

Copyright 2012 Securities Research Company

Bonds $504.0 Mil Com 1737.272 Mil BV 7.11 /sh P/E 5.54 (Ind CMPTR P/E 10.41) Ctry US

104

DELTA NATURAL GAS COMPANY, INCORPORATED (DGAS)

Provides gas to retail customers in central and southeastern Kentucky

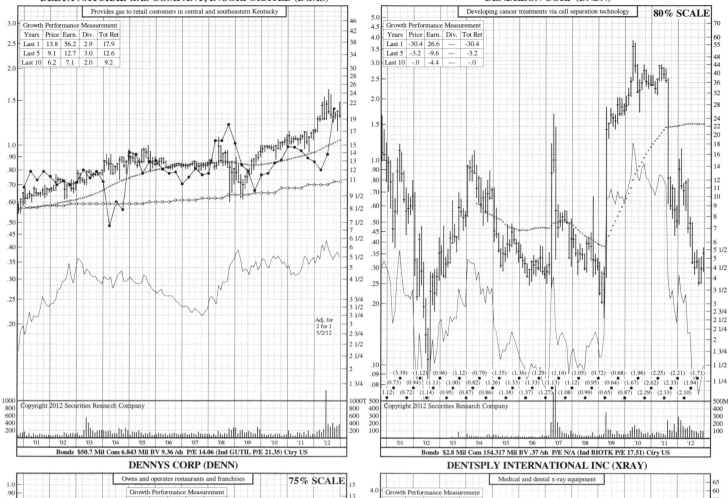

Copyright 2012 Securities Research Company

Bonds $50.7 Mil Com 6.843 Mil BV 9.36 /sh P/E 14.06 (Ind GUTIL P/E 21.35) Ctry US

DENDREON CORP (DNDN)

Developing cancer treatments via cell separation technology

80% SCALE

Copyright 2012 Securities Research Company

Bonds $2.8 Mil Com 154.317 Mil BV .37 /sh P/E N/A (Ind BIOTK P/E 17.51) Ctry US

DENNYS CORP (DENN)

Owns and operates restaurants and franchises

75% SCALE

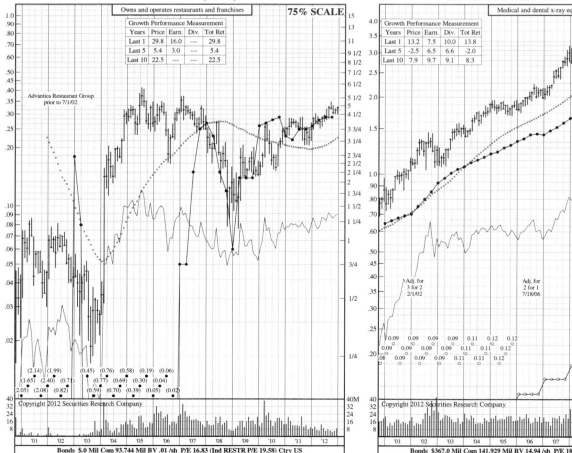

Copyright 2012 Securities Research Company

Bonds $.0 Mil Com 93.744 Mil BV .01 /sh P/E 16.83 (Ind RESTR P/E 19.58) Ctry US

DENTSPLY INTERNATIONAL INC (XRAY)

Medical and dental x-ray equipment

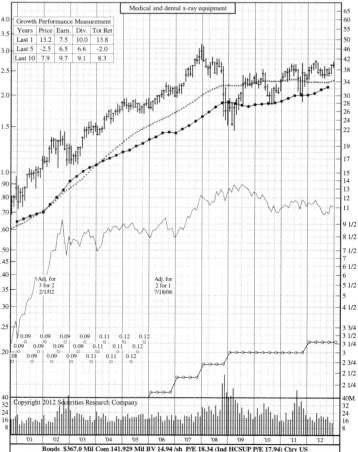

Copyright 2012 Securities Research Company

Bonds $367.0 Mil Com 141.929 Mil BV 14.94 /sh P/E 18.34 (Ind HCSUP P/E 17.94) Ctry US

DEPOMED INC (DEPO)

Gastric Retention System for oral delivery of time-released drugs

Growth Performance Measurement				
Years	Price	Earn.	Div.	Tot Ret
Last 1	19.5	---	---	19.5
Last 5	13.7	3.9	---	13.7
Last 10	12.0	9.8	---	12.0

(1.80) (1.87) (0.83) (1.23) (0.91) (0.73) (0.65) (0.97) (0.88) (0.70) (0.63) (0.62) (0.02) (0.72)
(1.57) (1.90) (0.92) (0.33) (0.97) (0.77) (0.64) (0.84) (0.99) (0.81) (0.75) (0.77) (0.22) (0.84)
(1.43) (1.81) (2.03) (0.62) (1.04) (0.78) (0.71) (0.72) (1.04) (0.75) (0.63) (0.73) (0.49) 1.20 (0.67)

Copyright 2012 Securities Research Company

Bonds $.4 Mil Com 56.103 Mil BV 1.53 /sh P/E N/A (Ind DRUGS P/E 12.73) Ctry US

DESTINATION MATERNITY CORP (DEST)

Specialty retailer of maternity

Growth Performance Measurement				
Years	Price	Earn.	Div.	Tot Ret
Last 1	29.0	-17.5	.0	33.2
Last 5	19.9	28.9	---	21.2
Last 10	2.0	3.1	---	2.6

Mother Works Prior to 12/9/08

Adj. for 2 for 1 3/2/11

0.04
0.01
0.07
(0.17)
(0.07) 0.12

Copyright 2012 Securities Research Company

Bonds $96.1 Mil Com 13.488 Mil BV 7.85 /sh P/E 14.77 (Ind RTAPP P/E 19.00) Ctry US

DESWELL INDS INC (DSWL)

Electronic products and plastic industrial parts

90% SCALE

Growth Performance Measurement				
Years	Price	Earn.	Div.	Tot Ret
Last 1	11.6	81.3	.0	18.6
Last 5	-16.9	---	-26.1	-11.9
Last 10	-13.0	---	-11.5	-4.3

Adj. for 3 for 2 7/23/02

Adj. for 3 for 2 3/30/05

Special $0.10

(0.07) (0.33) (0.36) (0.09)
0.025 (0.29) (0.50) (0.09)
(0.03) (0.17) (0.52) (0.32) (0.06)

Copyright 2012 Securities Research Company

Bonds $.0 Mil Com 16.635 Mil BV 6.37 /sh P/E N/A (Ind EEQPM P/E 16.88) Ctry Hong Kong

DIALOGIC INC (DLGC)

Offer voice-over-Internet-protocol services

55% SCALE

Growth Performance Measurement				
Years	Price	Earn.	Div.	Tot Ret
Last 1	-77.3	81.5	---	-77.3
Last 5	-59.2	21.6	---	-59.2
Last 10	---	---	---	---

Veraz Networks prior to 10/1/10

Dialogic Inc. merged 10/1/10

Adj. for 1 for 5 9/17/12

Adj. for 1 for 5 10/4/10

(8.25) (11.80) (15.10) (29.50) (35.25) (12.50) (2.75) (11.25) (5.00) (9.25) (11.20) (7.00) (1.63)
(5.50) (11.40) (12.50) (22.05) (33.50) (21.50) (3.00) (9.50) (7.25) (7.50) (8.35) (3.25)
(2.75) (11.00) (12.20) (20.20) (33.50) (26.00) (21.50) (6.00) (11.25) (6.50) (10.45) (9.40) (4.65)

Copyright 2012 Securities Research Company

Bonds $.0 Mil Com 14.403 Mil BV -7.41 /sh P/E N/A (Ind APPSF P/E 24.69) Ctry US

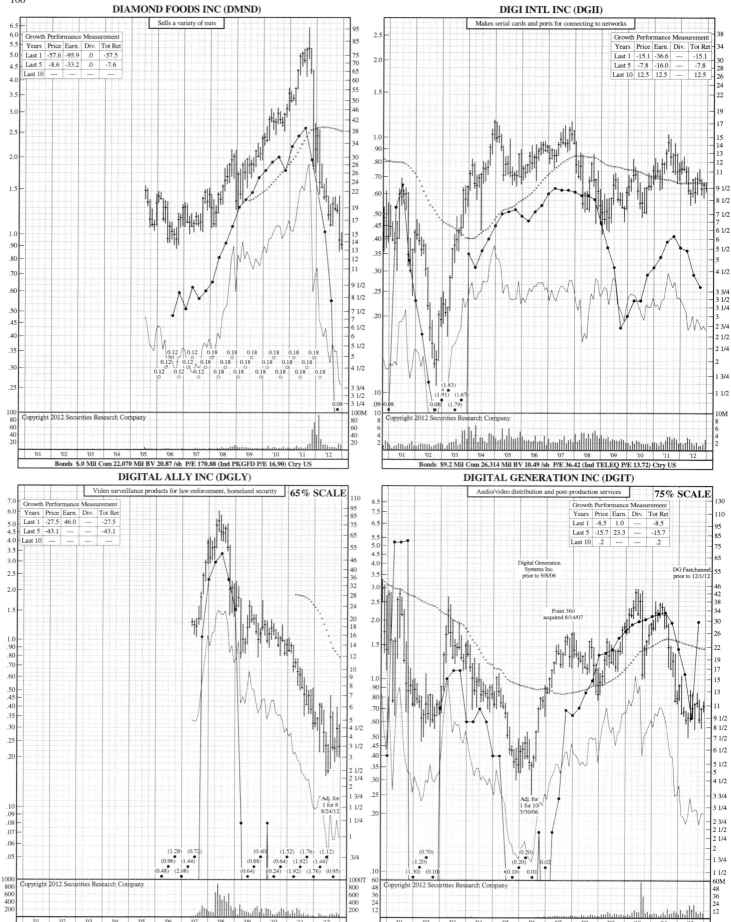

DIAMOND FOODS INC (DMND)

Sells a variety of nuts

Growth Performance Measurement				
Years	Price	Earn.	Div.	Tot Ret
Last 1	-57.6	-95.9	.0	-57.5
Last 5	-8.6	-33.2	.0	-7.6
Last 10	---	---	---	---

0.12 0.12 0.18 0.18 0.18 0.18 0.18 0.18
0.12 0.12 0.18 0.18 0.18 0.18 0.18 0.18
0.12 0.12 0.18 0.18 0.18 0.18 0.18 0.18 0.18
0.08

Copyright 2012 Securities Research Company

Bonds $.0 Mil Com 22.070 Mil BV 20.87 /sh P/E 170.88 (Ind PKGFD P/E 16.90) Ctry US

DIGI INTL INC (DGII)

Makes serial cards and ports for connecting to networks

Growth Performance Measurement				
Years	Price	Earn.	Div.	Tot Ret
Last 1	-15.1	-36.6	---	-15.1
Last 5	-7.8	-16.0	---	-7.8
Last 10	12.5	12.5	---	12.5

(1.83)
(1.91) (1.67)
.09 .08 0.08 (1.79)

Copyright 2012 Securities Research Company

Bonds $9.2 Mil Com 26.314 Mil BV 10.49 /sh P/E 36.42 (Ind TELEQ P/E 13.72) Ctry US

DIGITAL ALLY INC (DGLY)

Video surveillance products for law enforcement, homeland security   **65% SCALE**

Growth Performance Measurement				
Years	Price	Earn.	Div.	Tot Ret
Last 1	-27.5	46.0	---	-27.5
Last 5	-43.1	---	---	-43.1
Last 10	---	---	---	---

(1.28) (0.72)
(0.96) (1.44)   (0.40)   (1.52) (1.76) (1.12)
(0.48) (2.08)   (0.64) (0.24) (1.92) (1.76) (0.95)
(0.64)   (1.92)

Adj. for
1 for 8
8/24/12

Copyright 2012 Securities Research Company

Bonds $.0 Mil Com 2.099 Mil BV 3.93 /sh P/E N/A (Ind ELEEQ P/E 15.50) Ctry US

DIGITAL GENERATION INC (DGIT)

Audio/video distribution and post-production services   **75% SCALE**

Growth Performance Measurement				
Years	Price	Earn.	Div.	Tot Ret
Last 1	-8.5	1.0	---	-8.5
Last 5	-15.7	23.3	---	-15.7
Last 10	.2	---	---	.2

Digital Generation
Systems Inc.
prior to 9/8/06

DG Fastchannel
prior to 12/1/12

Point 360
acquired 8/14/07

(0.70)
(1.20)   (0.20)
(1.30) (0.10)   (0.20) 0.02
(0.10) 0.01

Adj. for
1 for 10
5/30/06

Copyright 2012 Securities Research Company

Bonds $15.7 Mil Com 27.634 Mil BV 11.16 /sh P/E 5.54 (Ind ADVER P/E 14.45) Ctry US

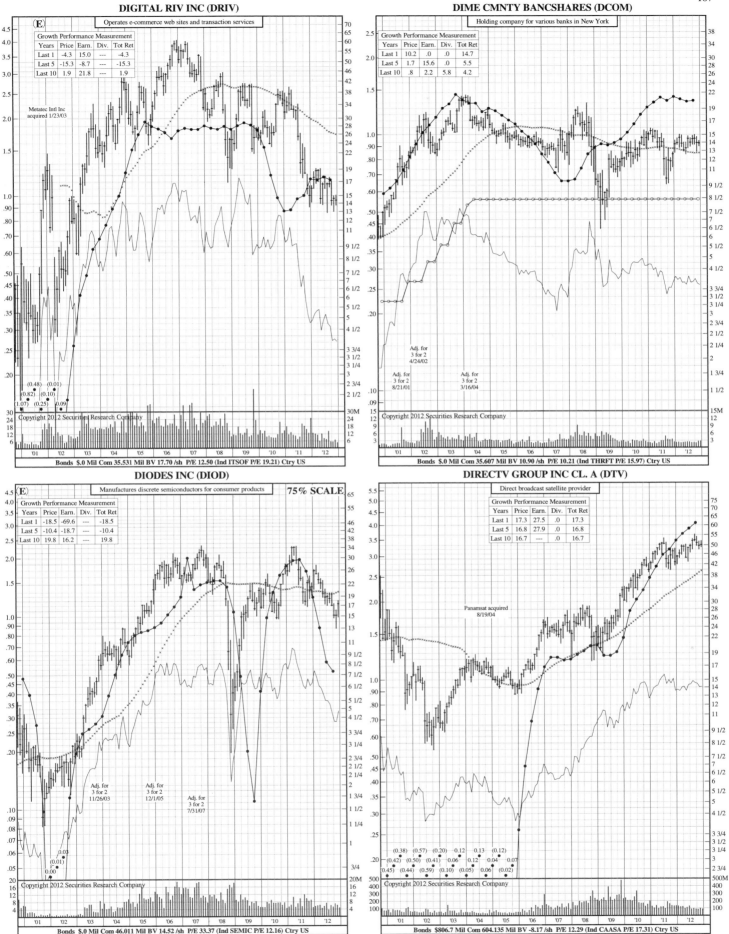

DIGITAL RIV INC (DRIV)

Operates e-commerce web sites and transaction services

(E)

Growth Performance Measurement

Years	Price	Earn.	Div.	Tot Ret
Last 1	-4.3	15.0	---	-4.3
Last 5	-15.3	-8.7	---	-15.3
Last 10	1.9	21.8	---	1.9

Metatec Intl Inc
acquired 1/23/03

(0.48) (0.01)
(0.82) (0.10)
(1.07) (0.25) 0.09

Copyright 2012 Securities Research Company

Bonds $.0 Mil Com 35.531 Mil BV 17.70 /sh P/E 12.50 (Ind ITSOF P/E 19.21) Ctry US

DIME CMNTY BANCSHARES (DCOM)

Holding company for various banks in New York

Growth Performance Measurement

Years	Price	Earn.	Div.	Tot Ret
Last 1	10.2	.0	.0	14.7
Last 5	1.7	15.6	.0	5.5
Last 10	.8	2.2	5.8	4.2

Adj. for
3 for 2
4/24/02

Adj. for
3 for 2
8/21/01

Adj. for
3 for 2
3/16/04

Copyright 2012 Securities Research Company

Bonds $.0 Mil Com 35.607 Mil BV 10.90 /sh P/E 10.21 (Ind THRFT P/E 15.97) Ctry US

DIODES INC (DIOD)

Manufactures discrete semiconductors for consumer products

75% SCALE

E

Growth Performance Measurement

Years	Price	Earn.	Div.	Tot Ret
Last 1	-18.5	-69.6	---	-18.5
Last 5	-10.4	-18.7	---	-10.4
Last 10	19.8	16.2	---	19.8

Adj. for
3 for 2
11/26/03

Adj. for
3 for 2
12/1/05

Adj. for
3 for 2
7/31/07

0.03
(0.01)
0.00

Copyright 2012 Securities Research Company

Bonds $.0 Mil Com 46.011 Mil BV 14.52 /sh P/E 33.37 (Ind SEMIC P/E 12.16) Ctry US

DIRECTV GROUP INC CL. A (DTV)

Direct broadcast satellite provider

Growth Performance Measurement

Years	Price	Earn.	Div.	Tot Ret
Last 1	17.3	27.5	.0	17.3
Last 5	16.8	27.9	.0	16.8
Last 10	16.7	---	.0	16.7

Panamsat acquired
8/19/04

(0.38) (0.57) (0.20) 0.12 0.13 (0.12)
(0.42) (0.50) 0.41 0.06 0.05 0.07
(0.45) (0.44) (0.59) (0.10) (0.05) 0.04 (0.02)

Copyright 2012 Securities Research Company

Bonds $806.7 Mil Com 604.135 Mil BV -8.17 /sh P/E 12.29 (Ind CAASA P/E 17.31) Ctry US

DISCOVERY COMMUNICATNS (DISCA)

Ascent Media Group, Inc.; Discovery Communications, Inc. (Discovery)

Discovery Holding Co
Prior to
9/18/08

Discovery Holding Company merged Discovery
Communications, LLC and Animal Planet L.P.
9/17/08

Growth Performance Measurement				
Years	Price	Earn.	Div.	Tot Ret
Last 1	54.9	12.9	---	54.9
Last 5	20.4	46.1	---	20.4
Last 10	---	---	---	---

Spun-off
from
Liberty Corp.
7/21/05

Dist. 0.05 shs. (Ascent Media Corp.
for ea. sh. held
9/17/08

(0.10)   (0.13)
0.12   (0.16)
0.00   (0.14)   0.08

Copyright 2012 Securities Research Company

Bonds $.0 Mil Com 144.968 Mil BV 24.18 /sh P/E 25.09 (Ind MEDIA P/E 18.56) Ctry US

DISCOVERY LABORATORIES INC N (DSCO)

Focuses on treatments for respiratory diseases

55% SCALE

Growth Performance Measurement				
Years	Price	Earn.	Div.	Tot Ret
Last 1	25.6	17.1	---	25.6
Last 5	-42.0	32.7	---	-42.0
Last 10	-25.9	20.0	---	-25.9

Adj. for
1 for 15
12/28/10

(9.90) (8.25) (9.75) (9.75) (11.85)   (12.00) (13.65) (9.15) (7.35) (6.90) (5.25) (3.45) (2.22) (1.17) (0.86)
(8.55)   (7.50) (9.60) (9.15) (11.40)   (11.85) (12.75) (11.10) (7.05) (6.90) (5.85) (4.05) (2.55) (1.42) (1.04)
(8.85)   (7.05) (9.00) (9.45) (10.65)   (12.00) (11.55) (12.75) (7.35) (7.05) (6.00) (4.50) (3.00) (1.68) (0.93) (0.97)

Copyright 2012 Securities Research Company

Bonds $.0 Mil Com 43.518 Mil BV .53 /sh P/E N/A (Ind DRUGS P/E 12.73) Ctry US

DISH NETWORK CORP (DISH)

Satellite TV dishes, receivers, and related equipment

70% SCALE

Echostar Communications
prior to 1/23/08

Special
$1.00

Special
$1.00

Special
$2.00

Growth Performance Measurement				
Years	Price	Earn.	Div.	Tot Ret
Last 1	27.8	1.2	---	34.8
Last 5	-.7	15.0	---	.4
Last 10	5.0	---	---	5.6

(0.99) (0.16) (0.41)
(1.27) (0.43) (0.45) (0.02)
(1.32) (0.69) (0.11) (0.21)

Copyright 2012 Securities Research Company

Bonds $5929.0 Mil Com 212.995 Mil BV .24 /sh P/E 11.10 (Ind CAASA P/E 17.31) Ctry US

DIXIE GROUP INC (DXYN)

Makes high-end carpet and rugs, and yarn

75% SCALE

Growth Performance Measurement				
Years	Price	Earn.	Div.	Tot Ret
Last 1	11.6	---	.0	11.6
Last 5	-17.0	---	.0	-17.0
Last 10	-1.5	---	.0	-1.5

(0.64)   (0.94) (0.48) (0.27)
(0.55) (0.07)   (0.77) (0.77) (0.46)   (0.04)
(0.49) (0.30)   (0.28) (1.00) (0.45) (0.02)   (0.04)

Copyright 2012 Securities Research Company

Bonds $143.4 Mil Com 12.174 Mil BV 4.87 /sh P/E N/A (Ind HMFRN P/E 19.93) Ctry US

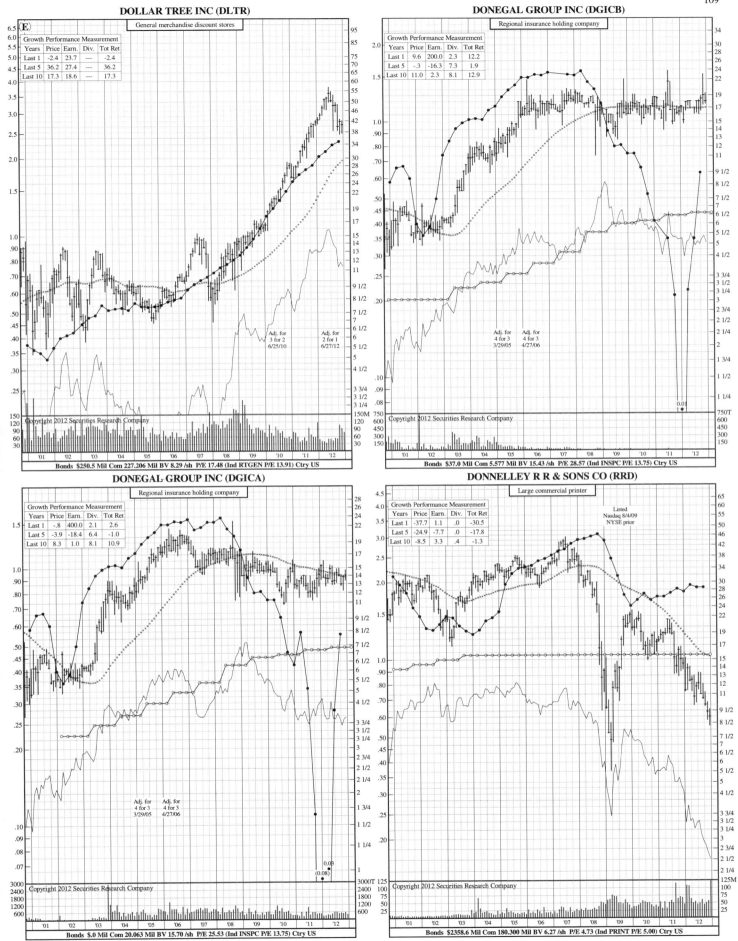

DOLLAR TREE INC (DLTR)

General merchandise discount stores

Growth Performance Measurement				
Years	Price	Earn.	Div.	Tot Ret
Last 1	-2.4	23.7	---	-2.4
Last 5	36.2	27.4	---	36.2
Last 10	17.3	18.6	---	17.3

Adj. for 3 for 2 6/25/10

Adj. for 2 for 1 6/27/12

Copyright 2012 Securities Research Company

Bonds $250.5 Mil Com 227.206 Mil BV 8.29 /sh P/E 17.48 (Ind RTGEN P/E 13.91) Ctry US

DONEGAL GROUP INC (DGICB)

Regional insurance holding company

Growth Performance Measurement				
Years	Price	Earn.	Div.	Tot Ret
Last 1	9.6	200.0	2.3	12.2
Last 5	-.3	-16.3	7.3	1.9
Last 10	11.0	2.3	8.1	12.9

Adj. for 4 for 3 3/29/05

Adj. for 4 for 3 4/27/06

0.01

Copyright 2012 Securities Research Company

Bonds $37.0 Mil Com 5.577 Mil BV 15.43 /sh P/E 28.57 (Ind INSPC P/E 13.75) Ctry US

DONEGAL GROUP INC (DGICA)

Regional insurance holding company

Growth Performance Measurement				
Years	Price	Earn.	Div.	Tot Ret
Last 1	-.8	400.0	2.1	2.6
Last 5	-3.9	-18.4	6.4	-1.0
Last 10	8.3	1.0	8.1	10.9

Adj. for 4 for 3 3/29/05

Adj. for 4 for 3 4/27/06

0.03 (0.08)

Copyright 2012 Securities Research Company

Bonds $.0 Mil Com 20.063 Mil BV 15.70 /sh P/E 25.53 (Ind INSPC P/E 13.75) Ctry US

DONNELLEY R R & SONS CO (RRD)

Large commercial printer

Growth Performance Measurement				
Years	Price	Earn.	Div.	Tot Ret
Last 1	-37.7	1.1	.0	-30.5
Last 5	-24.9	-7.7	.0	-17.8
Last 10	-8.5	3.3	.4	-1.3

Listed Nasdaq 8/4/09 NYSE prior

Copyright 2012 Securities Research Company

Bonds $2358.6 Mil Com 180.300 Mil BV 6.27 /sh P/E 4.73 (Ind PRINT P/E 5.00) Ctry US

110

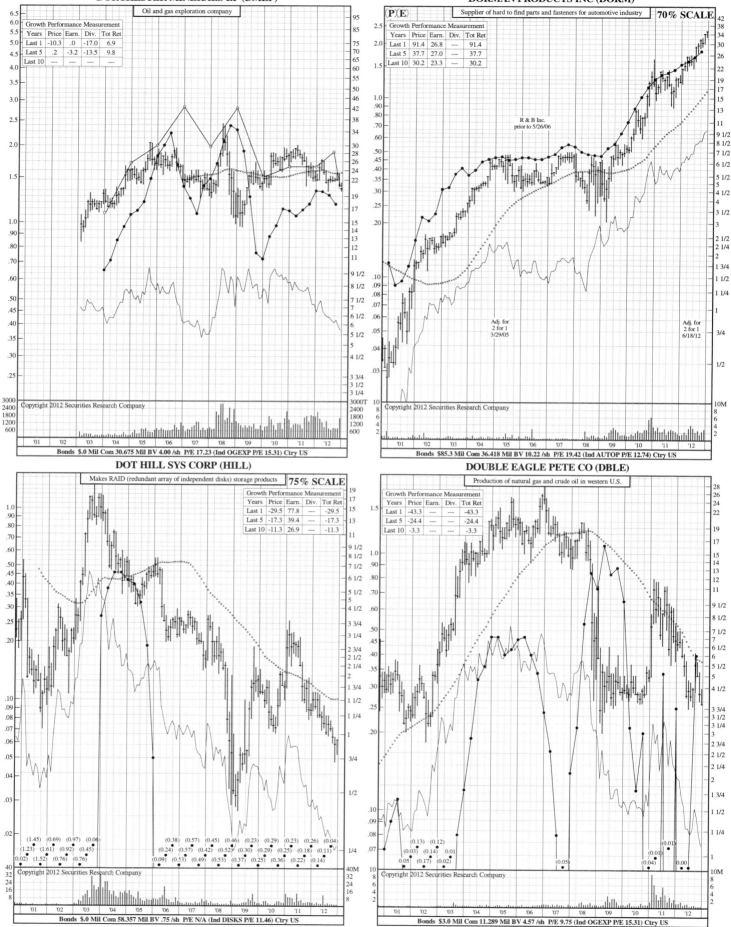

DORCHESTER MINERALS LP (DMLP)

Oil and gas exploration company

Growth Performance Measurement

Years	Price	Earn.	Div.	Tot Ret
Last 1	-10.3	.0	-17.0	6.9
Last 5	.2	-3.2	-13.5	9.8
Last 10	---	---	---	---

Copyright 2012 Securities Research Company

Bonds $.0 Mil Com 30.675 Mil BV 4.00 /sh P/E 17.23 (Ind OGEXP P/E 15.31) Ctry US

DORMAN PRODUCTS INC (DORM)

Supplier of hard to find parts and fasteners for automotive industry   70% SCALE

Growth Performance Measurement

Years	Price	Earn.	Div.	Tot Ret
Last 1	91.4	26.8	---	91.4
Last 5	37.7	27.0	---	37.7
Last 10	30.2	23.3	---	30.2

R & B Inc.
prior to 5/26/06

Adj. for
2 for 1
3/29/05

Adj. for
2 for 1
6/18/12

Copyright 2012 Securities Research Company

Bonds $85.3 Mil Com 36.418 Mil BV 10.22 /sh P/E 19.42 (Ind AUTOP P/E 12.74) Ctry US

DOT HILL SYS CORP (HILL)

Makes RAID (redundant array of independent disks) storage products   75% SCALE

Growth Performance Measurement

Years	Price	Earn.	Div.	Tot Ret
Last 1	-29.5	77.8		-29.5
Last 5	-17.3	39.4	---	-17.3
Last 10	-11.3	26.9	---	-11.3

(1.45) (0.69) (0.97) (0.06)   (0.38) (0.57) (0.45) (0.46) (0.23) (0.29) (0.23) (0.26) (0.04)
(1.23) (1.61) (0.92) (0.45)   (0.24) (0.57) (0.42) (0.52) (0.30) (0.29) (0.25) (0.18) (0.11)
(0.02) (1.52) (0.76) (0.76)   (0.09) (0.53) (0.49) (0.53) (0.37) (0.25) (0.36) (0.22) (0.14)

Copyright 2012 Securities Research Company

Bonds $.0 Mil Com 58.357 Mil BV .75 /sh P/E N/A (Ind DISKS P/E 11.46) Ctry US

DOUBLE EAGLE PETE CO (DBLE)

Production of natural gas and crude oil in western U.S.

Growth Performance Measurement

Years	Price	Earn.	Div.	Tot Ret
Last 1	-43.3	---	---	-43.3
Last 5	-24.4	---	---	-24.4
Last 10	-3.3	---	---	-3.3

(0.13) (0.12)
(0.03) (0.14) 0.01   (0.01)
(0.05) (0.17) (0.02)   (0.05)   (0.01)   0.00
                                              (0.04)

Copyright 2012 Securities Research Company

Bonds $3.0 Mil Com 11.289 Mil BV 4.57 /sh P/E 9.75 (Ind OGEXP P/E 15.31) Ctry US

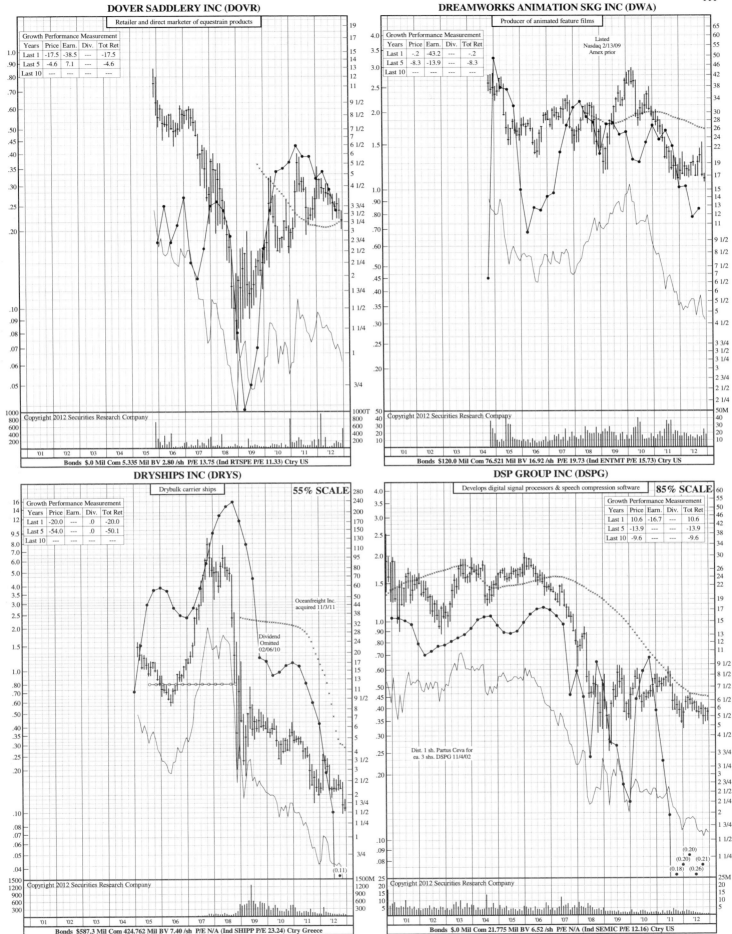

DOVER SADDLERY INC (DOVR)

Retailer and direct marketer of equestrain products

Growth Performance Measurement

Years	Price	Earn.	Div.	Tot Ret
Last 1	-17.5	-38.5	---	-17.5
Last 5	-4.6	7.1	---	-4.6
Last 10	---	---	---	---

Copyright 2012 Securities Research Company

Bonds $.0 Mil Com 5.335 Mil BV 2.80 /sh P/E 13.75 (Ind RTSPE P/E 11.33) Ctry US

DREAMWORKS ANIMATION SKG INC (DWA)

Producer of animated feature films

Listed
Nasdaq 2/13/09
Amex prior

Growth Performance Measurement

Years	Price	Earn.	Div.	Tot Ret
Last 1	-.2	-43.2	---	-.2
Last 5	-8.3	-13.9	---	-8.3
Last 10	---	---	---	---

Copyright 2012 Securities Research Company

Bonds $120.0 Mil Com 76.521 Mil BV 16.92 /sh P/E 19.73 (Ind ENTMT P/E 15.73) Ctry US

DRYSHIPS INC (DRYS)

Drybulk carrier ships

55% SCALE

Growth Performance Measurement

Years	Price	Earn.	Div.	Tot Ret
Last 1	-20.0	---	.0	-20.0
Last 5	-54.0	---	.0	-50.1
Last 10	---	---	---	---

Oceanfreight Inc.
acquired 11/3/11

Dividend
Omitted
02/06/10

(0.11)

Copyright 2012 Securities Research Company

Bonds $587.3 Mil Com 424.762 Mil BV 7.40 /sh P/E N/A (Ind SHIPP P/E 23.24) Ctry Greece

DSP GROUP INC (DSPG)

Develops digital signal processors & speech compression software

85% SCALE

Growth Performance Measurement

Years	Price	Earn.	Div.	Tot Ret
Last 1	10.6	-16.7	---	10.6
Last 5	-13.9	---	---	-13.9
Last 10	-9.6	---	---	-9.6

Dist. 1 sh. Partus Ceva for
ea. 3 shs. DSPG 11/4/02

(0.20)
(0.20) (0.21)
(0.18) (0.26)

Copyright 2012 Securities Research Company

Bonds $.0 Mil Com 21.775 Mil BV 6.52 /sh P/E N/A (Ind SEMIC P/E 12.16) Ctry US

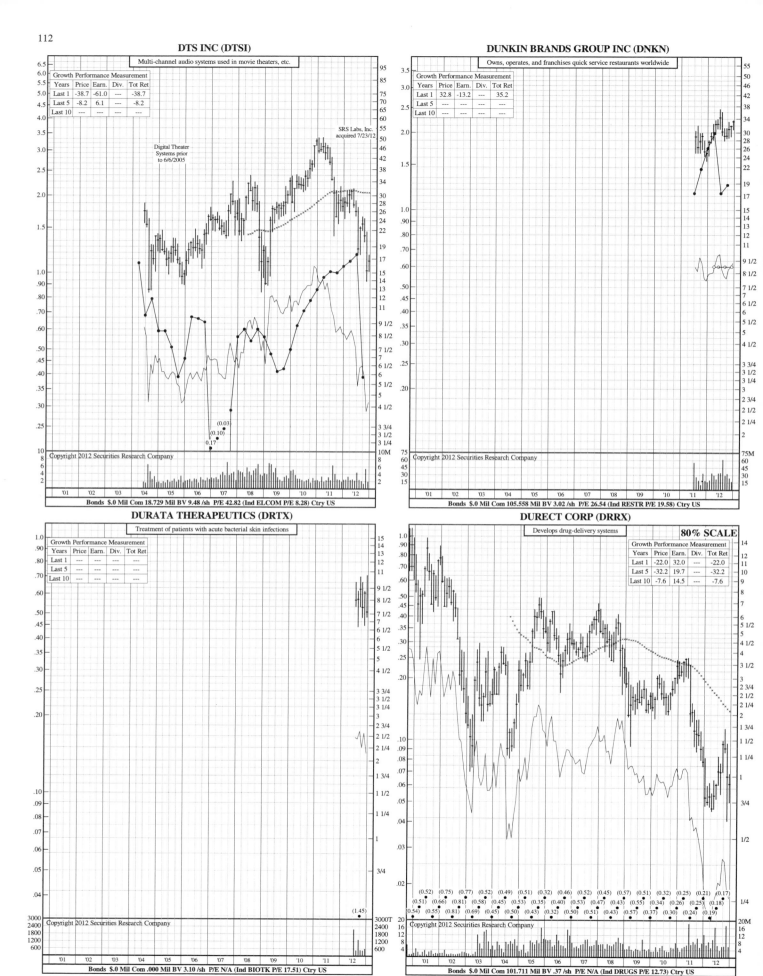

DTS INC (DTSI)

Multi-channel audio systems used in movie theaters, etc.

Growth Performance Measurement				
Years	Price	Earn.	Div.	Tot Ret
Last 1	-38.7	-61.0	---	-38.7
Last 5	-8.2	6.1	---	-8.2
Last 10	---	---	---	---

SRS Labs, Inc.
acquired 7/23/12

Digital Theater
Systems prior
to 6/6/2005

(0.03)
(0.10)
0.17

Copyright 2012 Securities Research Company

Bonds $.0 Mil Com 18.729 Mil BV 9.48 /sh P/E 42.82 (Ind ELCOM P/E 8.28) Ctry US

DUNKIN BRANDS GROUP INC (DNKN)

Owns, operates, and franchises quick service restaurants worldwide

Growth Performance Measurement				
Years	Price	Earn.	Div.	Tot Ret
Last 1	32.8	-13.2	---	35.2
Last 5	---	---	---	---
Last 10	---	---	---	---

Copyright 2012 Securities Research Company

Bonds $.0 Mil Com 105.558 Mil BV 3.02 /sh P/E 26.54 (Ind RESTR P/E 19.58) Ctry US

DURATA THERAPEUTICS (DRTX)

Treatment of patients with acute bacterial skin infections

Growth Performance Measurement				
Years	Price	Earn.	Div.	Tot Ret
Last 1	---	---	---	---
Last 5	---	---	---	---
Last 10	---	---	---	---

(1.45)

Copyright 2012 Securities Research Company

Bonds $.0 Mil Com .000 Mil BV 3.10 /sh P/E N/A (Ind BIOTK P/E 17.51) Ctry US

DURECT CORP (DRRX)

Develops drug-delivery systems

80% SCALE

Growth Performance Measurement				
Years	Price	Earn.	Div.	Tot Ret
Last 1	-22.0	32.0	---	-22.0
Last 5	-32.2	19.7	---	-32.2
Last 10	-7.6	14.5	---	-7.6

(0.52) (0.75) (0.77) (0.52) (0.49) (0.51) (0.32) (0.46) (0.52) (0.45) (0.57) (0.51) (0.32) (0.25) (0.21) (0.17)
(0.51) (0.66) (0.81) (0.58) (0.45) (0.53) (0.35) (0.40) (0.53) (0.47) (0.43) (0.55) (0.34) (0.26) (0.25) (0.18)
(0.54) (0.55) (0.81) (0.69) (0.45) (0.50) (0.43) (0.32) (0.50) (0.51) (0.43) (0.57) (0.37) (0.30) (0.24) (0.19)

Copyright 2012 Securities Research Company

Bonds $.0 Mil Com 101.711 Mil BV .37 /sh P/E N/A (Ind DRUGS P/E 12.73) Ctry US

DXP ENTERPRISES INC (DXPE)

Distributes MRO products, equipment and integrated services

55% SCALE

(P)(E)

Growth Performance Measurement				
Years	Price	Earn.	Div.	Tot Ret
Last 1	52.4	63.4	---	52.4
Last 5	16.0	19.7	---	16.0
Last 10	56.8	34.7	---	56.8

Adj. for
2 for 1
10/1/08

(0.96)
(0.97)
(0.92) (0.95)

Copyright 2012 Securities Research Company

'01 '02 '03 '04 '05 '06 '07 '08 '09 '10 '11 '12

Bonds $36.8 Mil Com 14.181 Mil BV 13.86 /sh P/E 16.14 (Ind TRADE P/E 25.46) Ctry US

DYAX CORP (DYAX)

A biopharmaceutical company

70% SCALE

Growth Performance Measurement				
Years	Price	Earn.	Div.	Tot Ret
Last 1	155.9	-23.3	---	155.9
Last 5	-1.0	24.7	---	-1.0
Last 10	6.8	11.9	---	6.8

(0.83) (1.08) (1.33) (1.13) (1.03) (1.09) (0.89) (0.87) (1.53) (1.03) (0.88) (0.64) (0.33) (0.36) (0.35) (0.37)
(0.93) (0.90) (1.32) (1.14) (1.02) (1.06) (1.05) (0.85) (1.36) (1.12) (1.03) (0.78) (0.51) (0.24) (0.30) (0.42)
(1.07) (0.80) (1.27) (1.28) (1.09) (1.03) (1.06) (0.88) (1.18) (1.53) (1.00) (0.89) (0.88) (0.29) (0.31) (0.34)

Copyright 2012 Securities Research Company

'01 '02 '03 '04 '05 '06 '07 '08 '09 '10 '11 '12

Bonds $.0 Mil Com 99.196 Mil BV -.49 /sh P/E N/A (Ind BIOTK P/E 17.51) Ctry US

DYNAMIC MATLS CORP (BOOM)

Uses explosives to bond metal plates

60% SCALE

(P)(E)

Growth Performance Measurement				
Years	Price	Earn.	Div.	Tot Ret
Last 1	-29.7	4.5	.0	-28.9
Last 5	-25.1	-10.1	-11.8	-24.2
Last 10	27.9	21.2	---	29.0

Adj. for
2 for 1
10/13/05

(0.12)
(0.25)

Copyright 2012 Securities Research Company

'01 '02 '03 '04 '05 '06 '07 '08 '09 '10 '11 '12

Bonds $.0 Mil Com 13.511 Mil BV 11.54 /sh P/E 11.98 (Ind MACHN P/E 14.49) Ctry US

DYNAVAX TECHNOLOGIES CORP (DVAX)

Focuses on the treatment of a variety of allergies

70% SCALE

Growth Performance Measurement				
Years	Price	Earn.	Div.	Tot Ret
Last 1	-14.2	35.3	---	-14.2
Last 5	-11.0	27.2	---	-11.0
Last 10	---	---	---	---

(3.94) (0.29) (0.79) (1.30) (1.55) (1.48) (0.52) (0.57) (0.71) (0.51) (0.35)
(2.82) (0.81) (0.69) (1.26) (1.44) (1.49) (0.89) (0.27) (0.83) (0.45) (0.35)
(9.06) (4.10) (0.56) (1.25) (1.41) (1.61) (1.18) (0.08) (1.01) (0.70) (0.40) (0.33)

Copyright 2012 Securities Research Company

'01 '02 '03 '04 '05 '06 '07 '08 '09 '10 '11 '12

Bonds $.0 Mil Com 178.707 Mil BV .73 /sh P/E N/A (Ind BIOTK P/E 17.51) Ctry US

114

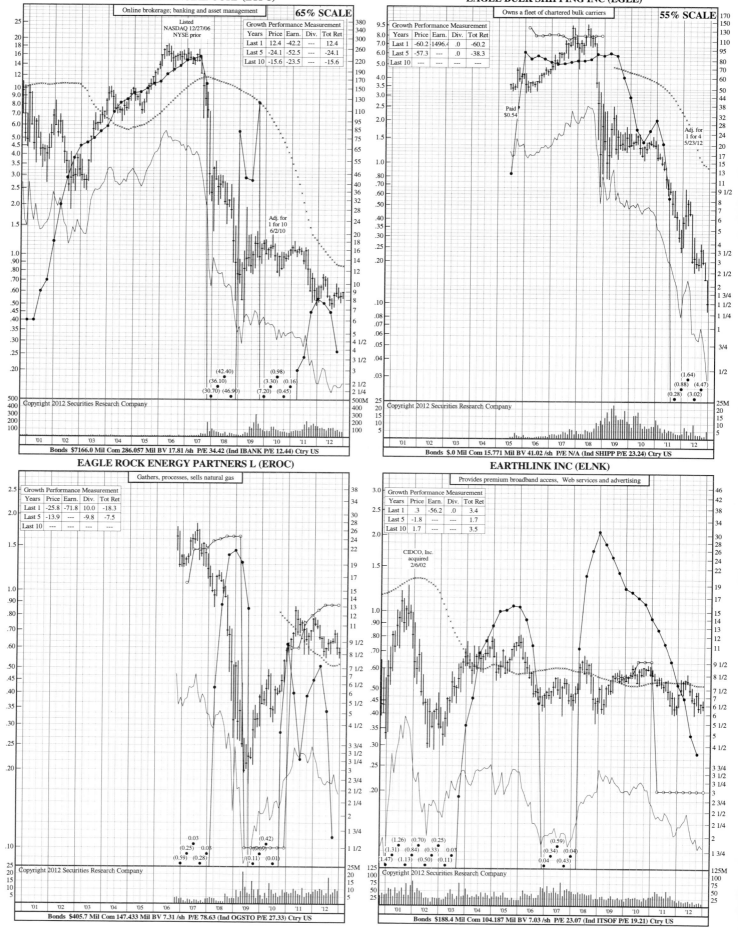

E TRADE FINANCIAL CORP (ETFC)

Online brokerage; banking and asset management

65% SCALE

Listed NASDAQ 12/27/06 NYSE prior

Growth Performance Measurement				
Years	Price	Earn.	Div.	Tot Ret
Last 1	12.4	-42.2	---	12.4
Last 5	-24.1	-52.5	---	-24.1
Last 10	-15.6	-23.5	---	-15.6

Adj. for 1 for 10 6/2/10

(42.40)
(36.10)
(30.70) (46.90)
(0.98)
(3.30) (0.16)
(7.20) (0.45)

Copyright 2012 Securities Research Company

Bonds $7166.0 Mil Com 286.057 Mil BV 17.81 /sh P/E 34.42 (Ind IBANK P/E 12.44) Ctry US

EAGLE BULK SHIPPING INC (EGLE)

Owns a fleet of chartered bulk carriers

55% SCALE

Growth Performance Measurement				
Years	Price	Earn.	Div.	Tot Ret
Last 1	-60.2	1496.4	.0	-60.2
Last 5	-57.3	---	.0	-38.3
Last 10	---	---	---	

Paid $0.54

Adj. for 1 for 4 5/23/12

(1.64)
(0.88) (4.47)
(0.28) (3.02)

Copyright 2012 Securities Research Company

Bonds $.0 Mil Com 15.771 Mil BV 41.02 /sh P/E N/A (Ind SHIPP P/E 23.24) Ctry US

EAGLE ROCK ENERGY PARTNERS L (EROC)

Gathers, processes, sells natural gas

Growth Performance Measurement				
Years	Price	Earn.	Div.	Tot Ret
Last 1	-25.8	-71.8	10.0	-18.3
Last 5	-13.9	---	-9.8	-7.5
Last 10	---	---	---	---

0.03
(0.25) 0.08
(0.59) (0.28)
(0.42)
(0.66)
(0.11) (0.01)

Copyright 2012 Securities Research Company

Bonds $405.7 Mil Com 147.433 Mil BV 7.31 /sh P/E 78.63 (Ind OGSTO P/E 27.33) Ctry US

EARTHLINK INC (ELNK)

Provides premium broadband access, Web services and advertising

Growth Performance Measurement				
Years	Price	Earn.	Div.	Tot Ret
Last 1	.3	-56.2	.0	3.4
Last 5	-1.8	---	---	1.7
Last 10	1.7	---	---	3.5

CIDCO, Inc. acquired 2/6/02

(1.26) (0.70) (0.25)
(1.31) (0.84) (0.33) 0.03
(1.47) (1.13) (0.50) (0.11)
(0.59)
0.04 (0.04)
(0.34) (0.43)

Copyright 2012 Securities Research Company

Bonds $188.4 Mil Com 104.187 Mil BV 7.03 /sh P/E 23.07 (Ind ITSOF P/E 19.21) Ctry US

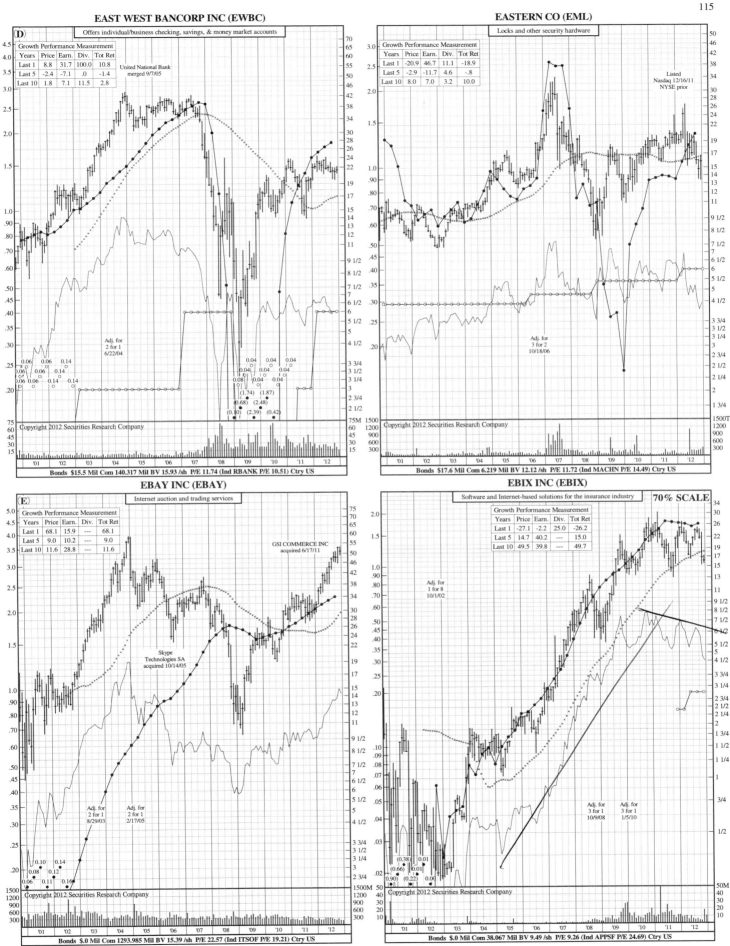

EAST WEST BANCORP INC (EWBC)

Offers individual/business checking, savings, & money market accounts

Growth Performance Measurement				
Years	Price	Earn.	Div.	Tot Ret
Last 1	8.8	31.7	100.0	10.8
Last 5	-2.4	-7.1	.0	-1.4
Last 10	1.8	7.1	11.5	2.8

United National Bank merged 9/7/05

Adj. for 2 for 1 6/22/04

Copyright 2012 Securities Research Company

Bonds $15.5 Mil Com 140.317 Mil BV 15.93 /sh P/E 11.74 (Ind RBANK P/E 10.51) Ctry US

EASTERN CO (EML)

Locks and other security hardware

Growth Performance Measurement				
Years	Price	Earn.	Div.	Tot Ret
Last 1	-20.9	46.7	11.1	-18.9
Last 5	-2.9	-11.7	4.6	-.8
Last 10	8.0	7.0	3.2	10.0

Listed Nasdaq 12/16/11 NYSE prior

Adj. for 3 for 2 10/18/06

Copyright 2012 Securities Research Company

Bonds $17.6 Mil Com 6.219 Mil BV 12.12 /sh P/E 11.72 (Ind MACHN P/E 14.49) Ctry US

EBAY INC (EBAY)

Internet auction and trading services

Growth Performance Measurement				
Years	Price	Earn.	Div.	Tot Ret
Last 1	68.1	15.9	---	68.1
Last 5	9.0	10.2	---	9.0
Last 10	11.6	28.8	---	11.6

GSI COMMERCE INC acquired 6/17/11

Skype Technologies SA acquired 10/14/05

Adj. for 2 for 1 8/29/03

Adj. for 2 for 1 2/17/05

Copyright 2012 Securities Research Company

Bonds $.0 Mil Com 1293.985 Mil BV 15.39 /sh P/E 22.57 (Ind ITSOF P/E 19.21) Ctry US

EBIX INC (EBIX)

Software and Internet-based solutions for the insurance industry   **70% SCALE**

Growth Performance Measurement				
Years	Price	Earn.	Div.	Tot Ret
Last 1	-27.1	-2.2	25.0	-26.2
Last 5	14.7	40.2	---	15.0
Last 10	49.5	39.8	---	49.7

Adj. for 1 for 8 10/1/02

Adj. for 3 for 1 10/9/08

Adj. for 3 for 1 1/5/10

Copyright 2012 Securities Research Company

Bonds $.0 Mil Com 38.067 Mil BV 9.49 /sh P/E 9.26 (Ind APPSF P/E 24.69) Ctry US

116

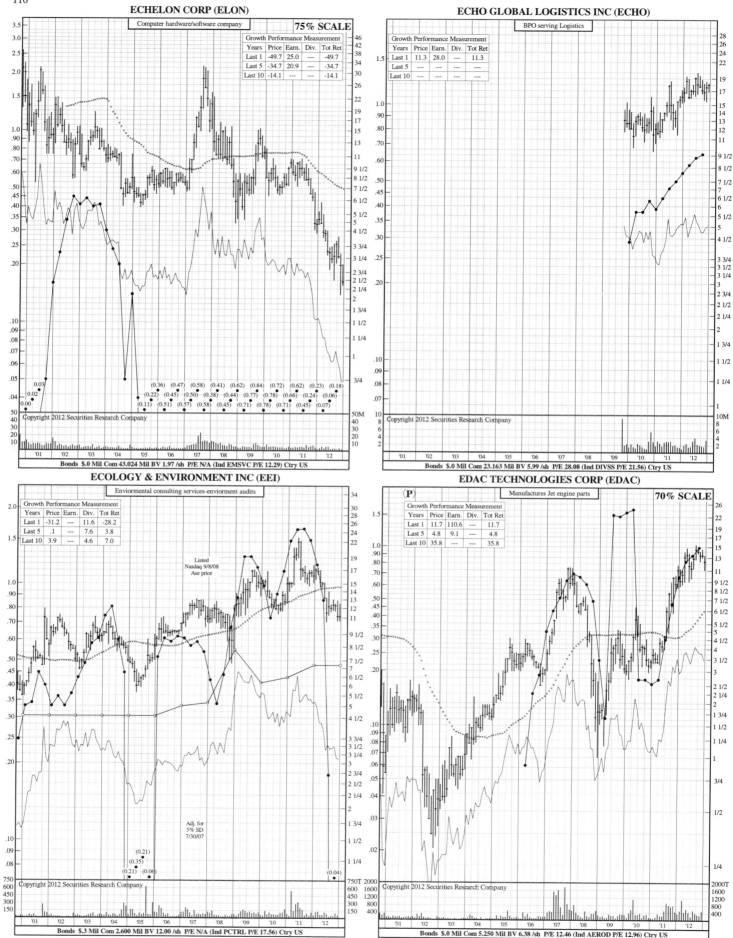

ECHELON CORP (ELON)

Computer hardware/software company

75% SCALE

Growth Performance Measurement				
Years	Price	Earn.	Div.	Tot Ret
Last 1	-49.7	25.0	---	-49.7
Last 5	-34.7	20.9	---	-34.7
Last 10	-14.1	---	---	-14.1

(0.36) (0.47) (0.58) (0.41) (0.62) (0.84) (0.72) (0.62) (0.23) (0.18)
(0.22) (0.45) (0.50) (0.38) (0.44) (0.77) (0.78) (0.66) (0.24) (0.06)
(0.11) (0.51) (0.57) (0.58) (0.45) (0.71) (0.78) (0.71) (0.45) (0.07)

0.03
0.02
0.00

Copyright 2012 Securities Research Company

Bonds $.0 Mil Com 43.024 Mil BV 1.97 /sh P/E N/A (Ind EMSVC P/E 12.29) Ctry US

ECHO GLOBAL LOGISTICS INC (ECHO)

BPO serving Logistics

Growth Performance Measurement				
Years	Price	Earn.	Div.	Tot Ret
Last 1	11.3	28.0	---	11.3
Last 5	---	---	---	---
Last 10	---	---	---	---

Copyright 2012 Securities Research Company

Bonds $.0 Mil Com 23.163 Mil BV 5.99 /sh P/E 28.08 (Ind DIVSS P/E 21.56) Ctry US

ECOLOGY & ENVIRONMENT INC (EEI)

Enviormental consulting services-enviorment audits

Growth Performance Measurement				
Years	Price	Earn.	Div.	Tot Ret
Last 1	-31.2	---	11.6	-28.2
Last 5	.1	---	7.6	3.8
Last 10	3.9	---	4.6	7.0

Listed
Nasdaq 9/8/08
Ase prior

Adj. for
5% SD
7/30/07

(0.21)
(0.35)
(0.21) (0.06)

(0.04)

Copyright 2012 Securities Research Company

Bonds $.3 Mil Com 2.600 Mil BV 12.00 /sh P/E N/A (Ind PCTRL P/E 17.56) Ctry US

EDAC TECHNOLOGIES CORP (EDAC)

(P)

Manufactures Jet engine parts

70% SCALE

Growth Performance Measurement				
Years	Price	Earn.	Div.	Tot Ret
Last 1	11.7	110.6	---	11.7
Last 5	4.8	9.1	---	4.8
Last 10	35.8	---	---	35.8

Copyright 2012 Securities Research Company

Bonds $.0 Mil Com 5.250 Mil BV 6.38 /sh P/E 12.46 (Ind AEROD P/E 12.96) Ctry US

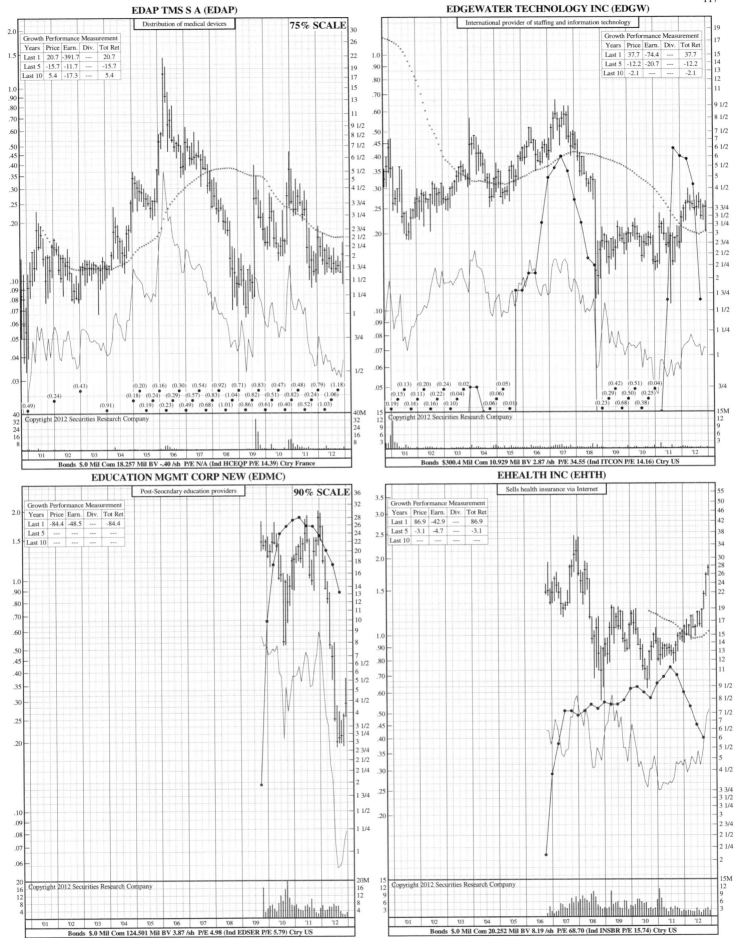

EDAP TMS S A (EDAP)

Distribution of medical devices

75% SCALE

Growth Performance Measurement

Years	Price	Earn.	Div.	Tot Ret
Last 1	20.7	-391.7	---	20.7
Last 5	-15.7	-11.7	---	-15.7
Last 10	5.4	-17.3	---	5.4

(0.49) (0.24) (0.43) (0.91) (0.20) (0.16) (0.30) (0.54) (0.92) (0.71) (0.83) (0.47) (0.48) (0.79) (1.18)
(0.18) (0.24) (0.29) (0.57) (0.83) (1.04) (0.82) (0.51) (0.82) (0.24) (1.06)
(0.19) (0.23) (0.49) (0.68) (1.01) (0.86) (0.61) (0.40) (0.52) (1.03)

Copyright 2012 Securities Research Company

Bonds $.0 Mil Com 18.257 Mil BV -.40 /sh P/E N/A (Ind HCEQP P/E 14.39) Ctry France

EDGEWATER TECHNOLOGY INC (EDGW)

International provider of staffing and information technology

Growth Performance Measurement

Years	Price	Earn.	Div.	Tot Ret
Last 1	37.7	-74.4	---	37.7
Last 5	-12.2	-20.7	---	-12.2
Last 10	-2.1	---	---	-2.1

(0.13) (0.20) (0.24) 0.02 (0.05) (0.42) (0.51) (0.04)
(0.15) (0.11) (0.22) (0.04) (0.06) (0.29) (0.50) (0.25)
(0.19) (0.16) (0.16) (0.10) (0.06) (0.01) (0.23) (0.68) (0.38)

Copyright 2012 Securities Research Company

Bonds $300.4 Mil Com 10.929 Mil BV 2.87 /sh P/E 34.55 (Ind ITCON P/E 14.16) Ctry US

EDUCATION MGMT CORP NEW (EDMC)

Post-Seocndary education providers

90% SCALE

Growth Performance Measurement

Years	Price	Earn.	Div.	Tot Ret
Last 1	-84.4	-48.5	---	-84.4
Last 5	---	---	---	---
Last 10	---	---	---	---

Copyright 2012 Securities Research Company

Bonds $.0 Mil Com 124.501 Mil BV 3.87 /sh P/E 4.98 (Ind EDSER P/E 5.79) Ctry US

EHEALTH INC (EHTH)

Sells health insurance via Internet

Growth Performance Measurement

Years	Price	Earn.	Div.	Tot Ret
Last 1	86.9	-42.9	---	86.9
Last 5	-3.1	-4.7	---	-3.1
Last 10	---	---	---	---

Copyright 2012 Securities Research Company

Bonds $.0 Mil Com 20.252 Mil BV 8.19 /sh P/E 68.70 (Ind INSBR P/E 15.74) Ctry US

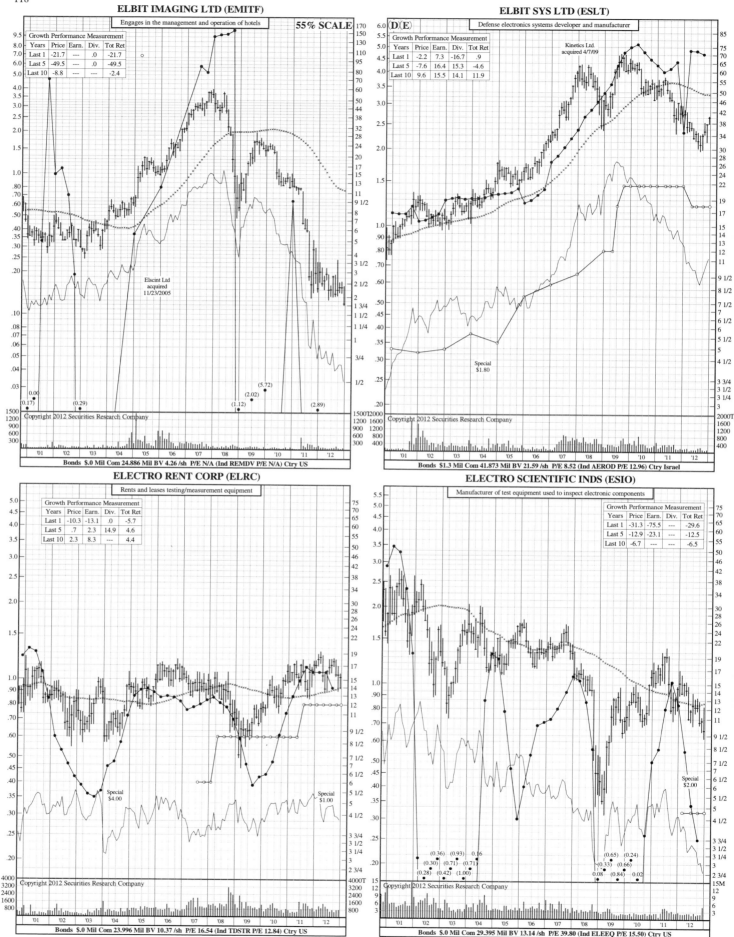

118

ELBIT IMAGING LTD (EMITF)

Engages in the management and operation of hotels

55% SCALE

Growth Performance Measurement

Years	Price	Earn.	Div.	Tot Ret
Last 1	-21.7	---	.0	-21.7
Last 5	-49.5	---	.0	-49.5
Last 10	-8.8	---	---	-2.4

Elscint Ltd
acquired
11/23/2005

0.00
(0.17)
(0.29)
(1.12)
(2.02)
(5.72)
(2.89)

Bonds $.0 Mil Com 24.886 Mil BV 4.26 /sh P/E N/A (Ind REMDV P/E N/A) Ctry US

ELBIT SYS LTD (ESLT)

Defense electronics systems developer and manufacturer

(D)(E)

Growth Performance Measurement

Years	Price	Earn.	Div.	Tot Ret
Last 1	-2.2	7.3	-16.7	.9
Last 5	-7.6	16.4	15.3	-4.6
Last 10	9.6	15.5	14.1	11.9

Kinetics Ltd.
acquired 4/7/09

Special
$1.80

Bonds $1.3 Mil Com 41.873 Mil BV 21.59 /sh P/E 8.52 (Ind AEROD P/E 12.96) Ctry Israel

ELECTRO RENT CORP (ELRC)

Rents and leases testing/measurement equipment

Growth Performance Measurement

Years	Price	Earn.	Div.	Tot Ret
Last 1	-10.3	-13.1	.0	-5.7
Last 5	.7	2.3	14.9	4.6
Last 10	2.3	8.3	---	4.4

Special
$4.00

Special
$1.00

Bonds $.0 Mil Com 23.996 Mil BV 10.37 /sh P/E 16.54 (Ind TDSTR P/E 12.84) Ctry US

ELECTRO SCIENTIFIC INDS (ESIO)

Manufacturer of test equipment used to inspect electronic components

Growth Performance Measurement

Years	Price	Earn.	Div.	Tot Ret
Last 1	-31.3	-75.5	---	-29.6
Last 5	-12.9	-23.1	---	-12.5
Last 10	-6.7	---	---	-6.5

Special
$2.00

(0.36) (0.93) .16
(0.30) (0.71) (0.71)
(0.28) (0.42) (1.00)
(0.65) (0.24)
(0.33) (0.66)
0.08 (0.84) 0.02

Bonds $.0 Mil Com 29.395 Mil BV 13.14 /sh P/E 39.80 (Ind ELEEQ P/E 15.50) Ctry US

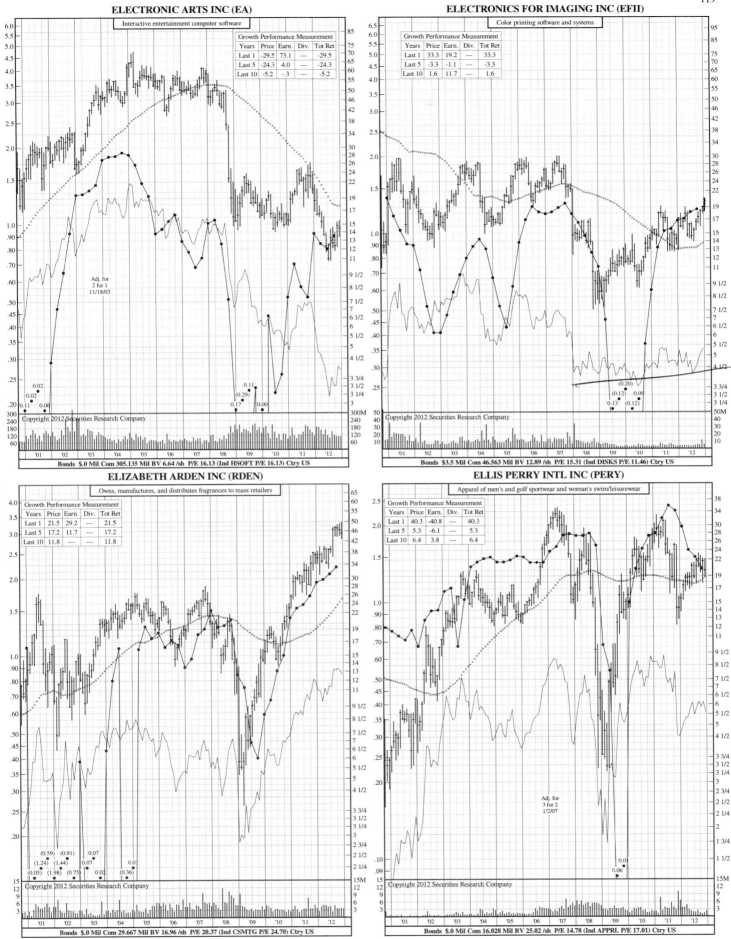

ELECTRONIC ARTS INC (EA)
Interactive entertainment computer software

Growth Performance Measurement				
Years	Price	Earn.	Div.	Tot Ret
Last 1	-29.5	73.1	---	-29.5
Last 5	-24.3	4.0	---	-24.3
Last 10	-5.2	-.3	---	-5.2

Adj. for
2 for 1
11/18/03

0.02
0.02
0.06
0.11

0.11
(0.29)
0.17   0.00

Copyright 2012 Securities Research Company

Bonds $.0 Mil Com 305.135 Mil BV 6.64 /sh P/E 16.13 (Ind HSOFT P/E 16.13) Ctry US

ELECTRONICS FOR IMAGING INC (EFII)
Color printing software and systems

Growth Performance Measurement				
Years	Price	Earn.	Div.	Tot Ret
Last 1	33.3	19.2	---	33.3
Last 5	-3.3	-1.1	---	-3.3
Last 10	1.6	11.7	---	1.6

(0.20)
(0.12)   0.09
0.13   (0.12)

Copyright 2012 Securities Research Company

Bonds $3.5 Mil Com 46.563 Mil BV 12.89 /sh P/E 15.31 (Ind DISKS P/E 11.46) Ctry US

ELIZABETH ARDEN INC (RDEN)
Owns, manufactures, and distributes fragrances to mass retailers

Growth Performance Measurement				
Years	Price	Earn.	Div.	Tot Ret
Last 1	21.5	29.2		21.5
Last 5	17.2	11.7		17.2
Last 10	11.8	---		11.8

(0.59)   (0.91)   0.07
(1.24)   (1.44)   0.07
(0.05) (1.98) (0.75) 0.02   (0.36)   0.01

Copyright 2012 Securities Research Company

Bonds $.0 Mil Com 29.667 Mil BV 16.96 /sh P/E 20.37 (Ind CSMTG P/E 24.70) Ctry US

ELLIS PERRY INTL INC (PERY)
Apparel of men's and golf sportwear and woman's swim/leisurewear

Growth Performance Measurement				
Years	Price	Earn.	Div.	Tot Ret
Last 1	40.3	-40.8	---	40.3
Last 5	5.3	-6.1	---	5.3
Last 10	6.4	3.8	---	6.4

Adj. for
3 for 2
1/2/07

0.01
0.06

Copyright 2012 Securities Research Company

Bonds $.0 Mil Com 16.028 Mil BV 25.02 /sh P/E 14.78 (Ind APPRL P/E 17.01) Ctry US

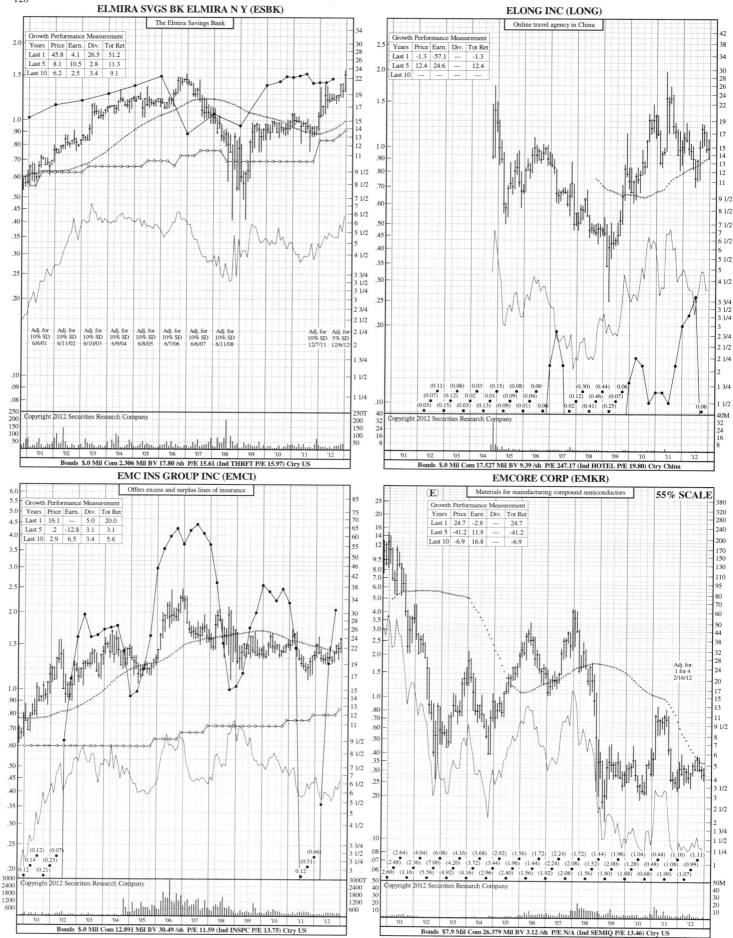

ELMIRA SVGS BK ELMIRA N Y (ESBK)

The Elmira Savings Bank

Growth Performance Measurement

Years	Price	Earn.	Div.	Tot Ret
Last 1	45.8	4.1	26.5	51.2
Last 5	8.1	10.5	2.8	11.3
Last 10	6.2	2.5	3.4	9.1

Adj. for 10% SD 6/6/01
Adj. for 10% SD 6/11/02
Adj. for 10% SD 6/10/03
Adj. for 10% SD 6/9/04
Adj. for 10% SD 6/8/05
Adj. for 10% SD 6/7/06
Adj. for 10% SD 6/6/07
Adj. for 10% SD 6/11/08
Adj. for 10% SD 12/7/11
Adj. for 5% SD 12/6/12

Copyright 2012 Securities Research Company

Bonds $.0 Mil Com 2.306 Mil BV 17.80 /sh P/E 15.61 (Ind THRFT P/E 15.97) Ctry US

ELONG INC (LONG)

Online travel agency in China

Growth Performance Measurement

Years	Price	Earn.	Div.	Tot Ret
Last 1	-1.3	-57.1	---	-1.3
Last 5	12.4	24.6	---	12.4
Last 10	---	---	---	---

(0.11) (0.08) 0.03 (0.15) (0.08) 0.00 (0.30) (0.44) 0.06
(0.07) (0.12) 0.02 0.01 (0.09) (0.04) (0.12) (0.46) (0.07)
(0.03) (0.15) (0.03) (0.13) (0.09) (0.01) 0.06 0.02 (0.41) (0.25) 0.06

Copyright 2012 Securities Research Company

Bonds $.0 Mil Com 17.527 Mil BV 9.39 /sh P/E 247.17 (Ind HOTEL P/E 19.80) Ctry China

EMC INS GROUP INC (EMCI)

Offers excess and surplus lines of insurance

Growth Performance Measurement

Years	Price	Earn.	Div.	Tot Ret
Last 1	16.1	---	5.0	20.0
Last 5	.2	-12.8	3.1	3.1
Last 10	2.9	6.5	3.4	5.6

(0.12) (0.07)
0.14 (0.23)
0.12 (0.21)

(0.66)
(0.51)
0.12

Copyright 2012 Securities Research Company

Bonds $.0 Mil Com 12.891 Mil BV 30.49 /sh P/E 11.59 (Ind INSPC P/E 13.75) Ctry US

EMCORE CORP (EMKR)

(E) Materials for manufacturing compound semiconductors   55% SCALE

Growth Performance Measurement

Years	Price	Earn.	Div.	Tot Ret
Last 1	24.7	-2.8		24.7
Last 5	-41.2	11.8	---	-41.2
Last 10	-6.9	16.8	---	-6.9

Adj. for 1 for 4 2/16/12

(2.64) (4.04) (6.08) (4.16) (3.68) (2.92) (1.56) (1.72) (2.24) (1.72) (1.44) (1.96) (1.44) (0.44) (1.16) (1.11)
(2.48) (2.36) (7.00) (4.20) (3.72) (3.44) (1.96) (1.44) (2.24) (2.08) (1.52) (2.00) (1.28) (0.48) (1.08) (0.99)
(2.60) (1.16) (5.56) (4.92) (4.16) (2.96) (2.40) (1.56) (1.92) (2.08) (1.56) (1.80) (1.88) (0.68) (1.00) (1.07)

Copyright 2012 Securities Research Company

Bonds $7.9 Mil Com 26.379 Mil BV 3.12 /sh P/E N/A (Ind SEMIQ P/E 13.46) Ctry US

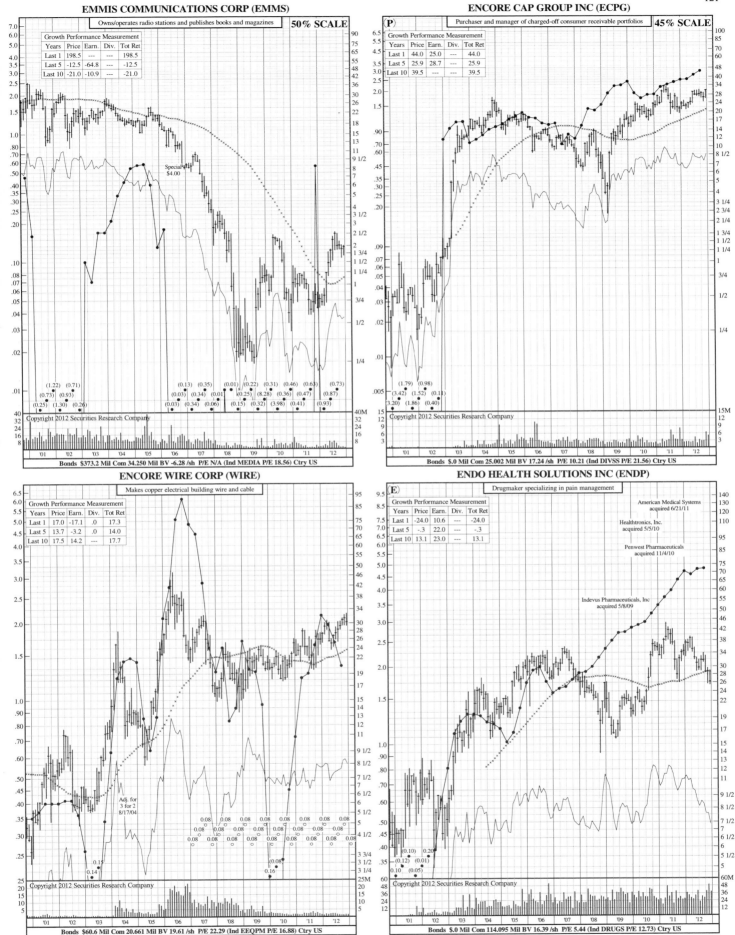

EMMIS COMMUNICATIONS CORP (EMMS)

Owns/operates radio stations and publishes books and magazines

50% SCALE

Growth Performance Measurement				
Years	Price	Earn.	Div.	Tot Ret
Last 1	198.5	---	---	198.5
Last 5	-12.5	-64.8	---	-12.5
Last 10	-21.0	-10.9	---	-21.0

Special $4.00

(1.22) (0.71)
(0.73) (0.93)
(0.25) (1.30) (0.26)

(0.13) (0.35) (0.01) (0.22) (0.31) (0.46) (0.63) (0.73)
(0.03) (0.34) (0.01) (0.25) (8.28) (0.36) (0.47) (0.87)
(0.03) (0.34) (0.06) (0.15) (0.32) (3.98) (0.41) (0.93)

Copyright 2012 Securities Research Company

Bonds $373.2 Mil Com 34.250 Mil BV -6.28 /sh P/E N/A (Ind MEDIA P/E 18.56) Ctry US

ENCORE CAP GROUP INC (ECPG)

Purchaser and manager of charged-off consumer receivable portfolios

45% SCALE

Growth Performance Measurement				
Years	Price	Earn.	Div.	Tot Ret
Last 1	44.0	25.0	---	44.0
Last 5	25.9	28.7	---	25.9
Last 10	39.5	---	---	39.5

(1.79) (0.98)
(3.42) (1.52) (0.11)
(3.20) (1.86) (0.40)

Copyright 2012 Securities Research Company

Bonds $.0 Mil Com 25.002 Mil BV 17.24 /sh P/E 10.21 (Ind DIVSS P/E 21.56) Ctry US

ENCORE WIRE CORP (WIRE)

Makes copper electrical building wire and cable

Growth Performance Measurement				
Years	Price	Earn.	Div.	Tot Ret
Last 1	17.0	-17.1	.0	17.3
Last 5	13.7	-3.2	.0	14.0
Last 10	17.5	14.2	---	17.7

Adj. for
3 for 2
8/17/04

0.08 0.08 0.08 0.08 0.08 0.08 0.08
0.08 0.08 0.08 0.08 0.08 0.08 0.08
0.15
0.14
0.08
0.16

Copyright 2012 Securities Research Company

Bonds $60.6 Mil Com 20.661 Mil BV 19.61 /sh P/E 22.29 (Ind EEQPM P/E 16.88) Ctry US

ENDO HEALTH SOLUTIONS INC (ENDP)

Drugmaker specializing in pain management

Growth Performance Measurement				
Years	Price	Earn.	Div.	Tot Ret
Last 1	-24.0	10.6	---	-24.0
Last 5	-.3	22.0	---	-.3
Last 10	13.1	23.0	---	13.1

American Medical Systems
acquired 6/21/11

Healthtronics, Inc.
acquired 5/5/10

Penwest Pharmaceuticals
acquired 11/4/10

Indevus Pharmaceuticals, Inc
acquired 5/8/09

(0.10) (0.20)
(0.12) (0.01)
0.10 (0.05)

Copyright 2012 Securities Research Company

Bonds $.0 Mil Com 114.095 Mil BV 16.39 /sh P/E 5.44 (Ind DRUGS P/E 12.73) Ctry US

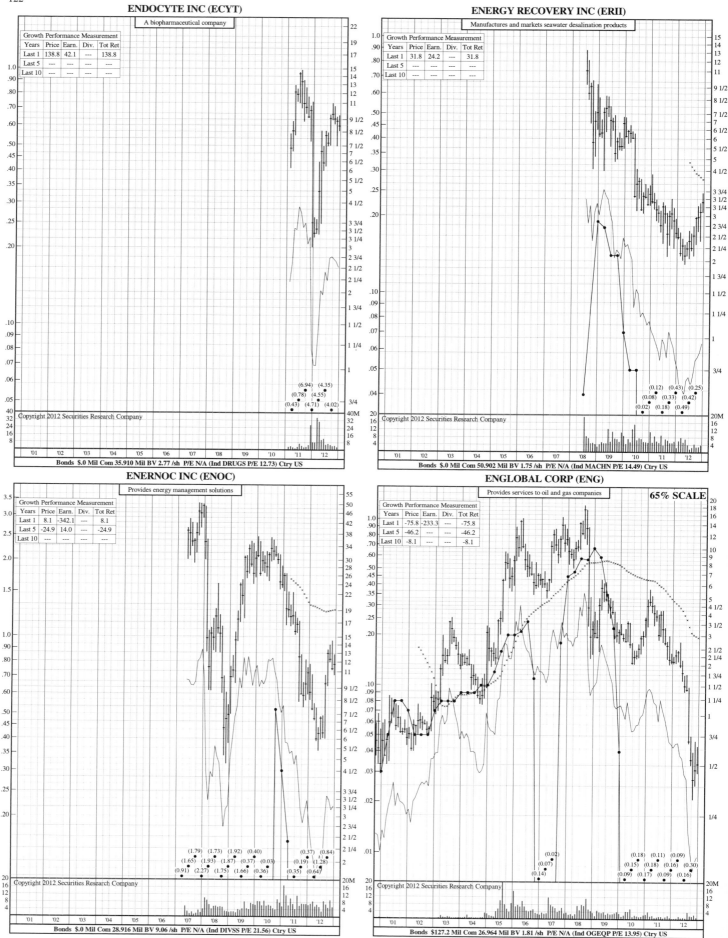

ENDOCYTE INC (ECYT)

A biopharmaceutical company

Growth Performance Measurement

Years	Price	Earn.	Div.	Tot Ret
Last 1	138.8	42.1	---	138.8
Last 5	---	---	---	---
Last 10	---	---	---	---

(6.94) (4.35)
(0.78) (4.55)
(0.43) (4.71) (4.02)

Copyright 2012 Securities Research Company

Bonds $.0 Mil Com 35.910 Mil BV 2.77 /sh P/E N/A (Ind DRUGS P/E 12.73) Ctry US

ENERGY RECOVERY INC (ERII)

Manufactures and markets seawater desalination products

Growth Performance Measurement

Years	Price	Earn.	Div.	Tot Ret
Last 1	31.8	24.2	---	31.8
Last 5	---	---	---	---
Last 10	---	---	---	---

(0.12) (0.43) (0.25)
(0.08) (0.33) (0.42)
(0.02) (0.18) (0.49)

Copyright 2012 Securities Research Company

Bonds $.0 Mil Com 50.902 Mil BV 1.75 /sh P/E N/A (Ind MACHN P/E 14.49) Ctry US

ENERNOC INC (ENOC)

Provides energy management solutions

Growth Performance Measurement

Years	Price	Earn.	Div.	Tot Ret
Last 1	8.1	-342.1	---	8.1
Last 5	-24.9	14.0	---	-24.9
Last 10	---	---	---	---

(1.79) (1.73) (1.92) (0.40)   (0.37) (0.84)
(1.65) (1.93) (1.87) (0.37) (0.03) (0.19) (1.28)
(0.91) (2.27) (1.75) (1.66) (0.36) (0.35) (0.64)

Copyright 2012 Securities Research Company

Bonds $.0 Mil Com 28.916 Mil BV 9.06 /sh P/E N/A (Ind DIVSS P/E 21.56) Ctry US

ENGLOBAL CORP (ENG)

Provides services to oil and gas companies

65% SCALE

Growth Performance Measurement

Years	Price	Earn.	Div.	Tot Ret
Last 1	-75.8	-233.3	---	-75.8
Last 5	-46.2	---	---	-46.2
Last 10	-8.1	---	---	-8.1

(0.02)   (0.18) (0.11) (0.09)
(0.07)   (0.15) (0.18) (0.16) (0.30)
(0.14)   (0.09) (0.17) (0.09) (0.16)

Copyright 2012 Securities Research Company

Bonds $127.2 Mil Com 26.964 Mil BV 1.81 /sh P/E N/A (Ind OGEQP P/E 13.95) Ctry US

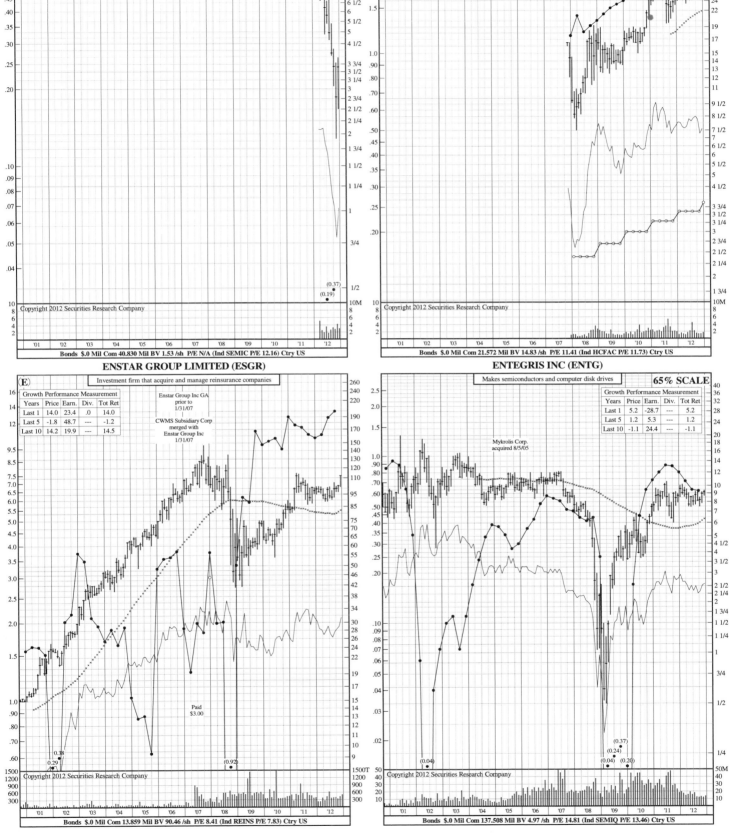

ENPHASE ENERGY INC (ENPH)

Microinverter systems for residential and commercial solar systems

Growth Performance Measurement

Years	Price	Earn.	Div.	Tot Ret
Last 1	---	---	---	---
Last 5	---	---	---	---
Last 10	---	---	---	---

(0.37)
(0.19)

Copyright 2012 Securities Research Company

Bonds $.0 Mil Com 40.830 Mil BV 1.53 /sh P/E N/A (Ind SEMIC P/E 12.16) Ctry US

ENSIGN GROUP INC (ENSG)

Provides nursing and rehabilitative care services

Growth Performance Measurement

Years	Price	Earn.	Div.	Tot Ret
Last 1	10.8	.0	9.1	11.8
Last 5	13.5	---	---	14.4
Last 10	---	---	---	---

Copyright 2012 Securities Research Company

Bonds $.0 Mil Com 21.572 Mil BV 14.83 /sh P/E 11.41 (Ind HCFAC P/E 11.73) Ctry US

ENSTAR GROUP LIMITED (ESGR)

(E)

Investment firm that acquire and manage reinsurance companies

Enstar Group Inc GA
prior to
1/31/07

CWMS Subsidiary Corp
merged with
Enstar Group Inc
1/31/07

Growth Performance Measurement

Years	Price	Earn.	Div.	Tot Ret
Last 1	14.0	23.4	.0	14.0
Last 5	-1.8	48.7	---	-1.2
Last 10	14.2	19.9	---	14.5

Paid
$3.00

0.38
0.29
(0.92)

Copyright 2012 Securities Research Company

Bonds $.0 Mil Com 13.859 Mil BV 90.46 /sh P/E 8.41 (Ind REINS P/E 7.83) Ctry US

ENTEGRIS INC (ENTG)

Makes semiconductors and computer disk drives

65% SCALE

Mykrolis Corp.
acquired 8/5/05

Growth Performance Measurement

Years	Price	Earn.	Div.	Tot Ret
Last 1	5.2	-28.7	---	5.2
Last 5	1.2	5.3	---	1.2
Last 10	-1.1	24.4	---	-1.1

(0.37)
(0.24)
(0.04)
(0.04) (0.20)

Copyright 2012 Securities Research Company

Bonds $.0 Mil Com 137.508 Mil BV 4.97 /sh P/E 14.81 (Ind SEMIQ P/E 13.46) Ctry US

124

ENTERPRISE BANCORP INC MASS (EBTC)

Full-service commercial bank

Growth Performance Measurement				
Years	Price	Earn.	Div.	Tot Ret
Last 1	15.5	12.6	4.8	18.6
Last 5	5.5	.5	6.6	7.9
Last 10	---	---	---	---

Adj. for
2 for 1
7/3/06

Copyright 2012 Securities Research Company

'01 '02 '03 '04 '05 '06 '07 '08 '09 '10 '11 '12

Bonds $.0 Mil Com 9.634 Mil BV 14.22 /sh P/E 13.22 (Ind RBANK P/E 10.51) Ctry US

ENTREMED INC (ENMD)

Develops drugs that inhibit the growth of new blood vessels

45% SCALE

Growth Performance Measurement				
Years	Price	Earn.	Div.	Tot Ret
Last 1	45.3	-62.5	---	45.3
Last 5	-36.3	25.6	---	-36.3
Last 10	-17.5	31.3	---	-17.5

Adj. for
1 for 11
7/1/10

(32.12) (26.84) (22.22) (8.80) (5.94) (3.96) (3.96) (3.08) (3.52) (3.19) (3.19) (1.32) (0.91) (0.68) (0.49) (0.78)
(32.34) (26.29) (33.11) (13.09) (6.71) (4.07) (3.63) (3.52) (3.41) (3.08) (3.30) (1.76) (1.09) (0.76) (0.48) (0.86)
33.44 (21.23) (23.43) (16.61) (6.93) (5.28) (3.63) (3.52) (3.41) (3.41) (3.30) (2.53) (1.21) (1.16) (0.59) (0.47)

Copyright 2012 Securities Research Company

'01 '02 '03 '04 '05 '06 '07 '08 '09 '10 '11 '12

Bonds $2.0 Mil Com 22.503 Mil BV .41 /sh P/E N/A (Ind BIOTK P/E 17.51) Ctry US

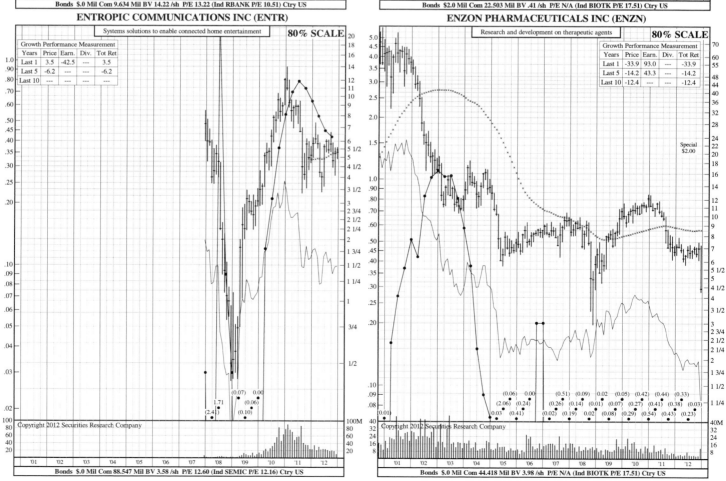

ENTROPIC COMMUNICATIONS INC (ENTR)

Systems solutions to enable connected home entertainment

80% SCALE

Growth Performance Measurement				
Years	Price	Earn.	Div.	Tot Ret
Last 1	3.5	-42.5	---	3.5
Last 5	-6.2	---	---	-6.2
Last 10	---	---	---	---

(0.07) 0.00
1.71 (0.06)
(2.4) (0.10)

Copyright 2012 Securities Research Company

'01 '02 '03 '04 '05 '06 '07 '08 '09 '10 '11 '12

Bonds $.0 Mil Com 88.547 Mil BV 3.58 /sh P/E 12.60 (Ind SEMIC P/E 12.16) Ctry US

ENZON PHARMACEUTICALS INC (ENZN)

Research and development on therapeutic agents

80% SCALE

Growth Performance Measurement				
Years	Price	Earn.	Div.	Tot Ret
Last 1	-33.9	93.0	---	-33.9
Last 5	-14.2	43.3	---	-14.2
Last 10	-12.4	---	---	-12.4

Special
$2.00

(0.06) 0.00 (0.51) (0.09) 0.02 (0.05) (0.42) (0.44) (0.33)
(2.06) (0.24) (0.26) (0.14) (0.01) (0.07) (0.27) (0.41) (0.03)
0.01 0.03 (0.41) 0.02 (0.19) 0.02 (0.08) (0.29) (0.54) (0.43) (0.23)

Copyright 2012 Securities Research Company

'01 '02 '03 '04 '05 '06 '07 '08 '09 '10 '11 '12

Bonds $.0 Mil Com 44.418 Mil BV 3.98 /sh P/E N/A (Ind BIOTK P/E 17.51) Ctry US

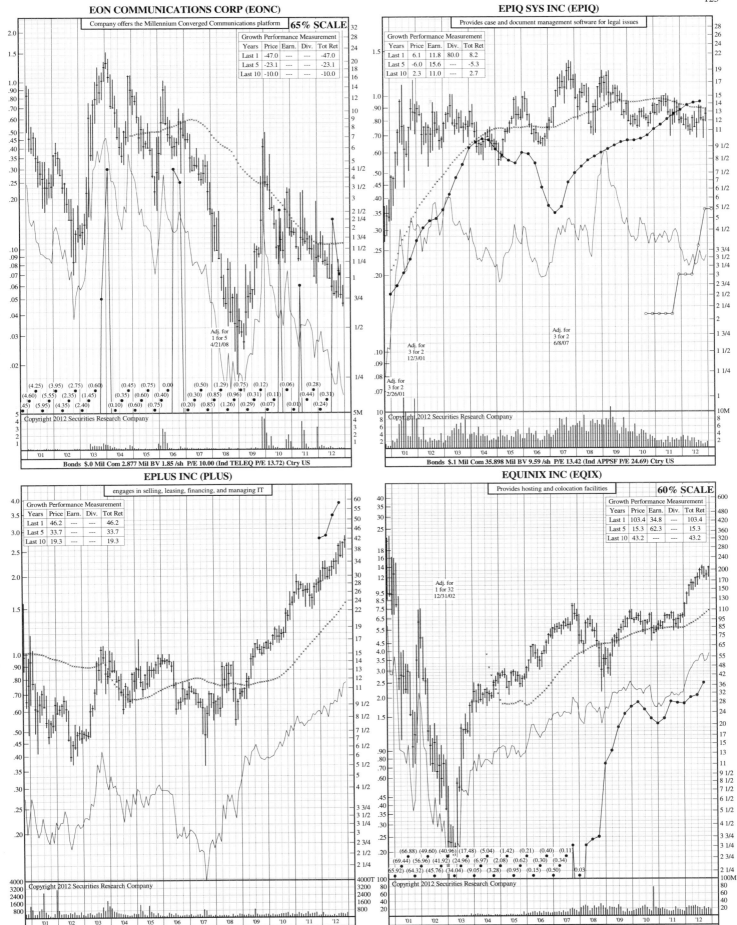

EON COMMUNICATIONS CORP (EONC)

Company offers the Millennium Converged Communications platform

65% SCALE

Growth Performance Measurement

Years	Price	Earn.	Div.	Tot Ret
Last 1	-47.0	---	---	-47.0
Last 5	-23.1	---	---	-23.1
Last 10	-10.0	---	---	-10.0

Adj. for
1 for 5
4/21/08

(4.25) (3.95) (2.75) (0.60) (0.45) (0.75) 0.00 (0.50) (1.29) (0.75) (0.12) (0.06) (0.28)
(4.60) (5.55) (2.35) (1.45) (0.35) (0.60) (0.40) (0.30) (0.85) (0.96) (0.31) (0.11) (0.44) (0.31)
.45) (5.95) (4.35) (2.40) (0.10) (0.60) (0.75) (0.20) (0.85) (1.26) (0.29) (0.07) (0.01) (0.24)

Copyright 2012 Securities Research Company

Bonds $.0 Mil Com 2.877 Mil BV 1.85 /sh P/E 10.00 (Ind TELEQ P/E 13.72) Ctry US

EPIQ SYS INC (EPIQ)

Provides case and document management software for legal issues

Growth Performance Measurement

Years	Price	Earn.	Div.	Tot Ret
Last 1	6.1	11.8	80.0	8.2
Last 5	-6.0	15.6	---	-5.3
Last 10	2.3	11.0	---	2.7

Adj. for
3 for 2
6/8/07

Adj. for
3 for 2
12/3/01

Adj. for
3 for 2
2/26/01

Copyright 2012 Securities Research Company

Bonds $.1 Mil Com 35.898 Mil BV 9.59 /sh P/E 13.42 (Ind APPSF P/E 24.69) Ctry US

EPLUS INC (PLUS)

engages in selling, leasing, financing, and managing IT

Growth Performance Measurement

Years	Price	Earn.	Div.	Tot Ret
Last 1	46.2	---	---	46.2
Last 5	33.7	---	---	33.7
Last 10	19.3	---	---	19.3

Copyright 2012 Securities Research Company

Bonds $.0 Mil Com 8.080 Mil BV 31.87 /sh P/E 10.65 (Ind APPSF P/E 24.69) Ctry US

EQUINIX INC (EQIX)

Provides hosting and colocation facilities

60% SCALE

Growth Performance Measurement

Years	Price	Earn.	Div.	Tot Ret
Last 1	103.4	34.8	---	103.4
Last 5	15.3	62.3	---	15.3
Last 10	43.2	---	---	43.2

Adj. for
1 for 32
12/31/02

(66.88) (49.60) (40.96) (17.48) (5.04) (1.42) (0.21) (0.40) (0.11)
(69.44) (56.96) (41.92) (24.96) (6.97) (2.08) (0.62) (0.30) (0.34)
65.92) (64.32) (45.76) (34.04) (9.05) (3.28) (0.95) (0.15) (0.50) 0.03

Copyright 2012 Securities Research Company

Bonds $.0 Mil Com 48.625 Mil BV 45.94 /sh P/E 83.15 (Ind ITSOF P/E 19.21) Ctry US

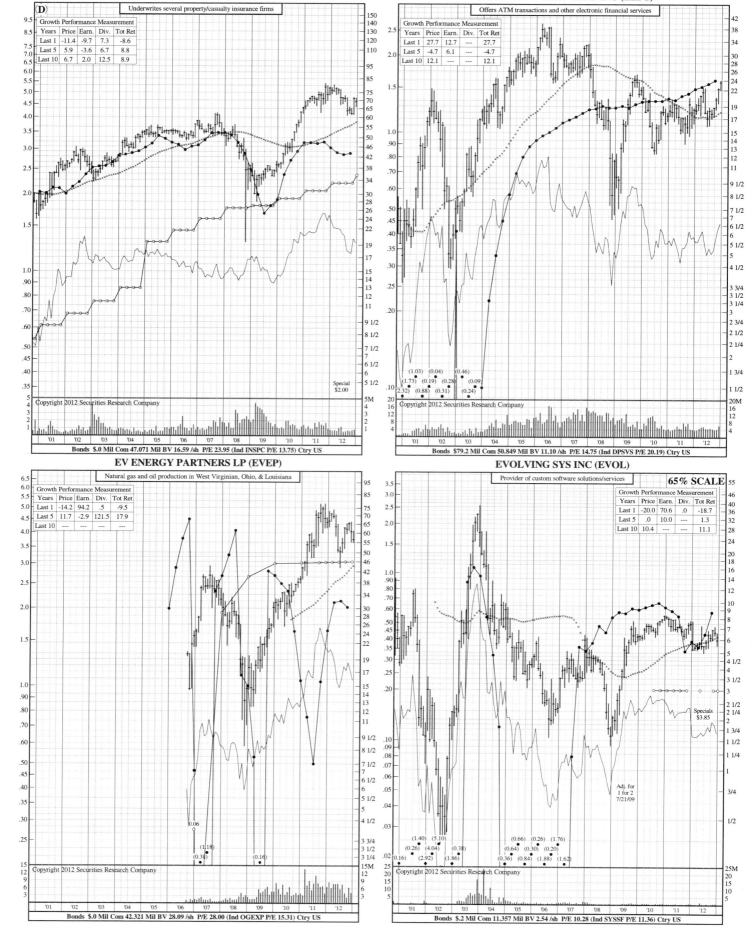

ERIE INDTY CO (ERIE)

Underwrites several property/casualty insurance firms

Growth Performance Measurement				
Years	Price	Earn.	Div.	Tot Ret
Last 1	-11.4	-9.7	7.3	-8.6
Last 5	5.9	-3.6	6.7	8.8
Last 10	6.7	2.0	12.5	8.9

Special $2.00

Copyright 2012 Securities Research Company

Bonds $.0 Mil Com 47.071 Mil BV 16.59 /sh P/E 23.95 (Ind INSPC P/E 13.75) Ctry US

EURONET WORLDWIDE INC (EEFT)

Offers ATM transactions and other electronic financial services

Growth Performance Measurement				
Years	Price	Earn.	Div.	Tot Ret
Last 1	27.7	12.7		27.7
Last 5	-4.7	6.1	---	-4.7
Last 10	12.1	---	---	12.1

(1.03) (0.04) (0.46)
(1.73) (0.19) (0.28) (0.09)
(2.32) (0.88) (0.31) (0.24)

Copyright 2012 Securities Research Company

Bonds $79.2 Mil Com 50.849 Mil BV 11.10 /sh P/E 14.75 (Ind DPSVS P/E 20.19) Ctry US

EV ENERGY PARTNERS LP (EVEP)

Natural gas and oil production in West Virginian, Ohio, & Louisiana

Growth Performance Measurement				
Years	Price	Earn.	Div.	Tot Ret
Last 1	-14.2	94.2	.5	-9.5
Last 5	11.7	-2.9	121.5	17.9
Last 10	---	---	---	---

0.06
(1.18)
(0.38)   (0.16)

Copyright 2012 Securities Research Company

Bonds $.0 Mil Com 42.321 Mil BV 28.09 /sh P/E 28.00 (Ind OGEXP P/E 15.31) Ctry US

EVOLVING SYS INC (EVOL)

Provider of custom software solutions/services

65% SCALE

Growth Performance Measurement				
Years	Price	Earn.	Div.	Tot Ret
Last 1	-20.0	70.6	.0	-18.7
Last 5	.0	10.0	---	1.3
Last 10	10.4	---	---	11.1

Specials $3.85

Adj. for 1 for 2 7/21/09

(1.40) (5.10)   (0.66) (0.26) (1.76)
(0.26) (4.04) (0.38) (0.64) (0.30) (0.20)
(0.16) (2.92) (1.86)   (0.36) (0.84) (1.88) (1.62)

Copyright 2012 Securities Research Company

Bonds $.2 Mil Com 11.357 Mil BV 2.54 /sh P/E 10.28 (Ind SYSSF P/E 11.36) Ctry US

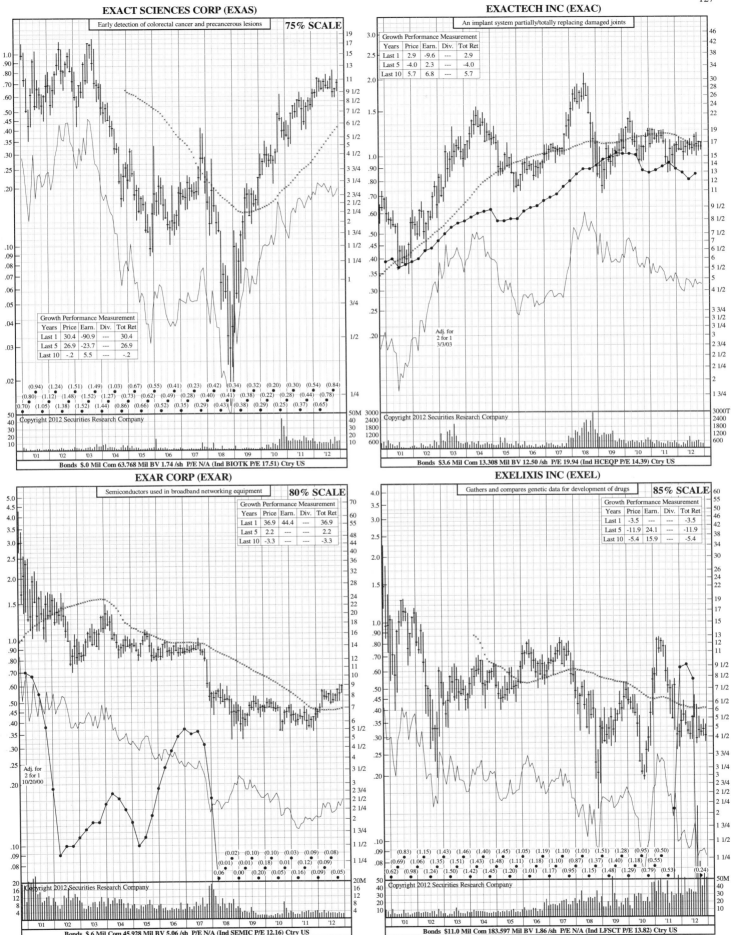

EXACT SCIENCES CORP (EXAS)
Early detection of colorectal cancer and precancerous lesions
75% SCALE

Growth Performance Measurement

Years	Price	Earn.	Div.	Tot Ret
Last 1	30.4	-90.9	---	30.4
Last 5	26.9	-23.7	---	26.9
Last 10	-.2	5.5	---	-.2

(0.94) (1.24) (1.51) (1.49) (1.03) (0.67) (0.55) (0.41) (0.23) (0.42) (0.34) (0.32) (0.20) (0.30) (0.54) (0.84)
(0.80) (1.12) (1.48) (1.52) (1.27) (0.73) (0.62) (0.49) (0.28) (0.40) (0.41) (0.38) (0.22) (0.28) (0.44) (0.78)
(0.70) (1.05) (1.38) (1.52) (1.44) (0.86) (0.66) (0.52) (0.35) (0.29) (0.43) (0.38) (0.29) (0.25) (0.37) (0.65)

Copyright 2012 Securities Research Company
Bonds $.0 Mil Com 63.768 Mil BV 1.74 /sh P/E N/A (Ind BIOTK P/E 17.51) Ctry US

EXACTECH INC (EXAC)
An implant system partially/totally replacing damaged joints

Growth Performance Measurement

Years	Price	Earn.	Div.	Tot Ret
Last 1	2.9	-9.6	---	2.9
Last 5	-4.0	2.3	---	-4.0
Last 10	5.7	6.8	---	5.7

Adj. for
2 for 1
3/3/03

Copyright 2012 Securities Research Company
Bonds $3.6 Mil Com 13.308 Mil BV 12.50 /sh P/E 19.94 (Ind HCEQP P/E 14.39) Ctry US

EXAR CORP (EXAR)
Semiconductors used in broadband networking equipment
80% SCALE

Growth Performance Measurement

Years	Price	Earn.	Div.	Tot Ret
Last 1	36.9	44.4	---	36.9
Last 5	2.2	---	---	2.2
Last 10	-3.3	---	---	-3.3

Adj. for
2 for 1
10/20/00

(0.02) (0.10) (0.10) (0.03) (0.09) (0.08)
(0.01) (0.01) (0.18) (0.01) (0.12) (0.09)
0.06 0.00 (0.20) (0.05) (0.16) (0.09) (0.05)

Copyright 2012 Securities Research Company
Bonds $.6 Mil Com 45.928 Mil BV 5.06 /sh P/E N/A (Ind SEMIC P/E 12.16) Ctry US

EXELIXIS INC (EXEL)
Gathers and compares genetic data for development of drugs
85% SCALE

Growth Performance Measurement

Years	Price	Earn.	Div.	Tot Ret
Last 1	-3.5	---	---	-3.5
Last 5	-11.9	24.1	---	-11.9
Last 10	-5.4	15.9	---	-5.4

(0.83) (1.15) (1.43) (1.46) (1.40) (1.45) (1.05) (1.19) (1.10) (1.01) (1.51) (1.28) (0.95) (0.50)
(0.69) (1.06) (1.35) (1.51) (1.43) (1.48) (1.11) (1.18) (1.10) (0.87) (1.37) (1.40) (1.18) (0.55)
(0.62) (0.98) (1.24) (1.50) (1.42) (1.45) (1.20) (1.01) (1.17) (0.95) (1.15) (1.48) (1.29) (0.79) (0.53) (0.24)

Copyright 2012 Securities Research Company
Bonds $11.0 Mil Com 183.597 Mil BV 1.86 /sh P/E N/A (Ind LFSCT P/E 13.82) Ctry US

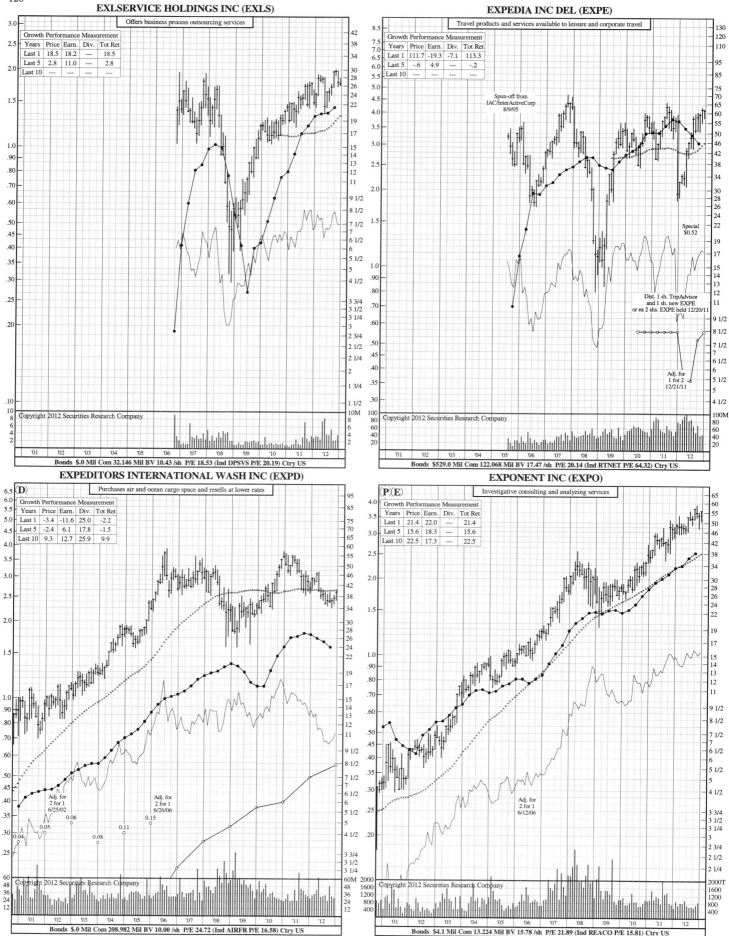

EXLSERVICE HOLDINGS INC (EXLS)

Offers business process outsourcing services

Growth Performance Measurement				
Years	Price	Earn.	Div.	Tot Ret
Last 1	18.5	18.2	---	18.5
Last 5	2.8	11.0	---	2.8
Last 10	---	---	---	---

Copyright 2012 Securities Research Company

Bonds $.0 Mil Com 32.146 Mil BV 10.43 /sh P/E 18.53 (Ind DPSVS P/E 20.19) Ctry US

EXPEDIA INC DEL (EXPE)

Travel products and services available to leisure and corporate travel

Growth Performance Measurement				
Years	Price	Earn.	Div.	Tot Ret
Last 1	111.7	-19.3	-7.1	113.3
Last 5	-.6	4.9	---	-.2
Last 10	---	---	---	---

Spun-off from
IAC/InterActiveCorp
8/9/05

Special
$0.52

Dist. 1 sh. TripAdvisor
and 1 sh. new EXPE
or ea 2 shs. EXPE held 12/20/11

Adj. for
1 for 2
12/21/11

Copyright 2012 Securities Research Company

Bonds $529.0 Mil Com 122.068 Mil BV 17.47 /sh P/E 20.14 (Ind RTNET P/E 64.32) Ctry US

EXPEDITORS INTERNATIONAL WASH INC (EXPD)

(D)   Purchases air and ocean cargo space and resells at lower rates

Growth Performance Measurement				
Years	Price	Earn.	Div.	Tot Ret
Last 1	-3.4	-11.6	25.0	-2.2
Last 5	-2.4	6.1	17.8	-1.5
Last 10	9.3	12.7	25.9	9.9

Adj. for
2 for 1
6/25/02

Adj. for
2 for 1
6/26/06

0.04   0.05   0.06   0.08   0.11   0.15

Copyright 2012 Securities Research Company

Bonds $.0 Mil Com 208.982 Mil BV 10.00 /sh P/E 24.72 (Ind AIRFR P/E 16.58) Ctry US

EXPONENT INC (EXPO)

(P/E)   Investigative consulting and analyzing services

Growth Performance Measurement				
Years	Price	Earn.	Div.	Tot Ret
Last 1	21.4	22.0	---	21.4
Last 5	15.6	18.3	---	15.6
Last 10	22.5	17.3	---	22.5

Adj. for
2 for 1
6/12/06

Copyright 2012 Securities Research Company

Bonds $4.1 Mil Com 13.224 Mil BV 15.78 /sh P/E 21.89 (Ind REACO P/E 15.81) Ctry US

EXPRESS SCRIPTS INC (ESRX)

Pharmacy benefit management services

75% SCALE

Growth Performance Measurement				
Years	Price	Earn.	Div.	Tot Ret
Last 1	20.8	20.2	---	20.8
Last 5	8.1	25.8	---	8.1
Last 10	24.6	28.3	---	24.6

Medco Health Solutions acquired 4/2/12

Priority Healthcare Corp. acquired 10/14/05

CuraScript Pharmacy acq. 1/2005

Adj. for 2 for 1 6/8/10

Adj. for 2 for 1 6/25/01

Adj. for 2 for 1 6/27/05

Adj. for 2 for 1 6/25/07

Copyright 2012 Securities Research Company

Bonds $1270.0 Mil Com 816.400 Mil BV 28.09 /sh P/E 15.65 (Ind HCSVS P/E 15.09) Ctry US

EXTREME NETWORKS INC (EXTR)

Designs and markets high-performance networking switches

60% SCALE

Growth Performance Measurement				
Years	Price	Earn.	Div.	Tot Ret
Last 1	24.7	187.5	---	24.7
Last 5	.6	---	---	.6
Last 10	1.1	19.1	---	1.1

0.00 (0.13) (0.03) (0.08)
(0.04) 0.04 (0.17) (0.10) (0.08) 0.0
(0.08) (0.15) (0.01) (0.03) 0.00 0.03

Copyright 2012 Securities Research Company

Bonds $.3 Mil Com 95.053 Mil BV 2.11 /sh P/E 15.83 (Ind TELEQ P/E 13.72) Ctry US

EZCORP INC (EZPW)

Operates pawnshops in Texas

55% SCALE

Growth Performance Measurement				
Years	Price	Earn.	Div.	Tot Ret
Last 1	-24.6	9.7	---	-24.6
Last 5	12.0	26.2	---	12.0
Last 10	33.4	45.4	---	33.4

Adj. for 3 for 1 12/12/06

(0.09)
(0.16) 0.01
(0.20) 0.00

Copyright 2012 Securities Research Company

Bonds $83.1 Mil Com 48.396 Mil BV 16.30 /sh P/E 7.05 (Ind FINAN P/E 11.42) Ctry US

F5 NETWORKS INC (FFIV)

Offers network products and services

75% SCALE

Growth Performance Measurement				
Years	Price	Earn.	Div.	Tot Ret
Last 1	-8.5	15.6	---	-8.5
Last 5	27.8	31.1	---	27.8
Last 10	33.6	---	---	33.6

Adj. for 2 for 1 8/21/07

(0.27) (0.14) (0.05) 0.07
(0.17) (0.20) (0.10) 0.04
0.02 (0.40) (0.15) (0.07)

Copyright 2012 Securities Research Company

Bonds $.0 Mil Com 79.050 Mil BV 16.88 /sh P/E 22.18 (Ind TELEQ P/E 13.72) Ctry US

130

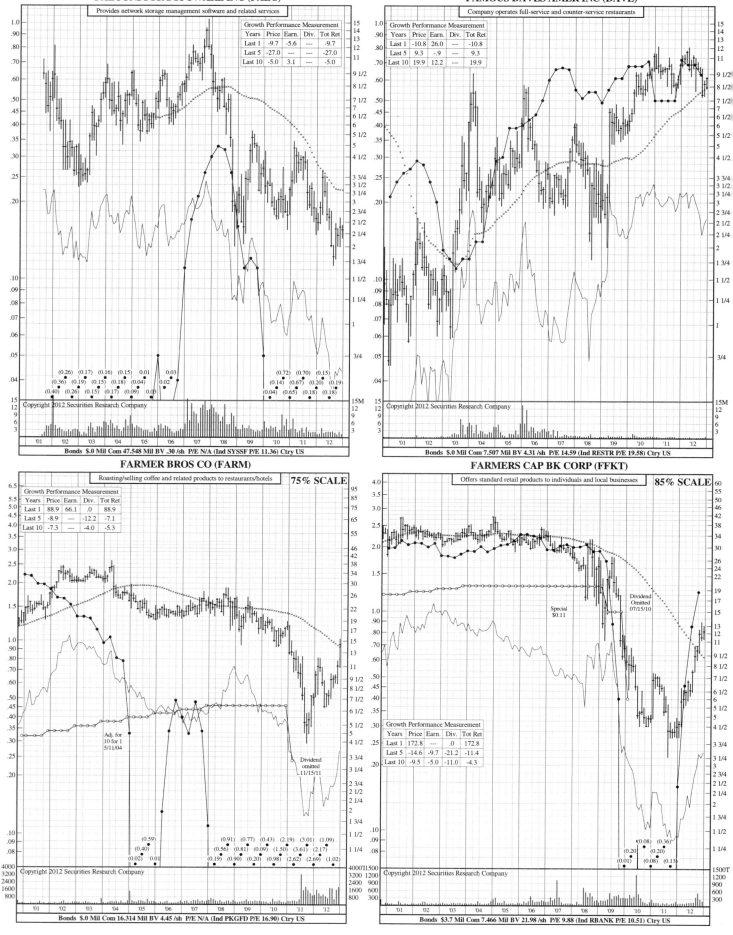

FALCONSTOR SOFTWARE INC (FALC)

Provides network storage management software and related services

Growth Performance Measurement				
Years	Price	Earn.	Div.	Tot Ret
Last 1	-9.7	-5.6	---	-9.7
Last 5	-27.0	---	---	-27.0
Last 10	-5.0	3.1	---	-5.0

(0.26) (0.17) (0.16) (0.15) 0.01   0.03   (0.72) (0.70) (0.15)
(0.36) (0.19) (0.15) (0.18) (0.04) 0.02   (0.14) (0.67) (0.20) (0.19)
(0.40) (0.26) (0.15) (0.17) (0.09) 0.03   (0.04) (0.65) (0.18) (0.18)

Copyright 2012 Securities Research Company

Bonds $.0 Mil Com 47.548 Mil BV .30 /sh P/E N/A (Ind SYSSF P/E 11.36) Ctry US

FAMOUS DAVES AMER INC (DAVE)

Company operates full-service and counter-service restaurants

Growth Performance Measurement				
Years	Price	Earn.	Div.	Tot Ret
Last 1	-10.8	26.0	---	-10.8
Last 5	9.3	-.9	---	9.3
Last 10	19.9	12.2	---	19.9

Copyright 2012 Securities Research Company

Bonds $.0 Mil Com 7.507 Mil BV 4.31 /sh P/E 14.59 (Ind RESTR P/E 19.58) Ctry US

FARMER BROS CO (FARM)   **75% SCALE**

Roasting/selling coffee and related products to restaurants/hotels

Growth Performance Measurement				
Years	Price	Earn.	Div.	Tot Ret
Last 1	88.9	66.1	.0	88.9
Last 5	-8.9	---	-12.2	-7.1
Last 10	-7.3	---	-4.0	-5.3

Adj. for
10 for 1
5/11/04

Dividend
omitted
11/15/11

(0.59)   (0.91) (0.77) (0.43) (2.19) (3.01) (1.09)
(0.40)   (0.56) (0.81) (0.09) (1.50) (3.61) (2.17)
(0.02) 0.01   (0.19) (0.90) (0.20) (0.98) (2.62) (2.69) (1.02)

Copyright 2012 Securities Research Company

Bonds $.0 Mil Com 16.314 Mil BV 4.45 /sh P/E N/A (Ind PKGFD P/E 16.90) Ctry US

FARMERS CAP BK CORP (FFKT)   **85% SCALE**

Offers standard retail products to individuals and local businesses

Special
$0.11

Dividend
Omitted
07/15/10

Growth Performance Measurement				
Years	Price	Earn.	Div.	Tot Ret
Last 1	172.8	---	.0	172.8
Last 5	-14.6	-9.7	-21.2	-11.4
Last 10	-9.5	-5.0	-11.0	-4.3

(0.08) (0.36)
(0.20) (0.20)
(0.01) (0.08) (0.13)

Copyright 2012 Securities Research Company

Bonds $3.7 Mil Com 7.466 Mil BV 21.98 /sh P/E 9.88 (Ind RBANK P/E 10.51) Ctry US

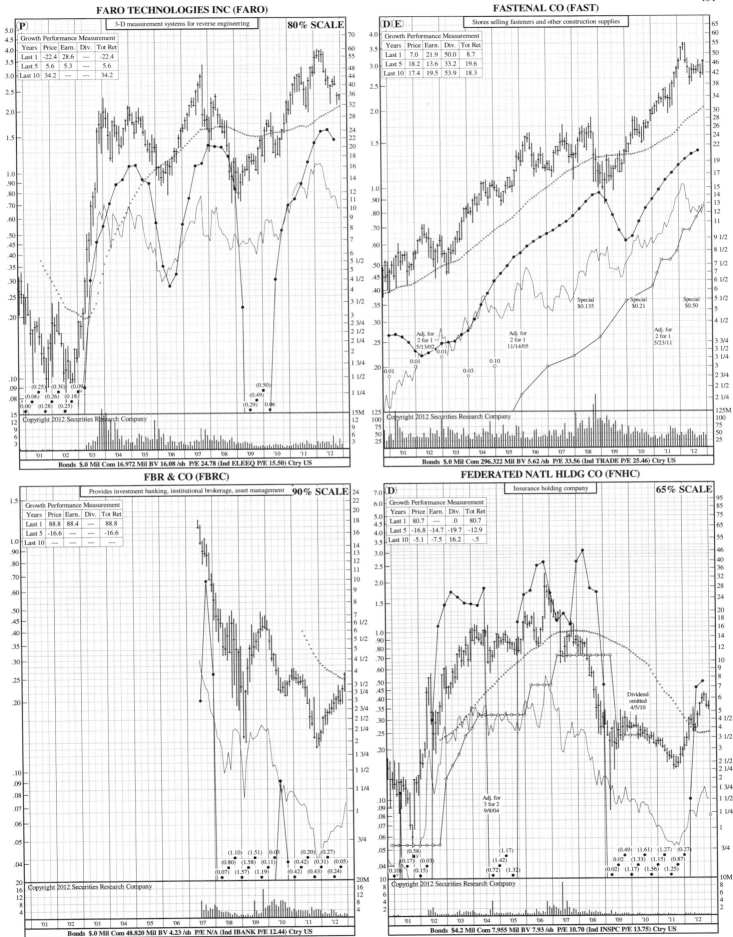

FARO TECHNOLOGIES INC (FARO)

3-D measurement systems for reverse engineering

80% SCALE

(P)

Growth Performance Measurement

Years	Price	Earn.	Div.	Tot Ret
Last 1	-22.4	28.6	---	-22.4
Last 5	5.6	5.3	---	5.6
Last 10	34.2	---	---	34.2

(0.25) (0.30) (0.09)
(0.06) (0.26) (0.18)
(0.00) (0.28) (0.25)
(0.50)
(0.49)
(0.29) 0.06

Copyright 2012 Securities Research Company

Bonds $.0 Mil Com 16.972 Mil BV 16.08 /sh P/E 24.78 (Ind ELEEQ P/E 15.50) Ctry US

FASTENAL CO (FAST)

Stores selling fasteners and other construction supplies

(D)(E)

Growth Performance Measurement

Years	Price	Earn.	Div.	Tot Ret
Last 1	7.0	21.9	50.0	8.7
Last 5	18.2	13.6	33.2	19.6
Last 10	17.4	19.5	53.9	18.3

Adj. for 2 for 1 5/13/02
0.01
0.01
Adj. for 2 for 1 11/14/05
0.10
0.03
0.01
Special $0.135
Special $0.21
Special $0.50
Adj. for 2 for 1 5/23/11

Copyright 2012 Securities Research Company

Bonds $.0 Mil Com 296.322 Mil BV 5.62 /sh P/E 33.56 (Ind TRADE P/E 25.46) Ctry US

FBR & CO (FBRC)

Provides investment banking, institutional brokerage, asset management

90% SCALE

Growth Performance Measurement

Years	Price	Earn.	Div.	Tot Ret
Last 1	88.8	88.4	---	88.8
Last 5	-16.6	---	---	-16.6
Last 10	---	---	---	---

(1.10) (1.51) 0.03 (0.20) (0.27)
(0.80) (1.58) (0.11) (0.42) (0.31) (0.05)
(0.07) (1.57) (1.19) (0.42) (0.43) (0.24)

Copyright 2012 Securities Research Company

Bonds $.0 Mil Com 48.820 Mil BV 4.23 /sh P/E N/A (Ind IBANK P/E 12.44) Ctry US

FEDERATED NATL HLDG CO (FNHC)

Insurance holding company

65% SCALE

(D)

Growth Performance Measurement

Years	Price	Earn.	Div.	Tot Ret
Last 1	80.7	---	.0	80.7
Last 5	-16.8	-14.7	-19.7	-12.9
Last 10	-5.1	-7.5	16.2	-.5

Adj. for 3 for 2 9/8/04

Dividend omitted 4/5/10

(0.58) (1.17) (0.49) (1.61) (1.27) (0.27)
(0.17) (0.03) (1.42) (0.02) (1.33) (1.15) (0.87)
(0.10) (0.15) (0.72) (1.32) (1.17) (1.56) (1.25)

Copyright 2012 Securities Research Company

Bonds $4.2 Mil Com 7.955 Mil BV 7.93 /sh P/E 10.70 (Ind INSPC P/E 13.75) Ctry US

132

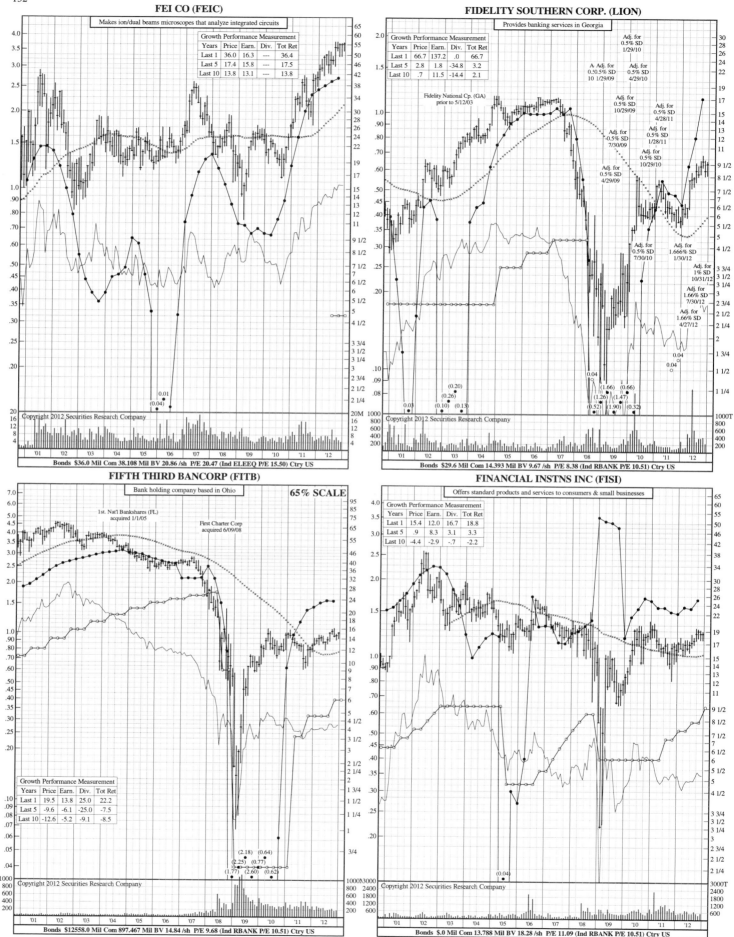

FEI CO (FEIC)

Makes ion/dual beams microscopes that analyze integrated circuits

Growth Performance Measurement				
Years	Price	Earn.	Div.	Tot Ret
Last 1	36.0	16.3	---	36.4
Last 5	17.4	15.8	---	17.5
Last 10	13.8	13.1	---	13.8

0.01
(0.04)

Copyright 2012 Securities Research Company

Bonds $36.0 Mil Com 38.108 Mil BV 20.86 /sh P/E 20.47 (Ind ELEEQ P/E 15.50) Ctry US

FIDELITY SOUTHERN CORP. (LION)

Provides banking services in Georgia

Growth Performance Measurement				
Years	Price	Earn.	Div.	Tot Ret
Last 1	66.7	137.2	.0	66.7
Last 5	2.8	1.8	-34.8	3.2
Last 10	.7	11.5	-14.4	2.1

Fidelity National Cp. (GA)
prior to 5/12/03

Adj. for
0.5% SD
1/29/10

A Adj. for
0.0.5% SD
10 1/29/09

Adj. for
0.5% SD
4/29/10

Adj. for
0.5% SD
10/29/09

Adj. for
0.5% SD
4/28/11

Adj. for
-0.5% SD
7/30/09

Adj. for
0.5% SD
1/28/11

Adj. for
0.5% SD
10/29/10

Adj. for
0.5% SD
4/29/09

Adj. for
0.5% SD
7/30/10

Adj. for
1.666% SD
1/30/12

Adj. for
1% SD
10/31/12

Adj. for
1.66% SD
7/30/12

Adj. for
1.66% SD
4/27/12

0.04

0.04

0.04

0.04

(1.66)   (0.66)
(1.26)   (1.47)
0.03   (0.20)   (0.52) (1.90) (0.32)
(0.10) (0.13)
(0.26)

Copyright 2012 Securities Research Company

Bonds $29.6 Mil Com 14.393 Mil BV 9.67 /sh P/E 8.38 (Ind RBANK P/E 10.51) Ctry US

FIFTH THIRD BANCORP (FITB)

Bank holding company based in Ohio

65% SCALE

1st. Nat'l Bankshares (FL)
acquired 1/1/05

First Charter Corp
acquired 6/09/08

Growth Performance Measurement				
Years	Price	Earn.	Div.	Tot Ret
Last 1	19.5	13.8	25.0	22.2
Last 5	-9.6	-6.1	-25.0	-7.5
Last 10	-12.6	-5.2	-9.1	-8.5

(2.18) (0.64)
(2.25) (0.77)
(1.77) (2.60) (0.62)

Copyright 2012 Securities Research Company

Bonds $12558.0 Mil Com 897.467 Mil BV 14.84 /sh P/E 9.68 (Ind RBANK P/E 10.51) Ctry US

FINANCIAL INSTNS INC (FISI)

Offers standard products and services to consumers & small businesses

Growth Performance Measurement				
Years	Price	Earn.	Div.	Tot Ret
Last 1	15.4	12.0	16.7	18.8
Last 5	.9	8.3	3.1	3.3
Last 10	-4.4	-2.9	-.7	-2.2

(0.04)

Copyright 2012 Securities Research Company

Bonds $.0 Mil Com 13.788 Mil BV 18.28 /sh P/E 11.09 (Ind RBANK P/E 10.51) Ctry US

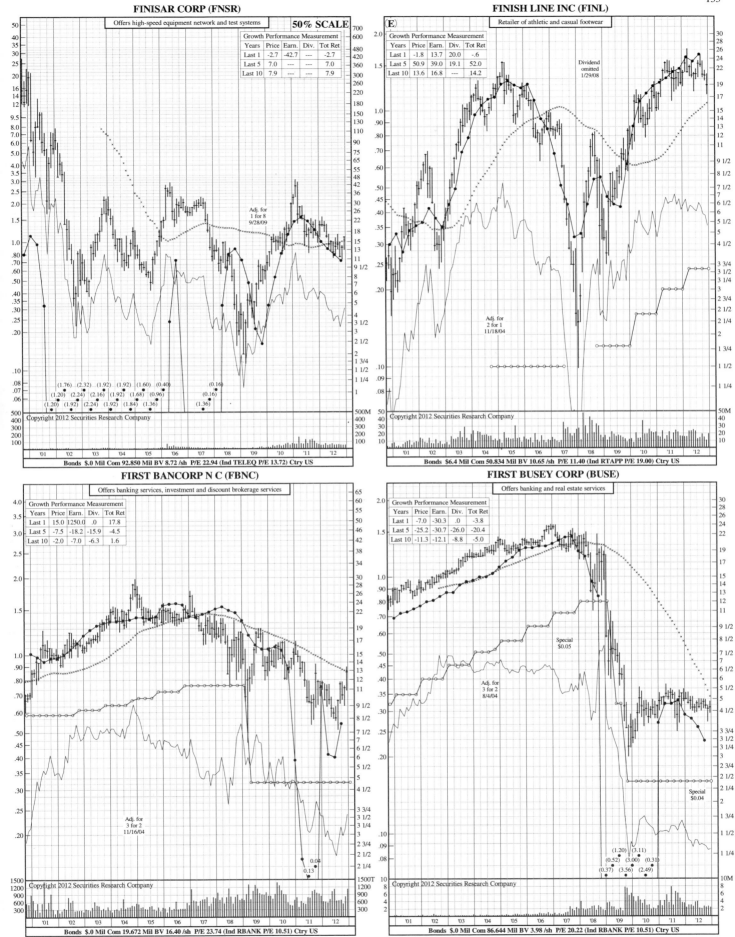

133

FINISAR CORP (FNSR)

Offers high-speed equipment network and test systems

50% SCALE

Growth Performance Measurement				
Years	Price	Earn.	Div.	Tot Ret
Last 1	-2.7	-42.7	---	-2.7
Last 5	7.0	---	---	7.0
Last 10	7.9	---	---	7.9

Adj. for
1 for 8
9/28/09

(1.76) (2.32) (1.92) (1.92) (1.60) (0.40) (0.16)
(1.20) (2.24) (2.16) (1.92) (1.68) (0.96) (0.16)
(1.20) (1.92) (2.24) (1.92) (1.84) (1.36) (1.36)

Copyright 2012 Securities Research Company

'01 '02 '03 '04 '05 '06 '07 '08 '09 '10 '11 '12

Bonds $.0 Mil Com 92.850 Mil BV 8.72 /sh P/E 22.94 (Ind TELEQ P/E 13.72) Ctry US

FINISH LINE INC (FINL)

(E) Retailer of athletic and casual footwear

Growth Performance Measurement				
Years	Price	Earn.	Div.	Tot Ret
Last 1	-1.8	13.7	20.0	-.6
Last 5	50.9	39.0	19.1	52.0
Last 10	13.6	16.8	---	14.2

Dividend
omitted
1/29/08

Adj. for
2 for 1
11/18/04

Copyright 2012 Securities Research Company

'01 '02 '03 '04 '05 '06 '07 '08 '09 '10 '11 '12

Bonds $6.4 Mil Com 50.834 Mil BV 10.65 /sh P/E 11.40 (Ind RTAPP P/E 19.00) Ctry US

FIRST BANCORP N C (FBNC)

Offers banking services, investment and discount brokerage services

Growth Performance Measurement				
Years	Price	Earn.	Div.	Tot Ret
Last 1	15.0	1250.0	.0	17.8
Last 5	-7.5	-18.2	-15.9	-4.5
Last 10	-2.0	-7.0	-6.3	1.6

Adj. for
3 for 2
11/16/04

0.04
0.13

Copyright 2012 Securities Research Company

'01 '02 '03 '04 '05 '06 '07 '08 '09 '10 '11 '12

Bonds $.0 Mil Com 19.672 Mil BV 16.40 /sh P/E 23.74 (Ind RBANK P/E 10.51) Ctry US

FIRST BUSEY CORP (BUSE)

Offers banking and real estate services

Growth Performance Measurement				
Years	Price	Earn.	Div.	Tot Ret
Last 1	-7.0	-30.3	.0	-3.8
Last 5	-25.2	-30.7	-26.0	-20.4
Last 10	-11.3	-12.1	-8.8	-5.0

Special
$0.05

Adj. for
3 for 2
8/4/04

Special
$0.04

(1.20) (3.11)
(0.52) (3.00) (0.31)
(0.37) (3.56) (2.49)

Copyright 2012 Securities Research Company

'01 '02 '03 '04 '05 '06 '07 '08 '09 '10 '11 '12

Bonds $.0 Mil Com 86.644 Mil BV 3.98 /sh P/E 20.22 (Ind RBANK P/E 10.51) Ctry US

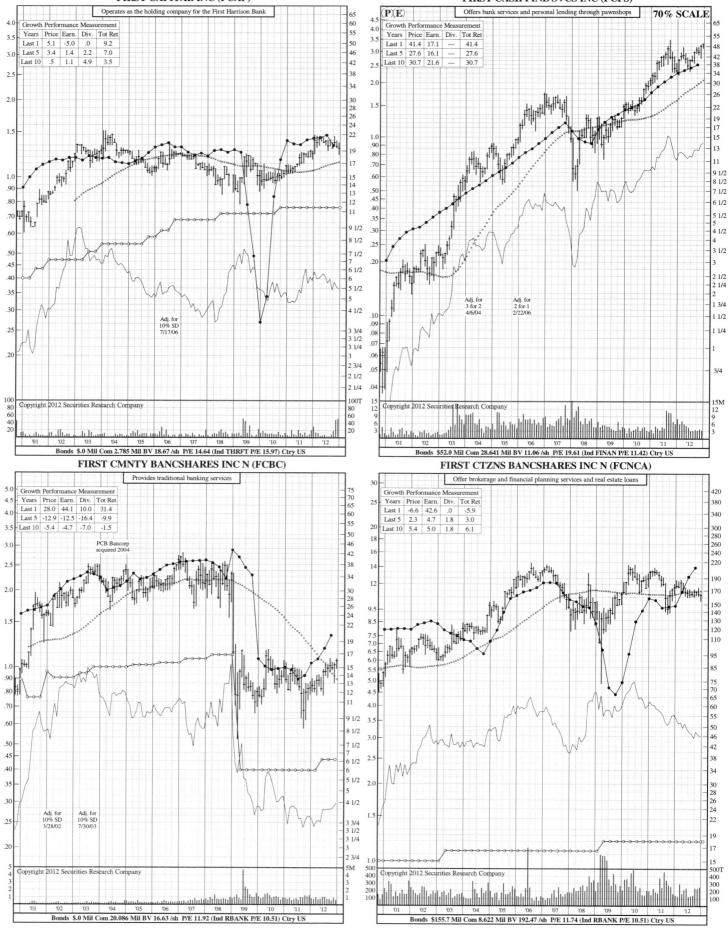

FIRST CAPITAL INC (FCAP)

Operates as the holding company for the First Harrison Bank

Growth Performance Measurement				
Years	Price	Earn.	Div.	Tot Ret
Last 1	5.1	-5.0	.0	9.2
Last 5	3.4	1.4	2.2	7.0
Last 10	.5	1.1	4.9	3.5

Adj. for
10% SD
7/17/06

Copyright 2012 Securities Research Company

Bonds $.0 Mil Com 2.785 Mil BV 18.67 /sh P/E 14.64 (Ind THRFT P/E 15.97) Ctry US

FIRST CASH FINL SVCS INC (FCFS)

Offers bank services and personal lending through pawnshops

70% SCALE

(P)(E)

Growth Performance Measurement				
Years	Price	Earn.	Div.	Tot Ret
Last 1	41.4	17.1	---	41.4
Last 5	27.6	16.1	---	27.6
Last 10	30.7	21.6	---	30.7

Adj. for
3 for 2
4/6/04

Adj. for
2 for 1
2/22/06

Copyright 2012 Securities Research Company

Bonds $52.0 Mil Com 28.641 Mil BV 11.06 /sh P/E 19.61 (Ind FINAN P/E 11.42) Ctry US

FIRST CMNTY BANCSHARES INC N (FCBC)

Provides traditional banking services

Growth Performance Measurement				
Years	Price	Earn.	Div.	Tot Ret
Last 1	28.0	44.1	10.0	31.4
Last 5	-12.9	-12.5	-16.4	-9.9
Last 10	-5.4	-4.7	-7.0	-1.5

PCB Bancorp
acquired 2004

Adj. for
10% SD
3/28/02

Adj. for
10% SD
7/30/03

Copyright 2012 Securities Research Company

Bonds $.0 Mil Com 20.086 Mil BV 16.63 /sh P/E 11.92 (Ind RBANK P/E 10.51) Ctry US

FIRST CTZNS BANCSHARES INC N (FCNCA)

Offer brokerage and financial planning services and real estate loans

Growth Performance Measurement				
Years	Price	Earn.	Div.	Tot Ret
Last 1	-6.6	42.6	.0	-5.9
Last 5	2.3	4.7	1.8	3.0
Last 10	5.4	5.0	1.8	6.1

Copyright 2012 Securities Research Company

Bonds $155.7 Mil Com 8.622 Mil BV 192.47 /sh P/E 11.74 (Ind RBANK P/E 10.51) Ctry US

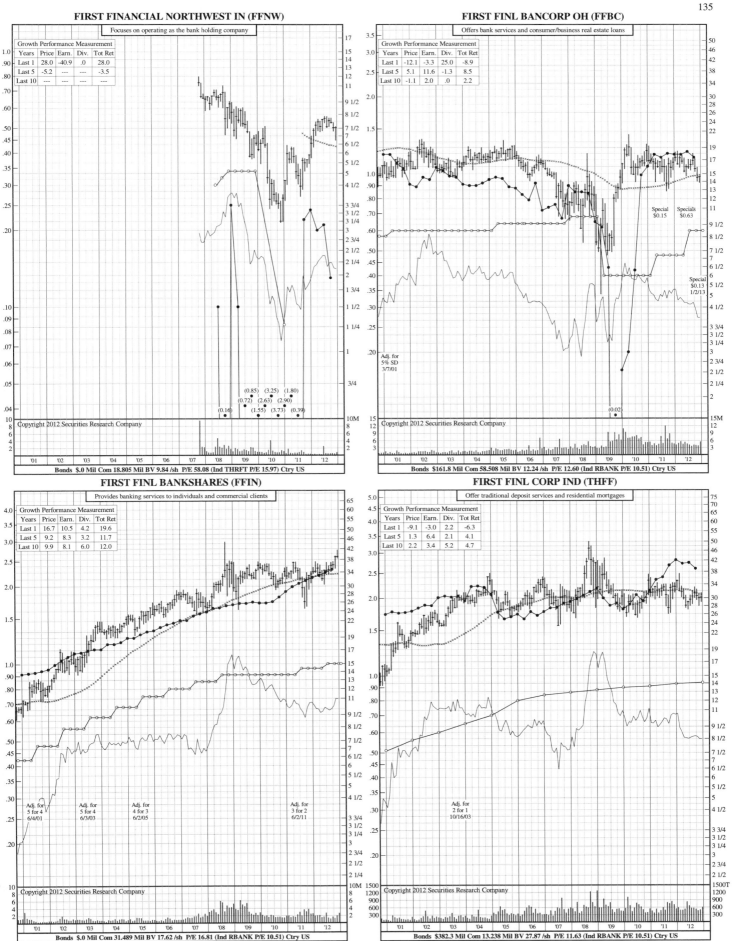

FIRST FINANCIAL NORTHWEST IN (FFNW)

Focuses on operating as the bank holding company

Growth Performance Measurement

Years	Price	Earn.	Div.	Tot Ret
Last 1	28.0	-40.9	.0	28.0
Last 5	-5.2	---	---	-3.5
Last 10	---	---	---	---

(0.85) (3.25) (1.80)
(0.72) (2.63) (2.90)
(0.16) (1.55) (3.73) (0.39)

Copyright 2012 Securities Research Company

Bonds $.0 Mil Com 18.805 Mil BV 9.84 /sh P/E 58.08 (Ind THRFT P/E 15.97) Ctry US

FIRST FINL BANCORP OH (FFBC)

Offers bank services and consumer/business real estate loans

Growth Performance Measurement

Years	Price	Earn.	Div.	Tot Ret
Last 1	-12.1	-3.3	25.0	-8.9
Last 5	5.1	11.6	-1.3	8.5
Last 10	-1.1	2.0	.0	2.2

Special
$0.15

Specials
$0.63

Special
$0.13
1/2/13

Adj. for
5% SD
3/7/01

(0.02)

Copyright 2012 Securities Research Company

Bonds $161.8 Mil Com 58.508 Mil BV 12.24 /sh P/E 12.60 (Ind RBANK P/E 10.51) Ctry US

FIRST FINL BANKSHARES (FFIN)

Provides banking services to individuals and commercial clients

Growth Performance Measurement

Years	Price	Earn.	Div.	Tot Ret
Last 1	16.7	10.5	4.2	19.6
Last 5	9.2	8.3	3.2	11.7
Last 10	9.9	8.1	6.0	12.0

Adj. for
5 for 4
6/4/01

Adj. for
5 for 4
6/3/03

Adj. for
4 for 3
6/2/05

Adj. for
3 for 2
6/2/11

Copyright 2012 Securities Research Company

Bonds $.0 Mil Com 31.489 Mil BV 17.62 /sh P/E 16.81 (Ind RBANK P/E 10.51) Ctry US

FIRST FINL CORP IND (THFF)

Offer traditional deposit services and residential mortgages

Growth Performance Measurement

Years	Price	Earn.	Div.	Tot Ret
Last 1	-9.1	-3.0	2.2	-6.3
Last 5	1.3	6.4	2.1	4.1
Last 10	2.2	3.4	5.2	4.7

Adj. for
2 for 1
10/16/03

Copyright 2012 Securities Research Company

Bonds $382.3 Mil Com 13.238 Mil BV 27.87 /sh P/E 11.63 (Ind RBANK P/E 10.51) Ctry US

136

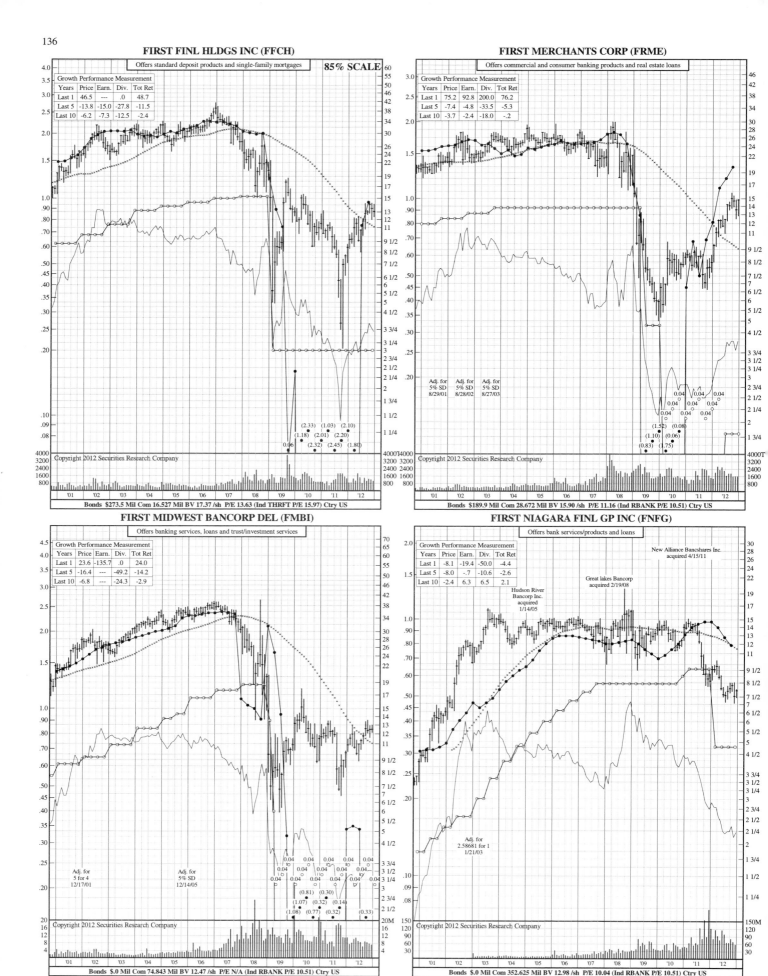

FIRST FINL HLDGS INC (FFCH)

Offers standard deposit products and single-family mortgages

85% SCALE

Growth Performance Measurement

Years	Price	Earn.	Div.	Tot Ret
Last 1	46.5	---	.0	48.7
Last 5	-13.8	-15.0	-27.8	-11.5
Last 10	-6.2	-7.3	-12.5	-2.4

(2.33) (1.03) (2.10)
(1.18) (2.01) (2.20)
0.06 (2.32) (2.45) (1.80)

Copyright 2012 Securities Research Company

Bonds $273.5 Mil Com 16.527 Mil BV 17.37 /sh P/E 13.63 (Ind THRFT P/E 15.97) Ctry US

FIRST MERCHANTS CORP (FRME)

Offers commercial and consumer banking products and real estate loans

Growth Performance Measurement

Years	Price	Earn.	Div.	Tot Ret
Last 1	75.2	92.8	200.0	76.2
Last 5	-7.4	-4.8	-33.5	-5.3
Last 10	-3.7	-2.4	-18.0	-.2

Adj. for 5% SD 8/29/01	Adj. for 5% SD 8/28/02	Adj. for 5% SD 8/27/03

0.04   0.04   0.04
0.04 0.04 0.04
0.04 0.04 0.04

(1.52) (0.08)
(1.10) (0.06)
(0.83) (1.75)

Copyright 2012 Securities Research Company

Bonds $189.9 Mil Com 28.672 Mil BV 15.90 /sh P/E 11.16 (Ind RBANK P/E 10.51) Ctry US

FIRST MIDWEST BANCORP DEL (FMBI)

Offers banking services, loans and trust/investment services

Growth Performance Measurement

Years	Price	Earn.	Div.	Tot Ret
Last 1	23.6	-135.7	.0	24.0
Last 5	-16.4	---	-49.2	-14.2
Last 10	-6.8	---	-24.3	-2.9

Adj. for 5 for 4 12/17/01	Adj. for 5% SD 12/14/05

0.04   0.04   0.04   0.04   0.04
0.04   0.04   0.04   0.04   0.04   0.04
0.04 0.04 0.04 0.04 0.04 0.04 0.03

(0.81) (0.30)
(1.07) (0.32) (0.14)
(1.08) (0.77) (0.32) (0.33)

Copyright 2012 Securities Research Company

Bonds $.0 Mil Com 74.843 Mil BV 12.47 /sh P/E N/A (Ind RBANK P/E 10.51) Ctry US

FIRST NIAGARA FINL GP INC (FNFG)

Offers bank services/products and loans

Growth Performance Measurement

Years	Price	Earn.	Div.	Tot Ret
Last 1	-8.1	-19.4	-50.0	-4.4
Last 5	-8.0	-.7	-10.6	-2.6
Last 10	-2.4	6.3	6.5	2.1

New Alliance Bancshares Inc. acquired 4/15/11

Great lakes Bancorp acquired 2/19/08

Hudson River Bancorp Inc. acquired 1/14/05

Adj. for 2.58681 for 1 1/21/03

Copyright 2012 Securities Research Company

Bonds $.0 Mil Com 352.625 Mil BV 12.98 /sh P/E 10.04 (Ind RBANK P/E 10.51) Ctry US

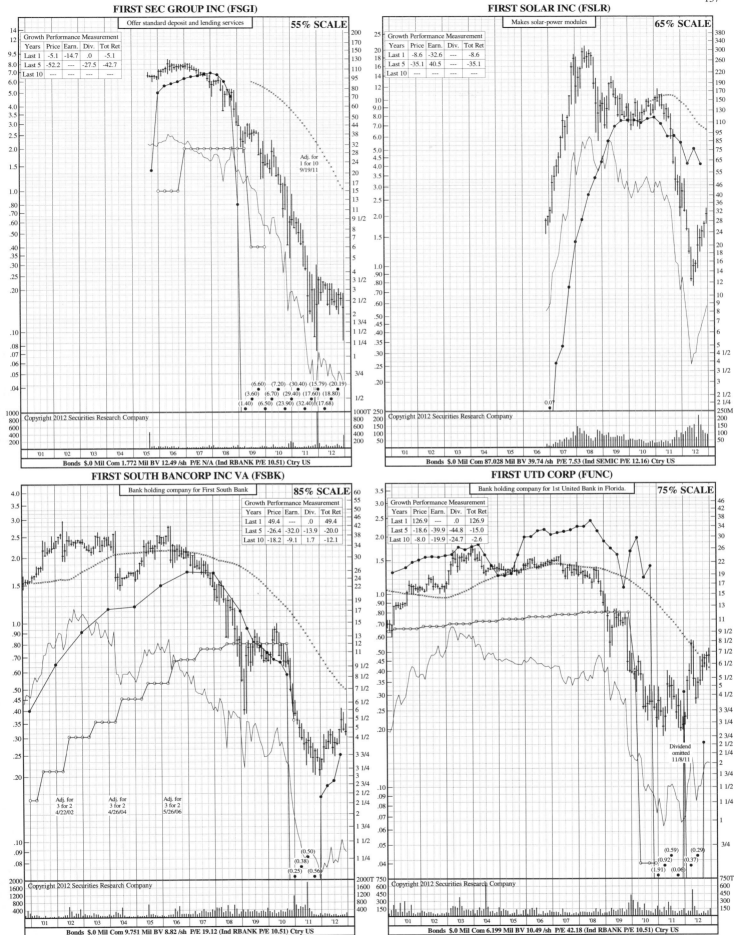

137

FIRST SEC GROUP INC (FSGI)

Offer standard deposit and lending services

55% SCALE

Growth Performance Measurement				
Years	Price	Earn.	Div.	Tot Ret
Last 1	-5.1	-14.7	.0	-5.1
Last 5	-52.2	---	-27.5	-42.7
Last 10	---	---	---	---

Adj. for
1 for 10
9/19/11

(6.60) (7.20) (30.40) (15.79) (20.19)
(3.60) (6.70) (29.40) (17.60) (18.80)
(1.40) (6.50) (23.90) (32.40) (17.68)

Copyright 2012 Securities Research Company

Bonds $.0 Mil Com 1.772 Mil BV 12.49 /sh P/E N/A (Ind RBANK P/E 10.51) Ctry US

FIRST SOLAR INC (FSLR)

Makes solar-power modules

65% SCALE

Growth Performance Measurement				
Years	Price	Earn.	Div.	Tot Ret
Last 1	-8.6	-32.6	---	-8.6
Last 5	-35.1	40.5	---	-35.1
Last 10	---	---	---	---

0.07

Copyright 2012 Securities Research Company

Bonds $.0 Mil Com 87.028 Mil BV 39.74 /sh P/E 7.53 (Ind SEMIC P/E 12.16) Ctry US

FIRST SOUTH BANCORP INC VA (FSBK)

Bank holding company for First South Bank

85% SCALE

Growth Performance Measurement				
Years	Price	Earn.	Div.	Tot Ret
Last 1	49.4	---	.0	49.4
Last 5	-26.4	-32.0	-13.9	-20.0
Last 10	-18.2	-9.1	1.7	-12.1

Adj. for
3 for 2
4/22/02

Adj. for
3 for 2
4/26/04

Adj. for
3 for 2
5/26/06

(0.50)
(0.38)
(0.25) (0.56)

Copyright 2012 Securities Research Company

Bonds $.0 Mil Com 9.751 Mil BV 8.82 /sh P/E 19.12 (Ind RBANK P/E 10.51) Ctry US

FIRST UTD CORP (FUNC)

Bank holding company for 1st United Bank in Florida.

75% SCALE

Growth Performance Measurement				
Years	Price	Earn.	Div.	Tot Ret
Last 1	126.9	---	.0	126.9
Last 5	-18.6	-39.9	-44.8	-15.0
Last 10	-8.0	-19.9	-24.7	-2.6

Dividend
omitted
11/8/11

(0.59) (0.29)
(0.92) (0.37)
(1.91) (0.06)

Copyright 2012 Securities Research Company

Bonds $.0 Mil Com 6.199 Mil BV 10.49 /sh P/E 42.18 (Ind RBANK P/E 10.51) Ctry US

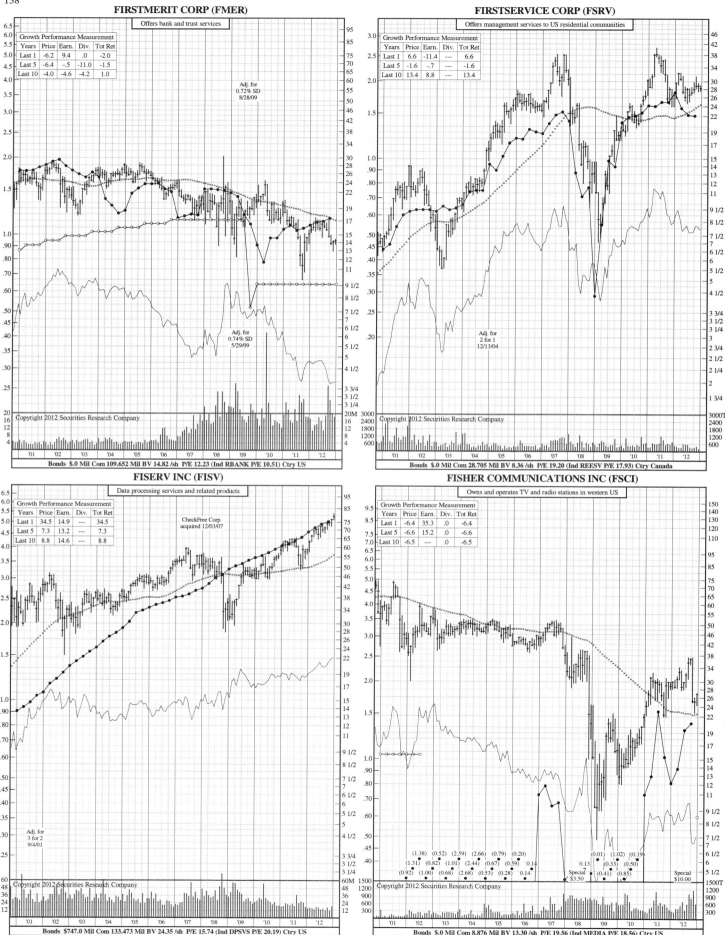

138

FIRSTMERIT CORP (FMER)

Offers bank and trust services

Growth Performance Measurement

Years	Price	Earn.	Div.	Tot Ret
Last 1	-6.2	9.4	.0	-2.0
Last 5	-6.4	-.5	-11.0	-1.5
Last 10	-4.0	-4.6	-4.2	1.0

Adj. for
0.72% SD
8/28/09

Adj. for
0.74% SD
5/29/09

Copyright 2012 Securities Research Company

Bonds $.0 Mil Com 109.652 Mil BV 14.82 /sh P/E 12.23 (Ind RBANK P/E 10.51) Ctry US

FIRSTSERVICE CORP (FSRV)

Offers management services to US residential communities

Growth Performance Measurement

Years	Price	Earn.	Div.	Tot Ret
Last 1	6.6	-11.4	---	6.6
Last 5	-1.6	-.7	---	-1.6
Last 10	13.4	8.8	---	13.4

Adj. for
2 for 1
12/13/04

Copyright 2012 Securities Research Company

Bonds $.0 Mil Com 28.705 Mil BV 8.36 /sh P/E 19.20 (Ind REESV P/E 17.93) Ctry Canada

FISERV INC (FISV)

Data processing services and related products

Growth Performance Measurement

Years	Price	Earn.	Div.	Tot Ret
Last 1	34.5	14.9	---	34.5
Last 5	7.3	13.2	---	7.3
Last 10	8.8	14.6	---	8.8

CheckFree Corp.
acquired 12/03/07

Adj. for
3 for 2
9/4/01

Copyright 2012 Securities Research Company

Bonds $747.0 Mil Com 133.473 Mil BV 24.35 /sh P/E 15.74 (Ind DPSVS P/E 20.19) Ctry US

FISHER COMMUNICATIONS INC (FSCI)

Owns and operates TV and radio stations in western US

Growth Performance Measurement

Years	Price	Earn.	Div.	Tot Ret
Last 1	-6.4	35.3	.0	-6.4
Last 5	-6.6	15.2	---	-6.6
Last 10	-6.5	---	.0	-6.5

(1.38) (0.52) (2.59) (2.66) (0.79) (0.20)   (0.01) (1.02) (0.19)
(1.31) (0.82) (1.01) (2.44) (0.67) (0.59) 0.14   0.13 (0.33) (0.50)
(0.92) (1.00) (0.68) (2.68) (0.53) (0.28) 0.14   Special (0.41) (0.85)   Special
                                                  $3.50 $10.00

Copyright 2012 Securities Research Company

Bonds $.0 Mil Com 8.876 Mil BV 13.30 /sh P/E 19.56 (Ind MEDIA P/E 18.56) Ctry US

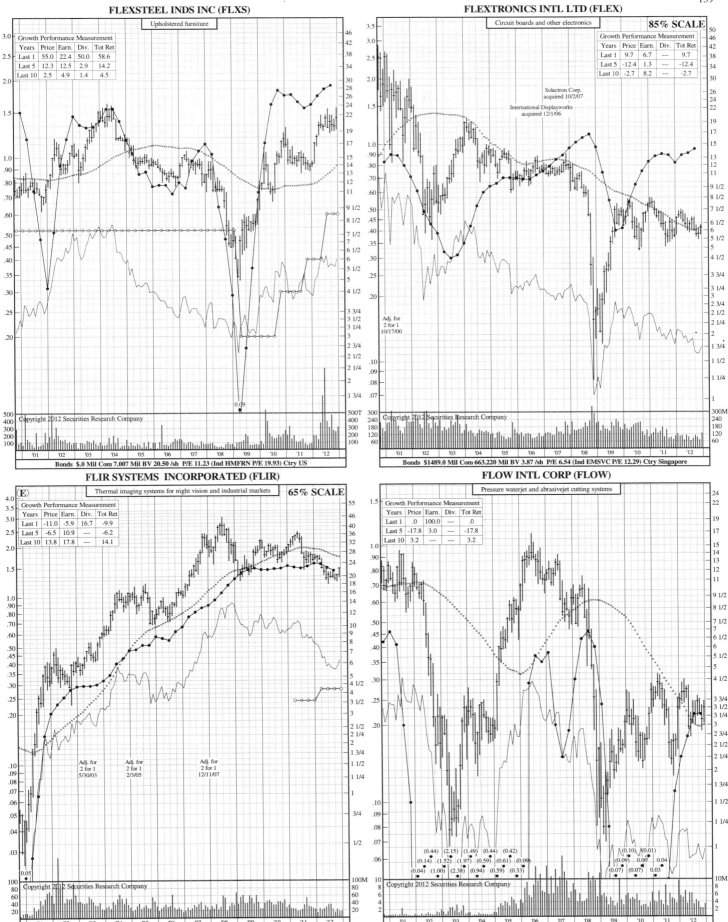

FLEXSTEEL INDS INC (FLXS)
Upholstered furniture

Growth Performance Measurement

Years	Price	Earn.	Div.	Tot Ret
Last 1	55.0	22.4	50.0	58.6
Last 5	12.3	12.5	2.9	14.2
Last 10	2.5	4.9	1.4	4.5

0.09

Copyright 2012 Securities Research Company

Bonds $.0 Mil Com 7.007 Mil BV 20.50 /sh P/E 11.23 (Ind HMFRN P/E 19.93) Ctry US

FLEXTRONICS INTL LTD (FLEX)
Circuit boards and other electronics

85% SCALE

Growth Performance Measurement

Years	Price	Earn.	Div.	Tot Ret
Last 1	9.7	6.7	---	9.7
Last 5	-12.4	1.3	---	-12.4
Last 10	-2.7	8.2	---	-2.7

Solectron Corp.
acquired 10/2/07

International Displayworks
acquired 12/1/06

Adj. for
2 for 1
10/17/00

Copyright 2012 Securities Research Company

Bonds $1489.0 Mil Com 663.220 Mil BV 3.87 /sh P/E 6.54 (Ind EMSVC P/E 12.29) Ctry Singapore

FLIR SYSTEMS INCORPORATED (FLIR)
(E) Thermal imaging systems for night vision and industrial markets

65% SCALE

Growth Performance Measurement

Years	Price	Earn.	Div.	Tot Ret
Last 1	-11.0	-5.9	16.7	-9.9
Last 5	-6.5	10.9	---	-6.2
Last 10	13.8	17.8		14.1

Adj. for
2 for 1
5/30/03

Adj. for
2 for 1
2/3/05

Adj. for
2 for 1
12/11/07

(0.05)

Copyright 2012 Securities Research Company

Bonds $1.5 Mil Com 150.026 Mil BV 10.68 /sh P/E 15.50 (Ind ELEEQ P/E 15.50) Ctry US

FLOW INTL CORP (FLOW)
Pressure waterjet and abrasivejet cutting systems

Growth Performance Measurement

Years	Price	Earn.	Div.	Tot Ret
Last 1	.0	100.0	---	.0
Last 5	-17.8	3.0	---	-17.8
Last 10	3.2	---		3.2

(0.44) (2.15) (1.49) (0.44) (0.42)   (0.10) (0.01)
(0.14) (1.52) (1.97) (0.59) (0.61) (0.09)   (0.09) (0.04)
(0.04) (1.00) (2.38) (0.94) (0.59) (0.33)   (0.07) (0.07) (0.03)

Copyright 2012 Securities Research Company

Bonds $70.4 Mil Com 48.417 Mil BV 2.09 /sh P/E 15.91 (Ind MACHN P/E 14.49) Ctry US

FLUSHING FINL CORP (FFIC)

Banking and loan services in New York state

Growth Performance Measurement				
Years	Price	Earn.	Div.	Tot Ret
Last 1	21.5	-6.8	.0	25.6
Last 5	-.9	.9	1.6	2.2
Last 10	3.5	1.4	8.0	6.1

Adj. for
3 for 2
8/31/01

Adj. for
3 for 2
12/16/03

Copyright 2012 Securities Research Company

Bonds $452.0 Mil Com 30.896 Mil BV 14.27 /sh P/E 13.95 (Ind THRFT P/E 15.97) Ctry US

FORMFACTOR INC (FORM)

Memory chip testing equipment

85% SCALE

Growth Performance Measurement				
Years	Price	Earn.	Div.	Tot Ret
Last 1	-9.9	10.2	---	-9.9
Last 5	-32.7	---	---	-32.7
Last 10	---	---	---	---

(1.62) (1.95) (2.50) (1.52) (1.13)
(1.40) (1.84) (2.35) (1.95) (1.16) (0.97)
(0.61) (1.70) (2.14) (2.33) (1.08) (1.01)

Copyright 2012 Securities Research Company

Bonds $.0 Mil Com 53.269 Mil BV 6.42 /sh P/E N/A (Ind SEMIQ P/E 13.46) Ctry US

FORRESTER RESH INC (FORR)

Technology research and consulting services

Growth Performance Measurement				
Years	Price	Earn.	Div.	Tot Ret
Last 1	-21.0	10.6	---	-19.8
Last 5	-.9	2.8	---	-.6
Last 10	5.6	7.8	---	5.7

Special
$3.00

Copyright 2012 Securities Research Company

Bonds $.0 Mil Com 22.295 Mil BV 13.28 /sh P/E 21.44 (Ind ITCON P/E 14.16) Ctry US

FORWARD AIR CORP (FWRD)

Provides transportation services to air freight forwarders

Growth Performance Measurement				
Years	Price	Earn.	Div.	Tot Ret
Last 1	9.2	14.5	42.9	10.2
Last 5	2.4	3.3	7.4	3.2
Last 10	10.5	11.5	---	11.1

Adj. for
3 for 2
4/4/05

Copyright 2012 Securities Research Company

Bonds $4.8 Mil Com 29.377 Mil BV 11.55 /sh P/E 20.12 (Ind AIRFR P/E 16.58) Ctry US

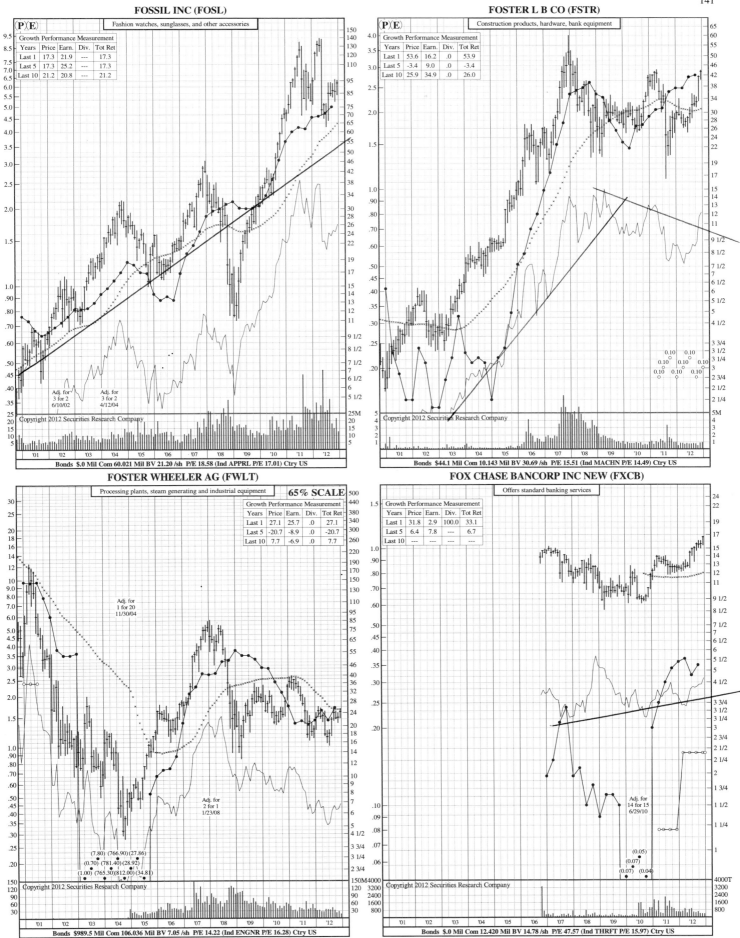

FOSSIL INC (FOSL)

Fashion watches, sunglasses, and other accessories

(P)(E)

Growth Performance Measurement				
Years	Price	Earn.	Div.	Tot Ret
Last 1	17.3	21.9	---	17.3
Last 5	17.3	25.2	---	17.3
Last 10	21.2	20.8	---	21.2

Adj. for
3 for 2
6/10/02

Adj. for
3 for 2
4/12/04

Copyright 2012 Securities Research Company

Bonds $.0 Mil Com 60.021 Mil BV 21.20 /sh P/E 18.58 (Ind APPRL P/E 17.01) Ctry US

FOSTER L B CO (FSTR)

Construction products, hardware, bank equipment

(P)(E)

Growth Performance Measurement				
Years	Price	Earn.	Div.	Tot Ret
Last 1	53.6	16.2	.0	53.9
Last 5	-3.4	9.0	.0	-3.4
Last 10	25.9	34.9	.0	26.0

0.10   0.10
0.10   0.10   0.10
0.10   0.10   0.10

Copyright 2012 Securities Research Company

Bonds $44.1 Mil Com 10.143 Mil BV 30.69 /sh P/E 15.51 (Ind MACHN P/E 14.49) Ctry US

FOSTER WHEELER AG (FWLT)

Processing plants, steam generating and industrial equipment

65% SCALE

Growth Performance Measurement				
Years	Price	Earn.	Div.	Tot Ret
Last 1	27.1	25.7	.0	27.1
Last 5	-20.7	-8.9	.0	-20.7
Last 10	7.7	-6.9	.0	7.7

Adj. for
1 for 20
11/30/04

Adj. for
2 for 1
1/23/08

(7.80) (766.90) (27.86)
(0.70) (781.40) (28.92)
(1.00) (765.30) (812.00) (34.81)

Copyright 2012 Securities Research Company

Bonds $989.5 Mil Com 106.036 Mil BV 7.05 /sh P/E 14.22 (Ind ENGNR P/E 16.28) Ctry US

FOX CHASE BANCORP INC NEW (FXCB)

Offers standard banking services

Growth Performance Measurement				
Years	Price	Earn.	Div.	Tot Ret
Last 1	31.8	2.9	100.0	33.1
Last 5	6.4	7.8	---	6.7
Last 10	---	---	---	---

Adj. for
14 for 15
6/29/10

(0.05)
(0.07)
(0.07) (0.04)

Copyright 2012 Securities Research Company

Bonds $.0 Mil Com 12.420 Mil BV 14.78 /sh P/E 47.57 (Ind THRFT P/E 15.97) Ctry US

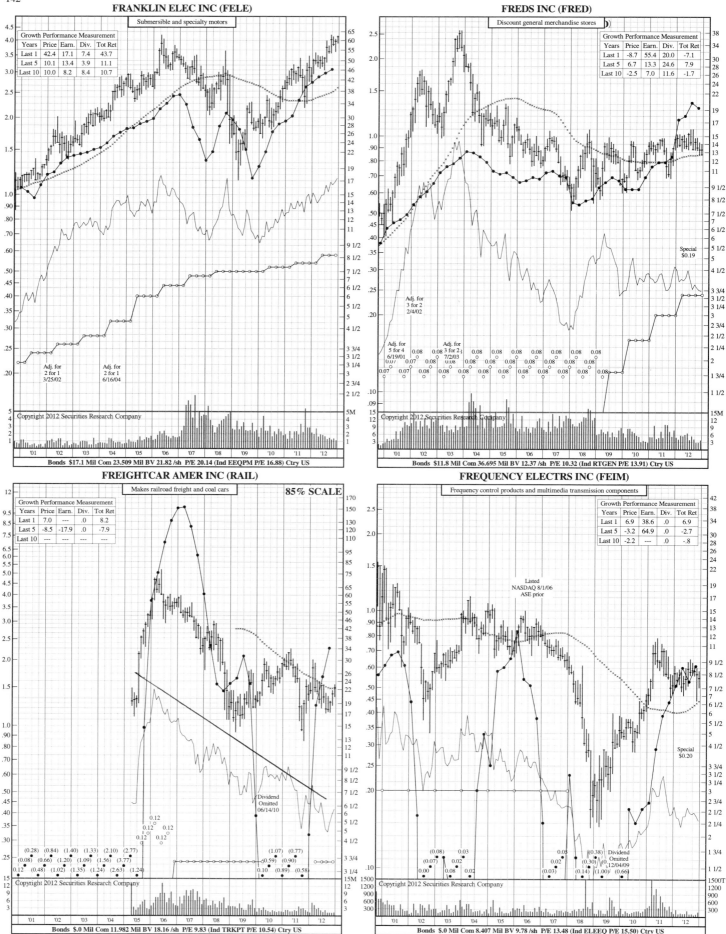

142

FRANKLIN ELEC INC (FELE)

Submersible and specialty motors

Growth Performance Measurement				
Years	Price	Earn.	Div.	Tot Ret
Last 1	42.4	17.1	7.4	43.7
Last 5	10.1	13.4	3.9	11.1
Last 10	10.0	8.2	8.4	10.7

Adj. for
2 for 1
3/25/02

Adj. for
2 for 1
6/16/04

Copyright 2012 Securities Research Company

Bonds $17.1 Mil Com 23.509 Mil BV 21.82 /sh P/E 20.14 (Ind EEQPM P/E 16.88) Ctry US

FREDS INC (FRED)

Discount general merchandise stores

Growth Performance Measurement				
Years	Price	Earn.	Div.	Tot Ret
Last 1	-8.7	55.4	20.0	-7.1
Last 5	6.7	13.3	24.6	7.9
Last 10	-2.5	7.0	11.6	-1.7

Special
$0.19

Adj. for
3 for 2
2/4/02

Adj. for
5 for 4
6/19/01

Adj. for
3 for 2
7/2/03

.07 .07   .07 .08 .08 .08 .08 .08 .08 .08 .08 .08 .08 .08
.07 .07   .08 .08 .08 .08 .08 .08 .08 .08 .08 .08 .08
.07 .07   .08

Copyright 2012 Securities Research Company

Bonds $11.8 Mil Com 36.695 Mil BV 12.37 /sh P/E 10.32 (Ind RTGEN P/E 13.91) Ctry US

FREIGHTCAR AMER INC (RAIL)

Makes railroad freight and coal cars

85% SCALE

Growth Performance Measurement				
Years	Price	Earn.	Div.	Tot Ret
Last 1	7.0	---	.0	8.2
Last 5	-8.5	-17.9	.0	-7.9
Last 10	---	---	---	---

Dividend
Omitted
06/14/10

.12 .12
.12 .12
.12 .12
.12 .12

(0.28) (0.84) (1.40) (1.33) (2.10) (2.77)   (1.07) (0.77)
(0.08) (0.66) (1.20) (1.09) (1.56) (3.77)   (0.59) (0.90)
.12 (0.48) (1.02) (1.35) (1.24) (2.63) (1.24)   .10 (0.89) (0.58)

Copyright 2012 Securities Research Company

Bonds $.0 Mil Com 11.982 Mil BV 18.16 /sh P/E 9.83 (Ind TRKPT P/E 10.54) Ctry US

FREQUENCY ELECTRS INC (FEIM)

Frequency control products and multimedia transmission components

Growth Performance Measurement				
Years	Price	Earn.	Div.	Tot Ret
Last 1	6.9	38.6	.0	6.9
Last 5	-3.2	64.9	.0	-2.7
Last 10	-2.2	---	.0	-.8

Listed
NASDAQ 8/1/06
ASE prior

Special
$0.20

Dividend
Omitted
12/04/09

(0.08) 0.03   0.05 (0.38)
(0.07) 0.02   0.02 (0.30) (1.00)
0.00 0.08 0.02   (0.03) (0.14) (1.00) (0.66)

Copyright 2012 Securities Research Company

Bonds $.0 Mil Com 8.407 Mil BV 9.78 /sh P/E 13.48 (Ind ELEEQ P/E 15.50) Ctry US

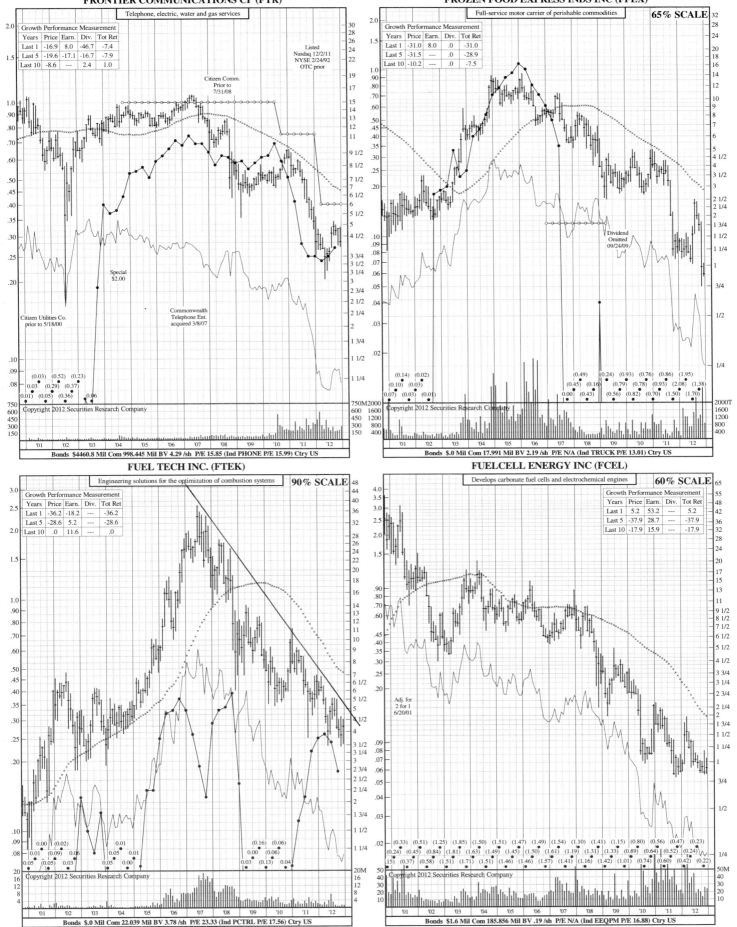

FRONTIER COMMUNICATIONS CP (FTR)

Telephone, electric, water and gas services

Growth Performance Measurement

Years	Price	Earn.	Div.	Tot Ret
Last 1	-16.9	8.0	-46.7	-7.4
Last 5	-19.6	-17.1	-16.7	-7.9
Last 10	-8.6	---	2.4	1.0

Listed
Nasdaq 12/2/11
NYSE 2/24/92
OTC prior

Citizen Comm.
Prior to
7/31/08

Special
$2.00

Citizen Utilities Co.
prior to 5/18/00

Commonwealth
Telephone Ent.
acquired 3/8/07

(0.03) (0.52) (0.23)
0.03 (0.29) (0.37)
(0.01) (0.05) (0.36) (0.06)

Copyright 2012 Securities Research Company

Bonds $4460.8 Mil Com 998.445 Mil BV 4.29 /sh P/E 15.85 (Ind PHONE P/E 15.99) Ctry US

FROZEN FOOD EXPRESS INDS INC (FFEX)

Full-service motor carrier of perishable commodities

65% SCALE

Growth Performance Measurement

Years	Price	Earn.	Div.	Tot Ret
Last 1	-31.0	8.0	.0	-31.0
Last 5	-31.5	---	.0	-28.9
Last 10	-10.2	---	.0	-7.5

Dividend
Omitted
09/24/09

(0.14) (0.02)   (0.49) (0.24) (0.93) (0.76) (0.86) (1.95)
(0.10) (0.03)   (0.45) (0.16) (0.79) (0.78) (0.93) (2.08) (1.38)
(0.07) (0.03) (0.01) 0.00 (0.43) (0.56) (0.82) (0.70) (1.50) (1.70)

Copyright 2012 Securities Research Company

Bonds $.0 Mil Com 17.991 Mil BV 2.19 /sh P/E N/A (Ind TRUCK P/E 13.01) Ctry US

FUEL TECH INC. (FTEK)

Engineering solutions for the optimization of combustion systems

90% SCALE

Growth Performance Measurement

Years	Price	Earn.	Div.	Tot Ret
Last 1	-36.2	-18.2	---	-36.2
Last 5	-28.6	5.2	---	-28.6
Last 10	.0	11.6	---	.0

0.00 (0.02)   (0.16) (0.06)
0.01 (0.09) 0.06   0.01   0.00 (0.06)
0.05 (0.05) 0.03 0.05 0.00 0.03 (0.13) 0.04

Copyright 2012 Securities Research Company

Bonds $.0 Mil Com 22.039 Mil BV 3.78 /sh P/E 23.33 (Ind PCTRL P/E 17.56) Ctry US

FUELCELL ENERGY INC (FCEL)

Develops carbonate fuel cells and electrochemical engines

60% SCALE

Growth Performance Measurement

Years	Price	Earn.	Div.	Tot Ret
Last 1	5.2	53.2	---	5.2
Last 5	-37.9	28.7	---	-37.9
Last 10	-17.9	15.9	---	-17.9

Adj. for
2 for 1
6/20/01

(0.33) (0.51) (1.25) (1.85) (1.50) (1.51) (1.47) (1.49) (1.54) (1.10) (1.41) (1.15) (0.80) (0.56) (0.47) (0.23)
(0.24) (0.45) (0.84) (1.81) (1.63) (1.49) (1.45) (1.50) (1.61) (1.19) (1.31) (1.33) (0.89) (0.64) (0.52) (0.24)
(15) (0.37) (0.58) (1.51) (1.71) (1.51) (1.46) (1.46) (1.57) (1.41) (1.16) (1.42) (1.01) (0.74) (0.60) (0.42) (0.22)

Copyright 2012 Securities Research Company

Bonds $1.6 Mil Com 185.856 Mil BV .19 /sh P/E N/A (Ind EEQPM P/E 16.88) Ctry US

144

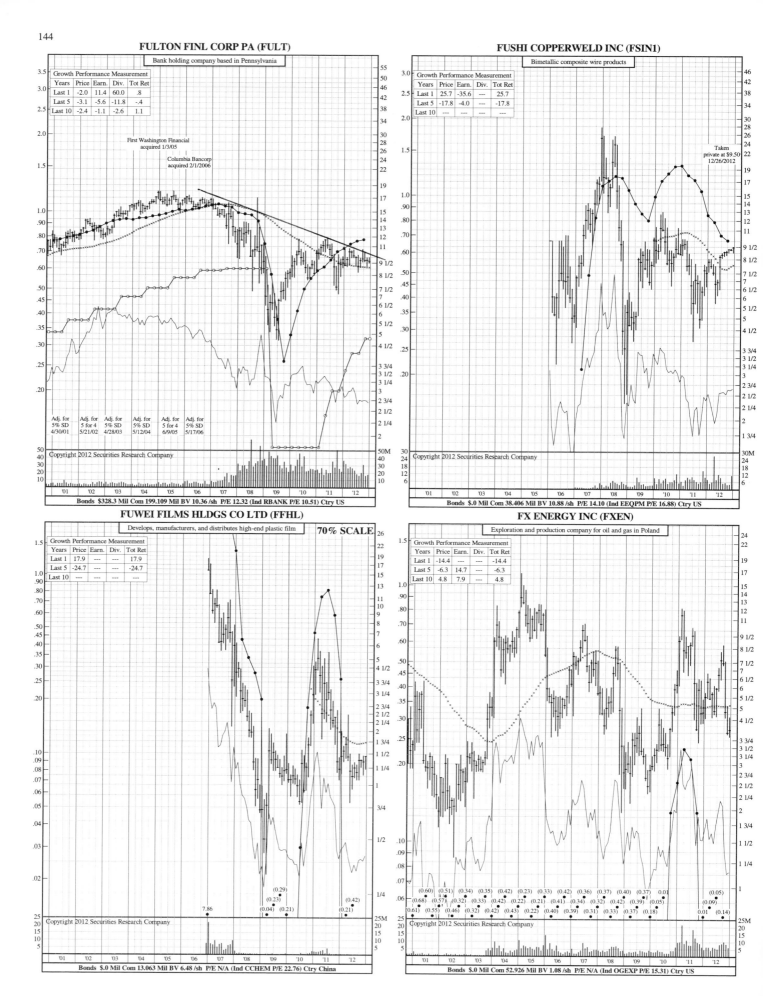

FULTON FINL CORP PA (FULT)

Bank holding company based in Pennsylvania

Growth Performance Measurement				
Years	Price	Earn.	Div.	Tot Ret
Last 1	-2.0	11.4	60.0	.8
Last 5	-3.1	-5.6	-11.8	-.4
Last 10	-2.4	-1.1	-2.6	1.1

First Washington Financial
acquired 1/3/05

Columbia Bancorp
acquired 2/1/2006

Adj. for 5% SD 4/30/01
Adj. for 5 for 4 5/21/02
Adj. for 5% SD 4/28/03
Adj. for 5% SD 5/12/04
Adj. for 5 for 4 6/9/05
Adj. for 5% SD 5/17/06

Copyright 2012 Securities Research Company

Bonds $328.3 Mil Com 199.109 Mil BV 10.36 /sh P/E 12.32 (Ind RBANK P/E 10.51) Ctry US

FUSHI COPPERWELD INC (FSIN1)

Bimetallic composite wire products

Growth Performance Measurement				
Years	Price	Earn.	Div.	Tot Ret
Last 1	25.7	-35.6	---	25.7
Last 5	-17.8	-4.0	---	-17.8
Last 10	---	---	---	---

Taken
private at $9.50
12/26/2012

Copyright 2012 Securities Research Company

Bonds $.0 Mil Com 38.406 Mil BV 10.88 /sh P/E 14.10 (Ind EEQPM P/E 16.88) Ctry US

FUWEI FILMS HLDGS CO LTD (FFHL)

Develops, manufacturers, and distributes high-end plastic film   **70% SCALE**

Growth Performance Measurement				
Years	Price	Earn.	Div.	Tot Ret
Last 1	17.9	---	---	17.9
Last 5	-24.7	---	---	-24.7
Last 10	---	---	---	---

7.86

(0.29)
(0.23)
(0.04) (0.21)

(0.42)
(0.21)

Copyright 2012 Securities Research Company

Bonds $.0 Mil Com 13.063 Mil BV 6.48 /sh P/E N/A (Ind CCHEM P/E 22.76) Ctry China

FX ENERGY INC (FXEN)

Exploration and production company for oil and gas in Poland

Growth Performance Measurement				
Years	Price	Earn.	Div.	Tot Ret
Last 1	-14.4	---	---	-14.4
Last 5	-6.3	14.7	---	-6.3
Last 10	4.8	7.9	---	4.8

(0.60) (0.51) (0.34) (0.35) (0.42) (0.23) (0.33) (0.42) (0.36) (0.37) (0.40) (0.37) 0.01 (0.05)
(0.68) (0.57) (0.32) (0.33) (0.42) (0.22) (0.21) (0.41) (0.32) (0.42) (0.39) (0.05) (0.09)
(0.61) (0.55) (0.46) (0.32) (0.42) (0.43) (0.22) (0.40) (0.39) (0.31) (0.33) (0.37) (0.18) 0.01 (0.14)

Copyright 2012 Securities Research Company

Bonds $.0 Mil Com 52.926 Mil BV 1.08 /sh P/E N/A (Ind OGEXP P/E 15.31) Ctry US

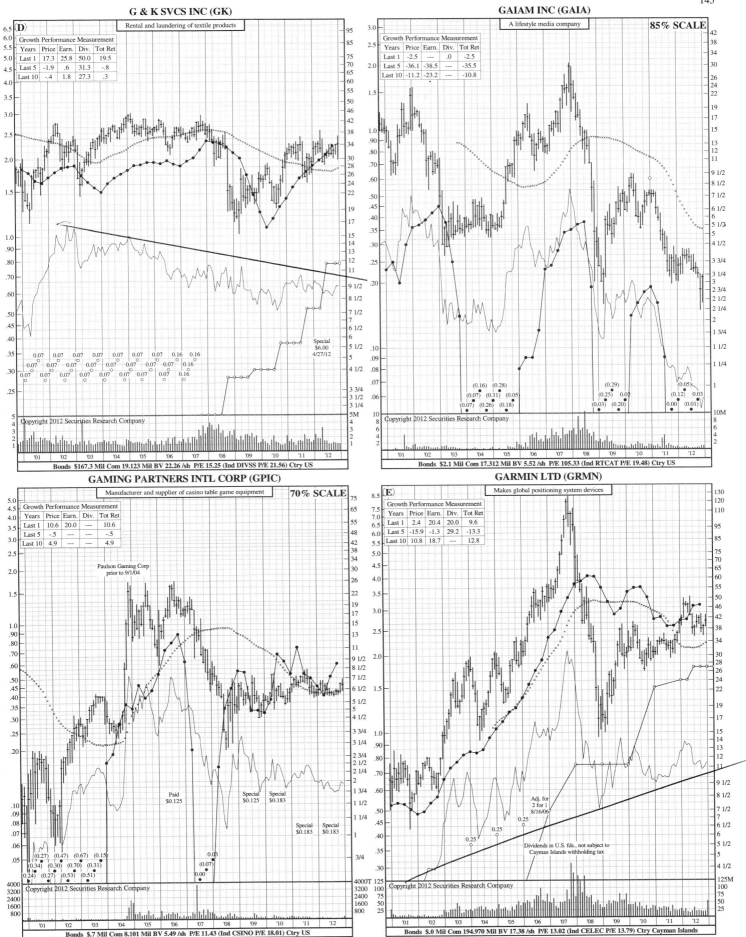

G & K SVCS INC (GK)

Rental and laundering of textile products

Growth Performance Measurement				
Years	Price	Earn.	Div.	Tot Ret
Last 1	17.3	25.8	50.0	19.5
Last 5	-1.9	.6	31.3	-.8
Last 10	-.4	1.8	27.3	.3

Special
$6.00
4/27/12

Copyright 2012 Securities Research Company

Bonds $167.3 Mil Com 19.123 Mil BV 22.26 /sh P/E 15.25 (Ind DIVSS P/E 21.56) Ctry US

GAIAM INC (GAIA)

A lifestyle media company

85% SCALE

Growth Performance Measurement				
Years	Price	Earn.	Div.	Tot Ret
Last 1	-2.5	---	.0	-2.5
Last 5	-36.1	-38.5	---	-35.5
Last 10	-11.2	-23.2	---	-10.8

Copyright 2012 Securities Research Company

Bonds $2.1 Mil Com 17.312 Mil BV 5.52 /sh P/E 105.33 (Ind RTCAT P/E 19.48) Ctry US

GAMING PARTNERS INTL CORP (GPIC)

Manufacturer and supplier of casino table game equipment

70% SCALE

Growth Performance Measurement				
Years	Price	Earn.	Div.	Tot Ret
Last 1	10.6	20.0	---	10.6
Last 5	-.5	---	---	-.5
Last 10	4.9	---	---	4.9

Paulson Gaming Corp
prior to 9/1/04

Paid
$0.125

Special
$0.125

Special
$0.183

Special
$0.183

Special
$0.183

Copyright 2012 Securities Research Company

Bonds $.7 Mil Com 8.101 Mil BV 5.49 /sh P/E 11.43 (Ind CSINO P/E 18.01) Ctry US

GARMIN LTD (GRMN)

Makes global positioning system devices

Growth Performance Measurement				
Years	Price	Earn.	Div.	Tot Ret
Last 1	2.4	20.4	20.0	9.6
Last 5	-15.9	-1.3	29.2	-13.3
Last 10	10.8	18.7	---	12.8

Adj. for
2 for 1
8/16/06

Dividends in U.S. fds., not subject to
Cayman Islands withholding tax

Copyright 2012 Securities Research Company

Bonds $.0 Mil Com 194.970 Mil BV 17.38 /sh P/E 13.02 (Ind CELEC P/E 13.79) Ctry Cayman Islands

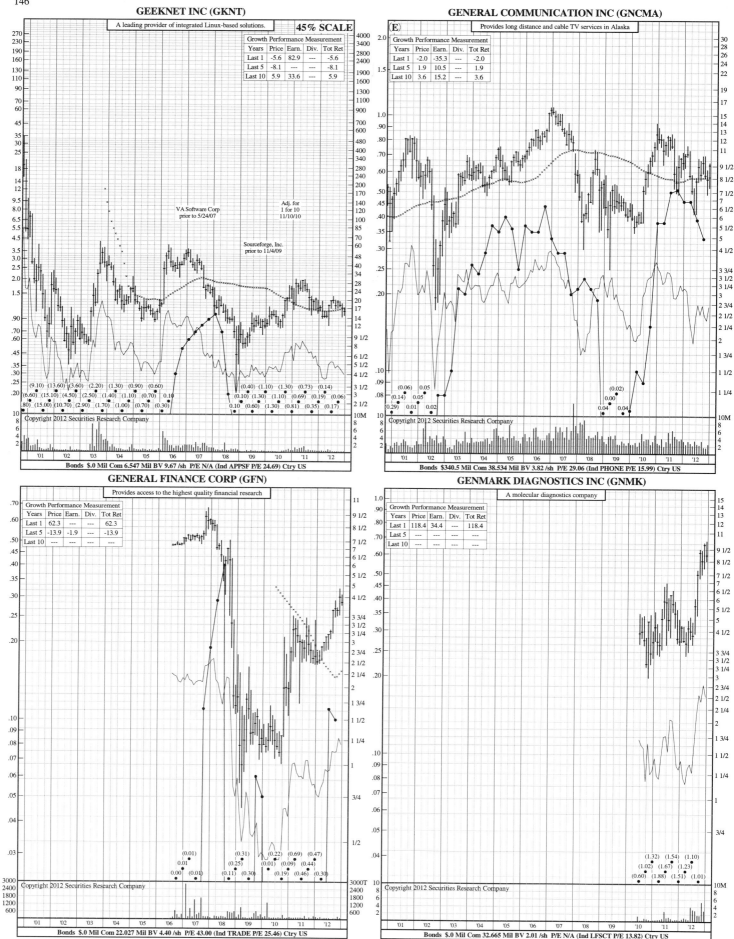

GEEKNET INC (GKNT)

A leading provider of integrated Linux-based solutions.

45% SCALE

Growth Performance Measurement				
Years	Price	Earn.	Div.	Tot Ret
Last 1	-5.6	82.9	---	-5.6
Last 5	-8.1	---	---	-8.1
Last 10	5.9	33.6	---	5.9

VA Software Corp
prior to 5/24/07

Adj. for
1 for 10
11/10/10

Sourceforge, Inc.
prior to 11/4/09

(9.10) (13.60) (3.60) (2.20) (1.30) (0.90) (0.60)   (0.40) (1.10) (1.30) (0.73) (0.14)
(6.60) (15.00) (4.50) (2.50) (1.40) (1.10) (0.70) 0.10   (0.10) (0.60) (0.19) (0.69) (0.06)
.80 (15.00) (10.70) (2.90) (1.70) (1.00) (0.70) (0.30) 0.10 (0.60) (1.30) (0.81) (0.35) (0.17)

Copyright 2012 Securities Research Company

'01 '02 '03 '04 '05 '06 '07 '08 '09 '10 '11 '12

Bonds $.0 Mil Com 6.547 Mil BV 9.67 /sh P/E N/A (Ind APPSF P/E 24.69) Ctry US

GENERAL COMMUNICATION INC (GNCMA)

(E)

Provides long distance and cable TV services in Alaska

Growth Performance Measurement				
Years	Price	Earn.	Div.	Tot Ret
Last 1	-2.0	-35.3	---	-2.0
Last 5	1.9	10.5	---	1.9
Last 10	3.6	15.2	---	3.6

(0.06) 0.05   (0.02)
(0.14) 0.05   0.00
(0.29) 0.01 0.02   0.04 0.04

Copyright 2012 Securities Research Company

'01 '02 '03 '04 '05 '06 '07 '08 '09 '10 '11 '12

Bonds $340.5 Mil Com 38.534 Mil BV 3.82 /sh P/E 29.06 (Ind PHONE P/E 15.99) Ctry US

GENERAL FINANCE CORP (GFN)

Provides access to the highest quality financial research

Growth Performance Measurement				
Years	Price	Earn.	Div.	Tot Ret
Last 1	62.3	---	---	62.3
Last 5	-13.9	-1.9	---	-13.9
Last 10	---	---	---	---

                (0.01)   (0.31)   (0.22) (0.69) (0.47)
                0.01   (0.25)   (0.01) (0.09) (0.44)
                0.00 (0.01)   (0.11) (0.30) (0.19) (0.46) (0.30)

Copyright 2012 Securities Research Company

'01 '02 '03 '04 '05 '06 '07 '08 '09 '10 '11 '12

Bonds $.0 Mil Com 22.027 Mil BV 4.40 /sh P/E 43.00 (Ind TRADE P/E 25.46) Ctry US

GENMARK DIAGNOSTICS INC (GNMK)

A molecular diagnostics company

Growth Performance Measurement				
Years	Price	Earn.	Div.	Tot Ret
Last 1	118.4	34.4	---	118.4
Last 5	---	---	---	---
Last 10	---	---	---	---

                              (1.32) (1.54) (1.10)
                              (1.02) (1.67) (1.23)
                              (0.60) (1.88) (1.51) (1.01)

Copyright 2012 Securities Research Company

'01 '02 '03 '04 '05 '06 '07 '08 '09 '10 '11 '12

Bonds $.0 Mil Com 32.665 Mil BV 2.01 /sh P/E N/A (Ind LFSCT P/E 13.82) Ctry US

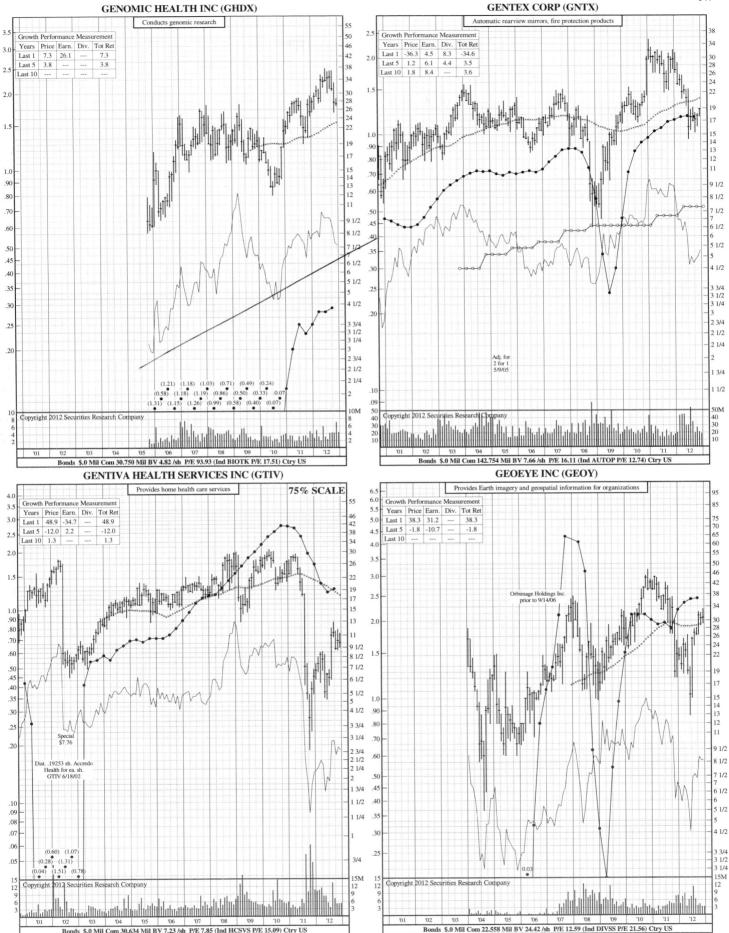

GENOMIC HEALTH INC (GHDX)

Conducts genomic research

Growth Performance Measurement

Years	Price	Earn.	Div.	Tot Ret
Last 1	7.3	26.1	---	7.3
Last 5	3.8	---	---	3.8
Last 10	---	---	---	---

(1.21) (1.18) (1.03) (0.71) (0.49) (0.24)
(0.58) (1.18) (1.19) (0.86) (0.50) (0.33) 0.07
(1.31) (1.15) (1.26) (0.99) (0.58) (0.40) (0.07)

Copyright 2012 Securities Research Company

Bonds $.0 Mil Com 30.750 Mil BV 4.82 /sh P/E 93.93 (Ind BIOTK P/E 17.51) Ctry US

GENTEX CORP (GNTX)

Automatic rearview mirrors, fire protection products

Growth Performance Measurement

Years	Price	Earn.	Div.	Tot Ret
Last 1	-36.3	4.5	8.3	-34.6
Last 5	1.2	6.1	4.4	3.5
Last 10	1.8	8.4	---	3.6

Adj. for
2 for 1
5/9/05

Copyright 2012 Securities Research Company

Bonds $.0 Mil Com 142.754 Mil BV 7.66 /sh P/E 16.11 (Ind AUTOP P/E 12.74) Ctry US

GENTIVA HEALTH SERVICES INC (GTIV)

Provides home health care services

75% SCALE

Growth Performance Measurement

Years	Price	Earn.	Div.	Tot Ret
Last 1	48.9	-34.7	---	48.9
Last 5	-12.0	2.2	---	-12.0
Last 10	1.3	---	---	1.3

Special
$7.76

Dist. .19253 sh. Accredo
Health for ea. sh.
GTIV 6/18/02

(0.60) (1.07)
(0.28) (1.31)
(0.04) (1.51) (0.78)

Copyright 2012 Securities Research Company

Bonds $.0 Mil Com 30.634 Mil BV 7.23 /sh P/E 7.85 (Ind HCSVS P/E 15.09) Ctry US

GEOEYE INC (GEOY)

Provides Earth imagery and geospatial information for organizations

Growth Performance Measurement

Years	Price	Earn.	Div.	Tot Ret
Last 1	38.3	31.2	---	38.3
Last 5	-1.8	-10.7	---	-1.8
Last 10	---	---	---	---

Orbimage Holdings Inc.
prior to 9/14/06

0.03

Copyright 2012 Securities Research Company

Bonds $.0 Mil Com 22.558 Mil BV 24.42 /sh P/E 12.59 (Ind DIVSS P/E 21.56) Ctry US

148

GEOSPACE TECHNOLOGIES CORP (GEOS)

Makes instruments and equipment for aquisition of seismic data

85% SCALE

Growth Performance Measurement			
Years	Price	Earn.	Div.	Tot Ret
Last 1	129.8	16.5	---	129.8
Last 5	18.7	12.5	---	18.7
Last 10	36.4	---	---	36.4

Adj. for 2 for 1 10/19/12

Copyright 2012 Securities Research Company

Bonds $4.0 Mil Com 12.828 Mil BV 16.79 /sh P/E 32.67 (Ind OGEQP P/E 13.95) Ctry US

GERMAN AMERN BANCORP INC (GABC)

Bank holding company based in Indiana

Growth Performance Measurement			
Years	Price	Earn.	Div.	Tot Ret
Last 1	19.4	24.2	.0	22.5
Last 5	11.3	17.7	.0	14.0
Last 10	3.9	9.6	1.0	6.3

Adj. fc 5% SI 11/28/01
Adj. for 5% SD 11/28/01
Adj. for 5% SD 11/26/02
Adj. for 5% SD 11/26/03

Copyright 2012 Securities Research Company

Bonds $122.9 Mil Com 12.631 Mil BV 14.49 /sh P/E 11.74 (Ind RBANK P/E 10.51) Ctry US

GERON CORP (GERN)

Stem cell and genetic nuclear transfer research

65% SCALE

Growth Performance Measurement			
Years	Price	Earn.	Div.	Tot Ret
Last 1	-4.7	18.4	---	-4.7
Last 5	-24.3	-1.0	---	-24.3
Last 10	-8.9	8.0	---	-8.9

Copyright 2012 Securities Research Company

Bonds $17.1 Mil Com 130.756 Mil BV .76 /sh P/E N/A (Ind BIOTK P/E 17.51) Ctry US

GEVO INC (GEVO)

A development stage renewable chemicals and biofuels company

80% SCALE

Growth Performance Measurement			
Years	Price	Earn.	Div.	Tot Ret
Last 1	-75.5	94.4	---	-75.5
Last 5	---	---	---	---
Last 10	---	---	---	---

Copyright 2012 Securities Research Company

Bonds $.0 Mil Com 39.408 Mil BV 2.79 /sh P/E N/A (Ind FERTL P/E 15.97) Ctry US

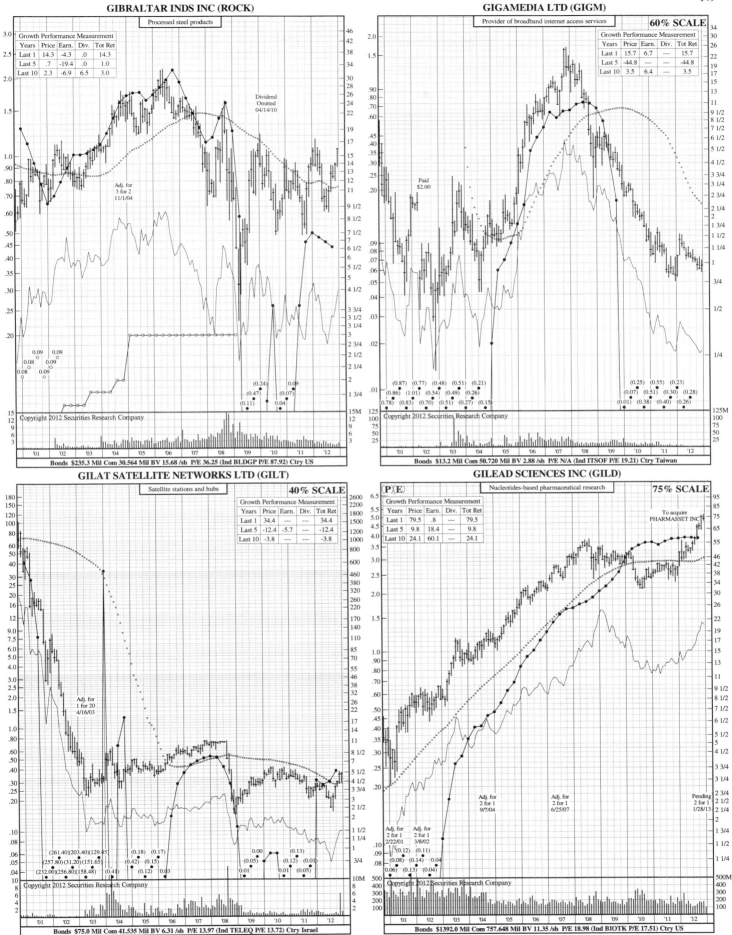

GIBRALTAR INDS INC (ROCK)

Processed steel products

Growth Performance Measurement

Years	Price	Earn.	Div.	Tot Ret
Last 1	14.3	-4.3	.0	14.3
Last 5	.7	-19.4	.0	1.0
Last 10	2.3	-6.9	6.5	3.0

Dividend Omitted 04/14/10

Adj. for 3 for 2 11/1/04

Copyright 2012 Securities Research Company

Bonds $235.3 Mil Com 30.564 Mil BV 15.68 /sh P/E 36.25 (Ind BLDGP P/E 87.92) Ctry US

GIGAMEDIA LTD (GIGM)

Provider of broadband internet access services

60% SCALE

Growth Performance Measurement

Years	Price	Earn.	Div.	Tot Ret
Last 1	15.7	6.7	---	15.7
Last 5	-44.8	---	---	-44.8
Last 10	3.5	6.4	---	3.5

Paid $2.00

Copyright 2012 Securities Research Company

Bonds $13.2 Mil Com 50.720 Mil BV 2.88 /sh P/E N/A (Ind ITSOF P/E 19.21) Ctry Taiwan

GILAT SATELLITE NETWORKS LTD (GILT)

Satellite stations and hubs

40% SCALE

Growth Performance Measurement

Years	Price	Earn.	Div.	Tot Ret
Last 1	34.4	---	---	34.4
Last 5	-12.4	-5.7	---	-12.4
Last 10	-3.8	---	---	-3.8

Adj. for 1 for 20 4/16/03

Copyright 2012 Securities Research Company

Bonds $75.0 Mil Com 41.535 Mil BV 6.31 /sh P/E 13.97 (Ind TELEQ P/E 13.72) Ctry Israel

GILEAD SCIENCES INC (GILD)

(P)(E) Nucleotides-based pharmaceutical research

75% SCALE

Growth Performance Measurement

Years	Price	Earn.	Div.	Tot Ret
Last 1	79.5	.8	---	79.5
Last 5	9.8	18.4	---	9.8
Last 10	24.1	60.1	---	24.1

To acquire PHARMASSET INC

Adj. for 2 for 1 9/7/04

Adj. for 2 for 1 6/25/07

Pending 2 for 1 1/28/13

Adj. for 2 for 1 2/22/01

Adj. for 2 for 1 3/8/02

Copyright 2012 Securities Research Company

Bonds $1392.0 Mil Com 757.648 Mil BV 11.35 /sh P/E 18.98 (Ind BIOTK P/E 17.51) Ctry US

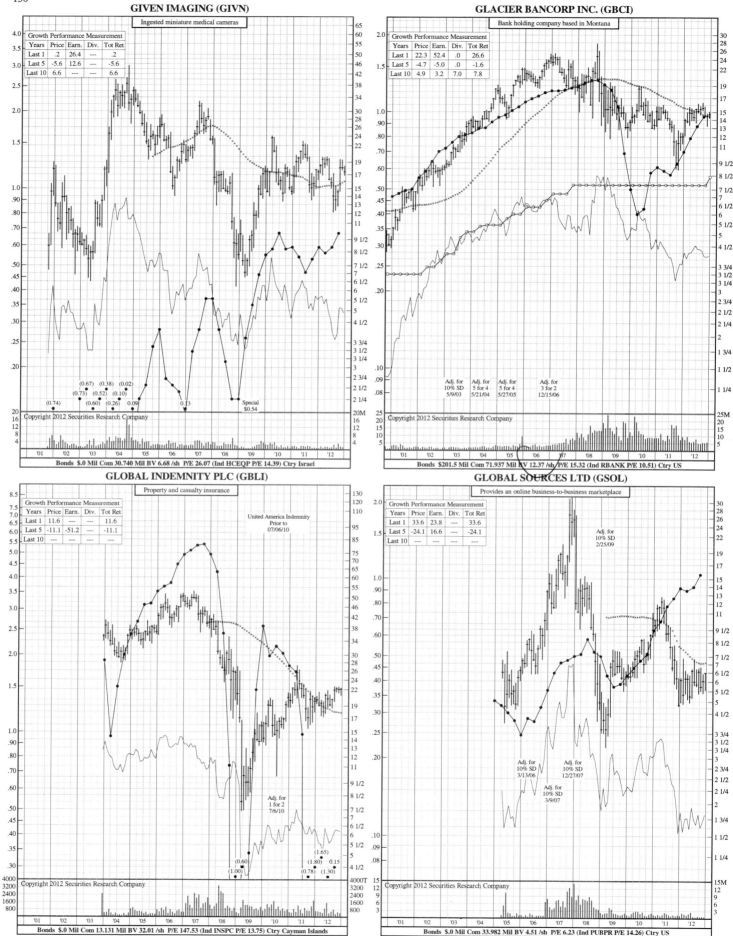

GIVEN IMAGING (GIVN)

Ingested miniature medical cameras

Copyright 2012 Securities Research Company

Growth Performance Measurement

Years	Price	Earn.	Div.	Tot Ret
Last 1	.2	26.4	---	.2
Last 5	-5.6	12.6	---	-5.6
Last 10	6.6	---	---	6.6

(0.74) (0.67) (0.38) (0.02)
(0.73) (0.52) (0.10)
(0.60) (0.26) 0.09 0.13

Special $0.54

Bonds $.0 Mil Com 30.740 Mil BV 6.68 /sh P/E 26.07 (Ind HCEQP P/E 14.39) Ctry Israel

GLACIER BANCORP INC. (GBCI)

Bank holding company based in Montana

Growth Performance Measurement

Years	Price	Earn.	Div.	Tot Ret
Last 1	22.3	52.4	.0	26.6
Last 5	-4.7	-5.0	.0	-1.6
Last 10	4.9	3.2	7.0	7.8

Adj. for 10% SD 5/9/03
Adj. for 5 for 4 5/21/04
Adj. for 5 for 4 5/27/05
Adj. for 3 for 2 12/15/06

Copyright 2012 Securities Research Company

Bonds $201.5 Mil Com 71.937 Mil BV 12.37 /sh P/E 15.32 (Ind RBANK P/E 10.51) Ctry US

GLOBAL INDEMNITY PLC (GBLI)

Property and casualty insurance

Growth Performance Measurement

Years	Price	Earn.	Div.	Tot Ret
Last 1	11.6	---	---	11.6
Last 5	-11.1	-51.2	---	-11.1
Last 10	---	---	---	---

United America Indemnity Prior to 07/06/10

Adj. for 1 for 2 7/6/10

(0.60) (1.65)
(1.00) (1.80) 0.15
(0.78) (1.30)

Copyright 2012 Securities Research Company

Bonds $.0 Mil Com 13.131 Mil BV 32.01 /sh P/E 147.53 (Ind INSPC P/E 13.75) Ctry Cayman Islands

GLOBAL SOURCES LTD (GSOL)

Provides an online business-to-business marketplace

Growth Performance Measurement

Years	Price	Earn.	Div.	Tot Ret
Last 1	33.6	23.8	---	33.6
Last 5	-24.1	16.6	---	-24.1
Last 10	---	---	---	---

Adj. for 10% SD 2/25/09

Adj. for 10% SD 3/13/06
Adj. for 10% SD 12/27/07
Adj. for 10% SD 3/9/07

Copyright 2012 Securities Research Company

Bonds $.0 Mil Com 33.982 Mil BV 4.51 /sh P/E 6.23 (Ind PUBPR P/E 14.26) Ctry US

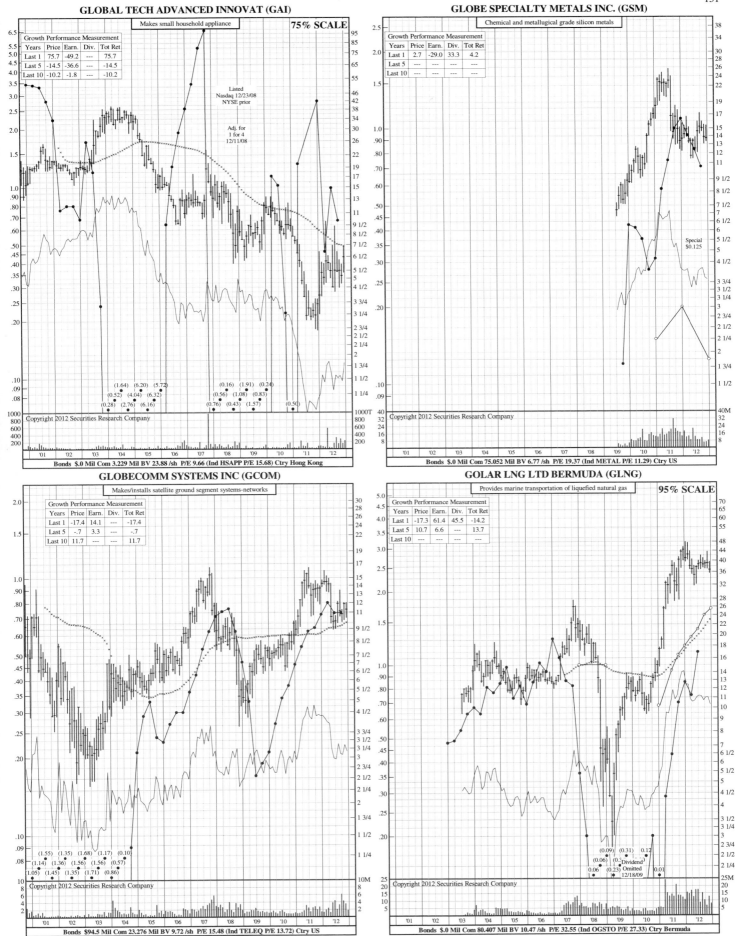

GLOBAL TECH ADVANCED INNOVAT (GAI)

Makes small household appliance

75% SCALE

Growth Performance Measurement

Years	Price	Earn.	Div.	Tot Ret
Last 1	75.7	-49.2	---	75.7
Last 5	-14.5	-36.6	---	-14.5
Last 10	-10.2	-1.8	---	-10.2

Listed
Nasdaq 12/23/08
NYSE prior

Adj. for
1 for 4
12/11/08

(1.64) (6.20) (5.72)
(0.52) (4.04) (6.32)
(0.28) (2.76) (6.16)

(0.16) (1.91) (0.24)
(0.56) (1.08) (0.83)
(0.76) (0.43) (1.57)
(0.50)

Copyright 2012 Securities Research Company

Bonds $.0 Mil Com 3.229 Mil BV 23.88 /sh P/E 9.66 (Ind HSAPP P/E 15.68) Ctry Hong Kong

GLOBE SPECIALTY METALS INC. (GSM)

Chemical and metallugical grade silicon metals

Growth Performance Measurement

Years	Price	Earn.	Div.	Tot Ret
Last 1	2.7	-29.0	33.3	4.2
Last 5	---	---	---	---
Last 10	---	---	---	---

Special
$0.125

Copyright 2012 Securities Research Company

Bonds $.0 Mil Com 75.052 Mil BV 6.77 /sh P/E 19.37 (Ind METAL P/E 11.29) Ctry US

GLOBECOMM SYSTEMS INC (GCOM)

Makes/installs satellite ground segment systems-networks

Growth Performance Measurement

Years	Price	Earn.	Div.	Tot Ret
Last 1	-17.4	14.1	---	-17.4
Last 5	-.7	3.3	---	-.7
Last 10	11.7	---	---	11.7

(1.55) (1.35) (1.68) (1.17) (0.10)
(1.14) (1.36) (1.56) (1.56) (0.57)
(1.05) (1.45) (1.35) (1.71) (0.86)

Copyright 2012 Securities Research Company

Bonds $94.5 Mil Com 23.276 Mil BV 9.72 /sh P/E 15.48 (Ind TELEQ P/E 13.72) Ctry US

GOLAR LNG LTD BERMUDA (GLNG)

Provides marine transportation of liquefied natural gas

95% SCALE

Growth Performance Measurement

Years	Price	Earn.	Div.	Tot Ret
Last 1	-17.3	61.4	45.5	-14.2
Last 5	10.7	6.6	---	13.7
Last 10	---	---	---	---

(0.09) (0.31) 0.12
(0.06) (0.2) Dividend
0.06 (0.23) Omitted
0.01
12/18/09

Copyright 2012 Securities Research Company

Bonds $.0 Mil Com 80.407 Mil BV 10.47 /sh P/E 32.55 (Ind OGSTO P/E 27.33) Ctry Bermuda

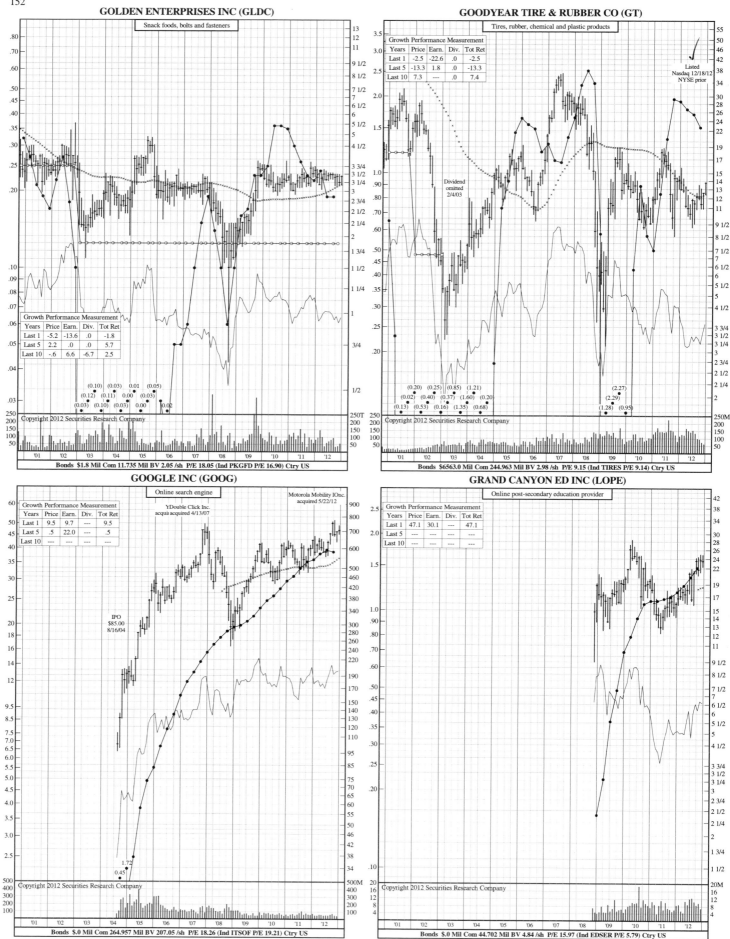

GOLDEN ENTERPRISES INC (GLDC)

Snack foods, bolts and fasteners

Growth Performance Measurement				
Years	Price	Earn.	Div.	Tot Ret
Last 1	-5.2	-13.6	.0	-1.8
Last 5	2.2	.0	.0	5.7
Last 10	-.6	6.6	-6.7	2.5

(0.10) (0.03) 0.01 (0.05)
(0.12) (0.11) 0.00 (0.03)
(0.03) (0.10) (0.03) 0.00 0.02

Copyright 2012 Securities Research Company

Bonds $1.8 Mil Com 11.735 Mil BV 2.05 /sh P/E 18.05 (Ind PKGFD P/E 16.90) Ctry US

GOODYEAR TIRE & RUBBER CO (GT)

Tires, rubber, chemical and plastic products

Growth Performance Measurement				
Years	Price	Earn.	Div.	Tot Ret
Last 1	-2.5	-22.6	.0	-2.5
Last 5	-13.3	1.8	.0	-13.3
Last 10	7.3	---	.0	7.4

Listed
Nasdaq 12/18/12
NYSE prior

Dividend
omitted
2/4/03

(0.20) (0.25) (0.85) (1.21)   (2.27)
(0.02) (0.40) (0.37) (1.60) (0.20)   (2.29)
(0.13) (0.53) (0.16) (1.35) (0.68)   (1.28) (0.95)

Copyright 2012 Securities Research Company

Bonds $6563.0 Mil Com 244.963 Mil BV 2.98 /sh P/E 9.15 (Ind TIRES P/E 9.14) Ctry US

GOOGLE INC (GOOG)

Online search engine

Growth Performance Measurement				
Years	Price	Earn.	Div.	Tot Ret
Last 1	9.5	9.7	---	9.5
Last 5	.5	22.0	---	.5
Last 10	---	---	---	---

YDouble Click Inc.
acquired acquired 4/13/07

Motorola Mobility IOnc.
acquired 5/22/12

IPO
$85.00
8/16/04

1.72
0.45

Copyright 2012 Securities Research Company

Bonds $.0 Mil Com 264.957 Mil BV 207.05 /sh P/E 18.26 (Ind ITSOF P/E 19.21) Ctry US

GRAND CANYON ED INC (LOPE)

Online post-secondary education provider

Growth Performance Measurement				
Years	Price	Earn.	Div.	Tot Ret
Last 1	47.1	30.1	---	47.1
Last 5	---	---	---	---
Last 10	---	---	---	---

Copyright 2012 Securities Research Company

Bonds $.0 Mil Com 44.702 Mil BV 4.84 /sh P/E 15.97 (Ind EDSER P/E 5.79) Ctry US

152

153

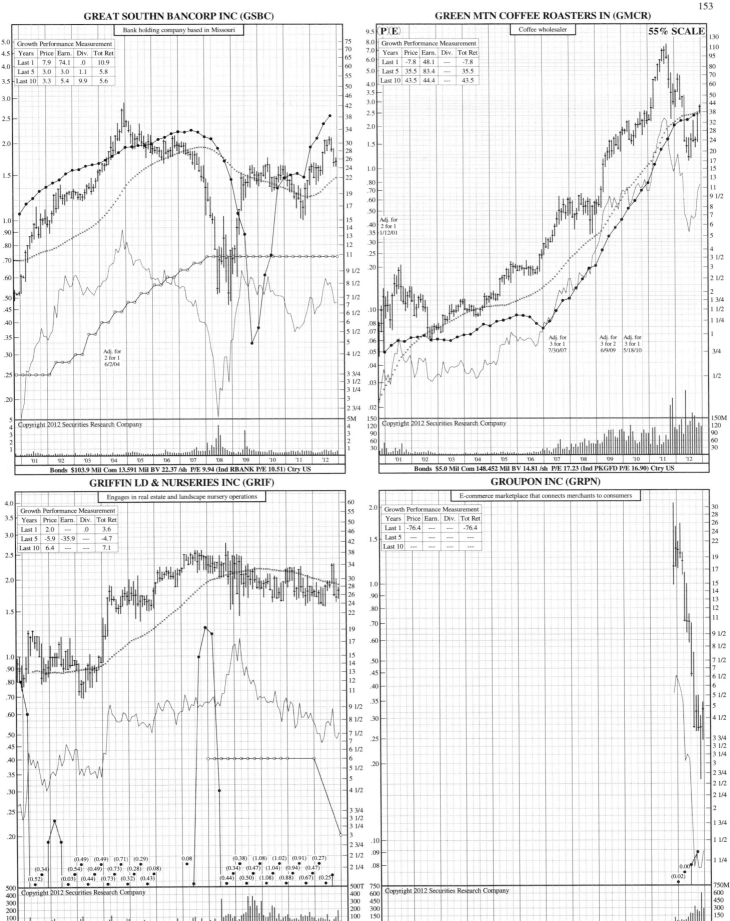

GREAT SOUTHN BANCORP INC (GSBC)

Bank holding company based in Missouri

Growth Performance Measurement				
Years	Price	Earn.	Div.	Tot Ret
Last 1	7.9	74.1	.0	10.9
Last 5	3.0	3.0	1.1	5.8
Last 10	3.3	5.4	9.9	5.6

Adj. for 2 for 1 6/2/04

Copyright 2012 Securities Research Company

Bonds $103.9 Mil Com 13.591 Mil BV 22.37 /sh P/E 9.94 (Ind RBANK P/E 10.51) Ctry US

GREEN MTN COFFEE ROASTERS IN (GMCR)

Coffee wholesaler   55% SCALE

Growth Performance Measurement				
Years	Price	Earn.	Div.	Tot Ret
Last 1	-7.8	48.1	---	-7.8
Last 5	35.5	83.4	---	35.5
Last 10	43.5	44.4	---	43.5

Adj. for 2 for 1 1/12/01

Adj. for 3 for 1 7/30/07

Adj. for 3 for 2 6/9/09

Adj. for 3 for 1 5/18/10

Copyright 2012 Securities Research Company

Bonds $5.0 Mil Com 148.452 Mil BV 14.81 /sh P/E 17.23 (Ind PKGFD P/E 16.90) Ctry US

GRIFFIN LD & NURSERIES INC (GRIF)

Engages in real estate and landscape nursery operations

Growth Performance Measurement				
Years	Price	Earn.	Div.	Tot Ret
Last 1	2.0	---	.0	3.6
Last 5	-5.9	-35.9	---	-4.7
Last 10	6.4	---	---	7.1

Copyright 2012 Securities Research Company

Bonds $50.6 Mil Com 5.140 Mil BV 20.43 /sh P/E 192.86 (Ind AGPRD P/E 12.62) Ctry US

GROUPON INC (GRPN)

E-commerce marketplace that connects merchants to consumers

Growth Performance Measurement				
Years	Price	Earn.	Div.	Tot Ret
Last 1	-76.4	---	---	-76.4
Last 5	---	---	---	---
Last 10	---	---	---	

Copyright 2012 Securities Research Company

Bonds $0.0 Mil Com 653.316 Mil BV 1.22 /sh P/E 54.00 (Ind RTNET P/E 64.32) Ctry US

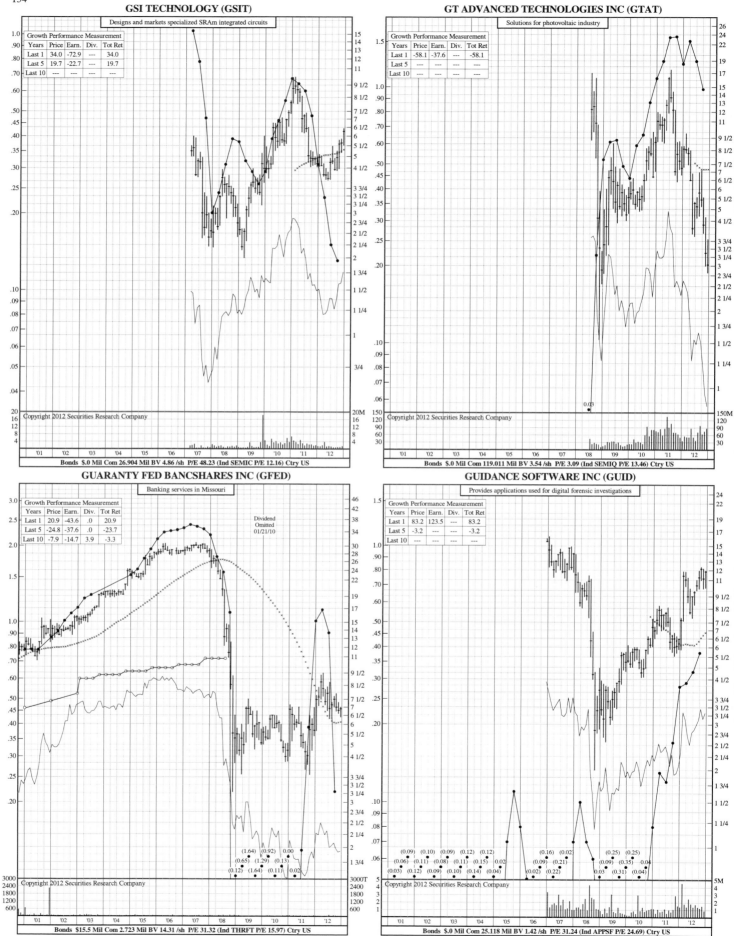

154

GSI TECHNOLOGY (GSIT)

Designs and markets specialized SRAm integrated circuits

Growth Performance Measurement				
Years	Price	Earn.	Div.	Tot Ret
Last 1	34.0	-72.9	---	34.0
Last 5	19.7	-22.7	---	19.7
Last 10	---	---	---	---

Copyright 2012 Securities Research Company

Bonds $.0 Mil Com 26.904 Mil BV 4.86 /sh P/E 48.23 (Ind SEMIC P/E 12.16) Ctry US

GT ADVANCED TECHNOLOGIES INC (GTAT)

Solutions for photovoltaic industry

Growth Performance Measurement				
Years	Price	Earn.	Div.	Tot Ret
Last 1	-58.1	-37.6	---	-58.1
Last 5	---	---	---	---
Last 10	---	---	---	---

0.03

Copyright 2012 Securities Research Company

Bonds $.0 Mil Com 119.011 Mil BV 3.54 /sh P/E 3.09 (Ind SEMIQ P/E 13.46) Ctry US

GUARANTY FED BANCSHARES INC (GFED)

Banking services in Missouri

Growth Performance Measurement				
Years	Price	Earn.	Div.	Tot Ret
Last 1	20.9	-43.6	.0	20.9
Last 5	-24.8	-37.6	.0	-23.7
Last 10	-7.9	-14.7	3.9	-3.3

Dividend
Omitted
01/21/10

(1.64) (0.92) 0.00
(0.65) (1.29) (0.13)
(0.12) (1.64) (0.11) 0.02

Copyright 2012 Securities Research Company

Bonds $15.5 Mil Com 2.723 Mil BV 14.31 /sh P/E 31.32 (Ind THRFT P/E 15.97) Ctry US

GUIDANCE SOFTWARE INC (GUID)

Provides applications used for digital forensic investigations

Growth Performance Measurement				
Years	Price	Earn.	Div.	Tot Ret
Last 1	83.2	123.5	---	83.2
Last 5	-3.2	---	---	-3.2
Last 10	---	---	---	---

(0.09) (0.10) (0.09) (0.12) (0.12)
(0.06) (0.11) (0.08) (0.11) (0.15) (0.04)
(0.03) (0.12) (0.09) (0.10) (0.14) (0.04)
(0.16) (0.02)
(0.09) (0.21)
(0.02) (0.22)
(0.25) (0.25)
(0.09) (0.35) 0.04
0.03 (0.31) (0.04)

Copyright 2012 Securities Research Company

Bonds $.0 Mil Com 25.118 Mil BV 1.42 /sh P/E 31.24 (Ind APPSF P/E 24.69) Ctry US

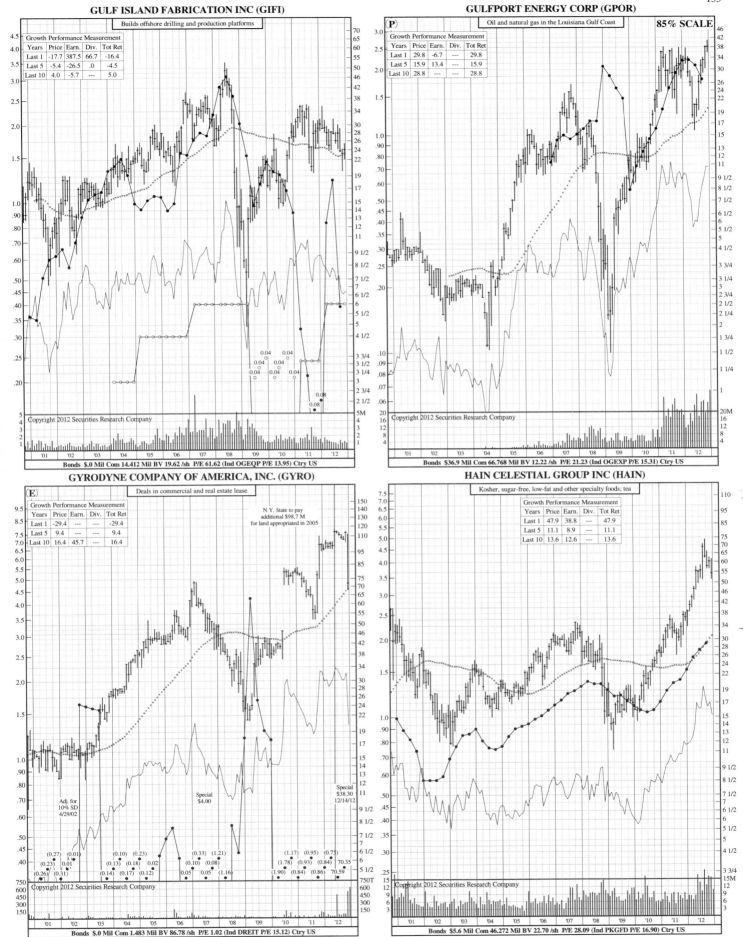

GULF ISLAND FABRICATION INC (GIFI)

Builds offshore drilling and production platforms

Growth Performance Measurement

Years	Price	Earn.	Div.	Tot Ret
Last 1	-17.7	387.5	66.7	-16.4
Last 5	-5.4	-26.5	.0	-4.5
Last 10	4.0	-5.7	---	5.0

Copyright 2012 Securities Research Company

0.04 0.04 0.04
0.04 0.04 0.04
0.04 0.04 0.04 0.04
0.08
0.08

Bonds $.0 Mil Com 14.412 Mil BV 19.62 /sh P/E 61.62 (Ind OGEQP P/E 13.95) Ctry US

GULFPORT ENERGY CORP (GPOR)

Oil and natural gas in the Louisiana Gulf Coast

85% SCALE

(P)

Growth Performance Measurement

Years	Price	Earn.	Div.	Tot Ret
Last 1	29.8	-6.7	---	29.8
Last 5	15.9	13.4	---	15.9
Last 10	28.8	---	---	28.8

Copyright 2012 Securities Research Company

Bonds $36.9 Mil Com 66.768 Mil BV 12.22 /sh P/E 21.23 (Ind OGEXP P/E 15.31) Ctry US

GYRODYNE COMPANY OF AMERICA, INC. (GYRO)

Deals in commercial and real estate lease

(E)

N.Y. State to pay
additional $98.7 M
for land appropriated in 2005

Growth Performance Measurement

Years	Price	Earn.	Div.	Tot Ret
Last 1	-29.4	---	---	-29.4
Last 5	9.4	---	---	9.4
Last 10	16.4	45.7	---	16.4

Special
$4.00

Special
$38.30
12/14/12

Adj. for
10% SD
4/29/02

Copyright 2012 Securities Research Company

(0.27) (0.01)
(0.23) 0.01
(0.26) (0.31)
(0.10) (0.23)
(0.13) (0.18)
(0.14) (0.17) (0.12)
0.02
(0.33) (1.21)
(0.10) (0.08)
0.05 0.05 (1.16)
(1.17) (0.95) (0.75)
(1.78) (0.93) (0.84) 70.35
(1.90) (0.84) (0.86) 70.59

Bonds $.0 Mil Com 1.483 Mil BV 86.78 /sh P/E 1.02 (Ind DREIT P/E 15.12) Ctry US

HAIN CELESTIAL GROUP INC (HAIN)

Kosher, sugar-free, low-fat and other specialty foods; tea

Growth Performance Measurement

Years	Price	Earn.	Div.	Tot Ret
Last 1	47.9	38.8	---	47.9
Last 5	11.1	8.9	---	11.1
Last 10	13.6	12.6	---	13.6

Copyright 2012 Securities Research Company

Bonds $5.6 Mil Com 46.272 Mil BV 22.70 /sh P/E 28.09 (Ind PKGFD P/E 16.90) Ctry US

156

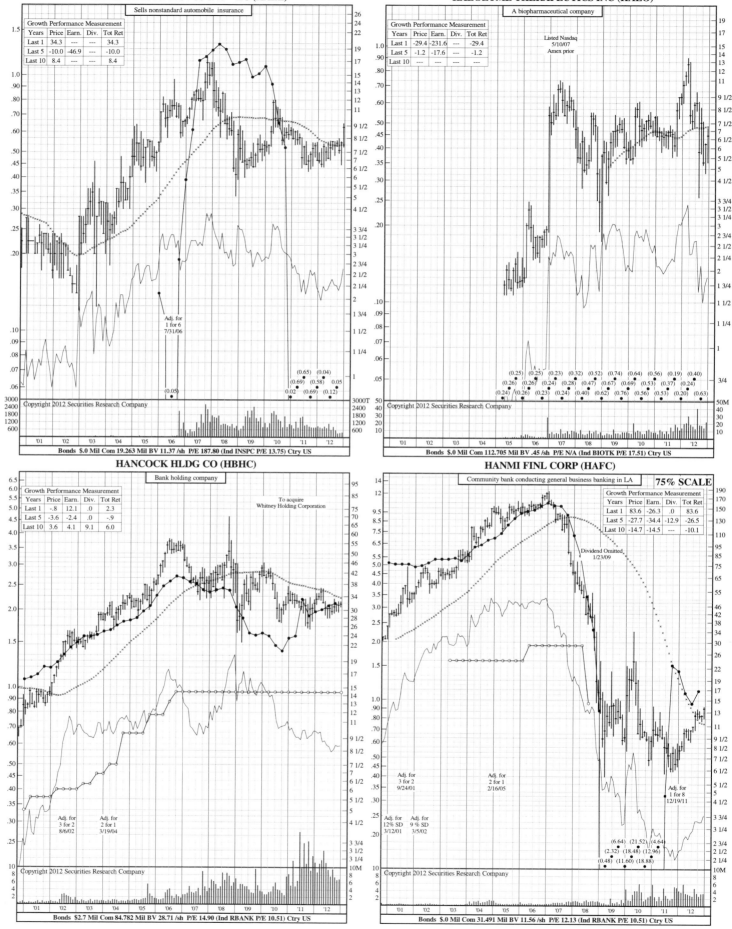

HALLMARK FINL SVCS INC   EC (HALL)

Sells nonstandard automobile insurance

Growth Performance Measurement				
Years	Price	Earn.	Div.	Tot Ret
Last 1	34.3	---	---	34.3
Last 5	-10.0	-46.9	---	-10.0
Last 10	8.4	---	---	8.4

Adj. for
1 for 6
7/31/06

(0.65) (0.04)
(0.69) (0.58) .05
.02 (0.69) (0.12)
(0.05)

3000   3000T
2400   2400
1800   1800
1200   1200
600   600

Copyright 2012 Securities Research Company

'01 '02 '03 '04 '05 '06 '07 '08 '09 '10 '11 '12

Bonds $.0 Mil Com 19.263 Mil BV 11.37 /sh P/E 187.80 (Ind INSPC P/E 13.75) Ctry US

HALOZYME THERAPEUTICS INC (HALO)

A biopharmaceutical company

Growth Performance Measurement				
Years	Price	Earn.	Div.	Tot Ret
Last 1	-29.4	-231.6	---	-29.4
Last 5	-1.2	-17.6	---	-1.2
Last 10	---	---	---	---

Listed Nasdaq
5/10/07
Amex prior

(0.25) (0.25) (0.23) (0.32) (0.52) (0.74) (0.64) (0.56) (0.19) (0.40)
(0.26) (0.26) (0.24) (0.28) (0.47) (0.67) (0.69) (0.53) (0.37) (0.24)
(0.24) (0.26) (0.23) (0.24) (0.40) (0.62) (0.76) (0.56) (0.53) (0.20) (0.63)

50M
40
30
20
10

Copyright 2012 Securities Research Company

'01 '02 '03 '04 '05 '06 '07 '08 '09 '10 '11 '12

Bonds $.0 Mil Com 112.705 Mil BV .45 /sh P/E N/A (Ind BIOTK P/E 17.51) Ctry US

HANCOCK HLDG CO (HBHC)

Bank holding company

Growth Performance Measurement				
Years	Price	Earn.	Div.	Tot Ret
Last 1	-.8	12.1	.0	2.3
Last 5	-3.6	-2.4	.0	-.9
Last 10	3.6	4.1	9.1	6.0

To acquire
Whitney Holding Corporation

Adj. for
3 for 2
8/6/02

Adj. for
2 for 1
3/19/04

10   10M
8   8
6   6
4   4
2   2

Copyright 2012 Securities Research Company

'01 '02 '03 '04 '05 '06 '07 '08 '09 '10 '11 '12

Bonds $2.7 Mil Com 84.782 Mil BV 28.71 /sh P/E 14.90 (Ind RBANK P/E 10.51) Ctry US

HANMI FINL CORP (HAFC)

Community bank conducting general business banking in LA   **75% SCALE**

Growth Performance Measurement				
Years	Price	Earn.	Div.	Tot Ret
Last 1	83.6	-26.3	.0	83.6
Last 5	-27.7	-34.4	-12.9	-26.5
Last 10	-14.7	-14.5	---	-10.1

Dividend Omitted
1/23/09

Adj. for
3 for 2
9/24/01

Adj. for
2 for 1
2/16/05

Adj. for
1 for 8
12/19/11

Adj. for
12% SD
3/12/01

Adj. for
9 % SD
3/5/02

(6.64) (21.52) (4.64)
(2.32) (18.48) (12.96)
(0.48) (11.60) (18.88)

10   10M
8   8
6   6
4   4
2   2

Copyright 2012 Securities Research Company

'01 '02 '03 '04 '05 '06 '07 '08 '09 '10 '11 '12

Bonds $.0 Mil Com 31.491 Mil BV 11.56 /sh P/E 12.13 (Ind RBANK P/E 10.51) Ctry US

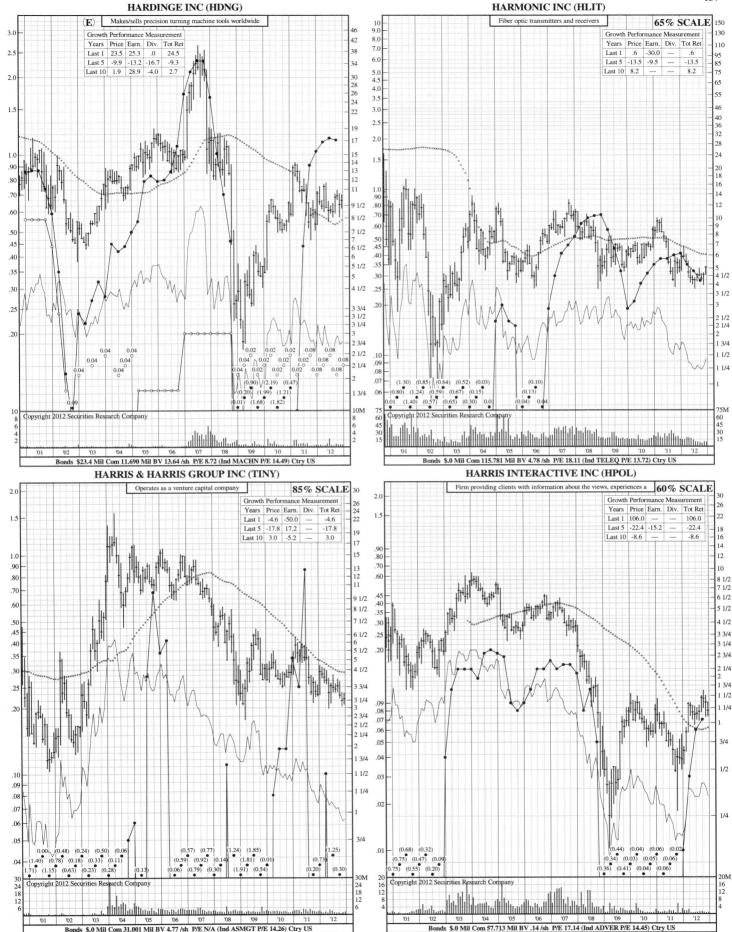

HARDINGE INC (HDNG)

(E) Makes/sells precision turning machine tools worldwide

Growth Performance Measurement

Years	Price	Earn.	Div.	Tot Ret
Last 1	23.5	25.3	.0	24.5
Last 5	-9.9	-13.2	-16.7	-9.3
Last 10	1.9	28.9	-4.0	2.7

Copyright 2012 Securities Research Company

Bonds $23.4 Mil Com 11.690 Mil BV 13.64 /sh P/E 8.72 (Ind MACHN P/E 14.49) Ctry US

HARMONIC INC (HLIT)

Fiber optic transmitters and receivers **65% SCALE**

Growth Performance Measurement

Years	Price	Earn.	Div.	Tot Ret
Last 1	.6	-30.0	---	.6
Last 5	-13.5	-9.5	---	-13.5
Last 10	8.2	---	---	8.2

Copyright 2012 Securities Research Company

Bonds $.0 Mil Com 115.781 Mil BV 4.78 /sh P/E 18.11 (Ind TELEQ P/E 13.72) Ctry US

HARRIS & HARRIS GROUP INC (TINY)

Operates as a venture capital company **85% SCALE**

Growth Performance Measurement

Years	Price	Earn.	Div.	Tot Ret
Last 1	-4.6	-50.0	---	-4.6
Last 5	-17.8	17.2	---	-17.8
Last 10	3.0	-5.2	---	3.0

Copyright 2012 Securities Research Company

Bonds $.0 Mil Com 31.001 Mil BV 4.77 /sh P/E N/A (Ind ASMGT P/E 14.26) Ctry US

HARRIS INTERACTIVE INC (HPOL)

Firm providing clients with information about the views, experiences a **60% SCALE**

Growth Performance Measurement

Years	Price	Earn.	Div.	Tot Ret
Last 1	106.0	---	---	106.0
Last 5	-22.4	-15.2	---	-22.4
Last 10	-8.6	---	---	-8.6

Copyright 2012 Securities Research Company

Bonds $.0 Mil Com 57.713 Mil BV .14 /sh P/E 17.14 (Ind ADVER P/E 14.45) Ctry US

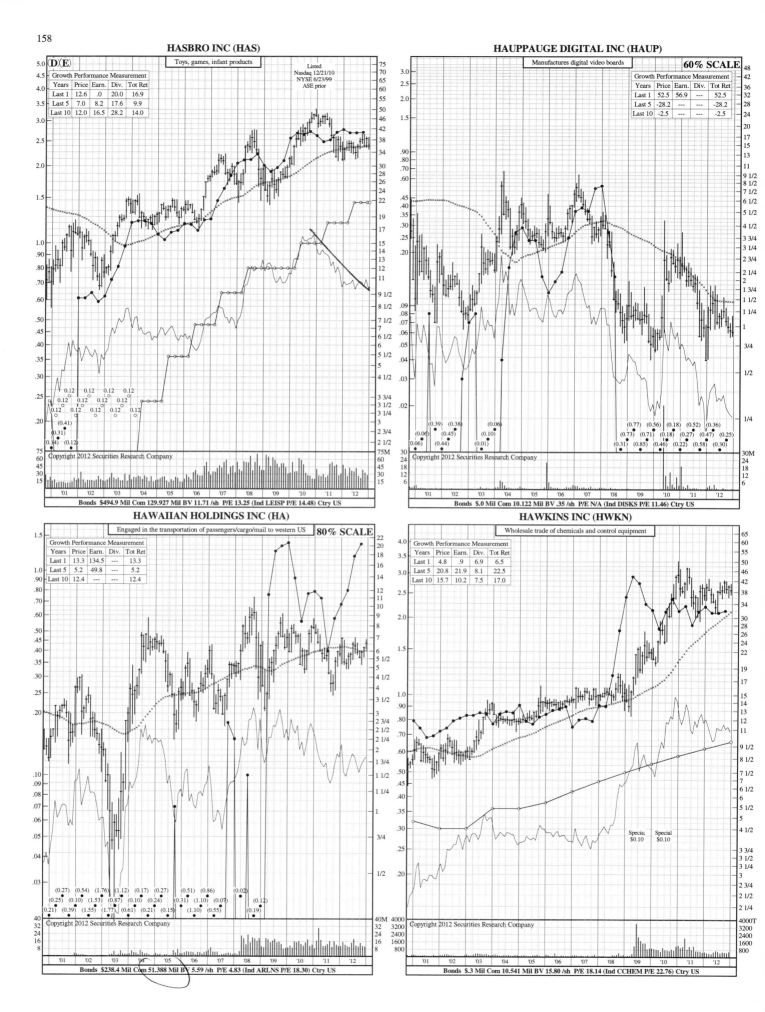

158

HASBRO INC (HAS)

Toys, games, infant products

Listed
Nasdaq 12/21/10
NYSE 6/23/99
ASE prior

(D)(E)

Growth Performance Measurement			
Years	Price	Earn.	Div.	Tot Ret
Last 1	12.6	.0	20.0	16.9
Last 5	7.0	8.2	17.6	9.9
Last 10	12.0	16.5	28.2	14.0

Copyright 2012 Securities Research Company

Bonds $494.9 Mil Com 129.927 Mil BV 11.71 /sh P/E 13.25 (Ind LEISP P/E 14.48) Ctry US

HAUPPAUGE DIGITAL INC (HAUP)

Manufactures digital video boards

60% SCALE

Growth Performance Measurement			
Years	Price	Earn.	Div.	Tot Ret
Last 1	52.5	56.9	---	52.5
Last 5	-28.2	---	---	-28.2
Last 10	-2.5	---	---	-2.5

Copyright 2012 Securities Research Company

Bonds $.0 Mil Com 10.122 Mil BV .35 /sh P/E N/A (Ind DISKS P/E 11.46) Ctry US

HAWAIIAN HOLDINGS INC (HA)

Engaged in the transportation of passengers/cargo/mail to western US

80% SCALE

Growth Performance Measurement			
Years	Price	Earn.	Div.	Tot Ret
Last 1	13.3	134.5	---	13.3
Last 5	5.2	49.8	---	5.2
Last 10	12.4	---	---	12.4

Copyright 2012 Securities Research Company

Bonds $238.4 Mil Com 51.388 Mil BV 5.59 /sh P/E 4.83 (Ind ARLNS P/E 18.30) Ctry US

HAWKINS INC (HWKN)

Wholesale trade of chemicals and control equipment

Growth Performance Measurement			
Years	Price	Earn.	Div.	Tot Ret
Last 1	4.8	.9	6.9	6.5
Last 5	20.8	21.9	8.1	22.5
Last 10	15.7	10.2	7.5	17.0

Special
$0.10

Special
$0.10

Copyright 2012 Securities Research Company

Bonds $.3 Mil Com 10.541 Mil BV 15.80 /sh P/E 18.14 (Ind CCHEM P/E 22.76) Ctry US

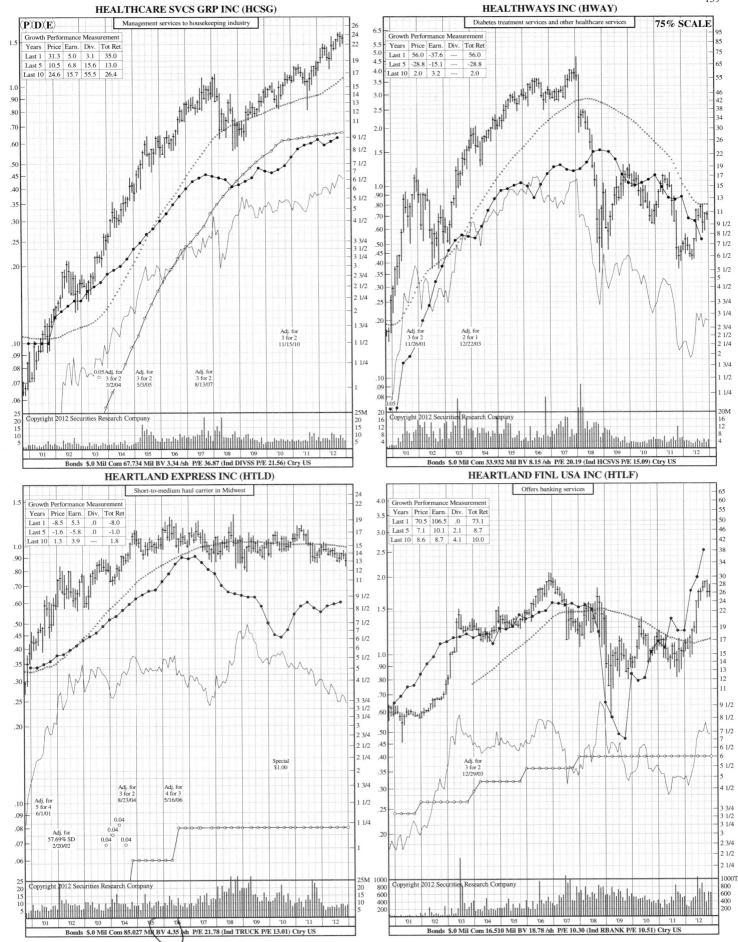

HEALTHCARE SVCS GRP INC (HCSG)

Management services to housekeeping industry

(P)(D)(E)

Growth Performance Measurement

Years	Price	Earn.	Div.	Tot Ret
Last 1	31.3	5.0	3.1	35.0
Last 5	10.5	6.8	15.6	13.0
Last 10	24.6	15.7	55.5	26.4

Adj. for
3 for 2
11/15/10

0.05 Adj. for
3 for 2
3/2/04

Adj. for
3 for 2
5/3/05

Adj. for
3 for 2
8/13/07

Copyright 2012 Securities Research Company

Bonds $.0 Mil Com 67.734 Mil BV 3.34 /sh P/E 36.87 (Ind DIVSS P/E 21.56) Ctry US

HEALTHWAYS INC (HWAY)

Diabetes treatment services and other healthcare services

75% SCALE

Growth Performance Measurement

Years	Price	Earn.	Div.	Tot Ret
Last 1	56.0	-37.6	---	56.0
Last 5	-28.8	-15.1	---	-28.8
Last 10	2.0	3.2	---	2.0

Adj. for
3 for 2
11/26/01

Adj. for
2 for 1
12/22/03

0.05

Copyright 2012 Securities Research Company

Bonds $.0 Mil Com 33.932 Mil BV 8.15 /sh P/E 20.19 (Ind HCSVS P/E 15.09) Ctry US

HEARTLAND EXPRESS INC (HTLD)

Short-to-medium haul carrier in Midwest

Growth Performance Measurement

Years	Price	Earn.	Div.	Tot Ret
Last 1	-8.5	5.3	.0	-8.0
Last 5	-1.6	-5.8	.0	-1.0
Last 10	1.3	3.9	---	1.8

Special
$1.00

Adj. for
3 for 2
8/23/04

Adj. for
4 for 3
5/16/06

Adj. for
5 for 4
6/1/01

0.04

Adj. for
57.69% SD
2/20/02

0.04

0.04   0.04

Copyright 2012 Securities Research Company

Bonds $.0 Mil Com 85.027 Mil BV 4.35 /sh P/E 21.78 (Ind TRUCK P/E 13.01) Ctry US

HEARTLAND FINL USA INC (HTLF)

Offers banking services

Growth Performance Measurement

Years	Price	Earn.	Div.	Tot Ret
Last 1	70.5	106.5	.0	73.1
Last 5	7.1	10.1	2.1	8.7
Last 10	8.6	8.7	4.1	10.0

Adj. for
3 for 2
12/29/03

Copyright 2012 Securities Research Company

Bonds $.0 Mil Com 16.510 Mil BV 18.78 /sh P/E 10.30 (Ind RBANK P/E 10.51) Ctry US

HEIDRICK & STRUGGLES INTL IN (HSII)

Provides executive recruiting services

Growth Performance Measurement				
Years	Price	Earn.	Div.	Tot Ret
Last 1	-29.2	390.9	.0	-26.7
Last 5	-16.3	-14.7	.0	-13.6
Last 10	.4	---	---	2.1

(0.63)
(0.60) 0.05
(0.17) (0.35)
(0.03)
(0.31)

Copyright 2012 Securities Research Company

'01 '02 '03 '04 '05 '06 '07 '08 '09 '10 '11 '12

Bonds $.0 Mil Com 17.971 Mil BV 14.06 /sh P/E 14.13 (Ind SRVEM P/E 22.28) Ctry US

HELEN OF TROY CORP LTD (HELE)

Electrical hair care products

Growth Performance Measurement				
Years	Price	Earn.	Div.	Tot Ret
Last 1	8.9	1.2	---	8.9
Last 5	14.3	14.3	---	14.3
Last 10	11.1	10.8	---	11.1

Copyright 2012 Securities Research Company

'01 '02 '03 '04 '05 '06 '07 '08 '09 '10 '11 '12

Bonds $55.0 Mil Com 31.807 Mil BV 28.27 /sh P/E 9.77 (Ind HSAPP P/E 15.68) Ctry US

HENRY JACK & ASSOC INC (JKHY)

D)

Integrated data processing systems

Growth Performance Measurement				
Years	Price	Earn.	Div.	Tot Ret
Last 1	16.8	12.8	9.5	18.1
Last 5	10.0	9.6	12.1	11.1
Last 10	12.5	12.1	12.6	13.3

0.10
Adj. for
2 for 1
3/5/01

Copyright 2012 Securities Research Company

'01 '02 '03 '04 '05 '06 '07 '08 '09 '10 '11 '12

Bonds $.3 Mil Com 86.073 Mil BV 12.17 /sh P/E 21.22 (Ind DPSVS P/E 20.19) Ctry US

HERCULES OFFSHORE INC (HERO)

Provides shallow-water drilling and liftboat services

70% SCALE

Growth Performance Measurement				
Years	Price	Earn.	Div.	Tot Ret
Last 1	39.0	-73.7	---	39.0
Last 5	-23.6	---	---	-23.6
Last 10	---	---	---	---

(0.84) (0.47) (0.38) (0.68)
(0.75) (0.67) (0.39) (0.67)
(0.10) (0.92) (0.45) (0.51) (0.66)

Copyright 2012 Securities Research Company

'01 '02 '03 '04 '05 '06 '07 '08 '09 '10 '11 '12

Bonds $.0 Mil Com 158.588 Mil BV 5.53 /sh P/E N/A (Ind OGDRL P/E 12.55) Ctry US

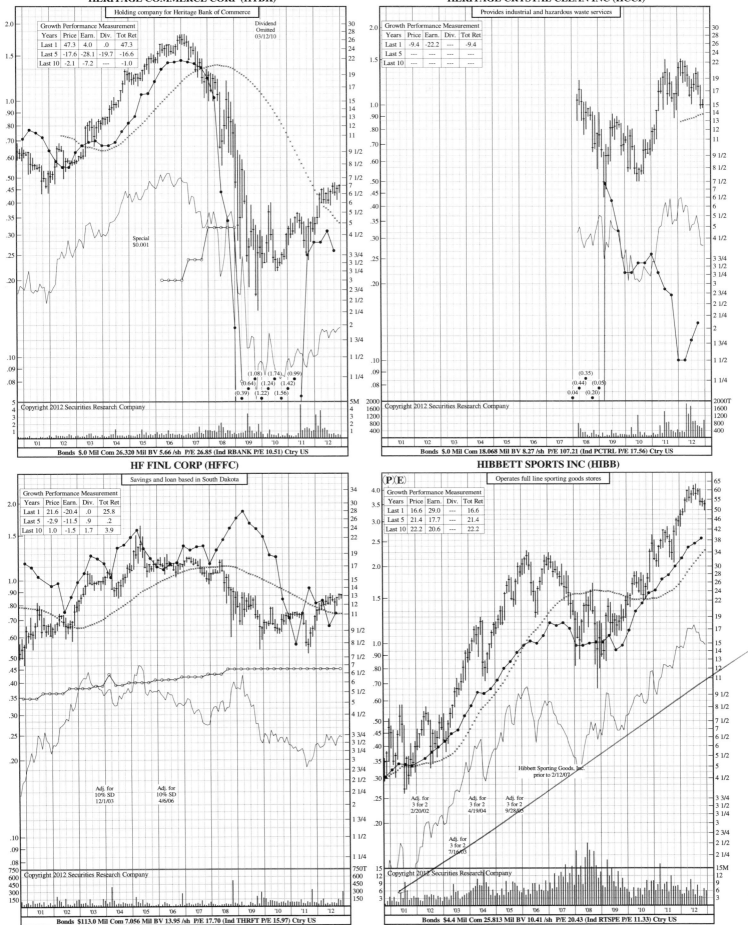

HERITAGE COMMERCE CORP (HTBK)
Holding company for Heritage Bank of Commerce

Growth Performance Measurement				
Years	Price	Earn.	Div.	Tot Ret
Last 1	47.3	4.0	.0	47.3
Last 5	-17.6	-28.1	-19.7	-16.6
Last 10	-2.1	-7.2	---	-1.0

Dividend Omitted 03/12/10

Special $0.001

(1.08) (1.74) (0.99)
(0.64) (1.24) (1.42)
(0.39) (1.22) (1.56)

Copyright 2012 Securities Research Company

Bonds $.0 Mil Com 26.320 Mil BV 5.66 /sh P/E 26.85 (Ind RBANK P/E 10.51) Ctry US

HERITAGE CRYSTAL CLEAN INC (HCCI)
Provides industrial and hazardous waste services

Growth Performance Measurement				
Years	Price	Earn.	Div.	Tot Ret
Last 1	-9.4	-22.2	---	-9.4
Last 5	---	---	---	---
Last 10	---	---	---	---

(0.35)
(0.44) (0.05)
0.04 (0.20)

Copyright 2012 Securities Research Company

Bonds $.0 Mil Com 18.068 Mil BV 8.27 /sh P/E 107.21 (Ind PCTRL P/E 17.56) Ctry US

HF FINL CORP (HFFC)
Savings and loan based in South Dakota

Growth Performance Measurement				
Years	Price	Earn.	Div.	Tot Ret
Last 1	21.6	-20.4	.0	25.8
Last 5	-2.9	-11.5	.9	.2
Last 10	1.0	-1.5	1.7	3.9

Adj. for
10% SD
12/1/03

Adj. for
10% SD
4/6/06

Copyright 2012 Securities Research Company

Bonds $113.0 Mil Com 7.056 Mil BV 13.95 /sh P/E 17.70 (Ind THRFT P/E 15.97) Ctry US

HIBBETT SPORTS INC (HIBB)
Operates full line sporting goods stores

(P)(E)

Growth Performance Measurement				
Years	Price	Earn.	Div.	Tot Ret
Last 1	16.6	29.0	---	16.6
Last 5	21.4	17.7	---	21.4
Last 10	22.2	20.6	---	22.2

Hibbett Sporting Goods, Inc.
prior to 2/12/07

Adj. for
3 for 2
2/20/02

Adj. for
3 for 2
4/19/04

Adj. for
3 for 2
9/28/05

Adj. for
3 for 2
7/16/03

Copyright 2012 Securities Research Company

Bonds $4.4 Mil Com 25.813 Mil BV 10.41 /sh P/E 20.43 (Ind RTSPE P/E 11.33) Ctry US

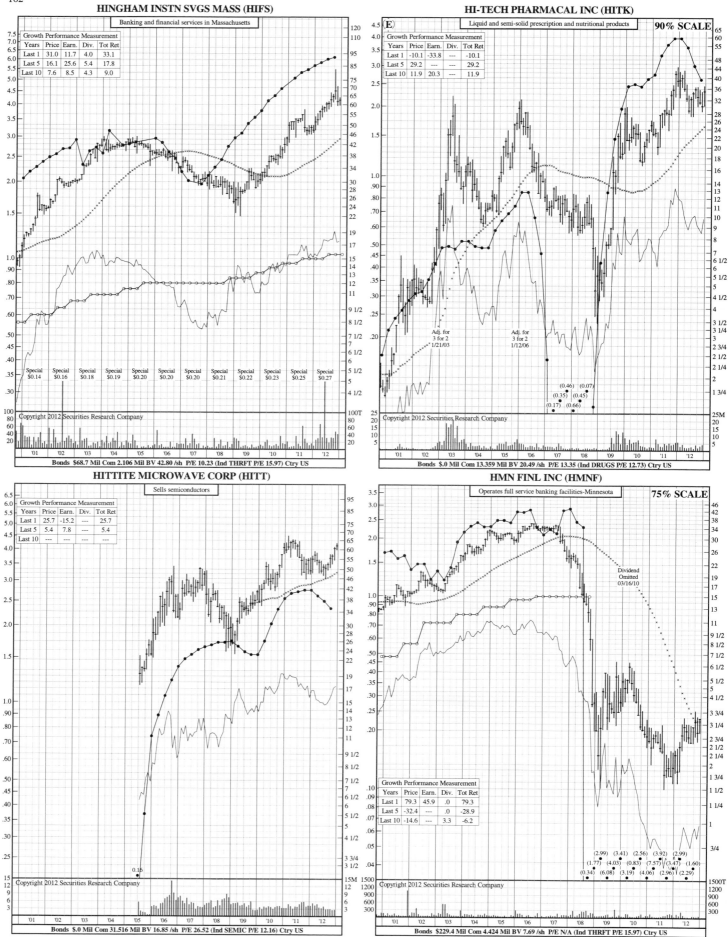

162

HINGHAM INSTN SVGS MASS (HIFS)

Banking and financial services in Massachusetts

Growth Performance Measurement				
Years	Price	Earn.	Div.	Tot Ret
Last 1	31.0	11.7	4.0	33.1
Last 5	16.1	25.6	5.4	17.8
Last 10	7.6	8.5	4.3	9.0

Special $0.14 Special $0.16 Special $0.18 Special $0.19 Special $0.20 Special $0.20 Special $0.20 Special $0.21 Special $0.22 Special $0.23 Special $0.25 Special $0.27

Copyright 2012 Securities Research Company

Bonds $68.7 Mil Com 2.106 Mil BV 42.80 /sh P/E 10.23 (Ind THRFT P/E 15.97) Ctry US

HI-TECH PHARMACAL INC (HITK)

(E) Liquid and semi-solid prescription and nutritional products **90% SCALE**

Growth Performance Measurement				
Years	Price	Earn.	Div.	Tot Ret
Last 1	-10.1	-33.8	---	-10.1
Last 5	29.2	---	---	29.2
Last 10	11.9	20.3	---	11.9

Adj. for 3 for 2 1/21/03

Adj. for 3 for 2 1/12/06

(0.46) (0.07)
(0.35) (0.45)
(0.17) (0.66)

Copyright 2012 Securities Research Company

Bonds $.0 Mil Com 13.359 Mil BV 20.49 /sh P/E 13.35 (Ind DRUGS P/E 12.73) Ctry US

HITTITE MICROWAVE CORP (HITT)

Sells semiconductors

Growth Performance Measurement				
Years	Price	Earn.	Div.	Tot Ret
Last 1	25.7	-15.2	---	25.7
Last 5	5.4	7.8	---	5.4
Last 10	---	---	---	---

0.15

Copyright 2012 Securities Research Company

Bonds $.0 Mil Com 31.516 Mil BV 16.85 /sh P/E 26.52 (Ind SEMIC P/E 12.16) Ctry US

HMN FINL INC (HMNF)

Operates full service banking facilities-Minnesota **75% SCALE**

Dividend Omitted 03/16/10

Growth Performance Measurement				
Years	Price	Earn.	Div.	Tot Ret
Last 1	79.3	45.9	.0	79.3
Last 5	-32.4	---	.0	-28.9
Last 10	-14.6	---	3.3	-6.2

(2.99) (3.41) (2.56) (3.92) (2.99)
(1.77) (4.03) (0.83) (7.57) (3.47) (1.60)
(0.34) (6.08) (3.19) (4.06) (2.96) (2.29)

Copyright 2012 Securities Research Company

Bonds $229.4 Mil Com 4.424 Mil BV 7.69 /sh P/E N/A (Ind THRFT P/E 15.97) Ctry US

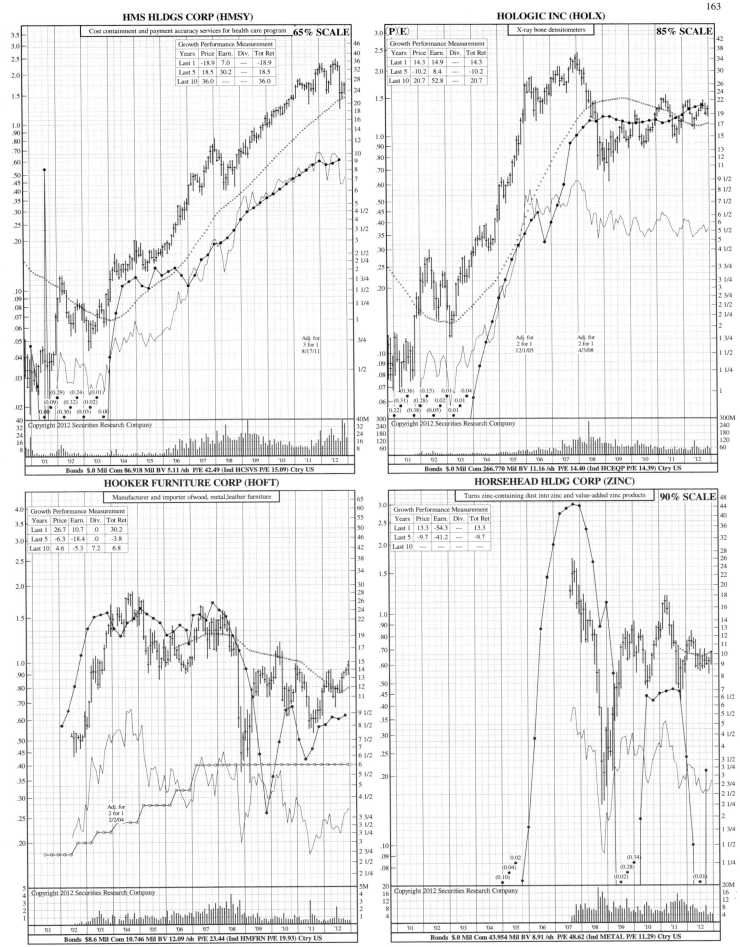

HMS HLDGS CORP (HMSY)

Cost containment and payment accuracy services for health care program **65% SCALE**

Years	Price	Earn.	Div.	Tot Ret
Last 1	-18.9	7.0	---	-18.9
Last 5	18.5	30.2	---	18.5
Last 10	36.0	---	---	36.0

Growth Performance Measurement

Adj. for
3 for 1
8/17/11

(0.29) (0.24) (0.01)
(0.09) (0.32) (0.02)
(0.00) (0.30) (0.03) 0.00

Copyright 2012 Securities Research Company

Bonds $.0 Mil Com 86.918 Mil BV 5.11 /sh P/E 42.49 (Ind HCSVS P/E 15.09) Ctry US

HOLOGIC INC (HOLX)

(P/E)   X-ray bone densitometers   **85% SCALE**

Years	Price	Earn.	Div.	Tot Ret
Last 1	14.3	14.9	---	14.3
Last 5	-10.2	8.4	---	-10.2
Last 10	20.7	52.8	---	20.7

Growth Performance Measurement

Adj. for   Adj. for
2 for 1   2 for 1
12/1/05   4/3/08

(0.36) (0.15) 0.01 0.04
(0.31) (0.28) 0.02 0.01
(0.22) (0.38) (0.05) 0.01

Copyright 2012 Securities Research Company

Bonds $.0 Mil Com 266.770 Mil BV 11.16 /sh P/E 14.40 (Ind HCEQP P/E 14.39) Ctry US

HOOKER FURNITURE CORP (HOFT)

Manufacturer and importer of wood, metal, leather furniture

Years	Price	Earn.	Div.	Tot Ret
Last 1	26.7	10.7	.0	30.2
Last 5	-6.3	-18.4	.0	-3.8
Last 10	4.6	-5.3	7.2	6.8

Growth Performance Measurement

Adj. for
2 for 1
2/2/04

Copyright 2012 Securities Research Company

Bonds $8.6 Mil Com 10.746 Mil BV 12.09 /sh P/E 23.44 (Ind HMFRN P/E 19.93) Ctry US

HORSEHEAD HLDG CORP (ZINC)

Turns zinc-containing dust into zinc and value-added zinc products **90% SCALE**

Years	Price	Earn.	Div.	Tot Ret
Last 1	13.3	-54.3	---	13.3
Last 5	-9.7	-41.2	---	-9.7
Last 10	---	---	---	---

Growth Performance Measurement

0.02   (0.34)
(0.04)   (0.28)
(0.10)   (0.02)   (0.01)

Copyright 2012 Securities Research Company

Bonds $.0 Mil Com 43.954 Mil BV 8.91 /sh P/E 48.62 (Ind METAL P/E 11.29) Ctry US

HOT TOPIC INC (HOTT)

Music-oriented apparel stores

Growth Performance Measurement				
Years	Price	Earn.	Div.	Tot Ret
Last 1	45.7	245.5	14.3	50.4
Last 5	10.6	5.6	---	12.2
Last 10	-4.5	-4.8	---	-3.8

Adj. for 2 for 1 12/28/00
Adj. for 3 for 2 2/7/02
Adj. for 3 for 2 9/3/03

Special $1.00

0.05
0.08
0.01

Copyright 2012 Securities Research Company

Bonds $.2 Mil Com 42.311 Mil BV 4.31 /sh P/E 25.34 (Ind RTAPP P/E 19.00) Ctry US

HOUSTON WIRE & CABLE CO (HWCC)

(E)

Distributes specialty wire and cable products

Growth Performance Measurement				
Years	Price	Earn.	Div.	Tot Ret
Last 1	-11.2	-19.1	.0	-8.6
Last 5	-2.8	-10.5	3.7	-.2
Last 10	---	19.5	---	---

0.00
0.04
0.08
0.05

Copyright 2012 Securities Research Company

Bonds $.0 Mil Com 17.831 Mil BV 5.95 /sh P/E 13.79 (Ind TRADE P/E 25.46) Ctry US

HUB GROUP INC (HUBG)

(P)(E)

Intermodal marketing company

80% SCALE

Growth Performance Measurement			
Years	Price	Earn.	Div.	Tot Ret
Last 1	3.6	24.8	---	3.6
Last 5	4.8	5.3	---	4.8
Last 10	39.5	48.4	---	39.5

Adj. for 2 for 1 5/12/05
Adj. for 2 for 1 6/7/06

0.05
0.04
0.04

Copyright 2012 Securities Research Company

Bonds $131.4 Mil Com 37.105 Mil BV 13.01 /sh P/E 18.56 (Ind AIRFR P/E 16.58) Ctry US

HUDSON CITY BANCORP (HCBK)

(D)

Bank holding company based in New Jersey

Growth Performance Measurement			
Years	Price	Earn.	Div.	Tot Ret
Last 1	30.1	-26.0	.0	35.2
Last 5	-11.6	-.4	-1.2	-6.8
Last 10	3.4	6.4	11.0	7.3

Adj. for 2 for 1 6/18/02
Adj. for 3.20600 for 1 6/7/05

0.06
0.06

Copyright 2012 Securities Research Company

Bonds $16973.0 Mil Com 528.194 Mil BV 8.92 /sh P/E 15.06 (Ind THRFT P/E 15.97) Ctry US

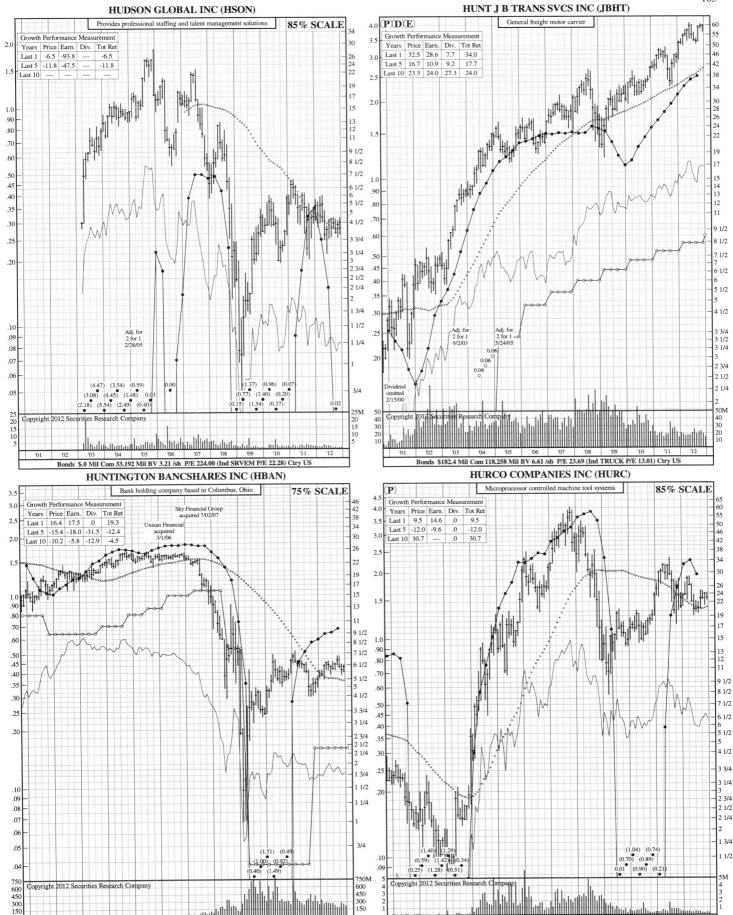

HUDSON GLOBAL INC (HSON)
Provides professional staffing and talent management solutions 85% SCALE

Growth Performance Measurement				
Years	Price	Earn.	Div.	Tot Ret
Last 1	-6.5	-93.8	---	-6.5
Last 5	-11.8	-47.5	---	-11.8
Last 10	---	---	---	---

Adj. for
2 for 1
2/28/05

(4.47) (3.54) (0.59) 0.00   (1.37) (0.96) (0.07)
(3.08) (4.45) (1.48) 0.03   (0.77) (1.40) (0.20)
(2.18) (5.54) (2.49) (0.40)   (0.15) (1.54) (0.37)   0.02

Copyright 2012 Securities Research Company

Bonds $.0 Mil Com 33.192 Mil BV 3.21 /sh P/E 224.00 (Ind SRVEM P/E 22.28) Ctry US

HUNT J B TRANS SVCS INC (JBHT)
General freight motor carrier

P D E

Growth Performance Measurement				
Years	Price	Earn.	Div.	Tot Ret
Last 1	32.5	28.6	7.7	34.0
Last 5	16.7	10.9	9.2	17.7
Last 10	23.3	24.0	27.3	24.0

Adj. for
2 for 1
9/2/03

Adj. for
2 for 1
5/24/05

0.06
0.06
0.06

Dividend
omitted
2/15/00

Copyright 2012 Securities Research Company

Bonds $182.4 Mil Com 118.258 Mil BV 6.61 /sh P/E 23.69 (Ind TRUCK P/E 13.01) Ctry US

HUNTINGTON BANCSHARES INC (HBAN)
Bank holding company based in Columbus, Ohio 75% SCALE

Growth Performance Measurement				
Years	Price	Earn.	Div.	Tot Ret
Last 1	16.4	17.5	.0	19.3
Last 5	-15.4	-18.0	-31.5	-12.4
Last 10	-10.2	-5.8	-12.9	-4.5

Sky Financial Group
acquired 7/02/07

Unizan Financial
acquired
3/1/06

(1.51) (0.49)
(1.00) (0.92)
(0.40) (1.49)

Copyright 2012 Securities Research Company

Bonds $4513.0 Mil Com 855.485 Mil BV 6.34 /sh P/E 9.54 (Ind RBANK P/E 10.51) Ctry US

HURCO COMPANIES INC (HURC)
Microprocessor controlled machine tool systems 85% SCALE

P

Growth Performance Measurement				
Years	Price	Earn.	Div.	Tot Ret
Last 1	9.5	14.6	.0	9.5
Last 5	-12.0	-9.6	.0	-12.0
Last 10	30.7	---	.0	30.7

(1.40) (1.29)
(0.59) (1.42) (0.34)
(0.25) (1.28) (0.51)

(1.04) (0.74)
(0.70) (0.89)
0.01 (0.90) (0.21)

Copyright 2012 Securities Research Company

Bonds $12.4 Mil Com 6.447 Mil BV 21.15 /sh P/E 11.73 (Ind MACHN P/E 14.49) Ctry US

166

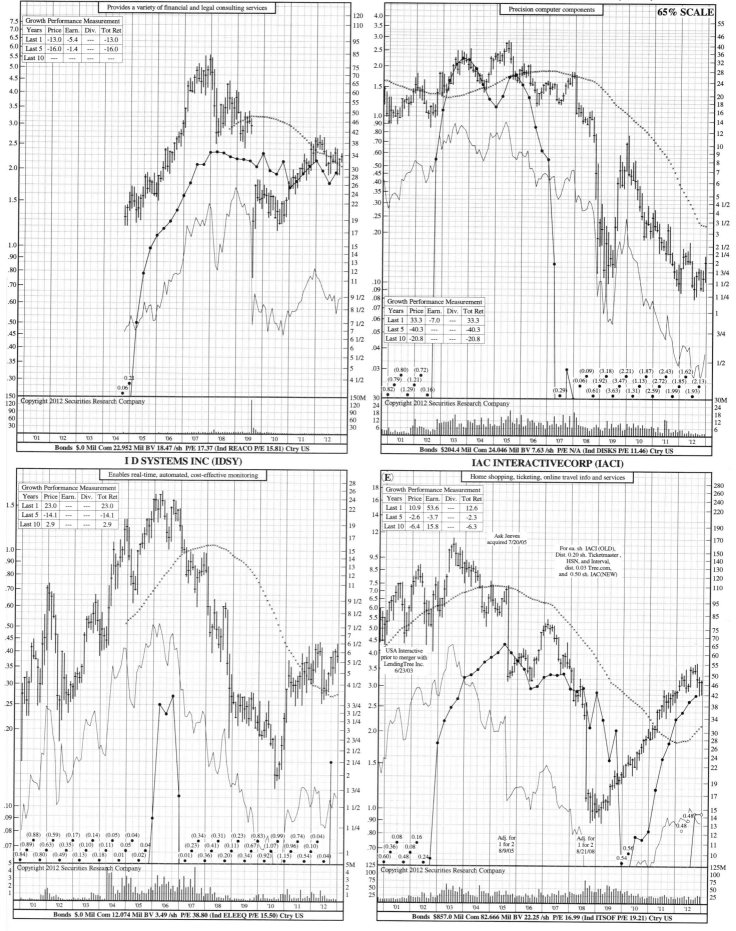

HURON CONSULTING GROUP INC (HURN)

Provides a variety of financial and legal consulting services

Growth Performance Measurement			
Years	Price	Earn.	Div.	Tot Ret
Last 1	-13.0	-5.4	---	-13.0
Last 5	-16.0	-1.4	---	-16.0
Last 10	---	---	---	---

0.21
0.06

Copyright 2012 Securities Research Company

Bonds $.0 Mil Com 22.952 Mil BV 18.47 /sh P/E 17.37 (Ind REACO P/E 15.81) Ctry US

HUTCHINSON TECHNOLOGY INC (HTCH)

Precision computer components   **65% SCALE**

Growth Performance Measurement			
Years	Price	Earn.	Div.	Tot Ret
Last 1	33.3	-7.0	---	33.3
Last 5	-40.3	---	---	-40.3
Last 10	-20.8	---	---	-20.8

(0.80) (0.72)
(0.79) (1.21)   (0.09) (3.18) (2.21) (1.87) (2.43) (1.62)
(0.82) (1.29) (0.16)   (0.06) (1.92) (3.47) (1.13) (2.72) (1.85) (2.13)
(0.29) (0.61) (3.63) (1.31) (2.59) (1.99) (1.93)

Copyright 2012 Securities Research Company

Bonds $204.4 Mil Com 24.046 Mil BV 7.63 /sh P/E N/A (Ind DISKS P/E 11.46) Ctry US

I D SYSTEMS INC (IDSY)

Enables real-time, automated, cost-effective monitoring

Growth Performance Measurement			
Years	Price	Earn.	Div.	Tot Ret
Last 1	23.0	---	---	23.0
Last 5	-14.1	---	---	-14.1
Last 10	2.9	---	---	2.9

(0.88) (0.59) (0.17) (0.14) (0.05) (0.04)   (0.34) (0.31) (0.23) (0.83) (0.99) (0.74) (0.04)
(0.89) (0.63) (0.35) (0.10) (0.11) 0.01 0.04   (0.23) (0.41) (0.11) (0.67) (1.07) (0.96) (0.04)
(0.84) (0.80) (0.49) (0.13) (0.18) 0.01 (0.02)   (0.01) (0.36) (0.20) (0.34) (0.92) (1.15) (0.54) (0.04)

Copyright 2012 Securities Research Company

Bonds $.0 Mil Com 12.074 Mil BV 3.49 /sh P/E 38.80 (Ind ELEEQ P/E 15.50) Ctry US

IAC INTERACTIVECORP (IACI)

(E)   Home shopping, ticketing, online travel info and services

Growth Performance Measurement			
Years	Price	Earn.	Div.	Tot Ret
Last 1	10.9	53.6	---	12.6
Last 5	-2.6	-3.7	---	-2.3
Last 10	-6.4	15.8	---	-6.3

Ask Jeeves
acquired 7/20/05

For ea. sh IACI (OLD),
Dist. 0.20 sh. Ticketmaster ,
HSN, and Interval,
dist. 0.03 Tree.com,
and 0.50 sh. IAC(NEW)

USA Interactive
prior to merger with
LendingTree Inc.
6/23/03

Adj. for
1 for 2
8/9/05

Adj. for
1 for 2
8/21/08

0.48 0.48
0.48

0.08 0.16   0.56
(0.36) 0.08   0.56
(0.60) 0.48 0.24   0.54

Copyright 2012 Securities Research Company

Bonds $857.0 Mil Com 82.666 Mil BV 22.25 /sh P/E 16.99 (Ind ITSOF P/E 19.21) Ctry US

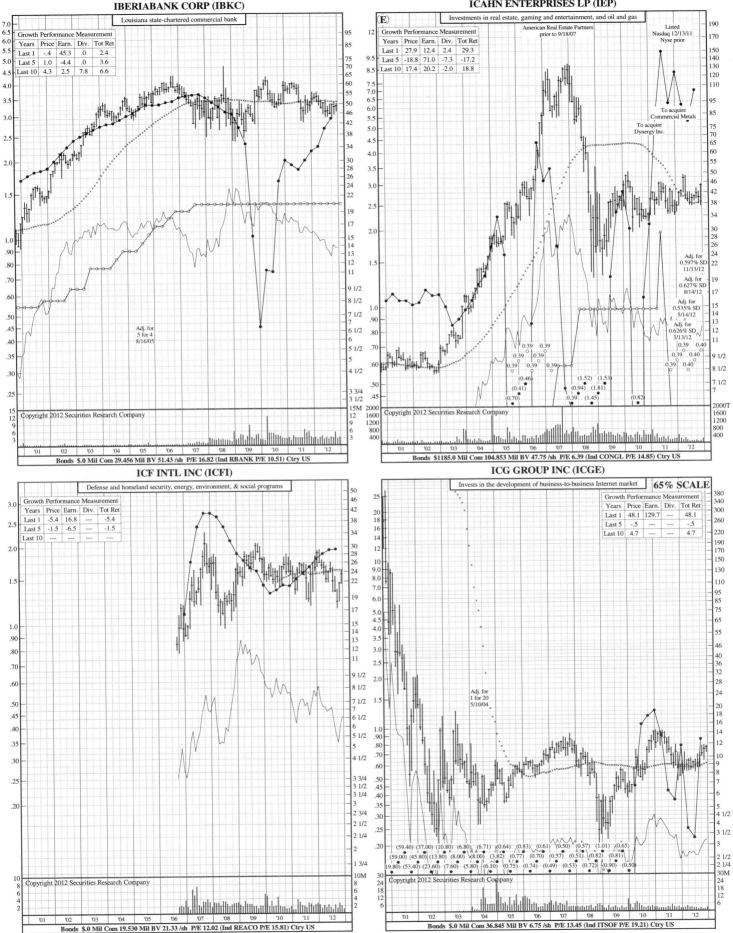

IBERIABANK CORP (IBKC)

Louisiana state-chartered commercial bank

Growth Performance Measurement

Years	Price	Earn.	Div.	Tot Ret
Last 1	-.4	45.3	.0	2.4
Last 5	1.0	-4.4	.0	3.6
Last 10	4.3	2.5	7.8	6.6

Adj. for
5 for 4
8/16/05

Copyright 2012 Securities Research Company

Bonds $.0 Mil Com 29.456 Mil BV 51.43 /sh P/E 16.82 (Ind RBANK P/E 10.51) Ctry US

ICAHN ENTERPRISES LP (IEP)

Investments in real estate, gaming and entertainment, and oil and gas

Growth Performance Measurement

Years	Price	Earn.	Div.	Tot Ret
Last 1	27.9	12.4	2.4	29.3
Last 5	-18.8	71.0	-7.3	-17.2
Last 10	17.4	20.2	-2.0	18.8

American Real Estate Partners
prior to 9/18/07

Listed
Nasdaq 12/13/11
Nyse prior

To acquire
Commercial Metals

To acquire
Dynergy Inc.

Adj. for
0.597% SD
11/13/12

Adj. for
0.627% SD
8/14/12

Adj. for
0.535% SD
5/14/12

Adj. for
0.626% SD
3/13/12

Copyright 2012 Securities Research Company

Bonds $1185.0 Mil Com 104.853 Mil BV 47.75 /sh P/E 6.39 (Ind CONGL P/E 14.85) Ctry US

ICF INTL INC (ICFI)

Defense and homeland security, energy, environment, & social programs

Growth Performance Measurement

Years	Price	Earn.	Div.	Tot Ret
Last 1	-5.4	16.8	---	-5.4
Last 5	-1.5	-6.5	---	-1.5
Last 10	---	---	---	---

Copyright 2012 Securities Research Company

Bonds $.0 Mil Com 19.530 Mil BV 21.33 /sh P/E 12.02 (Ind REACO P/E 15.81) Ctry US

ICG GROUP INC (ICGE)

Invests in the development of business-to-business Internet market

65% SCALE

Growth Performance Measurement

Years	Price	Earn.	Div.	Tot Ret
Last 1	48.1	129.7	---	48.1
Last 5	-.5	---	---	-.5
Last 10	4.7	---	---	4.7

Adj. for
1 for 20
5/10/04

Copyright 2012 Securities Research Company

Bonds $.0 Mil Com 36.845 Mil BV 6.75 /sh P/E 13.45 (Ind ITSOF P/E 19.21) Ctry US

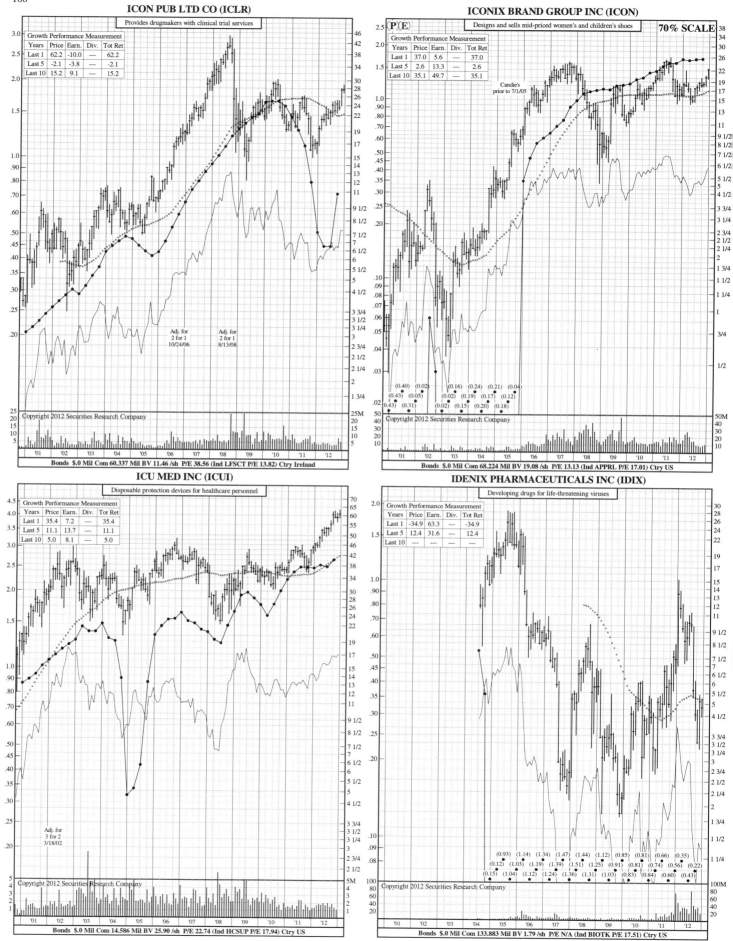

168

ICON PUB LTD CO (ICLR)

Provides drugmakers with clinical trial services

Growth Performance Measurement

Years	Price	Earn.	Div.	Tot Ret
Last 1	62.2	-10.0	---	62.2
Last 5	-2.1	-3.8	---	-2.1
Last 10	15.2	9.1	---	15.2

Adj. for 2 for 1 10/24/06   Adj. for 2 for 1 8/13/08

Copyright 2012 Securities Research Company

Bonds $.0 Mil Com 60.337 Mil BV 11.46 /sh P/E 38.56 (Ind LFSCT P/E 13.82) Ctry Ireland

ICONIX BRAND GROUP INC (ICON)

(P)(E)   70% SCALE

Designs and sells mid-priced women's and children's shoes

Growth Performance Measurement

Years	Price	Earn.	Div.	Tot Ret
Last 1	37.0	5.6	---	37.0
Last 5	2.6	13.3	---	2.6
Last 10	35.1	49.7	---	35.1

Candie's prior to 7/1/05

(0.40) (0.02)   (0.16) (0.24) (0.21) (0.04)
(0.43) (0.05)   (0.02) (0.19) (0.17) (0.12)
(0.43) (0.31)   (0.02) (0.15) (0.20) (0.18)

Copyright 2012 Securities Research Company

Bonds $.0 Mil Com 68.224 Mil BV 19.08 /sh P/E 13.13 (Ind APPRL P/E 17.01) Ctry US

ICU MED INC (ICUI)

Disposable protection devices for healthcare personnel

Growth Performance Measurement

Years	Price	Earn.	Div.	Tot Ret
Last 1	35.4	7.2	---	35.4
Last 5	11.1	13.7	---	11.1
Last 10	5.0	8.1	---	5.0

Adj. for 3 for 2 3/18/02

Copyright 2012 Securities Research Company

Bonds $.0 Mil Com 14.586 Mil BV 25.90 /sh P/E 22.74 (Ind HCSUP P/E 17.94) Ctry US

IDENIX PHARMACEUTICALS INC (IDIX)

Developing drugs for life-threatening viruses

Growth Performance Measurement

Years	Price	Earn.	Div.	Tot Ret
Last 1	-34.9	63.3	---	-34.9
Last 5	12.4	31.6	---	12.4
Last 10	---	---	---	---

(0.93) (1.14) (1.34) (1.47) (1.44) (1.12) (0.85) (0.81) (0.66) (0.35)
(0.12) (1.03) (1.19) (1.39) (1.51) (1.25) (0.91) (0.81) (0.74) (0.56) (0.22)
(0.15) (1.04) (1.12) (1.24) (1.36) (1.31) (1.03) (0.83) (0.84) (0.60) (0.43)

Copyright 2012 Securities Research Company

Bonds $.0 Mil Com 133.883 Mil BV 1.79 /sh P/E N/A (Ind BIOTK P/E 17.51) Ctry US

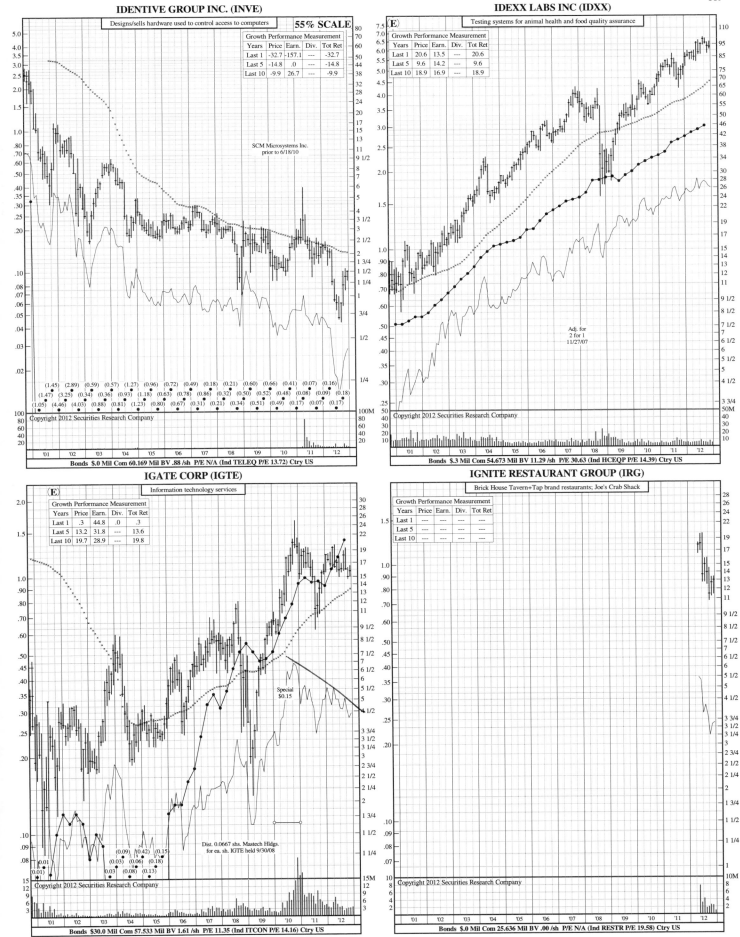

169

IDENTIVE GROUP INC. (INVE)

Designs/sells hardware used to control access to computers

55% SCALE

SCM Microsystems Inc. prior to 6/18/10

Growth Performance Measurement				
Years	Price	Earn.	Div.	Tot Ret
Last 1	-32.7	-157.1	---	-32.7
Last 5	-14.8	.0	---	-14.8
Last 10	-9.9	26.7	---	-9.9

(1.45) (2.89) (0.59) (0.57) (1.27) (0.96) (0.72) (0.49) (0.18) (0.21) (0.60) (0.66) (0.41) (0.07) (0.16)
(1.47) (3.25) (0.34) (0.36) (0.93) (1.18) (0.63) (0.78) (0.86) (0.32) (0.50) (0.52) (0.48) (0.08) (0.09) (0.18)
(1.05) (4.46) (4.03) (0.88) (0.81) (1.23) (0.80) (0.67) (0.31) (0.21) (0.34) (0.51) (0.49) (0.17) (0.07) (0.17)

Copyright 2012 Securities Research Company

Bonds $.0 Mil Com 60.169 Mil BV .88 /sh P/E N/A (Ind TELEQ P/E 13.72) Ctry US

IDEXX LABS INC (IDXX)

Testing systems for animal health and food quality assurance

(E)

Growth Performance Measurement				
Years	Price	Earn.	Div.	Tot Ret
Last 1	20.6	13.5	---	20.6
Last 5	9.6	14.2	---	9.6
Last 10	18.9	16.9	---	18.9

Adj. for 2 for 1 11/27/07

Copyright 2012 Securities Research Company

Bonds $.3 Mil Com 54.673 Mil BV 11.29 /sh P/E 30.63 (Ind HCEQP P/E 14.39) Ctry US

IGATE CORP (IGTE)

Information technology services

(E)

Growth Performance Measurement				
Years	Price	Earn.	Div.	Tot Ret
Last 1	.3	44.8	.0	.3
Last 5	13.2	31.8	---	13.6
Last 10	19.7	28.9	---	19.8

Special $0.15

Dist. 0.0667 shs. Mastech Hldgs. for ea. sh. IGTE held 9/30/08

0.01
0.01
(0.09) (0.42) (0.15)
(0.03) (0.06) (0.18)
(0.03) (0.08) (0.13)

Copyright 2012 Securities Research Company

Bonds $30.0 Mil Com 57.533 Mil BV 1.61 /sh P/E 11.35 (Ind ITCON P/E 14.16) Ctry US

IGNITE RESTAURANT GROUP (IRG)

Brick House Tavern+Tap brand restaurants; Joe's Crab Shack

Growth Performance Measurement				
Years	Price	Earn.	Div.	Tot Ret
Last 1	---	---	---	---
Last 5	---	---	---	---
Last 10	---	---	---	---

Copyright 2012 Securities Research Company

Bonds $.0 Mil Com 25.636 Mil BV .00 /sh P/E N/A (Ind RESTR P/E 19.58) Ctry US

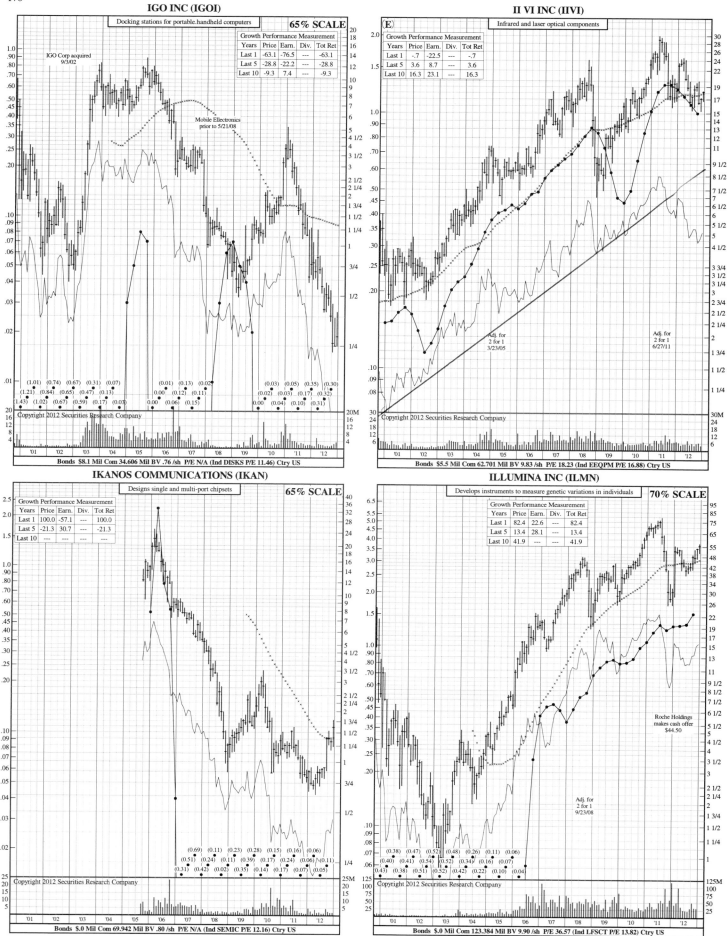

IGO INC (IGOI)

Docking stations for portable.handheld computers

65% SCALE

IGO Corp acquired 9/3/02

Mobile Ellectronics prior to 5/21/08

Growth Performance Measurement				
Years	Price	Earn.	Div.	Tot Ret
Last 1	-63.1	-76.5	---	-63.1
Last 5	-28.8	-22.2	---	-28.8
Last 10	-9.3	7.4	---	-9.3

(1.01) (0.74) (0.67) (0.31) (0.07) (0.01) (0.13) (0.02) (0.03) (0.05) (0.35) (0.30)
(1.21) (0.84) (0.65) (0.47) (0.13) 0.00 (0.12) (0.11) (0.02) (0.03) (0.17) (0.32)
(1.43) (1.02) (0.67) (0.59) (0.17) (0.03) 0.00 (0.06) (0.15) 0.00 (0.04) (0.10) (0.31)

Copyright 2012 Securities Research Company

'01 '02 '03 '04 '05 '06 '07 '08 '09 '10 '11 '12

Bonds $8.1 Mil Com 34.606 Mil BV .76 /sh P/E N/A (Ind DISKS P/E 11.46) Ctry US

II VI INC (IIVI)

(E) Infrared and laser optical components

Growth Performance Measurement				
Years	Price	Earn.	Div.	Tot Ret
Last 1	-.7	-22.5	---	-.7
Last 5	3.6	8.7	---	3.6
Last 10	16.3	23.1	---	16.3

Adj. for 2 for 1 3/23/05

Adj. for 2 for 1 6/27/11

Copyright 2012 Securities Research Company

'01 '02 '03 '04 '05 '06 '07 '08 '09 '10 '11 '12

Bonds $5.5 Mil Com 62.701 Mil BV 9.83 /sh P/E 18.23 (Ind EEQPM P/E 16.88) Ctry US

IKANOS COMMUNICATIONS (IKAN)

Designs single and multi-port chipsets

65% SCALE

Growth Performance Measurement				
Years	Price	Earn.	Div.	Tot Ret
Last 1	100.0	-57.1	---	100.0
Last 5	-21.3	30.7	---	-21.3
Last 10	---	---	---	---

(0.69) (0.11) (0.23) (0.28) (0.15) (0.16) (0.06)
(0.51) (0.24) (0.11) (0.39) (0.17) (0.24) (0.06) (0.11)
(0.31) (0.02) (0.02) (0.35) (0.14) (0.17) (0.07) (0.05)

Copyright 2012 Securities Research Company

'01 '02 '03 '04 '05 '06 '07 '08 '09 '10 '11 '12

Bonds $.0 Mil Com 69.942 Mil BV .80 /sh P/E N/A (Ind SEMIC P/E 12.16) Ctry US

ILLUMINA INC (ILMN)

Develops instruments to measure genetic variations in individuals

70% SCALE

Growth Performance Measurement				
Years	Price	Earn.	Div.	Tot Ret
Last 1	82.4	22.6	---	82.4
Last 5	13.4	28.1	---	13.4
Last 10	41.9	---	---	41.9

Roche Holdings makes cash offer $44.50

Adj. for 2 for 1 9/23/08

(0.38) (0.47) (0.52) (0.48) (0.26) (0.11) (0.06)
(0.40) (0.41) (0.54) (0.52) (0.34) (0.16) (0.07)
(0.43) (0.38) (0.51) (0.52) (0.42) (0.22) (0.10) (0.04)

Copyright 2012 Securities Research Company

'01 '02 '03 '04 '05 '06 '07 '08 '09 '10 '11 '12

Bonds $.0 Mil Com 123.384 Mil BV 9.90 /sh P/E 36.57 (Ind LFSCT P/E 13.82) Ctry US

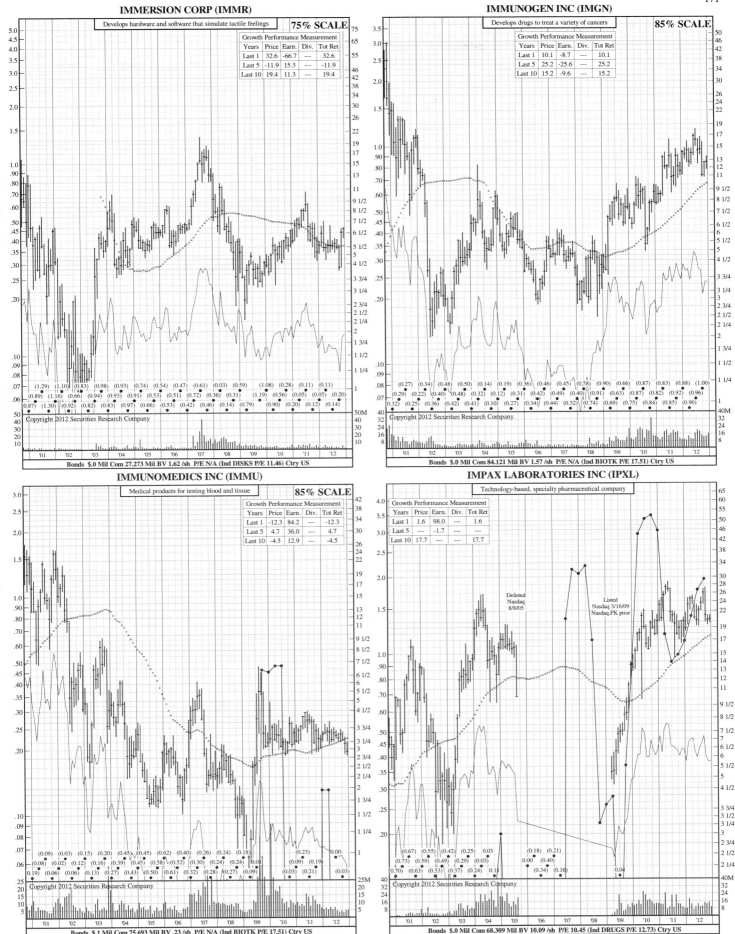

IMMERSION CORP (IMMR)

Develops hardware and software that simulate tactile feelings

75% SCALE

Growth Performance Measurement

Years	Price	Earn.	Div.	Tot Ret
Last 1	32.6	-66.7	---	32.6
Last 5	-11.9	15.3	---	-11.9
Last 10	19.4	11.3	---	19.4

(1.29) (1.10) (0.83) (0.98) (0.93) (0.74) (0.54) (0.47) (0.61) (0.03) (0.59) (1.08) (0.28) (0.11) (0.11)
(0.89) (1.16) (0.66) (0.94) (0.91) (0.53) (0.51) (0.72) (0.36) (0.31) (1.19) (0.56) (0.05) (0.05) (0.20)
(0.87) (1.30) (0.92) (0.82) (0.83) (0.97) (0.66) (0.53) (0.42) (0.46) (0.14) (0.79) (0.90) (0.20) (0.12) (0.14)

Copyright 2012 Securities Research Company

Bonds $.0 Mil Com 27.273 Mil BV 1.62 /sh P/E N/A (Ind DISKS P/E 11.46) Ctry US

IMMUNOGEN INC (IMGN)

Develops drugs to treat a variety of cancers

85% SCALE

Growth Performance Measurement

Years	Price	Earn.	Div.	Tot Ret
Last 1	10.1	-8.7	---	10.1
Last 5	25.2	-25.6	---	25.2
Last 10	15.2	-9.6	---	15.2

(0.27) (0.34) (0.48) (0.50) (0.14) (0.19) (0.36) (0.46) (0.45) (0.58) (0.90) (0.66) (0.87) (0.83) (0.88) (1.00)
(0.29) (0.22) (0.40) (0.48) (0.32) (0.12) (0.31) (0.42) (0.49) (0.40) (0.91) (0.63) (0.87) (0.82) (0.92) (0.96)
(0.32) (0.25) (0.36) (0.42) (0.41) (0.10) (0.27) (0.34) (0.44) (0.32) (0.74) (0.69) (0.75) (0.84) (0.85) (0.90)

Copyright 2012 Securities Research Company

Bonds $.0 Mil Com 84.121 Mil BV 1.57 /sh P/E N/A (Ind BIOTK P/E 17.51) Ctry US

IMMUNOMEDICS INC (IMMU)

Medical products for testing blood and tissue

85% SCALE

Growth Performance Measurement

Years	Price	Earn.	Div.	Tot Ret
Last 1	-12.3	84.2	---	-12.3
Last 5	4.7	36.0	---	4.7
Last 10	-4.5	12.9	---	-4.5

(0.09) (0.03) (0.15) (0.20) (0.45) (0.45) (0.62) (0.40) (0.26) (0.24) (0.18) (0.23) 0.00
(0.08) (0.02) (0.12) (0.16) (0.39) (0.45) (0.58) (0.52) (0.30) (0.24) (0.21) (0.09) (0.19)
(0.19) (0.06) (0.06) (0.13) (0.27) (0.43) (0.50) (0.61) (0.32) (0.28) (0.27) (0.09) (0.03) (0.21) (0.03)

Copyright 2012 Securities Research Company

Bonds $.1 Mil Com 75.693 Mil BV .23 /sh P/E N/A (Ind BIOTK P/E 17.51) Ctry US

IMPAX LABORATORIES INC (IPXL)

Technology-based, specialty pharmaceutical company

Growth Performance Measurement

Years	Price	Earn.	Div.	Tot Ret
Last 1	1.6	98.0	---	1.6
Last 5	---	-1.7	---	---
Last 10	17.7	---	---	17.7

Delisted
Nasdaq
8/8/05

Listed
Nasdaq 3/16/09
Nasdaq.PK prior

(0.67) (0.55) (0.42) (0.25) 0.03 (0.18) (0.21)
(0.73) (0.59) (0.65) (0.29) 0.03 0.00 (0.40)
(0.70) (0.63) (0.53) (0.37) (0.29) 0.11 (0.34) (0.16) 0.04

Copyright 2012 Securities Research Company

Bonds $.0 Mil Com 68.309 Mil BV 10.09 /sh P/E 10.45 (Ind DRUGS P/E 12.73) Ctry US

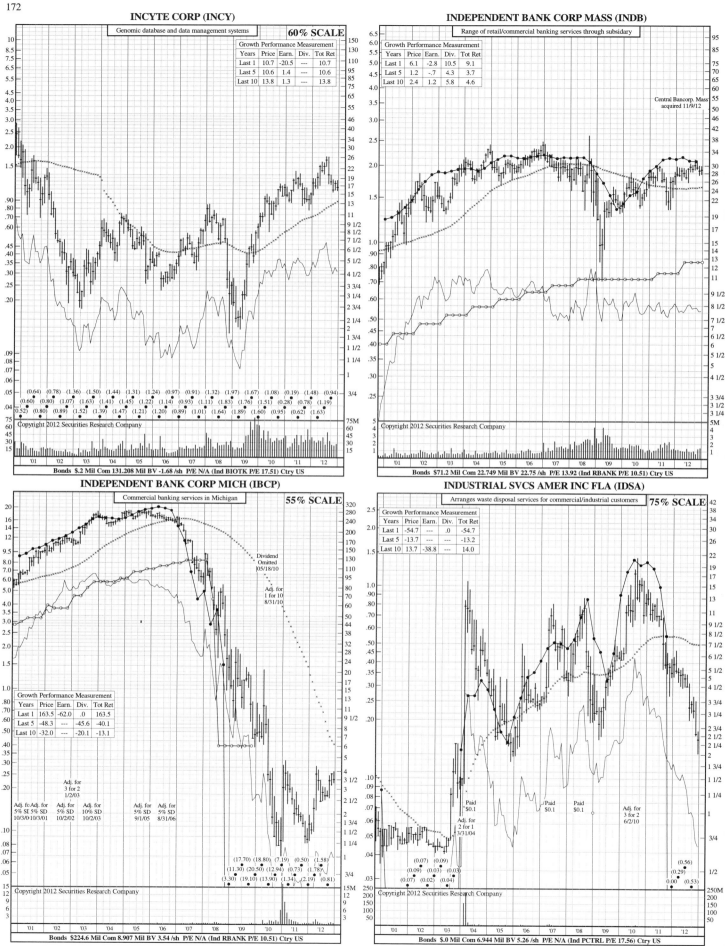

172

INCYTE CORP (INCY)

Genomic database and data management systems **60% SCALE**

Growth Performance Measurement

Years	Price	Earn.	Div.	Tot Ret
Last 1	10.7	-20.5	---	10.7
Last 5	10.6	1.4	---	10.6
Last 10	13.8	1.3	---	13.8

(0.64) (0.78) (1.36) (1.50) (1.44) (1.31) (1.24) (0.97) (0.91) (1.32) (1.97) (1.67) (1.08) (0.19) (1.48) (0.94)
(0.60) (0.80) (1.07) (1.63) (1.41) (1.45) (1.22) (1.14) (0.93) (1.11) (1.83) (1.76) (1.51) (0.28) (0.78) (1.19)
(0.52) (0.80) (0.89) (1.52) (1.39) (1.47) (1.21) (1.20) (0.89) (1.01) (1.64) (1.89) (1.60) (0.95) (0.62) (1.63)

Copyright 2012 Securities Research Company

'01 '02 '03 '04 '05 '06 '07 '08 '09 '10 '11 '12

Bonds $.2 Mil Com 131.208 Mil BV -1.68 /sh P/E N/A (Ind BIOTK P/E 17.51) Ctry US

INDEPENDENT BANK CORP MASS (INDB)

Range of retail/commercial banking services through subsidiary

Growth Performance Measurement

Years	Price	Earn.	Div.	Tot Ret
Last 1	6.1	-2.8	10.5	9.1
Last 5	1.2	-.7	4.3	3.7
Last 10	2.4	1.2	5.8	4.6

Central Bancorp. Mass
acquired 11/9/12

Copyright 2012 Securities Research Company

'01 '02 '03 '04 '05 '06 '07 '08 '09 '10 '11 '12

Bonds $71.2 Mil Com 22.749 Mil BV 22.75 /sh P/E 13.92 (Ind RBANK P/E 10.51) Ctry US

INDEPENDENT BANK CORP MICH (IBCP)

Commercial banking services in Michigan **55% SCALE**

Dividend
Omitted
05/18/10

Adj. for
1 for 10
8/31/10

Growth Performance Measurement

Years	Price	Earn.	Div.	Tot Ret
Last 1	163.5	-62.0	.0	163.5
Last 5	-48.3	---	-45.6	-40.1
Last 10	-32.0	---	-20.1	-13.1

Adj. for
3 for 2
1/2/03

Adj. fo Adj. for   Adj. for   Adj. for   Adj. for Adj. for
5% SE 5% SD   5% SD   10% SD   5% SD   5% SD
10/3/0 10/3/01   10/2/02   10/2/03   9/1/05   8/31/06

(17.70) (18.80) (7.19) (0.50) (1.58)
(11.30) (20.50) (12.94) (0.73) (1.78)
(3.30) (19.10) (13.90) (1.34) (2.19) (0.81)

Copyright 2012 Securities Research Company

'01 '02 '03 '04 '05 '06 '07 '08 '09 '10 '11 '12

Bonds $224.6 Mil Com 8.907 Mil BV 3.54 /sh P/E N/A (Ind RBANK P/E 10.51) Ctry US

INDUSTRIAL SVCS AMER INC FLA (IDSA)

Arranges waste disposal services for commercial/industrial customers **75% SCALE**

Growth Performance Measurement

Years	Price	Earn.	Div.	Tot Ret
Last 1	-54.7	---	.0	-54.7
Last 5	-13.7	---	---	-13.2
Last 10	13.7	-38.8	---	14.0

Paid
$0.1

Paid
$0.1

Paid
$0.1

Adj. for
3 for 2
6/2/10

Adj. for
2 for 1
3/31/04

(0.07) (0.09)   (0.56)
(0.09) (0.03) (0.03)   (0.29)
(0.07) (0.02) (0.04)   0.00 (0.53)

Copyright 2012 Securities Research Company

'01 '02 '03 '04 '05 '06 '07 '08 '09 '10 '11 '12

Bonds $.0 Mil Com 6.944 Mil BV 5.26 /sh P/E N/A (Ind PCTRL P/E 17.56) Ctry US

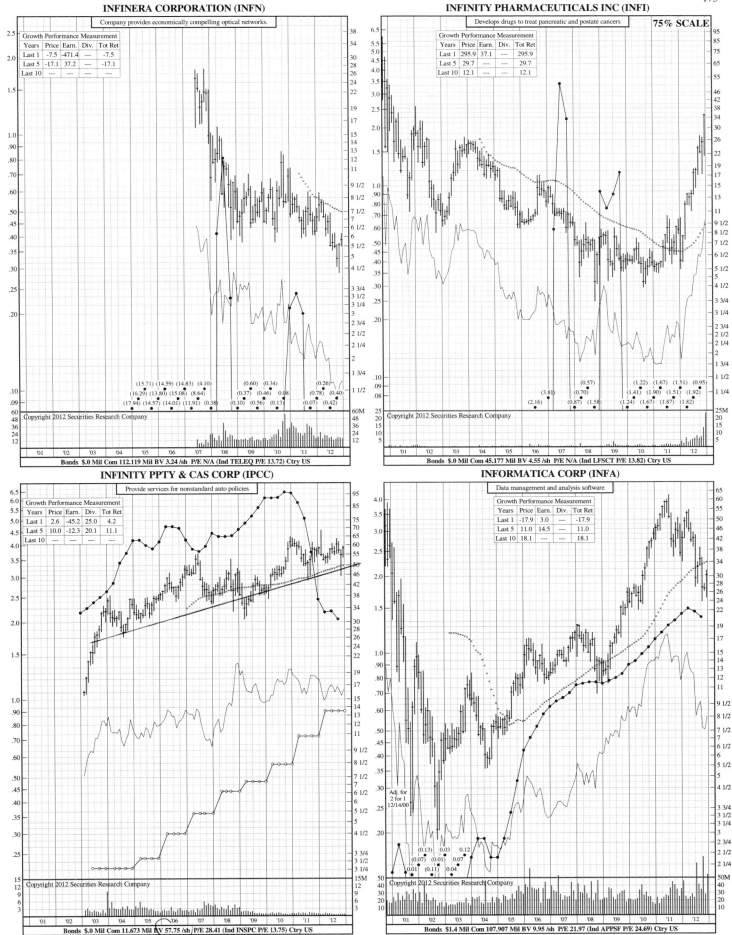

INFINERA CORPORATION (INFN)

Company provides economically compelling optical networks.

Growth Performance Measurement				
Years	Price	Earn.	Div.	Tot Ret
Last 1	-7.5	-471.4	---	-7.5
Last 5	-17.1	37.2	---	-17.1
Last 10	---	---	---	---

(15.71) (14.59) (14.83) (4.10)   (0.60) (0.34)   (0.26)
(16.29) (13.80) (15.08) (8.64)   (0.37) (0.46) 0.08   (0.78) (0.40)
(17.94) (14.57) (14.01) (11.91) 0.38 (0.10) (0.56) (0.13) (0.07) (0.42)

Copyright 2012 Securities Research Company

Bonds $.0 Mil Com 112.119 Mil BV 3.24 /sh P/E N/A (Ind TELEQ P/E 13.72) Ctry US

INFINITY PHARMACEUTICALS INC (INFI)

Develops drugs to treat pancreatic and postate cancers.   **75% SCALE**

Growth Performance Measurement				
Years	Price	Earn.	Div.	Tot Ret
Last 1	295.9	37.1	---	295.9
Last 5	29.7	---	---	29.7
Last 10	12.1	---	---	12.1

(3.81)   (0.57)   (1.22) (1.67) (1.51) (0.95)
              (0.70)   (1.41) (1.90) (1.51) (1.92)
(2.16)   (0.87) (1.58) (1.24) (1.67) (1.87) (1.82)

Copyright 2012 Securities Research Company

Bonds $.0 Mil Com 45.177 Mil BV 4.55 /sh P/E N/A (Ind LFSCT P/E 13.82) Ctry US

INFINITY PPTY & CAS CORP (IPCC)

Provide services for nonstandard auto policies

Growth Performance Measurement				
Years	Price	Earn.	Div.	Tot Ret
Last 1	2.6	-45.2	25.0	4.2
Last 5	10.0	-12.3	20.1	11.1
Last 10	---	---	---	---

Copyright 2012 Securities Research Company

Bonds $.0 Mil Com 11.673 Mil BV 57.75 /sh P/E 28.41 (Ind INSPC P/E 13.75) Ctry US

INFORMATICA CORP (INFA)

Data management and analysis software

Growth Performance Measurement				
Years	Price	Earn.	Div.	Tot Ret
Last 1	-17.9	3.0	---	-17.9
Last 5	11.0	14.5	---	11.0
Last 10	18.1	---	---	18.1

Adj. for
2 for 1
12/14/00

       (0.13) 0.03 0.12
       (0.07) (0.01) 0.07
0.01   (0.11) 0.04

Copyright 2012 Securities Research Company

Bonds $1.4 Mil Com 107.907 Mil BV 9.95 /sh P/E 21.97 (Ind APPSF P/E 24.69) Ctry US

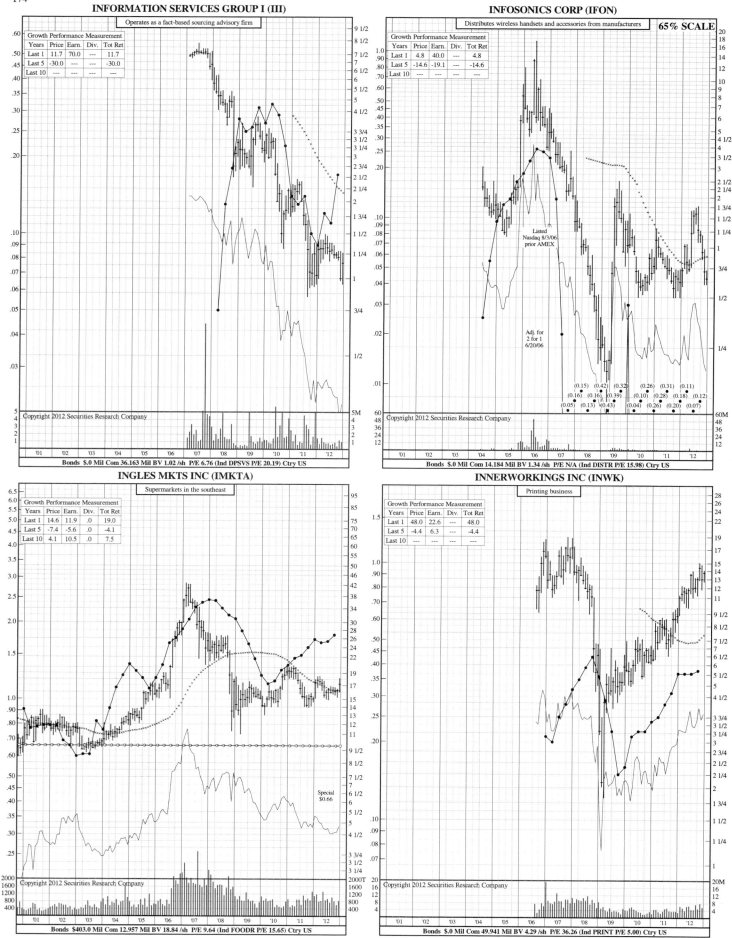

174

INFORMATION SERVICES GROUP I (III)

Operates as a fact-based sourcing advisory firm

Growth Performance Measurement				
Years	Price	Earn.	Div.	Tot Ret
Last 1	11.7	70.0	---	11.7
Last 5	-30.0	---	---	-30.0
Last 10	---	---	---	---

Copyright 2012 Securities Research Company

Bonds $.0 Mil Com 36.163 Mil BV 1.02 /sh P/E 6.76 (Ind DPSVS P/E 20.19) Ctry US

INFOSONICS CORP (IFON)

Distributes wireless handsets and accessories from manufacturers

65% SCALE

Growth Performance Measurement				
Years	Price	Earn.	Div.	Tot Ret
Last 1	4.8	40.0	---	4.8
Last 5	-14.6	-19.1	---	-14.6
Last 10	---	---	---	---

Listed
Nasdaq 8/3/06
prior AMEX

Adj. for
2 for 1
6/20/06

(0.15) (0.42) (0.32)   (0.26) (0.31) (0.11)
(0.16) (0.16) (0.39)   (0.10) (0.28) (0.18) (0.12)
(0.05) (0.13) (0.43)   (0.04) (0.26) (0.20) (0.07)

Copyright 2012 Securities Research Company

Bonds $.0 Mil Com 14.184 Mil BV 1.34 /sh P/E N/A (Ind DISTR P/E 15.98) Ctry US

INGLES MKTS INC (IMKTA)

Supermarkets in the southeast

Growth Performance Measurement				
Years	Price	Earn.	Div.	Tot Ret
Last 1	14.6	11.9	.0	19.0
Last 5	-7.4	-5.6	.0	-4.1
Last 10	4.1	10.5	.0	7.5

Special
$0.66

Copyright 2012 Securities Research Company

Bonds $403.0 Mil Com 12.957 Mil BV 18.84 /sh P/E 9.64 (Ind FOODR P/E 15.65) Ctry US

INNERWORKINGS INC (INWK)

Printing business

Growth Performance Measurement				
Years	Price	Earn.	Div.	Tot Ret
Last 1	48.0	22.6	---	48.0
Last 5	-4.4	6.3	---	-4.4
Last 10	---	---	---	---

Copyright 2012 Securities Research Company

Bonds $.0 Mil Com 49.941 Mil BV 4.29 /sh P/E 36.26 (Ind PRINT P/E 5.00) Ctry US

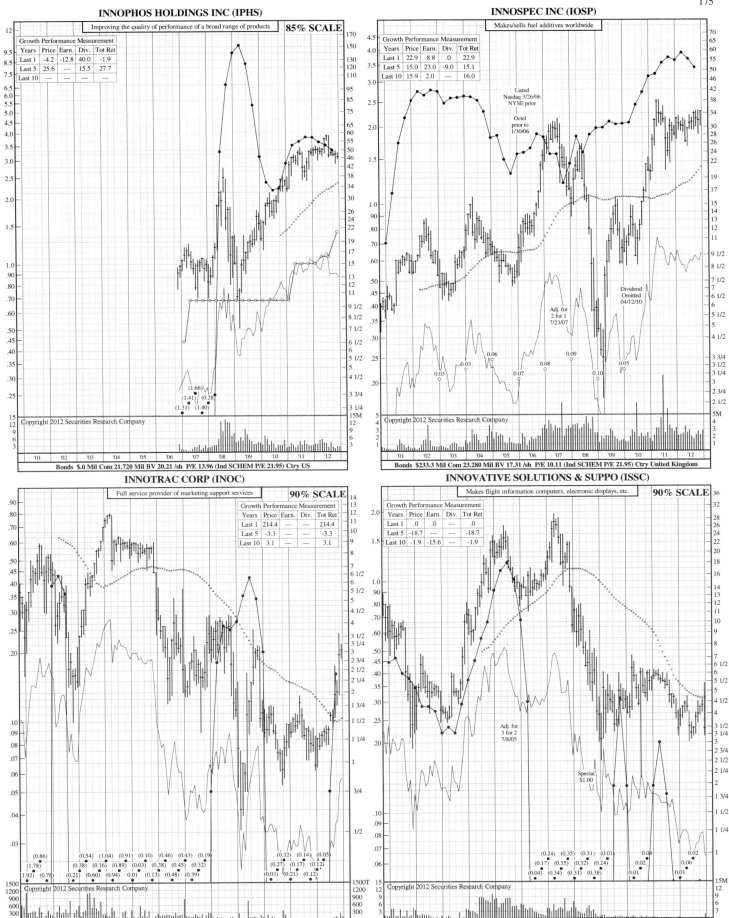

INNOPHOS HOLDINGS INC (IPHS)

Improving the quality of performance of a broad range of products

85% SCALE

Growth Performance Measurement

Years	Price	Earn.	Div.	Tot Ret
Last 1	-4.2	-12.8	40.0	-1.9
Last 5	25.6	---	15.5	27.7
Last 10	---	---	---	---

(1.66)
(1.41) (0.28)
(1.31) (1.40)

Copyright 2012 Securities Research Company

Bonds $.0 Mil Com 21.720 Mil BV 20.21 /sh P/E 13.96 (Ind SCHEM P/E 21.95) Ctry US

INNOSPEC INC (IOSP)

Makes/sells fuel additives worldwide

Growth Performance Measurement

Years	Price	Earn.	Div.	Tot Ret
Last 1	22.9	-8.8	.0	22.9
Last 5	15.0	23.0	-9.0	15.1
Last 10	15.9	2.0	---	16.0

Listed
Nasdaq 3/26/06
NYSE prior

Octel
prior to
1/30/06

Adj. for
2 for 1
7/23/07

Dividend
Omitted
04/12/10

0.03   0.06   0.09
0.03   0.07   0.08   0.05
                           0.10

Copyright 2012 Securities Research Company

Bonds $233.3 Mil Com 23.280 Mil BV 17.31 /sh P/E 10.11 (Ind SCHEM P/E 21.95) Ctry United Kingdom

INNOTRAC CORP (INOC)

Full service provider of marketing support services

90% SCALE

Growth Performance Measurement

Years	Price	Earn.	Div.	Tot Ret
Last 1	214.4	---		214.4
Last 5	-3.3	---	---	-3.3
Last 10	3.1	---	---	3.1

(0.86)   (0.54) (1.04) (0.91) (0.10) (0.46) (0.43) (0.19)   (0.32) (0.14) (0.05)
(1.78)   (0.38) (0.16) (0.89) (0.03) (0.38) (0.45) (0.32)   (0.27) (0.17) (0.12)
(1.92) (0.78)   (0.21) (0.60) (0.94) (0.01) (0.13) (0.48) (0.39)   (0.03) (0.21) (0.12)

Copyright 2012 Securities Research Company

Bonds $.0 Mil Com 13.155 Mil BV 1.60 /sh P/E 19.06 (Ind DIVSS P/E 21.56) Ctry US

INNOVATIVE SOLUTIONS & SUPPO (ISSC)

Makes flight information computers, electronic displays, etc.

90% SCALE

Growth Performance Measurement

Years	Price	Earn.	Div.	Tot Ret
Last 1	.0	.0		.0
Last 5	-18.7	---	---	-18.7
Last 10	-1.9	-15.6	---	-1.9

Adj. for
3 for 2
7/8/05

Special
$1.00

(0.24) (0.35) (0.31) (0.01)   0.04   0.02
(0.17) (0.35) (0.32) (0.24)   0.02   0.00
(0.04) (0.34) (0.31) (0.38)   0.01   0.01

Copyright 2012 Securities Research Company

Bonds $.0 Mil Com 16.583 Mil BV 3.27 /sh P/E 68.80 (Ind AEROD P/E 12.96) Ctry US

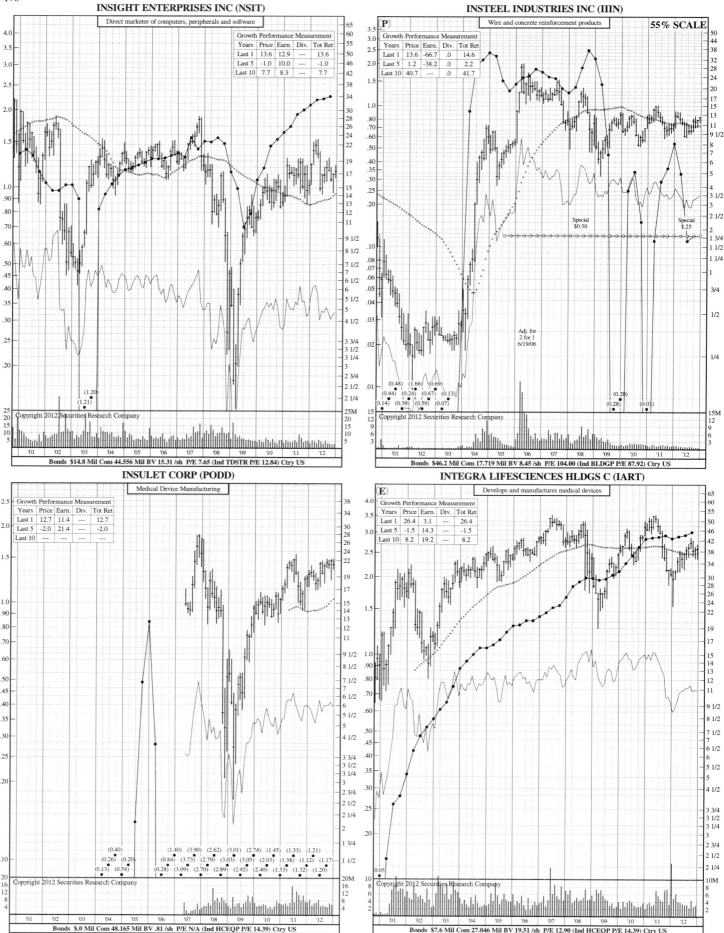

INSIGHT ENTERPRISES INC (NSIT)

Direct marketer of computers, peripherals and software

Growth Performance Measurement				
Years	Price	Earn.	Div.	Tot Ret
Last 1	13.6	12.9	---	13.6
Last 5	-1.0	10.0	---	-1.0
Last 10	7.7	8.3	---	7.7

(1.20)
(1.21)

Copyright 2012 Securities Research Company

Bonds $14.8 Mil Com 44.556 Mil BV 15.31 /sh P/E 7.65 (Ind TDSTR P/E 12.84) Ctry US

INSTEEL INDUSTRIES INC (IIIN)

(P)

Wire and concrete reinforcement products

55% SCALE

Growth Performance Measurement				
Years	Price	Earn.	Div.	Tot Ret
Last 1	13.6	-66.7	.0	14.6
Last 5	1.2	-38.2	.0	2.2
Last 10	40.7	---	.0	41.7

Special
$0.50

Special
$.25

Adj. for
2 for 1
6/19/06

(0.48) (1.66) (0.69)
(0.44) (0.24) (0.67) (0.13)
(0.14) (0.39) (0.59) (0.07)

(0.20)
(0.28)   (0.03)

Copyright 2012 Securities Research Company

Bonds $46.2 Mil Com 17.719 Mil BV 8.45 /sh P/E 104.00 (Ind BLDGP P/E 87.92) Ctry US

INSULET CORP (PODD)

Medical Device Manufacturing

Growth Performance Measurement				
Years	Price	Earn.	Div.	Tot Ret
Last 1	12.7	11.4	---	12.7
Last 5	-2.0	21.4	---	-2.0
Last 10	---	---	---	---

(0.40)
(0.26) (0.20)   (1.40) (3.90) (2.62) (3.01) (2.74) (1.45) (1.33) (1.21)
(0.13) (0.54)   (0.84) (3.73) (2.79) (3.05) (2.03) (1.38) (1.12) (1.17)
(0.28) (3.09) (2.70) (2.89) (2.92) (2.40) (1.53) (1.32) (1.20)

Copyright 2012 Securities Research Company

Bonds $.0 Mil Com 48.165 Mil BV .81 /sh P/E N/A (Ind HCEQP P/E 14.39) Ctry US

INTEGRA LIFESCIENCES HLDGS C (IART)

(E)

Develops and manufactures medical devices

Growth Performance Measurement				
Years	Price	Earn.	Div.	Tot Ret
Last 1	26.4	3.1	---	26.4
Last 5	-1.5	14.3	---	-1.5
Last 10	8.2	19.2	---	8.2

0.05

Copyright 2012 Securities Research Company

Bonds $7.6 Mil Com 27.046 Mil BV 19.51 /sh P/E 12.90 (Ind HCEQP P/E 14.39) Ctry US

INTEGRATED DEVICE TECHNOLOGY (IDTI)

Large scale integrated circuits

75% SCALE

Growth Performance Measurement				
Years	Price	Earn.	Div.	Tot Ret
Last 1	33.7	-45.1	---	33.7
Last 5	-8.4	-22.2	---	-8.4
Last 10	-1.4	---	---	-1.4

(0.19) (0.47)
(0.25) (0.45) (0.25)
(0.22) (0.28) (0.49)

Copyright 2012 Securities Research Company

Bonds $179.6 Mil Com 144.180 Mil BV 4.53 /sh P/E 26.07 (Ind SEMIC P/E 12.16) Ctry US

INTEGRATED SILICON SOLUTION (ISSI)

High performance memory for computer components

90% SCALE

Growth Performance Measurement				
Years	Price	Earn.	Div.	Tot Ret
Last 1	-1.5	-21.9	---	-1.5
Last 5	6.3	20.5	---	6.3
Last 10	7.5	---	---	7.5

(1.89) (1.79) (0.52) (0.10) (0.26) (0.38)
(1.12) (1.88) (0.86) (0.05) (0.27) (0.25) (0.34)
(0.45) (1.94) (1.09) (0.17) (0.33) (0.31) (0.02) (0.22)

Copyright 2012 Securities Research Company

Bonds $.0 Mil Com 27.778 Mil BV 8.80 /sh P/E 10.11 (Ind SEMIC P/E 12.16) Ctry US

INTEL CORP (INTC)

Semiconductors, microprocessors, microcomputers

Growth Performance Measurement				
Years	Price	Earn.	Div.	Tot Ret
Last 1	-15.0	-2.0	7.1	-10.5
Last 5	-5.0	18.5	14.9	-2.0
Last 10	2.8	17.0	27.4	5.0

Xircom, Inc. acq. 3/13/01

McAfee Inc. acquired 2/28/11

0.08 0.08 0.08 0.08 0.16
0.08 0.08 0.08 0.08 0.16 0.16
0.08 0.08 0.08 0.08 0.16 0.16

Copyright 2012 Securities Research Company

Bonds $1848.0 Mil Com 4963.000 Mil BV 9.89 /sh P/E 8.56 (Ind SEMIC P/E 12.16) Ctry US

INTELIQUENT (IQNT)

Tandem interconnection services including wireless, wireline etc

Growth Performance Measurement				
Years	Price	Earn.	Div.	Tot Ret
Last 1	-76.0	-1.3	---	-76.0
Last 5	-33.0	---	---	-33.0
Last 10	---	---	---	---

Neutral Tandem Inc, prior to 2/7/12

Copyright 2012 Securities Research Company

Bonds $.0 Mil Com 32.223 Mil BV 8.59 /sh P/E 3.34 (Ind TLALT P/E N/A) Ctry US

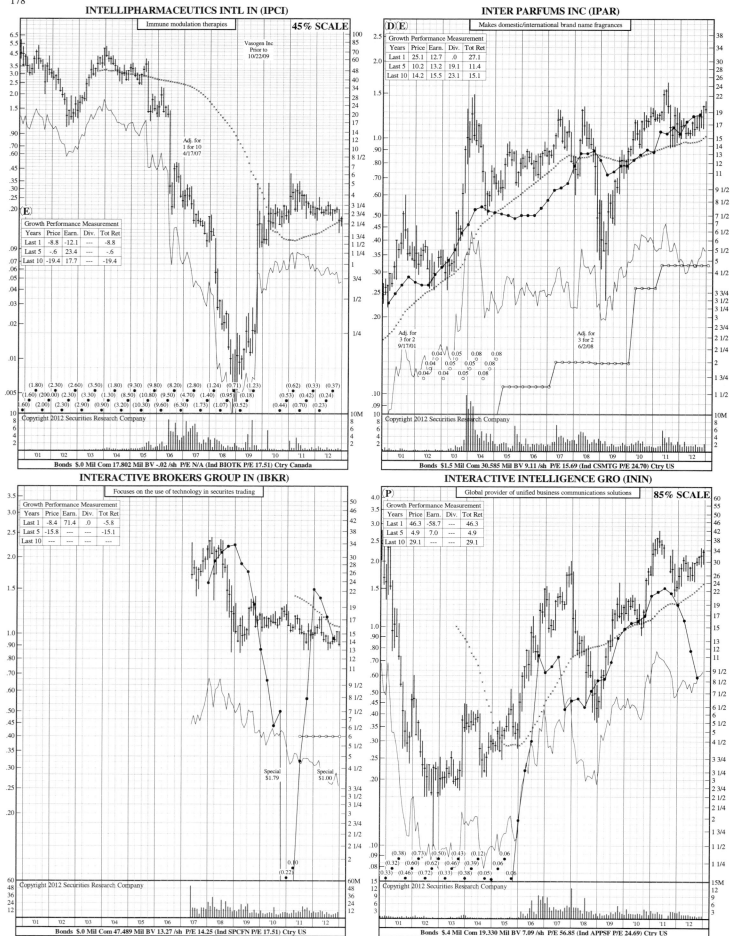

178

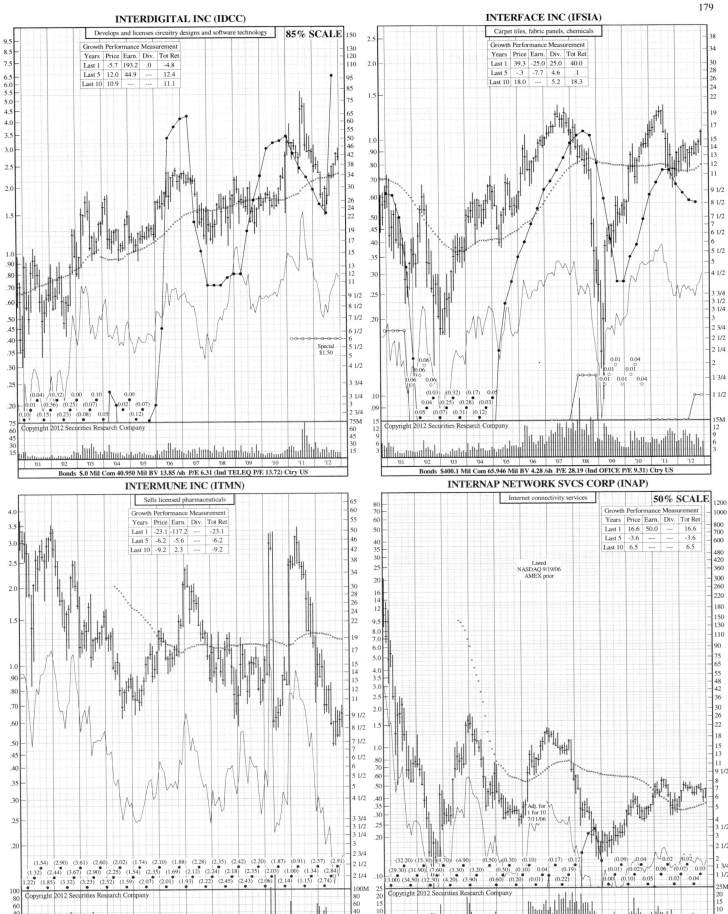

INTERDIGITAL INC (IDCC)

Develops and licenses circuitry designs and software technology

85% SCALE

Growth Performance Measurement				
Years	Price	Earn.	Div.	Tot Ret
Last 1	-5.7	193.2	.0	-4.8
Last 5	12.0	44.9	---	12.4
Last 10	10.9	---		11.1

Special $1.50

(0.04) (0.32) 0.00 0.10 0.00
0.01 (0.36) (0.25) (0.07) 0.02 (0.07)
0.10 (0.15) (0.23) (0.08) 0.05 (0.12)

Copyright 2012 Securities Research Company

Bonds $.0 Mil Com 40.950 Mil BV 13.85 /sh P/E 6.31 (Ind TELEQ P/E 13.72) Ctry US

INTERFACE INC (IFSIA)

Carpet tiles, fabric panels, chemicals

Growth Performance Measurement				
Years	Price	Earn.	Div.	Tot Ret
Last 1	39.3	-25.0	25.0	40.0
Last 5	-.3	-7.7	4.6	.1
Last 10	18.0	---	5.2	18.3

0.06 0.01 0.04
0.06 0.06 0.01 0.01
0.06 0.01 0.04
(0.03) (0.32) (0.17) 0.05
0.04 (0.25) (0.28) (0.03)
0.05 (0.07) (0.31) (0.12)

Copyright 2012 Securities Research Company

Bonds $400.1 Mil Com 65.946 Mil BV 4.28 /sh P/E 28.19 (Ind OFICE P/E 9.31) Ctry US

INTERMUNE INC (ITMN)

Sells licensed pharmaceuticals

Growth Performance Measurement				
Years	Price	Earn.	Div.	Tot Ret
Last 1	-23.1	-117.2	---	-23.1
Last 5	-6.2	-5.6	---	-6.2
Last 10	-9.2	2.3	---	-9.2

(1.54) (2.90) (3.61) (2.60) (2.02) (1.74) (2.10) (1.88) (2.28) (2.35) (2.42) (2.20) (1.87) (0.91) (2.57) (2.91)
(1.32) (2.44) (3.67) (2.90) (2.25) (1.54) (2.35) (1.69) (2.12) (2.24) (2.18) (2.35) (2.03) (1.00) (1.34) (2.84)
(1.22) (1.85) (3.32) (3.23) (2.52) (1.59) (2.07) (2.01) (1.93) (2.22) (2.45) (2.43) (2.06) (2.14) (1.15) (2.74)

Copyright 2012 Securities Research Company

Bonds $1.6 Mil Com 66.016 Mil BV 1.84 /sh P/E N/A (Ind BIOTK P/E 17.51) Ctry US

INTERNAP NETWORK SVCS CORP (INAP)

Internet connectivity services

50% SCALE

Growth Performance Measurement				
Years	Price	Earn.	Div.	Tot Ret
Last 1	16.6	50.0	---	16.6
Last 5	-3.6	---	---	-3.6
Last 10	6.5	---	---	6.5

Listed
NASDAQ 9/19/06
AMEX prior

Adj. for
1 for 10
7/11/06

(32.20) (15.30) (4.70) (4.90) (0.50) (0.30) (0.10) (0.17) (0.12) (0.09) -0.04 0.02 0.02
(29.30) (31.90) (7.60) (3.30) (3.20) (0.50) (0.10) 0.04 (0.19) (0.01) (0.02) 0.06 (0.02) 0.03
(13.00) (34.50) (12.30) (4.20) (3.90) (0.60) (0.20) (0.01) (0.22) 0.00 (0.10) 0.05 0.02 0.04

Copyright 2012 Securities Research Company

Bonds $14.4 Mil Com 53.456 Mil BV 3.63 /sh P/E 230.87 (Ind ITSOF P/E 19.21) Ctry US

180

INTERNATIONAL BANCSHARES COR (IBOC)

A bank holding company

Growth Performance Measurement

Years	Price	Earn.	Div.	Tot Ret
Last 1	-1.3	-13.1	5.6	.7
Last 5	-2.9	-.7	-9.8	-.5
Last 10	-.1	1.2	2.4	2.3

Adj. for 5 for 4 6/18/01
Adj. for 5 for 4 6/17/02
Adj. for 5 for 4 6/17/03
Adj. for 5 for 4 6/1/04
Adj. for 5 for 4 6/1/05
Adj. for 10% SD 5/17/07

Copyright 2012 Securities Research Company

'01 '02 '03 '04 '05 '06 '07 '08 '09 '10 '11 '12

Bonds $.0 Mil Com 67.223 Mil BV 21.30 /sh P/E 12.39 (Ind RBANK P/E 10.51) Ctry US

INTERNATIONAL SPEEDWAY CORP (ISCA)

(D) Promoter of motorsports activities in US

Growth Performance Measurement

Years	Price	Earn.	Div.	Tot Ret
Last 1	9.1	-5.6	25.0	10.6
Last 5	-7.7	-11.8	20.1	-7.1
Last 10	-2.9	-2.7	12.8	-2.5

Action Performance acquired 12/10/05

0.06 0.06 0.06 0.06 0.06 0.08 0.10 0.14 0.16 0.20
0.06 0.12 0.18

Copyright 2012 Securities Research Company

'01 '02 '03 '04 '05 '06 '07 '08 '09 '10 '11 '12

Bonds $496.1 Mil Com 26.354 Mil BV 26.53 /sh P/E 18.19 (Ind LEISF P/E 17.17) Ctry US

INTERNET GOLD-GOLDEN LINES L (IGLD)

Provides a wide array of internet services to meet the needs of reside

65% SCALE

Growth Performance Measurement

Years	Price	Earn.	Div.	Tot Ret
Last 1	-69.6	---	---	-69.6
Last 5	-22.3	---	---	-22.3
Last 10	11.5	---	---	11.5

(0.91) (0.05)
(0.99) (0.24)
(1.03) (0.57)
(3.55)
(3.36)

Copyright 2012 Securities Research Company

'01 '02 '03 '04 '05 '06 '07 '08 '09 '10 '11 '12

Bonds $3.6 Mil Com 19.203 Mil BV -1.67 /sh P/E N/A (Ind ITSOF P/E 19.21) Ctry US

INTERNET PATENTS CORP (PTNT)

Operates an online insurance marketplace

80% SCALE

Growth Performance Measurement

Years	Price	Earn.	Div.	Tot Ret
Last 1	-56.4	---	---	-56.4
Last 5	-17.0	---	---	-17.0
Last 10	8.2	11.3	---	8.2

Insweb,Inc. prior to 10/31/11

(4.74) (3.09) (1.37) (0.96) (1.75) (1.77) (1.42) (1.74) (0.28) (0.61) (0.01) (0.38)
(5.88) (3.52) (1.82) (0.98) (1.51) (1.89) (1.87) (1.69) (0.81) (0.61) (0.18) (0.50)
(6.96) (3.96) (2.45) (1.06) (1.19) (1.91) (1.50) (1.53) (1.31) (0.39) (0.59) (0.56) (0.55)

Special $5.00

Copyright 2012 Securities Research Company

'01 '02 '03 '04 '05 '06 '07 '08 '09 '10 '11 '12

Bonds $.0 Mil Com 7.752 Mil BV 4.36 /sh P/E N/A (Ind ITSOF P/E 19.21) Ctry US

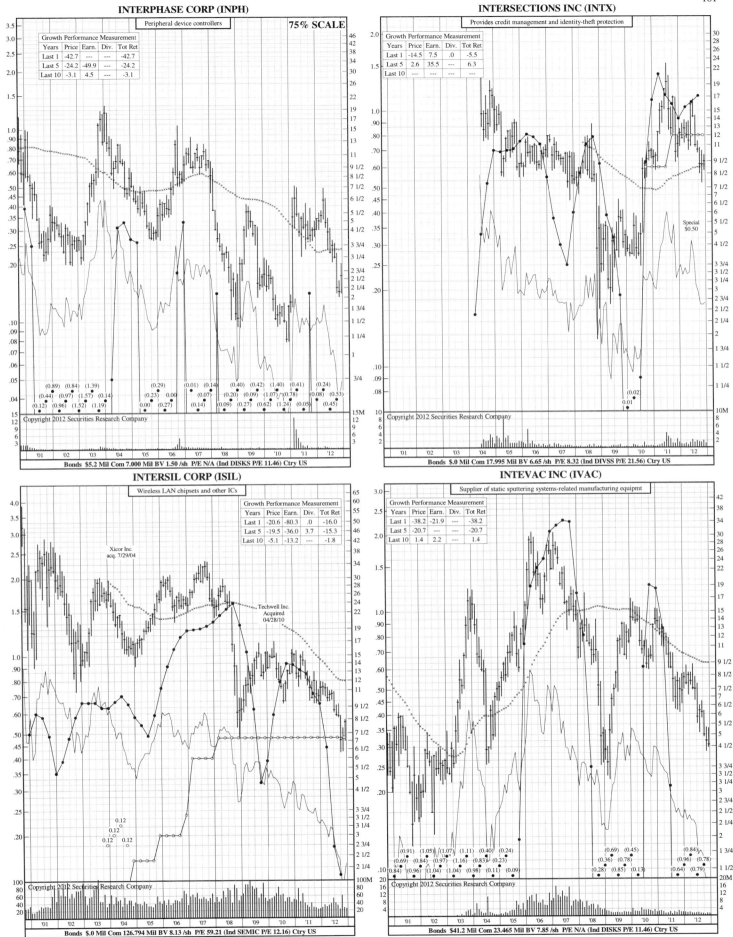

INTERPHASE CORP (INPH)
Peripheral device controllers
75% SCALE

Growth Performance Measurement

Years	Price	Earn.	Div.	Tot Ret
Last 1	-42.7	---	---	-42.7
Last 5	-24.2	-49.9	---	-24.2
Last 10	-3.1	4.5	---	-3.1

(0.89) (0.84) (1.39)　　　(0.29)　　　(0.01) (0.14)　(0.40) (0.42) (1.40) (0.41)　(0.24)
(0.44) (0.97) (1.57) (0.14)　　(0.23) 0.00 (0.07)　(0.20) (0.09) (1.07) (0.78) (0.08) (0.53)
(0.12) (0.96) (1.52) (1.19)　0.00 (0.27) (0.14) (0.09) (0.27) (0.62) (1.24) (0.05) (0.45)

Copyright 2012 Securities Research Company

Bonds $5.2 Mil Com 7.000 Mil BV 1.50 /sh P/E N/A (Ind DISKS P/E 11.46) Ctry US

INTERSECTIONS INC (INTX)
Provides credit management and identity-theft protection

Growth Performance Measurement

Years	Price	Earn.	Div.	Tot Ret
Last 1	-14.5	7.5	.0	-5.5
Last 5	2.6	35.5		6.3
Last 10	---	---	---	---

Special
$0.50

(0.02)
0.01

Copyright 2012 Securities Research Company

Bonds $.0 Mil Com 17.995 Mil BV 6.65 /sh P/E 8.32 (Ind DIVSS P/E 21.56) Ctry US

INTERSIL CORP (ISIL)
Wireless LAN chipsets and other ICs

Xicor Inc.
acq. 7/29/04

Techwell Inc.
Acquired
04/28/10

Growth Performance Measurement

Years	Price	Earn.	Div.	Tot Ret
Last 1	-20.6	-80.3	.0	-16.0
Last 5	-19.5	-36.0	3.7	-15.3
Last 10	-5.1	-13.2	---	-1.8

0.12
0.12
0.12
0.12　　0.12

Copyright 2012 Securities Research Company

Bonds $.0 Mil Com 126.794 Mil BV 8.13 /sh P/E 59.21 (Ind SEMIC P/E 12.16) Ctry US

INTEVAC INC (IVAC)
Supplier of static sputtering systems-related manufacturing equipmt

Growth Performance Measurement

Years	Price	Earn.	Div.	Tot Ret
Last 1	-38.2	-21.9	---	-38.2
Last 5	-20.7	---	---	-20.7
Last 10	1.4	2.2	---	1.4

(0.91) (1.05) (1.07) (1.11) (0.40) (0.24)　　(0.69) (0.45)　　(0.84)
(0.69) (0.84) (0.97) (1.16) (0.83) (0.23)　(0.36) (0.78)　(0.96) (0.78)
(0.84) (0.96) (1.04) (1.04) (0.98) (0.11) (0.09)　(0.28) (0.85) (0.13)　(0.64) (0.79)

Copyright 2012 Securities Research Company

Bonds $41.2 Mil Com 23.465 Mil BV 7.85 /sh P/E N/A (Ind DISKS P/E 11.46) Ctry US

182

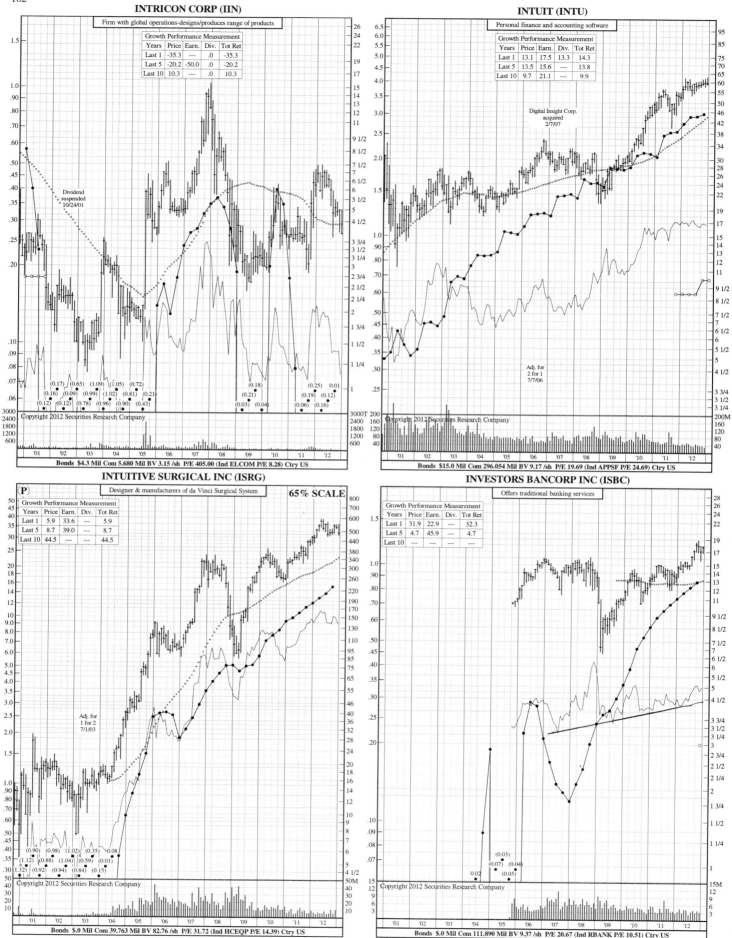

INTRICON CORP (IIN)

Firm with global operations-designs/produces range of products

Growth Performance Measurement				
Years	Price	Earn.	Div.	Tot Ret
Last 1	-35.3	---	.0	-35.3
Last 5	-20.2	-50.0	.0	-20.2
Last 10	10.3	---	.0	10.3

Dividend suspended 10/24/01

(0.17) (0.65) (1.09) (1.05) (0.72)
(0.16) (0.09) (0.99) (1.02) (0.81) (0.21)
(0.12) (0.12) (0.78) (0.96) (0.90) (0.43)
(0.18)
(0.21)
(0.03) (0.04)
(0.25) (0.01)
(0.19) (0.12)
(0.06) (0.16)

Copyright 2012 Securities Research Company

'01 '02 '03 '04 '05 '06 '07 '08 '09 '10 '11 '12

Bonds $4.3 Mil Com 5.680 Mil BV 3.15 /sh P/E 405.00 (Ind ELCOM P/E 8.28) Ctry US

INTUIT (INTU)

Personal finance and accounting software

Growth Performance Measurement				
Years	Price	Earn.	Div.	Tot Ret
Last 1	13.1	17.5	13.3	14.3
Last 5	13.5	15.6	---	13.8
Last 10	9.7	21.1	---	9.9

Digital Insight Corp. acquired 2/7/07

Adj. for 2 for 1 7/7/06

Copyright 2012 Securities Research Company

'01 '02 '03 '04 '05 '06 '07 '08 '09 '10 '11 '12

Bonds $15.0 Mil Com 296.054 Mil BV 9.17 /sh P/E 19.69 (Ind APPSF P/E 24.69) Ctry US

INTUITIVE SURGICAL INC (ISRG)

(P)

Designer & manufacturers of da Vinci Surgical System

65% SCALE

Growth Performance Measurement				
Years	Price	Earn.	Div.	Tot Ret
Last 1	5.9	33.6	---	5.9
Last 5	8.7	39.0	---	8.7
Last 10	44.5	---	---	44.5

Adj. for 1 for 2 7/1/03

(0.90) (0.98) (1.02) (0.35) 0.08
(1.12) (0.88) (1.04) (0.59) (0.01)
(1.32) (0.92) (0.94) (0.84) (0.15)

Copyright 2012 Securities Research Company

'01 '02 '03 '04 '05 '06 '07 '08 '09 '10 '11 '12

Bonds $.0 Mil Com 39.763 Mil BV 82.76 /sh P/E 31.72 (Ind HCEQP P/E 14.39) Ctry US

INVESTORS BANCORP INC (ISBC)

Offers traditional banking services

Growth Performance Measurement				
Years	Price	Earn.	Div.	Tot Ret
Last 1	31.9	22.9	---	32.3
Last 5	4.7	45.9	---	4.7
Last 10	---	---	---	---

(0.03)
(0.07) (0.04)
0.02 (0.05)

Copyright 2012 Securities Research Company

'01 '02 '03 '04 '05 '06 '07 '08 '09 '10 '11 '12

Bonds $.0 Mil Com 111.890 Mil BV 9.37 /sh P/E 20.67 (Ind RBANK P/E 10.51) Ctry US

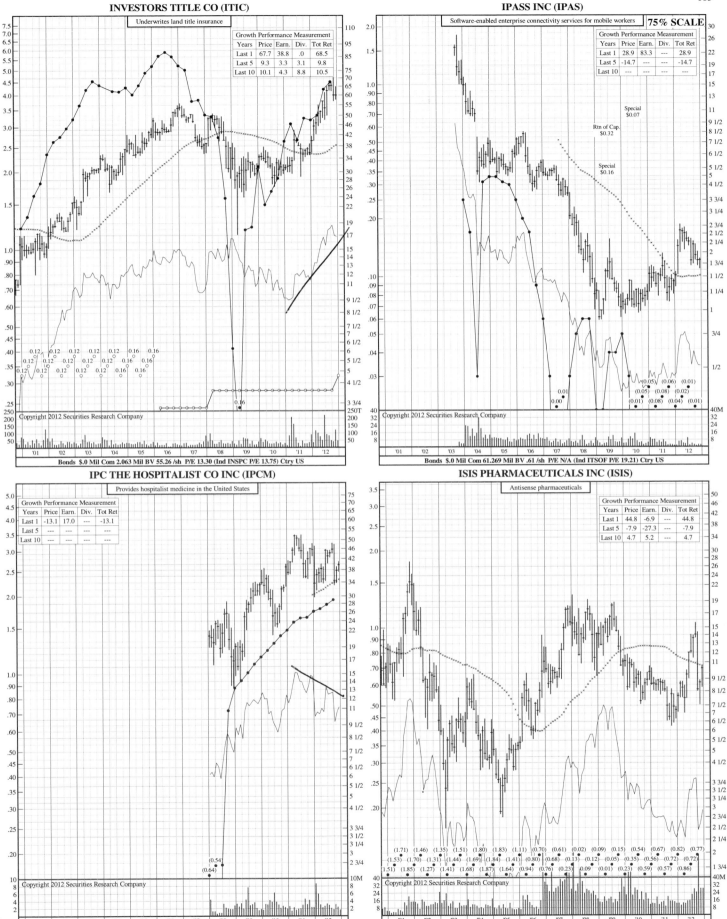

INVESTORS TITLE CO (ITIC)

Underwrites land title insurance

Growth Performance Measurement				
Years	Price	Earn.	Div.	Tot Ret
Last 1	67.7	38.8	.0	68.5
Last 5	9.3	3.3	3.1	9.8
Last 10	10.1	4.3	8.8	10.5

0.12 0.12 0.12 0.12 0.12 0.16 0.16
0.12 0.12 0.12 0.12 0.12 0.16 0.16
0.12 0.12 0.12 0.12 0.16 0.16
0.16

Copyright 2012 Securities Research Company

Bonds $.0 Mil Com 2.063 Mil BV 55.26 /sh P/E 13.30 (Ind INSPC P/E 13.75) Ctry US

IPASS INC (IPAS)

Software-enabled enterprise connectivity services for mobile workers **75% SCALE**

Growth Performance Measurement				
Years	Price	Earn.	Div.	Tot Ret
Last 1	28.9	83.3	---	28.9
Last 5	-14.7	---	---	-14.7
Last 10	---	---	---	---

Special $0.07

Rtn of Cap. $0.32

Special $0.16

0.01
0.00

(0.05) (0.06) (0.01)
(0.05) (0.08) (0.02)
(0.01) (0.08) (0.04) (0.01)

Copyright 2012 Securities Research Company

Bonds $.0 Mil Com 61.269 Mil BV .61 /sh P/E N/A (Ind ITSOF P/E 19.21) Ctry US

IPC THE HOSPITALIST CO INC (IPCM)

Provides hospitalist medicine in the United States

Growth Performance Measurement				
Years	Price	Earn.	Div.	Tot Ret
Last 1	-13.1	17.0	---	-13.1
Last 5	---	---	---	---
Last 10	---	---	---	---

(0.54)
(0.64)

Copyright 2012 Securities Research Company

Bonds $.0 Mil Com 16.683 Mil BV 14.75 /sh P/E 20.58 (Ind HCSVS P/E 15.09) Ctry US

ISIS PHARMACEUTICALS INC (ISIS)

Antisense pharmaceuticals

Growth Performance Measurement				
Years	Price	Earn.	Div.	Tot Ret
Last 1	44.8	-6.9	---	44.8
Last 5	-7.9	-27.3	---	-7.9
Last 10	4.7	5.2	---	4.7

(1.71) (1.46) (1.35) (1.51) (1.80) (1.83) (1.11) (0.70) (0.61) (0.02) (0.09) (0.15) (0.54) (0.67) (0.82) (0.77)
(1.53) (1.70) (1.31) (1.44) (1.69) (1.84) (1.41) (0.80) (0.68) (0.13) (0.12) (0.05) (0.35) (0.56) (0.72) (0.72)
(1.51) (1.85) (1.27) (1.41) (1.68) (1.87) (1.64) (0.94) (0.76) (0.23) (0.09) (0.01) (0.23) (0.59) (0.57) (0.86)

Copyright 2012 Securities Research Company

Bonds $87.3 Mil Com 101.211 Mil BV 1.68 /sh P/E N/A (Ind BIOTK P/E 17.51) Ctry US

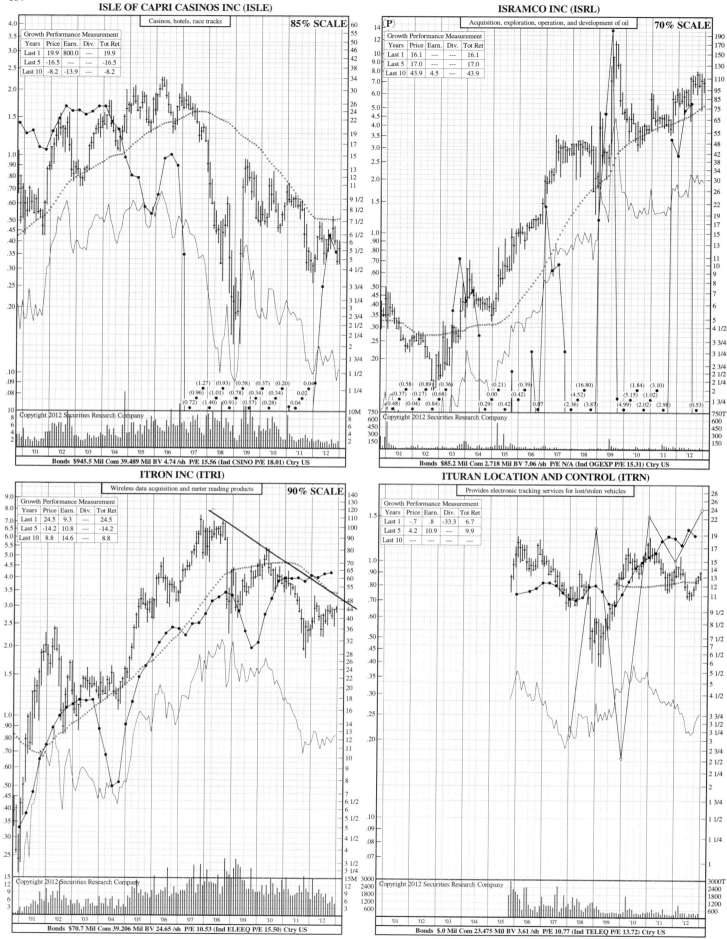

184

ISLE OF CAPRI CASINOS INC (ISLE)

Casinos, hotels, race tracks

85% SCALE

Growth Performance Measurement				
Years	Price	Earn.	Div.	Tot Ret
Last 1	19.9	800.0	---	19.9
Last 5	-16.5	---	---	-16.5
Last 10	-8.2	-13.9	---	-8.2

(1.27) (0.93) (0.58) (0.37) (0.20) 0.04
(0.96) (1.01) (0.78) (0.34) (0.34) 0.02
(0.72) (1.40) (0.91) (0.57) (0.28) 0.04

Copyright 2012 Securities Research Company

Bonds $945.5 Mil Com 39.489 Mil BV 4.74 /sh P/E 15.56 (Ind CSINO P/E 18.01) Ctry US

ISRAMCO INC (ISRL)

Acquisition, exploration, operation, and development of oil

70% SCALE

(P)

Growth Performance Measurement				
Years	Price	Earn.	Div.	Tot Ret
Last 1	16.1	---	---	16.1
Last 5	17.0	---	---	17.0
Last 10	43.9	4.5	---	43.9

(0.58) (0.89) (0.36)   (0.21) (0.39)   (16.80)   (1.84) (3.10)
(0.37) (0.17) (0.68)   0.00 (0.42)   (4.52)   (5.15) (1.02)
(0.48) (0.04) (0.84)   (0.29)(0.42) 0.07 (2.36)(3.87) (4.99)(2.02)(2.98) (0.53)

Copyright 2012 Securities Research Company

Bonds $85.2 Mil Com 2.718 Mil BV 7.06 /sh P/E N/A (Ind OGEXP P/E 15.31) Ctry US

ITRON INC (ITRI)

Wireless data acquisition and meter reading products

90% SCALE

Growth Performance Measurement				
Years	Price	Earn.	Div.	Tot Ret
Last 1	24.5	9.3	---	24.5
Last 5	-14.2	10.8	---	-14.2
Last 10	8.8	14.6	---	8.8

Copyright 2012 Securities Research Company

Bonds $70.7 Mil Com 39.206 Mil BV 24.65 /sh P/E 10.53 (Ind ELEEQ P/E 15.50) Ctry US

ITURAN LOCATION AND CONTROL (ITRN)

Provides electronic tracking services for lost/stolen vehicles

Growth Performance Measurement				
Years	Price	Earn.	Div.	Tot Ret
Last 1	-.7	.8	-33.3	6.7
Last 5	4.2	10.9	---	9.9
Last 10	---	---	---	

Copyright 2012 Securities Research Company

Bonds $.0 Mil Com 23.475 Mil BV 3.61 /sh P/E 10.77 (Ind TELEQ P/E 13.72) Ctry US

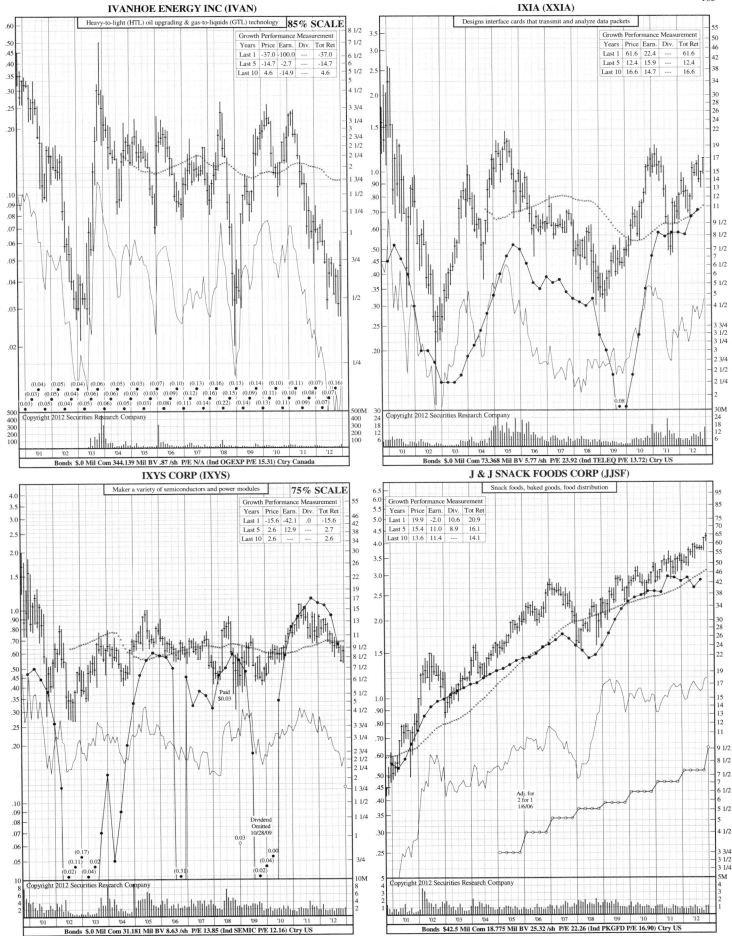

IVANHOE ENERGY INC (IVAN)

Heavy-to-light (HTL) oil upgrading & gas-to-liquids (GTL) technology   **85% SCALE**

Growth Performance Measurement				
Years	Price	Earn.	Div.	Tot Ret
Last 1	-37.0	-100.0	---	-37.0
Last 5	-14.7	-2.7	---	-14.7
Last 10	4.6	-14.9	---	4.6

Copyright 2012 Securities Research Company

Bonds $.0 Mil Com 344.139 Mil BV .87 /sh P/E N/A (Ind OGEXP P/E 15.31) Ctry Canada

IXIA (XXIA)

Designs interface cards that transmit and analyze data packets

Growth Performance Measurement				
Years	Price	Earn.	Div.	Tot Ret
Last 1	61.6	22.4	---	61.6
Last 5	12.4	15.9	---	12.4
Last 10	16.6	14.7	---	16.6

Copyright 2012 Securities Research Company

Bonds $.0 Mil Com 73.368 Mil BV 5.77 /sh P/E 23.92 (Ind TELEQ P/E 13.72) Ctry US

IXYS CORP (IXYS)   **75% SCALE**

Maker a variety of semiconductors and power modules

Growth Performance Measurement				
Years	Price	Earn.	Div.	Tot Ret
Last 1	-15.6	-42.1	.0	-15.6
Last 5	2.6	12.9	---	2.7
Last 10	2.6	---	---	2.6

Paid $0.03

Dividend Omitted 10/28/09

Copyright 2012 Securities Research Company

Bonds $.0 Mil Com 31.181 Mil BV 8.63 /sh P/E 13.85 (Ind SEMIC P/E 12.16) Ctry US

J & J SNACK FOODS CORP (JJSF)

Snack foods, baked goods, food distribution

Growth Performance Measurement				
Years	Price	Earn.	Div.	Tot Ret
Last 1	19.9	-2.0	10.6	20.9
Last 5	15.4	11.0	8.9	16.1
Last 10	13.6	11.4	---	14.1

Adj. for 2 for 1 1/6/06

Copyright 2012 Securities Research Company

Bonds $42.5 Mil Com 18.775 Mil BV 25.32 /sh P/E 22.26 (Ind PKGFD P/E 16.90) Ctry US

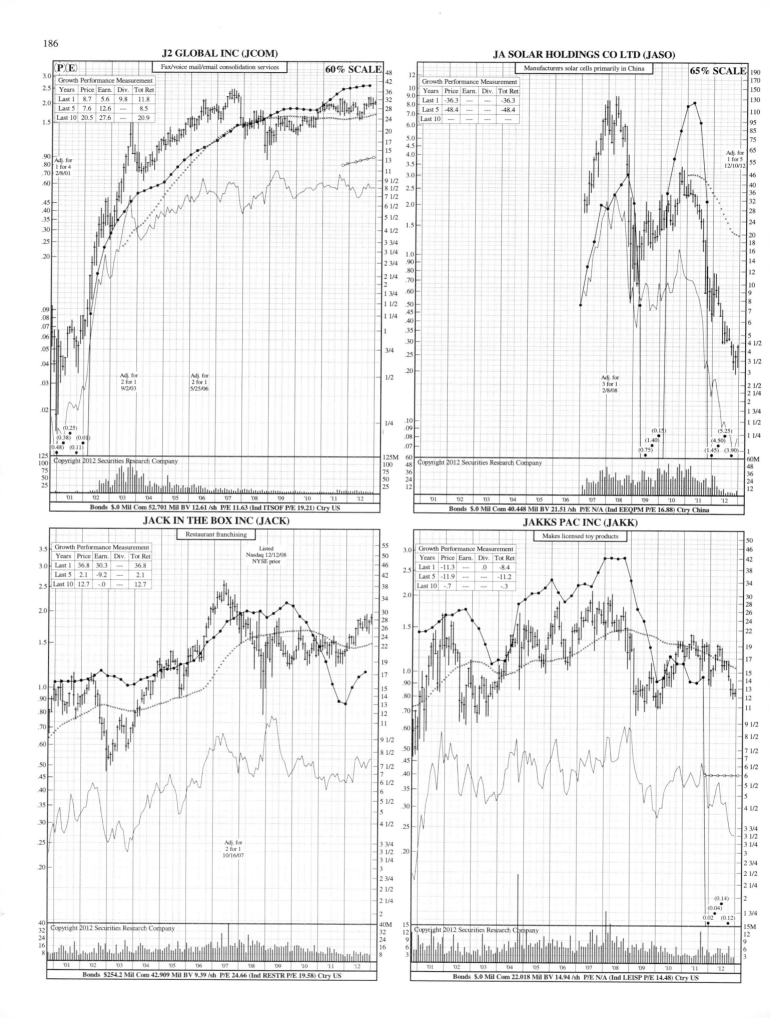

J2 GLOBAL INC (JCOM)

Fax/voice mail/email consolidation services

60% SCALE

Growth Performance Measurement				
Years	Price	Earn.	Div.	Tot Ret
Last 1	8.7	5.6	9.8	11.8
Last 5	7.6	12.6	---	8.5
Last 10	20.5	27.6	---	20.9

Adj. for
1 for 4
2/8/01

Adj. for
2 for 1
9/2/03

Adj. for
2 for 1
5/25/06

(0.25)
(0.38) (0.01)
(0.48) (0.11)

Copyright 2012 Securities Research Company

Bonds $.0 Mil Com 52.701 Mil BV 12.61 /sh P/E 11.63 (Ind ITSOF P/E 19.21) Ctry US

JA SOLAR HOLDINGS CO LTD (JASO)

Manufacturers solar cells primarily in China

65% SCALE

Growth Performance Measurement				
Years	Price	Earn.	Div.	Tot Ret
Last 1	-36.3	---	---	-36.3
Last 5	-48.4	---	---	-48.4
Last 10	---	---	---	---

Adj. for
1 for 5
12/10/12

Adj. for
3 for 1
2/8/08

(0.15)   (5.25)
(1.40)   (4.50)
(0.75)   (1.45) (3.90)

Copyright 2012 Securities Research Company

Bonds $.0 Mil Com 40.448 Mil BV 21.51 /sh P/E N/A (Ind EEQPM P/E 16.88) Ctry China

JACK IN THE BOX INC (JACK)

Restaurant franchising

Listed
Nasdaq 12/12/08
NYSE prior

Growth Performance Measurement				
Years	Price	Earn.	Div.	Tot Ret
Last 1	36.8	30.3	---	36.8
Last 5	2.1	-9.2	---	2.1
Last 10	12.7	-.0	---	12.7

Adj. for
2 for 1
10/16/07

Copyright 2012 Securities Research Company

Bonds $254.2 Mil Com 42.909 Mil BV 9.39 /sh P/E 24.66 (Ind RESTR P/E 19.58) Ctry US

JAKKS PAC INC (JAKK)

Makes licensed toy products

Growth Performance Measurement				
Years	Price	Earn.	Div.	Tot Ret
Last 1	-11.3	---	.0	-8.4
Last 5	-11.9	---	---	-11.2
Last 10	-.7	---	---	-.3

(0.14)
(0.04)
0.02   (0.12)

Copyright 2012 Securities Research Company

Bonds $.0 Mil Com 22.018 Mil BV 14.94 /sh P/E N/A (Ind LEISP P/E 14.48) Ctry US

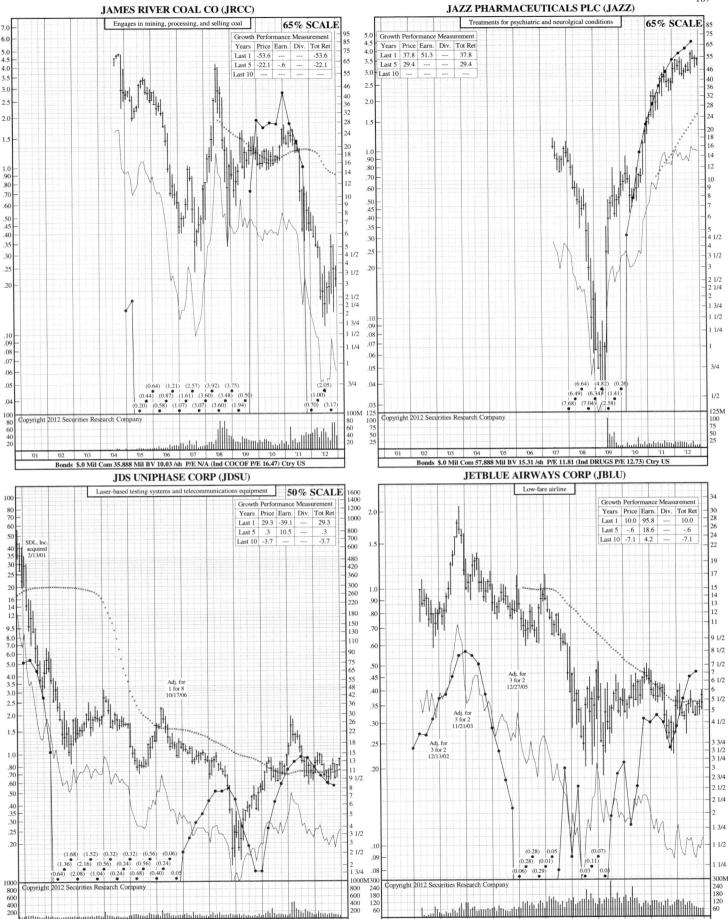

JAMES RIVER COAL CO (JRCC)

Engages in mining, processing, and selling coal

65% SCALE

Growth Performance Measurement				
Years	Price	Earn.	Div.	Tot Ret
Last 1	-53.6	---	---	-53.6
Last 5	-22.1	-.6	---	-22.1
Last 10	---	---	---	---

(0.64) (1.21) (2.57) (3.92) (3.75)   (2.05)
(0.44) (0.87) (1.61) (3.60) (3.48) (0.50)   (1.00)
(0.20) (0.58) (1.07) (3.07) (3.60) (1.94)   (0.70) (3.17)

Copyright 2012 Securities Research Company

Bonds $.0 Mil Com 35.888 Mil BV 10.03 /sh P/E N/A (Ind COCOF P/E 16.47) Ctry US

JAZZ PHARMACEUTICALS PLC (JAZZ)

Treatments for psychiatric and neurolgical conditions

65% SCALE

Growth Performance Measurement				
Years	Price	Earn.	Div.	Tot Ret
Last 1	37.8	51.3	---	37.8
Last 5	29.4	---	---	29.4
Last 10	---	---	---	---

(6.64) (4.82) (0.26)
(6.49) (6.34) (1.41)
(7.68) (7.04) (2.58)

Copyright 2012 Securities Research Company

Bonds $.0 Mil Com 57.888 Mil BV 15.31 /sh P/E 11.81 (Ind DRUGS P/E 12.73) Ctry US

JDS UNIPHASE CORP (JDSU)

Laser-based testing systems and telecommunications equipment

50% SCALE

Growth Performance Measurement				
Years	Price	Earn.	Div.	Tot Ret
Last 1	29.3	-39.1	---	29.3
Last 5	.3	10.5	---	.3
Last 10	-3.7	---	---	-3.7

SDL, Inc.
acquired
2/13/01

Adj. for
1 for 8
10/17/06

(1.68) (1.52) (0.32) (0.32) (0.56) (0.06)
(1.36) (2.16) (0.56) (0.24) (0.56) (0.24)
(0.64) (2.08) (1.04) (0.24) (0.48) (0.40) 0.05

Copyright 2012 Securities Research Company

Bonds $900.0 Mil Com 230.099 Mil BV 4.64 /sh P/E 24.11 (Ind TELEQ P/E 13.72) Ctry US

JETBLUE AIRWAYS CORP (JBLU)

Low-fare airline

Growth Performance Measurement				
Years	Price	Earn.	Div.	Tot Ret
Last 1	10.0	95.8	---	10.0
Last 5	-.6	18.6	---	-.6
Last 10	-7.1	4.2	---	-7.1

Adj. for
3 for 2
12/27/05

Adj. for
3 for 2
11/21/03

Adj. for
3 for 2
12/13/02

(0.28) 0.05   (0.07)
(0.28) (0.01)   (0.11)
(0.06) (0.29)   0.03 0.05

Copyright 2012 Securities Research Company

Bonds $2626.0 Mil Com 284.298 Mil BV 6.69 /sh P/E 12.17 (Ind ARLNS P/E 18.30) Ctry US

188

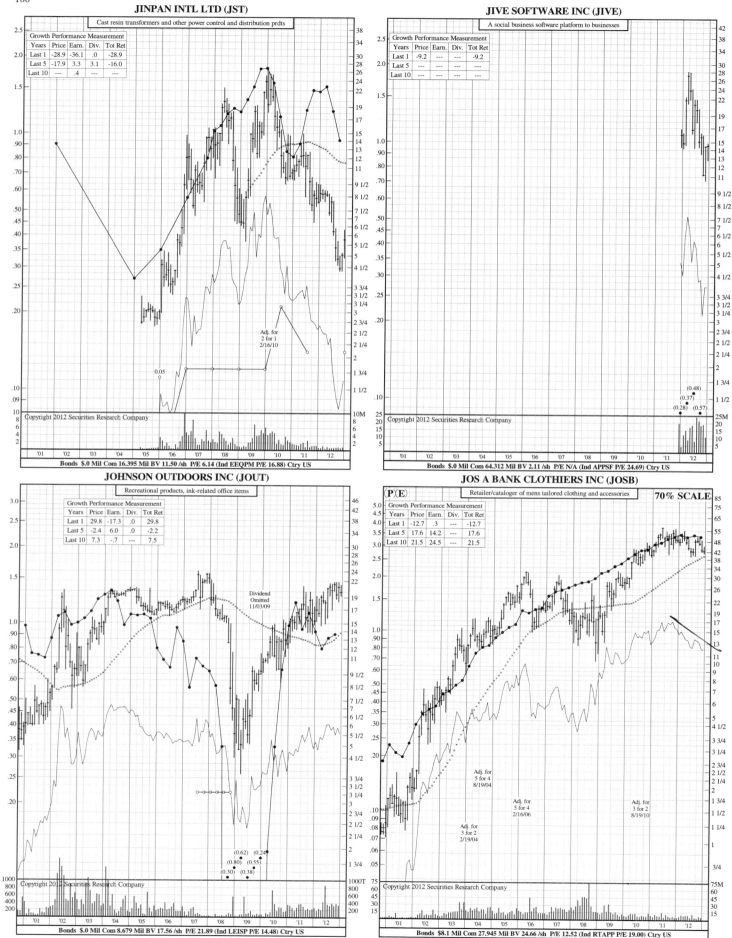

JINPAN INTL LTD (JST)
Cast resin transformers and other power control and distribution prdts

Growth Performance Measurement				
Years	Price	Earn.	Div.	Tot Ret
Last 1	-28.9	-36.1	.0	-28.9
Last 5	-17.9	3.3	3.1	-16.0
Last 10	---	.4	---	---

Adj. for
2 for 1
2/16/10

0.05

Copyright 2012 Securities Research Company

'01 '02 '03 '04 '05 '06 '07 '08 '09 '10 '11 '12

Bonds $.0 Mil Com 16.395 Mil BV 11.50 /sh P/E 6.14 (Ind EEQPM P/E 16.88) Ctry US

JIVE SOFTWARE INC (JIVE)
A social business software platform to businesses

Growth Performance Measurement				
Years	Price	Earn.	Div.	Tot Ret
Last 1	-9.2	---	---	-9.2
Last 5	---	---	---	---
Last 10	---	---	---	---

(0.48)
(0.37)
(0.28) (0.57)

Copyright 2012 Securities Research Company

'01 '02 '03 '04 '05 '06 '07 '08 '09 '10 '11 '12

Bonds $.0 Mil Com 64.312 Mil BV 2.11 /sh P/E N/A (Ind APPSF P/E 24.69) Ctry US

JOHNSON OUTDOORS INC (JOUT)
Recreational products, ink-related office items

Growth Performance Measurement				
Years	Price	Earn.	Div.	Tot Ret
Last 1	29.8	-17.3	.0	29.8
Last 5	-2.4	6.0	.0	-2.2
Last 10	7.3	-.7	---	7.5

Dividend
Omitted
11/03/09

(0.62) (0.24)
(0.80) (0.55)
(0.30) (0.38)

Copyright 2012 Securities Research Company

'01 '02 '03 '04 '05 '06 '07 '08 '09 '10 '11 '12

Bonds $.0 Mil Com 8.679 Mil BV 17.56 /sh P/E 21.89 (Ind LEISP P/E 14.48) Ctry US

JOS A BANK CLOTHIERS INC (JOSB)
Retailer/cataloger of mens tailored clothing and accessories

(P/E)   **70% SCALE**

Growth Performance Measurement				
Years	Price	Earn.	Div.	Tot Ret
Last 1	-12.7	.3	---	-12.7
Last 5	17.6	14.2	---	17.6
Last 10	21.5	24.5	---	21.5

Adj. for
5 for 4
8/19/04

Adj. for
5 for 4
2/16/06

Adj. for
3 for 2
8/19/10

Adj. for
3 for 2
2/19/04

Copyright 2012 Securities Research Company

'01 '02 '03 '04 '05 '06 '07 '08 '09 '10 '11 '12

Bonds $8.1 Mil Com 27.945 Mil BV 24.66 /sh P/E 12.52 (Ind RTAPP P/E 19.00) Ctry US

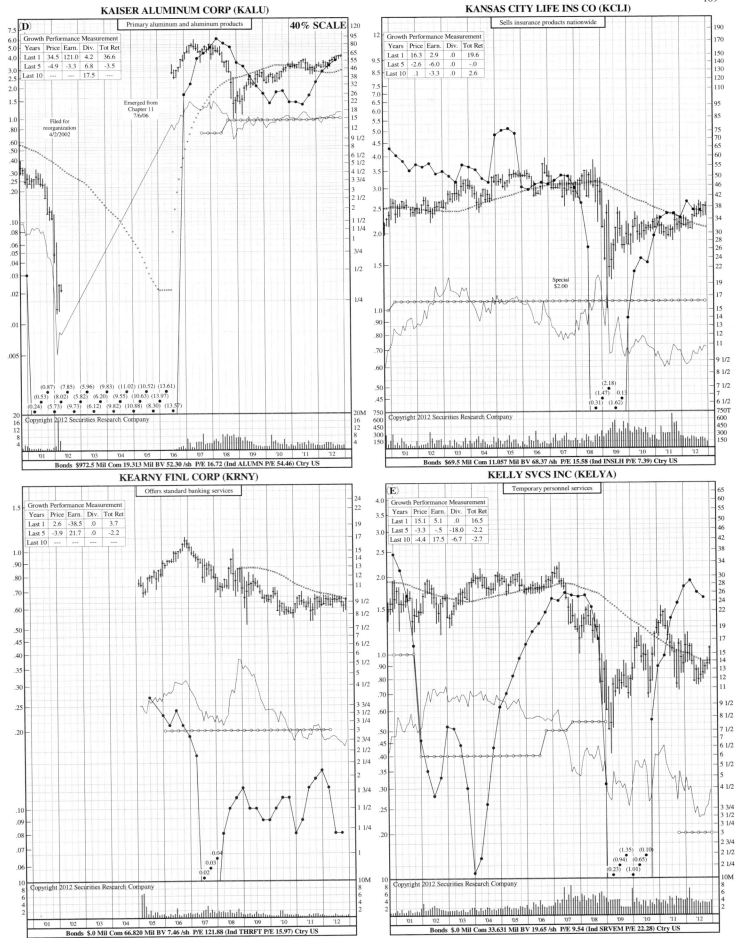

KAISER ALUMINUM CORP (KALU)

Primary aluminum and aluminum products

40% SCALE

Growth Performance Measurement				
Years	Price	Earn.	Div.	Tot Ret
Last 1	34.5	121.0	4.2	36.6
Last 5	-4.9	-3.3	6.8	-3.5
Last 10	---	---	17.5	---

Emerged from Chapter 11 7/6/06

Filed for reorganization 4/2/2002

(0.87) (7.85) (5.96) (9.83) (11.02) (10.52) (13.61)
(0.53) (8.02) (5.82) (6.20) (9.55) (10.63) (13.97)
(0.24) (5.73) (9.73) (6.12) (9.82) (10.88) (8.30) (13.57)

Copyright 2012 Securities Research Company

Bonds $972.5 Mil Com 19.313 Mil BV 52.30 /sh P/E 16.72 (Ind ALUMN P/E 54.46) Ctry US

KANSAS CITY LIFE INS CO (KCLI)

Sells insurance products nationwide

Growth Performance Measurement				
Years	Price	Earn.	Div.	Tot Ret
Last 1	16.3	2.9	.0	19.6
Last 5	-2.6	-6.0	.0	-.0
Last 10	.1	-3.3	.0	2.6

Special $2.00

(2.18)
(1.47) 0.13
(0.31) (1.62)

Copyright 2012 Securities Research Company

Bonds $69.5 Mil Com 11.057 Mil BV 68.37 /sh P/E 15.58 (Ind INSLH P/E 7.39) Ctry US

KEARNY FINL CORP (KRNY)

Offers standard banking services

Growth Performance Measurement				
Years	Price	Earn.	Div.	Tot Ret
Last 1	2.6	-38.5	.0	3.7
Last 5	-3.9	21.7	.0	-2.2
Last 10	---	---	---	---

0.04
0.03
0.02

Copyright 2012 Securities Research Company

Bonds $.0 Mil Com 66.820 Mil BV 7.46 /sh P/E 121.88 (Ind THRFT P/E 15.97) Ctry US

KELLY SVCS INC (KELYA)

Temporary personnel services

Growth Performance Measurement				
Years	Price	Earn.	Div.	Tot Ret
Last 1	15.1	5.1	.0	16.5
Last 5	-3.3	-.5	-18.0	-2.2
Last 10	-4.4	17.5	-6.7	-2.7

(1.35) (0.10)
(0.94) (0.65)
(0.23) (1.01)

Copyright 2012 Securities Research Company

Bonds $.0 Mil Com 33.631 Mil BV 19.65 /sh P/E 9.54 (Ind SRVEM P/E 22.28) Ctry US

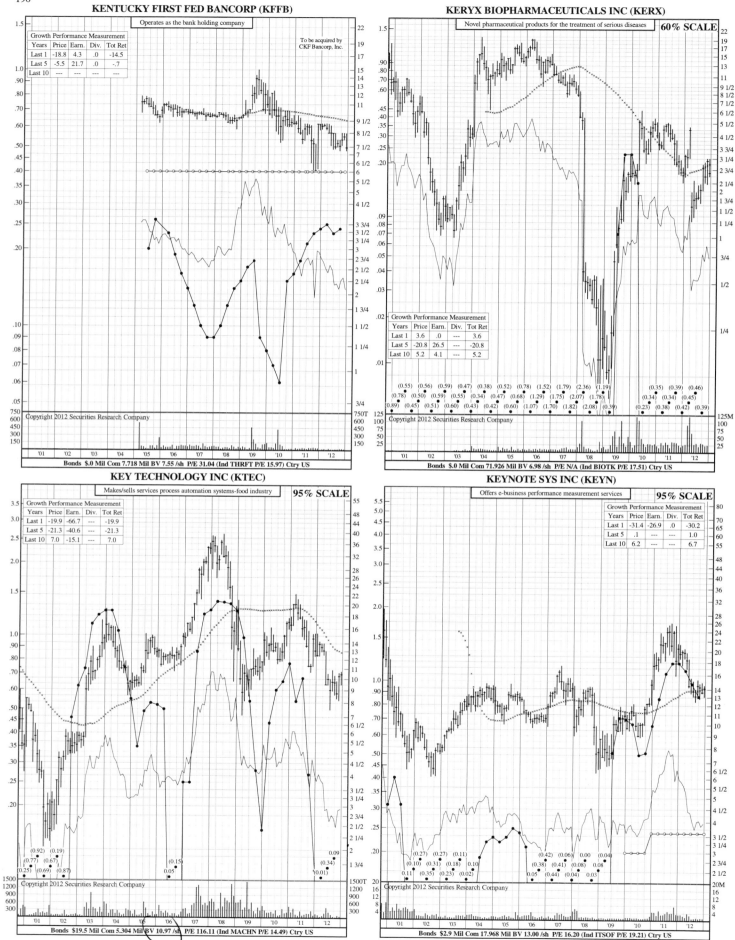

190

KENTUCKY FIRST FED BANCORP (KFFB)

Operates as the bank holding company

To be acquired by CKF Bancorp, Inc.

Growth Performance Measurement				
Years	Price	Earn.	Div.	Tot Ret
Last 1	-18.8	4.3	.0	-14.5
Last 5	-5.5	21.7	.0	-.7
Last 10	---	---	---	---

Copyright 2012 Securities Research Company

Bonds $.0 Mil Com 7.718 Mil BV 7.55 /sh P/E 31.04 (Ind THRFT P/E 15.97) Ctry US

KERYX BIOPHARMACEUTICALS INC (KERX)

Novel pharmaceutical products for the treatment of serious diseases

60% SCALE

Growth Performance Measurement				
Years	Price	Earn.	Div.	Tot Ret
Last 1	3.6	.0	---	3.6
Last 5	-20.8	26.5	---	-20.8
Last 10	5.2	4.1	---	5.2

(0.55) (0.56) (0.59) (0.47) (0.38) (0.52) (0.78) (1.52) (1.79) (2.36) (1.19)   (0.35) (0.39) (0.46)
(0.78) (0.50) (0.59) (0.55) (0.34) (0.47) (0.68) (1.29) (1.75) (2.07) (1.78)   (0.34) (0.34) (0.45)
(0.89) (0.45) (0.51) (0.60) (0.43) (0.42) (0.60) (1.07) (1.70) (1.82) (2.08) (0.39)   (0.23) (0.38) (0.42) (0.39)

Copyright 2012 Securities Research Company

Bonds $.0 Mil Com 71.926 Mil BV 6.98 /sh P/E N/A (Ind BIOTK P/E 17.51) Ctry US

KEY TECHNOLOGY INC (KTEC)

Makes/sells services process automation systems-food industry

95% SCALE

Growth Performance Measurement				
Years	Price	Earn.	Div.	Tot Ret
Last 1	-19.9	-66.7	---	-19.9
Last 5	-21.3	-40.6	---	-21.3
Last 10	7.0	-15.1	---	7.0

(0.92) (0.19)   0.09
(0.77) (0.67)   (0.15)   (0.34)
(0.25) (0.69) (0.87)   0.05   (0.01)

Copyright 2012 Securities Research Company

Bonds $19.5 Mil Com 5.304 Mil BV 10.97 /sh P/E 116.11 (Ind MACHN P/E 14.49) Ctry US

KEYNOTE SYS INC (KEYN)

Offers e-business performance measurement services

95% SCALE

Growth Performance Measurement				
Years	Price	Earn.	Div.	Tot Ret
Last 1	-31.4	-26.9	---	-30.2
Last 5	.1	---	---	1.0
Last 10	6.2	---	---	6.7

(0.27) (0.27) (0.11)   (0.42) (0.06) 0.00 (0.04)
(0.10) (0.31) (0.18) (0.10)   (0.38) (0.41) (0.08) 0.08
(0.11) (0.35) (0.23) (0.02)   0.05 (0.44) (0.04) 0.03

Copyright 2012 Securities Research Company

Bonds $2.9 Mil Com 17.968 Mil BV 13.00 /sh P/E 16.20 (Ind ITSOF P/E 19.21) Ctry US

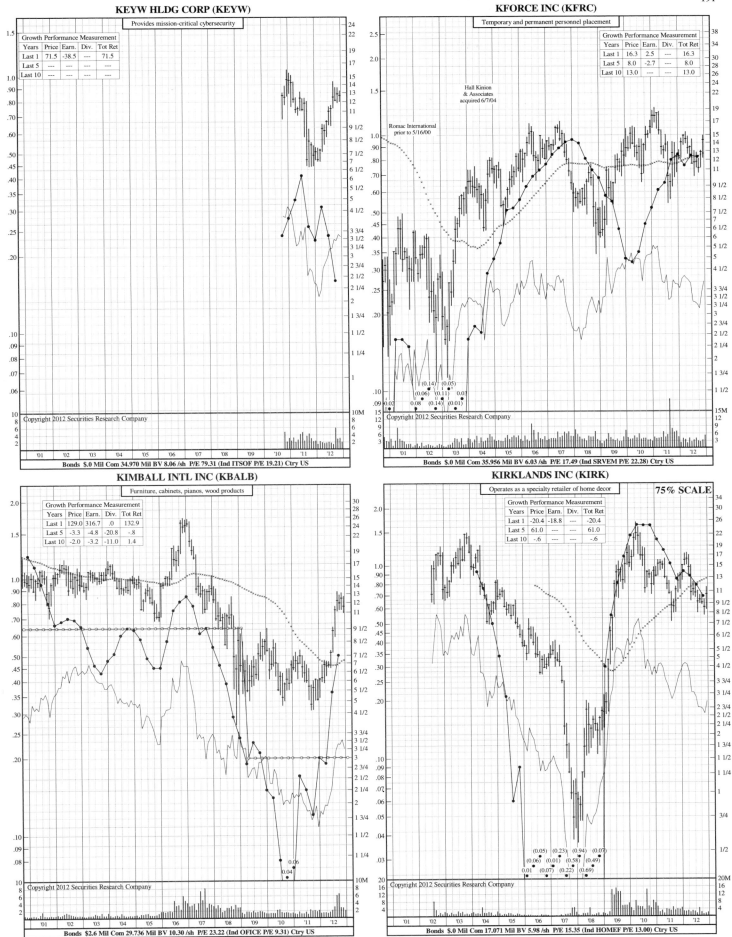

KEYW HLDG CORP (KEYW)

Provides mission-critical cybersecurity

Growth Performance Measurement

Years	Price	Earn.	Div.	Tot Ret
Last 1	71.5	-38.5	---	71.5
Last 5	---	---	---	---
Last 10	---	---	---	---

Copyright 2012 Securities Research Company

Bonds $.0 Mil Com 34.970 Mil BV 8.06 /sh P/E 79.31 (Ind ITSOF P/E 19.21) Ctry US

KFORCE INC (KFRC)

Temporary and permanent personnel placement

Growth Performance Measurement

Years	Price	Earn.	Div.	Tot Ret
Last 1	16.3	2.5	---	16.3
Last 5	8.0	-2.7	---	8.0
Last 10	13.0	---	---	13.0

Hall Kinion
& Associates
acquired 6/7/04

Romac International
prior to 5/16/00

Copyright 2012 Securities Research Company

Bonds $.0 Mil Com 35.956 Mil BV 6.03 /sh P/E 17.49 (Ind SRVEM P/E 22.28) Ctry US

KIMBALL INTL INC (KBALB)

Furniture, cabinets, pianos, wood products

Growth Performance Measurement

Years	Price	Earn.	Div.	Tot Ret
Last 1	129.0	316.7	.0	132.9
Last 5	-3.3	-4.8	-20.8	-.8
Last 10	-2.0	-3.2	-11.0	1.4

Copyright 2012 Securities Research Company

Bonds $2.6 Mil Com 29.736 Mil BV 10.30 /sh P/E 23.22 (Ind OFICE P/E 9.31) Ctry US

KIRKLANDS INC (KIRK)

Operates as a specialty retailer of home decor

75% SCALE

Growth Performance Measurement

Years	Price	Earn.	Div.	Tot Ret
Last 1	-20.4	-18.8	---	-20.4
Last 5	61.0	---	---	61.0
Last 10	-.6	---	---	-.6

Copyright 2012 Securities Research Company

Bonds $.0 Mil Com 17.071 Mil BV 5.98 /sh P/E 15.35 (Ind HOMEF P/E 13.00) Ctry US

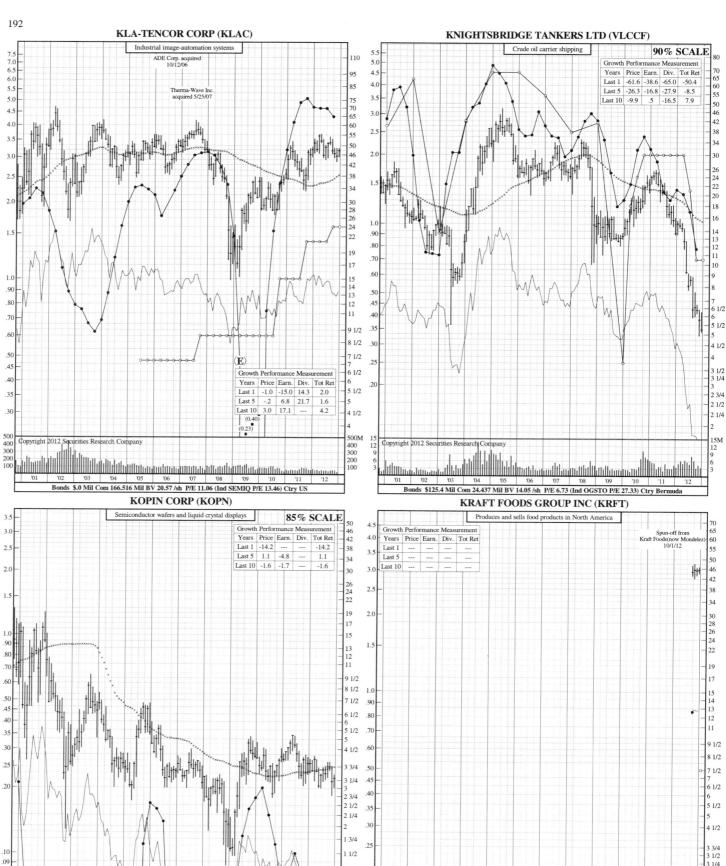

KLA-TENCOR CORP (KLAC)

Industrial image-automation systems

ADE Corp. acquired
10/12/06

Therma-Wave Inc.
acquired 5/25/07

(E)

Growth Performance Measurement				
Years	Price	Earn.	Div.	Tot Ret
Last 1	-1.0	-15.0	14.3	2.0
Last 5	-.2	6.8	21.7	1.6
Last 10	3.0	17.1	---	4.2

(0.40)
(0.23)

Copyright 2012 Securities Research Company

Bonds $.0 Mil Com 166.516 Mil BV 20.57 /sh P/E 11.06 (Ind SEMIQ P/E 13.46) Ctry US

KNIGHTSBRIDGE TANKERS LTD (VLCCF)

Crude oil carrier shipping

90% SCALE

Growth Performance Measurement				
Years	Price	Earn.	Div.	Tot Ret
Last 1	-61.6	-38.6	-65.0	-50.4
Last 5	-26.3	-16.8	-27.9	-8.5
Last 10	-9.9	.5	-16.5	7.9

Copyright 2012 Securities Research Company

Bonds $125.4 Mil Com 24.437 Mil BV 14.05 /sh P/E 6.73 (Ind OGSTO P/E 27.33) Ctry Bermuda

KOPIN CORP (KOPN)

Semiconductor wafers and liquid crystal displays

85% SCALE

Growth Performance Measurement				
Years	Price	Earn.	Div.	Tot Ret
Last 1	-14.2	---	---	-14.2
Last 5	1.1	-4.8	---	1.1
Last 10	-1.6	-1.7	---	-1.6

(0.58) (0.16) (0.06) (0.12) (0.12)   (0.05)   (0.08)
(0.43) (0.31) (0.07) (0.10) (0.11) (0.01)   (0.11) 0.02   0.02
(0.22) (0.53) (0.09) (0.11) (0.14) (0.05)   (0.15) (0.01)   0.05 (0.19)

Copyright 2012 Securities Research Company

Bonds $2.6 Mil Com 66.295 Mil BV 2.40 /sh P/E N/A (Ind SEMIC P/E 12.16) Ctry US

KRAFT FOODS GROUP INC (KRFT)

Produces and sells food products in North America

Spun-off from
Kraft Foods(now Mondelez)
10/1/12

Growth Performance Measurement				
Years	Price	Earn.	Div.	Tot Ret
Last 1	---	---	---	---
Last 5	---	---	---	---
Last 10	---	---	---	---

Copyright 2012 Securities Research Company

Bonds $.0 Mil Com 592.542 Mil BV 12.59 /sh P/E 54.13 (Ind PKGFD P/E 16.90) Ctry US

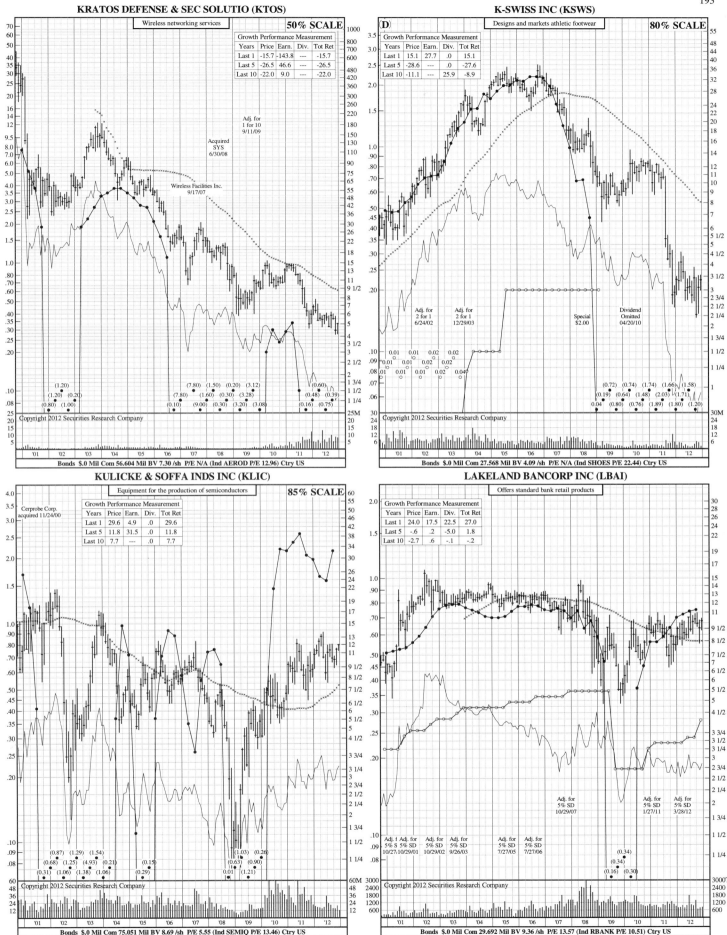

KRATOS DEFENSE & SEC SOLUTIO (KTOS)

Wireless networking services

50% SCALE

Growth Performance Measurement				
Years	Price	Earn.	Div.	Tot Ret
Last 1	-15.7	-143.8	---	-15.7
Last 5	-26.5	46.6	---	-26.5
Last 10	-22.0	9.0	---	-22.0

Adj. for
1 for 10
9/11/09

Acquired
SYS
6/30/08

Wireless Facilities Inc.
9/17/07

(1.20)
(1.20)   (0.20)
(0.80)   (1.00)

(7.80)   (1.50) (0.20) (3.12)
(7.80)   (1.60) (0.30) (3.28)
(0.10)   (9.00) (0.30) (3.20) (3.08)

(0.60)
(0.48) (0.39)
(0.16) (0.75)

Copyright 2012 Securities Research Company

Bonds $.0 Mil Com 56.604 Mil BV 7.30 /sh P/E N/A (Ind AEROD P/E 12.96) Ctry US

K-SWISS INC (KSWS)

D

Designs and markets athletic footwear

80% SCALE

Growth Performance Measurement				
Years	Price	Earn.	Div.	Tot Ret
Last 1	15.1	27.7	.0	15.1
Last 5	-28.6	.0	---	-27.6
Last 10	-11.1	---	25.9	-8.9

Adj. for
2 for 1
6/24/02

Adj. for
2 for 1
12/29/03

Special
$2.00

Dividend
Omitted
04/20/10

0.01   0.01   0.02   0.02
0.01   0.01   0.02   0.02
0.01   0.01   0.02   0.02 0.04
0.01   0.01   0.02   0.02 0.04

(0.72) (0.74) (1.74) (1.66) (1.58)
(0.19) (0.64) (1.48) (2.03) (1.71)
0.04   (0.80) (0.76) (1.89) (1.80) (1.20)

Copyright 2012 Securities Research Company

Bonds $.0 Mil Com 27.568 Mil BV 4.09 /sh P/E N/A (Ind SHOES P/E 22.44) Ctry US

KULICKE & SOFFA INDS INC (KLIC)

Equipment for the production of semiconductors

85% SCALE

Cerprobe Corp.
acquired 11/24/00

Growth Performance Measurement				
Years	Price	Earn.	Div.	Tot Ret
Last 1	29.6	4.9	.0	29.6
Last 5	11.8	31.5	.0	11.8
Last 10	7.7	---	.0	7.7

(0.87) (1.29) (1.54)
(0.68) (1.25) (4.93) (0.21)
(0.31) (1.06) (1.38) (1.06)

(0.15)
(0.29)

(1.03) (0.26)
(0.63) (0.90)
0.01   (1.21)

Copyright 2012 Securities Research Company

Bonds $.0 Mil Com 75.051 Mil BV 8.69 /sh P/E 5.55 (Ind SEMIQ P/E 13.46) Ctry US

LAKELAND BANCORP INC (LBAI)

Offers standard bank retail products

Growth Performance Measurement				
Years	Price	Earn.	Div.	Tot Ret
Last 1	24.0	17.5	22.5	27.0
Last 5	-.6	.2	-5.0	1.8
Last 10	-2.7	.6	-.1	-.2

Adj. for
5% SD
10/29/07

Adj. for
5% SD
1/27/11

Adj. for
5% SD
3/28/12

Adj. t   Adj. for   Adj. for Adj. for
5% S   5% SD   5% SD   5% SD
10/27 10/29/01 10/29/02 9/26/03

Adj. for   Adj. for
5% SD   5% SD
7/27/05   7/27/06

(0.34)
(0.34)
(0.16) (0.30)

Copyright 2012 Securities Research Company

Bonds $.0 Mil Com 29.692 Mil BV 9.36 /sh P/E 13.57 (Ind RBANK P/E 10.51) Ctry US

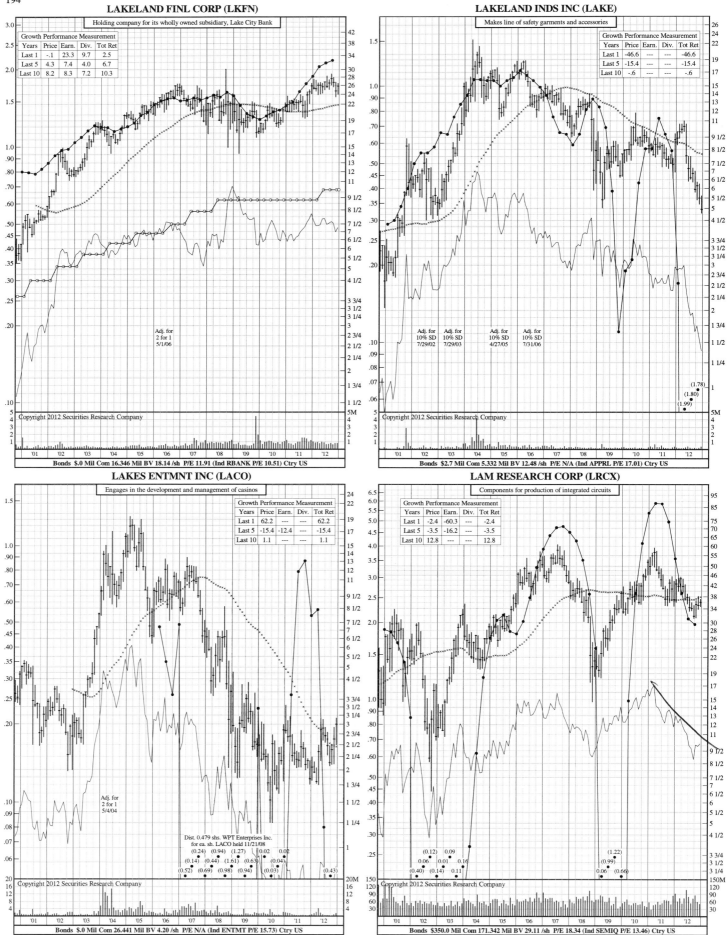

194

LAKELAND FINL CORP (LKFN)

Holding company for its wholly owned subsidiary, Lake City Bank

Growth Performance Measurement

Years	Price	Earn.	Div.	Tot Ret
Last 1	-.1	23.3	9.7	2.5
Last 5	4.3	7.4	4.0	6.7
Last 10	8.2	8.3	7.2	10.3

Adj. for
2 for 1
5/1/06

Copyright 2012 Securities Research Company

Bonds $.0 Mil Com 16.346 Mil BV 18.14 /sh P/E 11.91 (Ind RBANK P/E 10.51) Ctry US

LAKELAND INDS INC (LAKE)

Makes line of safety garments and accessories

Growth Performance Measurement

Years	Price	Earn.	Div.	Tot Ret
Last 1	-46.6	---	---	-46.6
Last 5	-15.4	---	---	-15.4
Last 10	-.6	---	---	-.6

Adj. for 10% SD 7/29/02	Adj. for 10% SD 7/29/03	Adj. for 10% SD 4/27/05	Adj. for 10% SD 7/31/06

(1.78)
(1.80)
(1.99)

Copyright 2012 Securities Research Company

Bonds $2.7 Mil Com 5.332 Mil BV 12.48 /sh P/E N/A (Ind APPRL P/E 17.01) Ctry US

LAKES ENTMNT INC (LACO)

Engages in the development and management of casinos

Growth Performance Measurement

Years	Price	Earn.	Div.	Tot Ret
Last 1	62.2	---	---	62.2
Last 5	-15.4	-12.4	---	-15.4
Last 10	1.1	---	---	1.1

Adj. for
2 for 1
5/4/04

Dist. 0.479 shs. WPT Enterprises Inc.
for ea. sh. LACO held 11/21/08
(0.24) (0.94) (1.27) 0.02 0.02
(0.14) (0.44) (1.61) (0.63) (0.04)
(0.52) (0.69) (0.98) (0.94) (0.03) (0.43)

Copyright 2012 Securities Research Company

Bonds $.0 Mil Com 26.441 Mil BV 4.20 /sh P/E N/A (Ind ENTMT P/E 15.73) Ctry US

LAM RESEARCH CORP (LRCX)

Components for production of integrated circuits

Growth Performance Measurement

Years	Price	Earn.	Div.	Tot Ret
Last 1	-2.4	-60.3	---	-2.4
Last 5	-3.5	-16.2	---	-3.5
Last 10	12.8	---	---	12.8

(0.12) 0.09
0.06 0.01 0.16
(0.40) (0.14) 0.11

(1.22)
(0.99)
0.06 (0.66)

Copyright 2012 Securities Research Company

Bonds $350.0 Mil Com 171.342 Mil BV 29.11 /sh P/E 18.34 (Ind SEMIQ P/E 13.46) Ctry US

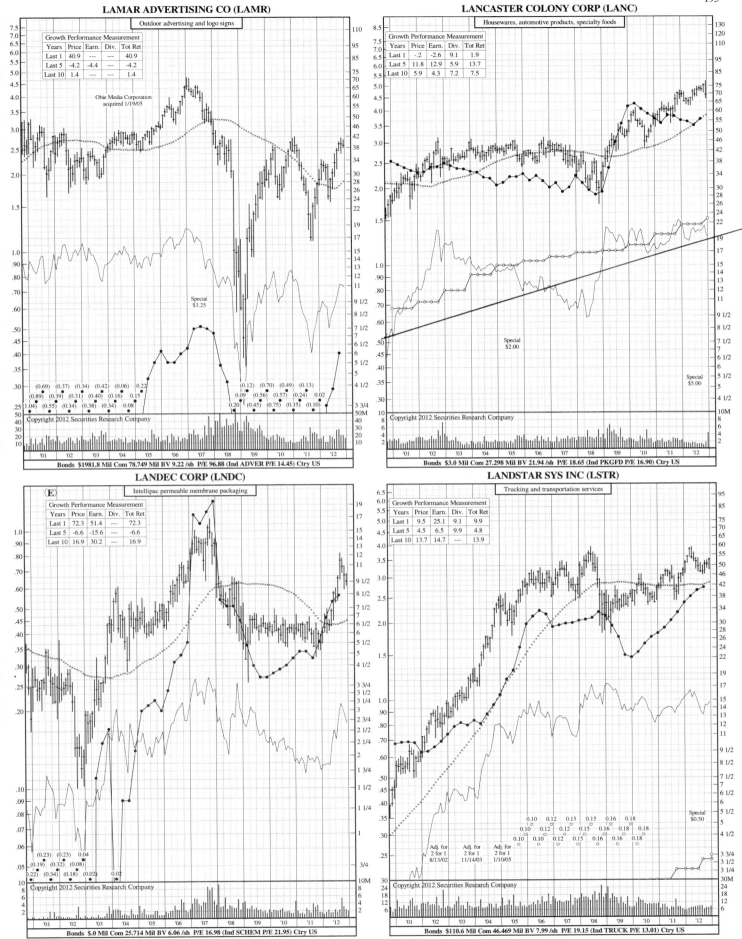

LAMAR ADVERTISING CO (LAMR)

Outdoor advertising and logo signs

Growth Performance Measurement				
Years	Price	Earn.	Div.	Tot Ret
Last 1	40.9	---	---	40.9
Last 5	-4.2	-4.4	---	-4.2
Last 10	1.4	---	---	1.4

Obie Media Corporation
acquired 1/19/05

Special
$3.25

(0.69) (0.37) (0.34) (0.42) (0.06)   (0.12) (0.70) (0.49) (0.13)
(0.89) (0.39) (0.31) (0.40) (0.16) 0.15   0.09 (0.56) (0.57) (0.24) 0.02
(1.04) (0.55) (0.34) (0.38) (0.34) 0.08 0.22 0.20 (0.45) (0.75) (0.35) (0.10)

Copyright 2012 Securities Research Company

'01 '02 '03 '04 '05 '06 '07 '08 '09 '10 '11 '12

Bonds $1981.8 Mil Com 78.749 Mil BV 9.22 /sh P/E 96.88 (Ind ADVER P/E 14.45) Ctry US

LANCASTER COLONY CORP (LANC)

Housewares, automotive products, specialty foods

Growth Performance Measurement				
Years	Price	Earn.	Div.	Tot Ret
Last 1	-.2	-2.6	9.1	1.9
Last 5	11.8	12.9	5.9	13.7
Last 10	5.9	4.3	7.2	7.5

Special
$2.00

Special
$5.00

Copyright 2012 Securities Research Company

'01 '02 '03 '04 '05 '06 '07 '08 '09 '10 '11 '12

Bonds $3.0 Mil Com 27.298 Mil BV 21.94 /sh P/E 18.65 (Ind PKGFD P/E 16.90) Ctry US

LANDEC CORP (LNDC)

(E)

Intellipac permeable membrane packaging

Growth Performance Measurement				
Years	Price	Earn.	Div.	Tot Ret
Last 1	72.3	51.4	---	72.3
Last 5	-6.6	-15.6	---	-6.6
Last 10	16.9	30.2	---	16.9

(0.23) (0.23) 0.04
(0.19) (0.32) (0.08)
(0.22) (0.34) (0.18) (0.02) 0.02

Copyright 2012 Securities Research Company

'01 '02 '03 '04 '05 '06 '07 '08 '09 '10 '11 '12

Bonds $.0 Mil Com 25.714 Mil BV 6.06 /sh P/E 16.98 (Ind SCHEM P/E 21.95) Ctry US

LANDSTAR SYS INC (LSTR)

Trucking and transportation services

Growth Performance Measurement				
Years	Price	Earn.	Div.	Tot Ret
Last 1	9.5	25.1	9.1	9.9
Last 5	4.5	6.5	9.9	4.8
Last 10	13.7	14.7	---	13.9

0.10 0.12 0.15 0.15 0.16 0.18   Special
0.10 0.12 0.12 0.15 0.16 0.18 0.18 $0.50
0.10 0.10 0.12 0.15 0.16 0.16 0.18

Adj. for   Adj. for   Adj. for
2 for 1   2 for 1   2 for 1
8/13/02   11/14/03   1/10/05

Copyright 2012 Securities Research Company

'01 '02 '03 '04 '05 '06 '07 '08 '09 '10 '11 '12

Bonds $110.6 Mil Com 46.469 Mil BV 7.99 /sh P/E 19.15 (Ind TRUCK P/E 13.01) Ctry US

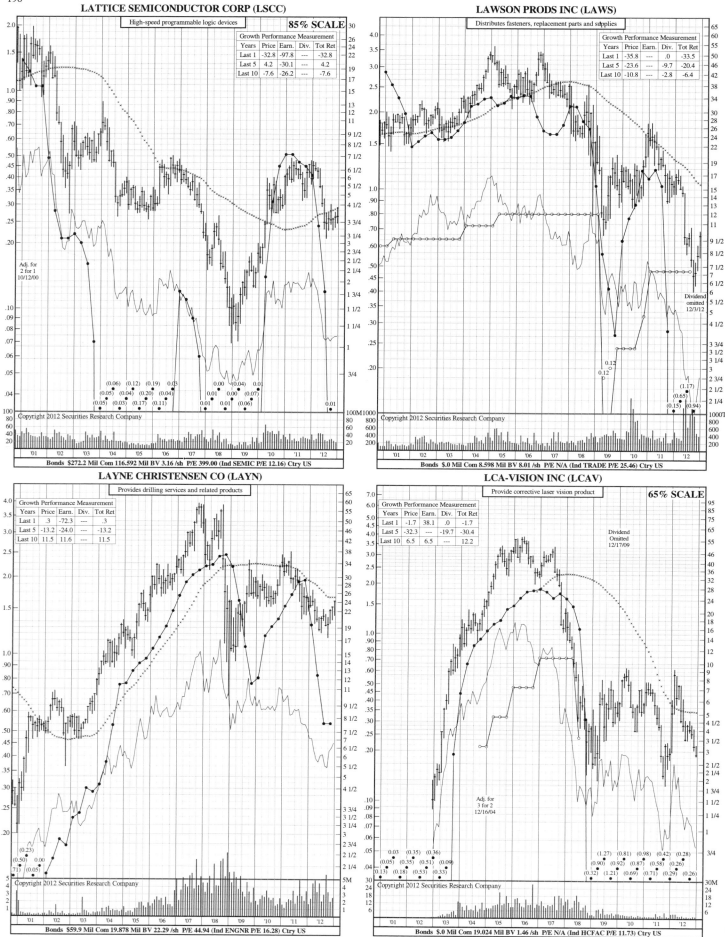

196

LATTICE SEMICONDUCTOR CORP (LSCC)

High-speed programmable logic devices

85% SCALE

Growth Performance Measurement				
Years	Price	Earn.	Div.	Tot Ret
Last 1	-32.8	-97.8	---	-32.8
Last 5	4.2	-30.1	---	4.2
Last 10	-7.6	-26.2	---	-7.6

Adj. for 2 for 1 10/12/00

(0.06) (0.12) (0.19) 0.03   0.00 (0.04) 0.0
(0.05) (0.04) (0.20) (0.04)   0.01 0.00 (0.07) 0.01
(0.05) (0.03) (0.17) (0.11)   0.01 0.01 (0.06)   0.01

Copyright 2012 Securities Research Company

Bonds $272.2 Mil Com 116.592 Mil BV 3.16 /sh P/E 399.00 (Ind SEMIC P/E 12.16) Ctry US

LAWSON PRODS INC (LAWS)

Distributes fasteners, replacement parts and supplies

Growth Performance Measurement				
Years	Price	Earn.	Div.	Tot Ret
Last 1	-35.8	---	.0	-33.5
Last 5	-23.6	---	-9.7	-20.4
Last 10	-10.8	---	-2.8	-6.4

Dividend omitted 12/3/12

0.12
0.12

(1.17)
(0.65)
(0.15) (0.94)

Copyright 2012 Securities Research Company

Bonds $.0 Mil Com 8.598 Mil BV 8.01 /sh P/E N/A (Ind TRADE P/E 25.46) Ctry US

LAYNE CHRISTENSEN CO (LAYN)

Provides drilling services and related products

Growth Performance Measurement				
Years	Price	Earn.	Div.	Tot Ret
Last 1	.3	-72.3	---	.3
Last 5	-13.2	-24.0	---	-13.2
Last 10	11.5	11.6	---	11.5

(0.23)
(0.50)   0.00
(.71) (0.05)

Copyright 2012 Securities Research Company

Bonds $59.9 Mil Com 19.878 Mil BV 22.29 /sh P/E 44.94 (Ind ENGNR P/E 16.28) Ctry US

LCA-VISION INC (LCAV)

Provide corrective laser vision product

65% SCALE

Growth Performance Measurement				
Years	Price	Earn.	Div.	Tot Ret
Last 1	-1.7	38.1	.0	-1.7
Last 5	-32.3	---	-19.7	-30.4
Last 10	6.5	6.5	---	12.2

Dividend Omitted 12/17/09

Adj. for 3 for 2 12/16/04

0.03 (0.35) (0.36)   (1.27) (0.81) (0.98) (0.42) (0.28)
(0.05) (0.35) (0.51) (0.09)   (0.90) (0.92) (0.87) (0.58) (0.26)
(0.13) (0.18) (0.53) (0.33)   (0.32) (1.21) (0.69) (0.71) (0.29) (0.26)

Copyright 2012 Securities Research Company

Bonds $.0 Mil Com 19.024 Mil BV 1.46 /sh P/E N/A (Ind HCFAC P/E 11.73) Ctry US

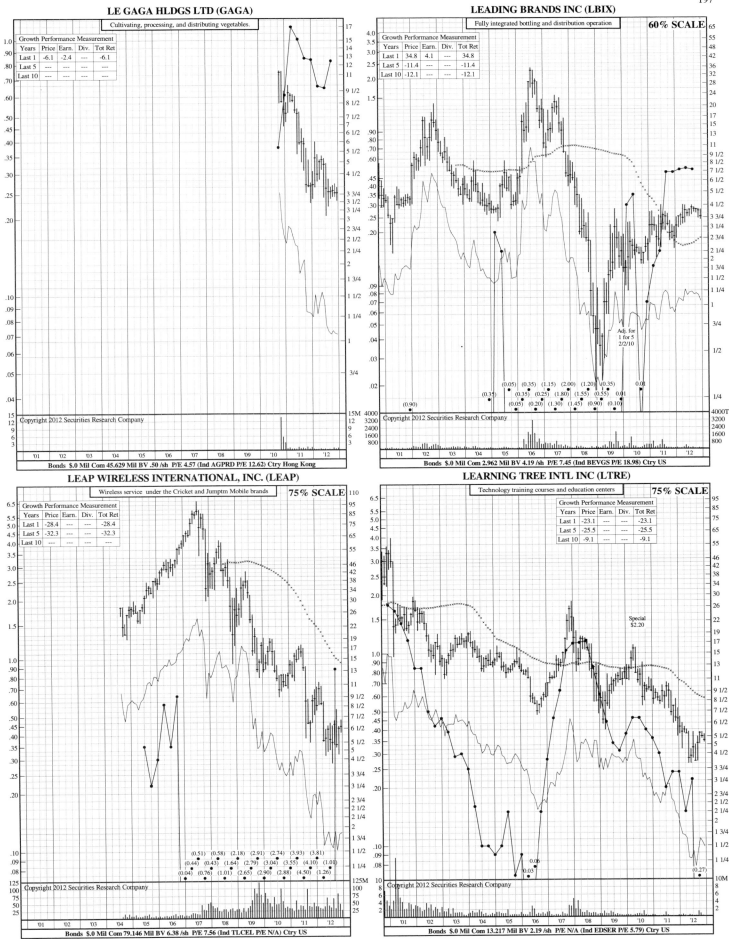

LE GAGA HLDGS LTD (GAGA)

Cultivating, processing, and distributing vegetables.

Growth Performance Measurement				
Years	Price	Earn.	Div.	Tot Ret
Last 1	-6.1	-2.4	---	-6.1
Last 5	---	---	---	---
Last 10	---	---	---	---

Copyright 2012 Securities Research Company

Bonds $.0 Mil Com 45.629 Mil BV .50 /sh P/E 4.57 (Ind AGPRD P/E 12.62) Ctry Hong Kong

LEADING BRANDS INC (LBIX)

Fully integrated bottling and distribution operation

60% SCALE

Growth Performance Measurement				
Years	Price	Earn.	Div.	Tot Ret
Last 1	34.8	4.1	---	34.8
Last 5	-11.4	---	---	-11.4
Last 10	-12.1	---	---	-12.1

Adj. for
1 for 5
2/2/10

(0.90)
(0.35) (0.05) (0.35) (1.15) (2.00) (1.20) (0.35) 0.01
(0.05) (0.20) (1.30) (1.45) (0.90) (0.10) 0.01
(0.35) (0.25) (1.80) (1.55) (0.55) (0.01) 0.01

Copyright 2012 Securities Research Company

Bonds $.0 Mil Com 2.962 Mil BV 4.19 /sh P/E 7.45 (Ind BEVGS P/E 18.98) Ctry US

LEAP WIRELESS INTERNATIONAL, INC. (LEAP)

Wireless service under the Cricket and Jumptm Mobile brands

75% SCALE

Growth Performance Measurement				
Years	Price	Earn.	Div.	Tot Ret
Last 1	-28.4	---	---	-28.4
Last 5	-32.3	---	---	-32.3
Last 10	---	---	---	---

(0.51) (0.58) (2.18) (2.91) (2.74) (3.93) (3.81)
(0.44) (0.43) (1.64) (2.79) (3.04) (3.55) (4.10) (1.01)
(0.04) (0.76) (1.01) (2.65) (2.90) (2.88) (4.50) (1.26)

Copyright 2012 Securities Research Company

Bonds $.0 Mil Com 79.146 Mil BV 6.38 /sh P/E 7.56 (Ind TLCEL P/E N/A) Ctry US

LEARNING TREE INTL INC (LTRE)

Technology training courses and education centers

75% SCALE

Growth Performance Measurement				
Years	Price	Earn.	Div.	Tot Ret
Last 1	-23.1	---	---	-23.1
Last 5	-25.5	---	---	-25.5
Last 10	-9.1	---	---	-9.1

Special
$2.20

0.06
0.03
(0.27)

Copyright 2012 Securities Research Company

Bonds $.0 Mil Com 13.217 Mil BV 2.19 /sh P/E N/A (Ind EDSER P/E 5.79) Ctry US

198

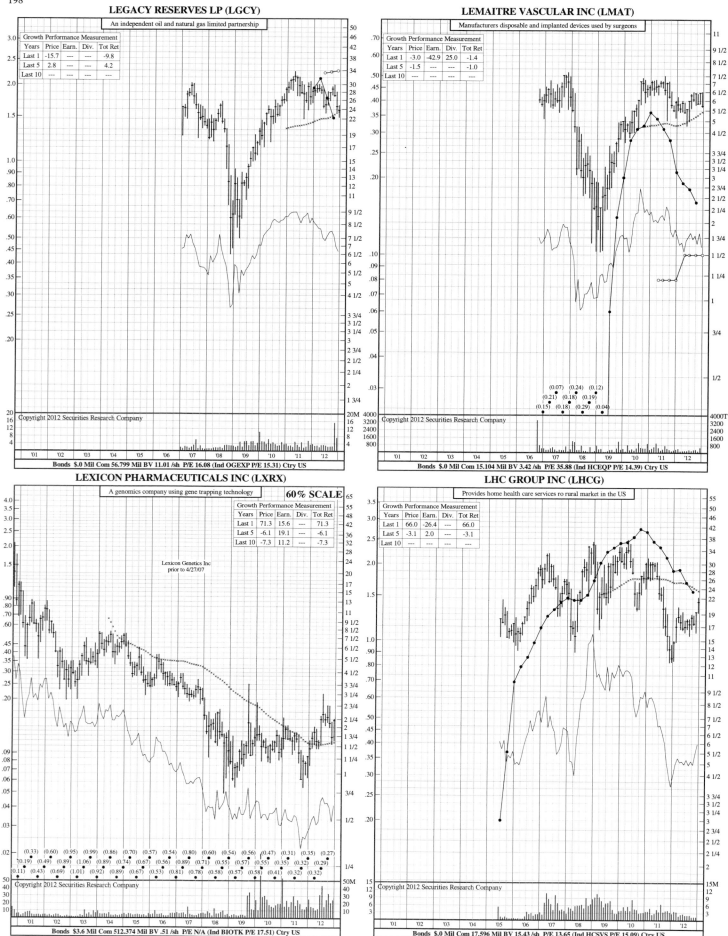

LEGACY RESERVES LP (LGCY)

An independent oil and natural gas limited partnership

Growth Performance Measurement

Years	Price	Earn.	Div.	Tot Ret
Last 1	-15.7	---	---	-9.8
Last 5	2.8	---	---	4.2
Last 10	---	---	---	---

Copyright 2012 Securities Research Company

Bonds $.0 Mil Com 56.799 Mil BV 11.01 /sh P/E 16.08 (Ind OGEXP P/E 15.31) Ctry US

LEMAITRE VASCULAR INC (LMAT)

Manufacturers disposable and implanted devices used by surgeons

Growth Performance Measurement

Years	Price	Earn.	Div.	Tot Ret
Last 1	-3.0	-42.9	25.0	-1.4
Last 5	-1.5	---	---	-1.0
Last 10	---	---	---	---

(0.07) (0.24) (0.12)
(0.21) (0.18) (0.19)
(0.15) (0.18) (0.29) (0.04)

Copyright 2012 Securities Research Company

Bonds $.0 Mil Com 15.104 Mil BV 3.42 /sh P/E 35.88 (Ind HCEQP P/E 14.39) Ctry US

LEXICON PHARMACEUTICALS INC (LXRX)

A genomics company using gene trapping technology

60% SCALE

Lexicon Genetics Inc
prior to 4/27/07

Growth Performance Measurement

Years	Price	Earn.	Div.	Tot Ret
Last 1	71.3	15.6	---	71.3
Last 5	-6.1	19.1	---	-6.1
Last 10	-7.3	11.2	---	-7.3

(0.33) (0.60) (0.95) (0.99) (0.86) (0.70) (0.57) (0.54) (0.80) (0.60) (0.54) (0.56) (0.47) (0.31) (0.35) (0.27)
(0.19) (0.49) (0.89) (1.06) (0.89) (0.74) (0.67) (0.56) (0.89) (0.71) (0.55) (0.57) (0.55) (0.35) (0.32) (0.29)
(0.11) (0.43) (0.69) (1.01) (0.92) (0.89) (0.67) (0.53) (0.81) (0.78) (0.58) (0.57) (0.58) (0.41) (0.32) (0.32)

Copyright 2012 Securities Research Company

Bonds $3.6 Mil Com 512.374 Mil BV .51 /sh P/E N/A (Ind BIOTK P/E 17.51) Ctry US

LHC GROUP INC (LHCG)

Provides home health care services ro rural market in the US

Growth Performance Measurement

Years	Price	Earn.	Div.	Tot Ret
Last 1	66.0	-26.4	---	66.0
Last 5	-3.1	2.0	---	-3.1
Last 10	---	---	---	---

Copyright 2012 Securities Research Company

Bonds $.0 Mil Com 17.596 Mil BV 15.43 /sh P/E 13.65 (Ind HCSVS P/E 15.09) Ctry US

LIBERTY GLOBAL INC (LBTYA)

199

LIFEPOINT HOSPITALS INC (LPNT)

Owns and operates rural hospitals

Province Healthcare Co. acquired 4/15/05

Growth Performance Measurement				
Years	Price	Earn.	Div.	Tot Ret
Last 1	1.6	.6	---	1.6
Last 5	4.9	6.4	---	4.9
Last 10	2.3	8.6	---	2.3

Copyright 2012 Securities Research Company

Bonds $257.1 Mil Com 49.349 Mil BV 32.52 /sh P/E 11.98 (Ind HCFAC P/E 11.73) Ctry US

LIFETIME BRANDS INC (LCUT)

Makes household cutlery under names Farberware and Hoffritz

80% SCALE

Susquehanna Pfaltzzgraff brands acquired 7/2005

Dividend Omitted 05/21/09

Lifetime Hoan Corp. prior to 6/30/05

Growth Performance Measurement				
Years	Price	Earn.	Div.	Tot Ret
Last 1	-12.6	-14.8	.0	-12.0
Last 5	-4.0	6.5	-16.7	-3.2
Last 10	8.3	13.3	-8.8	9.9

(0.54)
(0.37) (0.08)
(0.03) (0.34)

Copyright 2012 Securities Research Company

Bonds $.0 Mil Com 12.571 Mil BV 12.23 /sh P/E 9.23 (Ind HSWRE P/E 13.33) Ctry US

LIGAND PHARMACEUTICALS INC (LGND)

Small-molecule pharmaceuticals

75% SCALE

Adj. for 1 for 6 11/19/10

Listed NASDAQ 6/12/06

Growth Performance Measurement				
Years	Price	Earn.	Div.	Tot Ret
Last 1	74.7	---	---	74.7
Last 5	-6.5	---	---	-6.5
Last 10	-4.3	---	---	-4.3

(5.04) (2.82) (2.64) (3.90) (2.58)   (2.94) 0.00   (1.50) (1.86) (1.26) (0.48)   0.00
(5.82) (3.60) (3.54) (2.46) (3.66)   0.00 (0.06) (1.56) (1.32) (0.66)   (0.07)
(6.18) (4.38) (2.58) (3.54) (2.70) (2.16) 0.00 (10.14) (1.74) (1.62) (0.84) (0.24)   0.08

Copyright 2012 Securities Research Company

Bonds $136.7 Mil Com 19.964 Mil BV 1.06 /sh P/E N/A (Ind BIOTK P/E 17.51) Ctry US

LIMELIGHT NETWORKS INC (LLNW)

Develops content delivery acceleration products to enterprises,

90% SCALE

Growth Performance Measurement				
Years	Price	Earn.	Div.	Tot Ret
Last 1	-25.0	-60.0	---	-25.0
Last 5	-20.3	---	---	-20.3
Last 10	---	---	---	---

(0.04) (0.07) (0.07)   (0.11) (0.16)
0.00 (0.08) (0.08)   (0.10) (0.13)
0.02 (0.08) (0.07) (0.01)   (0.02) (0.13)

Copyright 2012 Securities Research Company

Bonds $.0 Mil Com 99.132 Mil BV 2.85 /sh P/E N/A (Ind ITSOF P/E 19.21) Ctry US

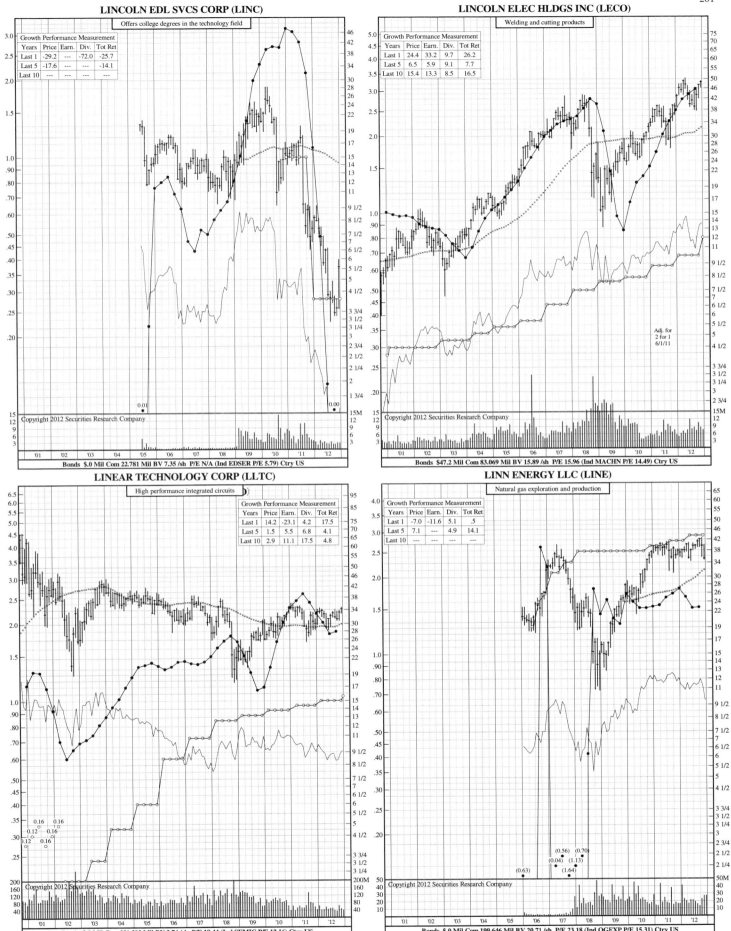

LINCOLN EDL SVCS CORP (LINC)

Offers college degrees in the technology field

Growth Performance Measurement

Years	Price	Earn.	Div.	Tot Ret
Last 1	-29.2	---	-72.0	-25.7
Last 5	-17.6	---	---	-14.1
Last 10	---	---	---	---

0.01

0.00

Copyright 2012 Securities Research Company

Bonds $.0 Mil Com 22.781 Mil BV 7.35 /sh P/E N/A (Ind EDSER P/E 5.79) Ctry US

LINCOLN ELEC HLDGS INC (LECO)

Welding and cutting products

Growth Performance Measurement

Years	Price	Earn.	Div.	Tot Ret
Last 1	24.4	33.2	9.7	26.2
Last 5	6.5	5.9	9.1	7.7
Last 10	15.4	13.3	8.5	16.5

Adj. for
2 for 1
6/1/11

Copyright 2012 Securities Research Company

Bonds $47.2 Mil Com 83.069 Mil BV 15.89 /sh P/E 15.96 (Ind MACHN P/E 14.49) Ctry US

LINEAR TECHNOLOGY CORP (LLTC)

High performance integrated circuits

Growth Performance Measurement

Years	Price	Earn.	Div.	Tot Ret
Last 1	14.2	-23.1	4.2	17.5
Last 5	1.5	5.5	6.8	4.1
Last 10	2.9	11.1	17.5	4.8

0.16   0.16
0.12   0.16
0.12 0.16

Copyright 2012 Securities Research Company

Bonds $.0 Mil Com 231.393 Mil BV 3.74 /sh P/E 18.44 (Ind SEMIC P/E 12.16) Ctry US

LINN ENERGY LLC (LINE)

Natural gas exploration and production

Growth Performance Measurement

Years	Price	Earn.	Div.	Tot Ret
Last 1	-7.0	-11.6	5.1	.5
Last 5	7.1	---	4.9	14.1
Last 10	---	---	---	---

(0.56)   (0.70)
(0.04) (1.13)
(1.64)
(0.63)

Copyright 2012 Securities Research Company

Bonds $.0 Mil Com 199.646 Mil BV 20.71 /sh P/E 23.18 (Ind OGEXP P/E 15.31) Ctry US

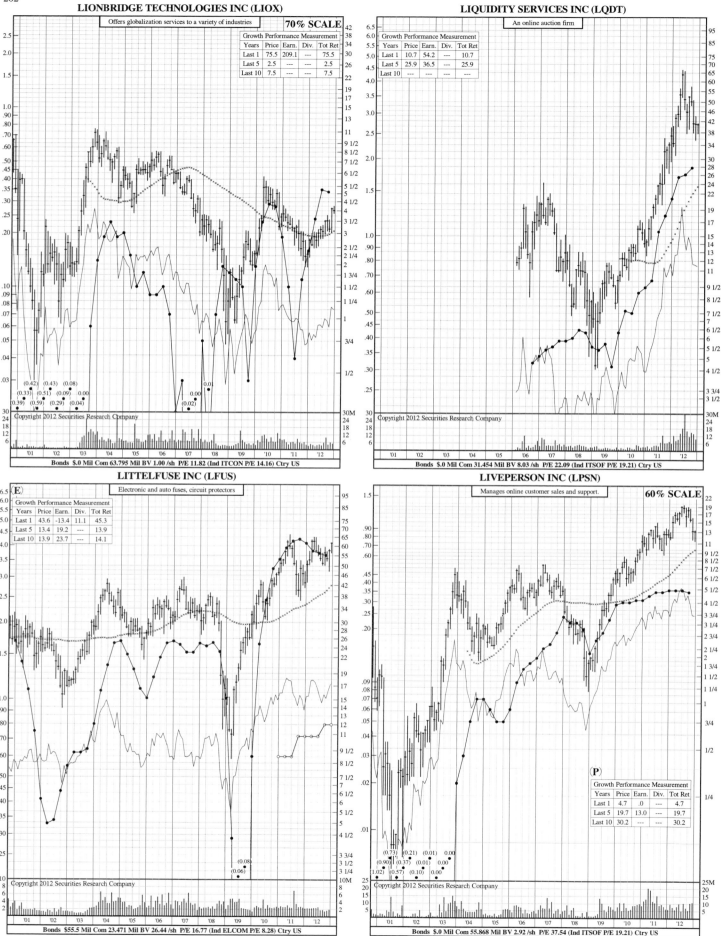

LIONBRIDGE TECHNOLOGIES INC (LIOX)

Offers globalization services to a variety of industries

70% SCALE

Growth Performance Measurement

Years	Price	Earn.	Div.	Tot Ret
Last 1	75.5	209.1	---	75.5
Last 5	2.5	---	---	2.5
Last 10	7.5	---	---	7.5

(0.42) (0.43) (0.08)
(0.33) (0.51) (0.09) 0.00
(0.39) (0.59) (0.29) (0.04)
0.00 0.01
(0.02)

Copyright 2012 Securities Research Company

Bonds $.0 Mil Com 63.795 Mil BV 1.00 /sh P/E 11.82 (Ind ITCON P/E 14.16) Ctry US

LIQUIDITY SERVICES INC (LQDT)

An online auction firm

Growth Performance Measurement

Years	Price	Earn.	Div.	Tot Ret
Last 1	10.7	54.2	---	10.7
Last 5	25.9	36.5	---	25.9
Last 10	---	---	---	---

Copyright 2012 Securities Research Company

Bonds $.0 Mil Com 31.454 Mil BV 8.03 /sh P/E 22.09 (Ind ITSOF P/E 19.21) Ctry US

LITTELFUSE INC (LFUS)

(E)

Electronic and auto fuses, circuit protectors

Growth Performance Measurement

Years	Price	Earn.	Div.	Tot Ret
Last 1	43.6	-13.4	11.1	45.3
Last 5	13.4	19.2	---	13.9
Last 10	13.9	23.7	---	14.1

(0.08)
(0.06)

Copyright 2012 Securities Research Company

Bonds $55.5 Mil Com 23.471 Mil BV 26.44 /sh P/E 16.77 (Ind ELCOM P/E 8.28) Ctry US

LIVEPERSON INC (LPSN)

Manages online customer sales and support.

60% SCALE

(P)

Growth Performance Measurement

Years	Price	Earn.	Div.	Tot Ret
Last 1	4.7	.0	---	4.7
Last 5	19.7	13.0	---	19.7
Last 10	30.2	---	---	30.2

(0.73) (0.21) (0.01) 0.00
(0.90) (0.37) (0.01) 0.00
(1.02) (0.57) (0.10) 0.00

Copyright 2012 Securities Research Company

Bonds $.0 Mil Com 55.868 Mil BV 2.92 /sh P/E 37.54 (Ind ITSOF P/E 19.21) Ctry US

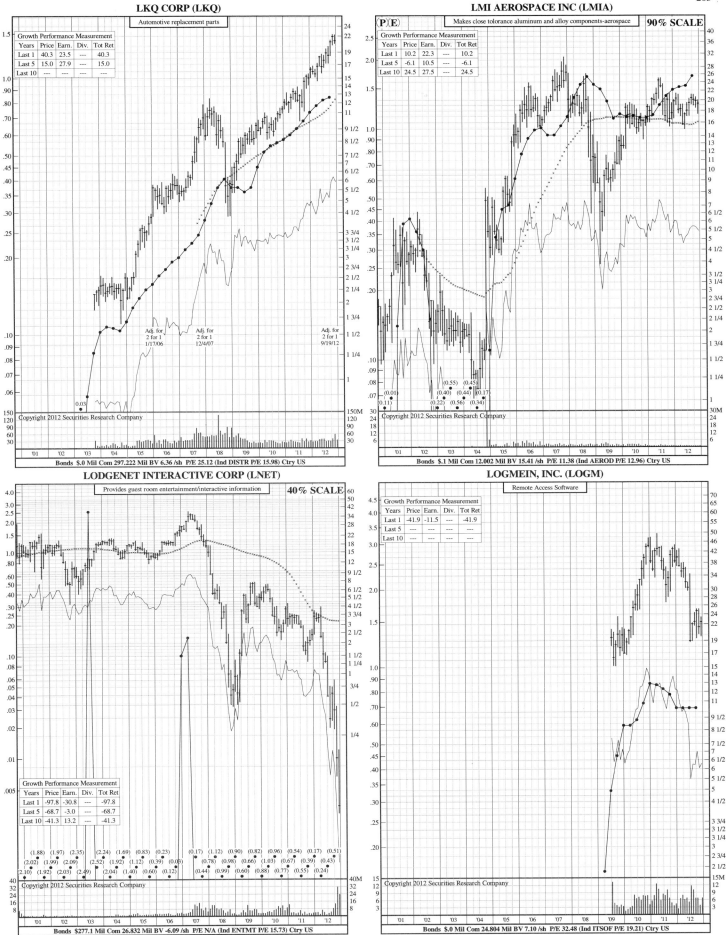

LKQ CORP (LKQ)

Automotive replacement parts

Growth Performance Measurement				
Years	Price	Earn.	Div.	Tot Ret
Last 1	40.3	23.5	---	40.3
Last 5	15.0	27.9	---	15.0
Last 10	---	---	---	---

Adj. for
2 for 1
1/17/06

Adj. for
2 for 1
12/4/07

Adj. for
2 for 1
9/19/12

0.03

Copyright 2012 Securities Research Company

Bonds $.0 Mil Com 297.222 Mil BV 6.36 /sh P/E 25.12 (Ind DISTR P/E 15.98) Ctry US

LMI AEROSPACE INC (LMIA)

(P)(E)   Makes close tolorance aluminum and alloy components-aerospace   90% SCALE

Growth Performance Measurement				
Years	Price	Earn.	Div.	Tot Ret
Last 1	10.2	22.3	---	10.2
Last 5	-6.1	10.5	---	-6.1
Last 10	24.5	27.5	---	24.5

(0.55) (0.45)
(0.40) (0.44) (0.17)
(0.01)
(0.11) (0.22) (0.56) (0.34)

Copyright 2012 Securities Research Company

Bonds $.1 Mil Com 12.002 Mil BV 15.41 /sh P/E 11.38 (Ind AEROD P/E 12.96) Ctry US

LODGENET INTERACTIVE CORP (LNET)

Provides guest room entertainment/interactive information   40% SCALE

Growth Performance Measurement				
Years	Price	Earn.	Div.	Tot Ret
Last 1	-97.8	-30.8	---	-97.8
Last 5	-68.7	-3.0	---	-68.7
Last 10	-41.3	13.2	---	-41.3

(1.88) (1.97) (2.35)   (2.24) (1.69) (0.83) (0.23)   (0.17) (1.12) (0.90) (0.82) (0.96) (0.54) (0.17) (0.51)
(2.02) (1.99) (2.09)   (2.52) (1.92) (1.12) (0.39) (0.03)   (0.78) (0.98) (0.66) (1.03) (0.67) (0.39) (0.43)
(2.10) (1.92) (2.03) (2.49)   (2.04) (1.40) (0.60) (0.12)   (0.44) (0.99) (0.60) (0.88) (0.77) (0.55) (0.24)

Copyright 2012 Securities Research Company

Bonds $277.1 Mil Com 26.832 Mil BV -6.09 /sh P/E N/A (Ind ENTMT P/E 15.73) Ctry US

LOGMEIN, INC. (LOGM)

Remote Access Software

Growth Performance Measurement				
Years	Price	Earn.	Div.	Tot Ret
Last 1	-41.9	-11.5	---	-41.9
Last 5	---	---	---	---
Last 10	---	---	---	---

Copyright 2012 Securities Research Company

Bonds $.0 Mil Com 24.804 Mil BV 7.10 /sh P/E 32.48 (Ind ITSOF P/E 19.21) Ctry US

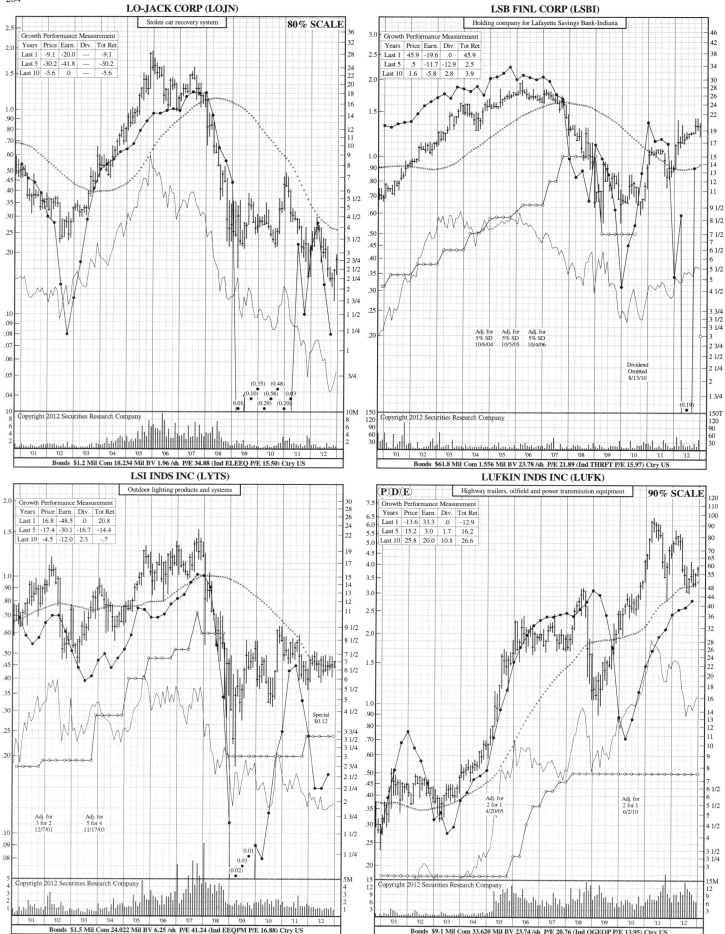

204

LO-JACK CORP (LOJN)

Stolen car recovery system

80% SCALE

Growth Performance Measurement

Years	Price	Earn.	Div.	Tot Ret
Last 1	-9.1	-20.0	---	-9.1
Last 5	-30.2	-41.8	---	-30.2
Last 10	-5.6	.0	---	-5.6

(0.35) (0.48)
(0.10) (0.56) 0.03
0.01 (0.29) (0.20)

Copyright 2012 Securities Research Company

Bonds $1.2 Mil Com 18.234 Mil BV 1.96 /sh P/E 34.88 (Ind ELEEQ P/E 15.50) Ctry US

LSB FINL CORP (LSBI)

Holding company for Lafayette Savings Bank-Indiana

Growth Performance Measurement

Years	Price	Earn.	Div.	Tot Ret
Last 1	45.9	-19.6	.0	45.9
Last 5	.5	-11.7	-12.9	2.5
Last 10	1.6	-5.8	2.8	3.9

Adj. for   Adj. for   Adj. for
5% SD   5% SD   5% SD
10/6/04   10/5/05   10/4/06

Dividend
Omitted
8/13/10

(0.19)

Copyright 2012 Securities Research Company

Bonds $61.8 Mil Com 1.556 Mil BV 23.78 /sh P/E 21.89 (Ind THRFT P/E 15.97) Ctry US

LSI INDS INC (LYTS)

Outdoor lighting products and systems

Growth Performance Measurement

Years	Price	Earn.	Div.	Tot Ret
Last 1	16.8	-48.5	.0	20.8
Last 5	-17.4	-30.1	-16.7	-14.4
Last 10	-4.5	-12.0	2.3	-.7

Special
$0.12

Adj. for   Adj. for
3 for 2   5 for 4
12/7/01   11/17/03

0.01
0.03
(0.02)

Copyright 2012 Securities Research Company

Bonds $1.5 Mil Com 24.022 Mil BV 6.25 /sh P/E 41.24 (Ind EEQPM P/E 16.88) Ctry US

LUFKIN INDS INC (LUFK)

(P)(D)(E)   Highway trailers, oilfield and power transmission equipment   90% SCALE

Growth Performance Measurement

Years	Price	Earn.	Div.	Tot Ret
Last 1	-13.6	33.3	.0	-12.9
Last 5	15.2	3.0	1.7	16.2
Last 10	25.8	20.0	10.8	26.6

Adj. for
2 for 1
4/20/05

Adj. for
2 for 1
6/2/10

Copyright 2012 Securities Research Company

Bonds $9.1 Mil Com 33.620 Mil BV 23.74 /sh P/E 20.76 (Ind OGEQP P/E 13.95) Ctry US

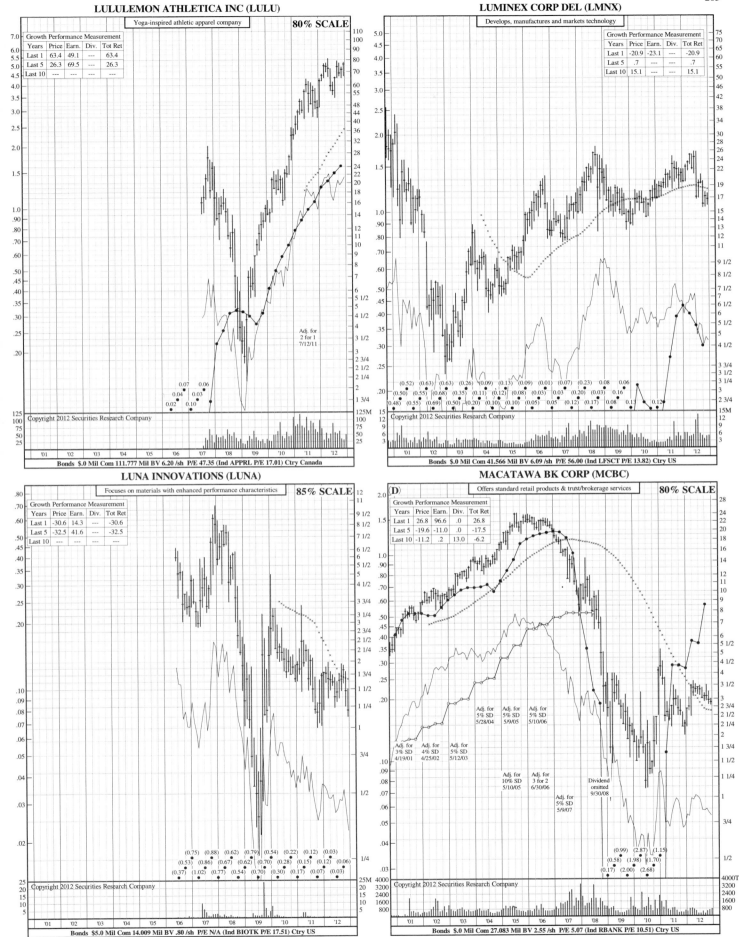

LULULEMON ATHLETICA INC (LULU)

Yoga-inspired athletic apparel company

80% SCALE

Growth Performance Measurement				
Years	Price	Earn.	Div.	Tot Ret
Last 1	63.4	49.1	---	63.4
Last 5	26.3	69.5	---	26.3
Last 10	---	---	---	---

Adj. for
2 for 1
7/12/11

0.07 0.06
0.04 0.03
0.02 0.10

Copyright 2012 Securities Research Company

Bonds $.0 Mil Com 111.777 Mil BV 6.20 /sh P/E 47.35 (Ind APPRL P/E 17.01) Ctry Canada

LUMINEX CORP DEL (LMNX)

Develops, manufactures and markets technology

Growth Performance Measurement				
Years	Price	Earn.	Div.	Tot Ret
Last 1	-20.9	-23.1	---	-20.9
Last 5	.7	---	---	.7
Last 10	15.1	---	---	15.1

(0.52) (0.63) (0.63) (0.26) (0.09) (0.13) (0.09) (0.01) (0.07) (0.23) 0.08 0.06
(0.50) (0.55) (0.68) (0.35) (0.11) (0.12) (0.08) (0.03) 0.03 (0.20) (0.03) 0.16
(0.48) (0.55) (0.69) (0.50) (0.20) (0.10) (0.10) (0.05) 0.05 (0.12) (0.17) 0.08 0.13 0.12

Copyright 2012 Securities Research Company

Bonds $.0 Mil Com 41.566 Mil BV 6.09 /sh P/E 56.00 (Ind LFSCT P/E 13.82) Ctry US

LUNA INNOVATIONS (LUNA)

Focuses on materials with enhanced performance characteristics

85% SCALE

Growth Performance Measurement				
Years	Price	Earn.	Div.	Tot Ret
Last 1	-30.6	14.3	---	-30.6
Last 5	-32.5	41.6	---	-32.5
Last 10	---	---	---	---

(0.75) (0.88) (0.62) (0.79) (0.54) (0.22) (0.12) (0.03)
(0.53) (0.86) (0.67) (0.62) (0.70) (0.28) (0.15) (0.12) (0.06)
(0.37) (1.02) (0.77) (0.54) (0.70) (0.30) (0.17) (0.07) (0.03)

Copyright 2012 Securities Research Company

Bonds $5.0 Mil Com 14.009 Mil BV .80 /sh P/E N/A (Ind BIOTK P/E 17.51) Ctry US

MACATAWA BK CORP (MCBC)

(D)

Offers standard retail products & trust/brokerage services

80% SCALE

Growth Performance Measurement				
Years	Price	Earn.	Div.	Tot Ret
Last 1	26.8	96.6	.0	26.8
Last 5	-19.6	-11.0	.0	-17.5
Last 10	-11.2	.2	13.0	-6.2

Adj. for
5% SD
5/28/04

Adj. for
5% SD
5/9/05

Adj. for
5% SD
5/10/06

Adj. for
3% SD
4/19/01

Adj. for
4% SD
4/25/02

Adj. for
5% SD
5/12/03

Adj. for
10% SD
5/10/06

Adj. for
3 for 2
6/30/06

Dividend
omitted
9/30/08

Adj. for
5% SD
5/9/07

(0.99) (2.87) (1.15)
(0.58) (1.98) (1.70)
(0.17) (2.00) (2.68)

Copyright 2012 Securities Research Company

Bonds $.0 Mil Com 27.083 Mil BV 2.55 /sh P/E 5.07 (Ind RBANK P/E 10.51) Ctry US

206

MADDEN STEVEN LTD (SHOO)

Designs and markets women's footwear

(P)(E)

Growth Performance Measurement				
Years	Price	Earn.	Div.	Tot Ret
Last 1	22.5	22.6	---	22.5
Last 5	36.6	26.7	---	36.6
Last 10	23.0	20.6	---	23.0

Adj. for
3 for 2
5/26/06

Special
$0.667

Special
$1.00

Adj. for
3 for 2
5/3/10

Adj. for
3 for 2
6/1/11

Copyright 2012 Securities Research Company

Bonds $.2 Mil Com 45.909 Mil BV 12.79 /sh P/E 16.26 (Ind SHOES P/E 22.44) Ctry US

MADISON SQUARE GARDEN CO (MSG)

Operates in the sports, entertainment, and media businesses

Growth Performance Measurement				
Years	Price	Earn.	Div.	Tot Ret
Last 1	54.9	28.3	---	54.9
Last 5	---	---	---	---
Last 10	---	---	---	---

Spun-Off
From
Cablevision Sys Corp.
2/9/10

Copyright 2012 Securities Research Company

Bonds $.0 Mil Com 62.055 Mil BV 18.02 /sh P/E 32.61 (Ind CAASA P/E 17.31) Ctry US

MAGAL SECURITY SYS LTD (MAGS)

Computerized security systems to detect and deter human intrusion   85% SCALE

Growth Performance Measurement				
Years	Price	Earn.	Div.	Tot Ret
Last 1	9.4	151.4	.0	9.4
Last 5	-8.4	---	.0	-8.4
Last 10	-3.1	12.0	-8.5	-3.0

Adj. for
3% SD
7/30/02

Adj. for
3% SD
8/7/03

Adj. for
5% SD
7/27/04

Paid
$0.116

Paid
$0.04

0.05   Dividends after Israel tax
to U.S. residents

(0.71)

0.00   (0.85)   (0.52)   (0.60)

Copyright 2012 Securities Research Company

Bonds $.0 Mil Com 16.053 Mil BV 3.26 /sh P/E 4.40 (Ind ELEEQ P/E 15.50) Ctry Israel

MAGELLAN HEALTH SVCS INC (MGLN)

Managed behavioral health care company

Growth Performance Measurement				
Years	Price	Earn.	Div.	Tot Ret
Last 1	-1.0	11.3	---	-1.0
Last 5	1.0	16.0	---	1.0
Last 10	---	---	---	---

Copyright 2012 Securities Research Company

Bonds $.0 Mil Com 27.400 Mil BV 35.92 /sh P/E 10.82 (Ind HCMAN P/E 9.74) Ctry US

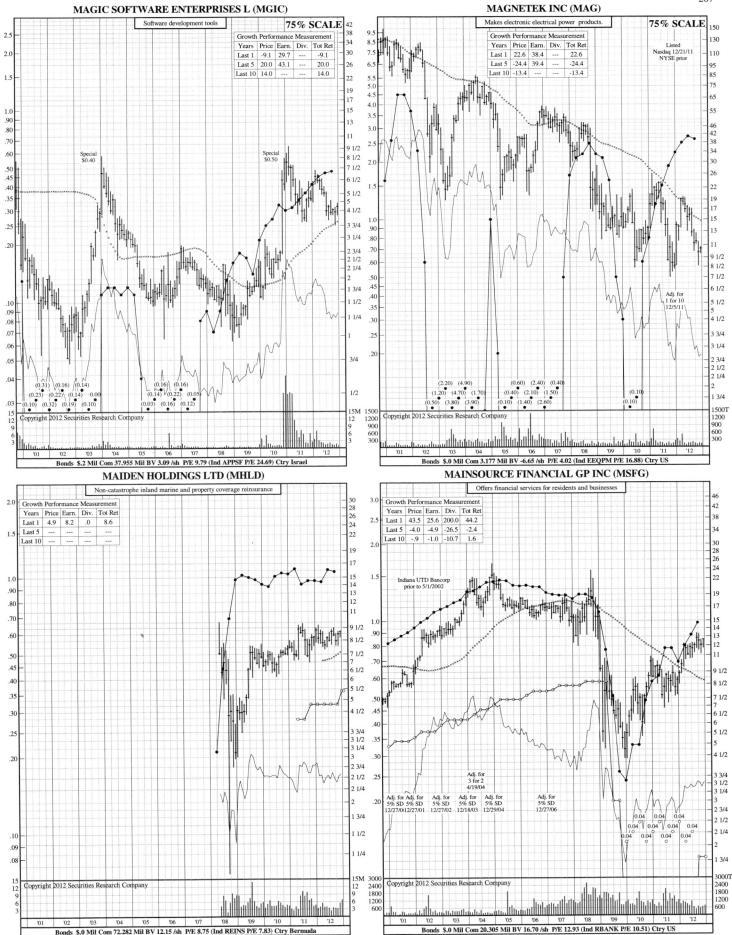

MAGIC SOFTWARE ENTERPRISES L (MGIC)

Software development tools

75% SCALE

Growth Performance Measurement				
Years	Price	Earn.	Div.	Tot Ret
Last 1	-9.1	29.7	---	-9.1
Last 5	20.0	43.1	---	20.0
Last 10	14.0	---	---	14.0

Special $0.40

Special $0.50

(0.31) (0.16) (0.14) 0.00
(0.23) (0.22) (0.14) (0.10)
(0.10) (0.32) (0.19) (0.10)
(0.16) (0.16)
(0.14) (0.22) (0.05)
(0.03) (0.16) (0.12)

Copyright 2012 Securities Research Company

Bonds $.2 Mil Com 37.955 Mil BV 3.09 /sh P/E 9.79 (Ind APPSF P/E 24.69) Ctry Israel

MAGNETEK INC (MAG)

Makes electronic electrical power products.

75% SCALE

Growth Performance Measurement				
Years	Price	Earn.	Div.	Tot Ret
Last 1	22.6	38.4	---	22.6
Last 5	-24.4	39.4	---	-24.4
Last 10	-13.4	---	---	-13.4

Listed Nasdaq 12/21/11 NYSE prior

Adj. for 1 for 10 12/5/11

(2.20) (4.90)
(1.20) (4.70) (1.70)
(0.50) (3.80) (3.90)
(0.60) (2.40) (0.40)
(0.40) (1.40) (1.50)
(0.10) (1.40) (2.60)
(0.10)
(0.10)

Copyright 2012 Securities Research Company

Bonds $.0 Mil Com 3.177 Mil BV -6.65 /sh P/E 4.02 (Ind EEQPM P/E 16.88) Ctry US

MAIDEN HOLDINGS LTD (MHLD)

Non-catastrophe inland marine and property coverage reinsurance

Growth Performance Measurement				
Years	Price	Earn.	Div.	Tot Ret
Last 1	4.9	8.2	.0	8.6
Last 5	---	---	---	---
Last 10	---	---	---	---

Copyright 2012 Securities Research Company

Bonds $.0 Mil Com 72.282 Mil BV 12.15 /sh P/E 8.75 (Ind REINS P/E 7.83) Ctry Bermuda

MAINSOURCE FINANCIAL GP INC (MSFG)

Offers financial services for residents and businesses

Growth Performance Measurement				
Years	Price	Earn.	Div.	Tot Ret
Last 1	43.5	25.6	200.0	44.2
Last 5	-4.0	-4.9	-26.5	-2.4
Last 10	-.9	-1.0	-10.7	1.6

Indiana UTD Bancorp prior to 5/1/2002

Adj. for 3 for 2 4/19/04

Adj. for 5% SD 12/27/01
Adj. for 5% SD 12/27/02
Adj. for 5% SD 12/18/03
Adj. for 5% SD 12/29/04
Adj. for 5% SD 12/27/06

0.04 0.04 0.04
0.04 0.04 0.04 0.04
0.04 0.04

Copyright 2012 Securities Research Company

Bonds $.0 Mil Com 20.305 Mil BV 16.70 /sh P/E 12.93 (Ind RBANK P/E 10.51) Ctry US

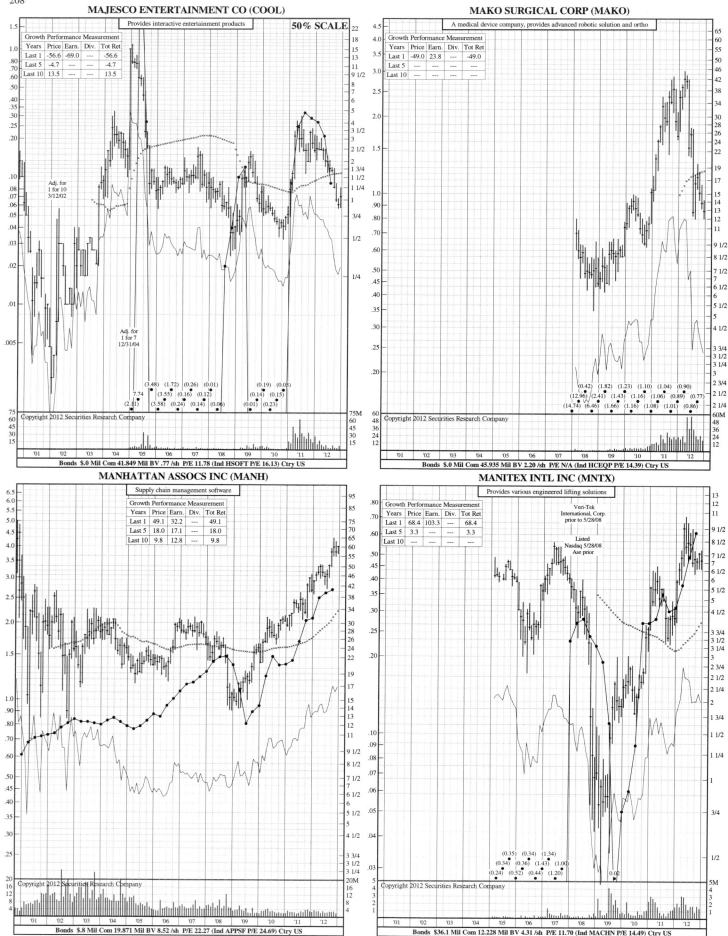

MAJESCO ENTERTAINMENT CO (COOL)

Provides interactive entertainment products

50% SCALE

Growth Performance Measurement

Years	Price	Earn.	Div.	Tot Ret
Last 1	-56.6	-69.0	---	-56.6
Last 5	-4.7	---	---	-4.7
Last 10	13.5	---	---	13.5

Adj. for
1 for 10
3/12/02

Adj. for
1 for 7
12/31/04

(3.48) (1.72) (0.26) (0.01)   (0.19) (0.08)
7.74   (0.14) (0.15)
(2.11) (3.58) (0.24) (0.14) (0.06) (0.01) (0.23)

Copyright 2012 Securities Research Company

Bonds $.0 Mil Com 41.849 Mil BV .77 /sh P/E 11.78 (Ind HSOFT P/E 16.13) Ctry US

MAKO SURGICAL CORP (MAKO)

A medical device company, provides advanced robotic solution and ortho

Growth Performance Measurement

Years	Price	Earn.	Div.	Tot Ret
Last 1	-49.0	23.8	---	-49.0
Last 5	---	---	---	---
Last 10	---	---	---	---

(0.42) (1.82) (1.23) (1.10) (1.04) (0.90)
(12.96) (2.41) (1.43) (1.16) (1.06) (0.89) (0.77)
(14.74) (6.46) (1.66) (1.16) (1.08) (1.01) (0.86)

Copyright 2012 Securities Research Company

Bonds $.0 Mil Com 45.935 Mil BV 2.20 /sh P/E N/A (Ind HCEQP P/E 14.39) Ctry US

MANHATTAN ASSOCS INC (MANH)

Supply chain management software

Growth Performance Measurement

Years	Price	Earn.	Div.	Tot Ret
Last 1	49.1	32.2	---	49.1
Last 5	18.0	17.1	---	18.0
Last 10	9.8	12.8	---	9.8

Copyright 2012 Securities Research Company

Bonds $.8 Mil Com 19.871 Mil BV 8.52 /sh P/E 22.27 (Ind APPSF P/E 24.69) Ctry US

MANITEX INTL INC (MNTX)

Provides various engineered lifting solutions

Veri-Tek
International, Corp.
prior to 5/28/08

Listed
Nasdaq 5/28/08
Ase prior

Growth Performance Measurement

Years	Price	Earn.	Div.	Tot Ret
Last 1	68.4	103.3	---	68.4
Last 5	3.3	---	---	3.3
Last 10	---	---	---	---

(0.35) (0.34) (1.34)
(0.34) (0.36) (1.43) (1.00)
(0.24) (0.52) (0.44) (1.20)   0.02

Copyright 2012 Securities Research Company

Bonds $36.1 Mil Com 12.228 Mil BV 4.31 /sh P/E 11.70 (Ind MACHN P/E 14.49) Ctry US

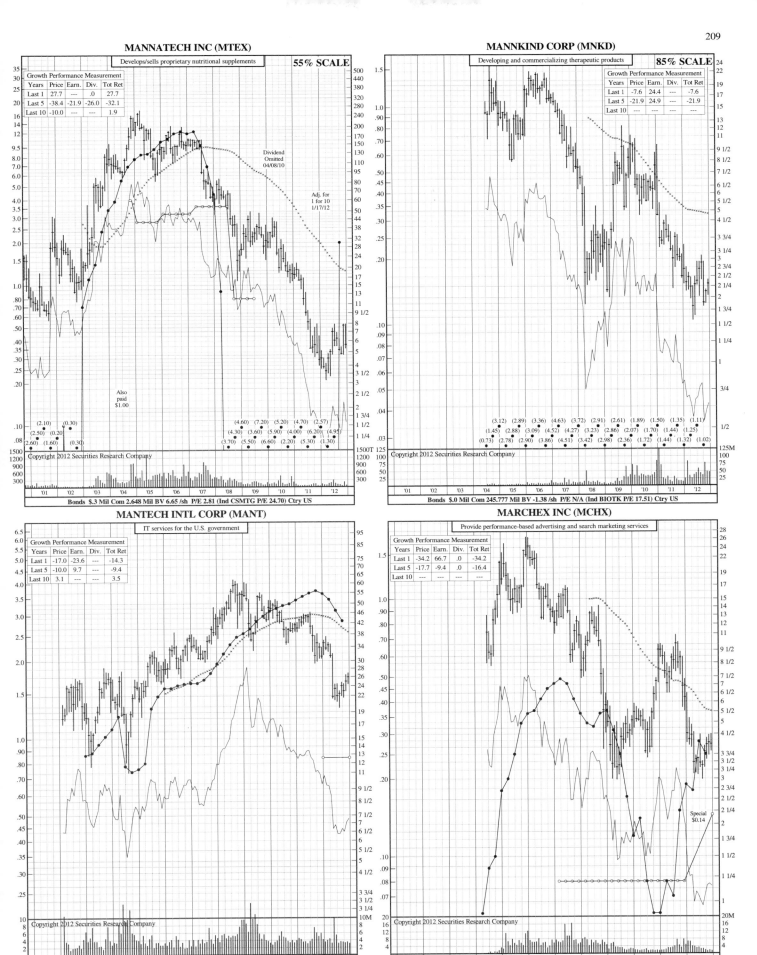

MANNATECH INC (MTEX)
Develops/sells proprietary nutritional supplements
55% SCALE

Growth Performance Measurement

Years	Price	Earn.	Div.	Tot Ret
Last 1	27.7	---	.0	27.7
Last 5	-38.4	-21.9	-26.0	-32.1
Last 10	-10.0	---	---	1.9

Dividend
Omitted
04/08/10

Adj. for
1 for 10
1/17/12

Also
paid
$1.00

(2.10) (0.30)
(2.50) (0.20)
(2.60) (1.60) (0.30)

(4.60) (7.20) (5.20) (4.70) (2.57)
(4.30) (3.60) (5.90) (4.00) (6.20) (4.95)
(3.70) (5.50) (6.60) (2.20) (5.30) (1.30)

Copyright 2012 Securities Research Company

Bonds $.3 Mil Com 2.648 Mil BV 6.65 /sh P/E 2.81 (Ind CSMTG P/E 24.70) Ctry US

MANNKIND CORP (MNKD)
Developing and commercializing therapeutic products
85% SCALE

Growth Performance Measurement

Years	Price	Earn.	Div.	Tot Ret
Last 1	-7.6	24.4	---	-7.6
Last 5	-21.9	24.9	---	-21.9
Last 10	---	---	---	---

(3.12) (2.89) (3.36) (4.63) (3.72) (2.91) (2.61) (1.89) (1.50) (1.35) (1.11)
(1.45) (2.88) (3.09) (4.52) (4.27) (3.23) (2.86) (2.07) (1.70) (1.44) (1.25)
(0.73) (2.78) (2.90) (3.86) (4.51) (3.42) (2.98) (2.36) (1.72) (1.44) (1.32) (1.02)

Copyright 2012 Securities Research Company

Bonds $.0 Mil Com 245.777 Mil BV -1.38 /sh P/E N/A (Ind BIOTK P/E 17.51) Ctry US

MANTECH INTL CORP (MANT)
IT services for the U.S. government

Growth Performance Measurement

Years	Price	Earn.	Div.	Tot Ret
Last 1	-17.0	-23.6	---	-14.3
Last 5	-10.0	9.7	---	-9.4
Last 10	3.1	---	---	3.5

Copyright 2012 Securities Research Company

Bonds $.0 Mil Com 23.811 Mil BV 31.03 /sh P/E 9.10 (Ind ITCON P/E 14.16) Ctry US

MARCHEX INC (MCHX)
Provide performance-based advertising and search marketing services

Growth Performance Measurement

Years	Price	Earn.	Div.	Tot Ret
Last 1	-34.2	66.7	.0	-34.2
Last 5	-17.7	-9.4	.0	-16.4
Last 10	---	---	---	---

Special
$0.14

Copyright 2012 Securities Research Company

Bonds $.0 Mil Com 28.102 Mil BV 4.40 /sh P/E 16.44 (Ind ITSOF P/E 19.21) Ctry US

210

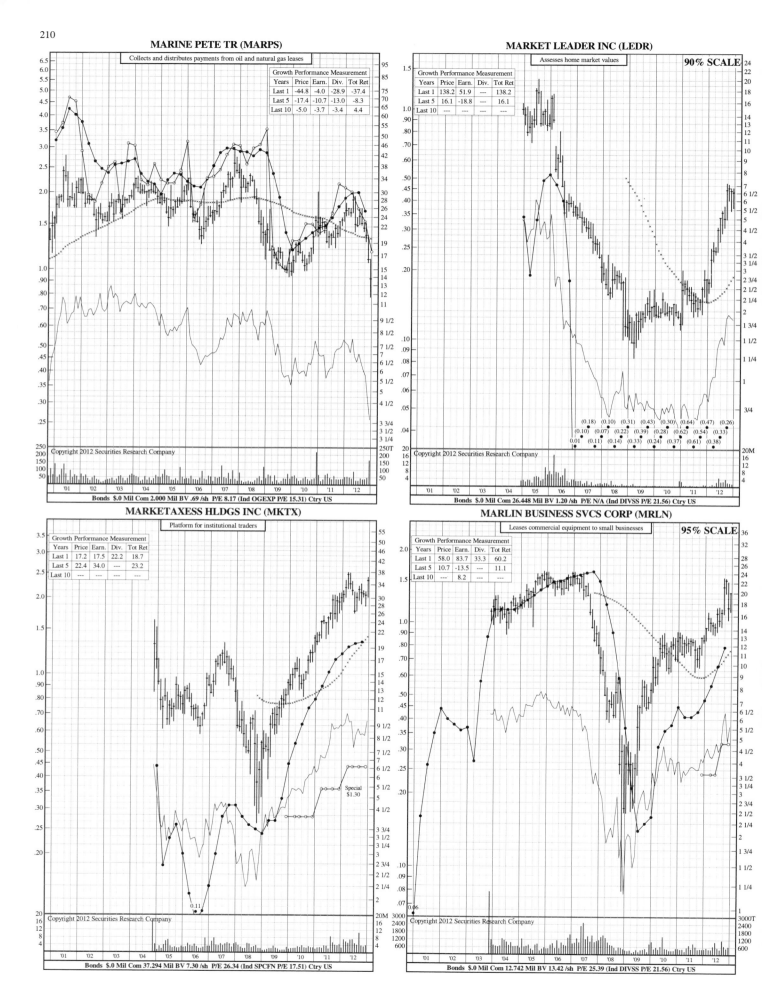

MARINE PETE TR (MARPS)

Collects and distributes payments from oil and natural gas leases

Growth Performance Measurement				
Years	Price	Earn.	Div.	Tot Ret
Last 1	-44.8	-4.0	-28.9	-37.4
Last 5	-17.4	-10.7	-13.0	-8.3
Last 10	-5.0	-3.7	-3.4	4.4

Copyright 2012 Securities Research Company

Bonds $.0 Mil Com 2.000 Mil BV .69 /sh P/E 8.17 (Ind OGEXP P/E 15.31) Ctry US

MARKET LEADER INC (LEDR)

Assesses home market values

90% SCALE

Growth Performance Measurement				
Years	Price	Earn.	Div.	Tot Ret
Last 1	138.2	51.9	---	138.2
Last 5	16.1	-18.8	---	16.1
Last 10	---	---	---	---

(0.18) (0.10) (0.31) (0.43) (0.30) (0.64) (0.47) (0.26)
(0.10) (0.07) (0.22) (0.39) (0.28) (0.62) (0.54) (0.33)
0.01 (0.11) (0.14) (0.33) (0.24) (0.37) (0.61) (0.38)

Copyright 2012 Securities Research Company

Bonds $.0 Mil Com 26.448 Mil BV 1.20 /sh P/E N/A (Ind DIVSS P/E 21.56) Ctry US

MARKETAXESS HLDGS INC (MKTX)

Platform for institutional traders

Growth Performance Measurement				
Years	Price	Earn.	Div.	Tot Ret
Last 1	17.2	17.5	22.2	18.7
Last 5	22.4	34.0	---	23.2
Last 10	---	---	---	---

Special $1.30

0.11

Copyright 2012 Securities Research Company

Bonds $.0 Mil Com 37.294 Mil BV 7.30 /sh P/E 26.34 (Ind SPCFN P/E 17.51) Ctry US

MARLIN BUSINESS SVCS CORP (MRLN)

Leases commercial equipment to small businesses

95% SCALE

Growth Performance Measurement				
Years	Price	Earn.	Div.	Tot Ret
Last 1	58.0	83.7	33.3	60.2
Last 5	10.7	-13.5	---	11.1
Last 10	---	8.2	---	---

0.06

Copyright 2012 Securities Research Company

Bonds $.0 Mil Com 12.742 Mil BV 13.42 /sh P/E 25.39 (Ind DIVSS P/E 21.56) Ctry US

MARTEN TRANS LTD (MRTN)

Specializes in protective service transportation of foods/chemicals

Growth Performance Measurement				
Years	Price	Earn.	Div.	Tot Ret
Last 1	2.2	23.0	25.0	2.7
Last 5	5.7	9.0	---	5.9
Last 10	12.6	10.3	---	12.7

Adj. for 3 for 2 7/25/03
Adj. for 3 for 2 12/27/05
Adj. for 3 for 2 12/8/03

Special $0.75

0.08 0.08
0.08 0.08
0.08 0.08 0.08

Copyright 2012 Securities Research Company

Bonds $63.6 Mil Com 22.071 Mil BV 15.32 /sh P/E 14.95 (Ind TRUCK P/E 13.01) Ctry US

MARTIN MIDSTREAM PRTNRS L P (MMLP)

Provides terminalling and storage services for petroleum products

Growth Performance Measurement				
Years	Price	Earn.	Div.	Tot Ret
Last 1	-9.8	.0	1.0	-1.0
Last 5	-2.6	-8.8	2.5	5.4
Last 10	5.8	---	---	11.8

Copyright 2012 Securities Research Company

Bonds $5.0 Mil Com 26.117 Mil BV 17.74 /sh P/E 28.76 (Ind OGSTO P/E 27.33) Ctry US

MARVELL TECHNOLOGY GROUP LTD (MRVL)

Integrated circuits for data storage/communications products

Growth Performance Measurement				
Years	Price	Earn.	Div.	Tot Ret
Last 1	-47.6	-37.4	---	-46.7
Last 5	-12.3	45.7	---	-12.0
Last 10	4.4	25.2	---	4.6

Galileo Technology Ltd. acquired 1/19/01

Adj. for 2 for 1 6/29/04
Adj. for 2 for 1 7/25/06

0.04 0.04
0.04 0.04 0.07
0.04 0.04 0.05

Copyright 2012 Securities Research Company

Bonds $24.4 Mil Com 535.000 Mil BV 9.33 /sh P/E 7.89 (Ind SEMIC P/E 12.16) Ctry US

MASIMO CORP (MASI)

Pioneered motion and low perfusion tolerant technology

Growth Performance Measurement				
Years	Price	Earn.	Div.	Tot Ret
Last 1	12.4	-7.2	---	12.4
Last 5	-11.8	4.7	---	-11.8
Last 10	---	---	---	---

Specials $2.75

Copyright 2012 Securities Research Company

Bonds $.0 Mil Com 57.232 Mil BV 5.44 /sh P/E 20.40 (Ind HCEQP P/E 14.39) Ctry US

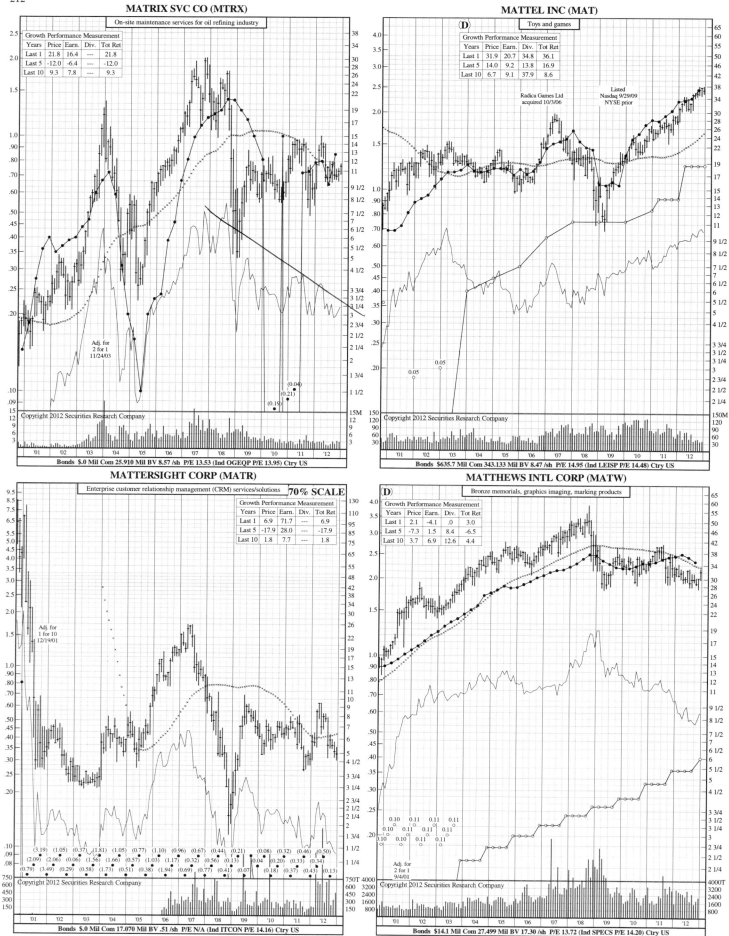

212

MATRIX SVC CO (MTRX)

On-site maintenance services for oil refining industry

Growth Performance Measurement

Years	Price	Earn.	Div.	Tot Ret
Last 1	21.8	16.4	---	21.8
Last 5	-12.0	-6.4	---	-12.0
Last 10	9.3	7.8	---	9.3

Adj. for
2 for 1
11/24/03

(0.04)
(0.21)
(0.19)

Copyright 2012 Securities Research Company

Bonds $.0 Mil Com 25.910 Mil BV 8.57 /sh P/E 13.53 (Ind OGEQP P/E 13.95) Ctry US

MATTEL INC (MAT)

(D)   Toys and games

Growth Performance Measurement

Years	Price	Earn.	Div.	Tot Ret
Last 1	31.9	20.7	34.8	36.1
Last 5	14.0	9.2	13.8	16.9
Last 10	6.7	9.1	37.9	8.6

Radica Games Ltd
acquired 10/3/06

Listed
Nasdaq 9/29/09
NYSE prior

0.05

0.05

Copyright 2012 Securities Research Company

Bonds $635.7 Mil Com 343.133 Mil BV 8.47 /sh P/E 14.95 (Ind LEISP P/E 14.48) Ctry US

MATTERSIGHT CORP (MATR)

Enterprise customer relationship management (CRM) services/solutions   **70% SCALE**

Growth Performance Measurement

Years	Price	Earn.	Div.	Tot Ret
Last 1	6.9	71.7	---	6.9
Last 5	-17.9	28.0	---	-17.9
Last 10	1.8	7.7	---	1.8

Adj. for
1 for 10
12/19/01

(3.19) (1.05) (0.37) (1.81) (1.05) (0.77) (1.10) (0.96) (0.67) (0.44) (0.21) (0.08) (0.32) (0.46) (0.50)
(2.09) (2.06) (0.06) (1.56) (1.66) (0.57) (1.03) (1.17) (0.32) (0.56) (0.13) (0.04) (0.20) (0.33) (0.34)
(0.79) (3.49) (0.29) (0.58) (1.73) (0.51) (0.38) (1.94) (0.69) (0.77) (0.41) (0.07) (0.18) (0.37) (0.43) (0.13)

Copyright 2012 Securities Research Company

Bonds $.0 Mil Com 17.070 Mil BV .51 /sh P/E N/A (Ind ITCON P/E 14.16) Ctry US

MATTHEWS INTL CORP (MATW)

(D)   Bronze memorials, graphics imaging, marking products

Growth Performance Measurement

Years	Price	Earn.	Div.	Tot Ret
Last 1	2.1	-4.1	.0	3.0
Last 5	-7.3	1.5	8.4	-6.5
Last 10	3.7	6.9	12.6	4.4

0.10 0.11 0.11 0.11
0.10 0.11 0.11 0.11
0.10 0.10 0.11 0.11

Adj. for
2 for 1
9/4/01

Copyright 2012 Securities Research Company

Bonds $14.1 Mil Com 27.499 Mil BV 17.30 /sh P/E 13.72 (Ind SPECS P/E 14.20) Ctry US

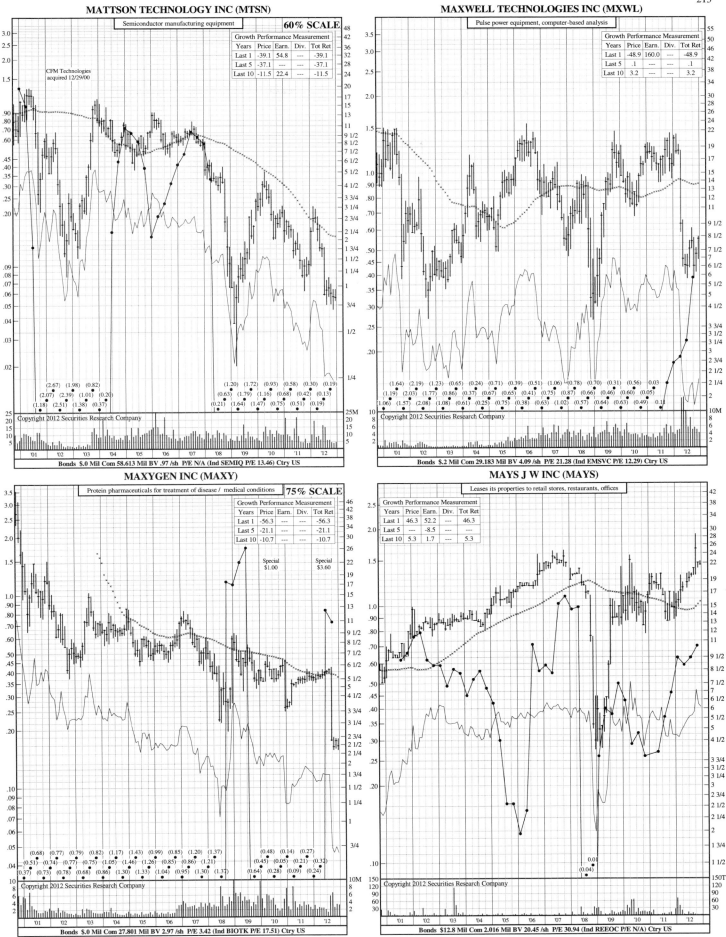

MATTSON TECHNOLOGY INC (MTSN)

Semiconductor manufacturing equipment

60% SCALE

CFM Technologies acquired 12/29/00

Growth Performance Measurement				
Years	Price	Earn.	Div.	Tot Ret
Last 1	-39.1	54.8	---	-39.1
Last 5	-37.1	---	---	-37.1
Last 10	-11.5	22.4	---	-11.5

(1.18) (2.51) (1.38) (0.37)
(2.07) (2.39) (1.01) (0.20)
(2.67) (1.98) (0.82)
(0.21) (1.64) (1.47) (0.75) (0.51) (0.19)
(0.63) (1.79) (1.16) (0.68) (0.42) (0.13)
(1.20) (1.72) (0.93) (0.58) (0.30) (0.19)

Copyright 2012 Securities Research Company

Bonds $.0 Mil Com 58.613 Mil BV .97 /sh P/E N/A (Ind SEMIQ P/E 13.46) Ctry US

MAXWELL TECHNOLOGIES INC (MXWL)

Pulse power equipment, computer-based analysis

Growth Performance Measurement				
Years	Price	Earn.	Div.	Tot Ret
Last 1	-48.9	160.0	---	-48.9
Last 5	.1	---	---	.1
Last 10	3.2	---	---	3.2

(1.06) (1.57) (2.08) (1.08) (0.61) (0.25) (0.75) (0.38) (0.63) (1.02) (0.57) (0.64) (0.63) (0.49) (0.11)
(1.19) (2.03) (1.77) (0.86) (0.37) (0.67) (0.65) (0.41) (0.75) (0.87) (0.66) (0.46) (0.60) (0.05)
(1.64) (2.19) (1.23) (0.65) (0.24) (0.71) (0.39) (0.51) (1.06) (0.78) (0.70) (0.31) (0.56) (0.03)

Copyright 2012 Securities Research Company

Bonds $.2 Mil Com 29.183 Mil BV 4.09 /sh P/E 21.28 (Ind EMSVC P/E 12.29) Ctry US

MAXYGEN INC (MAXY)

Protein pharmaceuticals for treatment of disease / medical conditions

75% SCALE

Growth Performance Measurement				
Years	Price	Earn.	Div.	Tot Ret
Last 1	-56.3	---	---	-56.3
Last 5	-21.1	---	---	-21.1
Last 10	-10.7	---	---	-10.7

Special $1.00   Special $3.60

(0.37) (0.73) (0.78) (0.68) (0.86) (1.30) (1.33) (1.04) (0.95) (1.30) (1.37)
(0.51) (0.74) (0.77) (0.75) (1.05) (1.46) (1.26) (0.85) (0.86) (1.21)
(0.68) (0.77) (0.79) (0.82) (1.17) (1.43) (0.99) (0.85) (1.20) (1.37)
(0.64) (0.28) (0.09) (0.24)
(0.45) (0.05) (0.21) (0.32)
(0.48) (0.14) (0.27)

Copyright 2012 Securities Research Company

Bonds $.0 Mil Com 27.801 Mil BV 2.97 /sh P/E 3.42 (Ind BIOTK P/E 17.51) Ctry US

MAYS J W INC (MAYS)

Leases its properties to retail stores, restaurants, offices

Growth Performance Measurement				
Years	Price	Earn.	Div.	Tot Ret
Last 1	46.3	52.2	---	46.3
Last 5	---	-8.5	---	---
Last 10	5.3	1.7	---	5.3

(0.04)
0.01

Copyright 2012 Securities Research Company

Bonds $12.8 Mil Com 2.016 Mil BV 20.45 /sh P/E 30.94 (Ind REEOC P/E N/A) Ctry US

214

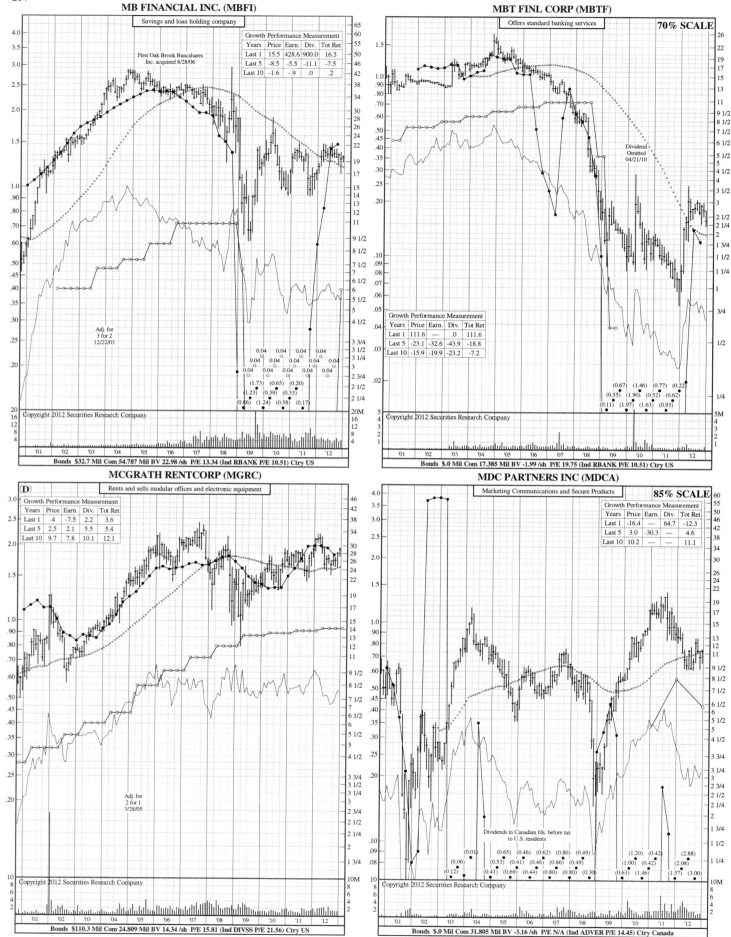

MB FINANCIAL INC. (MBFI)
Savings and loan holding company

First Oak Brook Bancshares Inc. acquired 8/28/06

Growth Performance Measurement				
Years	Price	Earn.	Div.	Tot Ret
Last 1	15.5	428.6	900.0	16.3
Last 5	-8.5	-5.5	-11.1	-7.5
Last 10	-1.6	-.9	.0	.2

Adj. for 3 for 2 12/22/03

0.04 0.04 0.04 0.04
0.04 0.04 0.04 0.04 0.04
0.04 0.04 0.04 0.04 0.04
(1.73) (0.65) (0.20)
(1.23) (0.39) (0.33)
(0.86) (1.24) (0.58) (0.17)

Copyright 2012 Securities Research Company

Bonds $32.7 Mil Com 54.787 Mil BV 22.98 /sh P/E 13.34 (Ind RBANK P/E 10.51) Ctry US

MBT FINL CORP (MBTF)
Offers standard banking services

70% SCALE

Dividend Omitted 04/21/10

Growth Performance Measurement				
Years	Price	Earn.	Div.	Tot Ret
Last 1	111.6	---	.0	111.6
Last 5	-23.1	-32.6	-43.9	-18.8
Last 10	-15.9	-19.9	-23.2	-7.2

(0.67) (1.46) (0.77) (0.22)
(0.55) (0.39) (1.90) (0.52) (0.62)
(0.11) (1.97) (1.63) (0.93)

Copyright 2012 Securities Research Company

Bonds $0.0 Mil Com 17.385 Mil BV -1.99 /sh P/E 19.75 (Ind RBANK P/E 10.51) Ctry US

MCGRATH RENTCORP (MGRC)
(D)
Rents and sells modular offices and electronic equipment

Growth Performance Measurement				
Years	Price	Earn.	Div.	Tot Ret
Last 1	.4	-7.5	2.2	3.6
Last 5	2.5	2.1	5.5	5.4
Last 10	9.7	7.8	10.1	12.1

Adj. for 2 for 1 3/28/05

Copyright 2012 Securities Research Company

Bonds $110.3 Mil Com 24.809 Mil BV 14.34 /sh P/E 15.81 (Ind DIVSS P/E 21.56) Ctry US

MDC PARTNERS INC (MDCA)
Marketing Communications and Secure Products

85% SCALE

Growth Performance Measurement				
Years	Price	Earn.	Div.	Tot Ret
Last 1	-16.4	---	64.7	-12.3
Last 5	3.0	-30.3	---	4.6
Last 10	10.2	---	---	11.1

Dividends in Canadian fds. before tax to U.S. residents

(0.01) (0.65) (0.46) (0.62) (0.80) (0.49) (1.20) (0.42) (2.88)
(0.06) (0.53) (0.41) (0.46) (0.86) (0.49) (1.00) (0.42) (2.08)
(0.12) (0.41) (0.69) (0.44) (0.80) (0.80) (0.30) (0.63) (1.46) (1.57) (3.00)

Copyright 2012 Securities Research Company

Bonds $0.0 Mil Com 31.805 Mil BV -3.16 /sh P/E N/A (Ind ADVER P/E 14.45) Ctry Canada

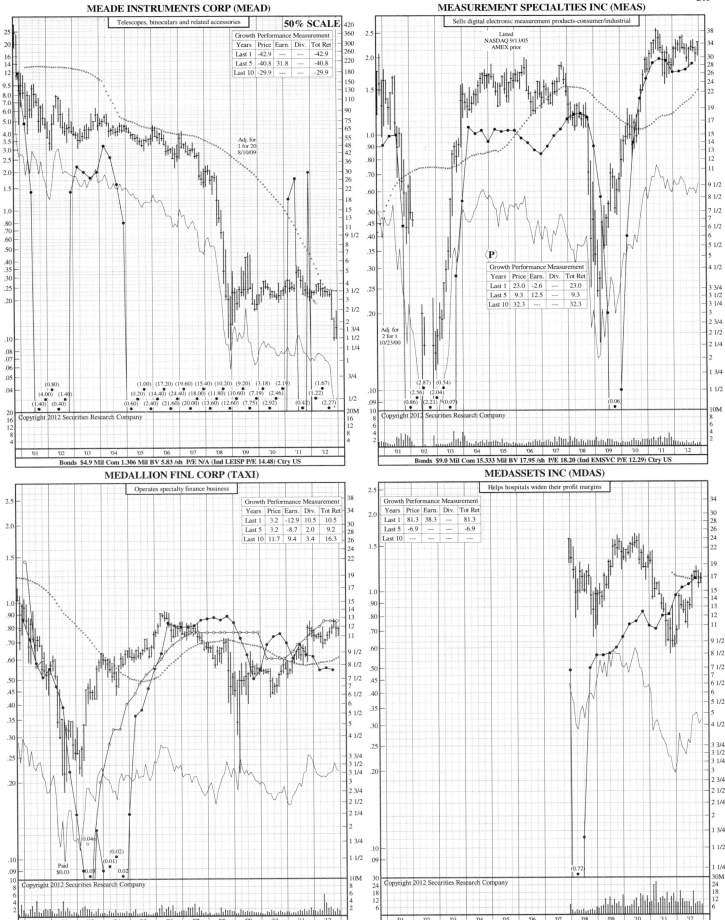

215

MEADE INSTRUMENTS CORP (MEAD)

Telescopes, binoculars and related accessories

50% SCALE

Growth Performance Measurement				
Years	Price	Earn.	Div.	Tot Ret
Last 1	-42.9	---	---	-42.9
Last 5	-40.8	31.8	---	-40.8
Last 10	-29.9	---	---	-29.9

Adj. for
1 for 20
8/10/09

(0.80)
(4.00) (1.40)
(1.40) (0.40)

(1.00) (17.20) (19.60) (15.40) (10.20) (9.20) (3.18) (2.19) (1.67)
(0.20) (14.40) (24.40) (18.00) (11.80) (10.60) (7.19) (2.46) (1.22)
(0.60) (2.40) (21.60) (20.00) (13.60) (12.60) (7.75) (2.92) (0.42) (2.27)

Copyright 2012 Securities Research Company

Bonds $4.9 Mil Com 1.306 Mil BV 5.83 /sh P/E N/A (Ind LEISP P/E 14.48) Ctry US

MEASUREMENT SPECIALTIES INC (MEAS)

Sells digital electronic measurement products-consumer/industrial

Listed
NASDAQ 9/13/05
AMEX prior

(P)

Growth Performance Measurement				
Years	Price	Earn.	Div.	Tot Ret
Last 1	23.0	-2.6	---	23.0
Last 5	9.3	12.5	---	9.3
Last 10	32.3	---	---	32.3

Adj. for
2 for 1
10/23/00

(2.87) (0.54)
(2.56) (2.04)
(0.86) (2.21) (0.07) (0.06)

Copyright 2012 Securities Research Company

Bonds $9.0 Mil Com 15.333 Mil BV 17.95 /sh P/E 18.20 (Ind EMSVC P/E 12.29) Ctry US

MEDALLION FINL CORP (TAXI)

Operates specialty finance business

Growth Performance Measurement				
Years	Price	Earn.	Div.	Tot Ret
Last 1	3.2	-12.9	10.5	10.5
Last 5	3.2	-8.7	2.0	9.2
Last 10	11.7	9.4	3.4	16.3

(0.04)
(0.02)
(0.01)
Paid 0.05 0.02
$0.03

Copyright 2012 Securities Research Company

Bonds $340.0 Mil Com 21.464 Mil BV 9.97 /sh P/E 10.99 (Ind SPCFN P/E 17.51) Ctry US

MEDASSETS INC (MDAS)

Helps hospitals widen their profit margins

Growth Performance Measurement				
Years	Price	Earn.	Div.	Tot Ret
Last 1	81.3	38.3	---	81.3
Last 5	-6.9	---	---	-6.9
Last 10	---	---	---	---

(0.72)

Copyright 2012 Securities Research Company

Bonds $.0 Mil Com 59.056 Mil BV 7.44 /sh P/E 14.97 (Ind HCTFC P/E 32.95) Ctry US

216

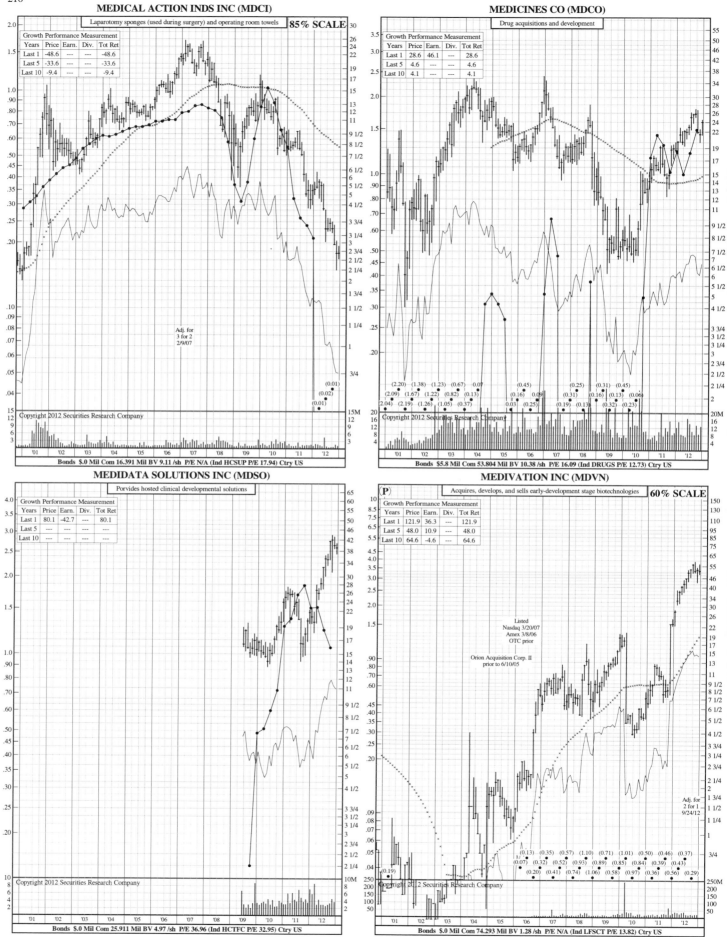

MEDICAL ACTION INDS INC (MDCI)
Laparotomy sponges (used during surgery) and operating room towels **85% SCALE**

Growth Performance Measurement

Years	Price	Earn.	Div.	Tot Ret
Last 1	-48.6	---	---	-48.6
Last 5	-33.6	---	---	-33.6
Last 10	-9.4	---	---	-9.4

Adj. for
3 for 2
2/9/07

(0.01)
(0.02)
(0.01)

Copyright 2012 Securities Research Company

Bonds $.0 Mil Com 16.391 Mil BV 9.11 /sh P/E N/A (Ind HCSUP P/E 17.94) Ctry US

MEDICINES CO (MDCO)
Drug acquisitions and development

Growth Performance Measurement

Years	Price	Earn.	Div.	Tot Ret
Last 1	28.6	46.1	---	28.6
Last 5	4.6	---	---	4.6
Last 10	4.1	---	---	4.1

(2.20) (1.38) (1.23) (0.67) 0.07 (0.45) (0.25) (0.31) (0.45)
(2.09) (1.67) (1.22) (0.82) (0.13) (0.16) 0.09 (0.31) (0.16) (0.13) (0.06)
(2.04) (2.19) (1.26) (1.05) (0.37) 0.03 (0.25) (0.19) (0.13) (0.32) (0.23)

Copyright 2012 Securities Research Company

Bonds $5.8 Mil Com 53.804 Mil BV 10.38 /sh P/E 16.09 (Ind DRUGS P/E 12.73) Ctry US

MEDIDATA SOLUTIONS INC (MDSO)
Porvides hosted clinical developmental solutions

Growth Performance Measurement

Years	Price	Earn.	Div.	Tot Ret
Last 1	80.1	-42.7	---	80.1
Last 5	---	---	---	---
Last 10	---	---	---	---

Copyright 2012 Securities Research Company

Bonds $.0 Mil Com 25.911 Mil BV 4.97 /sh P/E 36.96 (Ind HCTFC P/E 32.95) Ctry US

MEDIVATION INC (MDVN)
(P) Acquires, develops, and sells early-development stage biotechnologies **60% SCALE**

Growth Performance Measurement

Years	Price	Earn.	Div.	Tot Ret
Last 1	121.9	36.3	---	121.9
Last 5	48.0	10.9	---	48.0
Last 10	64.6	-4.6	---	64.6

Listed
Nasdaq 3/20/07
Amex 3/8/06
OTC prior

Orion Acquisition Corp. II
prior to 6/10/05

Adj. for
2 for 1
9/24/12

(0.19)
(0.13) (0.35) (0.57) (1.10) (0.71) (1.01) (0.50) (0.46) (0.37)
(0.07) (0.32) (0.52) (0.93) (0.89) (0.85) (0.84) (0.39) (0.43)
(0.20) (0.41) (0.74) (1.06) (0.58) (0.97) (0.36) (0.56) (0.29)

Copyright 2012 Securities Research Company

Bonds $.0 Mil Com 74.293 Mil BV 1.28 /sh P/E N/A (Ind LFSCT P/E 13.82) Ctry US

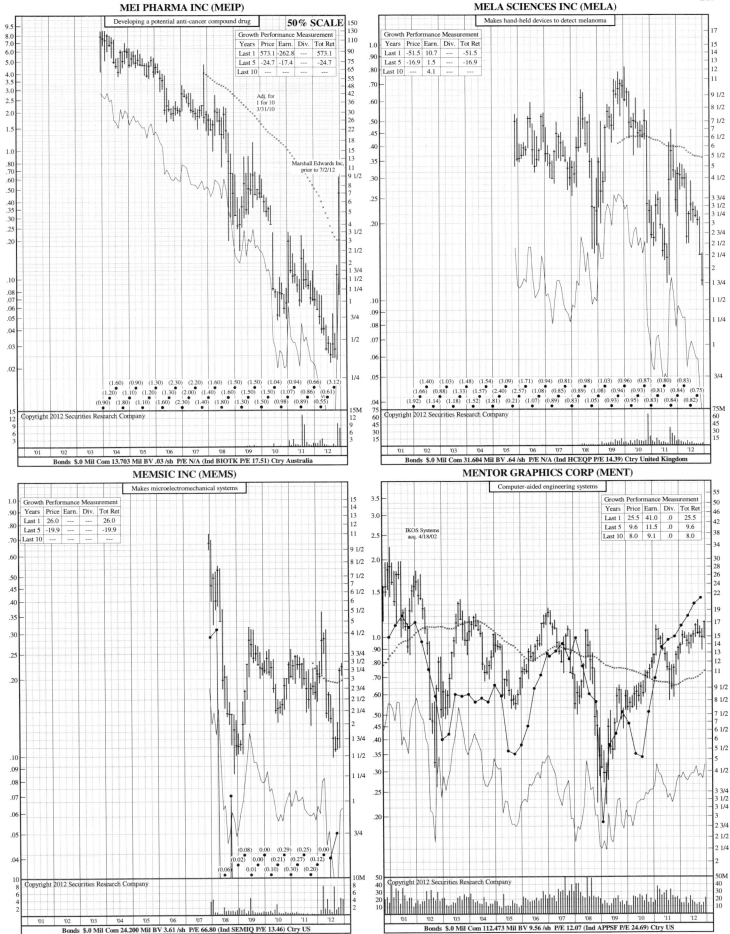

MEI PHARMA INC (MEIP)

Developing a potential anti-cancer compound drug

50% SCALE

Growth Performance Measurement				
Years	Price	Earn.	Div.	Tot Ret
Last 1	573.1	-262.8	---	573.1
Last 5	-24.7	-17.4	---	-24.7
Last 10	---	---	---	---

Adj. for
1 for 10
3/31/10

Marshall Edwards Inc,
prior to 7/2/12

(1.60) (0.90) (1.30) (2.30) (2.20) (1.60) (1.50) (1.50) (1.04) (0.94) (0.66) (3.12)
(1.20) (1.10) (1.20) (1.30) (2.00) (1.40) (1.60) (1.50) (1.50) (1.07) (0.86) (0.61)
(0.90) (1.80) (1.10) (1.60) (2.30) (1.40) (1.80) (1.30) (1.50) (0.98) (0.89) (0.55)

Copyright 2012 Securities Research Company

Bonds $.0 Mil Com 13.703 Mil BV .03 /sh P/E N/A (Ind BIOTK P/E 17.51) Ctry Australia

MELA SCIENCES INC (MELA)

Makes hand-held devices to detect melanoma

Growth Performance Measurement				
Years	Price	Earn.	Div.	Tot Ret
Last 1	-51.5	10.7	---	-51.5
Last 5	-16.9	1.5	---	-16.9
Last 10	---	4.1	---	---

(1.40) (1.03) (1.48) (1.54) (3.09) (1.71) (0.94) (0.81) (0.98) (1.03) (0.96) (0.87) (0.80) (0.83)
(1.66) (0.88) (1.33) (1.57) (2.40) (2.57) (1.08) (0.85) (0.89) (1.08) (0.94) (0.93) (0.81) (0.84) (0.75)
(1.92) (1.14) (1.18) (1.52) (1.81) (0.21) (1.07) (0.89) (0.83) (1.05) (0.93) (0.95) (0.83) (0.84) (0.82)

Copyright 2012 Securities Research Company

Bonds $.0 Mil Com 31.604 Mil BV .64 /sh P/E N/A (Ind HCEQP P/E 14.39) Ctry United Kingdom

MEMSIC INC (MEMS)

Makes microelectromechanical systems

Growth Performance Measurement				
Years	Price	Earn.	Div.	Tot Ret
Last 1	26.0	---	---	26.0
Last 5	-19.9	---	---	-19.9
Last 10	---	---	---	---

(0.08) 0.00 (0.29) (0.25) 0.00
(0.02) 0.00 (0.21) (0.27) (0.12)
(0.06) 0.01 (0.10) (0.30) (0.20)

Copyright 2012 Securities Research Company

Bonds $.0 Mil Com 24.200 Mil BV 3.61 /sh P/E 66.80 (Ind SEMIQ P/E 13.46) Ctry US

MENTOR GRAPHICS CORP (MENT)

Computer-aided engineering systems

IKOS Systems
acq. 4/18/02

Growth Performance Measurement				
Years	Price	Earn.	Div.	Tot Ret
Last 1	25.5	41.0	.0	25.5
Last 5	9.6	11.5	.0	9.6
Last 10	8.0	9.1	.0	8.0

Copyright 2012 Securities Research Company

Bonds $.0 Mil Com 112.473 Mil BV 9.56 /sh P/E 12.07 (Ind APPSF P/E 24.69) Ctry US

218

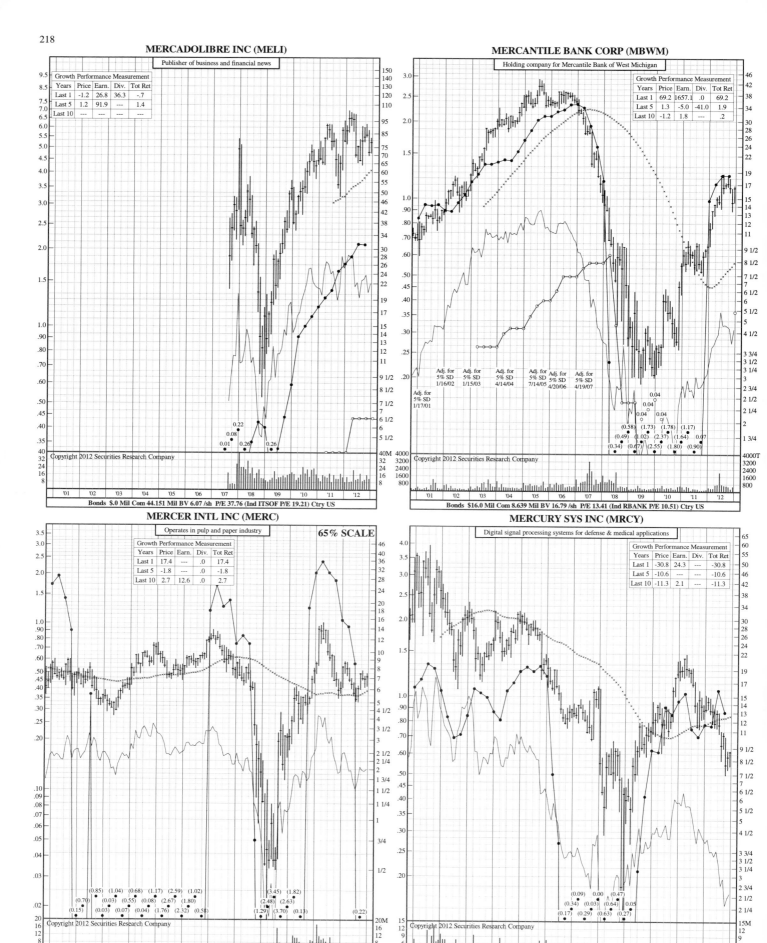

MERCADOLIBRE INC (MELI)

Publisher of business and financial news

Bonds $.0 Mil Com 44.151 Mil BV 6.07 /sh P/E 37.76 (Ind ITSOF P/E 19.21) Ctry US

MERCANTILE BANK CORP (MBWM)

Holding company for Mercantile Bank of West Michigan

Bonds $16.0 Mil Com 8.639 Mil BV 16.79 /sh P/E 13.41 (Ind RBANK P/E 10.51) Ctry US

MERCER INTL INC (MERC)

Operates in pulp and paper industry

65% SCALE

Bonds $1163.9 Mil Com 55.816 Mil BV 6.95 /sh P/E N/A (Ind PPROD P/E 17.65) Ctry US

MERCURY SYS INC (MRCY)

Digital signal processing systems for defense & medical applications

Bonds $14.1 Mil Com 32.242 Mil BV 10.86 /sh P/E 10.57 (Ind EMSVC P/E 12.29) Ctry US

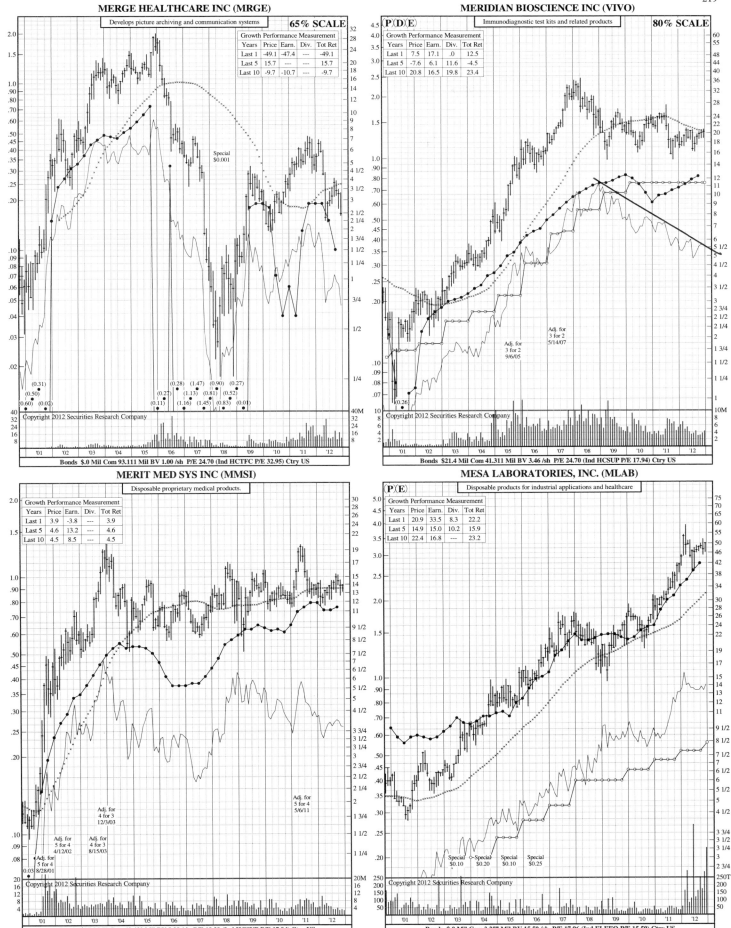

MERGE HEALTHCARE INC (MRGE)

Develops picture archiving and communication systems

65% SCALE

Growth Performance Measurement

Years	Price	Earn.	Div.	Tot Ret
Last 1	-49.1	-47.4	---	-49.1
Last 5	15.7	---	---	15.7
Last 10	-9.7	-10.7	---	-9.7

Special $0.001

(0.31)
(0.50) (0.02)
(0.60)

(0.28) (1.47) (0.90) (0.27)
(0.27) (1.13) (0.81) (0.52)
(0.11) (1.16) (1.45) (0.83) (0.01)

Copyright 2012 Securities Research Company

Bonds $.0 Mil Com 93.111 Mil BV 1.00 /sh P/E 24.70 (Ind HCTFC P/E 32.95) Ctry US

MERIDIAN BIOSCIENCE INC (VIVO)

(P)(D)(E)

Immunodiagnostic test kits and related products

80% SCALE

Growth Performance Measurement

Years	Price	Earn.	Div.	Tot Ret
Last 1	7.5	17.1	.0	12.5
Last 5	-7.6	6.1	11.6	-4.5
Last 10	20.8	16.5	19.8	23.4

Adj. for
3 for 2
5/14/07

Adj. for
3 for 2
9/6/05

(0.26)

Copyright 2012 Securities Research Company

Bonds $21.4 Mil Com 41.311 Mil BV 3.46 /sh P/E 24.70 (Ind HCSUP P/E 17.94) Ctry US

MERIT MED SYS INC (MMSI)

Disposable proprietary medical products.

Growth Performance Measurement

Years	Price	Earn.	Div.	Tot Ret
Last 1	3.9	-3.8	---	3.9
Last 5	4.6	13.2	---	4.6
Last 10	4.5	8.5	---	4.5

Adj. for
4 for 3
12/3/03

Adj. for
5 for 4
5/6/11

Adj. for
5 for 4
4/12/02

Adj. for
4 for 3
8/15/03

Adj. for
5 for 4
8/28/01

0.03

Copyright 2012 Securities Research Company

Bonds $27.8 Mil Com 42.432 Mil BV 8.98 /sh P/E 18.29 (Ind HCSUP P/E 17.94) Ctry US

MESA LABORATORIES, INC. (MLAB)

(P)(E)

Disposable products for industrial applications and healthcare

Growth Performance Measurement

Years	Price	Earn.	Div.	Tot Ret
Last 1	20.9	33.5	8.3	22.2
Last 5	14.9	15.0	10.2	15.9
Last 10	22.4	16.8	---	23.2

Special
$0.10

Special
$0.20

Special
$0.10

Special
$0.25

Copyright 2012 Securities Research Company

Bonds $.0 Mil Com 3.357 Mil BV 15.50 /sh P/E 17.96 (Ind ELEEQ P/E 15.50) Ctry US

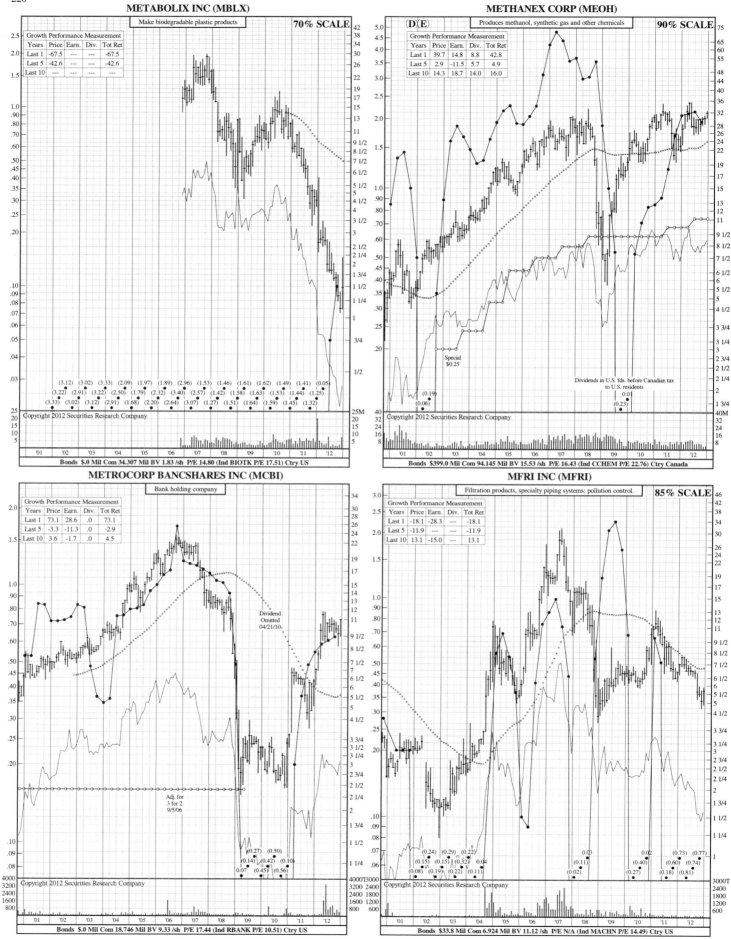

METABOLIX INC (MBLX)

Make biodegradable plastic products

70% SCALE

Growth Performance Measurement				
Years	Price	Earn.	Div.	Tot Ret
Last 1	-67.5	---	---	-67.5
Last 5	-42.6	---	---	-42.6
Last 10	---	---	---	---

(3.12) (3.02) (3.33) (2.09) (1.97) (1.89) (2.96) (1.53) (1.46) (1.61) (1.62) (1.49) (1.41) (0.05)
(3.22) (2.91) (3.22) (2.50) (1.79) (2.32) (2.32) (2.57) (1.42) (1.58) (1.63) (1.53) (1.44) (1.25)
(3.33) (3.02) (3.12) (2.91) (1.68) (2.20) (2.64) (3.07) (1.27) (1.51) (1.64) (1.59) (1.45) (1.32)

Copyright 2012 Securities Research Company

Bonds $.0 Mil Com 34.307 Mil BV 1.83 /sh P/E 14.80 (Ind BIOTK P/E 17.51) Ctry US

METHANEX CORP (MEOH)

(D)(E)   Produces methanol, synthetic gas and other chemicals

90% SCALE

Growth Performance Measurement				
Years	Price	Earn.	Div.	Tot Ret
Last 1	39.7	14.8	8.8	42.8
Last 5	2.9	-11.5	5.7	4.9
Last 10	14.3	18.7	14.0	16.0

Special
$0.25

Dividends in U.S. fds. before Canadian tax
to U.S. residents

0.01
(0.19)
(0.06)   (0.23)

Copyright 2012 Securities Research Company

Bonds $399.0 Mil Com 94.145 Mil BV 15.53 /sh P/E 16.43 (Ind CCHEM P/E 22.76) Ctry Canada

METROCORP BANCSHARES INC (MCBI)

Bank holding company

Growth Performance Measurement				
Years	Price	Earn.	Div.	Tot Ret
Last 1	73.1	28.6	.0	73.1
Last 5	-3.3	-11.3	.0	-2.9
Last 10	3.6	-1.7	.0	4.5

Dividend
Omitted
04/21/10

Adj. for
3 for 2
9/5/06

(0.27) (0.50)
(0.14) (0.42) (0.10)
0.07 (0.45) (0.56)

Copyright 2012 Securities Research Company

Bonds $.0 Mil Com 18.746 Mil BV 9.33 /sh P/E 17.44 (Ind RBANK P/E 10.51) Ctry US

MFRI INC (MFRI)

Filtration products, specialty piping systems; pollution control.

85% SCALE

Growth Performance Measurement				
Years	Price	Earn.	Div.	Tot Ret
Last 1	-18.1	-28.3	---	-18.1
Last 5	-11.9	-15.0	---	-11.9
Last 10	13.1	-15.0	---	13.1

(0.24) (0.29) (0.22)   0.03   0.02   (0.73) (0.77)
(0.15) (0.15) (0.32) 0.04   (0.11)   (0.40)   (0.60) (0.74)
(0.08) (0.19) (0.22) (0.11)   (0.02) (0.27) (0.18) (0.81)

Copyright 2012 Securities Research Company

Bonds $33.8 Mil Com 6.924 Mil BV 11.12 /sh P/E N/A (Ind MACHN P/E 14.49) Ctry US

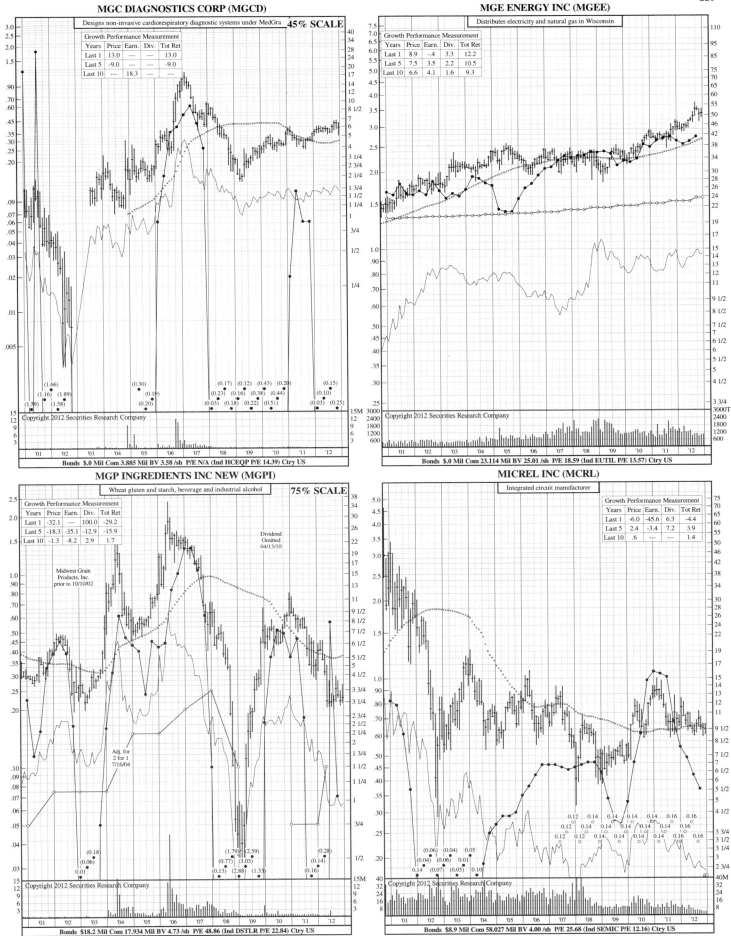

222

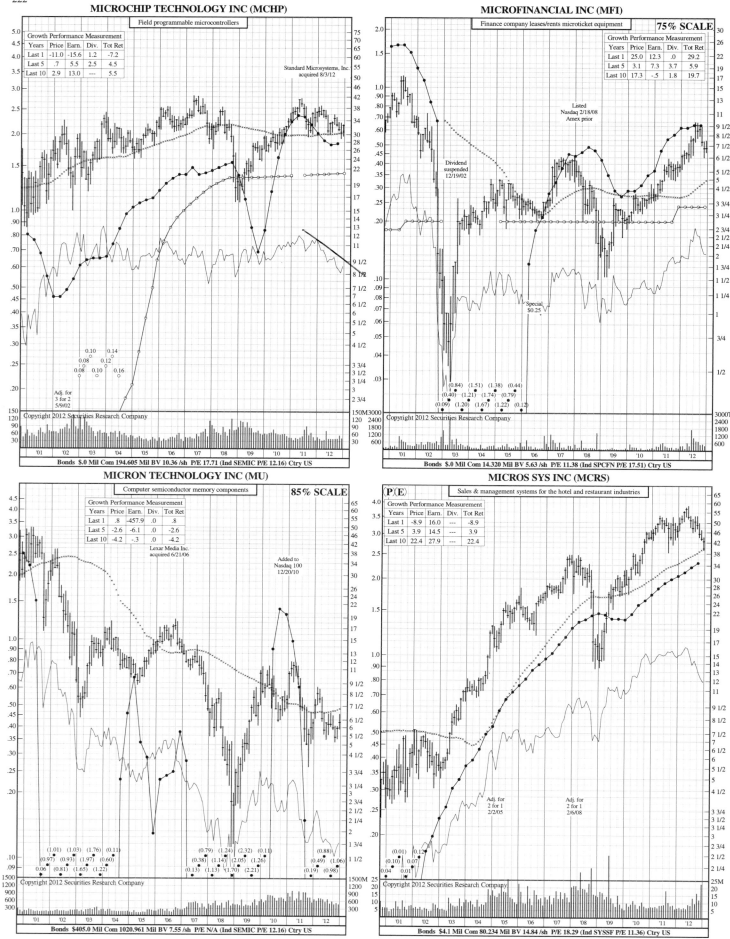

MICROCHIP TECHNOLOGY INC (MCHP)

Field programmable microcontrollers

Standard Microsystems, Inc. acquired 8/3/12

Growth Performance Measurement				
Years	Price	Earn.	Div.	Tot Ret
Last 1	-11.0	-15.6	1.2	-7.2
Last 5	.7	5.5	2.5	4.5
Last 10	2.9	13.0	---	5.5

0.10 0.14
0.08 0.12
0.08 0.10 0.16

Adj. for
3 for 2
5/9/02

Copyright 2012 Securities Research Company

Bonds $.0 Mil Com 194.605 Mil BV 10.36 /sh P/E 17.71 (Ind SEMIC P/E 12.16) Ctry US

MICROFINANCIAL INC (MFI)

Finance company leases/rents microticket equipment

75% SCALE

Listed
Nasdaq 2/18/08
Amex prior

Growth Performance Measurement				
Years	Price	Earn.	Div.	Tot Ret
Last 1	25.0	12.3	.0	29.2
Last 5	3.1	7.3	3.7	5.9
Last 10	17.3	-.5	1.8	19.7

Dividend
suspended
12/19/02

Special
$0.25

(0.84) (1.51) (1.38) (0.44)
(0.40) (1.21) (1.74) (0.79)
(0.09) (1.20) (1.67) (1.22) (0.12)

Copyright 2012 Securities Research Company

Bonds $.0 Mil Com 14.320 Mil BV 5.63 /sh P/E 11.38 (Ind SPCFN P/E 17.51) Ctry US

MICRON TECHNOLOGY INC (MU)

Computer semiconductor memory components

85% SCALE

Lexar Media Inc.
acquired 6/21/06

Added to
Nasdaq 100
12/20/10

Growth Performance Measurement				
Years	Price	Earn.	Div.	Tot Ret
Last 1	.8	-457.9	.0	.8
Last 5	-2.6	-6.1	.0	-2.6
Last 10	-4.2	-.3	.0	-4.2

(1.01) (1.03) (1.76) (0.11)   (0.79) (1.24) (2.32) (0.11)   (0.88)
(0.97) (0.93) (1.97) (0.60)   (0.38) (1.14) (2.05) (1.26)   (0.49) (1.06)
0.06   (0.81) (1.65) (1.22)   (0.13) (1.13) (1.70) (2.21)   (0.19) (0.98)

Copyright 2012 Securities Research Company

Bonds $405.0 Mil Com 1020.961 Mil BV 7.55 /sh P/E N/A (Ind SEMIC P/E 12.16) Ctry US

MICROS SYS INC (MCRS)

(P)(E)

Sales & management systems for the hotel and restaurant industries

Growth Performance Measurement				
Years	Price	Earn.	Div.	Tot Ret
Last 1	-8.9	16.0	---	-8.9
Last 5	3.9	14.5	---	3.9
Last 10	22.4	27.9	---	22.4

Adj. for
2 for 1
2/2/05

Adj. for
2 for 1
2/6/08

(0.01) 0.12
(0.10) 0.07
0.04   0.01

Copyright 2012 Securities Research Company

Bonds $4.1 Mil Com 80.234 Mil BV 14.84 /sh P/E 18.29 (Ind SYSSF P/E 11.36) Ctry US

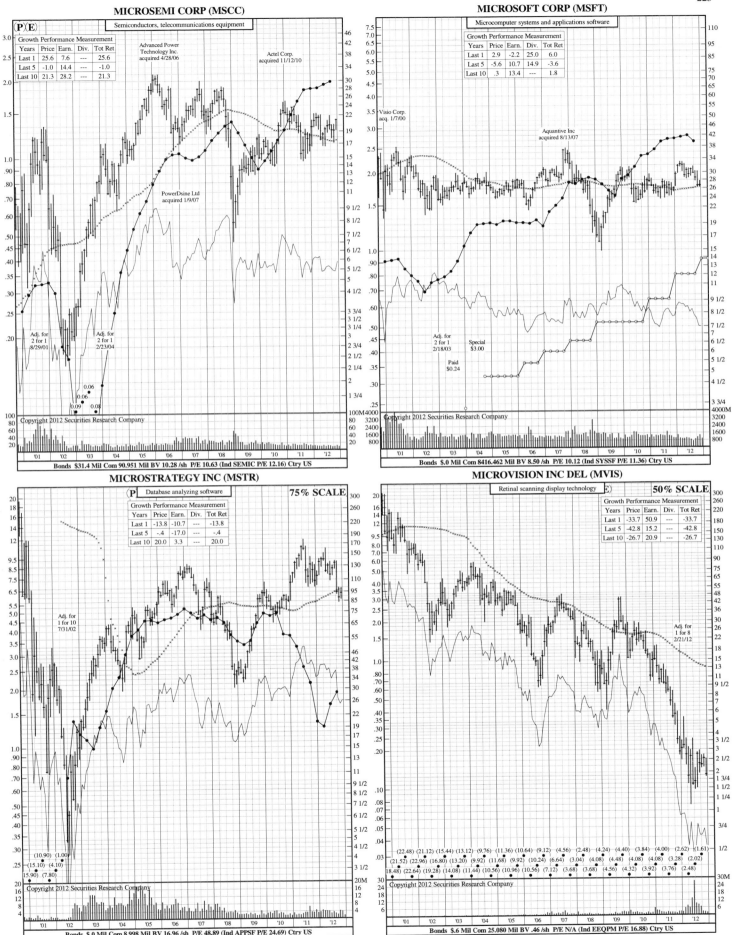

223

MICROSEMI CORP (MSCC)

Semiconductors, telecommunications equipment

(P)(E)

Growth Performance Measurement				
Years	Price	Earn.	Div.	Tot Ret
Last 1	25.6	7.6	---	25.6
Last 5	-1.0	14.4	---	-1.0
Last 10	21.3	28.2	---	21.3

Advanced Power Technology Inc. acquired 4/28/06

Actel Corp. acquired 11/12/10

PowerDsine Ltd acquired 1/9/07

Adj. for 2 for 1 8/29/01

Adj. for 2 for 1 2/23/04

0.06
0.06
0.09 0.08

Copyright 2012 Securities Research Company

Bonds $31.4 Mil Com 90.951 Mil BV 10.28 /sh P/E 10.63 (Ind SEMIC P/E 12.16) Ctry US

MICROSOFT CORP (MSFT)

Microcomputer systems and applications software

Growth Performance Measurement				
Years	Price	Earn.	Div.	Tot Ret
Last 1	2.9	-2.2	25.0	6.0
Last 5	-5.6	10.7	14.9	-3.6
Last 10	.3	13.4	---	1.8

Visio Corp. acq. 1/7/00

Aquantive Inc acquired 8/13/07

Adj. for 2 for 1 2/18/03

Special $3.00

Paid $0.24

Copyright 2012 Securities Research Company

Bonds $.0 Mil Com 8416.462 Mil BV 8.50 /sh P/E 10.12 (Ind SYSSF P/E 11.36) Ctry US

MICROSTRATEGY INC (MSTR)

Database analyzing software

75% SCALE

(P)

Growth Performance Measurement				
Years	Price	Earn.	Div.	Tot Ret
Last 1	-13.8	-10.7	---	-13.8
Last 5	-.4	-17.0	---	-.4
Last 10	20.0	3.3	---	20.0

Adj. for 1 for 10 7/31/02

(10.90) (1.00)
(15.10) (4.10)
15.90 (7.80)

Copyright 2012 Securities Research Company

Bonds $.0 Mil Com 8.998 Mil BV 16.96 /sh P/E 48.89 (Ind APPSF P/E 24.69) Ctry US

MICROVISION INC DEL (MVIS)

Retinal scanning display technology

(E) 50% SCALE

Growth Performance Measurement				
Years	Price	Earn.	Div.	Tot Ret
Last 1	-33.7	50.9	---	-33.7
Last 5	-42.8	15.2	---	-42.8
Last 10	-26.7	20.9	---	-26.7

Adj. for 1 for 8 2/21/12

(22.48) (21.12) (15.44) (13.12) (9.76) (11.36) (10.64) (9.12) (4.56) (2.48) (4.24) (4.40) (3.84) (4.00) (2.62) (1.61)
(21.52) (22.96) (16.80) (13.20) (9.92) (11.68) (9.92) (10.24) (6.64) (3.04) (4.08) (4.48) (4.08) (4.08) (3.28) (2.02)
18.48 (22.64) (19.28) (14.08) (11.44) (10.56) (10.96) (10.56) (7.12) (3.68) (3.68) (4.56) (4.32) (3.92) (3.76) (2.08)

Copyright 2012 Securities Research Company

Bonds $.6 Mil Com 25.080 Mil BV .46 /sh P/E N/A (Ind EEQPM P/E 16.88) Ctry US

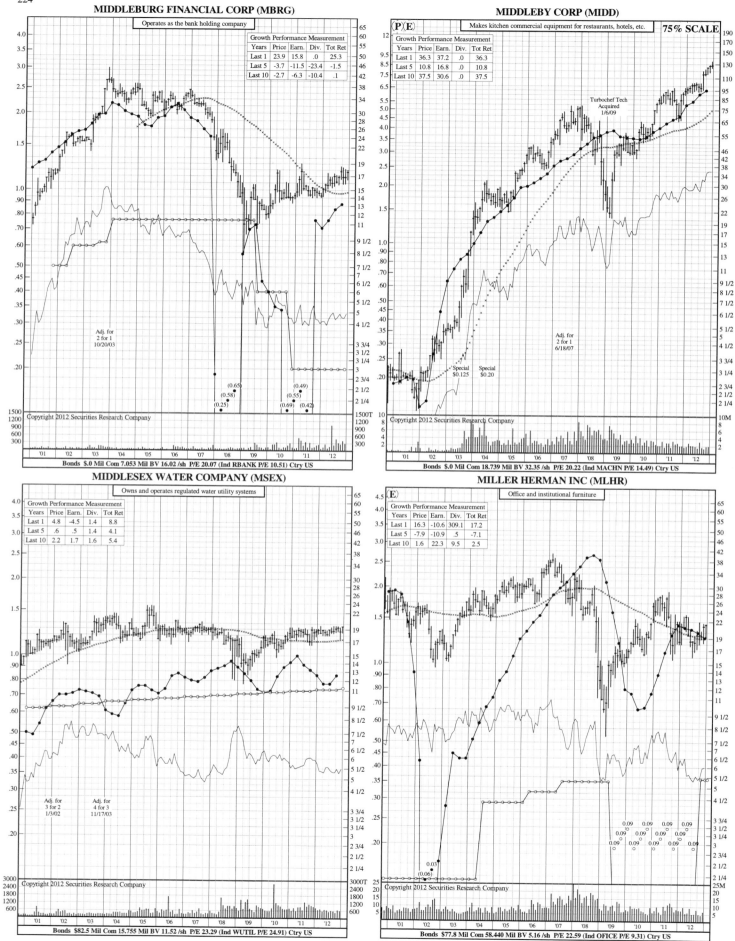

224

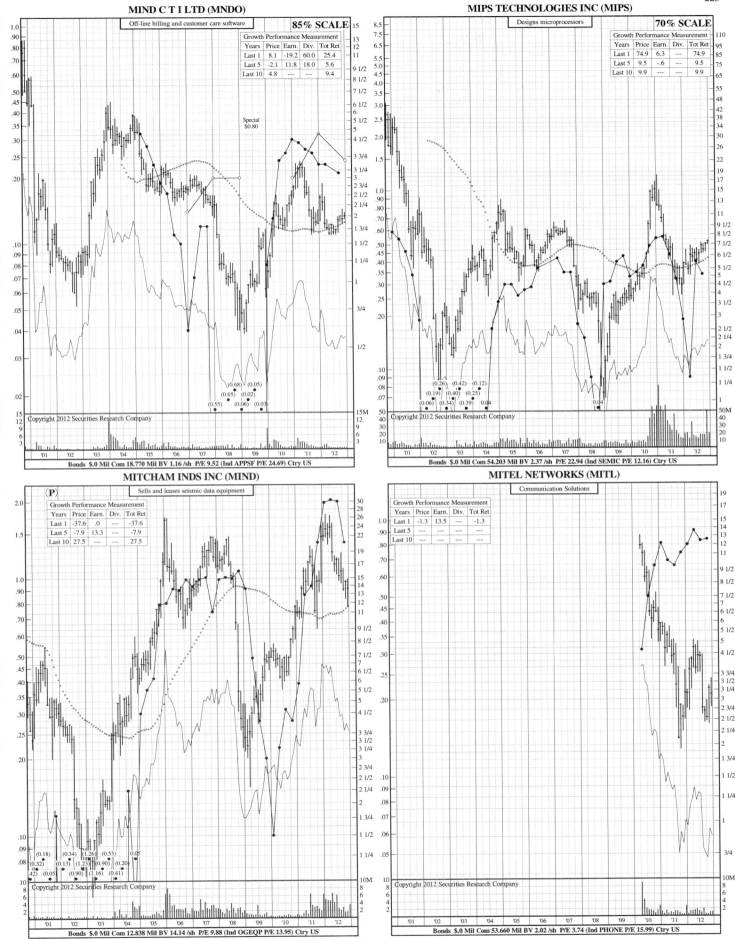

MIND C T I LTD (MNDO)

Off-line billing and customer care software

85% SCALE

Growth Performance Measurement

Years	Price	Earn.	Div.	Tot Ret
Last 1	8.1	-19.2	60.0	25.4
Last 5	-2.1	11.8	18.0	5.6
Last 10	4.8	---	---	9.4

Special $0.80

(0.68) (0.05)
(0.65) (0.02)
(0.55) (0.06) (0.03)

Copyright 2012 Securities Research Company

Bonds $.0 Mil Com 18.770 Mil BV 1.16 /sh P/E 9.52 (Ind APPSF P/E 24.69) Ctry US

MIPS TECHNOLOGIES INC (MIPS)

Designs microprocessors

70% SCALE

Growth Performance Measurement

Years	Price	Earn.	Div.	Tot Ret
Last 1	74.9	6.3	---	74.9
Last 5	9.5	-.6	---	9.5
Last 10	9.9	---	---	9.9

(0.26) (0.42) (0.12)
(0.19) (0.40) (0.25)
(0.06) (0.34) (0.39) 0.04
0.04

Copyright 2012 Securities Research Company

Bonds $.0 Mil Com 54.203 Mil BV 2.37 /sh P/E 22.94 (Ind SEMIC P/E 12.16) Ctry US

MITCHAM INDS INC (MIND)

(P)

Sells and leases seismic data equipment

Growth Performance Measurement

Years	Price	Earn.	Div.	Tot Ret
Last 1	-37.6	.0	---	-37.6
Last 5	-7.9	13.3	---	-7.9
Last 10	27.5	---	---	27.5

(0.18) (0.34) (1.26) (0.55) 0.05
(0.32) (0.13) (1.23) (0.90) (0.20)
.42) (0.05) (0.90) (1.16) (0.41)

Copyright 2012 Securities Research Company

Bonds $.0 Mil Com 12.838 Mil BV 14.14 /sh P/E 9.88 (Ind OGEQP P/E 13.95) Ctry US

MITEL NETWORKS (MITL)

Communication Solutions

Growth Performance Measurement

Years	Price	Earn.	Div.	Tot Ret
Last 1	-1.3	13.5	---	-1.3
Last 5	---	---	---	---
Last 10	---	---	---	---

Copyright 2012 Securities Research Company

Bonds $.0 Mil Com 53.660 Mil BV 2.02 /sh P/E 3.74 (Ind PHONE P/E 15.99) Ctry US

226

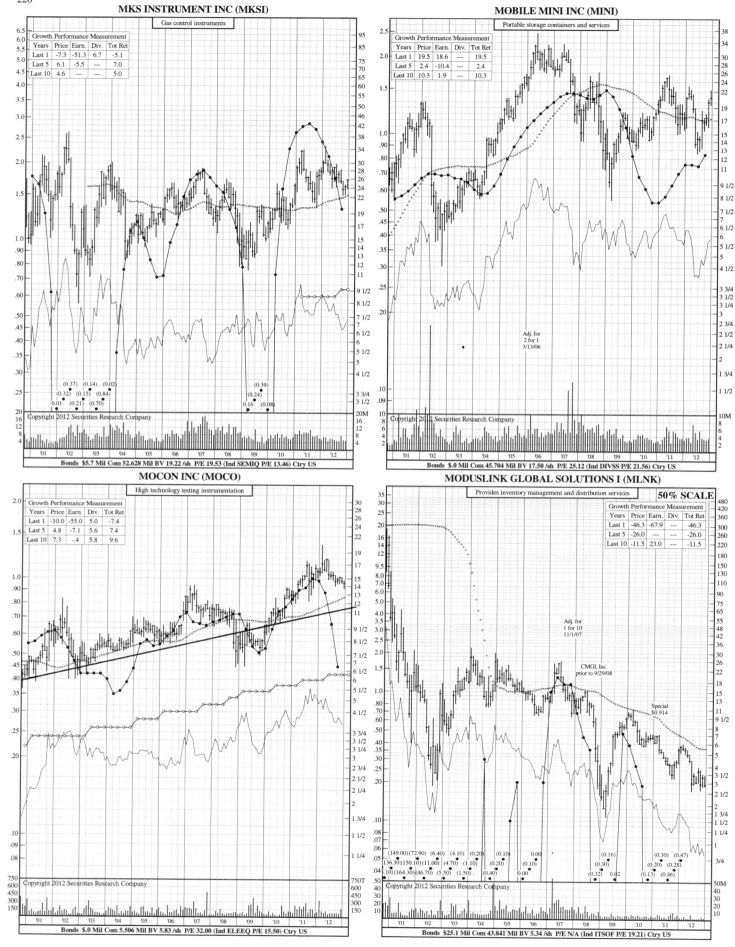

MKS INSTRUMENT INC (MKSI)

Gas control instruments

Growth Performance Measurement				
Years	Price	Earn.	Div.	Tot Ret
Last 1	-7.3	-51.3	6.7	-5.1
Last 5	6.1	-5.5	---	7.0
Last 10	4.6	---	---	5.0

(0.37) (0.14) (0.02)
(0.32) (0.15) (0.84)
0.01 (0.21) (0.70)

(0.39)
(0.24)
0.16 (0.08)

Copyright 2012 Securities Research Company

Bonds $5.7 Mil Com 52.628 Mil BV 19.22 /sh P/E 19.53 (Ind SEMIQ P/E 13.46) Ctry US

MOBILE MINI INC (MINI)

Portable storage containers and services

Growth Performance Measurement				
Years	Price	Earn.	Div.	Tot Ret
Last 1	19.5	18.6	---	19.5
Last 5	2.4	-10.4	---	2.4
Last 10	10.3	1.9	---	10.3

Adj. for
2 for 1
3/13/06

Copyright 2012 Securities Research Company

Bonds $.0 Mil Com 45.704 Mil BV 17.50 /sh P/E 25.12 (Ind DIVSS P/E 21.56) Ctry US

MOCON INC (MOCO)

High technology testing instrumentation

Growth Performance Measurement				
Years	Price	Earn.	Div.	Tot Ret
Last 1	-10.0	-55.0	5.0	-7.4
Last 5	4.8	-7.1	5.6	7.4
Last 10	7.3	-.4	5.8	9.6

Copyright 2012 Securities Research Company

Bonds $.0 Mil Com 5.506 Mil BV 5.83 /sh P/E 32.00 (Ind ELEEQ P/E 15.50) Ctry US

MODUSLINK GLOBAL SOLUTIONS I (MLNK)

Provides inventory management and distribution services

50% SCALE

Growth Performance Measurement				
Years	Price	Earn.	Div.	Tot Ret
Last 1	-46.3	-67.9	---	-46.3
Last 5	-26.0	---	---	-26.0
Last 10	-11.5	23.0	---	-11.5

Adj. for
1 for 10
11/1/07

CMGI, Inc.
prior to 9/29/08

Special
$0.914

(149.00) (72.90) (6.40) (4.10) (0.20) (0.10) 0.00 (0.16) (0.30) (0.47)
136.30 (150.10) (11.00) (4.70) (1.10) (0.20) (0.10) (0.30) (0.20) (0.28)
.10 (164.30) (46.70) (5.50) (1.50) (0.40) 0.00 (0.32) 0.02 (0.13) (0.46)

Copyright 2012 Securities Research Company

Bonds $25.1 Mil Com 43.841 Mil BV 5.34 /sh P/E N/A (Ind ITSOF P/E 19.21) Ctry US

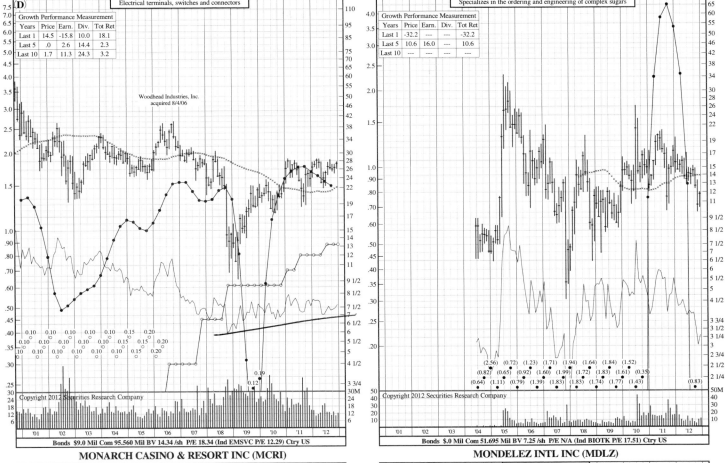

MOLEX INC (MOLX)

Electrical terminals, switches and connectors

Growth Performance Measurement				
Years	Price	Earn.	Div.	Tot Ret
Last 1	14.5	-15.8	10.0	18.1
Last 5	.0	2.6	14.4	2.3
Last 10	1.7	11.3	24.3	3.2

Woodhead Industries, Inc.
acquired 8/4/06

0.10 0.10 0.10 0.10 0.10 0.15 0.20
0.10 0.10 0.10 0.10 0.15 0.20
0.10 0.10 0.10 0.15 0.20
0.19
0.12

Copyright 2012 Securities Research Company

Bonds $9.0 Mil Com 95.560 Mil BV 14.34 /sh P/E 18.34 (Ind EMSVC P/E 12.29) Ctry US

MOMENTA PHARMACEUTICALS INC (MNTA)

Specializes in the ordering and engineering of complex sugars

Growth Performance Measurement				
Years	Price	Earn.	Div.	Tot Ret
Last 1	-32.2	---	---	-32.2
Last 5	10.6	16.0	---	10.6
Last 10	---	---	---	---

(2.56) (0.72) (1.23) (1.71) (1.94) (1.64) (1.84) (1.52)
(0.82) (0.65) (0.92) (1.60) (1.99) (1.72) (1.83) (1.61) (0.35)
(0.64) (1.11) (0.79) (1.39) (1.83) (1.83) (1.74) (1.77) (1.43) (0.83)

Copyright 2012 Securities Research Company

Bonds $.0 Mil Com 51.695 Mil BV 7.25 /sh P/E N/A (Ind BIOTK P/E 17.51) Ctry US

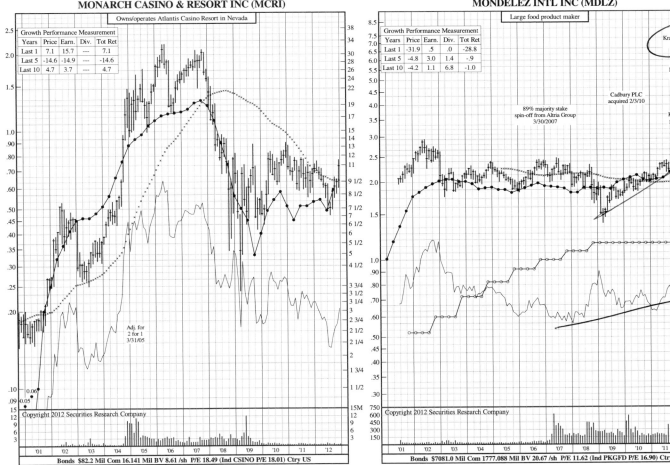

MONARCH CASINO & RESORT INC (MCRI)

Owns/operates Atlantis Casino Resort in Nevada

Growth Performance Measurement				
Years	Price	Earn.	Div.	Tot Ret
Last 1	7.1	15.7	---	7.1
Last 5	-14.6	-14.9	---	-14.6
Last 10	4.7	3.7	---	4.7

Adj. for
2 for 1
3/31/05

0.06
0.09 0.05

Copyright 2012 Securities Research Company

Bonds $82.2 Mil Com 16.141 Mil BV 8.61 /sh P/E 18.49 (Ind CSINO P/E 18.01) Ctry US

MONDELEZ INTL INC (MDLZ)

Large food product maker

Growth Performance Measurement				
Years	Price	Earn.	Div.	Tot Ret
Last 1	-31.9	.5	---	-28.8
Last 5	-4.8	3.0	1.4	-.9
Last 10	-4.2	1.1	6.8	-1.0

Spun-off
Kraft Foods Group
10/1/12

Listed
Nasdaq 6/27/12
NYSE prior

Cadbury PLC
acquired 2/3/10

Kraft Foods, Inc.
prior to 10/1/12

89% majority stake
spin-off from Altria Group
3/30/2007

Copyright 2012 Securities Research Company

Bonds $7081.0 Mil Com 1777.088 Mil BV 20.67 /sh P/E 11.62 (Ind PKGFD P/E 16.90) Ctry US

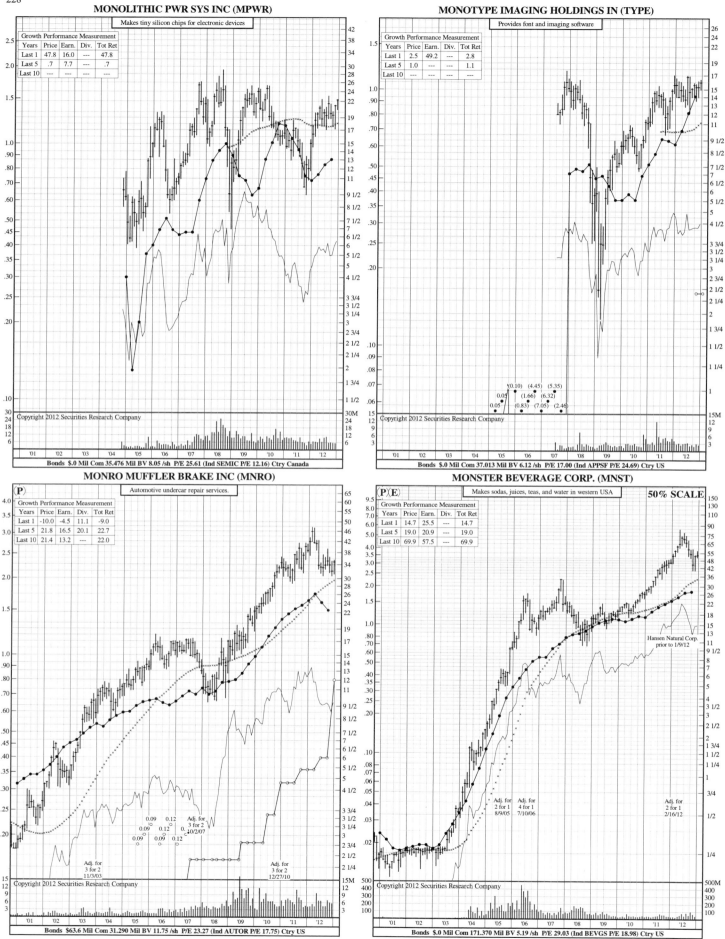

MONOLITHIC PWR SYS INC (MPWR)

Makes tiny silicon chips for electronic devices

Growth Performance Measurement				
Years	Price	Earn.	Div.	Tot Ret
Last 1	47.8	16.0	---	47.8
Last 5	.7	7.7	---	.7
Last 10	---	---	---	---

Copyright 2012 Securities Research Company

Bonds $.0 Mil Com 35.476 Mil BV 8.05 /sh P/E 25.61 (Ind SEMIC P/E 12.16) Ctry Canada

MONOTYPE IMAGING HOLDINGS IN (TYPE)

Provides font and imaging software

Growth Performance Measurement				
Years	Price	Earn.	Div.	Tot Ret
Last 1	2.5	49.2	---	2.8
Last 5	1.0	---	---	1.1
Last 10	---	---	---	---

Copyright 2012 Securities Research Company

Bonds $.0 Mil Com 37.013 Mil BV 6.12 /sh P/E 17.00 (Ind APPSF P/E 24.69) Ctry US

MONRO MUFFLER BRAKE INC (MNRO)

(P)

Automotive undercar repair services.

Growth Performance Measurement				
Years	Price	Earn.	Div.	Tot Ret
Last 1	-10.0	-4.5	11.1	-9.0
Last 5	21.8	16.5	20.1	22.7
Last 10	21.4	13.2	---	22.0

0.09   0.12   Adj. for
0.09   0.12   3 for 2
0.09   0.09   0.12   10/2/07
0.09   0.09   0.12

Adj. for
3 for 2
11/3/03

Adj. for
3 for 2
12/27/10

Copyright 2012 Securities Research Company

Bonds $63.6 Mil Com 31.290 Mil BV 11.75 /sh P/E 23.27 (Ind AUTOR P/E 17.75) Ctry US

MONSTER BEVERAGE CORP. (MNST)

(P)(E)

Makes sodas, juices, teas, and water in western USA   50% SCALE

Growth Performance Measurement				
Years	Price	Earn.	Div.	Tot Ret
Last 1	14.7	25.5	---	14.7
Last 5	19.0	20.9	---	19.0
Last 10	69.9	57.5	---	69.9

Hansen Natural Corp.
prior to 1/9/12

Adj. for   Adj. for
2 for 1   4 for 1
8/9/05   7/10/06

Adj. for
2 for 1
2/16/12

Copyright 2012 Securities Research Company

Bonds $.0 Mil Com 171.370 Mil BV 5.19 /sh P/E 29.03 (Ind BEVGS P/E 18.98) Ctry US

MORGANS HOTEL GROUP CO (MHGC)

Owns and manages luxury boutique hotels NY, CA, FL, and London

Growth Performance Measurement			
Years	Price	Earn.	Div.	Tot Ret
Last 1	-6.1	-37.8	---	-6.1
Last 5	-22.1	-90.5	---	-22.1
Last 10	---	---	---	---

(0.99)
(0.02)
(0.59) (1.70) (2.16) (2.61) (3.11) (1.88) (2.26)
(0.36) (0.71) (2.11) (2.22) (2.84) (1.64) (1.69)
(0.09) (0.64) (1.81) (1.85) (3.35) (2.75) (1.52)

Copyright 2012 Securities Research Company

'01 '02 '03 '04 '05 '06 '07 '08 '09 '10 '11 '12

Bonds $.0 Mil Com 31.242 Mil BV -6.24 /sh P/E N/A (Ind HOTEL P/E 19.80) Ctry US

MORNINGSTAR INC (MORN)

Offers financial information to individual and professional investors

Growth Performance Measurement			
Years	Price	Earn.	Div.	Tot Ret
Last 1	5.7	22.4	100.0	6.4
Last 5	-4.2	8.1	---	-4.0
Last 10	---	---	---	---

0.05

Copyright 2012 Securities Research Company

'01 '02 '03 '04 '05 '06 '07 '08 '09 '10 '11 '12

Bonds $.0 Mil Com 47.131 Mil BV 15.91 /sh P/E 30.21 (Ind PUBPR P/E 14.26) Ctry US

MOSYS INC (MOSY)

Licenses embedded memory chips

Growth Performance Measurement			
Years	Price	Earn.	Div.	Tot Ret
Last 1	-17.1	10.9	---	-17.1
Last 5	-6.4	-52.2	---	-6.4
Last 10	-11.7	---	---	-11.7

Monolithic System
Technology Inc.
prior to 5/25/06

0.02 (0.10) (0.15) (0.02) (0.32) (0.47) (0.50) (0.52) (0.59) (0.50) (0.49)
(0.04) (0.12) (0.14) (0.09) (0.22) (0.50) (0.46) (0.53) (0.60) (0.55) (0.53)
0.01 0.03 (0.09) (0.09) (0.06) (0.46) (0.46) (0.51) (0.57) (0.57) (0.51)

Copyright 2012 Securities Research Company

'01 '02 '03 '04 '05 '06 '07 '08 '09 '10 '11 '12

Bonds $.0 Mil Com 39.907 Mil BV 1.78 /sh P/E N/A (Ind SEMIC P/E 12.16) Ctry US

MOVE INC (MOVE)

Real estate from the Internet

60% SCALE

Growth Performance Measurement			
Years	Price	Earn.	Div.	Tot Ret
Last 1	19.8	580.0	---	19.8
Last 5	-5.0	---	---	-5.0
Last 10	8.3	---	---	8.3

Homestore Inc.
prior to 5/3/06

Adj. for
1 for 4
11/21/11

(0.64) (5.80) (4.12) (0.16) (0.12) 0.00 (0.04)
(2.32) (4.60) (8.44) (0.68) 0.00 (0.20) (0.12) (0.04) (0.04)
3.88 (0.12) (7.68) (0.20) (1.28) (0.16) (0.04) (0.24) (0.08) 0.00 0.00

Copyright 2012 Securities Research Company

'01 '02 '03 '04 '05 '06 '07 '08 '09 '10 '11 '12

Bonds $.6 Mil Com 39.325 Mil BV 2.39 /sh P/E 22.26 (Ind ITSOF P/E 19.21) Ctry US

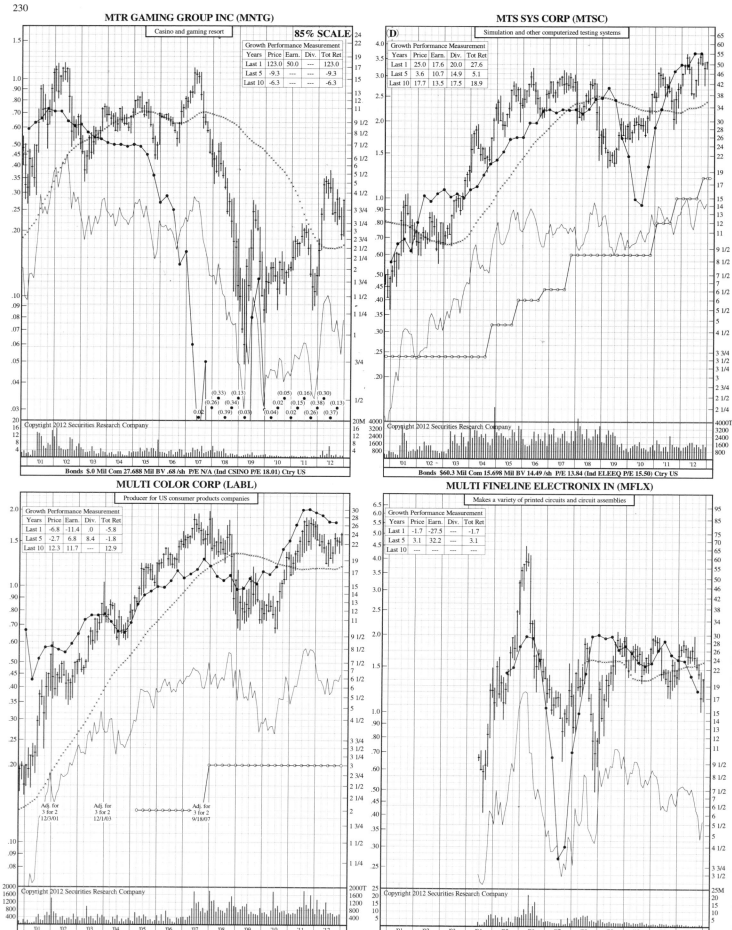

MTR GAMING GROUP INC (MNTG)

Casino and gaming resort

85% SCALE

Growth Performance Measurement

Years	Price	Earn.	Div.	Tot Ret
Last 1	123.0	50.0	---	123.0
Last 5	-9.3	---	---	-9.3
Last 10	-6.3	---	---	-6.3

(0.33) (0.13) (0.05) (0.16) (0.30)
(0.26) (0.34) 0.02 (0.15) (0.38) (0.13)
0.02 (0.39) (0.03) (0.04) 0.02 (0.26) (0.37)

Copyright 2012 Securities Research Company

Bonds $.0 Mil Com 27.688 Mil BV .68 /sh P/E N/A (Ind CSINO P/E 18.01) Ctry US

MTS SYS CORP (MTSC)

(D) Simulation and other computerized testing systems

Growth Performance Measurement

Years	Price	Earn.	Div.	Tot Ret
Last 1	25.0	17.6	20.0	27.6
Last 5	3.6	10.7	14.9	5.1
Last 10	17.7	13.5	17.5	18.9

Copyright 2012 Securities Research Company

Bonds $60.3 Mil Com 15.698 Mil BV 14.49 /sh P/E 13.84 (Ind ELEEQ P/E 15.50) Ctry US

MULTI COLOR CORP (LABL)

Producer for US consumer products companies

Growth Performance Measurement

Years	Price	Earn.	Div.	Tot Ret
Last 1	-6.8	-11.4	.0	-5.8
Last 5	-2.7	6.8	8.4	-1.8
Last 10	12.3	11.7	---	12.9

Adj. for
3 for 2
12/3/01

Adj. for
3 for 2
12/1/03

Adj. for
3 for 2
9/18/07

Copyright 2012 Securities Research Company

Bonds $.0 Mil Com 16.147 Mil BV 17.28 /sh P/E 13.48 (Ind PRINT P/E 5.00) Ctry US

MULTI FINELINE ELECTRONIX IN (MFLX)

Makes a variety of printed circuits and circuit assemblies

Growth Performance Measurement

Years	Price	Earn.	Div.	Tot Ret
Last 1	-1.7	-27.5	---	-1.7
Last 5	3.1	32.2	---	3.1
Last 10	---	---	---	---

Copyright 2012 Securities Research Company

Bonds $.0 Mil Com 23.766 Mil BV 18.60 /sh P/E 16.70 (Ind EMSVC P/E 12.29) Ctry US

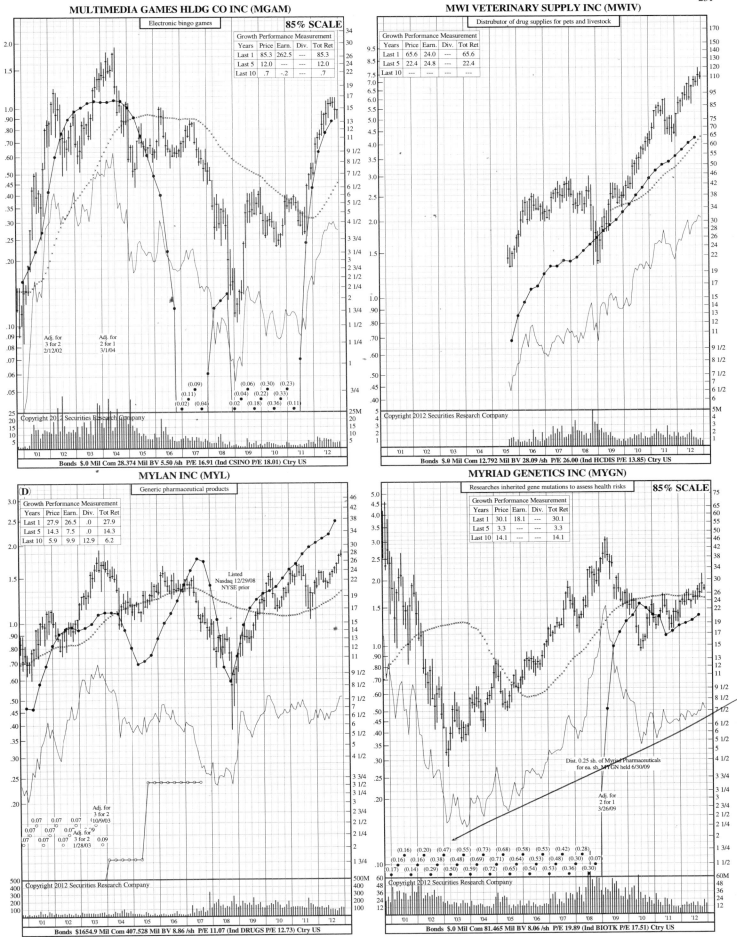

MULTIMEDIA GAMES HLDG CO INC (MGAM)

Electronic bingo games

85% SCALE

Growth Performance Measurement				
Years	Price	Earn.	Div.	Tot Ret
Last 1	85.3	262.5	---	85.3
Last 5	12.0	---	---	12.0
Last 10	.7	-.2	---	.7

Adj. for
3 for 2
2/12/02

Adj. for
2 for 1
3/1/04

(0.09)
(0.11)
(0.02) 0.04

(0.06) (0.30) (0.23)
(0.04) (0.22) (0.33)
0.02 (0.18) (0.36) (0.11)

Copyright 2012 Securities Research Company

Bonds $.0 Mil Com 28.374 Mil BV 5.50 /sh P/E 16.91 (Ind CSINO P/E 18.01) Ctry US

MWI VETERINARY SUPPLY INC (MWIV)

Distrubutor of drug supplies for pets and livestock

Growth Performance Measurement				
Years	Price	Earn.	Div.	Tot Ret
Last 1	65.6	24.0	---	65.6
Last 5	22.4	24.8	---	22.4
Last 10	---	---	---	---

Copyright 2012 Securities Research Company

Bonds $.0 Mil Com 12.792 Mil BV 28.09 /sh P/E 26.00 (Ind HCDIS P/E 13.85) Ctry US

MYLAN INC (MYL)

(D)

Generic pharmaceutical products

Growth Performance Measurement				
Years	Price	Earn.	Div.	Tot Ret
Last 1	27.9	26.5	.0	27.9
Last 5	14.3	7.5	.0	14.3
Last 10	5.9	9.9	12.9	6.2

Listed
Nasdaq 12/29/08
NYSE prior

0.07 0.07 0.07
0.07   0.09
0.07   0.07
0.07   0.09

Adj. for
3 for 2
10/9/03

Adj. for
3 for 2
1/28/03

Copyright 2012 Securities Research Company

Bonds $1654.9 Mil Com 407.528 Mil BV 8.86 /sh P/E 11.07 (Ind DRUGS P/E 12.73) Ctry US

MYRIAD GENETICS INC (MYGN)

Researches inherited gene mutations to assess health risks

85% SCALE

Growth Performance Measurement				
Years	Price	Earn.	Div.	Tot Ret
Last 1	30.1	18.1	---	30.1
Last 5	3.3	---	---	3.3
Last 10	14.1	---	---	14.1

Dist. 0.25 sh. of Myriad Pharmaceuticals
for ea. sh. MYGN held 6/30/09

Adj. for
2 for 1
3/26/09

(0.16) (0.20) (0.47) (0.55) (0.73) (0.68) (0.58) (0.53) (0.42) (0.28)
(0.16) (0.16) (0.38) (0.48) (0.69) (0.71) (0.64) (0.53) (0.48) (0.30) (0.07)
(0.17) (0.14) (0.29) (0.50) (0.59) (0.72) (0.65) (0.54) (0.53) (0.36) (0.30)

Copyright 2012 Securities Research Company

Bonds $.0 Mil Com 81.465 Mil BV 8.06 /sh P/E 19.89 (Ind BIOTK P/E 17.51) Ctry US

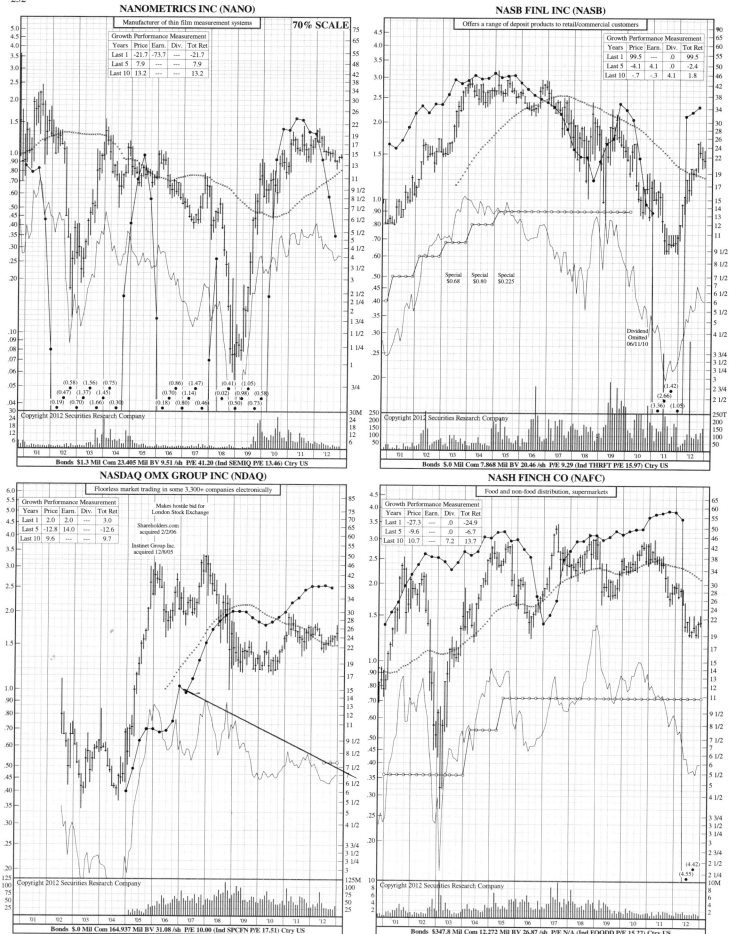

232

NANOMETRICS INC (NANO)
Manufacturer of thin film measurement systems
70% SCALE

Growth Performance Measurement				
Years	Price	Earn.	Div.	Tot Ret
Last 1	-21.7	-73.7	---	-21.7
Last 5	7.9	---	---	7.9
Last 10	13.2	---	---	13.2

(0.58) (1.56) (0.75)
(0.47) (1.37) (1.45)
(0.19) (0.70) (1.66) (0.30)
(0.86) (1.47)
(0.70) (1.14)
(0.18) (0.80) (0.46)
(0.41) (1.05)
(0.02) (0.98) (0.58)
(0.50) (0.73)

Copyright 2012 Securities Research Company

Bonds $1.3 Mil Com 23.405 Mil BV 9.51 /sh P/E 41.20 (Ind SEMIQ P/E 13.46) Ctry US

NASB FINL INC (NASB)
Offers a range of deposit products to retail/commercial customers

Growth Performance Measurement				
Years	Price	Earn.	Div.	Tot Ret
Last 1	99.5	---	.0	99.5
Last 5	-4.1	4.1	.0	-2.4
Last 10	-.7	-.3	4.1	1.8

Special $0.68   Special $0.80   Special $0.225

Dividend Omitted 06/11/10

(1.42)
(2.66)
(3.36) (1.05)

Copyright 2012 Securities Research Company

Bonds $.0 Mil Com 7.868 Mil BV 20.46 /sh P/E 9.29 (Ind THRFT P/E 15.97) Ctry US

NASDAQ OMX GROUP INC (NDAQ)
Floorless market trading in some 3,300+ companies electronically

Growth Performance Measurement				
Years	Price	Earn.	Div.	Tot Ret
Last 1	2.0	2.0	---	3.0
Last 5	-12.8	14.0	---	-12.6
Last 10	9.6	---	---	9.7

Makes hostile bid for London Stock Exchange

Shareholders.com acquired 2/2/06

Instinet Group Inc. acquired 12/8/05

Copyright 2012 Securities Research Company

Bonds $.0 Mil Com 164.937 Mil BV 31.08 /sh P/E 10.00 (Ind SPCFN P/E 17.51) Ctry US

NASH FINCH CO (NAFC)
Food and non-food distribution, supermarkets

Growth Performance Measurement				
Years	Price	Earn.	Div.	Tot Ret
Last 1	-27.3	---	.0	-24.9
Last 5	-9.6	---	.0	-6.7
Last 10	10.7	---	7.2	13.7

(4.42)
(4.55)

Copyright 2012 Securities Research Company

Bonds $347.8 Mil Com 12.272 Mil BV 26.87 /sh P/E N/A (Ind FOODD P/E 15.22) Ctry US

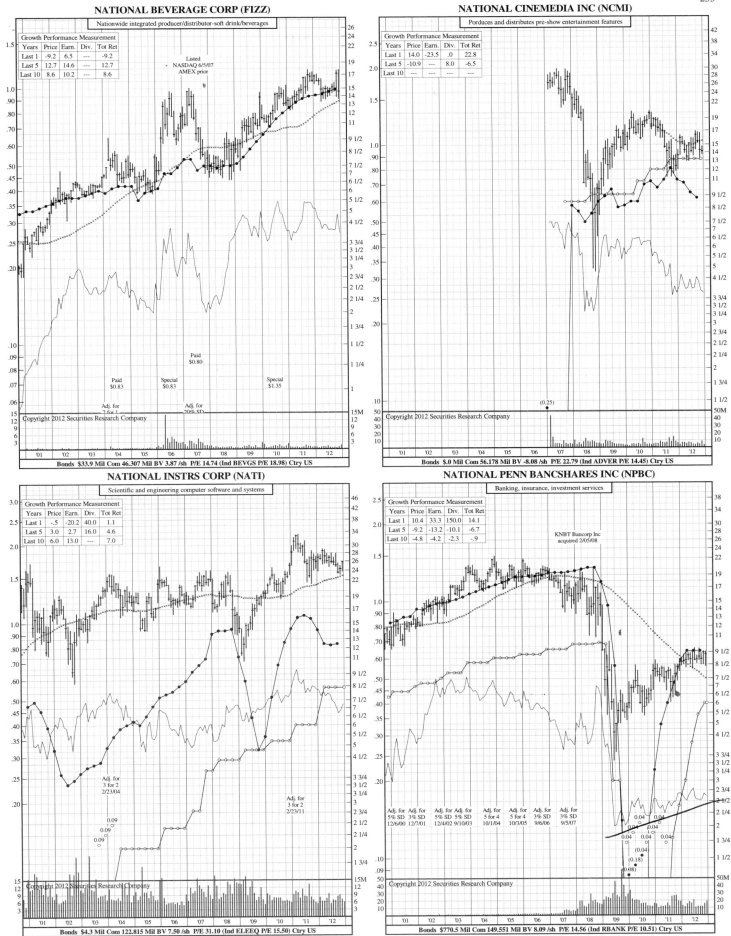

NATIONAL BEVERAGE CORP (FIZZ)

Nationwide integrated producer/distributor-soft drink/beverages

Growth Performance Measurement				
Years	Price	Earn.	Div.	Tot Ret
Last 1	-9.2	6.5	---	-9.2
Last 5	12.7	14.6	---	12.7
Last 10	8.6	10.2	---	8.6

Listed
- NASDAQ 6/5/07
AMEX prior

Paid
$0.80

Paid
$0.83

Special
$0.83

Special
$1.35

Adj. for
2 for 1

Adj. for
20% SD

Copyright 2012 Securities Research Company

Bonds $33.9 Mil Com 46.307 Mil BV 3.87 /sh P/E 14.74 (Ind BEVGS P/E 18.98) Ctry US

NATIONAL CINEMEDIA INC (NCMI)

Porduces and distributes pre-show entertainment features

Growth Performance Measurement				
Years	Price	Earn.	Div.	Tot Ret
Last 1	14.0	-23.5	.0	22.8
Last 5	-10.9	---	8.0	-6.5
Last 10	---	---	---	---

(0.25)

Copyright 2012 Securities Research Company

Bonds $.0 Mil Com 56.178 Mil BV -8.08 /sh P/E 22.79 (Ind ADVER P/E 14.45) Ctry US

NATIONAL INSTRS CORP (NATI)

Scientific and engineering computer software and systems

Growth Performance Measurement				
Years	Price	Earn.	Div.	Tot Ret
Last 1	-.5	-20.2	40.0	1.1
Last 5	3.0	2.7	16.0	4.6
Last 10	6.0	13.0	---	7.0

Adj. for
3 for 2
2/23/04

Adj. for
3 for 2
2/23/11

0.09
0.09
0.09

Copyright 2012 Securities Research Company

Bonds $4.3 Mil Com 122.815 Mil BV 7.50 /sh P/E 31.10 (Ind ELEEQ P/E 15.50) Ctry US

NATIONAL PENN BANCSHARES INC (NPBC)

Banking, insurance, investment services

Growth Performance Measurement				
Years	Price	Earn.	Div.	Tot Ret
Last 1	10.4	33.3	150.0	14.1
Last 5	-9.2	-13.2	-10.1	-6.7
Last 10	-4.8	-4.2	-2.3	-.9

KNBT Bancorp Inc
acquired 2/05/08

Adj. for
5% SD
12/6/00

Adj. for
3% SD
12/7/01

Adj. for
5% SD
12/4/02

Adj. for
5% SD
9/10/03

Adj. for
5 for 4
10/1/04

Adj. for
5 for 4
10/3/05

Adj. for
3% SD
9/6/06

Adj. for
3% SD
9/5/07

0.04
0.04
0.04
0.04
0.04
0.04
(0.04)
(0.18)
(0.08)

Copyright 2012 Securities Research Company

Bonds $770.5 Mil Com 149.551 Mil BV 8.09 /sh P/E 14.56 (Ind RBANK P/E 10.51) Ctry US

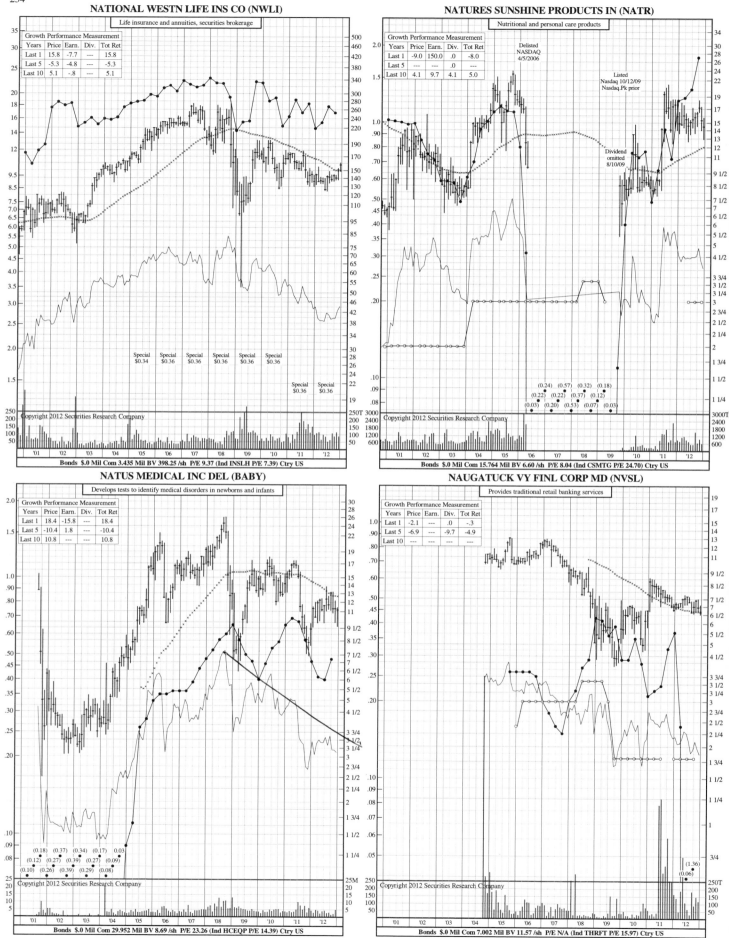

234

NATIONAL WESTN LIFE INS CO (NWLI)

Life insurance and annuities, securities brokerage

Growth Performance Measurement

Years	Price	Earn.	Div.	Tot Ret
Last 1	15.8	-7.7	---	15.8
Last 5	-5.3	-4.8	---	-5.3
Last 10	5.1	-.8	---	5.1

Special $0.34 Special $0.36 Special $0.36 Special $0.36 Special $0.36 Special $0.36 Special $0.36 Special $0.36

Copyright 2012 Securities Research Company

Bonds $.0 Mil Com 3.435 Mil BV 398.25 /sh P/E 9.37 (Ind INSLH P/E 7.39) Ctry US

NATURES SUNSHINE PRODUCTS IN (NATR)

Nutritional and personal care products

Growth Performance Measurement

Years	Price	Earn.	Div.	Tot Ret
Last 1	-9.0	150.0	.0	-8.0
Last 5	---	---	.0	---
Last 10	4.1	9.7	4.1	5.0

Delisted NASDAQ 4/5/2006

Listed Nasdaq 10/12/09 Nasdaq.Pk prior

Dividend omitted 8/10/09

(0.24) (0.57) (0.32) (0.18)
(0.22) (0.22) (0.37) (0.12)
(0.03) (0.20) (0.53) (0.07) (0.03)

Copyright 2012 Securities Research Company

Bonds $.0 Mil Com 15.764 Mil BV 6.60 /sh P/E 8.04 (Ind CSMTG P/E 24.70) Ctry US

NATUS MEDICAL INC DEL (BABY)

Develops tests to identify medical disorders in newborns and infants

Growth Performance Measurement

Years	Price	Earn.	Div.	Tot Ret
Last 1	18.4	-15.8	---	18.4
Last 5	-10.4	1.8	---	-10.4
Last 10	10.8	---	---	10.8

(0.18) (0.37) (0.34) (0.17) 0.03
(0.12) (0.26) (0.39) (0.27) (0.09)
(0.10) (0.26) (0.39) (0.29) (0.08)

Copyright 2012 Securities Research Company

Bonds $.0 Mil Com 29.952 Mil BV 8.69 /sh P/E 23.26 (Ind HCEQP P/E 14.39) Ctry US

NAUGATUCK VY FINL CORP MD (NVSL)

Provides traditional retail banking services

Growth Performance Measurement

Years	Price	Earn.	Div.	Tot Ret
Last 1	-2.1	.0	---	-.3
Last 5	-6.9	---	-9.7	-4.9
Last 10	---	---	---	---

(1.36)
(0.06)

Copyright 2012 Securities Research Company

Bonds $.0 Mil Com 7.002 Mil BV 11.57 /sh P/E N/A (Ind THRFT P/E 15.97) Ctry US

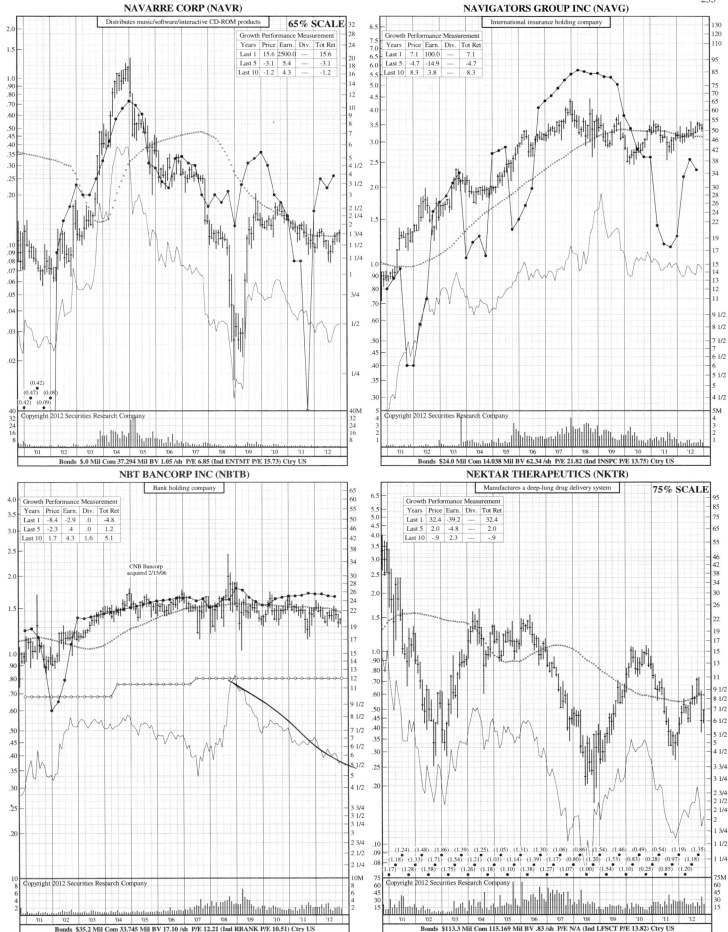

NAVARRE CORP (NAVR)

Distributes music/software/interactive CD-ROM products

65% SCALE

Growth Performance Measurement				
Years	Price	Earn.	Div.	Tot Ret
Last 1	15.6	2500.0	---	15.6
Last 5	-3.1	5.4	---	-3.1
Last 10	-1.2	4.3	---	-1.2

(0.42)
(0.47) (0.05)
(0.42) (0.09)

Copyright 2012 Securities Research Company

Bonds $.0 Mil Com 37.294 Mil BV 1.05 /sh P/E 6.85 (Ind ENTMT P/E 15.73) Ctry US

NAVIGATORS GROUP INC (NAVG)

International insurance holding company

Growth Performance Measurement				
Years	Price	Earn.	Div.	Tot Ret
Last 1	7.1	100.0	---	7.1
Last 5	-4.7	-14.9	---	-4.7
Last 10	8.3	3.8	---	8.3

Copyright 2012 Securities Research Company

Bonds $24.0 Mil Com 14.038 Mil BV 62.34 /sh P/E 21.82 (Ind INSPC P/E 13.75) Ctry US

NBT BANCORP INC (NBTB)

Bank holding company

Growth Performance Measurement				
Years	Price	Earn.	Div.	Tot Ret
Last 1	-8.4	-2.9	.0	-4.8
Last 5	-2.3	.4	.0	1.2
Last 10	1.7	4.3	1.6	5.1

CNB Bancorp
acquired 2/15/06

Copyright 2012 Securities Research Company

Bonds $35.2 Mil Com 33.745 Mil BV 17.10 /sh P/E 12.21 (Ind RBANK P/E 10.51) Ctry US

NEKTAR THERAPEUTICS (NKTR)

Manufactures a deep-lung drug delivery system

75% SCALE

Growth Performance Measurement				
Years	Price	Earn.	Div.	Tot Ret
Last 1	32.4	-39.2	---	32.4
Last 5	2.0	-4.8	---	2.0
Last 10	-.9	2.3	---	-.9

(1.24) (1.48) (1.86) (1.39) (1.25) (1.05) (1.31) (1.30) (1.06) (0.86) (1.54) (1.46) (0.49) (0.54) (1.19) (1.35)
(1.18) (1.33) (1.71) (1.54) (1.21) (1.03) (1.14) (1.39) (1.17) (0.80) (1.20) (1.53) (0.83) (0.28) (0.97) (1.18)
(1.17) (1.28) (1.58) (1.75) (1.26) (1.18) (1.10) (1.38) (1.27) (1.07) (1.00) (1.54) (1.10) (0.25) (0.85) (1.20)

Copyright 2012 Securities Research Company

Bonds $113.3 Mil Com 115.169 Mil BV .83 /sh P/E N/A (Ind LFSCT P/E 13.82) Ctry US

236

NEOGEN CORP (NEOG)

Makes/sells diverse line of products related to food and safe animals

(P)(E)

Growth Performance Measurement				
Years	Price	Earn.	Div.	Tot Ret
Last 1	47.9	10.8	---	47.9
Last 5	20.7	16.2	---	20.7
Last 10	23.9	15.1	---	23.9

Adj. for
5 for 4
1/2/04

Adj. for
3 for 2
9/5/07

Adj. for
3 for 2
12/16/09

Copyright 2012 Securities Research Company

Bonds $.0 Mil Com 23.862 Mil BV 10.18 /sh P/E 44.00 (Ind HCSUP P/E 17.94) Ctry US

NET 1 UEPS TECHNOLOGIES INC (UEPS)

Provides universal electronic payment systems

90% SCALE

Growth Performance Measurement				
Years	Price	Earn.	Div.	Tot Ret
Last 1	-33.4	-20.7	---	-33.4
Last 5	-29.5	.5	---	-29.5
Last 10	-2.5	---	---	-2.5

Adj. for
1 for 6
6/13/05

Copyright 2012 Securities Research Company

Bonds $.0 Mil Com 45.600 Mil BV 7.75 /sh P/E 4.29 (Ind APPSF P/E 24.69) Ctry South Africa

NETAPP INC (NTAP)

Network data storage devices

(E) **70% SCALE**

Growth Performance Measurement				
Years	Price	Earn.	Div.	Tot Ret
Last 1	-7.5	-5.2	---	-7.5
Last 5	6.1	14.3	---	6.1
Last 10	12.9	28.3	---	12.9

Copyright 2012 Securities Research Company

Bonds $134.0 Mil Com 358.284 Mil BV 13.05 /sh P/E 15.46 (Ind DISKS P/E 11.46) Ctry US

NETEASE INC (NTES)

Chinese web portal services

(P) **50% SCALE**

Growth Performance Measurement				
Years	Price	Earn.	Div.	Tot Ret
Last 1	-5.2	18.7	---	-5.2
Last 5	17.5	29.5	---	17.5
Last 10	31.0	---	---	31.0

Trading suspended
8/31/01 to 12/31/01

Adj. for
4 for 1
3/28/06

Copyright 2012 Securities Research Company

Bonds $.0 Mil Com 129.854 Mil BV 19.31 /sh P/E 9.98 (Ind ITSOF P/E 19.21) Ctry China

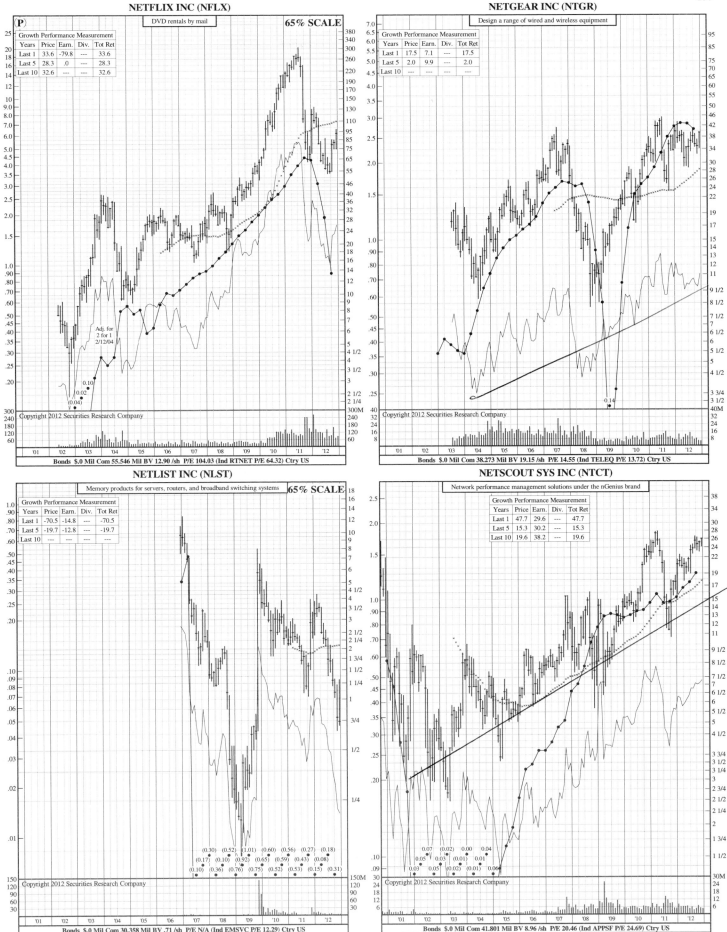

237

NETFLIX INC (NFLX)

DVD rentals by mail

65% SCALE

(P)

Growth Performance Measurement				
Years	Price	Earn.	Div.	Tot Ret
Last 1	33.6	-79.8	---	33.6
Last 5	28.3	.0	---	28.3
Last 10	32.6	---	---	32.6

Adj. for
2 for 1
2/12/04

0.10
0.02
(0.04)

Copyright 2012 Securities Research Company

Bonds $.0 Mil Com 55.546 Mil BV 12.90 /sh P/E 104.03 (Ind RTNET P/E 64.32) Ctry US

NETGEAR INC (NTGR)

Design a range of wired and wireless equipment

Growth Performance Measurement				
Years	Price	Earn.	Div.	Tot Ret
Last 1	17.5	7.1	---	17.5
Last 5	2.0	9.9	---	2.0
Last 10	---	---	---	---

(0.14)

Copyright 2012 Securities Research Company

Bonds $.0 Mil Com 38.273 Mil BV 19.15 /sh P/E 14.55 (Ind TELEQ P/E 13.72) Ctry US

NETLIST INC (NLST)

Memory products for servers, routers, and broadband switching systems

65% SCALE

Growth Performance Measurement				
Years	Price	Earn.	Div.	Tot Ret
Last 1	-70.5	-14.8	---	-70.5
Last 5	-19.7	-12.8	---	-19.7
Last 10	---	---	---	---

(0.30) (0.52) (1.01) (0.60) (0.56) (0.27) (0.18)
(0.17) (0.10) (0.92) (0.65) (0.59) (0.43) (0.08)
(0.10) (0.36) (0.76) (0.75) (0.52) (0.53) (0.15) (0.31)

Copyright 2012 Securities Research Company

Bonds $.0 Mil Com 30.358 Mil BV .71 /sh P/E N/A (Ind EMSVC P/E 12.29) Ctry US

NETSCOUT SYS INC (NTCT)

Network performance management solutions under the nGenius brand

Growth Performance Measurement				
Years	Price	Earn.	Div.	Tot Ret
Last 1	47.7	29.6	---	47.7
Last 5	15.3	30.2	---	15.3
Last 10	19.6	38.2	---	19.6

0.07 (0.02) 0.00 0.04
0.05   0.03 (0.01) 0.01
0.03   0.05 (0.02) (0.01) 0.06

Copyright 2012 Securities Research Company

Bonds $.0 Mil Com 41.801 Mil BV 8.96 /sh P/E 20.46 (Ind APPSF P/E 24.69) Ctry US

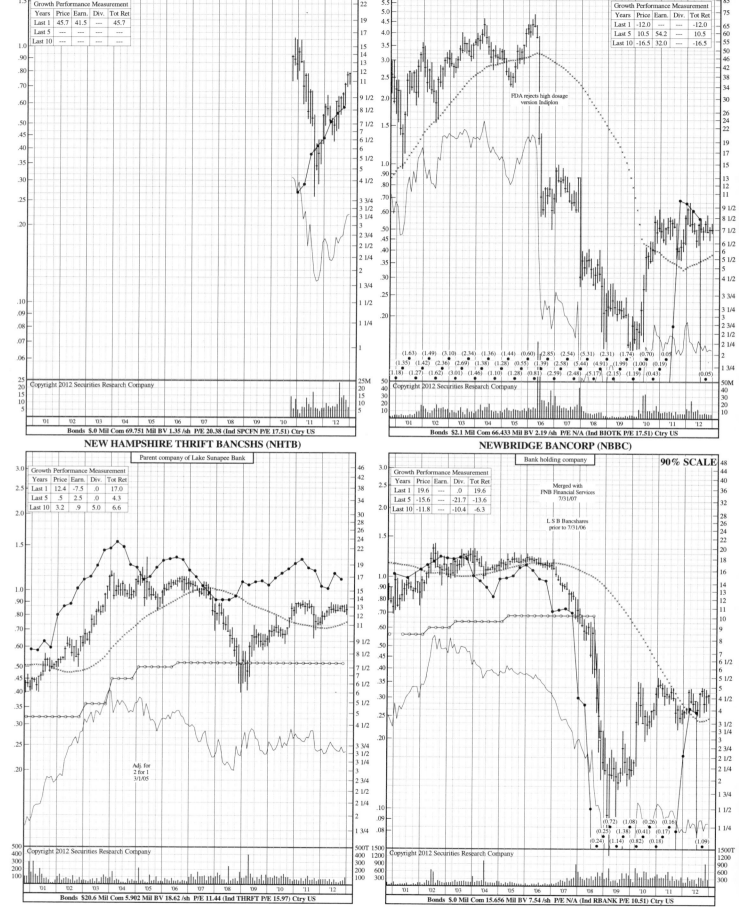

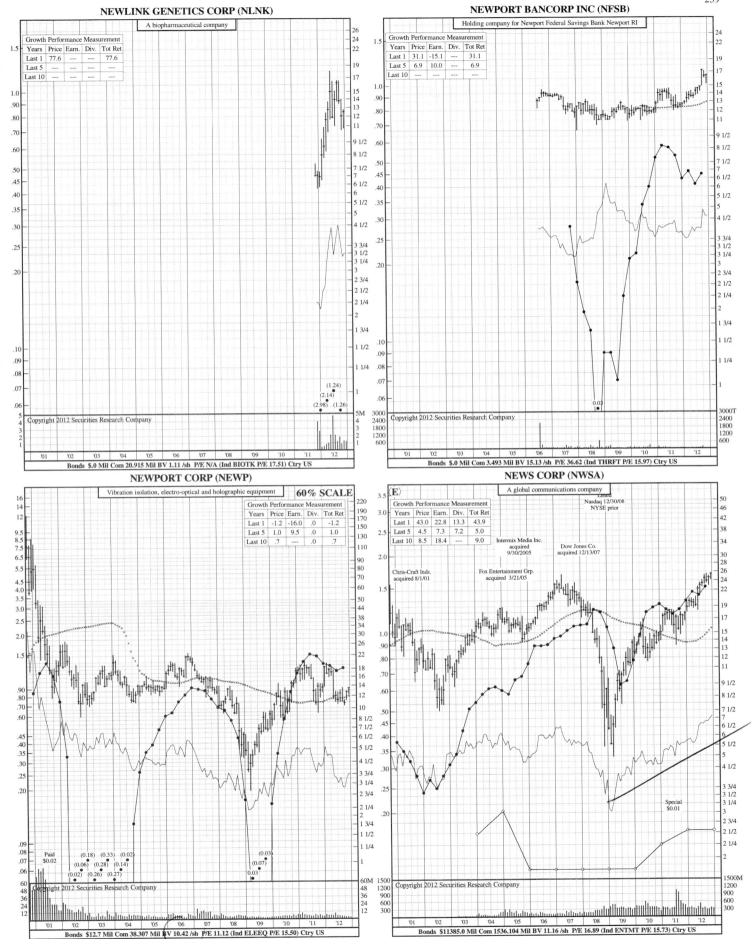

NEWLINK GENETICS CORP (NLNK)

A biopharmaceutical company

Growth Performance Measurement				
Years	Price	Earn.	Div.	Tot Ret
Last 1	77.6	---	---	77.6
Last 5	---	---	---	---
Last 10	---	---	---	---

(1.24)
(2.14)
(2.98) (1.26)

Copyright 2012 Securities Research Company

Bonds $.0 Mil Com 20.915 Mil BV 1.11 /sh P/E N/A (Ind BIOTK P/E 17.51) Ctry US

NEWPORT BANCORP INC (NFSB)

Holding company for Newport Federal Savings Bank Newport RI

Growth Performance Measurement				
Years	Price	Earn.	Div.	Tot Ret
Last 1	31.1	-15.1	---	31.1
Last 5	6.9	10.0	---	6.9
Last 10	---	---	---	---

0.02

Copyright 2012 Securities Research Company

Bonds $.0 Mil Com 3.493 Mil BV 15.13 /sh P/E 36.62 (Ind THRFT P/E 15.97) Ctry US

NEWPORT CORP (NEWP)

Vibration isolation, electro-optical and holographic equipment

60% SCALE

Growth Performance Measurement				
Years	Price	Earn.	Div.	Tot Ret
Last 1	-1.2	-16.0	.0	-1.2
Last 5	1.0	9.5	.0	1.0
Last 10	.7	---	.0	.7

Paid
$0.02

(0.18) (0.33) (0.02)
(0.06) (0.28) (0.14)
(0.02) (0.26) (0.27)

(0.03)
(0.07)
0.03

Copyright 2012 Securities Research Company

Bonds $12.7 Mil Com 38.307 Mil BV 10.42 /sh P/E 11.12 (Ind ELEEQ P/E 15.50) Ctry US

NEWS CORP (NWSA)

(E)

A global communications company

Listed
Nasdaq 12/30/08
NYSE prior

Growth Performance Measurement				
Years	Price	Earn.	Div.	Tot Ret
Last 1	43.0	22.8	13.3	43.9
Last 5	4.5	7.3	7.2	5.0
Last 10	8.5	18.4	---	9.0

Intermix Media Inc.
acquired
9/30/2005

Dow Jones Co.
acquired 12/13/07

Chris-Craft Inds.
acquired 8/1/01

Fox Entertainment Grp.
acquired 3/21/05

Special
$0.01

Copyright 2012 Securities Research Company

Bonds $11385.0 Mil Com 1536.104 Mil BV 11.16 /sh P/E 16.89 (Ind ENTMT P/E 15.73) Ctry US

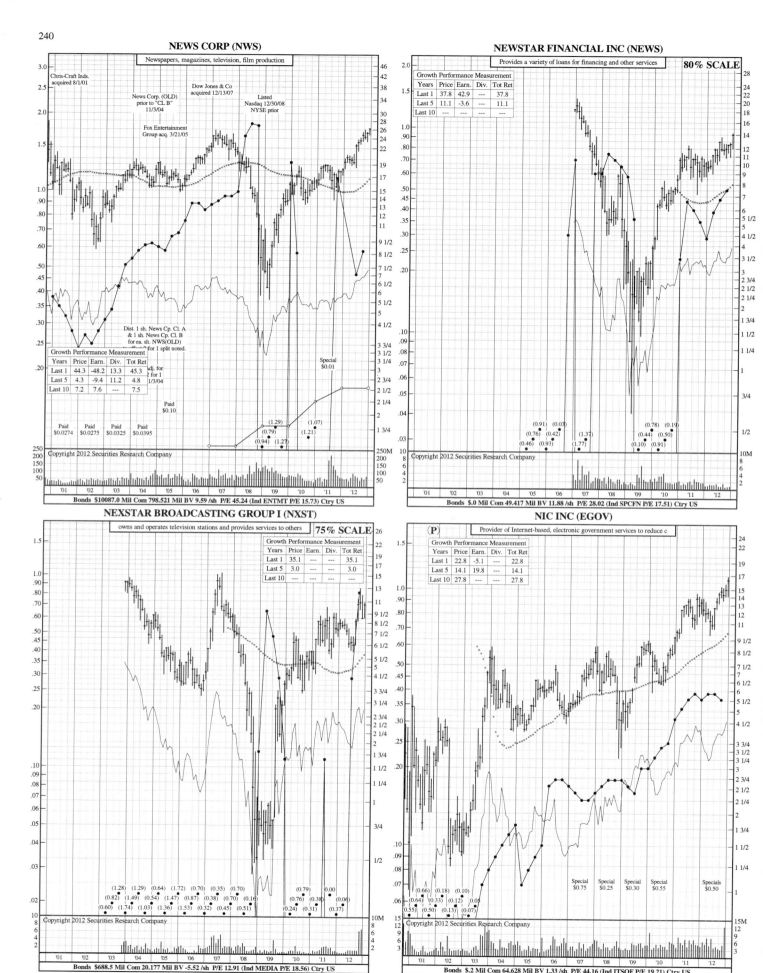

NEWS CORP (NWS)

Newspapers, magazines, television, film production

Chris-Craft Inds. acquired 8/1/01

News Corp. (OLD) prior to "CL B" 11/3/04

Fox Entertainment Group acq. 3/21/05

Dow Jones & Co acquired 12/13/07

Listed Nasdaq 12/30/08 NYSE prior

Dist. 1 sh. News Cp. Cl. A & 1 sh. News Cp. Cl. B for ea. sh. NWS(OLD) 2 for 1 split noted.

Growth Performance Measurement				
Years	Price	Earn.	Div.	Tot Ret
Last 1	44.3	-48.2	13.3	45.3
Last 5	4.3	-9.4	11.2	4.8
Last 10	7.2	7.6	---	7.5

adj. for 2 for 1 1/3/04

Special $0.01

Paid $0.10

Paid $0.0274   Paid $0.0275   Paid $0.0325   Paid $0.0395

(1.29)   (1.07)
(0.79)   (1.21)
(0.94)   (1.27)

Bonds $10087.0 Mil Com 798.521 Mil BV 9.59 /sh P/E 45.24 (Ind ENTMT P/E 15.73) Ctry US

NEWSTAR FINANCIAL INC (NEWS)

Provides a variety of loans for financing and other services

80% SCALE

Growth Performance Measurement				
Years	Price	Earn.	Div.	Tot Ret
Last 1	37.8	42.9	---	37.8
Last 5	11.1	-3.6	---	11.1
Last 10	---	---	---	---

(0.91) (0.03)   (0.78) (0.19)
(0.76) (0.42)   (1.37)   (0.44) (0.50)
(0.46) (0.93)   (1.77)   (0.10) (0.91)

Bonds $.0 Mil Com 49.417 Mil BV 11.88 /sh P/E 28.02 (Ind SPCFN P/E 17.51) Ctry US

NEXSTAR BROADCASTING GROUP I (NXST)

owns and operates television stations and provides services to others

75% SCALE

Growth Performance Measurement				
Years	Price	Earn.	Div.	Tot Ret
Last 1	35.1	---	---	35.1
Last 5	3.0	---	---	3.0
Last 10	---	---	---	---

(1.28) (1.29) (0.64) (1.72) (0.70) (0.35) (0.70)   (0.79)   (0.00)
(0.82) (1.49) (0.54) (1.47) (0.87) (0.38) (0.70) (0.16)   (0.76) (0.38)   (0.06)
(0.60) (1.74) (1.03) (1.36) (1.53) (0.32) (0.45) (0.51)   (0.24) (0.31)   (0.37)

Bonds $688.5 Mil Com 20.177 Mil BV -5.52 /sh P/E 12.91 (Ind MEDIA P/E 18.56) Ctry US

NIC INC (EGOV)

(P)

Provider of Internet-based, electronic government services to reduce c

Growth Performance Measurement				
Years	Price	Earn.	Div.	Tot Ret
Last 1	22.8	-5.1	---	22.8
Last 5	14.1	19.8	---	14.1
Last 10	27.8	---	---	27.8

(0.66) (0.18) (0.10)   Special   Special   Special   Special   Specials
(0.64) (0.33) (0.12) 0.05 $0.75 $0.25 $0.30 $0.55 $0.50
(0.55) (0.50) (0.13) (0.07)

Bonds $.2 Mil Com 64.628 Mil BV 1.33 /sh P/E 44.16 (Ind ITSOF P/E 19.21) Ctry US

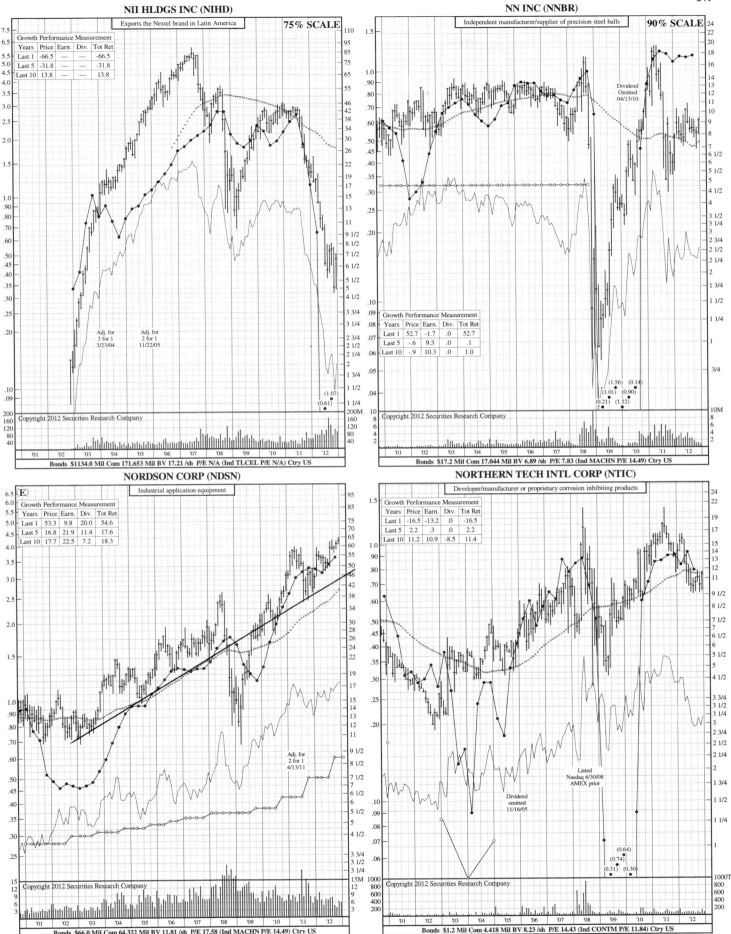

NII HLDGS INC (NIHD)

Exports the Nextel brand in Latin America

75% SCALE

Growth Performance Measurement				
Years	Price	Earn.	Div.	Tot Ret
Last 1	-66.5	---	---	-66.5
Last 5	-31.8	---	---	-31.8
Last 10	13.8	---	---	13.8

Adj. for 3 for 1 3/23/04

Adj. for 2 for 1 11/22/05

(1.07)
(0.61)

Copyright 2012 Securities Research Company

Bonds $1134.0 Mil Com 171.653 Mil BV 17.21 /sh P/E N/A (Ind TLCEL P/E N/A) Ctry US

NN INC (NNBR)

Independent manufacturer/supplier of precision steel balls

90% SCALE

Dividend Omitted 04/13/10

Growth Performance Measurement				
Years	Price	Earn.	Div.	Tot Ret
Last 1	52.7	-1.7	.0	52.7
Last 5	-.6	9.3	.0	.1
Last 10	-.9	10.3	.0	1.0

(1.56) (0.14)
(1.01) (0.90)
(0.21) (1.52)

Copyright 2012 Securities Research Company

Bonds $17.2 Mil Com 17.044 Mil BV 6.89 /sh P/E 7.83 (Ind MACHN P/E 14.49) Ctry US

NORDSON CORP (NDSN)

(E)

Industrial application equipment

Growth Performance Measurement				
Years	Price	Earn.	Div.	Tot Ret
Last 1	53.3	9.8	20.0	54.6
Last 5	16.8	21.9	11.4	17.6
Last 10	17.7	22.5	7.2	18.3

Adj. for 2 for 1 4/13/11

Copyright 2012 Securities Research Company

Bonds $66.0 Mil Com 64.322 Mil BV 11.81 /sh P/E 17.58 (Ind MACHN P/E 14.49) Ctry US

NORTHERN TECH INTL CORP (NTIC)

Developer/manufacturer or proprietary corrosion inhibiting products

Growth Performance Measurement				
Years	Price	Earn.	Div.	Tot Ret
Last 1	-16.5	-13.2	.0	-16.5
Last 5	2.2	.3	.0	2.2
Last 10	11.2	10.9	-8.5	11.4

Listed Nasdaq 6/30/08 AMEX prior

Dividend omitted 11/16/05

(0.64)
(0.74)
(0.31) (0.30)

Copyright 2012 Securities Research Company

Bonds $1.2 Mil Com 4.418 Mil BV 8.23 /sh P/E 14.43 (Ind CONTM P/E 11.84) Ctry US

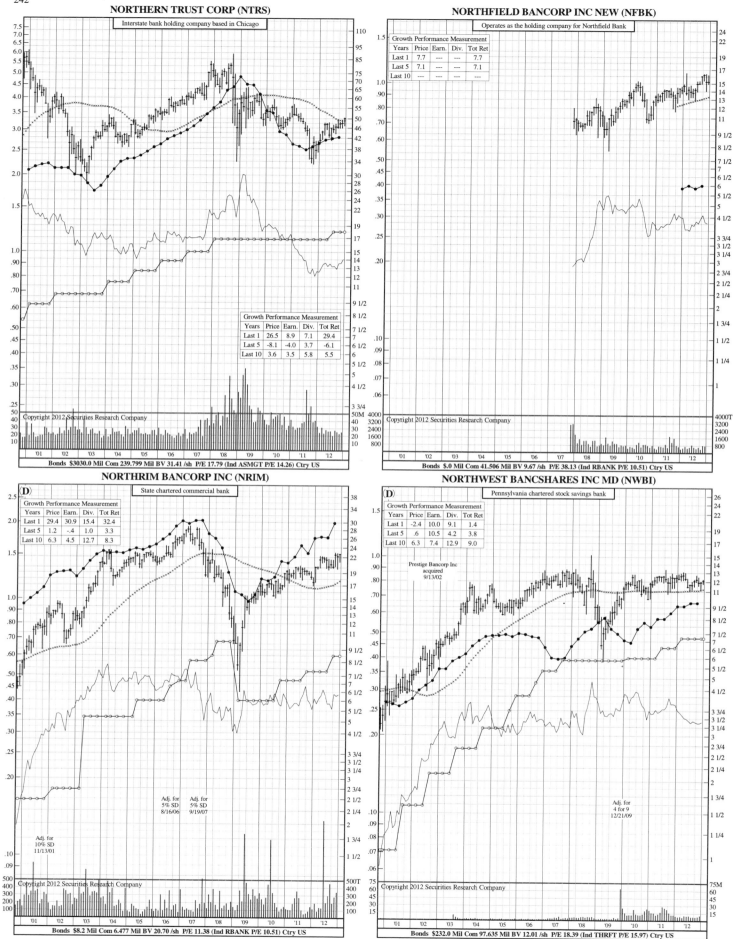

242

NORTHERN TRUST CORP (NTRS)

Interstate bank holding company based in Chicago

Growth Performance Measurement				
Years	Price	Earn.	Div.	Tot Ret
Last 1	26.5	8.9	7.1	29.4
Last 5	-8.1	-4.0	3.7	-6.1
Last 10	3.6	3.5	5.8	5.5

Copyright 2012 Securities Research Company

Bonds $3030.0 Mil Com 239.799 Mil BV 31.41 /sh P/E 17.79 (Ind ASMGT P/E 14.26) Ctry US

NORTHFIELD BANCORP INC NEW (NFBK)

Operates as the holding company for Northfield Bank

Growth Performance Measurement				
Years	Price	Earn.	Div.	Tot Ret
Last 1	7.7	---	---	7.7
Last 5	7.1	---	---	7.1
Last 10	---	---	---	---

Copyright 2012 Securities Research Company

Bonds $.0 Mil Com 41.506 Mil BV 9.67 /sh P/E 38.13 (Ind RBANK P/E 10.51) Ctry US

NORTHRIM BANCORP INC (NRIM)

State chartered commercial bank

Growth Performance Measurement				
Years	Price	Earn.	Div.	Tot Ret
Last 1	29.4	30.9	15.4	32.4
Last 5	1.2	-.4	1.0	3.3
Last 10	6.3	4.5	12.7	8.3

Adj. for
5% SD
8/16/06

Adj. for
5% SD
9/19/07

Adj. for
10% SD
11/13/01

Copyright 2012 Securities Research Company

Bonds $8.2 Mil Com 6.477 Mil BV 20.70 /sh P/E 11.38 (Ind RBANK P/E 10.51) Ctry US

NORTHWEST BANCSHARES INC MD (NWBI)

Pennsylvania chartered stock savings bank

Growth Performance Measurement				
Years	Price	Earn.	Div.	Tot Ret
Last 1	-2.4	10.0	9.1	1.4
Last 5	.6	10.5	4.2	3.8
Last 10	6.3	7.4	12.9	9.0

Prestige Bancorp Inc
acquired
9/13/02

Adj. for
4 for 9
12/21/09

Copyright 2012 Securities Research Company

Bonds $232.0 Mil Com 97.635 Mil BV 12.01 /sh P/E 18.39 (Ind THRFT P/E 15.97) Ctry US

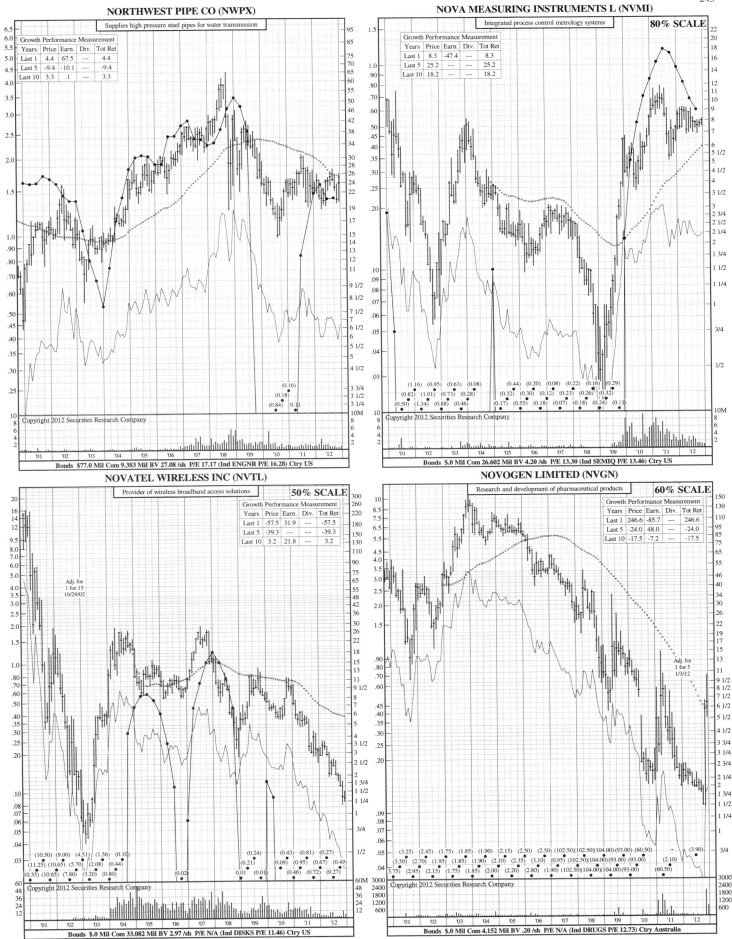

NORTHWEST PIPE CO (NWPX)

Supplies high pressure steel pipes for water transmission

Growth Performance Measurement

Years	Price	Earn.	Div.	Tot Ret
Last 1	4.4	67.5	---	4.4
Last 5	-9.4	-10.1	---	-9.4
Last 10	3.3	.1	---	3.3

(0.16)
(0.18)
(0.84) 0.11

Copyright 2012 Securities Research Company

Bonds $77.0 Mil Com 9.383 Mil BV 27.08 /sh P/E 17.17 (Ind ENGNR P/E 16.28) Ctry US

NOVA MEASURING INSTRUMENTS L (NVMI)

Integrated process control metrology systems

80% SCALE

Growth Performance Measurement

Years	Price	Earn.	Div.	Tot Ret
Last 1	8.3	-47.4	---	8.3
Last 5	25.2	---	---	25.2
Last 10	18.2	---	---	18.2

(1.16) (0.95) (0.63) (0.08)   (0.44) (0.20) (0.08) (0.22) (0.16) (0.29)
(0.82) (1.01) (0.73) (0.28)   (0.32) (0.30) (0.12) (0.23) (0.26) (0.32)
(0.50) (1.34) (0.88) (0.46)   (0.17) (0.55) (0.18) (0.07) (0.18) (0.24) (0.11)

Copyright 2012 Securities Research Company

Bonds $.0 Mil Com 26.602 Mil BV 4.20 /sh P/E 13.30 (Ind SEMIQ P/E 13.46) Ctry US

NOVATEL WIRELESS INC (NVTL)

Provider of wireless broadband access solutions

50% SCALE

Adj. for
1 for 15
10/29/02

Growth Performance Measurement

Years	Price	Earn.	Div.	Tot Ret
Last 1	-57.5	31.9	---	-57.5
Last 5	-39.3	---	---	-39.3
Last 10	3.2	21.8	---	3.2

(10.50) (9.00) (4.51) (1.56) (0.10)   (0.24)   (0.43) (0.81) (0.27)
(11.25) (10.65) (5.70) (2.08) (0.44)   (0.21)   0.09 (0.95) (0.67) (0.49)
(10.35) (10.65) (7.80) (3.20) (0.80)   (0.02)   0.01 0.01 (0.46) (0.72) (0.27)

Copyright 2012 Securities Research Company

Bonds $.0 Mil Com 33.082 Mil BV 2.97 /sh P/E N/A (Ind DISKS P/E 11.46) Ctry US

NOVOGEN LIMITED (NVGN)

Research and development of pharmaceutical products

60% SCALE

Growth Performance Measurement

Years	Price	Earn.	Div.	Tot Ret
Last 1	246.6	-85.7	---	246.6
Last 5	-24.0	48.0	---	-24.0
Last 10	-17.5	-7.2	---	-17.5

Adj. for
1 for 5
1/3/12

(3.25) (2.45) (1.75) (1.85) (1.90) (2.15) (2.50) (2.50) 102.50) 102.50)(104.00) (93.00) (60.50)   (3.90)
(3.50) (2.70) (1.95) (1.85) (1.90) (2.35) (3.10) 0.95) 102.50)(104.00)(93.00) (93.00)   (2.10)
3.75) (2.95) (2.15) (1.75) (1.85) (2.00) (2.10) (2.20) (2.80) (1.90) 102.50)104.00)(93.00)(93.00)   (60.50)
10.35) (10.65) (7.80) (3.20) (0.80)

Copyright 2012 Securities Research Company

Bonds $.0 Mil Com 4.152 Mil BV .20 /sh P/E N/A (Ind DRUGS P/E 12.73) Ctry Australia

NPS PHARMACEUTICALS INC (NPSP)

Research & development of treatments for central nervous system   **90% SCALE**

Growth Performance Measurement				
Years	Price	Earn.	Div.	Tot Ret
Last 1	38.1	---	---	38.1
Last 5	18.9	---	---	18.9
Last 10	-9.7	---	---	-9.7

(1.26) (2.20) (2.79) (3.05) (4.01) (4.63) (4.14) (3.09) (1.32) 0.03   (0.18) (0.37) (0.59) (0.43) (0.08)
(1.05) (1.67) (2.49) (2.86) (3.60) (4.43) (4.54) (3.59) (1.90) 0.02   (0.19) (0.41) (0.63) (0.55) (0.23)
(1.29) (1.43) (2.36) (2.86) (3.44) (4.24) (4.61) (3.83) (2.43) (0.69) (0.31) (0.33) (0.53) (0.59) (0.24) 0.02

Copyright 2012 Securities Research Company

Bonds $1.9 Mil Com 86.647 Mil BV -.54 /sh P/E 455.00 (Ind BIOTK P/E 17.51) Ctry US

NTELOS HLDGS CORP (NTLS)

Supply phone services and Internet access to residents of Virginia

Growth Performance Measurement				
Years	Price	Earn.	Div.	Tot Ret
Last 1	-35.7	-51.2	-25.0	-27.4
Last 5	-26.1	-8.4	7.0	-17.3
Last 10	---	---	---	---

Adj. for
1 for 2
11/1/11

Dist. 1 sh.Lumos Networks Cp
for ea. post sh. NTLS
10/31/11

(1.90)
(2.56)
(2.20) (0.50)

Copyright 2012 Securities Research Company

Bonds $.0 Mil Com 21.750 Mil BV 2.26 /sh P/E 12.37 (Ind TLCEL P/E N/A) Ctry US

NUANCE COMMUNICATIONS INC (NUAN)

Digital imaging and speech recognition software   **75% SCALE**

E

Growth Performance Measurement				
Years	Price	Earn.	Div.	Tot Ret
Last 1	-11.3	26.3	---	-11.3
Last 5	3.6	24.9	---	3.6
Last 10	15.7	21.8	---	15.7

ScanSoft Inc.
prior to
10/18/2005

Nuance Communications
merged 09/16/2005

Transcend Services Inc.
acquired 4/27/12

Ditech Networks
acquired 12/4/12

(0.09)
(0.21)

Copyright 2012 Securities Research Company

Bonds $.0 Mil Com 313.577 Mil BV 8.86 /sh P/E 12.90 (Ind APPSF P/E 24.69) Ctry US

NUPATHE INC (PATH)

Therapeutics for neurological and psychiatric disorders

Growth Performance Measurement				
Years	Price	Earn.	Div.	Tot Ret
Last 1	83.7	-1.2	---	83.7
Last 5	---	---	---	---
Last 10	---	---	---	---

(2.13) (1.76)
8.4 (1.59) (1.65)
(4.39) (1.63) (1.74)

Copyright 2012 Securities Research Company

Bonds $.0 Mil Com 14.755 Mil BV .09 /sh P/E N/A (Ind DRUGS P/E 12.73) Ctry US

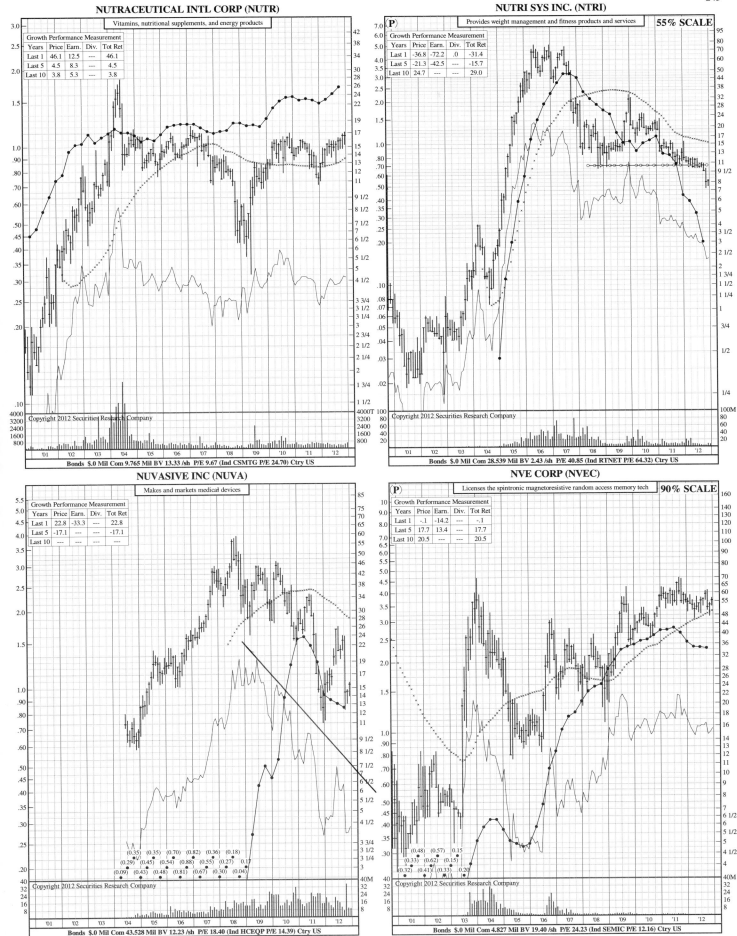

NUTRACEUTICAL INTL CORP (NUTR)

Vitamins, nutritional supplements, and energy products

Growth Performance Measurement

Years	Price	Earn.	Div.	Tot Ret
Last 1	46.1	12.5	---	46.1
Last 5	4.5	8.3	---	4.5
Last 10	3.8	5.3	---	3.8

Copyright 2012 Securities Research Company

Bonds $.0 Mil Com 9.765 Mil BV 13.33 /sh P/E 9.67 (Ind CSMTG P/E 24.70) Ctry US

NUTRI SYS INC. (NTRI)

(P)

Provides weight management and fitness products and services

55% SCALE

Growth Performance Measurement

Years	Price	Earn.	Div.	Tot Ret
Last 1	-36.8	-72.2	.0	-31.4
Last 5	-21.3	-42.5	---	-15.7
Last 10	24.7	---	---	29.0

Copyright 2012 Securities Research Company

Bonds $.0 Mil Com 28.539 Mil BV 2.43 /sh P/E 40.85 (Ind RTNET P/E 64.32) Ctry US

NUVASIVE INC (NUVA)

Makes and markets medical devices

Growth Performance Measurement

Years	Price	Earn.	Div.	Tot Ret
Last 1	22.8	-33.3	---	22.8
Last 5	-17.1	---	---	-17.1
Last 10	---	---	---	---

Copyright 2012 Securities Research Company

(0.35) (0.35) (0.70) (0.82) (0.36) (0.18)
(0.29) (0.45) (0.54) (0.88) (0.55) (0.27) (0.17)
(0.09) (0.43) (0.48) (0.81) (0.67) (0.30) (0.04)

Bonds $.0 Mil Com 43.528 Mil BV 12.23 /sh P/E 18.40 (Ind HCEQP P/E 14.39) Ctry US

NVE CORP (NVEC)

(P)

Licenses the spintronic magnetoresistive random access memory tech

90% SCALE

Growth Performance Measurement

Years	Price	Earn.	Div.	Tot Ret
Last 1	-.1	-14.2	---	-.1
Last 5	17.7	13.4	---	17.7
Last 10	20.5	---	---	20.5

Copyright 2012 Securities Research Company

(0.48) (0.57) 0.15
(0.33) (0.62) 0.15
(0.32) (0.41) (0.33) 0.20

Bonds $.0 Mil Com 4.827 Mil BV 19.40 /sh P/E 24.23 (Ind SEMIC P/E 12.16) Ctry US

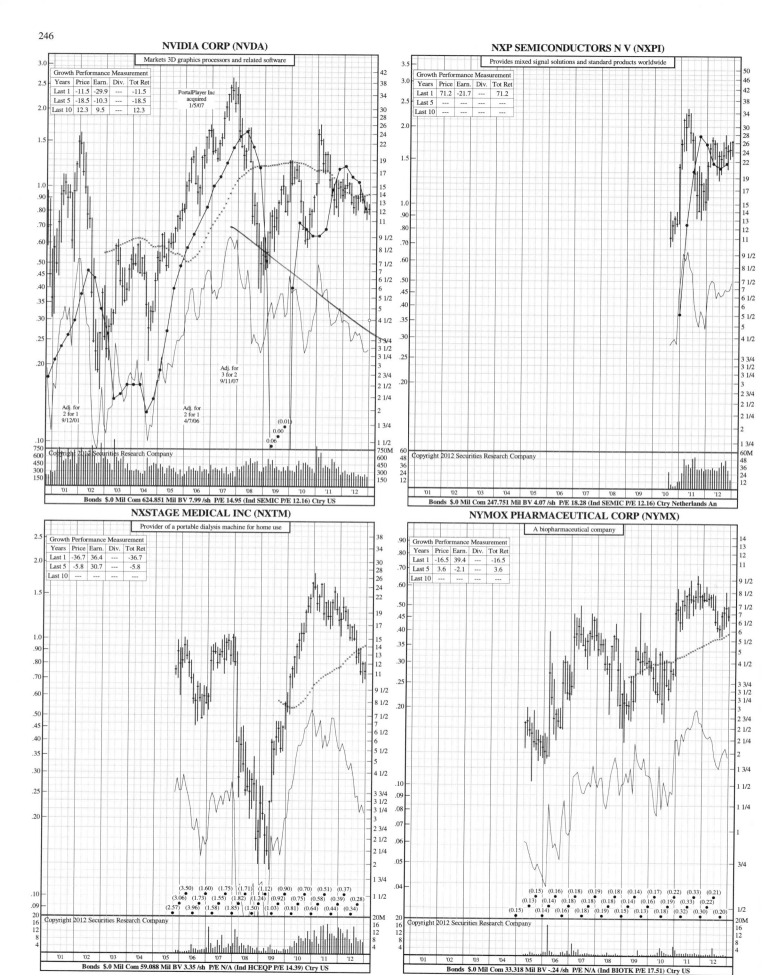

NVIDIA CORP (NVDA)

Markets 3D graphics processors and related software

Growth Performance Measurement				
Years	Price	Earn.	Div.	Tot Ret
Last 1	-11.5	-29.9	---	-11.5
Last 5	-18.5	-10.3	---	-18.5
Last 10	12.3	9.5	---	12.3

PortalPlayer Inc
acquired
1/5/07

Adj. for
3 for 2
9/11/07

Adj. for
2 for 1
9/12/01

Adj. for
2 for 1
4/7/06

(0.01)
0.00
0.06

Copyright 2012 Securities Research Company

Bonds $.0 Mil Com 624.851 Mil BV 7.99 /sh P/E 14.95 (Ind SEMIC P/E 12.16) Ctry US

NXP SEMICONDUCTORS N V (NXPI)

Provides mixed signal solutions and standard products worldwide

Growth Performance Measurement				
Years	Price	Earn.	Div.	Tot Ret
Last 1	71.2	-21.7	---	71.2
Last 5	---	---	---	---
Last 10	---	---	---	---

Copyright 2012 Securities Research Company

Bonds $.0 Mil Com 247.751 Mil BV 4.07 /sh P/E 18.28 (Ind SEMIC P/E 12.16) Ctry Netherlands An

NXSTAGE MEDICAL INC (NXTM)

Provider of a portable dialysis machine for home use

Growth Performance Measurement				
Years	Price	Earn.	Div.	Tot Ret
Last 1	-36.7	36.4	---	-36.7
Last 5	-5.8	30.7	---	-5.8
Last 10	---	---	---	---

(3.50) (1.60) (1.75) (1.71) (1.12) (0.90) (0.70) (0.51) (0.37)
(3.06) (1.73) (1.55) (1.82) (1.24) (0.92) (0.75) (0.58) (0.39) (0.28)
(2.57) (3.96) (1.58) (1.85) (1.50) (1.03) (0.81) (0.64) (0.44) (0.34)

Copyright 2012 Securities Research Company

Bonds $.0 Mil Com 59.088 Mil BV 3.35 /sh P/E N/A (Ind HCEQP P/E 14.39) Ctry US

NYMOX PHARMACEUTICAL CORP (NYMX)

A biopharmaceutical company

Growth Performance Measurement				
Years	Price	Earn.	Div.	Tot Ret
Last 1	-16.5	39.4	---	-16.5
Last 5	3.6	-2.1	---	3.6
Last 10	---	---	---	---

(0.15) (0.16) (0.18) (0.19) (0.18) (0.14) (0.17) (0.22) (0.33) (0.21)
(0.13) (0.14) (0.18) (0.18) (0.18) (0.14) (0.16) (0.19) (0.33) (0.22)
(0.15) (0.14) (0.16) (0.18) (0.19) (0.15) (0.13) (0.18) (0.32) (0.30) (0.20)

Copyright 2012 Securities Research Company

Bonds $.0 Mil Com 33.318 Mil BV -.24 /sh P/E N/A (Ind BIOTK P/E 17.51) Ctry US

O REILLY AUTOMOTIVE INC NEW (ORLY)

Retail stores selling auto parts, tools, and accessories

Growth Performance Measurement

Years	Price	Earn.	Div.	Tot Ret
Last 1	11.8	26.8	---	11.8
Last 5	22.5	22.0	---	22.5
Last 10	21.6	19.9	---	21.6

Adj. for
2 for 1
6/16/05

Copyright 2012 Securities Research Company

Bonds $90.7 Mil Com 114.622 Mil BV 19.46 /sh P/E 19.70 (Ind AUTOR P/E 17.75) Ctry US

OAK RIDGE FINL SVCS INC (BKOR)

Operates as the holding company for Bank of Oak Ridge

Growth Performance Measurement

Years	Price	Earn.	Div.	Tot Ret
Last 1	64.8	-366.7	---	64.8
Last 5	-15.1	---	---	-15.1
Last 10	---	---	---	---

(0.15) (0.69)
(0.13) (0.19)
(0.19) (0.16) (0.70)

Copyright 2012 Securities Research Company

Bonds $.0 Mil Com 1.809 Mil BV .00 /sh P/E N/A (Ind RBANK P/E 10.51) Ctry US

OBAGI MEDICAL PRODUCTS INC (OMPI)

Creates, distributes, and sells topical skin care/restoration prods

Growth Performance Measurement

Years	Price	Earn.	Div.	Tot Ret
Last 1	33.8	3.7	---	33.8
Last 5	-5.8	5.5	---	-5.8
Last 10	---	---	---	---

Copyright 2012 Securities Research Company

Bonds $.0 Mil Com 17.413 Mil BV 3.09 /sh P/E 15.99 (Ind DRUGS P/E 12.73) Ctry US

OCEAN SHORE HLDG CO NEW (OSHC)

Offers banking services to individual, businesses, government entities

Growth Performance Measurement

Years	Price	Earn.	Div.	Tot Ret
Last 1	44.2	6.8	.0	46.6
Last 5	8.4	20.6	---	9.8
Last 10	---	---	---	---

Copyright 2012 Securities Research Company

Bonds $.0 Mil Com 6.933 Mil BV 14.75 /sh P/E 18.73 (Ind THRFT P/E 15.97) Ctry US

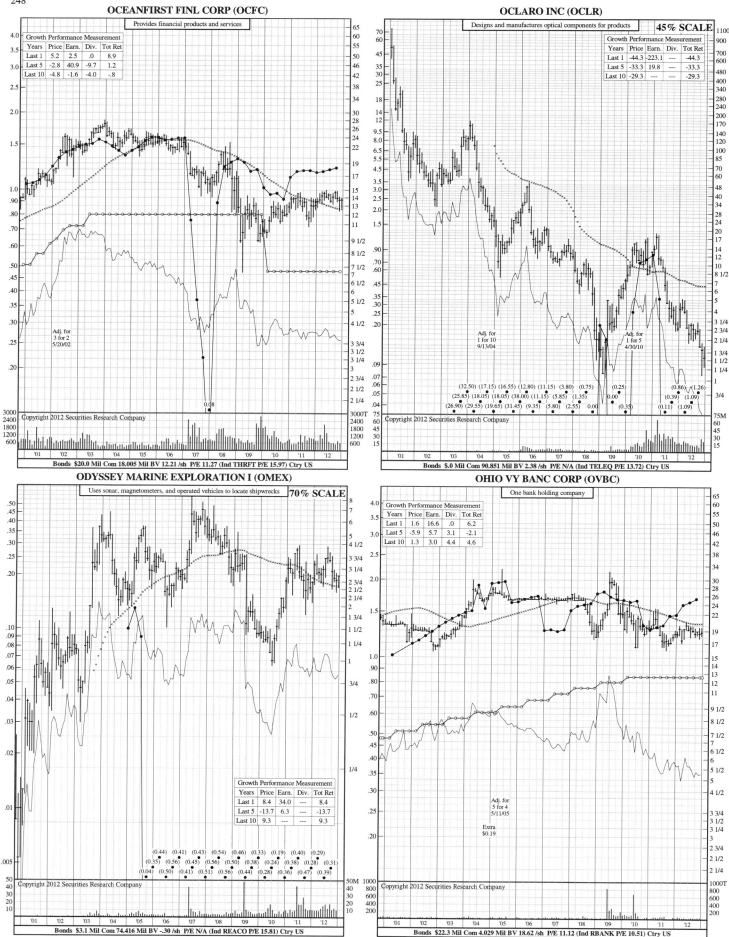

248

OCEANFIRST FINL CORP (OCFC)

Provides financial products and services

Growth Performance Measurement				
Years	Price	Earn.	Div.	Tot Ret
Last 1	5.2	2.5	.0	8.9
Last 5	-2.8	40.9	-9.7	1.2
Last 10	-4.8	-1.6	-4.0	-.8

Adj. for
3 for 2
5/20/02

0.08

Copyright 2012 Securities Research Company

Bonds $20.0 Mil Com 18.005 Mil BV 12.21 /sh P/E 11.27 (Ind THRFT P/E 15.97) Ctry US

OCLARO INC (OCLR)

Designs and manufactures optical components for products

45% SCALE

Growth Performance Measurement				
Years	Price	Earn.	Div.	Tot Ret
Last 1	-44.3	-223.1	---	-44.3
Last 5	-33.3	19.8	---	-33.3
Last 10	-29.3	---	---	-29.3

Adj. for
1 for 10
9/13/04

Adj. for
1 for 5
4/30/10

(32.50) (17.15) (16.55) (12.80) (11.15) (3.80) (0.75)   (0.25)   (0.86) (1.26)
(25.85) (18.05) (18.05) (38.00) (11.15) (5.85) (1.35)   0.00   (0.39) (1.09)
(26.90) (29.55) (19.65) (31.45) (9.35) (5.80) (2.55) 0.00   (0.35)   (0.11) (1.09)

Copyright 2012 Securities Research Company

Bonds $.0 Mil Com 90.851 Mil BV 2.38 /sh P/E N/A (Ind TELEQ P/E 13.72) Ctry US

ODYSSEY MARINE EXPLORATION I (OMEX)

Uses sonar, magnetometers, and operated vehicles to locate shipwrecks

70% SCALE

(0.44) (0.41) (0.43) (0.54) (0.46) (0.33) (0.19) (0.40) (0.29)
(0.35) (0.56) (0.45) (0.56) (0.50) (0.38) (0.24) (0.38) (0.28) (0.31)
(0.04) (0.50) (0.41) (0.51) (0.56) (0.44) (0.28) (0.36) (0.47) (0.39)

Growth Performance Measurement				
Years	Price	Earn.	Div.	Tot Ret
Last 1	8.4	34.0	---	8.4
Last 5	-13.7	6.3	---	-13.7
Last 10	9.3	---	---	9.3

Copyright 2012 Securities Research Company

Bonds $3.1 Mil Com 74.416 Mil BV -.30 /sh P/E N/A (Ind REACO P/E 15.81) Ctry US

OHIO VY BANC CORP (OVBC)

One bank holding company

Growth Performance Measurement				
Years	Price	Earn.	Div.	Tot Ret
Last 1	1.6	16.6	.0	6.2
Last 5	-5.9	5.7	3.1	-2.1
Last 10	1.3	3.0	4.4	4.6

Adj. for
5 for 4
5/11/05

Extra
$0.19

Copyright 2012 Securities Research Company

Bonds $22.3 Mil Com 4.029 Mil BV 18.62 /sh P/E 11.12 (Ind RBANK P/E 10.51) Ctry US

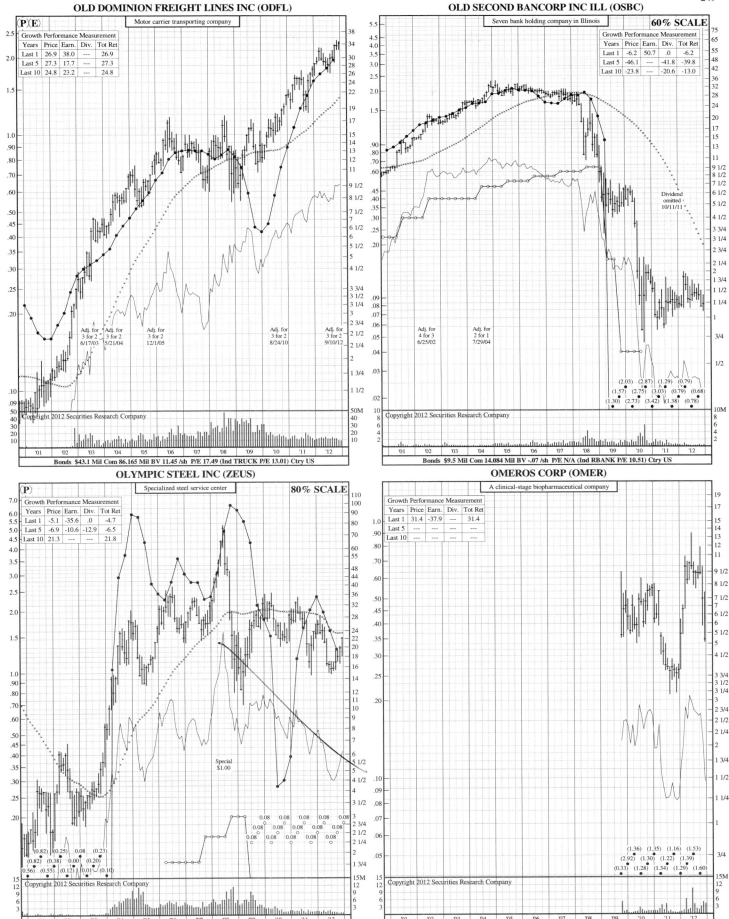

OLD DOMINION FREIGHT LINES INC (ODFL)

Motor carrier transporting company

Growth Performance Measurement				
Years	Price	Earn.	Div.	Tot Ret
Last 1	26.9	38.0	---	26.9
Last 5	27.3	17.7	---	27.3
Last 10	24.8	23.2	---	24.8

Adj. for 3 for 2 6/17/03
Adj. for 3 for 2 5/21/04
Adj. for 3 for 2 12/1/05
Adj. for 3 for 2 8/24/10
Adj. for 3 for 2 9/10/12

Copyright 2012 Securities Research Company

Bonds $43.1 Mil Com 86.165 Mil BV 11.45 /sh P/E 17.49 (Ind TRUCK P/E 13.01) Ctry US

OLD SECOND BANCORP INC ILL (OSBC)

Seven bank holding company in Illinois

60% SCALE

Growth Performance Measurement				
Years	Price	Earn.	Div.	Tot Ret
Last 1	-6.2	50.7	.0	-6.2
Last 5	-46.1	---	-41.8	-39.8
Last 10	-23.8	---	-20.6	-13.0

Dividend omitted 10/11/11

Adj. for 4 for 3 6/25/02
Adj. for 2 for 1 7/29/04

(2.03) (2.87) (1.29) (0.79)
(1.57) (2.75) (3.03) (0.79) (0.68)
(1.30) (2.73) (3.42) (1.38) (0.78)

Copyright 2012 Securities Research Company

Bonds $9.5 Mil Com 14.084 Mil BV -.07 /sh P/E N/A (Ind RBANK P/E 10.51) Ctry US

OLYMPIC STEEL INC (ZEUS)

Specialized steel service center

80% SCALE

Growth Performance Measurement				
Years	Price	Earn.	Div.	Tot Ret
Last 1	-5.1	-35.6	.0	-4.7
Last 5	-6.9	-10.6	-12.9	-6.5
Last 10	21.3	---	---	21.8

Special $1.00

0.08 0.08 0.08 0.08 0.08
0.08 0.08 0.08 0.08 0.08
0.08 0.08 0.08 0.08 0.08

(0.82) (0.25) 0.08 (0.23)
(0.82) (0.38) 0.00 (0.20)
(0.56) (0.55) (0.12) 0.01 (0.10)

Copyright 2012 Securities Research Company

Bonds $87.4 Mil Com 10.918 Mil BV 27.46 /sh P/E 17.03 (Ind STEEL P/E 15.22) Ctry US

OMEROS CORP (OMER)

A clinical-stage biopharmaceutical company

Growth Performance Measurement				
Years	Price	Earn.	Div.	Tot Ret
Last 1	31.4	-37.9	---	31.4
Last 5	---	---	---	---
Last 10	---	---	---	---

(1.36) (1.35) (1.16) (1.53)
(2.92) (1.30) (1.22) (1.39)
(0.33) (1.28) (1.34) (1.29) (1.60)

Copyright 2012 Securities Research Company

Bonds $.0 Mil Com 25.887 Mil BV -.03 /sh P/E N/A (Ind DRUGS P/E 12.73) Ctry US

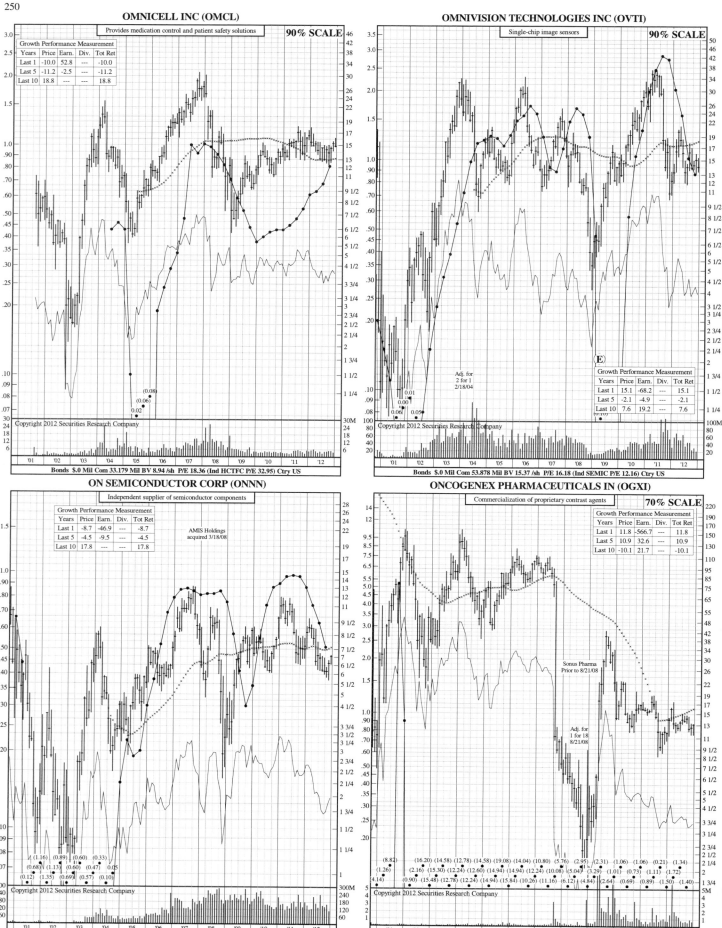

250

OMNICELL INC (OMCL)

Provides medication control and patient safety solutions

90% SCALE

Growth Performance Measurement				
Years	Price	Earn.	Div.	Tot Ret
Last 1	-10.0	52.8	---	-10.0
Last 5	-11.2	-2.5	---	-11.2
Last 10	18.8	---	---	18.8

(0.08)
(0.06)
0.02

Copyright 2012 Securities Research Company

Bonds $.0 Mil Com 33.179 Mil BV 8.94 /sh P/E 18.36 (Ind HCTFC P/E 32.95) Ctry US

OMNIVISION TECHNOLOGIES INC (OVTI)

Single-chip image sensors

90% SCALE

Adj. for
2 for 1
2/18/04

0.01
0.00
0.06 0.05

(E)

Growth Performance Measurement				
Years	Price	Earn.	Div.	Tot Ret
Last 1	15.1	-68.2	---	15.1
Last 5	-2.1	-4.9	---	-2.1
Last 10	7.6	19.2	---	7.6

Copyright 2012 Securities Research Company

Bonds $.0 Mil Com 53.878 Mil BV 15.37 /sh P/E 16.18 (Ind SEMIC P/E 12.16) Ctry US

ON SEMICONDUCTOR CORP (ONNN)

Independent supplier of semiconductor components

Growth Performance Measurement				
Years	Price	Earn.	Div.	Tot Ret
Last 1	-8.7	-46.9	---	-8.7
Last 5	-4.5	-9.5	---	-4.5
Last 10	17.8	---	---	17.8

AMIS Holdings
acquired 3/18/08

(1.16) (0.89) (0.60) (0.33)
(0.68) (1.13) (0.60) (0.47) 0.05
(0.12) (1.35) (0.69) (0.57) (0.10)

Copyright 2012 Securities Research Company

Bonds $1295.3 Mil Com 448.294 Mil BV 3.35 /sh P/E 13.82 (Ind SEMIC P/E 12.16) Ctry US

ONCOGENEX PHARMACEUTICALS IN (OGXI)

Commercialization of proprietary contrast agents

70% SCALE

Growth Performance Measurement				
Years	Price	Earn.	Div.	Tot Ret
Last 1	11.8	-566.7	---	11.8
Last 5	10.9	32.6	---	10.9
Last 10	-10.1	21.7	---	-10.1

Sonus Pharma
Prior to 8/21/08

Adj. for
1 for 18
8/21/08

(8.82) (16.20) (14.58) (12.78) (14.58) (19.08) (14.04) (10.80) (5.76) (2.95) (2.31) (1.06) (1.06) (0.21) (1.34)
(1.26) (2.16) (15.30) (12.24) (12.60) (14.94) (14.94) (12.24) (10.08) (5.04) (3.29) (1.01) (0.73) (1.11) (1.72)
(4.14) (0.90) (15.48) (12.78) (12.24) (14.94) (15.84) (14.26) (11.16) (6.12) (4.84) (2.64) (0.69) (0.89) (1.50) (1.40)

Copyright 2012 Securities Research Company

Bonds $.0 Mil Com 14.657 Mil BV 4.76 /sh P/E N/A (Ind BIOTK P/E 17.51) Ctry US

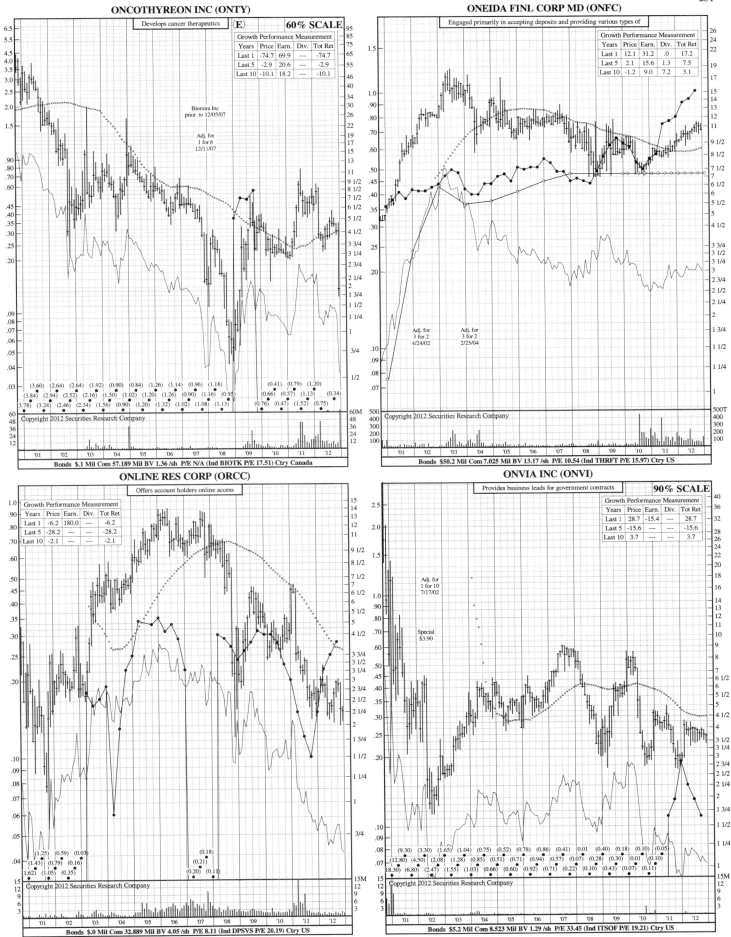

ONCOTHYREON INC (ONTY)

Develops cancer therapeutics   (E)   **60% SCALE**

Growth Performance Measurement				
Years	Price	Earn.	Div.	Tot Ret
Last 1	-74.7	69.9	---	-74.7
Last 5	-2.9	20.6	---	-2.9
Last 10	-10.1	18.2	---	-10.1

Biomira Inc
prior to 12/05/07

Adj. for
1 for 6
12/11/07

(3.60) (2.64) (2.64) (1.92) (0.90) (0.84) (1.26) (1.14) (0.96) (1.18)   (0.41) (0.79) (1.20)
(3.84) (2.94) (2.52) (2.16) (1.50) (1.02) (1.02) (1.26) (0.90) (1.16) (0.95)   (0.66) (0.57) (1.13) (0.34)
(3.78) (3.24) (2.46) (2.34) (1.56) (0.90) (1.20) (1.32) (1.02) (1.08) (1.13)   (0.76) (0.47) (1.52) (0.75)

Copyright 2012 Securities Research Company

Bonds $.1 Mil Com 57.189 Mil BV 1.36 /sh P/E N/A (Ind BIOTK P/E 17.51) Ctry Canada

ONEIDA FINL CORP MD (ONFC)

Engaged primarily in accepting deposits and providing various types of

Growth Performance Measurement				
Years	Price	Earn.	Div.	Tot Ret
Last 1	12.1	31.2	.0	17.2
Last 5	2.1	15.6	1.3	7.5
Last 10	-1.2	9.0	7.2	3.1

Adj. for
3 for 2
4/24/02

Adj. for
3 for 2
2/25/04

Copyright 2012 Securities Research Company

Bonds $50.2 Mil Com 7.025 Mil BV 13.17 /sh P/E 10.54 (Ind THRFT P/E 15.97) Ctry US

ONLINE RES CORP (ORCC)

Offers account holders online access

Growth Performance Measurement				
Years	Price	Earn.	Div.	Tot Ret
Last 1	-6.2	180.0	---	-6.2
Last 5	-28.2	---	---	-28.2
Last 10	-2.1	---	---	-2.1

(1.25) (0.59) (0.03)   (0.18)
(1.43) (0.79) (0.16)   (0.21)
(1.62) (1.05) (0.35)   (0.20) (0.11)

Copyright 2012 Securities Research Company

Bonds $.0 Mil Com 32.889 Mil BV 4.05 /sh P/E 8.11 (Ind DPSVS P/E 20.19) Ctry US

ONVIA INC (ONVI)

Provides business leads for government contracts   **90% SCALE**

Growth Performance Measurement				
Years	Price	Earn.	Div.	Tot Ret
Last 1	28.7	-15.4	---	28.7
Last 5	-15.6	---	---	-15.6
Last 10	3.7	---	---	3.7

Adj. for
1 for 10
7/17/02

Special
$3.90

(9.30) (3.30) (1.65) (1.04) (0.75) (0.52) (0.78) (0.86) (0.41) (0.01) (0.40) (0.18) (0.10) (0.05)
(12.80) (4.50) (1.28) (0.85) (0.71) (0.94) (0.57) (0.07) (0.28) (0.01) (0.10)
(18.30) (6.80) (2.47) (1.55) (1.03) (0.66) (0.60) (0.92) (0.71) (0.07) (0.10) (0.43) (0.07) (0.11)

Copyright 2012 Securities Research Company

Bonds $5.2 Mil Com 8.523 Mil BV 1.29 /sh P/E 33.45 (Ind ITSOF P/E 19.21) Ctry US

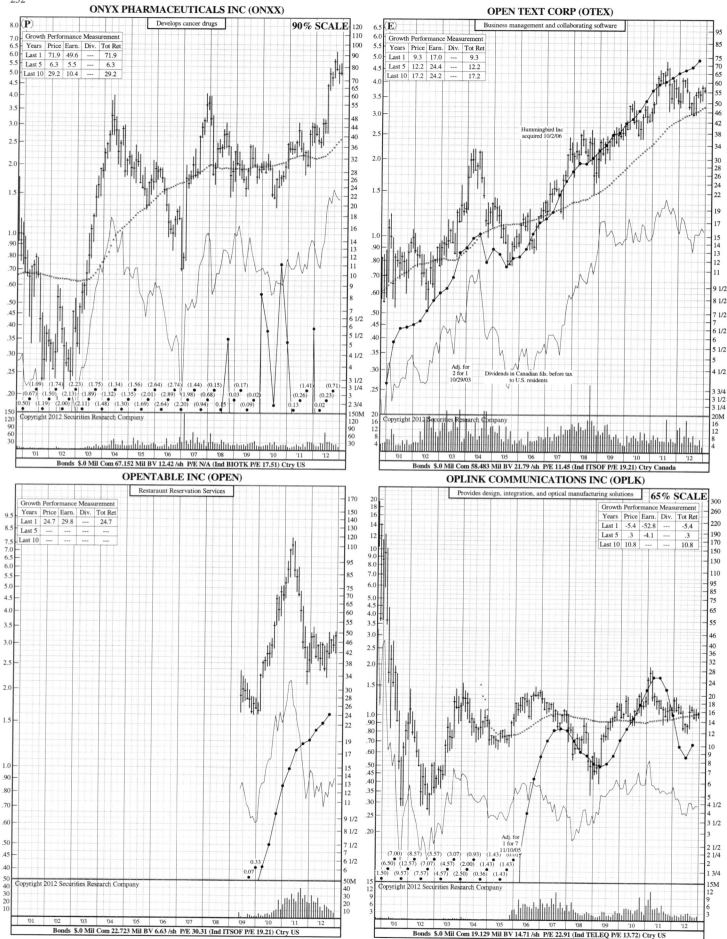

252

ONYX PHARMACEUTICALS INC (ONXX)

Develops cancer drugs

90% SCALE

Growth Performance Measurement

Years	Price	Earn.	Div.	Tot Ret
Last 1	71.9	49.6	---	71.9
Last 5	6.3	5.5	---	6.3
Last 10	29.2	10.4	---	29.2

Copyright 2012 Securities Research Company

Bonds $.0 Mil Com 67.152 Mil BV 12.42 /sh P/E N/A (Ind BIOTK P/E 17.51) Ctry US

OPEN TEXT CORP (OTEX)

Business management and collaborating software

Growth Performance Measurement

Years	Price	Earn.	Div.	Tot Ret
Last 1	9.3	17.0	---	9.3
Last 5	12.2	24.4	---	12.2
Last 10	17.2	24.2	---	17.2

Hummingbird Inc
acquired 10/2/06

Adj. for
2 for 1
10/29/03

Dividends in Canadian fds. before tax
to U.S. residents

Copyright 2012 Securities Research Company

Bonds $.0 Mil Com 58.483 Mil BV 21.79 /sh P/E 11.45 (Ind ITSOF P/E 19.21) Ctry Canada

OPENTABLE INC (OPEN)

Restaraunt Reservation Services

Growth Performance Measurement

Years	Price	Earn.	Div.	Tot Ret
Last 1	24.7	29.8	---	24.7
Last 5	---	---	---	---
Last 10	---	---	---	---

Copyright 2012 Securities Research Company

Bonds $.0 Mil Com 22.723 Mil BV 6.63 /sh P/E 30.31 (Ind ITSOF P/E 19.21) Ctry US

OPLINK COMMUNICATIONS INC (OPLK)

Provides design, integration, and optical manufacturing solutions

65% SCALE

Growth Performance Measurement

Years	Price	Earn.	Div.	Tot Ret
Last 1	-5.4	-52.8	---	-5.4
Last 5	.3	-4.1	---	.3
Last 10	10.8	---	---	10.8

Adj. for
1 for 7
11/10/05

Copyright 2012 Securities Research Company

Bonds $.0 Mil Com 19.129 Mil BV 14.71 /sh P/E 22.91 (Ind TELEQ P/E 13.72) Ctry US

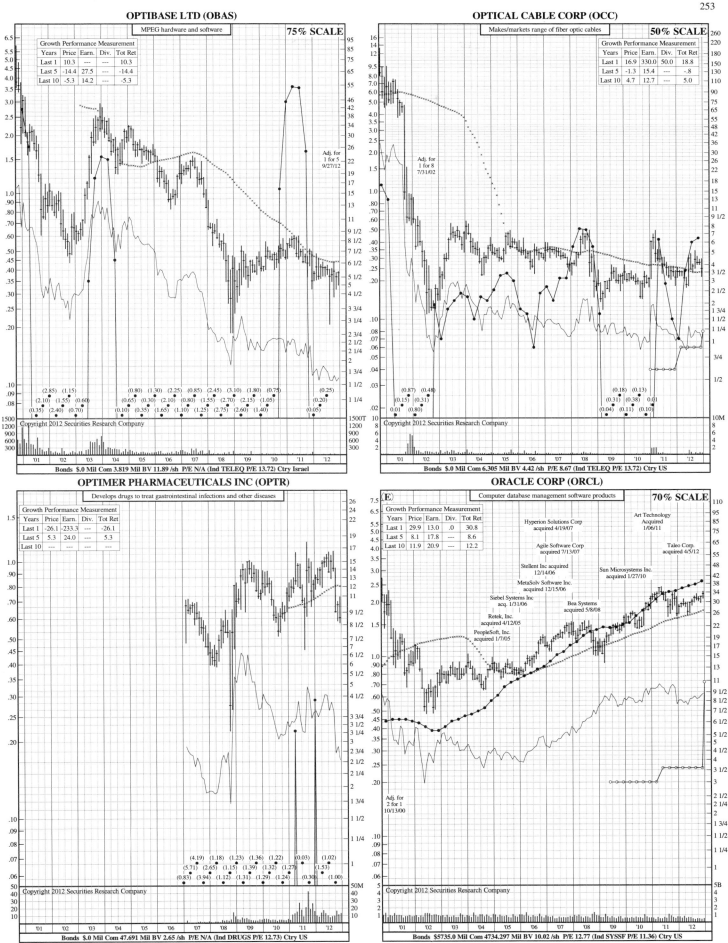

OPTIBASE LTD (OBAS)

MPEG hardware and software

75% SCALE

Growth Performance Measurement				
Years	Price	Earn.	Div.	Tot Ret
Last 1	10.3	---	---	10.3
Last 5	-14.4	27.5	---	-14.4
Last 10	-5.3	14.2	---	-5.3

Adj. for
1 for 5
9/27/12

(2.85) (1.15)
(2.10) (1.55) (0.60)
(0.35) (2.40) (0.70)
(0.80) (1.30) (2.25) (0.85) (2.45) (3.10) (1.80) (0.75)
(0.65) (0.30) (2.10) (0.80) (1.55) (2.70) (2.15) (1.05)
(0.10) (0.35) (1.65) (1.10) (1.25) (2.75) (2.60) (1.40)
(0.20) (0.25)
(0.05)

Copyright 2012 Securities Research Company

Bonds $.0 Mil Com 3.819 Mil BV 11.89 /sh P/E N/A (Ind TELEQ P/E 13.72) Ctry Israel

OPTICAL CABLE CORP (OCC)

Makes/markets range of fiber optic cables

50% SCALE

Growth Performance Measurement				
Years	Price	Earn.	Div.	Tot Ret
Last 1	16.9	330.0	50.0	18.8
Last 5	-1.3	15.4	---	-.8
Last 10	4.7	12.7	---	5.0

Adj. for
1 for 8
7/31/02

(0.87) (0.48)
(0.15) (0.31)
(0.01) (0.80)
(0.18) (0.13)
(0.31) (0.38) (0.01)
(0.04) (0.11) (0.10)

Copyright 2012 Securities Research Company

Bonds $.0 Mil Com 6.305 Mil BV 4.42 /sh P/E 8.67 (Ind TELEQ P/E 13.72) Ctry US

OPTIMER PHARMACEUTICALS INC (OPTR)

Develops drugs to treat gastrointestinal infections and other diseases

Growth Performance Measurement				
Years	Price	Earn.	Div.	Tot Ret
Last 1	-26.1	-233.3	---	-26.1
Last 5	5.3	24.0	---	5.3
Last 10	---	---	---	---

(4.19) (1.18) (1.23) (1.36) (1.22) (0.03) (1.02)
(5.71) (2.65) (1.15) (1.39) (1.32) (1.27) (1.53)
(0.83) (3.94) (1.12) (1.31) (1.29) (1.24) (0.30) (1.00)

Copyright 2012 Securities Research Company

Bonds $.0 Mil Com 47.691 Mil BV 2.65 /sh P/E N/A (Ind DRUGS P/E 12.73) Ctry US

ORACLE CORP (ORCL)

Computer database management software products

70% SCALE

(E)

Growth Performance Measurement				
Years	Price	Earn.	Div.	Tot Ret
Last 1	29.9	13.0	.0	30.8
Last 5	8.1	17.8	---	8.6
Last 10	11.9	20.9	---	12.2

Hyperion Solutions Corp
acquired 4/19/07

Art Technology
Acquired
1/06/11

Agile Software Corp
acquired 7/13/07

Taleo Corp.
acquired 4/5/12

Stellent Inc acquired
12/14/06

Sun Microsystems Inc.
acquired 1/27/10

MetaSolv Software Inc.
acquired 12/15/06

Siebel Systems Inc
acq. 1/31/06

Bea Systems
acquired 5/8/08

Retek, Inc.
acquired 4/12/05

PeopleSoft, Inc.
acquired 1/7/05

Adj. for
2 for 1
10/13/00

Copyright 2012 Securities Research Company

Bonds $5735.0 Mil Com 4734.297 Mil BV 10.02 /sh P/E 12.77 (Ind SYSSF P/E 11.36) Ctry US

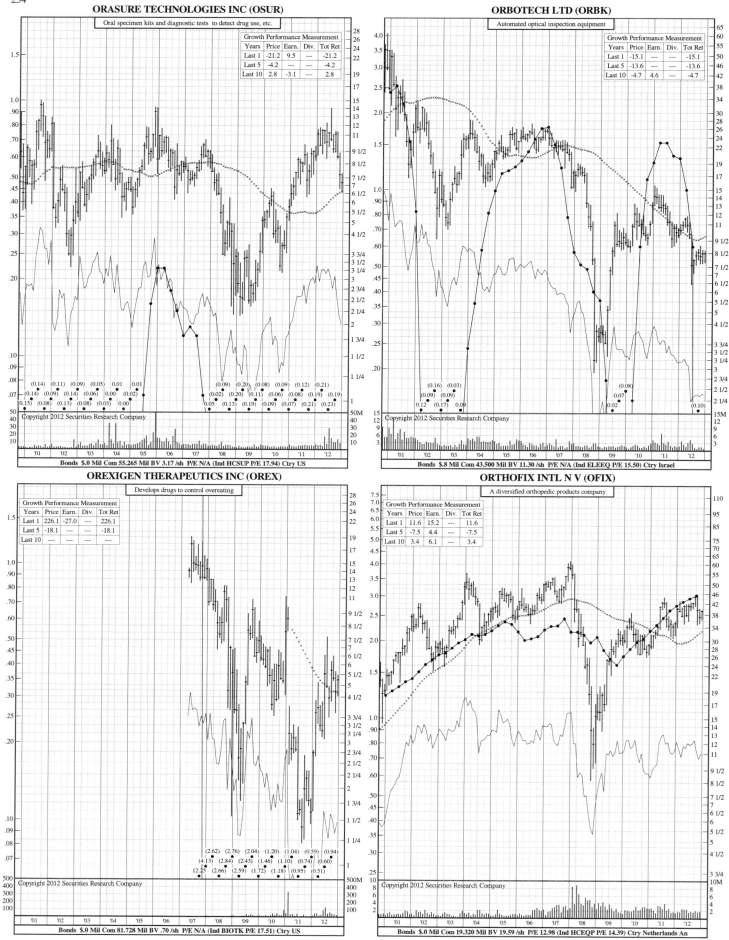

254

ORASURE TECHNOLOGIES INC (OSUR)
Oral specimen kits and diagnostic tests to detect drug use, etc.

Growth Performance Measurement

Years	Price	Earn.	Div.	Tot Ret
Last 1	-21.2	9.5	---	-21.2
Last 5	-4.2	---	---	-4.2
Last 10	2.8	-3.1	---	2.8

(0.14) (0.11) (0.09) (0.05) 0.01 0.01 (0.09) (0.20) (0.08) (0.09) (0.12) (0.21)
(0.14) (0.14) (0.06) 0.00 (0.02) (0.02) (0.20) (0.11) (0.06) (0.08) (0.19) (0.19)
(0.15) (0.08) (0.13) (0.08) (0.03) 0.00 0.05 (0.13) (0.19) (0.09) (0.07) (0.21) (0.23)

Copyright 2012 Securities Research Company

'01 '02 '03 '04 '05 '06 '07 '08 '09 '10 '11 '12

Bonds $.0 Mil Com 55.265 Mil BV 3.17 /sh P/E N/A (Ind HCSUP P/E 17.94) Ctry US

ORBOTECH LTD (ORBK)
Automated optical inspection equipment

Growth Performance Measurement

Years	Price	Earn.	Div.	Tot Ret
Last 1	-15.1	---	---	-15.1
Last 5	-13.6	---	---	-13.6
Last 10	-4.7	4.6	---	-4.7

(0.16) (0.03) (0.08)
0.07
0.12 (0.17) 0.09 0.02 (0.10)

Copyright 2012 Securities Research Company

'01 '02 '03 '04 '05 '06 '07 '08 '09 '10 '11 '12

Bonds $.8 Mil Com 43.500 Mil BV 11.30 /sh P/E N/A (Ind ELEEQ P/E 15.50) Ctry Israel

OREXIGEN THERAPEUTICS INC (OREX)
Develops drugs to control overeating

Growth Performance Measurement

Years	Price	Earn.	Div.	Tot Ret
Last 1	226.1	-27.0	---	226.1
Last 5	-18.1	---	---	-18.1
Last 10	---	---	---	---

(2.62) (2.76) (2.04) (1.20) (1.04) (0.59) (0.94)
(4.13) (2.84) (2.43) (1.46) (1.10) (0.74) (0.60)
12.25 (2.66) (2.59) (1.72) (1.18) (0.95) (0.51)

Copyright 2012 Securities Research Company

'01 '02 '03 '04 '05 '06 '07 '08 '09 '10 '11 '12

Bonds $.0 Mil Com 81.728 Mil BV .70 /sh P/E N/A (Ind BIOTK P/E 17.51) Ctry US

ORTHOFIX INTL N V (OFIX)
A diversified orthopedic products company

Growth Performance Measurement

Years	Price	Earn.	Div.	Tot Ret
Last 1	11.6	15.2	---	11.6
Last 5	-7.5	4.4	---	-7.5
Last 10	3.4	6.1	---	3.4

Copyright 2012 Securities Research Company

'01 '02 '03 '04 '05 '06 '07 '08 '09 '10 '11 '12

Bonds $.0 Mil Com 19.320 Mil BV 19.59 /sh P/E 12.98 (Ind HCEQP P/E 14.39) Ctry Netherlands An

255

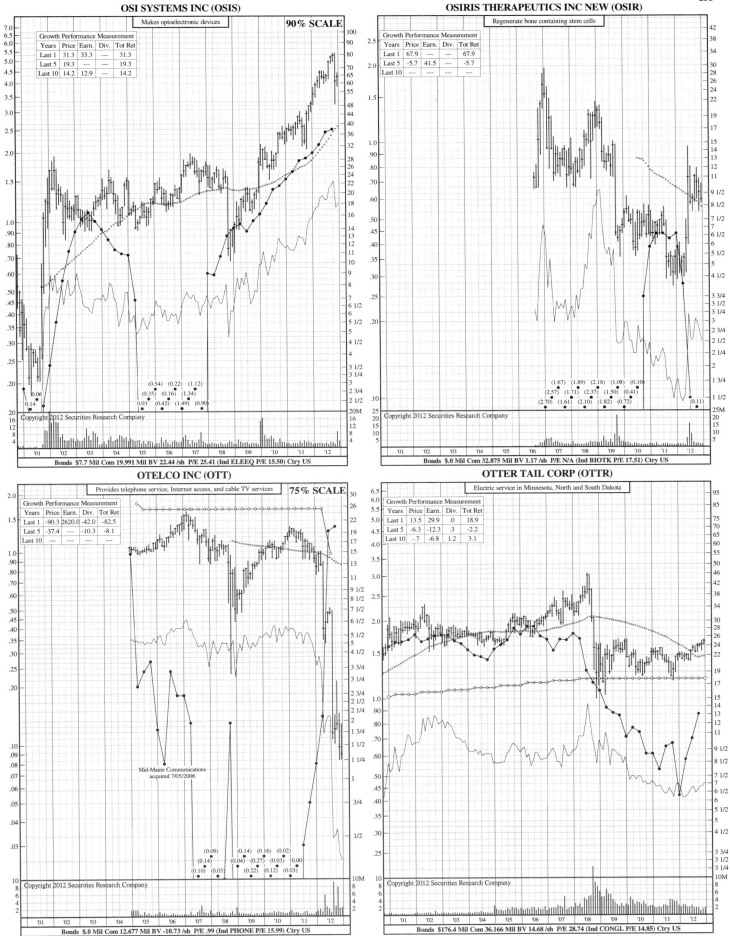

OSI SYSTEMS INC (OSIS)
Makes optoelectronic devices — 90% SCALE

Growth Performance Measurement

Years	Price	Earn.	Div.	Tot Ret
Last 1	31.3	33.3	---	31.3
Last 5	19.3	---	---	19.3
Last 10	14.2	12.9	---	14.2

(0.54) (0.22) (1.12)
(0.35) (0.16) (1.34)
0.06
0.14
0.03 (0.42) (1.49) (0.90)

Copyright 2012 Securities Research Company

Bonds $7.7 Mil Com 19.991 Mil BV 22.44 /sh P/E 25.41 (Ind ELEEQ P/E 15.50) Ctry US

OSIRIS THERAPEUTICS INC NEW (OSIR)
Regenerate bone containing stem cells

Growth Performance Measurement

Years	Price	Earn.	Div.	Tot Ret
Last 1	67.9	---	---	67.9
Last 5	-5.7	41.5	---	-5.7
Last 10	---	---	---	---

(1.67) (1.89) (2.18) (1.08) (0.10)
(2.57) (1.71) (2.37) (1.50) (0.41)
(2.70) (1.61) (2.10) (1.82) (0.72) (0.11)

Copyright 2012 Securities Research Company

Bonds $.0 Mil Com 32.875 Mil BV 1.17 /sh P/E N/A (Ind BIOTK P/E 17.51) Ctry US

OTELCO INC (OTT)
Provides telephone service, Internet access, and cable TV services — 75% SCALE

Growth Performance Measurement

Years	Price	Earn.	Div.	Tot Ret
Last 1	-90.3	2620.0	-42.0	-82.5
Last 5	-37.4	---	-10.3	-8.1
Last 10	---	---	---	---

Mid-Maine Communications
acquired 7/05/2006

(0.09)
(0.14) (0.14) (0.16) (0.02)
(0.10) (0.04) (0.27) (0.03) 0.00
(0.03) (0.22) (0.12) (0.03)

Copyright 2012 Securities Research Company

Bonds $.0 Mil Com 12.677 Mil BV -10.73 /sh P/E .99 (Ind PHONE P/E 15.99) Ctry US

OTTER TAIL CORP (OTTR)
Electric service in Minnesota, North and South Dakota

Growth Performance Measurement

Years	Price	Earn.	Div.	Tot Ret
Last 1	13.5	29.9	.0	18.9
Last 5	-6.3	-12.3	.3	-2.2
Last 10	-.7	-6.8	1.2	3.1

Copyright 2012 Securities Research Company

Bonds $176.4 Mil Com 36.166 Mil BV 14.68 /sh P/E 28.74 (Ind CONGL P/E 14.85) Ctry US

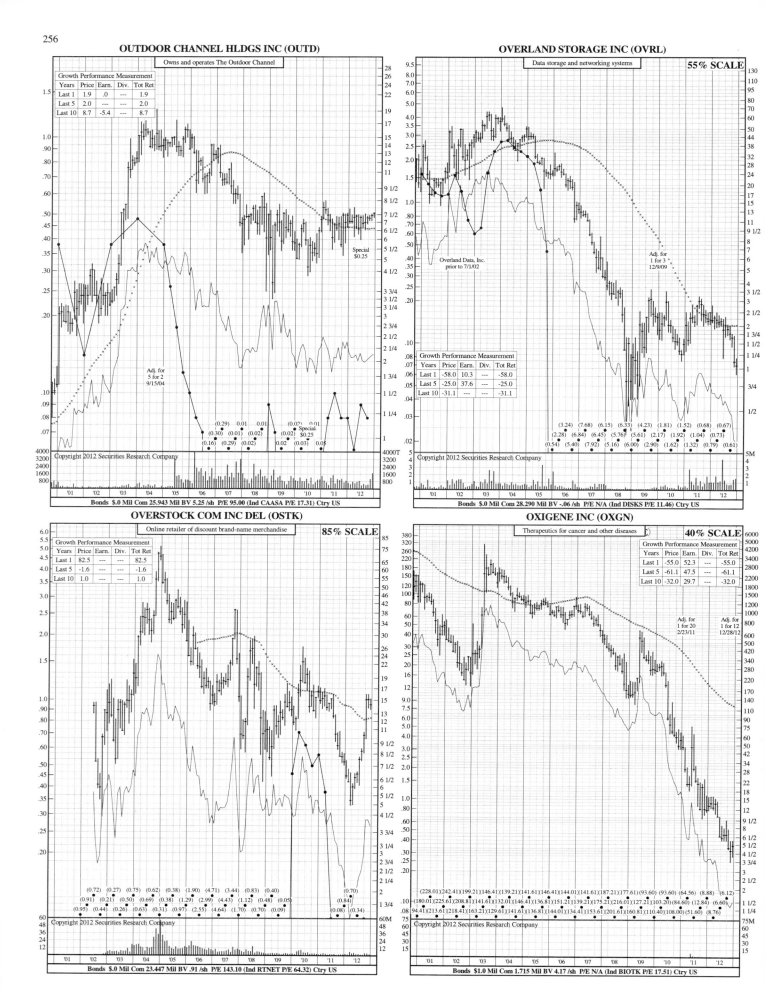

OUTDOOR CHANNEL HLDGS INC (OUTD)

Owns and operates The Outdoor Channel

Growth Performance Measurement				
Years	Price	Earn.	Div.	Tot Ret
Last 1	1.9	.0	---	1.9
Last 5	2.0	---	---	2.0
Last 10	8.7	-5.4	---	8.7

Special $0.25

Adj. for 5 for 2 9/15/04

(0.29) .01 .01
(0.30) (0.01) (0.02)
(0.16) (0.29) (0.02)

(0.02) .01
(0.02) Special $0.25
.02 (0.03) .05

Copyright 2012 Securities Research Company

Bonds $.0 Mil Com 25.943 Mil BV 5.25 /sh P/E 95.00 (Ind CAASA P/E 17.31) Ctry US

OVERLAND STORAGE INC (OVRL)

Data storage and networking systems

55% SCALE

Overland Data, Inc. prior to 7/1/02

Adj. for 1 for 3 12/9/09

Growth Performance Measurement				
Years	Price	Earn.	Div.	Tot Ret
Last 1	-58.0	10.3	---	-58.0
Last 5	-25.0	37.6	---	-25.0
Last 10	-31.1	---	---	-31.1

(3.24) (7.68) (6.15) (6.33) (4.23) (1.81) (1.52) (0.68) (0.67)
(2.28) (6.84) (6.45) (5.76) (5.61) (2.17) (1.92) (1.04) (0.73)
(0.54) (5.40) (7.92) (5.16) (6.00) (2.90) (1.62) (1.32) (0.79) (0.61)

Copyright 2012 Securities Research Company

Bonds $.0 Mil Com 28.290 Mil BV -.06 /sh P/E N/A (Ind DISKS P/E 11.46) Ctry US

OVERSTOCK COM INC DEL (OSTK)

Online retailer of discount brand-name merchandise

85% SCALE

Growth Performance Measurement				
Years	Price	Earn.	Div.	Tot Ret
Last 1	82.5	---	---	82.5
Last 5	-1.6	---	---	-1.6
Last 10	1.0	---	---	1.0

(0.72) (0.27) (0.75) (0.62) (0.38) (1.90) (4.71) (3.44) (0.83) (0.40)   (0.70)
(0.91) (0.21) (0.50) (0.69) (1.29) (2.99) (1.12) (0.48) (0.05)   (0.84)
(0.95) (0.44) (0.26) (0.63) (0.31) (0.97) (2.55) (4.64) (1.70) (0.70) (0.09)   (0.08) (0.34)

Copyright 2012 Securities Research Company

Bonds $.0 Mil Com 23.447 Mil BV .91 /sh P/E 143.10 (Ind RTNET P/E 64.32) Ctry US

OXIGENE INC (OXGN)

Therapeutics for cancer and other diseases

40% SCALE

Growth Performance Measurement				
Years	Price	Earn.	Div.	Tot Ret
Last 1	-55.0	52.3	---	-55.0
Last 5	-61.1	47.5	---	-61.1
Last 10	-32.0	29.7	---	-32.0

Adj. for 1 for 20 2/23/11

Adj. for 1 for 12 12/28/12

(228.01)(242.41)(199.21)(146.41)(139.21)(141.61)(146.41)(144.01)(141.61)(187.21)(177.61) (93.60) (93.60) (64.56) (8.88) (6.12)
(180.01)(225.61)(208.81)(141.61)(132.01)(146.41)(136.81)(151.21)(139.21)(175.21)(216.01)(127.21)(103.20) (84.60) (12.84) (6.60)
(94.41)(213.61)(218.41)(163.21)(129.61)(141.61)(136.81)(144.01)(134.41)(153.61)(201.61)(160.81)(110.40)(108.00) (51.60) (8.76)

Copyright 2012 Securities Research Company

Bonds $1.0 Mil Com 1.715 Mil BV 4.17 /sh P/E N/A (Ind BIOTK P/E 17.51) Ctry US

257

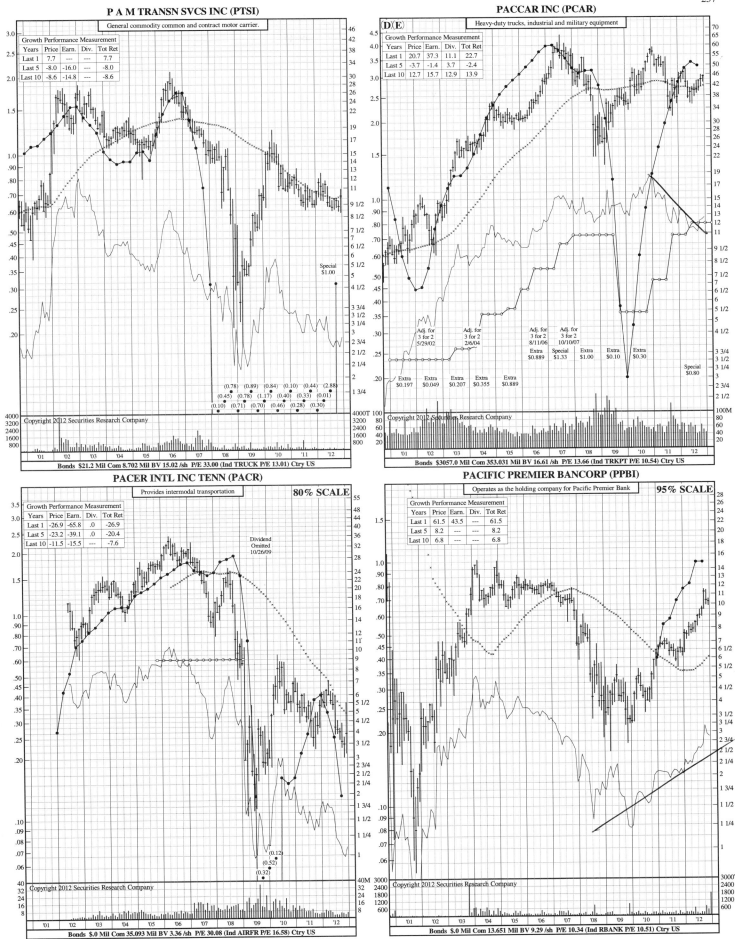

P A M TRANSN SVCS INC (PTSI)
General commodity common and contract motor carrier.

Growth Performance Measurement

Years	Price	Earn.	Div.	Tot Ret
Last 1	7.7	---	---	7.7
Last 5	-8.0	-16.0	---	-8.0
Last 10	-8.6	-14.8	---	-8.6

Special $1.00

(0.78) (0.89) (0.84) (0.10) (0.44) (2.88)
(0.45) (0.78) (1.17) (0.40) (0.33) (0.01)
(0.10) (0.71) (0.70) (0.46) (0.28) (0.30)

Copyright 2012 Securities Research Company

Bonds $21.2 Mil Com 8.702 Mil BV 15.02 /sh P/E 33.00 (Ind TRUCK P/E 13.01) Ctry US

PACCAR INC (PCAR)
Heavy-duty trucks, industrial and military equipment

(D)(E)

Growth Performance Measurement

Years	Price	Earn.	Div.	Tot Ret
Last 1	20.7	37.3	11.1	22.7
Last 5	-3.7	-1.4	3.7	-2.4
Last 10	12.7	15.7	12.9	13.9

Adj. for 3 for 2 5/29/02
Adj. for 3 for 2 2/6/04
Adj. for 3 for 2 8/11/06
Adj. for 3 for 2 10/10/07

Extra $0.889
Special $1.33
Extra $1.00
Extra $0.10
Extra $0.30
Special $0.80

Extra $0.197
Extra $0.049
Extra $0.207
Extra $0.355
Extra $0.889

Copyright 2012 Securities Research Company

Bonds $3057.0 Mil Com 353.031 Mil BV 16.61 /sh P/E 13.66 (Ind TRKPT P/E 10.54) Ctry US

PACER INTL INC TENN (PACR)
Provides intermodal transportation

80% SCALE

Growth Performance Measurement

Years	Price	Earn.	Div.	Tot Ret
Last 1	-26.9	-65.8	.0	-26.9
Last 5	-23.2	-39.1	.0	-20.4
Last 10	-11.5	-15.5	---	-7.6

Dividend Omitted 10/26/09

(0.12)
(0.52)
(0.32)

Copyright 2012 Securities Research Company

Bonds $.0 Mil Com 35.093 Mil BV 3.36 /sh P/E 30.08 (Ind AIRFR P/E 16.58) Ctry US

PACIFIC PREMIER BANCORP (PPBI)
Operates as the holding company for Pacific Premier Bank

95% SCALE

Growth Performance Measurement

Years	Price	Earn.	Div.	Tot Ret
Last 1	61.5	43.5	---	61.5
Last 5	8.2	---	---	8.2
Last 10	6.8	---	---	6.8

Copyright 2012 Securities Research Company

Bonds $.0 Mil Com 13.651 Mil BV 9.29 /sh P/E 10.34 (Ind RBANK P/E 10.51) Ctry US

258

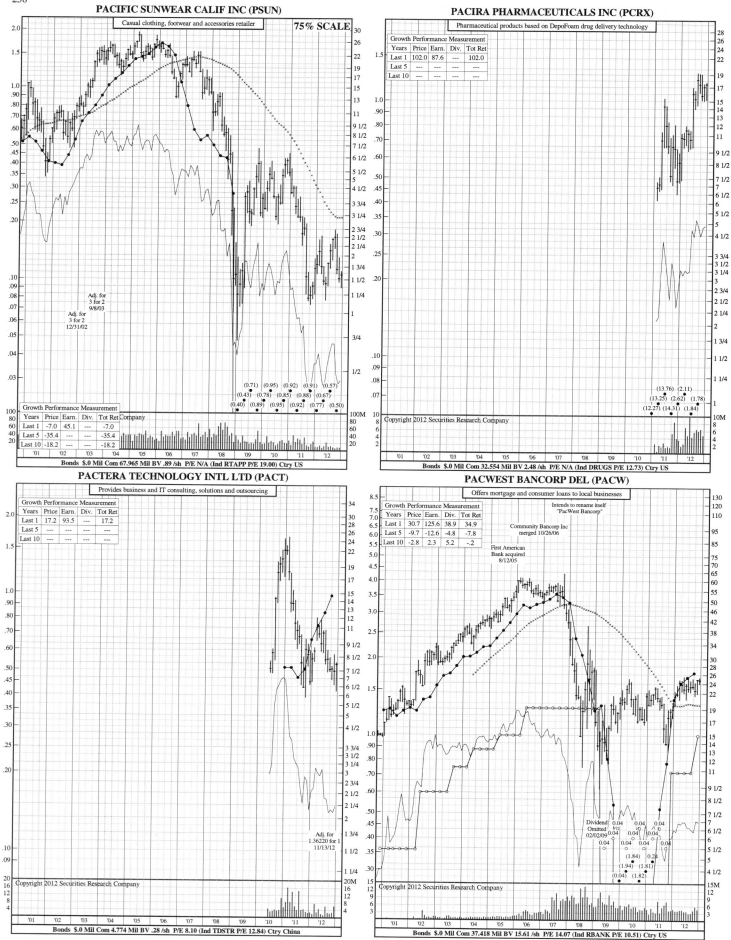

PACIFIC SUNWEAR CALIF INC (PSUN)

Casual clothing, footwear and accessories retailer

75% SCALE

Adj. for
3 for 2
9/8/03

Adj. for
3 for 2
12/31/02

(0.71) (0.95) (0.92) (0.91) (0.57)
(0.43) (0.78) (0.85) (0.88) (0.67)
(0.40) (0.89) (0.95) (0.92) (0.77) (0.50)

Growth Performance Measurement				
Years	Price	Earn.	Div.	Tot Ret
Last 1	-7.0	45.1	---	-7.0
Last 5	-35.4	---	---	-35.4
Last 10	-18.2	---	---	-18.2

Bonds $.0 Mil Com 67.965 Mil BV .89 /sh P/E N/A (Ind RTAPP P/E 19.00) Ctry US

PACIRA PHARMACEUTICALS INC (PCRX)

Pharmaceutical products based on DepoFoam drug delivery technology

Growth Performance Measurement				
Years	Price	Earn.	Div.	Tot Ret
Last 1	102.0	87.6	---	102.0
Last 5	---	---	---	---
Last 10	---	---	---	---

(13.76) (2.11)
(13.25) (2.62) (1.78)
(12.27) (14.31) (1.84)

Copyright 2012 Securities Research Company

Bonds $.0 Mil Com 32.554 Mil BV 2.48 /sh P/E N/A (Ind DRUGS P/E 12.73) Ctry US

PACTERA TECHNOLOGY INTL LTD (PACT)

Provides business and IT consulting, solutions and outsourcing

Growth Performance Measurement				
Years	Price	Earn.	Div.	Tot Ret
Last 1	17.2	93.5	---	17.2
Last 5	---	---	---	---
Last 10	---	---	---	---

Adj. for
1.36220 for 1
11/13/12

Copyright 2012 Securities Research Company

Bonds $.0 Mil Com 4.774 Mil BV .28 /sh P/E 8.10 (Ind TDSTR P/E 12.84) Ctry China

PACWEST BANCORP DEL (PACW)

Offers mortgage and consumer loans to local businesses

Intends to rename itself
"PacWest Bancorp"

Community Bancorp Inc
merged 10/26/06

First American
Bank acquired
8/12/05

Growth Performance Measurement				
Years	Price	Earn.	Div.	Tot Ret
Last 1	30.7	125.6	38.9	34.9
Last 5	-9.7	-12.6	-4.8	-7.8
Last 10	-2.8	2.3	5.2	-.2

Dividend   0.04   0.04   0.04
Omitted   0.04   0.04
02/02/09   0.04   0.04   0.04
             0.04   0.04   0.04
             (1.84) 0.28
             (1.94) (1.81)
             (0.04) (1.82)

Copyright 2012 Securities Research Company

Bonds $.0 Mil Com 37.418 Mil BV 15.61 /sh P/E 14.07 (Ind RBANK P/E 10.51) Ctry US

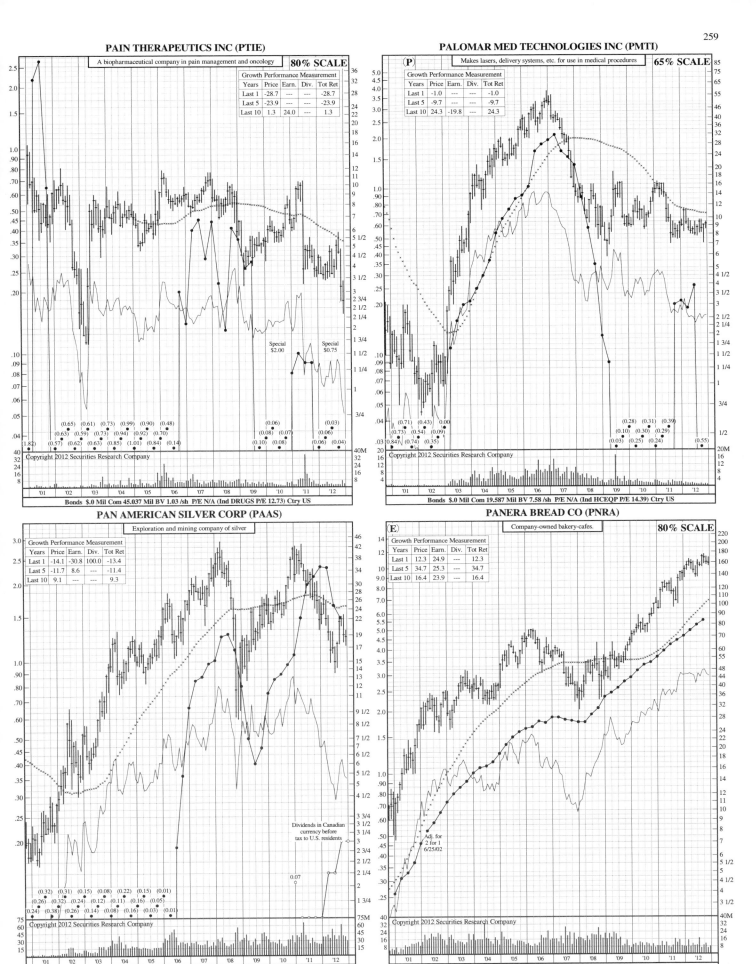

PAIN THERAPEUTICS INC (PTIE)

A biopharmaceutical company in pain management and oncology

80% SCALE

Growth Performance Measurement				
Years	Price	Earn.	Div.	Tot Ret
Last 1	-28.7	---	---	-28.7
Last 5	-23.9	---	---	-23.9
Last 10	1.3	24.0	---	1.3

Special $2.00   Special $0.75

(0.65) (0.61) (0.73) (0.99) (0.90) (0.48)   (0.06)   (0.03)
(0.63) (0.59) (0.73) (0.94) (0.92) (0.70) (0.08) (0.07) (0.06)
(1.82) (0.57) (0.62) (0.63) (0.85) (1.01) (0.84) (0.14) (0.10) (0.08) (0.06) (0.04)

Copyright 2012 Securities Research Company

'01 '02 '03 '04 '05 '06 '07 '08 '09 '10 '11 '12

Bonds $.0 Mil Com 45.037 Mil BV 1.03 /sh P/E N/A (Ind DRUGS P/E 12.73) Ctry US

PALOMAR MED TECHNOLOGIES INC (PMTI)

(P) Makes lasers, delivery systems, etc. for use in medical procedures

65% SCALE

Growth Performance Measurement				
Years	Price	Earn.	Div.	Tot Ret
Last 1	-1.0	---	---	-1.0
Last 5	-9.7	---	---	-9.7
Last 10	24.3	-19.8	---	24.3

(0.71) (0.43) 0.00   (0.28) (0.31) (0.39)
(0.73) (0.54) (0.09) (0.10) (0.30) (0.29)
(0.84) (0.74) (0.35) (0.03) (0.25) (0.24)   (0.55)

Copyright 2012 Securities Research Company

'01 '02 '03 '04 '05 '06 '07 '08 '09 '10 '11 '12

Bonds $.0 Mil Com 19.587 Mil BV 7.58 /sh P/E N/A (Ind HCEQP P/E 14.39) Ctry US

PAN AMERICAN SILVER CORP (PAAS)

Exploration and mining company of silver

Growth Performance Measurement				
Years	Price	Earn.	Div.	Tot Ret
Last 1	-14.1	-30.8	100.0	-13.4
Last 5	-11.7	8.6	---	-11.4
Last 10	9.1	---	---	9.3

Dividends in Canadian
currency before
tax to U.S. residents

0.07

(0.32) (0.31) (0.15) (0.08) (0.22) (0.15) (0.01)
(0.26) (0.32) (0.24) (0.12) (0.11) (0.16) (0.05)
(0.24) (0.38) (0.26) (0.14) (0.08) (0.16) (0.03) (0.01)

Copyright 2012 Securities Research Company

'01 '02 '03 '04 '05 '06 '07 '08 '09 '10 '11 '12

Bonds $.0 Mil Com 152.356 Mil BV 18.04 /sh P/E 12.66 (Ind METAL P/E 11.29) Ctry Canada

PANERA BREAD CO (PNRA)

(E) Company-owned bakery-cafes.

80% SCALE

Growth Performance Measurement				
Years	Price	Earn.	Div.	Tot Ret
Last 1	12.3	24.9	---	12.3
Last 5	34.7	25.3	---	34.7
Last 10	16.4	23.9	---	16.4

Adj. for
2 for 1
6/25/02

Copyright 2012 Securities Research Company

'01 '02 '03 '04 '05 '06 '07 '08 '09 '10 '11 '12

Bonds $.0 Mil Com 28.360 Mil BV 26.45 /sh P/E 28.57 (Ind RESTR P/E 19.58) Ctry US

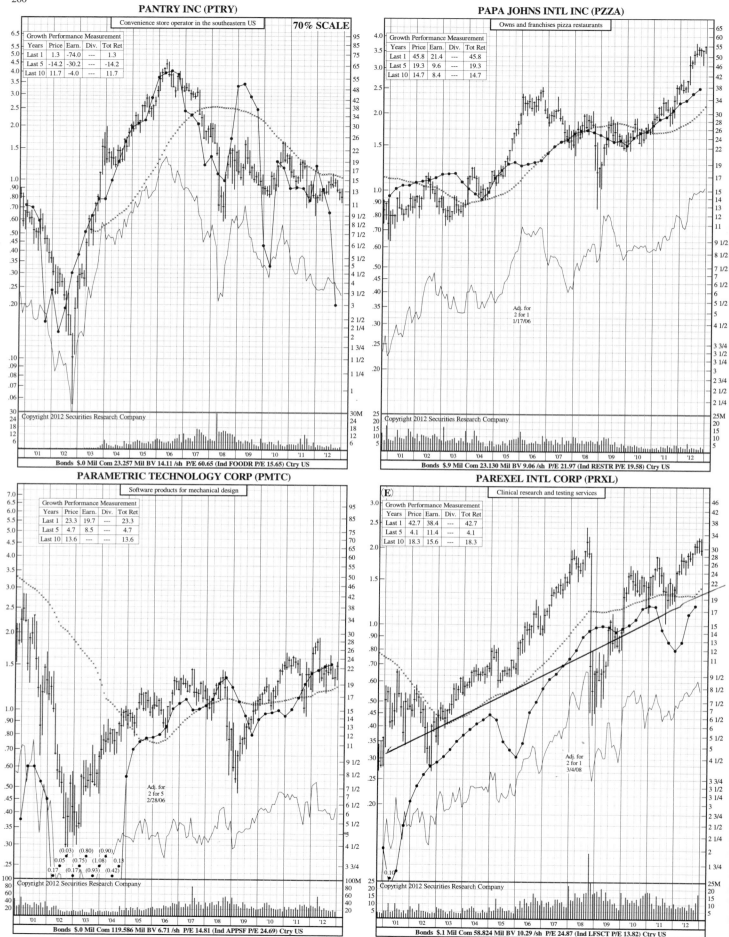

260

PANTRY INC (PTRY)

Convenience store operator in the southeastern US

70% SCALE

Growth Performance Measurement

Years	Price	Earn.	Div.	Tot Ret
Last 1	1.3	-74.0	---	1.3
Last 5	-14.2	-30.2	---	-14.2
Last 10	11.7	-4.0	---	11.7

Bonds $.0 Mil Com 23.257 Mil BV 14.11 /sh P/E 60.65 (Ind FOODR P/E 15.65) Ctry US

PAPA JOHNS INTL INC (PZZA)

Owns and franchises pizza restaurants

Growth Performance Measurement

Years	Price	Earn.	Div.	Tot Ret
Last 1	45.8	21.4	---	45.8
Last 5	19.3	9.6	---	19.3
Last 10	14.7	8.4	---	14.7

Adj. for
2 for 1
1/17/06

Bonds $.9 Mil Com 23.130 Mil BV 9.06 /sh P/E 21.97 (Ind RESTR P/E 19.58) Ctry US

PARAMETRIC TECHNOLOGY CORP (PMTC)

Software products for mechanical design

Growth Performance Measurement

Years	Price	Earn.	Div.	Tot Ret
Last 1	23.3	19.7	---	23.3
Last 5	4.7	8.5	---	4.7
Last 10	13.6	---	---	13.6

Adj. for
2 for 5
2/28/06

0.17 (0.17) (0.93) (0.42)
0.05 (0.75) (1.08) 0.1
(0.03) (0.80) (0.90)

Bonds $.0 Mil Com 119.586 Mil BV 6.71 /sh P/E 14.81 (Ind APPSF P/E 24.69) Ctry US

PAREXEL INTL CORP (PRXL)

Clinical research and testing services

E

Growth Performance Measurement

Years	Price	Earn.	Div.	Tot Ret
Last 1	42.7	38.4	---	42.7
Last 5	4.1	11.4	---	4.1
Last 10	18.3	15.6	---	18.3

Adj. for
2 for 1
3/4/08

0.10

Bonds $.1 Mil Com 58.824 Mil BV 10.29 /sh P/E 24.87 (Ind LFSCT P/E 13.82) Ctry US

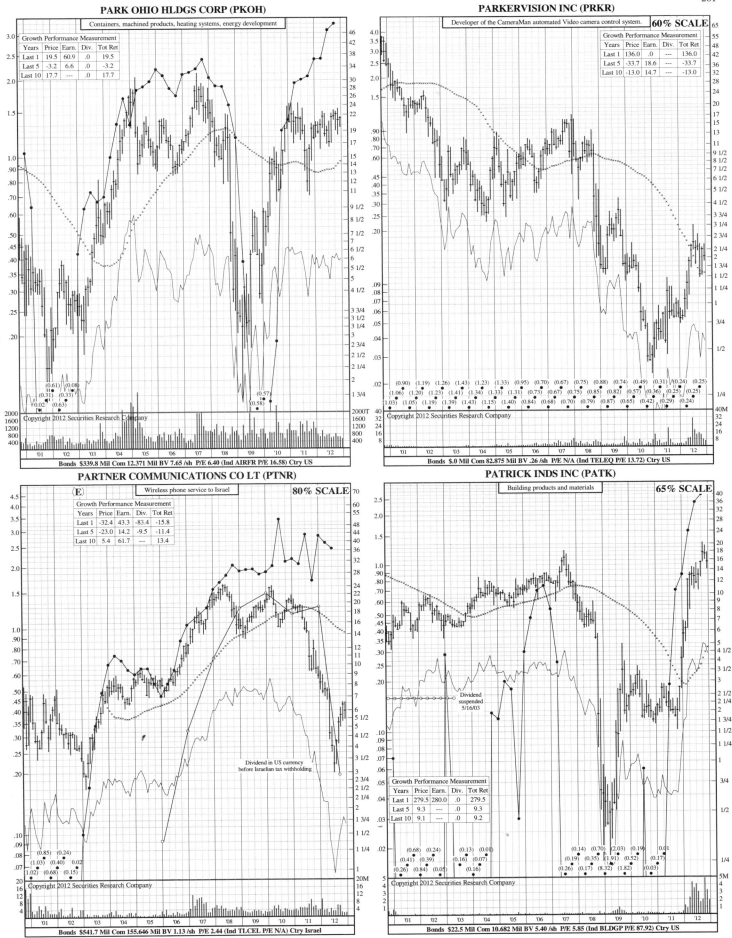

PARK OHIO HLDGS CORP (PKOH)

Containers, machined products, heating systems, energy development

Growth Performance Measurement				
Years	Price	Earn.	Div.	Tot Ret
Last 1	19.5	60.9	.0	19.5
Last 5	-3.2	6.6	.0	-3.2
Last 10	17.7	---	.0	17.7

(0.61) (0.08)
(0.31) (0.33)
(0.02) (0.63)
(0.57)
(0.58)

Copyright 2012 Securities Research Company

Bonds $339.8 Mil Com 12.371 Mil BV 7.65 /sh P/E 6.40 (Ind AIRFR P/E 16.58) Ctry US

PARKERVISION INC (PRKR)

Developer of the CameraMan automated Video camera control system. **60% SCALE**

Growth Performance Measurement				
Years	Price	Earn.	Div.	Tot Ret
Last 1	136.0	.0	---	136.0
Last 5	-33.7	18.6	---	-33.7
Last 10	-13.0	14.7	---	-13.0

(0.90) (1.19) (1.26) (1.43) (1.23) (1.33) (0.95) (0.70) (0.67) (0.75) (0.88) (0.74) (0.49) (0.31) (0.24) (0.25)
(1.06) (1.20) (1.23) (1.41) (1.34) (1.33) (1.31) (0.73) (0.67) (0.75) (0.85) (0.82) (0.57) (0.36) (0.25) (0.25)
(1.03) (1.05) (1.19) (1.39) (1.43) (1.15) (1.40) (0.84) (0.68) (0.70) (0.79) (0.87) (0.65) (0.42) (0.29) (0.24)

Copyright 2012 Securities Research Company

Bonds $.0 Mil Com 82.875 Mil BV .26 /sh P/E N/A (Ind TELEQ P/E 13.72) Ctry US

PARTNER COMMUNICATIONS CO LT (PTNR)

(E)   Wireless phone service to Israel   **80% SCALE**

Growth Performance Measurement				
Years	Price	Earn.	Div.	Tot Ret
Last 1	-32.4	43.3	-83.4	-15.8
Last 5	-23.0	14.2	-9.5	-11.4
Last 10	5.4	61.7	---	13.4

Dividend in US currency
before Israelian tax withholding

(0.85) (0.24)
(1.03) (0.40) (0.02)
(1.02) (0.68) (0.15)
(0.26)

Copyright 2012 Securities Research Company

Bonds $541.7 Mil Com 155.646 Mil BV 1.13 /sh P/E 2.44 (Ind TLCEL P/E N/A) Ctry Israel

PATRICK INDS INC (PATK)

Building products and materials   **65% SCALE**

Dividend
suspended
5/16/03

Growth Performance Measurement				
Years	Price	Earn.	Div.	Tot Ret
Last 1	279.5	280.0	.0	279.5
Last 5	9.3	---	.0	9.3
Last 10	9.1	---	.0	9.2

(0.68) (0.24) (0.13) (0.01) (0.14) (0.70) (2.03) (0.19) 0.01
(0.41) (0.39) (0.16) (0.07) (0.19) (0.35) (1.91) (0.52) (0.17)
(0.26) (0.84) (0.05) (0.16) (0.26) (0.17) (8.32) (1.82) (0.03)

Copyright 2012 Securities Research Company

Bonds $22.5 Mil Com 10.682 Mil BV 5.40 /sh P/E 5.85 (Ind BLDGP P/E 87.92) Ctry US

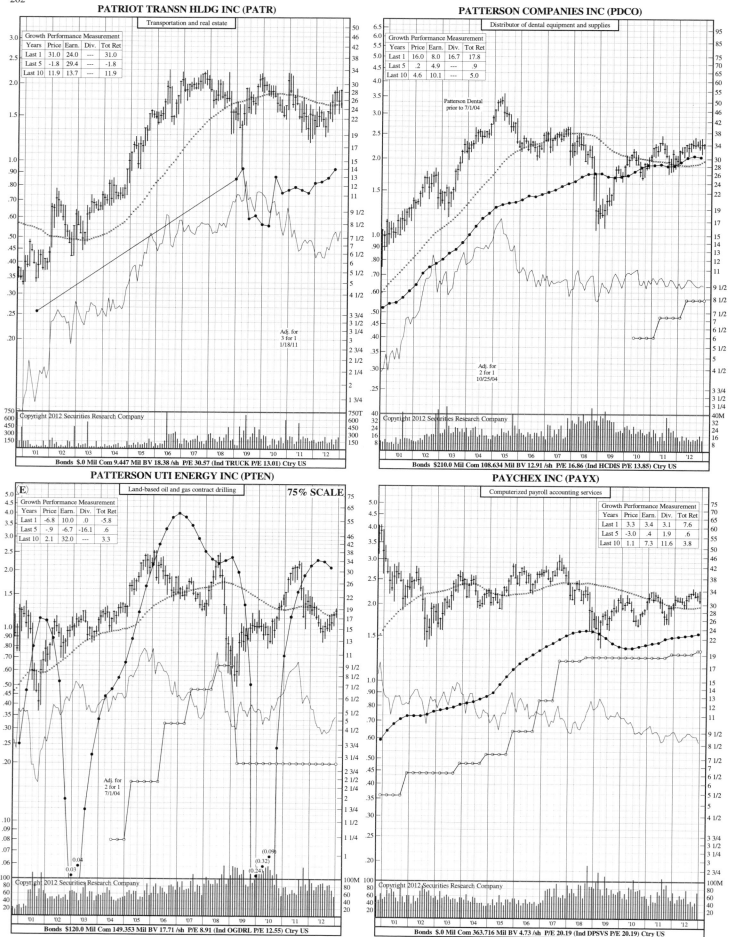

PATRIOT TRANSN HLDG INC (PATR)

Transportation and real estate

Growth Performance Measurement

Years	Price	Earn.	Div.	Tot Ret
Last 1	31.0	24.0	---	31.0
Last 5	-1.8	29.4	---	-1.8
Last 10	11.9	13.7	---	11.9

Adj. for
3 for 1
1/18/11

Bonds $.0 Mil Com 9.447 Mil BV 18.38 /sh P/E 30.57 (Ind TRUCK P/E 13.01) Ctry US

PATTERSON COMPANIES INC (PDCO)

Distributor of dental equipment and supplies

Growth Performance Measurement

Years	Price	Earn.	Div.	Tot Ret
Last 1	16.0	8.0	16.7	17.8
Last 5	.2	4.9	---	.9
Last 10	4.6	10.1	---	5.0

Patterson Dental
prior to 7/1/04

Adj. for
2 for 1
10/25/04

Bonds $210.0 Mil Com 108.634 Mil BV 12.91 /sh P/E 16.86 (Ind HCDIS P/E 13.85) Ctry US

PATTERSON UTI ENERGY INC (PTEN)

(E)   Land-based oil and gas contract drilling   75% SCALE

Growth Performance Measurement

Years	Price	Earn.	Div.	Tot Ret
Last 1	-6.8	10.0	.0	-5.8
Last 5	-.9	-6.7	-16.1	.6
Last 10	2.1	32.0	---	3.3

Adj. for
2 for 1
7/1/04

0.04
0.03
0.0

(0.09)
(0.32)
(0.24)

Bonds $120.0 Mil Com 149.353 Mil BV 17.71 /sh P/E 8.91 (Ind OGDRL P/E 12.55) Ctry US

PAYCHEX INC (PAYX)

Computerized payroll accounting services

Growth Performance Measurement

Years	Price	Earn.	Div.	Tot Ret
Last 1	3.3	3.4	3.1	7.6
Last 5	-3.0	.4	1.9	.6
Last 10	1.1	7.3	11.6	3.8

Bonds $.0 Mil Com 363.716 Mil BV 4.73 /sh P/E 20.19 (Ind DPSVS P/E 20.19) Ctry US

262

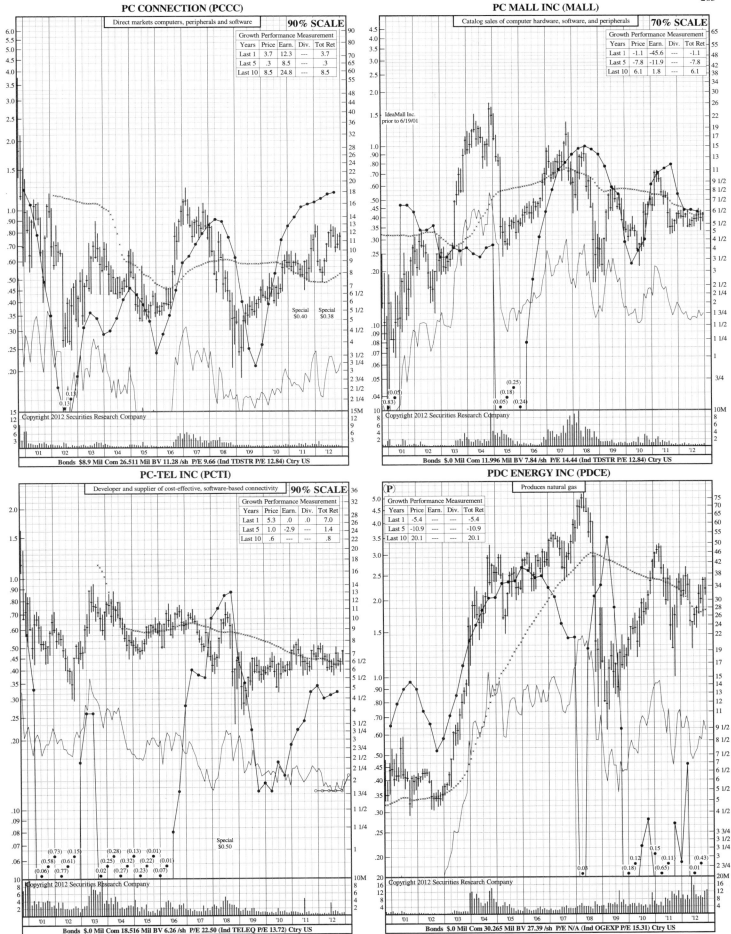

PC CONNECTION (PCCC)

Direct markets computers, peripherals and software

90% SCALE

Growth Performance Measurement				
Years	Price	Earn.	Div.	Tot Ret
Last 1	3.7	12.3	---	3.7
Last 5	.3	8.5	---	.3
Last 10	8.5	24.8	---	8.5

Special $0.40   Special $0.38

0.13
0.13

Copyright 2012 Securities Research Company

Bonds $8.9 Mil Com 26.511 Mil BV 11.28 /sh P/E 9.66 (Ind TDSTR P/E 12.84) Ctry US

PC MALL INC (MALL)

Catalog sales of computer hardware, software, and peripherals

70% SCALE

Growth Performance Measurement				
Years	Price	Earn.	Div.	Tot Ret
Last 1	-1.1	-45.6	---	-1.1
Last 5	-7.8	-11.9	---	-7.8
Last 10	6.1	1.8	---	6.1

IdeaMall Inc.
prior to 6/19/01

(0.25)
(0.18)
(0.05) (0.24)
(0.05)
(0.83)

Copyright 2012 Securities Research Company

Bonds $.0 Mil Com 11.996 Mil BV 7.84 /sh P/E 14.44 (Ind TDSTR P/E 12.84) Ctry US

PC-TEL INC (PCTI)

Developer and supplier of cost-effective, software-based connectivity

90% SCALE

Growth Performance Measurement				
Years	Price	Earn.	Div.	Tot Ret
Last 1	5.3	.0	.0	7.0
Last 5	1.0	-2.9	---	1.4
Last 10	.6	---	---	.8

Special $0.50

(0.73) (0.15)
(0.58) (0.61)   (0.28) (0.13) (0.01)
(0.06) (0.77)   (0.25) (0.32) (0.22) (0.01)
                 0.02   (0.27) (0.23) (0.07)

Copyright 2012 Securities Research Company

Bonds $.0 Mil Com 18.516 Mil BV 6.26 /sh P/E 22.50 (Ind TELEQ P/E 13.72) Ctry US

PDC ENERGY INC (PDCE)

(P)

Produces natural gas

Growth Performance Measurement				
Years	Price	Earn.	Div.	Tot Ret
Last 1	-5.4	---	---	-5.4
Last 5	-10.9	---	---	-10.9
Last 10	20.1	---	---	20.1

0.15
0.12   (0.11)
0.08 (0.18) (0.65) 0.01 (0.43)

Copyright 2012 Securities Research Company

Bonds $.0 Mil Com 30.265 Mil BV 27.39 /sh P/E N/A (Ind OGEXP P/E 15.31) Ctry US

264

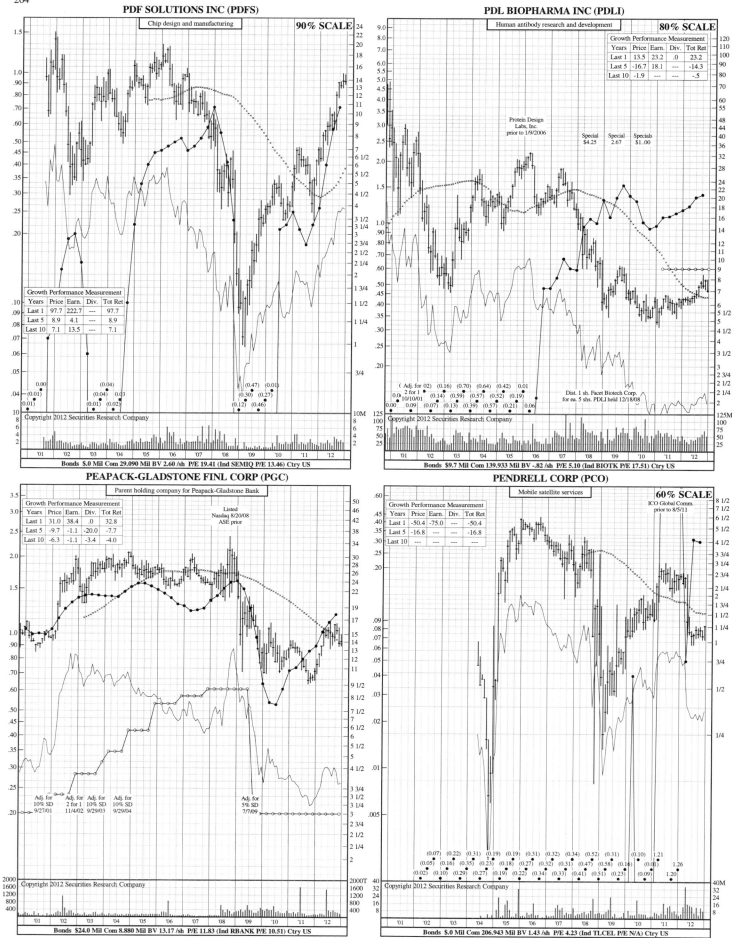

PDF SOLUTIONS INC (PDFS)

Chip design and manufacturing

90% SCALE

Growth Performance Measurement				
Years	Price	Earn.	Div.	Tot Ret
Last 1	97.7	222.7	---	97.7
Last 5	8.9	4.1	---	8.9
Last 10	7.1	13.5	---	7.1

(0.01)
0.00
(0.01)
(0.04) 0.03
(0.04)
(0.01) (0.02)
(0.47) (0.01)
(0.30) (0.27)
(0.12) (0.46)

Copyright 2012 Securities Research Company

Bonds $.0 Mil Com 29.090 Mil BV 2.60 /sh P/E 19.41 (Ind SEMIQ P/E 13.46) Ctry US

PDL BIOPHARMA INC (PDLI)

Human antibody research and development

80% SCALE

Growth Performance Measurement				
Years	Price	Earn.	Div.	Tot Ret
Last 1	13.5	23.2	.0	23.2
Last 5	-16.7	18.1	---	-14.3
Last 10	-1.9	---	---	-.5

Protein Design
Labs, Inc.
prior to 1/9/2006

Special $4.25   Special 2.67   Specials $1..00

(Adj. for 02)
2 for 1
10/10/01
0.00
(0.16) (0.70) (0.64) (0.42) 0.01
(0.14) (0.59) (0.57) (0.52) (0.19)
0.09 (0.07) (0.13) (0.39) (0.57) (0.21) 0.06

Dist. 1 sh. Facet Biotech Corp.
for ea. 5 shs. PDLI held 12/18/08

Copyright 2012 Securities Research Company

Bonds $9.7 Mil Com 139.933 Mil BV -.82 /sh P/E 5.10 (Ind BIOTK P/E 17.51) Ctry US

PEAPACK-GLADSTONE FINL CORP (PGC)

Parent holding company for Peapack-Gladstone Bank

Growth Performance Measurement				
Years	Price	Earn.	Div.	Tot Ret
Last 1	31.0	38.4	.0	32.8
Last 5	-9.7	-1.1	-20.0	-7.7
Last 10	-6.3	-1.1	-3.4	-4.0

Listed
Nasdaq 8/20/08
ASE prior

Adj. for
10% SD
9/27/01

Adj. for
2 for 1
11/4/02

Adj. for
10% SD
9/29/03

Adj. for
10% SD
9/29/04

Adj. for
5% SD
7/7/09

Copyright 2012 Securities Research Company

Bonds $24.0 Mil Com 8.880 Mil BV 13.17 /sh P/E 11.83 (Ind RBANK P/E 10.51) Ctry US

PENDRELL CORP (PCO)

Mobile satellite services

60% SCALE

ICO Global Comm.
prior to 8/5/11

Growth Performance Measurement				
Years	Price	Earn.	Div.	Tot Ret
Last 1	-50.4	-75.0	---	-50.4
Last 5	-16.8	---	---	-16.8
Last 10	---	---	---	---

(0.07) (0.22) (0.31) (0.19) (0.19) (0.31) (0.32) (0.34) (0.52) (0.31)   (0.10) 1.21
(0.05) (0.16) (0.35) (0.23) (0.18) (0.27) (0.32) (0.31) (0.47) (0.58) (0.16)   (0.01) 1.26
(0.02) (0.10) (0.29) (0.27) (0.19) (0.22) (0.34) (0.33) (0.41) (0.51) (0.23)   (0.09) 1.20

Copyright 2012 Securities Research Company

Bonds $.0 Mil Com 206.943 Mil BV 1.43 /sh P/E 4.23 (Ind TLCEL P/E N/A) Ctry US

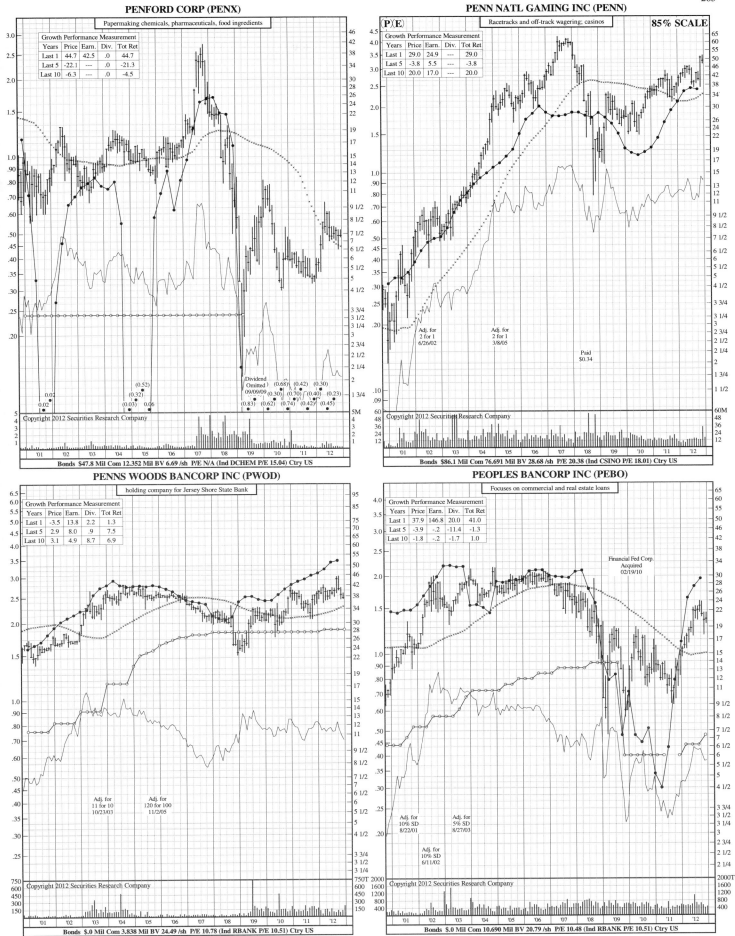

PENFORD CORP (PENX)

Papermaking chemicals, pharmaceuticals, food ingredients

Growth Performance Measurement				
Years	Price	Earn.	Div.	Tot Ret
Last 1	44.7	42.5	.0	44.7
Last 5	-22.1	---	.0	-21.3
Last 10	-6.3	---	.0	-4.5

Dividend Omitted 09/09/09 (0.68) (0.42) (0.30)
(0.52) (0.30) (0.70) (0.40) (0.23)
(0.32)
0.02 (0.03) 0.06 (0.83) (0.62) (0.74) (0.42) (0.45)
0.02

Copyright 2012 Securities Research Company

Bonds $47.8 Mil Com 12.352 Mil BV 6.69 /sh P/E N/A (Ind DCHEM P/E 15.04) Ctry US

PENN NATL GAMING INC (PENN)

Racetracks and off-track wagering; casinos

85% SCALE

(P)(E)

Growth Performance Measurement				
Years	Price	Earn.	Div.	Tot Ret
Last 1	29.0	24.9	---	29.0
Last 5	-3.8	5.5	---	-3.8
Last 10	20.0	17.0	---	20.0

Adj. for 2 for 1 6/26/02
Adj. for 2 for 1 3/8/05
Paid $0.34

Copyright 2012 Securities Research Company

Bonds $86.1 Mil Com 76.691 Mil BV 28.68 /sh P/E 20.38 (Ind CSINO P/E 18.01) Ctry US

PENNS WOODS BANCORP INC (PWOD)

holding company for Jersey Shore State Bank

Growth Performance Measurement				
Years	Price	Earn.	Div.	Tot Ret
Last 1	-3.5	13.8	2.2	1.3
Last 5	2.9	8.0	.9	7.5
Last 10	3.1	4.9	8.7	6.9

Adj. for 11 for 10 10/23/03
Adj. for 120 for 100 11/2/05

Copyright 2012 Securities Research Company

Bonds $.0 Mil Com 3.838 Mil BV 24.49 /sh P/E 10.78 (Ind RBANK P/E 10.51) Ctry US

PEOPLES BANCORP INC (PEBO)

Focuses on commercial and real estate loans

Growth Performance Measurement				
Years	Price	Earn.	Div.	Tot Ret
Last 1	37.9	146.8	20.0	41.0
Last 5	-3.9	-.2	-11.4	-1.3
Last 10	-1.8	-.2	-1.7	1.0

Financial Fed Corp. Acquired 02/19/10

Adj. for 10% SD 8/22/01
Adj. for 5% SD 8/27/03
Adj. for 10% SD 6/11/02

Copyright 2012 Securities Research Company

Bonds $.0 Mil Com 10.690 Mil BV 20.79 /sh P/E 10.48 (Ind RBANK P/E 10.51) Ctry US

266

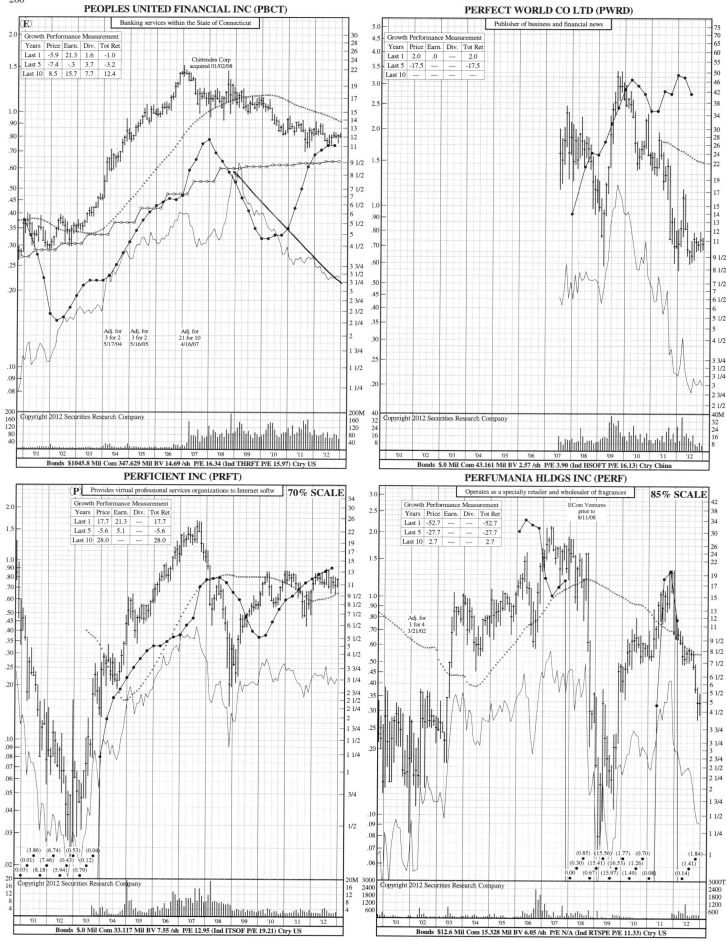

PEOPLES UNITED FINANCIAL INC (PBCT)

Banking services within the State of Connecticut

(E)

Growth Performance Measurement				
Years	Price	Earn.	Div.	Tot Ret
Last 1	-5.9	21.3	1.6	-1.0
Last 5	-7.4	-.3	3.7	-3.2
Last 10	8.5	15.7	7.7	12.4

Chittenden Corp
acquired 01/02/08

Adj. for
3 for 2
5/17/04

Adj. for
3 for 2
5/16/05

Adj. for
21 for 10
4/16/07

Copyright 2012 Securities Research Company

Bonds $1045.8 Mil Com 347.629 Mil BV 14.69 /sh P/E 16.34 (Ind THRFT P/E 15.97) Ctry US

PERFECT WORLD CO LTD (PWRD)

Publisher of business and financial news

Growth Performance Measurement				
Years	Price	Earn.	Div.	Tot Ret
Last 1	2.0	.0	---	2.0
Last 5	-17.5	---	---	-17.5
Last 10	---	---	---	---

Copyright 2012 Securities Research Company

Bonds $.0 Mil Com 43.161 Mil BV 2.57 /sh P/E 3.90 (Ind HSOFT P/E 16.13) Ctry China

PERFICIENT INC (PRFT)

Provides virtual professional services organizations to Internet softw

70% SCALE

P

Growth Performance Measurement				
Years	Price	Earn.	Div.	Tot Ret
Last 1	17.7	21.3	---	17.7
Last 5	-5.6	5.1	---	-5.6
Last 10	28.0	---	---	28.0

(3.86) (6.74) (0.53) (0.04)
(0.01) (7.46) (0.43) (0.12)
(0.03) (8.18) (5.94) (0.79)

Copyright 2012 Securities Research Company

Bonds $.0 Mil Com 33.117 Mil BV 7.55 /sh P/E 12.95 (Ind ITSOF P/E 19.21) Ctry US

PERFUMANIA HLDGS INC (PERF)

Operates as a specialty retailer and wholesaler of fragrances

85% SCALE

ECom Ventures
prior to
8/11/08

Growth Performance Measurement				
Years	Price	Earn.	Div.	Tot Ret
Last 1	-52.7	---	---	-52.7
Last 5	-27.7	---	---	-27.7
Last 10	2.7	---	---	2.7

Adj. for
1 for 4
3/21/02

(0.85) (15.56) (1.77) (0.70)   (1.84)
(0.30) (15.41) (16.53) (1.26)   (1.41)
0.00 (0.67) (15.97) (1.49) (0.08)   (0.14)

Copyright 2012 Securities Research Company

Bonds $12.6 Mil Com 15.328 Mil BV 6.05 /sh P/E N/A (Ind RTSPE P/E 11.33) Ctry US

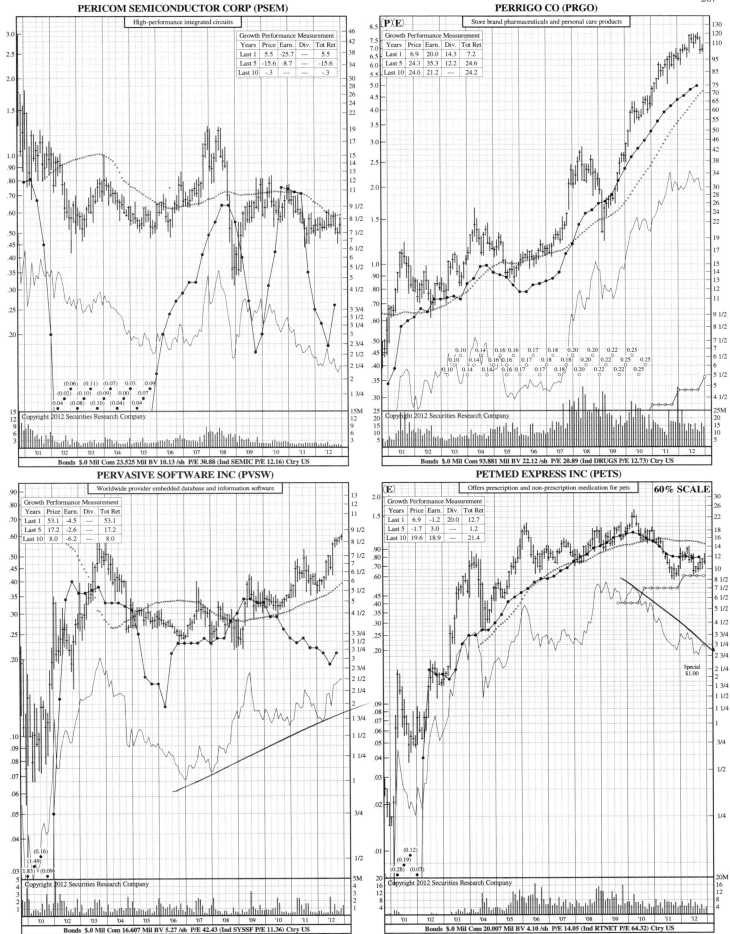

PERICOM SEMICONDUCTOR CORP (PSEM)

High-performance integrated circuits

Growth Performance Measurement				
Years	Price	Earn.	Div.	Tot Ret
Last 1	5.5	-25.7	---	5.5
Last 5	-15.6	-8.7	---	-15.6
Last 10	-.3	---	---	-.3

(0.06) (0.11) (0.07) 0.03 0.09
(0.02) (0.10) (0.10) 0.00 0.07
0.04 (0.08) (0.10) (0.04) 0.04

Copyright 2012 Securities Research Company

Bonds $.0 Mil Com 23.525 Mil BV 10.13 /sh P/E 30.88 (Ind SEMIC P/E 12.16) Ctry US

PERRIGO CO (PRGO)

Store brand pharmaceuticals and personal care products

(P)(E)

Growth Performance Measurement				
Years	Price	Earn.	Div.	Tot Ret
Last 1	6.9	20.0	14.3	7.2
Last 5	24.3	35.3	12.2	24.6
Last 10	24.0	21.2	---	24.2

0.10 0.14 0.16 0.16 0.17 0.18 0.20 0.20 0.22 0.25
0.10 0.14 0.16 0.16 0.17 0.18 0.18 0.22 0.25 0.25
0.10 0.14 0.14 0.16 0.17 0.17 0.18 0.20 0.22 0.22 0.25

Copyright 2012 Securities Research Company

Bonds $.0 Mil Com 93.881 Mil BV 22.12 /sh P/E 20.89 (Ind DRUGS P/E 12.73) Ctry US

PERVASIVE SOFTWARE INC (PVSW)

Worldwide provider embedded database and information software

Growth Performance Measurement				
Years	Price	Earn.	Div.	Tot Ret
Last 1	53.1	-4.5	---	53.1
Last 5	17.2	-2.6	---	17.2
Last 10	8.0	-6.2	---	8.0

(0.16)
(1.49)
(1.83) (0.09)

Copyright 2012 Securities Research Company

Bonds $.0 Mil Com 16.607 Mil BV 5.27 /sh P/E 42.43 (Ind SYSSF P/E 11.36) Ctry US

PETMED EXPRESS INC (PETS)

Offers prescription and non-prescription medication for pets

60% SCALE

(E)

Growth Performance Measurement				
Years	Price	Earn.	Div.	Tot Ret
Last 1	6.9	-1.2	20.0	12.7
Last 5	-1.7	3.0	---	1.2
Last 10	19.6	18.9	---	21.4

Special $1.00

(0.12)
(0.19)
(0.28) (0.07)

Copyright 2012 Securities Research Company

Bonds $.0 Mil Com 20.007 Mil BV 4.10 /sh P/E 14.05 (Ind RTNET P/E 64.32) Ctry US

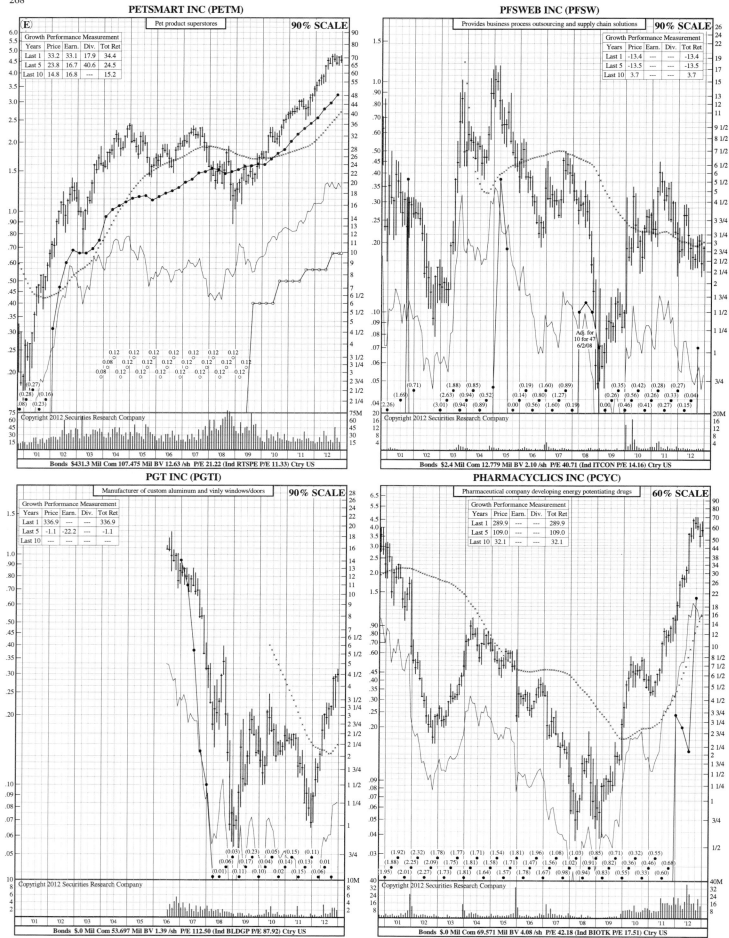

268

PETSMART INC (PETM)
Pet product superstores — 90% SCALE

Growth Performance Measurement

Years	Price	Earn.	Div.	Tot Ret
Last 1	33.2	33.1	17.9	34.4
Last 5	23.8	16.7	40.6	24.5
Last 10	14.8	16.8	---	15.2

Copyright 2012 Securities Research Company

Bonds $431.3 Mil Com 107.475 Mil BV 12.63 /sh P/E 21.22 (Ind RTSPE P/E 11.33) Ctry US

PFSWEB INC (PFSW)
Provides business process outsourcing and supply chain solutions — 90% SCALE

Growth Performance Measurement

Years	Price	Earn.	Div.	Tot Ret
Last 1	-13.4	---	---	-13.4
Last 5	-13.5	---	---	-13.5
Last 10	3.7	---	---	3.7

Adj. for 10 for 47 6/2/08

Copyright 2012 Securities Research Company

Bonds $2.4 Mil Com 12.779 Mil BV 2.10 /sh P/E 40.71 (Ind ITCON P/E 14.16) Ctry US

PGT INC (PGTI)
Manufacturer of custom aluminum and vinly windows/doors — 90% SCALE

Growth Performance Measurement

Years	Price	Earn.	Div.	Tot Ret
Last 1	336.9	---	---	336.9
Last 5	-1.1	-22.2	---	-1.1
Last 10	---	---	---	---

Copyright 2012 Securities Research Company

Bonds $.0 Mil Com 53.697 Mil BV 1.39 /sh P/E 112.50 (Ind BLDGP P/E 87.92) Ctry US

PHARMACYCLICS INC (PCYC)
Pharmaceutical company developing energy potentiating drugs — 60% SCALE

Growth Performance Measurement

Years	Price	Earn.	Div.	Tot Ret
Last 1	289.9	---	---	289.9
Last 5	109.0	---	---	109.0
Last 10	32.1	---	---	32.1

Copyright 2012 Securities Research Company

Bonds $.0 Mil Com 69.571 Mil BV 4.08 /sh P/E 42.18 (Ind BIOTK P/E 17.51) Ctry US

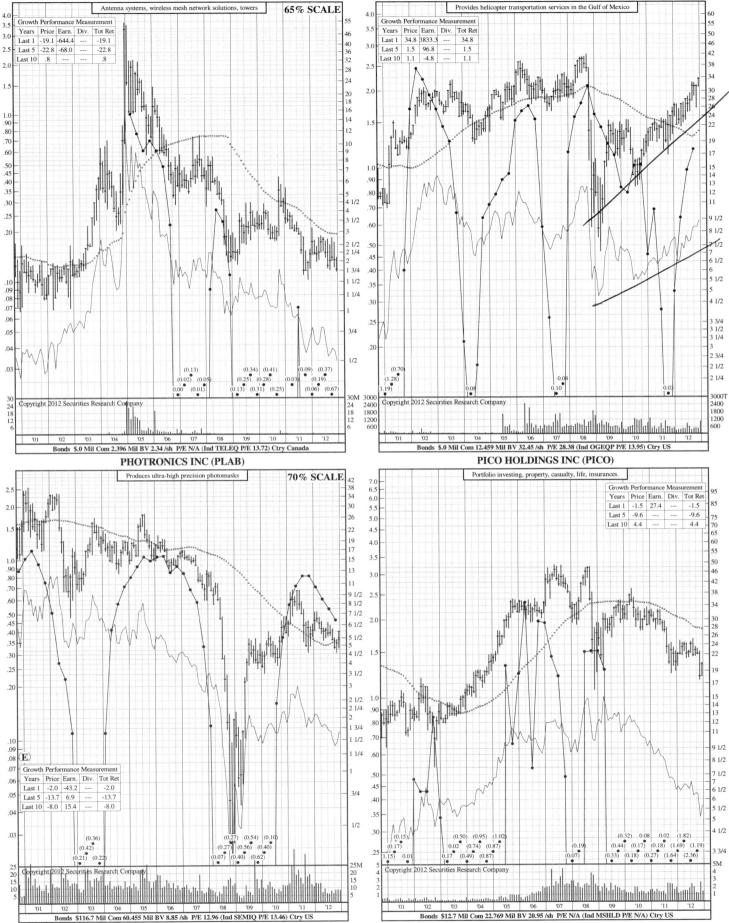

PHAZAR CORP (ANTP)

Antenna systems, wireless mesh network solutions, towers

65% SCALE

Growth Performance Measurement

Years	Price	Earn.	Div.	Tot Ret
Last 1	-19.1	-644.4	---	-19.1
Last 5	-22.8	-68.0	---	-22.8
Last 10	.8	---	---	.8

(0.13)
(0.02) (0.05)   (0.34) (0.41)   (0.09) (0.37)
0.00 (0.01)   (0.25) (0.28)   (0.03) (0.19)
                (0.13) (0.31) (0.25)   (0.06) (0.67)

Copyright 2012 Securities Research Company

'01 '02 '03 '04 '05 '06 '07 '08 '09 '10 '11 '12

Bonds $.0 Mil Com 2.396 Mil BV 2.34 /sh P/E N/A (Ind TELEQ P/E 13.72) Ctry Canada

PHI INC (PHIIK)

Provides helicopter transportation services in the Gulf of Mexico

Growth Performance Measurement

Years	Price	Earn.	Div.	Tot Ret
Last 1	34.8	3833.3	---	34.8
Last 5	1.5	96.8	---	1.5
Last 10	1.1	-4.8	---	1.1

(0.70)
(1.28)   0.04
(1.19)   0.08   0.10   0.03

Copyright 2012 Securities Research Company

'01 '02 '03 '04 '05 '06 '07 '08 '09 '10 '11 '12

Bonds $.0 Mil Com 12.459 Mil BV 32.45 /sh P/E 28.38 (Ind OGEQP P/E 13.95) Ctry US

PHOTRONICS INC (PLAB)

Produces ultra-high precision photomasks

70% SCALE

E)

Growth Performance Measurement

Years	Price	Earn.	Div.	Tot Ret
Last 1	-2.0	-43.2	---	-2.0
Last 5	-13.7	6.9	---	-13.7
Last 10	-8.0	15.4	---	-8.0

(0.36)
(0.42)   (0.27) (0.54) (0.10)
(0.21) (0.22)   (0.27) (0.56) (0.40)
                  (0.07) (0.40) (0.62)

Copyright 2012 Securities Research Company

'01 '02 '03 '04 '05 '06 '07 '08 '09 '10 '11 '12

Bonds $116.7 Mil Com 60.455 Mil BV 8.85 /sh P/E 12.96 (Ind SEMIQ P/E 13.46) Ctry US

PICO HOLDINGS INC (PICO)

Portfolio investing, property, casualty, life, insurances.

Growth Performance Measurement

Years	Price	Earn.	Div.	Tot Ret
Last 1	-1.5	27.4	---	-1.5
Last 5	-9.6	---	---	-9.6
Last 10	4.4	---	---	4.4

(0.15)
(0.17)   (0.50) (0.95) (1.02)   (0.32) 0.08 0.02 (1.82)
0.01   0.02 (0.74) 0.87   (0.19)   (0.44) (0.17) (0.18) (1.69) (1.19)
              0.17 (0.49) (0.87)   (0.07)   (0.33) (0.18) (0.27) (1.64) (2.36)

Copyright 2012 Securities Research Company

'01 '02 '03 '04 '05 '06 '07 '08 '09 '10 '11 '12

Bonds $12.7 Mil Com 22.769 Mil BV 20.95 /sh P/E N/A (Ind MSHLD P/E N/A) Ctry US

PIXELWORKS INC (PXLW)

Designer, developer and marketer of semiconductors and software for el **50% SCALE**

Growth Performance Measurement				
Years	Price	Earn.	Div.	Tot Ret
Last 1	-7.4	86.4	---	-7.4
Last 5	-.4	39.2	---	-.4
Last 10	-18.5	---	---	-18.5

Adj. for 1 for 3 6/4/08

Copyright 2012 Securities Research Company

Bonds $.6 Mil Com 18.401 Mil BV .93 /sh P/E N/A (Ind SEMIC P/E 12.16) Ctry US

PLANAR SYS INC (PLNR)

Makes high performance electronic display products **65% SCALE**

Growth Performance Measurement				
Years	Price	Earn.	Div.	Tot Ret
Last 1	-25.1	---	---	-25.1
Last 5	-25.9	-20.8	---	-25.9
Last 10	-23.4	---	---	-23.4

Copyright 2012 Securities Research Company

Bonds $15.6 Mil Com 20.945 Mil BV 2.50 /sh P/E N/A (Ind ELEEQ P/E 15.50) Ctry US

PLEXUS CORP (PLXS)

Electronic components and assemblies **75% SCALE**

Growth Performance Measurement				
Years	Price	Earn.	Div.	Tot Ret
Last 1	-5.8	3.9	---	-5.8
Last 5	-.4	10.7	---	-.4
Last 10	11.4	30.3	---	11.4

Copyright 2012 Securities Research Company

Bonds $141.4 Mil Com 34.968 Mil BV 18.49 /sh P/E 10.79 (Ind EMSVC P/E 12.29) Ctry US

PLUG POWER INC (PLUG)

Develops on-site power generation systems **40% SCALE**

Growth Performance Measurement				
Years	Price	Earn.	Div.	Tot Ret
Last 1	-75.5	44.8	---	-75.5
Last 5	-58.3	29.6	---	-58.3
Last 10	-36.2	19.8	---	-36.2

Adj. for 1 for 10 5/20/11

Copyright 2012 Securities Research Company

Bonds $5.7 Mil Com 38.125 Mil BV .87 /sh P/E N/A (Ind EEQPM P/E 16.88) Ctry US

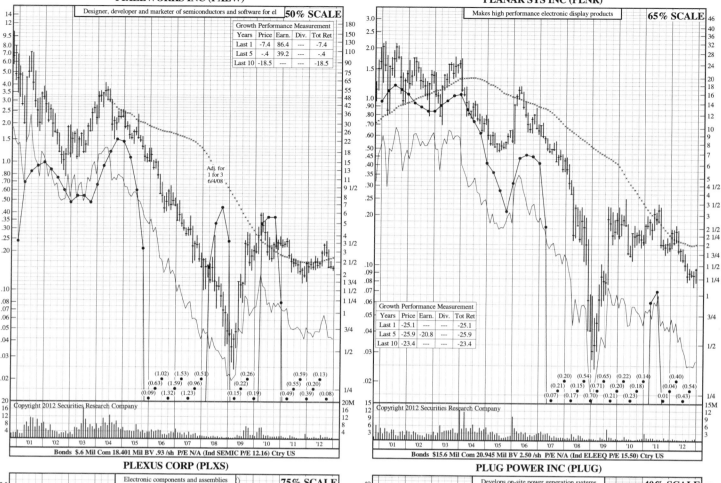

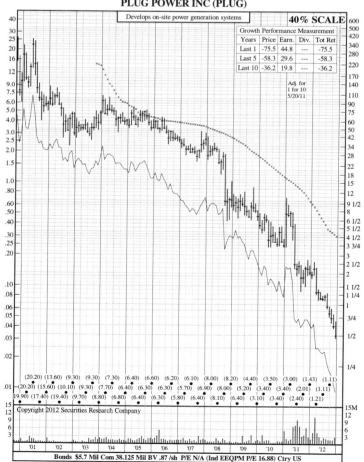

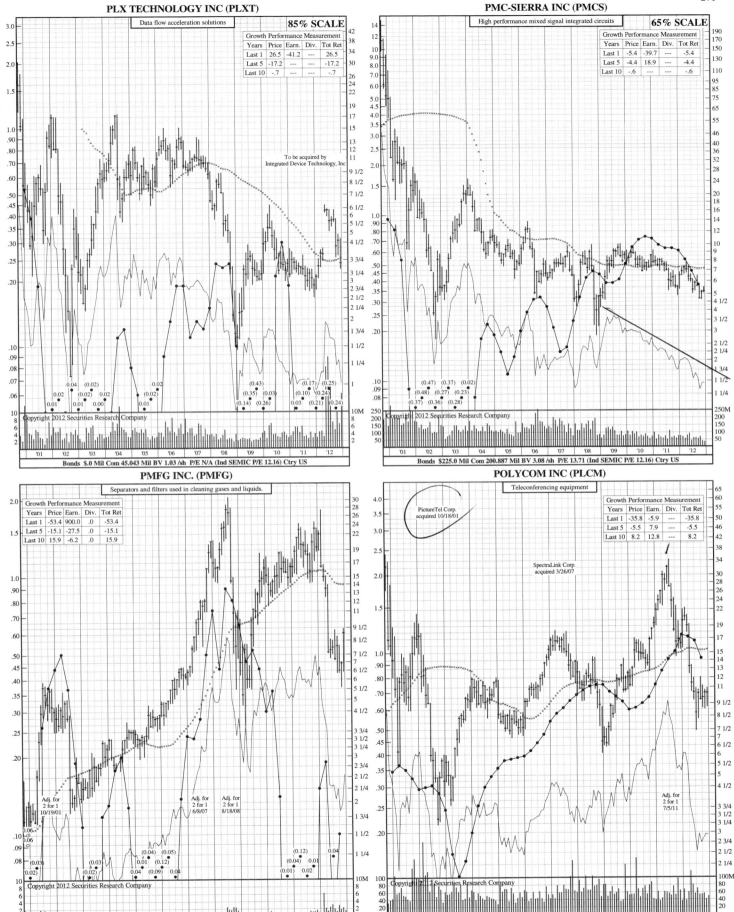

PLX TECHNOLOGY INC (PLXT)

Data flow acceleration solutions

85% SCALE

To be acquired by
Integrated Device Technology, Inc

Growth Performance Measurement				
Years	Price	Earn.	Div.	Tot Ret
Last 1	26.5	-41.2	---	26.5
Last 5	-17.2	---	---	-17.2
Last 10	-.7	---	---	-.7

Copyright 2012 Securities Research Company

Bonds $.0 Mil Com 45.043 Mil BV 1.03 /sh P/E N/A (Ind SEMIC P/E 12.16) Ctry US

PMC-SIERRA INC (PMCS)

High performance mixed signal integrated circuits

65% SCALE

Growth Performance Measurement				
Years	Price	Earn.	Div.	Tot Ret
Last 1	-5.4	-39.7	---	-5.4
Last 5	-4.4	18.9	---	-4.4
Last 10	-.6	---	---	-.6

Copyright 2012 Securities Research Company

Bonds $225.0 Mil Com 200.887 Mil BV 3.08 /sh P/E 13.71 (Ind SEMIC P/E 12.16) Ctry US

PMFG INC. (PMFG)

Separators and filters used in cleaning gases and liquids.

Growth Performance Measurement				
Years	Price	Earn.	Div.	Tot Ret
Last 1	-53.4	900.0	.0	-53.4
Last 5	-15.1	-27.5	.0	-15.1
Last 10	15.9	-6.2	.0	15.9

Adj. for
2 for 1
10/19/01

Adj. for
2 for 1
6/8/07

Adj. for
2 for 1
8/18/08

Copyright 2012 Securities Research Company

Bonds $1.4 Mil Com 20.920 Mil BV 6.20 /sh P/E 90.90 (Ind MACHN P/E 14.49) Ctry US

POLYCOM INC (PLCM)

Teleconferencing equipment

PictureTel Corp.
acquired 10/18/01

SpectraLink Corp.
acquired 3/26/07

Growth Performance Measurement				
Years	Price	Earn.	Div.	Tot Ret
Last 1	-35.8	-5.9	---	-35.8
Last 5	-5.5	7.9	---	-5.5
Last 10	8.2	12.8	---	8.2

Adj. for
2 for 1
7/5/11

Copyright 2012 Securities Research Company

Bonds $.0 Mil Com 175.433 Mil BV 7.97 /sh P/E 11.01 (Ind TELEQ P/E 13.72) Ctry US

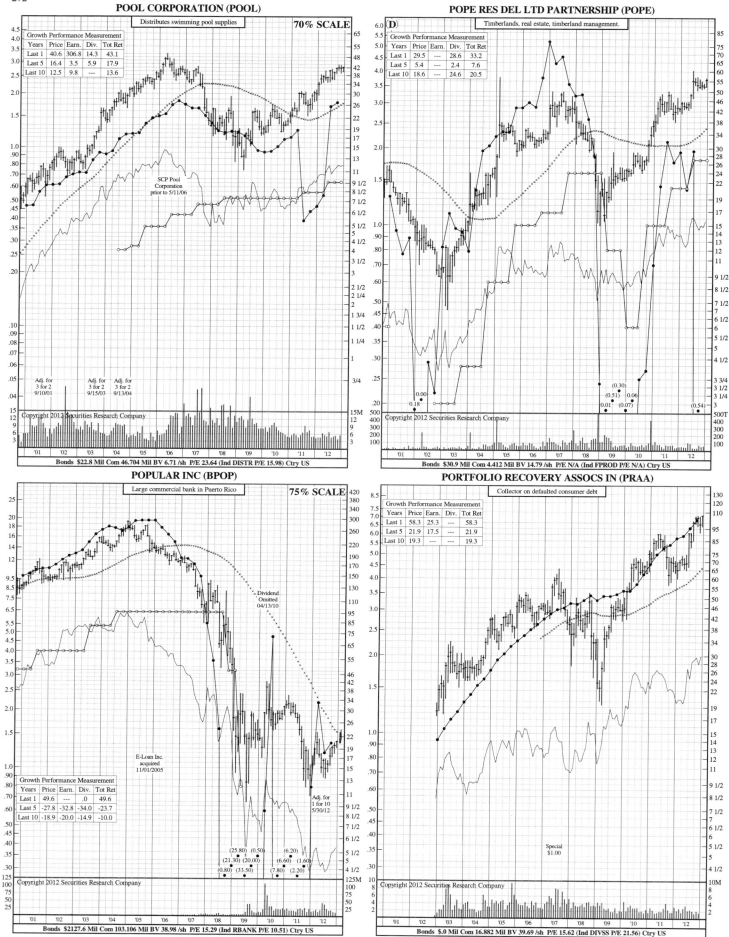

272

POOL CORPORATION (POOL)

Distributes swimming pool supplies

70% SCALE

Growth Performance Measurement				
Years	Price	Earn.	Div.	Tot Ret
Last 1	40.6	306.8	14.3	43.1
Last 5	16.4	3.5	5.9	17.9
Last 10	12.5	9.8	---	13.6

SCP Pool
Corporation
prior to 5/11/06

Adj. for
3 for 2
9/10/01

Adj. for
3 for 2
9/15/03

Adj. for
3 for 2
9/13/04

Copyright 2012 Securities Research Company

Bonds $22.8 Mil Com 46.704 Mil BV 6.71 /sh P/E 23.64 (Ind DISTR P/E 15.98) Ctry US

POPE RES DEL LTD PARTNERSHIP (POPE)

(D)

Timberlands, real estate, timberland management.

Growth Performance Measurement				
Years	Price	Earn.	Div.	Tot Ret
Last 1	29.5	---	28.6	33.2
Last 5	5.4	---	2.4	7.6
Last 10	18.6	---	24.6	20.5

(0.30)

(0.51) 0.06

0.00 0.01 (0.07)

0.18 (0.54)

Copyright 2012 Securities Research Company

Bonds $30.9 Mil Com 4.412 Mil BV 14.79 /sh P/E N/A (Ind FPROD P/E N/A) Ctry US

POPULAR INC (BPOP)

Large commercial bank in Puerto Rico

75% SCALE

Dividend
Omitted
04/13/10

E-Loan Inc.
acquired
11/01/2005

Adj. for
1 for 10
5/30/12

Growth Performance Measurement				
Years	Price	Earn.	Div.	Tot Ret
Last 1	49.6	---	.0	49.6
Last 5	-27.8	-32.8	-34.0	-23.7
Last 10	-18.9	-20.0	-14.9	-10.0

(25.80) (0.50) (6.20)
(21.30) (20.00) (6.60) (1.60)
(0.80) (33.50) (7.80) (2.20)

Copyright 2012 Securities Research Company

Bonds $2127.6 Mil Com 103.106 Mil BV 38.98 /sh P/E 15.29 (Ind RBANK P/E 10.51) Ctry US

PORTFOLIO RECOVERY ASSOCS IN (PRAA)

Collector on defaulted consumer debt

Growth Performance Measurement				
Years	Price	Earn.	Div.	Tot Ret
Last 1	58.3	25.3	---	58.3
Last 5	21.9	17.5	---	21.9
Last 10	19.3	---	---	19.3

Special
$1.00

Copyright 2012 Securities Research Company

Bonds $.0 Mil Com 16.882 Mil BV 39.69 /sh P/E 15.62 (Ind DIVSS P/E 21.56) Ctry US

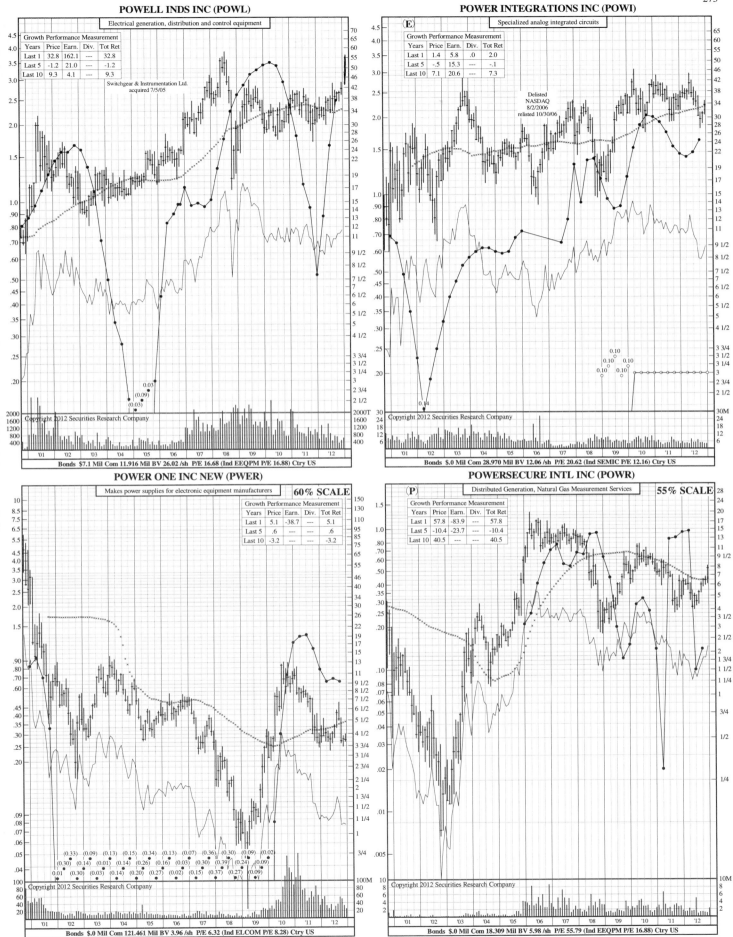

POWELL INDS INC (POWL)

Electrical generation, distribution and control equipment

Growth Performance Measurement				
Years	Price	Earn.	Div.	Tot Ret
Last 1	32.8	162.1	---	32.8
Last 5	-1.2	21.0	---	-1.2
Last 10	9.3	4.1	---	9.3

Switchgear & Instrumentation Ltd.
acquired 7/5/05

0.03
(0.09)
(0.03)

Copyright 2012 Securities Research Company

Bonds $7.1 Mil Com 11.916 Mil BV 26.02 /sh P/E 16.68 (Ind EEQPM P/E 16.88) Ctry US

POWER INTEGRATIONS INC (POWI)

Specialized analog integrated circuits

Growth Performance Measurement				
Years	Price	Earn.	Div.	Tot Ret
Last 1	1.4	5.8	.0	2.0
Last 5	-.5	15.3	---	-.1
Last 10	7.1	20.6	---	7.3

Delisted
NASDAQ
8/2/2006
relisted 10/30/06

0.10
0.10   0.10
0.10   0.10

0.14

Copyright 2012 Securities Research Company

Bonds $.0 Mil Com 28.970 Mil BV 12.06 /sh P/E 20.62 (Ind SEMIC P/E 12.16) Ctry US

POWER ONE INC NEW (PWER)

Makes power supplies for electronic equipment manufacturers

60% SCALE

Growth Performance Measurement				
Years	Price	Earn.	Div.	Tot Ret
Last 1	5.1	-38.7	---	5.1
Last 5	.6	---	---	.6
Last 10	-3.2	---	---	-3.2

(0.33) (0.09) (0.13) (0.15) (0.34) (0.13) (0.07) (0.36) (0.30) (0.09) (0.02)
(0.30) (0.14) (0.01) (0.26) (0.16) (0.03) (0.03) (0.39) (0.24) (0.09)
0.01 (0.30) (0.03) (0.14) (0.20) (0.27) (0.02) (0.15) (0.37) (0.27) (0.09)

Copyright 2012 Securities Research Company

Bonds $.0 Mil Com 121.461 Mil BV 3.96 /sh P/E 6.32 (Ind ELCOM P/E 8.28) Ctry US

POWERSECURE INTL INC (POWR)

Distributed Generation, Natural Gas Measurement Services

55% SCALE

Growth Performance Measurement				
Years	Price	Earn.	Div.	Tot Ret
Last 1	57.8	-83.9	---	57.8
Last 5	-10.4	-23.7	---	-10.4
Last 10	40.5	---	---	40.5

Copyright 2012 Securities Research Company

Bonds $.0 Mil Com 18.309 Mil BV 5.98 /sh P/E 55.79 (Ind EEQPM P/E 16.88) Ctry US

POWERWAVE TECHNOLOGIES INC (PWAV)

Supplies wireless solutions for wireless communications networks **40% SCALE**

Growth Performance Measurement

Years	Price	Earn.	Div.	Tot Ret
Last 1	-85.1	1256.8	---	-85.1
Last 5	-56.6	-8.8	---	-56.6
Last 10	-36.0	---	---	-36.0

Adj. for
1 for 5
10/31/11

(0.35)   (2.00) (0.85)   (3.25) (1.55)   0.00   (2.97)
(1.30)   (1.50) (1.45)   (1.80) (2.60)   (0.10)   (1.77) (5.02)
(0.40)   (0.45) (1.75) (0.20)   (0.65) (3.30) (0.55)   0.00   (0.37) (4.32)

'01 '02 '03 '04 '05 '06 '07 '08 '09 '10 '11 '12

Bonds $.0 Mil Com 31.771 Mil BV -4.13 /sh P/E N/A (Ind TELEQ P/E 13.72) Ctry US

POZEN INC (POZN)

Treats migraines with combinations of triptans/anti-inflammatory drugs **85% SCALE**

Growth Performance Measurement

Years	Price	Earn.	Div.	Tot Ret
Last 1	26.8	---	---	26.8
Last 5	-16.0	39.0	---	-16.0
Last 10	-.3	---	---	-.3

(0.49) (0.85) (0.79) (0.53)   (0.18) 0.77   (0.11) (0.35)   (0.22) (0.18) (0.05)   (0.03)
(0.32) (0.77) (0.87) (0.66)   0.04 (0.81)   (0.13) (0.51)   (0.22) (0.66) (0.21)   (0.08)
(0.16) (0.68) (0.87) (0.72) 0.44   0.29   0.02 (0.66)   (0.04) (0.09) (0.23)

'01 '02 '03 '04 '05 '06 '07 '08 '09 '10 '11 '12

Bonds $.0 Mil Com 30.309 Mil BV 2.96 /sh P/E 3.58 (Ind DRUGS P/E 12.73) Ctry US

PREFERRED BK LOS ANGELES CA (PFBC)

Operates as an independent commercial bank in California **65% SCALE**

Growth Performance Measurement

Years	Price	Earn.	Div.	Tot Ret
Last 1	90.6	---	.0	90.6
Last 5	-35.8	-61.4	-14.0	-33.5
Last 10	-15.2	---	---	-10.4

Dividend
Omitted
03/01/010

Adj. for
3 for 2
2/21/07

Adj. for
1 for 5
6/20/11

(9.25) (3.50) (4.52)
(7.60) (5.90) (5.65)
(0.25) (7.60) (4.70) (0.12)

'01 '02 '03 '04 '05 '06 '07 '08 '09 '10 '11 '12

Bonds $.0 Mil Com 13.188 Mil BV 13.75 /sh P/E 129.09 (Ind RBANK P/E 10.51) Ctry US

PREFORMED LINE PRODS CO (PLPC)

E Formed wire products

Growth Performance Measurement

Years	Price	Earn.	Div.	Tot Ret
Last 1	-.4	16.7	.0	.9
Last 5	-.2	16.7	.0	1.1
Last 10	13.6	20.9	.0	15.0

Special
$0.40

'01 '02 '03 '04 '05 '06 '07 '08 '09 '10 '11 '12

Bonds $.0 Mil Com 5.313 Mil BV 44.31 /sh P/E 9.76 (Ind EEQPM P/E 16.88) Ctry US

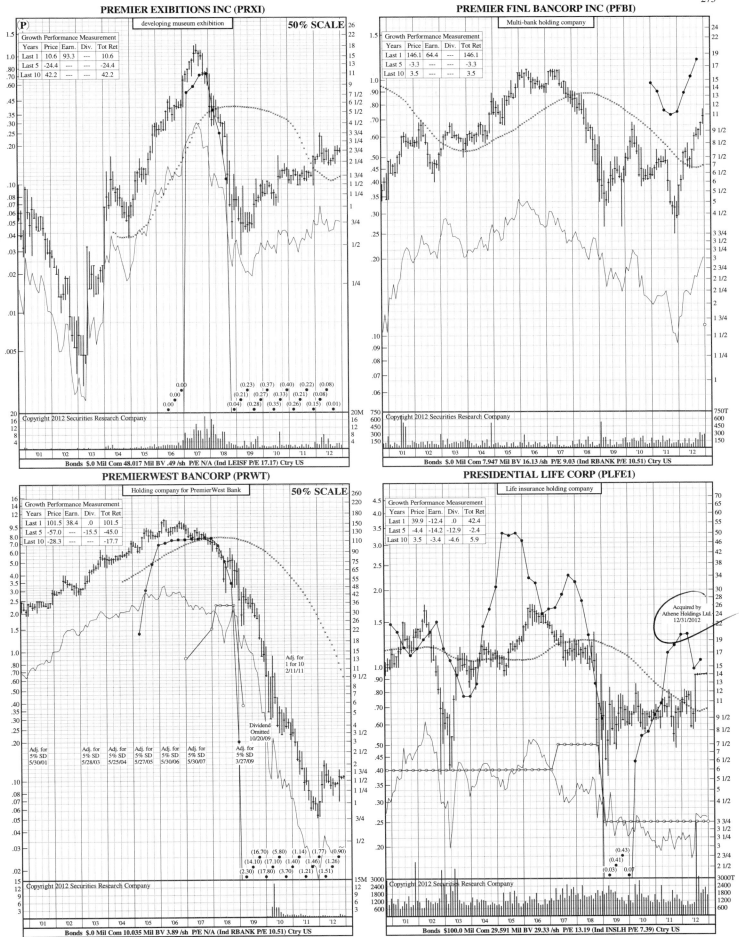

PREMIER EXIBITIONS INC (PRXI)
developing museum exhibition — 50% SCALE

Growth Performance Measurement				
Years	Price	Earn.	Div.	Tot Ret
Last 1	10.6	93.3	---	10.6
Last 5	-24.4	---	---	-24.4
Last 10	42.2	---	---	42.2

(0.23) (0.37) (0.40) (0.22) (0.08)
0.00
0.00 (0.21) (0.27) (0.33) (0.26) (0.08)
0.00 (0.04) (0.28) (0.35) (0.26) (0.15) (0.01)

Copyright 2012 Securities Research Company

Bonds $.0 Mil Com 48.017 Mil BV .49 /sh P/E N/A (Ind LEISF P/E 17.17) Ctry US

PREMIER FINL BANCORP INC (PFBI)
Multi-bank holding company

Growth Performance Measurement				
Years	Price	Earn.	Div.	Tot Ret
Last 1	146.1	64.4	---	146.1
Last 5	-3.3	---	---	-3.3
Last 10	3.5	---	---	3.5

Copyright 2012 Securities Research Company

Bonds $.0 Mil Com 7.947 Mil BV 16.13 /sh P/E 9.03 (Ind RBANK P/E 10.51) Ctry US

PREMIERWEST BANCORP (PRWT)
Holding company for PremierWest Bank — 50% SCALE

Growth Performance Measurement				
Years	Price	Earn.	Div.	Tot Ret
Last 1	101.5	38.4	.0	101.5
Last 5	-57.0	---	-15.5	-45.0
Last 10	-28.3	---	---	-17.7

Adj. for
1 for 10
2/11/11

Dividend
Omitted
10/20/09

Adj. for   Adj. for   Adj. for   Adj. for   Adj. for   Adj. for   Adj. for
5% SD   5% SD   5% SD   5% SD   5% SD   5% SD   5% SD
5/30/01   5/28/03   5/25/04   5/27/05   5/30/06   5/30/07   3/27/09

(16.70) (5.80) (1.14) (1.77) (0.90)
(14.10) (17.10) (1.40) (1.46) (1.26)
(2.30) (17.80) (3.70) (1.21) (1.51)

Copyright 2012 Securities Research Company

Bonds $.0 Mil Com 10.035 Mil BV 3.89 /sh P/E N/A (Ind RBANK P/E 10.51) Ctry US

PRESIDENTIAL LIFE CORP (PLFE1)
Life insurance holding company

Growth Performance Measurement				
Years	Price	Earn.	Div.	Tot Ret
Last 1	39.9	-12.4	.0	42.4
Last 5	-4.4	-14.2	-12.9	-2.4
Last 10	3.5	-3.4	-4.6	5.9

Acquired by
Athene Holdings Ltd.
12/31/2012

(0.43)
(0.41)
(0.03) 0.07

Copyright 2012 Securities Research Company

Bonds $100.0 Mil Com 29.591 Mil BV 29.33 /sh P/E 13.19 (Ind INSLH P/E 7.39) Ctry US

PRGX GLOBAL INC (PRGX)

Provider of accounts payable and other audit services

55% SCALE

Growth Performance Measurement

Years	Price	Earn.	Div.	Tot Ret
Last 1	8.4	-21.4	---	8.4
Last 5	-5.5	---	---	-5.5
Last 10	-23.1	-27.0	---	-23.1

Adj. for 1 for 10 8/14/06

(3.60) (0.20) (0.45)
(2.60) (2.28) (0.50) 0.04
(0.50) (3.10) (0.62) (0.60)

Copyright 2012 Securities Research Company

Bonds $95.3 Mil Com 27.906 Mil BV 2.65 /sh P/E 29.32 (Ind DIVSS P/E 21.56) Ctry US

PRICE T ROWE GROUP INC (TROW)

Investment advice to mutual funds and other clients

(D)(E)

Growth Performance Measurement

Years	Price	Earn.	Div.	Tot Ret
Last 1	14.3	13.8	9.7	16.7
Last 5	1.4	6.9	14.9	3.0
Last 10	16.9	15.0	15.6	18.3

T. Rowe Price Assoc. prior to 12/28/00

Adj. for 2 for 1 6/26/06

.26

Copyright 2012 Securities Research Company

Bonds $.0 Mil Com 254.865 Mil BV 15.14 /sh P/E 20.74 (Ind ASMGT P/E 14.26) Ctry US

PRICELINE COM INC (PCLN)

Web-based "name your own price" services

60% SCALE

(P)(E)

Growth Performance Measurement

Years	Price	Earn.	Div.	Tot Ret
Last 1	32.6	34.6	---	32.6
Last 5	40.1	50.9	---	40.1
Last 10	51.7	52.3	---	51.7

Adj. for 1 for 6 6/16/03

0.15
0.13
0.25

(0.90)
(1.26)
(1.32) (0.66)

Copyright 2012 Securities Research Company

Bonds $.0 Mil Com 49.865 Mil BV 71.75 /sh P/E 21.44 (Ind RTNET P/E 64.32) Ctry US

PRICESMART INC (PSMT)

Club retailing stores in Central America and the Caribbean

95% SCALE

Growth Performance Measurement

Years	Price	Earn.	Div.	Tot Ret
Last 1	10.6	8.7	20.0	11.5
Last 5	20.7	21.8	---	21.4
Last 10	12.9	12.7	---	13.2

(0.41)
(0.95)
(1.26)

(3.41) (4.12) (2.56) (0.07)
(2.25) (4.24) (2.92) (0.35)
(0.04) (4.20) (3.37) (0.64)

Copyright 2012 Securities Research Company

Bonds $.0 Mil Com 30.216 Mil BV 13.87 /sh P/E 34.22 (Ind HYPMK P/E 16.40) Ctry US

276

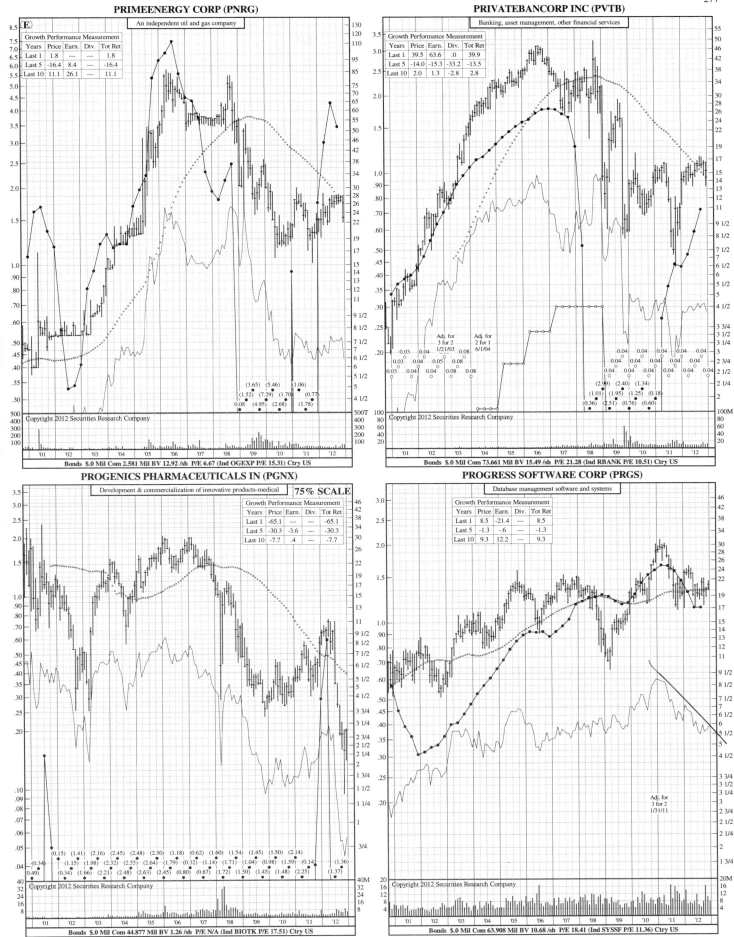

PRIMEENERGY CORP (PNRG)

An independent oil and gas company

(E)

Growth Performance Measurement				
Years	Price	Earn.	Div.	Tot Ret
Last 1	1.8	---	---	1.8
Last 5	-16.4	8.4	---	-16.4
Last 10	11.1	26.1	---	11.1

(3.65) (5.46) (1.06)
(1.52) (7.29) (1.70) (0.77)
0.08 (4.95) (2.68) (1.78)

Copyright 2012 Securities Research Company

Bonds $.0 Mil Com 2.581 Mil BV 12.92 /sh P/E 6.67 (Ind OGEXP P/E 15.31) Ctry US

PRIVATEBANCORP INC (PVTB)

Banking, asset management, other financial services

Growth Performance Measurement				
Years	Price	Earn.	Div.	Tot Ret
Last 1	39.5	63.6	.0	39.9
Last 5	-14.0	-15.3	-33.2	-13.5
Last 10	2.0	1.3	-2.8	2.8

Adj. for
3 for 2
1/21/03

Adj. for
2 for 1
6/1/04

0.03 0.04 0.08 0.08
0.03 0.04 0.05 0.08
0.03 0.04 0.08 0.08

0.04 0.04 0.04 0.04 0.04
0.04 0.04 0.04 0.04 0.04
0.04 0.04 0.04 0.04

(2.99) (2.40) (1.34)
(1.01) (1.95) (1.25) (0.18)
(0.36) (2.51) (0.76) (0.60)

Copyright 2012 Securities Research Company

Bonds $.0 Mil Com 73.661 Mil BV 15.49 /sh P/E 21.28 (Ind RBANK P/E 10.51) Ctry US

PROGENICS PHARMACEUTICALS IN (PGNX)

Development & commercialization of innovative products-medical   **75% SCALE**

Growth Performance Measurement				
Years	Price	Earn.	Div.	Tot Ret
Last 1	-65.1	---	---	-65.1
Last 5	-30.3	-3.6	---	-30.3
Last 10	-7.7	.4	---	-7.7

(0.15) (1.41) (2.16) (2.45) (2.48) (2.50) (1.18) (0.62) (1.60) (1.54) (1.45) (1.50) (2.14) (1.36)
(0.34) (1.15) (1.98) (2.32) (2.55) (2.64) (1.79) (0.32) (1.14) (1.71) (1.04) (0.98) (1.59) (0.14) (1.37)
(0.49) (0.34) (1.66) (2.21) (2.48) (2.63) (2.45) (0.80) (0.67) (1.72) (1.50) (1.45) (1.48) (2.25)

Copyright 2012 Securities Research Company

Bonds $.0 Mil Com 44.877 Mil BV 1.26 /sh P/E N/A (Ind BIOTK P/E 17.51) Ctry US

PROGRESS SOFTWARE CORP (PRGS)

Database management software and systems

Growth Performance Measurement				
Years	Price	Earn.	Div.	Tot Ret
Last 1	8.5	-21.4	---	8.5
Last 5	-1.3	-.6	---	-1.3
Last 10	9.3	12.2	---	9.3

Adj. for
3 for 2
1/31/11

Copyright 2012 Securities Research Company

Bonds $.0 Mil Com 63.908 Mil BV 10.68 /sh P/E 18.41 (Ind SYSSF P/E 11.36) Ctry US

278

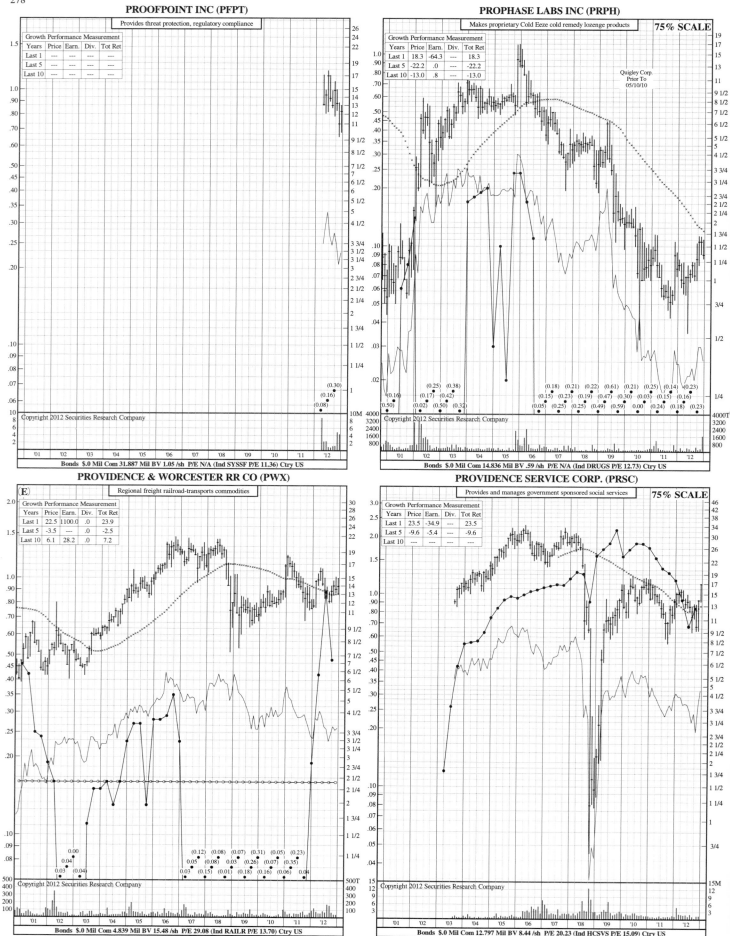

PROOFPOINT INC (PFPT)

Provides threat protection, regulatory compliance

Growth Performance Measurement

Years	Price	Earn.	Div.	Tot Ret
Last 1	---	---	---	---
Last 5	---	---	---	---
Last 10	---	---	---	---

(0.30)
(0.16)
(0.08)

Bonds $.0 Mil Com 31.887 Mil BV 1.05 /sh P/E N/A (Ind SYSSF P/E 11.36) Ctry US

PROPHASE LABS INC (PRPH)

Makes proprietary Cold Eeze cold remedy lozenge products

75% SCALE

Growth Performance Measurement

Years	Price	Earn.	Div.	Tot Ret
Last 1	18.3	-64.3	---	18.3
Last 5	-22.2	.0	---	-22.2
Last 10	-13.0	.8	---	-13.0

Quigley Corp.
Prior To
05/10/10

(0.16) (0.25) (0.38) (0.18) (0.21) (0.22) (0.61) (0.21) (0.25) (0.14) (0.23)
(0.17) (0.42) (0.15) (0.23) (0.19) (0.47) (0.30) (0.03) (0.15) (0.16)
(0.50) (0.02) (0.50) (0.32) (0.05) (0.25) (0.25) (0.49) (0.59) .00 (0.24) (0.18) (0.23)

Bonds $.0 Mil Com 14.836 Mil BV .59 /sh P/E N/A (Ind DRUGS P/E 12.73) Ctry US

PROVIDENCE & WORCESTER RR CO (PWX)

(E)

Regional freight railroad-transports commodities

Growth Performance Measurement

Years	Price	Earn.	Div.	Tot Ret
Last 1	22.5	1100.0	.0	23.9
Last 5	-3.5	---	.0	-2.5
Last 10	6.1	28.2	.0	7.2

0.00
0.04   (0.12) (0.08) (0.07) (0.31) (0.05) (0.23)
0.03   0.05 (0.08) 0.03 (0.26) (0.07) (0.35)
0.03 (0.04) 0.03 (0.15) (0.01) (0.18) (0.16) (0.06) 0.04

Bonds $.0 Mil Com 4.839 Mil BV 15.48 /sh P/E 29.08 (Ind RAILR P/E 13.70) Ctry US

PROVIDENCE SERVICE CORP. (PRSC)

Provides and manages government sponsored social services

75% SCALE

Growth Performance Measurement

Years	Price	Earn.	Div.	Tot Ret
Last 1	23.5	-34.9	---	23.5
Last 5	-9.6	-5.4	---	-9.6
Last 10	---	---	---	---

Bonds $.0 Mil Com 12.797 Mil BV 8.44 /sh P/E 20.23 (Ind HCSVS P/E 15.09) Ctry US

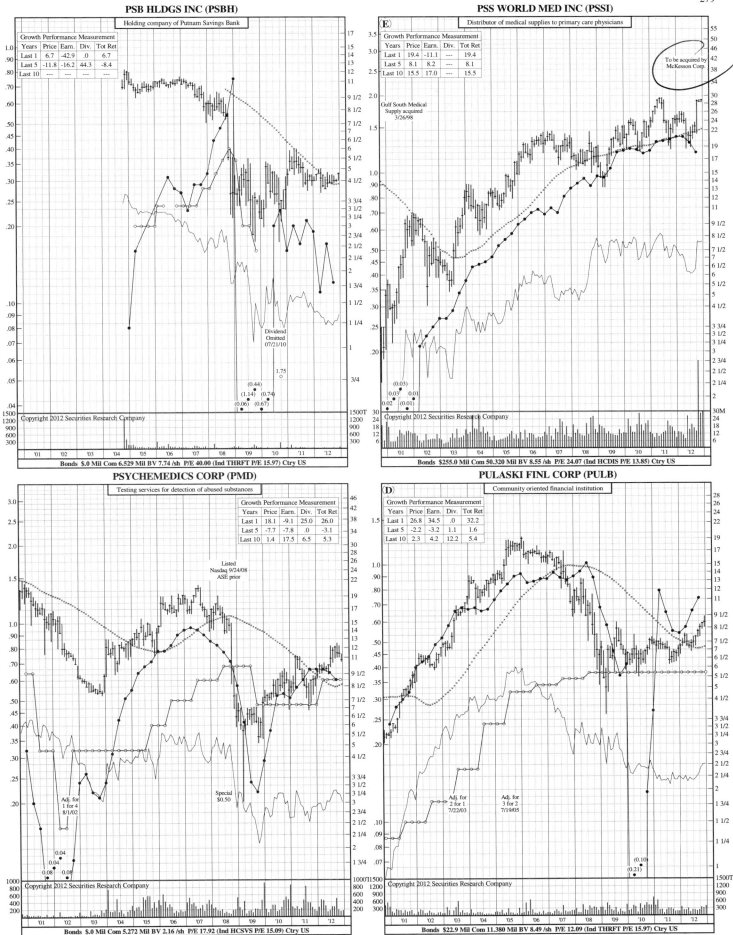

279

PSB HLDGS INC (PSBH)

Holding company of Putnam Savings Bank

Growth Performance Measurement				
Years	Price	Earn.	Div.	Tot Ret
Last 1	6.7	-42.9	.0	6.7
Last 5	-11.8	-16.2	44.3	-8.4
Last 10	---	---	---	---

Dividend
Omitted
07/21/10

1.75

(0.44)
(1.14) (0.74)
(0.06) (0.67)

Copyright 2012 Securities Research Company

Bonds $.0 Mil Com 6.529 Mil BV 7.74 /sh P/E 40.00 (Ind THRFT P/E 15.97) Ctry US

PSS WORLD MED INC (PSSI)

(E)   Distributor of medical supplies to primary care physicians

Growth Performance Measurement				
Years	Price	Earn.	Div.	Tot Ret
Last 1	19.4	-11.1	---	19.4
Last 5	8.1	8.2	---	8.1
Last 10	15.5	17.0	---	15.5

To be acquired by
McKesson Corp.

Gulf South Medical
Supply acquired
3/26/98

(0.03)
(0.03) (0.01)
0.02 (0.01)

Copyright 2012 Securities Research Company

Bonds $255.0 Mil Com 50.320 Mil BV 8.55 /sh P/E 24.07 (Ind HCDIS P/E 13.85) Ctry US

PSYCHEMEDICS CORP (PMD)

Testing services for detection of abused substances

Growth Performance Measurement				
Years	Price	Earn.	Div.	Tot Ret
Last 1	18.1	-9.1	25.0	26.0
Last 5	-7.7	-7.8	.0	-3.1
Last 10	1.4	17.5	6.5	5.3

Listed
Nasdaq 9/24/08
ASE prior

Special
$0.50

Adj. for
1 for 4
8/1/02

0.04
0.04
0.08 0.08

Copyright 2012 Securities Research Company

Bonds $.0 Mil Com 5.272 Mil BV 2.16 /sh P/E 17.92 (Ind HCSVS P/E 15.09) Ctry US

PULASKI FINL CORP (PULB)

(D)   Community oriented financial institution

Growth Performance Measurement				
Years	Price	Earn.	Div.	Tot Ret
Last 1	26.8	34.5	.0	32.2
Last 5	-2.2	-3.2	1.1	1.6
Last 10	2.3	4.2	12.2	5.4

Adj. for
2 for 1
7/22/03

Adj. for
3 for 2
7/19/05

(0.10)
(0.21)

Copyright 2012 Securities Research Company

Bonds $22.9 Mil Com 11.380 Mil BV 8.49 /sh P/E 12.09 (Ind THRFT P/E 15.97) Ctry US

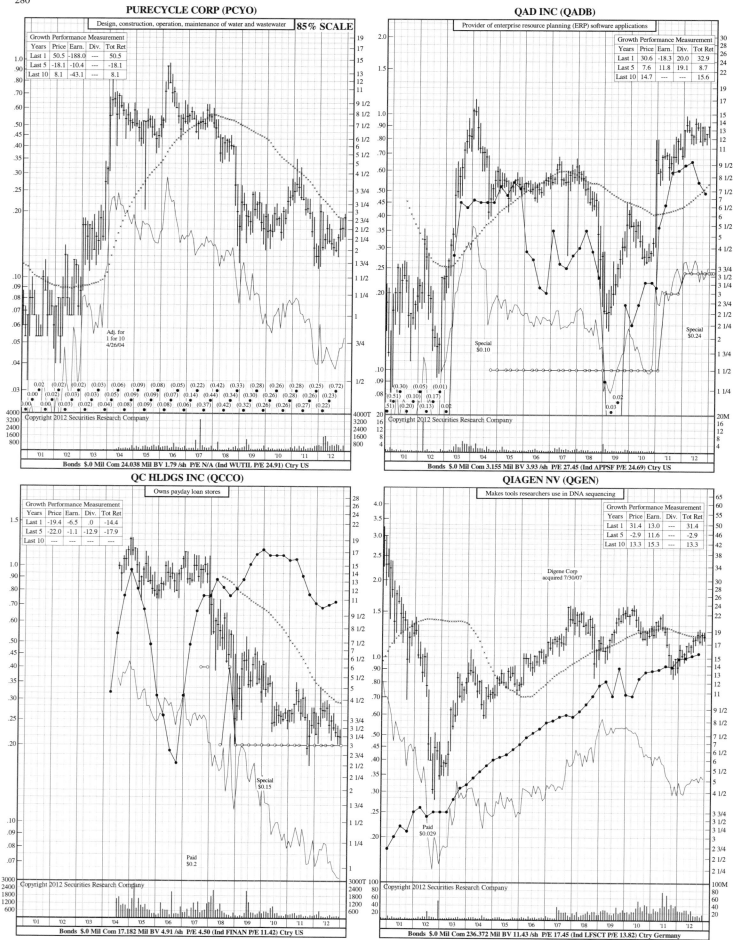

280

PURECYCLE CORP (PCYO)

Design, construction, operation, maintenance of water and wastewater

85% SCALE

Growth Performance Measurement

Years	Price	Earn.	Div.	Tot Ret
Last 1	50.5	-188.0	---	50.5
Last 5	-18.1	-10.4	---	-18.1
Last 10	8.1	-43.1	---	8.1

Adj. for
1 for 10
4/26/04

(0.02) (0.02) (0.02) (0.03) (0.06) (0.09) (0.08) (0.05) (0.22) (0.42) (0.33) (0.28) (0.26) (0.28) (0.25) (0.72)
0.00 (0.02) (0.03) (0.03) (0.05) (0.09) (0.09) (0.07) (0.14) (0.44) (0.34) (0.30) (0.26) (0.28) (0.26) (0.23)
0.00 0.00 (0.03) (0.04) (0.08) (0.09) (0.08) (0.06) (0.37) (0.42) (0.32) (0.26) (0.28) (0.27) (0.22)

Bonds $.0 Mil Com 24.038 Mil BV 1.79 /sh P/E N/A (Ind WUTIL P/E 24.91) Ctry US

QAD INC (QADB)

Provider of enterprise resource planning (ERP) software applications

Growth Performance Measurement

Years	Price	Earn.	Div.	Tot Ret
Last 1	30.6	-18.3	20.0	32.9
Last 5	7.6	11.8	19.1	8.7
Last 10	14.7	---	---	15.6

Special
$0.10

Special
$0.24

(0.30) (0.05) (0.01)
(0.51) (0.10) (0.17)   0.02
(.51)   (0.20) (0.13) 0.02   0.03

Bonds $.0 Mil Com 3.155 Mil BV 3.93 /sh P/E 27.45 (Ind APPSF P/E 24.69) Ctry US

QC HLDGS INC (QCCO)

Owns payday loan stores

Growth Performance Measurement

Years	Price	Earn.	Div.	Tot Ret
Last 1	-19.4	-6.5	.0	-14.4
Last 5	-22.0	-1.1	-12.9	-17.9
Last 10	---	---	---	---

Special
$0.15

Paid
$0.2

Bonds $.0 Mil Com 17.182 Mil BV 4.91 /sh P/E 4.50 (Ind FINAN P/E 11.42) Ctry US

QIAGEN NV (QGEN)

Makes tools researchers use in DNA sequencing

Growth Performance Measurement

Years	Price	Earn.	Div.	Tot Ret
Last 1	31.4	13.0	---	31.4
Last 5	-2.9	11.6	---	-2.9
Last 10	13.3	15.3	---	13.3

Digene Corp
acquired 7/30/07

Paid
$0.029

Bonds $.0 Mil Com 236.372 Mil BV 11.43 /sh P/E 17.45 (Ind LFSCT P/E 13.82) Ctry Germany

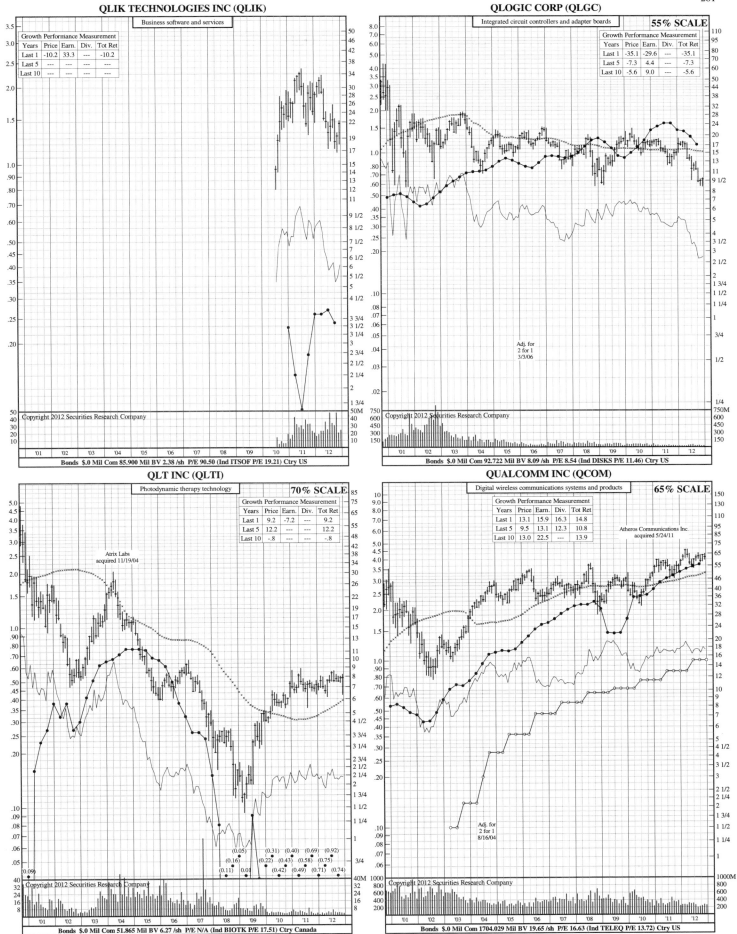

QLIK TECHNOLOGIES INC (QLIK)

Business software and services

Growth Performance Measurement				
Years	Price	Earn.	Div.	Tot Ret
Last 1	-10.2	33.3	---	-10.2
Last 5	---	---	---	---
Last 10	---	---	---	---

Copyright 2012 Securities Research Company

Bonds $.0 Mil Com 85.900 Mil BV 2.38 /sh P/E 90.50 (Ind ITSOF P/E 19.21) Ctry US

QLOGIC CORP (QLGC)

Integrated circuit controllers and adapter boards

55% SCALE

Growth Performance Measurement				
Years	Price	Earn.	Div.	Tot Ret
Last 1	-35.1	-29.6	---	-35.1
Last 5	-7.3	4.4	---	-7.3
Last 10	-5.6	9.0	---	-5.6

Adj. for
2 for 1
3/3/06

Copyright 2012 Securities Research Company

Bonds $.0 Mil Com 92.722 Mil BV 8.09 /sh P/E 8.54 (Ind DISKS P/E 11.46) Ctry US

QLT INC (QLTI)

Photodynamic therapy technology

70% SCALE

Growth Performance Measurement				
Years	Price	Earn.	Div.	Tot Ret
Last 1	9.2	-7.2	---	9.2
Last 5	12.2	---	---	12.2
Last 10	-.8	---	---	-.8

Atrix Labs
acquired 11/19/04

(0.09)

(0.05)   (0.31) (0.40) (0.69) (0.92)
(0.16)   (0.22) (0.43) (0.58) (0.75)
(0.11) 0.01   (0.42) (0.49) (0.71) (0.74)

Copyright 2012 Securities Research Company

Bonds $.0 Mil Com 51.865 Mil BV 6.27 /sh P/E N/A (Ind BIOTK P/E 17.51) Ctry Canada

QUALCOMM INC (QCOM)

Digital wireless communications systems and products

65% SCALE

Growth Performance Measurement				
Years	Price	Earn.	Div.	Tot Ret
Last 1	13.1	15.9	16.3	14.8
Last 5	9.5	13.1	12.3	10.8
Last 10	13.0	22.5	---	13.9

Atheros Communications Inc.
acquired 5/24/11

Adj. for
2 for 1
8/16/04

Copyright 2012 Securities Research Company

Bonds $.0 Mil Com 1704.029 Mil BV 19.65 /sh P/E 16.63 (Ind TELEQ P/E 13.72) Ctry US

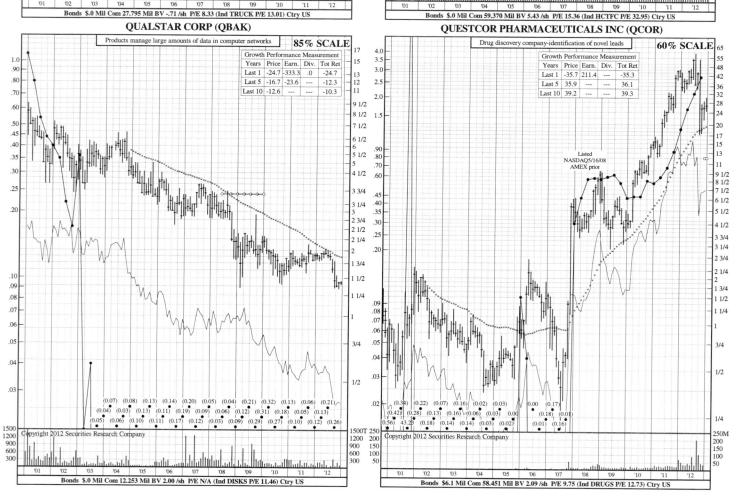

282

QUALITY DISTR INC FLA (QLTY)

Transports bulk chemical products

95% SCALE

Growth Performance Measurement

Years	Price	Earn.	Div.	Tot Ret
Last 1	-46.7	18.0	---	-46.7
Last 5	6.2	21.7	---	6.2
Last 10	---	---	---	---

(0.06)
(0.06)
0.00

Copyright 2012 Securities Research Company

Bonds $.0 Mil Com 27.795 Mil BV -.71 /sh P/E 8.33 (Ind TRUCK P/E 13.01) Ctry US

QUALITY SYS INC (QSII)

(P)E

Health care information management software

70% SCALE

Growth Performance Measurement

Years	Price	Earn.	Div.	Tot Ret
Last 1	-53.1	-13.1	.0	-51.2
Last 5	2.6	12.0	7.0	6.1
Last 10	21.3	24.6	---	23.5

Paid
$0.75

Adj. for
2 for 1
3/28/05

Adj. for
2 for 1
3/27/06

Adj. for
2 for 1
10/27/11

Copyright 2012 Securities Research Company

Bonds $.0 Mil Com 59.370 Mil BV 5.43 /sh P/E 15.36 (Ind HCTFC P/E 32.95) Ctry US

QUALSTAR CORP (QBAK)

Products manage large amounts of data in computer networks

85% SCALE

Growth Performance Measurement

Years	Price	Earn.	Div.	Tot Ret
Last 1	-24.7	-333.3	.0	-24.7
Last 5	-16.7	-23.6	---	-12.3
Last 10	-12.6	---	---	-10.3

(0.07) (0.08) (0.13) (0.14) (0.20) (0.05) (0.04) (0.21) (0.32) (0.13) (0.06) (0.21)
(0.04) (0.03) (0.13) (0.11) (0.19) (0.09) (0.06) (0.12) (0.31) (0.18) (0.05) (0.13)
(0.05) (0.06) (0.10) (0.11) (0.17) (0.12) (0.03) (0.09) (0.29) (0.27) (0.10) (0.12) (0.26)

Copyright 2012 Securities Research Company

Bonds $.0 Mil Com 12.253 Mil BV 2.00 /sh P/E N/A (Ind DISKS P/E 11.46) Ctry US

QUESTCOR PHARMACEUTICALS INC (QCOR)

Drug discovery company-identification of novel leads

60% SCALE

Growth Performance Measurement

Years	Price	Earn.	Div.	Tot Ret
Last 1	-35.7	211.4	---	-35.3
Last 5	35.9	---	---	36.1
Last 10	39.2	---	---	39.3

Listed
NASDAQ 5/16/08
AMEX prior

(0.34) (0.22) (0.07) (0.16) (0.02) (0.03) 0.00 (0.17)
(0.42) (0.28) (0.13) (0.16) (0.06) (0.03) (0.18) (0.01)
(0.56) 43.25 (0.18) (0.14) (0.14) (0.03) (0.02) (0.01) (0.16)

Copyright 2012 Securities Research Company

Bonds $6.1 Mil Com 58.451 Mil BV 2.09 /sh P/E 9.75 (Ind DRUGS P/E 12.73) Ctry US

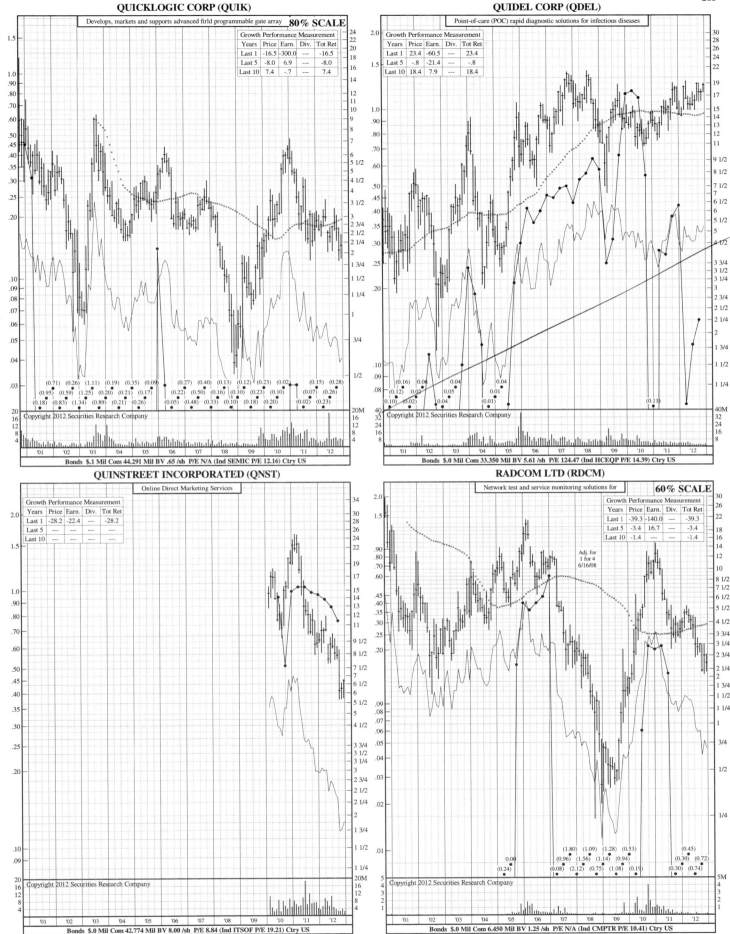

283

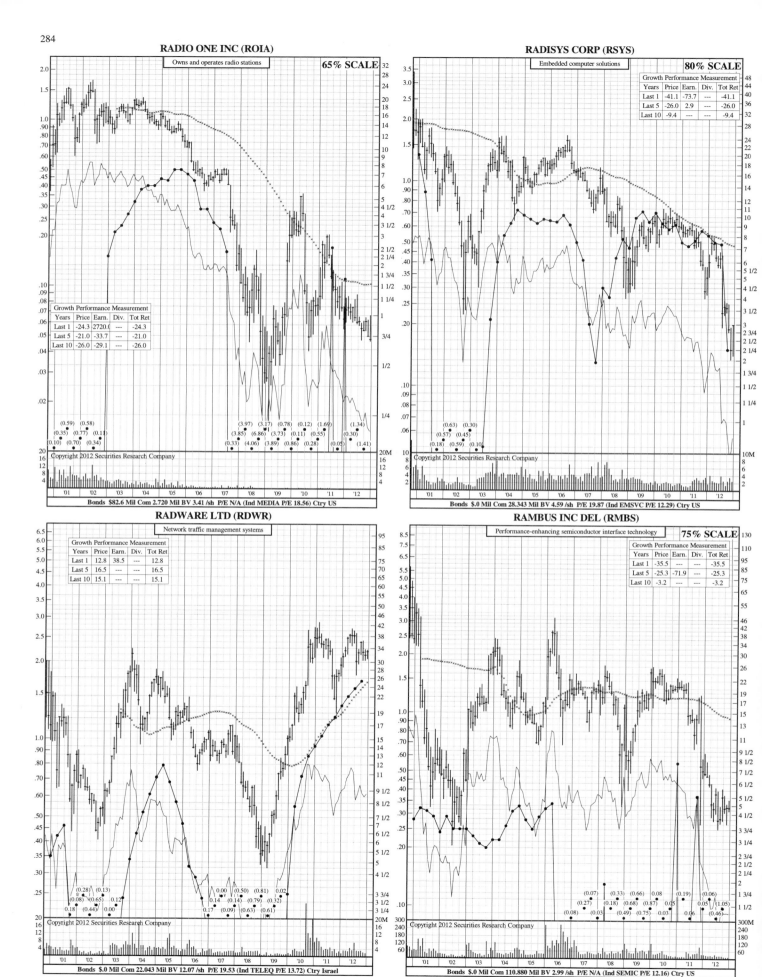

RADIO ONE INC (ROIA)
Owns and operates radio stations
65% SCALE

Growth Performance Measurement			
Years	Price	Earn.	Div.	Tot Ret
Last 1	-24.3	2720.0	---	-24.3
Last 5	-21.0	-33.7	---	-21.0
Last 10	-26.0	-29.1	---	-26.0

(0.59) (0.58)
(0.35) (0.77) (0.11)
(0.10) (0.70) (0.34)
(3.97) (3.17) (0.78) (0.12) (1.69) (1.34)
(3.85) (6.86) (3.73) (0.11) (0.55) (0.30)
(0.33) (4.06) (3.89) (0.86) (0.28) (0.05) (1.41)

Copyright 2012 Securities Research Company
Bonds $82.6 Mil Com 2.720 Mil BV 3.41 /sh P/E N/A (Ind MEDIA P/E 18.56) Ctry US

RADISYS CORP (RSYS)
Embedded computer solutions
80% SCALE

Growth Performance Measurement			
Years	Price	Earn.	Div.	Tot Ret
Last 1	-41.1	-73.7	---	-41.1
Last 5	-26.0	2.9	---	-26.0
Last 10	-9.4	---	---	-9.4

(0.63) (0.30)
(0.57) (0.45)
(0.18) (0.59) (0.10)

Copyright 2012 Securities Research Company
Bonds $.0 Mil Com 28.343 Mil BV 4.59 /sh P/E 19.87 (Ind EMSVC P/E 12.29) Ctry US

RADWARE LTD (RDWR)
Network traffic management systems

Growth Performance Measurement			
Years	Price	Earn.	Div.	Tot Ret
Last 1	12.8	38.5	---	12.8
Last 5	16.5	---	---	16.5
Last 10	15.1	---	---	15.1

(0.28) (0.13)
(0.08) (0.65) (0.12)
(0.18) (0.44) (0.00)
0.00 (0.50) (0.81) 0.02
0.14 (0.14) (0.79) (0.32)
0.17 (0.09) (0.63) (0.61)

Copyright 2012 Securities Research Company
Bonds $.0 Mil Com 22.043 Mil BV 12.07 /sh P/E 19.53 (Ind TELEQ P/E 13.72) Ctry Israel

RAMBUS INC DEL (RMBS)
Performance-enhancing semiconductor interface technology
75% SCALE

Growth Performance Measurement			
Years	Price	Earn.	Div.	Tot Ret
Last 1	-35.5	---	---	-35.5
Last 5	-25.3	-71.9	---	-25.3
Last 10	-3.2	---	---	-3.2

(0.07) (0.33) (0.66) 0.08 (0.19) (0.06)
(0.27) (0.18) (0.68) (0.87) 0.05 0.05 (1.05)
(0.08) (0.03) (0.49) (0.75) (0.03) 0.06 (0.46)

Copyright 2012 Securities Research Company
Bonds $.0 Mil Com 110.880 Mil BV 2.99 /sh P/E N/A (Ind SEMIC P/E 12.16) Ctry US

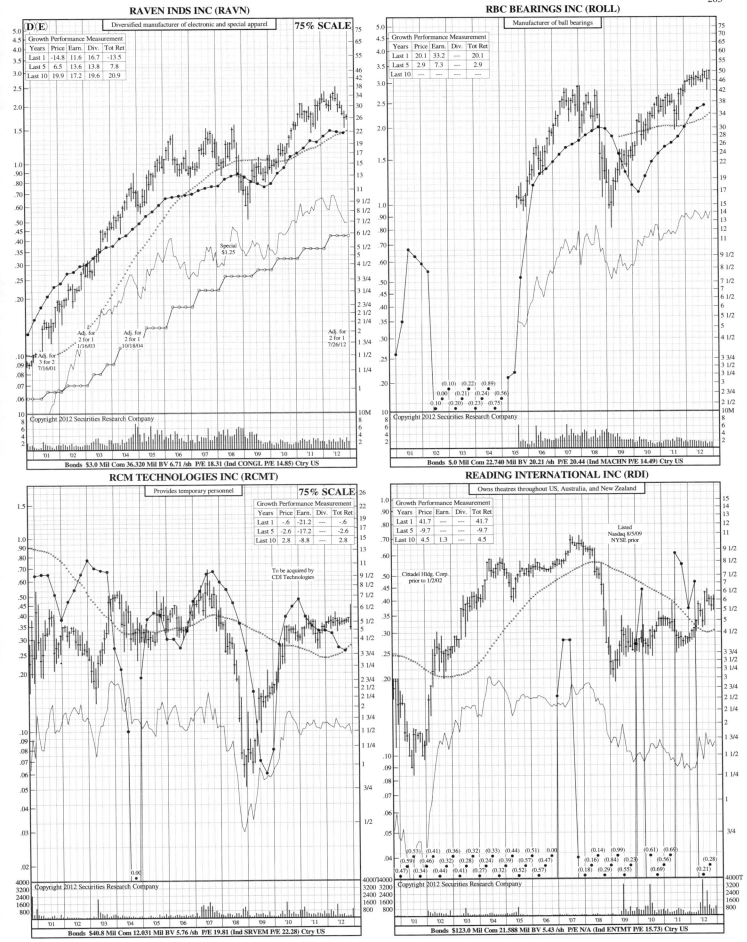

RAVEN INDS INC (RAVN)

(D)(E) | Diversified manufacturer of electronic and special apparel | **75% SCALE**

Growth Performance Measurement

Years	Price	Earn.	Div.	Tot Ret
Last 1	-14.8	11.6	16.7	-13.5
Last 5	6.5	13.6	13.8	7.8
Last 10	19.9	17.2	19.6	20.9

Special $1.25

Adj. for 3 for 2 7/16/01

Adj. for 2 for 1 1/16/03

Adj. for 2 for 1 10/18/04

Adj. for 2 for 1 7/26/12

Copyright 2012 Securities Research Company

Bonds $3.0 Mil Com 36.320 Mil BV 6.71 /sh P/E 18.31 (Ind CONGL P/E 14.85) Ctry US

RBC BEARINGS INC (ROLL)

Manufacturer of ball bearings

Growth Performance Measurement

Years	Price	Earn.	Div.	Tot Ret
Last 1	20.1	33.2	---	20.1
Last 5	2.9	7.3	---	2.9
Last 10	---	---	---	---

(0.10) (0.22) (0.89)
0.00 (0.21) (0.24) (0.56)
(0.10) (0.20) (0.23) (0.75)

Copyright 2012 Securities Research Company

Bonds $.0 Mil Com 22.740 Mil BV 20.21 /sh P/E 20.44 (Ind MACHN P/E 14.49) Ctry US

RCM TECHNOLOGIES INC (RCMT)

Provides temporary personnel | **75% SCALE**

Growth Performance Measurement

Years	Price	Earn.	Div.	Tot Ret
Last 1	-.6	-21.2	---	-.6
Last 5	-2.6	-17.2	---	-2.6
Last 10	2.8	-8.8	---	2.8

To be acquired by CDI Technologies

0.00

Copyright 2012 Securities Research Company

Bonds $40.8 Mil Com 12.031 Mil BV 5.76 /sh P/E 19.81 (Ind SRVEM P/E 22.28) Ctry US

READING INTERNATIONAL INC (RDI)

Owns theatres throughout US, Australia, and New Zealand

Growth Performance Measurement

Years	Price	Earn.	Div.	Tot Ret
Last 1	41.7	---	---	41.7
Last 5	-9.7	---	---	-9.7
Last 10	4.5	1.3	---	4.5

Listed Nasdaq 8/5/09 NYSE prior

Cittadel Hldg. Corp. prior to 1/2/02

(0.53) (0.41) (0.36) (0.32) (0.33) (0.44) (0.51) 0.00 (0.14) (0.99) (0.61) (0.69)
(0.59) (0.46) (0.32) (0.28) (0.24) (0.39) (0.57) (0.47) (0.16) (0.84) (0.23) (0.56) (0.28)
(0.47) (0.34) (0.44) (0.41) (0.27) (0.32) (0.52) (0.57) (0.18) (0.29) (0.55) (0.69) (0.21)

Copyright 2012 Securities Research Company

Bonds $123.0 Mil Com 21.588 Mil BV 5.43 /sh P/E N/A (Ind ENTMT P/E 15.73) Ctry US

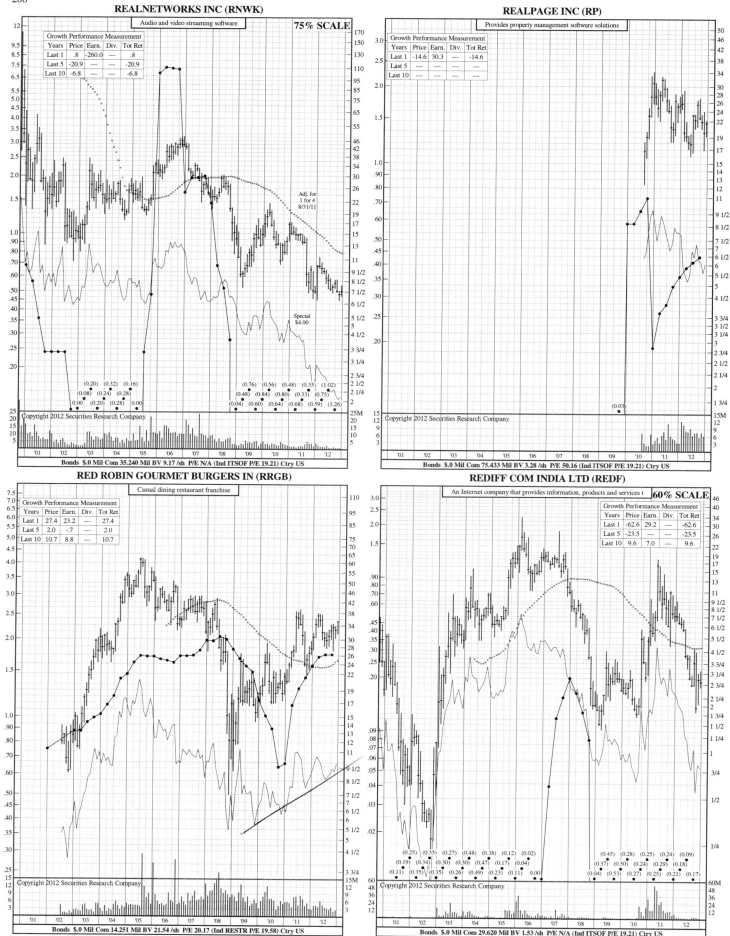

286

REALNETWORKS INC (RNWK)
Audio and video streaming software
75% SCALE

Growth Performance Measurement

Years	Price	Earn.	Div.	Tot Ret
Last 1	.8	-260.0	---	.8
Last 5	-20.9	---	---	-20.9
Last 10	-6.8	---	---	-6.8

Adj. for
1 for 4
8/31/11

Special
$4.00

(0.20) (0.32) (0.16)   (0.76) (0.56) (0.48) (0.35) (1.02)
(0.08) (0.24) (0.28)   (0.48) (0.84) (0.80) (0.33) (0.75)
0.00 (0.20) (0.28) 0.00   (0.04) (0.60) (0.64) (0.68) (0.59) (1.26)

Copyright 2012 Securities Research Company

Bonds $.0 Mil Com 35.240 Mil BV 9.17 /sh P/E N/A (Ind ITSOF P/E 19.21) Ctry US

REALPAGE INC (RP)
Provides property management software solutions

Growth Performance Measurement

Years	Price	Earn.	Div.	Tot Ret
Last 1	-14.6	30.3	---	-14.6
Last 5	---	---	---	---
Last 10	---	---	---	---

(0.03)

Copyright 2012 Securities Research Company

Bonds $.0 Mil Com 75.433 Mil BV 3.28 /sh P/E 50.16 (Ind ITSOF P/E 19.21) Ctry US

RED ROBIN GOURMET BURGERS IN (RRGB)
Casual dining restaurant franchise

Growth Performance Measurement

Years	Price	Earn.	Div.	Tot Ret
Last 1	27.4	23.2	---	27.4
Last 5	2.0	-.7	---	2.0
Last 10	10.7	8.8	---	10.7

Copyright 2012 Securities Research Company

Bonds $.0 Mil Com 14.251 Mil BV 21.54 /sh P/E 20.17 (Ind RESTR P/E 19.58) Ctry US

REDIFF COM INDIA LTD (REDF)
An Internet company that provides information, products and services t
60% SCALE

Growth Performance Measurement

Years	Price	Earn.	Div.	Tot Ret
Last 1	-62.6	29.2	---	-62.6
Last 5	-23.5	---	---	-23.5
Last 10	9.6	7.0	---	9.6

(0.25) (0.35) (0.27) (0.48) (0.38) (0.12) (0.02)   (0.45) (0.28) (0.25) (0.24) (0.09)
(0.19) (0.34) (0.30) (0.30) (0.47) (0.17) (0.04)   (0.37) (0.50) (0.24) (0.29) (0.18)
(0.11) (0.35) (0.35) (0.26) (0.49) (0.23) (0.11) 0.00   (0.04) (0.53) (0.27) (0.25) (0.21) (0.17)

Copyright 2012 Securities Research Company

Bonds $.0 Mil Com 29.620 Mil BV 1.53 /sh P/E N/A (Ind ITSOF P/E 19.21) Ctry US

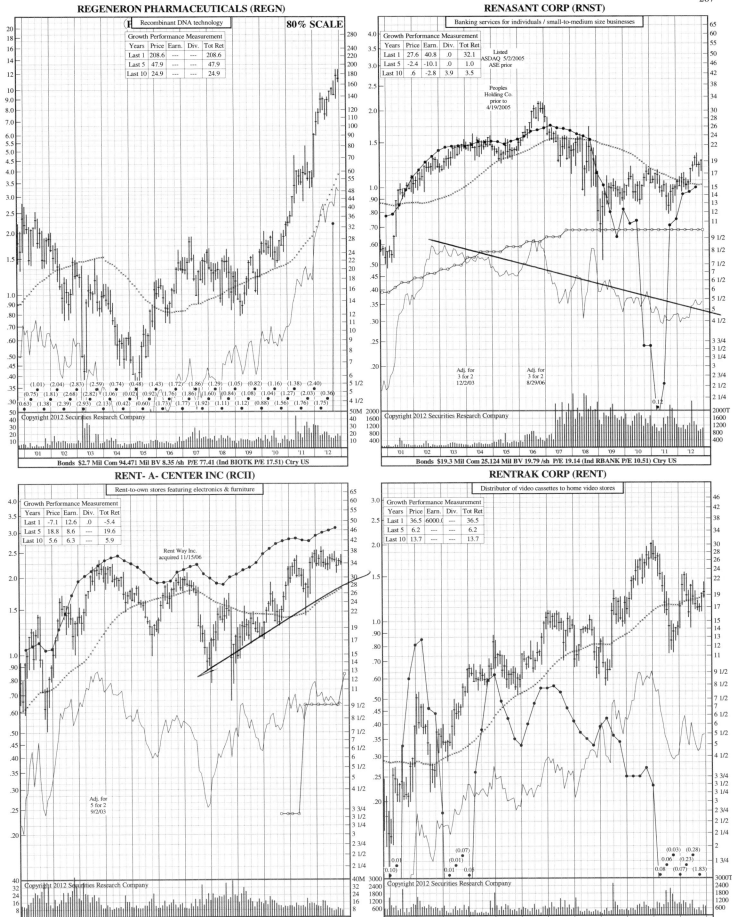

REGENERON PHARMACEUTICALS (REGN)

Recombinant DNA technology

80% SCALE

Growth Performance Measurement				
Years	Price	Earn.	Div.	Tot Ret
Last 1	208.6	---	---	208.6
Last 5	47.9	---	---	47.9
Last 10	24.9	---	---	24.9

(1.01) (2.04) (2.83) (2.59) (0.74) (0.48) (1.43) (1.72) (1.86) (1.29) (1.05) (0.82) (1.16) (1.38) (2.40)
(0.75) (1.81) (2.68) (2.82) (1.06) (0.02) (0.92) (1.76) (1.86) (1.60) (0.84) (1.08) (1.04) (1.27) (2.03) (0.36)
(0.63) (1.38) (2.39) (2.93) (2.13) (0.42) (0.60) (1.73) (1.77) (1.92) (1.11) (1.12) (0.88) (1.56) (1.76) (1.75)

Copyright 2012 Securities Research Company

Bonds $2.7 Mil Com 94.471 Mil BV 8.35 /sh P/E 77.41 (Ind BIOTK P/E 17.51) Ctry US

RENASANT CORP (RNST)

Banking services for individuals / small-to-medium size businesses

Growth Performance Measurement				
Years	Price	Earn.	Div.	Tot Ret
Last 1	27.6	40.8	.0	32.1
Last 5	-2.4	-10.1	.0	1.0
Last 10	.6	-2.8	3.9	3.5

Listed
ASDAQ 5/2/2005
ASE prior

Peoples
Holding Co.
prior to
4/19/2005

Adj. for
3 for 2
12/2/03

Adj. for
3 for 2
8/29/06

0.12

Copyright 2012 Securities Research Company

Bonds $19.3 Mil Com 25.124 Mil BV 19.79 /sh P/E 19.14 (Ind RBANK P/E 10.51) Ctry US

RENT- A- CENTER INC (RCII)

Rent-to-own stores featuring electronics & furniture

Growth Performance Measurement				
Years	Price	Earn.	Div.	Tot Ret
Last 1	-7.1	12.6	.0	-5.4
Last 5	18.8	8.6	---	19.6
Last 10	5.6	6.3		5.9

Rent Way Inc.
acquired 11/15/06

Adj. for
5 for 2
9/2/03

Copyright 2012 Securities Research Company

Bonds $672.2 Mil Com 58.841 Mil BV 24.83 /sh P/E 10.98 (Ind RTCOM P/E 4.59) Ctry US

RENTRAK CORP (RENT)

Distributor of video cassettes to home video stores

Growth Performance Measurement				
Years	Price	Earn.	Div.	Tot Ret
Last 1	36.5	6000.0	---	36.5
Last 5	6.2	---	---	6.2
Last 10	13.7	---	---	13.7

0.01
(0.10)

(0.07)
(0.01)
0.01   0.05

(0.03) (0.28)
0.06   (0.23)
0.08   (0.07) (1.83)

Copyright 2012 Securities Research Company

Bonds $.0 Mil Com 11.844 Mil BV 2.50 /sh P/E N/A (Ind ENTMT P/E 15.73) Ctry US

288

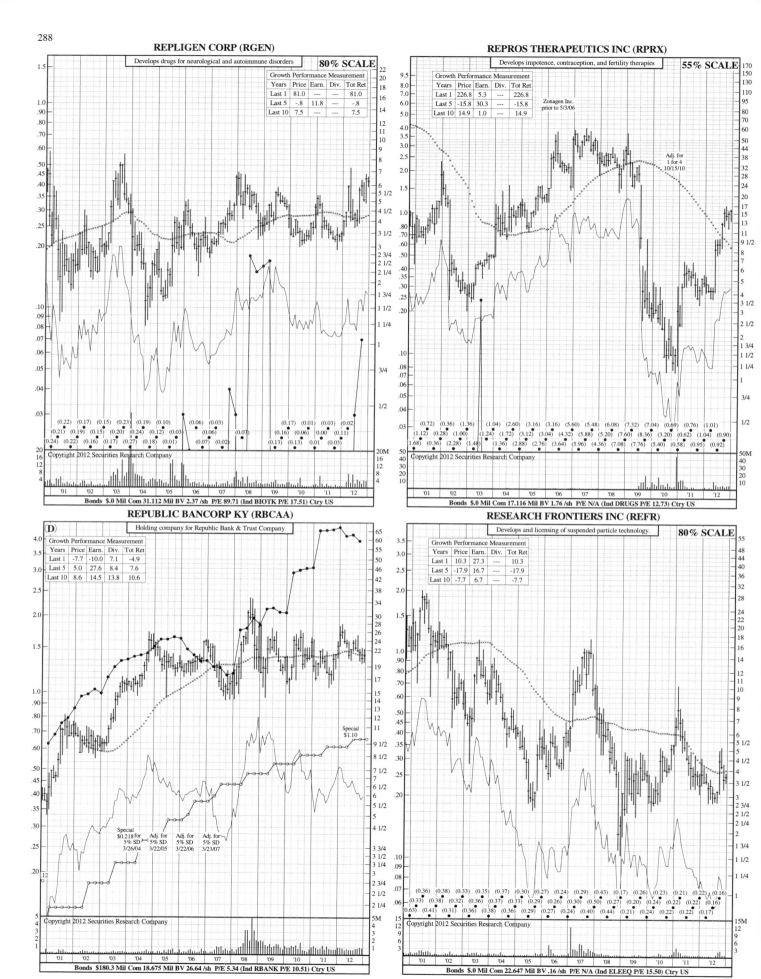

REPLIGEN CORP (RGEN)

Develops drugs for neurological and autoimmune disorders

80% SCALE

Growth Performance Measurement				
Years	Price	Earn.	Div.	Tot Ret
Last 1	81.0	---	---	81.0
Last 5	-.8	11.8	---	-.8
Last 10	7.5	---	---	7.5

Copyright 2012 Securities Research Company

Bonds $.0 Mil Com 31.112 Mil BV 2.37 /sh P/E 89.71 (Ind BIOTK P/E 17.51) Ctry US

REPROS THERAPEUTICS INC (RPRX)

Develops impotence, contraception, and fertility therapies

55% SCALE

Growth Performance Measurement				
Years	Price	Earn.	Div.	Tot Ret
Last 1	226.8	5.3	---	226.8
Last 5	-15.8	30.3	---	-15.8
Last 10	14.9	1.0	---	14.9

Zonagen Inc. prior to 5/3/06

Adj. for 1 for 4 10/15/10

Copyright 2012 Securities Research Company

Bonds $.0 Mil Com 17.116 Mil BV 1.76 /sh P/E N/A (Ind DRUGS P/E 12.73) Ctry US

REPUBLIC BANCORP KY (RBCAA)

(D)

Holding company for Republic Bank & Trust Company

Growth Performance Measurement				
Years	Price	Earn.	Div.	Tot Ret
Last 1	-7.7	-10.0	7.1	-4.9
Last 5	5.0	27.6	8.4	7.6
Last 10	8.6	14.5	13.8	10.6

Special $1.10

Special $0.218 for 5% SD 3/26/04

Adj. for 5% SD 3/22/05

Adj. for 5% SD 3/22/06

Adj. for 5% SD 3/23/07

Copyright 2012 Securities Research Company

Bonds $180.3 Mil Com 18.675 Mil BV 26.64 /sh P/E 5.34 (Ind RBANK P/E 10.51) Ctry US

RESEARCH FRONTIERS INC (REFR)

Develops and licensing of suspended particle technology.

80% SCALE

Growth Performance Measurement				
Years	Price	Earn.	Div.	Tot Ret
Last 1	10.3	27.3	---	10.3
Last 5	-17.9	16.7	---	-17.9
Last 10	-7.7	6.7	---	-7.7

Copyright 2012 Securities Research Company

Bonds $.0 Mil Com 22.647 Mil BV .16 /sh P/E N/A (Ind ELEEQ P/E 15.50) Ctry US

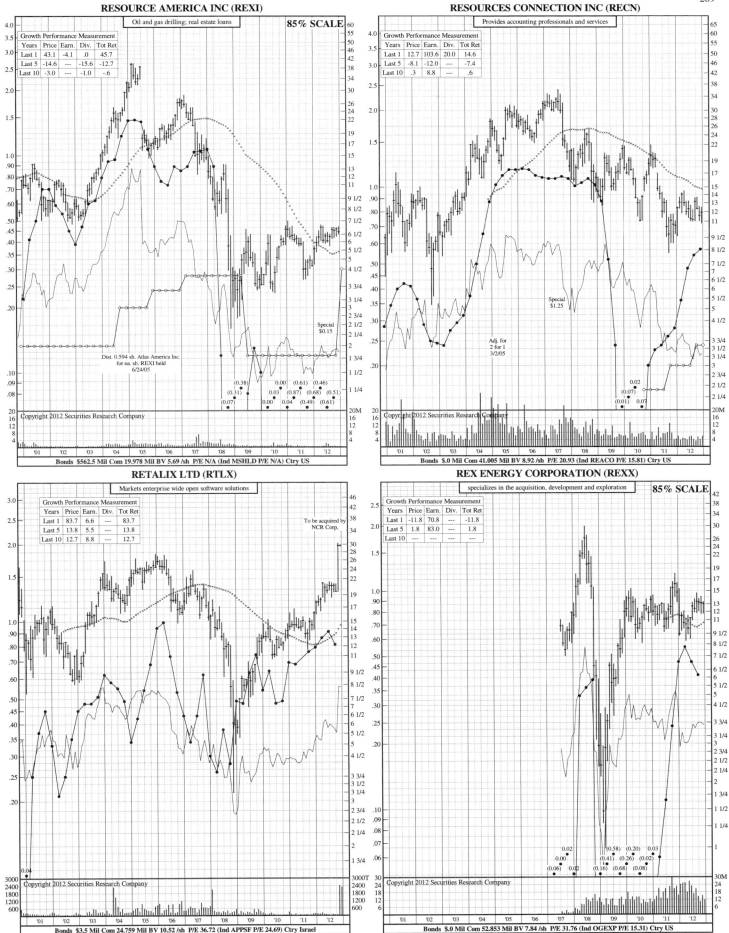

RESOURCE AMERICA INC (REXI)

Oil and gas drilling; real estate loans

85% SCALE

Growth Performance Measurement

Years	Price	Earn.	Div.	Tot Ret
Last 1	43.1	-4.1	.0	45.7
Last 5	-14.6	---	-15.6	-12.7
Last 10	-3.0	---	-1.0	-.6

Special $0.15

Dist. 0.594 sh. Atlas America Inc. for ea. sh. REXI held 6/24/05

(0.38)   0.00   (0.61) (0.46)
(0.31)   0.03 (0.87) (0.68) (0.51)
(0.07)   0.00   0.04 (0.49) (0.61)

Copyright 2012 Securities Research Company

Bonds $562.5 Mil Com 19.978 Mil BV 5.69 /sh P/E N/A (Ind MSHLD P/E N/A) Ctry US

RESOURCES CONNECTION INC (RECN)

Provides accounting professionals and services

Growth Performance Measurement

Years	Price	Earn.	Div.	Tot Ret
Last 1	12.7	103.6	20.0	14.6
Last 5	-8.1	-12.0	---	-7.4
Last 10	.3	8.8	---	.6

Special $1.25

Adj. for 2 for 1 3/2/05

0.02
(0.07)
(0.01)   0.07

Copyright 2012 Securities Research Company

Bonds $.0 Mil Com 41.005 Mil BV 8.92 /sh P/E 20.93 (Ind REACO P/E 15.81) Ctry US

RETALIX LTD (RTLX)

Markets enterprise wide open software solutions

Growth Performance Measurement

Years	Price	Earn.	Div.	Tot Ret
Last 1	83.7	6.6	---	83.7
Last 5	13.8	5.5	---	13.8
Last 10	12.7	8.8	---	12.7

To be acquired by NCR Corp.

0.04

Copyright 2012 Securities Research Company

Bonds $3.5 Mil Com 24.759 Mil BV 10.52 /sh P/E 36.72 (Ind APPSF P/E 24.69) Ctry Israel

REX ENERGY CORPORATION (REXX)

specializes in the acquisition, development and exploration

85% SCALE

Growth Performance Measurement

Years	Price	Earn.	Div.	Tot Ret
Last 1	-11.8	70.8	---	-11.8
Last 5	1.8	83.0	---	1.8
Last 10	---	---	---	---

0.02   (0.58) (0.20) 0.03
0.00 (0.41) (0.26) (0.02)
(0.06) 0.02 (0.16) (0.68) (0.08)

Copyright 2012 Securities Research Company

Bonds $.0 Mil Com 52.853 Mil BV 7.84 /sh P/E 31.76 (Ind OGEXP P/E 15.31) Ctry US

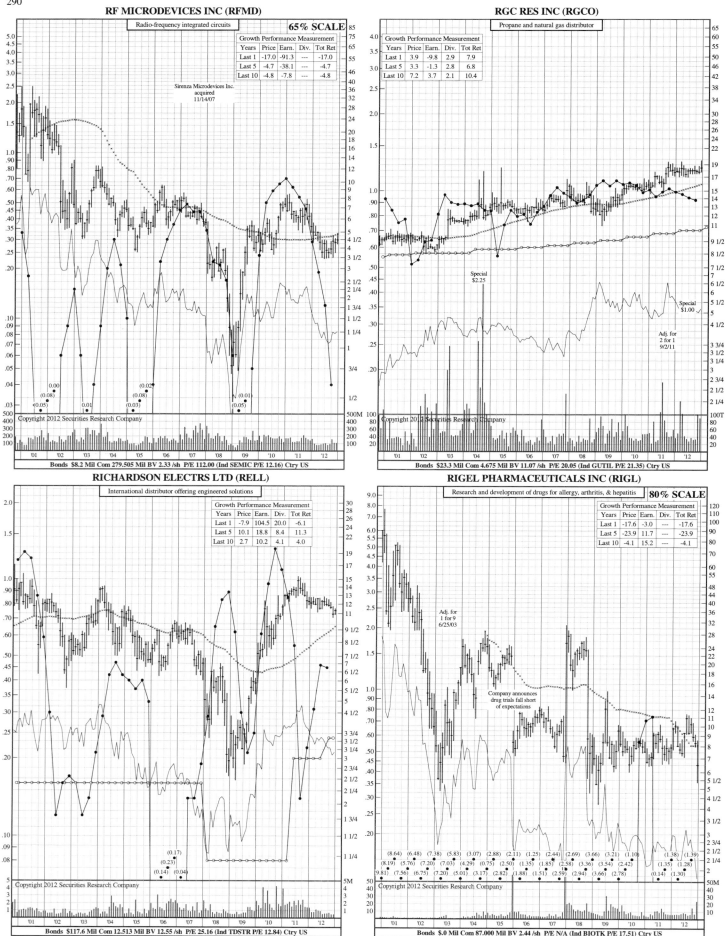

RF MICRODEVICES INC (RFMD)

Radio-frequency integrated circuits

65% SCALE

Growth Performance Measurement

Years	Price	Earn.	Div.	Tot Ret
Last 1	-17.0	-91.3	---	-17.0
Last 5	-4.7	-38.1	---	-4.7
Last 10	-4.8	-7.8	---	-4.8

Sirenza Microdevices Inc.
acquired
11/14/07

0.00
(0.08)
(0.05)   0.01
(0.08)
(0.03)

0.029

(0.01)
(0.05)

Copyright 2012 Securities Research Company

Bonds $8.2 Mil Com 279.505 Mil BV 2.33 /sh P/E 112.00 (Ind SEMIC P/E 12.16) Ctry US

RGC RES INC (RGCO)

Propane and natural gas distributor

Growth Performance Measurement

Years	Price	Earn.	Div.	Tot Ret
Last 1	3.9	-9.8	2.9	7.9
Last 5	3.3	-1.3	2.8	6.8
Last 10	7.2	3.7	2.1	10.4

Special
$2.25

Special
$1.00

Adj. for
2 for 1
9/2/11

Copyright 2012 Securities Research Company

Bonds $23.3 Mil Com 4.675 Mil BV 11.07 /sh P/E 20.05 (Ind GUTIL P/E 21.35) Ctry US

RICHARDSON ELECTRS LTD (RELL)

International distributor offering engineered solutions

Growth Performance Measurement

Years	Price	Earn.	Div.	Tot Ret
Last 1	-7.9	104.5	20.0	-6.1
Last 5	10.1	18.8	8.4	11.3
Last 10	2.7	10.2	4.1	4.0

(0.17)
(0.23)
(0.14)   (0.04)

Copyright 2012 Securities Research Company

Bonds $117.6 Mil Com 12.513 Mil BV 12.55 /sh P/E 25.16 (Ind TDSTR P/E 12.84) Ctry US

RIGEL PHARMACEUTICALS INC (RIGL)

Research and development of drugs for allergy, arthritis, & hepatitis

80% SCALE

Growth Performance Measurement

Years	Price	Earn.	Div.	Tot Ret
Last 1	-17.6	-3.0	---	-17.6
Last 5	-23.9	11.7	---	-23.9
Last 10	-4.1	15.2	---	-4.1

Adj. for
1 for 9
6/25/03

Company announces
drug trials fall short
of expectations

(8.64) (6.48) (7.38) (5.83) (3.07) (2.88) (2.11) (1.25) (2.44) (2.69) (3.66) (3.21) (1.10)   (1.38) (1.39)
(8.19) (5.76) (7.20) (7.03) (4.29) (0.75) (1.85) (2.58) (3.36) (3.54) (2.42)   (1.35) (1.28)
(9.81) (7.56) (6.75) (7.20) (5.01) (3.17) (2.82) (1.88) (1.51) (2.59) (2.94) (3.66) (2.78)   (0.14) (1.30)

Copyright 2012 Securities Research Company

Bonds $.0 Mil Com 87.000 Mil BV 2.44 /sh P/E N/A (Ind BIOTK P/E 17.51) Ctry US

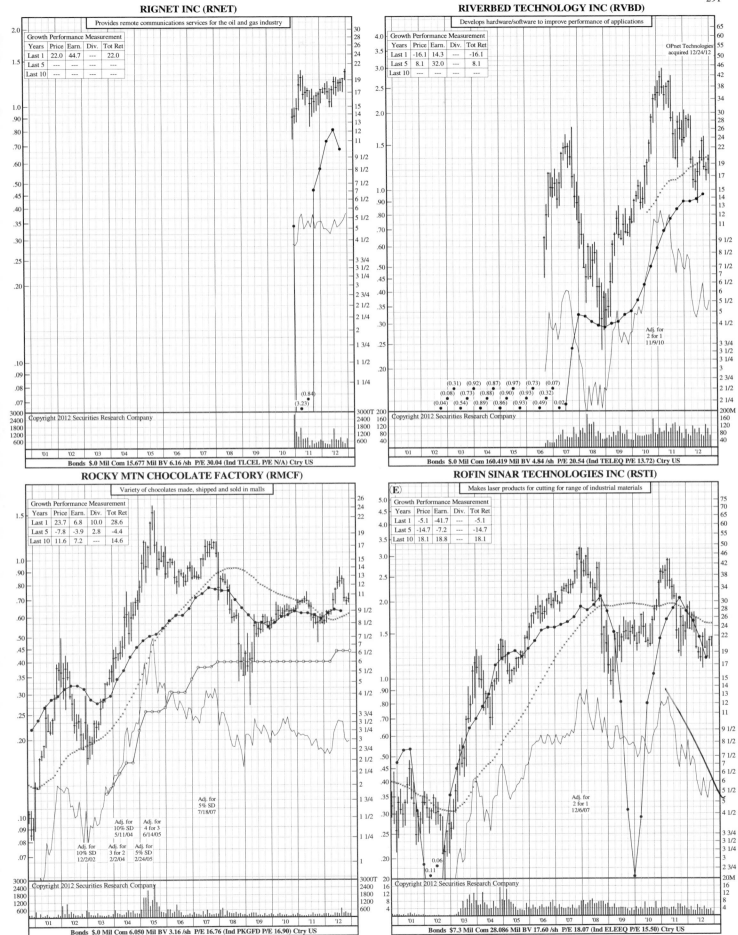

RIGNET INC (RNET)

Provides remote communications services for the oil and gas industry

Growth Performance Measurement

Years	Price	Earn.	Div.	Tot Ret
Last 1	22.0	44.7	---	22.0
Last 5	---	---	---	---
Last 10	---	---	---	---

(0.84)
(3.23)

Copyright 2012 Securities Research Company

Bonds $.0 Mil Com 15.677 Mil BV 6.16 /sh P/E 30.04 (Ind TLCEL P/E N/A) Ctry US

RIVERBED TECHNOLOGY INC (RVBD)

Develops hardware/software to improve performance of applications

OPnet Technologies
acquired 12/24/12

Growth Performance Measurement

Years	Price	Earn.	Div.	Tot Ret
Last 1	-16.1	14.3	---	-16.1
Last 5	8.1	32.0	---	8.1
Last 10	---	---	---	---

Adj. for
2 for 1
11/9/10

(0.31) (0.92) (0.87) (0.97) (0.73) (0.07)
(0.08) (0.73) (0.88) (0.90) (0.93) (0.32)
(0.04) (0.54) (0.89) (0.86) (0.93) (0.49) 0.02

Copyright 2012 Securities Research Company

Bonds $.0 Mil Com 160.419 Mil BV 4.84 /sh P/E 20.54 (Ind TELEQ P/E 13.72) Ctry US

ROCKY MTN CHOCOLATE FACTORY (RMCF)

Variety of chocolates made, shipped and sold in malls

Growth Performance Measurement

Years	Price	Earn.	Div.	Tot Ret
Last 1	23.7	6.8	10.0	28.6
Last 5	-7.8	-3.9	2.8	-4.4
Last 10	11.6	7.2	---	14.6

Adj. for
5% SD
7/18/07

Adj. for
10% SD
5/11/04

Adj. for
4 for 3
6/14/05

Adj. for
10% SD
12/2/02

Adj. for
3 for 2
2/2/04

Adj. for
5% SD
2/24/05

Copyright 2012 Securities Research Company

Bonds $.0 Mil Com 6.050 Mil BV 3.16 /sh P/E 16.76 (Ind PKGFD P/E 16.90) Ctry US

ROFIN SINAR TECHNOLOGIES INC (RSTI)

(E)   Makes laser products for cutting for range of industrial materials

Growth Performance Measurement

Years	Price	Earn.	Div.	Tot Ret
Last 1	-5.1	-41.7	---	-5.1
Last 5	-14.7	-7.2	---	-14.7
Last 10	18.1	18.8	---	18.1

Adj. for
2 for 1
12/6/07

0.06
0.11

Copyright 2012 Securities Research Company

Bonds $7.3 Mil Com 28.086 Mil BV 17.60 /sh P/E 18.07 (Ind ELEEQ P/E 15.50) Ctry US

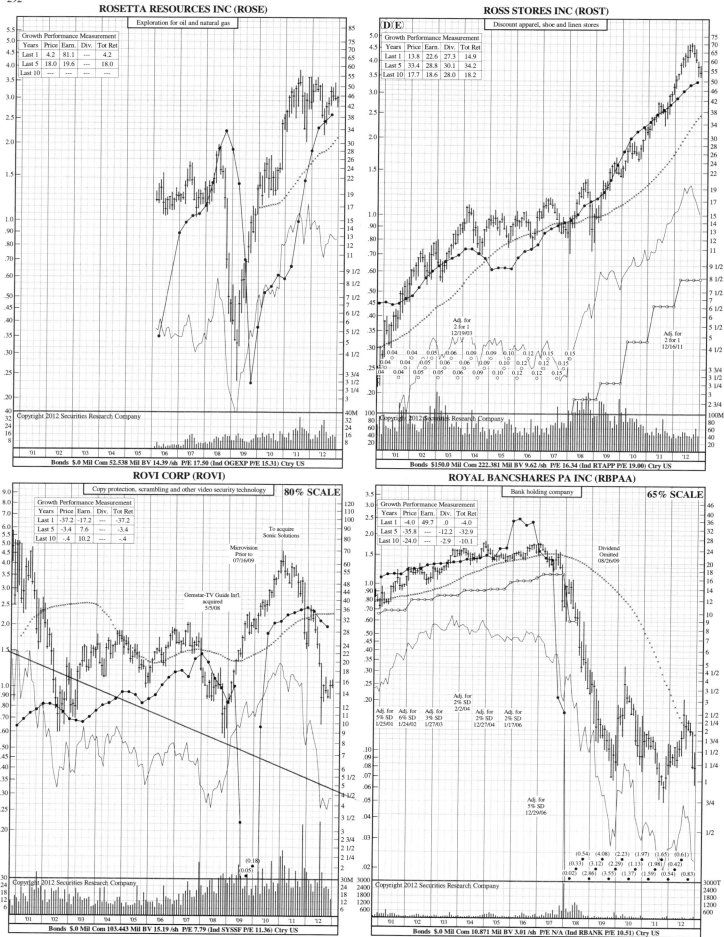

ROSETTA RESOURCES INC (ROSE)

Exploration for oil and natural gas

Growth Performance Measurement				
Years	Price	Earn.	Div.	Tot Ret
Last 1	4.2	81.1	---	4.2
Last 5	18.0	19.6	---	18.0
Last 10	---	---	---	---

Copyright 2012 Securities Research Company

Bonds $.0 Mil Com 52.538 Mil BV 14.39 /sh P/E 17.50 (Ind OGEXP P/E 15.31) Ctry US

ROSS STORES INC (ROST)

(D)(E)

Discount apparel, shoe and linen stores

Growth Performance Measurement				
Years	Price	Earn.	Div.	Tot Ret
Last 1	13.8	22.6	27.3	14.9
Last 5	33.4	28.8	30.1	34.2
Last 10	17.7	18.6	28.0	18.2

Adj. for 2 for 1 12/19/03

Adj. for 2 for 1 12/16/11

0.04 0.04 0.05 0.06 0.09 0.09 0.10 0.12 0.15 0.15
0.04 0.04 0.05 0.06 0.06 0.09 0.10 0.12 0.12 0.15
0.04 0.04 0.05 0.06 0.09 0.10 0.12 0.12 0.15

Copyright 2012 Securities Research Company

Bonds $150.0 Mil Com 222.381 Mil BV 9.62 /sh P/E 16.34 (Ind RTAPP P/E 19.00) Ctry US

ROVI CORP (ROVI)

80% SCALE

Copy protection, scrambling and other video security technology

Growth Performance Measurement				
Years	Price	Earn.	Div.	Tot Ret
Last 1	-37.2	-17.2	---	-37.2
Last 5	-3.4	7.6	---	-3.4
Last 10	-.4	10.2	---	-.4

To acquire Sonic Solutions

Microvision Prior to 07/16/09

Gemstar-TV Guide Int'l. acquired 5/5/08

(0.18)
(0.05)

Copyright 2012 Securities Research Company

Bonds $.0 Mil Com 103.443 Mil BV 15.19 /sh P/E 7.79 (Ind SYSSF P/E 11.36) Ctry US

ROYAL BANCSHARES PA INC (RBPAA)

65% SCALE

Bank holding company

Growth Performance Measurement				
Years	Price	Earn.	Div.	Tot Ret
Last 1	-4.0	49.7	.0	-4.0
Last 5	-35.8	---	-12.2	-32.9
Last 10	-24.0	---	-2.9	-10.1

Dividend Omitted 08/26/09

Adj. for 2% SD 2/2/04

Adj. for 5% SD 1/25/01

Adj. for 6% SD 1/24/02

Adj. for 3% SD 1/27/03

Adj. for 2% SD 12/27/04

Adj. for 2% SD 1/17/06

Adj. for 5% SD 12/29/06

(0.54) (4.08) (2.23) (1.97) (1.65) (0.61)
(0.33) (3.12) (2.29) (1.13) (1.98) (0.42)
(0.02) (2.86) (3.55) (1.37) (1.59) (0.54) (0.83)

Copyright 2012 Securities Research Company

Bonds $.0 Mil Com 10.871 Mil BV 3.01 /sh P/E N/A (Ind RBANK P/E 10.51) Ctry US

ROYAL GOLD INC (RGLD)

Royalty interests in gold mining operations

80% SCALE

(E)

Growth Performance Measurement

Years	Price	Earn.	Div.	Tot Ret
Last 1	20.7	8.1	36.4	21.5
Last 5	21.7	15.6	18.2	22.3
Last 10	12.6	16.5	---	13.0

Paid $0.05

Paid $0.075

Paid $0.10

0.13
0.09
0.13

Copyright 2012 Securities Research Company

Bonds $.0 Mil Com 64.354 Mil BV 31.53 /sh P/E 50.53 (Ind GOLDM P/E 12.48) Ctry US

RTI BIOLOGICS INC (RTIX)

Bone allografts, tissue processing

Growth Performance Measurement

Years	Price	Earn.	Div.	Tot Ret
Last 1	-3.8	12.5	---	-3.8
Last 5	-13.2	---	---	-13.2
Last 10	-8.3	---	---	-8.3

(0.89) (0.42)
(0.34) (0.51)   (0.21) (0.20) (0.10) 0.05
(0.25) (0.87)   (0.09) (0.21) (0.16) 0.02
              0.03 (0.20) (0.20) (0.04)

Copyright 2012 Securities Research Company

Bonds $.0 Mil Com 55.957 Mil BV 3.23 /sh P/E 23.72 (Ind HCSUP P/E 17.94) Ctry US

RUDOLPH TECHNOLOGIES INC (RTEC)

Process control systems for semiconductor manufacturing

Growth Performance Measurement

Years	Price	Earn.	Div.	Tot Ret
Last 1	45.1	-28.7	---	45.1
Last 5	3.5	.0	---	3.5
Last 10	-3.5	17.0	---	-3.5

0.09
0.13
0.13   0.11   (0.08) (0.57)
                (0.45) (0.22)
            0.03 (0.30) (0.55)

Copyright 2012 Securities Research Company

Bonds $.0 Mil Com 32.343 Mil BV 7.43 /sh P/E 18.67 (Ind SEMIQ P/E 13.46) Ctry US

RUSH ENTERPRISES INC (RUSHB)

Retailer of premium transportation and construction equipment

(P/E)

Growth Performance Measurement

Years	Price	Earn.	Div.	Tot Ret
Last 1	1.6	46.6	---	1.6
Last 5	-.6	3.4	---	-.6
Last 10	21.7	20.4	---	21.7

Adj. for
3 for 2
10/11/07

Copyright 2012 Securities Research Company

Bonds $.0 Mil Com 10.792 Mil BV 15.28 /sh P/E 10.16 (Ind TRADE P/E 25.46) Ctry US

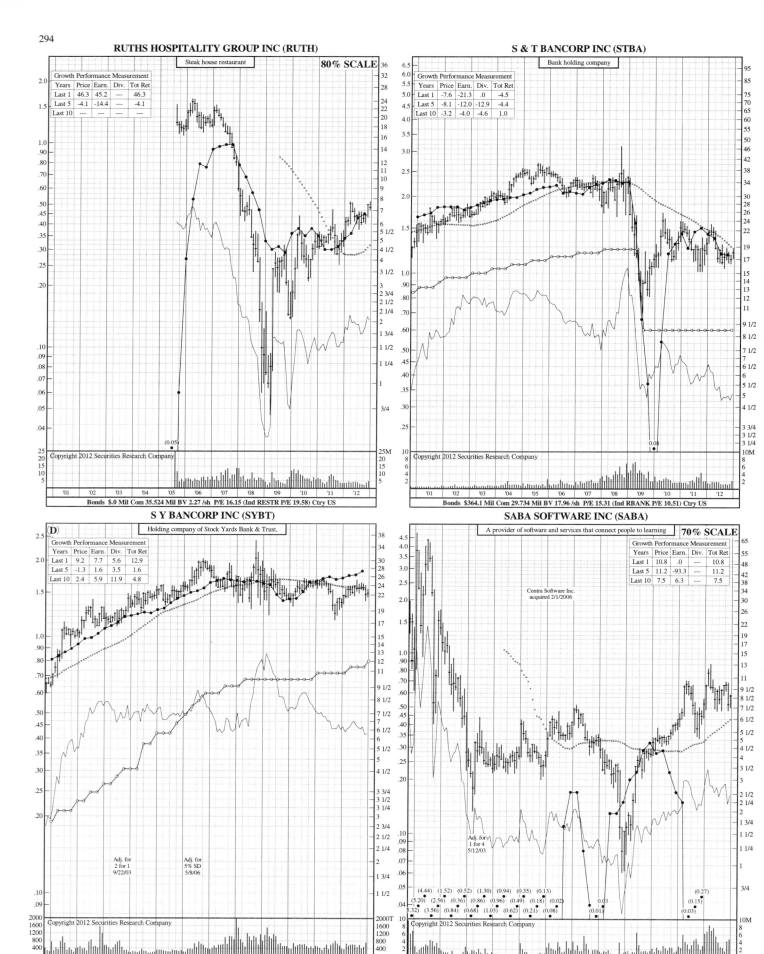

294

RUTHS HOSPITALITY GROUP INC (RUTH)

Steak house restaurant

80% SCALE

Growth Performance Measurement				
Years	Price	Earn.	Div.	Tot Ret
Last 1	46.3	45.2	---	46.3
Last 5	-4.1	-14.4	---	-4.1
Last 10	---	---	---	---

(0.05)

Copyright 2012 Securities Research Company

Bonds $.0 Mil Com 35.524 Mil BV 2.27 /sh P/E 16.15 (Ind RESTR P/E 19.58) Ctry US

S & T BANCORP INC (STBA)

Bank holding company

Growth Performance Measurement				
Years	Price	Earn.	Div.	Tot Ret
Last 1	-7.6	-21.3	.0	-4.5
Last 5	-8.1	-12.0	-12.9	-4.4
Last 10	-3.2	-4.0	-4.6	1.0

0.08

Copyright 2012 Securities Research Company

Bonds $364.1 Mil Com 29.734 Mil BV 17.96 /sh P/E 15.31 (Ind RBANK P/E 10.51) Ctry US

S Y BANCORP INC (SYBT)

(D) Holding company of Stock Yards Bank & Trust,

Growth Performance Measurement				
Years	Price	Earn.	Div.	Tot Ret
Last 1	9.2	7.7	5.6	12.9
Last 5	-1.3	1.6	3.5	1.6
Last 10	2.4	5.9	11.9	4.8

Adj. for
2 for 1
9/22/03

Adj. for
5% SD
5/8/06

Copyright 2012 Securities Research Company

Bonds $.0 Mil Com 13.916 Mil BV 14.47 /sh P/E 12.32 (Ind RBANK P/E 10.51) Ctry US

SABA SOFTWARE INC (SABA)

A provider of software and services that connect people to learning

70% SCALE

Growth Performance Measurement				
Years	Price	Earn.	Div.	Tot Ret
Last 1	10.8	.0	---	10.8
Last 5	11.2	-93.3	---	11.2
Last 10	7.5	6.3	---	7.5

Centra Software Inc.
acquired 2/1/2006

Adj. for
1 for 4
5/12/03

(4.44) (1.52) (0.52) (1.30) (0.94) (0.35) (0.13)   (0.27)
(5.20) (2.56) (0.36) (0.86) (0.96) (0.49) (0.18) (0.02)   0.03   (0.15)
(5.32) (3.56) (0.84) (1.03) (0.62) (0.21) (0.08)   (0.01)   (0.03)

Copyright 2012 Securities Research Company

Bonds $3.1 Mil Com 29.786 Mil BV 1.21 /sh P/E N/A (Ind ITSOF P/E 19.21) Ctry US

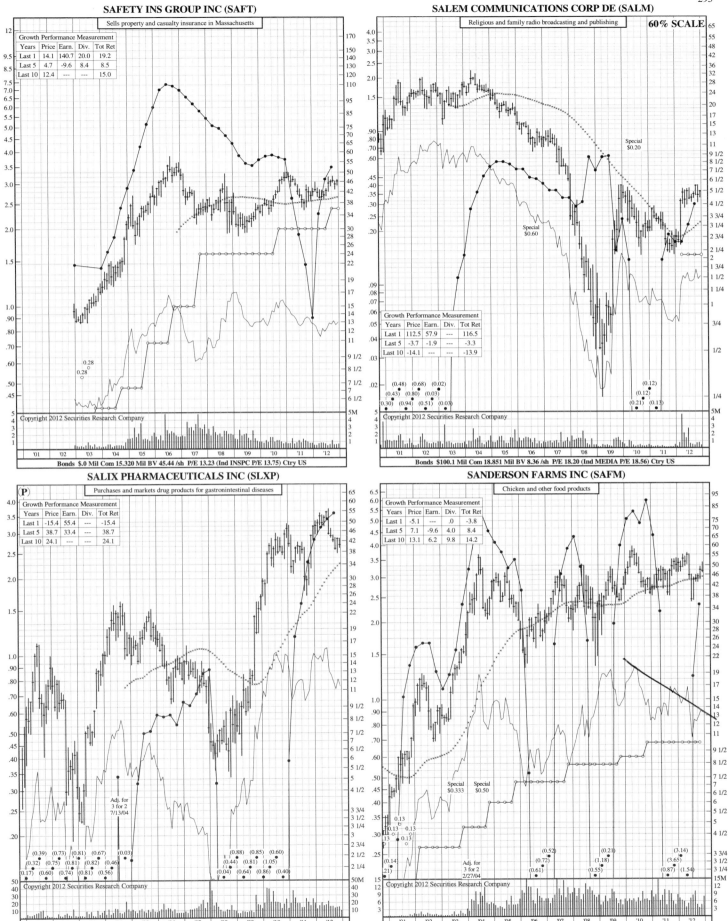

SAFETY INS GROUP INC (SAFT)

Sells property and casualty insurance in Massachusetts

Growth Performance Measurement				
Years	Price	Earn.	Div.	Tot Ret
Last 1	14.1	140.7	20.0	19.2
Last 5	4.7	-9.6	8.4	8.5
Last 10	12.4	---	---	15.0

0.28
0.28

Copyright 2012 Securities Research Company

Bonds $.0 Mil Com 15.320 Mil BV 45.44 /sh P/E 13.23 (Ind INSPC P/E 13.75) Ctry US

SALEM COMMUNICATIONS CORP DE (SALM)

Religious and family radio broadcasting and publishing

60% SCALE

Special
$0.20

Special
$0.60

Growth Performance Measurement				
Years	Price	Earn.	Div.	Tot Ret
Last 1	112.5	57.9	---	116.5
Last 5	-3.7	-1.9		-3.3
Last 10	-14.1	---		-13.9

(0.48) (0.68) (0.02)   (0.12)
(0.43) (0.80) (0.03)   (0.12)
(0.30) (0.94) (0.51) (0.03)   (0.21) (0.13)

Copyright 2012 Securities Research Company

Bonds $100.1 Mil Com 18.851 Mil BV 8.36 /sh P/E 18.20 (Ind MEDIA P/E 18.56) Ctry US

SALIX PHARMACEUTICALS INC (SLXP)

(P)

Purchases and markets drug products for gastrointestinal diseases

Growth Performance Measurement				
Years	Price	Earn.	Div.	Tot Ret
Last 1	-15.4	55.4	---	-15.4
Last 5	38.7	33.4	---	38.7
Last 10	24.1	---		24.1

Adj. for
3 for 2
7/13/04

(0.39) (0.73) (0.81) (0.67) (0.03)   (0.88) (0.85) (0.60)
(0.32) (0.75) (0.81) (0.82) (0.46)   (0.44) (0.81) (1.05)
(0.17) (0.60) (0.74) (0.81) (0.56)   (0.04) (0.64) (0.86) (0.40)

Copyright 2012 Securities Research Company

Bonds $.0 Mil Com 58.842 Mil BV 9.05 /sh P/E 11.27 (Ind DRUGS P/E 12.73) Ctry US

SANDERSON FARMS INC (SAFM)

Chicken and other food products

Growth Performance Measurement				
Years	Price	Earn.	Div.	Tot Ret
Last 1	-5.1	---	.0	-3.8
Last 5	7.1	-9.6	4.0	8.4
Last 10	13.1	6.2	9.8	14.2

Special
$0.333

Special
$0.50

Adj. for
3 for 2
2/27/04

0.13
0.13 0.13
13
0.13

0.13
0.13

(0.14)   (0.52)   (0.21)   (3.14)
(0.21)   (0.72)   (1.18)   (3.65)
               (0.61)   (0.55)   (0.87) (1.54)

Copyright 2012 Securities Research Company

Bonds $104.7 Mil Com 22.969 Mil BV 23.66 /sh P/E 20.32 (Ind PKGFD P/E 16.90) Ctry US

'01 '02 '03 '04 '05 '06 '07 '08 '09 '10 '11 '12

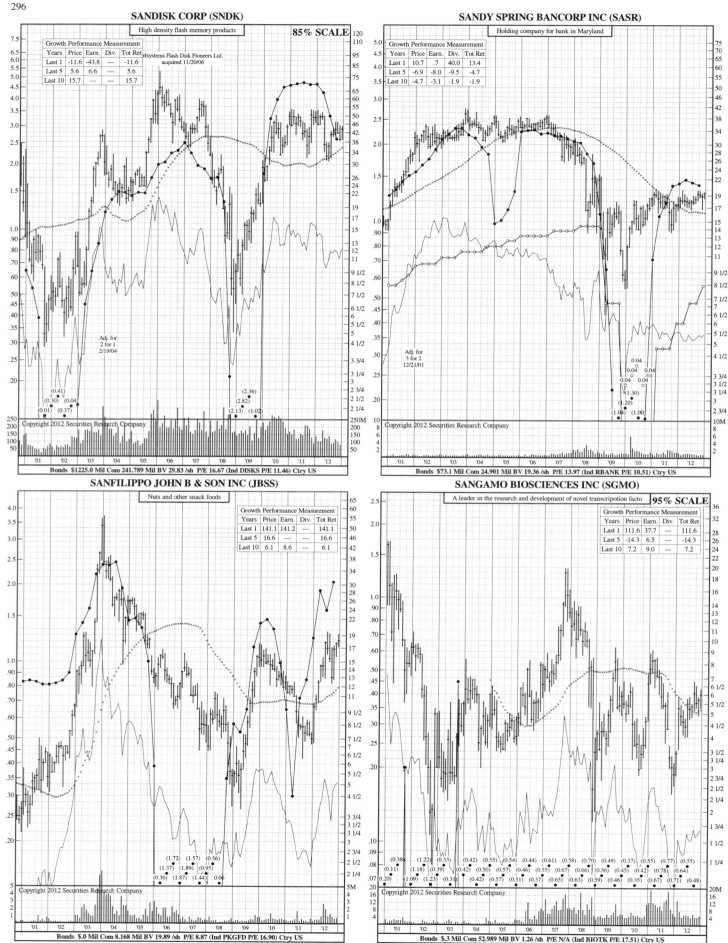

SANDISK CORP (SNDK)
High density flash memory products
85% SCALE

SANDY SPRING BANCORP INC (SASR)
Holding company for bank in Maryland

SANFILIPPO JOHN B & SON INC (JBSS)
Nuts and other snack foods

SANGAMO BIOSCIENCES INC (SGMO)
A leader in the research and development of novel transcripotion facto
95% SCALE

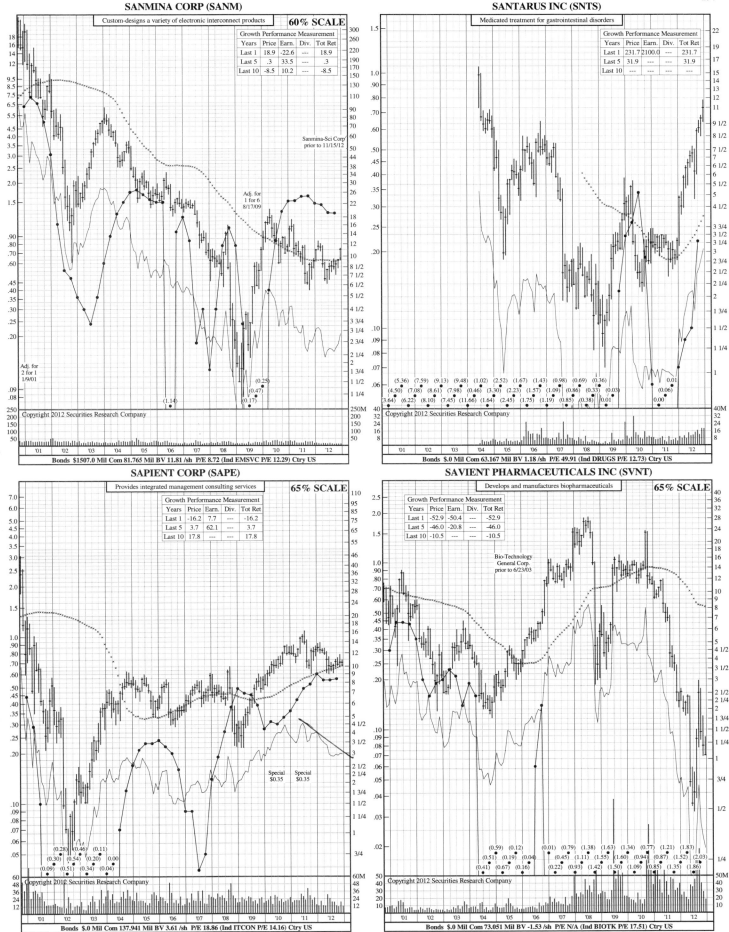

SANMINA CORP (SANM)

Custom-designs a variety of electronic interconnect products

60% SCALE

Growth Performance Measurement				
Years	Price	Earn.	Div.	Tot Ret
Last 1	18.9	-22.6	---	18.9
Last 5	.3	33.5	---	.3
Last 10	-8.5	10.2	---	-8.5

Sanmina-Sci Corp prior to 11/15/12

Adj. for 1 for 6 8/17/09

Adj. for 2 for 1 1/9/01

(1.14)   (0.25)   (0.47)   (0.17)

Copyright 2012 Securities Research Company

Bonds $1507.0 Mil Com 81.765 Mil BV 11.81 /sh P/E 8.72 (Ind EMSVC P/E 12.29) Ctry US

SANTARUS INC (SNTS)

Medicated treatment for gastrointestinal disorders

Growth Performance Measurement				
Years	Price	Earn.	Div.	Tot Ret
Last 1	231.7	2100.0	---	231.7
Last 5	31.9	---	---	31.9
Last 10	---	---	---	---

(5.36) (7.59) (9.13) (9.48) (1.02) (2.52) (1.67) (1.43) (0.98) (0.69) (0.36)   (0.01)
(4.50) (7.08) (8.61) (7.98) (0.46) (3.30) (2.23) (1.57) (1.09) (0.86) (0.33) (0.03)   (0.06)
(3.64) (6.22) (8.10) (7.45) (11.66) (1.64) (2.45) (1.75) (1.19) (0.85) (0.38) (0.01)   0.00

Copyright 2012 Securities Research Company

Bonds $.0 Mil Com 63.167 Mil BV 1.18 /sh P/E 49.91 (Ind DRUGS P/E 12.73) Ctry US

SAPIENT CORP (SAPE)

Provides integrated management consulting services

65% SCALE

Growth Performance Measurement				
Years	Price	Earn.	Div.	Tot Ret
Last 1	-16.2	7.7	---	-16.2
Last 5	3.7	62.1	---	3.7
Last 10	17.8	---	---	17.8

Special $0.35   Special $0.35

(0.28) (0.46) (0.11)
(0.30) (0.54) (0.20) (0.00)
(0.09) (0.51) (0.34) (0.04)

Copyright 2012 Securities Research Company

Bonds $.0 Mil Com 137.941 Mil BV 3.61 /sh P/E 18.86 (Ind ITCON P/E 14.16) Ctry US

SAVIENT PHARMACEUTICALS INC (SVNT)

Develops and manufactures biopharmaceuticals

65% SCALE

Growth Performance Measurement				
Years	Price	Earn.	Div.	Tot Ret
Last 1	-52.9	-50.4	---	-52.9
Last 5	-46.0	-20.8	---	-46.0
Last 10	-10.5	---	---	-10.5

Bio-Technology General Corp. prior to 6/23/03

(0.59) (0.12)   (0.01) (0.79) (1.38) (1.63) (1.34) (0.77) (1.21) (1.83)
(0.51) (0.19) (0.04) (0.45) (1.11) (1.55) (1.60) (0.94) (0.87) (1.52) (2.03)
(0.41) (0.67) (0.16) (0.22) (0.93) (1.42) (1.50) (1.09) (0.85) (1.35) (1.86)

Copyright 2012 Securities Research Company

Bonds $.0 Mil Com 73.051 Mil BV -1.53 /sh P/E N/A (Ind BIOTK P/E 17.51) Ctry US

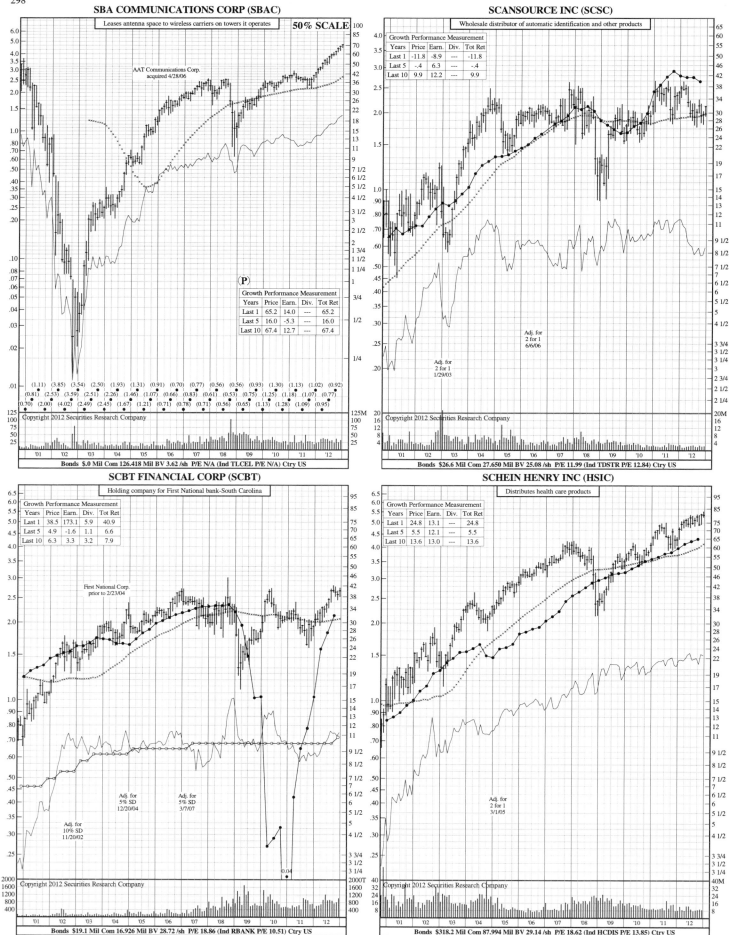

298

SBA COMMUNICATIONS CORP (SBAC)

Leases antenna space to wireless carriers on towers it operates

50% SCALE

AAT Communications Corp.
acquired 4/28/06

(P)

Growth Performance Measurement				
Years	Price	Earn.	Div.	Tot Ret
Last 1	65.2	14.0	---	65.2
Last 5	16.0	-5.3	---	16.0
Last 10	67.4	12.7	---	67.4

(1.11) (3.85) (3.54) (2.50) (1.93) (1.31) (0.91) (0.70) (0.77) (0.56) (0.56) (0.93) (1.30) (1.13) (1.02) (0.92)
(0.81) (2.53) (3.59) (2.51) (2.26) (1.46) (1.07) (0.66) (0.83) (0.61) (0.53) (0.75) (1.25) (1.18) (1.07) (0.77)
(0.70) (2.00) (4.02) (2.49) (2.45) (1.67) (1.21) (0.71) (0.78) (0.71) (0.56) (0.65) (1.13) (1.28) (1.09) (0.95)

Copyright 2012 Securities Research Company

'01 '02 '03 '04 '05 '06 '07 '08 '09 '10 '11 '12

Bonds $.0 Mil Com 126.418 Mil BV 3.62 /sh P/E N/A (Ind TLCEL P/E N/A) Ctry US

SCANSOURCE INC (SCSC)

Wholesale distributor of automatic identification and other products

Growth Performance Measurement				
Years	Price	Earn.	Div.	Tot Ret
Last 1	-11.8	-8.9	---	-11.8
Last 5	-.4	6.3	---	-.4
Last 10	9.9	12.2	---	9.9

Adj. for
2 for 1
6/6/06

Adj. for
2 for 1
1/29/03

Copyright 2012 Securities Research Company

'01 '02 '03 '04 '05 '06 '07 '08 '09 '10 '11 '12

Bonds $26.6 Mil Com 27.650 Mil BV 25.08 /sh P/E 11.99 (Ind TDSTR P/E 12.84) Ctry US

SCBT FINANCIAL CORP (SCBT)

Holding company for First National bank-South Carolina

Growth Performance Measurement				
Years	Price	Earn.	Div.	Tot Ret
Last 1	38.5	173.1	5.9	40.9
Last 5	4.9	-1.6	1.1	6.6
Last 10	6.3	3.3	3.2	7.9

First National Corp.
prior to 2/23/04

Adj. for
5% SD
12/20/04

Adj. for
5% SD
3/7/07

Adj. for
10% SD
11/20/02

0.04

Copyright 2012 Securities Research Company

'01 '02 '03 '04 '05 '06 '07 '08 '09 '10 '11 '12

Bonds $19.1 Mil Com 16.926 Mil BV 28.72 /sh P/E 18.86 (Ind RBANK P/E 10.51) Ctry US

SCHEIN HENRY INC (HSIC)

Distributes health care products

Growth Performance Measurement				
Years	Price	Earn.	Div.	Tot Ret
Last 1	24.8	13.1	---	24.8
Last 5	5.5	12.1	---	5.5
Last 10	13.6	13.0	---	13.6

Adj. for
2 for 1
3/1/05

Copyright 2012 Securities Research Company

'01 '02 '03 '04 '05 '06 '07 '08 '09 '10 '11 '12

Bonds $318.2 Mil Com 87.994 Mil BV 29.14 /sh P/E 18.62 (Ind HCDIS P/E 13.85) Ctry US

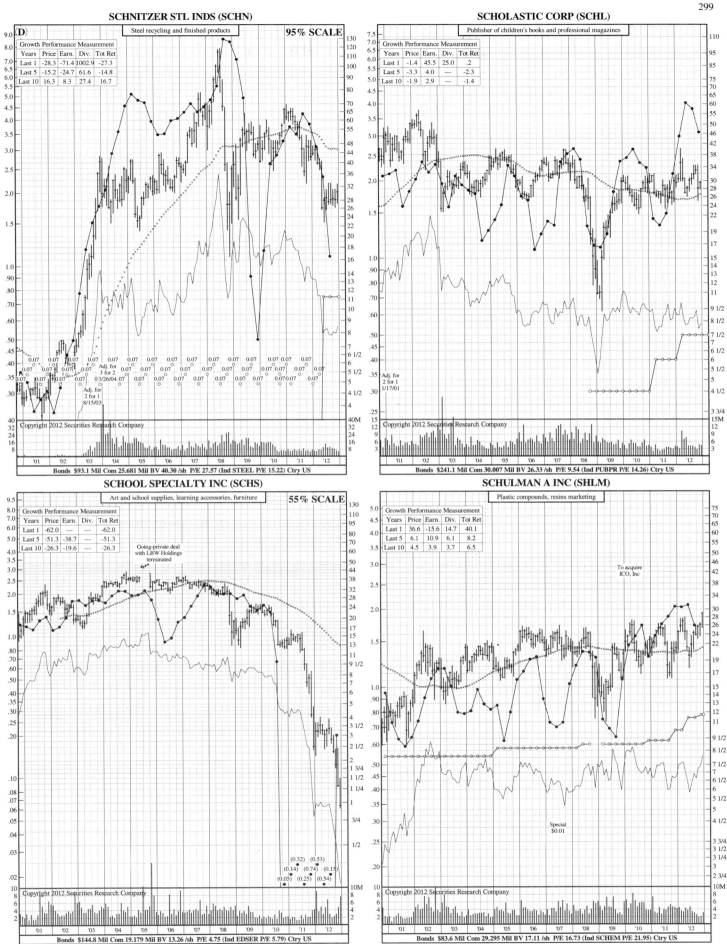

SCHNITZER STL INDS (SCHN)

Steel recycling and finished products

95% SCALE

(D)

Growth Performance Measurement

Years	Price	Earn.	Div.	Tot Ret
Last 1	-28.3	-71.4	1002.9	-27.3
Last 5	-15.2	-24.7	61.6	-14.8
Last 10	16.3	8.3	27.4	16.7

Adj. for 3 for 2 03/26/04

Adj. for 2 for 1 8/15/03

Copyright 2012 Securities Research Company

Bonds $93.1 Mil Com 25.681 Mil BV 40.30 /sh P/E 27.57 (Ind STEEL P/E 15.22) Ctry US

SCHOLASTIC CORP (SCHL)

Publisher of children's books and professional magazines

Growth Performance Measurement

Years	Price	Earn.	Div.	Tot Ret
Last 1	-1.4	45.5	25.0	.2
Last 5	-3.3	4.0	---	-2.3
Last 10	-1.9	2.9	---	-1.4

Adj. for 2 for 1 1/17/01

Copyright 2012 Securities Research Company

Bonds $241.1 Mil Com 30.007 Mil BV 26.33 /sh P/E 9.54 (Ind PUBPR P/E 14.26) Ctry US

SCHOOL SPECIALTY INC (SCHS)

Art and school supplies, learning accessories, furniture

55% SCALE

Growth Performance Measurement

Years	Price	Earn.	Div.	Tot Ret
Last 1	-62.0	---	---	-62.0
Last 5	-51.3	-38.7	---	-51.3
Last 10	-26.3	-19.6	---	-26.3

Going-private deal with LBW Holdings terminated

(0.32) (0.53)
(0.14) (0.74) (0.15)
(0.05) (0.25) (0.54)

Copyright 2012 Securities Research Company

Bonds $144.8 Mil Com 19.179 Mil BV 13.26 /sh P/E 4.75 (Ind EDSER P/E 5.79) Ctry US

SCHULMAN A INC (SHLM)

Plastic compounds, resins marketing

Growth Performance Measurement

Years	Price	Earn.	Div.	Tot Ret
Last 1	36.6	-15.6	14.7	40.1
Last 5	6.1	10.9	6.1	8.2
Last 10	4.5	3.9	3.7	6.5

To acquire ICO, Inc

Special $0.01

Copyright 2012 Securities Research Company

Bonds $83.6 Mil Com 29.295 Mil BV 17.11 /sh P/E 16.73 (Ind SCHEM P/E 21.95) Ctry US

300

SCICLONE PHARMACEUTICALS INC (SCLN)

Acquires pharmaceuticals for worldwide marketing

80% SCALE

	Growth Performance Measurement			
Years	Price	Earn.	Div.	Tot Ret
Last 1	.5	72.1	---	.5
Last 5	15.9	---	---	15.9
Last 10	3.1	---	---	3.1

(0.14) (0.29) (0.29) (0.09) (0.32) (0.27) (0.17) (0.15) (0.12) (0.33) (0.18)
(0.09) (0.29) (0.27) (0.06) (0.12) (0.31) (0.20) (0.19) (0.10) (0.22) (0.19)
(0.05) (0.15) (0.32) (0.30) (0.13) (0.35) (0.25) (0.19) (0.14) (0.17) (0.28) (0.06)

Copyright 2012 Securities Research Company

'01 '02 '03 '04 '05 '06 '07 '08 '09 '10 '11 '12

Bonds $.0 Mil Com 55.247 Mil BV 2.60 /sh P/E 5.82 (Ind BIOTK P/E 17.51) Ctry US

SCIENTIFIC GAMES CORP (SGMS)

Sells instant and online lottery tickets and services

85% SCALE

	Growth Performance Measurement			
Years	Price	Earn.	Div.	Tot Ret
Last 1	-10.6	85.3	---	-10.6
Last 5	-23.6	---	---	-23.6
Last 10	1.8	---	---	1.8

(0.43) 0.05   (1.51) (0.06)
(0.43) (0.06)   (1.37) 0.01
(0.36) (0.13)   (1.27) (1.56) (0.23)

Copyright 2012 Securities Research Company

'01 '02 '03 '04 '05 '06 '07 '08 '09 '10 '11 '12

Bonds $.0 Mil Com 85.078 Mil BV 4.61 /sh P/E N/A (Ind CSINO P/E 18.01) Ctry US

SEACHANGE INTL INC (SEAC)

Digital advertisement systems for the television industry

	Growth Performance Measurement			
Years	Price	Earn.	Div.	Tot Ret
Last 1	37.6	-51.0	---	37.6
Last 5	6.0	---	---	6.0
Last 10	4.6	14.9	---	4.6

(0.04) 0.02 0.06 0.00   (0.42) (0.27) (0.32)
(0.03) (0.13) 0.03 (0.05)   (0.40) (0.30) (0.23) 0.03
.06 (0.09) 0.02 (0.06) 0.07 (0.20) (0.55) (0.28) (0.17)   0.08

Copyright 2012 Securities Research Company

'01 '02 '03 '04 '05 '06 '07 '08 '09 '10 '11 '12

Bonds $1.2 Mil Com 32.291 Mil BV 6.15 /sh P/E 40.29 (Ind TELEQ P/E 13.72) Ctry US

SEACOAST BKG CORP FLA (SBCF)

Offers array of retail banking services

70% SCALE

	Growth Performance Measurement			
Years	Price	Earn.	Div.	Tot Ret
Last 1	5.9	81.8	.0	5.9
Last 5	-31.0	---	-42.6	-27.1
Last 10	-21.1	---	-19.8	-11.8

Dividend
Omitted
04/13/10

Adj. for   Adj. for
3 for 1   10% SD
7/16/02   7/30/03

(2.16) (3.30) (2.23) (0.47) 0.01
(1.11) (2.23) (2.78) (0.50) (0.11)
(0.87) (2.55) (3.04) (1.07) (0.22) (0.02)

Copyright 2012 Securities Research Company

'01 '02 '03 '04 '05 '06 '07 '08 '09 '10 '11 '12

Bonds $25.0 Mil Com 94.811 Mil BV 1.25 /sh P/E N/A (Ind RBANK P/E 10.51) Ctry US

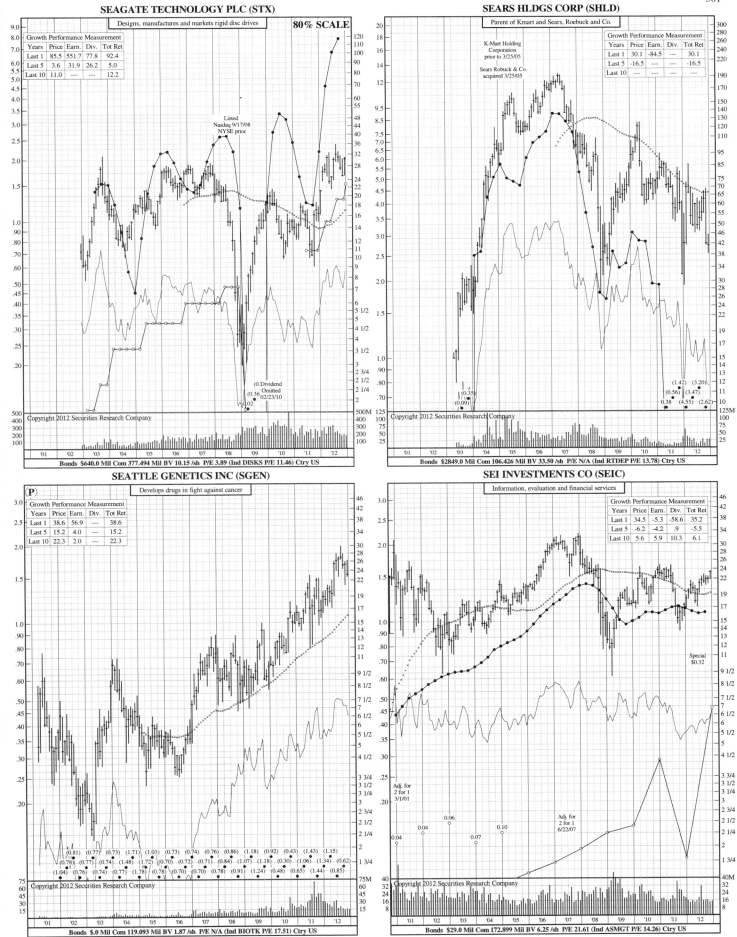

SEAGATE TECHNOLOGY PLC (STX)

Designs, manufactures and markets rigid disc drives

80% SCALE

Growth Performance Measurement				
Years	Price	Earn.	Div.	Tot Ret
Last 1	85.5	551.7	77.8	92.4
Last 5	3.6	31.9	26.2	5.0
Last 10	11.0	---	---	12.2

Listed
Nasdaq 9/17/08
NYSE prior

(0.Dividend
Omitted
02/23/10
(0.36)
0.02

Copyright 2012 Securities Research Company

Bonds $640.0 Mil Com 377.494 Mil BV 10.15 /sh P/E 3.89 (Ind DISKS P/E 11.46) Ctry US

SEARS HLDGS CORP (SHLD)

Parent of Kmart and Sears, Roebuck and Co.

K-Mart Holding
Corporation
prior to 3/25/05

Sears Robuck & Co.
acquired 3/25/05

Growth Performance Measurement				
Years	Price	Earn.	Div.	Tot Ret
Last 1	30.1	-84.5	---	30.1
Last 5	-16.5	---	---	-16.5
Last 10	---	---	---	---

(0.35)
(0.09)

(1.42) (3.20)
(0.56) (3.47)
0.38 (4.55) (2.62)

Copyright 2012 Securities Research Company

Bonds $2849.0 Mil Com 106.426 Mil BV 33.50 /sh P/E N/A (Ind RTDEP P/E 13.78) Ctry US

SEATTLE GENETICS INC (SGEN)

(P)

Develops drugs in fight against cancer

Growth Performance Measurement				
Years	Price	Earn.	Div.	Tot Ret
Last 1	38.6	56.9	---	38.6
Last 5	15.2	4.0	---	15.2
Last 10	22.3	2.0	---	22.3

(0.81) (0.77) (0.73) (1.71) (1.03) (0.73) (0.74) (0.76) (0.86) (1.18) (0.92) (0.43) (1.43) (1.15)
(0.78) (0.77) (0.74) (1.48) (1.72) (0.70) (0.72) (0.71) (1.07) (1.18) (0.30) (1.06) (1.34) (0.62)
(1.04) (0.76) (0.74) (0.77) (1.78) (0.78) (0.70) (0.70) (0.78) (0.91) (1.24) (0.48) (0.65) (1.44) (0.85)

Copyright 2012 Securities Research Company

Bonds $.0 Mil Com 119.093 Mil BV 1.87 /sh P/E N/A (Ind BIOTK P/E 17.51) Ctry US

SEI INVESTMENTS CO (SEIC)

Information, evaluation and financial services

Growth Performance Measurement				
Years	Price	Earn.	Div.	Tot Ret
Last 1	34.5	-5.3	-58.6	35.2
Last 5	-6.2	-4.2	.9	-5.5
Last 10	5.6	5.9	10.3	6.1

Special
$0.32

Adj. for
2 for 1
3/1/01

Adj. for
2 for 1
6/22/07

0.04
0.06
0.07
0.10

Copyright 2012 Securities Research Company

Bonds $29.0 Mil Com 172.899 Mil BV 6.25 /sh P/E 21.61 (Ind ASMGT P/E 14.26) Ctry US

302

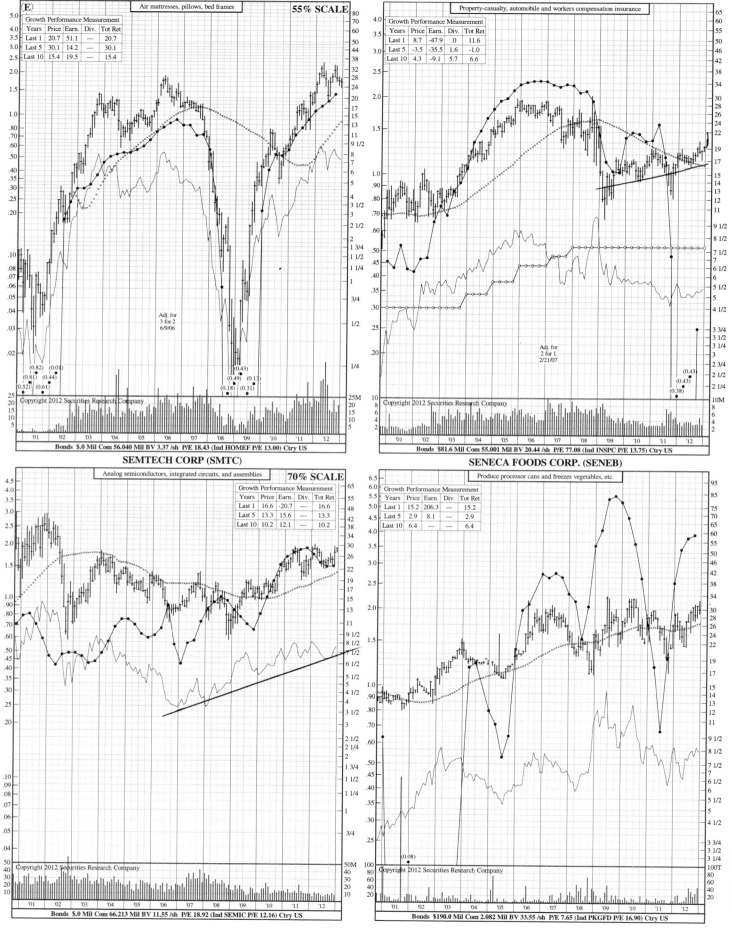

SELECT COMFORT CORP (SCSS)

Air mattresses, pillows, bed frames

55% SCALE

(E)

Growth Performance Measurement

Years	Price	Earn.	Div.	Tot Ret
Last 1	20.7	51.1	---	20.7
Last 5	30.1	14.2	---	30.1
Last 10	15.4	19.5	---	15.4

Adj. for
3 for 2
6/9/06

(0.82) (0.01)
(0.81) (0.44)
(0.52) (0.61)

(0.43)
(0.49) (0.13)
(0.18) (0.31)

Copyright 2012 Securities Research Company

Bonds $.0 Mil Com 56.040 Mil BV 3.37 /sh P/E 18.43 (Ind HOMEF P/E 13.00) Ctry US

SELECTIVE INS GROUP INC (SIGI)

Property-casualty, automobile and workers compensation insurance

Growth Performance Measurement

Years	Price	Earn.	Div.	Tot Ret
Last 1	8.7	-47.9	.0	11.6
Last 5	-3.5	-35.5	1.6	-1.0
Last 10	4.3	-9.1	5.7	6.6

Adj. for
2 for 1
2/21/07

(0.43)
(0.43)
(0.38)

Copyright 2012 Securities Research Company

Bonds $81.6 Mil Com 55.001 Mil BV 20.44 /sh P/E 77.08 (Ind INSPC P/E 13.75) Ctry US

SEMTECH CORP (SMTC)

Analog semiconductors, integrated circuits, and assemblies

70% SCALE

Growth Performance Measurement

Years	Price	Earn.	Div.	Tot Ret
Last 1	16.6	-20.7	---	16.6
Last 5	13.3	15.6	---	13.3
Last 10	10.2	12.1	---	10.2

Copyright 2012 Securities Research Company

Bonds $.0 Mil Com 66.213 Mil BV 11.55 /sh P/E 18.92 (Ind SEMIC P/E 12.16) Ctry US

SENECA FOODS CORP. (SENEB)

Produce processor cans and freezes vegetables, etc.

Growth Performance Measurement

Years	Price	Earn.	Div.	Tot Ret
Last 1	15.2	206.3	---	15.2
Last 5	2.9	8.1	---	2.9
Last 10	6.4	---	---	6.4

(0.08)

Copyright 2012 Securities Research Company

Bonds $190.0 Mil Com 2.082 Mil BV 33.55 /sh P/E 7.65 (Ind PKGFD P/E 16.90) Ctry US

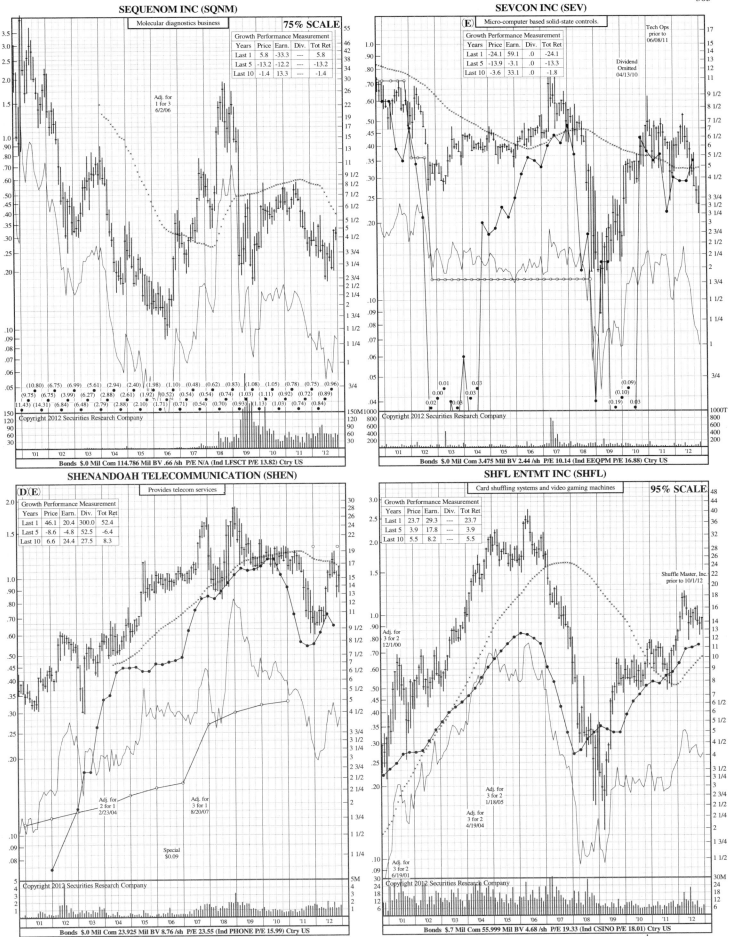

SEQUENOM INC (SQNM)

Molecular diagnostics business

75% SCALE

Growth Performance Measurement

Years	Price	Earn.	Div.	Tot Ret
Last 1	5.8	-33.3	---	5.8
Last 5	-13.2	-12.2	---	-13.2
Last 10	-1.4	13.3	---	-1.4

Adj. for 1 for 3 6/2/06

(10.80) (6.75) (6.99) (5.61) (2.94) (2.40) (1.98) (1.10) (0.48) (0.62) (0.83) (1.08) (1.05) (0.78) (0.75) (0.96)
(9.75) (6.75) (3.99) (6.27) (2.88) (2.61) (1.92) (0.52) (0.54) (0.54) (0.74) (1.03) (1.11) (0.92) (0.72) (0.89)
(11.43) (14.31) (6.84) (6.48) (2.79) (2.88) (2.10) (1.71) (0.71) (0.54) (0.70) (0.93) (1.13) (1.03) (0.74) (0.84)

Copyright 2012 Securities Research Company

Bonds $.0 Mil Com 114.786 Mil BV .66 /sh P/E N/A (Ind LFSCT P/E 13.82) Ctry US

SEVCON INC (SEV)

(E) Micro-computer based solid-state controls.

Tech Ops prior to 06/08/11

Growth Performance Measurement

Years	Price	Earn.	Div.	Tot Ret
Last 1	-24.1	59.1	.0	-24.1
Last 5	-13.9	-3.1	.0	-13.3
Last 10	-3.6	33.1	.0	-1.8

Dividend Omitted 04/13/10

0.01 0.03
0.00 0.03 (0.09)
0.02 0.03 (0.10)
0.05 (0.19) 0.03

Copyright 2012 Securities Research Company

Bonds $.0 Mil Com 3.475 Mil BV 2.44 /sh P/E 10.14 (Ind EEQPM P/E 16.88) Ctry US

SHENANDOAH TELECOMMUNICATION (SHEN)

(D)(E) Provides telecom services

Growth Performance Measurement

Years	Price	Earn.	Div.	Tot Ret
Last 1	46.1	20.4	300.0	52.4
Last 5	-8.6	-4.8	52.5	-6.4
Last 10	6.6	24.4	27.5	8.3

Adj. for 2 for 1 2/23/04

Adj. for 3 for 1 8/20/07

Special $0.09

Copyright 2012 Securities Research Company

Bonds $.0 Mil Com 23.925 Mil BV 8.76 /sh P/E 23.55 (Ind PHONE P/E 15.99) Ctry US

SHFL ENTMT INC (SHFL)

Card shuffling systems and video gaming machines

95% SCALE

Growth Performance Measurement

Years	Price	Earn.	Div.	Tot Ret
Last 1	23.7	29.3	---	23.7
Last 5	3.9	17.8	---	3.9
Last 10	5.5	8.2	---	5.5

Shuffle Master, Inc. prior to 10/1/12

Adj. for 3 for 2 12/1/00

Adj. for 3 for 2 1/18/05

Adj. for 3 for 2 4/19/04

Adj. for 3 for 2 6/19/01

Copyright 2012 Securities Research Company

Bonds $.7 Mil Com 55.999 Mil BV 4.68 /sh P/E 19.33 (Ind CSINO P/E 18.01) Ctry US

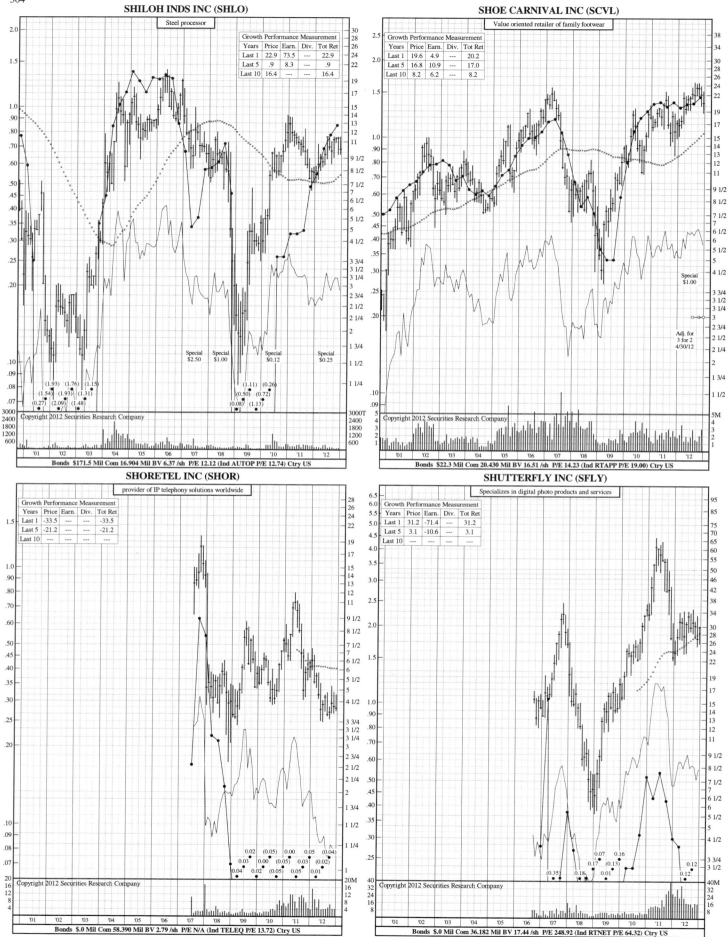

304

SHILOH INDS INC (SHLO)

Steel processor

Growth Performance Measurement				
Years	Price	Earn.	Div.	Tot Ret
Last 1	22.9	73.5	---	22.9
Last 5	.9	8.3	---	.9
Last 10	16.4	---	---	16.4

Special $2.50   Special $1.00   Special $0.12   Special $0.25

(1.93) (1.76) (1.15)
(1.54) (1.93) (1.31)   (1.11) (0.26)
(0.27) (2.09) (1.48)   (0.50) (0.72)
                         (0.08) (1.13)

Copyright 2012 Securities Research Company

Bonds $171.5 Mil Com 16.904 Mil BV 6.37 /sh P/E 12.12 (Ind AUTOP P/E 12.74) Ctry US

SHOE CARNIVAL INC (SCVL)

Value oriented retailer of family footwear

Growth Performance Measurement				
Years	Price	Earn.	Div.	Tot Ret
Last 1	19.6	4.9	---	20.2
Last 5	16.8	10.9	---	17.0
Last 10	8.2	6.2	---	8.2

Special $1.00

Adj. for 3 for 2 4/30/12

Copyright 2012 Securities Research Company

Bonds $22.3 Mil Com 20.430 Mil BV 16.51 /sh P/E 14.23 (Ind RTAPP P/E 19.00) Ctry US

SHORETEL INC (SHOR)

provider of IP telephony solutions worldwide

Growth Performance Measurement				
Years	Price	Earn.	Div.	Tot Ret
Last 1	-33.5	---	---	-33.5
Last 5	-21.2	---	---	-21.2
Last 10	---	---	---	---

0.02 (0.05) 0.00 0.05 (0.04)
0.03 0.00 (0.05) 0.03 (0.02)
0.04 0.02 (0.05) 0.05 0.01

Copyright 2012 Securities Research Company

Bonds $.0 Mil Com 58.390 Mil BV 2.79 /sh P/E N/A (Ind TELEQ P/E 13.72) Ctry US

SHUTTERFLY INC (SFLY)

Specializes in digital photo products and services

Growth Performance Measurement				
Years	Price	Earn.	Div.	Tot Ret
Last 1	31.2	-71.4	---	31.2
Last 5	3.1	-10.6	---	3.1
Last 10	---	---	---	---

0.07 0.16
0.17 (0.13)
(0.35) 0.18 0.01   0.12
                      0.12

Copyright 2012 Securities Research Company

Bonds $.0 Mil Com 36.182 Mil BV 17.44 /sh P/E 248.92 (Ind RTNET P/E 64.32) Ctry US

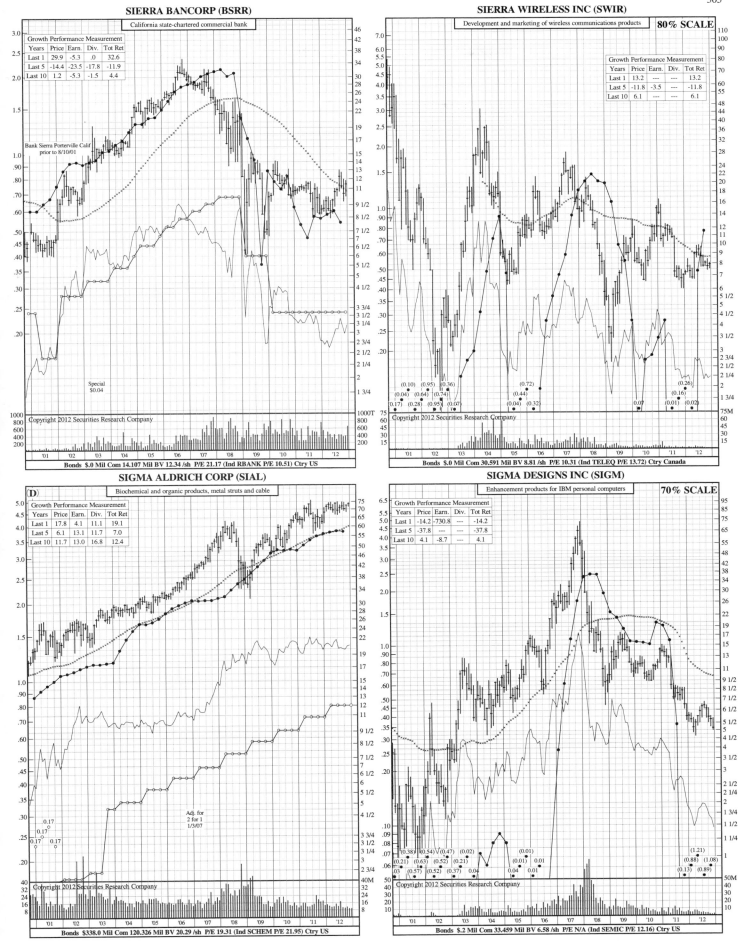

SIERRA BANCORP (BSRR)
California state-chartered commercial bank

Growth Performance Measurement				
Years	Price	Earn.	Div.	Tot Ret
Last 1	29.9	-5.3	.0	32.6
Last 5	-14.4	-23.5	-17.8	-11.9
Last 10	1.2	-5.3	-1.5	4.4

Bank Sierra Porterville Calif
prior to 8/10/01

Special
$0.04

Copyright 2012 Securities Research Company

Bonds $.0 Mil Com 14.107 Mil BV 12.34 /sh P/E 21.17 (Ind RBANK P/E 10.51) Ctry US

SIERRA WIRELESS INC (SWIR)
Development and marketing of wireless communications products

80% SCALE

Growth Performance Measurement				
Years	Price	Earn.	Div.	Tot Ret
Last 1	13.2	---	---	13.2
Last 5	-11.8	-3.5	---	-11.8
Last 10	6.1	---	---	6.1

(0.10) (0.95) (0.36)   (0.72)   (0.26)
(0.04) (0.64) (0.74)   (0.44)   (0.16)
(0.17) (0.28) (0.95) (0.07) (0.04) (0.32)   0.07 (0.01) (0.02)

Copyright 2012 Securities Research Company

Bonds $.0 Mil Com 30.591 Mil BV 8.81 /sh P/E 10.31 (Ind TELEQ P/E 13.72) Ctry Canada

SIGMA ALDRICH CORP (SIAL)
Biochemical and organic products, metal struts and cable

(D)

Growth Performance Measurement				
Years	Price	Earn.	Div.	Tot Ret
Last 1	17.8	4.1	11.1	19.1
Last 5	6.1	13.1	11.7	7.0
Last 10	11.7	13.0	16.8	12.4

Adj. for
2 for 1
1/3/07

0.17
0.17
0.17 0.17

Copyright 2012 Securities Research Company

Bonds $338.0 Mil Com 120.326 Mil BV 20.29 /sh P/E 19.31 (Ind SCHEM P/E 21.95) Ctry US

SIGMA DESIGNS INC (SIGM)
Enhancement products for IBM personal computers

70% SCALE

Growth Performance Measurement				
Years	Price	Earn.	Div.	Tot Ret
Last 1	-14.2	-730.8	---	-14.2
Last 5	-37.8	---	---	-37.8
Last 10	4.1	-8.7	---	4.1

(0.38) (0.54) V(0.47) (0.02)   (0.01)   (1.21)
(0.21) (0.63) (0.52) (0.21)   (0.01) 0.01   (0.88) (1.08)
0.03 (0.57) (0.52) (0.37) 0.04   0.04 0.01   (0.13) (0.89)

Copyright 2012 Securities Research Company

Bonds $.2 Mil Com 33.459 Mil BV 6.58 /sh P/E N/A (Ind SEMIC P/E 12.16) Ctry US

306

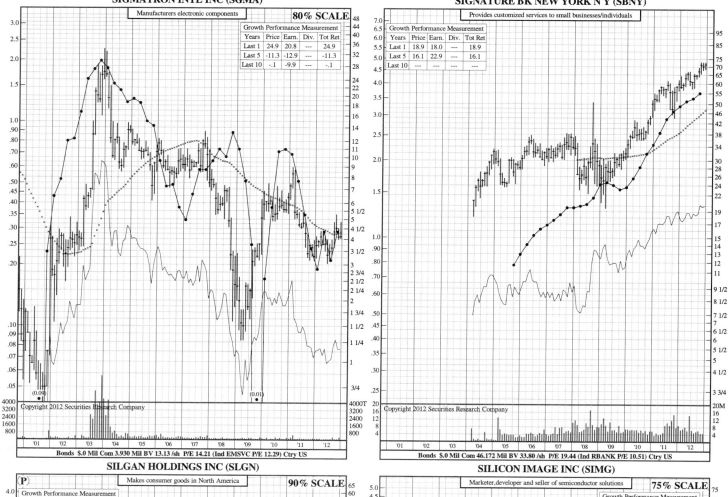

SIGMATRON INTL INC (SGMA)

Manufacturers electronic components

80% SCALE

Growth Performance Measurement				
Years	Price	Earn.	Div.	Tot Ret
Last 1	24.9	20.8	---	24.9
Last 5	-11.3	-12.9	---	-11.3
Last 10	-.1	-9.9	---	-.1

(0.09)　　　(0.01)

Copyright 2012 Securities Research Company

Bonds $.0 Mil Com 3.930 Mil BV 13.13 /sh P/E 14.21 (Ind EMSVC P/E 12.29) Ctry US

SIGNATURE BK NEW YORK N Y (SBNY)

Provides customized services to small businesses/individuals

Growth Performance Measurement				
Years	Price	Earn.	Div.	Tot Ret
Last 1	18.9	18.0	---	18.9
Last 5	16.1	22.9	---	16.1
Last 10	---	---	---	---

Copyright 2012 Securities Research Company

Bonds $.0 Mil Com 46.172 Mil BV 33.80 /sh P/E 19.44 (Ind RBANK P/E 10.51) Ctry US

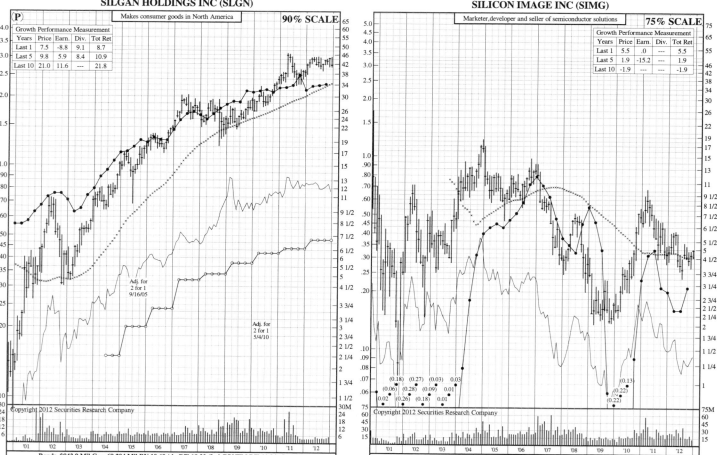

SILGAN HOLDINGS INC (SLGN)

(P)　　　Makes consumer goods in North America

90% SCALE

Growth Performance Measurement				
Years	Price	Earn.	Div.	Tot Ret
Last 1	7.5	-8.8	9.1	8.7
Last 5	9.8	5.9	8.4	10.9
Last 10	21.0	11.6	---	21.8

Adj. for
2 for 1
9/16/05

Adj. for
2 for 1
5/4/10

Copyright 2012 Securities Research Company

Bonds $843.9 Mil Com 69.204 Mil BV 10.60 /sh P/E 18.22 (Ind CONTM P/E 11.84) Ctry US

SILICON IMAGE INC (SIMG)

Marketer,developer and seller of semiconductor solutions

75% SCALE

Growth Performance Measurement				
Years	Price	Earn.	Div.	Tot Ret
Last 1	5.5	.0	---	5.5
Last 5	1.9	-15.2	---	1.9
Last 10	-1.9	---	---	-1.9

(0.18)　(0.27)　(0.09)　0.03
(0.06)　(0.28)　(0.09)　0.01　　　　　　　(0.13)
0.02　(0.26)　(0.18)　0.01　　　　　　　　(0.22)
　　　　　　　　　　　　　　　　　　　(0.22)

Copyright 2012 Securities Research Company

Bonds $.5 Mil Com 82.267 Mil BV 2.49 /sh P/E 23.62 (Ind SEMIC P/E 12.16) Ctry US

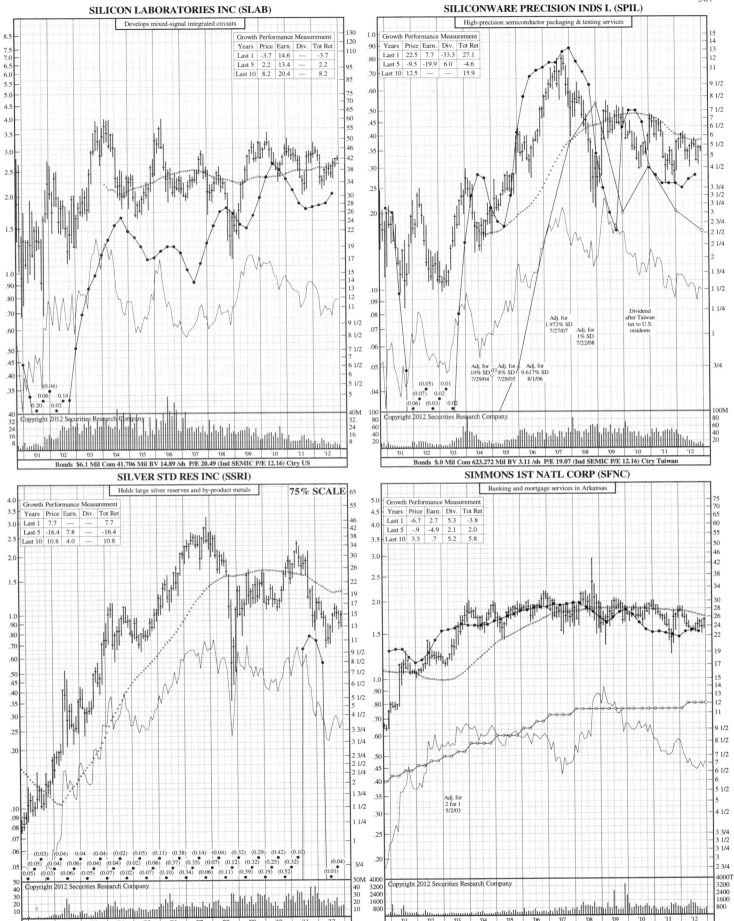

SILICON LABORATORIES INC (SLAB)
Develops mixed-signal integrated circuits

Growth Performance Measurement				
Years	Price	Earn.	Div.	Tot Ret
Last 1	-3.7	14.6	---	-3.7
Last 5	2.2	13.4	---	2.2
Last 10	8.2	20.4	---	8.2

(0.04)
(0.06)
0.20 0.14
0.02

Copyright 2012 Securities Research Company

Bonds $6.1 Mil Com 41.706 Mil BV 14.89 /sh P/E 20.49 (Ind SEMIC P/E 12.16) Ctry US

SILICONWARE PRECISION INDS L (SPIL)
High-precision semiconductor packaging & testing services

Growth Performance Measurement				
Years	Price	Earn.	Div.	Tot Ret
Last 1	22.5	7.7	-33.3	27.1
Last 5	-9.5	-19.9	6.0	-4.6
Last 10	12.5	---	---	15.9

Adj. for
1.972% SD
7/27/07

Adj. for
1% SD
7/22/08

Dividend
after Taiwan
tax to U.S.
residents

Adj. for
10% SD 8% SD 9.617% SD
7/29/04 7/28/05 8/1/06

.03

(0.05) 0.01
(0.07) 0.02
(0.06) (0.03) 0.02

Copyright 2012 Securities Research Company

Bonds $.0 Mil Com 623.272 Mil BV 3.11 /sh P/E 19.07 (Ind SEMIC P/E 12.16) Ctry Taiwan

SILVER STD RES INC (SSRI)
Holds large silver reserves and by-product metals

75% SCALE

Growth Performance Measurement				
Years	Price	Earn.	Div.	Tot Ret
Last 1	7.7	---		7.7
Last 5	-16.4	7.8		-16.4
Last 10	10.8	4.0	---	10.8

(0.03) (0.04) 0.04 (0.04) (0.02) (0.05) (0.11) (0.38) (0.14) (0.04) (0.32) 0.29 (0.42) (0.10)
(0.05) (0.04) (0.06) (0.04) (0.04) (0.02) (0.06) (0.37) (0.35) (0.07) (0.12) (0.32) (0.25) (0.32) (0.04)
(0.05) (0.03) (0.06) (0.05) (0.07) (0.04) (0.07) (0.10) (0.34) (0.06) (0.11) (0.39) (0.19) (0.52) (0.01)

Copyright 2012 Securities Research Company

Bonds $.0 Mil Com 80.748 Mil BV 12.64 /sh P/E N/A (Ind METAL P/E 11.29) Ctry Canada

SIMMONS 1ST NATL CORP (SFNC)
Banking and mortgage services in Arkansas

Growth Performance Measurement				
Years	Price	Earn.	Div.	Tot Ret
Last 1	-6.7	2.7	5.3	-3.8
Last 5	-.9	-4.9	2.1	2.0
Last 10	3.3	.7	5.2	5.8

Adj. for
2 for 1
5/2/03

Copyright 2012 Securities Research Company

Bonds $46.2 Mil Com 16.647 Mil BV 24.25 /sh P/E 16.68 (Ind RBANK P/E 10.51) Ctry US

308

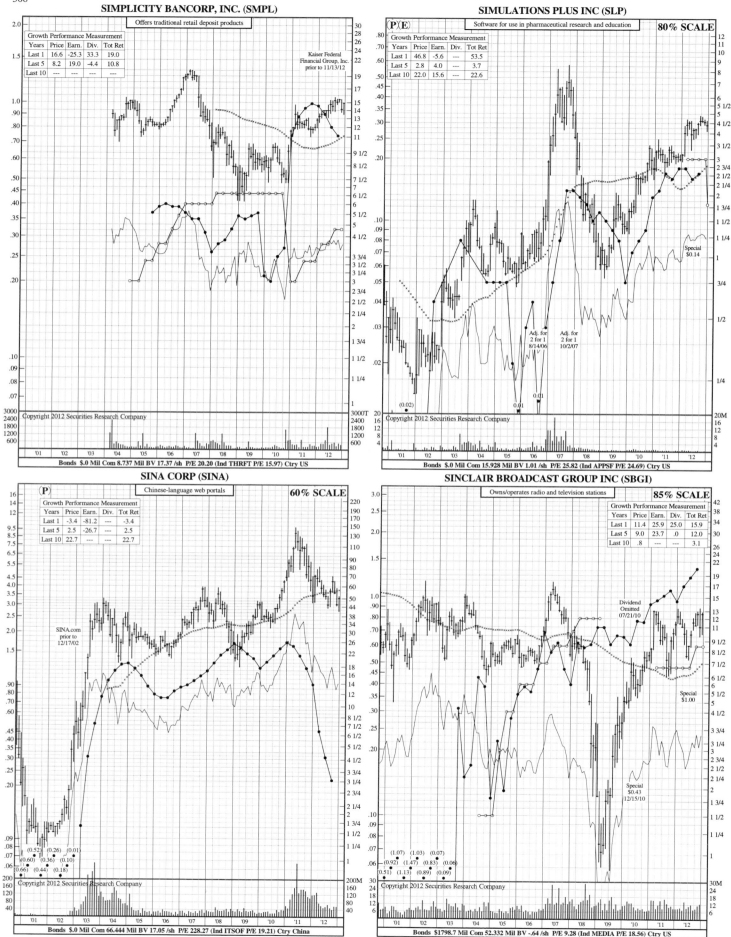

SIMPLICITY BANCORP, INC. (SMPL)

Offers traditional retail deposit products

Kaiser Federal
Financial Group, Inc.
prior to 11/13/12

Growth Performance Measurement

Years	Price	Earn.	Div.	Tot Ret
Last 1	16.6	-25.3	33.3	19.0
Last 5	8.2	19.0	-4.4	10.8
Last 10	---	---	---	---

Copyright 2012 Securities Research Company

Bonds $.0 Mil Com 8.737 Mil BV 17.37 /sh P/E 20.20 (Ind THRFT P/E 15.97) Ctry US

SIMULATIONS PLUS INC (SLP)

Software for use in pharmaceutical research and education

80% SCALE

(P)(E)

Growth Performance Measurement

Years	Price	Earn.	Div.	Tot Ret
Last 1	46.8	-5.6	---	53.5
Last 5	2.8	4.0	---	3.7
Last 10	22.0	15.6	---	22.6

Special
$0.14

Adj. for
2 for 1
8/14/06

Adj. for
2 for 1
10/2/07

0.01

(0.02)   0.01

Copyright 2012 Securities Research Company

Bonds $.0 Mil Com 15.928 Mil BV 1.01 /sh P/E 25.82 (Ind APPSF P/E 24.69) Ctry US

SINA CORP (SINA)

Chinese-language web portals

60% SCALE

(P)

Growth Performance Measurement

Years	Price	Earn.	Div.	Tot Ret
Last 1	-3.4	-81.2	---	-3.4
Last 5	2.5	-26.7	---	2.5
Last 10	22.7	---	---	22.7

SINA.com
prior to
12/17/02

(0.52) (0.26) (0.01)
(0.60) (0.36) (0.10)
(0.66) (0.44) (0.18)

Copyright 2012 Securities Research Company

Bonds $.0 Mil Com 66.444 Mil BV 17.05 /sh P/E 228.27 (Ind ITSOF P/E 19.21) Ctry China

SINCLAIR BROADCAST GROUP INC (SBGI)

Owns/operates radio and television stations

85% SCALE

Growth Performance Measurement

Years	Price	Earn.	Div.	Tot Ret
Last 1	11.4	25.9	25.0	15.9
Last 5	9.0	23.7	.0	12.0
Last 10	.8	---	---	3.1

Dividend
Omitted
07/21/10

Special
$1.00

Special
$0.43
12/15/10

(1.07) (1.03) (0.07)
(0.92) (1.47) (0.83) (0.06)
(0.51) (1.13) (0.89) (0.09)

Copyright 2012 Securities Research Company

Bonds $1798.7 Mil Com 52.332 Mil BV -.64 /sh P/E 9.28 (Ind MEDIA P/E 18.56) Ctry US

SIRIUS XM RADIO INC (SIRI)

Developing a satellite-based subscription radio service

45% SCALE

Growth Performance Measurement				
Years	Price	Earn.	Div.	Tot Ret
Last 1	58.8	-12.5	---	58.8
Last 5	-.9	---	---	-.9
Last 10	16.3	---	---	16.3

XM Satellite Radio
acquired 7/30/08

(4.94) (5.25) (6.03) (2.74) (0.48) (0.61) (0.65) (0.84) (0.48) (0.35) (0.30) (0.16)
(4.70) (5.36) (5.99) (4.16) (0.48) (0.57) (0.63) (0.86) (0.55) (0.38) (0.33) (0.25) 0.00
(4.71) (5.03) (5.52) (5.67) (1.22) (0.51) (0.63) (0.83) (0.78) (0.44) (0.32) (0.30) (0.08)

Copyright 2012 Securities Research Company

'01 '02 '03 '04 '05 '06 '07 '08 '09 '10 '11 '12

Bonds $1068.0 Mil Com 5207.146 Mil BV .80 /sh P/E 41.29 (Ind CAASA P/E 17.31) Ctry US

SKYWEST INC (SKYW)

Regional airline based in Utah

Growth Performance Measurement				
Years	Price	Earn.	Div.	Tot Ret
Last 1	-1.0	-33.9	.0	.2
Last 5	-14.2	-29.9	5.9	-13.2
Last 10	-.5	-10.4	7.2	.5

Adj. for
2 for 1
12/18/00   0.08   0.08   0.08
    0.08 0.08   0.08   0.08   0.08
0.08   0.08

(0.13)
(0.33)

Copyright 2012 Securities Research Company

'01 '02 '03 '04 '05 '06 '07 '08 '09 '10 '11 '12

Bonds $48.3 Mil Com 51.256 Mil BV 26.77 /sh P/E 31.95 (Ind ARLNS P/E 18.30) Ctry US

SKYWORKS SOLUTIONS INC (SWKS)

Integrated circuits and electrical ceramics

85% SCALE

Growth Performance Measurement				
Years	Price	Earn.	Div.	Tot Ret
Last 1	25.2	1.1	.0	25.2
Last 5	19.0	31.8	.0	19.0
Last 10	8.9	---	.0	8.9

Alpha Inds., Inc.
prior to 6/26/02

(0.32) (0.15) (0.07)
(0.31) (0.26) (0.12)
(0.11) (0.29) (0.08) (0.01)

Copyright 2012 Securities Research Company

'01 '02 '03 '04 '05 '06 '07 '08 '09 '10 '11 '12

Bonds $.3 Mil Com 194.321 Mil BV 9.91 /sh P/E 10.63 (Ind SEMIC P/E 12.16) Ctry US

SLM CORP (SLM)

Student loan financial services

Growth Performance Measurement				
Years	Price	Earn.	Div.	Tot Ret
Last 1	27.8	-2.3	25.0	31.4
Last 5	-3.2	-1.8	-12.9	-2.4
Last 10	-6.8	3.8	6.5	-4.7

USA Education
prior to 5/17/02

Listed
Nasdaq 12/12/11
NYSE prior

Dividend
Omitted
10/18/07

Adj. for
3 for 1
6/23/03

Copyright 2012 Securities Research Company

'01 '02 '03 '04 '05 '06 '07 '08 '09 '10 '11 '12

Bonds $104558.5 Mil Com 462.159 Mil BV 9.47 /sh P/E 8.04 (Ind FINAN P/E 11.42) Ctry US

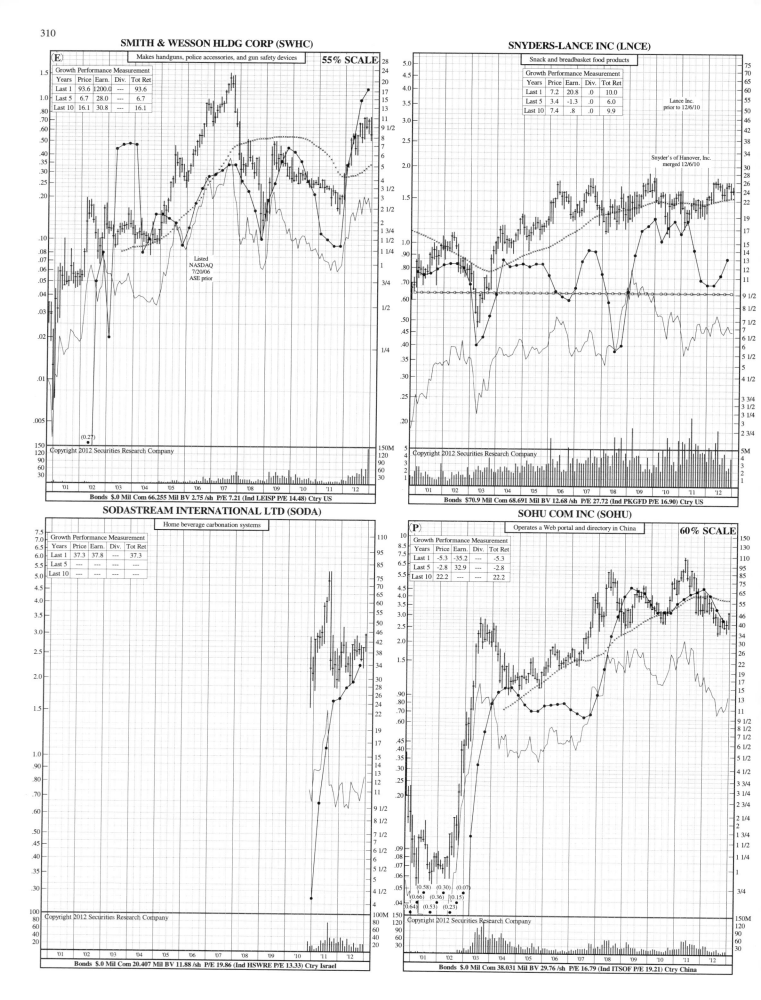

SMITH & WESSON HLDG CORP (SWHC)

Makes handguns, police accessories, and gun safety devices

55% SCALE

Growth Performance Measurement				
Years	Price	Earn.	Div.	Tot Ret
Last 1	93.6	1200.0	---	93.6
Last 5	6.7	28.0	---	6.7
Last 10	16.1	30.8	---	16.1

Listed NASDAQ 7/20/06 ASE prior

(0.27)

Copyright 2012 Securities Research Company

Bonds $.0 Mil Com 66.255 Mil BV 2.75 /sh P/E 7.21 (Ind LEISP P/E 14.48) Ctry US

SNYDERS-LANCE INC (LNCE)

Snack and breadbasket food products

Growth Performance Measurement				
Years	Price	Earn.	Div.	Tot Ret
Last 1	7.2	20.8	.0	10.0
Last 5	3.4	-1.3	.0	6.0
Last 10	7.4	.8	.0	9.9

Lance Inc. prior to 12/6/10

Snyder's of Hanover, Inc. merged 12/6/10

Copyright 2012 Securities Research Company

Bonds $70.9 Mil Com 68.691 Mil BV 12.68 /sh P/E 27.72 (Ind PKGFD P/E 16.90) Ctry US

SODASTREAM INTERNATIONAL LTD (SODA)

Home beverage carbonation systems

Growth Performance Measurement				
Years	Price	Earn.	Div.	Tot Ret
Last 1	37.3	37.8	---	37.3
Last 5	---	---	---	---
Last 10	---	---	---	---

Copyright 2012 Securities Research Company

Bonds $.0 Mil Com 20.407 Mil BV 11.88 /sh P/E 19.86 (Ind HSWRE P/E 13.33) Ctry Israel

SOHU COM INC (SOHU)

Operates a Web portal and directory in China

60% SCALE

Growth Performance Measurement				
Years	Price	Earn.	Div.	Tot Ret
Last 1	-5.3	-35.2	---	-5.3
Last 5	-2.8	32.9	---	-2.8
Last 10	22.2	---	---	22.2

(0.58) (0.30) (0.07)
(0.66) (0.36) (0.15)
(0.64) (0.53) (0.23)

Copyright 2012 Securities Research Company

Bonds $.0 Mil Com 38.031 Mil BV 29.76 /sh P/E 16.79 (Ind ITSOF P/E 19.21) Ctry China

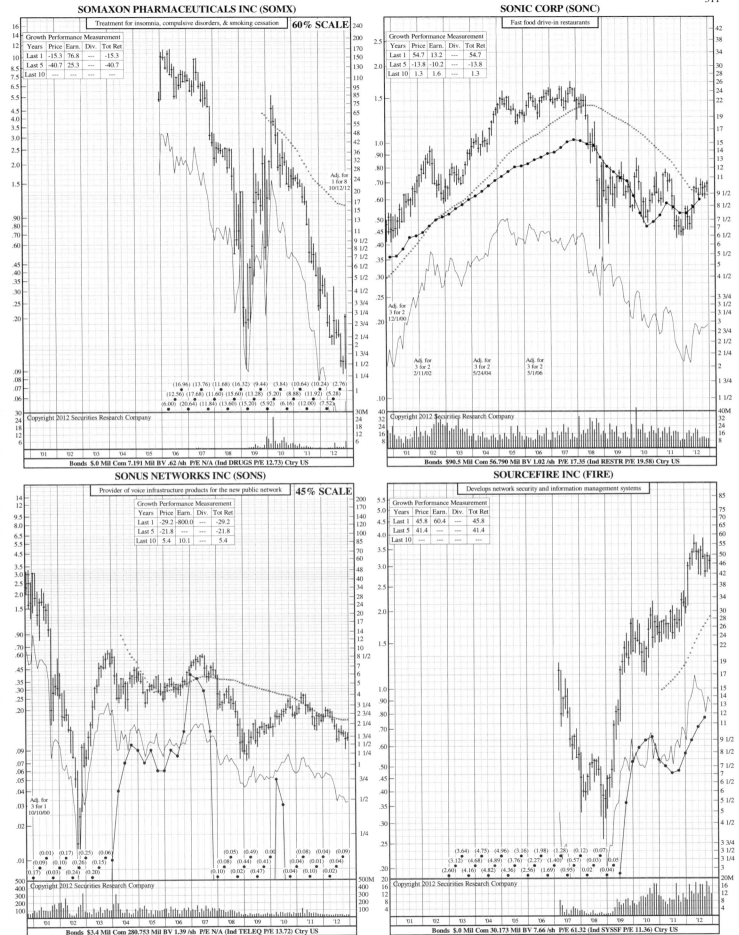

SOMAXON PHARMACEUTICALS INC (SOMX)

Treatment for insomnia, compulsive disorders, & smoking cessation

60% SCALE

Growth Performance Measurement				
Years	Price	Earn.	Div.	Tot Ret
Last 1	-15.3	76.8	---	-15.3
Last 5	-40.7	25.3	---	-40.7
Last 10	---	---	---	---

Adj. for
1 for 8
10/12/12

(16.96) (13.76) (11.68) (16.32) (9.44) (3.84) (10.64) (10.24) (2.76)
(12.56) (17.68) (11.60) (15.60) (13.28) (5.20) (8.88) (11.92) (5.28)
(6.00) (20.64) (11.84) (13.60) (15.20) (5.92) (6.16) (12.00) (7.52)

Copyright 2012 Securities Research Company

Bonds $.0 Mil Com 7.191 Mil BV .62 /sh P/E N/A (Ind DRUGS P/E 12.73) Ctry US

SONIC CORP (SONC)

Fast food drive-in restaurants

Growth Performance Measurement				
Years	Price	Earn.	Div.	Tot Ret
Last 1	54.7	13.2	---	54.7
Last 5	-13.8	-10.2	---	-13.8
Last 10	1.3	1.6	---	1.3

Adj. for
3 for 2
12/1/00

Adj. for   Adj. for   Adj. for
3 for 2   3 for 2   3 for 2
2/11/02   5/24/04   5/1/06

Copyright 2012 Securities Research Company

Bonds $90.5 Mil Com 56.790 Mil BV 1.02 /sh P/E 17.35 (Ind RESTR P/E 19.58) Ctry US

SONUS NETWORKS INC (SONS)

Provider of voice infrastructure products for the new public network

45% SCALE

Growth Performance Measurement				
Years	Price	Earn.	Div.	Tot Ret
Last 1	-29.2	-800.0	---	-29.2
Last 5	-21.8	---	---	-21.8
Last 10	5.4	10.1	---	5.4

Adj. for
3 for 1
10/10/00

(0.01) (0.17) (0.25) (0.06)   (0.05) (0.49) 0.00   (0.08) (0.04) (0.09)
(0.09) (0.10) (0.26) (0.15)   (0.08) (0.44) (0.41) (0.04) (0.01) (0.04)
(0.17) (0.03) (0.24) (0.20)   (0.10) (0.02) (0.47) (0.04) (0.10) (0.02)

Copyright 2012 Securities Research Company

Bonds $3.4 Mil Com 280.753 Mil BV 1.39 /sh P/E N/A (Ind TELEQ P/E 13.72) Ctry US

SOURCEFIRE INC (FIRE)

Develops network security and information management systems

Growth Performance Measurement				
Years	Price	Earn.	Div.	Tot Ret
Last 1	45.8	60.4	---	45.8
Last 5	41.4	---	---	41.4
Last 10	---	---	---	---

(3.64) (4.75) (4.96) (3.16) (1.98) (1.28) (0.12) (0.07)
(3.12) (4.68) (4.89) (3.76) (2.27) (1.40) (0.57) (0.03) 0.05
(2.60) (4.16) (4.82) (4.36) (2.56) (1.69) (0.95) (0.04)

Copyright 2012 Securities Research Company

Bonds $.0 Mil Com 30.173 Mil BV 7.66 /sh P/E 61.32 (Ind SYSSF P/E 11.36) Ctry US

312

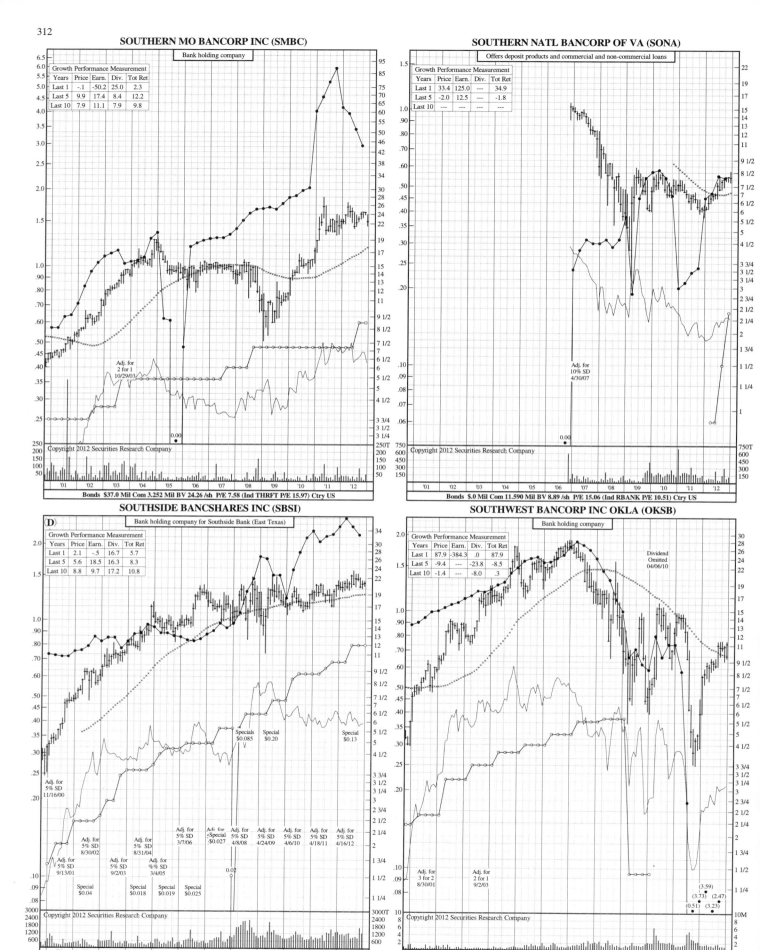

SOUTHERN MO BANCORP INC (SMBC)

Bank holding company

Growth Performance Measurement

Years	Price	Earn.	Div.	Tot Ret
Last 1	-.1	-50.2	25.0	2.3
Last 5	9.9	17.4	8.4	12.2
Last 10	7.9	11.1	7.9	9.8

Adj. for
2 for 1
10/29/03

0.00

Copyright 2012 Securities Research Company

Bonds $37.0 Mil Com 3.252 Mil BV 24.26 /sh P/E 7.58 (Ind THRFT P/E 15.97) Ctry US

SOUTHERN NATL BANCORP OF VA (SONA)

Offers deposit products and commercial and non-commercial loans

Growth Performance Measurement

Years	Price	Earn.	Div.	Tot Ret
Last 1	33.4	125.0	---	34.9
Last 5	-2.0	12.5	---	-1.8
Last 10	---	---	---	---

Adj. for
10% SD
4/30/07

0.00

Copyright 2012 Securities Research Company

Bonds $.0 Mil Com 11.590 Mil BV 8.89 /sh P/E 15.06 (Ind RBANK P/E 10.51) Ctry US

SOUTHSIDE BANCSHARES INC (SBSI)

(D)

Bank holding company for Southside Bank (East Texas)

Growth Performance Measurement

Years	Price	Earn.	Div.	Tot Ret
Last 1	2.1	-.5	16.7	5.7
Last 5	5.6	18.5	16.3	8.3
Last 10	8.8	9.7	17.2	10.8

Adj. for
5% SD
11/16/00

Adj. for
5% SD
9/13/01

Adj. for
5% SD
8/30/02

Adj. for
5% SD
9/2/03

Adj. for
%% SD
3/4/05

Adj. for
5% SD
8/31/04

Adj. for
5% SD
3/7/06

Adj. for
Special
$0.027

Adj. for
5% SD
4/8/08

Adj. for
5% SD
4/24/09

Adj. for
5% SD
4/6/10

Adj. for
5% SD
4/18/11

Adj. for
5% SD
4/16/12

Specials
$0.085

Special
$0.20

Special
$0.13

0.02

Special
$0.04

Special
$0.018

Special
$0.019

Special
$0.025

Copyright 2012 Securities Research Company

Bonds $.0 Mil Com 17.374 Mil BV 15.94 /sh P/E 9.66 (Ind RBANK P/E 10.51) Ctry US

SOUTHWEST BANCORP INC OKLA (OKSB)

Bank holding company

Growth Performance Measurement

Years	Price	Earn.	Div.	Tot Ret
Last 1	87.9	-384.3	.0	87.9
Last 5	-9.4	---	-23.8	-8.5
Last 10	-1.4	---	-8.0	.3

Dividend
Omitted
04/06/10

Adj. for
3 for 2
8/30/01

Adj. for
2 for 1
9/2/03

(3.59)
(3.73)   (2.47)
(0.51)
(3.23)

Copyright 2012 Securities Research Company

Bonds $25.0 Mil Com 19.448 Mil BV 12.85 /sh P/E N/A (Ind RBANK P/E 10.51) Ctry US

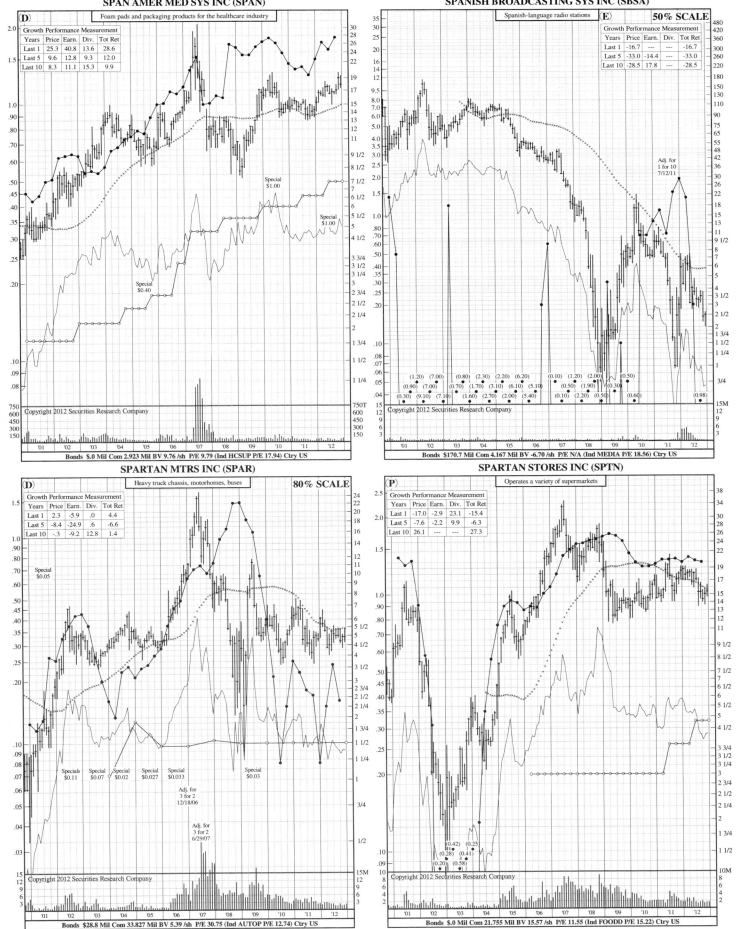

SPAN AMER MED SYS INC (SPAN)

Foam pads and packaging products for the healthcare industry

(D)

Growth Performance Measurement				
Years	Price	Earn.	Div.	Tot Ret
Last 1	25.3	40.8	13.6	28.6
Last 5	9.6	12.8	9.3	12.0
Last 10	8.3	11.1	15.3	9.9

Special $1.00

Special $1.00

Special $0.40

Copyright 2012 Securities Research Company

Bonds $.0 Mil Com 2.923 Mil BV 9.76 /sh P/E 9.79 (Ind HCSUP P/E 17.94) Ctry US

SPANISH BROADCASTING SYS INC (SBSA)

Spanish-language radio stations

50% SCALE

(E)

Growth Performance Measurement				
Years	Price	Earn.	Div.	Tot Ret
Last 1	-16.7	---	---	-16.7
Last 5	-33.0	-14.4	---	-33.0
Last 10	-28.5	17.8	---	-28.5

Adj. for 1 for 10 7/12/11

(1.20) (7.00) (0.80) (2.30) (2.20) (6.20)   (0.10) (1.20) (2.00)   (0.50)
(0.90) (7.00) (0.70) (1.70) (3.10) (6.10) (5.10) (0.50) (1.90) (0.30) (0.60)   (0.98)
(0.30) (9.10) (7.10) (1.60) (2.70) (2.00) (5.40) (0.10) (2.20) (0.50)

Copyright 2012 Securities Research Company

Bonds $170.7 Mil Com 4.167 Mil BV -6.70 /sh P/E N/A (Ind MEDIA P/E 18.56) Ctry US

SPARTAN MTRS INC (SPAR)

Heavy truck chassis, motorhomes, buses

80% SCALE

(D)

Growth Performance Measurement				
Years	Price	Earn.	Div.	Tot Ret
Last 1	2.3	-5.9	.0	4.4
Last 5	-8.4	-24.9	.6	-6.6
Last 10	-.3	-9.2	12.8	1.4

Special $0.05

Specials $0.11   Special $0.07   Special $0.02   Special $0.027   Special $0.033   Special $0.03

Adj. for 3 for 2 12/18/06

Adj. for 3 for 2 6/29/07

Copyright 2012 Securities Research Company

Bonds $28.8 Mil Com 33.827 Mil BV 5.39 /sh P/E 30.75 (Ind AUTOP P/E 12.74) Ctry US

SPARTAN STORES INC (SPTN)

Operates a variety of supermarkets

(P)

Growth Performance Measurement				
Years	Price	Earn.	Div.	Tot Ret
Last 1	-17.0	-2.9	23.1	-15.4
Last 5	-7.6	-2.2	9.9	-6.3
Last 10	26.1	---	---	27.3

(0.42) (0.25)
(0.28) (0.41)
(0.20) (0.58)

Copyright 2012 Securities Research Company

Bonds $.0 Mil Com 21.755 Mil BV 15.57 /sh P/E 11.55 (Ind FOODD P/E 15.22) Ctry US

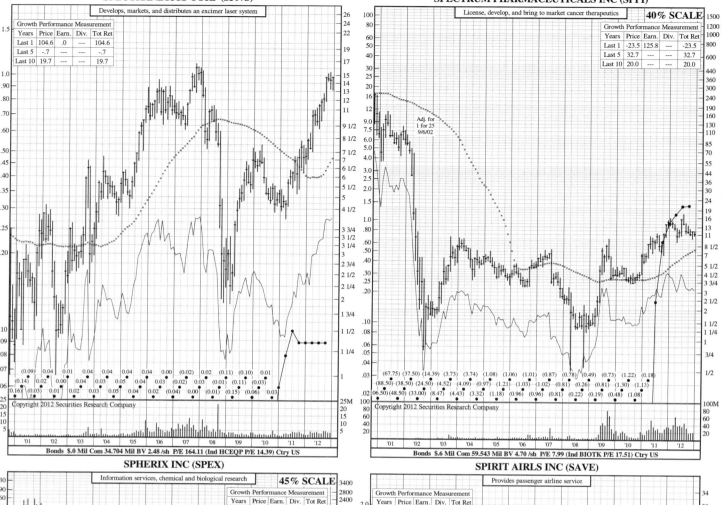
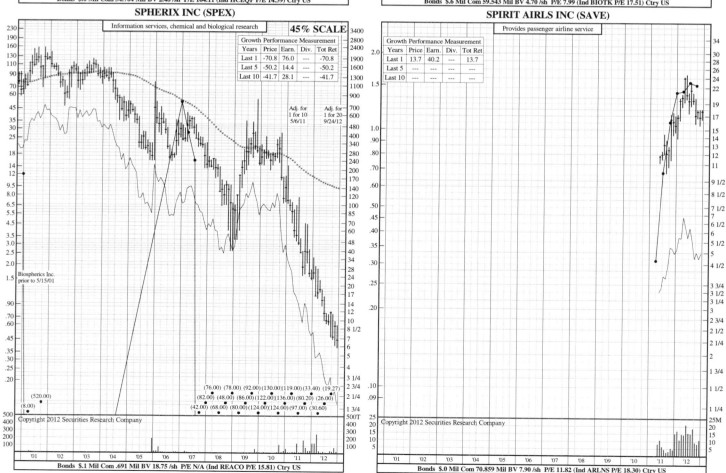

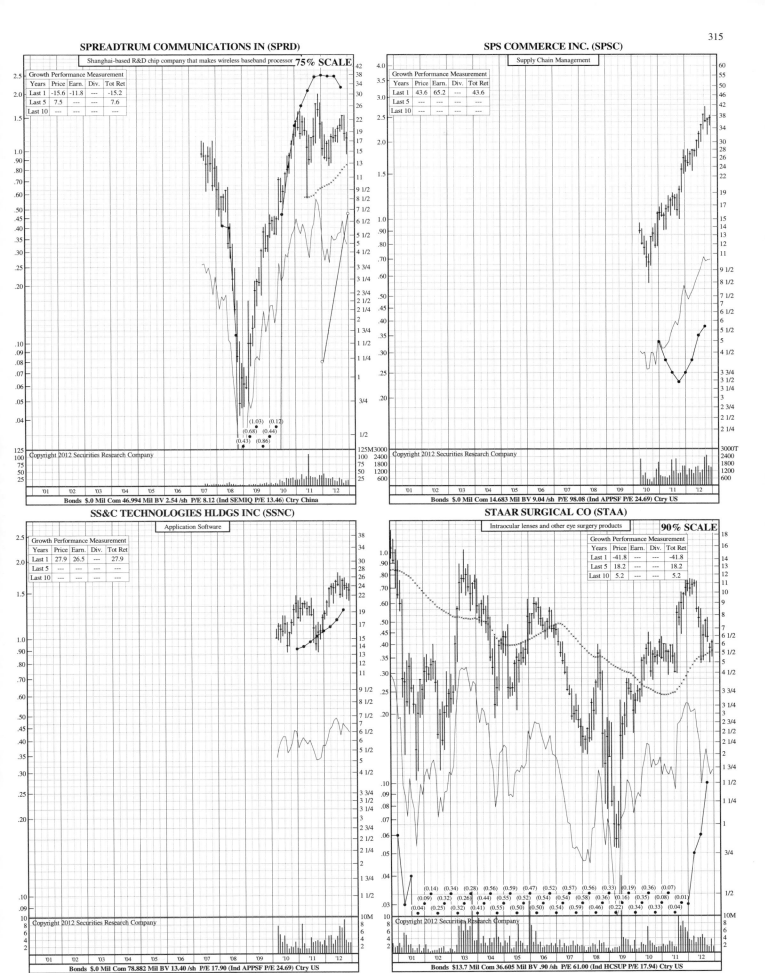

SPREADTRUM COMMUNICATIONS IN (SPRD)

Shanghai-based R&D chip company that makes wireless baseband processor **75% SCALE**

Growth Performance Measurement				
Years	Price	Earn.	Div.	Tot Ret
Last 1	-15.6	-11.8	---	-15.2
Last 5	7.5	---	---	7.6
Last 10	---	---	---	---

(1.03) (0.12)
(0.68) (0.44)
(0.43) (0.86)

Copyright 2012 Securities Research Company

Bonds $.0 Mil Com 46.994 Mil BV 2.54 /sh P/E 8.12 (Ind SEMIQ P/E 13.46) Ctry China

SPS COMMERCE INC. (SPSC)

Supply Chain Management

Growth Performance Measurement				
Years	Price	Earn.	Div.	Tot Ret
Last 1	43.6	65.2	---	43.6
Last 5	---	---	---	---
Last 10	---	---	---	---

Copyright 2012 Securities Research Company

Bonds $.0 Mil Com 14.683 Mil BV 9.04 /sh P/E 98.08 (Ind APPSF P/E 24.69) Ctry US

SS&C TECHNOLOGIES HLDGS INC (SSNC)

Application Software

Growth Performance Measurement				
Years	Price	Earn.	Div.	Tot Ret
Last 1	27.9	26.5	---	27.9
Last 5	---	---	---	---
Last 10	---	---	---	---

Copyright 2012 Securities Research Company

Bonds $.0 Mil Com 78.882 Mil BV 13.40 /sh P/E 17.90 (Ind APPSF P/E 24.69) Ctry US

STAAR SURGICAL CO (STAA)

Intraocular lenses and other eye surgery products **90% SCALE**

Growth Performance Measurement				
Years	Price	Earn.	Div.	Tot Ret
Last 1	-41.8	---	---	-41.8
Last 5	18.2	---	---	18.2
Last 10	5.2	---	---	5.2

(0.14) (0.34) (0.28) (0.56) (0.59) (0.47) (0.52) (0.57) (0.56) (0.33) (0.19) (0.36) (0.07)
(0.09) (0.32) (0.26) (0.44) (0.52) (0.55) (0.54) (0.54) (0.58) (0.36) (0.16) (0.35) (0.08) (0.01)
(0.04) (0.25) (0.32) (0.41) (0.55) (0.50) (0.50) (0.54) (0.59) (0.46) (0.22) (0.34) (0.33) (0.04)

Copyright 2012 Securities Research Company

Bonds $13.7 Mil Com 36.605 Mil BV .90 /sh P/E 61.00 (Ind HCSUP P/E 17.94) Ctry US

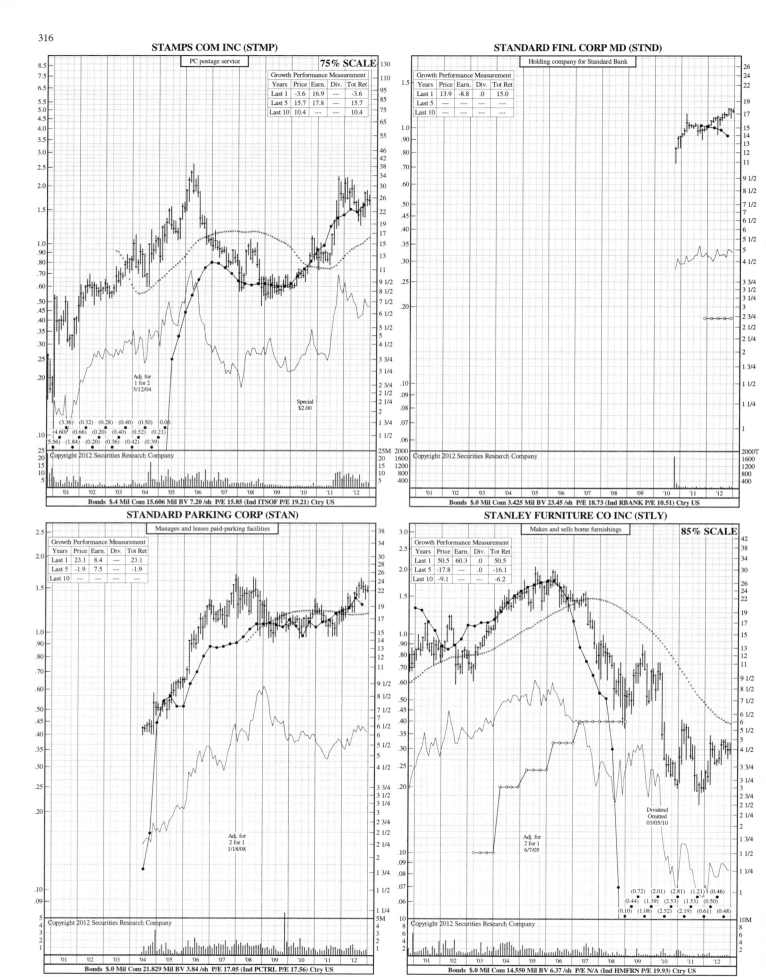

STAMPS COM INC (STMP)

PC postage service

75% SCALE

Growth Performance Measurement

Years	Price	Earn.	Div.	Tot Ret
Last 1	-3.6	16.9	---	-3.6
Last 5	15.7	17.8	---	15.7
Last 10	10.4	---	---	10.4

Adj. for
1 for 2
5/12/04

Special
$2.00

(3.36) (0.32) (0.28) (0.40) (0.50) 0.06
(4.60) (0.66) (0.20) (0.40) (0.52) (0.21)
(5.56) (1.84) (0.20) (0.36) (0.42) (0.39)

Copyright 2012 Securities Research Company

Bonds $.4 Mil Com 15.606 Mil BV 7.20 /sh P/E 15.85 (Ind ITSOF P/E 19.21) Ctry US

STANDARD FINL CORP MD (STND)

Holding company for Standard Bank

Growth Performance Measurement

Years	Price	Earn.	Div.	Tot Ret
Last 1	13.9	-8.8	.0	15.0
Last 5	---	---	---	---
Last 10	---	---	---	---

Copyright 2012 Securities Research Company

Bonds $.0 Mil Com 3.425 Mil BV 23.45 /sh P/E 18.73 (Ind RBANK P/E 10.51) Ctry US

STANDARD PARKING CORP (STAN)

Manages and leases paid-parking facilities

Growth Performance Measurement

Years	Price	Earn.	Div.	Tot Ret
Last 1	23.1	8.4	---	23.1
Last 5	-1.9	7.5	---	-1.9
Last 10	---	---	---	---

Adj. for
2 for 1
1/18/08

Copyright 2012 Securities Research Company

Bonds $.0 Mil Com 21.829 Mil BV 3.84 /sh P/E 17.05 (Ind PCTRL P/E 17.56) Ctry US

STANLEY FURNITURE CO INC (STLY)

Makes and sells home furnishings

85% SCALE

Growth Performance Measurement

Years	Price	Earn.	Div.	Tot Ret
Last 1	50.5	60.3	.0	50.5
Last 5	-17.8	---	.0	-16.1
Last 10	-9.1	---	---	-6.2

Adj. for
2 for 1
6/7/05

Dividend
Omitted
03/05/10

(0.72) (2.01) (2.81) (1.21) (0.46)
(0.44) (1.39) (2.53) (1.53) (0.50)
(0.10) (1.08) (2.52) (2.19) (0.61) (0.48)

Copyright 2012 Securities Research Company

Bonds $.0 Mil Com 14.550 Mil BV 6.37 /sh P/E N/A (Ind HMFRN P/E 19.93) Ctry US

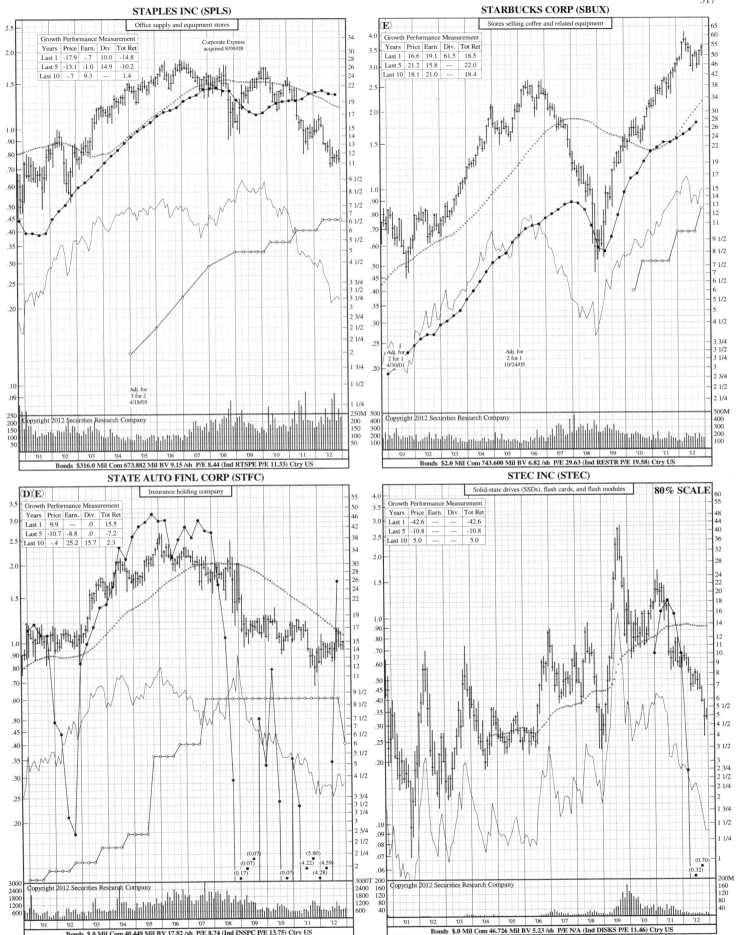

STAPLES INC (SPLS)

Office supply and equipment stores

Corporate Express acquired 8/08/08

Growth Performance Measurement				
Years	Price	Earn.	Div.	Tot Ret
Last 1	-17.9	-.7	10.0	-14.8
Last 5	-13.1	-1.0	14.9	-10.2
Last 10	-.7	9.3	---	1.4

Adj. for 3 for 2 4/18/05

Copyright 2012 Securities Research Company

Bonds $316.0 Mil Com 673.882 Mil BV 9.15 /sh P/E 8.44 (Ind RTSPE P/E 11.33) Ctry US

STARBUCKS CORP (SBUX)

Stores selling coffee and related equipment

Growth Performance Measurement				
Years	Price	Earn.	Div.	Tot Ret
Last 1	16.6	19.1	61.5	18.5
Last 5	21.2	15.8	---	22.0
Last 10	18.1	21.0	---	18.4

Adj. for 2 for 1 4/30/01

Adj. for 2 for 1 10/24/05

Copyright 2012 Securities Research Company

Bonds $2.0 Mil Com 743.600 Mil BV 6.82 /sh P/E 29.63 (Ind RESTR P/E 19.58) Ctry US

STATE AUTO FINL CORP (STFC)

(D)(E)

Insurance holding company

Growth Performance Measurement				
Years	Price	Earn.	Div.	Tot Ret
Last 1	9.9	---	.0	15.5
Last 5	-10.7	-8.8	.0	-7.2
Last 10	-.4	25.2	15.7	2.3

(0.07)
(0.07)
(0.17)

(5.80)
(4.22) (4.59)
(0.07) (4.28)

Copyright 2012 Securities Research Company

Bonds $.0 Mil Com 40.449 Mil BV 17.82 /sh P/E 8.74 (Ind INSPC P/E 13.75) Ctry US

STEC INC (STEC)

Solid-state drives (SSDs), flash cards, and flash modules

80% SCALE

Growth Performance Measurement				
Years	Price	Earn.	Div.	Tot Ret
Last 1	-42.6	---	---	-42.6
Last 5	-10.8	---	---	-10.8
Last 10	5.0	---	---	5.0

(0.70)
(0.32)

Copyright 2012 Securities Research Company

Bonds $.0 Mil Com 46.726 Mil BV 5.23 /sh P/E N/A (Ind DISKS P/E 11.46) Ctry US

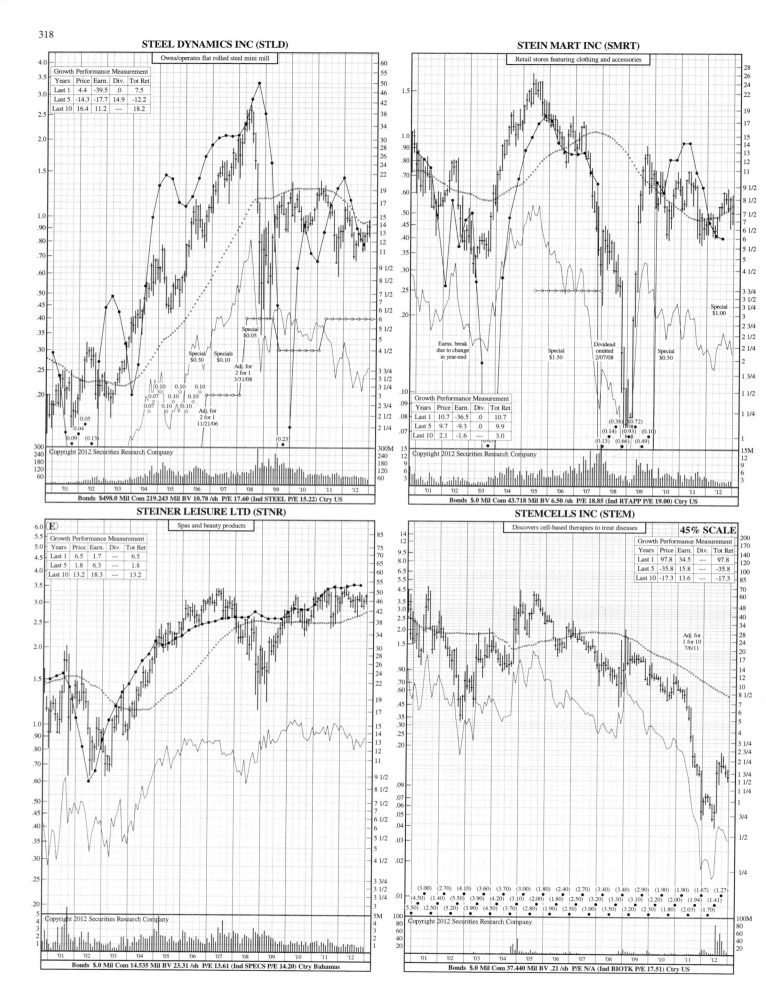

STEEL DYNAMICS INC (STLD)

Owns/operates flat rolled steel mini mill

Growth Performance Measurement				
Years	Price	Earn.	Div.	Tot Ret
Last 1	4.4	-39.5	.0	7.5
Last 5	-14.3	-17.7	14.9	-12.2
Last 10	16.4	11.2	---	18.2

Special $0.05
Special $0.30
Specials $0.10
Adj. for 2 for 1 3/31/08
0.10 0.10 0.10 0.10
0.07 0.10 0.10 0.10
0.07 0.10 0.10
Adj. for 2 for 1 11/21/06
0.05
0.04
0.09 (0.13)
(0.23)

Copyright 2012 Securities Research Company

Bonds $498.0 Mil Com 219.243 Mil BV 10.78 /sh P/E 17.60 (Ind STEEL P/E 15.22) Ctry US

STEIN MART INC (SMRT)

Retail stores featuring clothing and accessories

Special $1.00
Earns. break due to change in year-end
Special $1.50
Dividend omitted 2/07/08
Special $0.50

Growth Performance Measurement				
Years	Price	Earn.	Div.	Tot Ret
Last 1	10.7	-36.5	.0	10.7
Last 5	9.7	-9.3	.0	9.9
Last 10	2.1	-1.6	---	3.0

(0.38) (0.72)
(0.14) (0.93) (0.10)
(0.13) (0.66) (0.49)
(0.05)

Copyright 2012 Securities Research Company

Bonds $.0 Mil Com 43.718 Mil BV 6.50 /sh P/E 18.85 (Ind RTAPP P/E 19.00) Ctry US

STEINER LEISURE LTD (STNR)

(E)
Spas and beauty products

Growth Performance Measurement				
Years	Price	Earn.	Div.	Tot Ret
Last 1	6.5	1.7	---	6.5
Last 5	1.8	6.3	---	1.8
Last 10	13.2	18.3	---	13.2

Copyright 2012 Securities Research Company

Bonds $.0 Mil Com 14.535 Mil BV 23.31 /sh P/E 13.61 (Ind SPECS P/E 14.20) Ctry Bahamas

STEMCELLS INC (STEM)

Discovers cell-based therapies to treat diseases

45% SCALE

Growth Performance Measurement				
Years	Price	Earn.	Div.	Tot Ret
Last 1	97.8	34.5	---	97.8
Last 5	-35.8	15.8	---	-35.8
Last 10	-17.3	13.6	---	-17.3

Adj. for 1 for 10 7/6/11

(3.00) (2.70) (4.10) (3.60) (3.70) (3.00) (1.80) (2.40) (2.70) (3.40) (3.40) (2.90) (1.90) (1.90) (1.67) (1.27)
(4.50) (1.40) (5.50) (3.90) (4.20) (3.10) (2.00) (2.20) (2.50) (3.20) (3.30) (3.10) (2.00) (1.94) (1.41)
(5.50) (2.50) (5.20) (3.90) (4.50) (3.70) (2.80) (1.90) (2.50) (3.20) (3.50) (2.30) (1.80) (2.03) (1.70)

Copyright 2012 Securities Research Company

Bonds $.0 Mil Com 37.440 Mil BV .21 /sh P/E N/A (Ind BIOTK P/E 17.51) Ctry US

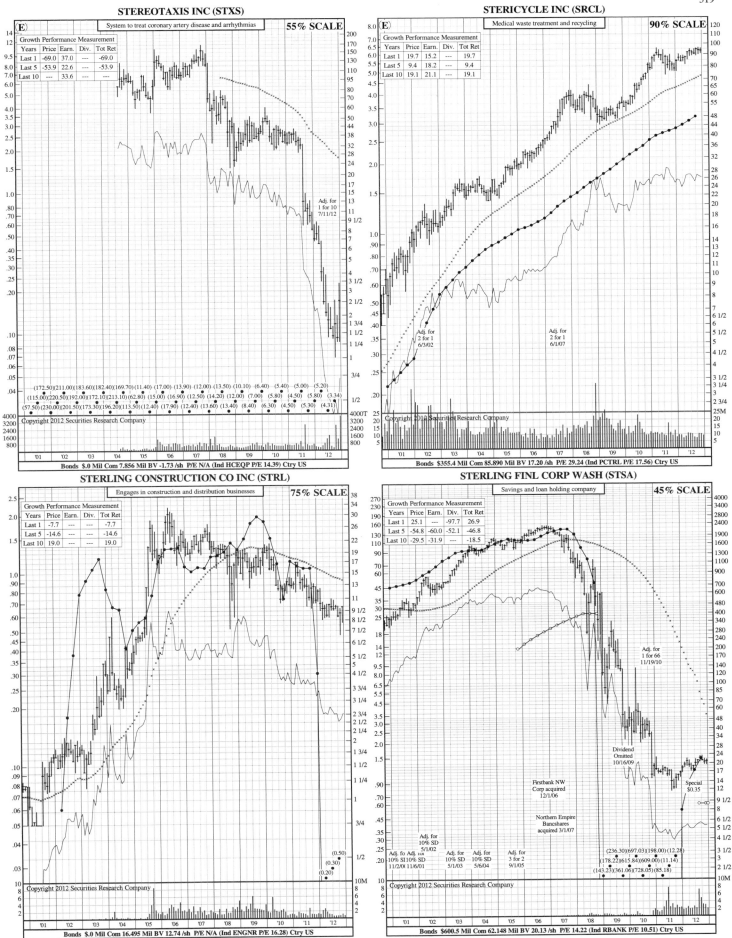

STEREOTAXIS INC (STXS)

System to treat coronary artery disease and arrhythmias

55% SCALE

(E)

Growth Performance Measurement

Years	Price	Earn.	Div.	Tot Ret
Last 1	-69.0	37.0	---	-69.0
Last 5	-53.9	22.6	---	-53.9
Last 10	---	33.6	---	---

Adj. for
1 for 10
7/11/12

(172.50)(211.00)(183.60)(182.40)(169.70)(11.40)(17.00)(13.90)(12.00)(13.50)(10.10)(6.40)(5.40)(5.00)(5.20)
(115.00)(220.50)(192.00)(172.10)(213.10)(62.80)(15.00)(16.90)(12.50)(14.20)(12.00)(7.00)(5.80)(4.50)(5.80)(3.34)
(57.50)(230.00)(201.50)(173.30)(196.20)(113.50)(12.40)(17.90)(12.40)(13.60)(13.40)(8.40)(6.30)(4.50)(5.30)(4.31)

Copyright 2012 Securities Research Company

Bonds $.0 Mil Com 7.856 Mil BV -1.73 /sh P/E N/A (Ind HCEQP P/E 14.39) Ctry US

STERICYCLE INC (SRCL)

Medical waste treatment and recycling

90% SCALE

(E)

Growth Performance Measurement

Years	Price	Earn.	Div.	Tot Ret
Last 1	19.7	15.2	---	19.7
Last 5	9.4	18.2	---	9.4
Last 10	19.1	21.1	---	19.1

Adj. for
2 for 1
6/3/02

Adj. for
2 for 1
6/1/07

Copyright 2012 Securities Research Company

Bonds $355.4 Mil Com 85.890 Mil BV 17.20 /sh P/E 29.24 (Ind PCTRL P/E 17.56) Ctry US

STERLING CONSTRUCTION CO INC (STRL)

Engages in construction and distribution businesses

75% SCALE

Growth Performance Measurement

Years	Price	Earn.	Div.	Tot Ret
Last 1	-7.7	---	---	-7.7
Last 5	-14.6	---	---	-14.6
Last 10	19.0	---	---	19.0

(0.50)
(0.30)
(0.20)

Copyright 2012 Securities Research Company

Bonds $.0 Mil Com 16.495 Mil BV 12.74 /sh P/E N/A (Ind ENGNR P/E 16.28) Ctry US

STERLING FINL CORP WASH (STSA)

Savings and loan holding company

45% SCALE

Growth Performance Measurement

Years	Price	Earn.	Div.	Tot Ret
Last 1	25.1	---	-97.7	26.9
Last 5	-54.8	-60.0	-52.1	-46.8
Last 10	-29.5	-31.9	---	-18.5

Adj. for
1 for 66
11/19/10

Dividend
Omitted
10/16/09

Special
$0.35

Firstbank NW
Corp acquired
12/1/06

Northern Empire
Bancshares
acquired 3/1/07

Adj. for
10% SD
5/1/02

Adj. fo Adj. for
10% SD 10% SD
11/2/0 11/6/01

Adj. for
10% SD
5/1/03

Adj. for
10% SD
5/6/04

Adj. for
3 for 2
9/1/05

(236.30)(697.03)(198.00)(12.28)
(178.22)(615.84)(609.00)(11.14)
(143.23)(361.06)(728.05)(85.18)

Copyright 2012 Securities Research Company

Bonds $600.5 Mil Com 62.148 Mil BV 20.13 /sh P/E 14.22 (Ind RBANK P/E 10.51) Ctry US

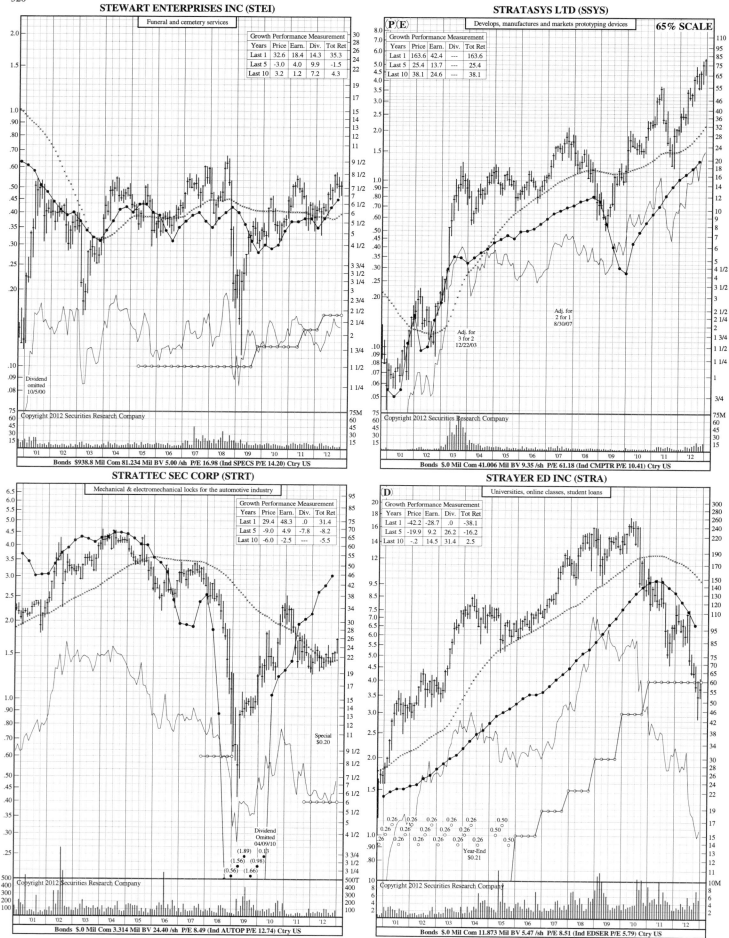

320

STEWART ENTERPRISES INC (STEI)

Funeral and cemetery services

Growth Performance Measurement				
Years	Price	Earn.	Div.	Tot Ret
Last 1	32.6	18.4	14.3	35.3
Last 5	-3.0	4.0	9.9	-1.5
Last 10	3.2	1.2	7.2	4.3

Dividend omitted 10/5/00

Copyright 2012 Securities Research Company

Bonds $938.8 Mil Com 81.234 Mil BV 5.00 /sh P/E 16.98 (Ind SPECS P/E 14.20) Ctry US

STRATASYS LTD (SSYS)

(P)(E)   Develops, manufactures and markets prototyping devices   65% SCALE

Growth Performance Measurement				
Years	Price	Earn.	Div.	Tot Ret
Last 1	163.6	42.4	---	163.6
Last 5	25.4	13.7	---	25.4
Last 10	38.1	24.6	---	38.1

Adj. for
2 for 1
8/30/07

Adj. for
3 for 2
12/22/03

Copyright 2012 Securities Research Company

Bonds $.0 Mil Com 41.006 Mil BV 9.35 /sh P/E 61.18 (Ind CMPTR P/E 10.41) Ctry US

STRATTEC SEC CORP (STRT)

Mechanical & electromechanical locks for the automotive industry

Growth Performance Measurement				
Years	Price	Earn.	Div.	Tot Ret
Last 1	29.4	48.3	.0	31.4
Last 5	-9.0	4.9	-7.8	-8.2
Last 10	-6.0	-2.5	---	-5.5

Special
$0.20

Dividend
Omitted
04/09/10

(1.89) 0.13
(1.56) (0.98)
(0.56) (1.66)

Copyright 2012 Securities Research Company

Bonds $.0 Mil Com 3.314 Mil BV 24.40 /sh P/E 8.49 (Ind AUTOP P/E 12.74) Ctry US

STRAYER ED INC (STRA)

(D)   Universities, online classes, student loans

Growth Performance Measurement				
Years	Price	Earn.	Div.	Tot Ret
Last 1	-42.2	-28.7	.0	-38.1
Last 5	-19.9	9.2	26.2	-16.2
Last 10	-.2	14.5	31.4	2.5

0.26 0.26 0.26 0.26 0.26   0.50
0.26 0.26 0.26 0.26 0.26 0.50
0.26 0.26 0.26 0.26 0.26 0.50

Year-End
$0.21

Copyright 2012 Securities Research Company

Bonds $.0 Mil Com 11.873 Mil BV 5.47 /sh P/E 8.51 (Ind EDSER P/E 5.79) Ctry US

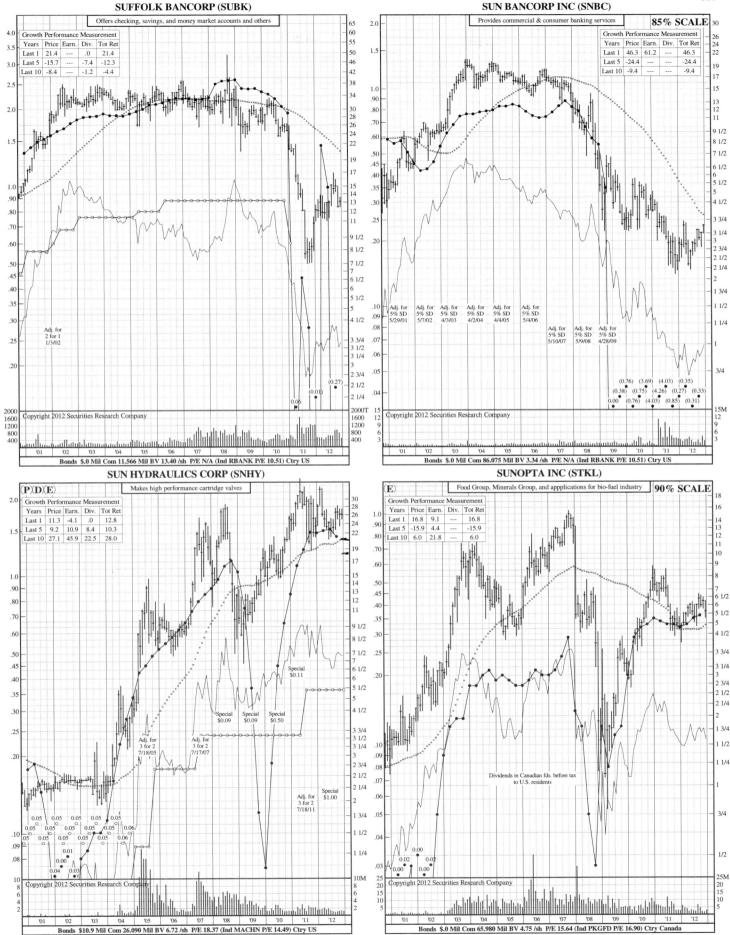

SUFFOLK BANCORP (SUBK)

Offers checking, savings, and money market accounts and others

Growth Performance Measurement				
Years	Price	Earn.	Div.	Tot Ret
Last 1	21.4	---	.0	21.4
Last 5	-15.7	---	-7.4	-12.3
Last 10	-8.4	---	-1.2	-4.4

Adj. for
2 for 1
1/3/02

(0.27)
(0.01)
0.06

Copyright 2012 Securities Research Company

Bonds $.0 Mil Com 11.566 Mil BV 13.40 /sh P/E N/A (Ind RBANK P/E 10.51) Ctry US

SUN BANCORP INC (SNBC)

Provides commercial & consumer banking services   **85% SCALE**

Growth Performance Measurement				
Years	Price	Earn.	Div.	Tot Ret
Last 1	46.3	61.2	---	46.3
Last 5	-24.4	---	---	-24.4
Last 10	-9.4	---	---	-9.4

Adj. for   Adj. for   Adj. for   Adj. for   Adj. for   Adj. for
5% SD   5% SD   5% SD   5% SD   5% SD   5% SD
5/29/01   5/7/02   4/3/03   4/2/04   4/4/05   5/4/06

Adj. for   Adj. for   Adj. for
5% SD   5% SD   5% SD
5/10/07   5/9/08   4/28/09

(0.76) (3.69) (4.03) (0.35)
(0.38) (0.75) (4.26) (0.27) (0.33)
0.00   (0.76) (4.03) (0.85) (0.31)

Copyright 2012 Securities Research Company

Bonds $.0 Mil Com 86.075 Mil BV 3.34 /sh P/E N/A (Ind RBANK P/E 10.51) Ctry US

SUN HYDRAULICS CORP (SNHY)

(P)(D)(E)   Makes high performance cartridge valves

Growth Performance Measurement				
Years	Price	Earn.	Div.	Tot Ret
Last 1	11.3	-4.1	.0	12.8
Last 5	9.2	10.9	8.4	10.3
Last 10	27.1	45.9	22.5	28.0

Special
$0.11

Special   Special   Special
$0.09 $0.09 $0.50

Adj. for
3 for 2
7/18/05

Adj. for
3 for 2
7/17/07

Adj. for
3 for 2
7/18/11

Special
$1.00

0.05   0.05   0.05   0.05   0.05
0.05   0.05   0.05   0.06/
0.05   0.05   0.05   0.05   0.06
0.05   0.05   0.06
0.01
0.00
0.04   0.03

Copyright 2012 Securities Research Company

Bonds $10.9 Mil Com 26.090 Mil BV 6.72 /sh P/E 18.37 (Ind MACHN P/E 14.49) Ctry US

SUNOPTA INC (STKL)

(E)   Food Group, Minerals Group, and appplications for bio-fuel industry   **90% SCALE**

Growth Performance Measurement				
Years	Price	Earn.	Div.	Tot Ret
Last 1	16.8	9.1	---	16.8
Last 5	-15.9	4.4	---	-15.9
Last 10	6.0	21.8	---	6.0

Dividends in Canadian fds. before tax
to U.S. residents

0.00
0.02   0.02
0.00   0.00

Copyright 2012 Securities Research Company

Bonds $.0 Mil Com 65.980 Mil BV 4.75 /sh P/E 15.64 (Ind PKGFD P/E 16.90) Ctry Canada

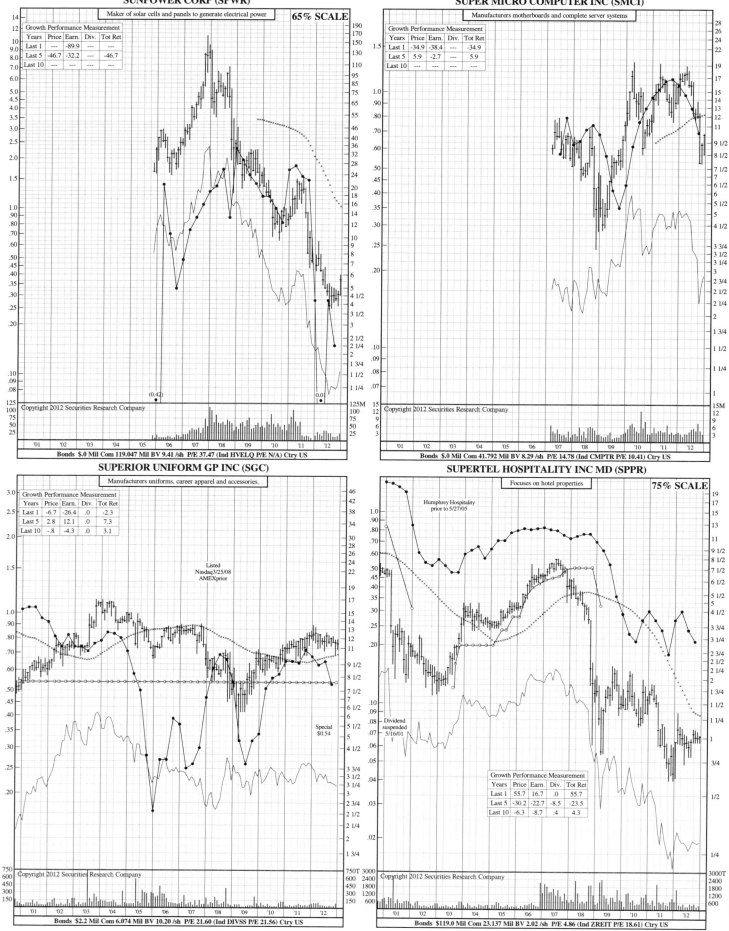

SUNPOWER CORP (SPWR)

Maker of solar cells and panels to generate electrical power

65% SCALE

Growth Performance Measurement

Years	Price	Earn.	Div.	Tot Ret
Last 1	---	-89.9	---	---
Last 5	-46.7	-32.2	---	-46.7
Last 10	---	---	---	---

(0.42)

0.0

Copyright 2012 Securities Research Company

Bonds $.0 Mil Com 119.047 Mil BV 9.41 /sh P/E 37.47 (Ind HVELQ P/E N/A) Ctry US

SUPER MICRO COMPUTER INC (SMCI)

Manufacturers motherboards and complete server systems

Growth Performance Measurement

Years	Price	Earn.	Div.	Tot Ret
Last 1	-34.9	-38.4	---	-34.9
Last 5	5.9	-2.7	---	5.9
Last 10	---	---	---	---

Copyright 2012 Securities Research Company

Bonds $.0 Mil Com 41.792 Mil BV 8.29 /sh P/E 14.78 (Ind CMPTR P/E 10.41) Ctry US

SUPERIOR UNIFORM GP INC (SGC)

Manufacturers uniforms, career apparel and accessories.

Growth Performance Measurement

Years	Price	Earn.	Div.	Tot Ret
Last 1	-6.7	-26.4	.0	-2.3
Last 5	2.8	12.1	.0	7.3
Last 10	-.8	-4.3	.0	3.1

Listed
Nasdaq3/25/08
AMEXprior

Special
$0.54

Copyright 2012 Securities Research Company

Bonds $2.2 Mil Com 6.074 Mil BV 10.20 /sh P/E 21.60 (Ind DIVSS P/E 21.56) Ctry US

SUPERTEL HOSPITALITY INC MD (SPPR)

Focuses on hotel properties

75% SCALE

Humphrey Hospitality
prior to 5/27/05

Dividend
suspended
5/16/01

Growth Performance Measurement

Years	Price	Earn.	Div.	Tot Ret
Last 1	55.7	16.7	.0	55.7
Last 5	-30.2	-22.7	-8.5	-23.5
Last 10	-6.3	-8.7	.4	4.3

Copyright 2012 Securities Research Company

Bonds $119.0 Mil Com 23.137 Mil BV 2.02 /sh P/E 4.86 (Ind ZREIT P/E 18.61) Ctry US

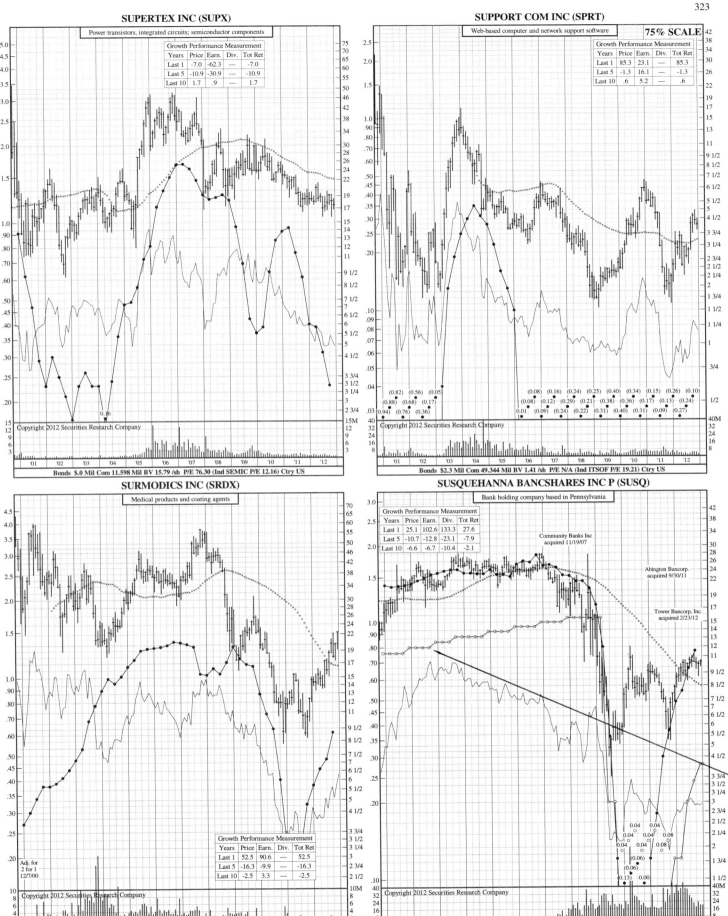

SUPERTEX INC (SUPX)

Power transistors, integrated circuits; semiconductor components

Growth Performance Measurement				
Years	Price	Earn.	Div.	Tot Ret
Last 1	-7.0	-62.3	---	-7.0
Last 5	-10.9	-30.9	---	-10.9
Last 10	1.7	.9	---	1.7

Copyright 2012 Securities Research Company

Bonds $.0 Mil Com 11.598 Mil BV 15.79 /sh P/E 76.30 (Ind SEMIC P/E 12.16) Ctry US

SUPPORT COM INC (SPRT)

Web-based computer and network support software

75% SCALE

Growth Performance Measurement				
Years	Price	Earn.	Div.	Tot Ret
Last 1	85.3	23.1	---	85.3
Last 5	-1.3	16.1	---	-1.3
Last 10	.6	5.2	---	.6

Copyright 2012 Securities Research Company

Bonds $2.3 Mil Com 49.344 Mil BV 1.41 /sh P/E N/A (Ind ITSOF P/E 19.21) Ctry US

SURMODICS INC (SRDX)

Medical products and coating agents

Growth Performance Measurement				
Years	Price	Earn.	Div.	Tot Ret
Last 1	52.5	90.6	---	52.5
Last 5	-16.3	-9.9	---	-16.3
Last 10	-2.5	3.3	---	-2.5

Adj. for 2 for 1 12/7/00

Copyright 2012 Securities Research Company

Bonds $.0 Mil Com 14.662 Mil BV 6.46 /sh P/E 36.66 (Ind HCEQP P/E 14.39) Ctry US

SUSQUEHANNA BANCSHARES INC P (SUSQ)

Bank holding company based in Pennsylvania

Growth Performance Measurement				
Years	Price	Earn.	Div.	Tot Ret
Last 1	25.1	102.6	133.3	27.6
Last 5	-10.7	-12.8	-23.1	-7.9
Last 10	-6.6	-6.7	-10.4	-2.1

Community Banks Inc acquired 11/19/07

Abington Bancorp. acquired 9/30/11

Tower Bancorp, Inc. acquired 2/23/12

Copyright 2012 Securities Research Company

Bonds $360.0 Mil Com 186.462 Mil BV 13.86 /sh P/E 13.61 (Ind RBANK P/E 10.51) Ctry US

324

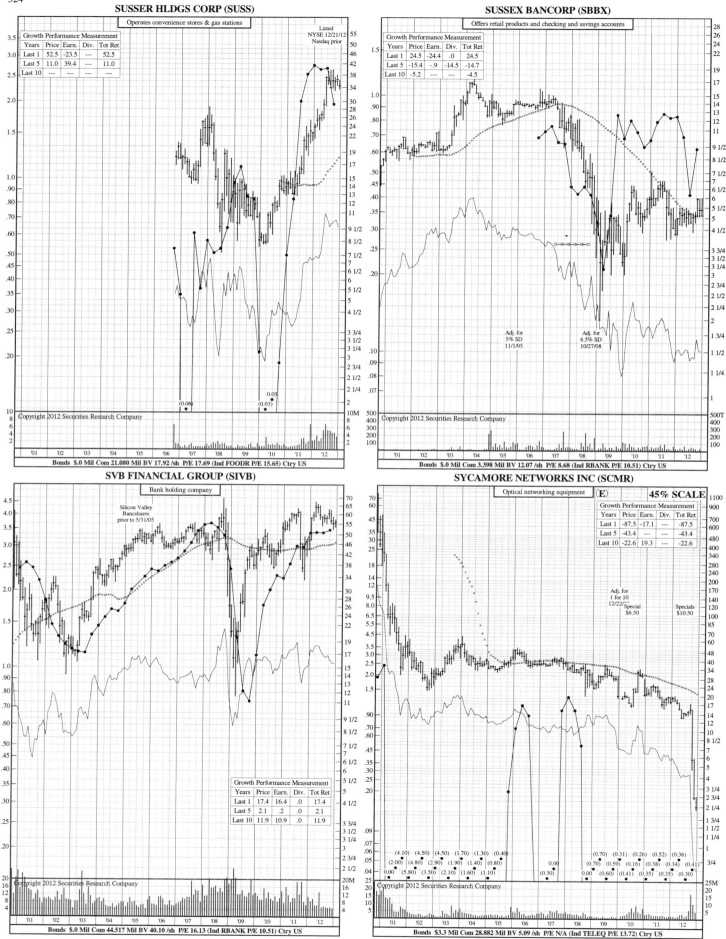

SUSSER HLDGS CORP (SUSS)

Operates convenience stores & gas stations

Listed
NYSE 12/21/12
Nasdaq prior

Growth Performance Measurement				
Years	Price	Earn.	Div.	Tot Ret
Last 1	52.5	-23.5	---	52.5
Last 5	11.0	39.4	---	11.0
Last 10	---	---	---	---

(0.06)
(0.03)
0.05

Copyright 2012 Securities Research Company

'01 '02 '03 '04 '05 '06 '07 '08 '09 '10 '11 '12

Bonds $.0 Mil Com 21.080 Mil BV 17.92 /sh P/E 17.69 (Ind FOODR P/E 15.65) Ctry US

SUSSEX BANCORP (SBBX)

Offers retail products and checking and savings accounts

Growth Performance Measurement				
Years	Price	Earn.	Div.	Tot Ret
Last 1	24.5	-24.4	.0	24.5
Last 5	-15.4	-.9	-14.5	-14.7
Last 10	-5.2	---	---	-4.5

Adj. for
5% SD
11/1/05

Adj. for
6.5% SD
10/27/08

Copyright 2012 Securities Research Company

'01 '02 '03 '04 '05 '06 '07 '08 '09 '10 '11 '12

Bonds $.0 Mil Com 3.398 Mil BV 12.07 /sh P/E 8.68 (Ind RBANK P/E 10.51) Ctry US

SVB FINANCIAL GROUP (SIVB)

Bank holding company

Silicon Valley
Bancshares
prior to 5/31/05

Growth Performance Measurement				
Years	Price	Earn.	Div.	Tot Ret
Last 1	17.4	16.4	.0	17.4
Last 5	2.1	.2	.0	2.1
Last 10	11.9	10.9	.0	11.9

Copyright 2012 Securities Research Company

'01 '02 '03 '04 '05 '06 '07 '08 '09 '10 '11 '12

Bonds $.0 Mil Com 44.517 Mil BV 40.10 /sh P/E 16.13 (Ind RBANK P/E 10.51) Ctry US

SYCAMORE NETWORKS INC (SCMR)

Optical networking equipment (E) 45% SCALE

Growth Performance Measurement				
Years	Price	Earn.	Div.	Tot Ret
Last 1	-87.5	-17.1	---	-87.5
Last 5	-43.4	---	---	-43.4
Last 10	-22.6	19.3	---	-22.6

Adj. for
1 for 10
12/22/GG
Special
$6.50

Specials
$10.50

(4.10) (4.50) (4.50) (1.70) (1.30) (0.40)   (0.70) (0.31) (0.26) (0.52) (0.36)
(2.00) (4.80) (2.90) (1.90) (1.40) (0.80) 0.00 (0.70) (0.59) (0.16) (0.38) (0.34) (0.41)
0.00 (5.80) (3.50) (2.10) (1.60) (1.10) (0.30) 0.00 (0.60) (0.41) (0.35) (0.35) (0.30)

Copyright 2012 Securities Research Company

'01 '02 '03 '04 '05 '06 '07 '08 '09 '10 '11 '12

Bonds $3.3 Mil Com 28.882 Mil BV 5.09 /sh P/E N/A (Ind TELEQ P/E 13.72) Ctry US

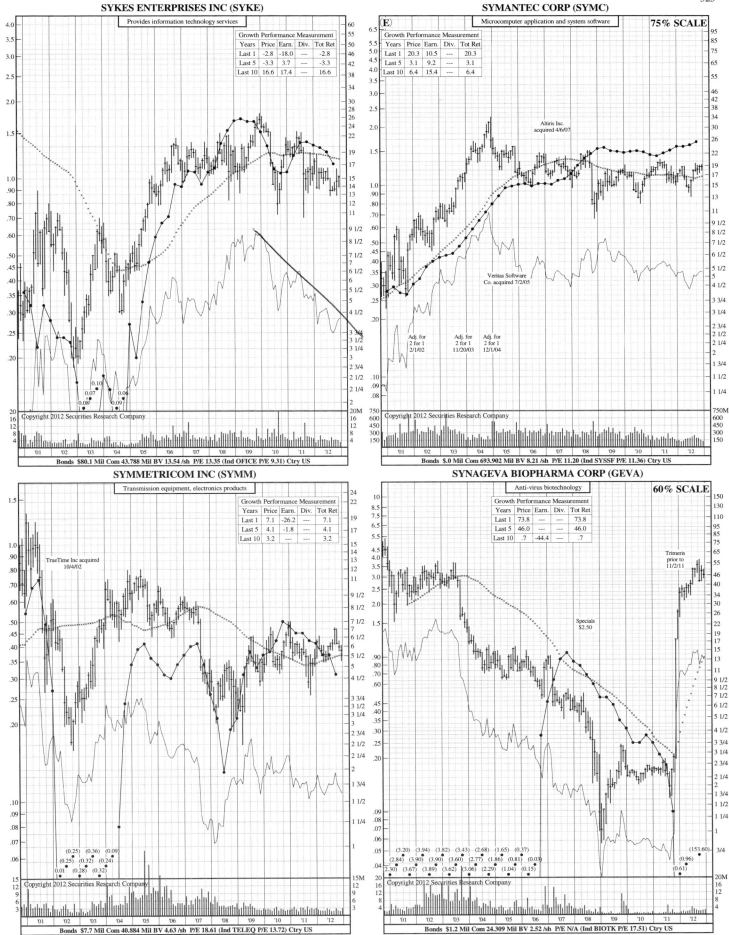

SYKES ENTERPRISES INC (SYKE)

Provides information technology services

Growth Performance Measurement

Years	Price	Earn.	Div.	Tot Ret
Last 1	-2.8	-18.0	---	-2.8
Last 5	-3.3	3.7	---	-3.3
Last 10	16.6	17.4	---	16.6

0.10
0.07   0.06
0.08   0.09

Copyright 2012 Securities Research Company

Bonds $80.1 Mil Com 43.788 Mil BV 13.54 /sh P/E 13.35 (Ind OFICE P/E 9.31) Ctry US

SYMANTEC CORP (SYMC)

(E)
Microcomputer application and system software
75% SCALE

Growth Performance Measurement

Years	Price	Earn.	Div.	Tot Ret
Last 1	20.3	10.5	---	20.3
Last 5	3.1	9.2	---	3.1
Last 10	6.4	15.4	---	6.4

Altiris Inc.
acquired 4/6/07

Veritas Software
Co. acquired 7/2/05

Adj. for   Adj. for   Adj. for
2 for 1   2 for 1   2 for 1
2/1/02   11/20/03   12/1/04

Copyright 2012 Securities Research Company

Bonds $.0 Mil Com 693.902 Mil BV 8.21 /sh P/E 11.20 (Ind SYSSF P/E 11.36) Ctry US

SYMMETRICOM INC (SYMM)

Transmission equipment, electronics products

Growth Performance Measurement

Years	Price	Earn.	Div.	Tot Ret
Last 1	7.1	-26.2	---	7.1
Last 5	4.1	-1.8	---	4.1
Last 10	3.2	---	---	3.2

TrueTime Inc acquired
10/4/02

(0.25) (0.36)   (0.09)
(0.25) (0.32) (0.24)
0.01 (0.28) (0.32)

Copyright 2012 Securities Research Company

Bonds $7.7 Mil Com 40.884 Mil BV 4.63 /sh P/E 18.61 (Ind TELEQ P/E 13.72) Ctry US

SYNAGEVA BIOPHARMA CORP (GEVA)

Anti-virus biotechnology
60% SCALE

Growth Performance Measurement

Years	Price	Earn.	Div.	Tot Ret
Last 1	73.8	---	---	73.8
Last 5	46.0	---	---	46.0
Last 10	.7	-44.4	---	.7

Trimeris
prior to
11/2/11

Specials
$2.50

(3.20) (3.94) (3.82) (3.43) (2.68) (1.65) (0.37)   (153.60)
(2.84) (3.90) (3.90) (3.60) (2.77) (1.86) (0.81) (0.03)   (0.96)
(2.30) (3.67) (3.89) (3.62) (3.06) (2.29) (1.04) (0.15)   (0.61)

Copyright 2012 Securities Research Company

Bonds $1.2 Mil Com 24.309 Mil BV 2.52 /sh P/E N/A (Ind BIOTK P/E 17.51) Ctry US

326

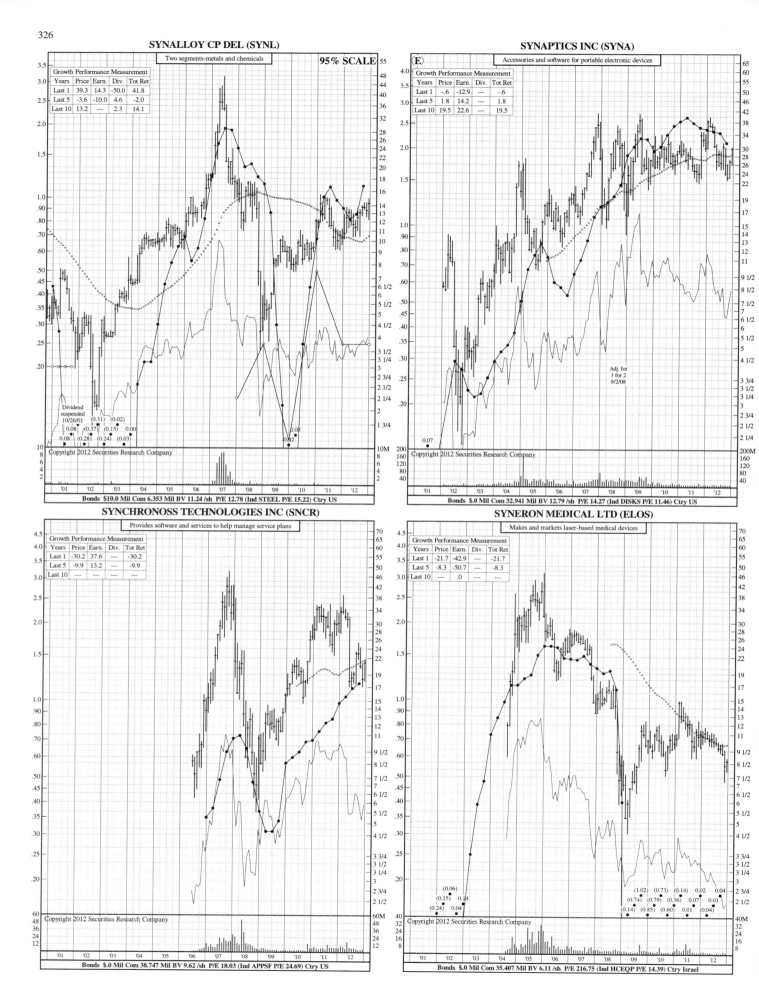

SYNALLOY CP DEL (SYNL)

Two segments-metals and chemicals

95% SCALE

Growth Performance Measurement				
Years	Price	Earn.	Div.	Tot Ret
Last 1	39.3	14.3	-50.0	41.8
Last 5	-3.6	-10.0	4.6	-2.0
Last 10	13.2	---	2.3	14.1

Dividend
suspended
10/26/01   (0.31) (0.02)
0.08   (0.37) (0.15) 0.00
0.08 (0.28) (0.24) (0.03)   0.05
0.92

Copyright 2012 Securities Research Company

'01 '02 '03 '04 '05 '06 '07 '08 '09 '10 '11 '12

Bonds $10.0 Mil Com 6.353 Mil BV 11.24 /sh P/E 12.78 (Ind STEEL P/E 15.22) Ctry US

SYNAPTICS INC (SYNA)

Accessories and software for portable electronic devices

(E)

Growth Performance Measurement				
Years	Price	Earn.	Div.	Tot Ret
Last 1	-.6	-12.9	---	-.6
Last 5	1.8	14.2	---	1.8
Last 10	19.5	22.6	---	19.5

Adj. for
3 for 2
9/2/08

0.07

Copyright 2012 Securities Research Company

'01 '02 '03 '04 '05 '06 '07 '08 '09 '10 '11 '12

Bonds $.0 Mil Com 32.941 Mil BV 12.79 /sh P/E 14.27 (Ind DISKS P/E 11.46) Ctry US

SYNCHRONOSS TECHNOLOGIES INC (SNCR)

Provides software and services to help manage service plans

Growth Performance Measurement				
Years	Price	Earn.	Div.	Tot Ret
Last 1	-30.2	37.6	---	-30.2
Last 5	-9.9	13.2	---	-9.9
Last 10	---	---	---	---

Copyright 2012 Securities Research Company

'01 '02 '03 '04 '05 '06 '07 '08 '09 '10 '11 '12

Bonds $.0 Mil Com 38.747 Mil BV 9.62 /sh P/E 18.03 (Ind APPSF P/E 24.69) Ctry US

SYNERON MEDICAL LTD (ELOS)

Makes and markets laser-based medical devices

Growth Performance Measurement				
Years	Price	Earn.	Div.	Tot Ret
Last 1	-21.7	-42.9	---	-21.7
Last 5	-8.3	-50.7	---	-8.3
Last 10	---	.0	---	---

(0.06)
(0.15)   0.14   (1.02) (0.73) (0.14) 0.02   0.04
(0.24) 0.04   (0.74) (0.79) (0.36) (0.07) 0.01
(0.14) (0.85) (0.60) 0.01 (0.04)

Copyright 2012 Securities Research Company

'01 '02 '03 '04 '05 '06 '07 '08 '09 '10 '11 '12

Bonds $.0 Mil Com 35.407 Mil BV 6.11 /sh P/E 216.75 (Ind HCEQP P/E 14.39) Ctry Israel

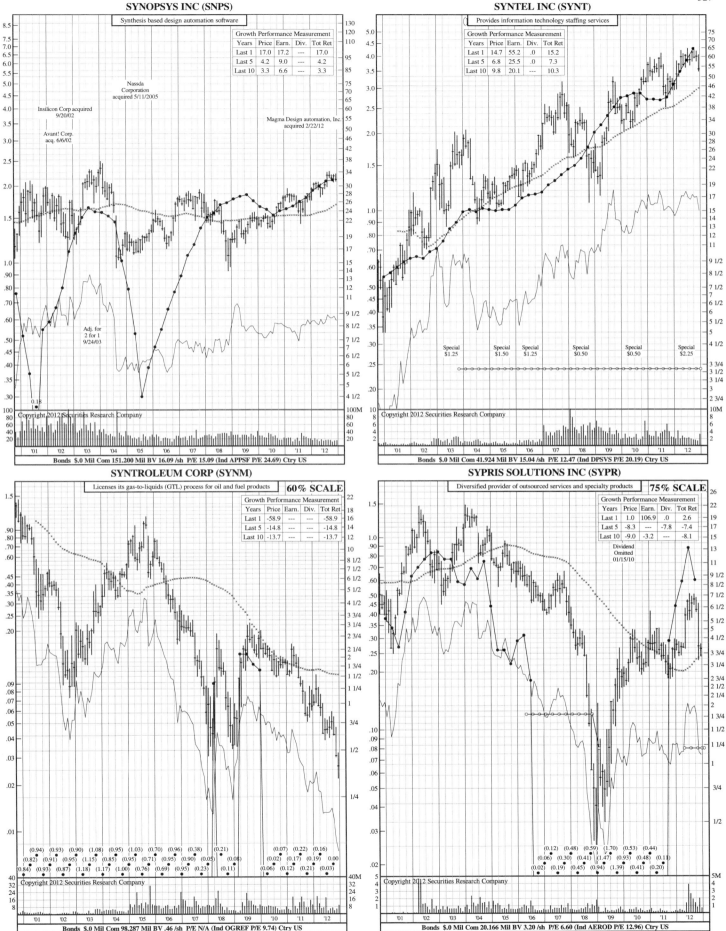

SYNOPSYS INC (SNPS)

Synthesis based design automation software

Growth Performance Measurement				
Years	Price	Earn.	Div.	Tot Ret
Last 1	17.0	17.2	---	17.0
Last 5	4.2	9.0	---	4.2
Last 10	3.3	6.6	---	3.3

Nassda
Corporation
acquired 5/11/2005

Insilicon Corp acquired
9/20/02

Avant! Corp.
acq. 6/6/02

Magma Design automation, Inc.
acquired 2/22/12

Adj. for
2 for 1
9/24/03

0.18

Copyright 2012 Securities Research Company

Bonds $.0 Mil Com 151.200 Mil BV 16.09 /sh P/E 15.09 (Ind APPSF P/E 24.69) Ctry US

SYNTEL INC (SYNT)

Provides information technology staffing services

Growth Performance Measurement				
Years	Price	Earn.	Div.	Tot Ret
Last 1	14.7	55.2	.0	15.2
Last 5	6.8	25.5	.0	7.3
Last 10	9.8	20.1	---	10.3

Special
$1.25

Special
$1.50

Special
$1.25

Special
$0.50

Special
$0.50

Special
$2.25

Copyright 2012 Securities Research Company

Bonds $.0 Mil Com 41.924 Mil BV 15.04 /sh P/E 12.47 (Ind DPSVS P/E 20.19) Ctry US

SYNTROLEUM CORP (SYNM)

Licenses its gas-to-liquids (GTL) process for oil and fuel products

60% SCALE

Growth Performance Measurement				
Years	Price	Earn.	Div.	Tot Ret
Last 1	-58.9	---	---	-58.9
Last 5	-14.8	---	---	-14.8
Last 10	-13.7	---	---	-13.7

(0.94) (0.93) (0.90) (1.08) (0.95) (1.03) (0.70) (0.96) (0.38)   (0.21)   (0.07) (0.22) (0.16)
(0.82) (0.91) (0.95) (1.15) (0.85) (0.95) (0.71) (0.95) (0.90) (0.05)   (0.08)   (0.02) (0.17) (0.19) 0.00
(0.84) (0.93) (0.87) (1.18) (1.17) (1.00) (0.76) (0.69) (0.95) (0.23)   (0.11)   (0.06) (0.12) (0.21) (0.03)

Copyright 2012 Securities Research Company

Bonds $.0 Mil Com 98.287 Mil BV .46 /sh P/E N/A (Ind OGREF P/E 9.74) Ctry US

SYPRIS SOLUTIONS INC (SYPR)

Diversified provider of outsourced services and specialty products

75% SCALE

Growth Performance Measurement				
Years	Price	Earn.	Div.	Tot Ret
Last 1	1.0	106.9	.0	2.6
Last 5	-8.3	---	-7.8	-7.4
Last 10	-9.0	-3.2	---	-8.1

Dividend
Omitted
01/15/10

(0.12) (0.48) (0.59) (1.70) (0.53) (0.44)
(0.06) (0.30) (0.41) (1.47) (0.93) (0.48) (0.11)
(0.02) (0.19) (0.45) (0.94) (1.39) (0.41) (0.20)

Copyright 2012 Securities Research Company

Bonds $.0 Mil Com 20.166 Mil BV 3.20 /sh P/E 6.60 (Ind AEROD P/E 12.96) Ctry US

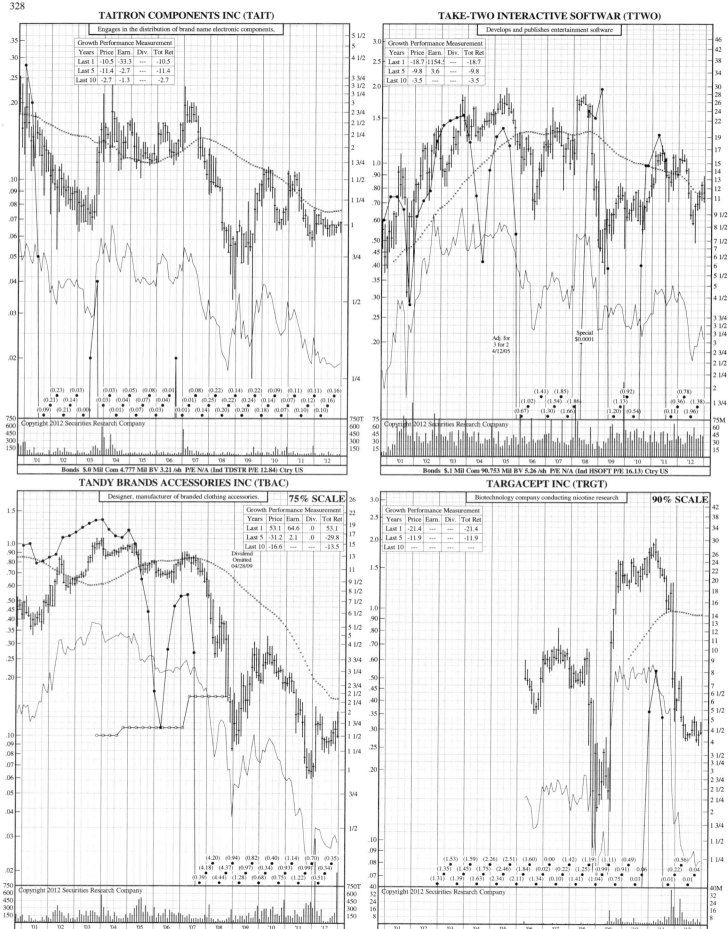

328

TAITRON COMPONENTS INC (TAIT)

Engages in the distribution of brand name electronic components,

Growth Performance Measurement				
Years	Price	Earn.	Div.	Tot Ret
Last 1	-10.5	-33.3	---	-10.5
Last 5	-11.4	-2.7	---	-11.4
Last 10	-2.7	-1.3	---	-2.7

(0.23) (0.03) (0.03) (0.05) (0.08) (0.01) (0.08) (0.22) (0.14) (0.22) (0.09) (0.11) (0.11) (0.16)
(0.21) (0.14) (0.03) (0.04) (0.07) (0.04) (0.01) (0.25) (0.22) (0.24) (0.18) (0.07) (0.12) (0.16)
(0.09) (0.21) (0.00) (0.01) (0.07) (0.03) (0.01) (0.01) (0.20) (0.20) (0.14) (0.07) (0.10) (0.10)

Copyright 2012 Securities Research Company

Bonds $.0 Mil Com 4.777 Mil BV 3.21 /sh P/E N/A (Ind TDSTR P/E 12.84) Ctry US

TAKE-TWO INTERACTIVE SOFTWAR (TTWO)

Develops and publishes entertainment software

Growth Performance Measurement				
Years	Price	Earn.	Div.	Tot Ret
Last 1	-18.7	1154.5	---	-18.7
Last 5	-9.8	3.6	---	-9.8
Last 10	-3.5	---	---	-3.5

Adj. for
3 for 2
4/12/05

Special
$0.0001

(1.41) (1.85) (0.92) (0.78)
(1.02) (1.54) (1.86) (1.13) (0.36) (1.38)
(0.67) (1.30) (1.66) (1.20) (0.54) (0.11) (1.96)

Copyright 2012 Securities Research Company

Bonds $.1 Mil Com 90.753 Mil BV 5.26 /sh P/E N/A (Ind HSOFT P/E 16.13) Ctry US

TANDY BRANDS ACCESSORIES INC (TBAC)

Designer, manufacturer of branded clothing accessories.

75% SCALE

Growth Performance Measurement				
Years	Price	Earn.	Div.	Tot Ret
Last 1	53.1	64.6	.0	53.1
Last 5	-31.2	2.1	.0	-29.8
Last 10	-16.6	---	---	-13.5

Dividend
Omitted
04/28/09

(4.20) (0.94) (0.82) (0.40) (1.14) (0.70) (0.35)
(4.18) (4.37) (0.97) (0.34) (0.93) (0.99) (0.34)
(0.39) (4.44) (1.28) (0.68) (0.75) (1.22) (0.51)

Copyright 2012 Securities Research Company

Bonds $41.1 Mil Com 7.134 Mil BV 3.63 /sh P/E N/A (Ind APPRL P/E 17.01) Ctry US

TARGACEPT INC (TRGT)

Biotechnology company conducting nicotine research

90% SCALE

Growth Performance Measurement				
Years	Price	Earn.	Div.	Tot Ret
Last 1	-21.4	---	---	-21.4
Last 5	-11.9	---	---	-11.9
Last 10	---	---	---	---

(1.53) (1.59) (2.26) (2.51) (1.60) (0.00) (1.42) (1.19) (1.11) (0.49) (0.56)
(1.35) (1.45) (1.75) (2.46) (1.84) (0.02) (0.22) (1.25) (0.99) (0.91) (0.06) (0.22) (0.04)
(1.31) (1.39) (1.63) (2.34) (2.11) (1.34) (0.10) (1.41) (1.04) (0.75) (0.03) (0.01) (0.01)

Copyright 2012 Securities Research Company

Bonds $.0 Mil Com 33.606 Mil BV 5.71 /sh P/E 109.50 (Ind BIOTK P/E 17.51) Ctry US

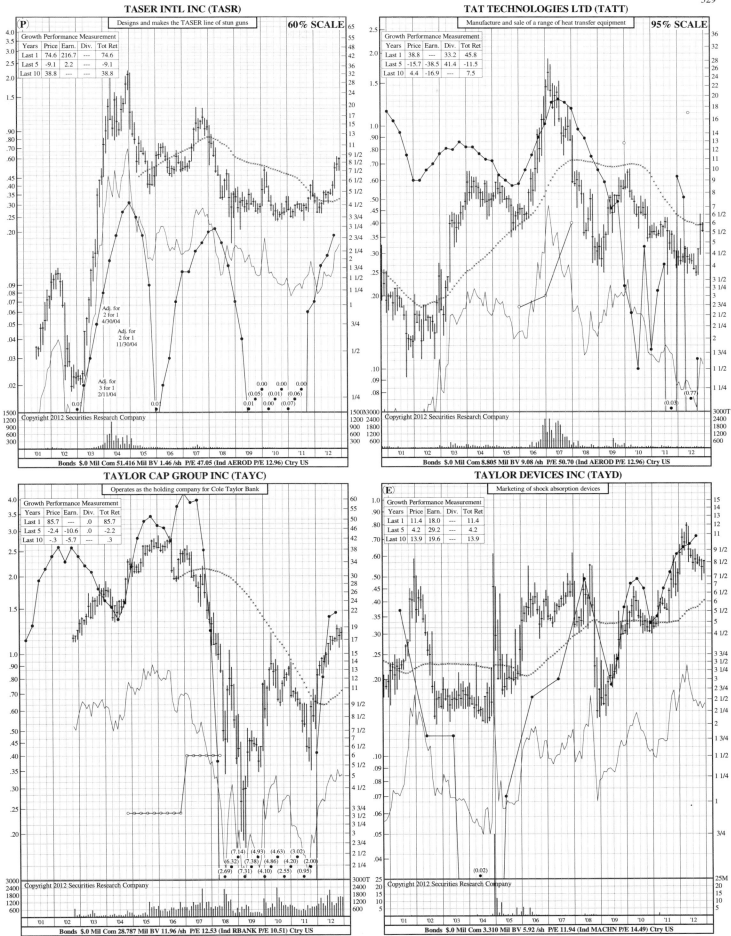

TASER INTL INC (TASR)
Designs and makes the TASER line of stun guns
60% SCALE

Growth Performance Measurement

Years	Price	Earn.	Div.	Tot Ret
Last 1	74.6	216.7	---	74.6
Last 5	-9.1	2.2	---	-9.1
Last 10	38.8	---		38.8

Adj. for
2 for 1
4/30/04

Adj. for
2 for 1
11/30/04

Adj. for
3 for 1
2/11/04

0.01

0.01

0.00 0.00 0.00
(0.05) (0.01) (0.06)
0.01 (0.07)

Copyright 2012 Securities Research Company

Bonds $.0 Mil Com 51.416 Mil BV 1.46 /sh P/E 47.05 (Ind AEROD P/E 12.96) Ctry US

TAT TECHNOLOGIES LTD (TATT)
Manufacture and sale of a range of heat transfer equipment
95% SCALE

Growth Performance Measurement

Years	Price	Earn.	Div.	Tot Ret
Last 1	38.8	---	33.2	45.8
Last 5	-15.7	-38.5	41.4	-11.5
Last 10	4.4	-16.9	---	7.5

(0.03)

(0.77)

Copyright 2012 Securities Research Company

Bonds $.0 Mil Com 8.805 Mil BV 9.08 /sh P/E 50.70 (Ind AEROD P/E 12.96) Ctry US

TAYLOR CAP GROUP INC (TAYC)
Operates as the holding company for Cole Taylor Bank

Growth Performance Measurement

Years	Price	Earn.	Div.	Tot Ret
Last 1	85.7	---	.0	85.7
Last 5	-2.4	-10.6	.0	-2.2
Last 10	-.3	-5.7	---	.3

(7.14) (4.93) (4.63) (3.02)
(6.32) (7.38) (4.86) (4.20) (2.00)
(2.69) (7.31) (4.10) (2.55) (0.95)

Copyright 2012 Securities Research Company

Bonds $.0 Mil Com 28.787 Mil BV 11.96 /sh P/E 12.53 (Ind RBANK P/E 10.51) Ctry US

TAYLOR DEVICES INC (TAYD)
Marketing of shock absorption devices

Growth Performance Measurement

Years	Price	Earn.	Div.	Tot Ret
Last 1	11.4	18.0	---	11.4
Last 5	4.2	29.2	---	4.2
Last 10	13.9	19.6	---	13.9

(0.02)

Copyright 2012 Securities Research Company

Bonds $.0 Mil Com 3.310 Mil BV 5.92 /sh P/E 11.94 (Ind MACHN P/E 14.49) Ctry US

330

TEARLAB CORP (TEAR)

Develops ophthalmic therapeutic treatments for eye diseases

50% SCALE

Growth Performance Measurement				
Years	Price	Earn.	Div.	Tot Ret
Last 1	266.1	-100.0	---	266.1
Last 5	15.4	34.3	---	15.4
Last 10	---	---	---	

SOLX, Inc.
acquired 9/1/06

Adj. for
1 for 25
10/9/08

(5.75) (11.00) (45.75) (7.00) (7.75) (2.86) (0.44) (0.59) (0.63) (0.87)
(3.75) (9.50) (137.75) (7.75) (8.00) (4.01) (1.03) (0.51) (0.41) (0.54) (0.86)
(3.75) (7.50) (11.50) (9.00) (8.75) (7.50) (1.96) (0.51) (0.47) (0.43) (0.64)

Copyright 2012 Securities Research Company

Bonds $.0 Mil Com 28.466 Mil BV .54 /sh P/E N/A (Ind HCSUP P/E 17.94) Ctry Canada

TECH DATA CORP (TECD)

Distributes computer related hardware products

Growth Performance Measurement				
Years	Price	Earn.	Div.	Tot Ret
Last 1	-7.9	1.2	---	-7.9
Last 5	3.8	17.9	---	3.8
Last 10	5.4	7.7	---	5.4

Copyright 2012 Securities Research Company

Bonds $316.8 Mil Com 37.761 Mil BV 51.93 /sh P/E 8.96 (Ind TDSTR P/E 12.84) Ctry US

TECHNE CORP (TECH)

Manufactures biological products

Growth Performance Measurement				
Years	Price	Earn.	Div.	Tot Ret
Last 1	.1	-.6	7.1	1.8
Last 5	.7	7.5	---	2.0
Last 10	9.1	12.7	---	9.8

Adj. for
2 for 1
12/4/00

Copyright 2012 Securities Research Company

Bonds $18.9 Mil Com 36.829 Mil BV 18.49 /sh P/E 21.49 (Ind LFSCT P/E 13.82) Ctry US

TECHTARGET INC (TTGT)

Operates web sites focused on information technology issues

Growth Performance Measurement				
Years	Price	Earn.	Div.	Tot Ret
Last 1	-5.0	3.7	---	-5.0
Last 5	-17.8	---	---	-17.8
Last 10	---	---	---	

Copyright 2012 Securities Research Company

Bonds $.0 Mil Com 39.490 Mil BV 4.96 /sh P/E 19.82 (Ind ITSOF P/E 19.21) Ctry US

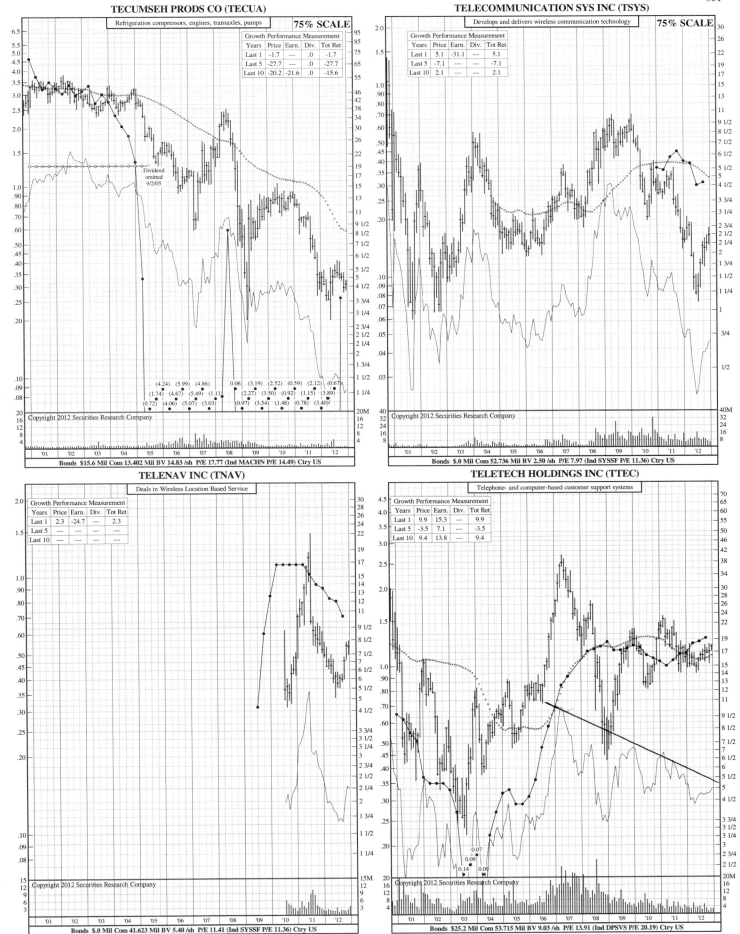

TECUMSEH PRODS CO (TECUA)

Refrigeration compressors, engines, transaxles, pumps

75% SCALE

Growth Performance Measurement				
Years	Price	Earn.	Div.	Tot Ret
Last 1	-1.7	---	.0	-1.7
Last 5	-27.7	---	.0	-27.7
Last 10	-20.2	-21.6	.0	-15.6

Dividend omitted 9/2/05

(4.24) (5.99) (4.86)   0.06 (3.19) (2.52) (0.59) (2.12) (0.67)
(1.74) (4.67) (5.49) (1.11)   (2.27) (3.50) (0.92) (1.15) (3.89)
(0.72) (4.06) (5.07) (3.03)   (0.97) (3.54) (1.48) (0.78) (3.40)

Copyright 2012 Securities Research Company

Bonds $15.6 Mil Com 13.402 Mil BV 14.83 /sh P/E 17.77 (Ind MACHN P/E 14.49) Ctry US

TELECOMMUNICATION SYS INC (TSYS)

Develops and delivers wireless communication technology

75% SCALE

Growth Performance Measurement				
Years	Price	Earn.	Div.	Tot Ret
Last 1	5.1	-31.1	---	5.1
Last 5	-7.1	---		-7.1
Last 10	2.1	---		2.1

Copyright 2012 Securities Research Company

Bonds $.0 Mil Com 52.736 Mil BV 2.50 /sh P/E 7.97 (Ind SYSSF P/E 11.36) Ctry US

TELENAV INC (TNAV)

Deals in Wireless Location Based Service

Growth Performance Measurement				
Years	Price	Earn.	Div.	Tot Ret
Last 1	2.3	-24.7	---	2.3
Last 5	---	---	---	---
Last 10	---	---	---	---

Copyright 2012 Securities Research Company

Bonds $.0 Mil Com 41.623 Mil BV 5.40 /sh P/E 11.41 (Ind SYSSF P/E 11.36) Ctry US

TELETECH HOLDINGS INC (TTEC)

Telephone- and computer-based customer support systems

Growth Performance Measurement				
Years	Price	Earn.	Div.	Tot Ret
Last 1	9.9	15.3	---	9.9
Last 5	-3.5	7.1	---	-3.5
Last 10	9.4	13.8	---	9.4

0.07
0.09
0.14   0.05

Copyright 2012 Securities Research Company

Bonds $25.2 Mil Com 53.715 Mil BV 9.03 /sh P/E 13.91 (Ind DPSVS P/E 20.19) Ctry US

332

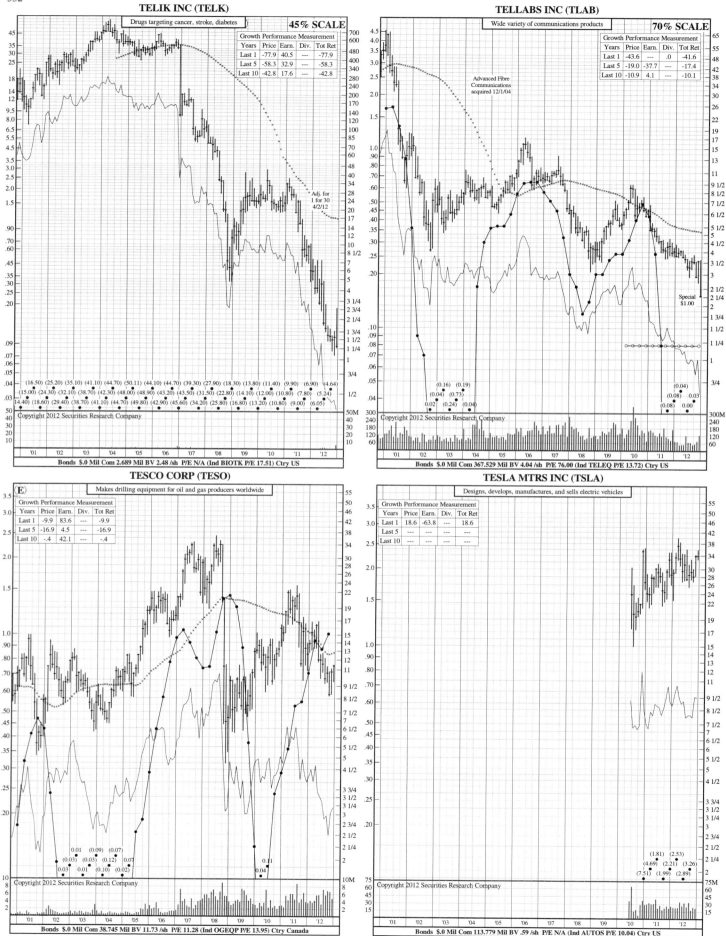

TELIK INC (TELK)

Drugs targeting cancer, stroke, diabetes

45% SCALE

Growth Performance Measurement				
Years	Price	Earn.	Div.	Tot Ret
Last 1	-77.9	40.5	---	-77.9
Last 5	-58.3	32.9	---	-58.3
Last 10	-42.8	17.6	---	-42.8

Adj. for 1 for 30 4/2/12

(16.50) (25.20) (35.10) (41.10) (44.70) (50.11) (44.10) (44.70) (39.30) (27.90) (18.30) (13.80) (11.40) (9.90) (6.90) (4.64)
(15.00) (24.30) (32.10) (38.70) (42.30) (48.00) (48.90) (43.20) (43.50) (31.50) (22.80) (14.10) (12.00) (10.80) (7.80) (5.24)
14.40) (18.60) (29.40) (38.70) (41.10) (44.70) (49.80) (42.90) (45.60) (34.20) (25.80) (16.80) (13.20) (10.80) (9.00) (6.05)

Copyright 2012 Securities Research Company

Bonds $.0 Mil Com 2.689 Mil BV 2.48 /sh P/E N/A (Ind BIOTK P/E 17.51) Ctry US

TELLABS INC (TLAB)

Wide variety of communications products

70% SCALE

Growth Performance Measurement				
Years	Price	Earn.	Div.	Tot Ret
Last 1	-43.6	---	.0	-41.6
Last 5	-19.0	-37.7	---	-17.4
Last 10	-10.9	4.1	---	-10.1

Advanced Fibre Communications acquired 12/1/04

Special $1.00

(0.16) (0.19)
(0.04) (0.73)
0.02 (0.24) (0.04)   (0.04)
                        0.03
(0.08) 0.00

Copyright 2012 Securities Research Company

Bonds $.0 Mil Com 367.529 Mil BV 4.04 /sh P/E 76.00 (Ind TELEQ P/E 13.72) Ctry US

TESCO CORP (TESO)

(E)

Makes drilling equipment for oil and gas producers worldwide

Growth Performance Measurement				
Years	Price	Earn.	Div.	Tot Ret
Last 1	-9.9	83.6	---	-9.9
Last 5	-16.9	4.5	---	-16.9
Last 10	-.4	42.1	---	-.4

0.01 (0.09) (0.07)
(0.03) (0.03) (0.12) 0.07
0.03) 0.01 (0.10) 0.02   0.11
                                0.04

Copyright 2012 Securities Research Company

Bonds $.0 Mil Com 38.745 Mil BV 11.73 /sh P/E 11.28 (Ind OGEQP P/E 13.95) Ctry Canada

TESLA MTRS INC (TSLA)

Designs, develops, manufactures, and sells electric vehicles

Growth Performance Measurement				
Years	Price	Earn.	Div.	Tot Ret
Last 1	18.6	-63.8	---	18.6
Last 5	---	---	---	---
Last 10	---	---	---	---

(1.81) (2.53)
(4.69) (2.21) (3.26)
(7.51) (1.99) (2.89)

Copyright 2012 Securities Research Company

Bonds $.0 Mil Com 113.779 Mil BV .59 /sh P/E N/A (Ind AUTOS P/E 10.04) Ctry US

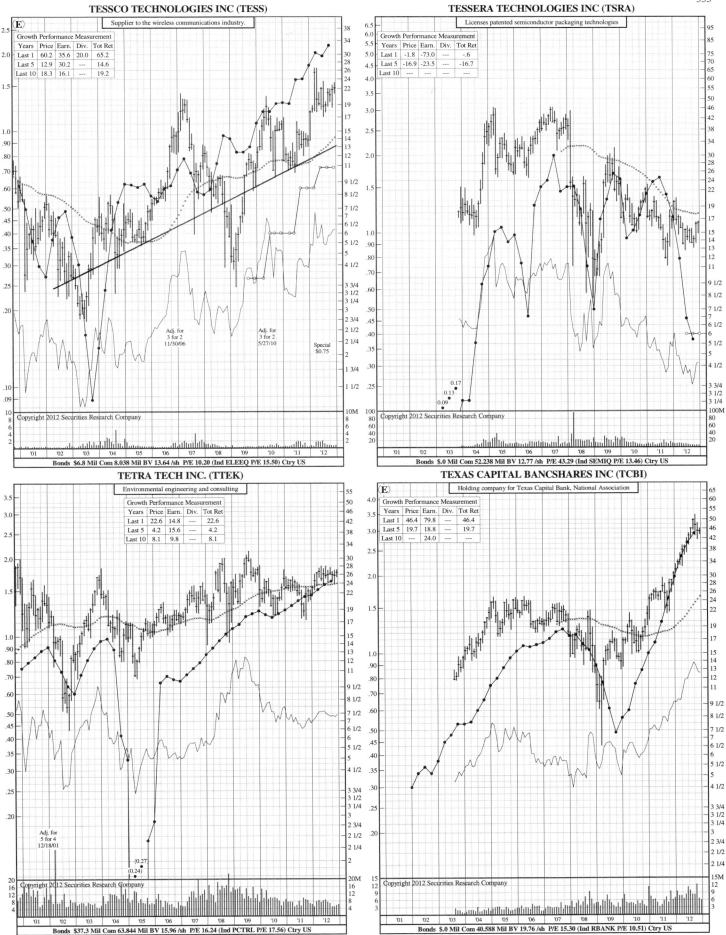

333

TESSCO TECHNOLOGIES INC (TESS)

Supplier to the wireless communications industry.

Growth Performance Measurement

Years	Price	Earn.	Div.	Tot Ret
Last 1	60.2	35.6	20.0	65.2
Last 5	12.9	30.2	---	14.6
Last 10	18.3	16.1	---	19.2

Adj. for 3 for 2 11/30/06

Adj. for 3 for 2 5/27/10

Special $0.75

Copyright 2012 Securities Research Company

Bonds $6.8 Mil Com 8.038 Mil BV 13.64 /sh P/E 10.20 (Ind ELEEQ P/E 15.50) Ctry US

TESSERA TECHNOLOGIES INC (TSRA)

Licenses patented semiconductor packaging technologies

Growth Performance Measurement

Years	Price	Earn.	Div.	Tot Ret
Last 1	-1.8	-73.0	---	-.6
Last 5	-16.9	-23.5	---	-16.7
Last 10	---	---	---	---

0.17
0.13
0.09

Copyright 2012 Securities Research Company

Bonds $.0 Mil Com 52.238 Mil BV 12.77 /sh P/E 43.29 (Ind SEMIQ P/E 13.46) Ctry US

TETRA TECH INC. (TTEK)

Environmental engineering and consulting

Growth Performance Measurement

Years	Price	Earn.	Div.	Tot Ret
Last 1	22.6	14.8	---	22.6
Last 5	4.2	15.6	---	4.2
Last 10	8.1	9.8	---	8.1

Adj. for 5 for 4 12/18/01

(0.27)
(0.24)

Copyright 2012 Securities Research Company

Bonds $37.3 Mil Com 63.844 Mil BV 15.96 /sh P/E 16.24 (Ind PCTRL P/E 17.56) Ctry US

TEXAS CAPITAL BANCSHARES INC (TCBI)

Holding company for Texas Capital Bank, National Association

Growth Performance Measurement

Years	Price	Earn.	Div.	Tot Ret
Last 1	46.4	79.8	---	46.4
Last 5	19.7	18.8	---	19.7
Last 10	---	24.0	---	---

Copyright 2012 Securities Research Company

Bonds $.0 Mil Com 40.588 Mil BV 19.76 /sh P/E 15.30 (Ind RBANK P/E 10.51) Ctry US

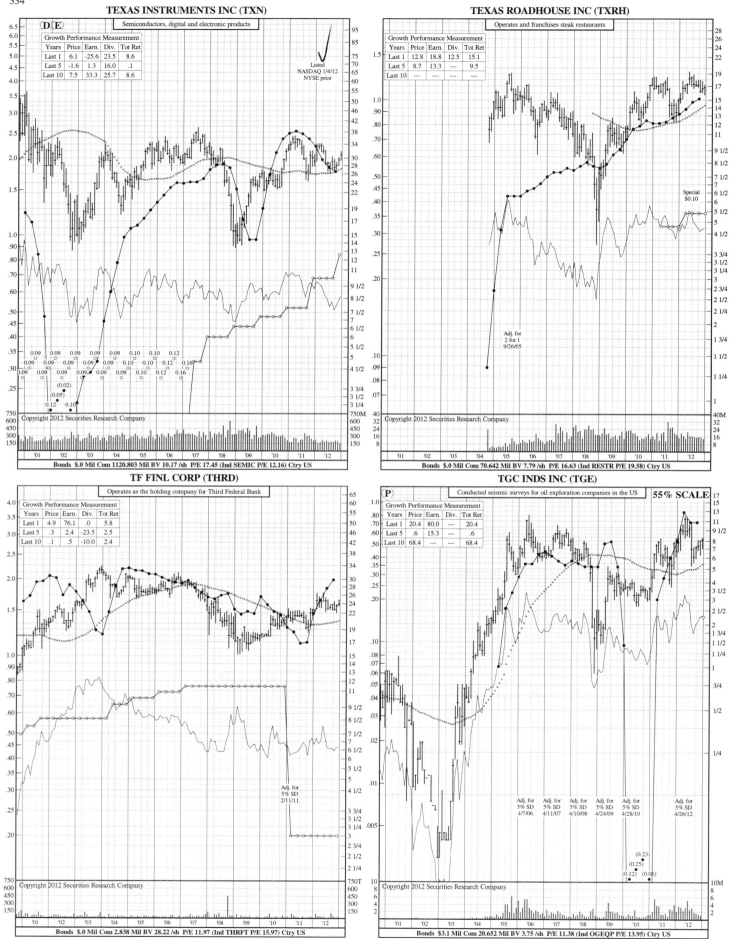

TEXAS INSTRUMENTS INC (TXN)

Semiconductors, digital and electronic products

D(E)

Growth Performance Measurement				
Years	Price	Earn.	Div.	Tot Ret
Last 1	6.1	-25.6	23.5	8.6
Last 5	-1.6	1.3	16.0	.1
Last 10	7.5	33.3	25.7	8.6

Listed NASDAQ 1/4/12 NYSE prior

0.09 0.09 0.09 0.09 0.09 0.10 0.10 0.12
0.09 0.09 0.09 0.09 0.09 0.10 0.10 0.12 0.16
0.09 0.09 0.09 0.09 0.09 0.10 0.10 0.12 0.16
(0.02)
(0.05)
0.12 0.10

Copyright 2012 Securities Research Company

Bonds $.0 Mil Com 1120.803 Mil BV 10.17 /sh P/E 17.45 (Ind SEMIC P/E 12.16) Ctry US

TEXAS ROADHOUSE INC (TXRH)

Operates and franchises steak restaurants

Growth Performance Measurement				
Years	Price	Earn.	Div.	Tot Ret
Last 1	12.8	18.8	12.5	15.1
Last 5	8.7	13.3	---	9.5
Last 10	---	---	---	---

Special $0.10

Adj. for 2 for 1 9/26/05

Copyright 2012 Securities Research Company

Bonds $.0 Mil Com 70.642 Mil BV 7.79 /sh P/E 16.63 (Ind RESTR P/E 19.58) Ctry US

TF FINL CORP (THRD)

Operates as the holding company for Third Federal Bank

Growth Performance Measurement				
Years	Price	Earn.	Div.	Tot Ret
Last 1	4.9	76.1	.0	5.8
Last 5	.3	2.4	-23.5	2.5
Last 10	.1	.5	-10.0	2.4

Adj. for 5% SD 2/11/11

Copyright 2012 Securities Research Company

Bonds $.0 Mil Com 2.838 Mil BV 28.22 /sh P/E 11.97 (Ind THRFT P/E 15.97) Ctry US

TGC INDS INC (TGE)

Conducted seismic surveys for oil exploration companies in the US

55% SCALE

P

Growth Performance Measurement				
Years	Price	Earn.	Div.	Tot Ret
Last 1	20.4	80.0	---	20.4
Last 5	.6	15.3	---	.6
Last 10	68.4	---	---	68.4

Adj. for 5% SD 4/7/06
Adj. for 5% SD 4/11/07
Adj. for 5% SD 4/10/08
Adj. for 5% SD 4/24/09
Adj. for 5% SD 4/28/10
Adj. for 5% SD 4/26/12

(0.23)
(0.25)
(0.12) (0.06)

Copyright 2012 Securities Research Company

Bonds $3.1 Mil Com 20.652 Mil BV 3.75 /sh P/E 11.38 (Ind OGEQP P/E 13.95) Ctry US

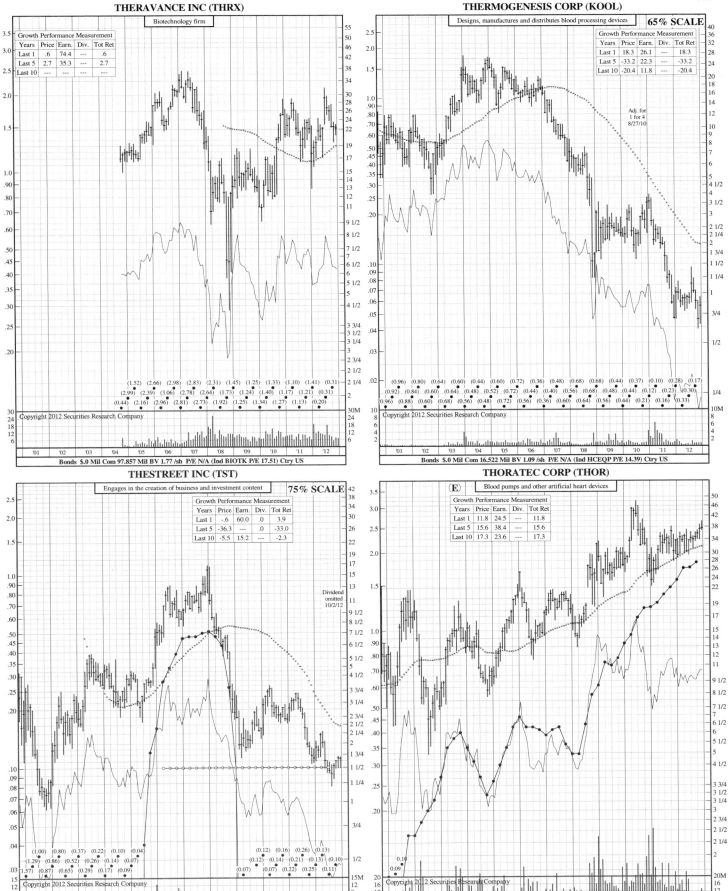

THERAVANCE INC (THRX)

Biotechnology firm

Growth Performance Measurement				
Years	Price	Earn.	Div.	Tot Ret
Last 1	.6	74.4	---	.6
Last 5	2.7	35.3	---	2.7
Last 10	---	---	---	---

(1.52) (2.66) (2.98) (2.83) (2.31) (1.45) (1.25) (1.33) (1.10) (1.41) (0.31)
(2.99) (2.39) (3.06) (2.78) (2.64) (1.73) (1.24) (1.40) (1.17) (1.21) (0.31)
(0.44) (2.16) (2.96) (2.81) (2.73) (1.92) (1.25) (1.34) (1.27) (1.13) (0.20)

Copyright 2012 Securities Research Company

Bonds $.0 Mil Com 97.857 Mil BV 1.77 /sh P/E N/A (Ind BIOTK P/E 17.51) Ctry US

THERMOGENESIS CORP (KOOL)

Designs, manufactures and distributes blood processing devices

65% SCALE

Growth Performance Measurement				
Years	Price	Earn.	Div.	Tot Ret
Last 1	18.3	26.1	---	18.3
Last 5	-33.2	22.3	---	-33.2
Last 10	-20.4	11.8	---	-20.4

Adj. for
1 for 4
8/27/10

(0.96) (0.80) (0.64) (0.60) (0.44) (0.60) (0.72) (0.36) (0.48) (0.68) (0.68) (0.44) (0.37) (0.10) (0.28) (0.17)
(0.92) (0.84) (0.60) (0.64) (0.48) (0.52) (0.72) (0.44) (0.40) (0.56) (0.68) (0.48) (0.44) (0.12) (0.23) (0.30)
(0.96) (0.88) (0.60) (0.68) (0.56) (0.48) (0.72) (0.56) (0.36) (0.60) (0.64) (0.56) (0.44) (0.21) (0.16) (0.33)

Copyright 2012 Securities Research Company

Bonds $.0 Mil Com 16.522 Mil BV 1.09 /sh P/E N/A (Ind HCEQP P/E 14.39) Ctry US

THESTREET INC (TST)

Engages in the creation of business and investment content

75% SCALE

Growth Performance Measurement				
Years	Price	Earn.	Div.	Tot Ret
Last 1	-.6	60.0	.0	3.9
Last 5	-36.3	---	.0	-33.0
Last 10	-5.5	15.2	---	-2.3

Dividend
omitted
10/2/12

(1.00) (0.80) (0.37) (0.22) (0.10) (0.04) (0.12) (0.16) (0.26) (0.13)
(1.29) (0.86) (0.52) (0.26) (0.14) (0.07) (0.12) (0.14) (0.21) (0.13) (0.10)
(1.57) (0.87) (0.65) (0.29) (0.17) (0.09) (0.07) (0.07) (0.22) (0.25) (0.11)

Copyright 2012 Securities Research Company

Bonds $.0 Mil Com 32.894 Mil BV 2.47 /sh P/E N/A (Ind ITSOF P/E 19.21) Ctry US

THORATEC CORP (THOR)

Ⓔ Blood pumps and other artificial heart devices

Growth Performance Measurement				
Years	Price	Earn.	Div.	Tot Ret
Last 1	11.8	24.5	---	11.8
Last 5	15.6	38.4	---	15.6
Last 10	17.3	23.6	---	17.3

0.10
0.09

Copyright 2012 Securities Research Company

Bonds $.0 Mil Com 58.757 Mil BV 11.45 /sh P/E 20.50 (Ind HCEQP P/E 14.39) Ctry US

336

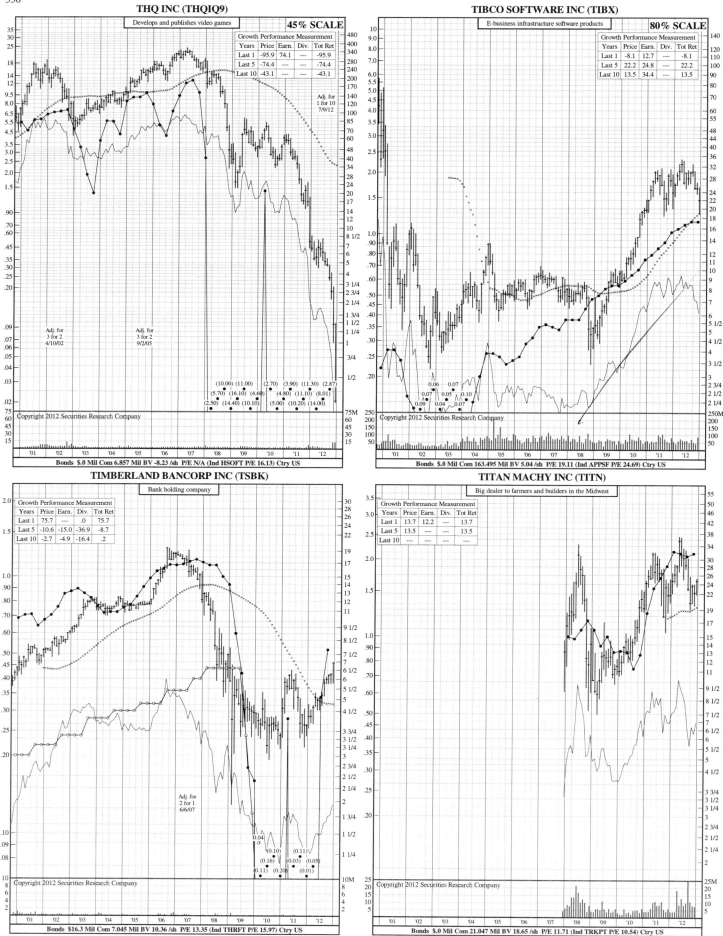

THQ INC (THQIQ9)

Develops and publishes video games

45% SCALE

Growth Performance Measurement

Years	Price	Earn.	Div.	Tot Ret
Last 1	-95.9	74.1	---	-95.9
Last 5	-74.4	---	---	-74.4
Last 10	-43.1	---	---	-43.1

Adj. for
1 for 10
7/9/12

Adj. for
3 for 2
4/10/02

Adj. for
3 for 2
9/2/05

(10.00) (11.00) (2.70) (3.90) (11.30) (2.87)
(5.70) (16.10) (4.60) (4.80) (11.10) (8.01)
(2.50) (14.40) (10.10) (5.00) (10.20) (14.00)

Copyright 2012 Securities Research Company

Bonds $.0 Mil Com 6.857 Mil BV -8.23 /sh P/E N/A (Ind HSOFT P/E 16.13) Ctry US

TIBCO SOFTWARE INC (TIBX)

E-business infrastructure software products

80% SCALE

Growth Performance Measurement

Years	Price	Earn.	Div.	Tot Ret
Last 1	-8.1	12.7	---	-8.1
Last 5	22.2	24.8	---	22.2
Last 10	13.5	34.4	---	13.5

0.06 0.07
0.07 0.05 0.10
0.09 0.04 0.07

Copyright 2012 Securities Research Company

Bonds $.0 Mil Com 163.495 Mil BV 5.04 /sh P/E 19.11 (Ind APPSF P/E 24.69) Ctry US

TIMBERLAND BANCORP INC (TSBK)

Bank holding company

Growth Performance Measurement

Years	Price	Earn.	Div.	Tot Ret
Last 1	75.7	---	.0	75.7
Last 5	-10.6	-15.0	-36.9	-8.7
Last 10	-2.7	-4.9	-16.4	.2

Adj. for
2 for 1
6/6/07

0.04

(0.10) (0.11)
(0.16) (0.03) (0.05)
(0.11) (0.20) (0.01)

Copyright 2012 Securities Research Company

Bonds $16.3 Mil Com 7.045 Mil BV 10.36 /sh P/E 13.35 (Ind THRFT P/E 15.97) Ctry US

TITAN MACHY INC (TITN)

Big dealer to farmers and builders in the Midwest

Growth Performance Measurement

Years	Price	Earn.	Div.	Tot Ret
Last 1	13.7	12.2	---	13.7
Last 5	13.5	---	---	13.5
Last 10	---	---	---	---

Copyright 2012 Securities Research Company

Bonds $.0 Mil Com 21.047 Mil BV 18.65 /sh P/E 11.71 (Ind TRKPT P/E 10.54) Ctry US

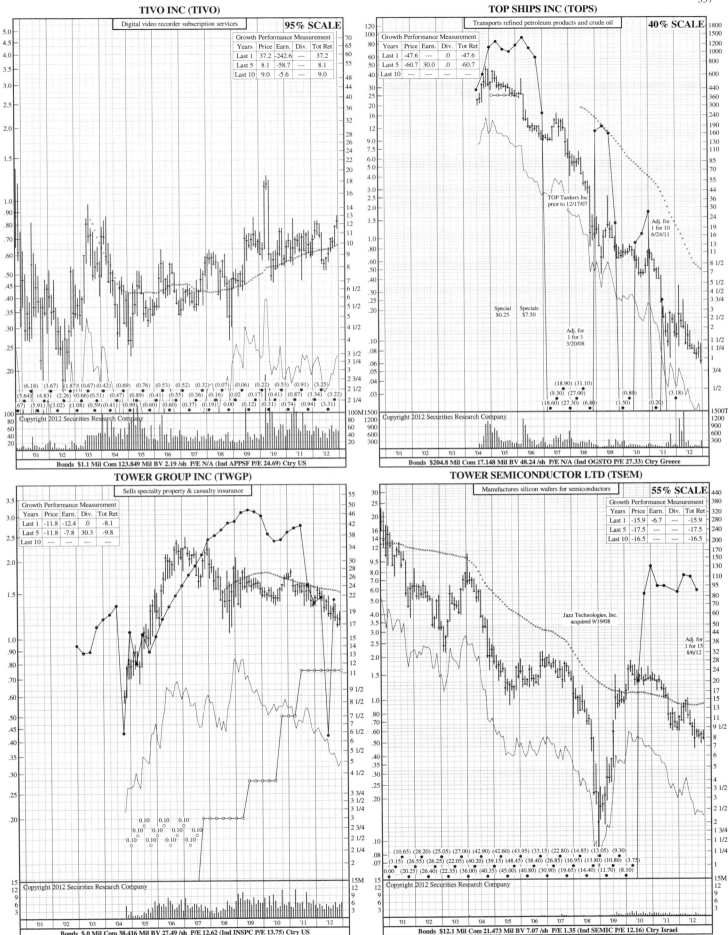

337

TIVO INC (TIVO)

Digital video recorder subscription services

95% SCALE

Growth Performance Measurement

Years	Price	Earn.	Div.	Tot Ret
Last 1	37.2	-242.6	---	37.2
Last 5	8.1	-58.7	---	8.1
Last 10	9.0	-5.6	---	9.0

(6.18) (3.67) (1.87) (0.67) (0.42) (0.69) (0.76) (0.53) (0.52) (0.32) (0.07) (0.06) (0.22) (0.53) (0.91) (3.25)
(5.64) (4.83) (2.26) (0.66) (0.51) (0.47) (0.89) (0.41) (0.55) (0.41) (0.16) (0.02) (0.17) (0.41) (3.34) (3.22)
(.67) (5.91) (3.02) (1.08) (0.59) (0.41) (0.60) (0.60) (0.41) (0.19) (0.11) (0.12) (0.31) (0.74) (0.94) (3.31)

Copyright 2012 Securities Research Company

Bonds $1.1 Mil Com 123.849 Mil BV 2.19 /sh P/E N/A (Ind APPSF P/E 24.69) Ctry US

TOP SHIPS INC (TOPS)

Transports refined petroleum products and crude oil

40% SCALE

Growth Performance Measurement

Years	Price	Earn.	Div.	Tot Ret
Last 1	-47.6	---	.0	-47.6
Last 5	-60.7	30.0	.0	-60.7
Last 10	---	---	---	

TOP Tankers Inc
prior to 12/17/07

Adj. for
1 for 10
6/24/11

Special
$0.25

Specials
$7.50

Adj. for
1 for 3
3/20/08

(18.90) (31.10)
(9.30) (27.00)   (0.80)   (3.18)
(18.60) (27.30) (6.80)   (1.50)   (0.20)

Copyright 2012 Securities Research Company

Bonds $204.8 Mil Com 17.148 Mil BV 48.24 /sh P/E N/A (Ind OGSTO P/E 27.33) Ctry Greece

TOWER GROUP INC (TWGP)

Sells specialty property & casualty insurance

Growth Performance Measurement

Years	Price	Earn.	Div.	Tot Ret
Last 1	-11.8	-12.4	.0	-8.1
Last 5	-11.8	-7.8	30.3	-9.8
Last 10	---	---	---	

0.10 0.10 0.10 0.10
0.10 0.10 0.10 0.10
0.10 0.10 0.10 0.10

Copyright 2012 Securities Research Company

Bonds $.0 Mil Com 38.416 Mil BV 27.49 /sh P/E 12.62 (Ind INSPC P/E 13.75) Ctry US

TOWER SEMICONDUCTOR LTD (TSEM)

Manufactures silicon wafers for semiconductors

55% SCALE

Growth Performance Measurement

Years	Price	Earn.	Div.	Tot Ret
Last 1	-15.9	-6.7	---	-15.9
Last 5	-17.5	---	---	-17.5
Last 10	-16.5	---	---	-16.5

Jazz Technologies, Inc.
acquired 9/19/08

Adj. for
1 for 15
8/6/12

(10.65) (28.20) (25.05) (27.00) (42.90) (42.60) (43.95) (33.15) (22.80) (14.85) (13.05) (9.30)
(3.15) (26.55) (26.25) (22.05) (40.20) (39.15) (48.45) (38.40) (26.85) (16.95) (10.80) (3.75)
0.00 (20.25) (26.40) (22.35) (36.00) (40.35) (45.00) (40.80) (30.90) (19.65) (14.40) (11.70) (8.10)

Copyright 2012 Securities Research Company

Bonds $12.1 Mil Com 21.473 Mil BV 7.07 /sh P/E 1.35 (Ind SEMIC P/E 12.16) Ctry Israel

338

TOWN SPORTS INTL HLDGS INC (CLUB)

Owns and operates full-service health clubs in NYC

Growth Performance Measurement				
Years	Price	Earn.	Div.	Tot Ret
Last 1	45.0	121.4	---	45.0
Last 5	2.2	-4.0	---	2.2
Last 10	---	---	---	---

(0.01)

0.03
0.04
0.05

Copyright 2012 Securities Research Company

Bonds $.0 Mil Com 23.632 Mil BV .67 /sh P/E 17.19 (Ind LEISF P/E 17.17) Ctry US

TRACTOR SUPPLY CO (TSCO)

P(E)

Farm supplies retailer

65% SCALE

Growth Performance Measurement				
Years	Price	Earn.	Div.	Tot Ret
Last 1	26.0	34.2	66.7	26.7
Last 5	37.5	25.3	---	37.9
Last 10	25.1	26.2	---	25.3

Adj. for
2 for 1
8/20/02

Adj. for
2 for 1
8/22/03

Adj. for
2 for 1
9/3/10

Copyright 2012 Securities Research Company

Bonds $54.7 Mil Com 70.437 Mil BV 14.94 /sh P/E 24.21 (Ind RTSPE P/E 11.33) Ctry US

TRANS WORLD ENTMT CORP (TWMC)

Retailer of records, cassettes, tapes, compact discs

80% SCALE

Musicland Holding Corp.
acquired 3/29/06

Growth Performance Measurement				
Years	Price	Earn.	Div.	Tot Ret
Last 1	37.6	---	---	37.6
Last 5	-6.6	---	---	-6.6
Last 10	-.4	5.3	---	-.4

(0.38) (0.03) (0.92) (1.72) (1.53) (1.49) (0.71)
(0.31) (0.04) (0.83) (1.67) (1.73) (1.56) (0.93) (0.01)
(0.16) (0.01) (0.06) (1.22) (1.78) (1.64) (1.29) (0.38)

Copyright 2012 Securities Research Company

Bonds $19.5 Mil Com 31.574 Mil BV 5.14 /sh P/E 7.40 (Ind RTSPE P/E 11.33) Ctry US

TRANS1 INC (TSON)

Proprietary surgical approach to treat degenerative disc disease

85% SCALE

Growth Performance Measurement				
Years	Price	Earn.	Div.	Tot Ret
Last 1	33.3	-1.2	---	33.3
Last 5	-31.5	25.0	---	-31.5
Last 10	---	-6.0	---	---

(0.47) (0.96) (1.36) (1.63) (2.09) (3.02) (3.83) (0.30) (0.75) (1.03) (1.13) (0.81) (0.83) (0.77)
(0.31) (0.80) (1.28) (1.54) (1.94) (2.44) (3.90) (3.55) (1.39) (0.96) (1.13) (0.87) (0.86) (0.74)
(0.15) (0.63) (1.12) (1.45) (1.79) (2.24) (3.45) (3.67) (1.49) (0.83) (1.07) (0.96) (0.82) (0.79) (0.84)

Copyright 2012 Securities Research Company

Bonds $.0 Mil Com 27.287 Mil BV 1.39 /sh P/E N/A (Ind HCSUP P/E 17.94) Ctry US

TRANSACT TECHNOLOGIES INC (TACT)

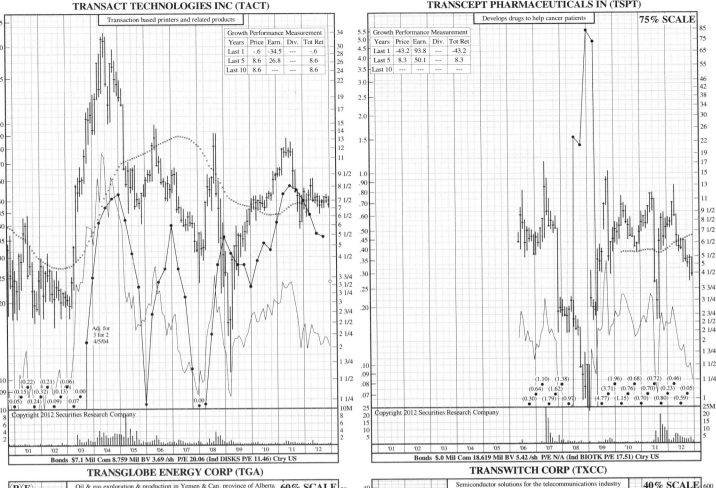

Transaction based printers and related products

Growth Performance Measurement				
Years	Price	Earn.	Div.	Tot Ret
Last 1	-.6	-34.5	---	-.6
Last 5	8.6	26.8	---	8.6
Last 10	8.6	---	---	8.6

Adj. for
3 for 2
4/5/04

(0.22) (0.21) (0.06)
(0.15) (0.32) (0.13) 0.00
(0.05) (0.24) (0.09) 0.07   0.00

Copyright 2012 Securities Research Company

Bonds $7.1 Mil Com 8.759 Mil BV 3.69 /sh P/E 20.06 (Ind DISKS P/E 11.46) Ctry US

TRANSCEPT PHARMACEUTICALS IN (TSPT)

75% SCALE

Develops drugs to help cancer patients

Growth Performance Measurement				
Years	Price	Earn.	Div.	Tot Ret
Last 1	-43.2	93.8	---	-43.2
Last 5	8.3	50.1	---	8.3
Last 10	---	---	---	---

(1.10) (1.38)   (1.96) (0.68) (0.72) (0.46)
(0.64) (1.62)   (3.71) (0.76) (0.70) (0.23) (0.05)
(0.30) (1.79) (0.97)   (4.77) (1.15) (0.70) (0.80) (0.59)

Copyright 2012 Securities Research Company

Bonds $.0 Mil Com 18.619 Mil BV 5.42 /sh P/E N/A (Ind BIOTK P/E 17.51) Ctry US

TRANSGLOBE ENERGY CORP (TGA)

(P)(E)   Oil & gas exploration & production in Yemen & Can. province of Alberta   **60% SCALE**

Growth Performance Measurement				
Years	Price	Earn.	Div.	Tot Ret
Last 1	18.9	25.3	---	18.9
Last 5	13.1	22.4	---	13.1
Last 10	37.1	32.4	---	37.1

Listed to
Nasdaq 1/21/08
Amex prior

(0.08)
0.00

Copyright 2012 Securities Research Company

Bonds $.0 Mil Com 73.780 Mil BV 5.25 /sh P/E 9.48 (Ind OGEXP P/E 15.31) Ctry Canada

TRANSWITCH CORP (TXCC)

Semiconductor solutions for the telecommunications industry   **40% SCALE**

Growth Performance Measurement				
Years	Price	Earn.	Div.	Tot Ret
Last 1	-80.9	-55.6	---	-80.9
Last 5	-38.7	11.6	---	-38.7
Last 10	-19.8	18.2	---	-19.8

Adj. for
1 for 8
11/24/09

(3.12) (5.36) (4.56) (3.84) (2.80) (1.36) (0.56) (1.04) (1.12) (0.80) (0.19) (0.11) (0.29) (0.53)
(2.88) (4.80) (5.12) (4.00) (2.96) (1.68) (0.56) (0.88) (1.12) (1.04) (0.38) (0.06) (0.12) (0.45) (0.56)
(1.20) (4.16) (5.68) (4.48) (3.84) (2.32) (0.96) (0.72) (1.12) (1.04) (0.56) (0.12) (0.03) (0.36) (0.59)

Copyright 2012 Securities Research Company

Bonds $.0 Mil Com 35.834 Mil BV .11 /sh P/E N/A (Ind SEMIC P/E 12.16) Ctry US

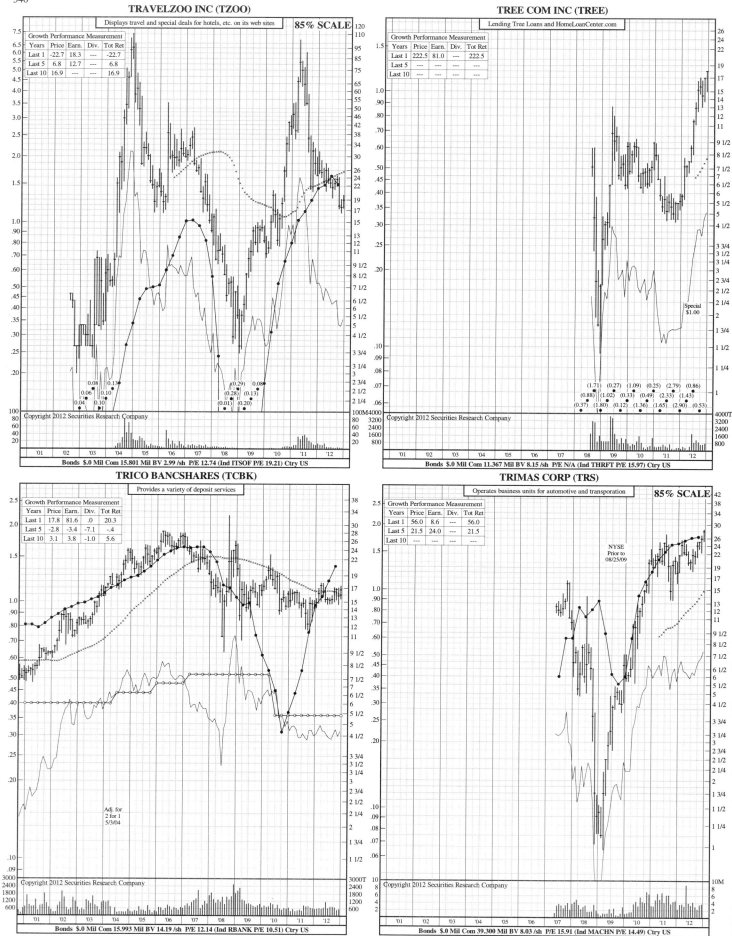

TRAVELZOO INC (TZOO)
Displays travel and special deals for hotels, etc. on its web sites   **85% SCALE**

Growth Performance Measurement				
Years	Price	Earn.	Div.	Tot Ret
Last 1	-22.7	18.3	---	-22.7
Last 5	6.8	12.7	---	6.8
Last 10	16.9	---	---	16.9

0.08   0.13
0.06   0.10   (0.29)   0.08
0.04   0.10   (0.28)   (0.13)
       (0.01)   (0.20)

Copyright 2012 Securities Research Company

Bonds $.0 Mil Com 15.801 Mil BV 2.99 /sh P/E 12.74 (Ind ITSOF P/E 19.21) Ctry US

TREE COM INC (TREE)
Lending Tree Loans and HomeLoanCenter.com

Growth Performance Measurement				
Years	Price	Earn.	Div.	Tot Ret
Last 1	222.5	81.0	---	222.5
Last 5	---	---	---	---
Last 10	---	---	---	---

Special
$1.00

(1.71)   (0.27)   (1.09)   (0.25)   (2.79)   (0.86)
(0.88)   (1.02)   (0.33)   (0.49)   (2.33)   (1.43)
(0.37)   (1.80)   (0.12)   (1.36)   (1.65)   (2.90)   (0.53)

Copyright 2012 Securities Research Company

Bonds $.0 Mil Com 11.367 Mil BV 8.15 /sh P/E N/A (Ind THRFT P/E 15.97) Ctry US

TRICO BANCSHARES (TCBK)
Provides a variety of deposit services

Growth Performance Measurement				
Years	Price	Earn.	Div.	Tot Ret
Last 1	17.8	81.6	.0	20.3
Last 5	-2.8	-3.4	-7.1	-.4
Last 10	3.1	3.8	-1.0	5.6

Adj. for
2 for 1
5/3/04

Copyright 2012 Securities Research Company

Bonds $.0 Mil Com 15.993 Mil BV 14.19 /sh P/E 12.14 (Ind RBANK P/E 10.51) Ctry US

TRIMAS CORP (TRS)
Operates business units for automotive and transporation   **85% SCALE**

Growth Performance Measurement				
Years	Price	Earn.	Div.	Tot Ret
Last 1	56.0	8.6	---	56.0
Last 5	21.5	24.0	---	21.5
Last 10	---	---	---	---

NYSE
Prior to
08/25/09

Copyright 2012 Securities Research Company

Bonds $.0 Mil Com 39.300 Mil BV 8.03 /sh P/E 15.91 (Ind MACHN P/E 14.49) Ctry US

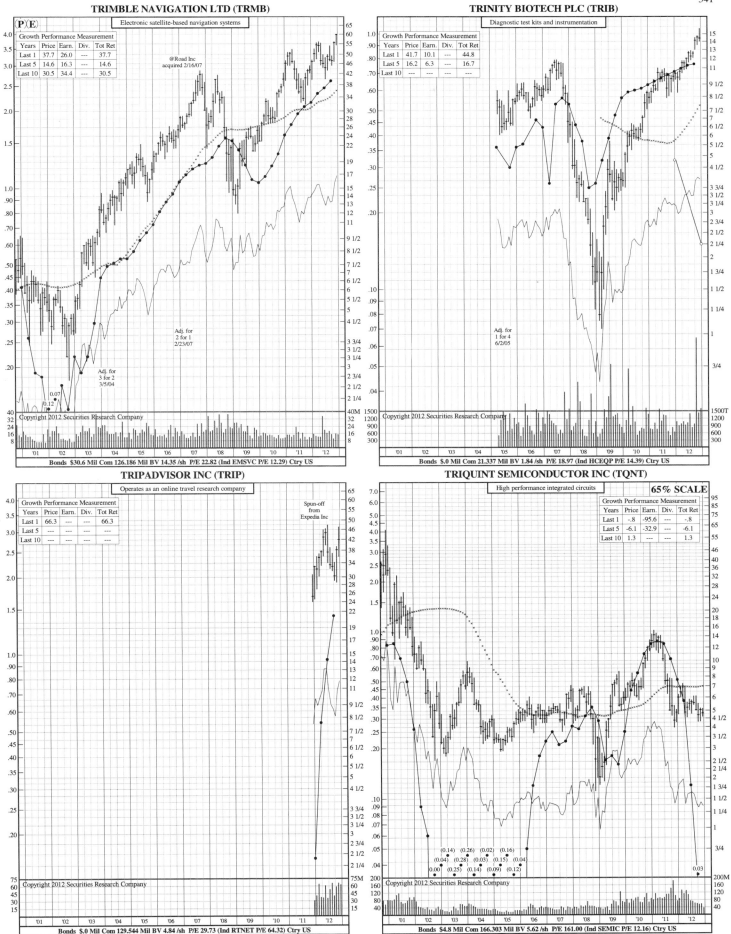

TRIMBLE NAVIGATION LTD (TRMB)

Electronic satellite-based navigation systems

Growth Performance Measurement			
Years	Price	Earn.	Div.	Tot Ret
Last 1	37.7	26.0	---	37.7
Last 5	14.6	16.3	---	14.6
Last 10	30.5	34.4	---	30.5

@Road Inc acquired 2/16/07

Adj. for 2 for 1 2/23/07

Adj. for 3 for 2 3/5/04

0.07
0.12

Copyright 2012 Securities Research Company

Bonds $30.6 Mil Com 126.186 Mil BV 14.35 /sh P/E 22.82 (Ind EMSVC P/E 12.29) Ctry US

TRINITY BIOTECH PLC (TRIB)

Diagnostic test kits and instrumentation

Growth Performance Measurement			
Years	Price	Earn.	Div.	Tot Ret
Last 1	41.7	10.1	---	44.8
Last 5	16.2	6.3	---	16.7
Last 10	---	---	---	---

Adj. for 1 for 4 6/2/05

Copyright 2012 Securities Research Company

Bonds $.0 Mil Com 21.337 Mil BV 1.84 /sh P/E 18.97 (Ind HCEQP P/E 14.39) Ctry US

TRIPADVISOR INC (TRIP)

Operates as an online travel research company

Growth Performance Measurement			
Years	Price	Earn.	Div.	Tot Ret
Last 1	66.3	---	---	66.3
Last 5	---	---	---	---
Last 10	---	---	---	---

Spun-off from Expedia Inc

Copyright 2012 Securities Research Company

Bonds $.0 Mil Com 129.544 Mil BV 4.84 /sh P/E 29.73 (Ind RTNET P/E 64.32) Ctry US

TRIQUINT SEMICONDUCTOR INC (TQNT)

High performance integrated circuits

65% SCALE

Growth Performance Measurement			
Years	Price	Earn.	Div.	Tot Ret
Last 1	-.8	-95.6	---	-.8
Last 5	-6.1	-32.9	---	-6.1
Last 10	1.3	---	---	1.3

(0.14) (0.26) (0.02) (0.16)
(0.04) (0.28) (0.03) (0.15) (0.04)
0.00 (0.25) (0.14) (0.09) (0.12)
0.03

Copyright 2012 Securities Research Company

Bonds $4.8 Mil Com 166.303 Mil BV 5.62 /sh P/E 161.00 (Ind SEMIC P/E 12.16) Ctry US

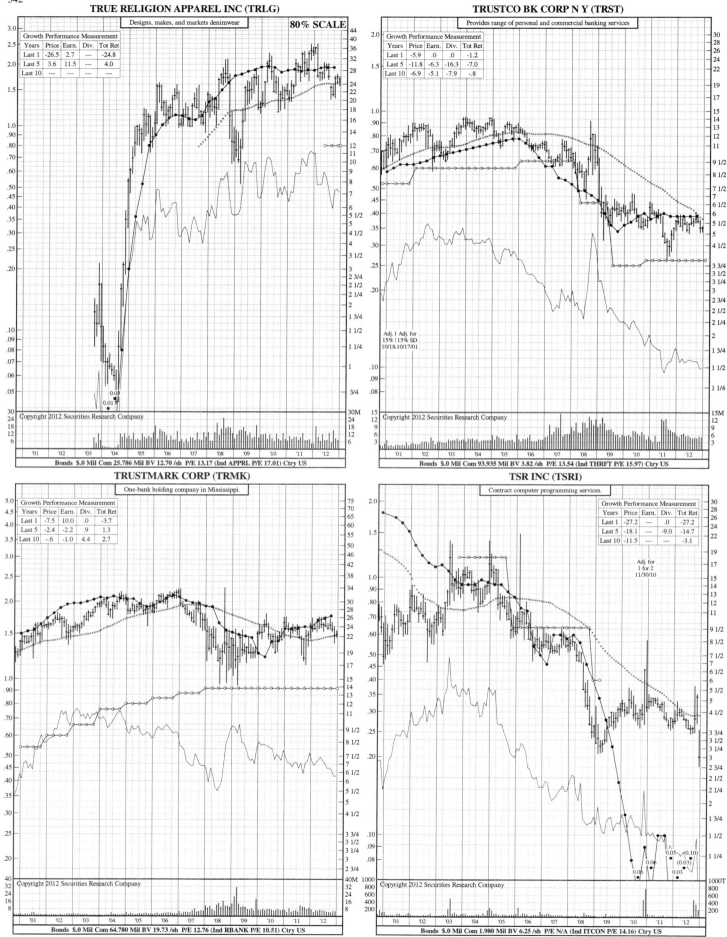

342

TRUE RELIGION APPAREL INC (TRLG)

Designs, makes, and markets denimwear

80% SCALE

Growth Performance Measurement

Years	Price	Earn.	Div.	Tot Ret
Last 1	-26.5	2.7	---	-24.8
Last 5	3.6	11.5	---	4.0
Last 10	---	---	---	---

Copyright 2012 Securities Research Company

Bonds $.0 Mil Com 25.786 Mil BV 12.70 /sh P/E 13.17 (Ind APPRL P/E 17.01) Ctry US

TRUSTCO BK CORP N Y (TRST)

Provides range of personal and commercial banking services

Growth Performance Measurement

Years	Price	Earn.	Div.	Tot Ret
Last 1	-5.9	.0	.0	-1.2
Last 5	-11.8	-6.3	-16.3	-7.0
Last 10	-6.9	-5.1	-7.9	-.8

Adj. 1 Adj. for
15% ; 15% SD
10/18;10/17/01

Copyright 2012 Securities Research Company

Bonds $.0 Mil Com 93.935 Mil BV 3.82 /sh P/E 13.54 (Ind THRFT P/E 15.97) Ctry US

TRUSTMARK CORP (TRMK)

One-bank holding company in Mississippi.

Growth Performance Measurement

Years	Price	Earn.	Div.	Tot Ret
Last 1	-7.5	10.0	.0	-3.7
Last 5	-2.4	-2.2	.9	1.3
Last 10	-.6	-1.0	4.4	2.7

Copyright 2012 Securities Research Company

Bonds $.0 Mil Com 64.780 Mil BV 19.73 /sh P/E 12.76 (Ind RBANK P/E 10.51) Ctry US

TSR INC (TSRI)

Contract computer programming services.

Growth Performance Measurement

Years	Price	Earn.	Div.	Tot Ret
Last 1	-27.2	---	.0	-27.2
Last 5	-18.1	---	-9.0	-14.7
Last 10	-11.5	---	---	-3.1

Adj. for
1 for 2
11/30/10

Copyright 2012 Securities Research Company

Bonds $.0 Mil Com 1.980 Mil BV 6.25 /sh P/E N/A (Ind ITCON P/E 14.16) Ctry US

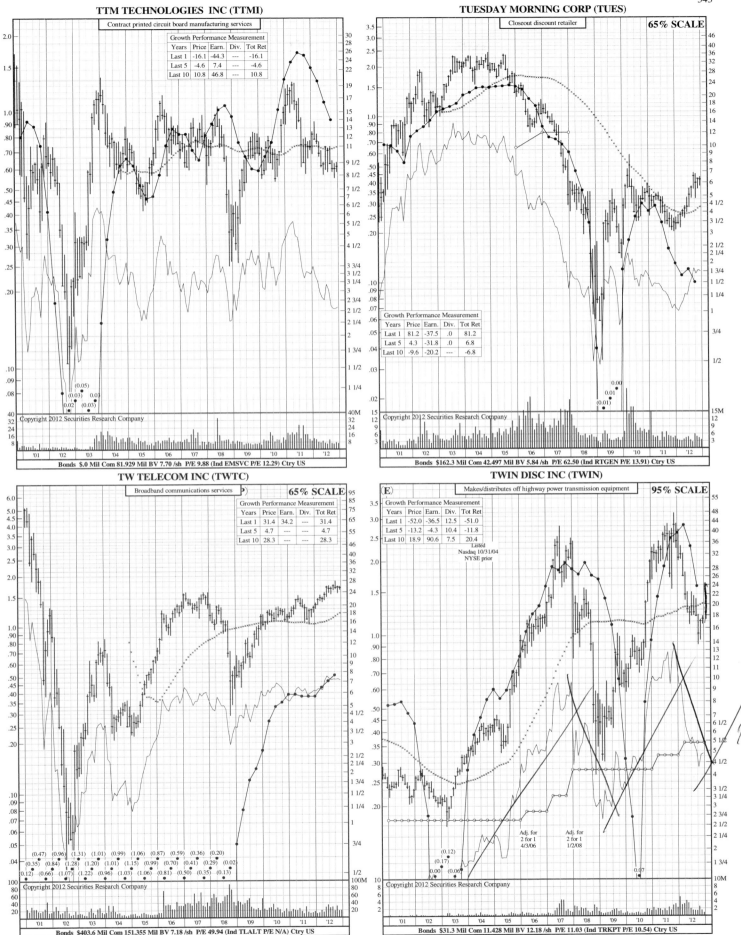

344

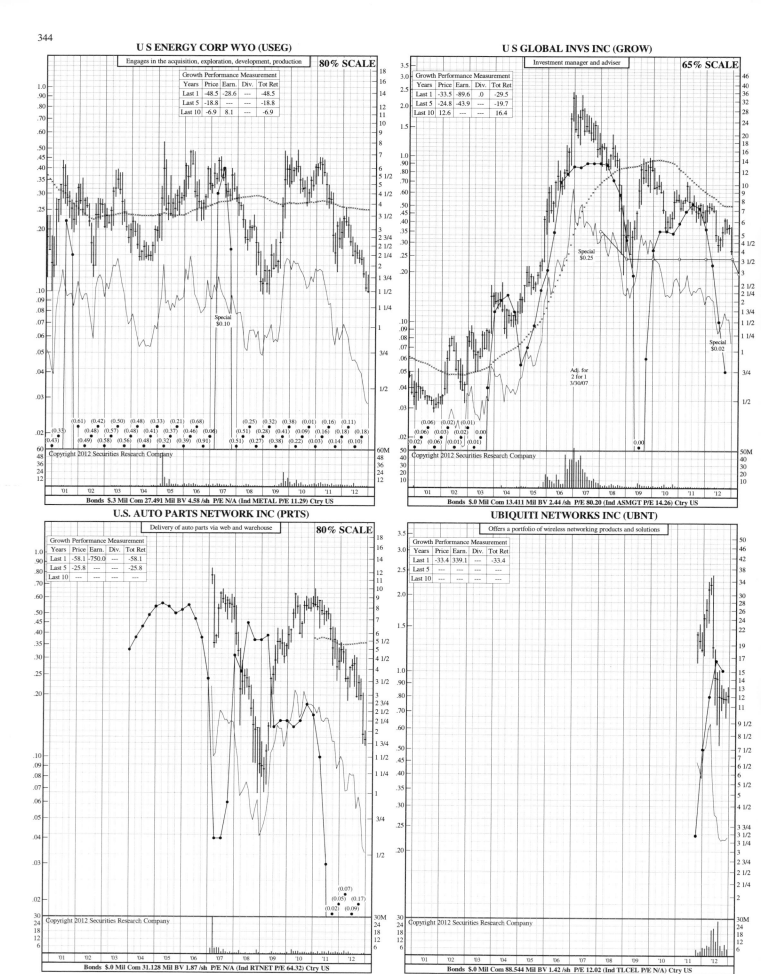

U S ENERGY CORP WYO (USEG)

Engages in the acquisition, exploration, development, production

80% SCALE

Growth Performance Measurement				
Years	Price	Earn.	Div.	Tot Ret
Last 1	-48.5	-28.6	---	-48.5
Last 5	-18.8	---	---	-18.8
Last 10	-6.9	8.1	---	-6.9

Special
$0.10

(0.61) (0.42) (0.50) (0.48) (0.33) (0.21) (0.68)   (0.25) (0.32) (0.38) (0.01) (0.16) (0.11)
(0.33) (0.48) (0.57) (0.48) (0.41) (0.37) (0.46) (0.06)   (0.51) (0.28) (0.41) (0.09) (0.16) (0.18) (0.18)
(0.43) (0.49) (0.58) (0.56) (0.48) (0.32) (0.39) (0.91)   (0.51) (0.27) (0.38) (0.22) (0.03) (0.14) (0.10)

Copyright 2012 Securities Research Company

'01 '02 '03 '04 '05 '06 '07 '08 '09 '10 '11 '12

Bonds $.3 Mil Com 27.491 Mil BV 4.58 /sh P/E N/A (Ind METAL P/E 11.29) Ctry US

U S GLOBAL INVS INC (GROW)

Investment manager and adviser

65% SCALE

Growth Performance Measurement				
Years	Price	Earn.	Div.	Tot Ret
Last 1	-33.5	-89.6	.0	-29.5
Last 5	-24.8	-43.9	---	-19.7
Last 10	12.6	---	---	16.4

Special
$0.25

Adj. for
2 for 1
3/30/07

Special
$0.02

(0.06) (0.02) (0.01)
(0.06) (0.03) (0.02) 0.00
(0.02) (0.06) (0.01) (0.01)   0.00

Copyright 2012 Securities Research Company

'01 '02 '03 '04 '05 '06 '07 '08 '09 '10 '11 '12

Bonds $.0 Mil Com 13.411 Mil BV 2.44 /sh P/E 80.20 (Ind ASMGT P/E 14.26) Ctry US

U.S. AUTO PARTS NETWORK INC (PRTS)

Delivery of auto parts via web and warehouse

80% SCALE

Growth Performance Measurement				
Years	Price	Earn.	Div.	Tot Ret
Last 1	-58.1	-750.0	---	-58.1
Last 5	-25.8	---	---	-25.8
Last 10	---	---	---	---

(0.07)
(0.05) (0.17)
(0.02) (0.09)

Copyright 2012 Securities Research Company

'01 '02 '03 '04 '05 '06 '07 '08 '09 '10 '11 '12

Bonds $.0 Mil Com 31.128 Mil BV 1.87 /sh P/E N/A (Ind RTNET P/E 64.32) Ctry US

UBIQUITI NETWORKS INC (UBNT)

Offers a portfolio of wireless networking products and solutions

Growth Performance Measurement				
Years	Price	Earn.	Div.	Tot Ret
Last 1	-33.4	339.1	---	-33.4
Last 5	---	---	---	---
Last 10	---	---	---	---

Copyright 2012 Securities Research Company

'01 '02 '03 '04 '05 '06 '07 '08 '09 '10 '11 '12

Bonds $.0 Mil Com 88.544 Mil BV 1.42 /sh P/E 12.02 (Ind TLCEL P/E N/A) Ctry US

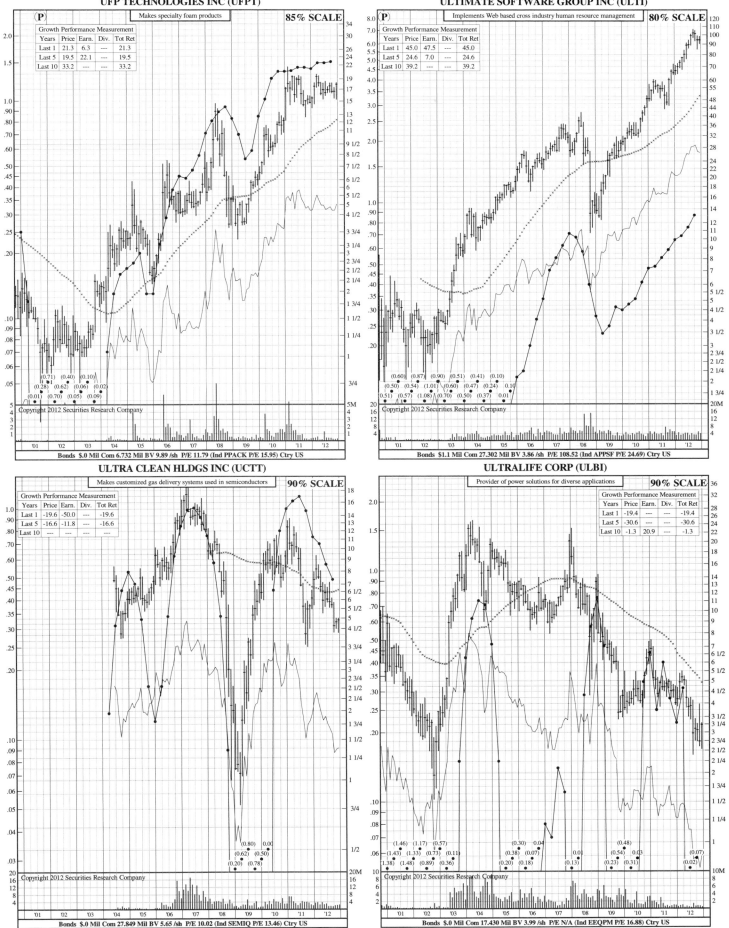

UFP TECHNOLOGIES INC (UFPT)

Makes specialty foam products

85% SCALE

Growth Performance Measurement

Years	Price	Earn.	Div.	Tot Ret
Last 1	21.3	6.3	---	21.3
Last 5	19.5	22.1	---	19.5
Last 10	33.2		---	33.2

(0.71) (0.40) (0.10)
(0.28) (0.62) (0.06) (0.02)
(0.01) (0.70) (0.05) (0.09)

Copyright 2012 Securities Research Company

Bonds $.0 Mil Com 6.732 Mil BV 9.89 /sh P/E 11.79 (Ind PPACK P/E 15.95) Ctry US

ULTIMATE SOFTWARE GROUP INC (ULTI)

Implements Web based cross industry human resource management

80% SCALE

Growth Performance Measurement

Years	Price	Earn.	Div.	Tot Ret
Last 1	45.0	47.5	---	45.0
Last 5	24.6	7.0	---	24.6
Last 10	39.2	---	---	39.2

(0.60) (0.87) (0.90) (0.51) (0.41) (0.10)
(0.50) (0.54) (1.01) (0.60) (0.47) (0.24) 0.10
(0.51) (0.57) (1.08) (0.70) (0.50) (0.37) 0.01

Copyright 2012 Securities Research Company

Bonds $1.1 Mil Com 27.302 Mil BV 3.86 /sh P/E 108.52 (Ind APPSF P/E 24.69) Ctry US

ULTRA CLEAN HLDGS INC (UCTT)

Makes customized gas delivery systems used in semiconductors

90% SCALE

Growth Performance Measurement

Years	Price	Earn.	Div.	Tot Ret
Last 1	-19.6	-50.0	---	-19.6
Last 5	-16.6	-11.8	---	-16.6
Last 10	---	---		---

(0.80) 0.00
(0.62) (0.50)
(0.20) (0.78)

Copyright 2012 Securities Research Company

Bonds $.0 Mil Com 27.849 Mil BV 5.65 /sh P/E 10.02 (Ind SEMIQ P/E 13.46) Ctry US

ULTRALIFE CORP (ULBI)

Provider of power solutions for diverse applications

90% SCALE

Growth Performance Measurement

Years	Price	Earn.	Div.	Tot Ret
Last 1	-19.4	---	---	-19.4
Last 5	-30.6	---	---	-30.6
Last 10	-1.3	20.9	---	-1.3

(1.46) (1.17) (0.57)   (0.30) 0.04   (0.48)   (0.07)
(1.43) (1.33) (0.73) (0.11)   (0.38) (0.07)   0.0   (0.54) 0.03   (0.02)
(1.38) (1.48) (0.89) (0.36)   (0.20) (0.18)   (0.13) (0.23) (0.31)

Copyright 2012 Securities Research Company

Bonds $.0 Mil Com 17.430 Mil BV 3.99 /sh P/E N/A (Ind EEQPM P/E 16.88) Ctry US

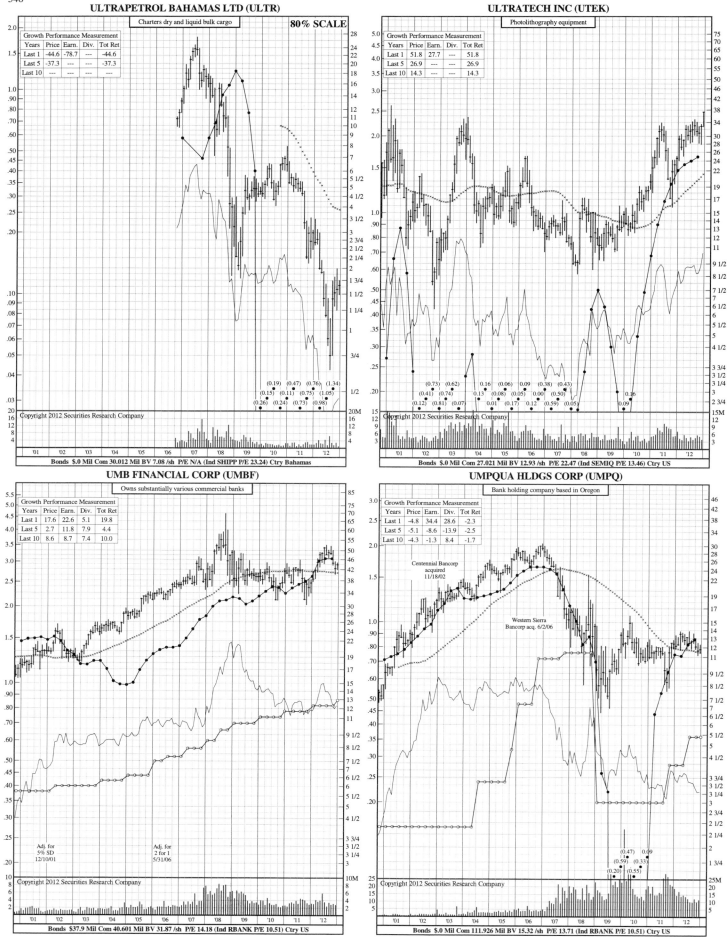

346

ULTRAPETROL BAHAMAS LTD (ULTR)

Charters dry and liquid bulk cargo

80% SCALE

Copyright 2012 Securities Research Company

Growth Performance Measurement				
Years	Price	Earn.	Div.	Tot Ret
Last 1	-44.6	-78.7	---	-44.6
Last 5	-37.3	---	---	-37.3
Last 10	---	---	---	---

(0.19) (0.47) (0.76) (1.34)
(0.15) (0.11) (0.75) (1.05)
(0.26) (0.24) (0.73) (0.98)

Bonds $.0 Mil Com 30.012 Mil BV 7.08 /sh P/E N/A (Ind SHIPP P/E 23.24) Ctry Bahamas

ULTRATECH INC (UTEK)

Photolithography equipment

Growth Performance Measurement				
Years	Price	Earn.	Div.	Tot Ret
Last 1	51.8	27.7	---	51.8
Last 5	26.9	---	---	26.9
Last 10	14.3	---	---	14.3

(0.73) (0.62)   0.16 (0.06) 0.09 (0.38) (0.43)   0.16
(0.41) (0.74)   0.13 (0.08) (0.05) 0.00 (0.50)   0.09
(0.12) (0.81) (0.07) 0.01 (0.17) 0.17 (0.59) (0.05)

Copyright 2012 Securities Research Company

Bonds $.0 Mil Com 27.021 Mil BV 12.93 /sh P/E 22.47 (Ind SEMIQ P/E 13.46) Ctry US

UMB FINANCIAL CORP (UMBF)

Owns substantially various commercial banks

Growth Performance Measurement				
Years	Price	Earn.	Div.	Tot Ret
Last 1	17.6	22.6	5.1	19.8
Last 5	2.7	11.8	7.9	4.4
Last 10	8.6	8.7	7.4	10.0

Adj. for
5% SD
12/10/01

Adj. for
2 for 1
5/31/06

Copyright 2012 Securities Research Company

Bonds $37.9 Mil Com 40.601 Mil BV 31.87 /sh P/E 14.18 (Ind RBANK P/E 10.51) Ctry US

UMPQUA HLDGS CORP (UMPQ)

Bank holding company based in Oregon

Growth Performance Measurement				
Years	Price	Earn.	Div.	Tot Ret
Last 1	-4.8	34.4	28.6	-2.3
Last 5	-5.1	-8.6	-13.9	-2.5
Last 10	-4.3	-1.3	8.4	-1.7

Centennial Bancorp
acquired
11/18/02

Western Sierra
Bancorp acq. 6/2/06

(0.47) 0.09
(0.59) (0.33)
(0.20) (0.55)

Copyright 2012 Securities Research Company

Bonds $.0 Mil Com 111.926 Mil BV 15.32 /sh P/E 13.71 (Ind RBANK P/E 10.51) Ctry US

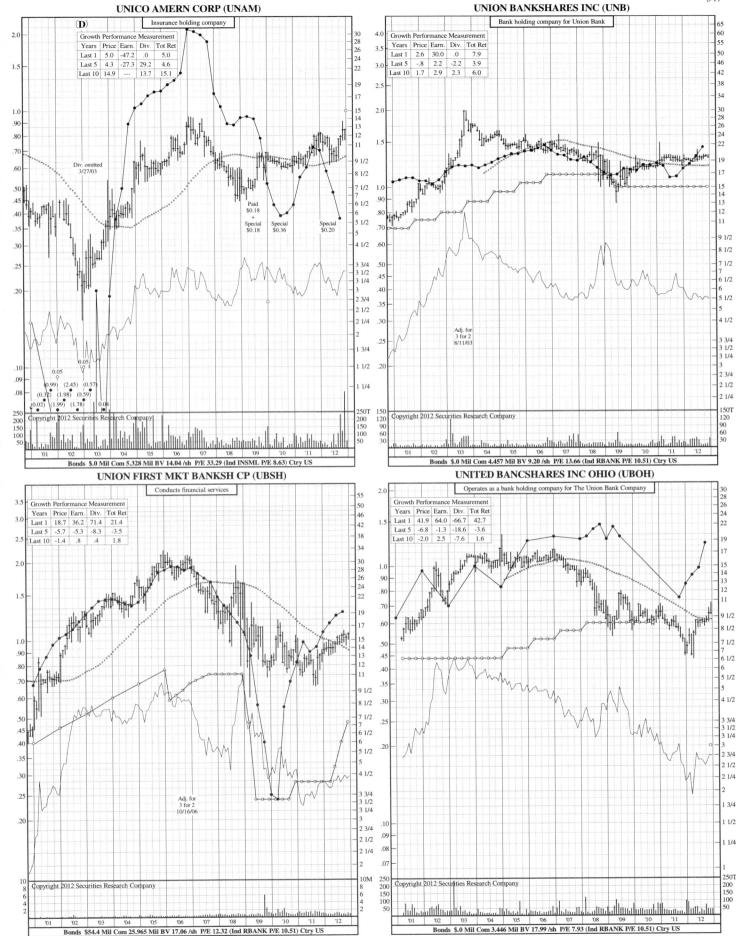

UNICO AMERN CORP (UNAM)

Insurance holding company

(D)

Growth Performance Measurement				
Years	Price	Earn.	Div.	Tot Ret
Last 1	5.0	-47.2	.0	5.0
Last 5	4.3	-27.3	29.2	4.6
Last 10	14.9	---	13.7	15.1

Div. omitted
3/27/03

Paid
$0.18

Special
$0.18

Special
$0.36

Special
$0.20

0.05
0.05
0.05
(0.99) (2.45) (0.57)
(0.32) (1.98) (0.59)
(0.02) (1.99) (1.78) 0.04

Copyright 2012 Securities Research Company

Bonds $.0 Mil Com 5.328 Mil BV 14.04 /sh P/E 33.29 (Ind INSML P/E 8.63) Ctry US

UNION BANKSHARES INC (UNB)

Bank holding company for Union Bank

Growth Performance Measurement				
Years	Price	Earn.	Div.	Tot Ret
Last 1	2.6	30.0	.0	7.9
Last 5	-.8	2.2	-2.2	3.9
Last 10	1.7	2.9	2.3	6.0

Adj. for
3 for 2
8/11/03

Copyright 2012 Securities Research Company

Bonds $.0 Mil Com 4.457 Mil BV 9.20 /sh P/E 13.66 (Ind RBANK P/E 10.51) Ctry US

UNION FIRST MKT BANKSH CP (UBSH)

Conducts financial services

Growth Performance Measurement				
Years	Price	Earn.	Div.	Tot Ret
Last 1	18.7	36.2	71.4	21.4
Last 5	-5.7	-5.3	-8.3	-3.5
Last 10	-1.4	.8	.4	1.8

Adj. for
3 for 2
10/16/06

Copyright 2012 Securities Research Company

Bonds $54.4 Mil Com 25.965 Mil BV 17.06 /sh P/E 12.32 (Ind RBANK P/E 10.51) Ctry US

UNITED BANCSHARES INC OHIO (UBOH)

Operates as a bank holding company for The Union Bank Company

Growth Performance Measurement				
Years	Price	Earn.	Div.	Tot Ret
Last 1	41.9	64.0	-66.7	42.7
Last 5	-6.8	-1.3	-18.6	-3.6
Last 10	-2.0	2.5	-7.6	1.6

Copyright 2012 Securities Research Company

Bonds $.0 Mil Com 3.446 Mil BV 17.99 /sh P/E 7.93 (Ind RBANK P/E 10.51) Ctry US

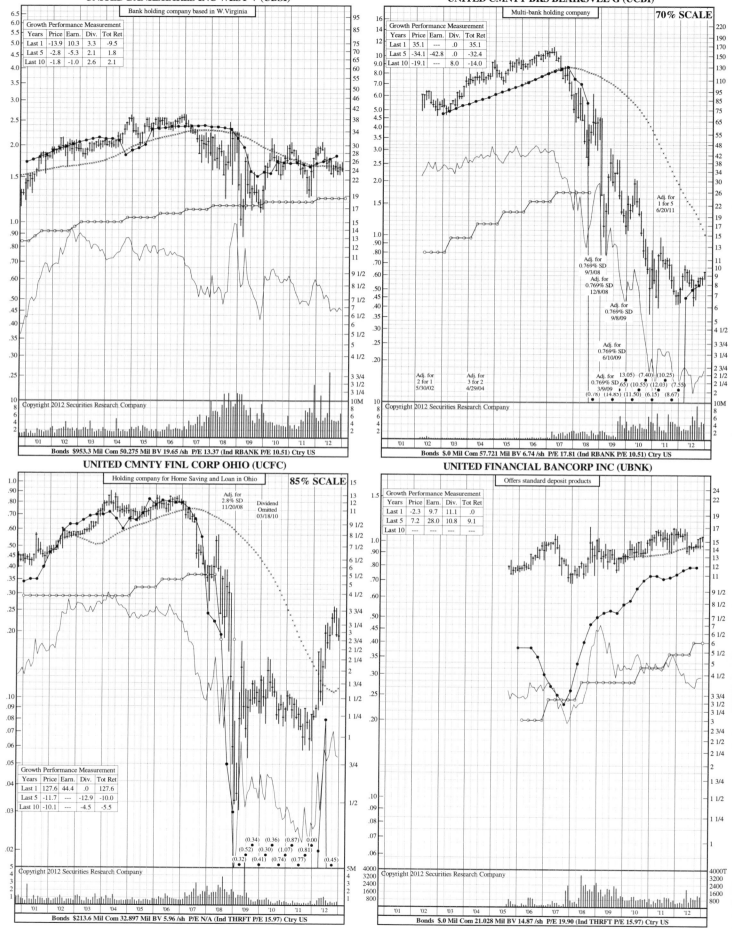

UNITED BANKSHARES INC WEST V (UBSI)

Bank holding company based in W.Virginia

Growth Performance Measurement

Years	Price	Earn.	Div.	Tot Ret
Last 1	-13.9	10.3	3.3	-9.5
Last 5	-2.8	-5.3	2.1	1.8
Last 10	-1.8	-1.0	2.6	2.1

Copyright 2012 Securities Research Company

Bonds $953.3 Mil Com 50.275 Mil BV 19.65 /sh P/E 13.37 (Ind RBANK P/E 10.51) Ctry US

UNITED CMNTY BKS BLAIRSVLE G (UCBI)

Multi-bank holding company

70% SCALE

Growth Performance Measurement

Years	Price	Earn.	Div.	Tot Ret
Last 1	35.1	---	.0	35.1
Last 5	-34.1	-42.8	.0	-32.4
Last 10	-19.1	---	8.0	-14.0

Adj. for 1 for 5 6/20/11

Adj. for 0.769% SD 9/3/08

Adj. for 0.769% SD 12/8/08

Adj. for 0.769% SD 9/8/09

Adj. for 0.769% SD 6/10/09

Adj. for 2 for 1 5/30/02

Adj. for 3 for 2 4/29/04

Adj. for 0.769% SD 3/9/09

13.05 (7.40) (10.25)
.65 (10.55) (12.03) (7.55)
(0.78) (14.85) (11.50) (6.15) (8.67)

Copyright 2012 Securities Research Company

Bonds $.0 Mil Com 57.721 Mil BV 6.74 /sh P/E 17.81 (Ind RBANK P/E 10.51) Ctry US

UNITED CMNTY FINL CORP OHIO (UCFC)

Holding company for Home Saving and Loan in Ohio

85% SCALE

Adj. for 2.8% SD 11/20/08

Dividend Omitted 03/18/10

Growth Performance Measurement

Years	Price	Earn.	Div.	Tot Ret
Last 1	127.6	44.4	.0	127.6
Last 5	-11.7	---	-12.9	-10.0
Last 10	-10.1	---	-4.5	-5.5

(0.34) (0.36) (0.87) 0.00
(0.52) (0.30) (1.07) (0.81)
(0.32) (0.41) (0.74) (0.77) (0.45)

Copyright 2012 Securities Research Company

Bonds $213.6 Mil Com 32.897 Mil BV 5.96 /sh P/E N/A (Ind THRFT P/E 15.97) Ctry US

UNITED FINANCIAL BANCORP INC (UBNK)

Offers standard deposit products

Growth Performance Measurement

Years	Price	Earn.	Div.	Tot Ret
Last 1	-2.3	9.7	11.1	.0
Last 5	7.2	28.0	10.8	9.1
Last 10	---	---	---	---

Copyright 2012 Securities Research Company

Bonds $.0 Mil Com 21.028 Mil BV 14.87 /sh P/E 19.90 (Ind THRFT P/E 15.97) Ctry US

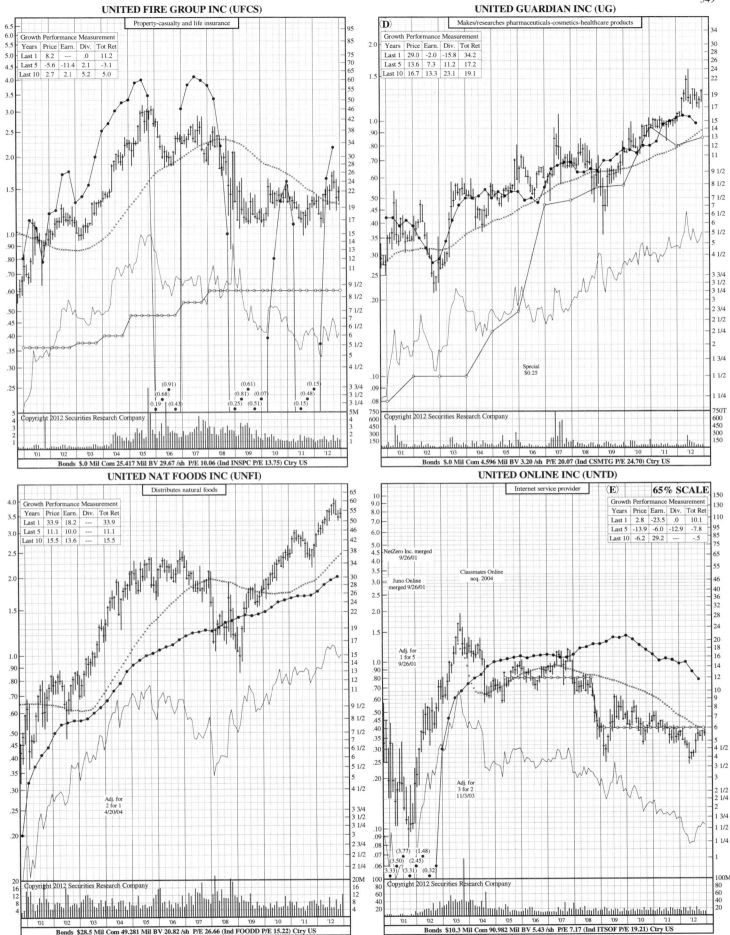

UNITED FIRE GROUP INC (UFCS)

Property-casualty and life insurance

Growth Performance Measurement				
Years	Price	Earn.	Div.	Tot Ret
Last 1	8.2	---	.0	11.2
Last 5	-5.6	-11.4	2.1	-3.1
Last 10	2.7	2.1	5.2	5.0

(0.91)
(0.68)
(0.61)
(0.81) (0.07)
0.19 (0.43)
(0.25) (0.51)
(0.15)
(0.48)
(0.15)

Copyright 2012 Securities Research Company

Bonds $.0 Mil Com 25.417 Mil BV 29.67 /sh P/E 10.06 (Ind INSPC P/E 13.75) Ctry US

UNITED GUARDIAN INC (UG)

(D)

Makes/researches pharmaceuticals-cosmetics-healthcare products

Growth Performance Measurement				
Years	Price	Earn.	Div.	Tot Ret
Last 1	29.0	-2.0	-15.8	34.2
Last 5	13.6	7.3	11.2	17.2
Last 10	16.7	13.3	23.1	19.1

Special
$0.25

Copyright 2012 Securities Research Company

Bonds $.0 Mil Com 4.596 Mil BV 3.20 /sh P/E 20.07 (Ind CSMTG P/E 24.70) Ctry US

UNITED NAT FOODS INC (UNFI)

Distributes natural foods

Growth Performance Measurement				
Years	Price	Earn.	Div.	Tot Ret
Last 1	33.9	18.2	---	33.9
Last 5	11.1	10.0	---	11.1
Last 10	15.5	13.6	---	15.5

Adj. for
2 for 1
4/20/04

Copyright 2012 Securities Research Company

Bonds $28.5 Mil Com 49.281 Mil BV 20.82 /sh P/E 26.66 (Ind FOODD P/E 15.22) Ctry US

UNITED ONLINE INC (UNTD)

Internet service provider

(E)   65% SCALE

Growth Performance Measurement				
Years	Price	Earn.	Div.	Tot Ret
Last 1	2.8	-23.5	.0	10.1
Last 5	-13.9	-6.0	-12.9	-7.8
Last 10	-6.2	29.2	---	-.5

NetZero Inc. merged
9/26/01

Juno Online
merged 9/26/01

Classmates Online
acq. 2004

Adj. for
1 for 5
9/26/01

Adj. for
3 for 2
11/3/03

(3.77) (1.48)
(3.50) (2.45)
3.33   (3.31) (0.32)

Copyright 2012 Securities Research Company

Bonds $10.3 Mil Com 90.982 Mil BV 5.43 /sh P/E 7.17 (Ind ITSOF P/E 19.21) Ctry US

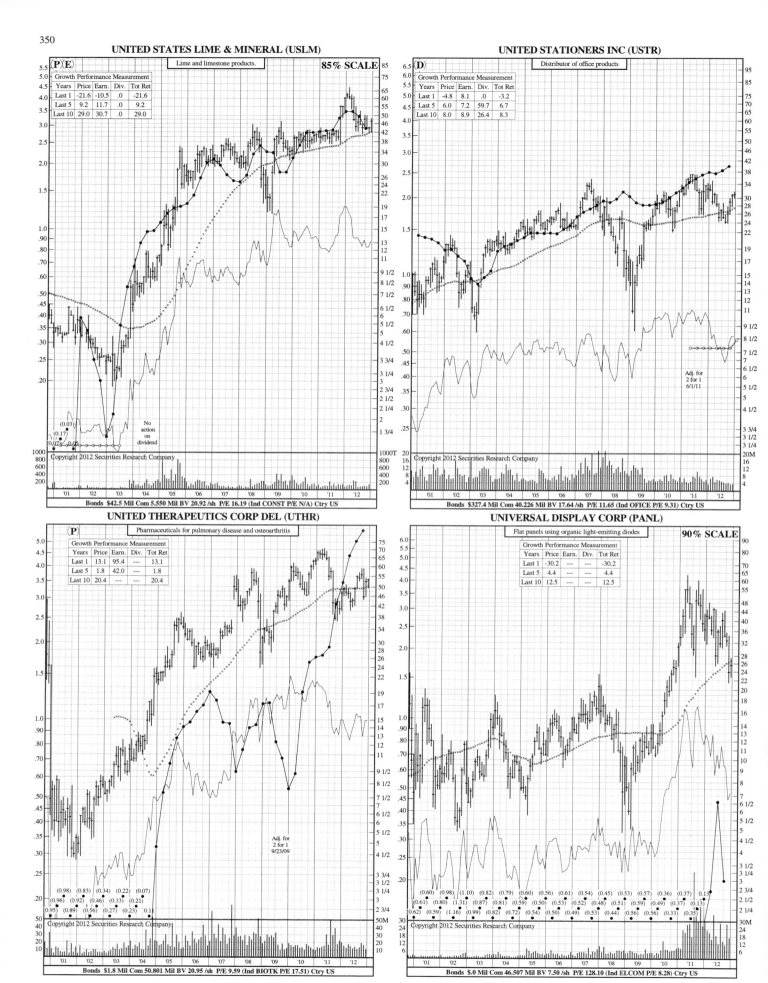

350

UNITED STATES LIME & MINERAL (USLM)
Lime and limestone products.
85% SCALE

Bonds $42.5 Mil Com 5.550 Mil BV 20.92 /sh P/E 16.19 (Ind CONST P/E N/A) Ctry US

UNITED STATIONERS INC (USTR)
Distributor of office products

Bonds $327.4 Mil Com 40.226 Mil BV 17.64 /sh P/E 11.65 (Ind OFICE P/E 9.31) Ctry US

UNITED THERAPEUTICS CORP DEL (UTHR)
Pharmaceuticals for pulmonary disease and osteoarthritis

Bonds $1.8 Mil Com 50.801 Mil BV 20.95 /sh P/E 9.59 (Ind BIOTK P/E 17.51) Ctry US

UNIVERSAL DISPLAY CORP (PANL)
Flat panels using organic light-emitting diodes
90% SCALE

Bonds $.0 Mil Com 46.507 Mil BV 7.50 /sh P/E 128.10 (Ind ELCOM P/E 8.28) Ctry US

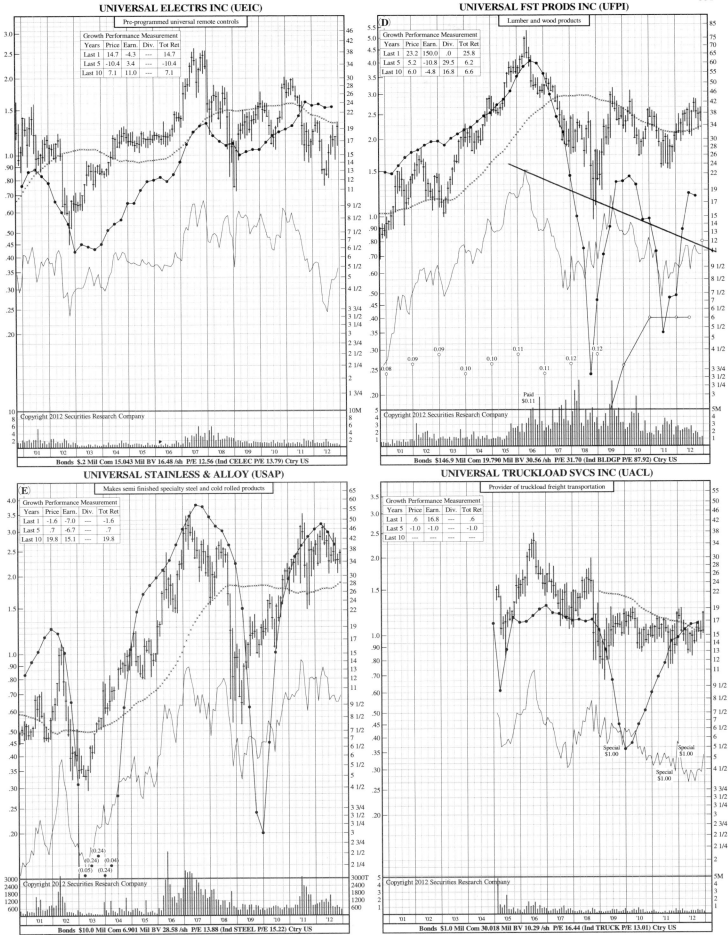

UNIVERSAL ELECTRS INC (UEIC)

Pre-programmed universal remote controls

Growth Performance Measurement				
Years	Price	Earn.	Div.	Tot Ret
Last 1	14.7	-4.3	---	14.7
Last 5	-10.4	3.4	---	-10.4
Last 10	7.1	11.0	---	7.1

Copyright 2012 Securities Research Company

Bonds $.2 Mil Com 15.043 Mil BV 16.48 /sh P/E 12.56 (Ind CELEC P/E 13.79) Ctry US

UNIVERSAL FST PRODS INC (UFPI)

Lumber and wood products

Growth Performance Measurement				
Years	Price	Earn.	Div.	Tot Ret
Last 1	23.2	150.0	.0	25.8
Last 5	5.2	-10.8	29.5	6.2
Last 10	6.0	-4.8	16.8	6.6

Copyright 2012 Securities Research Company

Bonds $146.9 Mil Com 19.790 Mil BV 30.56 /sh P/E 31.70 (Ind BLDGP P/E 87.92) Ctry US

UNIVERSAL STAINLESS & ALLOY (USAP)

Makes semi finished specialty steel and cold rolled products

Growth Performance Measurement				
Years	Price	Earn.	Div.	Tot Ret
Last 1	-1.6	-7.0	---	-1.6
Last 5	.7	-6.7	---	.7
Last 10	19.8	15.1	---	19.8

Copyright 2012 Securities Research Company

Bonds $10.0 Mil Com 6.901 Mil BV 28.58 /sh P/E 13.88 (Ind STEEL P/E 15.22) Ctry US

UNIVERSAL TRUCKLOAD SVCS INC (UACL)

Provider of truckload freight transportation

Growth Performance Measurement				
Years	Price	Earn.	Div.	Tot Ret
Last 1	.6	16.8	---	.6
Last 5	-1.0	-1.0	---	-1.0
Last 10	---	---	---	---

Copyright 2012 Securities Research Company

Bonds $1.0 Mil Com 30.018 Mil BV 10.29 /sh P/E 16.44 (Ind TRUCK P/E 13.01) Ctry US

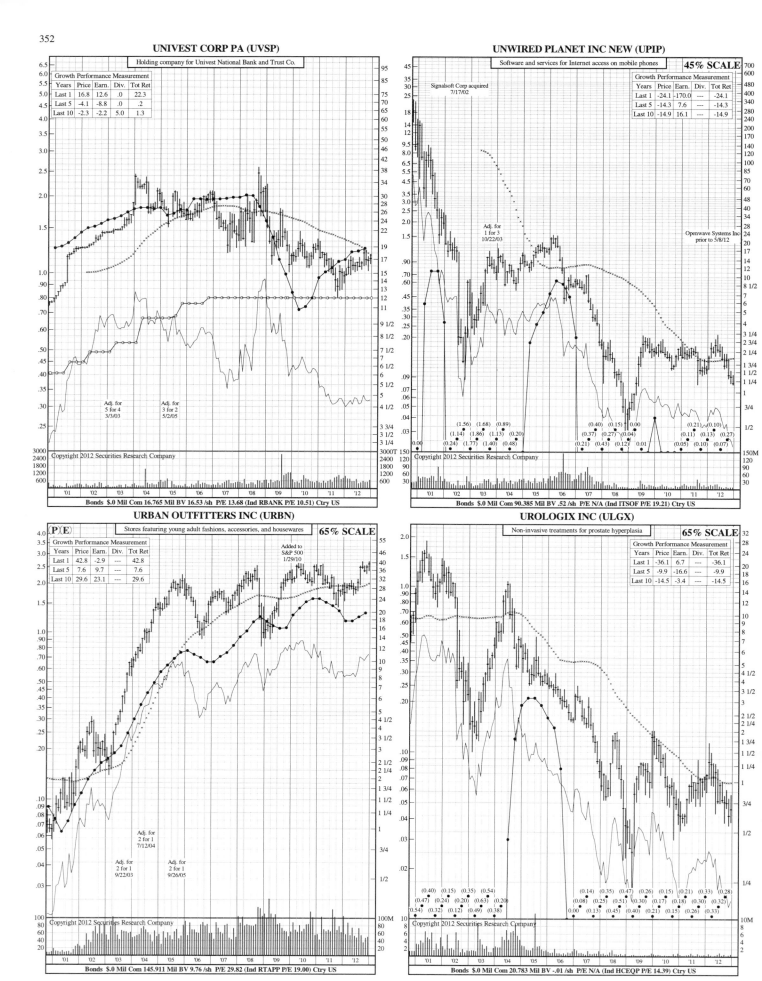

UNIVEST CORP PA (UVSP)

Holding company for Univest National Bank and Trust Co.

Growth Performance Measurement

Years	Price	Earn.	Div.	Tot Ret
Last 1	16.8	12.6	.0	22.3
Last 5	-4.1	-8.8	.0	.2
Last 10	-2.3	-2.2	5.0	1.3

Adj. for
5 for 4
3/3/03

Adj. for
3 for 2
5/2/05

Copyright 2012 Securities Research Company

Bonds $.0 Mil Com 16.765 Mil BV 16.53 /sh P/E 13.68 (Ind RBANK P/E 10.51) Ctry US

UNWIRED PLANET INC NEW (UPIP)

Software and services for Internet access on mobile phones

45% SCALE

Signalsoft Corp acquired
7/17/02

Growth Performance Measurement

Years	Price	Earn.	Div.	Tot Ret
Last 1	-24.1	-170.0	---	-24.1
Last 5	-14.3	7.6	---	-14.3
Last 10	-14.9	16.1	---	-14.9

Adj. for
1 for 3
10/22/03

Openwave Systems Inc
prior to 5/8/12

(1.56) (1.68) (0.89)   (0.40) (0.15) 0.00   (0.21) (0.10)
(1.14) (1.86) (1.13) (0.20)   (0.37) (0.27) (0.04)   (0.11) (0.13) (0.27)
0.00 (0.24) (1.77) (1.40) (0.48)   (0.21) (0.43) (0.12) 0.01   (0.05) (0.10) (0.07)

Copyright 2012 Securities Research Company

Bonds $.0 Mil Com 90.385 Mil BV .52 /sh P/E N/A (Ind ITSOF P/E 19.21) Ctry US

URBAN OUTFITTERS INC (URBN)

(P)E

Stores featuring young adult fashions, accessories, and housewares

65% SCALE

Growth Performance Measurement

Years	Price	Earn.	Div.	Tot Ret
Last 1	42.8	-2.9		42.8
Last 5	7.6	9.7		7.6
Last 10	29.6	23.1	---	29.6

Added to
S&P 500
1/29/10

Adj. for
2 for 1
7/12/04

Adj. for
2 for 1
9/26/05

Adj. for
2 for 1
9/22/03

Copyright 2012 Securities Research Company

Bonds $.0 Mil Com 145.911 Mil BV 9.76 /sh P/E 29.82 (Ind RTAPP P/E 19.00) Ctry US

UROLOGIX INC (ULGX)

Non-invasive treatments for prostate hyperplasia

65% SCALE

Growth Performance Measurement

Years	Price	Earn.	Div.	Tot Ret
Last 1	-36.1	6.7	---	-36.1
Last 5	-9.9	-16.6	---	-9.9
Last 10	-14.5	-3.4	---	-14.5

(0.40) (0.15) (0.35) (0.54)   (0.14) (0.35) (0.47) (0.26) (0.15) (0.21) (0.33) (0.28)
(0.47) (0.24) (0.20) (0.63) (0.20)   (0.08) (0.25) (0.51) (0.30) (0.17) (0.18) (0.30) (0.32)
(0.54) (0.32) (0.49) (0.38)   0.00 (0.13) (0.45) (0.40) (0.21) (0.15) (0.26) (0.33)

Copyright 2012 Securities Research Company

Bonds $.0 Mil Com 20.783 Mil BV -.01 /sh P/E N/A (Ind HCEQP P/E 14.39) Ctry US

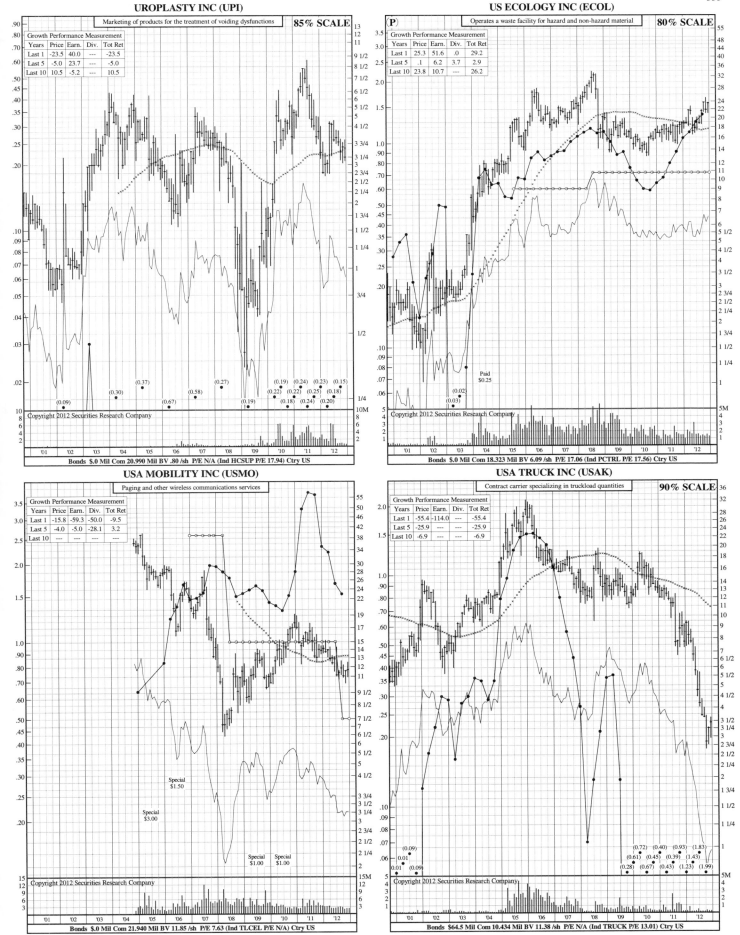

353

UROPLASTY INC (UPI)

Marketing of products for the treatment of voiding dysfunctions

85% SCALE

Bonds $.0 Mil Com 20.990 Mil BV .80 /sh P/E N/A (Ind HCSUP P/E 17.94) Ctry US

Growth Performance Measurement

Years	Price	Earn.	Div.	Tot Ret
Last 1	-23.5	40.0	---	-23.5
Last 5	-5.0	23.7	---	-5.0
Last 10	10.5	-5.2	---	10.5

(0.09) (0.30) (0.37) (0.67) (0.58) (0.27) (0.19) (0.19) (0.22) (0.18) (0.24) (0.22) (0.23) (0.25) (0.24) (0.20) (0.15) (0.18)

US ECOLOGY INC (ECOL)

(P) Operates a waste facility for hazard and non-hazard material

80% SCALE

Growth Performance Measurement

Years	Price	Earn.	Div.	Tot Ret
Last 1	25.3	51.6	.0	29.2
Last 5	.1	6.2	3.7	2.9
Last 10	23.8	10.7	---	26.2

Paid $0.25

(0.02) (0.03)

Bonds $.0 Mil Com 18.323 Mil BV 6.09 /sh P/E 17.06 (Ind PCTRL P/E 17.56) Ctry US

USA MOBILITY INC (USMO)

Paging and other wireless communications services

Growth Performance Measurement

Years	Price	Earn.	Div.	Tot Ret
Last 1	-15.8	-59.3	-50.0	-9.5
Last 5	-4.0	-5.0	-28.1	3.2
Last 10	---	---	---	---

Special $1.50

Special $3.00

Special $1.00   Special $1.00

Bonds $.0 Mil Com 21.940 Mil BV 11.85 /sh P/E 7.63 (Ind TLCEL P/E N/A) Ctry US

USA TRUCK INC (USAK)

Contract carrier specializing in truckload quantities

90% SCALE

Growth Performance Measurement

Years	Price	Earn.	Div.	Tot Ret
Last 1	-55.4	-114.0	---	-55.4
Last 5	-25.9	---	---	-25.9
Last 10	-6.9	---	---	-6.9

(0.09) (0.01) (0.09) (0.72) (0.61) (0.28) (0.40) (0.45) (0.67) (0.93) (0.39) (0.43) (1.83) (1.43) (1.23) (1.99)

Bonds $64.5 Mil Com 10.434 Mil BV 11.38 /sh P/E N/A (Ind TRUCK P/E 13.01) Ctry US

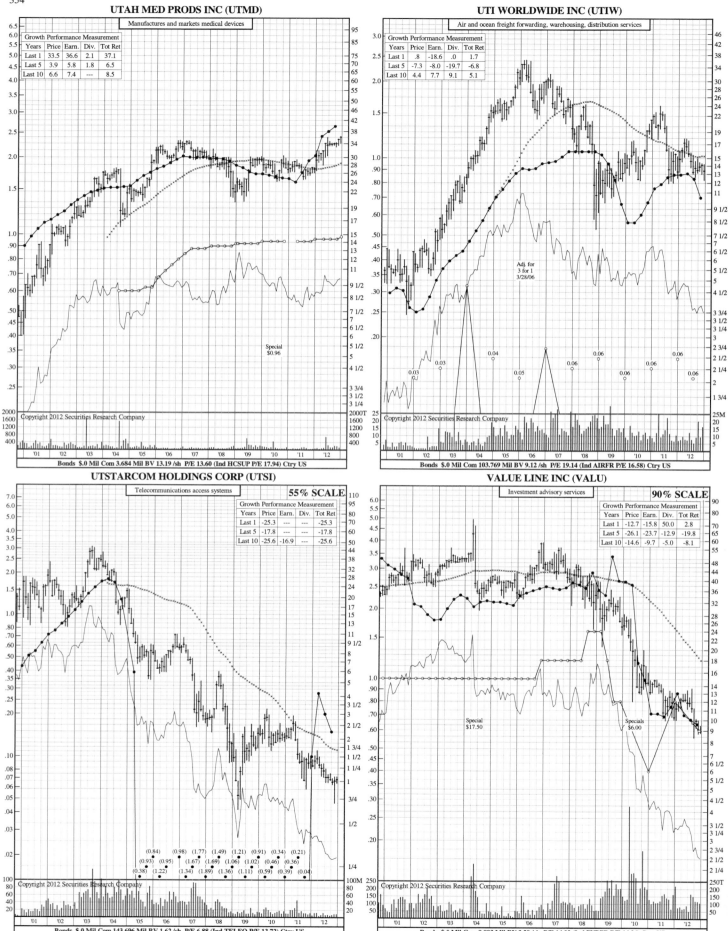

UTAH MED PRODS INC (UTMD)

Manufactures and markets medical devices

Growth Performance Measurement				
Years	Price	Earn.	Div.	Tot Ret
Last 1	33.5	36.6	2.1	37.1
Last 5	3.9	5.8	1.8	6.5
Last 10	6.6	7.4	---	8.5

Special
$0.96

Copyright 2012 Securities Research Company

Bonds $.0 Mil Com 3.684 Mil BV 13.19 /sh P/E 13.60 (Ind HCSUP P/E 17.94) Ctry US

UTI WORLDWIDE INC (UTIW)

Air and ocean freight forwarding, warehousing, distribution services

Growth Performance Measurement				
Years	Price	Earn.	Div.	Tot Ret
Last 1	.8	-18.6	.0	1.7
Last 5	-7.3	-8.0	-19.7	-6.8
Last 10	4.4	7.7	9.1	5.1

Adj. for
3 for 1
3/28/06

0.03
0.03
0.04
0.05
0.06
0.06
0.06
0.06
0.06

Copyright 2012 Securities Research Company

Bonds $.0 Mil Com 103.769 Mil BV 9.12 /sh P/E 19.14 (Ind AIRFR P/E 16.58) Ctry US

UTSTARCOM HOLDINGS CORP (UTSI)

Telecommunications access systems

55% SCALE

Growth Performance Measurement				
Years	Price	Earn.	Div.	Tot Ret
Last 1	-25.3	---	---	-25.3
Last 5	-17.8	---	---	-17.8
Last 10	-25.6	-16.9	---	-25.6

(0.84) (0.98) (1.77) (1.49) (1.21) (0.91) (0.34) (0.21)
(0.93) (0.95) (1.67) (1.69) (1.06) (1.02) (0.46) (0.36)
(0.38) (1.22) (1.34) (1.89) (1.36) (1.11) (0.59) (0.39) (0.04)

Copyright 2012 Securities Research Company

Bonds $.0 Mil Com 143.696 Mil BV 1.62 /sh P/E 6.88 (Ind TELEQ P/E 13.72) Ctry US

VALUE LINE INC (VALU)

Investment advisory services

90% SCALE

Growth Performance Measurement				
Years	Price	Earn.	Div.	Tot Ret
Last 1	-12.7	-15.8	50.0	2.8
Last 5	-26.1	-23.7	-12.9	-19.8
Last 10	-14.6	-9.7	-5.0	-8.1

Special
$17.50

Specials
$6.00

Copyright 2012 Securities Research Company

Bonds $.0 Mil Com 9.893 Mil BV 3.29 /sh P/E 14.02 (Ind PUBPR P/E 14.26) Ctry US

354

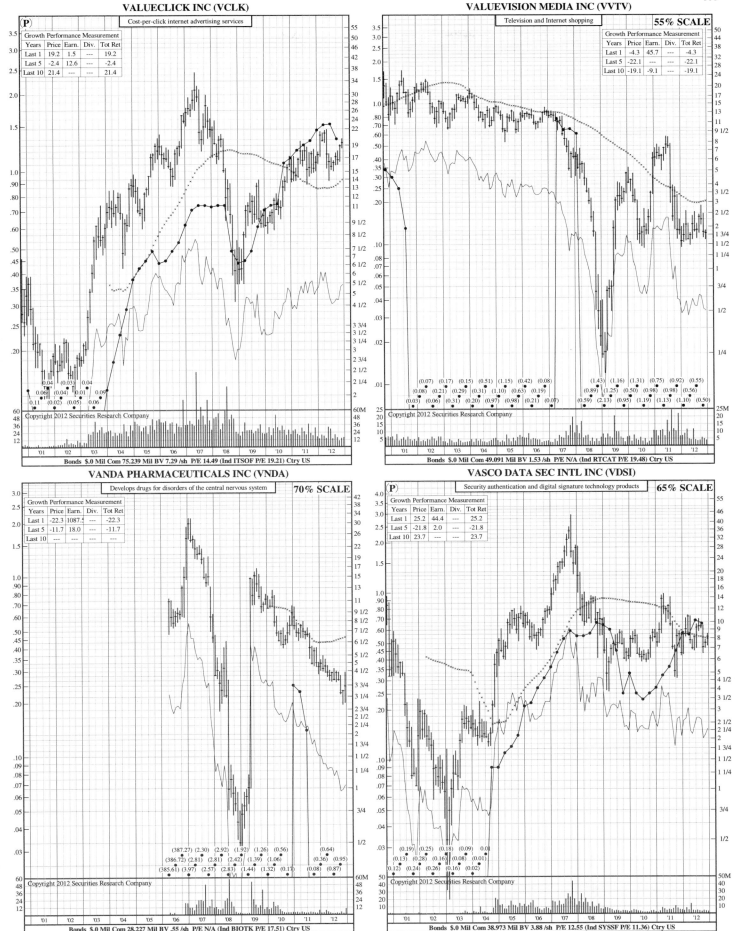

VALUECLICK INC (VCLK)

Cost-per-click internet advertising services

(P)

Growth Performance Measurement				
Years	Price	Earn.	Div.	Tot Ret
Last 1	19.2	1.5	---	19.2
Last 5	-2.4	12.6	---	-2.4
Last 10	21.4	---	---	21.4

0.04   (0.03)   0.04
0.06   (0.04)   0.01   0.09
0.11   0.02   (0.05)   0.06

Copyright 2012 Securities Research Company

Bonds $.0 Mil Com 75.239 Mil BV 7.29 /sh P/E 14.49 (Ind ITSOF P/E 19.21) Ctry US

VALUEVISION MEDIA INC (VVTV)

Television and Internet shopping

55% SCALE

Growth Performance Measurement				
Years	Price	Earn.	Div.	Tot Ret
Last 1	-4.3	45.7	---	-4.3
Last 5	-22.1	---	---	-22.1
Last 10	-19.1	-9.1	---	-19.1

(0.07) (0.17) (0.15) (0.51) (1.15) (0.42) (0.08)   (1.43) (1.16) (1.31) (0.75) (0.92) (0.55)
(0.08) (0.21) (0.29) (0.31) (1.10) (0.63) (0.19)   (0.89) (1.25) (0.50) (0.98) (0.98) (0.56)
(0.03) (0.06) (0.31) (0.20) (0.97) (0.98) (0.21) (0.07) (0.59) (2.13) (0.95) (1.19) (1.13) (1.10) (0.50)

Copyright 2012 Securities Research Company

Bonds $.0 Mil Com 49.091 Mil BV 1.53 /sh P/E N/A (Ind RTCAT P/E 19.48) Ctry US

VANDA PHARMACEUTICALS INC (VNDA)

Develops drugs for disorders of the central nervous system

70% SCALE

Growth Performance Measurement				
Years	Price	Earn.	Div.	Tot Ret
Last 1	-22.3	1087.5	---	-22.3
Last 5	-11.7	18.0	---	-11.7
Last 10	---	---	---	---

(387.27) (2.30) (2.92) (1.92) (1.26) (0.56)   (0.64)
(386.72) (2.81) (2.81) (2.42) (1.39) (1.06)   (0.36) (0.95)
(385.61) (3.97) (2.57) (2.83) (1.44) (1.32) (0.17) (0.08) (0.87)

Copyright 2012 Securities Research Company

Bonds $.0 Mil Com 28.227 Mil BV .55 /sh P/E N/A (Ind BIOTK P/E 17.51) Ctry US

VASCO DATA SEC INTL INC (VDSI)

Security authentication and digital signature technology products

65% SCALE

(P)

Growth Performance Measurement				
Years	Price	Earn.	Div.	Tot Ret
Last 1	25.2	44.4	---	25.2
Last 5	-21.8	2.0	---	-21.8
Last 10	23.7	---	---	23.7

(0.19) (0.25) (0.18) (0.09) 0.01
(0.13) (0.28) (0.16) (0.08) (0.01)
(0.12) (0.24) (0.26) (0.16) (0.02)

Copyright 2012 Securities Research Company

Bonds $.0 Mil Com 38.973 Mil BV 3.88 /sh P/E 12.55 (Ind SYSSF P/E 11.36) Ctry US

356

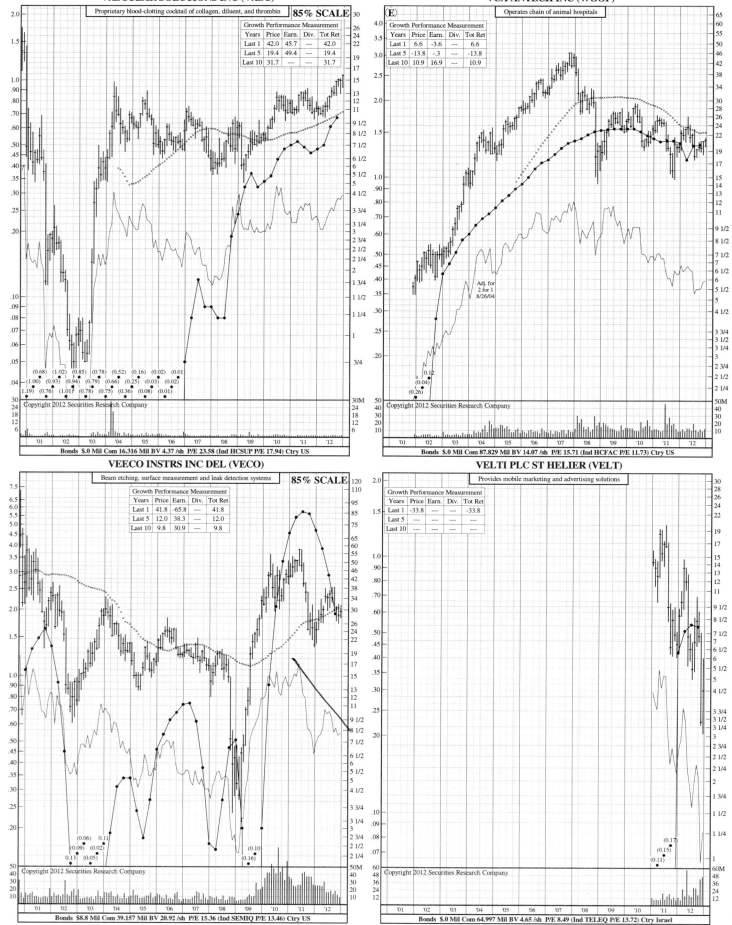

VASCULAR SOLUTIONS INC (VASC)

Proprietary blood-clotting cocktail of collagen, diluent, and thrombin **85% SCALE**

Growth Performance Measurement

Years	Price	Earn.	Div.	Tot Ret
Last 1	42.0	45.7	---	42.0
Last 5	19.4	49.4	---	19.4
Last 10	31.7	---	---	31.7

(0.68) (1.02) (0.85) (0.78) (0.52) (0.16) (0.02) (0.01)
(1.00) (0.93) (0.94) (0.79) (0.66) (0.25) (0.03) (0.02)
(1.19) (0.76) (1.01) (0.78) (0.75) (0.36) (0.08) (0.01)

Copyright 2012 Securities Research Company

Bonds $.0 Mil Com 16.316 Mil BV 4.37 /sh P/E 23.58 (Ind HCSUP P/E 17.94) Ctry US

VCA ANTECH INC (WOOF)

(E) Operates chain of animal hospitals

Growth Performance Measurement

Years	Price	Earn.	Div.	Tot Ret
Last 1	6.6	-3.6	---	6.6
Last 5	-13.8	-.3	---	-13.8
Last 10	10.9	16.9	---	10.9

Adj. for
2 for 1
8/26/04

0.12
(0.04)
(0.26)

Copyright 2012 Securities Research Company

Bonds $.0 Mil Com 87.829 Mil BV 14.07 /sh P/E 15.71 (Ind HCFAC P/E 11.73) Ctry US

VEECO INSTRS INC DEL (VECO)

Beam etching, surface measurement and leak detection systems **85% SCALE**

Growth Performance Measurement

Years	Price	Earn.	Div.	Tot Ret
Last 1	41.8	-65.8	---	41.8
Last 5	12.0	38.3	---	12.0
Last 10	9.8	30.9	---	9.8

(0.06) 0.11
(0.09) (0.02)
0.13 (0.05)
(0.10)
(0.16)

Copyright 2012 Securities Research Company

Bonds $8.8 Mil Com 39.157 Mil BV 20.92 /sh P/E 15.36 (Ind SEMIQ P/E 13.46) Ctry US

VELTI PLC ST HELIER (VELT)

Provides mobile marketing and advertising solutions

Growth Performance Measurement

Years	Price	Earn.	Div.	Tot Ret
Last 1	-33.8	---	---	-33.8
Last 5	---	---	---	---
Last 10	---	---	---	---

0.17
(0.15)
(0.11)

Copyright 2012 Securities Research Company

Bonds $.0 Mil Com 64.997 Mil BV 4.65 /sh P/E 8.49 (Ind TELEQ P/E 13.72) Ctry Israel

VERISIGN INC (VRSN)

E-commerce authentication systems and services

80% SCALE

Growth Performance Measurement				
Years	Price	Earn.	Div.	Tot Ret
Last 1	8.7	26.4	---	8.7
Last 5	.6	22.9	---	.6
Last 10	17.1	9.9	---	17.1

Special $3.00   Special $2.75

Copyright 2012 Securities Research Company

Bonds $138.0 Mil Com 155.257 Mil BV -.17 /sh P/E 21.93 (Ind ITSOF P/E 19.21) Ctry US

VERASTEM INC (VSTM)

A biopharmaceutical company focusing on small molecule drugs

Growth Performance Measurement				
Years	Price	Earn.	Div.	Tot Ret
Last 1	---	---	---	---
Last 5	---	---	---	---
Last 10	---	---	---	---

(5.64)
(0.68)
(0.34)

Copyright 2012 Securities Research Company

Bonds $.0 Mil Com 21.255 Mil BV 4.50 /sh P/E N/A (Ind BIOTK P/E 17.51) Ctry US

VERENIUM CORP (VRNM)

(E)

Global leader in discovering and developing novel enzymes

45% SCALE

Growth Performance Measurement				
Years	Price	Earn.	Div.	Tot Ret
Last 1	-.9	-7.1	---	-.9
Last 5	-48.5	39.8	---	-48.5
Last 10	-32.4	21.3	---	-32.4

Merged with
Celunol Corp 6/20/07

Diversa Corp
prior to 6/20/07

Adj. for
1 for 12
9/10/09

(0.60) (7.20) (9.48) (12.00) (9.36) (9.60) (11.88) (8.16) (8.28) (15.00) (14.16) (7.40) (1.65) (0.74) (0.90)
(1.32) (5.28) (9.84) (11.16) (10.80) (9.24) (11.16) (10.44) (13.80) (15.84) (11.16) (4.27) (2.25) (0.84) (0.36)
(2.88) (2.76) (8.88) (10.32) (11.16) (8.76) (10.44) (11.40) (7.32) (11.40) (15.00) (12.60) (5.50) (2.27) (1.50) (0.36)

Copyright 2012 Securities Research Company

Bonds $2.7 Mil Com 12.783 Mil BV 3.03 /sh P/E N/A (Ind LFSCT P/E 13.82) Ctry US

VERA BRADLEY INC (VRA)

Functional accessories for women

Growth Performance Measurement				
Years	Price	Earn.	Div.	Tot Ret
Last 1	-22.2	18.8	---	-22.2
Last 5	---	---	---	---
Last 10	---	---	---	---

Copyright 2012 Securities Research Company

Bonds $.0 Mil Com 40.562 Mil BV 4.81 /sh P/E 15.89 (Ind APPRL P/E 17.01) Ctry US

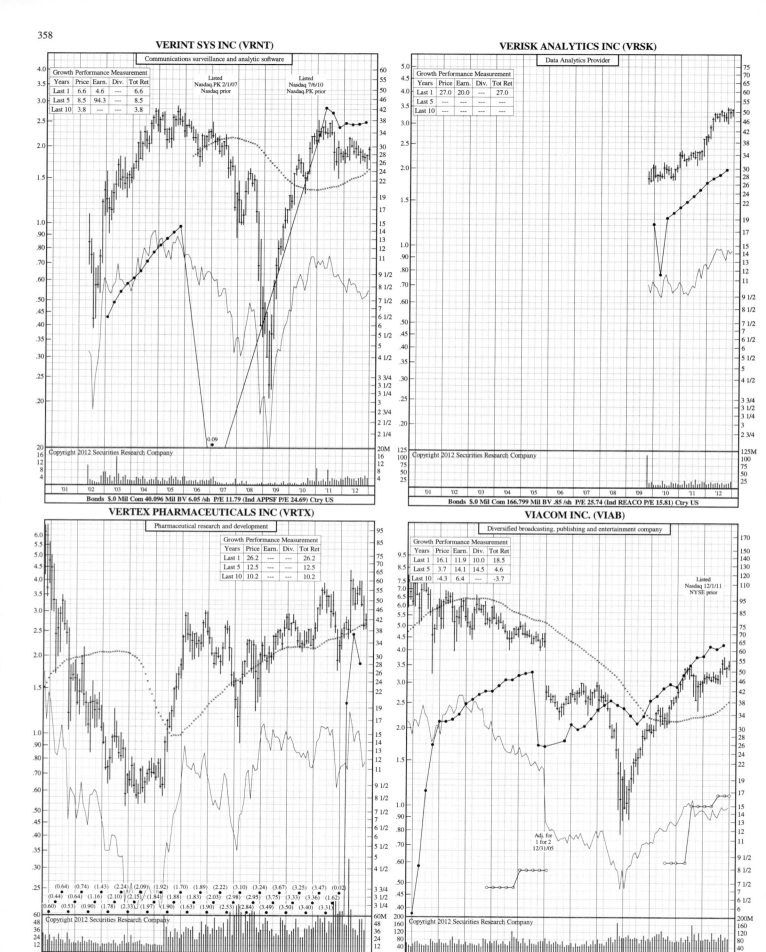

358

VERINT SYS INC (VRNT)

Communications surveillance and analytic software

Copyright 2012 Securities Research Company

Growth Performance Measurement				
Years	Price	Earn.	Div.	Tot Ret
Last 1	6.6	4.6	---	6.6
Last 5	8.5	94.3	---	8.5
Last 10	3.8	---	---	3.8

Listed
Nasdaq.PK 2/1/07
Nasdaq prior

Listed
Nasdaq 7/6/10
Nasdaq.PK prior

0.09

Bonds $.0 Mil Com 40.096 Mil BV 6.05 /sh P/E 11.79 (Ind APPSF P/E 24.69) Ctry US

VERISK ANALYTICS INC (VRSK)

Data Analytics Provider

Growth Performance Measurement				
Years	Price	Earn.	Div.	Tot Ret
Last 1	27.0	20.0	---	27.0
Last 5	---	---	---	---
Last 10	---	---	---	---

Copyright 2012 Securities Research Company

Bonds $.0 Mil Com 166.799 Mil BV .85 /sh P/E 25.74 (Ind REACO P/E 15.81) Ctry US

VERTEX PHARMACEUTICALS INC (VRTX)

Pharmaceutical research and development

Growth Performance Measurement				
Years	Price	Earn.	Div.	Tot Ret
Last 1	26.2	---	---	26.2
Last 5	12.5	---	---	12.5
Last 10	10.2	---	---	10.2

(0.64) (0.74) (1.43) (2.24) (2.09) (1.92) (1.70) (1.89) (2.22) (3.10) (3.24) (3.67) (3.25) (3.47) (0.02)
(0.44) (0.64) (1.16) (2.10) (2.15) (1.84) (1.88) (1.83) (2.03) (2.98) (2.95) (3.75) (3.33) (3.36) (1.62)
(0.60) (0.53) (0.90) (1.78) (2.33) (1.97) (1.90) (1.63) (1.90) (2.53) (2.84) (3.49) (3.50) (3.40) (3.31)

Copyright 2012 Securities Research Company

Bonds $20.0 Mil Com 216.827 Mil BV 4.75 /sh P/E 22.29 (Ind BIOTK P/E 17.51) Ctry US

VIACOM INC. (VIAB)

Diversified broadcasting, publishing and entertainment company

Growth Performance Measurement				
Years	Price	Earn.	Div.	Tot Ret
Last 1	16.1	11.9	10.0	18.5
Last 5	3.7	14.1	14.5	4.6
Last 10	-4.3	6.4	---	-3.7

Listed
Nasdaq 12/1/11
NYSE prior

Adj. for
1 for 2
12/31/05

Copyright 2012 Securities Research Company

Bonds $7584.0 Mil Com 451.026 Mil BV 14.69 /sh P/E 12.50 (Ind ENTMT P/E 15.73) Ctry US

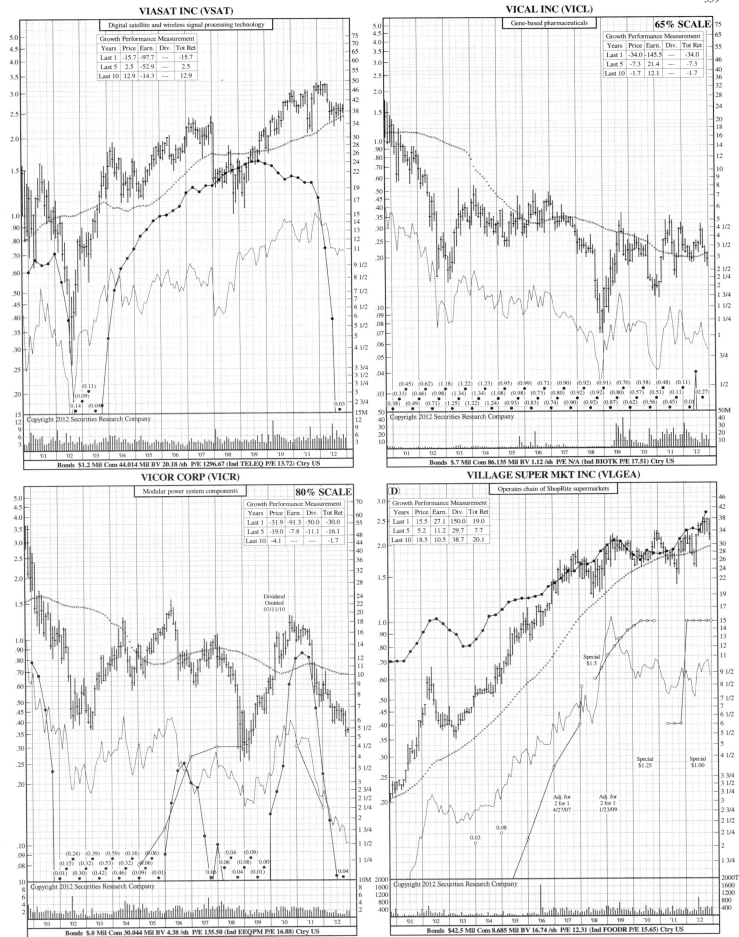

VIASAT INC (VSAT)

Digital satellite and wireless signal processing technology

Growth Performance Measurement			
Years	Price	Earn.	Div.	Tot Ret
Last 1	-15.7	-97.7	---	-15.7
Last 5	2.5	-52.9	---	2.5
Last 10	12.9	-14.3	---	12.9

(0.11)
(0.09)
0.14 0.04
0.03

Copyright 2012 Securities Research Company

Bonds $1.2 Mil Com 44.014 Mil BV 20.18 /sh P/E 1296.67 (Ind TELEQ P/E 13.72) Ctry US

VICAL INC (VICL)

Gene-based pharmaceuticals

65% SCALE

Growth Performance Measurement			
Years	Price	Earn.	Div.	Tot Ret
Last 1	-34.0	-145.5	---	-34.0
Last 5	-7.3	21.4	---	-7.3
Last 10	-1.7	12.1	---	-1.7

(0.45) (0.62) (1.18) (1.22) (1.23) (0.95) (0.99) (0.71) (0.90) (0.92) (0.91) (0.70) (0.58) (0.48) (0.11)
(0.33) (0.46) (0.98) (1.34) (1.34) (1.08) (0.98) (0.73) (0.80) (0.92) (0.92) (0.80) (0.57) (0.51) (0.11) (0.27)
(0.38) (0.49) (0.71) (1.25) (1.22) (1.24) (0.93) (0.83) (0.74) (0.90) (0.92) (0.87) (0.62) (0.56) (0.45) 0.01

Copyright 2012 Securities Research Company

Bonds $.7 Mil Com 86.135 Mil BV 1.12 /sh P/E N/A (Ind BIOTK P/E 17.51) Ctry US

VICOR CORP (VICR)

Modular power system components

80% SCALE

Growth Performance Measurement			
Years	Price	Earn.	Div.	Tot Ret
Last 1	-31.9	-91.3	-50.0	-30.0
Last 5	-19.0	-7.8	-11.1	-16.1
Last 10	-4.1	---	---	-1.7

Dividend
Omitted
03/11/10

(0.24) (0.39) (0.59) (0.16) 0.06 0.04 (0.09)
(0.15) (0.32) (0.53) (0.32) (0.06) 0.06 (0.08) 0.00
(0.01) (0.30) (0.42) (0.46) (0.09) (0.01) 0.05 0.04 (0.01) 0.04

Copyright 2012 Securities Research Company

Bonds $.0 Mil Com 30.044 Mil BV 4.38 /sh P/E 135.50 (Ind EEQPM P/E 16.88) Ctry US

(D) VILLAGE SUPER MKT INC (VLGEA)

Operates chain of ShopRite supermarkets

Growth Performance Measurement			
Years	Price	Earn.	Div.	Tot Ret
Last 1	15.5	27.1	150.0	19.0
Last 5	5.2	11.2	29.7	7.7
Last 10	18.5	10.5	38.7	20.1

Special
$1.5

Special
$1.25

Special
$1.00

Adj. for
2 for 1
4/27/07

Adj. for
2 for 1
1/23/09

0.03 0.08

Copyright 2012 Securities Research Company

Bonds $42.5 Mil Com 8.685 Mil BV 16.74 /sh P/E 12.31 (Ind FOODR P/E 15.65) Ctry US

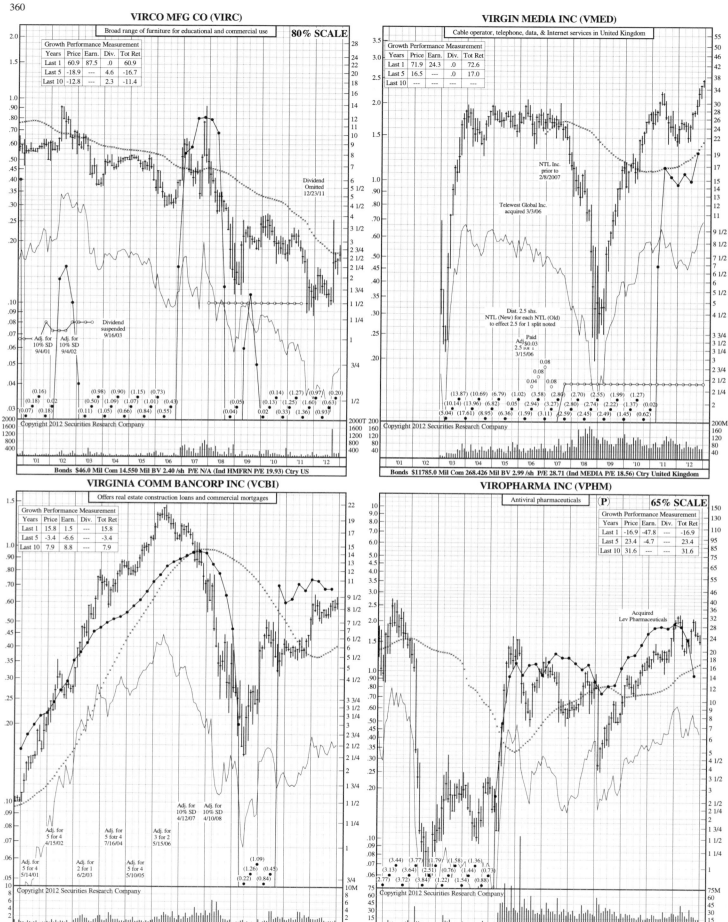

VIRCO MFG CO (VIRC)

Broad range of furniture for educational and commercial use

80% SCALE

Growth Performance Measurement				
Years	Price	Earn.	Div.	Tot Ret
Last 1	60.9	87.5	.0	60.9
Last 5	-18.9	---	4.6	-16.7
Last 10	-12.8	---	2.3	-11.4

Dividend Omitted 12/23/11

Adj. for 10% SD 9/4/01

Adj. for 10% SD 9/4/02

Dividend suspended 9/16/03

(0.16) (0.98) (0.90) (1.15) (0.73) (0.14) (1.27) (0.97) (0.20)
(0.18) 0.02 (0.50) (1.09) (1.07) (1.01) (0.43) (0.13) (1.25) (1.60) (0.63)
(0.07) (0.18) (0.11) (1.05) (0.66) (0.84) (0.55) (0.04) 0.02 (0.33) (1.36) (0.93) 0.05

Copyright 2012 Securities Research Company

Bonds $46.0 Mil Com 14.550 Mil BV 2.40 /sh P/E N/A (Ind HMFRN P/E 19.93) Ctry US

VIRGIN MEDIA INC (VMED)

Cable operator, telephone, data, & Internet services in United Kingdom

Growth Performance Measurement				
Years	Price	Earn.	Div.	Tot Ret
Last 1	71.9	24.3	.0	72.6
Last 5	16.5	---	.0	17.0
Last 10	---	---	---	---

NTL Inc. prior to 2/8/2007

Telewest Global Inc. acquired 3/3/06

Dist. 2.5 shs.
NTL (New) for each NTL (Old) to effect 2.5 for 1 split noted

Adj Paid
2.5 for 1 $0.03
3/15/06

0.08
0.08
0.04 0.08

(13.87) (10.69) (6.79) (1.02) (3.58) (2.80) (2.70) (2.55) (1.99) (1.27)
(10.14) (13.96) (6.82) (0.05) (2.94) (3.27) (2.80) (2.74) (2.22) (1.37) (0.02)
(5.04) (17.61) (8.95) (6.36) (1.59) (3.11) (2.59) (2.45) (2.49) (1.45) (0.62)

Copyright 2012 Securities Research Company

Bonds $11785.0 Mil Com 268.426 Mil BV 2.99 /sh P/E 28.71 (Ind MEDIA P/E 18.56) Ctry United Kingdom

VIRGINIA COMM BANCORP INC (VCBI)

Offers real estate construction loans and commercial mortgages

Growth Performance Measurement				
Years	Price	Earn.	Div.	Tot Ret
Last 1	15.8	1.5	---	15.8
Last 5	-3.4	-6.6	---	-3.4
Last 10	7.9	8.8	---	7.9

Adj. for 10% SD 4/12/07

Adj. for 10% SD 4/10/08

Adj. for 5 for 4 4/15/02

Adj. for 5 fotr 4 7/16/04

Adj. for 3 for 2 5/15/06

Adj. for 5 for 4 5/14/01

Adj. for 2 for 1 6/2/03

Adj. for 5 for 4 5/10/05

(1.09)
(1.26) (0.45)
(0.22) (0.84)

Copyright 2012 Securities Research Company

Bonds $.0 Mil Com 30.825 Mil BV 7.64 /sh P/E 13.16 (Ind RBANK P/E 10.51) Ctry US

VIROPHARMA INC (VPHM)

Antiviral pharmaceuticals **(P)** **65% SCALE**

Growth Performance Measurement				
Years	Price	Earn.	Div.	Tot Ret
Last 1	-16.9	-47.8	---	-16.9
Last 5	23.4	-4.7	---	23.4
Last 10	31.6	---	---	31.6

Acquired Lev Pharmaceuticals

(3.44) (3.77) (1.79) (1.58) (1.36)
(3.13) (3.64) (2.51) (0.76) (1.44) (0.73)
(2.77) (3.72) (3.84) (1.22) (1.54) (0.88)

Copyright 2012 Securities Research Company

Bonds $.5 Mil Com 65.908 Mil BV 11.87 /sh P/E 23.96 (Ind DRUGS P/E 12.73) Ctry US

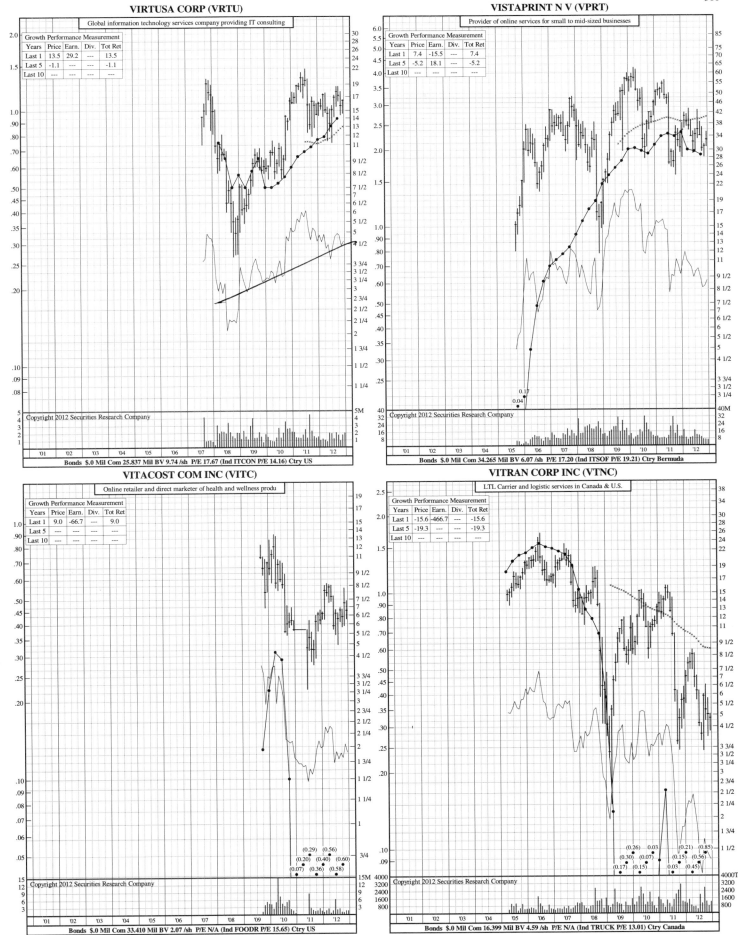

VIRTUSA CORP (VRTU)
Global information technology services company providing IT consulting

Growth Performance Measurement				
Years	Price	Earn.	Div.	Tot Ret
Last 1	13.5	29.2	---	13.5
Last 5	-1.1	---	---	-1.1
Last 10	---	---	---	---

Copyright 2012 Securities Research Company

Bonds $.0 Mil Com 25.837 Mil BV 9.74 /sh P/E 17.67 (Ind ITCON P/E 14.16) Ctry US

VISTAPRINT N V (VPRT)
Provider of online services for small to mid-sized businesses

Growth Performance Measurement				
Years	Price	Earn.	Div.	Tot Ret
Last 1	7.4	-15.5	---	7.4
Last 5	-5.2	18.1	---	-5.2
Last 10	---	---	---	---

0.17
0.04

Copyright 2012 Securities Research Company

Bonds $.0 Mil Com 34.265 Mil BV 6.07 /sh P/E 17.20 (Ind ITSOF P/E 19.21) Ctry Bermuda

VITACOST COM INC (VITC)
Online retailer and direct marketer of health and wellness produ

Growth Performance Measurement				
Years	Price	Earn.	Div.	Tot Ret
Last 1	9.0	-66.7	---	9.0
Last 5	---	---	---	---
Last 10	---	---	---	---

(0.29) (0.56)
(0.20) (0.40) (0.60)
(0.07) (0.36) (0.58)

Copyright 2012 Securities Research Company

Bonds $.0 Mil Com 33.410 Mil BV 2.07 /sh P/E N/A (Ind FOODR P/E 15.65) Ctry US

VITRAN CORP INC (VTNC)
LTL Carrier and logistic services in Canada & U.S.

Growth Performance Measurement				
Years	Price	Earn.	Div.	Tot Ret
Last 1	-15.6	-466.7	---	-15.6
Last 5	-19.3	---	---	-19.3
Last 10	---	---	---	---

(0.26) 0.03 (0.21) (0.85)
(0.30) (0.07) (0.15) (0.56)
(0.17) (0.15) 0.03 (0.45)

Copyright 2012 Securities Research Company

Bonds $.0 Mil Com 16.399 Mil BV 4.59 /sh P/E N/A (Ind TRUCK P/E 13.01) Ctry Canada

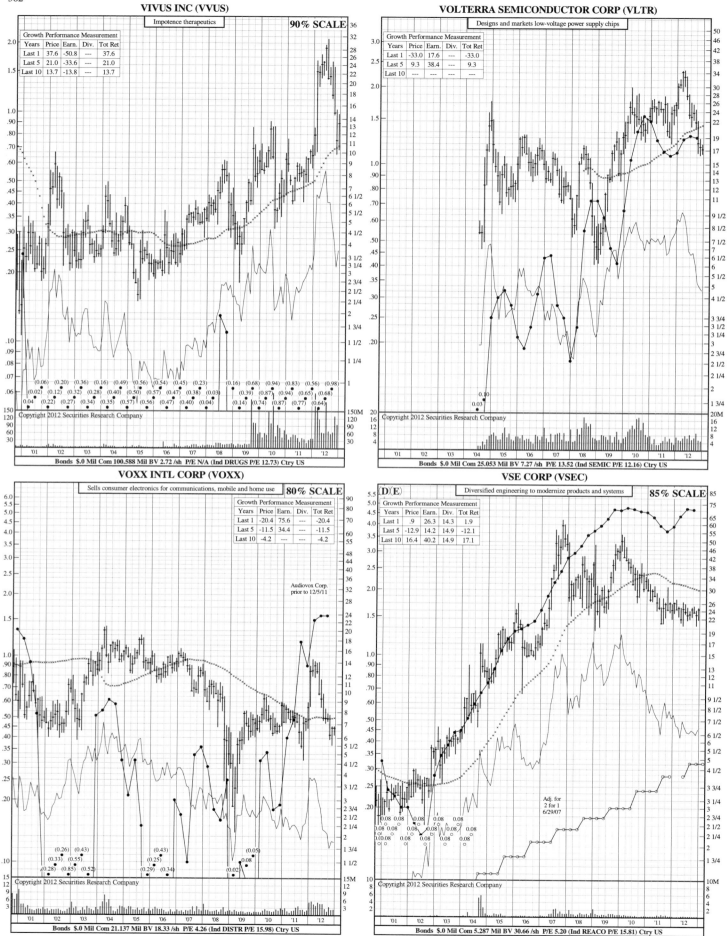

362

VIVUS INC (VVUS)

Impotence therapeutics

90% SCALE

Growth Performance Measurement

Years	Price	Earn.	Div.	Tot Ret
Last 1	37.6	-50.8	---	37.6
Last 5	21.0	-33.6	---	21.0
Last 10	13.7	-13.8	---	13.7

(0.06) (0.20) (0.36) (0.16) (0.49) (0.56) (0.54) (0.45) (0.23)   (0.16) (0.68) (0.94) (0.83) (0.56) (0.98)
(0.02) (0.12) (0.32) (0.28) (0.40) (0.50) (0.57) (0.47) (0.38) (0.03)   (0.39) (0.87) (0.94) (0.65) (0.68)
0.04 (0.22) (0.27) (0.34) (0.35) (0.57) (0.56) (0.47) (0.40) (0.04)   (0.14) (0.74) (0.87) (0.77) (0.64)

Copyright 2012 Securities Research Company

Bonds $.0 Mil Com 100.588 Mil BV 2.72 /sh P/E N/A (Ind DRUGS P/E 12.73) Ctry US

VOLTERRA SEMICONDUCTOR CORP (VLTR)

Designs and markets low-voltage power supply chips

Growth Performance Measurement

Years	Price	Earn.	Div.	Tot Ret
Last 1	-33.0	17.6	---	-33.0
Last 5	9.3	38.4	---	9.3
Last 10	---	---	---	---

0.10
0.03

Copyright 2012 Securities Research Company

Bonds $.0 Mil Com 25.053 Mil BV 7.27 /sh P/E 13.52 (Ind SEMIC P/E 12.16) Ctry US

VOXX INTL CORP (VOXX)

Sells consumer electronics for communications, mobile and home use

80% SCALE

Growth Performance Measurement

Years	Price	Earn.	Div.	Tot Ret
Last 1	-20.4	75.6	---	-20.4
Last 5	-11.5	34.4	---	-11.5
Last 10	-4.2	---	---	-4.2

Audiovox Corp.
prior to 12/5/11

(0.26) (0.43)   (0.43)   (0.05)
(0.33) (0.55)   (0.25)   0.08
(0.28) (0.85) (0.52)   (0.29) (0.34)   (0.02)

Copyright 2012 Securities Research Company

Bonds $.0 Mil Com 21.137 Mil BV 18.33 /sh P/E 4.26 (Ind DISTR P/E 15.98) Ctry US

VSE CORP (VSEC)

(D)(E)

Diversified engineering to modernize products and systems

85% SCALE

Growth Performance Measurement

Years	Price	Earn.	Div.	Tot Ret
Last 1	.9	26.3	14.3	1.9
Last 5	-12.9	14.2	14.9	-12.1
Last 10	16.4	40.2	14.9	17.1

Adj. for
2 for 1
6/29/07

0.08 0.08 0.08 0.08 0.08
0.08   0.08   0.08 0.08
0.0 0.08   0.08   0.08

Copyright 2012 Securities Research Company

Bonds $.0 Mil Com 5.287 Mil BV 30.66 /sh P/E 5.20 (Ind REACO P/E 15.81) Ctry US

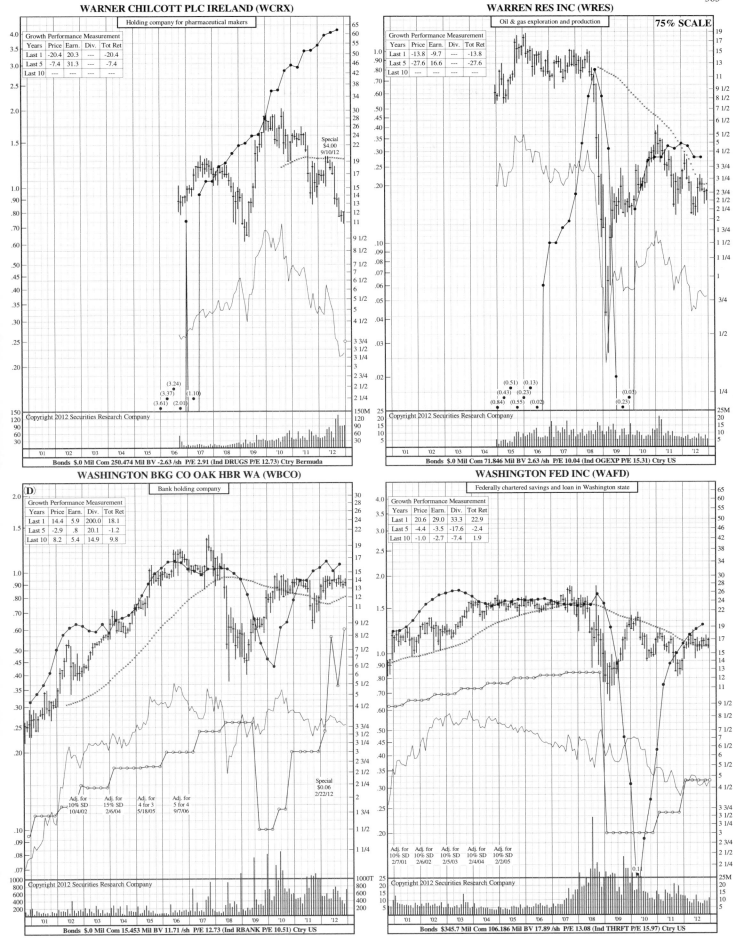

WARNER CHILCOTT PLC IRELAND (WCRX)

Holding company for pharmaceutical makers

Growth Performance Measurement				
Years	Price	Earn.	Div.	Tot Ret
Last 1	-20.4	20.3	---	-20.4
Last 5	-7.4	31.3	---	-7.4
Last 10	---	---	---	---

Special $4.00 9/10/12

(3.24)
(3.37)   (1.10)
(3.61) (2.01)

Copyright 2012 Securities Research Company

Bonds $.0 Mil Com 250.474 Mil BV -2.63 /sh P/E 2.91 (Ind DRUGS P/E 12.73) Ctry Bermuda

WARREN RES INC (WRES)

Oil & gas exploration and production

75% SCALE

Growth Performance Measurement				
Years	Price	Earn.	Div.	Tot Ret
Last 1	-13.8	-9.7	---	-13.8
Last 5	-27.6	16.6	---	-27.6
Last 10	---	---	---	---

(0.51)   (0.13)
(0.43) (0.23)   (0.03)
(0.84) (0.55) (0.02)   (0.23)

Copyright 2012 Securities Research Company

Bonds $.0 Mil Com 71.846 Mil BV 2.63 /sh P/E 10.04 (Ind OGEXP P/E 15.31) Ctry US

WASHINGTON BKG CO OAK HBR WA (WBCO)

(D)

Bank holding company

Growth Performance Measurement				
Years	Price	Earn.	Div.	Tot Ret
Last 1	14.4	5.9	200.0	18.1
Last 5	-2.9	.8	20.1	-1.2
Last 10	8.2	5.4	14.9	9.8

Special $0.06 2/22/12

Adj. for 10% SD 10/4/02

Adj. for 15% SD 2/6/04

Adj. for 4 for 3 5/18/05

Adj. for 5 for 4 9/7/06

Copyright 2012 Securities Research Company

Bonds $.0 Mil Com 15.453 Mil BV 11.71 /sh P/E 12.73 (Ind RBANK P/E 10.51) Ctry US

WASHINGTON FED INC (WAFD)

Federally chartered savings and loan in Washington state

Growth Performance Measurement				
Years	Price	Earn.	Div.	Tot Ret
Last 1	20.6	29.0	33.3	22.9
Last 5	-4.4	-3.5	-17.6	-2.4
Last 10	-1.0	-2.7	-7.4	1.9

Adj. for 10% SD 2/7/01

Adj. for 10% SD 2/6/02

Adj. for 10% SD 2/5/03

Adj. for 10% SD 2/4/04

Adj. for 10% SD 2/2/05

0.1

Copyright 2012 Securities Research Company

Bonds $345.7 Mil Com 106.186 Mil BV 17.89 /sh P/E 13.08 (Ind THRFT P/E 15.97) Ctry US

WASHINGTON TR BANCORP (WASH)

Bank holding company

Growth Performance Measurement				
Years	Price	Earn.	Div.	Tot Ret
Last 1	10.3	18.2	9.1	14.1
Last 5	.8	2.6	3.7	4.1
Last 10	3.0	4.7	5.5	5.8

Copyright 2012 Securities Research Company

Bonds $138.8 Mil Com 16.371 Mil BV 18.20 /sh P/E 12.65 (Ind RBANK P/E 10.51) Ctry US

WAYSIDE TECHNOLOGY GROUP INC (WSTG)

Design and programming software

Growth Performance Measurement				
Years	Price	Earn.	Div.	Tot Ret
Last 1	-9.1	8.9	.0	-3.9
Last 5	4.3	8.5	1.3	9.5
Last 10	18.9	---	---	23.7

Programmer's Paradise, Inc
prior to 8/22/06

(3.49) (0.79) (0.01)
(3.59) (0.84) (0.55) (0.06)
(3.70) (3.49) (0.59) (0.02)

Copyright 2012 Securities Research Company

Bonds $.0 Mil Com 4.762 Mil BV 6.47 /sh P/E 9.09 (Ind APPSF P/E 24.69) Ctry US

WD-40 CO (WDFC)

Produces WD-40 lubricant and rust preventive

Growth Performance Measurement				
Years	Price	Earn.	Div.	Tot Ret
Last 1	16.6	8.4	7.4	19.5
Last 5	4.4	3.4	3.0	6.6
Last 10	6.0	4.0	3.8	7.9

Copyright 2012 Securities Research Company

Bonds $9.5 Mil Com 15.716 Mil BV 11.82 /sh P/E 21.41 (Ind HSHLD P/E 17.60) Ctry US

WEB COM GROUP INC (WWWW)

Provides Web site building software, custom design consulting & more

Growth Performance Measurement				
Years	Price	Earn.	Div.	Tot Ret
Last 1	29.3	42.0	---	29.3
Last 5	5.0	21.8	---	5.0
Last 10	---	---	---	---

0.03

Copyright 2012 Securities Research Company

Bonds $.2 Mil Com 49.130 Mil BV 4.29 /sh P/E 10.42 (Ind ITSOF P/E 19.21) Ctry US

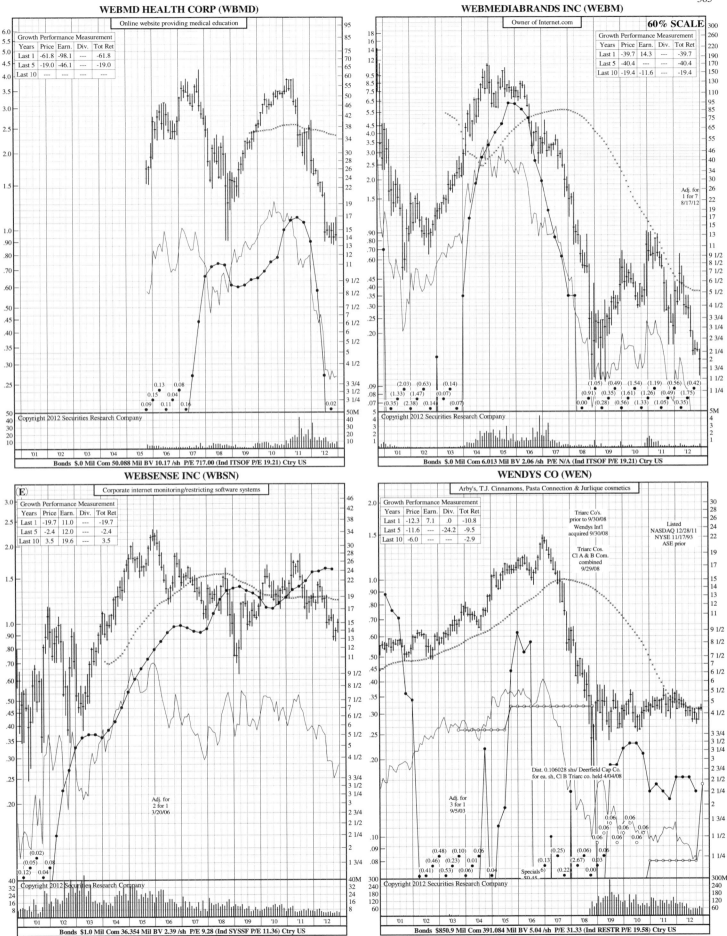

WEBMD HEALTH CORP (WBMD)

Online website providing medical education

Growth Performance Measurement				
Years	Price	Earn.	Div.	Tot Ret
Last 1	-61.8	-98.1	---	-61.8
Last 5	-19.0	-46.1	---	-19.0
Last 10	---	---	---	---

Copyright 2012 Securities Research Company

Bonds $.0 Mil Com 50.088 Mil BV 10.17 /sh P/E 717.00 (Ind ITSOF P/E 19.21) Ctry US

WEBMEDIABRANDS INC (WEBM)

Owner of Internet.com

60% SCALE

Growth Performance Measurement				
Years	Price	Earn.	Div.	Tot Ret
Last 1	-39.7	14.3	---	-39.7
Last 5	-40.4	---	---	-40.4
Last 10	-19.4	-11.6	---	-19.4

Adj. for
1 for 7
8/17/12

Copyright 2012 Securities Research Company

Bonds $.0 Mil Com 6.013 Mil BV 2.06 /sh P/E N/A (Ind ITSOF P/E 19.21) Ctry US

WEBSENSE INC (WBSN)

(E)

Corporate internet monitoring/restricting software systems

Growth Performance Measurement				
Years	Price	Earn.	Div.	Tot Ret
Last 1	-19.7	11.0	---	-19.7
Last 5	-2.4	12.0	---	-2.4
Last 10	3.5	19.6	---	3.5

Adj. for
2 for 1
3/20/06

Copyright 2012 Securities Research Company

Bonds $1.0 Mil Com 36.354 Mil BV 2.39 /sh P/E 9.28 (Ind SYSSF P/E 11.36) Ctry US

WENDYS CO (WEN)

Arby's, T.J. Cinnamons, Pasta Connection & Jurlique cosmetics

Growth Performance Measurement				
Years	Price	Earn.	Div.	Tot Ret
Last 1	-12.3	7.1	.0	-10.8
Last 5	-11.6	---	-24.2	-9.5
Last 10	-6.0	---	---	-2.9

Triarc Co's.
prior to 9/30/08
Wendys Int'l
acquired 9/30/08

Triarc Cos.
Cl A & B Com.
combined
9/29/08

Listed
NASDAQ 12/28/11
NYSE 11/17/93
ASE prior

Dist. 0.106028 shs/ Deerfield Cap Co.
for ea. sh, Cl B Triarc co. held 4/04/08

Adj. for
3 for 1
9/5/03

Specials
$0.45

Copyright 2012 Securities Research Company

Bonds $850.9 Mil Com 391.084 Mil BV 5.04 /sh P/E 31.33 (Ind RESTR P/E 19.58) Ctry US

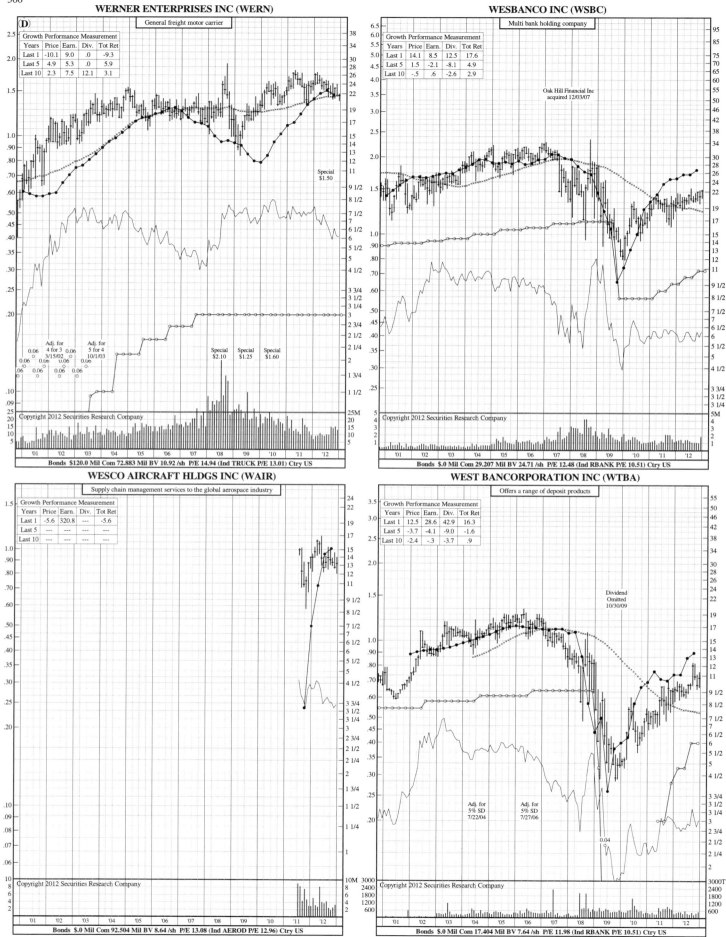

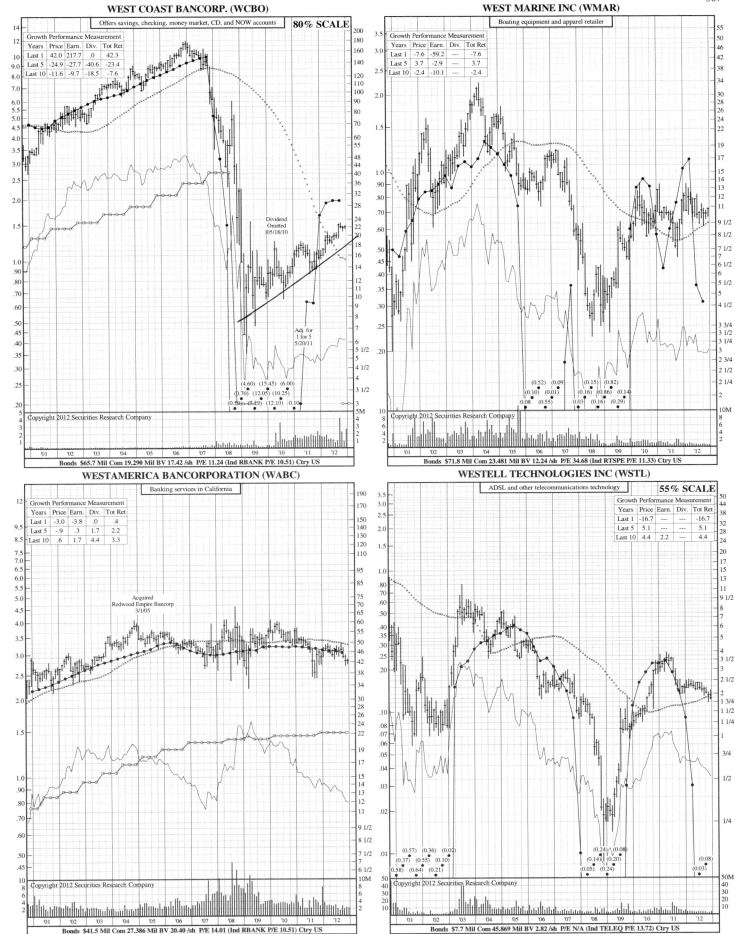

367

WEST COAST BANCORP. (WCBO)

Offers savings, checking, money market, CD, and NOW accounts

80% SCALE

Growth Performance Measurement

Years	Price	Earn.	Div.	Tot Ret
Last 1	42.0	217.7	.0	42.3
Last 5	-24.9	-27.7	-40.6	-23.4
Last 10	-11.6	-9.7	-18.5	-7.6

Dividend
Omitted
05/18/10

Adj. for
1 for 5
5/20/11

(4.60) (15.45) (6.00)
(0.70) (12.05) (10.25)
(0.99) (7.55) (12.10) -0.10

Copyright 2012 Securities Research Company

Bonds $65.7 Mil Com 19.290 Mil BV 17.42 /sh P/E 11.24 (Ind RBANK P/E 10.51) Ctry US

WEST MARINE INC (WMAR)

Boating equipment and apparel retailer

Growth Performance Measurement

Years	Price	Earn.	Div.	Tot Ret
Last 1	-7.6	-59.2	---	-7.6
Last 5	3.7	-2.9	---	3.7
Last 10	-2.4	-10.1	---	-2.4

(0.52) (0.09)   (0.15) (0.82)
(0.10) (0.01)   (0.16) (0.86) (0.14)
0.08 (0.55)   0.03 (0.16) (0.29)

Copyright 2012 Securities Research Company

Bonds $71.8 Mil Com 23.481 Mil BV 12.24 /sh P/E 34.68 (Ind RTSPE P/E 11.33) Ctry US

WESTAMERICA BANCORPORATION (WABC)

Banking services in California

Growth Performance Measurement

Years	Price	Earn.	Div.	Tot Ret
Last 1	-3.0	-3.8	.0	.4
Last 5	-.9	.3	1.7	2.2
Last 10	.6	1.7	4.4	3.3

Acquired
Redwood Empire Bancorp
3/1/05

Copyright 2012 Securities Research Company

Bonds $41.5 Mil Com 27.386 Mil BV 20.40 /sh P/E 14.01 (Ind RBANK P/E 10.51) Ctry US

WESTELL TECHNOLOGIES INC (WSTL)

ADSL and other telecommunications technology

55% SCALE

Growth Performance Measurement

Years	Price	Earn.	Div.	Tot Ret
Last 1	-16.7	---	---	-16.7
Last 5	5.1	---	---	5.1
Last 10	4.4	2.2	---	4.4

(0.57) (0.36) (0.02)   (0.24) (0.08)
(0.37) (0.55) (0.10)   (0.14) (0.20)   (0.08)
(0.58) (0.64) (0.21)   (0.05) (0.24)   (0.03)

Copyright 2012 Securities Research Company

Bonds $7.7 Mil Com 45.869 Mil BV 2.82 /sh P/E N/A (Ind TELEQ P/E 13.72) Ctry US

368

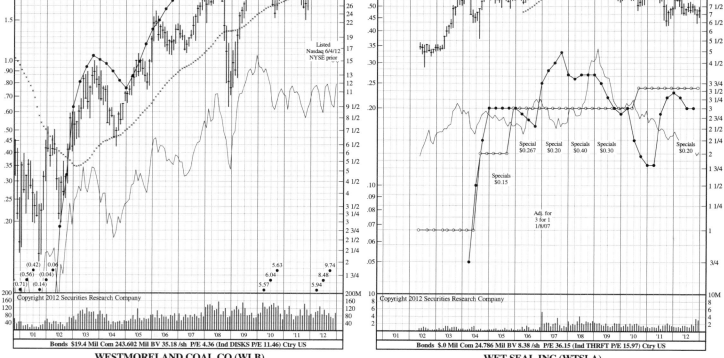

WESTERN DIGITAL CORP (WDC)

Computer management and control devices

90% SCALE

Growth Performance Measurement				
Years	Price	Earn.	Div.	Tot Ret
Last 1	37.3	175.9	---	38.1
Last 5	7.1	34.4	---	7.2
Last 10	20.9	40.7	---	20.9

Listed
Nasdaq 6/4/12
NYSE prior

(0.42) 0.06
(0.56) (0.04)
(0.71) (0.14)

5.63   9.74
6.04   8.48
5.57   5.94

Copyright 2012 Securities Research Company

Bonds $19.4 Mil Com 243.602 Mil BV 35.18 /sh P/E 4.36 (Ind DISKS P/E 11.46) Ctry US

WESTFIELD FINANCIAL INC. (WFD)

Operates as the holding company for Westfield Bank

Growth Performance Measurement				
Years	Price	Earn.	Div.	Tot Ret
Last 1	-1.8	-9.1	.0	1.5
Last 5	-5.7	-9.5	3.7	-3.0
Last 10	3.4	---	13.7	5.8

Special   Special   Specials   Specials   Specials
$0.267 $0.20 $0.40 $0.30 $0.20

Specials
$0.15

Adj. for
3 for 1
1/8/07

Copyright 2012 Securities Research Company

Bonds $.0 Mil Com 24.786 Mil BV 8.38 /sh P/E 36.15 (Ind THRFT P/E 15.97) Ctry US

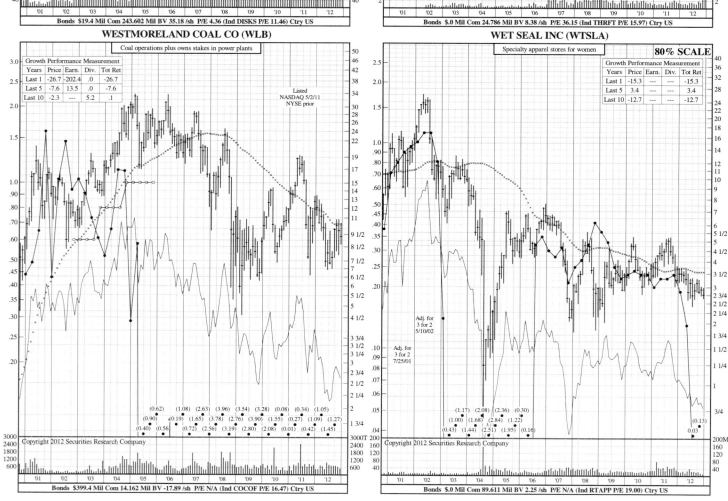

WESTMORELAND COAL CO (WLB)

Coal operations plus owns stakes in power plants

Growth Performance Measurement				
Years	Price	Earn.	Div.	Tot Ret
Last 1	-26.7	-202.4	.0	-26.7
Last 5	-7.6	13.5	.0	-7.6
Last 10	-2.3	---	5.2	.1

Listed
NASDAQ 5/2/11
NYSE prior

(0.62)   (1.08) (2.63) (3.96) (3.54) (3.28) (0.08) (0.34) (1.05)
(0.90) (0.19) (1.65) (3.78) (2.76) (3.90) (1.55) (0.27) (1.09) (1.27)
(0.40) (0.56) (0.72) (2.56) (3.19) (2.80) (2.08) (0.01) (0.42) (1.45)

Copyright 2012 Securities Research Company

Bonds $399.4 Mil Com 14.162 Mil BV -17.89 /sh P/E N/A (Ind COCOF P/E 16.47) Ctry US

WET SEAL INC (WTSLA)

Specialty apparel stores for women

80% SCALE

Growth Performance Measurement				
Years	Price	Earn.	Div.	Tot Ret
Last 1	-15.3	---	---	-15.3
Last 5	3.4	---	---	3.4
Last 10	-12.7	---	---	-12.7

Adj. for
3 for 2
5/10/02

Adj. for
3 for 2
7/25/01

(1.17) (2.08) (2.36) (0.30)
(1.00) (1.68) (2.84) (1.22)
(0.43) (1.44) (2.51) (1.95) (0.16)   (0.13)
                                                                    0.03

Copyright 2012 Securities Research Company

Bonds $.0 Mil Com 89.611 Mil BV 2.25 /sh P/E N/A (Ind RTAPP P/E 19.00) Ctry US

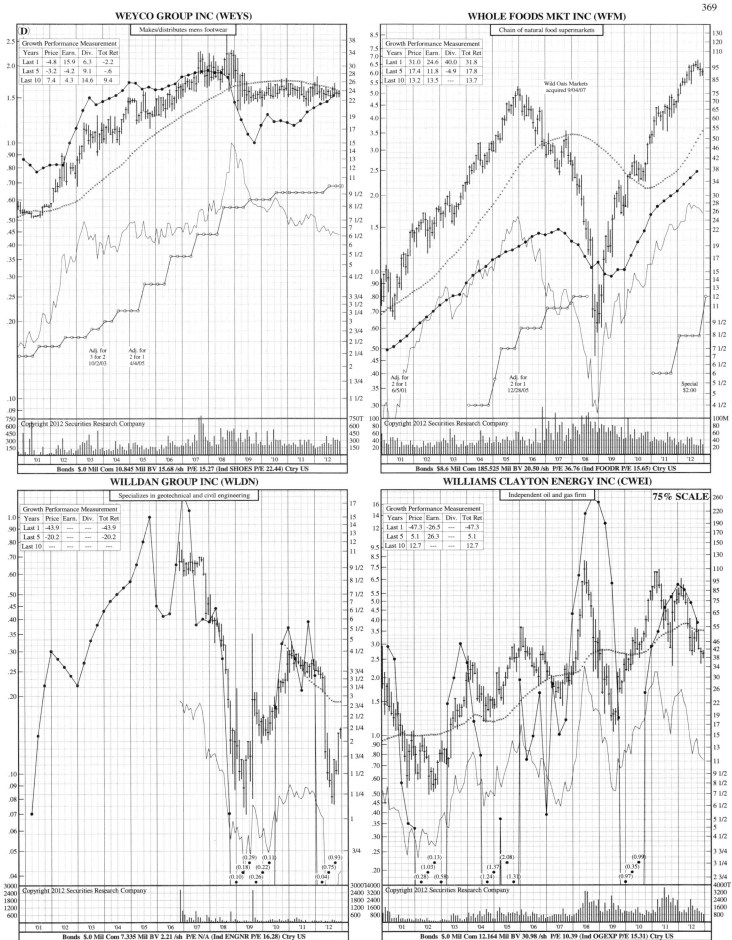

WEYCO GROUP INC (WEYS)
Makes/distributes mens footwear

(D)

Growth Performance Measurement				
Years	Price	Earn.	Div.	Tot Ret
Last 1	-4.8	15.9	6.3	-2.2
Last 5	-3.2	-4.2	9.1	-.6
Last 10	7.4	4.3	14.6	9.4

Adj. for 3 for 2 10/2/03

Adj. for 2 for 1 4/4/05

Copyright 2012 Securities Research Company

Bonds $.0 Mil Com 10.845 Mil BV 15.68 /sh P/E 15.27 (Ind SHOES P/E 22.44) Ctry US

WHOLE FOODS MKT INC (WFM)
Chain of natural food supermarkets

Growth Performance Measurement				
Years	Price	Earn.	Div.	Tot Ret
Last 1	31.0	24.6	40.0	31.8
Last 5	17.4	11.8	-4.9	17.8
Last 10	13.2	13.5	---	13.7

Wild Oats Markets acquired 9/04/07

Adj. for 2 for 1 6/5/01

Adj. for 2 for 1 12/28/05

Special $2.00

Copyright 2012 Securities Research Company

Bonds $8.6 Mil Com 185.525 Mil BV 20.50 /sh P/E 36.76 (Ind FOODR P/E 15.65) Ctry US

WILLDAN GROUP INC (WLDN)
Specializes in geotechnical and civil engineering

Growth Performance Measurement				
Years	Price	Earn.	Div.	Tot Ret
Last 1	-43.9	---	---	-43.9
Last 5	-20.2	---	---	-20.2
Last 10	---	---	---	---

(0.29) (0.11)
(0.18) (0.22)
(0.10) (0.26)

(0.93)
(0.75)
(0.04)

Copyright 2012 Securities Research Company

Bonds $.0 Mil Com 7.335 Mil BV 2.21 /sh P/E N/A (Ind ENGNR P/E 16.28) Ctry US

WILLIAMS CLAYTON ENERGY INC (CWEI)
Independent oil and gas firm

75% SCALE

Growth Performance Measurement				
Years	Price	Earn.	Div.	Tot Ret
Last 1	-47.3	-26.5	---	-47.3
Last 5	5.1	26.3	---	5.1
Last 10	12.7	---	---	12.7

(0.13)
(1.03)
(0.28) (0.58)

(2.08)
(1.37)
(1.24) (1.31)

(0.99)
(0.35)
(0.97)

Copyright 2012 Securities Research Company

Bonds $.0 Mil Com 12.164 Mil BV 30.98 /sh P/E 10.39 (Ind OGEXP P/E 15.31) Ctry US

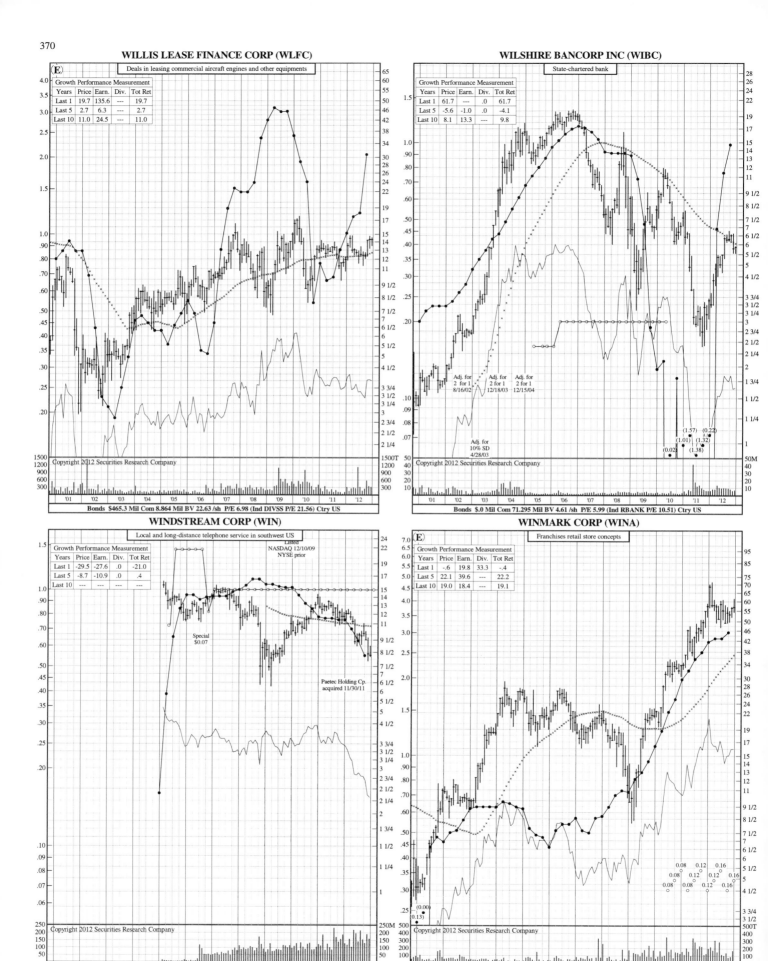

WILLIS LEASE FINANCE CORP (WLFC)

(E) Deals in leasing commercial aircraft engines and other equipments

Growth Performance Measurement

Years	Price	Earn.	Div.	Tot Ret
Last 1	19.7	135.6	---	19.7
Last 5	2.7	6.3	---	2.7
Last 10	11.0	24.5	---	11.0

Copyright 2012 Securities Research Company

Bonds $465.3 Mil Com 8.864 Mil BV 22.63 /sh P/E 6.98 (Ind DIVSS P/E 21.56) Ctry US

WILSHIRE BANCORP INC (WIBC)

State-chartered bank

Growth Performance Measurement

Years	Price	Earn.	Div.	Tot Ret
Last 1	61.7	---	.0	61.7
Last 5	-5.6	-1.0	.0	-4.1
Last 10	8.1	13.3	---	9.8

Adj. for
2 for 1
8/16/02

Adj. for
2 for 1
12/18/03

Adj. for
2 for 1
12/15/04

Adj. for
10% SD
4/28/03

(1.57) (0.22)
(1.01) (1.32)
(0.02) (1.38)

Copyright 2012 Securities Research Company

Bonds $.0 Mil Com 71.295 Mil BV 4.61 /sh P/E 5.99 (Ind RBANK P/E 10.51) Ctry US

WINDSTREAM CORP (WIN)

Local and long-distance telephone service in southwest US

Listed
NASDAQ 12/10/09
NYSE prior

Growth Performance Measurement

Years	Price	Earn.	Div.	Tot Ret
Last 1	-29.5	-27.6	.0	-21.0
Last 5	-8.7	-10.9	.0	.4
Last 10	---	---	---	---

Special
$0.07

Paetec Holding Cp.
acquired 11/30/11

Copyright 2012 Securities Research Company

Bonds $5456.2 Mil Com 588.127 Mil BV 2.12 /sh P/E 15.05 (Ind PHONE P/E 15.99) Ctry US

WINMARK CORP (WINA)

(E) Franchises retail store concepts

Growth Performance Measurement

Years	Price	Earn.	Div.	Tot Ret
Last 1	-.6	19.8	33.3	-.4
Last 5	22.1	39.6	---	22.2
Last 10	19.0	18.4	---	19.1

0.08 0.12 0.16
0.08 0.12 0.12 0.16
0.08 0.08 0.12 0.16

(0.00)
0.13

Copyright 2012 Securities Research Company

Bonds $12.1 Mil Com 4.987 Mil BV 3.42 /sh P/E 18.87 (Ind RTSPE P/E 11.33) Ctry US

WINTRUST FINANCIAL CORP (WTFC)

Multibank holding company engaged in business and real estate loans

Growth Performance Measurement				
Years	Price	Earn.	Div.	Tot Ret
Last 1	30.8	36.6	.0	31.5
Last 5	2.1	-2.6	-8.5	2.8
Last 10	1.6	3.9	6.8	2.2

Adj. for
3 for 2
3/15/02

0.05
0.09
0.12
0.16
(0.06)
(0.35)
(1.11) 0.3

Copyright 2012 Securities Research Company

Bonds $.0 Mil Com 36.441 Mil BV 43.53 /sh P/E 17.56 (Ind RBANK P/E 10.51) Ctry US

WIRELESS RONIN TECHNOLOGIES (RNIN)

Electronic display products

75% SCALE

Growth Performance Measurement				
Years	Price	Earn.	Div.	Tot Ret
Last 1	-66.7	32.4	---	-66.7
Last 5	-32.8	39.5	---	-32.8
Last 10	---	---	---	---

Adj. for
1 for 5
12/17/12

(24.20) (3.95) (5.90) (5.10) (2.90) (1.90) (1.70) (1.15)
(37.80) (4.05) (5.95) (5.80) (3.20) (2.10) (1.70) (1.30)
(48.55) (14.20) (5.20) (6.60) (3.40) (2.35) (1.65) (1.40)

Copyright 2012 Securities Research Company

Bonds $.0 Mil Com 4.998 Mil BV .69 /sh P/E N/A (Ind ELEEQ P/E 15.50) Ctry US

WOODWARD INC (WWD)

Makes hydromechanical & electronic fuel controls/delivery systems

Growth Performance Measurement				
Years	Price	Earn.	Div.	Tot Ret
Last 1	-6.8	4.7	14.3	-6.1
Last 5	2.3	9.5	7.8	3.0
Last 10	18.1	11.2	7.5	18.7

Adj. for
3 for 1
2/15/06

Adj. for
2 for 1
2/15/08

Copyright 2012 Securities Research Company

Bonds $139.0 Mil Com 68.427 Mil BV 14.67 /sh P/E 18.97 (Ind MACHN P/E 14.49) Ctry US

WORLD ACCEP CORP DEL (WRLD)

Short-term loans, tax preparation, other financial services

(P)E

Growth Performance Measurement				
Years	Price	Earn.	Div.	Tot Ret
Last 1	1.4	19.4	---	1.4
Last 5	22.5	21.0	---	22.5
Last 10	25.6	20.2	---	25.6

Copyright 2012 Securities Research Company

Bonds $78.4 Mil Com 12.925 Mil BV 34.07 /sh P/E 10.37 (Ind FINAN P/E 11.42) Ctry US

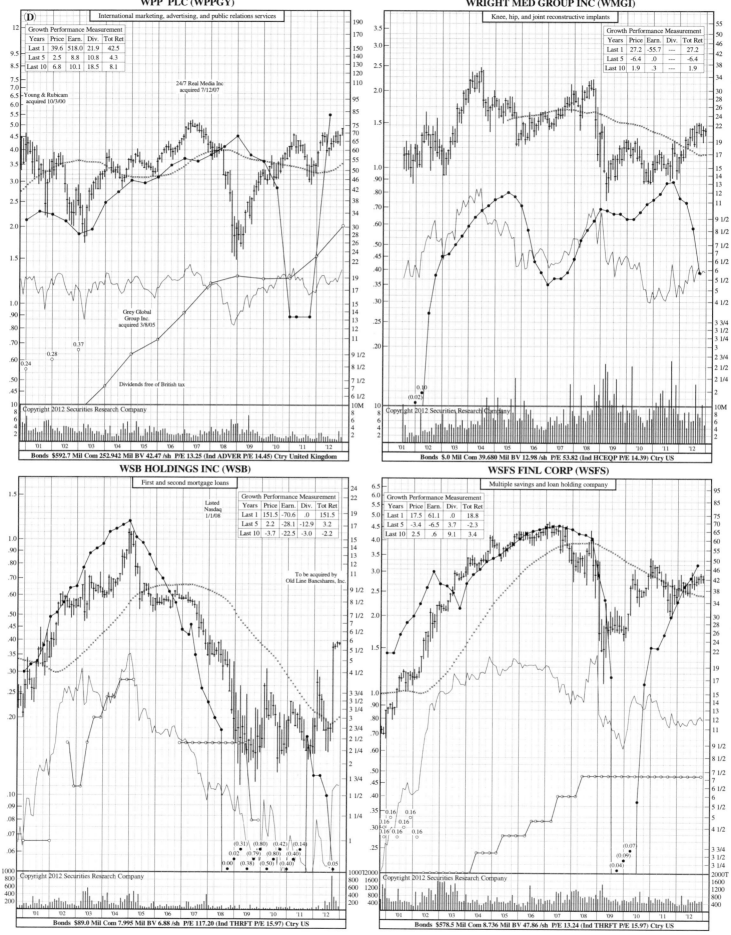

WPP PLC (WPPGY)

International marketing, advertising, and public relations services

Growth Performance Measurement				
Years	Price	Earn.	Div.	Tot Ret
Last 1	39.6	518.0	21.9	42.5
Last 5	2.5	8.8	10.8	4.3
Last 10	6.8	10.1	18.5	8.1

Young & Rubicam acquired 10/3/00

24/7 Real Media Inc acquired 7/12/07

Grey Global Group Inc. acquired 3/8/05

Dividends free of British tax

Copyright 2012 Securities Research Company

Bonds $592.7 Mil Com 252.942 Mil BV 42.47 /sh P/E 13.25 (Ind ADVER P/E 14.45) Ctry United Kingdom

WRIGHT MED GROUP INC (WMGI)

Knee, hip, and joint reconstructive implants

Growth Performance Measurement				
Years	Price	Earn.	Div.	Tot Ret
Last 1	27.2	-55.7	---	27.2
Last 5	-6.4	.0	---	-6.4
Last 10	1.9	.3	---	1.9

Copyright 2012 Securities Research Company

Bonds $.0 Mil Com 39.680 Mil BV 12.98 /sh P/E 53.82 (Ind HCEQP P/E 14.39) Ctry US

WSB HOLDINGS INC (WSB)

First and second mortgage loans

Listed Nasdaq 1/1/08

Growth Performance Measurement				
Years	Price	Earn.	Div.	Tot Ret
Last 1	151.5	-70.6	.0	151.5
Last 5	2.2	-28.1	-12.9	3.2
Last 10	-3.7	-22.5	-3.0	-2.2

To be acquired by Old Line Bancshares, Inc.

Copyright 2012 Securities Research Company

Bonds $89.0 Mil Com 7.995 Mil BV 6.88 /sh P/E 117.20 (Ind THRFT P/E 15.97) Ctry US

WSFS FINL CORP (WSFS)

Multiple savings and loan holding company

Growth Performance Measurement				
Years	Price	Earn.	Div.	Tot Ret
Last 1	17.5	61.1	.0	18.8
Last 5	-3.4	-6.5	3.7	-2.3
Last 10	2.5	.6	9.1	3.4

Copyright 2012 Securities Research Company

Bonds $578.5 Mil Com 8.736 Mil BV 47.86 /sh P/E 13.24 (Ind THRFT P/E 15.97) Ctry US

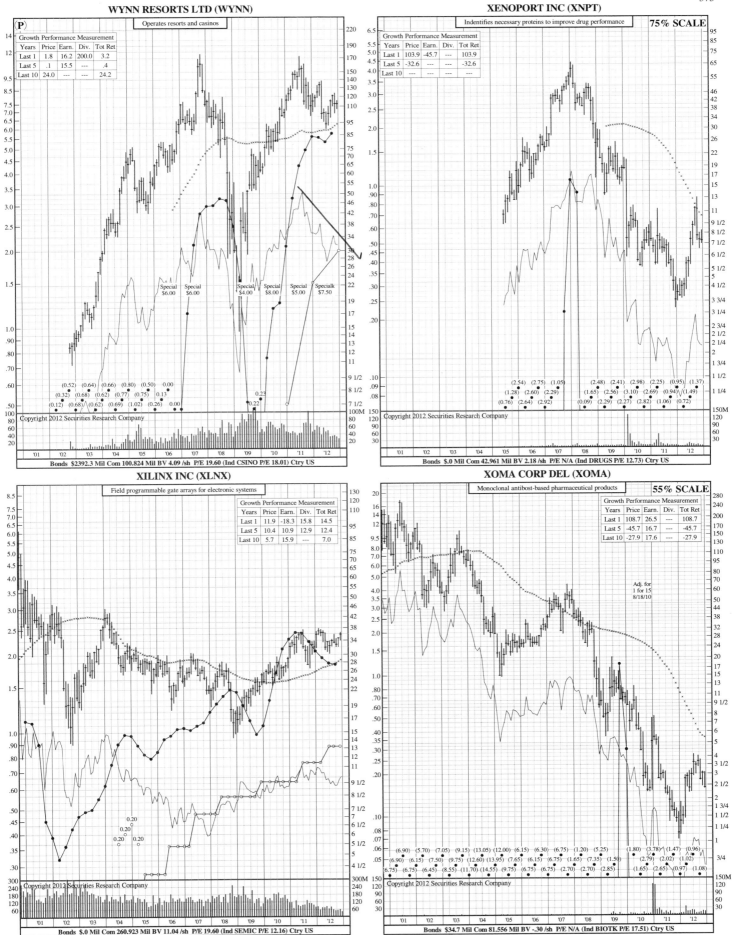

WYNN RESORTS LTD (WYNN)

Operates resorts and casinos

Growth Performance Measurement				
Years	Price	Earn.	Div.	Tot Ret
Last 1	1.8	16.2	200.0	3.2
Last 5	.1	15.5	---	.4
Last 10	24.0	---	---	24.2

Special $6.00 Special $6.00 Special $4.00 Special $8.00 Special $5.00 Specialk $7.50

(0.52) (0.64) (0.66) (0.80) (0.50) 0.00
(0.32) (0.68) (0.62) (0.77) (0.75) 0.13   0.23
(0.12) (0.68) (0.62) (0.69) (1.02) (0.26) 0.00   0.22

Copyright 2012 Securities Research Company

Bonds $2392.3 Mil Com 100.824 Mil BV 4.09 /sh P/E 19.60 (Ind CSINO P/E 18.01) Ctry US

XENOPORT INC (XNPT)

Indentifies necessary proteins to improve drug performance **75% SCALE**

Growth Performance Measurement				
Years	Price	Earn.	Div.	Tot Ret
Last 1	103.9	-45.7	---	103.9
Last 5	-32.6	---	---	-32.6
Last 10	---	---	---	---

(2.54) (2.75) (1.05)   (2.48) (2.41) (2.98) (2.25) (0.95) (1.37)
(1.28) (2.60) (2.29)   (1.65) (2.56) (3.10) (2.69) (0.94) (1.49)
(0.76) (2.64) (2.92)   (0.09) (2.29) (2.27) (2.82) (1.06) (0.72)

Copyright 2012 Securities Research Company

Bonds $.0 Mil Com 42.961 Mil BV 2.18 /sh P/E N/A (Ind DRUGS P/E 12.73) Ctry US

XILINX INC (XLNX)

Field programmable gate arrays for electronic systems

Growth Performance Measurement				
Years	Price	Earn.	Div.	Tot Ret
Last 1	11.9	-18.3	15.8	14.5
Last 5	10.4	10.9	12.9	12.4
Last 10	5.7	15.9	---	7.0

0.20
0.20
0.20 0.20
0.20 0.20

Copyright 2012 Securities Research Company

Bonds $.0 Mil Com 260.923 Mil BV 11.04 /sh P/E 19.60 (Ind SEMIC P/E 12.16) Ctry US

XOMA CORP DEL (XOMA)

Monoclonal antibost-based pharmaceutical products **55% SCALE**

Growth Performance Measurement				
Years	Price	Earn.	Div.	Tot Ret
Last 1	108.7	26.5	---	108.7
Last 5	-45.7	16.7	---	-45.7
Last 10	-27.9	17.6	---	-27.9

Adj. for
1 for 15
8/18/10

(6.90) (5.70) (7.05) (9.15) (13.05) (12.00) (6.15) (6.30) (6.75) (1.20) (5.25)   (1.80) (3.78) (1.47) (0.96)
(6.90) (6.15) (7.50) (9.75) (12.60) (13.95) (7.65) (6.15) (6.75) (1.65) (7.35) (1.50)   (2.79) (2.02) (1.02)
(6.75) (6.75) (6.45) (8.55) (11.70) (14.55) (9.75) (6.75) (6.75) (2.70) (2.70) (2.85)   (1.65) (2.65) (0.97) (1.08)

Copyright 2012 Securities Research Company

Bonds $34.7 Mil Com 81.556 Mil BV -.30 /sh P/E N/A (Ind BIOTK P/E 17.51) Ctry US

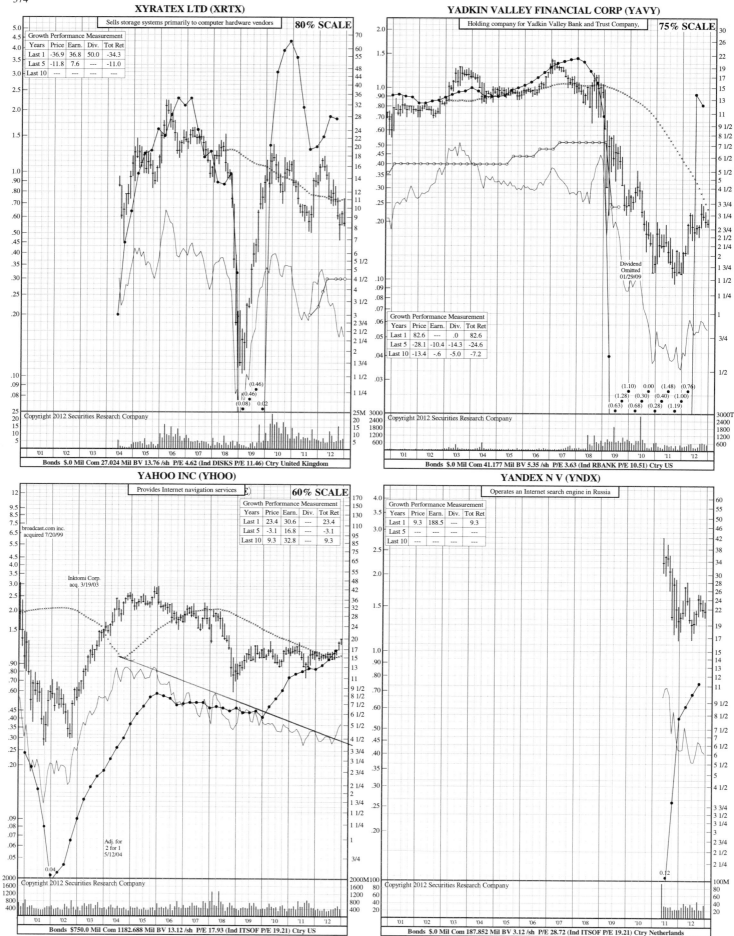

XYRATEX LTD (XRTX)

Sells storage systems primarily to computer hardware vendors

80% SCALE

Growth Performance Measurement

Years	Price	Earn.	Div.	Tot Ret
Last 1	-36.9	36.8	50.0	-34.3
Last 5	-11.8	7.6	---	-11.0
Last 10	---	---	---	---

(0.46)
(0.46)
(0.08)   0.02

Copyright 2012 Securities Research Company

Bonds $.0 Mil Com 27.024 Mil BV 13.76 /sh P/E 4.62 (Ind DISKS P/E 11.46) Ctry United Kingdom

YADKIN VALLEY FINANCIAL CORP (YAVY)

Holding company for Yadkin Valley Bank and Trust Company,

75% SCALE

Dividend
Omitted
01/29/09

Growth Performance Measurement

Years	Price	Earn.	Div.	Tot Ret
Last 1	82.6	---	.0	82.6
Last 5	-28.1	-10.4	-14.3	-24.6
Last 10	-13.4	-.6	-5.0	-7.2

(1.10)   0.00   (1.48)   (0.76)
(1.28)   (0.30)   (0.40)   (1.00)
(0.63)   (0.68)   (0.28)   (1.19)

Copyright 2012 Securities Research Company

Bonds $.0 Mil Com 41.177 Mil BV 5.35 /sh P/E 3.63 (Ind RBANK P/E 10.51) Ctry US

YAHOO INC (YHOO)

Provides Internet navigation services

60% SCALE

broadcast.com inc.
acquired 7/20/99

Inktomi Corp.
acq. 3/19/03

Growth Performance Measurement

Years	Price	Earn.	Div.	Tot Ret
Last 1	23.4	30.6	---	23.4
Last 5	-3.1	16.8	---	-3.1
Last 10	9.3	32.8	---	9.3

Adj. for
2 for 1
5/12/04

0.04

Copyright 2012 Securities Research Company

Bonds $750.0 Mil Com 1182.688 Mil BV 13.12 /sh P/E 17.93 (Ind ITSOF P/E 19.21) Ctry US

YANDEX N V (YNDX)

Operates an Internet search engine in Russia

Growth Performance Measurement

Years	Price	Earn.	Div.	Tot Ret
Last 1	9.3	188.5	---	9.3
Last 5	---	---	---	---
Last 10	---	---	---	---

0.12

Copyright 2012 Securities Research Company

Bonds $.0 Mil Com 187.852 Mil BV 3.12 /sh P/E 28.72 (Ind ITSOF P/E 19.21) Ctry Netherlands

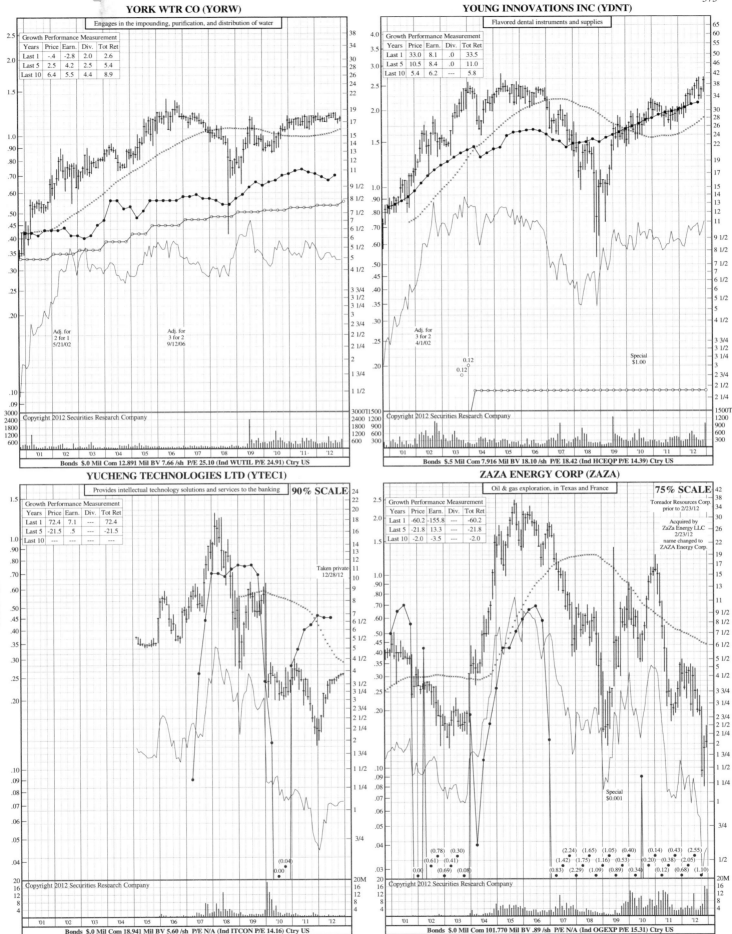

YORK WTR CO (YORW)

Engages in the impounding, purification, and distribution of water

Growth Performance Measurement				
Years	Price	Earn.	Div.	Tot Ret
Last 1	-.4	-2.8	2.0	2.6
Last 5	2.5	4.2	2.5	5.4
Last 10	6.4	5.5	4.4	8.9

Adj. for
2 for 1
5/21/02

Adj. for
3 for 2
9/12/06

Copyright 2012 Securities Research Company

Bonds $.0 Mil Com 12.891 Mil BV 7.66 /sh P/E 25.10 (Ind WUTIL P/E 24.91) Ctry US

YOUNG INNOVATIONS INC (YDNT)

Flavored dental instruments and supplies

Growth Performance Measurement				
Years	Price	Earn.	Div.	Tot Ret
Last 1	33.0	8.1	.0	33.5
Last 5	10.5	8.4	.0	11.0
Last 10	5.4	6.2	---	5.8

Adj. for
3 for 2
4/1/02

0.12
0.12

Special
$1.00

Copyright 2012 Securities Research Company

Bonds $.5 Mil Com 7.916 Mil BV 18.10 /sh P/E 18.42 (Ind HCEQP P/E 14.39) Ctry US

YUCHENG TECHNOLOGIES LTD (YTEC1)

Provides intellectual technology solutions and services to the banking

90% SCALE

Growth Performance Measurement				
Years	Price	Earn.	Div.	Tot Ret
Last 1	72.4	7.1	---	72.4
Last 5	-21.5	.5	---	-21.5
Last 10	---	---	---	---

Taken private
12/28/12

(0.04)
0.00

Copyright 2012 Securities Research Company

Bonds $.0 Mil Com 18.941 Mil BV 5.60 /sh P/E N/A (Ind ITCON P/E 14.16) Ctry US

ZAZA ENERGY CORP (ZAZA)

Oil & gas exploration, in Texas and France

75% SCALE

Toreador Resources Corp.
prior to 2/23/12

Acquired by
ZaZa Energy LLC
2/23/12
name changed to
ZAZA Energy Corp.

Growth Performance Measurement				
Years	Price	Earn.	Div.	Tot Ret
Last 1	-60.2	-155.8	---	-60.2
Last 5	-21.8	13.3	---	-21.8
Last 10	-2.0	-3.5	---	-2.0

(0.78) (0.30)   (2.24) (1.65) (1.05) (0.40)   (0.14) (0.43) (2.55)
(0.61) (0.41)   (1.75) (1.16) (0.53)   (0.20) (0.38) (2.05)
0.00   (0.69) (0.08)   (0.83) (2.29) (0.89) (0.34)   (0.12) (0.68) (1.10)

Special
$0.001

Copyright 2012 Securities Research Company

Bonds $.0 Mil Com 101.770 Mil BV .89 /sh P/E N/A (Ind OGEXP P/E 15.31) Ctry US

ZEBRA TECHNOLOGIES CORP (ZBRA)
Computerized label and ticket printing systems

Growth Performance Measurement				
Years	Price	Earn.	Div.	Tot Ret
Last 1	9.9	8.3	---	9.9
Last 5	2.5	8.8	---	2.5
Last 10	4.4	9.9	---	4.4

Adj. for 3 for 2 8/22/03   Adj. for 3 for 2 8/26/04

Copyright 2012 Securities Research Company

Bonds $.6 Mil Com 50.858 Mil BV 16.25 /sh P/E 15.79 (Ind OFCEL P/E 6.38) Ctry US

ZILLOW INC (Z)
Operates an online real estate information market

Growth Performance Measurement				
Years	Price	Earn.	Div.	Tot Ret
Last 1	23.4	122.2	---	23.4
Last 5	---	---	---	---
Last 10	---	---	---	---

0.09
0.00   0.18
0.00   0.12

Copyright 2012 Securities Research Company

Bonds $.0 Mil Com 25.909 Mil BV 8.27 /sh P/E 138.75 (Ind REESV P/E 17.93) Ctry US

ZION OIL & GAS INC (ZN)
Oil & gas production and exploration

85% SCALE

Growth Performance Measurement				
Years	Price	Earn.	Div.	Tot Ret
Last 1	-19.9	79.8	---	-19.9
Last 5	-23.4	-12.6	---	-23.4
Last 10	---	---	---	---

Listed Nasdaq 9/3/09 NYSE prior

(0.21) (0.46) (0.37) (0.39) (0.36) (0.26) (0.40)
(0.14) (0.41) (0.39) (0.34) (0.34) (0.35) (0.41) (0.38)
(0.07) (0.38) (0.47) (0.37) (0.38) (1.29) (1.88) (1.85)

Copyright 2012 Securities Research Company

Bonds $.0 Mil Com 32.314 Mil BV .64 /sh P/E N/A (Ind OGEXP P/E 15.31) Ctry US

ZIONS BANCORPORATION (ZION)
Multibank holding company based in Utah

Growth Performance Measurement				
Years	Price	Earn.	Div.	Tot Ret
Last 1	31.4	37.9	.0	31.7
Last 5	-14.4	-24.9	-52.9	-13.0
Last 10	-5.9	-9.7	-25.9	-2.6

Amegy Bancorp acquired 12/3/05

0.04 0.04 0.04 0.04 0.04
0.16 0.04 0.04 0.04 0.04
0.16 0.04 0.04 0.04 0.04 0.04
(3.32) (2.18) 0.22
(2.75) (3.69) (1.02)
(0.31) (3.12) (1.47)

Copyright 2012 Securities Research Company

Bonds $2715.3 Mil Com 184.182 Mil BV 26.05 /sh P/E 16.34 (Ind RBANK P/E 10.51) Ctry US

377

ZIPCAR INC (ZIP)

Zipcar is the world's leading car-sharing service

Growth Performance Measurement

Years	Price	Earn.	Div.	Tot Ret
Last 1	-38.6	---	---	-38.6
Last 5	---	---	---	---
Last 10	---	---	---	---

(1.10) 0.05
(1.12) (0.13)
(0.95) (1.01)

Copyright 2012 Securities Research Company

Bonds $.0 Mil Com 40.063 Mil BV 5.78 /sh P/E 63.38 (Ind TRUCK P/E 13.01) Ctry US

ZIX CORP (ZIXI)

Marketing/distribution of music and other digital data

55% SCALE

Zixlt Corp. prior to 8/13/02

Growth Performance Measurement

Years	Price	Earn.	Div.	Tot Ret
Last 1	-1.1	6.3	.0	-1.1
Last 5	-9.5	---	.0	-9.5
Last 10	-4.5	---	.0	-4.5

(2.45) (2.27) (2.08) (1.33) (1.17) (1.24) (1.09) (0.57) (0.21) (0.13) (0.08) (0.06)
(2.38) (2.51) (2.09) (1.72) (1.17) (1.24) (1.17) (0.77) (0.28) (0.13) (0.09) (0.07) 0.00
(2.30) (2.84) (2.06) (1.87) (1.23) (1.19) (1.21) (0.93) (0.39) (0.17) (0.10) (0.07) (0.04)

Copyright 2012 Securities Research Company

Bonds $.0 Mil Com 61.265 Mil BV .93 /sh P/E 16.41 (Ind ITSOF P/E 19.21) Ctry US

ZOGENIX INC (ZGNX)

Products for the treatment of central nervous system disorders/pain

Growth Performance Measurement

Years	Price	Earn.	Div.	Tot Ret
Last 1	-40.1	45.0	---	-40.1
Last 5	---	---	---	---
Last 10	---	---	---	---

(0.90) (1.59)
(0.73) (1.99) (0.99)
(0.17) (1.80) (1.29)

Copyright 2012 Securities Research Company

Bonds $.0 Mil Com 100.666 Mil BV .13 /sh P/E N/A (Ind DRUGS P/E 12.73) Ctry US

ZOLTEK COS INC (ZOLT)

Carbon fiber composites

75% SCALE

Growth Performance Measurement

Years	Price	Earn.	Div.	Tot Ret
Last 1	1.7	---	---	1.7
Last 5	-29.0	.6	---	-29.0
Last 10	13.4	---	---	13.4

(0.66) (0.43) (0.63) (0.91) (0.91) (1.55) (0.44)   (0.33) (0.28) (0.02)
(0.48) (0.45) (0.21) (0.76) (0.92) (0.81) (0.66) (0.22)   (0.16) (0.27) (0.24)
(0.30) (0.83) (0.35) (0.71) (0.95) (0.67) (0.31) (0.43)   (0.04) (0.30) (0.24)

Copyright 2012 Securities Research Company

Bonds $5.4 Mil Com 34.355 Mil BV 8.76 /sh P/E 10.76 (Ind SCHEM P/E 21.95) Ctry US

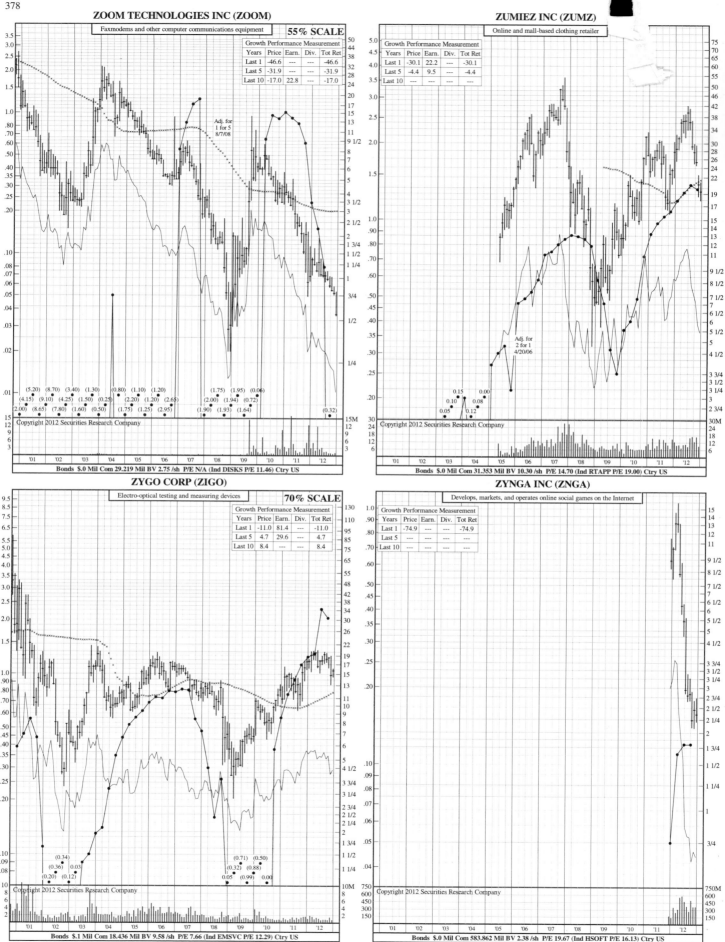

378

ZOOM TECHNOLOGIES INC (ZOOM)

Faxmodems and other computer communications equipment

55% SCALE

Growth Performance Measurement				
Years	Price	Earn.	Div.	Tot Ret
Last 1	-46.6	---	---	-46.6
Last 5	-31.9	---	---	-31.9
Last 10	-17.0	22.8	---	-17.0

Adj. for
1 for 5
8/7/08

(5.20) (8.70) (3.40) (1.30)   (0.80) (1.10) (1.20)   (1.75) (1.95) (0.06)
(4.15) (9.10) (4.25) (1.50) (0.25) (2.20) (1.20) (2.65)   (2.00) (1.94) (0.72)
(2.00) (8.65) (7.80) (1.60) (0.50) (1.75) (1.25) (2.95)   (1.90) (1.93) (1.64)   (0.32)

Copyright 2012 Securities Research Company

Bonds $.0 Mil Com 29.219 Mil BV 2.75 /sh P/E N/A (Ind DISKS P/E 11.46) Ctry US

ZUMIEZ INC (ZUMZ)

Online and mall-based clothing retailer

Growth Performance Measurement				
Years	Price	Earn.	Div.	Tot Ret
Last 1	-30.1	22.2	---	-30.1
Last 5	-4.4	9.5	---	-4.4
Last 10	---	---	---	---

Adj. for
2 for 1
4/20/06

0.15   0.00
0.10   0.08
0.05   0.12

Copyright 2012 Securities Research Company

Bonds $.0 Mil Com 31.353 Mil BV 10.30 /sh P/E 14.70 (Ind RTAPP P/E 19.00) Ctry US

ZYGO CORP (ZIGO)

Electro-optical testing and measuring devices

70% SCALE

Growth Performance Measurement				
Years	Price	Earn.	Div.	Tot Ret
Last 1	-11.0	81.4	---	-11.0
Last 5	4.7	29.6	---	4.7
Last 10	8.4	---	---	8.4

(0.34)   (0.71) (0.50)
(0.36) 0.03   (0.32) (0.88)
(0.20) (0.12)   0.05 (0.99) 0.00

Copyright 2012 Securities Research Company

Bonds $.1 Mil Com 18.436 Mil BV 9.58 /sh P/E 7.66 (Ind EMSVC P/E 12.29) Ctry US

ZYNGA INC (ZNGA)

Develops, markets, and operates online social games on the Internet

Growth Performance Measurement				
Years	Price	Earn.	Div.	Tot Ret
Last 1	-74.9	---	---	-74.9
Last 5	---	---	---	---
Last 10	---	---	---	---

Copyright 2012 Securities Research Company

Bonds $.0 Mil Com 583.862 Mil BV 2.38 /sh P/E 19.67 (Ind HSOFT P/E 16.13) Ctry US